Sons of United

A Chronicle of the Manchester United Youth Team

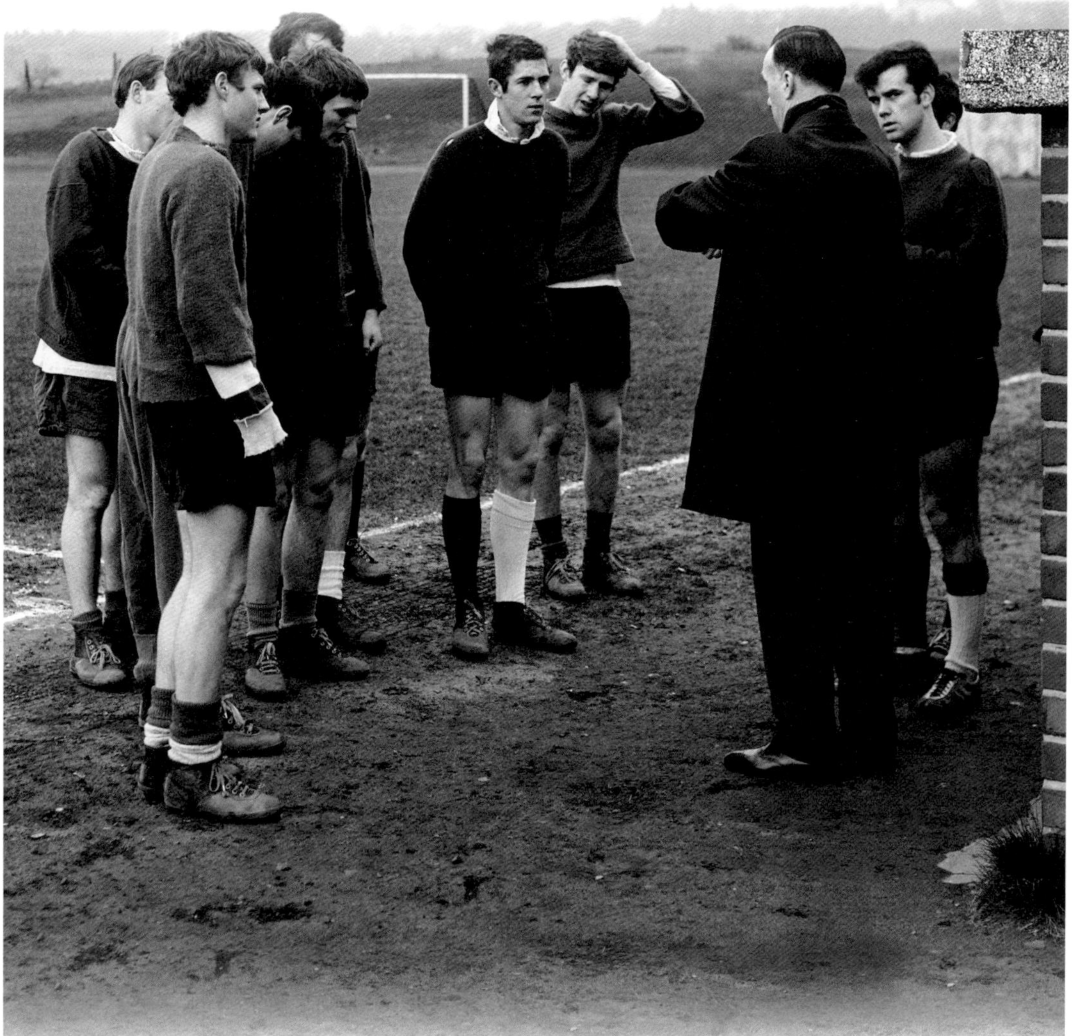

Steve Hobin & Tony Park

Copyright © Popular Side publications 2012

Published and distributed by Popular Side publications

Printed at: Deanprint Limited, Cheadle Heath Works, Stockport Road, Stockport, SK3 0PR.

Website: www.sonsofunited.com

All rights reserved. Apart from any use permitted under UK copyright law, this publication may only be reproduced, stored or transmitted, in any form, or by any means, with prior permission in writing of the publishers or, in the case of reprographic production, in accordance with the terms of licences issued by the Copyright Licensing Agency.

While every endeavour has been made to contact owners of copyright material produced in this book, we have not always been successful. In the event of a copyright query, the authors and publisher will be happy to rectify any omissions and credit individuals at the earliest opportunity.

IBSN: 978 0 9574564 0 2

Authors: Steve Hobin and Tony Park

Initial artwork concept: Annik Associates

Redesign, image restoration, cover and layout: Matthew Hobin

Enquiries: sonsofunited@yahoo.co.uk

Steve Hobin grew up in Gorton and was educated at Old Hall Drive Junior School and Central High School for Boys in Longsight. He attended his first game at Old Trafford in January 1967 and has now watched Manchester United play in fifteen different countries.

Having worked in the financial services industry since 1980, a job promotion entailed him relocating to the Midlands in 1988 and since 2000 he has operated his own financial advice practice in Droitwich in Worcestershire.

Steve would like to dedicate his efforts towards the book to his parents, Jean and Ernest Hobin.

Born in Stevenage in Hertfordshire, Tony Park grew up in the sunny climes of Sydney, Australia. He got his love of Manchester United through his father who was a fanatical Celtic and Denis Law fan, and watched the Reds for the first time against Liverpool on Boxing Day 1978.

Upon returning to the UK in 1987, he worked in Human Resources for numerous companies and now runs his own business as a Management Consultant. A season ticket holder in the old Popular Side (Sir Alex Ferguson Stand), Tony lives in Marple Bridge in Cheshire. He would like to dedicate this book to his parents Bob and Jo, and his two sisters Veronica and Marion.

The authors would also like to commemorate the work of Jimmy Murphy, without a shadow of a doubt the greatest youth coach the British game has ever known. Murphy's efforts in building the Manchester United youth team to attain such remarkable success during the 1950's & 1960's was one of the key foundations of the club's standing today. This book has been inspired by his incredible achievements.

CONTENTS

Preface — v
League History — vi
Acknowledgements — vii
'Foreword' by Wilf McGuinness — viii

Chapter One: Rocca's Revolution — *The pre-F.A. Youth Cup era* — 1

Introduction: The Manchester United Youth Team — 2
Last of the MUJACs: An interview with Jack 'Crasher' White — 5
Introduction: The F.A. Youth Cup — 11

Chapter Two: Murphy's Marvels — *October 1952 - April 1958* — 15

Irish Tour 1953 — 28
Swiss Tour 1954 — 46
The Tomlinson Trophy 1953, 1954 & 1955 — 64

Chapter Three: Rebirth & Glory — *October 1958 - February 1968* — 121

Chapter Four: Dark Days — *December 1968 - March 1981* — 209

Tour of Jamaica 1973 — 237

Chapter Five: Harrison's Hopefuls — *November 1981 - April 1991* — 289

Grossi-Morera Tournament 1989 — 334

Chapter Six: Harrison's Heroes — *November 1991 - December 1997* — 365

Lancashire F.A. Youth Cup 1970-1985 & 1989-1998 — 387

Chapter Seven: Global Strategy — *December 1998 - May 2011* — 425

Malaysia - Champions Youth Cup 2007 — 482

Chapter Eight: Sons of United — 523

Youth Programmes — 560
Youth Coaches — 562
Talent of Tomorrow — 563
Roll of Honour — 564
Dream Team — 568

Preface

While Manchester United has frequently hit the headlines with numerous high-profile signings over the past seven or eight decades, the club's youth system has quietly continued to produce a steady stream of material for the first-team. The history of the Reds' youth set-up not only makes for fascinating reading, it also gives an insight into the importance of grooming young talent as a strategy for any professional football club. Having visionaries such as Matt Busby and Alex Ferguson at the helm has made the club one of the most consistent developers of soccer talent the football world has known and it is no coincidence that two of the most successful periods in United's history have coincided with their stewardships.

Since 1945, when Busby first took charge at Old Trafford, over 200 juniors have made it into the senior side, which equates to about 50% of the number of first-team debutants. Of the top 40 appearance totals in the club's history, half of them belong to ex-juniors, and in respect of United's all-time top ten goalscorers, six of them have also come through the ranks.

At the time of writing, the Reds' youth system has developed over 90 internationals from countries all over the globe. A more staggering statistic is that since October 1937, at least one of the club's youth players has been included in every single competitive United squad and, with only a solitary exception, a minimum of at least one of them has made an appearance. It is a unique record in English football and, considering trends at the top level of the sport, one which is unlikely to be repeated.

In addition, the Reds hold numerous records in the F.A. Youth Cup, and the most trophy wins, highest goalscorer, biggest victory, longest sequence without defeat and the most victories are amongst them. Over 500 players have taken part in the Youth Cup on behalf of United, with 32% breaking through to the first-team and 38% going on to find employment in the Football League or Premier League. A 70% success rate is a highly satisfying result and the figure provides much encouragement for the current generation of the club's teenagers.

'Sons of United' is fundamentally made up of two main components.

Firstly, it uses the club's involvement in the F.A. Youth Cup as a central theme, from the competition's commencement in October 1952 right through to United's record-breaking tenth trophy triumph in 2011. However, because of the importance of other youth games, tournaments and friendly matches at home and overseas, a number of those have also been included. The book also covers the inception and development of the Reds' youth set-up from the early 1930's onwards and provides details about how the Youth Cup came into existence.

Every one of the Youth Cup ties United have featured in to May 2011 has at least one dedicated page. Details include the date and kick-off times of all matches, line-ups of both teams, scores and goalscorers, a match report, other relevant data and, frequently, visual material. Great care has been taken to ensure complete accuracy with all the information contained within these pages, but as so often happens with publications of this nature, mistakes may occur and we would appreciate any feedback to help us to correct them for future reference. There is also a small amount of information missing, which will become clear as the pages are turned, though this, we hope, you will feel is outweighed by the huge volume of completely new material. We are sure the reader will appreciate that some facts are simply unobtainable, and after researching the subject for over eighteen years, the authors feel they have now exhausted all the avenues available to them.

In regards to crowds, the vast majority of attendances noted are official. In a small number of cases we have two differing attendances and in those instances we have attempted to give the one we believe is correct. There are also a number of games for which we have been unable to ascertain a crowd and the newspaper match report has come to our rescue by supplying an approximation of those inside the stadium.

The reader should be aware that newspaper match reports from 40, 50 or 60 years ago are often not the same as those of today because, for example, printing techniques differed, as did the grammar used. However, the authors wanted to use a number of original reports as it was felt they would give the readership a flavour for football of the period, though it should be pointed out that the print in some of the reports reproduced from old newspapers is not as clear as it would be from modern publications.

There are occasions where names appear in newspaper match reports that are wrong, so they have been corrected in the team line-ups at the top of the page. We have also spotted a tiny number of mistakes contained in the United Review match summaries and, again, these have been put right in the information bars.

A few of the substitute details have been particularly difficult to nail down because when they were initially introduced in the 1960's, their involvement or otherwise often wasn't noted. Even so, we believe that all the information given about United's substitutes are correct, while a little detail in respect of our opponents' bench is still lacking. In the team line-ups, a ◊ (diamond) besides a substitute's name denotes that we do not know whether or not he got on, whereas the symbol ‡ means that the substitute was used but we are unsure as to who he replaced.

In the chapter detailing the Reds' involvement in the Tomlinson Trophy, the team that our opponents normally played for is given in parenthesis next to their name. For example, Sheffield & Hallamshire's Jack Fowler has his name followed by (OF) because he was involved with Oaks Fold. All of the main clubs of the remaining players should be clear from the text.

The book's second major element is the inclusion of 114 players biographies. These profiles have been painstakingly compiled through literally thousands of hours of (mainly library-based) research during which a number of inaccuracies found in other sources have been corrected.

To give just four examples of the many mistakes we have discovered, Alex Dawson does not have a middle name (given as Downie in other publications) while 'Shay' Brennan was given just one Christian name at birth (James), and we have copies of their birth certificates as proof. Also, Jimmy Nicholl's month of birth is December 1956 (often noted as February 1956) and Carlo Sartori was born in Caderzone (not Calderzone) in Italy.

The main factor that sets the biographies in this book apart from any others is that the majority of the players concerned have been given the opportunity to amend what has been written about them. Because of our approach in contacting said players, a few of whom have since sadly passed away, we have been able to obtain numerous anecdotes, which have the dual effect of adding another dimension to the text, as well as providing information not available elsewhere. The reader should note that some of the quotes included in the book were given to the press at the time, some are pre-match and some post-match, while others have been obtained by the authors in more recent years.

Besides their accuracy, the authors would also describe the biographies as 'reasonably comprehensive'. They set out how the subjects began in football and later progressed through the club's ranks and beyond. This is a completely different take on any player biographies in any other publication and helps to demonstrate just what a young footballer is expected to go through in order to make a career out of the game.

Of course, some of those concerned spent much the greater part of their time in football away from Old Trafford and we realised that in order to paint a complete picture of a player's efforts in the game, it was sometimes necessary to include an amount of 'non-United' facts. As it was always our intention to make the profiles as complete as possible, just as much work has been put into researching these sections of the biographies as any other.

Contained within each profile is the individual's name alongside the season or seasons they appeared in the Youth Cup for United in addition to their place and date of birth. Details of the subject's height and weight are based on those correct while they were eligible for selection for the youth team and position(s) noted relate to those that the player operated in during their tenure in the Reds' under-18 side.

There are a number of abbreviations in the career section of the biographies and those in regards to overseas countries should be evident from the text. In the same section, c/s means close season, (NC) stands for non-contract and (L) represents a loan period. In addition, App. is short for apprentice, Ass. is the abbreviation for associate, Pro. means professional, Am. is a shortened version of amateur and (T) indicates a trial period.

In regards to the biographies, it was decided to include those of all the 48 players who contributed towards United winning the trophy for five consecutive seasons from 1952/53 to 1956/57, every one of the subsequent starting captains and a small number of others whose story we hope will be of interest to the reader. There are only two 'captains' who do not have a profile and they are Danny Rose and Ryan Tunnicliffe, because they assumed the armband part-way through a game when the skipper who began the match was substituted. Rose took over the captaincy against Sunderland at Durham in January 2006 and Tunnicliffe briefly led the under-18's at Burnley four years later. The only information lacking about captains relates to Nobby Stiles and Barry Smith in the 1958/59 campaign. We know the latter began the season as skipper while the former had taken over by the end of the cup run. When exactly the captaincy switched over we are unable to pinpoint, and the players concerned cannot recollect the event all these years later.

Finally, we would like to point out that the book wasn't put together to be read as a narrative from the first page to the last. Because the publication is heavy on facts, it is viewed by the authors as more akin to an encyclopaedia, which can be 'dipped' in and out of or even used as a work of reference given the amount of information contained within its pages. Whichever way the reader chooses to approach the book, the authors sincerely hope that they enjoy and find some merit in their work.

LEAGUE HISTORY

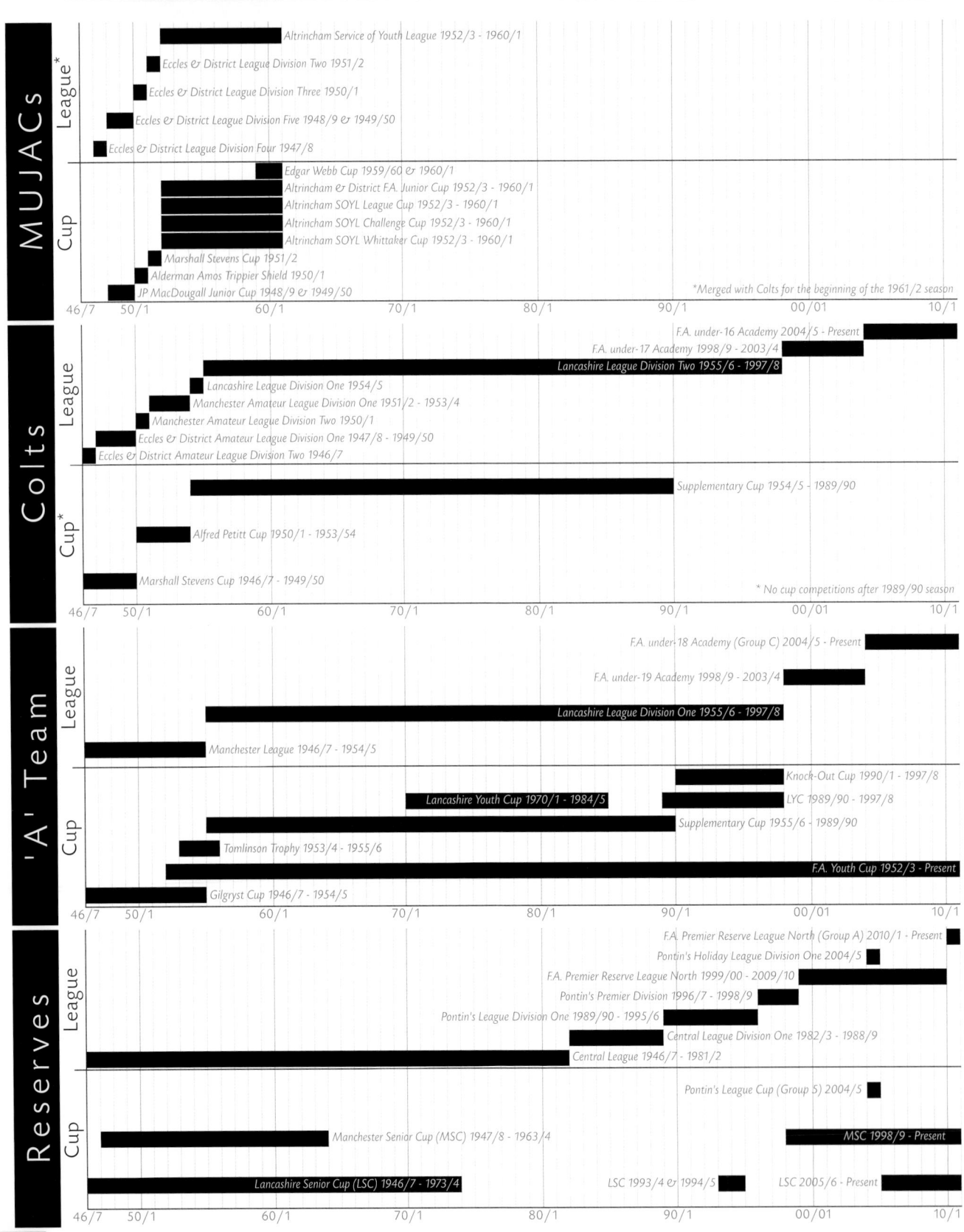

Acknowledgements

Writing a book of this magnitude would have been impossible without the help and support of many people and we wish to thank the numerous club historians who have provided us with the details we required.

In that regard we would like to offer our eternal gratitude for the generosity of the assistance and hospitality provided by Mike Cox, one of United's premier statisticians/historians, whose input towards this project has been absolutely immense.

Other historians we wish to record grateful thanks to for their contributions include the following:

David Bull and Gary Chalk (both Southampton), Matt Hill (Peterborough), Gerald Mortimer (Derby County), the late John Maddox (Manchester City), Andy Porter (Tottenham Hotspur), Tony Matthews (West Bromwich Albion), Colin Cameron (Charlton Athletic), Phil Hollow (Plymouth Argyle), Harry Glasper (Middlesbrough), Iain Cook (Arsenal), Simon Marland (Bolton Wanderers), John Helliar (West Ham United), Ron Hockings (Chelsea), John D. Cross (Blackpool), Bob Graham (Sunderland), Paul Joannou (Newcastle United), Mike Jackman (Blackburn Rovers), David Salmon (Kent), Martin Bartley (Brentford), Malcolm Hartley (Bradford Park Avenue), Steve Durham (Workington), Terry Frost (Bradford City), Chas Sumner (Chester City), Peter Cullen (Bury), Garth Dykes and Stewart Beckett (both Oldham Athletic), Gordon Neale and Dave Windross (both York City), Lawrence Bland (Preston North End and Morecambe), Jim Brown (Coventry City), Trefor Jones (Watford), Dave Smith (Leicester City), Stuart Basson (Chesterfield), Gordon Macey (Queen's Park Rangers), Peter Bishop and Gilbert Upton (both Tranmere Rovers), Denis Clarebrough (Sheffield United), Ivan Barnsley (Birmingham City), Geoff Allman (Walsall), Donald Nannestad (Lincoln City), Richard Wells (Aldershot), Terry Surridge (Altrincham), Gordon Dickson (Berwick Rangers), Phil Chadwick (Witton Albion), Ray Simpson (Burnley), Tim Carder (Brighton & Hove Albion), Neil Harvey (Cambridge City), John Smith (Wolverhampton Wanderers), Frank Tweddle (Darlington), Ian Cruddas (Buxton), Barry Hewitt (Everton), Barry Worsley (Banbury Spencer), Alex White (Fulham), Peter Evans (Hednesford Town), Ian Thomas (Huddersfield Town), Brian Ellis (Luton Town), Tony Ambrosen (Newport County), Tony Brown (Notts County), S. Lunt and Jeff Rourke (both Wigan Athletic), Phil Sherwin (Port Vale), Peter Jeffs (Portsmouth), David Downs (Reading), Kenneth Lowry (Ards), Stewart Fell (Radcliffe Borough), Paul Gilligan (Doncaster Rovers), Gerry Somerton and Barry Dalby (both Rotherham United), Keith Smith (Canterbury City), Mick Renshaw (Sheffield Wednesday), R. Briggs (Grimsby Town), Tom Spence (Tonbridge), Mike Braham (Southport), Mike Blackstone (Exeter City), Wade Martin (Stoke City), the late Professor D.H. Farmer (Swansea City), Dave Topping (Sankeys of Wellington), Geraint Parry and Peter Jones (both Wrexham), Dave Siddall (Droylsden), John Litster (Raith Rovers), William Hughes (Northwich Victoria), Paul Clayton (Shamrock Rovers) and, finally, Barry Stephenson (Bedford Town).

The majority of the photographic material contained herein has been sourced from Getty Images, Action Images, Colorsport, Mirrorpix, the Press Association and Howard Talbot, although due to the sheer quantity involved we have been unable to find the space to list each picture individually.

We also wish to express our gratitude to a number of freelance photographers who have supplied us with images, namely Tom Morris, Steven Bridge, Brian Tonks and Alan Cozzi, and we are similarly indebted to John Cocks, Liverpool Football Club's former official photographer.

We would additionally like to record our appreciation to the many newspapers that have allowed us to reproduce headlines, match reports, cartoons and advertisements from their back-issues. The source of the vast majority of match reports and passages are noted within the text and the reader should be aware that the newspapers involved are mainly referred to by the name they were known by at that time.

The main exception to this is the Manchester Evening News which, upon its merger with the Evening Chronicle on 27th July 1963, was known as the Manchester Evening News & Chronicle for several years after which the 'Chronicle' part was dropped. The former-named newspaper is referred to throughout as either the Manchester Evening News or simply the Evening News.

Those newspapers that have also given us their permission to include their photographs are as follows:

(Wolverhampton) Express & Star, Southern Daily Echo, Bolton News, Bury Times, Oldham Chronicle, Wrexham & North Wales Guardian, Sheffield Star, Kentish Times, Barnsley Chronicle, Birmingham Mail, Sunderland Echo, Derbyshire Times, (Stoke-on-Trent) Sentinel, Huddersfield Examiner, Lancashire Telegraph, Irish Times, Lancashire Evening Post, Newcastle Chronicle, Chester Chronicle, Coventry Evening Telegraph, Islington Gazette, Liverpool Echo, Derby Telegraph, Middlesbrough Gazette, Watford Observer, Croydon Advertiser, Scunthorpe Telegraph, Nottingham Post, Eastern Daily Press, Reading Chronicle, News & Star (Cumbria) and the Manchester Evening News.

For numerous of the other pictures which enhance this publication, we sincerely thank Johnny Fuggle, James Thomas, Alan Kirke and Ray Adler, in addition to those obtained from Leslie Millman's collection, as all five of those named have allowed us access to their personal troves. We are also indebted to Steve Erskine for the same reason.

The authors also wish to express their appreciation to the many former players and their families who often came to our assistance when images were required.

In the early years of our research, John Treleven provided us with much valuable assistance. John's access to Youth Cup information from the Football Association's headquarters, particularly in relation to how the competition was formed, proved absolutely invaluable. John shared his findings freely and for that the authors are eternally grateful.

We would also like to express our appreciation to the staff members at Tameside Library, Sheffield Central Library, Bolton Central Library, Bury Library, Manchester Central Library and the British Newspaper Library at Colindale in London.

Additionally, a word of thanks goes out to Edwin Ferris of the Northern Ireland Schools' F.A. while Ceri Stennett at the Football Association of Wales also lent invaluable support in providing details of international schoolboy and youth matches.

For their assistance in proof reading, we wish to acknowledge the time-consuming effort put in by Iain McCartney, James Thomas, Eifion Evans, Matthew Hobin, Jenny Watson and Ian Brunton, and the long hours and effort spent typing the text by Julie Street and Karen Webley is also greatly appreciated. Iain, James, Eifion and Kevin Burthem deserve special mention as they supplied much of the material which got the project underway in the initial period of our research and they have been a great source of support and encouragement ever since.

For their help in tracking down players, we are deeply indebted to Les Kershaw and the scouting staff at Manchester United, while Mark Wylie, the club's museum curator, kindly allowed us access to archival records. Dave Ryan, Paul McGuinness and other members of the club's staff also provided help, information and material whenever it was requested, as did David Sadler and other members of the Association of Former Manchester United Players.

The authors also wish to thank Wilf McGuinness for kindly agreeing to write the foreword for us. To have someone with Wilf's incredible background and immense knowledge on board spurred us on and filled us both with a huge sense of pride.

We gratefully acknowledge the work Andy Alldridge of Annik Associates in Worcester has put in on the design and layout of the book and his originality in creating the match templates. Andy's quite superb efforts were followed by the hard graft, technical competence and hundreds of man-hours put in by Matthew Hobin, whose skills have gone a long way in making this book so visually powerful. Quite simply, without Matthew's input and drive this publication might never have reached a conclusion.

The authors would also like to thank the numerous subscribers who have waited patiently for a publication date. They are:

Alan Tyler, the late Mike Dobbin, Pete Hargreaves, Hal Hargreaves, James Thomas, Norman Horridge, David Horridge, Paul Brown, Dave Pearce, David Price, Johnny Fuggle, Geoff Theobold, D. Boult, Peter Higham, Colin Jones, Michael Pike, Alan Appleby, Brian Keighley, Paul Entwistle, Derek Leonard, Robert Brimicombe, John Kelly, Brian Pendlebury, Michael Passmore, M.G. Weldon, Colin Buckley, Bryan Buckley, Kevin Herlihy, Billy O'Neill, Alan Bradshaw, David Humberston, David N. Robertson, David Platt, Chris Fenlon, Ged Pole, John Moore, Gary Wynne, Derek Clarke, John Tuckett, Michael Grayson, Kevin Burthem, Ian Jones, the late W.J. Jones, Jim Bailey and Paul A. Tansley.

Most importantly, during the course of their research, the authors have interviewed in excess of 400 former or current youth team players, or members of their families, and we feel it appropriate to record here the time and patience they took to answer our questions and allow us into their homes. In a similar vein, we were also fortunate to spend time with former United youth coach Frank Blunstone and ex-manager Tommy Docherty. To them all, a most sincere thank you.

Finally, as keen historians and collectors of anything to do with Manchester United's youth team, if any reader holds any information about same not contained in this book, or has any related memorabilia they would like to share with the authors, such as tickets, team sheets, photos, medals, trophies, programmes, selection cards or letters, we would be delighted to hear from you.

FOREWORD

By Wilf McGuinness

The pleasure this book gives in bringing back a lot of fond memories is wonderful. Not only for myself but for the players, the coaching staff and, of course, the fans who have been involved with the youth team over such a long period of time and has made the name of Manchester United famous around the world. The likes of Duncan Edwards, Bobby Charlton, George Best, David Beckham and Ryan Giggs are known in virtually every country I visit and lend substance to a fantastic legacy that was first created over 80 years ago.

So many things that people don't know about the football club have been brought to life in this book. The records, the statistics, the young players and how the success of the youth team has helped to create the culture that is Manchester United.

Back in 1952 I was still a schoolboy and, even though I was a United fan, I was actually a Manchester fan and regularly watched both of the city's two major teams. I played for and captained Manchester Boys and I was being chased by a whole host of clubs. Then I watched the youth team in action against Nantwich at The Cliff and I looked at Duncan Edwards and John Doherty, who were great feeders, but there were players scoring all over the place. I had never seen an exhibition like it, every move seemed to end in a goal. This was the way football should have been played, and it was definitely the way I wanted to play football.

Watching the youth team that night really swung it for me. Later that season I went to Old Trafford and saw the final against Wolves, who were one of the top clubs in the country at the time, but United thrashed them 7-1 and that was the final push that made my mind up. I just had to join this club.

The following season I joined Manchester United and was told by Jimmy Murphy, one of the greatest ever coaches, that *'I wasn't at school any more and I was entering a man's world'*. The do's and don'ts were hammered home to me and whenever I played, Jimmy's voice was in the background.

There were some wonderful people who supported Jimmy. Men like Bert Whalley, Arthur Powell, Jack Pauline, Joe Travis, Bert Fishburn and later, Johnny Aston. Even the trainers, Tom Curry and Bill Inglis, they all had a positive bearing on my success as a young footballer. All of them were extremely capable and they all played their roles to perfection, not only in my eyes but in the eyes of all the players coming through.

In the youth team we had players who not only had Central League experience, but also First Division experience, and with the incomparable Duncan Edwards, even international experience.

The first thing I realised was how different it was from schoolboy football. The training, the coaching, it was all high tempo and the players were always being encouraged. Even though we got knocked down on occasions, we were reminded how good we were and to always believe in ourselves.

I competed in the Youth Cup for three consecutive campaigns, captaining the team to success in the 1955/56 season and becoming one of only five players to win a full set of three winner's plaques. I played in 27 ties in total and of all the games I took part in during my career, it was those youth matches that were the most exciting.

There was the final at Wolves in 1954; we drew the first leg 4-4 at Old Trafford and Wolves were so bullish about beating us down at Molineux. Then one of their lads gave away a penalty and David Pegg won us the cup. I'll never forget Stan Cullis at the end of the match giving the lad who gave the penalty away one almighty kick up the backside.

Then there was a game at Maine Road played in terrible fog. Steve Fleet was the Manchester City goalkeeper back then and our paths still cross from time to time. Duncan scored our winner with a shot from outside the penalty box but Steve still tells me he would have saved the shot only for the fog. I keep reminding him that you couldn't save Duncan's piledrivers.

I remember in my second season going down to London to face Chelsea at Stamford Bridge in the Youth Cup semi-final. Before the game Jimmy Murphy told everyone to *'play a team game and use the ball like you have been taught'*. Duncan scored twice in the second half to win us the match, he was such a fantastic talent.

In my final season in the Youth Cup I was lucky to see one of the best goals to grace Old Trafford when Bobby Charlton scored with an overhead kick against Bexleyheath. If I didn't know already, that goal made me realise just how good Bobby was.

We went on to reach the final and faced Chesterfield, and we really cocked it up in the first leg. After being 3-0 up we let them back in the game and it ended up at 3-2 so we knew it was going to be a tough game at their place. It was my last ever game in the youth side and I had already played in the first-team. Then the relatively unknown Dennis Fidler scored from an acute angle to help us retain the trophy. It wasn't all about the Charlton's and the Edwards', everyone played their part in the youth team.

Fortunately for me there were other trophies to win. We also went over to Switzerland regularly to play in the Blue Stars Tournament. They were proud moments for us, representing the club abroad, and for many of the lads it was their first ever time outside of our own country. In the first year we went there the Swiss were making preparations as hosts for the 1954 World Cup Finals and I remember the Brazilians approaching Matt Busby as they wanted to take Billy Whelan back to Brazil with them. Billy had been sensational in all our games.

The feeling we got playing in the youth team was that it was the most important game of our lives. The coaching staff treated us like we were the best players in the world. They lifted us when we needed lifting, and we got lifted so far. Those lessons were not just about football but also about life, and that is what playing for Manchester United is all about.

Moving on, we had a few players of real quality in the 1964 side, people like Bestie, John Aston, John Fitzpatrick and David Sadler, and the team just got better and better as the tournament went on. I think that is one of the major benefits of the Youth Cup because it helped those players to grow up as footballers by getting the chance to appear in big stadiums and to know what it means to follow in the footsteps of so many others.

When I took over as chief coach, the youth players we had were all good technically, but you need more than that when stepping up into the first-team. The first characteristic I looked for was self-belief, without that a player won't make it. I also looked at their temperament, vision and knowledge of the game. When they needed to be strong, when to be direct and when to slow the game down. Unfortunately when I assessed all those young lads they weren't all Manchester United quality and it would take years before the youth system was re-established as the best in the country.

It goes in cycles like that sometimes and our scouting probably wasn't at its best in the late 1960's. Many of the scouts were coming to the end of their careers and other clubs were much more competitive. They had copied the Manchester United way and had very good youth systems in place. Clubs like Chelsea and West Ham now had excellent set-ups while Arsenal were starting to scout in Ireland where United had held a very strong presence up to that point. Although the likes of Frank Stapleton had trials with us he eventually chose Arsenal, we were finding it much harder and lost a bit of focus in the early 1970's.

There is nothing better than having stability and the history of United has shown that a player coming through the ranks is more likely to understand the history and culture of the club rather than someone who has cost a fee. For a spell in the 1970's and 1980's we didn't have that permanence and it showed in the results at youth level. Of course, all that changed when Eric Harrison joined the club and he took us to Youth Cup finals in 1982 and 1986 although, unfortunately, we eventually lost them both.

Understandably, it then took a little time for Alex Ferguson to bed in, but after his first few years there was an improvement right through the club. At last we started to look like the real Manchester United again. He planted the seeds and got the right people around him with the result that Fergie's Fledglings started to fly. They are still soaring today.

Under Alex Ferguson we have had so many good things happen at Old Trafford and like Matt Busby before him, he gave youth a chance and continues to do so to this day. It's no wonder that we want him to go on for many more years, with the same pattern and plan.

I am very proud and thrilled for my son Paul, who reached the Reserves as a player and has been associated with the club for nearly 30 years, when he won the F.A. Youth Cup as team manager in 2011.

I am Manchester born and bred and so many former players still live in the area. We meet at numerous functions and recall incidents from our memorable life in football.

I feel so happy to have been involved with this great football club and I am sure you will find this book not only fascinating reading but a lasting record of all the fantastic highs and some of the lows of some of the players who have represented the club over the last 80 years.

These are our memories of where it all began.

Mujac's Young Team of Scoring Stars

Chapter One
ROCCA'S REVOLUTION

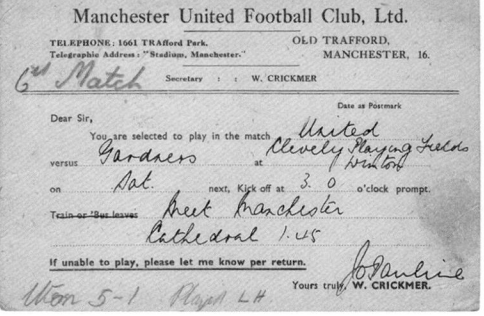

W. CRICKMER

INTRODUCTION

The Manchester United Youth Team

The name Walter Whittaker probably means nothing to the vast number of Manchester United supporters around the world and yet it is he who holds the distinction of being the first ever youth player to appear for the club.

A goalkeeper of some physical presence, who was procured from local outfit Molyneaux F.C. when aged just seventeen years-old, Whittaker debuted for Newton Heath against Grimsby Town in March 1896. Born at nearby Openshaw in 1878, the same year that Newton Heath (Lancashire & Yorkshire Railway) formed, he only managed three first-team starts before his contract was allowed to lapse. Whittaker moved on to a number of other clubs, clocking up an impressive 428 Football League and Southern League appearances, and so it could be claimed that he was one who got away.

Up to that point, Newton Heath had regularly mined for prospects north of the border, plundering the Scottish junior football circles of Annbank, Stenhousemuir and, in particular, Dundee in search of the budding talent that they planned would become the building blocks of a successful team. While this was clearly a strategy of minimising transfer fees and perhaps obtaining the services of a gifted youngster on the cheap, it could hardly be described as a genuine youth policy given that the majority of those who came under consideration were amateurs and held other jobs which paid for their keep.

The real origins of youth football at Manchester United were first evidenced in the Manchester Guardian in 1909, seven years after the club's rebirth and change of name, when the directors discussed putting together a team made up purely of Manchester-born players. Yet little was achieved behind the scenes towards this aim, even though the Reds topped the Central League in the 1912/13 season in only the second year of the division's existence.

Some considerable time later, a second player burst through to the first-team scene when Sidney Tyler was recruited from Stourbridge F.C. in May 1922. A native of Wolverhampton, the seventeen year-old full-back made a solitary appearance against Leicester City in November 1923 before going on to carve out a more notable career in the game with Wolves, Gillingham and Millwall.

In September 1930, yet another seventeen year-old, Tom Manley, joined United from Northwich Victoria and not only made his way into the senior side but notched up an impressive 195 league and cup starts before World War Two intervened to curtail a promising career. To that effect, Manley was a bona fide youth product, by joining the club prior to his 18th birthday and having never previously represented another Football League club. Manley was groomed at Old Trafford and remained to give dedicated service to the Reds, which was a notable exception to the rule of most other competitors who may well have developed juniors and then commonly sold them on.

The early 1930's saw United as by far the poorer of Manchester's two major football clubs and James Gibson was keen to bring about a swing in fortunes. An undoubted visionary, the Reds' chairman had bankrolled the club throughout his tenure, but times were tough in the depression years and so he sought a pioneering strategy for improvement. Reasoning that if United couldn't afford to buy the big names of the day, then perhaps they could cultivate their own through the medium of a structured youth system, and with that aim in mind, the far-sighted Gibson set out to find someone who could turn his dream into a reality.

Some 80 years or so after Gibson began to implement his master plan, no-one knows for sure whether he acted on his own volition or how much some of the other major figures at Old Trafford, such as chief scout Louis Rocca or secretary Walter Crickmer, influenced his thinking. It is known that both Rocca and Crickmer were highly supportive of the venture and it is safe to assume that they would have had a huge input in setting up a system to develop home grown talent. Indeed, one of them might even have thought of the idea before sharing it with their receptive chairman.

Scott Duncan, Manchester United's manager from June 1932 to November 1937

Meanwhile, up in Scotland, Cowdenbeath had won promotion to the Scottish First Division in 1924 and appointed Scott Duncan as secretary/manager. With a team made up predominantly of local youngsters, Duncan won plaudits as Cowdenbeath regularly finished in the top half of the table. So, in 1932, Gibson concluded that here was the man to take his plan forward and offered the former Newcastle United striker the opportunity of replicating his success in Lancashire.

That same year, the Reds entered a side known as Manchester United 'A' in the Manchester League. The 'A' team was the club's third string and, operating at a level below the Reserves, it was often made up of seventeen and eighteen year-olds. With Gibson, Rocca and Crickmer acting as architects of the new enterprise, and Duncan employed as the builder, the foundations of United's youth team were laid. One week before a new campaign commenced, Duncan looked on as the 'Reds and Stripes' battled out a 5-5 draw in a public practice match and in his weekly Manchester Evening Chronicle column he commented:

I have watched the United players closely in their training, and while I do not want to individualise, I consider that we have some young players who are destined for high honours. I have been immensely pleased with them in their practice games, and I have also noticed a great enthusiasm amongst young amateur players who have written to the United asking for trials. By running a team in the Manchester

Long-term employee and talent-spotter Louis Rocca, who was responsible for many youngsters joining United in the 1930's

League we shall be able to give all likely juniors a chance of showing their paces and the United hope to discover from their number more than average finds.

I am convinced that there is, in the Manchester district, many a young international in the making. The United will do all they can to encourage the young player who feels, and shows, that he is likely to develop with training. No junior need have fear that he will not be given a proper chance. I have had too much experience of searching for young players, and what success I have met with in the past I hope to repeat while with Manchester United.

Juniors are, to a certain extent, themselves to blame. They imagine that, because their talents have secured them a transfer from a junior club to a senior side, that they are ready for better football as seen as they step inside their new quarters. They sulk when they are not chosen to fill the place of a man who has been injured; they become discontented and lose heart and interest. If they would appreciate the fact they were being held in reserve to develop their talents, develop their muscles and build up their frame so that in time they could step in and do themselves justice, how different it would be!

To hurry along a youngster is a big mistake, but the junior must be assured that his time will come. I know of several instances of young, promising players who have gone out of the game because they have been put into senior football a year or two before they should have done. That is why today the demand for good footballers exceeds the supply. And that is why I am glad the United have become members of the Manchester League in which they can train their own young players. That is the stepping stone, and it will always be my desire not to put a young footballer into a higher class of football until he is ready for it.

The 'A' team created a little piece of history for the club when facing Ashfield at home on the 22nd August 1932. Ironically, the match was staged at Altrincham's Moss Lane, a ground that would eventually become the home venue of United's Reserves in the 2000's.

Containing names such as Hall in goal, Rawlinson at right-back, Coode at right-half and forwards Littler, Bulger and Howarth, the young Reds led 3-1 at half-time before eventually losing their first ever match 5-4. A couple of weeks later, goals from the likes of Anderson, McFarlane and Hadfield contributed towards a 6-0 win over Stockport County in United's maiden Gilgryst Cup tie.

The players were aged between seventeen and nineteen, and it wasn't long before the likes of Vose, Hall and Coode were promoted into the Reserves. In fact, George Vose went on to become a fans' favourite at Old Trafford when chosen for over 200 first-team games, an early and encouraging indication that the plans could work as envisaged.

Unfortunately, the conveyor belt took a little while to produce a meaningful output because, with United struggling in the Second Division, results were paramount and there were many comings and goings at the club. Duncan was under pressure almost from day one and forays into the transfer market became the main focus in his search for a winning formula. With the Reds living a yo-yo like existence between the top two divisions during the 1930's, Duncan's plans appeared to be built on quicksand rather than solid ground and after winning only five out of the opening fourteen games of the 1937/38 term, he resigned in early November to take up a post at Ipswich.

While his record at first-team level could be described as modest at best, behind the scenes young hopefuls were coming through and the likes of Johnny Carey, Jackie Wassall, Johnny Hanlon and Stan Pearson had all progressed from the 'A' team into the senior eleven. It is interesting to ponder what might have happened if Duncan had remained at Old Trafford a little while longer, particularly as the first-team managed to turn things around and win promotion back to the top division at the end of that campaign.

Five months prior to Duncan's departure, on the 1st June 1937 to be precise, a board meeting took place in which it was decided *'to give special attention to the coaching of youth players'*, while in February 1938 reference was made *'to the formation of a junior athletic club for cultivating young players after they leave school'*.

The following month, it was announced by Tom Jackson, the Manchester Evening News' reporter who penned a column in United's official programme, that the MUJACs were about to come into being. Jackson wrote that a *'schoolboy football scheme which the club have formed in co-operation with local educational authorities will be known as the Manchester United Junior Athletic Club'* and he went on to reveal that *'the club will be co-operating with teachers in providing coaching and training facilities for boys when they leave school'*.

One of the schoolmasters involved was a United supporter by the name of John Bill. Writing a serial entitled *'The Story of United as Never Told Before,'* which was published in a Supporters' Club Newsletter in the late 1960's, Mr. Bill reminisced:

The year after the commission of enquiry, I had a request from Mr. Crickmer to meet him to discuss the subject of youth football. With the help of a committee of fifteen schoolmasters and other people interested in schoolboy and junior football.........he proposed to cover the whole of the area in seeking potential young players.

Having obtained the most promising boys it was intended to run them in local leagues, and by coaching and training with the co-operation of Mr. Tom Curry, Jim McClelland and other members of the United staff to improve their football with an eye on the future.

All club facilities were placed at our disposal and by the start of the 1938/39 season we had weeded out our players to produce two teams.

There was, though, the problematic issue of suitable training facilities. In his 1960 book, *'The History of a Great Football Club,'* author Percy M. Young recorded, *'On 3rd May (1938), the chairman emphasised the necessity for a pitch for practice games and for the 'A' team, and stated that he had been making enquiries about a tenancy of the old Broughton Rangers rugby ground. By 21st June this tenancy was secured'*. In between the dates mentioned, at United's AGM held on the 17th June, Gibson mentioned that *'the education authorities were a committee of teachers and instructors from the University of Manchester'*.

Wasting no time in making full use of their new facility, which was known as The Cliff, trials and training sessions took place there throughout that August in preparation for the forthcoming season. One of those who undertook assessments was none other than future United stalwart John Aston. Thus the MUJACs, Manchester United's first ever true 'youth teams' were formed and henceforth provided the bedrock for the club's junior development for the next 70-odd years.

The very first day of the MUJAC trials in August 1938 included future full England international Johnny Aston (eighth from the right) and trainer Arthur Powell (far right)

3

The Manchester Evening Chronicle's Alf Clarke perfectly summed up the feelings of those who had worked behind the scenes to bring the new venture to fruition in his United Review column dated 3rd September 1938:

History was created in Manchester United football circles today. This afternoon there are no fewer than five United teams on duty. They are the senior side, Central League eleven, 'A' team, MUJAC first-team and MUJAC second eleven. Never before have the United had so many sides representing them. I need scarcely add that MUJAC stands for Manchester United Junior Athletic Club, and represents the schoolboy players who are now in training at Old Trafford and from whom it is hoped will spring a Manchester United senior team of the future – and all local boys.

No club in the country is better served with junior players than Manchester United, and it is very pleasing to record that many teachers in the Manchester, Salford and Stretford areas, who are sponsoring the scheme, give many hours of their leisure time looking after the welfare of the junior players.

Chairman Gibson was keen to stress that the club didn't have prior claim on any of the youngsters by saying, *'We only tell them we hope that if as a result of what the club has done they rise to anything like fame, they will bear the club in mind......'*

The MUJAC firsts operated in the Chorlton Amateur League and opened their campaign with a 7-0 victory at Manchester Zion. Later coming up against the likes of St. Cuthbert's, Hockney Social and McPherson's, they won their first 26 games, scoring over 180 goals and conceding only 24 in the process, before losing 4-1 to Range Rovers in March 1939.

However, it wasn't only the kids who were hitting the headlines because the Reds' Central League side won the title for the first time since 1921, making it a double when collecting the Manchester Senior Cup, and there was even more to crow about when the 'A' team topped the Manchester Amateur League and reached the final of the Gilgryst Cup. With such an impressive infrastructure in place, talented boys such as Sammy Lynn, Johnny Hanlon and others felt the benefit of moving from one successful side up to the next while developing their skills and knowledge on their way to eventually becoming first-team regulars.

Additionally, those in the Reds' scouting network supplemented the quest for local prospects by making forays out of the area to sign talents such as Allenby Chilton from Seaham Colliery in the North-East and Charlie Mitten from Scottish junior club Strathallan Hawthorn. Thus, the youth system United supporters recognise today was fully operational in 1938 and the effect on the club's fortunes was almost immediate. The first-team consolidated their place in the top flight, finishing in 14th position, and the future appeared infinitely rosier than it had for a long time.

Then, with that season's divisional commitments drawing to a close, the MUJACs were tasked with facing a completely different class of opposition, as John Bill later recalled when writing:

The United organised friendly matches against other League club's junior teams, a pioneering practice at the time, with the young United side pitting themselves against Everton Boys and Preston Boys as 'special attractions'.

Laid out beneath a banner headed 'MUJACs YOUNG TEAM OF SCORING STARS', an Alf Clarke article appeared in the Manchester Evening Chronicle on Saturday, 15th April 1939 in order to spotlight the opener:

Meanwhile, I want to draw your attention to the match at Old Trafford on Monday evening (kick-off 6.30) between the MUJAC eleven versus Everton 'A'.

The Manchester United Junior Athletic Club came into formation this season and they have been a big success. They are virtually champions of the Chorlton Amateur League, having lost only one league game. So a challenge was thrown out by Everton 'A' to play the MUJAC in home and away games. The challenge was accepted and Monday's game is the first of the two.

Everton 'A' have not lost a match in the league in which they play. But whereas Everton compete in an average-age league, the MUJAC figure in an open-age competition.

It may seem invidious to make distinctions in this grand MUJAC team, which has scored 223 goals this season, but as goalscoring seems to be a lost art by the United senior team forwards I want to draw attention to the three inside-forwards of the MUJAC who have been doing all the damage. There is Aston, inside-right, who possesses fine ball control and can work in a very small space. He is also clever with his head. He was a member of the Ravensbury Street school team, and also played for the city boys. His goals total 47.

Centre-forward is White, who used to play centre half-back. He has scored 60 goals, while Mears, inside-left, who three seasons ago formed a brilliant city boys' left wing triangle with Healy and Brennan, is the possessor of a brilliant left-foot shot. His goals number 44.

It will be seen that these three young players have, between them, scored 151 goals this season. I am hoping that some day we shall see these three local lads figuring in Manchester United's senior team.

I am informed that they are just seventeen years of age, though whether they will become professional footballers is another matter.

No boy, unless he desires, will be asked to sign professional forms. In fact, the Manchester United club have no control whatever over the boys, who are under the jurisdiction of local schoolteachers. The boys are allowed facilities to do their training at the United ground on two evenings a week. United's attitude is simply to foster a 'keep fit' campaign among boys in the years following their schooldays. The MUJAC now covers a long-felt want.

A report of the clash was given in the Liverpool Daily Post:

EVERTON "B" SIDE'S FIRST DEFEAT

MANCHESTER JUNIORS PREVAIL

BY STORK

Everton B team, which had gone throughout the season without a defeat, met a reverse at Old Trafford, Manchester, last night, when they were beaten 3-0 by the Mujacs, which is equivalent to the B team of Manchester United. But although defeated they were far from disgraced, for they upheld the traditions of the Everton club by their high-class football. By comparison, the Mujacs were more forceful. They were older boys in fact, yet I would not say that their football was quite so neat as that of the Everton lads. To some extent the game was spoiled by a high wind which the Everton team had to face in the first half, and I feel that this took so much out of them that they were somewhat tired in the second session.

White, the Mujacs centre forward, scored two goals in the first half when they were on top. But Everton returned the compliment in the second half, and had they finished with any sort of accuracy they would at least have shared the honour. The three inside men had ample opportunities, but their marksmanship was all wrong. They either lifted the ball over the bar or outside the upright. Nevertheless Everton had given a good account of themselves, but towards the end the Manchester lads obtained a third goal in rather an uncommon way. Bearwood, in making a clearance shot the ball on to Atkins and it rebounded into the goal. Everton's best players were goalkeeper Canavan, Dugdale, Bailey, and Atkins. Much was expected of Dean, but he was rather a disappointment, while Simmons was too easily brushed aside to be effective.

Lyon produced some good football and so, for that matter, did several of the Manchester lads. It was a most interesting game and was thoroughly enjoyed by the 1,400 people.

The Reds' line-up that night was: Higgins, Curless, Haslam, Cookson, Howcroft, Healy, Lockwood, Aston, White, Mears and Brennan.

Expectations surrounding the return at Goodison Park nine days later were captured in an official Everton programme with the following lines:

This game has been looked forward to with a great deal of interest, and our boys have a score to wipe out, for last Monday we met with the first reverse of the season, when at Old Trafford we lost by three goals to nothing. Those fortunate enough to be present at Manchester were treated to an exhibition by these youthful prodigies, and tonight's game should be no exception. Our lads play in the true traditional Everton style, and will be all out to show us that the result at Manchester was all wrong.

Both teams have schoolboy internationals, barring accidents there are a number that, in the space of two or three years, will be wearing the first-team jerseys of their clubs.

With the writer of that piece gaining his wish about the score in Manchester being proved *all wrong*, Everton triumphing by a 5-3 margin, his prediction about future senior stars proved prophetic when the MUJAC's number eight ended up as a fixture in United's senior side. Additionally, George Curless had made it to the brink of the Reserves and was being touted as the best full-back on the club's books with a fine career ahead of him, while left full-back Harry Haslam progressed to become a professional footballer prior to making a name for himself as Luton Town's manager in the 1970's.

LAST OF THE MUJACs

An interview with Jack 'Crasher' White

WHITE, John Stanley

Born: Trafford Park, Manchester, 16th September 1921
Role: Centre-half or centre-forward
Career: **Trafford Park Council School/ Stretford Boys/ Manchester United Junior Athletic Club** August 1938/ **Manchester United** August and September 1939

On any given Saturday morning in the football season at the Carrington Training Centre, there are numerous young hopefuls going through their drills, facing each other in small-sided contests, playing practice matches or turning out for one of the Academy sides. Each has his own complete kit, training bag, all-weather coat and two pairs of boots which, of course, are all paid for by the club. By the time they reach under-16 level, the boys will invariably have had media attention, as well as sponsorship deals, personal teaching programmes at a local school, agents and, in some cases, the promise of a professional contract.

When the teenage Jack White was first approached to join the Manchester United Junior Athletic Club in 1938, the world was a vastly different place. In February 2012, the 90 year-old answered a few questions about how he became a junior at the club and what it was like to play for the MUJACs in their first ever groundbreaking season.

When did you first get involved in football?
I was about eight years-old when I started playing for my school. We played all the schools in the local Stretford and Gorse Hill areas. It wasn't a league as such, we took part in friendly games organised by our teacher, a Mr. Luby, who was also the sports master. When I was about twelve I turned out for the local church team, St. Cuthbert's.
A couple of years later Harry Wardle and a teacher called Marsden looked after the Stretford area and they took a liking to me. They pushed me along and then picked me for the Stretford Boys team.

Who were your football idols as a young boy?
We couldn't afford newspapers in those days as my father had six kids to support, so I knew nothing about other teams. We lived in Trafford Park, which is just down the road from Old Trafford, and I remember Tom Manley, Billy Bryant, George Roughton and Bill McKay. The players in that team were my idols as I was a keen United fan, but they were awful and nearly got relegated to the Third Division a few years earlier.
I was all United, not even City drew my interest because Old Trafford was on my doorstep. I basically lived on top of the ground. There weren't many supporters going to the games in those days, and it was only a few coppers to get in, but more often than not I would get into the ground for free when they opened the gates at half-time.

How did you first hear about the MUJACs?
It was through the teachers who ran Stretford Boys. Harry Wardle was a headmaster at one of the schools and married the daughter of our next door neighbour. He knew I was a good player from the Stretford Boys team.
There were quite a few teachers involved from all over Manchester, and they explained that they were putting a junior team together and picking the best local footballers to play in a league.

How did you actually make the team?
We all went for trials and then they selected lads to come back. Myself and John Phoenix both played for Stretford Boys and we kept getting picked to play, John at full-back and me at centre-half, although I also played centre-forward as well. They narrowed it down to about twenty boys and we were all more or less the same age, sixteen years-old.
They organised proper games during the trials. Mr. McClelland, who was an ex-United player, and Arthur Powell were based at the Warwick Road stadium and they were always around. I knew I had a chance because they kept picking me.

Where did you train?
We went down to The Cliff once a week for training, but we had no money so the club paid for our bus fares. The home games were played at The Cliff on Saturday afternoons and it was a right trek to get there in those days. All the away games were in the Chorlton district so we didn't have to go too far.
We played in an open-age league and we found ourselves up against some good footballers who were much older lads. We got kicked to death in some matches, but as the results showed we held our own and won the Chorlton & District Amateur League in the 1938/39 season.

What was it like playing for the MUJACs?
I was thrilled to bits about playing for Manchester United. I thought I was the 'bees knees' and looked forward to every game. A little later when they moved me upfront I used to score six or seven goals in a game and when I got home and told people they would often rib me by asking, 'Who were you playing today? Henshaws?' (A local school for the visually impaired).

Why were you moved from centre-half to centre-forward?
Early in the season, I don't know how it happened, but they signed Harry Howcroft, who was from Wigan. I was one of the tallest in the team so the teachers wanted me to play centre-forward. The team was so good it was quite easy to score either with my head or simple tap-ins.
Mickey Mears and Johnny Aston were very good inside-forwards and we really played some wonderful football, no wonder we scored fourteen or fifteen goals regularly. John Healey was our left-half and captain, he was a very encouraging player. Funnily enough, parents were very rarely seen at any of the games. I suppose they were working or looking after their children.
The exception was Harry Haslam's mother and father, who came to every single match, and it stood out. In the end I scored over 80 goals in that (1938/39) season and earned the nickname 'Crasher'. I can't remember why, though.

What do you remember about the challenge matches against Everton and Preston North End at the end of the season?
We really looked forward to the Everton games because we didn't even know that they had a junior team. Everton was a big game, and it was my first match at Old Trafford. I was a little nervous and worked up a bit as all my mates from school came along as well as my brother Roy.
I'd been to Old Trafford before to get treatment, and that's when I met Tom Curry and Bert Whalley for the first time. I scored two that night and should have scored a hat-trick, but my shot went off a defender. It was a good hard fought game but I really enjoyed it.
Then we went to Goodison and I think Everton put a couple of older lads in from their 'A' team because they didn't want to lose the home game. Charlie Mitten came on as a substitute for us in the second half and scored a great goal after I fluffed my shot. The ball came in from the right wing and I mis-kicked it, and before I knew it the ball was in the back of the net. Charlie was tremendous, but Mickey Mears was streets ahead of everyone, he was some player. I recall we lost the first game at Preston 2-1, but I don't remember the return at Old Trafford at all.

What happened at the end of the season?
They got us back to Old Trafford and took a photo of the team and all the trophies. Not long after, the war broke out and when Old Trafford was bombed all the trophies were destroyed.

Were you invited back for the following season?
Yes, I went back for pre-season and played a couple of times for the 'A' team until war was declared in early September and they cancelled all the games. I was an apprentice engineer with my father at F. Hills & Sons in Trafford Park and as there was no more organised football I just continued my apprenticeship until I got called up.

So then what happened?
Well, when I was a little older I started playing again for St. Cuthbert's and I finally got called up in 1942. As I was an engineer I was put in the Navy and did my training at Gosport and Portsmouth. I often saw players down in Portsmouth, but I didn't turn out myself.
I saw active service as a mine sweeper in the North Sea and in the English Channel. I was also at the forefront of the Normandy D-Day invasion, clearing mines ready for the landing.

What sort of football did you play once you returned from active service?
I turned out again for St. Cuthbert's and a couple of local teams well into my mid-30's. I had a family to support, though, so I packed it in and then when I retired I moved to Poulton-le-Fylde with my wife.

What are your fondest memories of your time at Manchester United?
Just playing some great football with some very good players. I have often wondered what happened to everyone. I know Harry Haslam managed Luton and Sheffield United and, of course, Johnny Aston had a great career with United. As for all the other players, if it wasn't for the war we could have made it in the game.

Pictured at an unkempt Old Trafford, the MUJACs won the Rusholme League Amateur Cup in 1944. Arthur Powell and Walter Crickmer are seen on the far right

The following term, 1939/40, saw Johnny Morris join the Reds from a Radcliffe outfit called St. John's and Joe Walton arrived from Queen's Street School in the Manchester suburb of Bradford. Unfortunately, both future first-teamers would have their time as juniors cut short by the events in Europe.

John Bill continued the story:

After one season we were convinced that the United Junior scheme was going to be a success. So we were all set for the second season when the blow fell – war was declared only a few weeks after training for 1939/40 had begun. The actual match programme had just opened. Of course, coming at such a time, World War Two dealt a shattering blow to all English clubs. Nevertheless, bearing in mind the circumstances, it certainly appeared that fate had treated Manchester United particularly unkindly.

If we review the position as it was in September 1939, we can easily see the optimism and confidence at Old Trafford.

The first-team, on its return to the First Division and having one of the youngest teams in the league, had obtained a very respectable position in the table. The Reserve team had won the championship of the Central League. The 'A' team with a team of seventeen year-olds had won the championship of the Manchester League. The MUJAC first-team had won their championship and the second eleven had carried all before them in their games.

To see his hopes dashed to the ground when their fulfilment seemed a matter of only a season or two away must have been a galling blow to Mr. Gibson, and all connected with United were intensely disappointed at the new turn of events.

Apart from compulsory loaning out their Broughton headquarters for at least part of the period when hostilities were taking place, one of the main problems encountered was that no less than eleven of the fifteen-man committee were called up for the national effort, while three of those remaining felt that they were unable to give their full commitment while war raged. As secretary Walter Crickmer was loathe to abandon the venture, the age limit of the MUJACs was dropped to fifteen, and, with John Bill installed as their secretary/manager, they continued by taking part in friendly fixtures.

That was until part-way into the season, when the secretary of the South Manchester & Wythenshawe League suggested to Bill that his team could fill out the remainder of the campaign with some competitive matches under their divisional umbrella. Upon Bill's acceptance, the MUJACs remained in that sphere until the war was over. The MUJACs also won the Rusholme League Amateur Cup and Wythenshawe League Junior Cup in the 1943/44 term, a time when they were commonly known as the 'Colts', which was then an unofficial moniker.

When Matt Busby was appointed manager of Manchester United in February 1945, he was faced with what many saw as an uphill task of rebuilding the club. Old Trafford had been severely damaged by bombs in the conflict and Busby found himself with no fit ground, hardly any money and yet was still saddled with high expectations. However, what he did inherit was fundamentally his first Manchester United youth team.

Busby could also call on a number of outstanding professionals, such as Carey, Chilton, Rowley and Pearson, all of whom had worked their way through the system to feature in the first-team before the war, and the manager was additionally aware that United possessed a band of exciting juniors who had represented the 'A' team and MUJACs in some capacity or other. Lads such as John Aston, John Anderson, Sammy Lynn, Joe Walton, Charlie Mitten and Johnny Morris were keen for action while others such as Jack Crompton and Henry Cockburn were attached to a side called Goslings, one of United's 'nursery' clubs.

With The Cliff previously requisitioned by the military authorities as a balloon site, by season 1946/47 normal football was back up and running. United's third eleven resumed in the Manchester League under the guidance of Harry Ablett, who had looked after the 'A' team before the war and remained with the club until the early 1970's. The newly-named Colts became the fourth team, finding success in that campaign's John Buckle Cup while operating in the Second Division of the Eccles & District Amateur League, and the MUJACs transformed into the Juniors.

By the end of that season, Jimmy Murphy had steered United's Reserves to the summit of the Central League, and after being congratulated by Busby on the achievement he commented that while the recognition was appreciated, it was his opinion that not one of the second string squad had what it took to graduate into the first-team.

Busby outlined United's *'structure and system'* in an October 1947 home match programme by mentioning that *'our system is as follows: MUJACs are outstanding boys fifteen to sixteen and a half years-old; Colts are sixteen and a half to eighteen years-old; 'A' team are eighteen to 21 years-old and then of course the Central League and League teams'.*

The MUJACs were then reformed under the auspices of Mr. M. Williams and won their first match 11-2 on 15th November 1947. Joining the Colts in the Eccles & District Amateur League, the MUJACs operated in a lower division than their club colleagues. Clearly some juniors would eventually buck the system in a big way, throwing Busby's age profiling out of the window by making it into the senior eleven as young as sixteen and seventeen.

At the start of the 1948/49 term the system changed slightly, with two MUJAC sides in operation. The MUJAC 'A' team, for boys aged between sixteen and a half and seventeen and a half, continued in the Eccles & District Amateur League while the MUJAC 'B' side took a place in the Levenshulme & District League. The lads in this group, aged between fifteen and half and sixteen and a half, faced Longsight's Crowcroft Villa in the Second Division League Cup final at Old Trafford on 2nd May 1949.

During the 1949 close season, Jimmy Murphy held a MUJAC 'Summer School', with participants including Bill Foulkes, Eddie Lewis, Mark Jones and other exceptional talents.

The Colts staged their matches at The Cliff in the 1949/50 season and the team was placed in the capable hands of secretary Jack Pauline, a dedicated individual who served and supported the junior sides with credit for many years. They were members of the Eccles & District Amateur League's First Division, while the MUJACs played their games almost next door to Old Trafford, at Gorse Hill School, in the Fifth Division of the same league.

Unfortunately, the summer sun of 1950 was temporarily blocked with a dark cloud when the news that Louis Rocca, the one-time supporter, tea-boy, talent scout, assistant manager and lead negotiator in obtaining Matt Busby's signature as manager, had passed away. Rocca was instrumental in bringing James Gibson to the club, assisted in co-managing the senior team before the arrival of Scott Duncan and discovered those of the quality of Johnny Carey and Stan Pearson amongst many others. Rocca was a key figure who ploughed the soil, planted the seeds, watered the tiny sapling that would eventually grow into the giant oak known as the Manchester United youth system, and his contribution to all the glories of the future was simply immense.

The following campaign saw the 'A' team win the Manchester League, with the likes of Dennis Viollet, Bill Foulkes, Les Olive, Frank Mooney, Geoff Bent and Jackie Blanchflower all prominent, while the first-team saw the introduction of juniors such as Cliff Birkett, Frank Clempson, Brian Birch and Jeff Whitefoot.

Since Busby had taken over at Old Trafford, crowds up and down the country had thronged to watch the Reds' buccaneering exploits. Eight players came through the ranks to feature in the 1948 F.A. Cup final and Busby's men also finished second in the First Division on four occasions. While there were additions to the team by way of those who cost fees in the shape of Reg Allen, Johnny Downie and Johnny Berry, United finally captured the league title in 1952 with mostly home grown talent, the likes of Roger Byrne, Don Gibson, Tom McNulty and Billy Redman progressing from the 'A' team to achieve what James Gibson had dreamt of twenty years earlier. Sadly, Gibson had passed away the previous September and never saw the house he so lovingly constructed and furnished finally throw open its doors to the First Division champions.

By 1952, United's youth system was in full swing and the Reds were the first club to look at Ireland as a source of young talent when fetching Tom Ritchie, Jackie Mooney, Johnny Scott, Paddy Kennedy, Noel McFarlane and Blanchflower across the water. Additionally, head scout Joe Armstrong was already targeting talented teenagers around the country who were impressing in county and international schoolboy games. Not only were United capturing the best of the bunch at local level, they were now attracting the finest prospects from places such as Yorkshire, the Midlands and the North-East. These were young lads, often only fifteen years-old, who it was planned would be developed in 'the United way'.

Matt Busby and sidekick Jimmy Murphy plan United's youth future

Jimmy Murphy's 1949 summer camp was an innovative scheme designed to attract young soccer talent from across the country

The Juniors in action at The Cliff in January 1951, one of the first ever football matches staged under floodlights in the North-West

At the commencement of the 1952/53 campaign, the MUJACs joined the Altrincham & District Junior League and became known simply as the Juniors. Thus, the hierarchy of the club's sides in descending order was now the seniors, Reserves, the 'A' team, the Colts, whose main commitments were in the First Division of the Manchester Amateur League, and, finally, the Juniors.

1952/53 was also the term that saw the introduction of the F.A. Youth Cup and both Murphy, Busby and their various capable helpers were keen to show off the shining young talent United possessed in their ranks. In the traditional curtain raiser to the season, Murphy took the opportunity to look at the likely prospects for Youth Cup duty in the annual 'Reds v. Blues' clash on the 16th August 1952, the line-ups reading as follows:

Reds: Clayton, Fulton, Bent, Whitehurst, Cope, Edwards, Morton, McFarlane, Hamilton, Bradshaw and Pegg.

Blues: O'Gorman, Kennedy, Rhodes, Evans, Taylor, Barrett, Birkett, Chapman, Lewis, Doherty and Scanlon.

A week later, the United Review made the following comments:

Once again a new season opens and all our junior teams are looking forward to a successful year. Last Saturday's public practice showed that there is a wealth of talent among the youngsters and many of them seem destined to make the first-team grade when they have the necessary experience. The match was played on a pitch that has never looked better, and under perfect weather conditions, and although the Reds won 5-0 there was not such a big margin between the teams. They played some really great football and fully deserved the applause and comments of appreciation from the spectators. Coaches Jimmy Murphy and Bert Whalley were very proud men after the game.

From the start both teams played fast moving football, keeping the ball on the ground and showing grand understanding between half-backs and inside-forwards. The Reds took the lead when Bradshaw scored with a good shot, and added to this before half-time through McFarlane. Two changes by the Blues at half-time brought in Colman at right half-back and Lowrie at inside-right, but it was the Reds who scored, when Bradshaw got the ball into the net following a scramble in the goalmouth. The same player added the fourth goal and completed his hat-trick when he hit the ball first time into the net following a brilliant run on the left wing by Pegg. McFarlane completed the scoring when he made no mistake with a penalty awarded for hands. The Blues were not outclassed, they combined well in midfield, but were up against a defence in which the half-back line proved too strong for them.

The match was significant in the respect that it was the first time Duncan Edwards pulled on a red shirt. The powerhouse half-back would go on to greater glory, not only for United but also on the international scene, yet for now he was just one of a number of talents who needed to compete for a place in one of the lesser teams. Each new term, the backroom staff identified and vetted scores of talented schoolboys who had the potential to become a Manchester United footballer, and Edwards wasn't the only arrival in the summer of 1952 of whom high expectations were held.

Tom Jackson, who took a close interest into the goings-on of the youngsters, articulated his views on the matter in the Evening News thus:

Yes, the search for young blood, plus all the essential facilities for coaching and training, is now a number one 'must' on the agendas of league clubs big and small. Small wonder, then, that the competition for schoolboy talent is as keen, if not keener, than for ready-made stars. Here at Old Trafford, however, this 'find 'em young' policy is not one newly-launched just to be in the fashion. Remember, the first seeds were planted with the formation of the MUJACs before the war, and since then it has developed to such a high degree that it is an integral part of United's long-term planning.

Matt Busby along with coaches Jimmy Murphy and Bert Whalley, and those unsung heroes, the club scouts, have roamed far and wide in building up United's playing resources for the new season. Their successes can be gauged by the fact that among the players on call for 1952/53 are some of the best youngsters in Britain – many of them fresh from the schoolboy international scene. There are many new names on United's list of 'promising juniors'. They include schools' internationals Gordon Clayton, a six-foot goalkeeper from Cannock; Duncan Edwards, left-half and captain of England Boys last season, from Dudley; Alan Morton, right winger from Tyneside; and Alan Rhodes, wing-half, from Chesterfield.

Colin Webster, a Welsh boy who has scored a lot of goals at centre-forward with RAF teams; youth international Walter Whitehurst, left-half, from Ryder Brow, Reddish; and Brian Lowry, inside-forward of Manchester Boys, are other newcomers whose names should be heard a-plenty in the near future.

In early October 1952, a spell when the seniors were floundering in the lower reaches of the First Division, Alf Clarke gave some interesting wider context in his United Review programme notes:

Perhaps the most interesting news recently in the affairs of the United club emerged from the annual meeting of the shareholders last week. For it was at this usual pleasant function that United director, Mr. W. Petherbridge, told the meeting the United, for the first time in their history had no mortgage on the ground.

The mortgage used to run into the thousands of pounds. And that is not many years ago. But the success of the club has coincided with the ability to repay the mortgage. Mr. Petherbridge also told the shareholders that he considered the purchase of The Cliff ground, at Lower Broughton, a grand stroke of business by the club. 'We now have adequate facilities for the training of our young players by evening as well as by day,' he said.

Matt Busby, too, gave us food for thought in his remarks to the shareholders. After paying tribute to the players for winning the league championship, especially after four years of disappointment as runners-up, he said, in his opinion, the young players on the United books were worth hundreds of thousands of pounds.

'In a couple of years time we shall have wonderful young material when it is needed most,' he said.

I suppose we can call this season a transitional period. Every club has its ups and downs. You cannot go on winning all the time. The time comes when the stars of yesterday make a gradual fade-out. But the club which comes back soonest to further honours is that which gradually brings up the young players ready to step into the league side.

This is a United policy. It is not the exclusive privilege of the Old Trafford club, of course. All clubs are concentrating on the younger element, but I do think that United have as many outstanding junior players as any other club in the country.

Busby had made a contentious statement because most of the younger element were untested at senior level and the competition in local soccer circles wasn't always a true gauge of the best ability. Coming up against the amateurs of Ball Haye Green, the junior teams of Bury and Stockport County, or the work sides of those such as Taylor Brothers, could only take the development of the starlets so far, so perhaps the new F.A. Youth Cup tournament would provide a more suitable test and prove the sceptics wrong.

In contrast with the first-team, the Juniors were undefeated in the Altrincham League, having already amassed more than sixty goals, the Colts led the way without loss in the Manchester Amateur League and the 'A' team were riding high in the Manchester League, as well as making progress in the Gilgryst Cup. The team that faced Leeds United at Old Trafford in October 1952 in the new national competition would turn out to be a composite of the two sides who had faced each other in the trial game back in August.

Jimmy Murphy's selection decisions were constrained by the competition's rules, which demanded that those competing needed to be under the age of eighteen on the 1st September at the beginning of a season. It meant that talented lads such as Mark Jones, Dennis Viollet, Freddie Goodwin and Jackie Blanchflower were already overage, and those who were slightly older still, such as Bill Foulkes, Brian Birch, Geoff Bent and Ian Greaves, would by then have been focusing their efforts on gaining as much first-team experience as they could.

It was far harder luck on Jeff Whitefoot, Cliff Birkett, Johnny Scott, Tommy Barrett and Ray Hampson, as they were only eighteen and featuring regularly in the 'A' team. Colin Webster and Walter Whitehurst probably felt the most disappointment because both of them missed out on eligibility by only a couple of months. Whereas Webster was a recent recruit, Whitehurst had been on the club's books for two seasons and he frequently figured alongside many of the lads who were in contention for places.

Optimism was undoubtedly high within the club that the under-18's were capable of making a name for themselves, though none could have imagined just how the F.A. Youth Cup would capture the attention of soccer fans across the country and revolutionise junior football, not only in England but also across the globe. What started as the dream of three men during the early 1930's became a reality in 1938, formed the basis of Matt Busby's triumphs in the late 1940's and early 1950's and now, in 1952, had developed into a fully operational production line of teenage talent.

It was the beginning of a practice that would be replicated in almost every country and, whereas some notable names within the sport went on to make great progress with their youth systems and policies over the years and decades, few have managed to integrate the ethos into the culture and fabric of their organisation to such an extent, and with so much success, as Manchester United.

The victorious 'Reds' prior to their clash with the 'Blues' in August 1952
Back row (l-r) Noel McFarlane, Bryce Fulton, Tommy Hamilton, Gordon Clayton, Duncan Edwards, Walter Whitehurst
Front row (l-r) Geoff Bent, Alan Morton, Ronnie Cope, Alan Bradshaw, David Pegg

A Butterworth cartoon from a United Review in September 1952 puts a comic slant on the increasing emphasis on youth prospects within the club

INTRODUCTION
The F.A. Youth Cup

The F.A. Youth Cup, or the Football Association Youth Challenge Cup Competition to coin its full title, came into existence in 1952. The Football Association's objective in establishing the competition was to provide a platform for young players to participate in a knock-out tournament that would help bridge a gap which they perceived existed between junior and adult football. As such it was hoped that it would attract substantial national as well as local interest.

The F.A. Youth Cup had a forerunner. The F.A. County Youth Challenge Cup Competition (County Youth Cup) was introduced towards the end of the Second World War and has been contested every year since.

The first winners of the County Youth Cup were Staffordshire, who narrowly defeated Wiltshire in the 1945 final on an aggregate of three goals to two. Even though the tournament provides an excellent forum for young footballers who have the honour to represent their respective counties, it does not have the same attraction as the F.A. Youth Cup.

This gulf in popularity is easily explained. The F.A. Youth Cup is, in the main, contested for amongst professional and non-league clubs that have established fan bases. The teams that make up the F.A. County Youth Cup do not enjoy the same benefit and, whereas the average fan who lives in, say, Southampton may take an interest if the Saints youth side were enjoying a decent run in the F.A. Youth Cup, it would be a lot less likely that he or she would have quite as much enthusiasm if Hampshire had made it as far as the later stages of the County Youth Cup. Also, because of the involvement of Premier League, Football League and sundry non-league clubs, the F.A. Youth Cup attracts far more media coverage than its County equivalent could ever hope for. In fact, so little publicity surrounds the County Youth Cup nowadays that our fan in Southampton probably wouldn't even be aware of Hampshire's progress, or lack of same, at any given time.

The finals of the County Youth Cup were played on a two-legged basis from 1945 to 1969 when they reverted to a single game. While home and away ties have become much more commonplace in more recent times, they were a fairly unusual feature in the 1940's.

One point worthy of mention regarding the County Youth Cup is that in the season prior to the commencement of the F.A. Youth Cup, 1951/52, all bar two games in the competition made a financial loss. It was then proposed at F.A. headquarters that from then on counties would still be invited to enter the County Youth Cup, but without a guarantee of their losses which, it can be assumed, had been the case previously.

So, while the County Youth Cup was already well established by the time of its introduction, and a whole number of regional Youth Cup competitions have sprung up subsequently, the F.A. Youth Cup has, since 1952, been the major standard-bearer for youth knock-out football in England and Wales.

The 1998/99 term saw the introduction of the F.A. Premier Academy League (FAPAL) and, while considered by some as another step forward in the development of youth football within these shores, it is played on a (mainly) regional league basis with play-offs for the leading clubs at the end of the season. Manchester United entered into two FAPALs initially, at under-17 and under-19 levels, with the two divisions replaced by a single under-18 league in 2004.

Being a national competition, the F.A. Youth Cup has a much broader base than the Academy League or its lower level equivalents and boasts a history that now stretches back seven decades, with most of the major clubs having captured it at some stage. It is, therefore, acknowledged as an extremely prestigious tournament to win and its overall contribution to the national game over the years would be impossible to measure.

In much the same way that the F.A. Challenge Cup is known simply as 'the Cup', due to its standing as the premier senior national knock-out competition, the F.A. Youth Cup is universally referred to as the 'the Youth Cup', and, henceforth, that is how it will frequently be referred to in this publication.

The finer details regarding exactly how the Youth Cup got off the ground are hard to pinpoint, although when the hard facts are mixed in with a sprinkling of probability most of the required pieces of the jigsaw fall into place. What is known with absolute certainty is that the concept was pioneered from the outset by a man of some considerable vision and influence, Joe Richards.

Born in the same year that the Football League was formed, 1888, he was the son of the Barnsley Main Colliery pit manager. Studying mining and commerce at Barnsley Technical College, as a youth he suffered the misfortune of having a leg crushed in a pit accident. He spent seven months in hospital and his injuries were such that they brought his days as a promising footballer to a premature end. Despite being required to call a halt to his playing activities, Richards retained his love of football and became a tireless worker for the good of the sport.

A lifelong practicing Christian, by 1919 he had been elected as a director of Barnsley Football Club and ten years later he joined Barnsley Town Council as an independent councillor. Simultaneously a freemason and a magistrate, he also served as a governor of Barnsley Grammar School, was chairman of the local juvenile court and sat on the probation committee for 22 years. Besides all of his conscientious efforts for the local community, he was also known to have interests in many other businesses. Becoming a director of Barnsley Main Colliery in 1933, by the following year he had begun a two-year tenure as chairman of Barnsley Football Club. Undoubtedly, Joe Richards was a pillar of society in the south Yorkshire pit town.

In 1948, he began a second term of office as Barnsley Football Club's chairman, on this occasion his stewardship lasting right through until 1966. Also elected to the Football League Management Committee in 1948, within twelve months he had formed the Northern Intermediate Football League (NIFL). It was a significant development in that part of the country as the NIFL was introduced specifically for fifteen to eighteen year-old players and was, until 1998 when the F.A. Premier Academy and Football League Alliances became fully operational, the junior league for professional clubs in and around Yorkshire and the North-East. It is hard to imagine just what those particular clubs would have done to attract and develop young talent in the intervening years without his foresight.

He was installed as the treasurer and president of the NIFL on its formation and was also the president of the Midland League for a quarter of a century. Richards held a similar position upon the formation of the North Midlands League whereupon he was elevated to the presidency of the Football League in 1957 after serving as vice-president for two years. It was a richly deserved honour and he was the first ever Yorkshireman to hold the post.

His first proposal as Football League president was to call for the formation of the Third and Fourth Divisions as they would come to exist for many years. Previously there were regional Third Divisions of North and South. The thinking behind creating the new format was to stimulate greater interest in the lower divisions and spread the wealth around, as it was always acknowledged that the southern section of the Third Division was much more prosperous than its northern counterpart due to larger attendances. His suggestions were not welcomed by all interested parties, yet by 1958 the new divisions were in place. Later a major influence in relation to the introduction of the Football League Cup in 1960, his support of the new venture certainly held great sway and it has survived under various sponsorship deals to this day.

He also served a four-year term of office as chairman of the England Under-23 committee and spent an identical duration as chairman of the England 'B' selection committee. Knighted for his services to football in June 1966, two months later he resigned his post as president of the Football League.

Joe Richards passed away in 1968 at the age of 80.

A year before his death, and in his capacity as Football League chairman, an elderly Joe Richards presents Denis Law with the 1966/67 First Division Championship trophy while club secretary Les Olive commentates on the occasion

He made mistakes during his term of office at the Football League and controversy never seemed to be far from his door, but no-one who knew him was ever in any doubt that he held the overall good of the game close to his heart. Many of the legacies he left to football are still with us and he is remembered with distinction as the man who did so much to drag the Football League into the modern era.

The story regarding the formation of the F.A. Youth Cup centres on a meeting of NIFL representatives in Yorkshire sometime in 1951 and it was at this gathering that Richards allegedly first suggested a knock-out competition for under eighteen year-olds. It is unclear how his proposal was greeted, and when he later touted Football League clubs with his idea he ran into a wall of apathy. Convinced that such a tournament could add real value to the development of youth football, he took his brainchild to the Football Association who agreed with the merits of his plans and set about putting them into place.

Records show that the F.A. Youth Committee met on the 17th December 1951, having convened exactly three months previously. Two of its members were delegated to attend an NIFL meeting, which was to take place in London, where a National Intermediate Cup Competition was discussed.

It is not clear from the minutes of the meeting whether the NIFL committee actually suggested a national tournament at the outset or whether they were proposing to introduce a knock-out competition for their own benefit and the Football Association considered it was such a worthwhile project that they felt compelled to expand the idea.

The F.A. were obviously satisfied with the proposals in principle as, by the end of the gathering, it was agreed that they would draw up rules for discussion at a later meeting, which was to be held on the 24th March 1952.

The drafted rules had been finalised by that date and were presented to the Football Association for approval at their next council meeting on the 2nd May 1952. The rules were adopted at that May assembly with only minor adjustments made to the proposals.

The Youth Cup Competition Standing Committee was appointed on the 4th July 1952 and it first sat just over a month later, on the 6th August. With everything finalised and rubber-stamped, the newly-inaugurated tournament was ready to begin.

The competition was set up in such a way as to resemble, with certain cosmetic differences, a 'junior' version of the F.A. Challenge Cup. The basic rules were that games would be decided on a knock-out basis, with the semi-finals and final entailing home and away legs.

It is known for definite that Joe Richards pressed for the final to be staged at Wembley, but in this instance he was overruled. His high ambition for the final venue was based on the certainty that using the National Stadium would draw much increased press coverage, which in turn should have seen a significant rise in the standing of the tournament.

The Youth Cup was open to all Football Association members, in addition to other applicants approved by the F.A. Council, with the entry fee set at ten shillings (50p) per club.

Participants needed to be aged at least fifteen as a minimum and eighteen as a maximum on the 1st September of the season of the competition. Games would last for a duration of 90 minutes, although on the agreement of both clubs beforehand they could be reduced to 80 minutes. Any replay had to take place within eight days of the original tie.

As floodlights were some way off for most clubs in 1952, and Sunday football was strictly taboo as far as the Football Association was concerned back then, participating clubs were encouraged, wherever possible, to stage Youth Cup ties on a Saturday rather than during the week. This usually entailed games taking place in the morning as the majority of participating clubs were Football League outfits whose pitch priorities on a Saturday afternoon lay with their first or Reserve team fixtures.

Games were required to be played on an enclosed ground which, preferably, would be the stadium used by the home club. The thinking behind the stadia rule was to ensure that the competition wasn't devalued by staging matches on, for example, public playing fields. Use of a proper ground was an important factor in the make-up of the tournament as it exposed the players to a 'big match' situation, which in turn instilled invaluable experience.

Of course, things would change as the 1950's progressed, with the majority of clubs installing floodlights as the decade ran its course. However, the rules laid down at the outset, and the suggestions of the Football Association, were designed to ensure that games would be staged at a time which would ensure a reasonable attendance and at a venue that befitted the name of the competition.

In summary, the overall framework was constructed in such a way as to give the new tournament a decent profile.

For the inaugural Youth Cup season, 93 clubs entered initially. There was one late withdrawal, Port Sunlight, who scratched after being drawn to face Bolton Wanderers at home, meaning that entry fees totalled £46 (92 x 10/-).

Naturally, the largest single contingent came from First Division clubs who provided fifteen entrants. The Second Division supplied fourteen participants and the Third Division (North) mustered a mere four entries while the wealthier clubs from the Southern section of the Third Division contributed twelve. The balance of clubs that went into the hat for the draw was made up of non-league and amateur sides.

The full composition of entrants is given on the opposite page and is followed by a list of Football League clubs that chose not to take part.

ENTRANTS BY LEAGUE

FIRST DIVISION

Blackpool
Bolton Wanderers
Chelsea
Derby County
Liverpool
Manchester United
Middlesbrough
Newcastle United
Portsmouth
Sheffield Wednesday
Stoke City
Sunderland
Tottenham Hotspur
West Bromwich Albion
Wolverhampton Wanderers

SECOND DIVISION

Barnsley
Birmingham City
Blackburn Rovers
Brentford
Bury
Doncaster Rovers
Everton
Huddersfield Town
Hull City
Leeds United
Luton Town
Nottingham Forest
Rotherham United
West Ham United

THIRD DIVISION (NORTH)

Bradford Park Avenue
Chester
Chesterfield
Oldham Athletic

THIRD DIVISION (SOUTH)

Aldershot
Bournemouth & Boscombe Athletic
Brighton & Hove Albion
Bristol City
Bristol Rovers
Crystal Palace
Exeter City
Gillingham
Leyton Orient
Queen's Park Rangers
Swindon Town
Walsall

ATHENIAN LEAGUE

Barnet
Hendon
Redhill
Walton & Hersham

BIRMINGHAM & DISTRICT LEAGUE

Brush Sports

CHESHIRE LEAGUE

Wellington Town

DELPHIAN LEAGUE

Woodford Town

ISTHMIAN LEAGUE

Leytonstone
Oxford City
Woking

MIDLAND LEAGUE

Scarborough

NORTHERN LEAGUE

Billingham Synthonia Recreation
Penrith
South Bank

SOUTHERN LEAGUE

Gravesend & Northfleet
Headington United
Worcester City

WESTERN LEAGUE

Trowbridge Town

OTHER NON-LEAGUE AND AMATEUR CLUBS

Bexleyheath & Welling
Bridlington Central United
Briggs Sports
Civil Service
Dawdon Colliery Welfare
Eastbourne United
Eynesbury Rovers
Gorleston
Great Yarmouth Town
Hereford Lads Club
Huntley & Palmers (Reading)
Kings Lynn
Leeds Wanderers
Longfleet St. Marys
Nantwich
Oak Villa Athletic (Plymouth)
Pinehurst Youth Centre (Swindon)
Pinner
Polytechnic (Chiswick)
Port Sunlight
Silksworth Colliery Welfare
South Liverpool
Stork (Cheshire)
Swanage Town
Tilbury
Twickenham
Vauxhall Motors
Welwyn Garden City
Wolverton Town & B.R.
Yorkshire Amateurs (Leeds)

FOOTBALL LEAGUE CLUBS THAT DID NOT ENTER

FIRST DIVISION

Arsenal
Aston Villa
Burnley
Cardiff City
Charlton Athletic
Manchester City
Preston North End

SECOND DIVISION

Fulham
Leicester City
Lincoln City
Notts County
Plymouth Argyle
Sheffield United
Southampton
Swansea Town

THIRD DIVISION (NORTH)

Accrington Stanley
Barrow
Bradford City
Carlisle United
Crewe Alexandra
Darlington
Gateshead
Grimsby Town
Halifax Town
Hartlepool United
Mansfield Town
Port Vale
Rochdale
Scunthorpe & Lindsey United
Southport
Stockport County
Tranmere Rovers
Workington
Wrexham
York City

THIRD DIVISION (SOUTH)

Colchester United
Coventry City
Ipswich Town
Millwall
Newport County
Northampton Town
Norwich City
Reading
Shrewsbury Town
Southend United
Torquay United
Watford

In order to save on travelling costs, the early rounds were contested between clubs in a particular geographical 'zone'. The reason that a club may have received a bye in the First Round came about if the zone contained an uneven number of participants. Zones were numbered one to nine for the opening two stages. For the Third Round, the zones were condensed down to five and were named as follows: North-West, North-East, Midlands, South-West and South-East. The Fourth Round was made up of just three zones, which were titled Northern, Midlands and Southern.

To use an example, Spurs were placed in Zone Seven for the First Round along with West Ham United, Woodford Town, Welwyn Garden City, Briggs Sports, Leyton Orient, Leytonstone and Tilbury.

Having successfully negotiated the first stage, Spurs remained in Zone Seven along with the survivors from the group. They then won their Second Round tie, which put them into the South-East Zone along with those still left in the competition from Zones Six, Seven and Eight. Another win in the Third Round thrust Spurs into the Southern Zone, a constitution of the remaining clubs from Zones Six, Seven, Eight and Nine. Had they won their Fourth Round game, Spurs would have entered the Fifth Round, or quarter-finals, at which stage the zoning system was dropped completely.

The Youth Cup was always regionalised in the early rounds, although there were modifications to the regions over the years.

There were 'play-by' dates imposed which, incidentally, all fell on Saturdays, although in mitigating circumstances the deadlines were known to have been extended. In the 1952/53 season all First and Second Round games had to be played by the 25th October 1952. Third Round ties should have been settled by the 29th November and the Fourth Round by the last day of January 1953. Fifth Round matches needed to be done and dusted by the 14th March and both legs of the semi-final by the 18th April. Both final games were to be contested by the 9th May 1953.

The system adopted in that first season continued until increased entries necessitated the introduction of a Preliminary Round for the 1956/57 campaign. The addition of a single Preliminary Round continued up to and including the 1961/62 season when there was a major overhaul to the structure of the tournament.

From 1962 onwards, based on previous results, 50 clubs were exempted to the First Round Proper with another 30 exempted to the Second Round Proper. The remaining clubs competed in eighteen geographical zones that consisted of two Qualifying Rounds. Two became three in the 1977/78 term when a Preliminary Qualifying Round was required.

In the lead up to the 1998/99 campaign there were still further alterations to the structure as all exemptions since then have been based on league status and not on previous performance. Consequently, the set-up now resembles more closely than ever the system used in the senior F.A. Cup.

Before a Premier League club enters the competition nowadays there are as many as six stages. Beginning with the Preliminary Round, there are then First, Second and Third Qualifying Rounds prior to the First and Second Rounds Proper.

The status ruling means that the 44 Premier League and Championship clubs are those that gain byes into the Third Round Proper. Football League Division Two and Three clubs qualify for 48 exempted places into the First Round Proper.

Substitutes were allowed for the first time in all Football Association competitions in season 1966/67, a year after they had been introduced by the Football League, while the 1986/87 campaign saw the two substitutes rule come into the Youth Cup. Two increased to three for the 1994/95 term, but of those named one had to be a goalkeeper. A year later the stipulated goalkeeper rule was dropped and from the 1998/99 season onwards the number of substitutes was extended to five. The authors can offer no explanation as to why Blackburn Rovers nominated six substitutes for the game at Ewood Park in March 2004.

The full rules of the Youth Cup can be found on the F.A.'s website, www.thefa.com, as well as all of the current season's entrants and results.

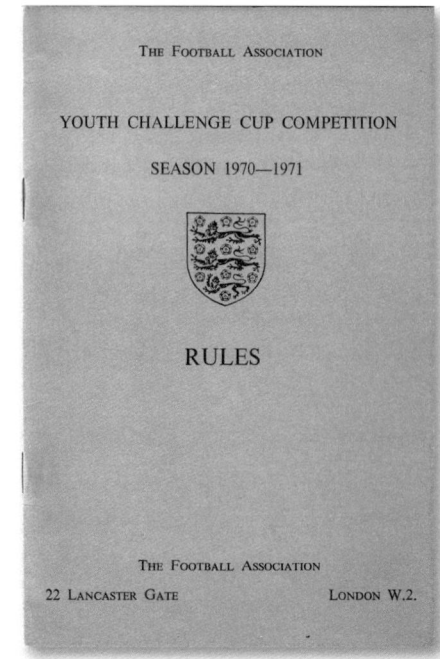

Blakeman hat trick in United Cup win

Chapter Two

MURPHY'S MARVELS

1952-53

1) Gordon Clayton	9) Eddie Lewis	1) Peter Barley	9) Billy Flitcroft
2) Bryce Fulton	10) David Pegg	2) Paul Hutchinson	10) Ernie Emmonds
3) Paddy Kennedy	11) Albert Scanlon	3) Fred Spridgeon	11) Ged Florence
4) Gordon Robbins		4) Peter McConnell	
5) Ronnie Cope		5) Jack Charlton	
6) Duncan Edwards		6) John Reynolds	
7) Noel McFarlane		7) Brian Tarrant	
8) John Doherty		8) Mick Evans	

OCTOBER 1952

MANCHESTER UNITED 4 v 0 LEEDS UNITED

Charlton (o.g.), Pegg, Scanlon (2)

first round

Wednesday 22nd
Kick-off 3.00 p.m.

The curtain went up on United's venture into the new tournament courtesy of an optimistic early omen. The Reds were fortunate enough to secure a home tie, with Leeds United providing the opposition, and so the game was arranged to be played at Old Trafford with an afternoon midweek kick-off.

Players and club officials alike would have been reasonably satisfied with the draw, as a home match is always useful in a knock-out competition, particularly at the opening stage, and their opponents wouldn't have been considered one of the stronger participants. The Leeds of 1952 weren't the power in the game that they would become over a decade later, as they had been relegated from the First Division at the end of the 1946/47 season and wouldn't regain their top-flight status until 1956.

It was rather fitting that they should be managed by the legendary Major Frank Buckley, as he had been born just a short distance from Old Trafford, at Urmston, and actually appeared three times for the Reds as long ago as the 1906/07 campaign. He would become much better known for his achievements as a manager than for his playing career, despite having been capped for England.

His considerable reputation was forged before the Second World War, when he took an ailing Wanderers from the depths of the Second Division to finish twice as runners-up in the First Division, and he also guided them to the 1939 F.A. Cup final, which ended in defeat at the hands of Portsmouth. It has long been acknowledged that the far-sighted Buckley laid the foundations at Molineux on which the great Wolverhampton sides of the 1940's and 1950's were built.

Much of the success the Major enjoyed during his tenancy at Wolves was based on selling proven players in order to balance the books while blooding promising youngsters in their places. It can be assumed then, that he, like his counterpart Matt Busby, would be wholly in favour of a competition that was conceived with the promotion of junior football in mind. Major Buckley had taken command at Elland Road in 1948 and he is generally regarded as having set up a robust youth system there.

There was also more than a little coincidence relating to one of those chosen by Frank Buckley to represent Leeds in this inaugural fixture. For the centre-half position he selected a strapping six-footer by the name of Jack Charlton. A member of the famous Milburn family of professional footballers who came from the North-East of England, Charlton would enjoy considerable success at Elland Road over a period of more than twenty years, as well as totalling a record number of appearances for the club and winning many caps for his country.

The Manchester United line-up for this historic first game was formidable even by 1952 standards and contained no less than six former schoolboy internationals. Goalkeeper Gordon Clayton, centre-half Ronnie Cope, forward David Pegg and half-back Duncan Edwards had all played for England, while full-back Paddy Kennedy and winger Noel McFarlane had represented the Republic of Ireland. Bryce Fulton, John Doherty, Eddie Lewis and Albert Scanlon were all from the Manchester vicinity, as was Bobby Harrop, and the latter was initially named in a squad of twelve until losing out to former Yorkshire Boys' captain Gordon Robbins for the number four jersey.

The pre-decimal prices of admission to view such a wonderful collection of teenage talent were 9d. (approximately 4p) for adults and 6d. (less than 3p) for children to stand on the Popular Side, or alternatively 1s. 3d. (about 6p) for a seat in the comfort of the Main Stand. Local referee Mr. A.R. Coupe of Urmston was paid a fee of one guinea (£1.05) for the responsibility of officiating the tie.

Both teams took to the field in their normal colours which, for United of course, meant their traditional strip of red shirts and white shorts. For Leeds in 1952, normal colours meant old gold and blue halved jerseys with black shorts.

The wily Major Buckley had identified one of the Reds' main strengths even before a ball was kicked. Leeds inside-forward Mick Evans recalled, *'I was switched from my normal inside-left (number ten) role to inside-right (number eight) in order to combat left-half Duncan Edwards as I am six feet, two inches tall. However, I didn't get a kick of the ball all the game.....'*

The Manchester Evening Chronicle reported that *'there were only about a couple of hundred spectators present when the game began.........pity that there was such a small crowd on a wet, dismal afternoon to see such splendid football'.*

The early part of the match saw most of the action centred around and about the Leeds goalmouth. A clever interchange between United's Pegg and Scanlon along the left flank was followed by a dangerous centre that fell to Doherty, who brought a smart save from visiting goalkeeper Peter Barley. Jack Charlton was kept busy and twice in quick succession cut out thrusts from the lively Lewis as he bore down on goal. Ernie Emmonds and Ged Florence combined to lead the first raid for the visitors, with the final pass proving too strong and the move coming to nothing.

Just on the quarter hour mark, the Manchester boys registered their opening goal in the competition, and what a super one it was to mark such an auspicious occasion. Albert Scanlon, who was described in one of the match reports as a *'go-ahead winger'*, gathered control of the ball on the left wing. He then cut inside sharply and drove a wicked cross-shot over the helpless Leeds 'keeper and into the far corner of the net.

The Reds almost had a second goal minutes later when McFarlane sent in a good effort that gave Leeds a fright, but the action then changed ends and the visitors' centre-forward, Stockport-born Billy Flitcroft, was only just beaten to the ball in front of goal by the safe hands of Clayton. At half-time, Scanlon's thunderous strike was all that separated the two sides.

The football in the second half was similar to the first, with United firmly in control and their efforts stubbornly resisted by a resolute Leeds defence. It seemed that the most the visitors could hope for was a breakaway equaliser, or a huge turn around in fortune, as their forwards had seen precious little of the ball. That was until a three-goals-in-seven-minutes barrage smashed any chances that Leeds held of a result and added a more realistic score to the proceedings. In that short time, the structure of Major Buckley's architecture was wantonly bulldozed into a tangled heap.

Firstly, on 74 minutes, Pegg doubled the Manchester advantage. Minutes later, the luckless Charlton, who had been such a sterling pivot for Leeds, turned a McFarlane shot past his own custodian to register a third goal for United. Those blasts were quickly followed in the 81st minute by another Scanlon strike which completed a convincing win for the home eleven. Scanlon displayed supreme skill and confidence when outfoxing Charlton with a 'nutmeg' during the run-up to his second goal.

The three-goal salvo was an early sign of the depth of junior ability at Old Trafford and of the devastating firepower that would carry the Busby Boys to many more victories over the ensuing years.

Various newspaper reports carried lines such as *'Manchester United showed some splendid football in attack'* and also mentioned that the Reds had *'monopolised play so much'*. One periodical accorded the opposition their due by noting that there *'was so much excellent Leeds defence, particularly from goalkeeper Peter Barley and centre-half Jack Charlton'*.

Alf Clarke, in his 'United Notebook' column in the Evening Chronicle, commented *'what a magnificent game it was......those who were there stayed right until the end and gave the fledglings a hearty round of applause as they returned to the dressing room. Nothing wrong with the United youth'*.

The eleven young men who represented Manchester United on that damp October day all those years ago had written the opening chapter of what would prove to be an enduring and largely successful story.

16

1) Brian Thorley	9) Brian Dodd	1) Gordon Clayton	9) Eddie Lewis
2) Ken Bebbington	10) Frank Stubbs	2) Bryce Fulton	10) David Pegg
3) Ernie Edwards	11) John Dean	3) Paddy Kennedy	11) Albert Scanlon
4) Colin Chesters		4) Bobby Harrop	
5) Don Latham		5) Ronnie Cope	
6) Maurice Capel		6) Duncan Edwards	
7) Maurice Ashcroft		7) Alan Morton	
8) Gordon Baxter		8) John Doherty	

1952-53

NANTWICH* 0 v 23 MANCHESTER UNITED
Doherty (5), Edwards D (5), Edwards E (o.g.), Lewis (4), Morton (2), Pegg (5), Scanlon

NOVEMBER 1952

Tuesday 4th

Kick-off 7.15 p.m.

Attendance 2,600

*Played at The Cliff

second round

Because several clubs had received a bye into the Second Round of the competition, the United boys had taken Leeds on in the knowledge that, if victorious, they would face the youth eleven of Nantwich Football Club as their next opponents.

The Nantwich Guardian, dated Friday, 10th October 1952, carried the following article under the headline 'FLOODLIGHT FOOTBALL':

If Manchester United beat Leeds United in the First Round of the national youth competition, Nantwich youth team will play Manchester United Youths by floodlight, at Broughton, Manchester.
On Monday, Nantwich F.C. committee accepted Manchester United's proposal to play the match at Manchester instead of Nantwich.

It was a brave but nonetheless sensible decision on the part of Nantwich to forfeit their home advantage. It gave them the opportunity to participate in a floodlit game, which was somewhat of a novelty in itself during the early part of the 1950's, with the virtual certainty of attracting a far larger attendance than they could have hoped to achieve if the match had been staged at their own ground. The game would also have attracted much more media attention by being switched to Manchester.

Realistically, though, it is highly likely that the underlying reason for Nantwich agreeing to United's suggestion of the change of venue was made largely due to financial considerations. Gate receipts eventually yielded the considerable sum of £216 and the Cheshire club's share would certainly have been a most welcome addition to their bank balance. Despite being only at youth level, it seemed even then that a game against Manchester United was considered to be the sporting equivalent of winning the football pools.

The Nantwich junior side was comprised of enthusiastic local lads, most of whom had completed a full working day before travelling to face United. Indeed, the Nantwich team coach actually made stops to pick up one or two players outside their places of work before heading north.

Once the coach arrived in Manchester, the driver confessed that he didn't have an inkling as to precisely where The Cliff was situated. Thinking it to be in close proximity to Old Trafford, he made his way down Chester Road and wrongly assumed that the floodlights seen in the distance was his destination. When later discovering that he was actually parked outside White City, where a greyhound race meeting was scheduled, it was quickly established that the bus needed to cross the swing-bridge over to Salford in order to reach the Broughton ground.

There were two changes to United's line-up from the First Round. Bobby Harrop was brought in for Gordon Robbins at right-half, while on the right wing one ex-schoolboy international, England's Alan Morton, was chosen to deputise for another, Eire's Noel McFarlane, who was injured.

Nantwich's strength seemed to rest on the four members of their side who had represented Crewe Boys. Goalkeeper Brian Thorley, forwards Brian Dodd and Gordon Baxter, along with full-back Ernie Edwards, had all seen service in the town team, as had United captain Ronnie Cope, who was well known to the opposition.

Curiously, around that time, whenever United staged a floodlit game at The Cliff, it became the practice to offer their opponents a set of amber shirts, which were sometimes noted as 'yellow' on the match programme. The Cliff's floodlights weren't particularly powerful, especially judged against modern standards, and the bright jerseys were used to enable the crowd to view the participants more easily.

Nantwich's officials were informed that the shirts had been obtained by United when the first-team toured the USA and Canada during the 1952 summer recess, and they obligingly agreed to the change of colours.

United also utilised special red tops of their own in floodlight games throughout that period, their use having been sanctioned by the forward-looking Matt Busby. The manager informed one source that he had been *'impressed with the effectiveness of similar fluorescent jerseys when we played under floodlights in America.'*

It had been raining heavily for most of the day in and around Manchester, which had the effect of leaving The Cliff's playing surface in an extremely heavy condition. Thankfully, there was never any danger of the game being postponed, as the downpour had subsided well before the kick-off, and a sizeable crowd assembled to view the 'David against Goliath' clash.

It must have been extremely unnerving for the Nantwich team to face the prospect of taking part in a competitive fixture under floodlights for the first time. In that respect, the United eleven held a distinct advantage, having played at least once a week under the arc lamps in midweek training sessions. Also, a watching audience of well over 2,000 partisan home supporters wouldn't have been an experience that most of the Nantwich lads had encountered before.

The writing seemed to be clearly on the wall for the non-leaguers when David Pegg opened the score for United after just three minutes of play. The Reds then claimed two more goals before six minutes had elapsed while Nantwich were left staggering at the continuous threat of quicksilver thrusts.

The regular additions to United's total was broken only by some spirited goalkeeping and desperate defending as the visitors withdrew almost their whole team to form a rearguard formation. At the end of a hopelessly one-sided 45 minutes, during which Nantwich had barely ventured out of their own half of the field, the Reds were already ten up.

Eddie Lewis, who was noted by one periodical as having been nominated as the first-team's 12th man on the previous Saturday at Spurs, staked a claim as Nantwich's chief tormentor with United's very first Youth Cup hat-trick, which included four out of the opening six goals.

In view of the muddy conditions, it was decided prior to the start of the game that two balls would be used. Periodically, as a ball went out of play, any excess mud was cleaned away while the other was put into use. However, the wags in the crowd reckoned the real reason for this practice was that even the balls needed a rest from United's shooting.

Some of the talk in the Nantwich dressing room at the break was that the Reds, having already put the result beyond doubt, would surely ease up in the second half. Unfortunately for them, easing up wasn't a philosophy that held much credence with coach Jimmy Murphy, who forcibly demanded his charges to make even greater efforts than they already had. One newspaper columnist was curious to know the comments that had been made behind the locked door and puzzled, *'What Jimmy Murphy said to his boys at half-time is anybody's guess, but they seemed to put more zest than ever into their play after the interval.'*

A ten-to-nothing scoreline would have been enough to satisfy all bar the most demanding managers or coaches but Murphy, ever the task-master, actually began his pep-talk by roaring *'you haven't won the game yet'* at the United team.

It has long since passed into legend that another thirteen goals hit the back of Nantwich's net after the resumption as a tide of red swarmed over, and finally submerged, the plucky amateurs. The Reds had completely crushed their opponents with a goal-crazy performance which was spiced with more than a dash of sheer football cruelty.

The 23-goal margin set up a Youth Cup record that is likely to stand forever, and it also created a record win for a Manchester United side in any grade of football up to that point in time.

Duncan Edwards added a further four second half goals to his early strike and in doing so he formed a group of three, along with David Pegg and John Doherty, to score five times. The Reds also contrived to hit the post on at least four occasions.

The Nantwich lads were totally out of their depth and had been subjected to the football equivalent of execution by machine gun fire. Nevertheless, their efforts weren't lost on the appreciative home crowd, who cheered and clapped them as they exited the pitch at the end of what must have seemed the longest 90 minutes of their lives.

It was later said that a great many supporters left The Cliff unsure as to exactly how many goals the Reds had actually piled up. One newspaper recorded that United goalkeeper Gordon Clayton touched the ball only nine times in the entire game, while the Daily Dispatch's brief summary claimed he *'hadn't a shot to save'*.

The Daily Mail reporter reckoned that Alan Morton was *'another Johnny Berry in miniature'* and Duncan Edwards represented *'the greatest junior soccer prospect I have ever seen'*. Edwards' passing was described as *'being the equal of anything I have seen from full international players'* by another hack, who went on to offer the view that United *'pounded their way through'* the match but *'produced the skill'* to go with their power.

The Mail correspondent was at pains to point out *'it was teamwork which gave the United juniors such a victory'* and suggested *'these goal hungry forwards will take a lot of stopping. Watch their progress to Wembley!'*

Despite the rout, Matt Busby was so taken by the heroics performed by Nantwich's goalkeeper Brian Thorley that he signed him immediately after the game, the youngster subsequently taking part in a number of junior matches for the Reds.

Even though they had been somewhat humbled by the heavy defeat, the visiting party of players and officials were sporting enough to give United captain Ronnie Cope a coach ride back to his home in Crewe en route to Nantwich.

The lowly Cheshire outfit would eventually extend their name to Nantwich Town Football Club.

17

1952-53

1) Gordon Clayton	9) Eddie Lewis	1) Roy Milton	9) Kendal
2) Bryce Fulton	10) David Pegg	2) Gordon Waring	10) Austin
3) Paddy Kennedy	11) Albert Scanlon	3) Henry Huddart	11) John Charnley
4) Noel McFarlane		4) Bill Whitehead	
5) Ronnie Cope		5) Brian Mitton	
6) Duncan Edwards		6) Bill Richardson	
7) Alan Morton		7) Roy Alker	
8) John Doherty		8) John Wright	

NOVEMBER 1952

MANCHESTER UNITED 2 v 0 BURY
Lewis (2)

Wednesday 26th
Kick-off 2.15 p.m.
Attendance 1,305

third round

Following the annihilation of poor Nantwich, it was a fair bet that United were now considered the adversaries that most, if not all, of the other competing clubs would have wanted to avoid. The next obstacle for the youngsters was provided by near neighbours Bury, who became the club's first Lancashire opposition in the Youth Cup when they made the short journey down the A56 from Gigg Lane into Manchester for an Old Trafford showdown.

The United management had initially sounded out their opponents in relation to staging the tie under floodlights at The Cliff. Bury felt the conditions would heavily favour the home side, who were more used to competing under artificial light, and so Old Trafford was used again while the match was given an early kick-off time.

Bury coach Dave Russell was prepared to tell anyone who would listen just how highly he rated his lads, and he received a pre-match boost from the Gigg Lane treatment room with the news that right-back Gordon Waring and right-half Bill Whitehead had both recovered from slight knocks and were passed fit to play. The Bury club were active recruiters of talent from the Newcastle-upon-Tyne area around that period of time, and with the exception of goalkeeper Roy Milton, who came from Brixham in Devon, their line-up was a mixture of locals and Tynesiders.

United announced only one personnel change from the previous round. With the availability of fit-again Noel McFarlane, the individual who could count himself unlucky to lose his place was Bobby Harrop. McFarlane resumed in Harrop's right-half spot, while Alan Morton retained his place at outside-right following his brace against Nantwich.

Those in the sparse crowd must have thought that they were going to witness another goal jamboree when the Reds took the lead with their first real attack in the seventh minute. It came about when powerhouse half-back Duncan Edwards sent in a typically booming shot on the Bury goal, which appeared to be going wide of an upright until, in a flash, centre-forward Eddie Lewis guided the stray ball past the startled Milton to gain his side an early advantage.

If the goal wasn't bad enough for Bury, they then suffered a further blow barely nine minutes later when outside-left John Charnley fell awkwardly in a tussle for possession near to the touchline. It was immediately obvious that he wouldn't be able to take any further part in the game and the winger was instead whisked off to Manchester Royal Infirmary where a fractured wrist was diagnosed and subsequently put in plaster.

The injury was desperately unfortunate, and the loss of a man was a burden Bury could surely have done without. Coming in the days well before substitutes were allowed, Charnley's absence meant that the Shakers' forward-line lacked full fire-power and it was the United attack which would begin to exert a strengthening grip on the contest.

The visiting defenders strove hard to keep their speedy opponents at bay and full-backs Huddart and Waring tackled and covered to keep Bury hopes flickering. Half-backs Whitehead and Richardson also slaved manfully for the cause, but they were employed almost exclusively in defensive duties, leaving little opportunity to lend support to their ball-starved front men.

The situation wasn't lost on the United lads. A goal ahead and an extra pair of legs gave them a significant advantage, a situation which allowed the boys to play confident, incisive football. In particular, Eddie Lewis tried desperately to add to his goal tally, missing a gilt-edged chance to do just that when slipping on the edge of the six-yard box with only Milton to beat.

Bury then survived another close shave when the Reds were awarded a free kick 25 yards from goal. Taken by John Doherty, the skilful inside-forward looked on in despair as his effort crashed against a post. Just before the half-time whistle sounded, the Reds again went near when the diminutive Alan Morton shot across the Shakers' goalmouth.

The home forwards remained on top during the second period, although the Bury boys demonstrated steely resolution and determination in the face of their predicament. The Shakers had a further injury scare to contend with when centre-half Brian Mitton was left dazed by a shot that struck him firmly in the face, but he was able to continue after a little attention from his trainer.

On 74 minutes, Milton frustrated United with a terrific stop, which was made from an equally good shot from David Pegg that he palmed around the post. Almost immediately after that save, the Reds struck again to install a crucial two-goal cushion and lift them into a virtually unassailable position, when a combined move culminated with Lewis stroking the ball home from close range following an astute Albert Scanlon pass.

With nothing to lose at 2-0 down, Bury charged forward in greater numbers, giving the crowd a glimpse of what could have been had their attack not suffered the handicap of the loss of Charnley. Centre-forward Kendal wasted a pair of good openings as the game drew to a close, and in the dying seconds of the contest the Shakers missed another great chance when Wright drilled a shot inches wide of Clayton's left-hand post.

Overall, it had been a plucky backs-to-the-wall display by the visitors and during an after-match interview, Matt Busby publicly paid tribute to their fighting qualities. It certainly stood as United's sternest test so far in the tournament, but the bottom line was that they were safely in the hat for the next round.

The abandon of youth! This ballet-like picture was taken during the F.A. National Youth Cup-tie between Bury and Manchester United at Old Trafford on Wednesday, when the young Shakers were beaten.

1) Gordon Clayton	9) Tommy Hamilton	1) Cyril Hatton	9) Jackie Keeley
2) Bryce Fulton	10) John Doherty	2) Ken Heyes	10) Alec Farrall
3) Paddy Kennedy	11) Albert Scanlon	3) Jimmy Irving	11) Derek Mayers
4) Eddie Colman		4) Ken Rea	
5) Ronnie Cope		5) Alan Favager	
6) Duncan Edwards		6) Gerry Joyce	
7) Alan Morton		7) Brian Harris	
8) Noel McFarlane		8) Peter Chamberlain	

MANCHESTER UNITED 1 v 0 EVERTON

Edwards

1952-53

FEBRUARY 1953

Wednesday 4th

Kick-off 2.30 p.m.

fourth round

Old Trafford was in the grip of 'cup fever' while the youth side prepared for their Fourth Round tie against Everton Youth. However, it wasn't the under-18's but the first-team that were grabbing the back page headlines, as they were due to meet the famous London non-league side Walthamstow Avenue at Arsenal's Highbury ground the following evening in an F.A. Cup Fourth Round Replay.

The Avenue had sensationally forced a deserved one-all draw at Old Trafford on the preceding Saturday and the replay was scheduled for Highbury, rather than Walthamstow's quaintly named Green Pond Road enclosure, in order to accommodate a much larger attendance.

The effect of Walthamstow's gutsy display, plus injury doubts to some senior men, prompted Matt Busby to withdraw David Pegg and two-goal hero against Bury in the last round, Eddie Lewis, from youth team duty in order to travel to the capital with the F.A. Cup squad. Those developments necessitated a call-up for Irish schoolboy Tommy Hamilton, who came into the youth side as a direct replacement for Lewis at centre-forward.

Hamilton had actually signed amateur forms for United in the summer of 1952 and then returned to Eire to complete his studies. He was as surprised as anyone when called to his headmaster's office one morning, with Jimmy Murphy waiting to speak to him on the other end of the telephone. Murphy wanted him to make the journey back to England in order that he could assist the youth team against Everton, a request that pleased the striker greatly.

There were three other changes to the team that had defeated Bury, two of which were positional. John Doherty switched from inside-right to inside-left, while Noel McFarlane regained a forward berth in the former position.

McFarlane's vacation of the right-half spot allowed a little Salford boy with a larger than life personality by the name of Eddie Colman to make his Youth Cup debut. The local youngster had been playing almost exclusively on the fifth rung of the club's ladder in the Juniors, with the only exception being on the 17th January when he went up two steps to take part in a 4-2 'A' team win at Mirrlees. It was obvious that he was being readied for the cup match, and there were those such as Paddy Kennedy, Gordon Clayton, Noel McFarlane and Albert Scanlon in the 'A' side to help him acclimatise to the increased demands of the higher standard.

Colman was now the fourth different right-half to be used in as many matches for the youth team, although any suggestions of it being a problem position were soon forgotten as he would establish himself as one of the Reds' greatest ever Youth Cup achievers over the next two and a half seasons.

Everton's juniors, along with United and Wolves, were now considered by most pundits to be amongst the favourites to win the trophy. The Toffees had scorched an impressive trail to Old Trafford by beating South Liverpool 7-0, Liverpool 3-0, and Blackpool 3-0, all away from home.

Even though the Merseysiders were situated in the Second Division at the time, as this was the second of their three consecutive post-war campaigns outside of the higher echelon, they were conscientiously building for the day when they would return to top flight football and their youth set-up was the envy of many other clubs.

The pairing of United and Everton threw up one of those strange quirks of coincidence that embroiders the rich tapestry which makes up association football. At inside-left for the Blues was a talented schemer by the name of Alec Farrall. Young Farrall came from the Wirral area, close to where a certain Joe Mercer lived. Mercer, who had enjoyed enormous success as a player with Arsenal, Everton and England, and would go on to further glories as a manager, most notably with Manchester City, was an old friend and trusted confidant of Matt Busby.

The two were discussing upcoming starlets one day when Busby remarked that he was keen to acquire Farrall for United. Mercer told Busby that he had no chance because he knew the lad's heart was set on signing for Everton, the club he had always supported. Mercer went on to recommend another option for Busby to consider whom he had seen in action for England Boys; the player that he referred to was Duncan Edwards.

Along with team-mate Derek Mayers, Farrall had been laid low with a heavy cold in the days leading up to the game, but both had recovered sufficiently to make the Everton line-up.

Among the crowd was wily Wolves manager Stan Cullis, who was there to see for himself how the United and Everton boys measured up to his own charges, particularly as they were now only one game away from a semi-final spot. While settling into his seat amongst a gathering given as 3,000 in one match report, there is no doubt that Mr. Cullis would surely have been quietly pleased that one of the strongest teams in the tournament was about to be eliminated.

From the moment the opening whistle sounded, it was apparent that the Goodison Park youths were not in the least bit intimidated by United's reputation and the game developed into a dour battle, of relatively few moments of excitement, fought out between two evenly matched contestants that sported defences with militant tendencies. Of the small number of scoring opportunities on offer, the best would fall to the guests.

The Reds survived an early fright when a cross was slightly misjudged by goalkeeper Clayton, whose blushes were spared when the ball was headed to safety. Everton centre-half Alan Favager was kept occupied and twice early on came to the rescue of his team with timely clearances.

With almost a third of the allotted time gone, the contest should have taken on a different complexion, when the Blues carved out the only clear-cut chance up to that point. The hard working Farrall, having been put clean through on goal following a sparkling run by Ken Rea, snatched at the opportunity and the ball, agonisingly for Everton, passed harmlessly outside the post with Clayton stranded. It was a let off United were only too thankful for.

Undeterred by that miss, the Toffees continued on the offensive and had two chances to score in one attacking thrust. Left-winger Mayers created mayhem in the home defence by centring across the gaping mouth of the goal, only there was no colleague in a suitable position to complete the job. The ball was then returned into the danger area from the opposite flank by Everton right-winger Brian Harris, and on this occasion United's full-back Bryce Fulton chose the safest option by simply whacking the ball away.

United were then required to manage with only ten men for several minutes due to an injury to Alan Morton.

As the half-time tea was being poured, it was the Reds who finished in a strong vein and the Merseysiders were grateful 'keeper Hatton remained in an alert mode. Hatton made successive saves from, firstly, John Doherty and, moments later, Alan Morton, who had just returned to the field, in order to keep the scoreboard blank at the break.

Continuing along the same lines as the first half, meaning a tough duel with few thrills, the game progressed with Everton still looking slightly the sharper of the two teams. Then, in the 56th minute, United scored with a fantastic effort to break the stalemate. It would prove to be the decisive goal and was stamped as a special piece of magic from an individual who would make a regular habit of drawing gasps of admiration from spectators, colleagues and opponents alike.

Everton custodian Cyril Hatton vividly recalled, *'In the dressing room before the game, our coach Gordon Watson told us all to keep an eye on the left-half (Edwards) as he'd played against Everton Reserves and scored two goals. It was proved correct how good he was by scoring the winner against us.*

The goal I can remember as if it was last week. A corner had been given away by Jimmy Irving on Manchester United's left wing. It was taken by Alan Morton. The ball was hit right across to the far side of the (penalty) area where Duncan Edwards arrived, trapping and hitting all in one movement. I never saw the ball and just heard it hit the back of the net. It was an absolutely brilliant goal.

We had enough chances to win the game. It's all about putting the ball in the back of the net, and that's just what Duncan Edwards did.'

It was certainly a superb strike by the young colossus, belted hard and low and through what the Daily Dispatch described as *'a forest of legs'*, and Edwards' effort was unanimously judged by various onlookers as worthy of winning any game.

For Everton, conceding for the only time in four Youth Cup games was a hammer blow to their hopes of continuing progress and it served to drain much of their previous enthusiasm away. Nevertheless, they continued to the bitter end in an effort to salvage something from the contest, although a late shot by centre-forward Jackie Keeley that went wide seemed to sum up their luck in front of goal.

A few of the daily newspapers made reference to the quality inherent in the two sides, which suggested they largely cancelled each other out. While one attempted to pinpoint a reason for the Reds' victory by claiming it was *'mainly because the left-wing pair of Doherty and Scanlon were in top form'*, another mentioned that *'a goalless first half was followed by a period in which continued United attacks were bound to gain a result'*.

If the visitors were disappointed at taking the knock-out, it was perfectly understandable that the United lads were elated with a victory over such highly rated opposition, even if the game had provided little in the way of entertainment. That the triumph was achieved without the services of star forwards Eddie Lewis and David Pegg made the success even sweeter for the Reds.

It proved to be a cup double for United, as the aforementioned Lewis and Pegg assisted the first-team to dispose of Walthamstow Avenue by a 5-2 margin the following evening, with the former adding to his growing reputation by knocking in one of the goals.

1952-53

1) Gordon Clayton	9) Eddie Lewis
2) Bryce Fulton	10) David Pegg
3) Paddy Kennedy	11) Albert Scanlon
4) Eddie Colman	
5) Ronnie Cope	
6) Duncan Edwards	
7) Noel McFarlane	
8) John Doherty	

1) Don Leeson	9) Bill Anderson
2) Eric Poole	10) Johnny Edgar
3) Peter Gillott	11) Arthur Breeze
4) Ted Brown	
5) Ollie Hopkins	
6) Trevor Archer	
7) Ron Riches	
8) Harold Sidebottom	

MARCH 1953

MANCHESTER UNITED 3 v 1 BARNSLEY

Doherty, McFarlane, Scanlon — *Sidebottom*

Saturday 21st

Kick-off 3.00 p.m.

Attendance 12,400

fifth round

The reputation of the youth side was growing rapidly, which was perfectly understandable considering their four straight victories and a goals tally that read: for, 30; against, 0.

The draw was kind to the Reds once more, favouring them with another home game, with the opposition provided by Barnsley who, along with Doncaster Rovers, were Yorkshire's two remaining representatives at the last eight stage.

Because United's senior team had no match, with scheduled opponents Tottenham Hotspur involved in an F.A. Cup semi-final against Blackpool at Villa Park, it was agreed that the Youth Cup tie should take place on the vacant Saturday. The time slot gave many of the United faithful an opportunity to see at first hand the cream of the club's young talent in the cut-and-thrust of the new national knock-out competition.

One person with more than a passing interest in the visiting team was Matt Busby's new record signing, centre-forward Tommy Taylor, who had joined United from the Oakwell club less than three weeks before. Taylor attended the game so that he could cast a professional eye over the United junior jewels he had heard so many good things about, and he would almost certainly have renewed acquaintances with the Barnsley officials, one of whom was chairman Mr. Joe Richards who, it should be remembered, had done so much to turn the idea of the Youth Cup into reality. Doubtless to say, it would have given Mr. Richards immense pleasure to see his beloved club's name become the first to be inscribed on the newly-minted trophy.

Barnsley arrived at Old Trafford full of confidence as, after a stalemate in Yorkshire in the previous round, they put North-East giants Newcastle United out of the tournament when securing an impressive 2-1 victory at St. James's Park in the replay. Following a bye at the opening stage, the Oakwell juniors had also eliminated Nottingham Forest and Oldham.

Missing from the Tykes' line-up was regular centre-forward Tommy Holmes, who had only just signed professional forms for the club. Holmes had been called up to the Army for his two-year dose of National Service in the week preceding the game and his absence meant a switch from the right wing to the centre of the attack for Bill Anderson. Those changes resulted in former United prospect Ron Riches taking Anderson's normal number seven shirt.

For the Reds, first-team experienced Eddie Lewis and David Pegg returned to the side, while Alan Morton and Tommy Hamilton made way and Noel McFarlane reverted to his more customary outside-right position. It was considered to be United's strongest youth team line-up, and to emphasise the importance Matt Busby and Jimmy Murphy placed on the game, a special training session was arranged for the Thursday before the tie.

In early 1953, three of United's under-18's found themselves the subject of a Butterworth cartoon for their achievements at first-team level

An expectant crowd of over 12,000 spectators was treated to a display of music and dancing by the St. John's Irish Pipers & Dancers from Benchill prior to the kick-off, which added some gaiety to the occasion, with the scores from the two F.A. Cup semi-finals being fought out that afternoon relayed over the public address system at fifteen-minute intervals.

The match commenced at a cracking pace as United's McFarlane whipped over an inviting cross that the Barnsley centre-half Hopkins did well to intercept. Storming straight down to the opposite end, Johnny Edgar had a chance for the Tykes that went begging when he hesitated slightly in front of goal and the United defenders were able to clear their lines. Both sides had served an early notice of their blatant intentions and it soon became obvious to all present that the game promised to be some punch-up.

Those in attendance were treated to a flowing and exciting game of football, which was in almost total contrast to the Everton game in the previous round. The Barnsley teenagers were forced mainly onto the back-foot, but, as a team, they never allowed themselves to be bullied or overawed. Their solid defenders weren't for buckling under pressure and, once in possession, they and their midfield colleagues were always on the lookout to release their speedy and direct front men on the offensive, with swift raids on the United goal.

Both forward-lines were slickness personified and the crowd simply lapped up the feast of à la carte junior soccer laid before them.

In the 43rd minute, the Reds gained a decisive edge when referee Jack Higham of Bury awarded them a free kick some 30 yards out from the Barnsley goal. Up strode left-half Duncan Edwards, who proceeded to smash a trademark piledriver of a shot, which looked every inch a goal with his name inscribed on it. That was until a deft touch via the head of John Doherty made doubly sure the ball was directed in-between the posts, leaving goalkeeper Leeson without a prayer of saving it.

Losing a goal at such a crucial time is often the pin that deflates a side's bubble, but the Yorkshire boys came out for the second period even more determined to demonstrate that they weren't simply going to roll over. With an hour on the clock, continuing competitive play between the two teams culminated when Barnsley breached the Reds' net for the first time in the competition with a well worked equaliser.

The goal was instigated by makeshift centre-forward Bill Anderson, who fed the ball to the player who had taken his normal position, right-winger Ron Riches. Holding possession down the touchline, Riches sent a pass inside to the unmarked Harold Sidebottom who, with calm and deadly precision, lifted the ball into the back of the goal past Clayton. United's goalkeeper had sensed the danger as the move developed, even advancing away from his line in an attempt to narrow the angle, only to no avail.

Naturally, the goal charged the Oakwell lads with a renewed sense of confidence and for a time it looked as though the Reds might lose control of the game entirely. It was the Barnsley kids who were calling the shots at that juncture, and it took what can only be described as a smash and grab breakaway for United to regain the lead.

Following some nice approach work, the ball fell to the twinkling feet of Irishman McFarlane, and not being one to need a written invitation in these matters, he showed his marker a clean pair of heels before cracking home a wicked shot to beat Leeson for the second time. It was a simple goal, albeit extremely smartly taken, and it came at a time when the clarity in the Reds' performance had started to become a little faded.

With the relief that the second goal brought, United fizzed back to life and would soon make the game safe with a further score, even though they were fortunate to do so.

In attempting to clear a home assault, Barnsley full-back Eric Poole kicked the ball against the chest of Albert Scanlon. Dropping invitingly at Scanlon's feet, he dispatched it clinically into Leeson's goal to give the Reds an unassailable lead and a precious place in the semi-final. The incident was a cruel piece of ill-luck from Barnsley's point of view and it was the deciding factor that finally curtailed their doughty challenge.

It had been a tremendous contest and, despite the result, must have delighted Joe Richards, who made his view known that his boys were a credit to Barnsley Football Club. Just as importantly, the contest received plenty of favourable comments in the sporting press, which caused the competition's prestige to leap a few places further forward.

The watching United supporters had certainly enjoyed good value for their entrance money and many of them would return to witness similar stirring victories by the teenage Reds over the coming years.

1) Gerry Cakebread
2) Roy Yeatman
3) Roy Hurrell
4) John Murray
5) Derek Reynolds
6) Bobby Halliday
7) Henry Bird
8) Dennis Heath
9) Vernon Avis
10) John Pearson
11) Charlie Hawes

1) Gordon Clayton
2) Bryce Fulton
3) Paddy Kennedy
4) Eddie Colman
5) Ronnie Cope
6) Duncan Edwards
7) Noel McFarlane
8) John Doherty
9) Eddie Lewis
10) David Pegg
11) Albert Scanlon

1952-53

BRENTFORD *1* v *2* MANCHESTER UNITED
Hawes   McFarlane, Scanlon

APRIL 1953

Saturday 11th

Kick-off 11.00 a.m.

Attendance 4,000

semi-final 1st leg

Busby boys a goal up

A Syd Jordan cartoon from the Brentford & Chiswick Times depicting the main events from the first leg of the Youth Cup semi-final at Griffin Park

1952-53

APRIL 1953

semi-final 1st leg

With five scalps under their belts, the Reds were now into the two-legged semi-final where two notable 'firsts' occurred. In Brentford, United faced opposition from the south of England, while the initial tie of the penultimate round represented a bona fide away game.

The Middlesex club had at its helm player/manager and former England goalscoring legend, Tommy Lawton. Their youth squad, whose full title at that time was Brentford Town Juniors, came under the stewardship of Alf Bew, who had seen his side defeat three non-league teams, Barnet, Hendon and Bexleyheath & Welling, along with two Football League outfits, Brighton & Hove Albion and Queen's Park Rangers, to reach the last four. It was proving to be a memorable season for the young Bees because, in all competitions, they boasted an imposing record of 35 victories and a draw from 42 games completed, and with a tremendous goal tally of 215 scored and 62 conceded.

A Saturday morning kick-off, preceding a Reserve fixture in the afternoon, ensured a bumper crowd of over 4,000 spectators at Griffin Park.

United fielded their most powerful line-up, as per the Barnsley match previously, with Jimmy Murphy having no injury worries to concern him.

The Brentford team contained several Middlesex Boys and Youth players, three of whom, Dennis Heath, Vernon Avis and John Pearson, were professionals. Right-back Roy Yeatman had represented England at schoolboy level on five occasions, while left-back and captain Roy Hurrell was selected for the England Youth team during a tour of Belgium.

Only Pearson had appeared in Brentford's first-team, however, and that merely in a friendly fixture. There was, therefore, a distinct difference in experience between the two sides, as the Reds were now able to boast four from the under-18 squad, namely Pegg, Doherty, Lewis and Edwards, that had made an impression in the club's senior set-up.

Whatever the differential was, the Brentford team started as if it counted for absolutely nothing, because at precisely three minutes past eleven, Griffin Park erupted like a waking volcano when the home side surged into an early lead.

It came about when a free kick awarded to the Bees was floated into United's penalty box. Reds' right-back Bryce Fulton seemed to have the situation under control and he sent a pass back to 'keeper Clayton, who appeared to fumble. Sensing the opportunity, Brentford's Charlie Hawes nipped smartly between the two and touched the ball through the goalie's legs and into the vacant net.

The setback forced United to take the game to their hosts, with wingers Scanlon and McFarlane soon coming to prominence by supplying rounds of potent ammunition for Pegg, Lewis and Doherty to fire. The Reds began to move crisply and the game would, in the main, slowly but surely become a defensive struggle for a Brentford side that tried desperately to hang onto its lead.

The home team did manage one other notable first half effort when Avis, who had been marked out of the game by Cope until that point, combined with Pearson only for the latter to blast in a strong shot that was blocked. When the rebound fell back at his feet, Pearson's reaction to the loose ball wasn't quick enough and the chance went begging. At the change of ends, Brentford still clung onto their solitary goal advantage.

If the crowd had enjoyed an explosive beginning to the opening half, they saw an even quicker start to the second period of play, only this time the successful strike would come from the away side. Barely two minutes had passed since the restart when, with Murphy's instructions no doubt still ringing in the team's ears, Noel McFarlane, who was enjoying a fine game for United, arrowed home a low drive from a difficult angle on the right-hand side of the penalty area. The ball slid just inside the near post and it clearly caught custodian Cakebread by surprise.

With the scores locked at one apiece, and the play having become a little ragged, Brentford ventured forward in one of their increasingly rare attacking moves. Fluttering into United's box went Bees' right-winger Henry Bird, who was sent sprawling over an outstretched defender's leg, and the referee instantly pointed his sharpest finger to the spot. Penalty!

The crowd roared with delight at the official's decision but, as skipper Hurrell tentatively placed the ball down on the twelve-yard mark, the noise inside the stadium lessened to an expectant hush. Face to face with Clayton in order to give his side the lead once more, and with some team-mates unable to look as the moment got the better of them, Hurrell took the short run-up only to sky the ball high and mighty over the bar.

It was a devastating miss, and the agony was compounded for Brentford when, moments later, Avis smacked a shot against a United post following a goalmouth scramble. Despite being well on top in terms of possession, the Reds had enjoyed a couple of huge slices of favour from Dame Fortune.

The game entered the final quarter of an hour with United's fitness and know-how once again beginning to unravel their hosts' tactics. Even though at that stage they would certainly have settled for bringing the Bees back to Old Trafford on level terms, it wasn't any great surprise when the Reds took the lead with just ten minutes to go. John Doherty was at the heart of a move in which he put the flying Albert Scanlon clear of a last Brentford defender, and the winger's clinical low drive beat the despairing Cakebread and simultaneously silenced the numbed crowd.

It was a goal that severely damaged Brentford's aspiration of reaching the final. A few of their side had displayed obvious signs of nerves, while individual and collective performances were accordingly adversely affected, and the lack of consistent fluidity in the home team even prompted one reporter to comment that 'the reputation of Manchester United had cast its shadow'. Most of those same players were faced with the daunting task of trying to turn the one-goal deficit around at Old Trafford just four days later.

If the Brentford boys were inhibited by their opponents' reputations, it was also acknowledged that it had been a far from vintage performance by United's standards. They had certainly bossed the show for long periods, only without creating their usual quota of chances. Nevertheless, Jimmy Murphy was well aware that his lads held the whip hand going into the second leg, and he would also have been pleased and proud with the character they had displayed in coming from behind for the only time in the competition.

In the confinement of the changing room, the Welshman dished out some special praise to skipper Ronnie Cope and Duncan Edwards, as he felt they had done more than most to put the Reds into such a promising position. With his customary verbal ferocity, Murphy was also perfectly correct in reminding the players that they were now just one more good performance away from a place in the final.

> *It helped a lot that the main defenders, myself, Bryce (Fulton), and Ron (Cope), along with Big Gordon (Clayton) in goal were there for all of the Youth Cup games because that stability and understanding means a lot to the side.*
>
> *In those days defenders were expected to defend first and foremost, the lads in the middle of the pitch came back to help when the other team attacked and created chances at the other end, while it was the job of the forwards to get goals. At that time it was unusual for me to venture much past the half-way line, and when I did I'd probably get a rollicking from Jimmy Murphy!*
>
> *The defence did a great job in that first Youth Cup season. We kept a few clean sheets, teams just couldn't break us down, and it was a great side to be a part of.*

PADDY KENNEDY

Brentford keeper G. Cakebread dives at the feet of Eddie Lewis, the Manchester centre forward, during an attack in the Brentford Juniors v. Manchester United Juniors game at Griffin Park to-day. On the left is Johnny Doherty, Manchester's inside-right.

1) Gordon Clayton	9) Eddie Lewis	1) Gerry Cakebread	9) Paul Bates
2) Bryce Fulton	10) David Pegg	2) Roy Yeatman	10) John Pearson
3) Paddy Kennedy	11) Albert Scanlon	3) Roy Hurrell	11) Charlie Hawes
4) Eddie Colman		4) Terry Garnier	
5) Ronnie Cope		5) Derek Reynolds	
6) Duncan Edwards		6) Vernon Avis	
7) Noel McFarlane		7) Henry Bird	
8) John Doherty		8) Dennis Heath	

1952-53

MANCHESTER UNITED 6 (8) V (1) 0 BRENTFORD
Doherty (2), Edwards, Lewis, McFarlane (pen), Scanlon

APRIL 1953

Wednesday 15th

Kick-off 4.45 p.m.

Attendance 5,877

semi-final 2nd leg

PLUCKY YOUNG "BEES" HAD TOO FORMIDABLE A TASK

Duncan Edwards training in the vastness of an empty Old Trafford

It was a miss that the Bees would rue almost immediately, as the Reds went straight down to the other end of the field to record a score. The goal kick that resulted from Hawes' miss was launched upfield by Clayton, with the ball then worked into the path of the scavenging Eddie Lewis, and the Harpurhey-raised lad raced away from his markers to plant it past the advancing Cakebread and put United two ahead on aggregate.

The cheers had barely died down for Lewis' goal when the Reds got another in the very next minute. Noel McFarlane directed a header in on target, which Cakebread did remarkably well to save but was unable to hold onto, and John Doherty, lurking with intent, was perfectly placed for, and had the simple job of, sticking in the rebound. The Reds' second goal meant that a task which had always seemed a steep one for Brentford now appeared to be positively vertical.

Following the double-barrelled salvo, United continued with relentless authority and it paid dividends once more before the interval when they were awarded a penalty for handball by makeshift left-half Avis. McFarlane had already been nominated to take any such spot kicks and he made no mistake to give the Reds their first Youth Cup penalty success.

The second period of the match developed into a display of exhibition football by the United eleven, who exuded the confidence of a team that was clearly the measure of their opponents in every sense. The game once again proved to be a good spectacle for a crowd that had braved the miserable weather, and they were treated to three further goals as the Brentford defence began to collapse under the strain of a continued pounding.

The Reds' fourth came when Doherty powered home a great header from a corner to register his second goal of the evening, and that feat was trumped by a classic Duncan Edwards goal, which came as a consequence of him hammering home a cannonball free kick. The rout was completed when Albert Scanlon registered number six with what was, for him, a rare headed effort.

By the end of the contest, the Brentford boys had been well and truly crushed

For the second instalment of the semi-final, Jimmy Murphy kept faith with the eleven who had wrested the initiative from Brentford in the opening leg.

The visiting team had changes forced upon them, because Bobby Halliday was injured in the game at Griffin Park and John Murray was unavailable. The Bees introduced Terry Garnier in place of Murray, with Vernon Avis moving to left-half to replace Halliday, and Paul Bates was brought in at centre-forward after being unable to train for three weeks due to an injury.

The kick-off was at the unusual time of a quarter to five, which, allied to some typical Manchester weather, rain falling before and all throughout the 90 minutes, produced a much lower than expected attendance. United's ground staff had also watered the pitch 24 hours prior to the match, which resulted in the wet playing surface turning extremely muddy soon after the game got underway, and those conditions meant that the endurance and stamina of the players, as well as their skill, would be put to the test.

Bearing in mind the quick goals at the start of both halves at Griffin Park, it was somewhat of a contrast for there to be no score at all in the Old Trafford encounter for almost half an hour as both teams began somewhat lethargically. On 28 minutes, a half-chance fell to Brentford's Hawes, but the opportunity to put his team level on aggregate was scorned when he placed his effort wide of United's goal.

FOOTBALL AT OLD TRAFFORD

★

F.A. National Youth Cup
Semi-Final Tie (2nd leg)

★

UNITED v. BRENTFORD

on Wednesday, 15th April
Kick-off 4-45 p.m.

★

Admission: Groundside 1/-, Juniors 6d.
Covered Terrace and Paddock 2/-
Grandstand 3/-

1952-53

APRIL 1953

semi-final 2nd leg

by a multi-talented force in full flow. The Bees had managed to create nothing more than the occasional scare for the home defence in the whole of the 90 minutes and there could be no serious complaints from them either at the result or the margin of it.

Brentford manager Tommy Lawton positively glowed in his admiration for the United side and was quoted after the game as saying, *'This is the greatest youth team I have ever seen and I have watched a lot. I cannot see any club beating them. Matt Busby must be the happiest manager in the world to have such material at his command.'*

Busby was indeed in clover when reflecting on the achievement of his young starlets in passing through to the final stage of the tournament. The wily Scot would also have gained huge satisfaction when pondering the enormous potential that they were capable of realising.

The Manchester Evening News' Tom Jackson reported *'it was an impressive display, but sixteen year-old Eddie Colman, ex-Salford Boys, was the 'star' of the occasion, playing a storming role behind a forward-line carrying young 'big guns' in Eddie Lewis, David Pegg and Doherty, all with first-team experience'.* Jackson's tribute was a tremendous accolade for tiny Colman, who was only introduced at the Fourth Round stage, and it gave an early pointer to his growing reputation as a creative and popular performer.

George Sands, writing for the County of Middlesex Chronicle, stated that *'in team-work and exploitation of the open spaces, Manchester were far superior. The ease and skill with which they slipped into position making them appear faster than they really were – and that was fast enough!'*

For United's two-goal hero John Doherty, there wasn't much time to dwell on the success because he was required to report to the Royal Air Force camp at Padgate the following day to begin his stint of National Service.

Of the defeated Brentford side, only Gerry Cakebread, Vernon Avis, John Pearson and Dennis Heath would progress into their first-team.

The Bees' centre-forward for the second leg, Paul Bates, went on to win England amateur international honours while later attached to Wycombe Wanderers whereas John Murray, who featured at right half-back at Griffin Park, would also play for England, at cricket, as well as keeping wicket for Middlesex for many years.

As Brentford goalkeeper Cakebread attempts to punch a high ball, John Doherty jumps to meet it while Eddie Lewis (centre) looks on

> *We had knitted together as a team by the time the Youth Cup semi-final came around and, should I say, we were quietly confident that we could go on and win it. That's not to say we were cock-sure or anything like that, but if you are going to win anything you have to have an inner belief that you can complete the job. Like most of the lads, I felt that if we could get a result down at Brentford then we would make it into the final. We would probably have settled for a draw before the game, although at the end of the match I would say there was definitely some disappointment that we hadn't brought a bigger lead back with us.*
>
> *They had no chance at Old Trafford, we were all over them. The thing about that side was there were so many attacking options. All of the lads upfront were capable of creating and scoring goals, and if we needed any assistance going forward, there was always Duncan......*

ALBERT SCANLON

1) Gordon Clayton	9) Eddie Lewis
2) Bryce Fulton	10) David Pegg
3) Paddy Kennedy	11) Albert Scanlon
4) Eddie Colman	
5) Ronnie Cope	
6) Duncan Edwards	
7) Noel McFarlane	
8) Billy Whelan	

1) Peter Owen	9) Harry Smith
2) Arthur Hodgkiss	10) Colin Booth
3) Eddie Clamp	11) Len Cooper
4) John Timmins	
5) Peter Russell	
6) Frank Bolton	
7) Brian Punter	
8) Bob Walker	

1952-53

MANCHESTER UNITED 7 v 1 WOLVERHAMPTON WANDERERS
Lewis (2), McFarlane (2), Pegg, Scanlon, Whelan — Smith

MAY 1953

Monday 4th
Kick-off 6.30 p.m.
Attendance 20,934

final 1st leg

The last obstacle standing between United and the prestige of becoming the inaugural winners of the F.A. Youth Cup was, almost inevitably, the mighty Wolverhampton Wanderers. Although many football clubs enjoyed their own particular memorable moments in the 1950's, none could match the sheer consistency of United and Wolves. Both would win the First Division title on three occasions during the decade, the Reds in seasons 1951/52, 1955/56 and 1956/57, while their great rivals breasted the championship winning line in the 1953/54, 1957/58 and 1958/59 campaigns.

Whenever the Wolves team was in town, great crowds would flock to see their star men clad in the famous old gold shirts. The Wolverhampton side was packed full of some of the greatest and most famous players of the era, many of whom were household names, and none more so than Billy Wright. Captain of both his club and country for so many years, Wright went on to become the first man to win 100 caps for England.

Wolves were also famed for their dangerous wingmen, Johnny Hancocks and Jimmy Mullen, and they could boast many other high class performers, including a number who were taken on at Molineux straight from school and nurtured through the club's junior teams.

In manager Stan Cullis they had a man who valued the principle of strength in depth as, only the week before the Youth Cup final, their Reserves had won the Central League championship for the third consecutive year. Cullis' belief that a quality junior section at his club would provide a natural extension to second string strength was a philosophy he shared with Matt Busby.

The Wolves Youth, having had a First Round bye, secured a resounding 5-0 victory in their initial game in the competition at Wellington Town. That success was followed by a couple of wins over close rivals, 2-0 against West Bromwich Albion at Molineux and an emphatic 5-0 mauling of Birmingham City at St. Andrews.

A meeting with Doncaster Rovers at the quarter-final stage resulted in a 6-0 home win and it led to a semi-final pairing with the junior side of Reading biscuit manufacturers, Huntley and Palmers. A 5-0 home victory for Wolves preceded a second leg win of 6-0, with the total sum of those scores giving the Midlanders a completely unblemished defensive record going into the final.

United were forced into changing the line-up of the semi-final side because John Doherty had been troubled with cartilage problems and was due to undergo corrective surgery in a military hospital. He was replaced by Billy Whelan and, having only recently been acquired from the Home Farm club of Dublin for a £10 signing-on fee, the opening tie of the final represented the inside-forward's debut as a Red.

The Wolverhampton team included ace marksman Harry Smith and former Manchester and England Boys' captain, Colin Booth. The Wanderers also boasted Eddie Clamp at left-back and Frank Bolton at left-half, both of whom had also represented England as schoolboys. Wolves' traditional strength down the flanks was illustrated by the fact that both Brian Punter at outside-right and left-winger Len Cooper had already been included in the England Youth eleven.

The scene was set for a fascinating contest, with the ultimate prize of winning the country's top youth trophy, and all the prestige that went with it, at stake.

It was hardly a shock, then, that a clash between what were unquestionably the two best teenage teams in the land should capture the imagination of United's followers, and on a bright spring evening, over 20,000 of them made their way to Old Trafford to witness the initial encounter.

Tom Jackson's view of the Reds' win was given in the Evening News:

At Old Trafford last night before 20,934 spectators, the United youths, all under-18 at the start of the season, beat the pride of Wolves' junior talent-spotters 7-1 in the first leg of the F.A. Youth Cup final.

The second leg will be played at Molineux on Saturday, and if the United lads go in with a feeling that the Cup is theirs for the mere taking who can blame them? Until they came under fire from what one soccer official, with nearly a lifetime's active association with boy players, described as the best young team he had ever seen, the Wolves prodigies had aggregated 29 goals without reply in six preliminary ties.

Gallantly as the Molineux boys fought, and despite their tremendous dash and enthusiasm, they were gradually torn to shreds by a United team that, say in three or four years' time, could be among the elite of First Division football.

Some of these boys have already made the headlines in United's first-team. Duncan Edwards, David Pegg and Eddie Lewis each have one foot firmly on the soccer ladder – yet there are others such as pint-sized Eddie Colman, a terrier at wing-half, outside-left Albert Scanlon, who has the guts and tenacity of an Eric Brook, and full-back Bryce Fulton.

Twenty thousand people, many of them who dashed straight from work without their teas to see this football treat, can't be wrong. It must have been real music in the ears of those behind the scenes at Old Trafford, who spend their days combing the junior fields for likely talent, to hear the prolonged and spontaneous applause at the end of this thriller.

What a pity, therefore, that the F.A., having gone out of their way to sponsor this new competition, should have deemed it unnecessary to be officially represented at the final stage. I can tell them now that they missed a great showpiece.

The Wolverhampton Express & Star's football correspondent went on to record the event so eloquently under a banner which proclaimed a rising star born of that locality:

Dudley boy the inspiration in Manchester United's Youth Cup lead

BEFORE they went to Old Trafford last night to meet Manchester United in the first game of the two-leg final of the F.A. Youth Cup, Wolves had not conceded a goal in the competition. Within three minutes of the start that cherished record had gone, and by the time the game ended six more goals had gone into the Wolves net, and they had scored once.

Neither they, nor the people from Wolverhampton who were among the 20,934 fortunate enough to see these games (writes "Commentator") will need me to remind them of the magnitude of the task which faces them in the return game at Molineux next Saturday. This United team, on this day's play, were, without any doubt, the finest youth side I have ever seen. That is why I say we were fortunate to be there.

Wolves have no need to look for excuses. Those who have seen them in their earlier games know that they, too, are a good junior side, and I shall be surprised, nay, astounded, if the game on Saturday is not much closer.

If I thought I was certain of seeing Duncan Edwards give another such polished display as he gave last night, wild horses would not keep me from Molineux. Edwards, whom I interviewed as a Dudley schoolboy along with Wolves Frank Bolton just 12 months ago, after they had played together for England, was, to all intents and purposes, the complete wing half-back.

SOMETHING TO REMEMBER

Strong man in a strong side, he failed only once in the whole game to make good use of the ball, and if for nothing else I would remember him for the uncanny accuracy of a series of long, raking passes across the field on the inside of the full-back, not to mention the urgency with which he played throughout.

Yet, for all this, Wolves had their moments, especially in the fifth minute of the game, when, within two minutes of McFarlane giving United their three-minute goal, Smith slipped through the middle to equalise with a fierce shot.

Three minutes later, however, Lewis, bringing some of his Division I. experience to his aid for the United, made it 2—1, and after 18 minutes another Division I. debutant, Pegg, took the United total to three.

WOLVES BEST EFFORT

It was then that Wolves made their best effort, and after 24 minutes Smith, brushing past centre-half Cope, brought the ball under control and again slammed it past former Cannock Boys goalkeeper, Clayton. A linesman, however, judged him to have brought the ball down with a hand and the point was lost.

Early in the second half a Clamp free kick hit the foot of a post, but the Wolves attack never came completely into the picture and Smith was left to make his valiant efforts largely on his own.

There were flashes of their normal competence from such as Timmins and Cooper, but there was never the smooth-working effectiveness we had come to associate with them. The most consistent display came from left back Clamp, who came to the rescue in more than one ticklish defensive situation and was always trying to use the ball to advantage.

F.A. COMPLIMENT

By contrast, the United became even more united as the game went on, and second-half goals from McFarlane (48 minutes), Lewis (58), Scanlon (73) and Whelan (85) meant that all five of their quick-thinking, quick-moving and quick-shooting attack got a goal, to leave everybody with nothing but the highest admiration for them.

Dudley - born DUNCAN EDWARDS, star of the Manchester United youth cup side.

The United boys had given some solid displays on the road to the final, as well as coming out on top in a couple of close calls, but to subject Wolves to such a big defeat underlined just how far in front of the rest they were. The margin of victory meant that the Reds could journey to Wolverhampton confident in the knowledge that nothing less than a soccer miracle would prevent them from returning to Manchester with the silverware.

25

1952-53

1) Peter Owen	9) Harry Smith	1) Gordon Clayton	9) Eddie Lewis
2) Arthur Hodgkiss	10) Ron Howells	2) Bryce Fulton	10) David Pegg
3) Eddie Clamp	11) Len Cooper	3) Paddy Kennedy	11) Albert Scanlon
4) John Timmins		4) Eddie Colman	
5) Peter Russell		5) Ronnie Cope	
6) Frank Bolton		6) Duncan Edwards	
7) Lionel Stephenson		7) Noel McFarlane	
8) Colin Booth		8) Billy Whelan	

MAY 1953

WOLVERHAMPTON WANDERERS 2 *(3)* v *(9)* 2 **MANCHESTER UNITED**

Smith (2)   Lewis, Whelan

final 2nd leg

Saturday 9th

Kick-off 3.00 p.m.

Attendance 14,208

F.A. YOUTH CUP FINAL
(2nd Leg)
WOLVERHAMPTON v. MANCHESTER UNITED
Manchester United announce that by arrangement with British Railways a special train will leave London Road Station at 12-25 p.m. to-morrow, Saturday, for Wolverhampton
Return fare 9'-
Roll up and cheer the boys

Upon arriving at Molineux for the second leg of the final, Jimmy Murphy was able to announce an unchanged side. Wolves, though, had injury problems stemming from the game at Old Trafford, which caused them to delay their team selection until just before the kick-off.

The Wolverhampton club's officials eventually chose Lionel Stephenson to replace Brian Punter at outside-right, with Colin Booth reverting from inside-left to inside-right at the expense of Bob Walker, while Ron Howells went into the side to take over the number ten shirt vacated by Booth.

The Reds were cheered on by a small band of United supporters who travelled down to the West Midlands. They had taken advantage of a British Railways football day trip to Wolverhampton that was laid on from the terminus now known as Piccadilly Station.

Molineux was bathed in glorious sunshine as the teams took to the field. The playing surface appeared in good condition, and was firm underfoot, which would have suited United's passing game.

When the contest started it was Wolves who created the early danger as they tried to shake off the effects of their heavy deficit. Following a quick burst down the left, Len Cooper brought a promising build-up to an end when volleying a long-range shot over United's bar.

Soon after, Gordon Clayton and Bryce Fulton combined to halt the speedy Harry Smith, and twice in successive raids Ronnie Cope was called upon to cut out menacing threats from the Wanderers. The Reds were then revived with a break that gave an opening to Albert Scanlon, who tried his luck from outside the box with an effort that flashed past an upright.

It was essential that Wolves scored as early in the game as possible if they were to stand any hope at all of making up the six-goal difference. That hope turned to reality after just six minutes, when a neat pass by Howells released

The two teams are presented to dignitaries, including Joe Richards, prior to the second leg of the final

26

1952-53

MAY 1953

Cooper on the left flank and his surging run was followed by a tantalising centre that leader Smith reached first. Smith brought the ball under control in the blink of an eye before powering in a hard drive, which registered as a goal after deflecting off United's full-back Paddy Kennedy prior to crossing the line.

The goal came as a huge morale booster to a home side that was soon bearing down on the Reds again. Smith almost made it two in as many minutes, on this occasion his shot striking 'keeper Clayton.

It had been a decidedly shaky opening by the Reds, although their early nerves would soon evaporate, and as one reporter put it, they suddenly *'began to show their claws'*.

A move involving Eddie Lewis, David Pegg and Scanlon culminated with the latter firing in a shot that cannoned away to safety. Lewis then came close for United when he headed against the woodwork, and in another attack Scanlon thudded a strike against the underside of the Wolverhampton bar with goalkeeper Owen well beaten. It was a let-off that Wolves couldn't afford to dwell on, and they countered quickly when the eye-catching Smith put in another shot that was charged away by Clayton.

With half-backs Duncan Edwards and Eddie Colman showing increasing prominence in the middle territory, and the forwards beginning to move with their usual co-ordination, the Reds claimed two goals in a decisive three-minute period to kill what slim chance there was of a Wolves comeback.

The equaliser came in the 34th minute following a pass from Noel McFarlane to Pegg, with Lewis meeting the latter's inviting centre by heading home in unstoppable fashion. It was a goal that carried the hallmark of consummate simplicity.

On 37 minutes, the Reds doubled their tally when an effort by Scanlon passed through a mass of bodies in the goalmouth and was deftly deflected into Owen's net by the alert Whelan.

Soon after the start of the second half, the away eleven almost added another score to their total, but Scanlon was denied when he hit the woodwork for the second time. His shot thumped against the inside of a post only to rebound across the face of the goal without crossing the line, and McFarlane followed up that near miss by sending a smashing effort whizzing over Wolves' crossbar.

The home side salvaged some pride in the 66th minute when they levelled the game. The goal was credited to the industrious Harry Smith and was described by Alf Clarke with a comment that *'it brought more laughs than many a stage comedian. A long ball from the Wolves' half was lobbed over the head of Cope. It was going harmlessly to Clayton, with not a Wolves player near the ball. Clayton, however, let it go under his hands and he fell into the ground'*.

It was a genuine howler by United's 'keeper. Nevertheless, with the team holding a six-goal aggregate lead and some excellent performances during the course of the cup run behind him, he was entitled to his mistake, even if his team-mates did rib him about it for months to come.

There were further flurries of action to follow the Wanderers' second goal but, with no more additions to the scoreline, the Reds had won by a margin of nine goals to three over the two legs. They were unquestionably worthy winners of the fledgling competition and, as such, they had carved out a memorable niche in the history of English youth football for Manchester United.

It was left to a proud and elated captain, Ronnie Cope, to receive the trophy on behalf of his colleagues. Presenting the silver cup, which was a gift donated by the Football League, was Joe Richards, the chairman of the Youth Cup committee. He congratulated both teams on their achievements, and in the course of his speech Richards raised the subject of making the final an annual event at Wembley once again.

final 2nd leg

The inaugural F.A. Youth Cup winners are pictured with the Tomlinson Trophy in September 1953
Back row (l-r) Billy Whelan, Eddie Colman, John Doherty, Gordon Clayton, Bryce Fulton, Paddy Kennedy, Duncan Edwards
Front row (l-r) Noel McFarlane, Eddie Lewis, Ronnie Cope, David Pegg, Albert Scanlon

1953 IRISH TOUR

MAY 1953

BOYLAND YOUTH CLUB, ALLIED UNION LEAGUE XI, BRAY WANDERERS/RATHFARNHAM SELECT XI

Monday 11th to Wednesday 20th

Although the United senior side lost six of their opening twelve games in the 1952/53 First Division campaign, and were actually in the lowly position of 18th in the league when the youth team met Leeds in their inaugural Youth Cup contest, they made a splendid recovery to finish in eighth place by the end of the season.

Lower down the club's rankings, there was much to shout about.

The 'A' team completed a double by winning both the Manchester League and Gilgryst Cup. The Colts headed the Manchester Amateur League Division One while the Juniors lifted the Altrincham Service of Youth League, the Whitaker Cup, the Altrincham & District F.A. Youth Cup and the Altrincham F.A. Junior Cup. On the local scene it was apparent that the Reds were virtually invincible at all levels.

Naturally, capturing the F.A. Youth Cup in 1953 also brought a number of the younger Manchester United playing staff to national prominence. The treasured honour of capturing that particular silver trophy was achieved by the youths displaying open, attractive football whenever possible, in true United traditions, and over the course of the competition they were called upon to defeat three of the strongest under-18 teams in the country.

While Brentford represented southern England's best hope, the Reds dashed their chances by defeating them both home and away. Wolves were the main torchbearers of the middle counties, but their fire was doused during a thrashing at Old Trafford. From the north, Everton were tipped by many to do well until the United kids put paid to their aspirations with a goal of some brilliance in a dour and closely fought encounter.

Even though Matt Busby, Jimmy Murphy and the other members of the backroom staff were only too happy to share in the euphoria of all the junior triumphs, they would also have looked at the situation in a long-term perspective. With so much precocious talent waiting in the wings, and the objective of bringing 'home grown' talent through the ranks running along the desired lines so far, it was then that the soccer wise men began to consider the next stage of their charges' development.

Prior to the Youth Cup final, the United management arranged for the youth squad, including three over-age additions, to take part in a ten-day long tour of Ireland, which would encompass three friendly matches.

The young Reds had actually been invited to take part in the Blue Stars (Ascension Day) International Youth Tournament in Zurich along with fellow Youth Cup finalists, Wolves. The Molineux club duly accepted the invitation of the competition's organisers whereas United declined, having already finalised the details of their Irish trip. Despite the Reds having taken part in a similar jaunt to the Emerald Isle two years previously, the 1953 tour was much more of a pivotal event in a number of ways.

For a start, it was the first such excursion made after the introduction of the Youth Cup, and as winners of the trophy the United boys travelled in the glare of the media's spotlight. Whereas the trip to Ulster in 1951 was probably regarded as something as a test case, the 1953 tour began a sequence that has seen the club's youngsters participate in literally dozens of overseas youth competitions since.

Also, with the inclusion of Duncan Edwards and Eddie Lewis, the Reds were able to boast of a couple first-team graduates in the touring party. David Pegg would have made up a trio of seniors, but he was required by Busby for United's

Manchester United's youth squad in Bangor, Northern Ireland
Back row (l-r) Ian Greaves, Walter Whitehurst, Tommy Barrett, Gordon Clayton, Alan Rhodes, Paddy Kennedy, Bryce Fulton, Hotel Manager
Middle row (l-r) Eddie Lewis, Bill Inglis (Trainer), Jimmy Murphy (Coach), Bert Whalley (Coach), Noel McFarlane
Front row (l-r) Sammy Chapman, Eddie Colman, Duncan Edwards, Billy Whelan, Albert Scanlon

1953

MAY 1953

Coronation Cup involvement north of the border. The Coronation Cup was an end of season tournament contested between four of the top teams from England, along with four of the best from Scotland, and it formed part of the Queen's coronation celebrations.

So, on the evening of Monday, 11th May 1953, just two days after the second leg of the Youth Cup final, Murphy and Bert Whalley accompanied a party of thirteen players on a flight to Belfast where a United Youth XI was due to meet a 'strengthened' Boyland Youth Club.

Staged at the Oval Football Ground 48 hours later with a 7.30 p.m. kick-off time, pre-match entertainment was supplied by the City of Belfast Ladies' Pipe Band.

United fielded the following side: Clayton, Fulton, Kennedy, Colman, Cope, Edwards, McFarlane, Whelan, Lewis, Whitehurst and Scanlon.

The Boyland team read: Rea (Banbridge Town), Marshall, Dickey, Downes (Banbridge Town), White (Coleraine Reserves), Ralph, Lowry (Banbridge Town), Douglas, Ervine, Hill (Carrickfergus Reserves) and Clint.

The Reds defeated the green and whites by three goals to nil.

The very next day, the Old Trafford delegation made their way south to the International Hotel in Bray for a week-long stay, and on the Friday evening a reception was given in their honour at the Arcadia Ballroom by the Rathfarnham Football Club.

It was said in a newspaper that *'Mr. P. Doran, Sec. of the sponsoring club, welcomed the visitors and paid a tribute to their prowess in football. The manager of the team (Mr. J. Murphy), then introduced the members of the team to the audience, who accorded them a great reception. Among the team members is Noel McFarlane, the former Bray player, who has fulfilled his earlier promise and is one of the most prominent forwards on the side'.*

Two days after, on Sunday, 17th May at 7.15 p.m. precisely, United squared up to an Allied Union League XI at Tolka Park. The Allied Union League team was actually a representative combination which was chosen from 130 junior teams in the Dublin vicinity.

There was only one line-up change from the Reds' earlier match in Belfast, with Ian Greaves deputising for Ronnie Cope at centre-half. It was a particularly memorable experience for Paddy Kennedy and Billy Whelan, coming as it did in their native city, and the event allowed the latter to renew acquaintances with two of his former Home Farm team-mates.

The Allied Union League consisted of: Lowry (St. Patrick's Athletic), Cullen (St. Patrick's Athletic), Williams (Goldenbridge), Mullen (Donore), McNally (St. Finbarr's), Slattery (Home Farm), Lowe (Johnville), Moloney (St. Finbarr's), Ryan (Home Farm) captain, Dunne (Johnville) and Nugent (St. Finbarr's).

United ran out victorious by a 4-1 margin, with Eddie Lewis grabbing himself a hat-trick while Albert Scanlon claimed the other goal.

The Dublin Times was full of praise for the tourists and its match report (see right) described the young Reds' victory.

The tour completed on the following Tuesday when, at the modest home of Bray Wanderers, the Reds signed off with a convincing victory over another combined side.

The Irish Times ran a report under a headline entitled 'EASY FOR MANCHESTER YOUTHS', which spelled yet another win for Murphy's boys:

A fair sized crowd at Carlisle ground, Bray, last night, saw a good exhibition of constructive, attacking football by the Manchester United Youths XI, who beat a Bray Wanderers & Rathfarnham Selection by 6-0.

Goals in the 35th and 36th minutes by Barrett and Lewis gave the Manchester side a 2-0 lead at the interval. McFarlane, from a penalty, and Lewis, in the fifth and sixth minutes of the second half, put Manchester further ahead. Nearing the end, Barrett and McFarlane added the last two goals.

It was a fitting finale to a fabulous season.

> *I recall the day we played at Bray's ground well enough. The hotel we stayed at was right opposite and as I looked out of my room I could see the groundsmen preparing the pitch in readiness for the match that evening. It was a great thrill for me, to be playing in my home town for United.*
>
> **NOEL McFARLANE**

STARS OF TO-MORROW WERE SHINING LAST NIGHT

MANCHESTER UNITED F.C. are known far and wide as top class and skilful exponents of the Soccer code. Dublin fans in large numbers got a glimpse yesterday at Tolka Park of how that great reputation was built up and how it is maintained when they saw the club's teenagers in action against a selection from Our Athletic Union League.

Coming with the proud reputation as English Youths Champions of 1952-53 they upheld that great honour with a magnificent display of football, well above their grade, splendid team work, and a sound knowledge of the best type of positional play that was a credit to their club.

Their combined work was the real factor that earned them a well deserved victory by four goals to one after a thoroughly entertaining game.

As with Jackie Carey and the Senior eleven, Ireland is well represented in the Youths' team, with Kennedy (left-full), McFarlane and Whelan (right wing pair) all hailing from Dublin. Each of these boys held his end up among the galaxy of budding stars, which included the 16-years-old 12 st. 6 lbs. and Schoolboy Youths English International, Edwards, the small but delightful right-half Coleman, and the burly pocket edition of Nat Lofthouse, centre-forward Lewis, to mention just some. Left winger Scanlon was another who is on the threshold of Soccer fame.

Stars in the making of the A.U.L. selection, who were up to their opponents' standard, were Lowe, a speedy and clever outside right, Dunne, a son of the late Jimmy Dunne, a good ball-playing inside left, McNally a promising centre-half, Moloney inside right, Slattery, Ryan and Nugent.

Though defeated the whole team put up a grand fight against worthy opposition.

An early warning of what was in store for the A.U.L. defenders came within two minutes of the start when the Manchester right half, Coleman, started the move that brought a grand goal before the home team had time to settle down. Sending a crisp pass out to Dubliner, McFarlane, the latter joined in a bout of interpassing on the right wing with ex-Home Farm colleague Whelan, which ended with McFarlane sending over a square, low centre which the burly centre-forward Lewis flashed past the helpless Lowry.

JIMMY DUNNE

Immediately after an equally brilliant piece of play by Lowe, the homesters' outside right, in which he beat the Lancashire defence, left Nugent with the goal at his mercy, but to the dismay of the crowd the left winger shot inches wide of the upright.

Lowry next brought off a smart save from Lewis before another Dubliner on the visiting team, Kennedy, left full, nipped in to head away for a corner a great shot from Lowe. This was well played by Moloney whose high centre was punched away by Clayton.

After Lowry had brought off two great saves at full length from Scanlon and McFarlane, the former got his revenge 5 minutes before the interval when he beat him with a right-footed shot that left the St. Pats goalie floundering on the ground.

Four minutes later the visiting centre-frward Lewis showed his real worth when he worked through the Irish defence on his own to beat Lowry from the back line for a really fine goal.

Signs of a thrilling fight back by the homesters came two minutes after the restart when they reduced the lead. This was also a well worked goal, initiated when Dunne split the defence open to send Nugent away. The latter ran on before crossing the ball over to the extreme flank for Lowe to close in and beat Clayton all ends up.

Ryan was unlucky minutes later when after seizing on a short pass by Fulton to Clayton he muffed his shot and Greaves cleared the danger.

This escape put the Lancashire boys on their mettle and with fifteen minutes left for play Lewis put the issue beyond doubt.

irish tour

1953-54

1) Alan Sloan	9) Jackie Keeley
2) Ken Heyes	10) Keith Williams
3) Ian Hillsdon	11) Charlie McDonnell
4) Johnny Clayton	
5) Alan Damen	
6) Brian Senior	
7) Stan McKay	
8) David Cox	

1) Gordon Clayton	9) Duncan Edwards
2) Ivan Beswick	10) Bobby Charlton
3) Alan Rhodes	11) David Pegg
4) Eddie Colman	
5) Bobby Harrop	
6) Wilf McGuinness	
7) Brian Lowry	
8) Sammy Chapman	

OCTOBER 1953

EVERTON 0 v 1 MANCHESTER UNITED

Colman

Saturday 24th
Kick-off 10.45 a.m.

first round

United's Youth Cup success at Everton

United's opening game in defence of the Youth Cup posed a stiff proposition - a trip to Goodison Park to take on Everton. Bearing in mind the close encounter that had taken place at Old Trafford only eight months previously, and on this occasion without the advantage of a home tie, the draw was certainly not one that the Reds would have chosen to open their new cup campaign.

Everton had just two players remaining from the February meeting, full-back Ken Heyes and centre-forward Jackie Keeley. Inside-forward Alec Farrall was still eligible for Everton, but was ruled out because of an injury, and his absence meant that the Toffees were forced to field a substantially different team to the one that had performed so well in defeat at Old Trafford.

For United, Gordon Clayton continued to form the last line of defence between the sticks, while in front of him there was a new pair of full-backs as Alan Rhodes and Ivan Beswick lined up for their Youth Cup debuts. There was also a first start at left-half for former Manchester and England Boys' captain Wilf McGuinness, with Eddie Colman remaining at right-half. A new number five was required to replace last season's skipper, Ronnie Cope, so Bobby Harrop came back into the side following his solitary outing in the massacre of Nantwich.

The forward-line carried three new faces. At outside-right was a local Ancoats boy, Brian Lowry, while Northern Ireland schoolboy international Sammy Chapman took the inside-right berth. Because of his versatility, Duncan Edwards was pushed up and into the centre-forward position and, with Albert Scanlon on the crocked list, David Pegg moved to outside-left.

Those alterations paved the way for the last of the newcomers, a highly rated prodigy who had made four appearances for England Boys earlier that year. He came from Ashington in Northumberland and would one day, through his fantastic skills and wonderful sportsmanship, become synonymous with Manchester United and all that is good in football. His name: Bobby Charlton.

Everton officials decided to stage the fixture on a Saturday and the game was allocated a morning kick-off slot, as the club's second string were due to meet Sheffield Wednesday Reserves on the Goodison Park pitch later in the day.

The home side began the tie in a bright and breezy fashion and took the play to United during the early minutes of the game. As it transpired, that was merely a show of bravado, because Everton were made to form a largely defensive stance once their initial attacking rush had subsided, and only wingers McKay and McDonnell were able to instil some trickery into a largely impotent attack.

While goalkeeper Sloan looked competent behind a steady defence, he was initially tested by United newcomer Lowry, whose smashing attempt on goal was finger-tipped over the crossbar. Lowry's effort was followed shortly after when Edwards, who was clearly enjoying an attacking role, made use of his enormous power by brushing past one defender, then another, and then a third, before unleashing a shot that he gave too much air to, the ball flying aimlessly into the stand behind the goal.

The Reds had built up a good head of steam and appeared more and more threatening with every raid. With ten minutes to the interlude, the goal that the Manchester side deserved finally arrived, and it would eventually see the Evertonians' exit from the cup for the second season in succession.

It developed when a driven centre delivered from the boot of David Pegg landed in the penalty area just in front of Sloan's goal. Pegg's dangerous cross caused pandemonium amongst the desperate Everton defenders, as well as a sense of heightened anticipation from the rushing forwards, and the home reargurd only managed to clear the ball as far as the edge of the box, where Colman was lurking with intent. The little wing-half didn't wait to bring the ball under control, instead electing to lash it on the volley, and it sailed like an accomplished archer's arrow into the top corner of Everton's net to leave Sloan as a virtual spectator as it passed him.

The second half was almost all United and, despite not being able to add to Colman's great goal, their creativity on the wet surface carved chunks out of the Blues' defence on several occasions. Everton did manage to get behind United's backs in the last quarter of an hour, with a couple of harmless crosses that were mopped up effectively, and they represented the last serious incidents of the proceedings.

The Liverpool Daily Post passed a few candid observations on the home team's performance when recording *'it was amazing that they were only defeated by a single goal'* and added *'Everton have to thank the fine work of Sloan, in goal, that they were not beaten by a greater margin'*.

The match was ultimately decided by the same scoreline as the earlier contest at Old Trafford, and in another similar vein, Eddie Colman's goal wasn't unlike Duncan Edwards' unstoppable shot which finally undid Everton's aspirations in the Manchester fixture back in February. There the similarities ended, as this particular contest was an entirely different kettle of fish to the previous fight.

The inspiration and promptings of last season's campaigners stood the younger element in the United side in great stead and was a considerable factor in the outcome of the game. It was, therefore, much more one-sided in the Reds' favour than the last match. Nevertheless, it could be safely assumed that Everton rued their luck in being drawn out of the hat with United twice in a row.

There was much praise for Bobby Harrop's performance, with the Liverpool Daily Post stating that *'the United pivot gave a good display'*, and the Manchester Evening News reporting he was *'responsible for breaking up many attacks'*.

The following extract, taken from the Everton v. Leicester City match programme dated 31st October 1953, summarised the Toffees' view of events:

Our early exit from the F.A. National Youth Challenge Cup Competition at the hands of Manchester United last Saturday morning at Goodison Park was, naturally, a big disappointment to us. We had hoped to do well in the competition even when we heard that the formidable Manchester United side were to be our opponents in the First Round.

We had met the United in the Fourth Round of the same competition last season at Old Trafford and were rather unfortunate to lose 1-0. So we had hopes of turning the tables this time. However, we received a setback by the untimely and unfortunate injury to Alec Farrall, who was eligible for our youth team, at Exeter in the floodlit match a short while ago. Our young centre-forward, Jimmy Gregory, was also out of action, and has been for some months, with a cartilage injury he received last season. Nevertheless, we still had high hopes of entering the Second Round of the Youth Competition.

Manchester United had other ideas, however, and proved to be the superior side on the day's play, although the game did not reach the high standard expected from these two teams.

Our defence took the major honours and are to be congratulated on limiting the score to 1-0. The goal came in the first half from United's right-half, Colman, who scored with a right-foot shot from the edge of the penalty area. We had our chances of scoring on more than one occasion but our forwards were off form and could not take advantage of the opportunities that were created.

Taking the game on the whole, United were full value for the win and it appeared that the experience of their young stars, Pegg and Edwards, did much to sway the game in their favour.

> *All of us new lads were aware that 'Big Gordon' (Clayton), David (Pegg), Duncan (Edwards) and Eddie (Colman) had helped to win the Youth Cup and we wanted to make sure that we won it again.*
>
> *It was a very exciting time. The competition was still in its infancy and lots of people were still talking about the (final) win over Wolves as it had only been just a few months before. We had another strong side and so I suppose some teams wouldn't have wanted to meet us whereas maybe one or two others might have fancied the challenge.*
>
> *I didn't feel any undue pressure when I made my Youth Cup debut and I would imagine that there was a lot more expected from the older ones than us new lads. They had done it before, so Jimmy (Murphy) and Bert (Whalley) would have wanted them to help us along as much as they could.*

ALAN RHODES

1) Gordon Clayton	9) Gordon Lester	1) Barry Davies	9) Bernard Evans
2) Ivan Beswick	10) David Pegg	2) Ken Jones	10) David Jackson
3) Alan Rhodes	11) Tommy Littler	3) Jimmy Fisher	11) Graham Williams
4) Eddie Colman		4) Peter Jackson	
5) Bobby Harrop		5) Alan Fox	
6) Wilf McGuinness		6) Denis Wilson	
7) Brian Lowry		7) Don Tomkins	
8) Bobby Charlton		8) Colin Roberts	

1953-54

MANCHESTER UNITED* 5 v 0 WREXHAM

Charlton (2), Littler, Lowry, Pegg

NOVEMBER 1953

Wednesday 11th

Kick-off 7.15 p.m.

* Played at The Cliff

second round

2nd Round F.A. Youth Cup

UNITED v. WREXHAM

will take place at the Cliff under floodlight on Wednesday next, 11th November, 1953

Kick-off 7-15 p.m.

With the Old Trafford hierarchy keen to continue their promotion of staging junior games under The Cliff's floodlights, a further opportunity arose when the Reds received a Second Round home engagement against Wrexham.

In was, in fact, the very first Youth Cup game for the Welsh club, whose senior team plied their trade in the Northern Section of the Third Division. Wrexham had decided against entering the competition in the 1952/53 season and were given a 'walkover' into the second stage of the 1953/54 tournament. Wrexham's bye resulted from the withdrawal of their proposed First Round opponents, Nantwich, whose reluctance to face the Racecourse Ground teenagers may have come about through fearing a repeat of the hammering they took against the Reds in their only other Youth Cup tie.

United made two changes to the side that had defeated Everton, both of which were in the forward-line. Duncan Edwards, who had been used in two consecutive first-team games against Arsenal and Huddersfield while deputising for the injured Henry Cockburn, was left out because Matt Busby felt he needed a rest. The manager had another Welsh team on his mind, as United's seniors were due to play Cardiff City at Ninian Park on the following Saturday and Edwards obviously figured in Busby's plans for that game.

Out of the side, too, went Sammy Chapman, and into his and Edwards' places came two former Cheshire Boys players, Gordon Lester and Tommy Littler. Lester, who had only recently signed up for service in the Royal Air Force, was brought in to fill the centre-forward berth while Littler was pencilled in at outside-left. Those inclusions meant positional changes for David Pegg, who moved to inside-left, and Bobby Charlton, who switched to inside-right.

The nucleus of the visiting team consisted of several lads who had featured in a very successful Wrexham Boys side that enjoyed many triumphs in the English and Welsh Schools' Trophies. In the spring of 1952, Wrexham Boys made it into the semi-final stages of those competitions only to be beaten on both occasions by an all-conquering Swansea Boys team.

Featured in the Wrexham eleven were David and Peter Jackson, twin sons of the club's manager, Peter Jackson senior. Far from carrying any fear about the prospect of meeting the current Youth Cup holders, the Welsh boys were delighted to have drawn such glamorous opposition and they travelled over the border in anticipation of putting an end to the Reds' interest in the competition. As Wrexham inside-left David Jackson recalled many years later, he and his colleagues *'fully expected that we would beat United.'*

The draw for the Third Round had already taken place by the time of Wrexham's arrival at The Cliff and the two contestants carried the added incentive of a home tie against Bradford Park Avenue as the prize of victory.

For the corresponding round of the 1952/53 season, the Reds invited their opponents to wear fluorescent jerseys for the viewing benefit of their supporters. Because Wrexham's normal strip is virtually identical to United's, and being the away side they were required to concede their usual 'colours', the Robins agreed, as Nantwich had done, to sport a plumage of amber on this occasion.

It was the only time up to that point that the influential Edwards had been absent for a Youth Cup game, but any doubts as to whether the Reds would be less potent without him were quickly dispelled. In a match that began quite timidly before developing into a fast flowing and hugely entertaining affair, the Reds accepted three of the many first half chances on offer to establish a commanding lead by the interval.

Two of the goals came from the impressive Charlton, while Pegg, who opened the scoring in the 33rd minute, grabbed the other. It is interesting to reflect that while Pegg and Charlton were team-mates in the same youth side, and were also close personal friends, there was actually a two-year gap in their ages. Even though Pegg had already accumulated 22 appearances in the First Division, such was the depth of United's playing staff just then that Charlton was still learning his craft in the club's fifth team.

The second period of the game passed with the Wrexham team unable to inflict any significant damage to the home defence while the Reds' corner count eventually moved well into double figures. Gordon Clayton was easily the most underemployed player on the field, as Bobby Harrop, Ivan Beswick and Alan Rhodes formed a virtual barricade, and there was simply too much movement, skill and enterprise from United's forwards and half-backs to allow Wrexham to force their way back into contention.

There was a goal each for wingers Lowry and Littler, the latter gaining just reward for a hugely encouraging debut, and with those contributions went the desired passage into stage three, as well as giving a more realistic look to the scoreline.

An observer representing the Daily Dispatch stated in a report that *'half-backs Colman and McGuinness, with excellent ball control and accurate passes, enabled an almost faultless forward-line to maintain a non-stop attack'*.

While the Robins revealed occasional glimpses of resistance, they lacked the required degree of bustle or quality to seriously trouble the Reds and in essence, it added up to a fairly comfortable win for United in the end.

There was an air of the inevitable in the match analysis contained in the Wrexham & North Wales Guardian newspaper, their report claiming the outcome *'was generally expected'*.

In only his second Youth Cup appearance, Wilf McGuinness' fine performance against Wrexham was noted in a number of newspaper reports

31

1953-54

1) Gordon Clayton	9) Sammy Chapman	1) Hough	9) John Taylor
2) Ivan Beswick	10) David Pegg	2) John Walker	10) Denis Miles
3) Alan Rhodes	11) Tommy Littler	3) Hobson	11) Brian Larvin
4) Eddie Colman		4) Les Thomas	
5) Bobby Harrop		5) Jim McPhee	
6) Wilf McGuinness		6) Peter Hall	
7) Brian Lowry		7) Sid Holdsworth	
8) Bobby Charlton		8) Ken Holdsworth	

DECEMBER 1953

MANCHESTER UNITED 6 v 0 BRADFORD PARK AVENUE

Chapman, Charlton, Littler, Pegg (3)

Wednesday 2nd
Kick-off 2.00 p.m.
Attendance 5,907

third round

PEGG'S THREE AND UNITED WIN THROUGH

For the second Youth Cup tie on the bounce, United welcomed the under-18 side of a Third Division (North) club, with Bradford Park Avenue becoming the next to try to topple the young Reds.

The beneficiaries of a First Round bye, Bradford had comfortably disposed of South Liverpool by six goals to nil at Park Avenue as a prelude to meeting United. The Avenue's manager, Norman Kirkman, travelled to Manchester with his side in the hope that they could return across the Pennines having put the brakes on the Reds' plans to retain the cup.

For Bradford's visit, club officials opted to utilise Old Trafford rather than The Cliff as they anticipated a much larger crowd than could comfortably be accommodated at their Salford training ground. Consequently, the game was pencilled in with an afternoon start time.

The cause of the expectancy was as a result of an engineers' strike in the Manchester area and it duly transpired that the gate would justify the time and choice of venue. Nearly 6,000 spectators passed through the turnstiles, yielding gate receipts of £353, and a large section of the crowd was in something of a holiday mood while enjoying a rare day of respite from the factory floor.

Jimmy Murphy made just the one alteration from the side that had beaten Wrexham in the previous round, with Sammy Chapman recalled in place of Gordon Lester at centre-forward.

Tom Jackson filed the following match report for the Evening News:

Manchester United's under-18 team qualified for the last sixteen in the F.A. Youth's Cup competition at Old Trafford this afternoon by easily defeating Bradford in the Third Round. A feature of the game was a brilliant first half hat-trick by David Pegg.

The crowd, about 5,000 at the start, saw United take the lead after two minutes with a goal from Pegg, who hit a grand shot into the roof of the net after Beswick and Littler had combined in a move on the left which split the Bradford defence.

Though the pitch was heavy, the boys displayed many grand touches with Colman prominent for United and Larvin unlucky with a shot that beat Clayton in the United goal but was cleared off the line by Rhodes.

Rhodes had to concede a corner to hold off a Bradford attack, but generally United had the better of the exchanges. Pegg shot wide from a good position, but subsequently Charlton (who hit the post), Littler, and Lowry showed the right ideas with some forceful shooting.

Bradford continued to be more concerned with defence, and it came as no surprise when Pegg increased United's lead after 36 minutes.

Eight minutes later Pegg completed his hat-trick, beating Hough all the way with a magnificent drive from 25 yards' range.

The second half saw United still in command, but Chapman had a goal disallowed and, after a Bradford breakaway, Hall forced Clayton to tip a long-range free kick over the bar.

United took a fourth goal after 67 minutes, Littler scoring after a raid by Lowry.

Chapman scored United's fifth goal after 87 minutes, and a minute later Charlton got a sixth.

The Bradford team could consider themselves unfortunate to meet up with a United forward combination who had their shooting boots fully loaded, although it was the all-round graft and commitment from the whole eleven that brought the widest smiles to the faces of Jimmy Murphy and Matt Busby.

Later in the week, Murphy explained to one reporter that *'we are always practising passing with the first emphasis on the men without the ball'* and he went on to say *'it is hard work but it is worth it.'* The same scribe also observed that against Bradford, *'young Wilf (McGuinness) hardly put a ball wrong'*.

There was fulsome praise for United's 'wide-boys' in an article which noted that *'two lively wingers, Brian Lowry and Tommy Littler, didn't let their many tricks impair their progressive play'*. The writer of the piece also claimed *'Littler's goal from Lowry's pass won the popularity prize'*.

With just a couple of minutes gone, David Pegg rifles home United's opening goal on the way to completing an impressive first half hat-trick

1953-54

DECEMBER 1953

That same goal was later credited as *'belonging to two fascinating wing men, with Littler worrying across-field like a terrier and pushing a pass to Lowry, who then jigged inside to give Littler a goal on a plate'*. Despite ending the game as the only home forward not to finish on the score sheet, Lowry was cited as the architect of three of the goals and probably ran a close second to hat-trick hero Pegg for the supporters' 'Man of the Match' award.

Because of the later demise of Bradford Park Avenue, the game remains as the one and only meeting between the two clubs in the Youth Cup. Park Avenue lost their Football League status in 1970, folded completely in 1974, only to reform as a non-league outfit in the 1980's.

The selection card above was sent to Bradford full-back John Walker

> *The Bradford match was a very, very exciting occasion for all of us. We knew there would be a good crowd because of the strike and, of course, I had to take a day off work, which my boss was good about. There were three wingers on our side, me, Brian Lowry and David (Pegg), four if you count Bobby Charlton.*
>
> *We just had too much for them and their defenders didn't know if they were coming or going. It was all over by half-time and we really expressed ourselves in the second half.*
>
> *I was fortunate to get a goal, something I'll never forget, scoring at Old Trafford. What a great feeling that was.*
>
> *It was fantastic to read about the game the next day. I must have bought about ten different newspapers.*
>
> **TOMMY LITTLER**

third round

The United side pose for a pre-match photograph prior to demolishing Bradford Park Avenue
Back row (l-r) Wilf McGuinness, Alan Rhodes, Gordon Clayton, Bobby Charlton, Sammy Chapman, Bobby Harrop
Front row (l-r) Ivan Beswick, Brian Lowry, David Pegg, Tommy Littler, Eddie Colman

1953-54

1) Bill Scrivens	9) Mel Ibbotson
2) Jim Willis	10) Peter Perry
3) Max Cook	11) Mick Saul
4) Albert Rhodes	
5) Gordon Robbins	
6) Tommy Seddon	
7) Barry Wainwright	
8) Glyn Jones	

1) Gordon Clayton	9) Sammy Chapman
2) Ivan Beswick	10) David Pegg
3) Alan Rhodes	11) Tommy Littler
4) Eddie Colman	
5) Bobby Harrop	
6) Wilf McGuinness	
7) Brian Lowry	
8) Bobby Charlton	

JANUARY 1954

ROTHERHAM UNITED 0 v 0 **MANCHESTER UNITED**
a.e.t.

Saturday 9th
Kick-off 2.15 p.m.
Attendance 7,200

fourth round

The reward for ousting one Yorkshire side in the Third Round was an engagement against another team from the White Rose county, only this time the Reds were required to travel. Their destination: Rotherham.

With the Millmoor juniors enjoying a good run of results in their own sphere, the youth game, which coincided with a very special day in the football calendar, that of the Third Round of the F.A. Cup, created a huge amount of local interest.

The Sheffield Star's John Piper painted an interesting background to the clash with the headline 'ROTHER BIRD'S FLEDGLINGS GREATEST TEST':

Six years ago, in a fantastic whirl of goal getting in the Sheffield Intermediate League, Rotherham United Junior team was born.

Tomorrow, the Millmoor mites embark on the greatest match of their happy existence – an existence in which has lain the sound and productive foundation of the sort of nursery side so essential to the clubs of today who are looking to tomorrow.

The Manchester United Juniors – the Busby Babes – are the Rotherham laddies' opponents in the tit-bit Fourth Round match of the F.A. National Youth Challenge Cup.

The boys from Trafford Park, who come to Millmoor tomorrow while the Rotherham United first-team are at Bristol in the full F.A. Cup, have been dubbed the greatest youth team in the country.

Here at Rotherham, where officials anticipate the best gate on record for local junior football, the youngsters, who train with self-imposed severity which would shame many full-time professionals, are all set for the occasion.

This is a team in which the exuberance of youth is blended among young men steeped in the natural footballing ability which so often characterises young South Yorkshire.

And behind the Rotherham Juniors, who quickly forsook the Sheffield Intermediate League to become a founder member of the now flourishing Northern Intermediate League, who won the League Cup in 1951 and who currently top the league table, undefeated in their last twelve games, is Rotherham schoolmaster Frank Williams, one of the all-too-few people in football solely for the love of the game.

Lucky Rotherham, to have as the guiding hand behind their nursery side a man of the Williams type. The meeting with Manchester United is undoubtedly the toughest and greatest game they have had to face.

'The lads would have asked for no other opponents', says Frank.

What of the members of the team – schoolboys, apprentices in painting and decorating, bricklaying, in steel and boiler smithing and, of course, where Rotherham football is concerned, a miner.

The singling-out of individuals from the juniors' ranks is unusual and not welcomed by those who know the value of 100 per cent team work, which is the basis of this side.

But among those who have been recognised in young representative football are Glyn Jones and Tommy Seddon, both members of the Sheffield & Hallamshire Football Association side which won the Youth County competition, while Jones has won the highest single honour – that of youth international.

Grammar schoolboy Micky Saul, whose fellow scholar Willis is right-back, is a schoolboy junior international. Cook, Robbins (former Barnsley schoolboy captain) and Jones and Saul again are county schoolboys.

Unlike many companion clubs in the Northern Intermediate League, Rotherham have no wide cross-country net for talent catching.

Practically all their players hail from Rotherham itself and the Rother Valley area.

Yet, through the juniors have graduated to the more senior Rotherham teams such players as Hussey, Bobby Williams, Silman, Reeson, Bentley, Jackson, Longden, Allott, Jenkins and others, most of whom seem assured of a bright career in the game, a career launched in the very best traditions of sportsmanship and the love of the game.

The Youth Cup clash provided some Saturday entertainment for those Rotherham followers not travelling to Ashton Gate, whereas United's Wembley hopes hinged on a tough proposal for the seniors at Burnley. Duncan Edwards was required by Matt Busby for the Turf Moor clash and so, with no injury problems to contend with, Jimmy Murphy was able to nominate a line-up identical to that which had convincingly k.o'd Bradford.

For Rotherham, Max Cook was sufficiently recovered from a recent injury to take his place at left-back.

It was only fifteen months since the Reds had met Leeds in their inaugural game in the Youth Cup and only one person, goalkeeper Gordon Clayton, had featured in all of the previous twelve contests. Therefore, it must have been a curious sight for him to see one of his team-mates from that game in the ranks of the opposition.

Gordon Robbins, who had taken the right-half berth in the Leeds match and found himself released from Old Trafford in March 1953, was now on Rotherham's books and he dearly desired to put one over his old club. Fortuitously still young enough to take part in the Youth Cup, the unpredictable hand of fate decreed that his current club would come up against his previous one with the prize of a quarter-final place at stake.

In the week leading up to the game, much of the country saw falls of snow. The welcome thaw that followed turned the Millmoor surface into an energy-sucking glue pot and the contest would develop into as much a test of lung and leg power as football technique.

As a result of the heavy conditions, it was agreed between the two Uniteds that a white ball should be used, a course of action that was taken in order to allow the spectators to spot the direction of the ball more easily in the soggy conditions. Even though it became normal practice to use a white ball many years ago, such an item was quite a novelty in 1954, when a much heavier brown ball, which soaked up water, was the usual choice.

Below a banner which read 'NO GOALS IN THRILLER AT MILLMOOR', the Rotherham Advertiser made the following observations:

Rotherham United Juniors delighted a crowd of more than 7,200 at Millmoor last Saturday, when they held Manchester United Juniors to a goalless draw, after extra-time played in semi-darkness.

The replay will be at Manchester on Wednesday, January 27th, under floodlights.

Rotherham, under no illusions as to the capabilities of their opponents, fought untiringly for success and matched just about everything Manchester could manage. The pace never flagged despite a very muddy pitch, and it says much for the fitness of the Rotherham team that they finished every bit as fresh as Manchester after a slogging two hours of football.

The two goalkeepers, Scrivens of Rotherham and Clayton for Manchester, were the heroes of a game that produced a lot of good football, and it would have been unfortunate if either of them had been beaten. Scrivens was injured in the last five minutes of extra-time while making a gallant save.

Rotherham had the better of the early play, and Clayton was in action, diving to save from Saul, and then a shot from Perry went just over the bar. Clayton made another grand save following a corner. Manchester called the tune when the second half opened, but Scrivens was given excellent cover by Willis and Cook, and the half-back line was in terrier-like mood.

Rotherham began to get on top again towards the end of normal time, and again did more of the attacking in extra-time. Perry was unfortunate not to score when he coolly back-heeled the ball and saw it stopped right on the line.

A star for Manchester was the diminutive Colman at wing-half, who played with all the assurance of a seasoned veteran, and McGuinness was also outstanding in a very accomplished defence. Along with Scrivens, Willis and Cook, best for Rotherham Juniors were Robbins at centre-half, and Perry among the forwards.

Peter Perry's back-heel effort, five minutes from the end of the contest, was hacked off the goal-line by United full-back Alan Rhodes, and David Pegg then countered for the Reds in the move which led to Rotherham goalie Scrivens receiving a nasty crack on the jaw. Despite being unable to continue, and just a few moments after he was led away for attention, the referee blew for full-time.

If the match at Rotherham underlined one fact for Jimmy Murphy, it was that there is never a proper substitute for installing a quality performer between the posts. While there hadn't been too much to occupy him in the previous two rounds, Gordon Clayton was a tower of strength for the Reds, and when one scribe wrote of the proceedings having *'hotted up to a rare tempo'* in the opening period, his report went on to claim that the *'keeper 'punched and dived to avert danger after danger'.*

It had been an all-action contest that positively thrilled the Millmoor crowd and totally belied the blank scoreline. As for the two teams, well, they would have to do it all over again in Manchester.

In the F.A. Cup, no replays were needed for the respective first-teams. Busby's men were beaten by five goals to three at Burnley but, with a splendid 3-1 win over Bristol City, Rotherham supporters had plenty to cheer about over that weekend.

34

1) Gordon Clayton	9) Peter Pearce
2) Ivan Beswick	10) Bobby Charlton
3) Alan Rhodes	11) David Pegg
4) Eddie Colman	
5) Bobby Harrop	
6) Wilf McGuinness	
7) Brian Lowry	
8) Duncan Edwards	

1) Bill Scrivens	9) Mel Ibbotson
2) Jim Willis	10) Peter Perry
3) Max Cook	11) Mick Saul
4) Albert Rhodes	
5) Gordon Robbins	
6) Tommy Seddon	
7) Barry Wainwright	
8) Glyn Jones	

1953-54

MANCHESTER UNITED* 3 v 1 ROTHERHAM UNITED

Edwards (3)   Ibbotson

JANUARY 1954

Wednesday 27th

Kick-off 7.00 p.m.

* Played at The Cliff

fourth round replay

The Cliff had already been pre-designated as the rematch venue even before a ball was kicked at Millmoor.

For the Millers, all of the eleven starters who had performed so well on their home patch were selected for the replay. Goalkeeper Bill Scriven's injury in the final moments at Rotherham was an unfortunate end to an otherwise great game, but thankfully he had sustained no lasting damage and was sufficiently recovered in time to take part in the next instalment.

There were changes for the Reds, with Duncan Edwards' recall to the youth side attracting most of the pre-match publicity. There was also a newcomer introduced to the United team, namely centre-forward Peter Pearce, and the attack was reorganised to accommodate both he and Edwards. With Sammy Chapman having returned to Northern Ireland, Tommy Littler was the only casualty of choice from the game at Millmoor.

United gave Rotherham the option of wearing the amber 'guest' jerseys but, possibly wary of the fate of previous wearers, Nantwich and Wrexham, they courteously declined, preferring instead to sport unfamiliar black and white striped shirts.

The Rotherham Advertiser's football correspondent penned the following match report:

F.A. Youth Cup, 4th Rd. Replay
MANCHESTER UNITED
v.
ROTHERHAM UNITED
by Floodlight, at The Cliff, Lower Broughton, on
Wednesday next, 27th Jan.
Kick-off 7 p.m.
Admission 1/-, Juniors 6d.

Cup Defeat At Manchester Was No Disgrace For United Juniors

ROTHERHAM United Juniors need not feel discouraged because of their 3-1 defeat by Manchester United Juniors at Manchester on Wednesday night, writes "Echo."

Rotherham, in this National Youth Cup-tie, came up against an even stronger Manchester side than that which visited Millmoor the other week, but fought pluckily throughout, and were not disgraced.

I think it was a pity that Manchester, in their eagerness to make sure of retaining this cup, which they won last season, found it necessary to bring into the side Duncan Edwards, who played in the England side against Italy last week, and has made 24 First Division appearances. I know Edwards is only 17, but I think it is against the basis of the Youth Cup to introduce professional players.

It was my first glimpse of Edwards, and indeed, he is an amazing player, almost of the John Charles stamp already. He was almost the entire reason for Manchester's superiority for not only did he score all their three goals but he dominated the play throughout. In addition Manchester had David Pegg and Bobby Charlton, both of whom have sampled First Division football, in their side.

Rotherham's team of local amateur —not recruited from the length and breadth of the country— had the added disadvantage of having to be at work all day Wednesday, and they found the bone-hard ground and the inadequate flood-lighting sore trials.

LOST THE BALL

Edwards scored the opening goal, 15 minutes after the start when he headed in from a corner, though Scrivens "lost" the ball in the semi-gloom. Scrivens later brought off a thrilling save from Charlton, and Pegg hit the upright, but Rotherham managed to do a fair share of the attacking in the first half, and were unlucky not to score when Rhodes kicked off the goal-line with the Manchester goalkeeper beaten.

For 20 minutes of the second half Rotherham more than held their own, and Jones was unfortunate with a great shot which Clayton saved at the foot of the upright. Then Edwards broke away, and with Rotherham defenders a little timid about going into the tackle, he threaded his way through to score with a brilliant shot. Undaunted, Rotherham fought back, and Ibbotson scored a fine goal from Wainwright's centre with 12 minutes to go, but in the last minute Edwards got a third goal for Manchester after the ball had rebounded from the cross-bar, Scrivens again misjudging the flight in the gloom.

The Rotherham defence fought hard to hold out, but the forwards seldom combined to bring any permanent relief. Scrivens did exceptionally well in goal, Robins was strong at centre-half, and Cook and Seddon also did useful work. Perry and Ibbotson were the best of the attack, Manchester's left-wing pair, Charlton and Pegg played some delightful football and Colman was best in defence. There were about 2,000 spectators with receipts of £96.

Despite the Reds conceding their first Youth Cup goal of the season, the power, skill, and determination of Edwards was principally the difference between the two sides.

The comments made by 'Echo' regarding Edwards' presence were totally uncalled for and sounded like a bad case of sour grapes. The Dudley lad had been on England under-23 duty in Italy just a week before facing Rotherham and that was a good enough reason to preclude him from further appearances in the tournament as far as the narrow-minded commentator was concerned.

One of the major benefits of the Youth Cup was to afford up-and-coming prospects the opportunity to pit their skills against the best of their contemporaries on a national stage. If it were left to 'Echo' who, it must be said, wasn't alone with his opinion on Edwards' inclusion, many of the finest prodigies in future years would have been prevented from taking part in the competition.

If the scribe had got his way, the Youth Cup stood to lose much of its credibility, as all the best individuals could have faced exclusion, and such a course of action would have turned the tournament into a distinctly second rate affair. Significantly, the Football Association shared the view that high calibre players, even full internationals, should be allowed to play their part in maintaining the highest possible standards in the competition.

Matt Busby wasn't slow to defend the club's decision to continue using Edwards in the tournament, and he aired his views on that very matter some time later in the Manchester Evening Chronicle:

A London friend told me that Manchester United were 'not playing fair' in their Youth Cup competition progress by including Duncan Edwards.

I was addressing a meeting of soccer referees the other night and the question cropped up. The general opinion was that Manchester United should not include him in their Youth Cup team.

So that's what people think. It amazes me! Duncan is eligible to participate in the Youth Cup and, what is more, is keen to play. He is no seeker of cups and medals, but he is just as anxious as any other United player to have the United name inscribed on the cup.

He may be 'outsize' in the juniors, but he will probably tell you that he has to work to the front the hard way. That is by constant training and coaching. The United youngster never needs to be told what to do – though he is not alone in that respect.

He, like others, is determined to make a success of his career as a footballer and is willing to listen to advice and put that advice into practice on the field.

Here is an eighteen year-old whose example can be a lesson to every soccer-thinking youth. There is no easy road to success in the game, not even if you have extra height and weight to help you.

I am happy to think that Duncan is getting so many honours from the game. I am glad to know that he remains as keen a player in junior soccer circles as in representative games.

Whatever the politics of the situation were, the score showed three goals to one in the United boys' favour and their ambition of retaining the trophy was now another step nearer to becoming a reality.

1953-54

1) Mick Topps	9) Johnny Sewell	
2) Eric Bingley	10) Terry Gill	
3) Roy Chorley	11) John West	
4) Trevor Edwards		
5) Ken Titcombe		
6) Keith Cox		
7) David Ruston		
8) Bernard Jarrold		

1) Gordon Clayton	9) Bobby Charlton	
2) Ivan Beswick	10) David Pegg	
3) Alan Rhodes	11) Albert Scanlon	
4) Eddie Colman		
5) Bobby Harrop		
6) Wilf McGuinness		
7) Brian Lowry		
8) Duncan Edwards		

MARCH 1954

BEXLEYHEATH & WELLING 1 v 2 MANCHESTER UNITED
Jarrold — *Charlton, Edwards*

fifth round

Saturday 13th
Kick-off 2.45 p.m.
Attendance 4,300

The opposition lying in waiting for the cup holders at the quarter-final stage was undeniably the surprise package of that season's competition. Almost unknown outside of football circles in the Home Counties, it is easy to picture United's officials scurrying to get hold of a map in order to ascertain precisely where they were situated once the draw was announced.

The pairing of the two sides created an event that, well over half a century later, has never been repeated during the Reds' participation in the Youth Cup. That is, they were required to play on the ground of non-league opponents.

The senior team of their hosts, Bexleyheath & Welling Football Club, were members of the Kent League Division One and the standard of football in that sphere in the 1950's was particularly good as almost all of the participating members were fully professional outfits.

At first glance, it appeared the draw had given United a rather 'soft' entry into the semi-final although, on closer inspection, two factors would totally dispel that theory. Firstly, at that period in time, Bexleyheath & Welling were the 'nursery' club of First Division side and near neighbours, Charlton Athletic. The arrangement between the two clubs was likely to be that, in return for some measure of financial support, Charlton would be given the first option of any of the Bexleyheath & Welling juniors who they felt were up to the required standard.

The Football League imposed restrictions on the number of juniors a club were permitted to sign at any given time, so the establishment of a 'nursery' circumvented that and other rules regarding the acquisition and development of promising youngsters. Curiously, 'nursery' clubs were much more common in the south of England than they were in the north.

The second consideration for United's management team was the impressive way in which Bexleyheath & Welling had reached the quarter-finals, dumping out the teenage representatives of two Football League clubs along the way.

Crystal Palace tasted defeat in the First Round, going down 5-3 in front of the Bexleyheath & Welling supporters, and victories over fellow non-leaguers, Longfleet (5-2 at home) and Woking (4-1, away), in the Second and Third Rounds respectively, brought First Division Chelsea's youth eleven to the compact Park View Road ground. There were wild scenes of delight at the end of a momentous victory for the Kent side when they finally overcame the fancied Londoners by winning 4-2 after extra-time.

Interest in the game against United was intense in and around the neighbouring towns and villages. In that respect, the club was to be applauded for their initiative in turning it into an occasion that still holds fond memories for many football followers in the locality.

Aware that the Manchester party faced a long journey back north after the match and extra-time, if necessary, needed to be accounted for, the start was brought forward slightly to a quarter to three. Tickets for the game were sold in advance, the gates opening promptly at 1.30 p.m., and members of the club's senior side acted as stewards for the day.

Prior to the match and at half-time, the Nicolson Pipe Band from Folkestone entertained the crowd, and shortly before kick-off the 22 participants and three officials were introduced to the Mayor of Bexley, Alderman M.J. Corr, J.P., who acted as president of the football club.

Bexleyheath & Welling even went to the trouble of advising their supporters not to use the club tea room that afternoon because it was designated strictly for the visitors. It was a most considerate gesture by the hosts, whose objective was to provide anyone who had travelled from Manchester to obtain refreshments with the minimum of waiting time.

The match programme produced for the tie proudly proclaimed within its cover, 'TOWN FOOTBALL CLUB OF KENT'S LARGEST BOROUGH'. That heading gave an indication as to the club's long-term ambition, as admission to the Football League was the top priority of Bexleyheath & Welling's stated objectives.

In his programme notes, manager Bert Johnson wrote, *'Considerable interest has focused on today's game. Had it been played a week earlier the BBC would have televised it.......'*

Just exactly why the BBC had proposed to screen the match on the previous

Gordon Clayton cuts an isolated figure while making a simple catch at a sloping Park View Road

Saturday and not on the scheduled date remains a mystery, but what fascinating viewing the clash would have made today had it been filmed and kept for posterity.

The Reds received a massive boost when Duncan Edwards was included for the replayed game against Rotherham and there was similar good news for the trip to Kent. Wing-wizard Albert Scanlon was back to full fitness after his cartilage problems and found himself named at number eleven, a development which saw Peter Pearce squeezed out of the line-up.

The seriousness that Matt Busby and Jimmy Murphy placed on the tie was underlined when Edwards was taken off senior duties to assist the youth side for the second successive game. Busby's decision to include Edwards was undoubtedly influenced by the recently announced news that the youth squad was booked to appear in an end of season international tournament in Switzerland.

It was Busby's intention that United should go there as England's premier youth side, and to achieve that honour it was essential to retain the Youth Cup. In the short-term at least, that meant seeing off the challenge of Bexleyheath & Welling.

If the Reds' injury news was good, the same couldn't be said for the home team as star forward and tormenter-in-chief of Chelsea in the previous round, Eddie Werge, had sustained a leg knock while playing for the Bexleyheath & Welling seniors. Werge's woes gave an opening to David Ruston, who came in at outside-right, while Bernard Jarrold moved into the position vacated by Werge's absence.

With the 'Full House' notices up all around the ground well before kick-off time, all was set for a keen duel.

Seen on the right, the Kentish Times delivered a balanced and informative report:

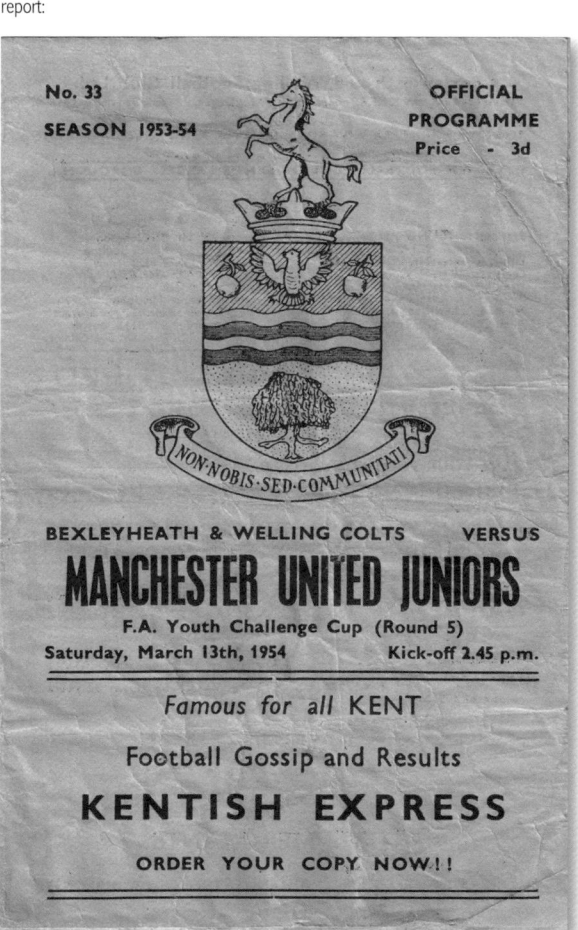

TOWN COLTS' CUP RUN ENDS

MANCHESTER UNITED WIN IN CLOSING MINUTES

BEXLEYHEATH and Welling Colts just failed to reach the semi-final of the much-coveted F.A. Youth Cup, losing to Manchester United Juniors by 2—1 in the fifth round at Park View-road ground, Welling, on Saturday. Town Colts held the northern boys to 1—1 until the 85th minute, when during a period of Town pressure United scored from a breakaway.

At least 4,300 saw a thrilling game, which swayed first in favour of one side and then the other. The attendance breaks the ground record, every corner being packed, and there was a large contingent from Manchester.

Manchester, the holders, are reputed to be the finest youth team in Britain. They included Duncan Edwards, who played in the "Young England" side at Bologna this season, inside-left Pegg, who has had considerable experience in Manchester United's first eleven, Charlton, a nephew of Jackie Milburn, who has also played in the first team, and McGuinness who, with Charlton, played for English Schools last season. Every Manchester boy was either a professional or is on the club's ground staff.

Yet Town Colts, by their determination and enthusiasm, made the northerners look ordinary, and victory was almost in their grasp. Town missed a penalty, but even so for most of the game the score was 1—1 and at any time the Colts might have snatched the winning goal instead of Manchester. It was touch and go all the way.

Manchester were the more dangerous in the front line, but the Colts had by far the better defence. United were faster on the ball, but the Colts covered so well and kicked so cleanly and accurately that nearly all the visitors' attacks broke down before they reached the danger area. Town's great handicap was the strange forward-line. Edwin Werge was badly missed and the line lacked cohesion. Their strength lay in the halves and backs, and Mick Topps was brilliant in goal.

Ken Titcombe was the outstanding player afield. He held Charlton in a tight grip and showed clever anticipation. Keith Cox also played one of his best games. His tackling completely upset the tall, well-built Edwards.

Town's move in bringing in Roy Chorley to partner Eric Bingley at back proved a feature of the game. Chorley fitted in perfectly. United's right-winger was speedy and clever, but this only served to draw out the best in Chorley, whose kicking, positioning and interception were faultless. Bingley proved again to be a polished defender just waiting for a chance to fit into the senior teams. Terry Gill was the liveliest of the forwards, but as a line they were disappointing.

Manchester scored first, after Topps had brought off two daring saves. Edwards received the ball and shot hard from 25yds, and Topps could only get his fingertips to the ball.

Town Colts fought back and stormed the United goal time after time. They gained their reward when from a corner Sewell's header was punched out by United's goalkeeper to Bernard Jarrold, who lobbed the ball over a crowd of players into the net.

From then on it was a ding-dong struggle, with either side likely to notch a winner. Tragedy came for Town when goalkeeper Clayton was penalised for what happened to be punching a Town forward. The referee pointed to the penalty spot, but after protests from United players he consulted the linesman and adhered to his decision. Titcombe shot straight at Clayton, who punched clear. Subsequently Titcombe prevented several likely goals and ended with enough glory to wipe out the memory of his penalty miss.

Clayton was prone to panic when harried and three times he dropped the ball dangerously because a Colt would not allow him an unchallenged kick. On one of these occasions the ball went loose with Clayton on the floor and the net empty, but no Colt was backing up.

Near the end United were defending most of the time. But they suddenly broke away and a long pass down the middle found Topps, Charlton and a defender racing for the ball. It seemed as if both Colts would get there first, but Charlton found a sudden spurt and just got a touch and the ball rolled into the empty net.

Town threw all caution to the winds and at one stage ten Colts could be counted in United's penalty box. Almost with the last kick Sewell sent over a high centre, but the chance went unaccepted.

And Town Colts' great run in the Youth Cup was over—but what a fright they gave the Manchester lads.

No. 33
SEASON 1953-54

OFFICIAL PROGRAMME
Price - 3d

BEXLEYHEATH & WELLING COLTS VERSUS

MANCHESTER UNITED JUNIORS

F.A. Youth Challenge Cup (Round 5)
Saturday, March 13th, 1954   Kick-off 2.45 p.m.

Famous for all KENT

Football Gossip and Results

KENTISH EXPRESS

ORDER YOUR COPY NOW!!

1953-54

MARCH 1954

fifth round

Duncan Edwards looks to challenge Bexleyheath 'keeper Mick Topps while Bobby Charlton (centre) stays alert

As the ball flashes across Bexleyheath & Welling's penalty area, United's complete forward-line is on view from left to right: Brian Lowry (partially hidden), David Pegg, Albert Scanlon, Bobby Charlton and Duncan Edwards

1953-54

MARCH 1954

fifth round

Syd Jordan Returns to the "K.T."

(cartoon by Syd Jordan, 1954, depicting the F.A. Youth Cup tie between Bexleyheath and Welling Colts and Manchester United Juniors, with captions including:)

- BUT OF COURSE MANCHESTER UNITED COLTS ARE ----
- WHEN THIS CUP TIE BECAME KNOWN SPORTS WRITERS BEGAN TO WRITE OFF THE TOWN COLTS CHANCES AND
- FOR A TIME THE MANCUNIAN BALL PLAY WAS BEWILDERING BUT SOON THE HOME COLTS
- GOT "STUCK IN" (WHATEVER THAT MIGHT MEAN) AND GAVE AS GOOD AS THEY RECEIVED.
- JOHNNY SEWELL WAS ALL SMILES BEFORE THE GAME BUT
- WHEN HE SAW THE OPPOSING CENTRE HALF JOHNNY WENT FOR HELP BUT IT MADE NO DIFFERENCE. THIS WAS THE ONLY WAY.
- ANOTHER BIG BOY FROM MANCHESTER WAS DUNCAN EDWARDS WHO FOUND HIS COLLEAGUES WITH CLEVER PASSES AND OPENED THE SCORE IN 22 MINUTES
- BUT BERNIE JARROLD PUT TOWN COLTS ON LEVEL TERMS 19 MINUTES LATER WITH A GREAT GOAL.
- TERRY GILL SKIPPERED TOWN COLTS AMONG WHOM MICK TOPPS WAS SAFE IN GOAL
- HOW FAR IS MANCHESTER? THERE WAS PLENTY OF VOCAL SUPPORT AND WHEN
- KEITH COX A WORKER AT WING HALF AND KEN TITCOMBE HELD THE MIDDLE WELL.
- ARRANGEMENTS WERE BEING MADE FOR THE REPLAY MANCHESTER SCORED FIVE MINUTES BEFORE — THE END.

Syd Jordan, well-known sports cartoonist—who began his career with the *Kentish Times* in 1919 and contributed his popular sketches to our columns for 20 years — has returned to us, and his work will appear regularly in appropriate papers in our series, according to the event visited. This week's cartoon deals with the F.A. Youth Cup tie between Bexleyheath and Welling Colts and Manchester United Juniors.

It had been a titanic tussle and United were grateful that they managed to survive Bexleyheath & Welling's bombardment in the later stages of the game. Towards the end of the tie, the home side gambled heavily on killing the Reds off without the need for a replay and paid the price with Charlton's winner.

Jimmy Murphy, in his 1968 book 'Matt....United......and me', declared that United *'were given a rough ride'* in the game and that he and Bert Whalley were heckled by a section of the crowd.

One rather loud gentleman shrieked down his ear *'Murphy, where is this great Edwards of yours? We ain't seen him yet.'* The coach went on to explain that Edwards chose that precise moment to pick the ball up in midfield and carry it forward a few paces before smashing it into the back of the Bexleyheath net. *'That is Edwards!'* replied Murphy, when turning to face the silenced supporter.

Of the Bexleyheath & Welling team, several made further progress in the game. Goalscorer Bernard Jarrold became an England Youth international while Terry Gill remained with the club and went on to become a prolific marksman in their senior eleven. David Ruston joined local Corinthian League amateur outfit, Erith & Belvedere.

No less than five of the side later signed for Charlton Athletic, three of whom made it into their first-team. Keith Cox put in fourteen appearances for the Addicks before emigrating in 1960 and John Sewell featured in over 200 league and cup starts for them before moving to Crystal Palace and then Leyton Orient.

Making his debut against Manchester United in February 1957, Trevor Edwards put in 66 appearances for Charlton prior to transferring to Cardiff City where he won two full caps for Wales. John West and Ken Titcombe served Charlton's Reserve and third teams while injury victim Eddie Werge also later played first-team football at The Valley.

1953-54

1) Geoff Barnsley	9) Brian Whitehouse
2) Don Howe	10) Alan Tranter
3) Jimmy Harris	11) Jimmy Garbett
4) Stan Purvis	
5) Jack Willetts	
6) Barry Cooke	
7) Mick Henson	
8) Tommy Watson	

1) Gordon Clayton	9) Peter Pearce
2) Ivan Beswick	10) Bobby Charlton
3) Alan Rhodes	11) David Pegg
4) Eddie Colman	
5) Bobby Harrop	
6) Wilf McGuinness	
7) Albert Scanlon	
8) Duncan Edwards	

MARCH 1954

WEST BROMWICH ALBION 1 v 3 MANCHESTER UNITED
Whitehouse — Pegg (2), Scanlon

Wednesday 31st
Kick-off 3.00 p.m.
Attendance 3,335

semi-final 1st leg

Scanlon's goal in Youth Cup

Now into the two-legged part of the competition, United's adversaries in the semi-final gave coach Jimmy Murphy a welcome opportunity to return to The Hawthorns, a ground where he was still held in the greatest of esteem from his playing days. If they were to reach the final for a second time, the Reds needed to beat a West Bromwich Albion team that had defeated, after a First Round bye, Chesterfield (1-0, away), Boldmere St. Michael's (7-2 at home), Sunderland (1-0, away) and Leeds United (3-1 at home).

The Albion were a club very much in the pink of health and Baggies' supporters were thoroughly enjoying one of their best ever campaigns. One of a group of chasers trailing Wolves for the First Division title, they had already booked a Wembley F.A. Cup final appearance against Preston on the first day of May.

Murphy made one adjustment to the eleven who had defeated Bexleyheath & Welling, Brian Lowry bowing out to allow Peter Pearce to regain his place at centre-forward. Positional changes meant that Albert Scanlon moved to outside-right, Bobby Charlton to inside-left and David Pegg to outside-left.

On a bright and largely mild afternoon, the Reds kicked off with the sun in their faces and wasted no time posing threats to the Albion defence. Arch schemer Eddie Colman slipped a neat pass into the area for Pearce to chase, with the ball plucked off his toenails by the out-rushing West Brom 'keeper.

The Reds pressed for a second time, and when Duncan Edwards spotted an opening, he drove a shot from just inside the box that brought the goalkeeper down on his knees in order to smother the moving ball.

United had set out an attacking stall that was based on the customary hard midfield graft demanded by Murphy, as well as lots of intelligent movement from the forwards.

Albion's best chance of the first half came about when Whitehouse climbed to beat Bobby Harrop to a cross. Harrop had intelligently positioned himself so that the West Brom leader couldn't make a proper connection with the ball and the covering defenders assisted him in ensuring the safety of their goal.

Albion then experienced a let off when Pegg slid a cunning pass into the feet of Edwards. The number eight was situated directly in front of goal, with the time and space to plant an easy shot past Geoff Barnsley, but an uncharacteristically tame effort flew straight into the arms of the grateful home goalie.

United certainly claimed the better part of the possession and displayed much the greater momentum going forward, although a second opening in as many attacks was wasted when Scanlon cut his way to goal only to thump a shot which was well wide.

With hardly time for West Brom to regroup, the Reds built yet another offensive movement, only this time, with 33 minutes gone, it ended with them taking a deserved lead. Despite operating in an unaccustomed right-wing role, Scanlon was prompting practically all of United's moves and he had temporarily switched across field into an area somewhere near to the inside-left spot. Gifted possession by Edwards, Scanlon took the ball forward a couple of paces before unleashing an unstoppable shot that shaved along the turf before nestling in the corner of the Albion net.

With no further incidents of note, that goal provided a 1-0 lead for the Old Trafford boys at the interlude.

The second session started in a heavy drizzle. The rain couldn't dampen the fire in the visitors' endeavours, though, and they were soon blazing at the Albion defensive door once more when a slick passing sequence, which involved every Manchester forward, ended with Scanlon's shot skimming barely inches wide of a post.

West Brom retaliated at last when left-winger Garbett won a rare corner that was cleared without ceremony by Ivan Beswick. The Reds quickly returned on the offensive via another move that gave Scanlon a clear sighting of goal, his effort again slashing off target.

With the second half midway through, United inflicted two further goals on the Baggies that were totally in keeping with the run of play. In the 64th minute, Edwards turned provider once again when finding an unmarked Pegg with a quick pass across the goalmouth. Exercising a coolness which constituted one of his trademarks, Pegg clipped the ball home to leave a startled Barnsley stranded.

Two minutes later Peter Pearce, who had drifted out wide to the right edge of the pitch, caught the West Brom defence off guard with a superb cross-field ball. Having moved inside once again, Scanlon cushioned a headed pass to Pegg who duly chested the ball down prior to picking his spot with a shot that saw Albion's goalkeeper forlornly fishing in the net.

In the latter part of the game, West Brom rose themselves to a rally in which centre-forward Whitehouse scored a fine individual goal. With thirteen minutes left to play, the Albion couldn't add to it and the game finished 3-1 in United's favour.

It represented a fine afternoon's work for the Reds, whose cute tactic of interchanging positions in the forward-line kept West Brom's rearguard mesmerised. There were also great displays from Harrop, Beswick and left full-back Alan Rhodes, a trio of snapping guard dogs at the back. Those named had largely kept the Albion danger men in check and deserved at least as much praise as those in front of them.

Wing-halves Colman and McGuinness also made immense contributions, most of United's moves stemming from their constant ball-winning and fluid distribution work.

The Reds' performance was unanimously praised in the press. One Midlands newspaper encapsulated the 90 minutes by stating that *'Manchester's brilliant wingers netted the goals at The Hawthorns on Wednesday in a display of football craft which would make many First Division sides look to their laurels'.*

Albert Scanlon, who scored the opener at The Hawthorns and paved United's way to the final

1) Gordon Clayton	9) Peter Pearce	
2) Ivan Beswick	10) Bobby Charlton	
3) Alan Rhodes	11) David Pegg	
4) Eddie Colman		
5) Bobby Harrop		
6) Wilf McGuinness		
7) Albert Scanlon		
8) Duncan Edwards		

1) Geoff Barnsley	9) Brian Whitehouse
2) Don Howe	10) Tommy Watson
3) Jack Willetts	11) Jimmy Garbett
4) Stan Purvis	
5) John Reynolds	
6) Barry Cooke	
7) Bob Townsend	
8) Alan Tranter	

1953-54

MANCHESTER UNITED 4 (7) v (1) 0 WEST BROMWICH ALBION

Colman, Edwards, Pearce, Scanlon

APRIL 1954

Monday 12th

Kick-off 5.45 p.m.

Attendance 9,451

semi-final 2nd leg

---

6   MANCHESTER EVENING NEWS, Monday, April 12, 1954.

DUNCAN EDWARDS IN TO-NIGHT'S BIG GAME

United's "bright boys" aim at Cup double

— BY — TOM JACKSON

DUNCAN EDWARDS, Manchester United's 17-year-old England "B" team player, will head an array of some of the brightest young soccer prospects in the country at Old Trafford to-night when he plays at inside-right in United's F.A. Youth Cup side now making a strong bid to repeat last season's success in winning the trophy.

United start their second-leg semi-final against West Bromwich Albion's up-and-coming youngsters two goals to the good. They won 3-1 at the Hawthorns last month and, as the winners of this tie qualify to meet Wolves, a repeat of last season's finals, which attracted big crowds, is on the cards.

Six schoolboy internationals will be in United's line-up unchanged from that which played in the first semi-final and which will again be captained by outside left David Pegg, who, like Edwards, has played in First Division football.

Other players to note in this parade of the young soccer idea are pint-sized Eddie Colman, ex-Salford Boys, right-half; Wilf McGuinness, the Manchester boy who has captained the England schools' side, at left half; and Bobby Charlton, inside left and schoolboy international nephew of Jackie Milburn, of Newcastle United.

With a lot of ground to make up in their attempt to emulate the achievement of their first-team in reaching a national cup final, West Brom plumped for changes in the second leg of the semi-final at Old Trafford. John Reynolds was brought in at centre-half for Jack Willetts, who moved to left-back, and Jimmy Harris lost his place in the side, as did Mick Henson, who was replaced at outside-right by Bob Townsend. Alan Tranter and Tommy Watson swapped the number eight and ten shirts.

The game started with United adopting a 'shoot-on-sight' policy and Albion's Geoff Barnsley had his hands warmed early in the game with a number of long-range drives, particularly from Duncan Edwards, which he did well to handle. The Reds saw most of the ball and, right from the off, their performance was positively sugar-coated.

With so much confidence and experience running through the home team, the tie quickly became a one-sided affair in which the Albion never quite made enough of an impression.

Despite working hard as a unit, West Brom were constantly pinned in their own half for sustained periods and it was something of a minor success that they lasted almost half an hour before conceding a goal. On 29 minutes, Peter Pearce broke the deadlock with an opener for the host team and five minutes later Eddie Colman made sure of a repeat United appearance in the final when grabbing number two.

Duncan Edwards was patently in no mood to be denied a goal of his own and he finally succeeded with one of his many power drives that almost broke the Baggies' net after 64 minutes.

Only nine minutes more passed before Albert Scanlon hit United's fourth and final goal of the game to conclude a scoreline of 4-0 on the day and an aggregate victory of 7-1 over both legs. The margin was very much an accurate reflection of the difference in ability between the two teams.

All throughout, Albion's forwards were unable to shake off the limpet-like grip of United's defenders and wing-halves. Similarly, their defenders never looked anything remotely resembling comfortable with the task at hand and they were in constant distress when trying to contain a slippery home attack.

West Brom were hit by a whirlwind display, and with all due credit for running themselves almost to a standstill in their attempts to make a fight of it, they had come up against a team who were in no mood for bargaining. Put simply, in terms of ability and know-how, the Old Trafford eleven were on a different level entirely.

Of the Albion side, right-back Don Howe went on to become easily the most famous. A stylish defender of the finest order, Howe made 23 full appearances for England before moving into the coaching side of the game where he was again involved in the national set-up for a number of years.

Albion centre-forward Brian Whitehouse also became a coach and was well known to Manchester United fans in that capacity during a spell at Old Trafford in the 1980's.

Despite the Albion youngsters' inability to make it to the last stage of the Youth Cup, the season ended on a glorious high note for the West Midlands club. The Baggies' senior side conquered Preston by three goals to two at Wembley to lift the F.A. Cup, additionally finishing in second place in the First Division to local rivals, Wolves.

41

1953-54

1) Tony Hawksworth
2) Ivan Beswick
3) Alan Rhodes
4) Eddie Colman
5) Bobby Harrop
6) Wilf McGuinness
7) Tommy Littler
8) Duncan Edwards
9) Bobby Charlton
10) David Pegg
11) Albert Scanlon

1) Geoff Sidebottom
2) Tony Griffiths
3) Gerry Harris
4) Frank Bolton
5) John Timmins
6) John Fallon
7) Stan Round
8) Bob Mason
9) Joe Bonson
10) Jimmy Murray
11) Len Cooper

APRIL 1954

MANCHESTER UNITED 4 v 4 WOLVERHAMPTON WANDERERS

Edwards (2), Pegg (2, 1 pen) — Bonson, Fallon, Mason, Murray

Friday 23rd
Kick-off 6.45 p.m.
Attendance 18,246

final 1st leg

FOOTBALL AT OLD TRAFFORD
TOMORROW (FRIDAY)
KICK-OFF 6-45 p.m.
F.A. Youth Cup Final
(FIRST LEG)
UNITED
(HOLDERS)
v.
WOLVES
ADMISSION:
Ground 1/-, Juniors 6d.
Covered Paddock & Terrace 2/-.
Grand Stand 3/-.

For the second season in succession, the side barring the way between United and the Youth Cup trophy, at the last stage of the tournament, was Wolverhampton Wanderers. The many-talented Wolves had blazed an equally impressive trail to the final as they did in the previous campaign and fairly rattled in the goals during their opening three ties.

After hammering Stoke City 7-0, they went on to inflict further drubbings of 8-0 on Derby County and 11-1 on Spalding United, all on home territory. Two close away victories followed, 1-0 at Nottingham Forest and 2-1 at Portsmouth, before a brilliant double over West Ham in the semi-final, 6-1 at Molineux and 2-1 at Upton Park, set up a repeat final as per twelve months previously.

Seven of those who featured in the 1953 final also took to the field in the 1954 version, with John Timmins, Frank Bolton and Len Cooper remaining for the Wanderers. That the Wolves had again managed to reach the tournament's showpiece with a side consisting of eight different faces was an indication of the tremendous strength in depth of their youth system at that time.

The Reds had Eddie Colman, Duncan Edwards, David Pegg and Albert Scanlon available, all of whom aspired to double their tally of silver plaques. There should have been one other participant from United's 1953 youth side on show but alas, after conceding only three goals in eight previous ties that season, goalkeeper Gordon Clayton was denied a place in the concluding games by a piece of wretched luck. Shortly before the final, the Cannock native sustained a broken wrist which robbed him of the opportunity of any further glory and the United youths of a popular, talented and experienced colleague in a key position.

Clayton's badly-timed injury meant an introduction for Tony Hawksworth, a sixteen year-old from Yorkshire who had only recently made his first appearance in the Central League. In a scenario similar to the year before, when John Doherty's misfortune created an opening for Billy Whelan in the starting line-up, Clayton's fracture brought about a tournament debut in the final for Hawksworth. Much as everyone concerned felt a great deal of sympathy for 'Big Gordon', Matt Busby and Jimmy Murphy wouldn't have lost any sleep over having to include Hawksworth in such an important game as they were simply replacing one former England Boys starlet with another.

There was one other change for the Reds, with the energetic Tommy Littler regaining his place at outside-right. The unfortunate individual who dropped out was Peter Pearce and, once again, the United offensive formation was reorganised accordingly.

With the memory of last season's heavy defeat at Old Trafford, where the 7-1 opening leg reverse reduced their chances of overhauling United to almost zero, Wolves chose to approach the match in Manchester with entirely changed tactics.

As the Wolverhampton Express & Star recorded, the outcome would also be considerably different:

WOLVES' BIG CHANCE TO TURN YOUTH CUP TABLES

WHAT a thriller there is in store for Wolves supporters on Monday when, at Molineux, the second leg of the F.A. Youth Cup final is played between Wolves and Manchester United. At Old Trafford last night, in the first set-to, Wolves shared eight goals with last year's cup winners in the first leg. With ordinary luck, Monday should see them holders of the trophy for the first time. The cup will be presented to the winners immediately after the game.

There was only one team in it in the first half, when Manchester were always struggling against a faster opposition.

The speed of the Wolves forwards gave the Old Trafford supporters the impression that the second leg would be a formality for Wolves, who hit back after a five-minute Manchester goal by Edwards, former Dudley schoolboy international, to score three goals through Bonson, Murray and Mason, and might easily have taken the total to five.

They peppered the Manchester defence into a state of near panic with their long accurate passes and strong shooting, and it was a very subdued 18,246 crowd who watched their favourites outplayed and outgeneralled.

In the second half, however, United moved England half-back Edwards, who plays inside-right for the youth team, to centre-forward. His strong bustling style set Wolves a problem they never really solved.

Previously they had been able to concentrate on attack for long periods, but the second half was another story. From a 3–1 interval lead it became 3–2 when Timmins handled an awkwardly-placed shot by Charlton for Pegg to score from the penalty spot. Then an Edwards header, a repeat of his goal in the first five minutes, brought the vocal encouragement from the spectators the Manchester team so sorely needed.

United's hopes slumped again as Wolves fought back with a beautiful goal—a 30-yard rising shot from left-half Fallon that was a goal from the moment it left his foot.

With the score 4–3 against them, the Old Trafford team threw everything into attack, for Pegg to score the final equaliser in a thrill-packed closing 20 minutes.

Never-still Bonson

Then the Wolves defence really came into its own.

Through all the thrills and fluctuations there ran the excellent team work of the Wolves. They showed far better combination than the home youths, and Murray and Mason, at inside-forward, used their wingers intelligently.

Cooper, on the left wing, was later handicapped with an ankle injury.

Centre-forward Bonson held the line together well, and his wanderings to the wings, especially in the first half, kept the United defence on tenterhooks. They did not know where he would appear next.

Bolton and Fallon, at wing half, kept the ball moving to their forwards in quick-fire style, and Timmins blotted Charlton out of the game when he was centre-forward.

Griffiths, at right-back, had a tough assignment in holding the lively Scanlon, but Harris never gave Littler any room, and the Manchester right-winger had a poor game in consequence.

The shrewd ploy of switching Duncan Edwards into the centre-forward role at the break was just the spark that was required to re-energise the Reds at a time when their prospects of success had faded to a pale shade of white. Clawing their way back to level the score was an achievement in itself, but it couldn't detract from a magnificent performance by the impressive Wanderers. In the view of many contemporary observers, United's failure to fully capitalise on their home advantage now meant that the scales were tipped considerably in favour of a victory for Wolves in the return tie at Molineux.

United's Chronicle correspondent Tom Jackson put forward his view of the evening's events under a strapline reading 'EDWARDS THE BULLDOZER SHOWED HOW':

1953-54

APRIL 1954

Thanks to a thrill-a-minute second-half recovery, Manchester United's under-18 team will begin the second leg of their F.A. Youth Cup final with Wolves at Molineux on Monday night with a 50-50 chance of retaining their hold on the trophy.

It looked as though the virile young Wolves, faster on the ball and deadly in their tackling, were going home with a handsome goal margin in their favour when they turned round leading 3-1 in the first instalment at Old Trafford last night. But how the Busby lads fought back!

With mighty Duncan Edwards bulldozing his way through the middle and David Pegg and Albert Scanlon teaming up perfectly on the left wing, United had the big-kicking Wolves defenders on tenterhooks.

From 1-3, Edwards and Pegg made it 3-all and the excitement mounted for the 18,246 spectators as Wolves again grabbed the lead only for Pegg to put the teams level within two minutes.

That's how they stand for Monday's return. It's still anybody's game, but if the young warriors put on a show only half as exciting as that second half at Old Trafford it will still be worth every mile of the journey to Molineux.

Wolves are strong - in fact they're a team moulded on the Stan Cullis tradition. They put the young ball artists such as Colman and Charlton out of their stride with their quick-fire tactics, but with McGuinness in good form at left-half and the forwards in better shape United found the way through.

Yes. It was great stuff all round.

With everyone in agreement with Jackson's last comment, all thoughts turned to the massive forthcoming task in Wolverhampton.

> "The home leg of the final against Wolves was a fantastic game, probably the best I ever played in. We didn't really deserve to be behind at half-time but they took their chances and we didn't.
>
> Jimmy (Murphy) and Bert (Whalley) encouraged us no end in the dressing room, told us how good we'd been and that there was everything to play for.
>
> In the second half we completely bombarded them. The ball seemed to keep coming to me from Duncan, in fact so often that I was completely knackered after about an hour. We got a corner and I called Duncan over, I told him to give the ball to someone else for a few minutes so that I could get my breath back. He was playing them on his own at times, and winning too. There are times in football when you have to accept defeat only nobody seemed to tell Duncan that was the case.
>
> Wolves were a really good side, they had a few who had played for England but, with a bit of help from the rest of us, Duncan gave us a chance going to Molineux."
>
> **TOMMY LITTLER**

final 1st leg

The Manchester United side ahead of the home leg of the 1953/54 Youth Cup final
Back row (l-r) Arthur Powell (Trainer), Ivan Beswick, Bobby Harrop, Duncan Edwards, Tony Hawksworth, Alan Rhodes, Albert Scanlon, Bobby Charlton
Front row (l-r) David Pegg, Tommy Littler, Eddie Colman, Wilf McGuinness

1953-54

1) Geoff Sidebottom
2) Tony Griffiths
3) Gerry Harris
4) Frank Bolton
5) John Timmins
6) John Fallon
7) Stan Round
8) Bob Mason
9) Joe Bonson
10) Jimmy Murray
11) Len Cooper

1) Tony Hawksworth
2) Ivan Beswick
3) Alan Rhodes
4) Eddie Colman
5) Bobby Harrop
6) Wilf McGuinness
7) Tommy Littler
8) Duncan Edwards
9) Bobby Charlton
10) David Pegg
11) Albert Scanlon

APRIL 1954

WOLVERHAMPTON WANDERERS 0(4) v (5)1 **MANCHESTER UNITED**

Pegg (pen)

Monday 26th

Kick-off 6.30 p.m.

Attendance 28,651

final 2nd leg

One of eleven winners' plaques supplied by the Football Association for the 1954 Youth Cup final - this one awarded to Tommy Littler

When the United squad arrived at Molineux to conclude their outstanding matter with Wolves, they were met by the atmosphere of a whole town in rapturous celebration. Just two days before the concluding instalment of the Youth Cup final, the Wanderers' senior team defeated Spurs to capture the First Division title in their last game of the season.

Of course, the players were left in no doubt as to the size of the task ahead of them by Jimmy Murphy and Bert Whalley, who explained that they should expect a full-blooded affair against a similarly talented team of teenagers. What the Reds' party probably hadn't bargained for was contending with the cauldron of noise and expectancy inside Molineux created by nearly 30,000 local supporters, who would be willing their youths on in the hope of ending an already triumphant campaign with a further trophy success.

The Wolverhampton Express & Star captured the prevailing mood in words with a preview of the evening's proceedings:

All the excitement available to Wolves and their followers was not expended in the scenes following the last championship match on Saturday. There is the prospect of more tonight with the certainty of seeing Football League president, Mr. Arthur Drewry, hand over to Wolves the championship cup and Mr. Joe Richards, of Barnsley, chairman of the F.A. Youth Cup committee, present the Youth Cup to the winners of the tie between Wolves and Manchester United.

Tonight's youth cup match is the second leg of their repeat of last season's Youth Cup final.

This season, however, there is a slight difference – a matter of six goals in fact. Whereas last season Wolves began the second game at Molineux lagging 7-1, they go into the field tonight able to start on level terms after creditably drawing 4-4 at Old Trafford in the first leg last Friday.

In the corresponding game at Molineux last season, Wolves held their own with a 2-2 draw. That, however, was not sufficient and the cup went back with United on the strength of a 9-3 aggregate win to Old Trafford. The young Wolves hope to wrest it from the holders tonight and set the seal on a season during which some of them have helped also to win the Birmingham League title.

With neither team carrying any injury problems forward, the same 22 personnel who had treated the Old Trafford crowd to a feast of eight goals would be on duty again at Molineux.

The Express & Star recorded the outcome, which didn't follow the majority of expectations, in the following considered way:

No triple triumph for the Molineux club

YOUNG WOLVES AGAIN FAIL IN BID FOR YOUTH CUP

EVERYTHING in the Molineux garden would have been lovely last night if only the Wolves youth eleven had succeeded in doing what all Wolverhampton hoped they would do and win the F.A. Youth Cup. They were beaten by Manchester United by the only goal (to give United the cup with a 5—4 aggregate and a second successive win) and this made it impossible for the exceptionally large crowd of supporters to see a triple presentation at the finish.

The youngsters did their best but (writes "Commentator") everything seemed to be against them from their own over-anxiety to do well to the fact that they caught the United on one of their best days. And this on the one day this season when Wolves did not play as well as they are able.

We ought, however, to pay the youngsters credit of saying that most of the 28,651 spectators turned up as much to see them as to stay for the subsequent presentation of the Football League Cup to Billy Wright by league president Mr. Arthur Drewry and the presentation of the Birmingham League Shield by Mr. J. T. Stone to Billy Crook.

How much happier their night would have been if the youth team could have managed a victory. It was not to be and to a large extent I thought their defeat by a penalty goal, which was something of a mystery, was a little hard on them.

It all happened so suddenly and surprisingly. In an attack on Wolves goal there was a scramble in the goalmouth. Timmins went up alongside Edwards and there was a stumble by both. The referee consulted the game and awarded a penalty. It was not until afterwards that I learned Timmins was judged to have handled the ball although, in fact, he did so quite accidentally.

THE SUPREME EFFORT

This and their own inability to find true form was rather more than the young Wolves could cope with. They hit back with tremendous vigour and gave the United a gruelling time, but they could not pierce a defence who seemed to improve as the game went on.

Furthermore, the penalty coming from Pegg after 34 minutes followed only six minutes after Wolves had made their supreme effort. They positively swarmed around the United goal and it was the wonder of the game that the ball did not get into the net.

It did everything but. A shot from Cooper hit the inside of a post and screwed along the goal-line before being hooked away; Bonson did almost the same thing and the ball was similarly cleared. The crowd simply roared the Wolves into action and there is no knowing what might have happened if a goal could have been obtained at this stage.

Whatever we may feel about the young Wolves let us give a lot of credit to the young United who, on this evening's play, were the better balanced and cooler side. There was the old-head-on-young shoulders look about such as Edwards (who from the start took over at centre-forward), Pegg and Scanlon and two virile displays from wing-halves Colman and McGuinness (fortunate to get away with a clear case of "hands" in his own penalty area).

They moved the ball wisely and quickly and worked the better as a team.

TRIED HARD, FARED WORSE

Wolves, in the absence of their customary smoothness, had to rely mainly on an unlimited supply of spirit and determination, but this was not enough and it seemed the harder they tried the more things went wrong for them, even down to the bounce of the ball.

Never mind, they did extremely well to get where they did—into the final for the second successive year, and some of them have time for yet another try.

Among the few who looked nearest to getting into their proper form were left-back Harris, centre-half Timmins, right-half Bolton (a bundle of excitable energy) and centre-forward Bonson, who kept plugging away against a most determined Harrop, and was foiled on several occasions only by a matter of inches and the skill of goalkeeper Hawksworth.

So, when the end came, it was to United captain that Mr. Joe Richards, chairman of the F.A. Youth Cup Committee, handed the trophy, for the second season in succession. This, he said, was not a patch on the first leg game (the 4—4 draw at Old Trafford on Friday), but it was, nevertheless, a tribute to both clubs.

Then came what most of the crowd had waited to see, the presentation of the Football League Cup to Billy Wright by Mr. Drewry.

It was the time for compliments, and Mr. Drewry paid them, to Wright in particular and Wolves players and club in general, when he said that this was the most difficult trophy in the world to win.

TWO REMEMBERED

When Wolves team appeared they were accompanied by former regular backs Roy Pritchard and Jack Short, to whom Wright made special reference for the large part they had played in the ultimate success. And he added: "It is going to take a darned good team to take this trophy from us."

Mr. Stanley Cullis appeared in response to the appeals of the crowd, who again crowded on the pitch in front of the Waterloo-road stand, and it was he who thanked the crowd for the support so loyally given during a difficult but successful season.

Billy Crook, receiving the Birmingham League Cup, mentioned that some of the lads who had taken part in the youth final had had a lot to do with winning it, and added: "Winning this cup was just as important to the Birmingham League side as the League Cup was to the first eleven."

So another happy night ended at Molineux, a night that might have been just a little happier if only the youngsters could have managed it.

1953-54

APRIL 1954

final 2nd leg

Under any circumstances, the game could not have been considered a spectacle and, indeed, the Molineux support was aggrieved that they had witnessed the poorest part of the final. It was, though, a truly stupendous performance by the boy Reds and even now, all these many years later, it can be viewed as one of United's most courageous and battling away performances in the Youth Cup.

The Manchester lads succeeded in subduing not only their lively opponents who, it has been suggested, made the fatal mistake of believing that they had completed the hard part of the task at Old Trafford, but they did so in the face of the massive expectations of the home crowd.

Those were the twin feats which underlined the huge amount of teamwork, resilience and character in the side that Jimmy Murphy, Bert Whalley and the other members of United's coaching staff had fashioned. On this particular occasion it was those very attributes which outshone the undoubted level of skill inherent in the team and led precisely to the reasons why the Wolves proved incapable of wrenching the cup away from them.

The final act was left to David Pegg, as captain, to hoist the silver trophy which would remain at Old Trafford for at least another year.

A few last printed words on the subject were given by Tom Jackson, who messaged a typical 'red-eyed' view of the event to his readers (see right):

Captain David Pegg, whose penalty conversion on his last appearance in the competition ensured that the Reds retained the Youth Cup

> "Jimmy Murphy warned us that Wolves would come after us, which is exactly what happened, but as the game went on their threat became less and less and we grew in confidence."
>
> **BOBBY HARROP**

TERRIFIC STUFF BY THE BUSBY BOYS

FOR the second year in succession the youngsters of Manchester United have triumphed in the F.A. Youth Cup for which 94 clubs competed this season. Their one-goal final victory at Molineux, the home of the League champions, after a 4-4 draw with the Wolves cubs at Old Trafford, was watched by 28,651 people in an atmosphere as tense as any ever experienced at Wembley.

United won because they played the type of constructive game that is bound to pay dividends in the long run.

Make no mistake, these Wolves lads were strong. They went into the tackle at lightning speed and their worrying tactics were always menacing. But the Busby hopes never scorned an opportunity to make the ball do the work and in Bobby Charlton, 16-year-old nephew of Jackie Milburn, they had a forward schemer with a delightful brand of football.

* * *

DUNCAN EDWARDS was once again the forager-in-chief in a tactical switch to centre forward, but for sheer spirit and determination I commend outside-right Tommy Littler, only 5ft. 4in. but a real bundle of energy, who chased everything in sight.

There was also a grand display from Wilf McGuinness, former Manchester Boys stalwart, at left-half, and Bobby Harrop never relaxed in a solid show at centre-half. And when things were hot for United, goalkeeper Tony Hawksworth, another England international, had the crowd at his feet with some magnificent saves.

Matt Busby should be a proud man to have such a wealth of young talent. Results speak for themselves, and with six of the team, including Edwards, eligible for this under-18s competition next season, hat-trick prospects are indeed rosy.

United's youths go to Switzerland next month as worthy representatives of youth football in this country.

1954

SWISS TOUR
BLUE STARS TOURNAMENT

MAY/JUNE 1954

YOUNG FELLOWS of ZURICH, BERNE BOYS, BLUE STARS of ZURICH, MTV MUNICH, RED STARS of ZURICH

Wednesday 26th to Tuesday 1st

swiss tour

In March 1954, the club's resident cartoonist took a humorous view of the young Reds' forthcoming tour in the United Review

46

So the name of Manchester United, having been the first to be inscribed on the Youth Cup trophy, was added for a second time.

Despite there being only one promotion from the younger ranks to the senior side during the course of the season, Noel McFarlane making his First Division bow in February 1954, two of the original graduates, Duncan Edwards and David Pegg, had accumulated a further 33 first-team appearances between them over the course of the campaign. Eddie Lewis made six further such starts that season, whereas John Doherty hadn't reappeared for the first eleven as he had the dual problems of his National Service and a troublesome knee to contend with.

The excitement wasn't quite over for the youth team.

On Wednesday, 26th May 1954, a month to the day since the victory at Molineux, a party of officials and sixteen players left Manchester's Ringway Airport, via London, bound for Zurich to take part in two friendly games and the Blue Stars International Youth Tournament.

The players who journeyed over to Switzerland were: Ivan Beswick, Bobby Charlton, Gordon Clayton, Eddie Colman, Duncan Edwards, Bryce Fulton, Bobby Harrop, Tony Hawksworth, Eddie Lewis, Tommy Littler, Wilf McGuinness, Peter Pearce, David Pegg, Alan Rhodes, Albert Scanlon and Billy Whelan. Coaches Bert Whalley and Jimmy Murphy, manager Matt Busby and long-serving trainer Arthur Powell made up the entourage.

For the majority of the youngsters, the trip represented the first time they had visited a foreign country and the 'working holiday' was set to last for seven days.

As the plane took off, standing on the tarmac waving goodbye was 70 year-old United supporter, Miss Ada Keane. The grand lady was living up to her name as she had risen at 5.00 a.m. before leaving her home at Sutton's flats in Pendleton to see the boys off three hours and twenty minutes later.

When asked about United's prospects in the youth tournament, Matt Busby, with obvious reference to the two recent heavy defeats suffered by the English national side, quipped, *'I think we shall have a good chance of winning – we don't have to play any Hungarians!'*

Matt Busby to write for you

MANCHESTER UNITED manager, Matt Busby, who left Manchester today with the United youth team for the World Youth Cup competition in Switzerland this week, will give his views on the games in the Evening Chronicle.

In addition, Matt Busby will give you his opinion on the future of European Soccer.

These articles will appear exclusively in the Evening Chronicle, so make sure you buy the Evening Chronicle.

Stadion Letzigrund in Zurich as it was in 1954

SWISS TOUR
FRIENDLY MATCHES

1954

MAY/JUNE 1954

BERNE SELECT XI, SWITZERLAND YOUTH XI

UNITED'S WORLD CUP WIN WAS A TRIUMPH OF TEAM WORK

Players, officials and airline staff board the plane at Heathrow on the second leg of their journey to Zurich

tournament success, and acted as a triumphant prelude to many more similar achievements over the ensuing decades.

Two days later, the Manchester squad travelled to Bienne to tackle a Berne Select youth side. Even though the home team took a shock lead by scoring twice in the opening minutes, success was achieved by a decisive 9-2 scoreline. The visitors led 3-2 at the break, with Whelan netting four in succession in the second half. United's goals came from Whelan (5) and Charlton (2), while Scanlon and Edwards claimed one each, and the line-up was: Clayton, Beswick, Fulton, Colman, Harrop, McGuinness, Charlton, Whelan, Edwards, Lewis and Scanlon.

Following an overnight stay in Bienne, the squad and officials then returned to Zurich where the youth team met the Swiss national youth side. Goals from Pegg (2), Whelan and Edwards gave the Reds a splendid 4-0 victory to bring the trip to a wonderful conclusion. United's formation was the same as that against Berne Select, except Hawksworth was in goal and Pegg played at inside-left.

The match against the Swiss Youths was staged prior to a full international between the host country and the Netherlands, as the World Cup finals were staged in Switzerland that year and the friendly with Holland formed part of the home nation's preparations. Both of United's games against the Berne Select and Switzerland Youth teams lasted 40 minutes each way.

Matt Busby was mightily impressed with the whole affair and the success of the tour is likely to have had a monumental bearing on his decision to lead the club into their European Cup adventure when the opportunity presented itself. The benefit gained by the boys of being exposed to, and succeeding against, the contrasting styles employed by the continentals was simply immeasurable. Also, the tremendous lift in morale the trip gave to every member of the party was another positive factor that Busby took from the foreign excursion.

On the following day, the Blue Stars tournament took place. All the games were of a 30-minutes duration (fifteen each way) with sixteen teams divided into four 'mini-leagues'. The team that topped each league then entered the semi-finals and, if victorious at that stage, the final.

United drew their opening contest 0-0 against Young Fellows of Zurich and in their following match defeated Berne Boys 2-0 with a goal apiece from Eddie Colman and Albert Scanlon. Requiring nothing less than a victory from their concluding group game, the Reds were locked at nil-nil with the host club, Blue Stars of Zurich, until the very last minute, when an Eddie Lewis goal put them into the last four.

After a 1-0 win over MTV Munich at the penultimate stage, which was courtesy of a Billy Whelan strike, United steamrollered Red Stars of Zurich 4-0 in the final with an Albert Scanlon goal and a hat-trick from Duncan Edwards. It gave England's sole representatives the Hermes Trophy, their first ever overseas youth

FUSSBALL-CLUB BLUE STARS ZÜRICH

XVI. Junioren-Turnier

Auffahrt. 27. Mai 1954

Stadion Letzigrund   Programm

48

1954

MAY/JUNE 1954

It is no coincidence that United and Wolverhampton Wanderers, both having seen their youth sides participate in the Blue Stars tournament, soon became the pioneers for English club football against overseas opposition. Even before the Reds qualified for the European Cup, Wolves had already contested friendly matches against continental opponents under the Molineux floodlights in front of massive crowds. Sensing that the demand was there, Busby took United into the European Cup just two years later, despite some fairly lengthy and bitter objections by the Football League.

The exercise was summarised in the Manchester Evening News by a 'Special Correspondent':

........(United's) performances have drawn unstinting praise from the Swiss newspapers and the general verdict here is that there is not much wrong with English football if these Busby boys are a sample of our future resources.

Particularly interested were the international selectors of Switzerland and Holland who were among the 42,000 crowd at the Zurich Grasshopper ground when the pick of the Swiss youths were out-speeded by United.

Altogether, United played seven games in four days. They won the youth tournament in Zurich with a record of four wins and a draw and on the tour scored 21 goals with only two against.

United's youth team were not only the cream of England, they finished the season as the talk of Europe. After a day of relaxation, the players returned home to a warm welcome and before their summer break could begin in earnest, they were fêted guests at a civic reception. Held at Manchester Town Hall, and hosted by no less than the Lord Mayor, Alderman R.S. Harper, the function was specifically arranged to honour their marvellous achievements at home and abroad.

Members of the tour party out and about enjoying the sights of Zurich

Albert Scanlon, Arthur Powell and Eddie Colman with the Hermes Cup outside Manchester Town Hall

swiss tour

49

1954-55

1) Willie Speight
2) Gerry Byrne
3) Arthur Daly
4) Bill O'Hara
5) John Price
6) Bobby Campbell
7) Con Phillips
8) Jimmy Melia
9) Frank O'Toole
10) Joe Fortune
11) K. Johnson

1) Gordon Clayton
2) John Walker
3) Alan Rhodes
4) Eddie Colman
5) Peter Jones
6) Wilf McGuinness
7) Ken Adams
8) Shay Brennan
9) Bobby English
10) Bobby Charlton
11) Ken Morgans

OCTOBER 1954

LIVERPOOL 1 v 4 MANCHESTER UNITED

Melia — Adams, Brennan (2), Colman

Saturday 30th
Kick-off 11.00 a.m.

first round

Just over a year had passed since United made their initial defence of the Youth Cup when a visit to Merseyside resulted in them putting paid to Everton's interest with a 1-0 victory. The draw for the opening round of the new term decreed that the Reds would return down the East Lancs Road, only on this occasion Liverpool provided the opposition. Similarly to the Everton fixture, a Saturday a.m. kick-off was preferred by the home club.

It was a decidedly mixed time for football fortunes in Liverpool just then. Evertonians were overjoyed at their club's recent return to the top echelon, which terminated a three-year sojourn in the Second Division.

Not so happy, though, was the red half of the city because Liverpool had finished rock bottom of the First Division at the same time as Everton's promotion and effectively took their neighbour's place in the lower division. Liverpool's exile was to last much longer than Everton's stay in the Second Division and it would be fully eight years before Anfield catered for the higher grade of football once more.

Making a welcome return between the sticks for United was Gordon Clayton, who reclaimed his place in the side following his enforced absence from last season's final. Defender Ivan Beswick had passed the competition age limit and his right-back place went to Harrogate-born John Walker. Alan Rhodes was still eligible, so he continued in the left-back role, as were Eddie Colman and Wilf McGuinness, both of whom remained in the wing-back berths. For the second season on the spin, a replacement centre-half was required and it meant that local boy Peter Jones was tasked with taking over from Bobby Harrop, whose performances made him such an outstanding pivot throughout his ten appearances in the last campaign.

United's attack was subject to radical changes. Tommy Littler, David Pegg and Albert Scanlon had all breached the age barrier, a development that found only Bobby Charlton and Duncan Edwards remaining. However, Edwards didn't figure in Jimmy Murphy's plans for the Anfield match because he was once again selected for the seniors.

Into the reckoning came a recently signed outside-right from Winsford United, Ken Adams, and locals Shay Brennan and Bobby English were included at inside-right and centre-forward respectively. On the left flank was another new face, a former Welsh schoolboy international called Ken Morgans.

It was, in fact, a quick return to Anfield for the United youth team as only just over a month had elapsed since they defeated the Liverpool County Youth side there in the Tomlinson Trophy. Three of the county team took up places in the Liverpool eleven, goalkeeper Willie Speight, half-back Bobby Campbell and ace marksman Jimmy Melia.

A wet welcome was in store for the Old Trafford lads, with a torrential overnight downpour making for a soggy playing surface. As the tie got underway, the rain relented only temporarily and dark clouds continued to threaten between heavy showers.

The game began in the best possible way for United, and especially for two of the new boys, when the opening goal was registered with less than a minute gone. Brennan initiated the damage inflicted on Liverpool when releasing Adams with a cute pass and the Warrington-based winger completed the job by firing the visitors ahead with a shot that went in off a post. The cup holders had started in a positive mode, with attacking intentions obvious, and soon after the goal Speight was required to be on his toes when saving further shots from Charlton and Adams.

Rain started to fall again just when Liverpool began exerting some pressure of their own, and they gained a corner that United cleared unceremoniously. Liverpool's Johnson then saw his shot saved by Clayton before Adams and Brennan, who seemed to share an uncanny understanding, linked again to make the score 2-0 after just twelve minutes. For that particular offensive, Adams acted as the provider when working an opening for Brennan, who made the most of a clear sight of goal by beating Speight's reach with a hard drive.

Despite the soaked ground making control of the ball difficult, the two teams displayed much gusto and opportunities continued to appear at both ends of the pitch. Overall, United's were the more substantial, and other narrow misses before the break by Charlton and English kept up the team's momentum. None of the many spectators massed at the Kop end of the ground could argue that the lead held by the away side at half-time wasn't fully deserved.

Liverpool came out full of fighting spirit for the start of the second half and after a swift break, Con Phillips was put through in a good position only to screw his shot wide with just Clayton between him and the goal frame.

United then whipped up another couple of half chances, but with ten minutes of the concluding period gone, Liverpool hit back to reduce their deficit. A long centre by O'Toole was brought under control by inside-right Melia and he scored with a finely executed shot from close quarters.

United's demeanour thereafter indicated they had taken offence at the setback and it didn't take long for them to revert to their earlier high quality. Displaying plenty of the passion and drive that made them the side every other one wanted to beat, McGuinness and Colman upped the chasing, harrying and distribution levels so that Liverpool's penalty box was turned into a siege area for a while.

For the third time, the eventual outcome was the productive Adams/Brennan partnership delivering the goods following a corner awarded to United with less than ten minutes to go. Adams leathered the flag kick across the six-yard box and his ball was met perfectly by partner Brennan, whose powerful header sailed home. With time now at a premium, the third United goal painted a picture for Liverpool that was as grim as the skyline.

Just four minutes later, it was left to one of the old hands, captain Eddie Colman, to perform the last rites on the Merseysiders when he put United into an unassailable lead by striking home a super shot from outside the box.

A 4-1 away win represented an excellent entrance to the new season's tournament for the boys and it was especially pleasing that three of the goals were shared between debutants Adams and Brennan.

Soon after receiving a few 'well done' comments from Jimmy Murphy and Bert Whalley in the dressing room, the United squad was ferried to a local hotel where they were treated to a meal with Matt Busby and the first-team. The seniors had a mid-afternoon engagement with Everton to look forward to and so both the youth and senior sides boarded a coach for Goodison Park shortly after lunching.

With a crowd of over 63,000 descending on the stadium, a highly harassed coach driver was unable to negotiate his way to the players' entrance and the entire United party was forced to walk most of the way down Goodison Road in order to complete their journey. Despite the presence of Duncan Edwards, Everton took the honours with a 4-2 victory.

Youth Cup novice Shay Brennan grabbed a brace at a soaked Anfield

1) Steve Fleet
2) Jack Harrabin
3) Vinny Vane
4) David Wall
5) Bill Chandley
6) Jack Swindells
7) Peter Lamb
8) Roy Beale
9) Vic Anderson
10) Jack Doyle
11) Peter Phoenix

1) Gordon Clayton
2) John Walker
3) Alan Rhodes
4) Eddie Colman
5) Peter Jones
6) Wilf McGuinness
7) Ken Adams
8) Shay Brennan
9) Duncan Edwards
10) Bobby Charlton
11) Ken Morgans

1954-55

MANCHESTER CITY 1 v 2 MANCHESTER UNITED
Lamb   Edwards (2)

NOVEMBER 1954

Wednesday 17th*

Kick-off 7.30 p.m.

Attendance 6,849

second round

The Reds' negotiation of the opening stage of the Youth Cup led them into a meeting that all Manchester football followers were hoping for; a City versus United derby match. Any clash between the two old adversaries is always a matter of fierce local prestige, and the fact that Jimmy Murphy's lads were twice winners and current favourites to win the tournament again only served to fuel City's incentive to put one over their nearest rivals.

For United, the prospect of losing their proud unbeaten record to the Light Blues, of all teams, provided the only spur that they required. City, on the other hand, positively relished the chance of ending the Reds' unbeaten Youth Cup run and a section of the editorial in the match programme indicated that they didn't feel the task was beyond them:

City, who got away to a good start with a 3-1 win at Everton, have several newcomers compared with the team that revealed great promise and scored plenty of goals before going down in the Fourth Round at Leeds last season when City made their bow in the competition. They showed useful quality at Everton, and while United undoubtedly have greater experience, the result is by no means a foregone conclusion.

As Maine Road was one of the first provincial football grounds to enjoy the benefits of floodlights, over four years before they were installed at Old Trafford, an evening start was a logical choice for the fixture. It was, therefore, the first floodlit Youth Cup game that the Reds were involved in away from The Cliff.

There was one significant difference to the United eleven from the game at Anfield, Duncan Edwards taking over at centre-forward in place of Bobby English. It was an opportune time to reintroduce Edwards to the youth team although, had the game taken place on the original date a week earlier, when a saturated Maine Road playing surface caused a postponement, he might not have featured.

Two days prior to the washed out fixture, on Monday, 8th November, Edwards was involved with an England Youth side that took on Wolves Youth at Molineux. Whether he would have turned out in the City match just 48 hours later can only be a matter of conjecture, but probably would have hinged on whether or not he remained free from injury.

In the light of events that later came to pass, it was certainly a stroke of fortune on United's part, and the outcome against City without Edwards' participation could have totally changed the course of the club's association with the Youth Cup.

The difference in the make-up of the two sides was notable. The team from Old Trafford was a real mixture of origins, with players from as far afield as the Midlands, the North-East, Wales, Yorkshire and Derbyshire, as well as a number of locals. That contrasted sharply with City's rather parochial composition, which was made up entirely of Manchester and Salford boys.

Unfortunately, the game was a virtual non-event for those hardy spectators who made their way to Maine Road that evening and it was caused by a phenomenon which was a regular and unwelcome occurrence in South-East Lancashire for many a long year.

On the day of the fixture, Manchester and the surrounding area was shrouded in a veil of fog. While it wasn't of the thick 'pea soup' variety the city was infamous for in those days, it was dense enough to ensure that the match was in doubt almost all day and practically until the start.

In light of the numbers who turned out for later Youth Cup derbies, it is certain that the prevailing weather badly affected the attendance and the tie might not have taken place at all had a crowd approaching 7,000 already paid at the gates by kick-off time.

As it was, referee Mr. A.R. Coupe of Urmston sanctioned the conditions as acceptable and play began in an eerie atmosphere, with the brightness of Maine Road's floodlights appearing to make a feeble attempt at breaking through the misty haze. Bearing in mind there had already been one deferment, and that a 'to be played by' date was hanging over the fixture, it would not be discourteous to Mr. Coupe to suggest that he might have been under some pressure to bring the tie to a conclusion.

City commenced with the fervour befitting the occasion and they took an

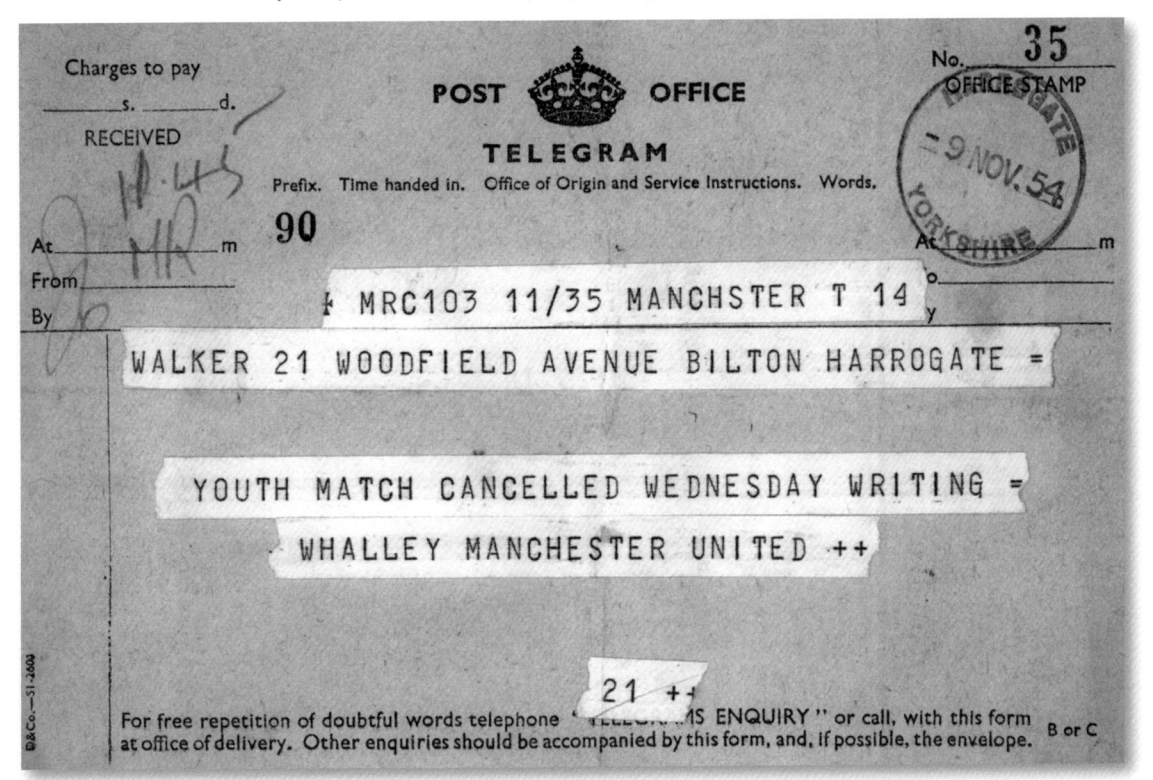

Coach Bert Whalley's telegram to John Walker notifying him of the postponed tie on the 10th November

This game was originally scheduled for Wednesday, November 10th but was postponed due to a waterlogged pitch

51

1954-55

NOVEMBER 1954

second round

unexpected lead just past the quarter-hour mark. The honour of registering the first goal in this historical all-Manchester Youth Cup contest went to City number seven, Peter Lamb.

United came back at City during the remainder of the opening half through concerted teamwork, only they just couldn't peg their neighbours back.

When the break arrived, Jimmy Murphy made a beeline for the referee's room. The Reds' coach let it be known in no uncertain terms that he felt the game should be abandoned when pointing out the lack of proper visibility wasn't conducive to football of that standard. Whether it was a genuine belief, or an act of gamesmanship, the truth probably falling somewhere between the two, the referee was unrelenting in his decision and stated that unless the conditions deteriorated still further, the game would be played to a conclusion.

Dismayed at the official's response, the coach returned to United's dressing room with the intention of reviving his charges for the second half. Certainly the most profound indication of the severity of the situation was given in his opening gambit, which the fired up Welshman commenced by stating, *'I believe you are a goal down.'*

After delivering his pep-talk and issuing new instructions, the team made their way to the tunnel and as Duncan Edwards was ready to leave, he reassured Murphy that *'things will be all right'.*

Not one given to idle boasts, Edwards personally forced the issue to make absolutely sure that things would eventually *'be all right'.* A pair of second half goals from him, the winner coming late on at the Platt Lane end of the ground, ensured that City's gloom at the final whistle was as palpable as the fog.

An unusual occurrence took place the following day, as neither the Evening News nor the Evening Chronicle carried reports of the game. The Manchester edition of the Daily Mail ran just a brief summary of events, part of which read that despite the Blues gaining an early incentive, *'United gradually gained the upper hand through the strong work of wing halves McGuinness and Colman'* even though *'fog blotted out the movement of the players for most of the game'.*

The only match description of any substance was contained in the northern edition of the Daily Dispatch and it began with a headline which proclaimed 'EDWARDS' TWO GOALS GIVE CUP-HOLDERS VICTORY':

In a mist-ruined game at Maine Road, Manchester United beat Manchester City in the Second Round of the F.A. Youth Challenge Cup competition, and will visit Barnsley in the next round.

United will have to show improved form if they are to progress in the competition to win the trophy as they have done in the last two seasons.

It was practically impossible to see across the ground, but visibility was good enough to see that City were the livelier team and quicker on the ball than United, who, in spite of the tireless work of Edwards, were obviously surprised by the strength of the opposition.

Certainly it was no more than they deserved when City took the lead in the 17th minute through Lamb, who, after a grand run by Beale, cracked a magnificent left-foot shot past Clayton.

City held this lead until the 65th minute, when Edwards equalised. The United centre-forward won the match twenty minutes later with another splendid individual effort.

United's bigger and more experienced team enjoyed long periods of superiority in the second half, admirably prompted by McGuinness, but Fleet, Harrabin and Chandley made several fine clearances.

Rhodes distinguished himself in the United defence in the first half when City were on top, but the home forwards, hard as they tried, were less effective in front of goal than their opponents.

In addition to which, of course, they hadn't an Edwards.

Certainly everyone in the Old Trafford camp was extremely pleased to come through a testing tie with another win on the board, having overcome the twin problems of a highly-charged set of opponents and the issue regarding improper visibility.

Happy that they were able to retain local bragging rights for at least a little while longer, it occurred to some United fans that even acts of nature were now unable to halt the young Reds' unrelenting progress.

The United Review's cartoonist, Butterworth, pokes a little fun at the expense of the club's scouting practices

1) Peter Hyde
2) Ron Dean
3) Eric Dent
4) Barry Barber
5) Brian Summerfield
6) Billy Houghton
7) Laurence Stafford
8) Joe Hooley
9) John Stainsby
10) Arthur Rowe
11) Jack Lunn

1) Gordon Clayton
2) John Walker
3) Alan Rhodes
4) Eddie Colman
5) Peter Jones
6) Wilf McGuinness
7) Ken Adams
8) Terry Beckett
9) Duncan Edwards
10) Bobby Charlton
11) Ken Morgans

1954-55

BARNSLEY 2 v 4 MANCHESTER UNITED

Stafford, Stainsby

Beckett (2), Edwards, Morgans

DECEMBER 1954

Saturday 11th

Kick-off 2.15 p.m.

third round

A trip to Oakwell to be entertained by Barnsley was the job at hand in Round Three, which meant for United that it was now their third consecutive away tie of the season.

Barnsley, it should be remembered, were the first team to score against the Reds in the Youth Cup. That quarter-final contest had taken place only 21 months previously and there were no surviving members from that Old Trafford match for the Tykes, though Gordon Clayton, Eddie Colman and Duncan Edwards remained for United.

The Yorkshire outfit had suffered the ignominy of relegation at the end of the 1952/53 season and as a Third Division (North) club, their first-team were contesting an F.A. Cup Second Round tie at Gateshead while United's seniors travelled to Burnley in order to fulfil a First Division engagement. Faced with an injury to senior centre-forward Tommy Taylor, Matt Busby kept faith with Colin Webster at Turf Moor, the Welsh striker's inclusion at Burnley meaning that Edwards was freed for Youth Cup action.

There was only one difference to the line-up from that which achieved victory over Manchester City, with former Manchester and England Boys' forward Terry Beckett drafted in at inside-right at the expense of Shay Brennan.

The game was broadcast live over the radio to all of the hospitals in the borough of Barnsley and it was promised that the running commentary would be interrupted occasionally so as to inform the patients, hospital staff and visitors how the Gateshead versus Barnsley match was progressing.

The Oakwell youngsters hardly needed any greater motivation for the visit of the Reds. Their club chairman, Joe Richards, still chaired the F.A. Youth Cup Committee, and that fact, added to the opportunity of lowering the colours of United in front of their own supporters, was a task the Tykes surely relished.

As the teams made their way out of the shade of the tunnel, on a cool, bright day, signs of the industrial landscape of South Yorkshire were clearly visible and in the distance, huge unsightly black mountains of coal waste from a nearby colliery met in contrast against a clear, blue sky.

The home side started like an angry whirlwind, blowing and gusting around their visitors at a terrific pace. With no time at all spent on ceremony, Barnsley's very first raid spelled out their intentions when inside-left Arthur Rowe shot against a United post. With no colleague on hand to capitalise on the situation, the loose ball was, as a newspaper report noted, *'hoofed out of the danger area.'*

One or two of United's forwards were guilty of straying offside on a couple of occasions as they tried to click into some sort of rhythm. Barnsley soon took up the offensive again, by carving the Reds wide open for a second time in a move which spelled danger when outside-left Jack Lunn found co-striker Rowe. He looped a ball into Clayton's penalty area that managed to evade all defenders and, unfortunately for Barnsley, his team-mates as well.

The Yorkshire eleven certainly showed the greater enterprise in the early stages and with fifteen minutes played, at no great surprise to the assembled onlookers, they went into the lead after slicing the Reds apart on a third occasion. A forward thrust from Barnsley ended when centre-forward John Stainsby put the finishing touch to a move which set the home fans, and many of the patients in the surrounding Barnsley hospitals, cheering vociferously.

A further shot by Rowe kept up the pressure on the United goal until, at last, a response was found when Edwards hammered a drive over Barnsley's bar. In the next move, a shot from new boy Terry Beckett was well handled by Hyde.

It proved to be a very watchable game, with both sides displaying their obvious capabilities for good football. In particular, Barnsley full-backs Ron Dean and Eric Dent built solid displays while the game progressed, as did centre-half Brian Summerfield, whose prominence had largely subdued Edwards to that point.

With a quarter of an hour still to go to the break, the Reds were dealt another hammer blow when conceding a second goal. It was a terribly sloppy affair from their perspective and came about when Barnsley were awarded a free kick which was taken by right-half Barry Barber. There was a plague of hesitation in the visitors' defence and as the ball came towards him, Tykes' outside-right Laurence Stafford was afforded enough space to hit it first time past Clayton.

The odds were stacking up against United, and when Bobby Charlton struck a shot against Barnsley's crossbar it seemed like their long unbeaten run was about to come off the rails. There could be no argument against the Barnsley Chronicle's claim that the home youngsters *'fully deserved their half-time lead'* because they *'were by far the superior side'* and so it was, therefore, a sorry bunch of Reds who trooped off at the interval to face a stern Jimmy Murphy in the locker room.

Whatever Murphy or his assistant Bert Whalley said to the team, it certainly had a profound effect as, right from the early moments of the second period, they began performing at a much improved level, both individually and collectively.

The magic words of wisdom imparted by the coaches paid dividends almost immediately when, just two minutes after the restart, United stormed back into the reckoning as Edwards and McGuinness linked to create space for Beckett, who gleefully placed a ground shot past Hyde.

Now imbued with a revived appetite for the challenge, the Reds began winning more of the ball in what must have seemed like a completely different game to the spectators. Edwards, especially, looked akin to the colossus who had already made 43 appearances in the First Division through leading from the front in his typically all-action way.

After going close twice more, United equalised just twelve minutes into the second half when Beckett finished a project in which Edwards operated as chief provider. Taking a pass from Ken Adams on the right touchline, Edwards clipped a cross that was met by Beckett, and his response was to thunder the ball into the top corner of the goal.

With Edwards now bossing the show, and the whole team looking yards faster in thought and movement than their adversaries, attacks by the home eleven diminished rapidly. When Barry Barber temporarily left the field for treatment to a knock, the Reds piled more misery onto Barnsley's plate by taking the lead less than ten minutes after drawing level. Needless to say, Edwards was on the scene, on this occasion taking on the role of executioner when pinning the ball past Hyde from an oblique angle.

It was a turnabout of grand proportions by the Reds, who continued to press on with their newly found advantage. A final goal was instigated by Edwards once again, the burly leader measuring another accurate cross that Ken Morgans headed beyond a flummoxed Hyde.

The action wasn't completely over as, despite being shackled for almost the entire second half, to their credit, Barnsley hadn't completely given up the ghost. Just as the final whistle was about to sound, John Stainsby only just failed to add to his earlier goal by placing an effort against a post.

All of the talk in the stands and on the terraces at Oakwell was of a brilliant transformation by United which had been prompted by the incredible Edwards, views that were later echoed in every match report. Quite rightly, everyone suggested that he had provided the spark to ignite a memorable win at a time when the tie was tightly clenched in the jaws of defeat.

There were plenty of goals and action for the crowd to enjoy, even if the outcome wasn't entirely to their liking. An outstanding performance by Edwards apart, the game was marked from a United standpoint by a splendid debut double by Terry Beckett and an opening goal at that level by Ken Morgans thrown in for good measure.

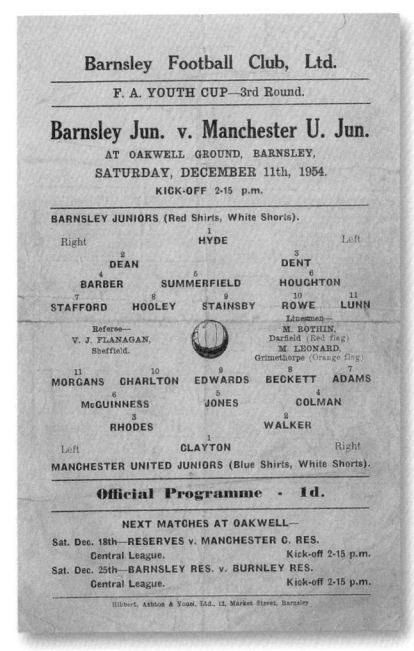

53

1954-55

1) Tony Hawksworth	9) Alan Blakeman
2) John Queenan	10) Shay Brennan
3) Alan Rhodes	11) Bobby Charlton
4) Eddie Colman	
5) Peter Jones	
6) Wilf McGuinness	
7) Ken Adams	
8) Terry Beckett	

1) Alan Hinchcliffe	9) Arthur Hukin
2) Barry Habershon	10) Tony Bates
3) John Hallatt	11) David Nevin
4) Terry Poole	
5) Peter Swan	
6) Brian Hill	
7) Frank Elliott	
8) Tony Kay	

FEBRUARY 1955

MANCHESTER UNITED 7 v 0 SHEFFIELD WEDNESDAY

Beckett, Blakeman (3), Brennan, Charlton (2)

Saturday 5th
Kick-off 11.00 a.m.

fourth round

New boys in Reds Cup XI

FOOTBALL at OLD TRAFFORD
F.A. YOUTH CUP (4th Round)

Manchester United (holders) v Sheffield Wednesday

Saturday, 5th February. Kick-off 11 a.m.

ADMISSION:
Ground 1/- • Boys 6d • Stand 2/6
ALL PAY

It had been the best part of ten months since Old Trafford staged a Youth Cup match when Sheffield Wednesday arrived in town to contest a Fourth Round tie on a typically grey and wintry Manchester day. With a United Reserves versus Huddersfield Town Reserves fixture to be accommodated on the same day, the youth contest was allocated the morning matinee slot while the Central League clash went ahead in the afternoon.

The junior Owls had beaten a path to Old Trafford by winning all of their previous Youth Cup ties away from Hillsborough. A 9-1 mauling of Derby County at the Baseball Ground in the opening round was preceded by a 2-1 win over Nottingham Forest next to the River Trent and a 4-1 victory at Middlesbrough. Those three successes completed quite an impressive list of victims and the Wednesday side were obviously a talented bunch with John Hallatt, a Rotherham boy, the star name amongst them. Hallatt had captained the national schoolboy eleven in 1954, a side which also featured United's Terry Beckett.

Jimmy Murphy was clearly unhappy with the Reds' performance at Barnsley, or more specifically the first half display, and as a result he took what he felt was the necessary remedial action. The impressive half-back line of Colman, Jones and McGuinness was left unaltered, but there were adjustments all around them. The main surprise amongst all of the changes was the dropping of Gordon Clayton from his job of guarding United's goal while Tony Hawksworth, who replaced him in last season's final, was brought back at his expense.

Murphy chose to draft John Queenan in at right-back, the former St. Gregory's School pupil taking over the place vacated by John Walker, who had left the club. The coach's axe also fell hard on Ken Morgans, whose omission came about despite his goalscoring feat at Oakwell.

Shay Brennan won a recall to the inside-left position, which prompted Bobby Charlton's move to outside-left, and as Duncan Edwards was with the seniors at Huddersfield, there was a call-up for sixteen year-old Alan Blakeman at centre-forward. In respect of the debutants, both Blakeman and Queenan hailed from Oldham's Chadderton suburb.

Bearing in mind Edwards' influence and scoring exploits at the last two stages of the tournament, the question on everyone's lips now seemed to be, 'How would the under-18's go on without him?'

The answer to that question was quite emphatic and deserved its full airing in a late edition of the Manchester Evening News:

Manchester United's youth team centre forward, Blakeman, leaps over a Sheffield Wednesday defender, but his shot hits the upright and goes out of play. Close behind him, in this F.A. Youth Cup fourth-round match at Old Trafford, is United's inside-right, Beckett.

CLEVER YOUNG REDS

MANCHESTER UNITED swamped Sheffield Wednesday in the fourth-round F.A. Youth Cup-tie at Old Trafford to-day by seven clear goals, six of them scored in the first half.

Charlton, McGuinness, and Colman were the stars in a United team that was never fully extended.

United scored after five minutes. BECKETT slamming one home after Swan had blocked a shot from Blakeman on the line.

Wednesday, despite their forceful midfield play, were kept in check and United were deservedly two up after 15 minutes when BLAKEMAN ran on to a through pass to score with a cross-shot.

Adams, with a pin-point centre, provided goal number three for BLAKEMAN, and then BRENNAN beat Hinchcliffe with a terrific shot for the fourth. Two further goals came just before half-time. BLAKEMAN forcing the ball through as he collided with Swan, and then CHARLTON scored the sixth with a terrific cross-shot.

Half-time: Manchester United 6, Sheffield Wednesday 0.

It was all United in the second half, too, but this time the goal rush was halted by some marvellous goalkeeping by Hinchcliffe. First a flying save to a 30-yard McGuinness drive and then a finger-tip effort under the bar to divert a curling shot from Charlton.

Hinchcliffe's best, however, was a one-handed save as Beckett drove the ball in from five yards. Wednesday, penned to defence, relied on individual forward rushes which had little success against strong-tackling Peter Jones.

Always there was a promise of further United goals with Charlton cutting in from the wing to give an added threat, but too many shots were wide of the mark.

Just before the end of the one-sided game CHARLTON scored United's seventh.

1954-55

FEBRUARY 1955

Wednesday were simply in the wrong place at the wrong time when finding the Old Trafford youngsters in an unstoppable goalscoring mood.

As usual, Jimmy Murphy's canny team selections and adjustments were fully vindicated. Not only had the Welshman's chosen permutation paid instant dividends in terms of a super victory, the introduction of new faces to the side, and the reintroduction of familiar ones, seemed to create just a little more competition for places for the next stage.

Alan Blakeman, the executor of a fine hat-trick, and Bobby Charlton, with his two goals, were the main contributors to Wednesday's downfall. Nevertheless, and as was normally the case, there were also superb performances in the hotbed of midfield from Colman and McGuinness. The two wing-halves supplied constant and countless passes to the forwards and their tackling and reading of potential danger gave the defence a comparatively easy time of it.

One report observed that *'McGuinness frequently joined the attack and with Colman kept the Wednesday defence on tenterhooks with their quick surges'*. The same account also intimated United could have undersold themselves by claiming *'it should have been a double figure score'*.

Even the Sheffield Star was moved to comment that *'the heavy score did not flatter Manchester, who were superior in all phases of the game'*.

> *I was scoring lots of goals for the juniors but my knee kept swelling up after each game. The club decided I needed an operation and so I was put into a private nursing home in Sale to be treated.*
>
> *It was just before the opening Youth Cup tie at Liverpool because I remember going on the team bus to Anfield with the other lads, we all went out for a meal after the game and then over to Goodison to watch the first-team. There was always a great team spirit.*
>
> *I was called to Old Trafford one Friday night and told to warm up with some of the other lads before getting a team talk from Murphy, Whalley and Busby in preparation for the Sheffield Wednesday game. I came in for Duncan and even though it was my first game at Old Trafford I wasn't nervous at all, the coaching staff used to tell us we were the best in England and that really built up our confidence.*

ALAN BLAKEMAN

fourth round

Spectators head for the cover of the Popular Side while the players pose for an obligatory team photo
Back row (l-r) Ken Adams, Wilf McGuinness, Alan Rhodes, Tony Hawksworth, Peter Jones, Shay Brennan
Front row (l-r) Terry Beckett, Bobby Charlton, Eddie Colman, Alan Blakeman, John Queenan

1954-55

1) Tony Hawksworth	9) Bobby English
2) John Queenan	10) Shay Brennan
3) Alan Rhodes	11) Bobby Charlton
4) Eddie Colman	
5) Duncan Edwards	
6) Wilf McGuinness	
7) Ken Morgans	
8) Terry Beckett	

1) Peter Dyer	9) Mike Kimberley
2) Ron Greet	10) Bernard Barnes
3) Russell Kevern	11) David Green
4) Reg Mitchell	
5) Ivor Lavers	
6) John Sample	
7) Ken Bradford	
8) Johnny Penny	

MARCH 1955

MANCHESTER UNITED 9 v 0 **PLYMOUTH ARGYLE**
Beckett, Brennan (3), Charlton (3, 1 pen)
Edwards, English

Saturday 12th
Kick-off 11.00 a.m.
Attendance 5,322

fifth round

1..2..3..4..5..6..7..8..9..!

United were now on the verge of the two-legged stage for the third time, so a home pairing with Plymouth Argyle was a most satisfactory draw under the circumstances. The meeting of the two clubs gave rise to an interesting connection, as ex-United favourite Jack 'Gunner' Rowley had been appointed as the Devon club's new manager less than a month before the Youth Cup meeting.

A West Country newspaper published two days prior to the game gave an indication as to the importance the Pilgrims attached to further progress in the tournament when revealing:

Argyle field their strongest team for the F.A. Youth Cup Fifth Round game....... the Argyle youngsters had a full scale practice match under the lights at Home Park this week. They travel to Manchester tomorrow.

An overnight stay in Manchester on the Friday was seen as a must for the Plymouth side as, for the second time in just over a month, a pre-noon start was required for an Old Trafford-staged youth tie. The early kick-off was needed because the club's Reserves were acting as hosts to Everton Reserves and the Central League contest was preferred for the afternoon kick-off.

The make-up of United's Reserves that day comprised of the following eleven: Crompton, Fulton, Bent, Goodwin, Cope, Blanchflower, McFarlane, Viollet, Lewis, Doherty and Pegg. It revealed that no less than six former Youth Cup participants, as well as four others (the exception being goalkeeper Jack Crompton) who joined the Reds straight from school and had graduated into the second string as a continuation of their football education.

Because United were already out of the F.A. Cup, the seniors were faced with the prospect of a vacant Saturday. Not wanting to have his stars idle at such an important time in the soccer calendar, Matt Busby arranged a friendly game at Lincoln where he took the opportunity to blood another former youth player in the first-team, with Billy Whelan making his senior entrance at Sincil Bank.

The match at Lincoln also provided a ray of good fortune for the current youth side. Peter Jones, who had made such a marvellous impression with his solid displays as a pivot, was on the injured list and so Jimmy Murphy slotted regular first-teamer Duncan Edwards straight into his position, centre-half being just another role that Edwards could comfortably fill with distinction.

Murphy implemented two other changes to the side that had obliterated Sheffield Wednesday. At outside-right, one Ken, namely Morgans, replaced another, Adams, while somewhat surprisingly considering his hat-trick performance against the Owls, Alan Blakeman was left out at the expense of the recalled Bobby English.

An already stretched Plymouth defence is unable to prevent Bobby Charlton (out of picture) from scoring United's first goal

1954-55

MARCH 1955

The Evening News noted the action in the following way:

Charlton and Brennan lead nine-goal revel

BY TOM JACKSON

BIDDING for a hat-trick of F.A. Youth Cup successes, Manchester United's Under-18 team had an easy passage into the semi-final when they overwhelmed Plymouth Youths 9-0 in the fifth round at Old Trafford to-day.

Charlton and Brennan both got hat-tricks in United's runaway victory but a big feature was the brilliant work of the half-backs, Colman, Edwards and McGuinness.

The Argyle boys put up strong resistance to several United raids cleverly engineered by wing-halves Colman and McGuinness. When Charlton broke through, however, he shot straight at the goalkeeper from a good position.

Plymouth took heart and Edwards twice had to come to the rescue when their attack moved dangerously before Kimberley had a fierce shot punched clear by Hawksworth.

United's attack was more persistent, and after 17 minutes a centre by Beckett resulted in CHARLTON scoring from close range.

Dyer the Plymouth goalkeeper showed brilliant anticipation when United exerted more pressure. But he was beaten again after 22 minutes, a shot by BRENNAN being deflected by a defender into the net.

Five minutes later a spectacular 20-yarder by CHARLTON put United three up.

Play continued to be largely in the United boys' favour, but Dyer foiled the attack on several occasions.

After 33 minutes, however, BRENNAN took a pass from McGuinness to score United's fourth goal with a low drive.

Rhodes cleared a shot by Kimberley in one of Argyle's few efforts at close quarters, but generally Edwards was the master in the middle.

Half-time: United Youths 4, Plymouth Argyle Youths 0.

Dyer was soon in action and one magnificent save from a header by Brennan foiled United of a further quick success.

The Plymouth attack could make little headway against the strong work of the United half-back line, and goal No. 5 came in the 53rd minute.

Beckett was brought down by Kevern as he was going through and from the penalty spot CHARLTON completed his hat-trick.

EIGHT UP

Plymouth never gave up trying and Green got a cheer from the 5,322 crowd for a spectacular drive which brought Hawksworth to a good save at the foot of the post.

But the United Boys, with Edwards the master at centre-half, commanded the all-round power and BRENNAN went on to complete his hat-trick after 67 minutes with a splendid drive.

BECKETT added United's seventh goal after 75 minutes.

Dyer was injured in saving from English, but no sooner had he resumed than a shot by ENGLISH was deflected into the net for United's eighth goal. This was after 81 minutes, and six minutes later EDWARDS ran through to register No. 9.

In a similar fashion to how they had treated Sheffield Wednesday a few weeks before, United completed a demolition job on their guests, with the result never seriously in doubt from the early minutes onwards. Bobby Charlton was again in rich goalscoring form and he and Shay Brennan claimed the lion's share of the applause for their three goals apiece.

There were enough accolades to go around the other team members and the industrious midfielders again grabbed a lot of attention. One report mentioned *'the architects of United's victory were undoubtedly wing-halves Eddie Colman and Wilf McGuinness'* and it went on to claim *'their distribution was superb and defensive play admirable'.*

Casting his mind back to the game over 40 years later in a newspaper article, Argyle's Reg Mitchell had no hesitation about where the source of most of his side's problems stemmed from when singling out one of their tormentor's for even more praise.

Mitchell recalled, *'Colman was United's captain that day and was brilliant in everything he did, his passing, work rate and skill were out of this world. In around 80 to 100 Combination (Reserve) League games with Argyle, often playing against well known First Division players, I never came across anyone again to match his talent. He was a total footballer.'*

The Plymouth Youth skipper summarised the Reds' performance that morning by saying, *'We'd never seen anything like it, it was as if they had come from another planet......'*

It is perhaps understandable that he was so taken aback by the gulf in class between the two sides. While the Reds had defeated the youth teams of three First Division clubs on their way to the Fifth Round, Argyle, following an opening stage bye, progressed to Old Trafford by disposing of Truro City, Swindon Town and Bristol City.

Three of the Plymouth team later reached first-team status, with John Penny, Bernard Barnes and Peter Dyer amassing just nineteen Football League appearances between them.

> *It was like a pack of dogs in the Plymouth game with everyone wanting to score. If we scored seven then we wanted eight, if we scored eight then we wanted nine.*
>
> *Jimmy Murphy made us that way and breathed fire into us. It seemed that every team we played he hated. On the bus going to the game he would come up to us and say, 'Liverpool? I hate Liverpool! Don't you hate Liverpool? Sheffield Wednesday? I hate Sheffield Wednesday!' and we would reply 'Yes Jimmy!'*
>
> *In that first season I think they were just giving me a taste of Youth Cup action early on. I mean, there were two full teams of lads older than me but it was great experience.*
>
> **BOBBY ENGLISH**

Eddie Colman's mesmerising form against the Pilgrims earned him rich praise from his opposite number

fifth round

1954-55

1) Brian Pickett	9) Les Allen	1) Tony Hawksworth	9) Shay Brennan
2) Roy Fergey	10) Tony Nicholas	2) John Queenan	10) Duncan Edwards
3) Terry Stacey	11) Bobby Laverick	3) Alan Rhodes	11) Bobby Charlton
4) Cliff Huxford		4) Eddie Colman	
5) Roy Cunningham		5) Peter Jones	
6) John Compton		6) Wilf McGuinness	
7) Colin Court		7) Ken Morgans	
8) Peter Brabrook		8) Terry Beckett	

APRIL 1955

CHELSEA 1 v 2 MANCHESTER UNITED

Laverick   Edwards (2)

Saturday 16th
Kick-off 3.00 p.m.
Attendance 9,000

semi-final 1st leg

The number of clubs left in the Youth Cup had now been whittled down to just four - United, West Bromwich Albion, Stoke City and Chelsea. The draw dictated that West Brom and Stoke would fight out an all-Staffordshire semi-final while the Reds had to face Chelsea in a Lancashire against London clash as well as having to travel to SW6 for the opening leg.

The Stamford Bridge faithful had already witnessed one great Chelsea versus United contest during the course of the season. Six months previously, in October 1954, the two clubs met in a First Division clash that would be talked about for years because of its thrills and spills, ups and downs, and twists and turns.

The game ended with Chelsea achieving a feat which few teams could come close to in the middle stages of the 1950's when putting five goals past United. Incredibly, however, they conceded six themselves in the process. It was a breathtaking victory for Matt Busby's team and quite understandably the epic match was still a vivid memory for both sets of supporters.

That early term defeat hadn't hampered Chelsea's progress to any great extent and the fashionable Londoners, who were celebrating the 50th season since their formation, were odds-on favourites for the First Division title. Seven days before United's youth team were due at Stamford Bridge, the Chelsea seniors defeated second-placed Wolves by a goal to nil to put them five points clear at the head of the table with only three fixtures left to fulfil.

The success Chelsea were enjoying just then was largely down to their shrewd manager Ted Drake, who did much during his time in charge of the Pensioners to throw off the 'under-achievers' image they had previously endured.

Drake wasn't slow to recognise the merits of the Old Trafford youth policy and for some time he had been employing an efficient and robust scouting system which came near to matching that of United's. Albeit that most of Chelsea's efforts were concentrated in the southern counties of England, they did have representatives in the north and a number of youngsters who signed on at Old Trafford around that time were also approached with an offer of employment by the Blues.

Over the weekend that their first-team were putting daylight between themselves and Wolves, the Chelsea teenagers took part in a tournament in Holland under the guidance of youth manager, Dick Foss. A 0-0 draw with Herder in their opening match was followed by a 6-0 win over DWS and a 6-1 victory against Spartaan. Those results, which included hat-tricks in both games by Les Allen, put them into a final in which they licked Arsenal Youth 2-0. Allen was again a scorer, and Arsenal's downfall gave Chelsea the double benefit of a cup to bring home as well as a lift to their confidence in the run up to meeting the Reds.

Their trail in the Youth Cup was a similar success story to United's. Queen's Park Rangers were smashed 8-0 and Fulham 6-2, both at home, prior to an 8-0 victory against Crystal Palace. Chelsea's win at Selhurst Park thrust them into a Fourth Round meeting with West Ham, a contest in which the Hammers found themselves next for the chop courtesy of a 3-0 defeat at Stamford Bridge. Following up that victory with a 5-1 win at Portsmouth, clearly Chelsea would take some stopping as they had turned some potentially difficult ties into a collection of very comfortable triumphs.

The Chelsea juniors also stood at the top of the South-East Counties League. Losing just once in sixteen matches, during those contests they scored a monstrous 77 goals and conceded a paltry fifteen.

Alongside Les Allen, one of the danger men in the Chelsea eleven was Peter Brabrook, a scheming inside-right who was an England Youth international and had already seen service in the First Division. The danger posed by the Blues wasn't just two-pronged because there was patently an undeniable strength running right through the side.

United possessed a few danger men of their own, none more so than Duncan Edwards, who now owned a full England cap due to his Wembley appearance against Scotland two weeks before.

There were plenty of football attractions in the capital on that particular Saturday afternoon with Spurs, QPR, Charlton, Fulham, West Ham and Crystal Palace all staging home games, but the news that Edwards was due for inclusion in the Reds' starting line-up invariably meant that a number of floating spectators made their way to Stamford Bridge.

With Peter Jones fit again, Edwards was back in the forward-line at inside-left. Ultimately, it was Bobby English who lost out to the big fellow, though Jimmy Murphy was satisfied he had his best side on view.

Under an almost unbroken spring sky, the game got underway.

The early minutes were spoilt by some nervousness, as both teams were clearly concerned about their opponents' reputation, and passes from red and blue jerseys alike found their way into the lost property department with some regularity. The first hint of good football came when Edwards attempted to force his way through the Chelsea penalty area with a tenacious run, despite the attention of two defenders, and a corner, which was easily dealt with, was the result.

Chelsea's opening gambit almost ended in grief for the Reds when 'keeper Hawksworth made a mess of a low shot. With the ball momentarily running loose, and to his relief, it was punted a long way up the pitch to safety.

As the play began to settle, United responded with a move between Shay Brennan and Terry Beckett, the two attackers weaving a neat pattern through the Blues' defence. Brennan's final pass asked a little too much of his colleague and the Chelsea defence regrouped immediately the ball came into their possession.

Within moments of that enterprising sortie, the Reds experienced at first hand why their opponents were so highly regarded when falling a goal behind in the 12th minute. A combination of passes unlocked the United defence, and when released with just Hawksworth to beat, winger Bobby Laverick gave him no hope with a hard drive that had 'goal' written all over it the second it left his foot.

For most of the remainder of the opening half, Chelsea gave a display which mixed the ingredients of speed and expert passing to cohesive teamwork. Their dominance backed United into a position they were hardly accustomed to, that of playing second fiddle for a prolonged period. Just before the break, Hawksworth made a superb and crucial save from a Tony Nicholas shot which could have made life much more difficult for the Reds than it already was.

Most of United's attackers simply weren't functioning with their usual fluency, despite promptings from Edwards, and it meant that Jimmy Murphy had some work to do in the interval.

As was normally the case, Murphy spent the opening 45 minutes making mental notes and his conclusions led him to dictate wholesale changes to the front runners for the second half, the alterations affecting every forward position. Moving Ken Morgans from the right to the left-wing while switching Terry Beckett to outside-right, he advised Bobby Charlton to slip into the inside-left spot and placed Edwards at centre-forward and Shay Brennan at inside-right.

In a similar scenario to the transformation that occurred earlier in the season at Barnsley, Murphy's shuffling produced an immediate and dramatic effect when United drew level within a minute of the restart. The move that produced the equaliser concluded when Edwards, who was situated on the edge of Chelsea's box with two defenders within touching distance, turned smartly to fire home a left-footed drive which scooted along the grass and into the back of the net.

The goal injected a fresh fluency and increased zest to the Reds' movement, and with the new roles established, plus the rush of confidence that a quick equaliser brought, they looked a totally rejuvenated bunch. At last, pistons turned as one, gears clicked into place, and the team mechanism was suddenly running smoothly because of Murphy's half-time 'service'.

In the 55th minute, United forged ahead. With several Chelsea defenders between him and the goal, Edwards went on a typical forward surge. Despite all attempts to interrupt his run, and with opponents seemingly bouncing off him as he tore past them, the Worcestershire lad launched a bombshell from 25 yards that hurtled past a dumbstruck goalkeeper.

It was now Chelsea's turn to try and catch shadows as red-shirted forwards ghosted in and around the home penalty area. With the balance now dramatically swung in United's favour, the Blues were left to rue the fact that they had failed to make their earlier superiority count to better effect.

When the referee called time, Murphy's boys had built the lead they desired. Nevertheless, the tie was far from over, and for United, the slender advantage meant that they wouldn't be able to take anything for granted in the second leg.

> *In the dressing room before the Youth Cup semi-final at Stamford Bridge, Jimmy Murphy told us not to have a 'Duncan Edwards complex'.*
>
> *He said that we were all great players in our own right and that we'd go on to play in United's first-team and maybe for England too. We were losing at half-time and so Jimmy decided to change things around.*
>
> *(Laughs) It was then that he encouraged us to give Duncan the ball as often as possible.*
>
> **WILF McGUINNESS**

1) Tony Hawksworth	9) Duncan Edwards	1) Brian Pickett	9) Les Allen
2) John Queenan	10) Bobby Charlton	2) Alan Hetherington	10) Tony Nicholas
3) Alan Rhodes	11) Ken Morgans	3) Roy Fergey	11) Bobby Laverick
4) Eddie Colman		4) Cliff Huxford	
5) Peter Jones		5) Roy Cunningham	
6) Wilf McGuinness		6) John Compton	
7) Terry Beckett		7) Colin Court	
8) Shay Brennan		8) Peter Brabrook	

1954-55

MANCHESTER UNITED 2 (4) v (2) 1 CHELSEA

Edwards (2, 1 pen) *Allen*

APRIL 1955

Monday 18th

Kick-off 6.00 p.m.

Attendance 15,868

With a section of the newspaper industry's membership exercising their right to take industrial action, and information in relation to sporting matters significantly diminished, there was little build-up to United's return Youth Cup fixture against Chelsea in the press. The splendid attendance, achieved despite yet another inconvenient kick-off time, was mostly down to the Stamford Bridge youngsters' deserved reputation for good football, their showing in the first leg, the closeness of the score and the supporters' anticipation of seeing a cracking match involving several of the brightest young stars of English soccer.

Jimmy Murphy picked the same eleven Reds who had fought back to claim the initiative in London, which caused the Evening Chronicle to mention that *'the front-line is switched to form that which reshuffled in the second half on Saturday'*. Chelsea made one personnel change, Alan Hetherington slotting in at number two while Roy Fergey changed full-back berths as a last minute replacement for Terry Stacey.

Duncan Edwards' appearance at Stamford Bridge brought an end to a three-match run in the first-team for the eighteen year-old and Matt Busby chose not to take him up to Newcastle, where the seniors had a First Division commitment on the very day that Chelsea were in Manchester. In view of Edwards' contribution to United's cause in the game, it would later be regarded as an astute decision on the manager's part.

Almost certainly as a result of their exertions just two days before, both teams initially appeared sluggish and the opinion formed by most of those present was that the first of them to find their usual fluency might just make their way through to the last two. As the Reds only required a draw to realise that feat, the onus was most definitely on the southerners to take the fight to United.

And they did; especially their exciting centre-forward Les Allen, who was compared to the club's boss when described as being *'built on the Ted Drake style'*. That same reporter went on to correctly predict to his readership that Chelsea's dynamic front man was someone *'you will be hearing a great deal about in a few years time'*.

Even though the Blues lived up to their pre-match billing by stamping a great impression on the crowd, and went close to equalising as many as half a dozen times, it was United that vastly increased their chances of a place in the final when they were awarded a penalty. Bobby Charlton had been nominated to take a spot kick in an earlier round against Plymouth, only on this occasion Edwards claimed the responsibility and he didn't disappoint too many folks inside the stadium when driving the ball past Brian Pickett.

The aggregate score stood at 3-1 to the Reds at half-time and the script was being acted out almost exactly as Jimmy Murphy would have wished.

The early part of Act Two made for the hardest viewing for United's coach, a scene in which the effervescent and effective Allen took centre stage by snatching an opportunist goal to put Chelsea back in the frame. With nerves on the bench stretched almost to breaking point, the irrepressible Edwards once again came up with a suitable response to calm everyone down.

The Reds won a corner, which was taken by Charlton, and he hit a high cross that dipped into Chelsea's penalty area where a mass of jostling bodies were waiting. Edwards was loitering just outside the box, and as the ball came across he made a dash towards goal. Despite there being numerous defenders and colleagues seemingly blocking his path, he timed his run and jump to perfection and bulleted an unstoppable header past all of them. The goal put United 2-1 up on the night, and 4-2 in credit overall, which meant that they were back in the final.

Even the usually partisan Alf Clarke, who disclosed that gate receipts totalled a huge £898, was forced into conceding Chelsea were *'a good young side'* who had given the Reds *'a real battle'*. Undoubtedly, though, the finest compliment Clarke could force himself to pay the boys from Stamford Bridge was that he had *'seen the United youngsters play better'*.

Contained in various match summaries were suitably glowing comments, such as the Blues had *'given United their toughest games in the tournament'* and that their *'speed, all-round skill and power would have tested many older sides'*.

The simple truth was that Chelsea, like many others before and after, were unable to find an answer to the incredible Edwards. Dudley's finest was well aware that his days in the youth team were numbered and it appeared he was determined to make the most of what was left of them.

Edwards had certainly been the difference between two exceptional young sides over a couple of tightly-contested scraps and he knew a repeat of that feat would end in him being part of a third Youth Cup winning triumph, an achievement which would take some matching but could never be beaten.

With the newspapers on strike and sporting events going without press coverage, the Review's cartoonist Butterworth focused on the Reds' impending tour to Switzerland and Germany

semi-final 2nd leg

59

1954-55

1) Tony Hawksworth	9) Duncan Edwards
2) John Queenan	10) Bobby Charlton
3) Alan Rhodes	11) Dennis Fidler
4) Eddie Colman	
5) Peter Jones	
6) Wilf McGuinness	
7) Terry Beckett	
8) Shay Brennan	

1) Mick Cashmore	9) Dick McCartney
2) Ray Whale	10) Alec Jackson
3) John Rogers	11) Graham Williams
4) Chuck Drury	
5) Barry Hughes	
6) Barry Cooke	
7) Dick Maynes	
8) Maurice Setters	

APRIL 1955

MANCHESTER UNITED 4 v 1 **WEST BROMWICH ALBION**

Charlton, Colman (2), Edwards — Hughes

final 1st leg

Wednesday 27th
Kick-off 6.30 p.m.
Attendance 16,696

United seek hat-trick

Football at Old Trafford
F.A. Youth Cup-Final
1st Leg
MANCHESTER UNITED (holders)
v.
WEST BROMWICH ALBION
Wednesday, 27th April,
Kick-off 6-30 p.m.
Admission:
Ground 1/- • Boys 6d
Terrace 2/- • Stand 3/-
— ALL PAY —

United now stood on the verge of an historic hat-trick of Youth Cup triumphs. By way of a change, their final foes weren't Wolverhampton Wanderers on this occasion but the Molineux club's close neighbours and fierce rivals, West Bromwich Albion.

There was, though, one significant consistency with the two previous finals, as United brought in yet another debutant to follow in the footsteps of Billy Whelan and Tony Hawksworth, and the new name on the team sheet was that of dashing left-winger, Stockport-born Dennis Fidler. Jimmy Murphy obviously hadn't been entirely at ease with the functionality of his forwards over the course of the season, a fact borne out by the numerous alterations he felt compelled to make to it over the previous seven games.

The individual who could class himself extremely unfortunate to lose out was Ken Morgans. Although naturally disappointed at his exclusion, the young Welsh lad was still eligible to take part in the tournament for the next two seasons and he had, after all, competed against, while featuring alongside, boys who were up to two years older and in their last Youth Cup term. As far as Jimmy Murphy was concerned, winning the trophy was about the here and now, whereas Morgans' undisguised potential combined with his tender age meant that he was more likely considered as one for the future by the management team.

West Brom and United had, of course, met just over a year before in the Youth Cup semi-final, the Reds winning 7-1 over two matches. Only one of the Baggies' side from those games was chosen for the first leg of this season's final and he was left-half Barry Cooke. To their obvious advantage, the Reds had five remaining, namely Alan Rhodes, Eddie Colman, Wilf McGuinness, Duncan Edwards and Bobby Charlton.

In front of an Old Trafford crowd approaching 17,000, which produced yet another substantial cash value at the turnstiles of £1,144, the battle commenced on a slippery surface.

Both sides began in an enterprising fashion without creating any clear-cut chances. West Brom weren't afraid to throw numbers into attack, but many of their thrusts, particularly down the centre of the park, floundered on the rock of centre-half Peter Jones. Colman, particularly, displayed all the confidence that came with not having finished on a losing side in the competition for three seasons and his flair for attempting the unexpected was greeted with howls of delight by the home support. However, for all his showmanship, Colman was usually up to the mark in finding a fellow Red when it came to releasing the ball.

Equally impressive in the half-back line was McGuinness. Always industrious, never afraid to shirk a tackle, he pushed, probed and persistently prompted his forwards into action. As the later stages of the first half approached, the Reds began to stretch the Albion defence and within a short spell Charlton was guilty of missing three chances of varying difficulty.

During the last five minutes of the initial period, United struck two rapier thrusts into the Albion's flesh. As the chief culprit of spurned chances so far, Charlton was instantly forgiven when putting the polish on a move that finished with him glancing a header into West Brom's goal.

Now that the scent of blood was in the air, the Reds went marauding again three minutes later and in a goalmouth mêlée the ball was emphatically banged home by Colman, the undoubted star of the half.

The crowd was mightily impressed by the quality of football on display and West Brom made a solid contribution to the game with a fair amount of possession.

Try as they might, the Albion couldn't force Hawksworth to make a save of note and at 2-0 in deficit they were now looking straight down the barrel of a smoking pistol.

Bobby Charlton, whose opener put the Reds in charge against West Brom

60

1954-55

APRIL 1955

final 1st leg

Peter Jones and his fellow defenders were mostly untroubled by Albion's attackers

The high entertainment value extended into the second section of the game but, even though West Brom continued to see their fair share of the ball, a combination of excellent defending by United and a lack of positive penetration from the visitors meant that Hawksworth remained largely idle.

As the half progressed, those present were given even further value for their admission fee when both sides appeared to redouble their efforts and netted within minutes of each other.

The Reds stormed down the Albion barricades for a third time, when the brilliant Colman hit another goal for the Reds, and West Brom retaliated from a corner in their next attack. Because the flag kick wasn't cleared effectively, centre-half Barry Hughes reduced the arrears, the ball seemingly glancing into the net off McGuinness before crossing the line.

Activity around the Albion's goalmouth reached fever pitch in the last few minutes as United went about them clearly determined to restore the three-goal leeway. After some wasteful approach work by the home inside-forwards, and with 85 minutes gone, the last meaningful act was left to Edwards, who fired home what the Daily Mail reporter reckoned was *'a fantastic goal'*.

Alf Clarke summarised the contest while also hinting at where he felt the venue should have been when recording:

It was a brilliant match on a rain-sodden ground yesterday, and the outstanding player on the field was probably the smallest - Eddie Colman, United's right-half, who crowned a great display by scoring twice.

West Bromwich proved themselves a grand side but faded in front of goal. But this first 'leg' final was good enough to grace Wembley itself.

In view of the Reds' commanding advantage, the overriding thought of most United supporters leaving the ground was that their youths already had one hand on the trophy.

"When we won the Youth Cup again in the 1954/55 season, the games were quite contrasting. I mean, they were either reasonably easy or very difficult. The team had a great understanding as we had Gordon (Clayton) or Tony (Hawksworth) in nets and then me and either John Walker or John Queenan in the full-back positions.

There were hardly any changes in the half-back line and the three of them were really consistent and dependable. Eddie (Colman) was in his third and last year in the youth team. It showed, too, as he and Wilf (McGuinness) were a much better wing-half pairing than any other we came across. They created loads of chances down at the other end of the pitch and then when we needed them in defence, they always seemed to be around to help out.

There may have been a bit of tinkering with the forward-line. I think that was more to do with keeping people on their toes than anything else. Bobby (Charlton) was there all the time and as everyone knows, he can play well in any position. Shay Brennan showed great form and then Terry (Beckett) came in and starting knocking in all these goals.

Kenny Morgans was really unlucky not to play in the final. I thought he did a smashing job for us in the earlier rounds, he was so fast no-one could catch him. I'm glad I didn't have to mark him, that's for sure.

Then there was Duncan. Well, what can you say. He was a full international by the time we'd won the cup and that is something I've always been very proud of, you know, to say that I played alongside a current England international. Not only that, one of the best there's ever been or likely to be.

We got off to a good start at Liverpool, that win did a lot for the confidence of the new lads. The pitch seemed to suit us because it was flat and fast, the wet surface made the ball go quicker.

One of our toughest games was at (Manchester) City. There was a lot of fog, and Jimmy Murphy said he could hardly see anything, but it didn't seem as bad out on the pitch. Obviously, there was quite a lot of local pride at stake, the lads from Manchester in the team wouldn't have wanted to lose that one.

We got past Barnsley, we were glad Duncan was with us for that one, and then we sailed through a couple of games when we scored loads and loads of goals.

In the semi-final, we all felt we had done the hard part by winning at Stamford Bridge, even though we knew we couldn't take it easy in the second leg. Chelsea really tested us at Old Trafford and it could have gone either way until Duncan put away his penalty.

They had two decent wingers, John (Queenan) had to look after a really tricky lad called Laverick who scored down at their place. Les Allen never gave us any peace, either. We were glad we met them in the semi-final, the two legs of the final were much, much easier in comparison.

All the lads used to really look forward to the Youth Cup matches and we couldn't wait to hear who we were playing when the draw was made. The games offered us the chance to play at grounds we'd never been to before, and usually in front of a good crowd. I can tell you, it was a bit different to playing for the Colts on some playing field in Timperley or Burnage.

Because we had this reputation, we knew everyone wanted to beat us and every game seemed to be an even greater challenge than the one before. Some players can respond to that and others can't. I used to think that if I defended well enough, there were enough goals in the side to win against any other team of our age group.

Bert (Whalley), Jimmy (Murphy) and Matt Busby were very serious about the Youth Cup. We had to take it seriously as well, because it was a massive thrill to be involved and nobody wanted to lose their place."

ALAN RHODES

61

1954-55

1) Mick Cashmore	1) Tony Hawksworth
2) Ray Whale	2) John Queenan
3) John Rogers	3) Alan Rhodes
4) Maurice Setters	4) Eddie Colman
5) Barry Hughes	5) Peter Jones
6) Barry Cooke	6) Wilf McGuinness
7) Dick Maynes	7) Terry Beckett
8) Jimmy Harris	8) Shay Brennan
9) Dick McCartney	9) Duncan Edwards
10) Alec Jackson	10) Bobby Charlton
11) Graham Williams	11) Dennis Fidler

APRIL 1955

WEST BROMWICH ALBION 0(1) v (7)3 **MANCHESTER UNITED**

Beckett, Brennan (2)

Saturday 30th
Kick-off 3.00 p.m.
Attendance 8,335

final 2nd leg

Third cup win for Man. U. Youths

For the second leg of the final at The Hawthorns just three days later, Jimmy Murphy stuck with the same eleven who had built up a healthy lead at Old Trafford. West Brom were forced to make changes, Chuck Drury dropping out through an injury he picked up in Manchester. Maurice Setters, who took the inside-right spot in the first leg, switched into Drury's right-half place while Jimmy Harris, who had featured in most of the previous rounds, was restored at number eight for the Baggies.

With the game's 3.00 p.m. kick-off requiring a Central League fixture between West Brom Reserves and Wolves Reserves to be brought forward to an 11.00 a.m. start, the concluding instalment of how the Reds held onto the Youth Cup for a further year was given in the Midland Chronicle & Free Press:

Manchester United Youths were flattered by the three-goals margin at The Hawthorns on Saturday but were undeniably the better side and retained the trophy by an aggregate of 7-1.

The three-goals deficit with which Albion started Saturday's game made them over-anxious and play was of an extremely poor standard for most of the first half. Manchester appeared nervous, too, and there were many unnecessary fouls.

Albion's forwards did not combine well and most of the thrills were at the other end. The home defence got through a lot of work and kept the dangerous United attack at bay until nineteen minutes from the end when right winger T. Beckett scored a fine goal following a clever left wing thrust between Fidler and Charlton.

The single goal was just about the measure of Manchester's slight superiority in attack but they grabbed two shock goals in the dying minutes of the game through inside-right Brennan. He hit the first from a Charlton pass and added the other less than a minute afterwards following a throw-in on the left.

It was the third successive year that United had won the cup and it will take a great team to beat them. Albion had conceded only five goals in their previous seven games – a tribute to the 'fire power' of the Manchester team which slammed them for seven in two matches.

The game produced a greater flow of traffic in and about United's penalty area and Hawksworth, who could easily have suffered from a case of acute loneliness

United's under-18 team are all smiles following their Youth Cup final defeat of West Brom
Back row (l-r) Duncan Edwards, Terry Beckett, Shay Brennan, Tony Hawksworth, Alan Rhodes, John Queenan
Front row (l-r) Peter Jones, Dennis Fidler, Eddie Colman, Wilf McGuinness, Bobby Charlton

1954-55

APRIL 1955

in the home leg, was called to respond to many more Albion attacks than had been the case at Old Trafford. During the opening 45 minutes alone, Hawksworth was forced to punch clear a long range shot from Cooke and a testing centre from Williams, as well as saving headers from both Jackson and Setters.

One of the main talking points of the second half was caused when the Albion's 'keeper completely missed a left-wing cross. The ball ran to Edwards, who instantly returned it to Charlton, and the latter's header beat the custodian only to see the ball scrambled off the goal-line.

United clearly had their work cut out early on, and prior to a definite pattern emerging there was what one reporter called *'a little over-eagerness with some questionable pushing and barging'* from both sides.

During the second period, any danger the Albion posed became less and less potent, and being in a position to play the patience game, the Reds showed two of their ace cards just when time was running out for the home team.

The outcome was never seriously in question after Terry Beckett bloodied the Albion's nose when opening the scoring. Beckett's deadliness had, to all intents and purposes, completely guillotined the Baggies' chance of glory and Shay Brennan then put the icing on the cake with his impressive contribution.

Immediately following the final whistle, skipper Eddie Colman proudly accepted the Youth Cup trophy on behalf of his team-mates from Councillor H. Hughes, vice president of the Football Association. A few seconds were then spent posing for a quick team photo before a bunch of jubilant players headed up the tunnel to receive the congratulations of Jimmy Murphy and Bert Whalley.

Murphy, who viewed the trophy presentations with a justifiable sense of pride and achievement, couldn't have worn a wider smile at United's victory celebrations as they provided him with yet another great memory of The Hawthorns, a ground where he had spent almost his entire playing career.

> *The toughest match that season was against Barnsley, but once we beat them I was really confident we would go on and win the Youth Cup. After the first leg of the final against West Brom and being 4-1 up I knew we would win it. There was no way they were going to score four goals against us.*
>
> *I remember running down the eighteen-yard line on the right wing and I just hit the ball across the 'keeper from an acute angle and the ball just flew past him into the corner of the net. I scored the first goal and it was all over really.*

TERRY BECKETT

Eddie Colman becomes the third United captain to receive the Youth Cup trophy

final 2nd leg

1953-55

SEPTEMBER 1954

Monday 20th
Kick-off 6.00 p.m.

the tomlinson trophy

1) Willie Speight (L)
2) John Parkes (E)
3) Ian Hillsdon (E)
4) Bobby Campbell (L)
5) Stan Billington (E)
6) Terry Stephens (E)
7) Jim Almond (L)
8) Jimmy Melia (L)
9) Jackie Keeley (E)
10) Jackie Kidd (E)
11) Harry Rudkin (SL)

1) Tony Hawksworth
2) Ivan Beswick
3) Alan Rhodes
4) Eddie Colman
5) Bobby Harrop
6) Wilf McGuinness
7) Tommy Littler
8) Bobby Charlton
9) Duncan Edwards
10) David Pegg
11) Albert Scanlon

LIVERPOOL COUNTY F.A. 0 — 3 MANCHESTER UNITED

Edwards (2), Scanlon

Three hundred and sixty four days since mercilessly crushing a talented Sheffield & Hallamshire eleven, United took part in the second such contest when they met Liverpool County.

The Merseysiders had beaten Gloucestershire 4-1 in the previous season's County Youth Cup final and were practically a combined Liverpool and Everton youth team, the exception being South Liverpool's Harry Rudkin.

The Reds fielded precisely the same side that had taken part in their final against Wolves five months earlier.

The match, which was viewed by what the Manchester Evening News described as a *'small attendance'*, was another triumph, in a long line of such highlights, for Duncan Edwards, and the big fellow just missed out on completing a hat-trick when one of his later efforts hit the back of the net only to be ruled out by referee Arthur Jones for an infringement.

The Liverpool Echo gave a fair account of the proceedings:

Manchester United Youths retained the Tomlinson Cup by defeating Liverpool County F.A. Youths at Anfield last night after a fast game in which the superiority of the visitors was most pronounced.

Duncan Edwards, the England 'B' international, was a grand leader for the United, and scored two splendid goals in the 16th and 21st minutes, Scanlon securing their third in the 60th minute.

Liverpool opened well, but once the visitors had taken the lead Liverpool faded. Liverpool, who were much slower than their opponents, were allowed few opportunities, Hawksworth never being seriously tested. Speight, the home goalkeeper, considering the heavy pressure brought to bear on him, did well.

Billington worked hard as a pivot for the home side, while Rudkin put over some nice centres.

The Daily Mail was emphatic in its observation about United winning *'the Tomlinson Trophy easily'*. The newspaper also claimed the victors *'were much more experienced, brilliant team workers, and faster on the ball'*, adding that *'Liverpool had only fighting spirit and endeavour'*.

The Mail also gave great credit to David Pegg, who they claimed *'was the maker of the openings'*.

YOUTH STARS IN ANFIELD DUEL

HIGHLIGHTS of the Youth battle between the Liverpool F.A. and Manchester United, at Anfield last night. Top: Manchester's first goal scored by their centre-forward Duncan Edwards.

1) Alan Collier (LT)	9) Brian Stapleton (LT)	1) Tony Hawksworth	9) Alex Dawson
2) Eric White (LT)	10) Tony Gregory (LT)	2) John Queenan	10) Bobby Charlton
3) Vic Moody (LT)	11) Michael Jordan (HT)	3) Peter Jones	11) Dennis Fidler
4) John Chambers (LT)		4) Bobby English	
5) Keith Underwood (LT)		5) Reg Holland	
6) David Hetherington (LT)		6) Wilf McGuinness	
7) John Kaye (LR)		7) Shay Brennan	
8) Brian Whitby (VM)		8) Mark Pearson	

1953-55

BEDFORDSHIRE COUNTY F.A. 3 v 4 MANCHESTER UNITED

Gregory (2), Stapleton — Brennan (2), Dawson (2)

NOVEMBER 1955

Monday 14th

Kick-off 7.15 p.m.

Attendance 1,699

FINE FIGHT BY COUNTY
Made United Go All The Way

The last of the trio of Tomlinson Trophy ties took place at Luton's Kenilworth Road ground in November 1955 when Bedfordshire acted as hosts. Bedfordshire had beaten Sheffield & Hallamshire 2-0 to claim the County Youth Cup title, thereby earning the right to a contest against the Reds, and eight of their lads were on the books of the home club. There was also one representative each from Vauxhall Motors, Hitchin Town and Leighton Rovers.

United made a departure from their decision of the previous year in fielding their full Youth Cup winning team, instead settling on what was essentially a mixture of their current and former youth sides.

Such a course of action was almost certainly taken because, unlike the two previous Tomlinson Trophy games, which had taken place only about three or four weeks into the new season, the current campaign was already well advanced by the time the match was contested.

Of the United side that trounced West Bromwich Albion in the 1955 Youth Cup final, Alan Rhodes' left-back responsibility passed to Peter Jones while Reg Holland slotted in at centre-half. Eddie Colman's place at right-half went to Bobby English, and in the attack, Terry Beckett and Duncan Edwards' places were filled by Alex Dawson and Mark Pearson.

There was a great expectancy in Luton that Edwards would make an appearance. Sadly for them, that wasn't possible and his omission from the line-up was probably due to National Service commitments, although he was in attendance at Kenilworth Road dressed in his squaddie's uniform.

As events transpired, Bedfordshire came the closest to wresting the trophy away from the Reds by virtue of a gutsy performance.

The following match report was given in the Luton News:

The all-conquering Manchester United youth team, winners of the F.A. Youth Cup three consecutive times, had something of a shock at Kenilworth Road on Monday by the strength of Bedfordshire's resistance in the meeting for the George Tomlinson Trophy.

Indeed, not until four minutes from the end did they secure the goal that made a replay unnecessary, or alternatively the cup being held jointly.

There was no disputing the fact that the United were the more polished, better-drilled team, and the fluency of their movements with each player seeming to know where the others were spoke of long practice together.

But Bedfordshire refused to be blinded by science and sheer determination and fighting spirit, interspersed with good football, kept them right in the game until the closing minutes.

With only ten minutes gone, they provided a shock when Gregory headed through, and what happened afterwards might have been a different story had the referee not disallowed what appeared to be a perfectly good goal by Whitby in the first minute.

Smooth work by United brought them goals from Brennan and Dawson, but the County kept at it and Stapleton equalised on the stroke of half-time.

With a brilliant left-wing causing a deal of trouble, Bedfordshire were thrown back on the defensive in the second half, but they fought hard though they could not prevent Brennan putting United ahead again.

Another goal by the long-striding Gregory levelled up things again and then came the winner by Dawson after the United defence had survived a jittery period.

In the pure football sense, United were the more able side and they kept to a policy of all-out attack for most of the game, with the wing-halves coming through with the ball.

This made things difficult for the home defence, who were often struggling gamely, and there were a number of great saves by Collier, who was in international form. Gregory was the best of a forward-line that had to rely on quick thrusts, and the left-wing was the more dangerous.

It was an exciting, attractive game which deserved to be watched by more than 1,699 people.

At the conclusion of the game, Mr. Maurice Love, current chairman of the Youth Cup committee, presented United with a specially inscribed plaque to commemorate their feat of winning the F.A. Youth Cup for three consecutive seasons on behalf of the Football Association.

Accepting the gift as the club's senior representative, Matt Busby, who was positively glowing with pride, revealed that the award came as a complete surprise to him and he went on to say that he was so pleased the Football Association had chosen to honour Manchester United and his players in such a way. All these years later, the club still holds the momento, which is seen below on the cover of an F.A. magazine and is periodically displayed in the museum at Old Trafford.

A year later, the Reds were due to take part in their fourth Tomlinson Trophy match, their potential opponents Middlesex having won the 1956 County Youth Cup by beating Staffordshire 3-2 in the two-legged final.

It was always assumed that Middlesex declined the offer to play United. However, more recent information from the Middlesex F.A. has indicated that might not have been the case and they have claimed that there is no firm evidence to suggest such a proposal was made. The person who acted as their match secretary in 1956 has been quoted as saying that he has no recollection whatsoever of any such game being muted.

It appears, then, that the Tomlinson Trophy was simply abandoned, possibly through a simple lack of interest, or maybe because of the logistical problems of bringing the County Youth Cup and F.A. Youth Cup winners together.

What a pity that was.

The Reds would have been up against a Middlesex Youth team containing not only future World Cup winner George Cohen of Fulham, but also Jimmy Greaves, Chelsea's teenage goal-machine.

Now that really could have been some game.

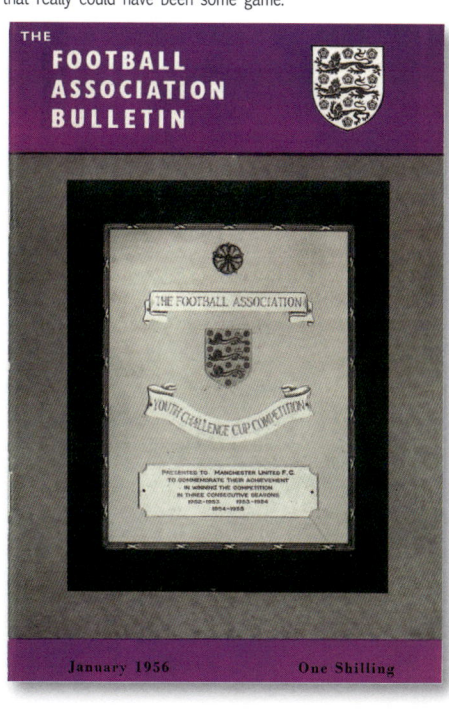

the tomlinson trophy

1955-56

1) Mike Lynne
2) Eric Nuttall
3) Ken Heywood
4) Jim Smith
5) Gordon Sheffield
6) Brian Parkinson
7) Tony Fairclough
8) Cliff Portwood
9) Keith Walkden
10) Mel Neil
11) Bill Norcross

1) Tony Hawksworth
2) John Queenan
3) Peter Jones
4) Bobby English
5) Reg Holland
6) Wilf McGuinness
7) Ken Morgans
8) Mark Pearson
9) Alex Dawson
10) Bobby Charlton
11) Dennis Fidler

OCTOBER 1955

PRESTON NORTH END 2 v 5 MANCHESTER UNITED

Neil, Portwood   Charlton (3, 1 pen), Dawson (2)

Monday 31st
Kick-off 7.00 p.m.

second round

Young Reds bid for Youth Cup

United's 1955/56 Youth Cup trail commenced with the rather unexpected piece of good news in that they had received their very first bye in the competition. Unfortunately, it wasn't all glad tidings because their Second Round tie was an away engagement, with Preston North End lying as the opposition in waiting.

Along with Maine Road, Deepdale was one of the earliest football grounds in the north of England to benefit from the installation of floodlights, from October 1953 onwards, and so it was, therefore, something of a no-brainer that the youth clash would be allocated an evening, rather than a weekend or afternoon, starting slot.

The Reds required to blood new players in order to fill the positions left vacant by those who were now ineligible from the previous season, principally three-times cup-winners Eddie Colman and Duncan Edwards, and a centre-half from Nottinghamshire by the name of Reg Holland was given the stopper responsibility while last term's number five, Peter Jones, relocated to the left full-back berth to accommodate him. Bobby English, who helped out by filling in at centre-forward on two occasions during the last cup run and was looking to gain a more permanent place in the side, found his wish realised when handed the right-half role previously held by Colman.

While English took over the little fellow's former position, Wilf McGuinness was honoured with succeeding Colman as team captain and Ken Morgans and Dennis Fidler were given the wing berths, adding to Bobby Charlton's experience in the front-line. There were two new additions to the forwards and both had recently been taken on at Old Trafford after shining in the white jersey of England as schoolboy internationals, namely inside-right Mark Pearson and centre-forward Alex Dawson.

Questions regarding whether the new boys might be as successful, skilful or single-minded as their predecessors in pursuit of national cup glory would probably have crossed the minds of the United management and coaching staff. The answers to those queries could, of course, only be provided by their performances on the park.

However, there was little room for any reservations regarding the quality of those chosen to represent United at Deepdale. The bare facts showed that the majority of them were already well versed in Youth Cup football and seven had been capped by their country as schoolboys for either England or Wales.

The match at Preston actually provided a relatively gentle introduction to the tournament for the new kids and not much more than a stroll in the park for those with previous participation in the competition.

After going in deficit in the early minutes of the tie, and then conceding again in the last seconds, when the thoughts of the players were perhaps straying as to who they might meet in the next round, in between the Reds managed to run in five scores of their own.

One news report summed up the 90 minutes by claiming *'supreme confidence marked everything that the Manchester boys did and they both overran and outplayed the home side'.*

That confidence was present right from the early moments when United ripped into Preston looking for an early advantage. To their sheer frustration, and after admonishing almost constant pressure from the kick-off, the Reds were staggered to fall behind as a result of some hesitancy from a corner in the ninth minute. When the ball was knocked into the danger area from the flag kick, United defenders were strung out like washing on a clothes line as it was prodded past Tony Hawksworth from close proximity.

The Reds responded in the best way they could, by demonstrating an increased sense of urgency which revealed the steely streak displayed in so many previous ties was still very much present. The industry demanded from his midfielders by Jimmy Murphy definitely heightened, prompting a reporter to note that *'McGuinness and English were strong attacking half-backs'* and that they *'repeatedly split the Preston defence wide open'.*

Only a few minutes after falling behind, the Reds levelled up the scores. With United's forwards converging on the North End goalmouth with some repetition, rookie Dawson broke loose of his shackles to go bearing in on goal. Just at the point when it looked as if he only had to guide the ball home, the centre-forward was unceremoniously flattened by Preston's goalie.

Adjudging that a foul had been committed, the referee awarded a penalty kick and the ball was placed on the spot by Bobby Charlton, who tucked his shot neatly past Lynne to make the score one-all.

There was hardly any time between United's opening goal and their second. Dawson continued to make a nuisance of himself amongst the Preston defenders and his labours were rewarded when he put the Reds into the lead. It was, in view of the number of Youth Cup goals he would eventually total, a somewhat historic strike and, for good measure, Dawson claimed another before the interval to stretch his side's lead to 3-1.

Only good work by the North End defence kept the score down to a respectable figure during the second half, and it appeared that Preston were left with only their pride still to play for when Charlton put United four goals to one in front.

One newspaper reporter reckoned North End 'keeper Lynne was one of the outstanding individuals on display, despite his penalty aberration, and justified that assertion by stating his *'brilliant point blank saves prevented the scores reaching double figures'.* Lynne could do nothing to stop Charlton completing a hat-trick midway through the second period, the number ten's third goal finalising United's scoring for the night.

With the match won, the Reds loosened their grip somewhat to let Preston back in for a spell of possession and North End were rewarded for continuing to battle away with their second successful strike in the last moments of the game.

It was an encouraging start to United's new cup campaign, and particularly so for the new boys, who all acquitted themselves well. Even so, the main contribution came from an old hand and the Daily Mail report claimed that the *'architect of Manchester's victory was inside-left Charlton, a brilliant schemer'.*

The Reds' new centre-half Reg Holland, whose maiden bow in the Youth Cup at Preston ended in an emphatic victory

1955-56

1) Tony Hawksworth	9) Alex Dawson
2) John Queenan	10) Bobby Charlton
3) Peter Jones	11) Dennis Fidler
4) Bobby English	
5) Reg Holland	
6) Wilf McGuinness	
7) Terry Beckett	
8) Mark Pearson	

1) Ronnie Routledge	9) Henry Rich
2) Henry McNally	10) Alan Hope
3) Allan Graham	11) Clive Bircham
4) Graham Reed	
5) George Morton	
6) Alan Carter	
7) Freddie Stansfield	
8) Frank Marshall	

MANCHESTER UNITED 4 v 0 SUNDERLAND

Charlton, Dawson (2), Pearson

DECEMBER 1955

Wednesday 14th

Kick-off 2.15 p.m.

Attendance 2,541

third round

Six weeks after the convincing victory at Deepdale, the draw for the Third Round brought Sunderland to Old Trafford and it represented the very first clash against a club that has become one of United's most regular Youth Cup foes over the intervening years.

On the day before the Wearsiders were due in town, the Manchester Evening News devoted a whole column, penned by Tom Jackson, entitled 'NOW UNITED BRING ON THE 15 YEAR-OLDS'. As the title suggested, the print space was devoted to introducing the junior Reds to the newspaper's readership.

Commenting on the number of former schoolboy internationals United were due to field against Sunderland, Jackson elaborated further on the emphasis that the club placed on nurturing its young stock:

All the youngsters are now going through the famous Busby 'nursery' at Old Trafford. Along with junior professionals such as Tony Hawksworth (goal), Peter Jones (full-back), Wilf McGuinness (wing-half) and Bobby Charlton (inside-left), they are proving that United's scouting system and methods of developing future first-team material is probably unsurpassed in big soccer.

Already this season, for instance, Charlton and Dawson have hit 58 goals between them. Charlton, a cousin to Newcastle United and England international Jackie Milburn, has scored 26 - including 20 in United's Reserve team - and Dawson 32, most of them in the fourth team.

Yet even these scoring feats are merely part of the club's reward for persevering with the young idea and scorning the transfer cheque book in preference to building up their own talent.

For the football served up by successive United youth teams in a three-year unbeaten spell in the F.A. competition goes to prove that the Reds' flow of highly-promising material is assured for years to come.

A few seasons ago, Matt Busby estimated that United possessed young players whose total future value was 'many thousands of pounds.'

Today, in the light of his first-team 'bloodings' and the successes of his young reserves, he might well be underestimating his Old Trafford stock even with a £250,000 assessment.

Sunderland's juniors won't be easy prey for this new United youth team. In the two previous rounds they won through with 9-2 victories - over South Bank (Middlesbrough's 'nursery' club) and Stockton Youths.

Alongside the preview of the Youth Cup game, the Evening News carried an article which noted that United's John Aston senior had reported back to Old Trafford after spending seventeen months in a North Wales sanatorium while recovering from illness. It claimed he was happy to be home, although Aston was forced to concede that, at the age of 34, his magnificent career as a footballer was over.

On the same day that the club's youngsters were receiving such glowing publicity in the press, he described Matt Busby's decision to keep him on the paid staff, despite his health problems, as *'a great gesture'*. It was, therefore, an opportune time to reflect on just what could be achieved in the game with the correct mixture of talent and dedication that the local man possessed.

Johnny Aston, it should be noted, was one of the first boys to sign for the MUJACs on their formation in 1938. Progressing through the grades at Old Trafford to become an established member of the first-team, the modest and unassuming defender assisted the club to win the 1948 F.A. Cup final and the First Division title in 1952 while earning himself seventeen full England caps and becoming the first Red to appear in the World Cup finals. What a fine and fitting example he was to any of United's new crop of hopefuls.

As Jimmy Murphy announced just a solitary alteration from the game at Preston, with Terry Beckett gaining the nod over Ken Morgans for the outside-right position, the Evening Chronicle's Alf Clarke described a spell of Manchester's infamous weather:

Conditions could not have been more miserable than they were at Old Trafford today for the Third Round F.A. Youth Cup tie between Manchester United and Sunderland.

The light was very bad and it was raining heavily just before the start.

In fact, it did not look at all possible that the match would be finished owing to the poor visibility.

Fortunately, the game progressed to a conclusion and the Evening News took up the story with the following match report under the headline 'CHARLTON SHINES FOR BRIGHT REDS':

MANCHESTER UNITED'S under-18 team gave a brilliant attacking display in the mud to gain a convincing victory over Sunderland Youths in the third round F.A. Youth Cup-tie at Old Trafford this afternoon.

A crowd cut down to 2,541 by the weather saw the United Boys, holders of the trophy for the last three years, monopolise the play, with Bobby Charlton having a part in their first three goals.

Sunderland won a corner-kick within seconds of the start, but United kept up the pressure and after a shot from Dawson had been cleared off the Sunderland goal line they took the lead in three minutes. A free kick on the right led to CHARLTON cleverly heading through to put United one up.

NEAR MISS

Sunderland had another escape when a low centre by Fidler slashed across their goalmouth, eluding both Charlton and Dawson. The ground began to churn up, but still the youngsters on both sides swung the heavy ball about with plenty of zest and enterprise.

Hawksworth conceded a free kick for over-carrying the ball, but went on to save well from Bircham, and then in another swift United raid a shot by Pearson was cleverly saved by Routledge.

McGuinness and Charlton were prominent in building up United raids.

After 29 minutes United's more forceful work was rewarded with a second goal. Charlton, who had earlier finished a brilliant run with a drive over the bar made the chance for DAWSON, who responded with a swift low shot into the net.

Five minutes before the interval United took a third goal, a pass from McGuinness resulting in Charlton laying on a perfect opening for DAWSON to drive the ball home from close range.

Half-time: Manchester United Youths 3, Sunderland 0.

The Sunderland forward had the spirit, but not the craft of the United attack which continued to create many fine openings. After 50 minutes, Dawson turned across a short centre for PEARSON to give United a four-goal lead.

FINE SAVE

Dawson was only just foiled from taking another chance when Routledge dived at his feet, and a few moments later the Sunderland goalkeeper excelled by turning a shot from Fidler round the post.

United threw away a chance of a fifth goal when Charlton missed from the penalty spot in the 60th minute, but later the Sunderland goal had escapes when English and Dawson hit the post and cross-bar with the goalkeeper beaten.

Sunderland staged a late rally, but they were twice foiled from scoring by Hawksworth. Then, just before the end, Charlton made two further brilliant efforts, from the second of which Routledge saved by turning the ball over the bar.

A near thing for the Sunderland Youth team. Routledge, their goalkeeper, fumbled this shot from Manchester United Youth centre-forward Dawson, but full-back McNally nipped in to clear the ball.

On a bog of a pitch, the Reds put on a powerhouse display to eliminate Sunderland from the competition. Alex Dawson and Bobby Charlton picked up the goalscoring mantle again, with only the woodwork denying the former a hat-trick. Charlton, too, could have helped himself to further goals, and it was only the heroics performed by the opposing goalkeeper, who pulled off several acrobatic saves, which denied him.

There was also the little matter of Charlton's rather uncharacteristic penalty miss. When the spot kick was given, the inside-left looked across to see his old Ashington school friend Ronnie Routledge attempting to bar the goalmouth. With the Reds already 4-0 up, Charlton failed to add to his third minute conversion by banging the ball practically straight into the arms of his pal.

The United Review concluded that the small number of spectators who braved the elements were *'treated to an exhibition of quick, methodical and controlled football'*, while the Sunderland Echo conceded their boys had been *'unable to do anything about the one-sided run of play'.*

69

1955-56

1) Tony Hawksworth
2) John Queenan
3) Peter Jones
4) Bobby English
5) Reg Holland
6) Wilf McGuinness
7) Terry Beckett
8) Mark Pearson
9) Alex Dawson
10) Bobby Charlton
11) Dennis Fidler

1) Alan Wilson
2) Bill Newson
3) Bobby Ferguson
4) Brian Wright
5) Jim Charlton
6) David Livingstone
7) Ron Thornton
8) Alan Spears
9) Stan Wynn
10) Peter Duffy
11) Reg Evans

JANUARY 1956

Saturday 28th
Kick-off 3.00 p.m.
Attendance 26,282

MANCHESTER UNITED 7 v 1 NEWCASTLE UNITED

Beckett, Charlton (2, 1 pen), Dawson (2), Fidler, McGuinness — Spears

fourth round

Manchester United's under-18's get ready to ruffle a few Magpie feathers
Back row (l-r) Bobby English, Dennis Fidler, Tony Hawksworth, Mark Pearson, Terry Beckett, Bobby Charlton
Front row (l-r) Reg Holland, Alex Dawson, Wilf McGuinness, Peter Jones, John Queenan

Following hard on the footsteps of their North-Eastern rivals in trying to halt the Reds' unerring cup progress, Newcastle United hit town on the last Saturday of January in 1956 confident in the expectation that they would be remembered as the team that finally ended the competition's one-club domination. As well as being Fourth Round Youth Cup day for the two Uniteds, it was also the same stage of the nation's senior knock-out tournament for those clubs left remaining.

Unfortunately, Matt Busby's first-team were not one of those still in contention as they had been subjected to an ignominious defeat at Bristol Rovers earlier in the month. To avoid a blank Saturday, Busby arranged a friendly fixture at Leeds, and because Manchester City were away at Southend in the F.A. Cup, it left the youth game as arguably the most appetising in and around the vicinity of Manchester.

The expectation of a large gate was evidenced as early as three days before Newcastle's arrival when an announcement from the Old Trafford ticket office gave notification that all reserved seats were sold.

In welcoming the Magpies to Old Trafford, the editor of the United Review pencilled the following notes in the match programme:

Our visitors represent a club who are renowned cup-fighters and we expect a very hard game today. At the time of writing two of their stars are doubtful starters, Thursby right half-back has been selected for the England Youth team at Sheffield while Bell has been injured and is not expected to be fit. They are, however, a big, strong side and last season were joint holders with Wolves of the Northern Intermediate League Cup. This season their record in the NIL is played 8, won 5 and lost 3.

Newcastle United commenced their nursery side in 1947-48 and are known in the North-East as the 'N's', they have produced some two dozen youths playing in league football today. The members of the present side were all born in the North-East and nine of them will be eligible to play in the competition next season. In the First Round they were drawn away to Seaton Delaval where they won 6-1, then followed two home draws against Middlesbrough (won 2-1) and North Shields (won 3-1). A feature of the game is that quite a number of the players have played together in schoolboy and representative matches and are well known to each other, so today's game is something of a reunion for them. Whatever the outcome of the game we are looking forward to an enjoyable match and may the best team win.

Newcastle fielded two changes from the team that appeared in the programme, with Brian Wright returning from injury in place of Eddie Egleton at right-half and Peter Duffy included at inside-left at the expense of Mike McWilliams. The dangermen in the Magpies' formation were ex-England schoolboy forwards Stan Wynn and Alan Spears, the two having shared a total of ten international caps between them prior to signing for the St. James's Park club.

Jimmy Murphy made no changes to the side that had beaten Sunderland and the two teams ran out to a welcome from a magnificent crowd of over 26,000 spectators. It was, to that point, by far the largest attendance for a youth game at Old Trafford and also a record for the tournament.

Newcastle, sporting their famous black and white strip, such a dramatic looking outfit which always seems to add another dimension of drama to the big occasion, got off on the wrong foot entirely, by almost conceding straight from the kick-off. Alex Dawson and chief accomplice Mark Pearson concocted a ruse in the opening foray that goalkeeper Alan Wilson read well when rushing out to pluck the ball away from the number nine. Wilson was also required to be bright-eyed a minute later, when Dawson threatened again with a run towards goal, and this time the Geordie goalie needed to sprint off his line to kick the ball clear of danger.

The early pressure Newcastle came under was relieved when they won a free kick that was taken by their number four and aimed into the box. The ball was headed to safety by a United defender, but another attack on the home goal followed when Duffy lashed a shot that went narrowly wide.

70

1955-56

JANUARY 1956

In their very next forward move, Newcastle silenced the Old Trafford masses by snatching the lead in the eighth minute when a cross from the left by winger Reg Evans was completely missed by Tony Hawksworth and inside-right Spears had the easiest of tasks just to roll the ball over the goal-line.

Moments later, a pass from Bobby Charlton found Mark Pearson in a favourable position, the inside-forward wasting the initiative by ballooning his shot over the bar with only Wilson to beat. Dennis Fidler got in on the act by producing a shot off target at the end of a terrific run, and Wilson then made a trio of excellent stops from Charlton, twice, and Bobby English.

The strain of trying to contain an increasingly effervescent forward force was beginning to have a detrimental effect on the Newcastle team and cracks in their defence were now widening with every United attack.

The 19th minute brought an inevitable equaliser when the Reds were awarded a free kick that was clipped towards the front of the goal. Darting out of a ruck of players assembled in front of Alan Wilson, who got the Reds off the mark with a header for the second game in succession.

More home advances followed, although Wilson proved a frustrating stumbling block by performing repeatedly good work. Newcastle's defenders were powerless to produce the pace, poise or protection necessary to hold a check on United's ceaseless offensive moves and just after the 33-minute mark, the Magpies conceded another. A beautifully struck long ball from the influential Charlton, a trademark for which he would soon become famous on much higher stages, was complemented by a neat piece of control by Terry Beckett and he scored with a shot which flew in off a post.

Within 60 seconds the Reds had increased their lead to 3-1 with an absolute peach of a goal when a meandering solo dribble by Dennis Fidler took him away from a couple of bemused opponents. Upon breaking clear, Fidler provided the finest moment of the match with a shot that fairly rocketed past Wilson and struck the underside of the crossbar prior to crossing the goal-line.

Only Wilson seemed able to hold the score back at that stage, and he made another stop, from Charlton once more, just prior to lemon-time.

Newcastle fell further behind in the 47th minute as a result of a penalty kick which was given when a Dawson header was handled by full-back Bobby Ferguson. Putting his miss from the spot in the previous round to the back of his mind, Charlton knocked the ball in for United's fourth goal.

There was hardly a let up for the crowd. Dawson fluffed a good opening later on when blasting high despite being well placed, and Newcastle then scorned an opportunity at the other end when Duffy cut a swathe into the Reds' area only to see Hawksworth pull off a fantastic save.

Hawksworth's block seemed to represent the point of no return for the St. James's Park boys and after Charlton volleyed a shot into the side netting, therefore unluckily missing out on a hat-trick against the club he supported as a boy, a move initiated by a Bobby English pass into the stride of Beckett ended when Dawson headed home the winger's centre from the improbable distance of just inside the eighteen-yard area.

With time and a considerable amount of enthusiasm running out for Newcastle, the Reds added number six just three minutes later following captain Wilf McGuinness' simple header from a Fidler corner.

By that stage of the proceedings, almost every Geordie had retreated into a defensive role in an attempt to keep the score down. They couldn't prevent chief tormentor Charlton running right through their ragged ranks to shoot wide, and with United in no particular mood to clock off early, Dawson registered his second goal to make the final score 7-1.

What a scintillating display of scorching soccer it was by the United lads and a delighted support was only too pleased to demonstrate their pleasure at the team's performance.

Up in the North-East, a local newspaper recorded bluntly that *'Newcastle United went the way of all the others against Manchester United youth'*. There was also a special mention for Bobby Charlton in the same report, with the observation that he was *'the outstanding personality on the field'* and that his contribution was framed within the context of *'a magnificent display of brilliant, constructive football'*.

In the Manchester Evening News, Tom Jackson's piece on the tie was headlined 'CHARLTON SHINES IN REDS' 'MAGYAR' TEAM' and he went on to expose that the performance had *'a real Hungarian stamp'* about it. Jackson ended his report by claiming *'no wonder these boys are favourites to win the cup for the fourth time in a row – and what a shame that Wembley's doors won't be opened for them – as yet!'*

Evening Chronicle cartoonist Edge's clever rhyme puts the Reds' bombardment of Newcastle in a comical context

1955-56

1) Tony Hawksworth	9) Alex Dawson	1) Andy Hamilton	9) Micky Chapman
2) John Queenan	10) Bobby Charlton	2) Henry Collison	10) Gerry Morgan
3) Peter Jones	11) Dennis Fidler	3) Alan Daniel	11) Pat Russell
4) Bobby English		4) George Page	
5) Reg Holland		5) Dave Sculley	
6) Wilf McGuinness		6) Larry Cook	
7) Terry Beckett		7) Michael Fuggle	
8) Mark Pearson		8) John Carey	

MARCH 1956

MANCHESTER UNITED 11 v 1 BEXLEYHEATH & WELLING

Beckett, Charlton (5), Dawson (3), Fidler, Pearson

Page

Saturday 17th
Kick-off 3.00 p.m.
Attendance 23,850

fifth round

FOOTBALL AT OLD TRAFFORD
SATURDAY, 17th MARCH

Central League Championship
UNITED Res.
(Top of League by four points)
v.
BOLTON W. Res.
(Won 1-0 at Burnden Park)
MORNING KICK-OFF 11 A.M.
7,631 spectators saw a most thrilling finish to the last game when the Reserves won 5-2 after being 2 goals down with 20 minutes to play.

F.A. YOUTH CUP—5th Round
UNITED YOUTH
(Undefeated in the competition—winners for last three years)
v.
BEXLEYHEATH & WELLING
(Charlton Nursery Club)
KICK-OFF 3-0 P.M.
Admission 1/-. Juniors 6d.
Stands: Unreserved 2/-; Juniors 1/-; Reserved 3/-.
1st team score v. Arsenal and F.A. Cup Semi-Finals will be given every 15 minutes.

With a semi-final place the prize of just one more victory, Old Trafford welcomed Bexleyheath & Welling, United's adversaries from the same stage of the tournament two years previously. In view of the fight that the supposed minnows had put up in the earlier encounter, there would have been no complacency in respect of the task which lay ahead of the Manchester boys if they were to reach the two-legged stage of the Youth Cup once again.

The circumstances surrounding the Bexleyheath game were not dissimilar to those prevailing in the last round against Newcastle, as the senior Reds had business outside of Manchester, in a league engagement at Arsenal, while Manchester City continued their fine F.A. Cup run in the semi-final against Spurs at Villa Park. There was one other game arranged at Old Trafford on the same day as the Bexleyheath fixture, United Reserves meeting Bolton in the Central League.

Because there was no senior team in action in Manchester, it was anticipated that another bumper crowd would pour through the turnstiles for the Youth Cup clash. When United sounded out their Lancashire neighbours regarding a change of time for the Reserve match, the Burnden Park club generously agreed to bring the fixture forward to an 11.00 a.m. start in order that the junior game could take centre stage with a three o'clock kick-off.

On the last occasion the Reds met Bexleyheath, the Kent club was a grooming ground for future Charlton Athletic stars. It was clear that a couple of years further on their ties with the Addicks were loosened, if not entirely cut. Bexleyheath had recruited, with one exception, all of their current youth squad from either the Kent or London areas and of the three individuals earmarked for Football League clubs, none would be heading for The Valley.

Right-half George Page's talents were spotted by Millwall, and while active for Bexleyheath he was concurrently a ground staff junior at The Den. Similarly, centre-forward Micky Chapman was on the books of Spurs as an amateur while inside-left Gerry Morgan was due to sign as a professional for Fulham at the end of Bexleyheath's Youth Cup run.

Bert Whalley and Jimmy Murphy agreed on an unchanged side for the third time in succession, which meant that Bobby Charlton and Wilf McGuinness were the only participants left from the tightly-fought scrap at Park View Road two years before, while Bexleyheath wore a completely new look.

The visiting side, which was supervised by club chairman and trainer George Stevens throughout their short stay in the north, were singularly carrying the banner for non-league football in Manchester as they were the sole representatives from outside the Football League left in the competition.

Demand for match tickets in the week leading up to the game was so strong that British Railways took the decision to operate a train service identical to the one provided for first-team matches from Central Station to the ground.

Bexleyheath, who sported a snazzy change strip of green and white quartered shirts and white shorts, conceded the kick-off at the toss-up and it gave the Reds an opportunity to go straight on the offensive. Within mere seconds of the start, Bobby Charlton had hammered a twenty-yard drive against the inside of a post only to see the ball bounce out. Despite the majority of supporters and most of the United team claiming a goal, Bolton referee Ken Dagnall waved play on. Visibly rattled by the early scare, the Bexleyheath side's subsequent loss of composure quickly became costly in terms of their inability to retain possession. In giving the ball away needlessly over those crucial opening minutes, they allowed their opponents to establish a superiority that never came under serious threat following an eleven-minute barrage which yielded three goals.

In the sixth minute, Dennis Fidler broke clear of their defence to fire his side ahead with a shot of such ferocity that it almost ripped a hole in the net. Bexleyheath immediately gifted the ball to the Reds from the restart, an error which allowed United to unbutton their defences again after a deft pass from Mark Pearson was cracked home by Charlton for the second. Goal number three arrived as early as the eleventh minute when, following on from excellent spadework by Wilf McGuinness, Charlton scored his second with some soccer sorcery for starters and a left-footed piledriver for the main course that tore into the top of the rigging.

Bexleyheath began to re-group and close ranks, tactics that temporarily held up United's flow of attacks. However, with so many players in red tops seemingly at the height of their form, it was only a matter of time before more damage would be inflicted on them and a fourth goal was registered in comedy fashion in the 20th minute when a half-hit Pearson effort wrong-footed sorrowful Bexleyheath goalie Andy Hamilton before trickling over the goal-line.

Unremitting attacks led to two further goal successes before the break. Alex Dawson registered number five with a humdinger of a drive from the eighteen-yard line, the goal keeping up his record of scoring in each of his Youth Cup appearances to date, and in the 44th minute Charlton completed his hat-trick to compound the doom and despair in Bexleyheath's dressing room at half-time.

The non-leaguers enjoyed their best spell of the game immediately following the resumption and it was a measure of their plucky spirit that they finally began to make some inroads into United territory. Centre-forward Chapman got clear of his shackles momentarily and moved ominously towards goal before Tony Hawksworth spotted the threat, the combination of his narrowing of the angles and firm block to Chapman's attempt snuffing out the chance. Bexleyheath came at the Reds again with a powerful run down the right by George Page, but the half-back ended up in a cul-de-sac when finding himself outnumbered by opponents.

United then scorned two quick chances; firstly, having already beaten Hamilton,

72

1955-56

MARCH 1956

fifth round

United goalie Tony Hawksworth foils a Bexleyheath attack while Reg Holland (to his right) and Wilf McGuinness (far right) appear relieved

Pearson's effort was blocked on the line by full-back Alan Daniel, and Charlton then narrowly missed the target with a hooked shot.

Bexleyheath hit back from those scares in the very best way, by scoring a goal themselves in the 61st minute. Full-back and captain Henry Collison set the right example by making a surging charge into unfamiliar territory, his weighted pass appearing to set up inside-right John Carey with an opening until he was baulked about twenty yards out.

Referee Dagnall awarded a direct free kick, whereupon a defensive wall of red was formed in an attempt to protect the goal, although neither that human structure nor United's goalie could do anything about the precision kick that Page flighted into the net to make the score 6-1.

Even at that stage, the goal represented a mere token for the visitors and the extent of the Reds' retribution was such that Charlton scored again almost before the euphoria had died down in the Bexleyheath camp. Dawson, Beckett and then Dawson again made it ten goals in total for United, and there were still as many minutes remaining on the clock.

If any of the crowd had decided that they had seen enough action for one day and left the stadium before full-time, they would have been unfortunate to miss easily the finest goal of the bunch. Deemed so spectacular that the Manchester Evening News even devoted a feature spot to it on the Monday following the game (see right), many years later the executor of that flamboyant strike claimed it to be the best he ever registered at Old Trafford.

It was an amazing win, with every United player making a telling contribution, and it left the impression that they wanted to make Bexleyheath pay dearly for some pre-match talk of *'revenge'* in relation to the Reds' victory in Kent two years earlier. Jimmy Murphy put a great emphasis on Bexleyheath's claims in the week leading up to the match and his charges responded with a dazzling performance which was peppered with moves straight off the training ground drawing board.

The Evening News 'Green Final' found space to comment that *'McGuinness was in grand form'* and the report went on to state *'United's bewildering high speed was too much for the visitors, whose goalkeeper Hamilton was constantly in action'*, as well as adding *'Bob Charlton was the chief menace with his craft and anticipation'*.

A TRULY AMAZING GOAL

This will go down in United's history

JACK ROWLEY used to hit 'em into the net with the speed of a rocket; Stan Pearson won a reputation as a crafty goal schemer. But to-day they're claiming a new slice of Manchester United history for 18-year-old Busby Boy, Bobby Charlton, who scored a phenomenal goal in United's 11-1 F.A. Youth Cup victory over Bexleyheath at Old Trafford on Saturday.

How did Charlton snatch this goal which was so unexpectedly and brilliantly taken, that even the Bexleyheath goalkeeper joined in the applause?

It was almost uncanny. The ball came across from the right wing towards Charlton, standing with his back to goal and just inside the penalty area.

The ball reached Bobby about chest-high and in a flash Bobby leapt up, did a sort of full-length "Western Roll" in mid-air, and completed a remarkable scissor-kick by slamming the ball high into the net with his right foot.

And he finished up by landing with both feet on the ground. That was Bobby's fifth goal of the game—and what a gem, to be sure!

73

1955-56

semi-final 1st leg

1) Tony Hawksworth	9) Alex Dawson
2) John Queenan	10) Bobby Charlton
3) Peter Jones	11) Dennis Fidler
4) Bobby English	
5) Reg Holland	
6) Wilf McGuinness	
7) Terry Beckett	
8) Mark Pearson	

1) Joe Dean	9) Alan Hart
2) Tom Wilson	10) Dennis Bannister
3) Bill Edisbury	11) Brian Riley
4) Graham Stanley	
5) Dick Oxtoby	
6) Malcolm Edwards	
7) Brian Birch	
8) Peter Deakin	

APRIL 1956

MANCHESTER UNITED 1 v 1 BOLTON WANDERERS

Charlton (pen) Birch

Wednesday 18th
Kick-off 5.45 p.m.
Attendance 22,269

PHEW! THIS WAS A REAL 'THRILLER'

With the season fast approaching its conclusion, the games representing the penultimate stage of the Youth Cup were initially arranged to be fought out on consecutive Wednesdays in April. The team blocking United's way to the final was Lancashire rivals Bolton Wanderers, who held what some felt was a slight psychological advantage in having to play their away leg first.

There was a complication surrounding the Burnden Park half of the contest as Alf Clarke, writing for the Evening Chronicle, revealed on the day prior to the Old Trafford tie:

There is a possibility that the second leg of the Youth Cup game, due to be played at Burnden Park on Wednesday evening, April 25, will be brought forward a day.

When I reminded Mr. Bill Ridley, manager of Bolton Wanderers, that this second leg clashed with the Johnny Aston testimonial match at Old Trafford on April 25, he said that he had completely overlooked it and would consult with Matt Busby, the United manager, on his return from Scotland, in the hope that the Burnden Park game could be brought forward.

Soon after Busby arrived back at his desk following his return from Glasgow, where the first-team had met Celtic in a friendly fixture, he came to an agreement with Burnden boss Ridley to stage the youth tie 48 hours earlier than the original date. Not only did the benefit match complicate the Youth Cup fixture, on the day prior to Aston's testimonial, United's 'A' team were due to entertain Blackpool 'A' in the Lancashire League Supplementary Cup final first leg at Old Trafford. As it so happened, the Blackpool game became a casualty of the congestion and was rescheduled for the following season.

On the eve of the opening match against the youthful Trotters, both of Manchester's evening papers ran previews of the forthcoming event, with Alf Clarke giving a prophetic assessment:

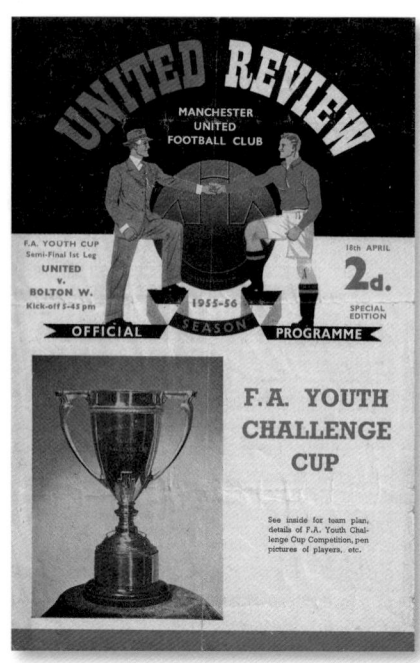

Dennis Fidler accidentally broke the nose of Bolton's Brian Birch

Bolton Wanderers make no secret of their hopes of defeating Manchester United in the Youth Cup semi-final tonight. This first leg at Old Trafford will be hard fought, and, despite United's brilliant record again this season, their forwards will have to do some precise shooting to beat Joe Dean, the Bolton goalkeeper, a native of Manchester who has just signed professional forms for the club.

The Wanderers had reached the last four by virtue of scoring a mere nine times. A First Round bye was followed by a one-nil win over Blackburn Rovers in Bolton at stage two, and a 2-1 winning margin against Liverpool at Anfield in the Third Round preceded a comfortable 4-0 passage past Everton at Burnden Park. Home advantage was utilised to the full in the quarter-final, where a highly creditable defeat of Wolves was achieved by registering twice without loss.

With only one goal recorded against them thus far, Bolton could justifiably boast of a mean defence, albeit some of the pre-match hype was focused on whether or not they would be able to shut out a free flowing United offence, whose 27-goal total was three times greater than that of their opponents.

The following match report appeared in the Bolton Evening News:

Only with the aid of a penalty kick after an hour's play could Manchester United's brilliant young holders of the F.A. Youth Cup - unbeaten in this country -

APRIL 1956

1955-56

semi-final 1st leg

save themselves from defeat last night, by the Bolton boys in a thrilling semi-final tie that had the 22,269 spectators roaring with excitement during the last twenty minutes when United put on heavy pressure.

The Wanderers' fighting form was a revelation and thoroughly earned a draw, only the third time United's youth team has drawn in 27 matches during the last four years.

By their speed and deadliness in the tackle, the Wanderers tore Manchester's teamwork to shreds, and, though raiding less often, they were also the more dangerous in attack. In the first minute, the Manchester goal escaped fortunately when Deakin's shot cannoned off an opponent onto a post. Then Hart, a fast and menacing centre-forward throughout the game, missed narrowly with a good opening.

This happy start put the Bolton lads in great heart for what they knew would be a big task, and when Birch put them in the lead with a fine shot, after passing all along the line, they played some grand cup-tie football in holding onto their lead.

United tried all they knew to master a strong Bolton middle-line in which Oxtoby never put a foot wrong at centre-half, and the crowd revelled in the thrusts of Charlton, an elusive inside-left, during many lively Manchester raids. Oxtoby saved an equaliser when Dean only parried a shot from outside-left Fidler, and both backs made last ditch clearances during a hectic defensive spell by the Wanderers.

Meantime, Birch, Hart and Riley made some threatening runs. It was the same in the second half - United attacking more often but failing at close range against the stubborn tackling and quick covering of the Bolton boys. Just on the hour United forced a corner and after the mêlée in front of Dean a Manchester forward lay on the grass and a linesman's flag signalled referee McCabe, of Sheffield, who promptly pointed to the penalty spot. Charlton swept a lovely shot past Dean - and then the fight was on.

First one attack looked like breaking through then the other, but despite many near things no more goals came. In a late collision with Fidler, Birch received a blow in the nose from a Manchester boy's head and examination in hospital revealed a fracture.

Practically every review of the action made references to the game's fiery incidents, the physical aspect of the contest seemingly giving off more heat than the average furnace.

With participants from both sides doing their level best to knock lumps out of each other, it was a wonder there were no serious injuries. Years later, one of the United side described the contest as *'a total kicking match'*, and he wasn't referring to what the players did with the ball.

There was a poor opinion of Mr. G. McCabe from both camps. The referee was criticised for failing to stamp his authority or admonishing certain individuals early in the game, with the effect that the general level of viciousness increased level upon level all through the 90 minutes.

In respect of the spiralling foul rate, it should be noted that both parties were similarly guilty, even though Bolton's Brian Birch, the player who suffered the worst experience of the conflict with a broken nose, was at least the victim of a complete accident.

Alf Clarke recorded that anyone watching the young Reds for the first time would have been disappointed with their display, as the *'rhythm with which they have waltzed through'* to the penultimate stage was often missing. Even so, Clarke felt United *'were much the better team'* at certain periods in the match and he concluded his piece by predicting that they *'will have learned a great deal'* and should *'benefit accordingly'* at Burnden Park.

The result left the Reds with a lot to do in a return fixture which was certain to be performed in front of another huge crowd, the majority of whom would have been expected to shout their all for a Bolton success.

Witty cartoonist Edge portrays a fiesty Old Trafford encounter in which United were knocked out of their stride by an uncompromising Bolton side

1955-56

1) Tony Hawksworth	9) Alex Dawson	1) Gordon Banks	9) Jim Mellors
2) John Queenan	10) Bobby Charlton	2) Jack Detchon	10) Harry Peck
3) Peter Jones	11) Dennis Fidler	3) Graham Whitehead	11) Charlie Rackstraw
4) Joe Carolan		4) Ged Graham	
5) Reg Holland		5) Peter Brent	
6) Wilf McGuinness		6) Johnny Brookes	
7) Ken Morgans		7) Peter Ledger	
8) Mark Pearson		8) Keith Havenhand	

APRIL 1956

MANCHESTER UNITED 3 v 2 CHESTERFIELD
Carolan, Charlton, Pearson   Ledger, Mellors

Monday 30th
Kick-off 6.30 p.m.
Attendance 24,544

final 1st leg

While United and Bolton Wanderers were battling for supremacy in one half of the Youth Cup semi-finals, a couple of less obvious clubs were contesting for the right to occupy the other vacant place in the last two.

In the opening leg of the penultimate stage, Chesterfield, on home soil, had recorded a slender 2-1 win over Bristol City, and in the return at Ashton Gate the Spireites hung on for a 1-1 draw. That result meant they were tasked with trying to stop the United train from thundering along the track towards its intended destination, which was retaining the silverware once again.

Chesterfield's route to the semi-final wasn't a particularly smooth one and they required replays in two of their earlier rounds. All the more impressive was the fact that they were required to win no less than five times while on tour.

When Chesterfield drew 1-1 against Sheffield United at Bramall Lane in the First Round, they were then redirected back to the same ground, where a 2-0 win ensued. Because Chesterfield didn't have floodlights, the replay wasn't staged at the Recreation Ground as both clubs agreed that an evening game was the most convenient option. The Second Round saw them pressing on the goals' accelerator for a 5-0 margin at Hull City and they followed that smart win with a 2-1 win over Port Vale in the Potteries.

A 0-0 draw at Doncaster Rovers came next, and the replay, which gave the Chesterfield fans a chance to see their youths in a home game at last, resulted in a marvellous 4-1 success. In the Fifth Round, the Derbyshire side found themselves paired away to Chelsea and they promptly upset all the odds by winning one-nil against a side containing six of those ousted by United in last season's semi-final.

It was a quite splendid and historic achievement for Chesterfield to reach the final. The resources available to a club in the Northern Section of the Third Division were infinitely less than those of United's and was emphasised by the tiny radius around the town that their youth squad had been recruited from.

Goalkeeper Gordon Banks, plus forwards Harry Peck and Charlie Rackstraw, were picked up from the Sheffield vicinity while centre-forward Jim Mellors hailed from Worksop. Right-half Ged Graham came from within the boundary of Chesterfield as did wingers Archie Smith and Peter Ledger.

Inside-right Keith Havenhand, already with first-team experience, made up the last of the Chesterfield locals whereas full-backs Jack Detchon and Graham Whitehead, centre-half Peter Brent and left-half Johnny Brookes were all culled from nearby Staveley. It represented a remarkable parade of talent from such a small proximity and now they were all on view in a national final.

On the Friday prior to the home leg, United published their list of retained players for the following season and in light of the tremendous success the club had enjoyed throughout the year, it was no surprise to learn that 39 professionals were to be kept on for the 1956/57 campaign. There were only three casualties, schoolteacher Laurie Cassidy, winger Noel McFarlane, and former England schoolboy starlet Cliff Birkett, all of whom were given free transfers.

McFarlane's departure was the least expected, as he had been a tremendous force when United captured the Youth Cup in 1953. However, having put in only one senior appearance and then finding it impossible to throw off some injury problems, the club saw fit to release him.

Wilf McGuinness and Bobby Charlton were again rested from Central League duties in readiness for the Youth Cup final. Two days before Chesterfield were expected in Manchester, United took part in a rearranged home Central League fixture against Everton as the original game in January had been abandoned after a quarter of an hour. The Everton game completed the Reserves' fulfilments for the season and when the game was over, having finished as champions, they were

United's Tony Hawksworth catches confidently as John Queenan (number two) races to cover the empty goalmouth

78

1955-56

APRIL 1956

presented with the Central League trophy by Mr. Stanley L. Blenkinson, the honorary treasurer of that association.

Some of those entitled to medals for their contribution to the title triumph were Albert Scanlon, Ronnie Cope, Billy Whelan and John Doherty, as well as the aforementioned McGuinness and Charlton. All of them, of course, were former Youth Cup winners.

The Manchester Evening News filed the following preview of Chesterfield's visit:

Tonight was THE NIGHT for the youngsters who comprise Manchester United's Youth eleven. They were meeting Chesterfield in the first leg of the F.A. Youth Cup final and in the team is a boy who has already been 'blooded' in First Division soccer. Last October, Wilf McGuinness was at left-half when Wolves provided the opposition at Old Trafford. Chesterfield provide severe opposition and if United are to make this their fourth win in succession a big effort is called for.

Arthur Ellis, England's No. 1 referee, is in charge of the game and prices range from 4s. in the B and C stands to 1s. for ground admission.

The second leg takes place at Chesterfield next Monday evening.

The smart money, of course, was riding on the home side to continue their unbeaten course of cup triumphs, but the grit shown by the Derbyshire youths made sure that the Reds' intention of taking a sizeable lead to Saltergate was dashed.

The Derbyshire Times commented on a match which provided plenty of incident to savour:

Chesterfield had a shock in the second minute when the United centre-forward missed an open goal after a well-engineered move by Pearson. But when Havenhand took the ball well in his stride to give the sprightly Ledger his first chance to show his paces - the United defence was hard pressed to clear the winger's cleverly-placed centre. Ledger, later marked assiduously by the home defenders, nearly paved the way for a Chesterfield goal in the eighth minute, when he put over a tantalising centre which had the defence in a real panic. There was a real sea of legs in the United goalmouth, and the ball was blocked several times before Havenhand shot wide.

The eleventh minute brought misfortune for Chesterfield and especially for goalkeeper Banks, who later redeemed himself time and time again with spectacular diving saves. Harassed by the centre-forward he allowed a long cross by right-half Carolan to twist through his hands into the net, and Chesterfield were unluckily one goal down.

This success, which set the crowd roaring, gave United added encouragement, and only a wonderful save by Banks prevented a second goal almost at once. The Chesterfield defence, in which centre-half Brent was outstanding, strove desperately to stem the tide of United attacks, but they were unable to stop the dangerous inside-left, Charlton, who used body-swerve to slide past three defenders before slipping the ball to Pearson, who gave Banks no chance.

That was in the 17th minute, and United went further ahead after half an hour when Charlton found the net with a perfectly-placed header from a Fidler centre. At this stage it looked as if Chesterfield would have little further interest in the final. With the inside-forwards falling well back to assist the harassed defence, there looked little chance of a Chesterfield goal and United supporters were beginning to anticipate a big score.

But Chesterfield held on grimly and began the second half in much more promising style - a delightful run by Havenhand, who then skimmed the bar with a header from a Ledger centre. That was the prelude to a determined retaliation by Chesterfield and it brought its reward in the 60th minute. A left-wing move between Rackstraw and Mellors tricked the United defence and the centre-forward was put through with only the goalkeeper to beat. He took his chance with the utmost coolness, shooting low into the net past the advancing 'keeper.

Three minutes later, Mellors might have scored again when he broke through on the left and cut in well towards goal. But he took the ball too far in seeking to gain a better position to shoot and was dispossessed.

There was still plenty of work for the Chesterfield defence, however, and especially for Banks, who was in brilliant form. Charlton hit the post when a goal looked certain, but this balanced a first half disappointment for Chesterfield when Mellors headed against the post.

With only two minutes to go, Ledger danced down the wing and put over one of his curling, close-to-goal specialities. The ball soared over the 'keeper's head and slid into the net by the far upright. And so Chesterfield had fought back to make the score 3-2. But there was a last-minute thrill when Banks dived daringly to the feet of two United forwards.

To succeed on Monday, Chesterfield will have to find a better answer to United's thrustful inside-forwards and also try to improve the shooting power of its own attack.

With the game almost over, Tony Hawksworth conceded a second goal to a speculative effort from Chesterfield's outside-right

That late goal from Peter Ledger was indeed a godsend for Chesterfield and even though it was hard to imagine United not scoring at the Recreation Ground the following week, the closeness of the margin now made the prospect of a home victory more of a likelihood.

The Daily Mail's Eric Thompson noted that Ledger *'hadn't been given more than this one chance by strong full-back Peter Jones'* and added that the Spireites' outside-right had hit the bull's-eye with *'the cutest lob I have seen all season'*.

Recounting the drama of United's opener, Thompson reasoned that *'goalkeeper Gordon Banks won't make another mistake like the early one that gave wing-half Carolan United's first goal'*. The Mail scribe went on to offer the opinion that the *'rest of his work suggested that he had not done it before'* and claimed the teenage custodian was a *'great young player'*.

Mentioning the Saltergate club's second goal now offered them *'a sporting chance of upsetting (the cup) holders'* and that the away team's half-time deficit was down to their inside-forwards having been *'tightly played by Carolan and the industrious McGuinness'*, as well as their wing halves being *'averse to adventure'*. Thompson also hinted tantalisingly at the possibility of an upset all United fans dreaded when querying *'why shouldn't Chesterfield have a chance in homelier surroundings?'*

final 1st leg

1955-56

1) Gordon Banks	9) Jim Mellors	1) Tony Hawksworth	9) Alex Dawson
2) Jack Detchon	10) Harry Peck	2) John Queenan	10) Bobby Charlton
3) Graham Whitehead	11) Archie Smith	3) Peter Jones	11) Dennis Fidler
4) Ged Graham		4) Joe Carolan	
5) Peter Brent		5) Reg Holland	
6) Johnny Brookes		6) Wilf McGuinness	
7) Peter Ledger		7) Ken Morgans	
8) Keith Havenhand		8) Mark Pearson	

MAY 1956

CHESTERFIELD 1 *(3)* v *(4)* 1 **MANCHESTER UNITED**
Havenhand — Fidler

Monday 7th
Kick-off 6.30 p.m.
Attendance 15,838

final 2nd leg

United win youth cup AGAIN!

In the week following Chesterfield's appearance at Old Trafford, the whole of the town famed worldwide for a certain crooked church spire was buzzing in anticipation of the mighty Manchester United's Youth Cup downfall.

There was only one change to report for either of the sides, which came in the Chesterfield ranks, and the Saltergate club took the precaution of naming fourteen players as there was the possibility of National Service calls on two or three members of their squad.

With regular outside-left Archie Smith now available, Charlie Rackstraw was left out of the team. Chesterfield officials went to the trouble of appealing for military leave for Smith, as well as Keith Havenhand and Jack Detchon, and were fortunate on all three counts, the inclusion of that trio giving them the boost of being able to field their best possible line-up.

Over in the United camp, Jimmy Murphy left well alone with what he considered to be his most efficient eleven.

The match programme contained the following editor's lines:

Today we make history so far as our Junior team is concerned by appearing in the F.A. Youth Challenge Cup final (second leg) against very redoubtable opponents indeed in Manchester United Juniors. Not only are they the holders of the cup, but they have won the trophy each year since the inauguration of the competition in 1953.

The first leg, played last Monday before nearly 25,000 spectators, appeared at half-time to be a foregone conclusion for the Manchester team, as they had established a three-goal lead.

However, to the credit of our lads, they fought back with determination and skill, and scored twice, to finish up 2-3.

So, today, we commence one goal down, but with a chance of winning the cup, although this will be no easy task against such opposition. If both teams play as good football, and with the same sportsmanship, as was displayed at Old Trafford last Monday, then whatever the result, the game will be well worthy of the occasion and a treat for the large crowd anticipated at the Recreation Ground.

Defying the close attention of goalkeeper Tony Hawksworth and Wilf McGuinness, Keith Havenhand heads home for Chesterfield while United's Peter Jones (far left), Reg Holland and John Queenan (far right) look on helplessly

1955-56

MAY 1956

We hope the best team wins, and may that team be Chesterfield.

After the match, the cup and mementoes will be presented by Mr. Joe Richards, chairman of the Youth Challenge Cup Committee, also chairman of Barnsley Football Club, and a vice president of the Football League.

The winners, besides receiving the cup, are to have silver plaques, while the losers receive bronze ones.

The Football Association will be represented at the match by Sir Stanley Rous, C.B.E., J.P., secretary.

With the finest of balances in the scoreline favouring the Reds, Chesterfield proved to be the masters of the play until suffering the most savage of blows right at the death.

The Derbyshire Times recorded the main events and dramatic ending thus:

> THE football season at Saltergate had a spectacular and dramatic ending on Monday evening when only cruel luck prevented Chesterfield Juniors wresting from Manchester United Juniors the F.A. Youth Cup—a trophy which United have won each year since the competition was inaugurated. They won the first "leg" 3–2 at Old Trafford last week, but Chesterfield were the much better team on Monday, and with a one-goal lead at the end of 90 minutes, and the aggregate score 3–3, another half-hour's play looked inevitable. But the referee, Mr. Arthur Ellis, had obviously allowed three minutes—some say four—for stoppages, and it was in the third minute of this injury time that United scored. There was just time for the ball to be kicked off again before the final whistle. So United retained the trophy most undeservedly, and there was no more unpopular man at Saltergate than Mr. Ellis who was loudly booed at the presentation ceremony.
>
> The game was packed with thrills, but it was not until the final minutes that the highlight in this Cup drama came. And those final minutes will provide a talking point for months to come. Injury time was in progress as Chesterfield left-back Whitehead moved to halt a United movement on the right flank. As the ball was pushed forward, the dark-haired Chesterfield defender stooped to his right and dropped his arm across the ball. Accidental or intentional, the handling led to a free-kick, from which Carolan, United's right-half, placed the ball perfectly for left-winger Fidler to score and so retain the trophy for United.
>
> Mr. Ellis, Halifax's world-famous referee, was most unpopular, for, according to the many watches timing this final period, he had let the game run three minutes into injury time before the deciding goal, and it was general opinion that stoppages for injuries had added up to nothing like three minutes' time.
>
> **"GIVE IT TO ELLIS"**
>
> Chesterfield supporters let the official know just how they felt as the teams lined up for the presentation by Mr. J. Richards, F.A. Youth Chairman. The tumult of acclaim for the defeated Chesterfield players filing past Mr. Richards died. And as the referee got up to walk down the gangway, it turned to a full-throated roar of disapproval. Yells of "Give it to Ellis" as United captain, Wilf McGuinness, received the trophy summed up the crowd's feelings.
>
> No wonder the crowd felt that injustice had been done, for the Chesterfield youngsters had dominated the United side for the greater part of the game. After a storming first half, there were fears that Chesterfield could not last. But they did, and 20 minutes after the interval they scored the goal that put them level.
>
> It was fitting that this goal should go to inside-right Keith Havenhand. He was the man of the match, and there was unquestionable class in everything he did. Combining perfectly with Ledger on the wing, he gave England Youth captain McGuinness and hefty left-back Peter Jones one of their hardest games in the competition. Havenhand had to score, it seemed, after he had hit the post with a shot that beat 'keeper Hawksworth all the way, and had bounced the ball on the bar in the first half.
>
> **HAVENHAND'S GOAL**
>
> And it was just as fitting that the goal should come from a free-kick by tall left-half Graham. He had had two previous long-range free-kicks tipped over the bar. The one that led to the goal was accurately placed from about 50 yards, curled over to the opposite side of the penalty area, and Havenhand's head did the rest from close range.
>
> Havenhand was only one of a hard-working Chesterfield line. Peter Ledger, on the wing, gave a fine display, and the other three forwards, Mellors in the middle, Peck and Smith on the left, strove gallantly for the full 90 minutes.
>
> In defence, it would be hard to fault any of the players, who were up against such a formidable attack. The United line included centre-forward Alec Dawson, selected this week for an F.A. international; clever, speedy inside-right Mark Pearson, former North East Derbyshire and England schoolboy representative; and schoolboy international Bobby Charlton at inside-left. But the Chesterfield defence had no regard for reputations. Hard, first-time tackling and a never-say-die spirit came out on top. Centre-half and skipper Peter Brent, left-half Johnny Brookes, right-half Gerald Graham and brilliant goalkeeper Gordon Banks all played splendidly.
>
> Although Chesterfield failed to take the Cup away from Manchester for the first time, it is a game that Chesterfield fans will remember for a long time.

So Dennis Fidler's stoppage time shot, which bobbled past an unsighted Gordon Banks from an acute angle, provided the goal that won United their fourth Youth Cup title.

To all intents and purposes, nobody with a nine bob note would have backed the Reds after Havenhand's 66th minute header burst into the back of Tony Hawksworth's net because until then United had been largely outmanoeuvred by an enterprising Chesterfield combination and were certainly well behind on the number of clear-cut chances.

Hawksworth, who 'excelled' according to one report, was one of the major reasons that the Reds were able to stay in contention. The goalkeeper's heroics were supplemented with a couple of strokes of good fortune, the ball twice ending up in safe areas after thudding the framework of his goal.

The after-match reaction of the crowd in booing referee Arthur Ellis was a lamentable prelude to the formalities of the handing over of the silverware to United captain Wilf McGuinness. But, as one wisecracking fan queried, was Joe Richards really presenting the cup, or was he simply handing it back?

With United already crowned as First Division champions and Manchester City the current F.A. Cup holders, the Evening News provided a suitable conclusion to the under-18's season with a short report:

Manchester's third major football trophy was won when United Youth team held Chesterfield Youth to a 1-1 draw after winning the first leg of the F.A. Youth Cup final 3-2. This is the fourth successive year they have won the cup.

In a storming game full of hard tackling and constructive play, Chesterfield were definitely the better side. Despite their fortune United must be praised for the way they fought throughout against a quick tackling, hard-hitting Chesterfield side.

Their star was skipper and left-half McGuinness, who drove and cajoled his men through 90 nerve-racking minutes.

Inside-forwards Pearson and Charlton also had their moments when both revealed tricky ball play and excellent constructive ideas, but in the main they were quietened by the first-time tackling of home wing halves Graham and Brookes.

Mr. Joe Richards, chairman of the F.A. Youth Committee, presents the F.A. Youth Cup to Wilf McGuinness, Manchester United Youth captain, after their final match at Chesterfield.

> "In the first leg we took our foot off the pedal and got a real roasting from Jimmy Murphy. We were 3-0 up and then they scored twice to bring it back to 3-2.
>
> When Joe Carolan took a free kick right at the end of the game at Chesterfield, I told him to knock it into the box. I had one eye on the ball and it was dropping so I thought about controlling it.
>
> Then, out of the corner of my eye, Dennis Fidler came from nowhere and hit it with his weaker right foot. It was a great goal and won us the match.
>
> Everyone came over and jumped all over Dennis, which was rare because we didn't do that sort of thing in those days."
>
> **ALEX DAWSON**

final 2nd leg

1956-57

1) David Gaskell	9) Alex Dawson	1) Alan Hodgkinson	9) Ian Lawson
2) Barry Smith	10) Mark Pearson	2) John Angus	10) Lewis Denham
3) Ray Maddison	11) Reg Hunter	3) John Calver	11) Ivan McAuley
4) Bobby English		4) Peter Simpson	
5) Reg Holland		5) John Talbut	
6) Harold Bratt		6) Bobby Baldwin	
7) Ken Morgans		7) Ian Towers	
8) Nobby Lawton		8) Jimmy Robson	

OCTOBER 1956

MANCHESTER UNITED* 5 v 2 BURNLEY

Dawson (5)   Denham, Lawson

Monday 8th

Kick-off 7.30 p.m.

Attendance 3,500

* Played at The Cliff

first round

Coach Bert Whalley (second right) is readied to take part in a training session with (l-r) David Gaskell, Alex Dawson, Mark Pearson, Jackie Hennessy and Reg Holland

By the time the First Round of the 1956/57 Youth Cup season was due to be contested, the names of some of the players who had indelibly written their names in the annals of the tournament's history had disappeared.

Gone were full-backs and twice winners John Queenan and Peter Jones. Also a recipient of two silver plaques, Dennis Fidler had now crossed over into open-age football for good. The names of three-time Youth Cup winners Tony Hawksworth, Bobby Charlton and Wilf McGuinness were also unavailable for selection due to their stepping past the age barrier, as was Joe Carolan, whose single competition success was achieved by courtesy of appearing in just three ties. Additionally, Terry Beckett, who was a member of the victorious 1954/55 side, had left to join Manchester City.

With such a dramatic drain of ability, and so much experience lost to United's new youth side, it meant that only Alex Dawson, Bobby English, Reg Holland, Ken Morgans and Mark Pearson remained to try and keep hold of a trophy that the club's personnel now looked upon as their own.

The new faces in the side were, firstly, Wigan-born David Gaskell, who was tasked with taking over from Hawksworth in goal, and for full-backs Queenan and Jones, now read Barry Smith and Ray Maddison. Even though their football pedigrees were vastly different, Smith and Maddison shared the distinction of growing up on the same side of Manchester.

The left-half position vacated by McGuinness was filled by a Salfordian, Harold Bratt, while in the forward-line, Newton Heath's Nobby Lawton was installed as the new inside-right. Reg Hunter, a prodigy who hailed from North Wales, was handed the left wing responsibility.

It was apparent that United's scouting and recruitment system was still in full flow and the evidence was verified by the fact that of the six new boys in the team, three of them, Gaskell, Smith and Bratt, had represented England at schoolboy football.

The opening round draw pitched the Reds up against Burnley, and for the first time in almost three years, The Cliff was designated as the preferred venue.

Any concerns regarding how the new boys might tackle the task asked of them were soon forgotten during a performance which suggested that United had hit on yet another fine blend of young players.

The United Review, which mentioned that a superb crowd of over 3,500 was in attendance, had a few words to convey in respect of the action at Lower Broughton:

The game opened very brightly, with each goal being in danger, but after ten minutes the Burnley team had the misfortune to lose the services of their left-back, who left the field with a suspected fracture of the leg. Despite this setback, Burnley were the first to score when Denham gave them the lead with a good shot after 28 minutes play. Two minutes later, the teams were on level terms when Dawson took a through pass from Lawton and went on to score.

Dawson put United ahead after 36 minutes following a corner kick and at half-time the score was 2-1. In the second half, Dawson added a third goal from close range after receiving the ball from Morgans and virtually sealed the match.

Two goals in five minutes, again by Dawson made the score 5-1, but Burnley were full of fight to the end and with two minutes remaining, Lawson reduced the arrears with a well taken goal.

The Reds fully utilised their superiority in terms of greater numbers to get on top while Burnley stuck hard to their task, despite the disadvantage of losing one of their number so early in the contest. Their full-back, Bobby Baldwin, had been subjected to a rather unfortunate and nasty injury in a coming together with Mark Pearson and was out of football for some weeks thereafter.

Not unnaturally, most of the plaudits for United's win went to Alex Dawson, whose personal caché of five goals was not only his best to date, it also equalled the same feat of previous nap hands completed in the Youth Cup by Bobby Charlton, John Doherty, Duncan Edwards and David Pegg.

From a historical point of view, the major significance of the game against Burnley was that it represented the fourth and final time The Cliff was used to stage such a tie.

1) Glyn Wilks	9) Rob Castle	1) David Gaskell	9) Alex Dawson
2) Stan Storton	10) Gordon Low	2) Barry Smith	10) Mark Pearson
3) Terry Caldwell	11) Mike Smith	3) Ray Maddison	11) Reg Hunter
4) Dennis Atkins		4) Bobby English	
5) Garbutt Richardson		5) Reg Holland	
6) Tony France		6) Harold Bratt	
7) Kevin McHale		7) Ken Morgans	
8) Denis Law		8) Nobby Lawton	

1956-57

HUDDERSFIELD TOWN* 2 v 4 **MANCHESTER UNITED**

Low, McHale   Dawson (2), English, Morgans

OCTOBER 1956

Monday 29th

Kick-off 7.00 p.m.

* Played at Beck Lane, Heckmondwike

TV Goalkeeper To Play Against Town Juniors

With the confidence of United's new entrants boosted by their relatively easy victory over Burnley, only three weeks passed before the Reds were handed what seemed a much more testing task with a tie at Huddersfield.

There were initial differences between the two parties in agreeing on a suitable date and it soon became clear that the Terriers preferred an evening game, which prompted United to suggest playing the fixture at The Cliff. The Huddersfield club, who wouldn't erect floodlights at their Leeds Road enclosure for a further four years, replied firmly in the negative. The prospect of giving up home advantage and travelling to Salford didn't curry any favour and so they responded by making arrangements to host the Reds at their training ground at Beck Lane in Heckmondwike.

The Town team included up-and-coming starlet Kevin McHale in their forward-line. The dashing McHale was an England Youth international, as well as the scorer of three goals in nine Second Division games, and he was partnered on the right side of Huddersfield's attack by a skinny, fair-haired sixteen year-old Scottish ground staff boy. The youngster's frail appearance hadn't hampered his soccer career to any degree as he had already appeared at Central League level for the Terriers. A world class striker in the making and a future icon in the history of Manchester United, he answered to the name of Denis Law.

On the day of the game, the Town added part-timer Mike Smith to their professional ranks. Normally utilised as an inside-forward, his first paid task was in switching to outside-left for the big game.

A couple of United's youth team goalkeepers, both past and present, were in the news leading up to the game over in Yorkshire as Tony Hawksworth and David Gaskell had made their first-team debuts within the last week. Gaskell received considerable media attention through his involvement in the Charity Shield game against Manchester City on the previous Wednesday when taking over the gloves from the injured Ray Wood at Maine Road.

At just turned sixteen years of age, Gaskell became an overnight sporting celebrity through the high profile game being televised and three days later, with Wood still unfit, Hawksworth was called on at short notice for a First Division fixture at Blackpool.

There was at least one encouraging sign for the Reds in that Alex Dawson, who had claimed a brace for the Reserves against Leeds at Old Trafford on the Saturday prior to the Youth Cup game, was still bang in form.

As the coach carrying the United squad sped over the Pennines, Jimmy Murphy reminded the players of their individual and collective duties and also delivered a briefing on some of their opponents. Murphy made special mention of Denis Law, directing that he should be closely watched, and gave the unenviable job of marking him to Harold Bratt.

When the Reds arrived at Heckmondwike, darkness was already falling and Murphy, Bert Whalley and the lads were greeted by cold, wet weather and a damp pitch lit by inadequate electric lamps. Despite the obvious discomfort, which Murphy recalled with horror for years afterwards, and a couple of early frights, United eventually came out on top.

The Huddersfield Examiner reported on the outcome:

> THREE goals scored in a twelve-minute period in the second half enabled Manchester United Juniors to run out comfortable 4-2 winners in an F.A. Youth Cup second round tie against Huddersfield Town Juniors under the Beck Lane floodlights last night.
>
> Town held a definite advantage midway through the first half in which United did not move smoothly owing to the half-backs' disinclination to part with the ball.
>
> Town were two up after twenty-five minutes through well-taken goals by Lowe and McHale, but right-half English reduced the lead two minutes before half-time with a powerful drive from twenty-five yards' range which left Wilkes helpless.
>
> There was a distinct improvement in United's play in the second half—an interval pep talk by former Welsh international Jimmy Murphy worked wonders —and they scored three goals in twelve minutes through centre-forward Dawson (2) and outside-right Morgans.
>
> Morgans and English were a constant threat to Town's defence in the second half and, with Town's forwards lacking finishing power, their team ran out good winners.
>
> Richardson, Law and McHale were prominent for Town in the first half.
>
> This was United's thirty-fifth consecutive win in the competition, the Lancashire club having won the trophy for four successive seasons.
>
> After about twenty-five minutes of the first half the referee, J. Russell, of Leeds, was hit in the face by the ball, which burst his nose, and he changed places with one of the linesmen, G. Kew, of Leeds, for the rest of the game.
>
> The attendance was just over 1,000.

One newspaper noted that the Reds appeared to 'gather momentum' as the match progressed while another posted a comment about them 'suddenly waking up to the task in hand'. Their goals were described as 'text book' by the Daily Mail and certainly none was more important or picturesque than the one that got them back into contention from Bobby English just before the break.

Dawson was involved in all of the other goals. Butting one in himself for the equaliser, courtesy of a Ken Morgans corner immediately after the second half got going, the roles were reversed ten minutes later when the centre-forward's cross was met by the head of Morgans to make it 3-2 to United. In the 57th minute, the prolific Dawson applied the coup de grâce when spectacularly heading home a free kick from English.

Assigned to shadow Denis Law, Harold Bratt gets on the case

second round

1956-57

1) David Gaskell	9) Alex Dawson
2) Barry Smith	10) Mark Pearson
3) Stuart Gibson	11) Reg Hunter
4) Bobby English	
5) Reg Holland	
6) Harold Bratt	
7) Ken Morgans	
8) Nobby Lawton	

1) Joe Johnson	9) Bert Llewellyn
2) Bryan Griffiths	10) Jimmy Blain
3) John O'Shaughnessy	11) Ken Price
4) John Connor	
5) George McNally	
6) Terry Gannon	
7) John Fielding	
8) Derek Temple	

FEBRUARY 1957

MANCHESTER UNITED 5 v 2 EVERTON

Dawson (2), Hunter, Lawton, Pearson   Llewellyn, Temple

Wednesday 27th
Kick-off 3.00 p.m.
Attendance 6,647

fourth round replay

Football at Old Trafford
F.A. YOUTH CUP
4TH ROUND REPLAY

UNITED YOUTH
Cup holders and unbeaten in the competition for four years

v

EVERTON YOUTH
(Strong opponents, confident of success)

Wednesday, 27th February
Kick-off 3-0 p.m.
Central League prices of admission

Everton's management applied a number of alterations to their side when the replay took place three weeks later at Old Trafford. While Murphy left the United team composition exactly as it was, suggesting he was satisfied with the showing put on by his boys in Liverpool, the Toffees imposed no less than six changes in structure, three of which were positional switches.

The Blues shifted Bryan Griffiths from left-back to right-back and John O'Shaughnessy into Griffiths' original position. George McNally was handed the pivot job and with it the uneasy task of looking after Alex Dawson. John Connor moved up to right-half from right-back, his new role meaning there was no place for Peter Redmond, and on the left-hand side of the forward-line, Everton brought in Jimmy Blain and Ken Price for Alec Ashworth and Ken Barton respectively.

A midweek afternoon start to the tie didn't deter a crowd of over six and a half thousand spectators from turning up to see a 'bonanza-of-goals' game and the Liverpool Daily Post delivered its verdict on the highlights as such:

Everton made a brave effort to hold Manchester United, the holders of the F.A. Youth Cup, in the Fourth Round replay at Old Trafford yesterday and at one time in the second half seemed likely to achieve their objective. But their defence could not find the answer to Manchester's clever attacks and defeat was sustained by five goals to two.

It was weak defensive play which allowed United to take an early lead and although Llewellyn and Temple, who were Everton's best forwards, contrived to gain an equaliser, the former being the scorer, Everton were again caught on the wrong foot when first Pearson and then Dawson added to an early goal by Lawton.

Everton concentrated on defence in the second half and after a breather their attack came back for Temple to make the score 3-2. They appeared to have a chance, but in a storming rally United gained command and Hunter and Dawson added further goals to give them the right to meet Blackburn Rovers in the Fifth Round.

United progressed at Everton's expense with the aid of a couple of superbly taken goals. Nobby Lawton's opener in the tenth minute was fashioned when dispossessing Gannon just inside the penalty area and he executed it by firing a left-footed shot into the corner of the net. Everton equalised just four minutes later, the Reds responding by regaining the advantage within 60 seconds when Mark Pearson found the target area after combining with Ken Morgans.

Dawson's first, and United's third, came when the deadly schemer directed the ball almost nonchalantly past Johnson with the side of his foot. Dawson had earlier warmed to the task when hitting the bar with a forceful drive.

When Temple scored a second for Everton, the tussle became white hot for a while and a killer blow was delivered for United when Morgans' right-wing run and cross was headed high into Johnson's goal by Reg Hunter. Captain Morgans helped to make the issue safe in the dying minutes when further clever wing play from him was followed by a second from Dawson, a typical diving header that flashed into the rigging.

The Liverpool Echo acknowledged that the *'Everton team could not complain about their dismissal'* because *'only for a short time did they match Manchester United in all round skill'*. The Echo felt that *'Manchester had a pull at wing-half and in defence, and even though Everton's goals, by Llewellyn and Temple, were well conceived, so were the five by the home club'*.

Nobby Lawton (top) and Reg Hunter, who were both on target with eye-catching goals against Everton

1) David Gaskell	9) Alex Dawson	1) Geoff Hickson	9) Peter Watson
2) Barry Smith	10) Mark Pearson	2) Alan Jones	10) Paddy Daly
3) Stuart Gibson	11) Reg Hunter	3) Len Hughes	11) Harry Downes
4) Bobby English		4) Malcolm Scott	
5) Reg Holland		5) Tommy Haworth	
6) Harold Bratt		6) Geoff Hindle	
7) Ken Morgans		7) Arthur Gill	
8) Nobby Lawton		8) Maurice Stuart	

1956-57

MANCHESTER UNITED 6 v 0 BLACKBURN ROVERS

Dawson (2), English, Hunter, Lawton, Morgans (pen)

MARCH 1957

Saturday 23rd

Kick-off 3.00 p.m.

Attendance 12,713

fifth round

There was another dose of double cup excitement in store for United's followers when Blackburn came to Manchester in search of glory and a Youth Cup semi-final spot. The first-team had already made it to the last four of the F.A. Cup and their big day coincided with the youth team's meeting with the Rovers. Matt Busby's seniors were in Sheffield to take on Birmingham City for the right to a day at Wembley and with the Reserves away at Aston Villa, Old Trafford was again available to host a Saturday afternoon Youth Cup match.

Blackburn were then under the astute stewardship of former United legend Johnny Carey who, in his time as manager at Ewood Park, followed Busby's example of promoting an efficient system of enlisting, developing and promoting young players. Their scouting network was active inside and outside the county and its scope could be evidenced by the fact that only three members of the Blackburn side were actually native to the Lancashire town. Others amongst their ranks came from places as diverse as Wrexham, the North-East, Blackpool, Crewe, and even from Manchester.

Because the Rovers were embroiled in a Second Division promotion race, Carey wasn't prepared to risk his ace forward Peter Dobing against United. Originally from the Chorlton district of Manchester, Dobing had already claimed a place in the senior side at Ewood Park and the eighteen year-old was the only absentee from the normal Blackburn youth team line-up.

Rovers' progress in the competition started with a 5-2 elimination of Preston North End in the First Round and continued with a 4-2 win over Liverpool at the second stage. A 3-3 draw with Blackpool completed a hat-trick of home ties and a satisfactory conclusion, by two goals to one at Bloomfield Road in the replay, was followed by a mammoth 10-0 scoreline against Spennymoor in the Fourth Round.

The United team was now beginning to pick itself and Jimmy Murphy made preparations for the game in the knowledge that the winners would meet Southampton in the semi-final. Even though hordes of United supporters would make the trek over to Hillsborough for the F.A. Cup tie, interest in the youth game was such that football train specials operated to Old Trafford from Central Station in the city centre once more.

The Reds went straight into Blackburn from the off and quickly forced a corner which was wasted. The Rovers then galloped down the field to win a flag kick of their own that was dealt with easily enough by the home defenders. Nobby Lawton later applied good vision to some nimble footwork when turning an inviting pass into the Blackburn penalty area, even though goalkeeper Hickson, who was on his toes and darted from his line to smother the ball, foiled that particular enterprise.

Lawton was again involved when the Reds took the lead in only the fifth minute, the inside-forward releasing Alex Dawson behind a temporarily snoozing defence. Instantly bringing the ball under control, Dawson confidently hit a left-foot drive and watched expectantly as his attempt cannoned against a post prior to crossing the goal-line.

Rovers retaliated through Paddy Daly, their most obviously gifted player, who escaped his markers to put in a shot that was inches off-target. With the Blackburn team appearing calm and collected in possession, even at that early stage they didn't look as if they possessed the manpower or wherewithal to pose much of a threat, Daly apart.

The Reds went close to scoring again in the 18th minute. Dawson was quicker than Blackburn's 'keeper to a stray ball, but the normally clinical marksman screwed his shot wide of the mark. Dawson plagued the Blackburn rearguard in another raid, when a crafty link-up between Morgans and Pearson seemed to set him up, and it was only some smart anticipation from centre-half Tommy Haworth which denied him the chance.

In the 23rd minute Blackburn conceded another goal, which was the result of a howler of gigantic proportions. A speculative long punt upfield by Bobby English was left for the visiting goalkeeper while his defenders stood appealing for an offside decision. Hickson came off his line by some distance and seemed to get caught up in the overall confusion. The custodian completely misread the bounce of the ball and when it sailed over his head and into the net for United goal number two, amused spectators were unsure whether to laugh or clap, so many did both.

Following that disappointment, Rovers steadied the ship somewhat by countering with moves that finally pinned United back for a time. David Gaskell was forced into a double save, with Daly testing him initially, and then again when Watson attempted to make something out of the rebound. Daly was once more at the cutting edge of a Blackburn assault and upon stealing a yard of space, he struck an inviting ball across the mouth of the United goal. With no-one to lend a hand in such an advanced position, Daly's good work fizzled into nothing.

At 2-0 up, the Reds emerged for the second period to produce their most sustained period of assault on Blackburn's goal. Rovers conceded a number of unnecessary free kicks during that uncomfortable spell, which only added to the amount of defending they were required to do.

With just seven minutes of the half gone, they were cracked open once again as a result of a mesmerising piece of skill by Morgans, when the Welsh wing wizard cleverly created a gap in the Blackburn rearguard and Dawson routinely converted the chance for his second goal of the match. The Ewood Park boys' prospects of taking a positive result from the game evaporated into the Manchester sky at that very moment.

Any resolve that the Rovers had demonstrated previously was totally absent throughout the remainder of the game as the Reds increased their volume of goals from three to six. Their fourth came about when some 'keep-ball' by Pearson and Hunter ended with a centre that Lawton mercilessly cracked beyond the helpless Hickson.

Blackburn's Haworth left the action for attention to an injury shortly after Lawton's goal, returning none the worse for wear and just in time to see Morgans confidently shoot home a penalty. In the very last minute, goal number six came from outside-left Reg Hunter, and it was seen as a just reward for someone who had toiled untiringly for the team effort and was involved in many of the Reds' best moves.

The applause accorded by the Old Trafford faithful at the full-time whistle was sustained and fully deserved for the victors. As they left the field, the smiles on the faces of the jubilant United teenagers was lined with a quiet ring of confidence.

Over at Hillsborough, the first-team defeated Birmingham City by courtesy of goals from Johnny Berry and Bobby Charlton, the two-nil result booking a place in the F.A. Cup final against Aston Villa.

Any of those United supporters who witnessed the youth team's scintillating display against Blackburn would have had little reason to doubt that yet another final for the youngsters was a very real possibility.

Alex Dawson challenges Blackburn goalie Geoff Hickson on his way to registering another couple of goals

1956-57

semi-final 1st leg

1) Tony Godfrey
2) Glen Walker
3) Mike Stickler
4) Peter Harley
5) Colin Holmes
6) David Scurr
7) Terry Paine
8) Terry Simpson
9) Wes Maughan
10) Peter Vine
11) John Sydenham

1) David Gaskell
2) Barry Smith
3) Stuart Gibson
4) Bobby English
5) Reg Holland
6) Harold Bratt
7) Ken Morgans
8) Nobby Lawton
9) Alex Dawson
10) Mark Pearson
11) Reg Hunter

APRIL 1957

SOUTHAMPTON **2 v 5** MANCHESTER UNITED
Maughan, Scurr — Dawson, English, Holmes (o.g.), Hunter, Pearson

Wednesday 3rd
Kick-off 7.30 p.m.
Attendance 19,320

Busby 'Babes' too good for young Saints

The order of the semi-final ties against Southampton was just as Jimmy Murphy and Bert Whalley would have wanted it, with the first leg at The Dell a preferred opener.

The young Saints had enjoyed an excellent run in the tournament and their goal record, having completed one game more than United, was virtually identical. An away tie at Trowbridge represented the start of Southampton's campaign and it was won in some style by seven goals to one. A titanic struggle with Cardiff City was in store for the Saints in the Second Round and following a 4-4 thriller at Ninian Park, progress was obtained by courtesy of a slender 3-2 win at The Dell.

Arch rivals Portsmouth were next to feel the blast of the Southampton forwards as they were brushed aside by a 3-0 defeat at Fratton Park. Saints then beat Bristol Rovers by courtesy of a two-one home win after initially drawing one-all.

Finally, in the Fifth Round and by way of a change, the Saints were drawn at home and they marked the occasion by putting on a display of their finest form which brought about a 6-0 hiding of Spurs. A goal from Terry Paine, plus two more from Terry Simpson and a hat-trick from centre-forward Wes Maughan, took Southampton's total of goals scored to 26, one more than United, while both teams had conceded nine apiece.

Prior to setting off on the long trek down to the south coast, Murphy named an unchanged side for the fourth consecutive time.

The match, which contained a multitude of talking points and got away to a most dramatic start that proved something of a let-off for the young Reds, was reported on by the Southern Daily Echo:

Only a soccer miracle will enable the Saints Colts to reach the final of the F.A. Youth Cup this season.

That is the conclusion I reached after watching them beaten 5-2 by the brilliant Manchester United side under the Dell floodlights last night in the first leg of the competition's semi-final.

They will, however, travel to Manchester on Monday for the second leg at Old Trafford, heartened by the knowledge that they had given Mr. Matt Busby's talented junior 'Babes' their hardest game in seven cup-ties this season.

That tribute to the local team's tenacity and fighting spirit came from the United manager himself, at the end of a capital game which drew a 19,320 crowd – a 'gate' only bettered three times this season at first-team matches on the ground.

This United side played with an assurance and maturity far beyond their years, and the Saints can take comfort from the fact that although well beaten, they did much to enhance the reputation of the club.

It was no disgrace to lose to a team that included three current England Youth internationals, a wing-half of the calibre of Bob English, and an outside-right, Ken Morgans, the Manchester skipper and Welsh schoolboy cap, who if I am not much mistaken will one day be playing for his native country in the international championship.

A goal down after only nine minutes, following the reprieve of a missed penalty in the first minute of the game, Manchester never lost their rhythm and purpose, and although their goal had some very narrow squeaks, even the most partisan Southampton supporter could not begrudge them their success.

The Saints, like Tottenham in the Fifth Round, never relaxed their efforts, but the final score did not flatter their opponents.

A number of the latecomers missed the game's dramatic opening for precisely 25 seconds after the Saints had kicked off towards the Archer's Road goal, referee N.C. Taylor was pointing to the penalty spot.

A centre from Terry Paine was handled by a Manchester defender as it floated over, but Terry Simpson lost a great chance of giving his side a tonic lead when his penalty kick struck the left-hand post and rebounded to the edge of the area.

Before a United player could get it away, David Scurr nipped in and cracked in a shot which England 'cap' David Gaskell saved at full stretch.

Then we had a glimpse of United's potential forward power with Tony Godfrey saving brilliantly from inside-left Mark Pearson, but in the ninth minute the Saints took the lead.

Again it was Paine with a perfect centre who made the opening, but it needed a gem of a header by centre-forward Wesley Maughan to steer the ball inches inside the far post.

The Saints might well have had a second goal but for Gaskell's timely deflection of Scurr's shot, and then in the 14th minute came the vital equaliser which set United surely on the road to victory.

Godfrey made his only mistake of the game when he dropped a centre from the right, and luckless Colin Holmes, trying to clear, steered the ball into his own net.

Before the Saints could recover, English, Manchester's very capable right-half, had smacked in a twenty-yard shot that went surely to its target and at half-time United led 2-1.

Another great effort by Godfrey kept out a Lawton 'special' early in the second half but he had no chance when, in the 57th minute, Pearson, after having one pile-driver blocked, made no mistake with his second attempt from the edge of the penalty area.

Then in a twinkling the Saints came right back into the game.

A free kick well placed by Peter Harley was never properly cleared and Scurr's deceptively easy left-foot shot caught Gaskell napping and was in the back of the net.

But Manchester's fast, clever attack was probing and widening the cracks in the home defence, and when centre-forward Alex Dawson was brought down 22 yards out, he himself took the free kick.

A tremendous one it was, too, and Godfrey did wonders in punching it away, only for Hunter to nip in and score off the crossbar.

Again the Saints hit back, and after a hectic scramble in United's goal Vine forced the ball over the line, but the goal was disallowed and, awarded a free kick, Manchester got out of trouble.

Dawson rounded off a polished display by getting United's fifth goal from Morgans' cross five minutes from the end, but the thrills did not end there, for in turn both Gaskell and Godfrey had to be on their toes to keep out good efforts.

There was pretty well universal agreement that the Reds were the better side on the night, with one report suggesting they *'lasted the pace better than Southampton'*. That said, United only managed to extend their lead following Peter Vine's disallowed effort and two goal-line clearances from Terry Simpson attempts.

All that now remained to be decided was whether Southampton had conceded United too great a margin for them to claw back. Moreover, would the Saints be capable of repeating some of the goalscoring form that blasted Spurs out of the tournament up at Old Trafford?

Only time would tell.

SOUTHAMPTON FOOTBALL CLUB
THE DELL — Phone 23408
Bus Routes 2 and 5.
TONIGHT, at 7.30 (gates open 6.45).
F.A. YOUTH CHALLENGE CUP — Semi-Final.
MANCHESTER UNITED
All pay at turnstiles.
Centre Stands 4/-. Wing Stands 3/-. Ground 2/- (Boys 1/-).

1) David Gaskell	9) Alex Dawson	1) Tony Godfrey	9) Wes Maughan
2) Barry Smith	10) Mark Pearson	2) Glen Walker	10) Peter Vine
3) Stuart Gibson	11) Reg Hunter	3) Mike Stickler	11) John Sydenham
4) Bobby English		4) Peter Harley	
5) Reg Holland		5) Colin Holmes	
6) Harold Bratt		6) David Scurr	
7) Ken Morgans		7) Terry Paine	
8) Nobby Lawton		8) Terry Simpson	

MANCHESTER UNITED 2 (7) v (5) 3 SOUTHAMPTON

Dawson (2)   Maughan (2), Paine

APRIL 1957

Monday 8th

Kick-off 7.30 p.m.

Attendance 16,876

semi-final 2nd leg

The return leg against Southampton was destined to be a landmark game in United's Youth Cup history even before a ball had been kicked.

For the first time ever, the Reds were able to put on a youth game under the recently erected Old Trafford floodlights. The significance of the new facility in the weeks, months and years to come meant that no longer would games have to be scheduled in midweek before sparse crowds that consisted mainly of schoolboys playing truant or factory workers from Trafford Park who were 'at a funeral'. It also signified that the days of The Cliff as a Youth Cup venue were over for good.

The new floodlights were used for the first time just 48 hours after the youngsters had beaten Blackburn Rovers in the Youth Cup Fifth Round tie and the United management decided that they would celebrate the grand switch-on by having a new set of red shirts made for when Bolton Wanderers paid a visit to contest a couple of First Division points.

The jerseys were manufactured from a material that had a special sheen and would supposedly create a 'glow' under artificial light. In that respect, they were similar in quality and effect to the amber jerseys which the Reds had previously offered to their guests when evening games were staged under The Cliff's floodlights.

The excitement of United's supporters was almost unbounded at that time as the visit of Southampton coincided with the week in which the seniors were preparing to fly off to Spain in order to tackle Real Madrid, then undisputedly the finest club side in the world. Matt Busby took a squad of seventeen players to the Spanish capital where they would meet the mighty Real in the first leg of the European Cup semi-final at the majestic Estadio Santiago Bernabéu.

Busby's men would be cheered on by 180 travelling United supporters whose trip, which included meals, accommodation and match tickets, cost a princely £35 per person. Included in Busby's party for Madrid were Bobby Charlton, Eddie Colman, Billy Whelan, Wilf McGuinness, Duncan Edwards, David Pegg and Gordon Clayton, all of whom, of course, were youth team graduates.

The Southampton game received the following preview in the Manchester Evening News:

Old Trafford's new £40,000 floodlights will be switched on tonight for the return F.A. Youth Cup semi-final between Manchester United and Southampton, which the Busby juniors will start with a three-goal advantage gained in the first leg.

A crowd of over 40,000 is anticipated for this youth game in which United will be seeking to retain the F.A. trophy for the fifth successive season.

There is a late doubt whether former England and Wigan schoolboy goalkeeper, sixteen year-old David Gaskell, will be fit to play. He is recovering from a sore throat and Bobby Allen, ex-Salford Boys, will be standing by to deputise.

The rest of the United side is unchanged from that which won at Southampton last week.

With the Saints also unaltered, except for their colours, and Gaskell given the okay to take his place at the last minute, the tie ended with a happy conclusion for the Reds. The result, though, was a completely new experience for the United youths and the events that led up to it were noted by the Southern Daily Echo:

Southampton can be proud of its Youth XI. They may be out of the F.A. Youth Cup but, under the new £40,000 Old Trafford floodlights last night, they made soccer history by doing what no other side had achieved in five years of the competition – they beat Manchester United, and beat them fairly and squarely.

The score was 3-2 and, as United had won the first leg of the semi-final 5-2 at the Dell last Wednesday, they now face West Ham or Sheffield Wednesday in their fifth successive final. But what a shake-up these brilliant Busby 'Babes' were given by the great-hearted young Saints.

It was a triumph which sent the prestige of the Southampton club soaring, and earned for Colin Holmes and his colleagues the admiration of 17,000 sporting and knowledgeable United fans. I wrote after last Wednesday's game that only a miracle could carry them into the final, but last night that miracle nearly happened.

With the exception of the opening minutes we saw in the first half the Manchester machine moving smoothly, effortlessly and remorselessly towards what one assumed was the inevitable conclusion, a triumph of skill over honest endeavour.

Yet, thanks to brilliant goalkeeping by Tony Godfrey, plus the luck you've got to have in this game, a goal after 26 minutes by centre-forward Alex Dawson was United's sole reward at half-time. And even that goal came from a rebound after Godfrey had made a miraculous save.

The crowd, however, sat back contentedly and expectantly during the interval waiting for the floodgates to open and swamp the Third Division 'minnows'.

But, within two minutes of the restart, the Saints, heartened by a reassuring word from Mr. Ted Bates, gave a hint of the dramatic change that was to come over this game.

A four-man move saw Wesley Maughan in possession for almost the first time, and England Youth goalkeeper Gaskell, who had not been bothered by a single first half shot, had to move smartly to stop the centre-forward's low drive.

In a flash, the Saints were moving with a new assurance. Gone was the earlier hesitancy and lack of 'bite', and they started to harry and test the United defence.

In the 53rd minute they won a corner on the left. Over came John Sydenham's accurate corner kick to the far post, and Terry Paine was there to scramble it in with his chest.

When Manchester, fighting back to retrieve lost ground, found the defence had bolted the door and barred it, Southampton, for the first time, looked as if they could pull the game out of the fire. And, in the 69th minute, they were in front, thanks to a glorious Maughan goal which was a model of its kind.

The young centre-forward picked up a pass from the left wing, 30 yards out, beat three men and then, with the coolness of a veteran, picked his spot and thumped a great cross shot low into the far corner of the net.

The crowd gave Maughan a great reception and thirteen minutes later were cheering him again when he put the Saints 3-1 up.

A gem of a pass from Terry Simpson to Paine; a quick centre, and centre-half Holland, another Youth cap, mis-kicked the inside-forward's through-pass.

Maughan, completely unmarked, was on the ball in a flash and another sure, right-foot shot was in the net. The United side, only a goal in front on aggregate and looking desperately worried, pulled out all the stops, but Godfrey, without a doubt the man of the match, performed prodigiously.

It was in injury-time, however, that United got a second and lucky goal which settled the issue. Barry Smith, their right-back, came crashing through the middle to unleash a shot which threatened to sweep Godfrey through the back of the net.

Somehow, Godfrey punched the ball clear but Dawson, ever the opportunist, nipped in to smack the ball home via the crossbar.

The game had hardly restarted before the final whistle went.

United are in the final and will probably win the trophy for the fifth time, but the glory had gone to the Saints. Their great fighting comeback was a tribute to their enthusiasm and their superior stamina, and it was a proud moment for them when United manager Mr. Matt Busby came into their dressing room afterwards to praise them for 'a great performance'.

After 44 matches, stretching back over four and a half years, Manchester United had finally lost a Youth Cup tie. The honour of reaching yet another final more than compensated for the defeat, although the invincibility United had enjoyed in the tournament was now gone forever.

The Daily Mail reckoned the Reds kept Southampton in *'complete subjection'* during the opening period and reasoned it was the absence of *'quick-fire tackling'*, a hallmark of United's early play, which triggered the Saints' remarkable transformation.

The Evening Chronicle also had a few words to convey:

Leading 5-2 from the first leg, they (United) played some dazzling soccer in the first half and looked likely to overrun Southampton.

They only scored once, through Dawson, before half-time, but there were some astonishing escapes in the Southampton goalmouth and a few equally astonishing saves by goalkeeper Godfrey.

Then Southampton fought back, knocking United out of their smooth stride. They got three well taken goals through winger Paine and centre-forward Maughan (2), and with the Busby boys clinging grimly to their one-goal aggregate lead it looked anybody's game until Dawson slammed in a rebound a minute from the end.

Of the Saints' personnel that brought an end to United's distinguished record, only full-backs Glen Walker and Mike Stickler, along with right-half Peter Harley, failed to break into the first-team at The Dell. Although Colin Holmes, David Scurr, Wes Maughan and Peter Vine aggregated barely ten senior games between them, Terry Simpson (22 league appearances), Tony Godfrey (141) and John Sydenham (341) all made their marks to some degree or other in Southampton's senior side.

Those figures were dwarfed by Terry Paine's magnificent record-breaking 713 Football League games for the Saints, which included the princely figure of 160 goals.

1956-57

1) Brian Goymer	9) George Fenn	1) David Gaskell	9) Alex Dawson
2) Joe Kirkup	10) John Cartwright	2) Barry Smith	10) Mark Pearson
3) Bert Howe	11) Terry McDonald	3) Ray Maddison	11) Reg Hunter
4) Clive Lewis		4) Bobby English	
5) Roy Walker		5) Reg Holland	
6) John Lyall		6) Harold Bratt	
7) Charlie Rowlands		7) Ken Morgans	
8) John Smith		8) Nobby Lawton	

MAY 1957

WEST HAM UNITED 2 v 3 MANCHESTER UNITED

Cartwright, Fenn (pen) — Dawson, Hunter, Lawton

Thursday 2nd
Kick-off 7.30 p.m.
Attendance 15,000

final 1st leg

Right from the time that United reached the final again, typical questions that were bandied about by supporters were a) could they actually win the cup again? and b) would Alex Dawson keep up his remarkable record of scoring in every round so far this season? Fellow finalists West Ham United felt they had a couple of answers of their own, and one in particular was free-scoring centre-forward George Fenn.

Under the guidance of former West Ham, Charlton and Sunderland number nine and current youth coach at Upton Park, Bill Robinson, Fenn had managed fifteen Youth Cup goals so far, having registered in all bar one game, and he seemed to provide the greatest source of danger to the Reds' continued aspirations. Along with the potential threat posed by Fenn, there were obvious examples of others who might have a say in the destiny of the trophy. Two of them were John Smith and Terry McDonald, both of whom had already contributed service in West Ham's first-team.

The young Hammers had easily k.o'd their first three opponents on their way to the final. Essex neighbours Dagenham were brushed aside 4-1, Briggs Sports later fell by fourteen goals to nil, and then Crystal Palace were eliminated 6-2, all at Upton Park.

West Ham then travelled to Reading, where a 4-2 success gave them another home engagement, on this occasion against an Arsenal side that was forced to taste a bitter defeat by a three to one scoreline. In the semi-final, the Hammers brought an excellent nil-nil result away from Hillsborough only to complete the job by beating Sheffield Wednesday 2-0 in the capital.

The West Ham match programme provided an excellent preview to the opening leg, which contained pen pictures of both sides and the previous results of the respective teams:

The first leg of the final of the F.A. Youth Cup for 1956-57 provides Londoners with the opportunity of seeing the Youth XI of Manchester United in action two days before their seniors take the field for the other national cup final at Wembley Stadium; but we know that although the Hammers' supporters will be cheering on their own favourites this evening, there will be many who will wish the best of luck to the Mancunians on Saturday in their efforts to complete the greatest 'double' in modern English football.

As the present holders of the youth trophy, the Manchester lads undoubtedly feel they must set their seniors an example by again scoring a success, but we can assure them that they will find us just as tough a proposition as their club-mates will find Aston Villa on Saturday. It will be observed, incidentally, that the Villa's colours are the same as our own!

From our own angle we probably feel very much as the Villa. On past performances the lads from Old Trafford will start favourites, but in cup finals such records rarely count for much, and the 'outsiders' often accomplish a performance which is labelled as a 'surprise'. Yet is it? After all, the Hammers have dismissed some very useful sides from the Youth Cup, and although these results may have received comparatively little publicity outside their own immediate circle, the young Hammers are well aware that a victory for them would not shock an extremely large number of fans who regard them as a 'dark horse'.

The Hammers have indeed already achieved one reward by becoming the first southern club to reach the final of this competition, and they are determined to grasp the opportunity of becoming the first team outside of Old Trafford to have their name inscribed on the trophy. The visitors' record in the competition is a remarkable one, but nevertheless it would not be out of place for the cup to start travelling around to other parts of the country for a change!

However, whatever may be the outcome of tonight's tussle, we say in conclusion that we sincerely hope that the better team will prove the eventual winners. It is a great start for a youngster's senior soccer career if he can say 'I was in the winning Youth Cup team', and with so many of tonight's players on the threshold of major competition there will be every incentive for them to put up a first-rate entertainment for 90 minutes.

But whatever may be the final score tonight, there is still the second leg to be played, and there may well be an even larger attendance present at Old Trafford next Tuesday evening.

The match programme also carried details of a British Railways special for West Ham fans wishing to travel to Manchester for the return tie. At a price of 24 shillings and nine pence (approximately £1.23), Hammers' followers would alight at Central Station an hour before kick-off and, even with a choice of return times, they couldn't expect to arrive back in London until 5.24 a.m. at the earliest.

On the fitness front, West Ham were able to name their first choice eleven. The Reds weren't quite as fortunate as they needed to contend with an injury problem to left-back Stuart Gibson, who had sustained a painful toe injury while training for the match.

Ray Maddison, United's left-back in the earlier ties against Burnley, Huddersfield and Sunderland, was the perfect deputy and he was brought in as a replacement for the unlucky Gibson. It really was a case of déjà vu for Bert Whalley and Jimmy Murphy as, for the third time in five years, following the earlier injuries to John Doherty and Gordon Clayton, the duo were forced to cope with the loss of one of their regulars for the final.

Matt Busby was in London at the time of the Youth Cup final, albeit he was indisposed on the evening of the game. Busby was acting as a guest speaker at a dinner celebration where the legendary Preston North End and England winger Tom Finney was due to be presented with the 'Footballer of the Year' award.

The *Boro' of West Ham Express* gave the following report on the events at Upton Park:

'Pitch favoured United,' says Hammers' Bill Robinson

MANCHESTER United's big, bustling youth team showed at Upton Park on Thursday last the sort of class that can keep the Old Trafford club on top for years to come. They played some brilliant football to beat West Ham Colts 3—2 in the first leg of the F.A. Youth Cup final.

Yet the young Hammers often outpaced but never outplayed—were great in defeat. They rocked the northerners right back on their heels with a 26th minute goal, only to lose the initiative in the vital opening stages of the second-half.

Coach Bill Robinson was far from disappointed with West Ham's display. He said afterwards: "Our compact pitch favoured United's use of the short pass. I think we'll shake them at Old Trafford."

The opening 25 minutes and the closing stages brought the best out of West Ham. It had them battling for an early lead and then fighting to pull back from a 3—2 deficit.

These young Hammers—a real credit to the club—played with poise and confidence in the early stages. But even the shock of being a goal down after 26 minutes couldn't upset the rhythm of a superbly fit United.

Out-manoeuvred

Gradually home wing-halves Charlie Lewis and John Lyall —"I didn't do so well in my first game as a professional"— found themselves being out-manoeuvred by Manchester's inside men.

Centre-forward Alec Dawson— surely a star of the not so distant future—was the real villain of the piece. Throughout he gave Roy Walker a gruelling time.

Salute the efforts of full-backs Charlie Howe and Joe Kirkup. Gallant Howe saved a certain goal 14 minutes from the finish when he kicked off the line with Brian Goymer, who made some fine saves, well beaten.

Fair-haired Johnny Cartwright notched West Ham's first goal. Charlie Rowlands, a nippy winger, mis-hit a shot 15 yards out and the ball went across for the inside-left to volley into the net.

Glancing header

United were on terms at the interval. DAWSON scoring with a glancing header in the 37th minute.

Two second-half goals inside a devastating three minutes ruined Hammers hopes. Lawton headed United into the lead after 52 minutes, then outside-left Hunter made it 3—1 after a dazzling run. Centre-forward George Fenn maintained his record of scoring in every round of the competition when he netted West Ham's second from the penalty spot in the 64th minute.

Fenn's penalty, given for 'hands', made for a frenetic finale to a fine contest which ebbed and flowed one way and then another in terms of each team's possessional superiority.

The *Manchester Evening Chronicle* conceded that West Ham were the Reds' *'equals in everything except an extra yard of pace'* while adding that the *'thrustful play of the United centre-forward Alex Dawson and his colleagues proved decisive'*.

90

1) David Gaskell
2) Barry Smith
3) Ray Maddison
4) Bobby English
5) Reg Holland
6) Harold Bratt
7) Ken Morgans
8) Nobby Lawton
9) Alex Dawson
10) Mark Pearson
11) Reg Hunter

1) Brian Goymer
2) Joe Kirkup
3) Bert Howe
4) Clive Lewis
5) Roy Walker
6) John Lyall
7) Charlie Rowlands
8) John Smith
9) George Fenn
10) John Cartwright
11) Terry McDonald

1956-57

MANCHESTER UNITED 5 (8) v (2) 0 WEST HAM UNITED

Dawson (2), Hunter, Pearson (2)

MAY 1957

Tuesday 7th

Kick-off 7.30 p.m.

Attendance 23,349

final 2nd leg

The United team that met West Ham at Old Trafford for the second leg of the 1956/57 Youth Cup final
Back row (l-r) Bobby English, Ray Maddison, Barry Smith, David Gaskell, Reg Hunter, Harold Bratt
Front row (l-r) Reg Holland, Alex Dawson, Ken Morgans, Mark Pearson, Nobby Lawton

Winning the away instalment of the final naturally placed United as everyone's favourites to clinch the cup victory that all at Old Trafford so badly wanted, although in the days leading up to the game Jimmy Murphy and Bert Whalley repeatedly pointed out to the players the pitfalls of resting on their first leg lead. The coaches reminded the squad that they had brought just a single goal advantage back to Manchester, whereas against Southampton they went through as a result of defending a three-goal superiority from the match at The Dell.

The consensus of a minority was that the error of leeway was too marginal and they could point to the simple fact that United had managed to concede two or more goals in seven out of their nine matches during the cup run. Conversely, they had averaged almost four goals a game at the other end of the pitch, with super-poacher Alex Dawson contributing approximately half of their total.

In other words, it was still all to play for.

The build-up to the second leg was completely dwarfed by the media's reactions to United's defeat in the F.A. Cup final on the previous Saturday, and in particular the controversial circumstances surrounding Aston Villa's victory.

The concluding leg of the Youth Cup final, therefore, gave an ideal opportunity to end the season on a high note, which the Manchester Evening News made due note of:

Although he had to wait 63 minutes for his first goal, it was bustling Manchester United centre-forward Alex Dawson who harassed West Ham United out of last night's second leg of the F.A. Youth Cup final at Old Trafford.

West Ham had felt the weight of this seventeen year-old centre-forward in last Thursday's first leg at West Ham when United gained a goal advantage with a 3-2 win.

Watching Dawson left them wondering what to do about Mark Pearson and Nobby Lawton, two coming inside-forward artists, whose passing and quick individual bursts tore holes in their defence.

United were on their way to their fifth F.A. Youth Cup – they have won every year since its inception – when Reg Hunter, collecting a long centre from Ken Morgans, rounded Kirkup and slammed the ball home after 24 minutes.

Goymer was nearly knocked over a minute later by a Dawson shot which he caught at the second attempt, and the goalkeeper was partly at fault with United's second goal in the 28th minute.

Dashing out to clear a long through pass, he could only push the ball to the advancing Pearson, who scored easily.

Pearson had a great shot finger-tipped over the bar before he scored a fine third goal for United in the 30th minute.

In the second half, West Ham never gave up trying but there was no punch about their forward play.

At last Dawson, who had tried so hard before the interval, came into his own. His goal in the 63rd minute was a simple push over the line from a low Morgans cross. It seemed to become all Dawson. Headers and high powered shots were fired in, and after he had collected United's fifth goal in the 70th minute, he went all out for his hat-trick.

91

1956-57

MAY 1957

final 2nd leg

Appeals go up for a penalty as Alex Dawson collapses under a heavy challenge in the West Ham goalmouth

And so it was that United collected the trophy for a fifth consecutive time, when skipper Ken Morgans acted as the smiling recipient of the Youth Cup on the steps of the Main Stand.

Capping a fine season for him personally, much the same could be said for all of his team-mates. Alex Dawson was rightly hailed for his goal in every game feat, although he would have been the first to acknowledge the assistance from all of those around him.

The very last words on United's incredible and truly historic feat were left to none other than Tom Jackson, whose one word headline perfectly summed up the feeling all around Old Trafford:

MAGNIFICENT!

IF manager Matt Busby wanted any consolation for Manchester United's tragic defeat at Wembley, he couldn't have wished for anything better than the brilliant performance of his under-18 team in winning the F.A. Youth Cup for the FIFTH successive season.

Here's a Cup record that may never be equalled. Every season since the F.A. decided to encourage junior players attached to League clubs by giving them their own knock-out competition United's bright youngsters have had a stranglehold on the trophy.

But it's also important to remember that each season there has been a different edition of this youth team, which has already helped to develop such established United players as Duncan Edwards, Billy Whelan, Eddie Colman, David Pegg, Bobby Charlton, and Wilf McGuinness to name a few.

United's successes in grooming schoolboy talent, thanks to the behind-the-scenes efforts of Matt Busby and his two great henchmen, Jimmy Murphy and Bert Whalley, were plain for all the 23,349 spectators to see at Old Trafford when the youth team had a nap hand of goals to add to the 3-2 victory gained in the first-leg final at West Ham.

It was a sparkling display of attacking football and teamwork that ensured the trophy staying at Old Trafford for at least another season. Alec Dawson, the Scots boy with the remarkable flair for goals, again led the forwards with great zest and skill, and he had two outstanding helpmates in inside-left Mark Pearson and right winger Ken Morgans.

1956-57

MAY 1957

final 2nd leg

Skipper Ken Morgans shows off the Youth Cup to an ecstatic Old Trafford crowd

1957-58

1) Peter Robinson	9) Alan Hart
2) Mick Henaghan	10) Ivan McAuley
3) Fenwick McLean	11) Trevor Lightbown
4) Bobby Baldwin	
5) John Talbut	
6) John Brier	
7) Ian Towers	
8) Ron Fenton	

1) David Gaskell	9) Nobby Lawton
2) Barry Smith	10) Mark Pearson
3) David Yeomans	11) Jimmy Elms
4) Jackie Hennessy	
5) Reg Holland	
6) Harold Bratt	
7) Tommy Spratt	
8) Johnny Giles	

OCTOBER 1957

BURNLEY 0 v 2 MANCHESTER UNITED

Elms, Lawton

first round

Saturday 19th

Kick-off 10.30 a.m.

The 1957/58 season, which ultimately proved so fateful and tragic for all those with an interest in Manchester United, swept in on a tidal wave of optimism. After the exploits of the recent past, manager Matt Busby was in sight of guiding his beloved Reds to a hat-trick of First Division championships, with the opportunity of emulating the feat of Huddersfield Town in the 1920's and Arsenal in the 1930's a very real one.

It was certain that Busby would have wanted to make a concerted attempt to gain a third successive league title and he was known to be eagerly anticipating a second assault at bringing the European Cup to Old Trafford. With the groundbreaking experiences of the recent past sure to stand them in good stead, the first-team squad was now a little older, and certainly much wiser, for their exposure to continental football and there was a lobby of pundits who felt that they were amply equipped to go the full distance this time around. A return to Wembley for the F.A. Cup final was also on the wish list of the management, players and supporters, as a quick revisit to the twin towers would have enabled the club's chance to redeem the injustice of losing to Aston Villa.

There were, therefore, incentives to succeed on all senior battlefields.

The under-18 squad, too, would require little motivation in the quest to prolong their Youth Cup winning sequence and the high expectations in that particular camp were not without good foundations. Even though Bobby English, Ken Morgans and Reg Hunter had been forced into 'retirement', and full-backs Ray Maddison and Stuart Gibson were no longer at the club, all of the remaining participants from the last campaign were still available and eager to continue the club's stranglehold on the competition.

Most ominously for those aspiring to end the red and white domination, Alex Dawson, who had already netted 31 Youth Cup goals, was still eligible and desperate to add to his staggering tally. With the amount of experience and talent left in the side, and mindful of United's almost faultless track record, it was plainly obvious that it would take one heck of a side to stop them.

For openers, the Reds were drawn away to Burnley, whom they had defeated at exactly the same stage a year earlier at The Cliff. The Clarets fielded four players from that meeting, with half-back Bobby Baldwin having returned to action since making a complete recovery from his leg break sustained at United's Lower Broughton enclosure.

Centre-forward Alan Hart hadn't represented Burnley in that specific game, but he had opposed the Reds before in the Youth Cup as a member of the Bolton side that succumbed to United in the semi-final some eighteen months before. Three of the Clarets side, Hart, Ron Fenton and Ivan McAuley, were professionally contracted to the Turf Moor club.

In order to rehearse their probable starting line-up against United, Burnley named a strong side to face Bury in a Lancashire League fixture on the preceding Saturday when the junior Clarets nicked the points with a win by the odd goal in five. The Burnley Express newspaper revealed that *'slight changes are entailed'* to the team because *'Trevor Lightbown, who played several Reserve matches at the start of the season, is available today after several weeks' absence through injury and study'*.

The visit of the Reds was actually the very first Youth Cup tie to be staged at Turf Moor as Burnley had only entered the tournament once before when, of course, their participation ended at The Cliff.

The Reds fielded a fresh defender in former Cheshire Boys left full-back David Yeomans, while at right-half Jackie Hennessy, a Dubliner with Republic of Ireland Boys representative honours to his credit, was also making his opening bow in the Youth Cup. With only the forward-line requiring a further injection of talent, a couple of new wingers were included. East Northumberland and England Boys star Tommy Spratt was situated at number seven while Jimmy Elms, who had already put in a previous Youth Cup appearance against Sunderland, occupied the left flank. A second Dubliner with Eire schoolboy international caps made up the team at inside-right, and what a precocious talent he was. The name: Johnny Giles.

As Alex Dawson was preferred for a First Division engagement with Portsmouth at Old Trafford, Jimmy Murphy gave the centre-forward job to a capable Mancunian understudy, Nobby Lawton.

The match highlights were recorded by the Burnley Express & News thus:

This First Round F.A. Youth Cup competition match was a keen contest, with the visitors the better team.

United, who have won the F.A. Youth Cup every year since its inception, included three youth internationals in their side – Holland, their centre-half, goalkeeper Gaskell, and inside-left Pearson.

During the first half they attacked consistently, worrying the Burnley defence

with short, accurate passes and intelligent positional play. Burnley's few attempts at attack were easily broken up by an unruffled defence.

It was not until United had scored their first goal that Burnley began to have their share of the attacking. The goal came in the 28th minute when left-winger Elms ran on to a Giles pass.

Burnley developed a more constructive attack. A McAuley shot gained a corner which was cleared, but almost immediately the ball was back in the visitors' penalty area. For the next few seconds, Burnley enjoyed a shooting-in session, during which five shots were blocked and returned by the desperate defenders before Gaskell had to concede a further corner.

Burnley continued to attack in the second half, favouring the long pass out to the wing whereas United continued their short passing game. McAuley and Lightbown co-operated well on the Burnley left wing. On the opposite side of the field, Towers, a lively outside-right, was also troublesome and tried Gaskell on more than one occasion.

Talbut was a prominent defender.

Lawton took advantage of an easy chance and netted United's second.

The victory represented nothing more than a solid start from the boy Reds, who saw attempts from Giles and Pearson rebound from the woodwork before the opening goal went in. While there had been some fine football from the wing-halves and forwards, it was actually United's full-backs who received most of the after-match accolades. They were required to work particularly hard to cope with the tricky Burnley wingers and their stubborn defending was a major factor in assisting to keep a blank 'goals against' account.

If Jimmy Murphy and Bert Whalley were at all dissatisfied, their only negative criticism would have been aimed at the touch of over-elaboration in front of goal by United's forwards, with much of the team's fast-flowing and constructive approach work nullified through that singular failing. Overall, the thought was that the youngsters had delivered an excellent result and through it they confirmed their intention to hold on to the trophy once again.

David Yeomans was given the number three jersey for the youth clash at Burnley

94

1) David Williams	9) Neil Turner	1) David Gaskell	9) Alex Dawson
2) David Jones	10) Mel Parsonage	2) Barry Smith	10) Mark Pearson
3) Tommy Singleton	11) Eddie Cobb	3) Les Cummings	11) Jimmy Elms
4) Johnny Walker		4) Jackie Hennessy	
5) Tommy Hall		5) Reg Holland	
6) Jimmy Gibbs		6) Harold Bratt	
7) Mandy Hill		7) Tommy Spratt	
8) Charlie Wroth		8) Johnny Giles	

BLACKPOOL 0 v 7 MANCHESTER UNITED

Dawson (5), Pearson (2)

1957-58

NOVEMBER 1957

Saturday 9th

Kick-off 11.00 a.m.

second round

The workmanlike win at Burnley earned the Old Trafford teenagers a trip to the seaside to face Blackpool in the Second Round. The Bloomfield Road outfit was an established and successful First Division club throughout the late 1940's and 1950's and had, in fact, finished in second place to United's senior side in the race for the First Division title just a matter of months before the Youth Cup tie.

Blackpool's under-18's had beaten Stockport County 3-1 at Edgeley Park to bring them into conflict with the Reds and one of their number, outside-left Eddie Cobb, was the son of Mr. John Cobb, a member of the club's office staff.

Bloomfield Road had already proved a fertile patch for the Reds that season, as United's first-team chalked up a 4-1 win there, and just a week after the seniors' win, the Reserves ran riot to claim both points with an 8-1 Central League victory.

For the youth clash, which was performed in the midst of a swirling, chilling gale that howled in furiously from the Irish Sea, Alex Dawson was brought back into the fold and despite sealing the earlier win at Turf Moor with his goal twelve minutes from time, Nobby Lawton was dropped to make way for him. There was just one other alteration, at left full-back, where Manchester lad Les Cummings was given the nod over David Yeomans. Cummings had joined United from Wythenshawe Boys Club and his credentials revealed that he had already represented the Manchester County F.A.

Two days prior to the Youth Cup contest, the Blackpool Gazette made mention of the game:

The gates will not be closed at Bloomfield Road on Saturday morning. There are still too few folk on a five-day week.

It is, however, a reasonable assumption that if the weather is fine a record attendance for a morning football match in Blackpool, except when Christmas Day has been celebrated on Saturday, will be created.

Visitors are the famous colts of Manchester United in the F.A. Youth Challenge Cup.

These 'Busby Babes' have seldom been challenged. Often in these ties they have hit up cricket scores.

Out of this team has graduated several of the players in the present League championship line-up.

And today, as Mr. Matt Busby's Academy for the Training of Young Footballers is still the finest football school in the land, the present eleven is considered as just about the best young football outfit in Britain.

Blackpool's colts will enter this weekend's match as second favourites.

But always there is the chance in a football match that the giants may be slain, and for that reason, apart entirely from the visitors' remarkable reputation, the turnstiles should be busy on Saturday morning.

That the ties in this tournament have an attraction for the public is established by the figures for the First Round match which Blackpool won at Stockport last month.

It was an evening game under floodlights and yet over 3,000 people watched it, and the receipts were £179.

A gulf in class which was wider than the Golden Mile prompted the following match report in the Manchester Evening News:

Manchester United youth eleven, holders of the F.A. Youth Cup, routed Blackpool 7-0 in the Second Round of the competition at Bloomfield Road. They were far too strong for Blackpool and their taller and heavier defenders dominated the game from start to finish.

Outstanding in a great forward-line was Alex Dawson, who scored five goals. Holding the ball close and moving into position with speed, all of his goals were brilliantly taken.

Blackpool were never in the hunt and were unable to contain the Babes' inside men, Giles and Pearson, who scored two extremely well-taken goals.

Gaskell in the Manchester goal was rarely troubled, due mainly to the fine covering of Holland and full-backs Cummings and Smith.

The Reds' emphatic win met with great approval from the noisy contingent of United followers inside a disappointingly near-empty Bloomfield Road. For the travelling supporters, the youth game represented the morning instalment of a double dose of football as they would soon be heading for the First Division clash between the senior Reds and Preston at Deepdale later that day.

Alex Dawson provided by far the most for them to shout about when deciding to provide his own illuminations for the seaside town. Getting off the mark by converting a free kick, he beat the Blackpool 'keeper in a chase for the ball before calmly slotting it home for his second goal. Dawson completed his hat-trick prior to half-time before he and Mark Pearson, who had instigated the majority of the most damaging moves in and around the Blackpool penalty area, shared out the bounty of four second half goals.

Such was United's almost total control of the proceedings that goalkeeper David Gaskell left the pitch feeling something similar to someone who had just served 90 minutes in solitary confinement. With almost no action at his end of the pitch to keep him occupied, Gaskell spent most of the game jumping up and down in the seclusion of his penalty box in order to keep himself from freezing.

The United Review felt that the Reds *'took time to settle down',* with the result that their *'early play was disjointed'.* The Review correspondent went on to record that after the interval *'the United boys put on a grand exhibition of attacking and forceful football which the home team were not able to counter'.*

One newspaper reckoned that Pearson was *'particularly effective'* while the Bloomfield Road club's back-line troubled to cope with a *'fast moving'* Giles. Another claimed that *'Matt Busby looked a very pleased man when he left the directors' box at the end of the game'.*

A reality check from Jimmy Murphy concluded with his view that Blackpool's defenders had offered only token resistance to United's onslaught throughout the contest. Often given to panicking, particularly in the second period when an increasingly gusting wind provided another factor they struggled to cope with, the Tangerines' rearguard never got to grips with opponents who were mainly a step or two ahead of them throughout.

Murphy was happy in the knowledge that his lads had completed the task in hand with the enthusiasm he always demanded, but by the same token he would have been aware that there were much tougher opponents waiting for the chance to lower the Reds' colours.

Already pining for home, Jackie Hennessy completed his second and last Youth Cup appearance at Bloomfield Road

1957-58

1) Finlay McDonnell	9) Tony Leighton
2) Keith Nussey	10) John Hawksby
3) Jimmy Trodden	11) Lenny Copp
4) Mel Durham	
5) Jim Simmons	
6) Jim Hansbro	
7) Jimmy Sheavills	
8) Clive Clark	

1) David Gaskell	9) Alex Dawson
2) Barry Smith	10) Mark Pearson
3) Les Cummings	11) Jimmy Elms
4) Nobby Stiles	
5) Reg Holland	
6) Harold Bratt	
7) Tommy Spratt	
8) Johnny Giles	

DECEMBER 1957

LEEDS UNITED 1 v 4 **MANCHESTER UNITED**

Leighton — Dawson (3), Spratt

Wednesday 18th
Kick-off 7.00 p.m.

third round

Busby juniors showed class

The Reds' Youth Cup travels continued at the next stage, with Elland Road the venue and Leeds United naturally providing the opposition.

The lead up to the tie was made against the headline hogging backdrop of Matt Busby's efforts to prize Northern Ireland's ace goalkeeper Harry Gregg away from Doncaster Rovers. Busby was reportedly prepared to stump up a phenomenal £22,500 for the dependable Ulsterman, which would have been a world record fee for a 'keeper, and the proposed transfer provided a field day for the back page banner writers.

Even though the first-team were handily placed in the race for the First Division title, they had uncharacteristically conceded four goals on three occasions already that season, as well as three goals in four matches. With a busy second half of the campaign to follow, which included F.A. Cup and European Cup commitments, there were obviously concerns about the side's defensive frailties within the confines of Old Trafford.

While the Gregg affair filled acres of newspaper columns, Jimmy Murphy and Bert Whalley's main concern was preparing their charges for the trip to Leeds and they chose to make just one alteration to the line-up that had burst Blackpool's bubble.

With Jackie Hennessy back home in Dublin, the Irish lad was replaced by a second player to represent United at youth level, following Terry Beckett, who had attended St. Patrick's School in Collyhurst. A dynamic, pocket-sized battleship who would one day display his determination, skill, commitment and lack of front teeth on the highest of world stages, he was Norbert Peter Stiles.

Any worries Murphy and Whalley harboured regarding their main striker proved unfounded when, after missing three Central League fixtures with an ankle knock, Alex Dawson was declared fit and ready to continue his astonishing goalscoring record in the competition.

Displaying something of a slight county bias, the Yorkshire Evening Post's match preview noted that 'although born in Aberdeen', Dawson had 'learned all his football on Humberside', and it went on to reveal that he and five other Reds, namely David Gaskell, Barry Smith, Reg Holland, Mark Pearson and Jimmy Elms, 'have won England Youth honours'.

On an evening when a set of thermal underwear and a good overcoat were regarded as essential items of clothing, the beaming Elland Road floodlights cascaded their glow onto the lush green stage below.

The United eleven, who were slightly older on average than their Yorkshire counterparts, wasted no time in asserting themselves on the game and within three minutes of the start, Tommy Spratt had already prized open the door of the home defence by pouncing on a short-range opportunity following a corner. With the confidence of taking the lead so early, the display of Spratt and his effervescent colleagues quickly developed into one which was all around cleverer, stronger, faster and more potent than their opponents could handle.

The Leeds lads tried hard enough, and actually weren't embarrassed in terms of overall possession, but they only caused problems for the Reds on a handful of occasions and were pushed back for lengthy periods of the match.

Once Alex Dawson had weighed in with a couple of goals, the outcome was no longer up for debate.

A smartly taken consolation from Leeds' centre-forward Tony Leighton, a rasping drive hit-on-the-run which Gaskell could only glance at, was soon followed by the completion of Dawson's hat-trick.

The press complimented the Reds on their performance, with one newspaper describing the impression they made as 'well-mixed, sharp, direct football, laced with flashes of individual skill as do their distinguished seniors in the First Division'. The report, which emanated from Yorkshire, went on to claim 'right-back Smith will probably be the next Johnny Carey, so classy was his display' and added that 'Pearson, their inside-left, was a model of everything an inside-forward should be'. That same scribe also felt that despite the 'heavy, wet pitch' and 'raw evening', the game had provided 'capital entertainment'.

Over at the Daily Mail, their summary stated 'on this showing it will be difficult for any side to prevent Manchester from carrying off the cup for the sixth time' while a rival newspaper was of the opinion that the Reds 'showed a fine understanding of passing, positioning and support play'.

Another scribe summarised the contest by simply declaring that 'Leeds were never in the hunt'.

The margin and the manner of the win greatly pleased the watching Matt Busby who, sometime later that evening, held a meeting with his Doncaster Rovers opposite number, Peter Doherty.

The Doncaster manager had been in attendance at Elland Road and as a result of that get-together, Busby tabled an increased offer for Harry Gregg. The following morning, the Rovers board hastily convened to discuss the situation and within a matter of days the Irish 'keeper became United property at the considerable cost of £25,000.

> "There were loads of physical games against the likes of Bolton Wanderers and Preston North End and you needed to be able to handle yourself. Jimmy (Murphy) wasn't big on team talks, he was just direct and to the point. He'd say, 'Lets get stuck in boys and get them beat!' He loved the youngsters but was always keen on working as a team.
>
> I would often come back and help out at corners, marking their centre-forward or the centre-half, particularly if they were big lads. We had good players in all the youth teams that I played in and my last year was no different.
>
> Mark (Pearson) was a wonderful player and we had such a good understanding on the pitch, but he never really got a chance later on. He was only small but you couldn't get the ball off him he was that strong. You could tell who would make it, Nobby Stiles, Nobby Lawton and Johnny Giles, he was a fantastic player. I just knew he would make it and thought that eventually he would take over from Billy Whelan. But all the players were quick learners and in tough games they knew how to dish it out when necessary.
>
> Personally I used to hate running work and Jimmy Murphy used to bang on at me all the time, 'the first fifteen yards Alex'. He also made me practice my heading so that I had good timing.
>
> I used to stand outside the eighteen-yard box and he used to tell the wingers to knock the ball in as hard as possible between the penalty spot and the six-yard line. Jimmy would say that he didn't mind one bit if they hit the corner flag, so long as their crosses were really belted over. I used to then run onto the ball and scored lots of goals that way. It was essential for me to have wingers and Jimmy Elms and Tommy Spratt did a really good job that season.
>
> I was also told about my movement off the ball to create space, it was the way United played. Tommy Taylor used to do magnificently for the first-team and Jimmy was always telling me to watch Tommy's play.
>
> I had a good scoring record in those days, if I could have kept all the balls from the hat-tricks I scored I would have had a house full. But you didn't do that back then, the ball was cleaned up for the next game."

ALEX DAWSON

1) David Gaskell
2) Barry Smith
3) Les Cummings
4) Nobby Stiles
5) Reg Holland
6) Harold Bratt
7) Tommy Spratt
8) Johnny Giles
9) Alex Dawson
10) Mark Pearson
11) Jimmy Elms

1) Billy Shipley
2) George Heslop
3) George Moy
4) Brian Wright
5) Billy Thompson
6) George Dalton
7) Grant Malcolm
8) Ken Hale
9) Graham Ross
10) Alan Smith
11) Mel Osmond

1957-58

MANCHESTER UNITED 8 v 0 NEWCASTLE UNITED

Dawson (4), Giles, Pearson (3)

JANUARY 1958

Saturday 4th

Kick-off 3.00 p.m.

Attendance 19,860

The youth team were finally glad of a home tie when the Fourth Round draw was made, especially after learning that their visitors would be Newcastle United. The junior Magpies had been on the thick end of a bad scoreline at Old Trafford two years before, although the tom-toms beating in the North-East suggested that this side would represent a totally different proposition.

There were unfortunate pre-match developments on the injury front for the Geordies with Jackie Bell, who had already appeared in the club's first-team and was the youth XI's regular left-half, and Alan Wilson, who would normally have taken the centre-forward spot, were declared unfit.

In contrast, Jimmy Murphy was much more fortunate in that he was able, and perfectly satisfied, to pin a 'no changes' team sheet on United's notice board.

With an empty space on the Old Trafford wall chart, the tie was allotted a Saturday afternoon kick-off. Both of Manchester's senior teams were drawn away in the Third Round of the F.A. Cup, United at Workington and City at West Bromwich Albion, and the indications were that the turnstiles would be clicking with some repetition for the youth encounter.

The visit of the Geordies represented the very first occasion that a youth game in Manchester was broadcast by live radio to local hospitals. Such transmissions were regular occurrences for senior fixtures, as they had been taking place ever since the United v. City 'derby' at Old Trafford in January 1954, and it was now the kids' turn to provide some action over the airwaves.

Once the game got underway, it didn't take long to reach a frantic pace and Newcastle were quickly put under the cosh, the Reds' initial attacking move ending when Alex Dawson failed to connect with a smart cross from Jimmy Elms. In the fourth minute Dawson was again at the centre of the action, when Newcastle goalie Shipley was unable to hold a shot from Elms. The ball dropped at the feet of the number nine, who hammered it goalwards, and with a super recovery Shipley somehow managed to get a palm behind the ball to deflect it for a corner which was cleared.

The Magpies replied with a twenty-yard drive from Smith that whistled over Gaskell's bar and United full-back Les Cummings was soon alert to another raid by the visitors that he dealt with calmly under pressure.

With the clock having ticked round to the 13th minute, it proved to be an unlucky one for Newcastle when they went behind to a contentious goal that certainly wouldn't have counted in the modern era. After conceding a corner, which was put over by Elms, their defence allowed Dawson to head the ball into Shipley's hands. Mark Pearson followed in with a rigorous *'old-fashioned shoulder charge'* and the goalkeeper ended up in the back of the net, still clutching the ball, which made it 1-0 to the Reds.

The development had the effect of turning the Magpies into lead statues and over the next half-hour, during which a further three goals were piled up by their tormentors, they were positively danced around by a cocky and unmerciful United.

Pearson notched his and the game's second by firing the ball home from an acute angle and a third came after Dawson crafted an opportunity for Johnny Giles to open his Youth Cup account. Within seconds of Giles' goal the Reds had twisted the knife in deeper still, when a Pearson 'assist' was gleefully converted by the deadly, dark and dangerous Dawson.

In order to give the game a proper sense of balance, the Reds matched their opening half total with an identical four-goal blast in the second period, Pearson snatching another while Dawson performed a trio of further successful raids to take his personal tally up to four. When United's 'goal-ometer' finally stuck on eight, the score perfectly gauged the splendour of their practically perfect and purring performance.

No-one in the crowd of almost 20,000 folk who were witness to those achievements could have foreseen that the two teenagers would never again participate in the under-18 tournament. The devastating events which followed dictated that Dawson and Pearson would soon be forced to bear far more football responsibility than competing in mere youth games..........

fourth round

United's under-18's prior to the kick-off against Newcastle
Back row (l-r) Harold Bratt, Nobby Stiles, David Gaskell, Barry Smith, Mark Pearson, Les Cummings
Front row (l-r) Tommy Spratt, Reg Holland, Alex Dawson, Johnny Giles, Jimmy Elms

MUNICH

THE FLOWERS OF MANCHESTER

FEBRUARY 1958

Just over a month after the marvellous Youth Cup win over Newcastle came the blackest day that Manchester United has ever known.

On Thursday, 6th February 1958, at four minutes past three in the afternoon, a British European Airways twin-engine Elizabethan aeroplane crashed on take-off from a snowbound Munich airport. The aircraft was returning from Belgrade en route to Manchester and had stopped at the German airfield for refuelling.

On board the craft were the Manchester United squad which was homeward bound from an action-packed European Cup quarter-final game against Red Star of Belgrade. A hard-fought 3-3 draw had been achieved in the Yugoslav capital, the result proving enough to see the Reds through to the last four on an aggregate of goals.

As a consequence of the crash, 23 people lost their lives. Eight of those killed were United players; Geoff Bent, Roger Byrne, Eddie Colman, Duncan Edwards, Mark Jones, David Pegg, Tommy Taylor and Billy Whelan. In a few moments of carnage, one of the greatest club sides Britain has ever produced was devastated.

Three members of the club's staff also perished; Walter Crickmer, trainer Tom Curry and coach Bert Whalley, all of whom were United to the core. Each of them was also a gentleman of the old school and their application, dedication and loyalty to the club's cause was unquestionable. Secretary Crickmer had served United for fully 28 years, while Whalley arrived at Old Trafford in May 1934 and 'Tosher' Curry followed him two months later.

Eight journalists were also killed. They were Alf Clarke (Manchester Evening Chronicle), Tom Jackson (Manchester Evening News), Don Davies (Manchester Guardian), George Fellows (Daily Herald), Archie Ledbrooke (Daily Mirror), Henry Rose (Daily Express), Eric Thompson (Daily Mail) and former Manchester City and England goalkeeper Frank Swift (News of the World). Two members of the aircraft crew and two other passengers also died.

There were also many other terrible repercussions as a result of the crash. Defender Jackie Blanchflower and winger Johnny Berry were so badly injured that they were unable to ever play football again. Manager Matt Busby, too, suffered injuries that were almost fatal and he was so close to death that he was given the last rites on three occasions.

Thankfully, through skilful and patient treatment by the surgeons and nursing staff of the Rechts der Isar Hospital in Munich, he pulled through. After a period of convalescence, Busby returned to football management but, understandably, it was a long time before he got back to his usual self.

Good pals as well as colleagues, Jimmy Murphy and Bert Whalley oversaw an unprecedented measure of success in the Youth Cup prior to the latter's tragic death at Munich

FEBRUARY 1958

From a football perspective, the tragedy was a loss of incalculable magnitude from United's point of view. The two youngest players to perish were Eddie Colman and Duncan Edwards, both just 21 years-old and already with nearly 300 first-team appearances between them. Billy Whelan and David Pegg were only a year older than Colman and Edwards, and they had shared almost 250 games in senior colours at the time of their deaths. Mark Jones, a rugged, dependable and likeable Yorkshireman, was only 24 when the tragedy struck. Jones had amassed 120 starts for the first-team, while Salford-born Geoff Bent was 25 and had gathered twelve First Division appearances prior to Munich.

Twenty-six year-old Tommy Taylor, then the club's record signing, had totalled an incredible 128 goals in just 189 appearances in United's number nine shirt. The oldest of the players who died was club captain Roger Byrne, who lost his life just two days away from his 29th birthday having amassed 277 games for the Reds.

On the international front, the demise of Taylor, Byrne and Edwards was a massive blow to England's hopes of winning the World Cup in Sweden later that year as all three were established internationals and had been automatic choices for England prior to their deaths. Also in receipt of a full England cap, David Pegg would almost certainly have added many more to his collection had he survived.

Billy Whelan's death robbed the Republic of Ireland of one of its rising stars, his fatality coming at a time when he was just beginning to stake a regular place in the Eire XI. Northern Ireland, too, suffered through the loss of Jackie Blanchflower's enforced retirement.

In human terms, the tragedy was of colossal proportions. The players who died or were badly injured were young men who played football for a living, and they were also husbands, fathers, fiancés, sons, brothers and friends. They were also like personal friends to the thousands of United supporters who thronged to Old Trafford every other Saturday, as well as the millions who could only follow their buccaneering exploits through the media.

Mercifully, several on board, including some of United's staff, survived the horrific smash as Ken Morgans, Bobby Charlton, Albert Scanlon, Harry Gregg, Bill Foulkes, Dennis Viollet, Blanchflower and Berry were all spared. Of those who were able to continue, it is generally regarded that Morgans would never reach his post-Munich potential whereas Scanlon and Viollet looked to have recovered their previous form initially only to then suffer from their experiences at a later date.

Forty-eight hours after the crash, the senior Reds were due to take on top-of-the-table Wolves at Old Trafford, a game which was postponed along with the Reserves' match at Aston Villa. The fixtures for United's 'A' and 'B' teams and Juniors were also cancelled as the Football Association and the Football League sympathetically allowed the club time to reorganise.

Jimmy Murphy was the man who was tasked with steering the United ship through those stormy waters. After visiting Munich to see the extent of the damage for himself, Murphy and the United directors decided that it would be in everyone's best interest to relocate the senior playing staff away from Manchester and so the Welshman accompanied those who could be considered for first-team duty, including some of the crash survivors, to the Norbreck Hydro Hotel in Blackpool.

Pictured below as it was in the 1950's, the object of moving to the hotel was in order to try to escape the intense interest shown by the national and international press in the tragedy.

It was Murphy's unenviable task to assemble a team to represent Manchester United when the authorities deemed that the time was right for them to resume their on-field commitments. Thirteen most sad and sorrowful days had passed, in which the depressing task of burying the dead was undertaken, when the Reds were plunged back into competitive action with a rearranged F.A. Cup tie against Sheffield Wednesday under floodlights. An emotionally fuelled Old Trafford was packed to bursting when a patched up team consisting of two emergency signings, Ernie Taylor from Blackpool and Stan Crowther from Aston Villa, two crash survivors, Harry Gregg and Bill Foulkes, and a mixture of Reserves and current youth team players emerged from the tunnel.

Besides Taylor and Crowther, twenty year-old Shay Brennan also made his first-team debut that evening. Stationed in the outside-left position, Brennan scored twice to assist the Reds into the Fifth Round, a victory completed by Alex Dawson's registering of a third United goal. When one-armed referee Alf Bond of London signalled 'time played', Murphy's patched-up marvels had assisted the club to take the first tentative step on the long haul back to recovery.

The club's Central League commitments resumed on the 22nd February, coincidentally against Sheffield Wednesday, when a side comprising of David Gaskell, Barry Smith, Les Cummings, Bobby English, Reg Holland, Harold Bratt, Tommy Spratt, Bobby Harrop, Jackie Mooney, Johnny Giles and Reg Hunter lost 4-0. All eleven had come through the Old Trafford junior ranks, their relative inexperience telling in the scoreline. Whereas the likes of Bratt, Smith, Hunter and Spratt had only made sporadic appearances in the Reserves, post-Munich they were utilised at that level much more frequently while others who had never before featured in the Central League found themselves competing in the higher grade.

In the week following the Reserves' defeat at Hillsborough, amateur internationals Warren Bradley, Bob Hardisty and Derek Lewin offered their services to United and the three Bishop Auckland players would prove a valuable addition to the club's second string resources. Bradley was a particularly fine acquisition, so much so that Matt Busby eventually persuaded him to sign professional forms and the striker went on to nail down a senior place in addition to winning full England honours.

The 'A' and 'B' teams also resumed on the 22nd February, the former with the likes of Spratt, Giles and Hunter missing from their ranks while the unfamiliar names of Cooper, Street, Baker and Gillespie appeared as names on the team sheet. With the 'A' side plunging to a 3-0 home defeat by Bury, the 'B' eleven enjoyed a much more satisfying result by winning 4-1 at Blackburn with newcomers Lee and White in the side.

It was as late as the 1st March before the Juniors got going again, when a 17-0 massacre of Timperley Methodists just edged the earlier 16-0 slamming of Knutsford to give them their biggest win of the season, and debutants Reavey and Birch both registered hat-tricks.

NORBRECK HYDRO & QUEENS DRIVE, NORBRECK.

1957-58

1) David Gaskell	9) Nobby Lawton
2) Barry Smith	10) Johnny Giles
3) Les Cummings	11) Jimmy Elms
4) Nobby Stiles	
5) Reg Holland	
6) Harold Bratt	
7) Graham Smith	
8) Tommy Spratt	

1) Billy Brough	9) Barry Walker
2) Roger Collinson	10) Archie Taylor
3) Geoff Palmer	11) Johnny Meredith
4) Keith Howarth	
5) Mike Quinlan	
6) Tony Cope	
7) Gerry Bedford	
8) Barry Dunn	

MARCH 1958

MANCHESTER UNITED 6 v 2 **DONCASTER ROVERS**

Elms, Lawton, Palmer (o.g.), Smith G., Spratt (2)

Collinson (pen), Meredith

fifth round

Wednesday 19th

Kick-off 7.30 p.m.

Attendance 16,899

United's Sputnik starts a rout

While everything was still in a state of flux due to the shattering circumstances of Munich, interest in the Youth Cup resumed six weeks after the air crash with the visit to Old Trafford of Doncaster Rovers.

Although the Yorkshire club have been forced to endure five seasons in the comparative wilderness of non-league football in recent years, in early 1958 their divisional status was only one step below that of top-flight football. The fact that their juniors had disposed of Grimsby Town (2-1, away), Nottingham Forest (1-0 at home), Barnsley (3-1 at home) and Sunderland (4-3, away) indicated that they possessed a youth system which stood comparison with most other clubs at that time.

Understandably, the Reds had a short-term need to channel all of their available resources into the requirements of the senior side and the consequence of that overriding priority meant that Alex Dawson and Mark Pearson were overlooked for selection. Jimmy Murphy needed to take into consideration United's involvement in the F.A. Cup semi-final against Fulham at Villa Park on the following Saturday and both Pearson and Dawson were firmly in his plans for that game.

Nobby Lawton was chosen as the obvious candidate to replace Dawson, but finding a successor for Pearson wasn't quite as straightforward. Murphy decided to throw a newcomer into the fray in order to solve that particular selection problem and he was Graham Smith, a winger who could operate on either side of the park. The Stockport wing-man's C.V. revealed that he had already spent a brief spell on the books of Blackburn and his and Lawton's inclusion brought about a re-jigging of the forward places.

The match programme for the Doncaster game contained a poignant transcript of a message from Matt Busby that had been recorded at his hospital bed in Munich. The manager relayed the news that both he and the players who were still hospitalised were now off the danger list and he went on to praise the work of Head Surgeon, Professor Maurer, and the staff of the Munich hospital where he had come so close to death.

Even at a time of immense personal grief and suffering, Busby said that *'it is wonderful to hear that the club have reached the semi-final of the F.A. Cup'*. He went on to extend his *'best wishes to everyone'* before concluding his message, in a way that only a great man can, with the sentence, *'Finally, may I just say God bless you all'*.

Totally ignoring their role as rank underdogs, the Rovers were right out of the blocks as the game got underway and in the first attack of note Archie Taylor's shot was almost turned over the goal-line by United's Les Cummings. The early stages undisputedly belonged to the visitors who, without severely testing Gaskell's goal again, were territorially well on top for almost half an hour.

In the 29th minute, it was down to United's wingers to shake off Doncaster's dominance when they conspired to bring about the opening goal. Debut boy Smith got the move underway when coming into possession and he beat a hasty track down the touchline. Smith made enough space for himself to centre precisely and the unmarked Jimmy Elms brought about a suitable conclusion when butting the ball beyond Brough.

The Reds had been badly in need of the fillip that Elms' conversion gave them and it came as their cue to take complete control of the game. Once the 'Goal This Way' sign had been discovered, the path along it was trodden more and more frequently and two more strikes from United counted on the score sheet in double-quick time, both resulting from Tommy Spratt efforts. Following a defence-splitting pass from Johnny Giles, the inside-right nipped in for the Reds' second with an expert use of his boot and Spratt was soon being congratulated again when measuring a neat and clinical header past Brough via a Nobby Lawton cross.

Four minutes after the resumption, the Rovers were staring at the end of their cup road when United racked up a fourth. A move started by one Nobby, Lawton, was completed by another, Stiles, whose strike was on its course into the netted enclosure despite glancing off Doncaster's Geoff Palmer before doing so.

The match's showpiece came right on three-quarter time. A dazzlingly memorable goal from the bubbling Smith it was too, when a determined run along the perimeter by United's number seven left three of the Doncaster team standing in his wake. Smith kept his flying momentum going while homing in on his intended target, and before any Doncaster defenders could get anywhere near to closing him down, and by now positioned on the edge of the visitors' penalty area, Smith rocketed the ball under a goalkeeper who could do no more than groan as it passed him. It was easily the highlight of the night and to a man, every spectator in the crowd stood to applaud an astonishing piece of virtuoso skill.

With everything now rosy in the garden, United allowed a touch of slackness into their game and 5-0 soon changed to 5-1 when they conceded to a Johnny Meredith goal. Nobby Lawton then hit back to make it 6-1 before Doncaster scored another through a Roger Collinson penalty to take the final score to 6-2.

In a game peppered with eight goals, the supporters were treated to a fine evening's entertainment and it meant, of course, that the youth team had now emulated the senior side by reaching a semi-final of their own.

Three days later, the first eleven drew 2-2 with Fulham in the penultimate stage of the F.A. Cup, an outcome which necessitated a replay at Highbury the following week. A hat-trick from Alex Dawson and one goal each from Shay Brennan and Bobby Charlton added up to more than Fulham's three, the result meaning that the senior Reds were at Wembley for the second year in succession.

Recent recruit Graham Smith opened his Youth Cup goal account with a fabulous individual effort which mesmerised the Doncaster defence

1) David Gaskell	9) Bernard Poole	1) John Cullen	9) Ted Farmer
2) Barry Smith	10) Johnny Giles	2) Phil Kelly	10) Brian Perry
3) Les Cummings	11) Jimmy Elms	3) Gordon Yates	11) Des Horne
4) Nobby Stiles		4) John Kirkham	
5) Reg Holland		5) Grenville Palin	
6) Harold Bratt		6) Les Cocker	
7) Graham Smith		7) Gerry Mannion	
8) Tommy Spratt		8) Cliff Durandt	

MANCHESTER UNITED 1 v 1 WOLVERHAMPTON WANDERERS

Spratt *Farmer*

1957-58

APRIL 1958

Tuesday 22nd

Kick-off 7.00 p.m.

Attendance 16,521

semi-final 1st leg

Now back in the Youth Cup semi-final for the sixth consecutive time, old foes would have to be disposed of if the club's unbroken run was to be extended still further, a direct result of United being drawn out of the hat right next to Wolves. It meant a third high level Youth Cup encounter between the two clubs in just six seasons and consistent with past meetings in the tournament, the opening leg was scheduled for Manchester. Because the make-up of one half of the final was already settled, with Chelsea waiting for the outcome of the United v. Wanderers encounters, the ties promised to be equally as engrossing as the previous four clashes.

Wolves hadn't figured as prominently in the Youth Cup since their appearances in the 1953 and 1954 finals and it was to their eternal credit that the Molineux production line seemed to have undergone a sharp upturn in terms of unearthing talent and consequent results on the pitch. It seemed only right, therefore, that the Wolverhampton club's continued faith in developing young blood received a proper acknowledgement from the editor of the programme for the initial game at Old Trafford:

Tonight the youth of the First Division Champions provide the opposition. Could this be a youthful prelude to a senior meeting in the F.A. Charity Shield?

Like our own club, the Wolves concentrate on youth as a foundation on which to build for ultimate strength. The post-war success of the Molineux club, coupled with that of United, is a high tribute to the fundamental soundness of this policy. There is no concealing the fact that the rivalry in searching for and recruiting stars of the future is no less keen than that of the clashes between our respective teams on the field.

Tonight's game recalls the finals of 1952/53 and 1953/54, the first two seasons of this competition. If it is anything akin in quality and excitement to those clashes, then the spectators are due for a real treat.

It had proved a hard slog to the semi-final for the Wanderers as they needed no less than three replays in order to progress at various stages.

Next door neighbours West Bromwich Albion became their first victims, falling 6-1 at Molineux after a 2-2 draw at The Hawthorns, and Aston Villa were later bounced out of the tournament by three to nothing at Villa Park. Stoke City were next to take a knock-out, 3-2 at the Victoria Ground after thinking they had done the hard work by forcing a 2-2 result in Wolverhampton. Leicester City then got a 9-0 panning at Molineux before Bolton Wanderers were ousted by a margin of 3-1 at Burnden Park following a 1-1 draw in the Midlands.

Despite over half of their side speaking with Black Country accents, the origins of the remaining members gave an indication as to the size of the net the club had cast in their quest for youthful talent. Goalkeeper John Cullen and right-back Phil Kelly were picked up while attached to Dublin clubs while Grenville Palin was a graduate of Wolves' famous Yorkshire 'nursery' side, Wath Wanderers.

Hailing from Burtonwood, Gerry Mannion was pinched from under the noses of a number of interested parties from the North-West. The real extent of the Molineux scouting system, though, was demonstrated by the inclusion in their forward-line of Cliff Durandt and Des Horne, both recruited from as far away as South Africa. There was an obvious strength down the left side of the team as half-back Les Cocker and inside-forward Brian Perry were already in receipt of England Youth honours.

Despite the importance of the game, there was still no release from first-team duty for either Alex Dawson or Mark Pearson because, with an F.A. Cup final looming into view, that course of action was considered quite necessary and wasn't at all unexpected.

If Jimmy Murphy hadn't been required to contend with enough problems over the past few weeks by having to run the football side of the club almost single-handedly, he was now faced with a selection headache when he could most have done without it. The coach's problem centred on Dawson's deputy Nobby Lawton, who was ruled out by a bout of pneumonia, and with options somewhat limited, Murphy elected to bring in Bernard Poole to fill the centre-forward position.

The Wolverhampton Express & Star recorded the thrills and spills of it all:

Just when it seemed certain that Wolves would end the first leg of their F.A. Youth Cup semi-final at Old Trafford last night a goal to the good, Manchester United, in extra-time allowed for injuries, made a last minute assault.

The ball flashed across the Wolves' goal, was kicked away, returned, and, in the ensuing mêlée, one of the United forwards sent in a point-blank shot. Down on the ball went goalkeeper Cullen, who had earlier brought off several daring saves. This time, however, he could only parry the ball, so fierce was the shot, and before he could even realise where it had dropped, inside-right Spratt had driven it into the net. The 16,521 spectators let out a roar of delight and the match ended 1-1.

The scene is thus set for another tremendous battle in the second leg at the Molineux Grounds tomorrow night for the right to meet Chelsea in the final.

It was the most closely contested youth game since the clubs met at Molineux in the competition four years ago.

Wolves took the lead just before the interval. Palin drove a long free kick into the Manchester area, where Perry headed on to Farmer. The tall centre-forward controlled as the ball dropped and drove first time past Gaskell, who had done well 24 hours earlier with the full might of the Wolves first eleven before him.

Wolves' lead gave the game fresh impetus in the second half, and as often as United went near to levelling, so Wolves went close to getting further ahead.

With the result, nobody could have cause for complaint, for these were evenly matched sides both playing a bright brand of football. Wolves' defenders in the United spell of pressure were magnificent. Palin was the cool commander in the side, and around him were henchmen of strength.

The football was never haphazard. Durandt and Perry ran themselves into the ground in the Wolves' attack, and there were flashes of quick-fire football from wingers Horne and Mannion, of whom, however, were facing stiffer opposition than usual.

The unanimous opinion of those inside Old Trafford was that the game had been an unqualified thriller. The Daily Mail match reporter was at pains to point out the qualities of the two sets of players and recorded that the second leg was set to be a classic *'if it is anything like last night's keen and exciting battle'.*

Highlighting opportunities scorned by the Reds in the first half, the Mail's scribe wrote *'the speedy dashes of home right winger Graham Smith laid on two good scoring chances, but first Jimmy Elms and then John Giles were faulty with their shooting'* and he then recorded *'Elms had the misfortune to hit a Wolves upright on another occasion, and in this hectic 36 minutes Smith also missed an open goal'.*

Later turning his comments to the away side, his article also stated *'Wolves, packing well in defence, withstood the assault, and began to create their own chances through dominant wing halves'* before revealing *'their goal, by centre-forward Ted Farmer, resulted from a defensive mistake by Norbert Stiles'.*

The piece ended with the Mail man offering the opinion that *'United enjoyed their second half supremacy and well earned their late reward'.*

Striker Bernard Poole, who was thrown in at the deep end against Wolves

103

1957-58

1) John Cullen	9) Ted Farmer
2) Phil Kelly	10) Brian Perry
3) Gordon Yates	11) Des Horne
4) John Kirkham	
5) Grenville Palin	
6) Les Cocker	
7) Gerry Mannion	
8) Cliff Durandt	

1) David Gaskell	9) Bernard Poole
2) Barry Smith	10) Johnny Giles
3) Les Cummings	11) Jimmy Elms
4) Nobby Stiles	
5) Reg Holland	
6) Harold Bratt	
7) Graham Smith	
8) Tommy Spratt	

APRIL 1958

WOLVERHAMPTON WANDERERS 3 (4) v (2) 1 **MANCHESTER UNITED**

Farmer, Horne, Mannion — Spratt

Thursday 24th
Kick-off 7.00 p.m.
Attendance 14,311

semi-final 2nd leg

UNITED YOUTHS RELEASE TROPHY GRIP AT LAST

With the two sets of combatants hardly finding the time to draw breath before the return game two days later, the following match preview appeared in the Wolverhampton Express & Star:

Prospects of tonight's F.A. Youth Cup semi-final second leg at Molineux being a repeat of Tuesday's 1-1 thriller at Old Trafford are brightened by the announcement that both Wolves and Manchester United are to field unchanged sides.

One effect of this is that goalkeeper Gaskell will have the unusual experience of playing against the Wolves for the third time in four days – he was also the goalkeeper in the First Division match on Monday.

Both teams include youth internationals, United counting Gaskell, Smith and Holland and Wolves having Cocker and Perry.

Gaskell and Smith were schoolboy internationals as was, in his native Eire, inside-left Giles, a most polished junior player.

In a game which bore comparison with any United had been involved in during their illustrious reign as five-times winners of the Youth Cup, spectators were privileged to see a performance of power, passion, pace and poise.

It was third time lucky for followers of the Wolves, who at last witnessed a victory over the young Reds, and the Wolverhampton Express & Star once again told it how it was:

All previous youth games at Molineux paled into something approaching insignificance by comparison with last night's super thriller which took the young Wolves, on a 4-2 aggregate, to their third F.A. Youth Cup final and, at the same time, brought the first defeat in the six years of the tournament to mighty Manchester United.

It was a double Wolves' achievement that at last brought the house down, and the after-match demonstration by youngsters who invaded the pitch could not have been more intense if the team had won the trophy itself.

Before they can celebrate this, however, they have to get the better of Chelsea, against whom they play a two-legged final next week – at Stamford Bridge next Tuesday (7.30), and at Molineux on Thursday (7.0).

Making last night's game so exciting was the way in which it rose to a second half crescendo after the first had fallen a little below what many of the 14,311 crowd had expected. It was as though these lads, playing their second tough game in three days, saved their best until last, as youngsters are wont to do. The result – a climax that simply bubbled with excitement, as during the last ten minutes Wolves turned a 1-1 draw into a 3-1 win.

Two devastating runs from South African left-winger Horne turned the tide. First, with ten minutes left to play, he scored himself, and then, in the last minute, he got clear to lay a pass at the feet of Mannion, who propelled the ball into the net from a narrow angle.

There can seldom have been more evenly matched sides than these, and both added something to the atmosphere by punctuating some intelligent football with bursts of impetuosity and overeagerness. United frequently moved the ball sweetly, with Giles the tactician. Wolves, the more direct, kept things going at the harder pace, thanks to some inspired driving power from wing-halves Kirkham and Cocker.

Because Wolves did most of the chasing, the goals seemed inevitable, but they had to wait until three minutes after the interval for Farmer to equalise Spratt's six-minute header which put United in such good fettle. Before the change-over, Palin missed a penalty.

And so it came to pass that with those two late goals, Wolverhampton Wanderers became the team to finally end Manchester United's total domination of the F.A. Youth Challenge Cup. The Reds' exit from the tournament severed a run which stretched back over a period of five and a half years and encompassed no less than 53 ties.

There were mixed responses to the Reds' defeat at Molineux. While some observers were only too happy to praise United's Youth Cup achievements, there were others who felt that it was about time the club's vice-like grip on the trophy was shaken off. Nevertheless, even in 1958 it was said that no other club would ever manage such a prolonged period of supremacy in the tournament, a prediction that has irrefutably turned into fact.

Within seven days of defeating United, Wolves had, somehow justifiably, gone on to win the trophy for themselves, even though the circumstances surrounding their triumph were absolutely remarkable.

The first leg of the final, at Stamford Bridge, was a nightmare for the Wanderers, who may just have been suffering somewhat slightly from their considerable exertions against United the week before. The Chelsea team, which contained a certain Jimmy Greaves, was in an unstoppable mood and sped into what any sane and reasonable football follower would have assumed to be an unassailable 5-1 lead.

In a comeback of almost unbelievable proportions, Wolves completely turned the tables on the Blues and eventually won the game with a 6-1 victory on their home patch. The aggregate, therefore, was 7-6, a result that at last placed Wolves on the winners' rostrum.

The game is rightly remembered as one of the greatest ever seen at Molineux and it marked a personal triumph for centre-forward Ted Farmer, whose four goals in the second game caused Chelsea the most pain. For their extraordinary feat, Farmer and his team-mates were each awarded a ten shillings (50p) win bonus.

There was hardly enough space for the Youth Cup in the Wolves' trophy cabinet, it being just one of six pieces of silverware the club claimed as their bounty for the season. With the exception of the F.A. Cup, the Wanderers had won every trophy they competed for as, while the seniors took the First Division championship, their Reserves claimed the Central League, the Wolves third eleven chipped in with the Birmingham & District League title and their fourth team stormed to a Worcestershire Combination League and Worcestershire Combination Cup double.

They were certainly happy days at the Molineux.

When the disappointment of losing their Youth Cup crown had subsided, the time came for the players, officials, supporters and other observers to reflect on whether United could have lifted the trophy for a sixth time. Naturally, there was a strong opinion that the loss of Mark Pearson and Alex Dawson had cost the Reds the chance of extending their fabulous winning sequence. Whether that view would have turned to reality can, of course, only ever be speculated on.

The facts, however, do tend to favour the theory in that United's management had been put into a position where they were unable to use what were arguably two of the most influential members of their side. Mark Pearson had featured in 22 consecutive Youth Cup ties before the Munich tragedy and although viewed as more of a provider of chances, the inside-forward actually managed to contribute twelve goals, an average that was better than one every two games. Dawson had taken part in one game less than Pearson, notching his name on various score sheets on no less than 43 occasions, which represented over two goals per game.

The inescapable fact was that the Reds lost their semi-final by a 4-2 aggregate margin. Could those two highly talented teenagers have contributed the difference over 180 minutes? On the balance of probability, most neutrals would almost certainly have answered 'yes' to that question and it would not be unfair on Wolves to suggest it was the absence of Dawson and Pearson that scuppered United's chance of a place in the final.

But it wasn't to be, and with over half of the team retaining their Youth Cup eligibility over the summer, there was always next season........

COPE, Ronald (1952/53)

Born: Crewe, 5th October 1934
Height: 5ft. 10ins., Weight: 11st. 7lbs.
Role: Centre-half
Career: The Borough School (Crewe)/ Crewe Boys/ Cheshire Boys/ England Boys/ **UNITED**: Am. May 1950 Pro. October 1951/ **Luton Town** August 1961/ **Northwich Victoria** December 1963/ **Winsford United** July 1968/ **Nantwich** October 1968 to April 1969

An archetypal stopper-style centre-half, strong in the air, hard in the tackle and possessing a well-built frame that enabled him to compete on equal terms with the powerful centre-forwards of the time, Ronnie Cope followed his father into the world of professional football. Prior to the Second World War, pivot George Cope was attached to Crewe Alexandra and his son obviously inherited his defending abilities. Employing a 'take no prisoners' ethic, George's uncompromising qualities earned him a most graphic nickname as he was known as 'Killer' Cope.

Young Ronnie passed through the stages of school, town and county football with flying colours before appearing four times for his country as a schoolboy in 1950, all of the games ending in English victories. Wales were crushed by six goals to one at Hillsborough while Eire put up stiff resistance before ultimately succumbing 3-2 in Dublin. England then completed a double over Scotland by winning 3-1 in Glasgow and 8-2 at Wembley.

His appearance at the Empire Stadium marked not only the first occasion that Wembley was utilised for an England schoolboy international fixture, it was also the first time that such a game was televised. That day's match programme noted that he *'had played for Crewe (Boys) for three years and Cheshire (Boys) for two'* and *'represented Cheshire last year in athletics'*.

Following the contest against Scotland in Glasgow, he learned of United's interest through a conversation with Bert Whalley, who handed him an envelope which was to be given to his father. The United coach, who was at the Ibrox game in order to run the rule over the boy's capabilities, relayed his findings back to Old Trafford and, shortly after, the fifteen year-old was astonished when Matt Busby and scout Louis Rocca pulled up outside his house in an Austin A7 car.

Having accepted the opportunity to sign as an amateur, over the next two years he developed in the junior and Manchester League teams and also saw a little action in the Central League. Nominated as captain for the opening Youth Cup tie in October 1952, he led the side through eight straight victories and a draw which climaxed on the 9th May 1953 at Molineux when, on behalf of the winners of the competition, he became the very first skipper to accept the trophy. A proud moment for him personally, besides being a truly historic day for Manchester United, as the oldest member of the team he was ineligible for the following season's tournament.

With Mark Jones doggedly holding down a place in the Reserves, he was forced to continue mainly in the junior sides for lengthy periods and it was only from March 1955 onwards, when Jones moved up to the seniors, that his promotion became more lasting.

Virtually ever-present the following term as the Reds won the Central League, in September 1956 Matt Busby concluded that the time was right to blood him in the First Division. His senior debut was against Arsenal at Highbury and, even though United beat the Gunners 2-1, it wasn't until the April of the following year before he sampled any more first-team fare. For his second shot in the higher sphere the outcome was another victory, the Reds defeating Burnley by two goals to nil at home.

Then returning to life in the Central League, at the beginning of the 1957/58 season Jones and Jackie Blanchflower haggled over the senior and Reserves' centre-half positions and so he was moved to right full-back. Even utilised at centre-forward, the experiment yielded four goals in three games, and he was on target in each and every one of those matches.

The events of the early weeks of 1958 dictated that he would take a more prominent role at the club. Because of Jones' death and the career-ending injuries to Blanchflower at Munich, he suddenly found himself as Jimmy Murphy's number one choice centre-half. He could just as easily have been a passenger on the fateful aeroplane, because club captain Roger Byrne was carrying a knock before the journey to Belgrade and the defender was initially nominated as his replacement. At the eleventh hour, Geoff Bent, a natural full-back understudy for Byrne, travelled instead and he was, sadly, one of the eight player casualties.

On the day of the crash Cope was shopping in Manchester city centre with his wife when news of the disaster broke. On that terrible afternoon he witnessed death at close quarters, watching in horror as an elderly lady was fatally struck by a bus.

He was thrust into the first-team immediately following the plane tragedy and missed only one fixture from then until the end of that term. With resources strained due to the fatalities and injuries caused at Munich, United picked up only nine further points in their league efforts but succeeded in knocking out Sheffield Wednesday, West Brom and Fulham to make it into the F.A. Cup final against Bolton. At age 23, a return to Wembley in May 1958 was the highest watermark of his football career and, despite losing the game, the players were rightly acknowledged as heroes for their achievement in reaching the end of season showpiece.

As the media glare over the disaster began to slowly fade away, the Reds' long-term recovery began in earnest. He played in one F.A. Cup and 32 league games in the 1958/59 campaign, when his invaluable contribution assisted in propelling the club to second spot in the table.

The 1959/60 season gave him his best appearance figures for United. After sitting out the opening two fixtures, which both ended in defeats, his recall encompassed all remaining 43 league and F.A. Cup matches with the club finishing in a creditable seventh position in the First Division.

Featuring in six out of the opening nine games of the next term, he lost his place when Busby switched Bill Foulkes from full-back into the middle of the defence, and a 3-1 home defeat by Wolves in September 1960 proved to be his last game in United's senior eleven. Including one Football League Cup and two European Cup ties, he had made 106 appearances for the first-team but, with a recall becoming less and less likely, he was transferred to Luton within a year for the considerable sum of £10,000.

One of a number of new signings made by Luton manager Sam Bartram in 1961, the fee involved meant that he was easily the most costly acquisition. Settling in the Dunstable area and immediately installed as club skipper, his first year was spent in the senior side at Kenilworth Road. Then, when Bartram left amid murmurings of interference from the board, events took a drastic turn for the worse.

Bartram penned a newspaper article shortly after in which it was claimed that most of the Luton directors hadn't wanted to back his decision to sign Cope. From that point on things began to go sour for the defender and when he made only three further starts in the 1962/63 campaign, it didn't take a genius to work out that his face simply didn't fit anymore.

With his prospects of regular first-team football having tumbled to zero, he was informed that he would be allowed to leave if a buyer willing to pay £5,000 for his signature could be found. Because no party was prepared to shell out that sort of money for someone who had spent most of the previous year in the Reserves, the situation became untenable and so he simply packed his bags and returned to his roots in Cheshire.

A move to Crewe looked the most likely outcome for a while but, after another article which described him as *'a footballer in chains'* appeared in the Daily Mail, the interest from Gresty Road suddenly cooled. The Mail feature was followed up in December 1963 with the news that he had chosen to become a part-time professional with Northwich Victoria. It was a suitable compromise as Northwich obtained a star man without having to open their cheque book and it also brought about an end to the animosity between Luton and their former captain.

Controversy did follow him for a little while longer, because his link-up with the Vics prompted a letter of complaint to the club from the Northwich Chronicle. The newspaper was unhappy over the lack of information they had been provided about the deal that took him from Luton to the Drill Field and the Vics responded by pointing out that the Professional Footballers' Association had, along with the Daily Mail, given them enormous assistance in what was quoted as a *'very delicate negotiation'*.

Making nearly 30 appearances for Northwich before the end of the season, they were followed up with approximately 50 starts in the 1964/65 campaign. His form during that period alerted several Football League clubs, who made tentative enquiries regarding his availability. In the weeks leading up to the kick-off of the 1965/66 term, Bradford City's approach fell flat when their target made it perfectly clear that he was happy to remain at the Drill Field. Between October 1965 and January 1966 he was called on to take temporary charge of team affairs and combined those duties with a further 50-plus games for the season.

In February 1968, Northwich decided to dispense with the services of their manager, an extremely unpopular decision that moved the entire playing staff to sign a petition requesting his immediate reinstatement. When their former boss burned his bridges by accepting an alternative post, Cope was widely tipped to get the job. The rumour was partly fact anyway as, with the help of a club director, he had taken over the mantle from the moment that the vacancy arose.

Instead, the Northwich hierarchy confounded everyone by giving the position to a one-time Eire international by the name of Noel Kelly, who decided to release the centre-back a few weeks later. He left having totalled 237 games, with fourteen goals scored, in a Northwich strip.

Then turning down offers from Holyhead Town and Sandbach Ramblers in order to join Northwich's near neighbours Winsford United, despite being made skipper he made barely a dozen appearances for them.

He then moved to Nantwich, where he was also installed as captain. There was, of course, a certain amount of irony in his signing for the Dabbers, as sixteen years previously he had led Manchester United's youth team to a record-breaking 23-0 victory over his new club's 1952 youth side. The final game of his spell with Nantwich was in April 1969 when the Cheshire side came back to win 4-2 after earlier trailing 2-0 to Frickley Colliery. Those 90 minutes were his last in that standard of football.

A month later he made a welcome return to Northwich Victoria as their trainer/coach, filling the position until December 1971 before later becoming Witton Albion's second team manager for approximately twelve months. Continuing in a playing capacity in a local Sunday league, he finally stopped at the age of 46.

After severing links with football entirely he was able to devote more time to his work in the insurance business. In 1989, the Cheshire resident retired having completed 26 years with the Prudential.

SCANLON, Albert Joseph (1952/53, 1953/54)

Born: Hulme, Manchester, 10th October 1935
Died: Salford, 22nd December 2009
Height: 5ft. 10ins., Weight: 10st. 9lbs.
Role: Outside-left or outside-right
Career: **St. Wilfred's School (Hulme)/ Xaverian Grammar School (Rusholme)/ Manchester Boys/ Lancashire Boys/ UNITED**: Am. May 1951 Pro. December 1952/ **Newcastle United** November 1960/ **Lincoln City** February 1962/ **Mansfield Town** April 1963/ **Belper Town** August and September 1966/ **Altrincham** December 1966

Manchester United have now been credited with scoring over seven hundred goals in the Youth Cup since initially entering the competition in 1952 and the distinguished honour of opening that formidable account will forever belong to one Albert Joseph Scanlon.

Raised just a couple of miles from Old Trafford, he harboured ambitions of making football his living from an early age. While at St. Winifred's School he was once introduced to Johnny Carey, who was a guest celebrity at a presentation ceremony, and when the Reds' captain asked him what his ambition was, Scanlon, in front of a mass of Manchester City supporters, responded simply and confidently, *'To play for United'*. His reply raised a huge howl from the watching teachers and pupils, but it was he who had the last laugh as he was on the payroll at Old Trafford for the majority of a dynamic decade.

A naturally left-footed winger who could seemingly glide past defenders with exceptional acceleration and close ball control, his attribute of being able to adapt on the right-hand side of the pitch when required came in useful at various times. His bursts of speed frequently caused panic amongst opposing defenders and often led to shooting opportunities for himself or his team-mates.

As one of the stars of a talented Hulme Lads' Club side, in 1950 he was included in a Manchester Boys team that contested the two-legged English Schools' Trophy final with Swansea. Having qualified for the final without him, due to a misunderstanding about his age, Manchester blew their chances when surprisingly losing 1-0 at home after registering a 0-0 draw in South Wales.

He later saw service with Lancashire Boys and was invited to join United at Easter in 1951 following a visit to his home by Jimmy Murphy. Solely representing the Juniors in his first term, he was in his second year at the club, and had already progressed from the Colts to the 'A' team, when the Reds met Leeds in that historic First Round Youth Cup tie in October 1952. He stamped his name in the record books with the opening goal only to follow it by, in his words, *'nutmeg(ging) Jack Charlton before planting the ball past the goalkeeper'* for his second.

Scoring against Nantwich and facing Bury in the Second and Third Rounds respectively in November 1952, during the following month he signed as a professional and gained a first crack at Central League football.

His input towards the Youth Cup run continued with a goal against Barnsley in the Fifth Round and others in each of the semi-final games against Brentford. The late winner he claimed at Griffin Park in the opening tie effectively put United in the driving seat to reach the last stage.

From a total goals tally of 50 scored by the Reds on the successful cup trail, his seven, which included one in the first leg of the final, proved to be an immense contribution and before the campaign was over he was able to add Manchester League and Gilgryst Cup medals to an expanding collection.

During the 1953 close season he was chosen for all three of the youth team's friendly games in Ireland. Prior to embarking on the short tour, all of the squad were awarded club blazers and he was so proud of his new item of clothing that he was known to stop people in the street to ask them how it looked on him.

A cartilage operation soon halted his progress, causing him to miss more than half of the 1953/54 term. Once back to fitness he got in two or three games before being plunged into the dramatic Youth Cup quarter-final tie at Bexleyheath & Welling, and he then proceeded to catch up on lost time by emulating his feat of the previous campaign by scoring in both legs of the semi-finals, on this occasion against West Brom.

A day after the second leg of the final against Wolves he was included in the side that defeated Stockport 'A' 3-2 in the Gilgryst Cup final, a success which sat nicely alongside a second Manchester League title.

Seven months after the young Reds retained the Youth Cup, Scanlon was in the first-team. He had served only the briefest of apprenticeships with the Central League side and was blooded against Arsenal at Old Trafford in November 1954 when United won by two goals to one. He kept his place for a 2-0 defeat at West Brom to then stand down until the following March when recalled for a 1-0 home win over Burnley. A fortnight later he notched his opening First Division goal in a 2-1 loss to Everton at Old Trafford.

The game against Burnley heralded the beginning of twelve consecutive starts which extended until the end of the season, his accumulation of fourteen first-team appearances bringing him four goals. He had also played nine times for the Central League side as well as contributing to yet another Manchester League title.

The nineteen year-old began the 1955/56 term where he left the last one, still with the seniors, and featured in the opening six games prior to dropping out at the expense of David Pegg. With time on his side, and the valuable experience gained so far, his continuing improvement was evidenced when he scored seven times in 33 matches as the second eleven tied up the Central League championship.

Out of the senior frame for over eighteen months in total, towards the end of the 1956/57 First Division title winning campaign he reappeared five times. He reverted to the Reserves again for the start of the 1957/58 season, but events soon began to change in his favour. After deputising for Johnny Berry on the right wing for clashes against Newcastle and Spurs in November 1957, he then won a more lasting recall the following month by taking part in nine consecutive league and F.A. Cup games prior to the European Cup match against Red Star in Belgrade on the 5th February 1958.

Following United's negotiation through a tricky tie in Yugoslavia, and with his form good, there was the possibility that a place in the senior side could have become a more permanent arrangement. Twenty-four hours later and events had conspired to dash any immediate ambitions, all of which were put into perspective with the heavy toll taken on the lives of his close friends and club colleagues at Munich. Scanlon lay in the Rechts der Isar Hospital for a period of recuperation with leg, head and internal injuries and missed what remained of the term.

His recovery was such that he got off to a tremendous start at the beginning of the 1958/59 campaign, and goals against Nottingham Forest and Blackburn were trumped by a wonderful hat-trick against West Ham at Old Trafford in September 1958. Within a few weeks he had earned the first of five England under-23 caps as Poland were defeated 4-1 at Hillsborough and a second was secured a month later when Czechoslovakia were beaten 3-0 at Norwich.

It was undoubtedly his best ever season for, not only did he compete in every United first-team game while scoring a very creditable sixteen goals as second place in the First Division was achieved, he then won his final two under-23 caps in the space of a week following the 1959 F.A. Cup final. Assisting England to a 3-0 victory over Italy in Milan and a 2-2 draw with West Germany in Bochum, he made a further 34 league and F.A. Cup appearances for the Reds in the 1959/60 term and was also honoured with selection for the Football League.

Despite his tremendous efforts of the past couple of years, things then unexpectedly started going sour for him. A dip in form allied to Matt Busby's decision to switch Bobby Charlton to a wide position put him somewhat out on a limb, and after clocking up a further eight games he was sold to Newcastle in November 1960 for the sum of £17,500.

Signed by former United forward Charlie Mitten, the Magpies' manager was later widely, and incorrectly, reported as being his uncle. Unfortunately, the move was an extremely bad one as it soon became obvious to the newcomer that the club was already on the wane. They were relegated to the Second Division in 1961 and as a result he never really established himself. Making only 27 appearances over a period of sixteen months, in February 1962 he was transferred to Lincoln for the bargain price of £2,000.

The winger fared rather better at Sincil Bank, hitting twelve goals in 54 matches, but a little over a year later he moved again, this time to Mansfield. He proved an inspired capture by manager Tommy Cummings as a few weeks later the Stags climbed into the Third Division. The more fluid football promoted by Cummings patently suited him better and his true class immediately became obvious to the Field Mill supporters. Then missing only a sprinkling of matches over the next two years while the club established themselves in the higher sphere, during his last Football League campaign he registered another twenty games before being released, at the age of 30, in April 1966.

Throughout the summer weeks spent at Mansfield he had worked in a bakery to supplement the lower earnings footballers were forced to endure during the shutdown period. Continuing in that capacity after his contract expired, at the opening of the 1966/67 season he also signed for Belper Town and over a period of two months made just four appearances for the Midland League club before moving back north.

He then played a solitary game for Altrincham Reserves before dropping out of the paid game entirely. Later giving a hand to factory side Massey Ferguson, in the period around 1968 he was a regular for Ashfield Labour Club in the Eccles & District League.

Albert Scanlon secured employment at Salford docks and later went through a particularly tough period of unemployment. After coming through that dark spell, he settled into a position at the Colgate Palmolive factory in Trafford Park for a number of years and in more recent times could sometimes be seen on MUTV in his role as a soccer pundit.

Admitted to Salford Royal Hospital in October 2009 with pneumonia and kidney problems, he was in intensive care for approximately four weeks before passing away two months later. Numerous past and present Manchester United staff attended his funeral, and the hearse carrying his coffin stopped under the Munich Memorial at Old Trafford for a few moments before making its way to All Saints Church in Weaste. There, Father Shaun Braiden told mourners, *'For the moment a true Red has come marching in, but the real saints are bidding him 'Welcome'.'*

McGUINNESS, Wilfred (1953/54, 1954/55, 1955/56)

Born: Collyhurst, Manchester, 25th October 1937
Height: 5ft. 8ins., Weight: 10st. 7lbs.
Role: Left half-back
Career: Mount Carmel School (Blackley)/ Manchester Boys/ Lancashire Boys/ England Boys/ UNITED: Am. June 1953 Pro. November 1954 to 1961, re-registered September 1966 to May 1967

One of the outstanding prospects of United's fabulous intake of junior talent in 1953, Wilf McGuinness was, following Duncan Edwards, the second former England Boys captain to join the club in just over a year.

Born in the distinctly working-class suburb of Collyhurst, his family moved to Blackley when he wasn't much more than a baby. His prowess for football initially developed in the Scouts, and while attending Mount Carmel School he was chosen to represent the city at both cricket and soccer.

His inclusion in Manchester's cricket team extended over a four-year period, although a preference and undisguised flair for the winter game also saw him installed as captain of the Lancashire Boys football side. During his formative years, McGuinness was guided by his father, Lawrence, as well as his sports teacher and headmaster at Mount Carmel, James Mulligan. With the encouragement of his dad and the practical advice of Mr. Mulligan, who himself was once a professional footballer, he debuted for England Boys, as skipper, in a win over Northern Ireland at York in 1952.

He captained Manchester Boys through an unbeaten 1952/53 season as well as picking up four further England caps, also as skipper, in recognition of his appearances against Wales (twice), Eire and Scotland. When Cheshire Boys were defeated 5-1 by Manchester Boys at the Birkenhead RFU ground in the last week of May 1953, a brilliant schoolboy career came to an end and he marked the occasion by scoring one of the goals claimed by the away side. Three weeks later, despite overtures from a multitude of clubs including Bolton, Wolves and Chelsea, he joined United.

His decision to sign for the Reds centred on an invitation received from chief scout Joe Armstrong to attend the Old Trafford leg of the 1953 Youth Cup final. While watching the goings-on, the fifteen year-old was struck by the thought that if United's coaches had played their part in the huge margin of victory with the lads they had at their disposal, a few of whom weren't of international schoolboy standard, then surely he, as captain of his city, county and country, must have a great chance of making his name in the sport under their direction.

In choosing United he also simultaneously spurned the opportunity to join Manchester City. Like many Mancunians at that time, when the Reds were stationed at Maine Road in the early post-war years, he grasped every opportunity to watch both sides.

He was undoubtedly a marvellous acquisition and a template could have been fashioned from his many attributes in order to build a complete half-back. Purposeful and positive when driving forward, tough and tenacious in defence, his Trojan-like capacity for work and exceptional qualities of leadership for one so young set him apart from most of his peers. Unarguably, though, the shaker in his cocktail was that rarest of qualities; the ability to exude a winning mentality.

His United career began in time-honoured fashion with the Juniors and, so that there was another option available should he fail to make the grade, for just over a year he also held employment with a textile company in Manchester. His club debut came in September 1953 and he remained on the lower level for only half a dozen games or so after which he sported the Colts' number six jersey for the majority of the term.

His tenure in the Reds' youth team lasted the maximum three campaigns, starting at Goodison Park in October 1953 and ending at the Recreation Ground in May 1956. Including those games against Everton and Chesterfield respectively, he completed 27 consecutive Youth Cup ties, a competition record he shares with Bobby Charlton. He was present for final wins on three occasions and had the honour of captaining the side in his final season. Also capped four times at England Youth level during the same period, he was initially utilised in the Central League as early as March 1955 in a 2-0 win at West Brom.

His first start for the seniors came in the October of that year and ended in a 4-3 home win over Wolves. The following week he retained his place for a 4-4 draw at Aston Villa and then needed to wait until the penultimate game of the term at Sunderland for another opportunity. He scored one of the goals at Roker Park as the Reds came away with a point courtesy of a 2-2 draw and also featured in 33 of the Reserves' fixtures that term.

Over the next couple of years he began to appear more regularly in the first-team, starting with thirteen Football League appearances in the 1956/57 campaign. During the 1957 close season he made his fourth and last trip to the Blue Stars tournament in Switzerland where, having already accumulated a silver and two gold medals on three previous visits, he again strode the victory podium as Augsberg were beaten 2-0 in the final.

Claiming only eight more starts for the first-team in the 1957/58 term, the main reason for his inability to fully establish himself in the seniors just then was that he was faced with one of the most thankless tasks in English football, that of trying to dislodge the incomparable Duncan Edwards from the side.

During the campaign after Edwards' death he missed only three league and cup matches out of the entire fixture list. One of the games he was absent from was a 4-0 defeat at Wolves in October 1958, just prior to his 21st birthday, and the reason he wasn't at Molineux was because he was making his full England debut in a 3-3 draw with Northern Ireland in Belfast. His endeavours assisted United to second spot in the First Division and also won him three appearances for the national under-23 side, as well as a second full cap in a 2-1 defeat by Mexico in Mexico City in May 1959.

He completed a run of nineteen straight appearances for the Reds from the start of the 1959/60 term and also played for England's under-23's against Hungary at Goodison Park. Despite the progress made on both the domestic and international scenes, McGuinness was experiencing some discomfort in his leg, with a precautionary X-ray failing to pinpoint any particular problem.

In December he decided to drop out of the first-team for a week of recuperation. Then choosing to have a painkilling injection prior to a game with Stoke's Reserves at Old Trafford, in a fairly innocuous collision with an opponent, he was the casualty of a broken right leg. His fracture was just about as bad as they come and, after undergoing a bone graft along with suffering numerous complications over a period of many months, he was eventually, and very regretfully, forced to admit that his playing days were over.

After the physical pain and mental anguish he inevitably suffered from the time of his injury right through 1960, his future had begun to look infinitely brighter by the following year when, firstly, Matt Busby gave him a job on the United coaching staff in order to principally look after the youths and, secondly, in July 1961, he married his sweetheart, Beryl.

He absolutely relished his new role and, possessed of a bountiful enthusiasm and alert football brain, helped to bring along many United youngsters who would later establish themselves in the senior side. His knack of developing talent was recognised in 1963 when he was invited to coach the England Youth side under manager Pat Whelton. It was certainly a purple period for the national side at that level, as they captured the European Youth Tournament that year and then went on to retain it in 1964.

Later put in charge of the Reserves at Old Trafford, in 1966 he was asked by Alf Ramsey to assist established England trainers Les Cocker and Harold Shepherdson to coach the World Cup squad at Lilleshall. On that never-to-be-forgotten day when England defeated West Germany to claim the Jules Rimet trophy at Wembley, McGuinness travelled on the team bus, was in the dressing room for the last minute preparations prior to the game, and also attended the post-match celebrations which heralded this country's most celebrated sporting victory.

That September he made an on-field comeback for the Reserves, which commenced with a 4-1 win at Manchester City. While retaining his coaching duties, over the course of the campaign he made a couple of dozen Central League appearances and in November 1966 was even named as an unused substitute for a senior fixture at Leicester. With a new crop of young talent coming through the Old Trafford system, once more he elected to resume his efforts solely in coaching and a year later also took on the added responsibility of coaching and training the England under-23 squad.

When Matt Busby relinquished the reigns at Old Trafford in June 1969 after sitting in the Old Trafford hot seat since 1945, there was some surprise when he handed them over to the 31 year-old. Given the title of chief coach, it was a profoundly proud moment for the local man, who had already spent over half of his life as a Manchester United employee, to be given the task of taking over from one of the greatest football managers ever to pin up a team sheet.

His first year went well enough, with a 2-0 friendly win over a Welsh XI at Bangor and a short pre-season continental tour setting the tone. A 7-2 success over a Copenhagen Select side flashed encouraging signs and two days later a resounding 9-1 win was secured over FC Zurich. As the curtain rose on the 1969/70 campaign, the Reds were asked to travel to Selhurst Park where hosts Crystal Palace were beginning their maiden term in the top flight. A 2-2 draw ensued, and on that very same day his wife gave birth to their second daughter, Clare.

Following the game at Palace, the Reds went on a three-match losing streak before stabilising. The performance of the team often varied from superb to very bad, and excellent wins against Liverpool, 4-1 at Anfield, and West Brom, 7-0 at Old Trafford, were offset by a 5-1 reverse at Newcastle and a 4-0 defeat at Manchester City. Even though United ended their divisional obligations in a reasonable eighth position, three places higher than in Busby's last season in charge, the campaign is often remembered for the disappointment of two semi-final knock-outs.

In the League Cup, Manchester City again held the upper hand over United by putting them out at the penultimate stage on a 4-3 aggregate. The Reds were certainly unfortunate to go out to the men from Maine Road, but it was the 1970 F.A. Cup semi-final exit to Leeds that was by far the most hurtful. A couple of goalless events were fought out by the two Uniteds, firstly at Hillsborough and then at Villa Park, before a Billy Bremner strike in the second replay at Burnden Park ended McGuinness' hopes of leading out his beloved Reds at Wembley.

Finally assuming the title of manager in June 1970, his transition from a coaching role was hindered by a number of factors. It couldn't have helped that neighbours City were going through their best ever post-war period, a development which left United in a somewhat unfamiliar role as the 'second' team in the area. Also, the club's finest on-field asset, the brilliant George Best, was gaining a dubious reputation for certain social activities while some other squad members were either past their best days or simply not up to the task.

He was also blocked by the board in his attempts to bring emerging talents to the club, such as Malcolm McDonald, Peter Shilton, Mick Mills and Colin Todd, all of whom were known to him through working with the England under-23 squad. McGuinness was forced into making do with what was already at his disposal and he gave those already at the club, for example Alan Gowling, Don Givens, Jimmy Rimmer, Paul Edwards and Willie Watson, the chance to prove themselves. Undoubtedly, however, the biggest burden he bore was simply living in the shadow of Busby's achievements.

Results deteriorated rapidly in the opening period of the 1970/71 term when only five league wins, plus more semi-final heartache, on this occasion to Third Division Aston Villa in the League Cup, hastened his departure. On the 28th December 1970, he was informed that United's directors had asked Busby to resume as manager while he would be given back his previous job as a coach. The situation soon became unbearable and, on the 27th February 1971, he said a few sad farewells before leaving.

It was then that he found out who one of his true friends was when receiving a call from Alf Ramsey, as the national football supremo wanted him to accompany an F.A. XI squad on a tour to Australia in addition to performing associated coaching duties.

Upon his return to England, and following a short spell out of work, an offer to manage Greek side Aris Salonika landed in his lap. Despite having four children, he and his wife reasoned that the job would give his career some impetus and, in July 1971, they set off for the warmth of the Mediterranean sun. After two years at Aris Salonika he took up a managerial role at Panachaiki of Patras for twelve months. There were other offers to remain in Greece when his contract finished at Panachaiki but, with a young family to consider, he and Beryl felt it best to head homewards.

Arriving back in England in August 1974, for several months he spent two days a week coaching at Everton and also assisted Toffees' boss Billy Bingham to assess the Goodison Park club's forthcoming opponents.

In February 1975 he was back on the managerial merry-go-round at York City Football Club. In what he later described as *'three very eventful years'*, the Minstermen suffered the misfortune of sliding down from the Second Division to the Fourth. The club was in a sorry state financially and the new boss was told he could only sign free transfer players, which eventually included Steve James and Tony Young from Manchester United. Later reflecting that he *'had very little to work with'* as York's directors kept the purse strings firmly closed, initially the signs were encouraging as his charges did enough to stave off the drop at the end of the 1974/75 season.

The club was relegated a year later, though, and in 1977 they finished bottom of the Third Division. When he was dismissed that October, the Bootham Crescent outfit was 22nd in the Fourth Division and, taking in the whole span of his tenure, of 113 league games, only 27 had ended in victory.

Another period of unemployment followed, but by the beginning of 1978 he had returned to football in another sunny climate. Having been jointly asked by the Football Association and the Foreign Office, he took up a coaching post with the Jordanian national military football squad, who were preparing for an Arab tournament to be held in Syria. The training and coaching took place largely in Amman, with the competition itself held in Damascus, and, all told, he was away for five months.

He was once more employed in the English game when a coaching position at Hull presented itself in July 1978. Informing the local newspaper that he was *'delighted to get the job because Hull are a club that can go places, unlike little York'*, further comments made in the article indicated that he was glad to be free from the strains of management.

He did, in fact, make a playing appearance for Hull when going on as substitute in a pre-season game in Holland in 1979. By the December of that year events at Boothferry Park had taken a turn for the worse and, with the team having won only four out of 26 games that term, manager Ken Houghton was sacked along with McGuinness and the club's chief scout. A 7-2 defeat at Brentford was the last straw for the Hull directors, who felt that a full managerial clear-out was required.

He was again without work for a spell and, after undergoing a period of the required training, was ready to take a completely different path by becoming a publican. Fortunately for the world of football, a call seemingly out of nowhere from Bury manager Jim Iley in August 1980 meant that he was soon back in the game.

Initially taking up the position of Reserves' coach, in June 1982 he was promoted to first-team trainer at Gigg Lane. He was further elevated up the club hierarchy in August 1983 when installed as assistant manager, a development that also finally earned him a contract.

Over the next few years he also assumed other responsibilities, including that of caretaker/manager for a few weeks when Iley was sacked in February 1984. A month later, Bury chose Martin Dobson as their new manager and another former Burnley star, Frank Casper, was appointed as his assistant. From that point, McGuinness was able to devote most of his time and effort into yet another role, that of club physiotherapist. It was a responsibility he had taken up in the later stages of Iley's reign when the Shakers operated just one team because of financial constraints.

The Dobson/Casper partnership instantly revived Bury's fortunes and they achieved promotion into the Third Division in 1985. Events surrounding the club meant that the success couldn't be sustained in the long-term and in April 1989 Dobson left. Along with Derek Fazakerley, the loyal McGuinness was again asked to fill the caretaker manager role for a few weeks until a new manager was found.

Resuming his duties as physiotherapist, in the 1991 close season, and at the age of 53, he retracted from the day-to-day involvement in the sport he had served so well. Having undergone a hip replacement operation, Bury brought in another physio, the development bringing an end to a career spanning 38 years that had been coloured with some incredible highs and a number of shattering lows. Throughout it all he managed to retain a keen sense of humour, an attribute that was to serve him well in the next stage of his life.

Back in August 1990, Bury granted him a richly deserved testimonial in which the opposition at Gigg Lane was the other football love of his life, Manchester United. The fact that it was the first game the Reds had been involved in since beating Crystal Palace in the F.A. Cup final that May ensured it was both a memorable and prosperous day for him, and nobody could have begrudged him either.

The Sale resident then carved himself a niche as an extremely successful and popular after-dinner speaker, whose often self-parodying sketches kept audiences in fits of laughter. He was re-employed by United on hospitality duties in 1992 and, as such, is usually seen at Old Trafford on matchdays.

LESTER, Gordon (1953/54)

Born: Holmes Chapel, 3rd November 1935
Died: Macclesfield, 19th October 2009
Height: 6ft., **Weight:** 11st. 7lbs.
Role: Centre-forward
Career: **Holmes Chapel Council School/ Crewe Grammar School/ Crewe Boys/ Cheshire Boys/ UNITED**: Am. June 1951 to December 1953/ **Ards** (NI) 1955/ **Ballymena United** (NI) 1955/ **Crewe Alexandra** November 1956 to c/s 1957

The captain of a successful Crewe Boys team that also included Ronnie Cope and future United coach Frank Blunstone in its ranks, Gordon Lester also went on to skipper the Cheshire county side at schoolboy level.

Tried as a pivot during his schooldays, he was much more at ease as a centre-forward and it was in the latter position that he came to the attention of the Old Trafford scouts. A robust leader of the line, whose style bore comparison to the great Nat Lofthouse, his greatest assets were speed off the mark and a stinging shot. Able to crack a ball with either foot, there was a slight preference to use his left 'peg'.

His first inclination of an interest from United came when a letter was received, which offered him an invitation to attend a trial at the playing fields of Henshaw's School for the Blind. The school was situated a short distance away from Old Trafford, just off Chester Road, and the assessment was watched by Matt Busby, Jimmy Murphy and Bert Whalley. Due to the favourable impression made, Lester was signed soon afterwards and he stayed on United's books as an amateur for a period of two and a half years.

During the 1951/52 season he spent the vast majority of his time in the Colts, with just the odd appearance for the Juniors. At that time the Juniors staged their home matches at Willcocks Farm, which was situated off Berwick Avenue in Burnage. He bagged numerous goals, including a hat-trick for the Colts from the outside-right position against Didsbury United in January 1952 and a haul of four against Lostock United that April.

Later in the year he notched another three, in the Juniors' pre-season warm up against Belvedere Works, and was then reinstated in the Colts. The striker made only about half a dozen starts up to September prior to disappearing from view entirely until November of the following year.

Utilised in just one Youth Cup match, his big opportunity marked a return to action against Wrexham under The Cliff's floodlights, and it came about because his room-mate in digs, Duncan Edwards, was being rested in preparation for a senior match.

He left Old Trafford with only a few more appearances to his name and in December 1953 joined the Royal Air Force. While keeping his fitness up with various station teams, he simultaneously learned the ropes as an air wireless fitter.

During his spell in the RAF, he was posted to the Aldergrove station in Northern Ireland. Soon picked up by the local Newtownards club, within his stay in Ulster he also made a few starts for Ballymena.

Upon returning to civilian life in the later stages of 1956, Crewe Alexandra took him onboard. He spent the remainder of the 1956/57 season in Crewe's 'A' (third) team but did earn just one promotion to their Reserves, in a game at Rhyl, in March 1957.

After giving up football entirely at the age of 21, his sporting activities were then mostly confined to the summer game. Over a period spanning more than twenty years, Holmes Chapel Cricket Club benefited from his on-field assistance, as well as his fiscal skills as the club's treasurer.

An engineer by profession, who spent the last 26 years of his working life at ICL in Kidsgrove, after retiring he was awarded an upper second honours degree in social sciences with politics and economics by the Open University, strove to improve his French and sang tenor in the Crewe Male Voice Choir.

Gordon Lester died in the East Cheshire Hospice in 2009.

ROBBINS, Gordon (1952/53)

Born: Barnsley, 7th February 1936
Died: Tenerife, Spain, 28th March 2006
Height: 5ft. 10ins., **Weight:** 11st. 7lbs.
Role: Right half-back
Career: **Ardsley Oaks School (Barnsley)/ Barnsley Boys/ Yorkshire Boys/ UNITED:** Am. May 1951 to March 1953/ **Rotherham United** May 1953/ **Goole Town** July 1956 to c/s 1957/ **Walsall** November 1958/ **Crewe Alexandra** December 1958 to June 1960/ **Denaby United** October 1960 to c/s 1961

Gordon Robbins was spotted by United scout Joe Armstrong while representing Yorkshire Boys at The Hawthorns. He subsequently joined the club straight from school having captained both Barnsley and Yorkshire and undergoing trials for England Boys.

The coaching staff initially saw him as a centre-half and it was as a pivot that he played in the Junior 'Reds v. Blues' trial game at Old Trafford in August 1951. He was later converted to the right-half position, where his main assets, those of strong tackling and constructive use of the ball, were used to their greatest effect. It was in the number four jersey that he made his solitary appearance in the Youth Cup for the Reds during their very first game in the tournament, against Leeds in October 1952.

Even though United cruised to a 4-0 victory, the right-half place went to Bobby Harrop for the next tie and he couldn't force his way back into the youth team once Eddie Colman had established himself in that position from the Fourth Round onwards.

Resident at Old Trafford for almost two years, despite being tried all along the half-back line and even twice at left full-back when making at least sixteen appearances for the Colts in the 1952/53 season, he was only ever used once in the 'A' team. His last known game was against Walkden Yard on the last day of January 1953 and tears flowed from the seventeen year-old when told that the club were releasing him, though he was soon consoled when Rotherham offered him a contract.

By a strange quirk of fate, the Reds were paired against Rotherham in the Youth Cup the following January and his selection for that game means he holds the distinction of becoming the first player ever to feature both for and against United in the competition. Because the Youth Cup was still in its infancy, it is almost certain he was the only participant to have represented two clubs in the tournament at that time. The Millmoor juniors provided tough opposition, the Reds proving successful only after a replay at The Cliff.

Without breaking into the first-team, he remained at Rotherham for over three years before making a perfectly timed move to Midland League outfit, Goole Town. The middle stages of the 1956/57 campaign were heady days for Goole as they became embroiled in a momentous F.A. Cup run that is still mentioned in the town to this day.

After ploughing through the qualifying hurdles, they put out fellow non-leaguers Wigan at Springfield Park in the First Round Proper and then eliminated Football League opposition by winning a replay at Workington. The Third Round draw gave them a plum tie at Nottingham Forest in January 1957 and, despite crashing to a 6-0 defeat, it had been a marvellous and profitable experience for the club. Robbins was with the Vikings for just the one season, and on top of all the F.A. Cup glory he was also a member of the side that captured the West Riding County Cup.

Following his exit from Goole, and by now stationed at Sutton Coldfield while serving his National Service in the RAF, he spent a period out of the game before signing for Walsall. It was to be a brief liaison as, after making his first appearance for their Reserves in a Birmingham League fixture at inside-right, his involvement with them stretched to only two more second string matches before he joined Crewe on the penultimate day of 1958.

He made four Football League appearances while at Gresty Road, his debut for the Alex on the 1st January 1959 resulting in a 2-0 win at Bradford Park Avenue. By the end of that month he had also been involved in a 0-0 draw at Aldershot and a 3-1 home defeat to Watford. The Yorkshireman then spent the majority of his time in Crewe's Reserves, the only exception was when taking the centre-half spot in a 1-1 draw at Darlington in March.

In October 1960, he made a final move when transferring to Central Alliance League club, Denaby United, his exit at the end of the season coinciding with a new managerial appointment.

Robbins then applied to return to amateur status in order that he could represent the Fire Service at football as he had, for some time, been combining his soccer with what would turn out to be a very successful working life in the Fire Brigade.

Representing the England Fire Service at football while in the early years of his chosen career, he took part in the annual fixtures against their Scottish counterparts and also the three military sides, the Army, the Navy and the Royal Air Force. Also chosen for the England Fire Service against the British Fire Service, the standard of football in those contests was quite high as a few of the English team were part-time professionals with non-league clubs. He captained the England Fire Service side until deciding to stop playing, and then reverted to the position of manager/coach right up until 1980.

Continuing to live in South Yorkshire, Gordon Robbins eventually rose to the rank of divisional officer in the Fire Service. He retired from duty in 1991 after a career spanning over 30 years and passed away while on holiday just a few weeks past his 70th birthday.

McFARLANE, William Noel (1952/53)

Born: Bray, Co. Wicklow, Eire, 20th December 1934
Height: 5ft. 8ins., **Weight:** 10st. 4lbs.
Role: Inside or outside-right or right half-back
Career: Bray National School/ Cualann Rovers/ Eire Boys/ **UNITED:** Am. June 1951 Pro. April 1952/ **Waterford** (Ire) June 1956/ **Altrincham** July 1957/ **Hyde United** October 1960 to November 1961

An old-fashioned touchline artist whose repertoire included electric bursts of speed, unselfish running and an enthusiastic willingness to get behind defences, the diversity of Noel McFarlane's skills brought him goals and glory, particularly early on in his football career.

He was raised just south of Dublin and, while not particularly bothered about playing Gaelic sports in his formative years, he took to football like a duck to water. Connecting with a renowned local club, Cualann Rovers, his performances for them in a schoolboy league that drew teams from in and around Dublin earned him international recognition.

The match programme produced for the game in which he starred for Eire Boys when they humbled England Boys at Goodison Park in 1951 mentioned that he needed *'very little space in which to carve out an opening'*, *'is very elusive'*, and could *'pass a ball to perfection'*.

Later finding himself talking to Bert Whalley on the homeward bound ship, due to that conversation the club official made his way to Bray in order to speak to his father. After an offer for his son to join United was accepted, Whalley and the fifteen year-old caught the next available boat back to England so that the boy could sign the required forms as soon as possible, the contract papers coming into effect that June.

Three months later he scored in the Juniors' 8-0 massacre of Boothstown. Promoted to the Colts later that month, by February 1952 the winger was performing with the 'A' team in the Manchester League and it was only a matter of weeks before United secured him as a professional.

His Youth Cup entrance came in his second year at the club, in October 1952, against Leeds. Following that historic win he was unavailable for the Nantwich game because of injury and, unable to dislodge Alan Morton, was included at right-half against Bury and then at number eight for the next two ties. Upon returning to the right wing for the quarter-final against Barnsley, he contributed his first goal in the tournament and then rattled another three into Brentford's net during the semi's. A brace from him in the first leg of the final against Wolves greatly assisted in ensuring that the trophy became a Manchester resident for the first twelve months of its existence.

It was a superb period for him personally, because towards the end of the 1952/53 season he also made an initial breakthrough into the Reserves.

With the Youth Cup successes still fresh in the memory, it was an especially big thrill for him to return home that summer when the club's youngsters played three games during a short tour of Ireland. Freshly invigorated,

Jack Pauline (in overcoat) and trainer Joe Travis are snapped with United's Colts prior to their 6-3 victory over Adelphi Lads' Club on 22nd September 1951
Back row (l-r) Philip Spiby, Walter Piggott, Tommy Barrett, Gordon Robbins, John Doherty, Roger Charlesworth
Front row (l-r) Noel McFarlane, Gordon Lester, Les Olive, Roger Wood, Ron Riches

he put in his best scoring performance for a United youth eleven by plundering a hat-trick in the home challenge match against Sheffield & Hallamshire in September 1953, which just happened to be his last appearance in that age group.

Getting the odd start for the Reserves while making himself almost a fixture in the Manchester League side that season, on the 13th February 1954, Matt Busby thrust him into the first-team as Johnny Berry's deputy when the Reds defeated Spurs 2-0 at Old Trafford. Still aged only nineteen, it was thought that he would one day succeed the consistent Berry.

Only nineteen months later, in September 1955, the winger was the victim of a particularly serious injury to his right leg in an 'A' team match at Bury. He required surgery and was on the sick list until the following March when returning for a Lancashire League home engagement with Rochdale Reserves. The damage was such that the management felt he could never regain his earlier fitness level and he was released soon after.

McFarlane was then forced to ask himself two questions; did he want to carry on playing and, if so, who with? The first was answered with a resounding 'yes', although he knew better than anyone that he would require a lesser standard than he had been used to, and the second part was completed when he was offered a deal with League of Ireland club, Waterford.

He made his entrance for the Blues in a Dublin City Cup game at home to Cork Athletic and, following a 7-3 win in which he scored once, a newspaper described him as a *'clever footballer'* who *'packs a useful shot'*. Hardly missing a game for Waterford all season, in the process he racked up over a dozen goals.

During the summer of 1957, he returned to Manchester in order to wed a Stretford lass who he became engaged to while with United and at almost the same time signed for Altrincham. His first game for them was at home to Mossley and following a 4-1 success a report claimed that his display was *'a revelation'*. He was Altrincham's top scorer in the 1957/58 campaign and remained a consistent performer for the Moss Lane side until October 1960 when he and four others left after a 25% wage cut was imposed.

Swiftly fixed up at Hyde, his debut for the Tigers was staged before a crowd of 2,100 and ended in a 5-1 win over Sankeys of Wellington which put them at the top of the Cheshire League table. A newspaper scribe was moved to mention that *'one of McFarlane's greatest assets is his ability to hold the ball'*.

Just a few fixtures into the 1961/62 season he underwent another leg operation that finished him as a footballer. Even though he had mended well enough for the start of the following campaign, with Hyde including him on their retained list, he declined the offer to continue.

From the time when he returned to the Manchester area, McFarlane had worked in his mother-in-law's wholesale fruit business, which was situated at the old Smithfield Market in the city centre. Managing the business until retiring in 2005, in the following February he underwent knee replacement surgery. Some nerves were damaged during the operation and resulted in the withdrawal of any further participation in golf, a long-time passion.

A Cheshire resident, his son, Ross, is a former golf professional who now acts as a commentator on the sport for Sky TV.

An old-fashioned inside-forward who was blessed with craft, tremendous passing skills and an expert ability to strike a ball, John Doherty grew up almost within earshot of Old Trafford in Stretford. Possessed with an acutely perceptive football brain, he could vary his technique from the subtle to the forceful in order to make the most of the prevailing match circumstances.

Doherty made the jump from school football to represent, firstly, Manchester Boys and, later, Lancashire Boys. In his early teens he was also involved with Benchill, a highly successful youth club side that contained a sprinkling of Manchester Boys players, and was then denied the opportunity to attend England Boys' trials through injury.

Signed for United straight from school by chief scout Louis Rocca, time in his early days at Old Trafford was divided between working in the club's offices or out on the pitch, where his talent for instigating and orchestrating attacks developed under the watchful eyes of the coaches.

DOHERTY, John Herbert (1952/53)

Born: Stretford, 12th March 1935
Died: Withington, Manchester, 13th November 2007
Height: 5ft. 10 ½ ins., Weight: 11st. 12lbs.
Role: Inside-forward
Career: Xaverian Grammar School (Rusholme)/ Manchester Boys/ Lancashire Boys/ UNITED: Am. May 1950 Pro. March 1952/ Leicester City October 1957/ Rugby Town player/ manager July 1958/ Altrincham September and October 1958

He scored a hat-trick for the Colts against Ferranti on the opening day of the 1950/51 campaign and was appearing regularly for the 'A' team by the second half of the season. Doherty remained with the Manchester League side during the following term, when he also made half a dozen starts in the Reserves.

At the age of seventeen he was the automatic choice at inside-right when United's Youth Cup story began in late 1952 and, despite not getting amongst the goals in the opening game, he compensated by finding the net five times in the Second Round match against Nantwich. *'All of my goals came in the second half,'* he pointed out. *'We were 10-0 up at half-time when Jimmy Murphy gave me a gentle reminder that I hadn't made a contribution and my goals came pretty quickly after we got going again.'*

Ten days after the Third Round win over Bury he made his First Division debut against Middlesbrough at Old Trafford. The United faithful went home smiling following a 3-2 win and the young Stretfordian retained his place for a further three matches, the second of which, a 3-2 victory at Chelsea, brought him his first two goals at senior level. Another appearance in a 1-1 home draw with Manchester City in January 1953 took his total number of First Division games to five for the season.

More Youth Cup goals, one against Barnsley in the Fifth Round and another two in the home leg of the semi-final against Brentford, helped propel the Reds into the final. Unfortunately, and even though his contribution in getting the team through seven consecutive victorious ties was huge, he was forced to miss those historic games against Wolves.

'After the game against Brentford, Eddie Lewis and I went to the Longford Cinema in Stretford to watch a Bob Hope, Bing Crosby and Dorothy Lamour film called 'The Road to Bali',' he recounted. *'When the lights went on at the end of the film I was in so much pain from my knee that I couldn't get out of my seat without some help.'* It was the start of a problem that would blight, and ultimately prematurely end, his football career.

The very next day he reported for his National Service term of duty at Padgate Royal Air Force camp near Warrington. Undergoing checks by military doctors soon after, they diagnosed a condition known as synovitis of the knee and such was the severity of his injury, the RAF medical staff informed him that he would never play competitively again. It was obvious that he couldn't take part in the Youth Cup final games, so United brought in Billy Whelan as his replacement. On the day after the Irishman knocked in one of the two goals against Wolves in the second leg of the final at Molinuex, Doherty checked into Altrincham General Hospital for a cartilage operation.

His dogged determination to disprove the doctors resulted in him being ready to start the next campaign, although he suffered a set-back in the opening Manchester League game and was missing until January 1954 when he got a run which lasted until the end of the season.

In the 1954/55 term he upped his Central League appearances to 29 while contributing nine goals. By the following season his form was such that not only did he score fifteen times in 24 starts for the table-topping Reserves, four goals from sixteen league games also earned him a First Division championship medal.

Gaining another success when the second string topped the Central League in 1957, he was absent from only two out of a total of 42 fixtures and his seventeen goals placed him as the team's third top scorer behind Bobby Charlton and Alex Dawson. However, due mainly to the exceptional form of Billy Whelan, he made little headway in first-team terms by adding only three appearances in the higher grade.

Still afflicted by his troublesome knee, he was absent for the opening weeks of the following campaign but then notched three goals in seven consecutive Reserve matches prior to winning a recall to First Division competition. That game, a 3-1 defeat at Wolves in September 1957 in which he scored the Reds' consolation goal, was his parting shot for the seniors and the following month he was sold to Leicester for a fee of £6,500.

His stay at Filbert Street was relatively brief. Introduced by the Foxes in a 2-2 home draw with Everton that October, he made six consecutive appearances, scoring twice, before missing a game through injury. It was apparent that his knee still wasn't fully functional and, even though he hit the net three times during another six-match consecutive run, the last of which was at Blackpool in December 1957, his exit from Filbert Street coincided with the end of the season.

Sensing that his knee wouldn't stand up to the rigours of football much longer, he took up the post of player/manager with Rugby Town, a club that had been promoted into the Southern League from the Birmingham League just weeks before his arrival. At the age of 23 he was by far the youngest manager in the division, but the Rugby directors saw his experience both on and off the field as crucial to consolidating their improved status.

Following the club's annual meeting in July 1958, his appointment was heralded with fanfares in the local newspaper. An article revealed he was to be engaged on a three-year, full-time contract and that he and his wife would be moving from Leicester to set up home in the area. Sensationally, with the new season just four games old, he unexpectedly quit. It was a remarkable turn of events in such a short space of time and his resignation was reluctantly accepted by the club's chairman. Of his decision, Doherty told the press, *'I have resigned for purely personal and domestic reasons. I don't think I am in a position to give of my best to the club or for the club. Although my stay has been short and sweet we have parted very good friends.'*

Later that month he returned to Manchester and was persuaded to sign for Altrincham by his old United youth team colleague, Noel McFarlane. Beginning just two games for the Cheshire League club, the first was a loss at Hyde and a week later, on the 4th October 1958, his second appearance ended in a 2-1 home defeat by Wrexham Reserves. At an age when most footballers have a good ten years to look forward to in the sport, electing to give it up was made in order to safeguard his long-term well-being.

Upon leaving football he worked in the motor trade for a time, and four years after last kicking a ball he was engaged as a coach at Hyde United under manager Frank Clempson, the two having remained friends since their days together at Old Trafford.

With a reporter claiming he was *'an insurance broker'*, Doherty was installed as Bangor City's part-time manager in August 1970 and he then disappeared off the scene entirely for approximately ten years before becoming a scout for Manchester City during the reign of John Bond. When Bond moved to Turf Moor in June 1983, he took up the mantle of chief scout there for just over twelve months.

In the ensuing years he held the chairmanship of the Association of Former Manchester United Players (AFMUP), who perform great work on behalf of charity. After his death from lung cancer in November 2007, United chief executive David Gill paid tribute by saying, *'John was a tireless leader of the AFMUP and a much loved and popular figure around Old Trafford. His work saw the group go from strength to strength. His quick wit and easy manner will be greatly missed. It was a special moment for him to be able to bring on the Premier League trophy at the end of last season, with his other friends from the Busby Babes' first title-winning team in 1956 for the presentation to the team, a role he performed with great pride and dignity.'*

EDWARDS, Duncan (1952/53, 1953/54, 1954/55)

Born: Dudley, 1st October 1936
Died: Munich, 21st February 1958
Height: 5ft. 10ins., **Weight:** 12st. 6lbs.
Role: Left half-back, centre-half or forward
Career: Priory Road Junior School (Dudley)/ Wolverhampton Street Secondary School (Dudley)/ Dudley Boys/ Worcestershire Boys/ Birmingham & District Boys/ Midland Counties Boys/ England Boys/
UNITED: Am. May 1952 Pro. October 1953 to his death

Arguably the greatest all-round player in Manchester United's history, Duncan Edwards died at the age of 21 as a result of the massive injuries he sustained in the Munich air disaster. Nicknamed 'Tank' by at least one of his United team-mates due to his immense physical presence and strength, contemporaries remember him as the most complete footballer of his era.

Equally at home defending as he was scoring or creating goals, even as a young boy he allied lion-hearted courage to the power in his game and, consequently, he rarely came second best in the tackle. Add those characteristics to a natural turn of speed, superb heading technique, an ability to distribute the ball as accurately over 50 yards as he could over short distances and an almost insatiable appetite for the game, it is hardly surprising that over half a century since his death, the name of Duncan Edwards is so revered by those who were fortunate enough to see him in full flow.

Hailing from the West Midlands town of Dudley, which as far as football geography goes, lies almost midway between The Hawthorns and Molineux, his progress as a schoolboy footballer was nothing less than startling. At the age of twelve he was included in a Dudley Boys team that was comprised of players who were generally two or three years older than him. Later captaining Worcestershire Boys, as well as representing the Birmingham & District Area and Midland Counties, his first appearance for England Boys was made when he was only thirteen.

He scored England's fifth goal on his international debut at Oldham in 1950 with another in the range of his considerable skills, a thunderbolt shot, and went on to win a further eight schoolboy caps over a period spanning 1951 and 1952. Skippering the national side in his last year, he remains the only person ever to represent England Boys for three years in succession.

With 'Captain of England Boys' on his C.V., the prized prodigy could have had his pick from any one of a number of professional clubs that coveted his signature. It says much for the set-up at Old Trafford, and the impression that Matt Busby made on him, that he chose to join United rather than one of the three Midlands giants, Wolves, West Brom or Aston Villa, that were on his doorstep. Such an acquisition hugely enriched Busby's happiness in the summer of 1952, coming as it did just weeks after the Reds had finally clinched the First Division championship and following their frustrating run of finishing as runners-up four times in the previous five years.

If Edwards' record as a schoolboy footballer was impressive, once he moved up north his enormous advancement began to read like fantasy.

He made his first competitive start in a Colts versus Heywood St. James clash at The Cliff in August 1952, the Reds running out comfortable winners by six goals to one. Early the following month he was promoted to the 'A' team and in the October he was chosen as left-half in United's 4-0 victory over Leeds in their first Youth Cup fixture. In November, his opening goals as a United player came when blasting five past Nantwich in the Second Round of the Youth Cup and by December he had made an initial outing at inside-right for the Reserves at Burnley.

Holding down a regular spot in the Central League side as from then, on the 1st April 1953 he was present in the 'A' side as they defeated Ashton United in the Gilgryst Cup final. Only three days later, at just sixteen years and 185 days old, he became a fully-fledged First Division footballer in a game against Cardiff at Old Trafford. Incredibly, his elevation from schoolboy football to the First Division had taken barely eleven months.

He had also been ever-present in the side that captured the inaugural Youth Cup. Reserving his best form for the tougher ties, there were rave reviews in most of the tabloids for his match-winning goal against Everton and his overall displays in both legs of the final against Wolves.

During the course of the 1953/54 campaign, Busby began the task of replacing some of the older men who gave the club such wonderful service in the early post-war period with the youngsters he had been nurturing for some time. Edwards began in the Reserves prior to establishing himself in the first-team in October and his senior responsibilities meant that he was absent from three out of the opening four rounds of the Youth Cup.

When he missed the Fourth Round tie at Rotherham in January 1954, it was because he was making his bow in the F.A. Cup at Burnley. The youth team managed a hard fought draw without him, but on his return in the replay he almost single-handedly destroyed the Millers with a hat-trick. He was present for all of the later rounds of the Youth Cup and gave a vintage display, which included scoring two goals, in the home leg of the final against Wolves as United clawed their way back from 3-1 down. A narrow victory at Molineux in the second leg gave him a winner's memento for the second time.

He had also added to his cap collection as the term unfolded, when chosen for England at under-23 level once and 'B' standard twice, on top of taking part in the annual international trial game, which consisted of a 'Young England' eleven facing a team of recognised England regulars. It was no secret that he was highly regarded by England manager Walter Winterbottom and his inclusion in the 'Young' team was a further step in his grooming as a future candidate for the full national side.

His experience of foreign football extended into the close season by helping United's youth team to win the Blue Stars tournament in Switzerland. After being switched from his normal left-half position to centre-forward for the later stages of the competition, he scored a magnificent hat-trick in the final against the local Red Stars team.

The 1954/55 campaign was, if anything, even busier for him than the two that had gone before. Besides featuring in 33 First Division games and three F.A. Cup ties for United, he was selected twice for the Football League and once for the England Youth team. He added to those honours with two further appearances for England under-23's and another for England 'B'.

Then, on the 2nd April 1955, the inevitable happened when, at the age of just eighteen years and 183 days, he became the youngest player to be capped as a full England international to that point in the 20th century, a record he held for over 40 years. Slotting into a side containing such legendary figures as Stanley Matthews, Billy Wright and Nat Lofthouse, England cruised to a fantastic 7-2 win over Scotland at Wembley.

For good measure he also helped to claim the Youth Cup for the third and, as far as he was concerned, last time. The two instalments of the semi-final saw him in devastating form, scoring all four goals against a top-class Chelsea outfit, and when taking to the field at Stamford Bridge for the opening leg, he became the first full international ever to put in an appearance in the Youth Cup.

Only just over a month since making his full England debut, Edwards took part in the national side's end of season tour of the continent, winning selection for all three games against Spain, France and Portugal. Soon after returning he received his National Service papers and for the next two years he was forced to juggle the extra responsibility along with those of club and country football commitments. While in the services he represented the British Army in many matches at home and in Europe, although a tug of war developed between United and the military selectors because the latter were keen to use him as often as possible.

As the 1955/56 term got underway his 19th birthday was still some weeks off, but that personal milestone came and went with his career still spiralling ever upwards. On the international front, further England honours came his way courtesy of starts for the under-23 and 'B' teams, and the only notable item that was missing from his massive trophy cabinet was a major domestic honour. That particular omission was satisfyingly put paid to as he made 33 appearances in United's charge to the First Division title, the championship being won in some style via an eleven points margin over second placed Blackpool.

Also picking up a further five England caps, three of them were earned on another post-season tour to northern Europe. In the concluding game of the tour against the current world champions West Germany, a blistering drive marked his first goal as a full international when the visitors secured an impressive 3-1 victory in Berlin.

His fifth campaign at Old Trafford got going with an extra buzz of excitement as the Reds became the first English representatives to enter the European Champions' Cup. Picking up valuable experience in the earlier rounds of the competition, United went out at the semi-final stage. That they lost to the acknowledged masters of European football, Real Madrid, whose team was packed with a veritable galaxy of star men, was no disgrace.

On the domestic front, though, the Reds were virtually invincible when wrapping up the First Division championship for the second term running, and they only failed to become the first team of the 20th century to win the 'double' when defeated in the F.A. Cup final by Aston Villa in highly controversial circumstances. Consoled somewhat with yet more representative honours, they amounted to a couple of games for the Football League as well as two more under-23 and six full England caps.

Shortly after the commencement of the 1957/58 season he celebrated his 21st birthday and within a matter of weeks of that date his total of full England appearances had edged up to eighteen. Recognition of his bourgeoning international reputation came in the form of his placing of third in the 1957 'European Footballer of the Year' stakes.

Additionally busied by assisting the Reds to their second tilt at the European Champions' Cup, it was on that particular adventure that his astonishing story came to a sad and premature end. When the fateful plane carrying the United party crashed after refuelling at Munich, Edwards suffered terrible injuries and following a monumental struggle for life which lasted fifteen days, he passed into eternal peace and immortality.

There are two stained glass windows depicting him, one in the red and white colours of United and another in the white and blue strip of England, at St. Francis' Church in Dudley, which serve to permanently preserve his memory. His broken body was laid to rest at the nearby Queen's Cross Cemetery.

There has been a display of his sporting mementoes on view in his home town for a number of years and in October 1999 Sir Bobby Charlton unveiled a statue of him in Dudley's busy Market Place. It acts as a focal point for the residents of the town, who still view him as their most famous sporting son.

Duncan Edwards was a unique schoolboy footballer whose incredible progress made him stand out as the dazzling diamond in a cluster of jewels that has been Manchester United's policy of producing 'home-grown' players since the 1930's. Winning three Youth Cups, two First Division championships, two Charity Shields, an F.A. Cup finalist's medal and virtually every representative honour available to him, but for his tragic death he would have played for his club and country for years to come.

Surely, we will never see his like again.

DUNCAN EDWARDS' COUNTY APPEARANCES

29th December 1949
Worcestershire Boys 2 Northamptonshire Boys 2 (Worcester)

11th April 1950
Worcestershire Boys 1 Staffordshire Boys 5 (Halesowen)

10th February 1951
Northamptonshire Boys 1 Worcestershire Boys 8 (Rushden)

27th March 1951
Worcestershire Boys 11 Bedfordshire Boys 1 (Worcester)

23rd April 1951
Gloucestershire Boys 3 Worcestershire Boys 2 (Stonehouse)

28th April 1951
Staffordshire Boys 2 Worcestershire Boys 1 (Brierley Hill)

21st May 1951
Worcestershire Boys 3 Derbyshire Boys 8 (Worcester)

22nd December 1951
Worcestershire Boys 2 Gloucestershire Boys 3 (Malvern)

2nd February 1952
Worcestershire Boys 3 Bedfordshire Boys 5 (Redditch)

DUNCAN EDWARDS' INTERNATIONAL APPEARANCES

6th May 1950
England Boys 5 Northern Ireland Boys 2 (Boundary Park, Oldham)

26th March 1951
Wales Boys 2 England Boys 2 (Somerton Park, Newport)

7th April 1951
England Boys 3 Wales Boys 0 (Wembley)

5th May 1951
England Boys 2 Scotland Boys 2 (Recreation Ground, Chesterfield)

11th May 1951
Northern Ireland Boys 1 England Boys 7 (Grosvenor Park, Belfast)

5th April 1952
England Boys 1 Scotland Boys 0 (Wembley)

26th April 1952
Scotland Boys 1 England Boys 4 (Pittodrie, Aberdeen)

3rd May 1952
England Boys 5 Wales Boys 1 (St. Andrews, Birmingham)

31st May 1952
Eire Boys 1 England Boys 0 (Dublin)

20th January 1954
Italy under-23's 3 England under-23's 0 (Bologna)

24th March 1954
West Germany 'B' 0 England 'B' 4 (Gelsenkirchen)

22nd May 1954
Switzerland 'B' 2 England 'B' 0 (Basle)

21st November 1954
Holland Youth 3 England Youth 2 (Arnhem)

19th January 1955
England under-23's 5 Italy under-23's 1 (Stamford Bridge, London)

8th February 1955
Scotland under-23's 0 England under-23's 6 (Shawfield, Glasgow)

23rd March 1955
England 'B' 1 West Germany 'B' 1 (Hillsborough, Sheffield)

2nd April 1955
England 7 Scotland 2 (Wembley)

15th May 1955
France 1 England 0 (Paris)

18th May 1955
Spain 1 England 1 (Madrid)

22nd May 1955
Portugal 3 England 1 (Oporto)

8th February 1956
England under-23's 3 Scotland under-23's 1 (Hillsborough, Sheffield)

21st March 1956
England 'B' 4 Switzerland 'B' 1 (The Dell, Southampton)

14th April 1956
Scotland 1 England 1 (Hampden Park, Glasgow)

9th May 1956
England 4 Brazil 2 (Wembley)

16th May 1956
Sweden 0 England 0 (Stockholm)

20th May 1956
Finland 1 England 5 (Helsinki)

26th May 1956
West Germany 1 England 3 (Berlin)

6th October 1956
Northern Ireland 1 England 1 (Windsor Park, Belfast)

5th December 1956
England 5 Denmark 2 (Molineux, Wolverhampton)

6th April 1957
England 2 Scotland 1 (Wembley)

8th May 1957
England 5 Eire 1 (Wembley)

15th May 1957
Denmark 1 England 4 (Copenhagen)

19th May 1957
Eire 1 England 1 (Dublin)

26th May 1957
Romania under-23's 0 England under-23's 1 (Bucharest)

30th May 1957
Czechoslovakia under-23's 0 England under-23's 2 (Bratislava)

19th October 1957
Wales 0 England 4 (Ninian Park, Cardiff)

6th November 1957
England 2 Northern Ireland 3 (Wembley)

27th November 1957
England 4 France 0 (Wembley)

MORGANS, Kenneth Godfrey
(1954/55, 1955/56, 1956/57)

Born: Swansea, 16th March 1939
Height: 5ft. 5ins., **Weight:** 9st. 2lbs.
Role: Outside-right or outside-left
Career: St. Thomas' Junior School (Swansea)/ Dan-y-Graig Secondary School (Swansea)/ Swansea Boys/ Wales Boys/ UNITED: Am. June 1954 Pro. March 1956/ **Swansea Town** March 1961/ **Newport County** June 1964/ **Cwmbran Town** player/manager June 1967 to 1970

When Ken Morgans won the first of his four international schoolboy caps he succeeded in emulating his father, who had also earned junior recognition for Wales in the inter-war years, and he later came to United's attention by starring for his country against England Boys at Maine Road in 1954. Matt Busby and Jimmy Murphy were in attendance and, liking what they saw in the boy from Swansea, they soon set about the task of making him United property.

Commencing service on the ground staff at Old Trafford that summer, the impression he might have formed in those early weeks was that football is a cakewalk because his Juniors' side ran in 32 goals in their three opening matches, including eight without loss against Knutsford Youth Club on the opening day of the season.

A tricky, two-footed individual whose essential assets of pace and close ball skills are so necessary to a wide attacker, his elevation into the Colts in late September lasted for the rest of that inaugural Lancashire League term, which meant that from then on he pitted himself against the younger element of Football League clubs on a regular basis.

His initial experience of the Youth Cup came at Anfield in October 1954. It was a rewarding one, a convincing display in a 4-1 win over Liverpool meaning that he retained his place for the next round at Manchester City. Producing a first tournament goal at Oakwell in a later tie, he then stood down for the following game.

Soon bouncing back, this time on the right flank for a thrashing of Plymouth, he also took part in both legs of the semi-final against Chelsea. Because of the introduction of Dennis Fidler, Morgans missed out for the final ties against West Brom, although he was awarded a plaque in recognition of his contribution during United's cup run. Along with scoring once in a 6-1 win over Preston in the Supplementary Cup final and the Colts' triumphant topping of their division, his on-field activities were almost perfect.

A couple of months into the 1955/56 campaign he took part in a 5-2 Youth Cup victory at Preston but was then unable to prise a wing spot away from either Fidler or Terry Beckett. His next chance came about due to the Reds' indifferent performance in the home leg of the semi-final in April 1956 when, by regaining the right wing position against Bolton at the expense of Beckett, the Welsh boy justified Jimmy Murphy's decision to include him by scoring one of the goals in a tremendous second leg win at Burnden Park.

He retained his place for both of the final games against Chesterfield and, with United's win over the Spireites, he felt the joy of taking home a second memento for his invaluable contribution. In divisional affairs he had been a mainstay of the Colts, for whom he operated on both flanks and once at centre-forward, and also appeared sparingly in the 'A' team.

His progress continued into the 1956/57 season when stretching his legs in both the Colts and the 'A' team prior to replacing Colin Webster at number seven for a 1-0 Central League home defeat by Blackpool in October. From then on he deputised several times for his fellow Welshman, whenever Webster was injured or on senior duty, as well as standing in for Albert Scanlon on occasions.

That term also saw him earmarked to represent Wales at youth level, and he was only overlooked through an unthinkable level of prejudice displayed by the national selectors. The reason given for his omission from his country's under-18 side was that he had committed the 'sin' of signing for an English Football League club.

In his third and final crack at the Youth Cup, he scored twice and was a permanent fixture at outside-right when the trophy was lifted once again via victories over West Ham. It was a particularly satisfying moment for United to complete their fifth such win in the competition and captain Morgans held the distinguished honour of accepting the silverware on behalf of his teammates in front of a crowd of 23,000.

At the start of the following campaign he made five appearances in the 'A' side before putting in twelve consecutive starts on the right wing for the Reserves. Some startling form allied to a superb goal at Huddersfield in mid-December 1957 meant that Busby couldn't overlook his claim for a senior berth any longer and so, with the seniors struggling to recapture their usual rhythm, he was drafted into a changed first-team forward-line against Leicester at Old Trafford at the expense of Johnny Berry. The Reds won easily, by putting four goals past the in-form Foxes without reply, and to much acclaim the new face fitted in with great success.

He then made seven further senior appearances in First Division and F.A. Cup games, and was beginning to establish himself, when he was chosen to travel to Yugoslavia for the European Cup fixture against Red Star of Belgrade in February 1958. Assisting United through a tough tie staged in cold and difficult conditions, that achievement was soon superseded by the events which unfolded on the homeward journey. Even though he was the last person to be found alive some hours after the crash at Munich, his injuries were relatively minor and following a short period of recuperation he was able to recommence in the Central League just five weeks later.

It was a harrowing time for everyone connected with Manchester United and for Morgans, his career at Old Trafford would never again live up to those pre-Munich expectations. Returning to senior duties in April to help the club establish some sort of stability by featuring in seven consecutive First Division fixtures, despite not being considered for the last league fixture and the F.A. Cup final against Bolton, nevertheless he was recalled for both European Cup meetings with AC Milan in May.

It soon became apparent that the plane crash had delivered him a huge psychological blow and he would total only four more first-team games for the Reds. He needed to wait until November 1958 for an initial recall, when taking up the outside-right spot in two consecutive fixtures, against Leeds at Elland Road and then at home to Burnley seven days later. The flanker then faded off the senior scene for some considerable time, during which he was party to a Central League championship in 1960.

He didn't step back up to the senior plate until February 1961 when helping the Reds to a 3-1 home win over Bolton, and he kept his place for the following game, a 3-2 reverse at Nottingham Forest which proved to be his last in the higher echelon. Another defeat, this time by 5-2 in a Reserve fixture at Manchester City in March, proved his final contribution for United and that same month he left for Swansea at a cost of £3,000.

While not having figured much in Busby's plans for almost three years, it was clear that he still possessed great talent. Besides representing 'The Rest' against the champions of the Central League, at international level he had been the recipient of two Welsh under-23 caps, both against Scotland, and therefore represented something of a major capture for Swansea.

He was introduced to the Second Division at Leeds in April 1961 and went on to play over 50 Football League, two F.A. Cup, two Football League Cup and a couple of Welsh Cup games for the Vetch Field club in a period spanning just over three seasons.

Moving to Fourth Division Newport County for what was mentioned in the newspapers as 'a small fee', his experience of the higher levels of football was obvious to one and all. He scored 44 goals in 125 league appearances while at Somerton Park, the highlight of which was when plundering four in October 1964 against Lincoln, and for those reasons he is remembered as a skilful and honest sort by County fans of a certain age.

Morgans exited the Football League by making the short journey to Welsh League members Cwmbran Town and while there combined the dual duties of player and manager for three campaigns. When he departed them in 1970 it signalled the end of a career in the game that had stretched to sixteen years.

With his playing days over, he was employed as a salesman and also became the licensee of the New Inn public house, which is situated in the village of New Inn, Pontypool.

Today living in his native Swansea, on the 50th anniversary of the Munich air disaster in 2008 he said of his later time at Old Trafford, *'I thought it would be the same as before the crash but it wasn't. I'd lost that extra yard (of pace) and I couldn't care if I was in the first-team or the Reserves.'*

COLMAN, Edward (1952/53, 1953/54, 1954/55)

Born: Ordsall, Salford, 1st November 1936
Died: Munich, 6th February 1958
Height: 5ft. 6ins., **Weight:** 9st. 7lbs.
Role: Right half-back
Career: Ordsall Council School/ Salford Boys/ Lancashire Boys/ UNITED: Am. May 1952 Pro. November 1953 to his death

Little Eddie Colman first saw the light of day amongst the vast ocean of terraced houses in the dockland area of Ordsall, Salford, just a short walking distance away from Old Trafford. An only child, the young Colman used sport as an outlet for his seemingly limitless energy and it was clear from an early age that he had been blessed with an abundance of talent which only seemed to be matched by his endearing sense of fun.

Growing up in the tough dock area instilled the firm working class values of friendship and loyalty into him and, while he would probably be referred to as 'streetwise' nowadays, his roguish demeanour couldn't mask his true personality, that of a likeable imp. As childhood gave way to adolescence, the rough edges fell away and he developed into a polite and charming young man who, nevertheless, found it impossible not to crack a joke or pull an amusing stunt whenever or wherever the opportunity arose. Moreover, he was one of a very small number of footballers who have been able to transpose their glowing personality onto the field of play and it was that rare quality which would make him such a firm favourite at Old Trafford, both with his colleagues and the United faithful.

After establishing himself as the star of his school teams at both football and cricket, he won representative honours for Salford and Lancashire at the two sports. Despite his name being bypassed when selection for England Boys soccer trials came around, it was generally believed locally that only his tiny frame cost him the chance.

Going on to captain the Salford Boys football team to the quarter-final of the English Schools' Trophy in the 1951/52 season, once Horwich, Farnworth, Leigh and Blackburn were disposed of, his side came up against the mighty Manchester, whose skipper was none other than Wilf McGuinness. Salford triumphed 1-0 over their near neighbours to progress into the last eight section where they faced Ilford over two legs. The Essex team gained a 2-2 draw in Salford and then, on the 29th March 1952, paved their way into the semi-final by defeating the northerners 4-2 at the Cricklewood Playing Fields in Ilford.

A few weeks later, on the 2nd May, he played in the opening leg of the Lancashire Schools' Trophy final at Maine Road, Salford having defeated Wigan, Skelmersdale, Southport, Bolton and Liverpool in order to get to the final where they again faced Manchester. The Mancunians turned the tables on his side to win the trophy by a 4-1 aggregate, with the concluding leg of the final taking place at Old Trafford just five days after the first instalment at Maine Road.

Colman initially came to United's attention through his involvement with Salford Boys. It was as a result of a knock he took while with the city side which indirectly led to the club procuring his signature, when Salford arranged for him to receive treatment from the Reds' medical staff. Sufficiently impressed with the care and attention received, and equally importantly the obvious conviviality at the club, offers of contracts were rejected from Wolves and Bolton. The exact date of signing was the 10th May 1952, just two weeks to the day after the Reds had captured their first post-war league title and only three days since his appearance at Old Trafford.

Matt Busby was in clover at securing his signature, for which the fifteen year-old received the obligatory ten quid, as he had undoubtedly added a fantastic talent to an already impressive stable of juniors. Also possessing an excellent temperament, the Salfordian may have only been a Mini in size but he had the c.c. of a Formula One engine and his ability to get stuck in when the need arose revealed fearless tackling abilities.

However, it was when in possession of the ball that the true range of his skills were displayed at their best. Quick of mind as well as feet, he could size up a situation in an instant and was able to thread passes through the eye of a proverbial needle into areas where colleagues could cause maximum damage. Also adept at bypassing opponents, not by the usual method of sheer speed but with a cute combination of ball control and a deceptive body swerve, the latter characteristic of being able to leave a man for 'dead' with a deceiving feint frequently caused crowds to cheer with delight. Significantly, it was also the trademark by which he earned his unique 'Snakehips' nickname.

His first appearance for United was made during a public practice match at Old Trafford in August 1952 when, going on for the second half of the game, his 'Blues' side lost by five goals to nil.

In his maiden season, Colman was a regular for the Juniors and frequently found himself with the responsibility of the captaincy. A popular skipper, he usually had team-mates in stitches with his jokes and the opposition in a tangle as a result of his wizardry on the park. As he led the team out of the dressing room, his last minute instructions, which became something of a standing joke, were to *'keep your high balls low and swing your low balls around!'*

Regular training and competitive matches, allied to the expert advice and experience passed on by the likes of Jimmy Murphy and Bert Whalley, brought his progress on in leaps and bounds. Although he was still comparatively lightweight in relation to most others of a similar age, it was the lack of physical size and strength which seems to offer the explanation as to his absence from the Youth Cup team until the tie against Everton in February 1953. The fourth player to be used in the right-half position in as many Youth Cup games, following that terrific tussle with the Toffees, which went United's way 1-0, he was ever-present until the age barrier finally caught up with him.

As the Reds marched to their first Youth Cup final win over Wolves, all of his blossoming talents were displayed to the full within a growing maturity and, developing a superb wing-half partnership with the more robust Duncan Edwards, his graft and trickery were integral parts of United's armoury. Off the field the two were the best of pals, even though he often risked death or serious injury as the giant Edwards was frequently the target of his good-natured humour.

Opening a second term of office in the Youth Cup team in October 1953 with the deciding goal at Everton, his next successful strike in the tournament came in the second leg of the semi-final against West Brom at Old Trafford. A measure of his soaring popularity on the terraces and in the stands was given in one of the match reports for that tie which read, *'Colman aroused as many roars for manoeuvring the ball with the sole of his boot, or performing 'kidology', as for his twenty-yard shot in the first half'*. The Reds went on to win the Youth Cup again in 1954 and over that summer European life was seen through his eyes for the first time when United's youth squad returned from Switzerland with the Blue Stars trophy.

In the scoring stakes again at the start of a third year in the youth side, his goal against Liverpool at Anfield in a First Round victory marked the beginning of his captaincy of the team. He then had to wait until the opening leg of the final to register again when his double blast, from a total of four, made the second leg at The Hawthorns somewhat of a formality.

That game at West Brom heralded the end of three magnificent years in the Youth Cup for the kid from Salford and there were smiles on the faces of all the United players as he collected the silverware from Football League representative Councillor H. Hughes on their behalf. Altogether, he had appeared in 25 Youth Cup matches of which 23 were won and two were drawn.

Besides being his last term in the youth team, the 1954/55 campaign also resulted in an introduction to the Central League eleven, his bow at that level falling in December 1954 in a 0-0 draw at Bury.

After making a further six consecutive appearances in the Reserves over the opening section of the following season, Busby deemed that the time was right to put him on show to a wider audience and with only eleven days gone since his 19th birthday, Colman was given his First Division baptism at Bolton in November 1955. Prior to his debut, the Daily Dispatch called him *'one of the best known footballers who has never played in a senior team'* and added that *'even in Manchester United's wonderful youth side he was conspicuous; likewise in this season's superb Reserve side'*.

Even though the Reds went down to a 3-1 defeat at Burnden Park, from then on no-one was able to wrest his place away from him. The Dispatch's match report revealed that he had shown *'an astonishing calm for a newcomer to the big game'* and described how he *'chose to concentrate on the ball, now back-heeling to beat his man, now indulging in a little dribble'*. Only on the losing side just four more times during a total of 26 senior matches as the Reds waltzed off with the First Division title, the pint-sized performer was a revelation and his dexterity and consistent form was a major factor in the championship charge.

Before the 1956/57 campaign began, the Reds were widely touted as one of the favourites to win the league again and aspirations increased amongst United followers when their idols won ten and drew two of their opening twelve domestic games. The retention of the title was eventually completed with the boys losing only six times, four of which came at the hands of Lancashire opposition, with Colman competing in 36 out of a maximum of 42 fixtures. He was also present for a run of six F.A. Cup ties which ended in defeat to the Villa at Wembley and found himself involved on the European stage with a trailblazing assault in the Champions' Cup.

Shortly into the 1957/58 season he passed the age of 21. United were yet again expected to be among the chasing pack for the First Division title and as the halfway stage loomed, a decent placing in the league table allied to challenges for the European Cup and F.A. Cup meant that he was in for a busy time, especially as he was still on National Service. In a football sense, 1958 began for him in the unlikely setting of Workington, where a Dennis Viollet hat-trick signalled an F.A. Cup Third Round exit for the local team. Seven days later he was at Elland Road, where another Viollet strike earned United a 1-1 draw with Leeds.

A midweek home European Cup game against Red Star of Belgrade was next up on the calendar and after going behind, the Reds scraped a 2-1 win, a rare senior goal from him, in the gloom of a weak Manchester fog, proving to be the winner. On the Saturday following the Red Star contest, United pulled out all the stops to crush Bolton by seven goals to two in a performance that had the Old Trafford masses sensing a third consecutive championship.

A week elapsed before the Reds' next game, a Fourth Round F.A. Cup fixture against Ipswich. Nobody at the time could have known that it would be the last appearance at Old Trafford for Colman, with the tie being won much more comfortably than the 2-0 margin suggested. On the first day of February 1958, Arsenal entertained United at Highbury and in a set-to of truly classic proportions, during which both sides were a credit to British football, the visitors took both points in a 5-4 win witnessed by 63,578 spectators. The victory, and the overall performance, put the team in good heart for their midweek trip to Belgrade.

The return leg of the European Cup tie, currently separated by his goal, was viewed with some trepidation but, with the Reds taking a three-goal lead in the Yugoslav capital, the home eleven were left with a seemingly impossible task. When they stormed back to make the score 3-3, Red Star showed what a fine side they obviously were. However, the referee's whistle came too soon for them and United went through on an aggregate of 5-4, with one newspaper reporter letting it be known that their right-half *'played magnificently throughout'*.

Less than 24 hours later he was dead, a victim of the horrific crash in Munich.

Football as a whole, and Manchester United in particular, were robbed of an outstanding individual whose continued good form would almost certainly have won him many more of the game's honours and, very likely, international recognition at some stage. At the time of his death he had already contributed towards two First Division championships, won a couple of Charity Shields and taken part in an F.A. Cup final.

Away from the game, too, there appeared to be a rosy future in front of him. Besides having loving parents who were extremely proud of their son's achievements, he was about to be engaged to Marjorie, an attractive and popular local girl who later married another former United youth team player, Bobby English.

The people of Salford turned out en masse when his funeral took place at Weaste Cemetery and it was a mark of respect they felt for one of their own. Today, the name of Eddie Colman is remembered within a halo of great memories. Never growing above five feet seven inches in height, as a footballer, and in terms of his larger-than-life character, he towered head and shoulders above most other players. On the field his shimmying, side-stepping style, which married subtlety with strength and stamina, left an indelible mark on those who saw him.

A plaque honouring his memory is to be found in Salford Lads' Club, and the City of Salford also named a block of flats after him. In Manchester, Eddie Colman Close can be found in the Newton Heath area, near to where United was originally formed.

HOLLAND, Eric Reginald
(1955/56, 1956/57, 1957/58)

Born: Stanton Hill, Nottinghamshire, 23rd January 1940
Height: 5ft. 10ins., **Weight:** 11st. 7lbs.
Role: Centre-half
Career: Healdswood Secondary School (Sutton-In-Ashfield)/ Sutton-in-Ashfield & District Boys/ Nottinghamshire Boys/ England Boys/ **UNITED:** Am. June 1955 Pro. May 1957/ **Wrexham** March 1960/ **Chester** March 1966/ **Altrincham** July to December 1967

Reg Holland initially came to United's attention due to being a member of the successful Sutton-in-Ashfield & District Boys side that reached the quarter-finals of the English Schools' Shield competition. Bearing in mind the resources available to them, making the last eight of the national tournament was a tremendous achievement as the Sutton team was chosen from only a handful of schools, whereas the 'big city' representatives had the benefit of drawing on talent from literally dozens of educational establishments. In fact, most of the Sutton side were pupils at the same school, Healdswood Secondary.

As fate would have it, Sutton Boys were paired against Manchester Boys in a match that should have taken place at Old Trafford but, due to a waterlogged surface, was switched to The Cliff. Inevitably, Joe Armstrong was there to cast a discerning eye over the talent and, despite Manchester Boys winning the game with some ease, the United scout had noted the centre-half's potential for the future.

Holland graduated to the England Boys side in 1955, a year in which he played four times for his country. Featuring in a resounding 9-1 win over Eire at Luton and a hard-fought 2-2 draw with Scotland at Goodison Park, he was also capped for his appearances against Wales, a 6-0 win in front of 90,000 at Wembley and a 6-2 victory at Ninian Park. The clashes against the Welsh were particularly memorable as the game in Cardiff represented a remarkable turnaround in fortune for the English boys, who trailed 2-0 at one stage, and with his selection for the game at Wembley, the defender became the very first representative of Nottinghamshire Boys to perform under the twin towers.

A naturally right-footed stopper, who had no problems using his left foot, he excelled in the air. His on-field authority caused one national reporter to make complimentary remarks prior to the boys version of the 'Auld Enemy' clash at Goodison Park by stating, *'In Holland, the Sutton-in-Ashfield centre-half, England possesses one of her greatest ever in that position. That is the general opinion of a lad who absolutely commands the centre of the field and uses the ball so well'*.

United's approach to his parents came via Bert Whalley, and from that moment there was never any danger that he would be tempted by any other club, despite him receiving concrete offers from both Notts County and West Ham. Fortunately for Whalley, he had been a follower of the Reds from afar since attending the 1948 F.A. Cup final with his father as an eight year-old.

He was given his first airing for the Blues in the annual 'Reds v. Blues' trial match in August 1955 and was deemed to be good enough to skip over the Juniors and straight into the Colts. Apart from a short spell in late September and early October, when he got a run at right full-back, his side finished second in the Lancashire League Division Two while he expanded his knowledge of defending from a central position.

It was in the number five jersey that he would make 25 consecutive appearances in United's youth team. Starting with a 5-2 win over Preston at Deepdale in October 1955 and concluding with the defeat by Wolves in April 1958, he assisted the youths to nineteen victories, four draws and only two reverses. Over the course of those games the Reds conceded just 31 goals while rattling 104 into the back of their various opponents' nets.

The loss to Wolves in the 1958 Youth Cup semi-final was a huge disappointment to everyone connected with the club but, in his last term in the team, the skipper felt the hurt more than most. Nevertheless, that defeat couldn't detract from his achievement of two final triumphs over Chesterfield and West Ham United, and the defeat of the latter in May 1957 rubber-stamped a professional contract for him that very same month.

Within the period when he was enjoying so much success in United's under-18 side, he was also capped at England Youth level. His first international youth start came in February 1957 with a 7-1 win over Wales in Cardiff and a month later his next appearance resulted in a fantastic 5-5 draw against the Dutch at Brentford. After gathering further caps against Scotland, a 3-1 win in Aberdeen, and West Germany, a 4-1 loss in Oberhausen, he took part in another amazing draw, this time 4-4 against Spain in Birmingham. Seeing service in three more England Youth fixtures at a tournament held in Barcelona, the Sutton lad was bestowed with the captaincy of the side against Greece after taking part in matches with

Holland and Austria.

Having been used occasionally in the 'A' team during the 1956/57 season while also taking part in the 'B' side's 2-1 Lancashire League Supplementary Cup final victory over Bolton, the trying events of the following campaign saw him filling in at left-half, left-back and centre-half for the Reserves from the time of his Central League debut on 22nd February 1958 until the end of that term.

Spending most of his time on 'A' team duty in the 1958/59 season, there were occasions when he was utilised in the Reserves for the usually preferred Bobby Harrop.

The 1959/60 campaign offered him better opportunities and, including the opening fixture, a 2-0 win over West Brom, he completed over twenty consecutive Central League matches at number two and occasionally got to wear the captain's armband before losing his place to Ian Greaves in January. By now recognised as a right full-back, and within days of appearing in a late February 2-1 'A' team win at Bury, Wrexham acquired his services through a free transfer.

Even though he had travelled as 12th man with the first-team on three occasions, the lack of chances to break through into the senior side made his decision to move to the Racecourse a relatively easy one. His stalled progress at Old Trafford came about largely due to the tremendous consistency of the senior full-back pairing of Bill Foulkes and Joe Carolan, as well as the potential shown by others such as Greaves. Right-back Foulkes didn't miss a solitary game during the 1959/60 term, while his left-sided partner Carolan was present for 41 out of a possible 42 First Division games.

Commenting on the transfer he later said, *'I was surprised when Matt Busby called me into his office to tell me I could leave as I thought I was doing okay. My only real regret is that I never got a game in the first-team.'*

Wrexham had only recently signed Reg Hunter from United and, shortly after, Peter Jones also contracted to the Welsh club to make up a trio of ex-Busby Babes at the Mold Road stadium.

Only a couple of months later, Holland won a Welsh Cup medal when Cardiff City were defeated in the final and two years further on he helped the Robins to win promotion to the Third Division.

The club couldn't sustain their elevated status, however, and only two years passed before they resumed in the Fourth Division following relegation. At the end of that season spent back in the basement division, the Robins reached the Welsh Cup final again, but their woes worsened in 1966 when suffering the ignominy of claiming the Football League's wooden spoon by way of finishing 92nd out of the 92 clubs.

Holland, though, had left just a few weeks before the term's final curtain fell when transferring to nearby Chester for what was reported to be a *'modest fee'*. Having totalled 145 games in all competitions for Wrexham over a six-year duration, he is fondly remembered as a loyal servant at the Racecourse.

The switch to Sealand Road wasn't a fruitful one, and in the space of just over a year only six league games and two Welsh Cup matches were added to his tally before he was given another free transfer.

Moving to Altrincham, his first Cheshire League game was completed in August 1967 and over the following two months he made nine appearances, the last of which came in an F.A. Cup Qualifying Round that October.

In 1968, he made a move that would soon see him as an England international once more, although no fee was involved because the switch was based on him joining Staffordshire Police. Life in the Police Force gave him the two-pronged benefits of carving out a worthwhile future while at the same time allowing him to continue playing regular, in fact almost daily, football.

Only 28 at the time of commencing his new career, after representing the County Force he progressed into the English Police Force side and, later, the British Police Force team. He also took part in games abroad for the Police, for example in Italy and Sweden, and when not on a soccer pitch he was the local bobby in the quaint Staffordshire twin villages of Little and Great Harwood.

Living close to his former place of work, Reg Holland retired from the constabulary at the age of 55.

PEGG, David (1952/53, 1953/54)

Born: Adwick-le-Street, Doncaster, 20th September 1935
Died: Munich, 6th February 1958
Height: 5ft. 9 ½ ins., Weight: 10st. 10lbs.
Role: Outside-left or inside-left
Career: **Highfields Modern School (Doncaster)/ Doncaster Technical School/ Doncaster Boys/ Yorkshire Boys/ England Boys/ UNITED**: Am. May 1951 Pro. September 1952 to his death

A most graceful and elegant footballer, whose dashing talent was a considerable cocktail containing deftness of touch, brilliant ball control and a terrific shot, David Pegg lived at 27, Coppice Road in the Highfields area of Doncaster. The house belonged to Brodsworth, a local colliery, which was known as the 'Queen's Pit' because it supplied coal to Buckingham Palace.

Equally at home on either flank or at inside-forward, he was naturally left-footed and able to score goals as well as provide them, in the latter instance particularly via his precision measured crosses.

During his formative years the youngster would often play football on a Saturday morning and then make his way to the Belle Vue ground to watch his local heroes, Doncaster Rovers, in the afternoon. Utilised in an inside-forward role after making his way into the Doncaster Boys side, when chosen to represent his county he was resituated on the left wing.

In 1950, he was selected for England Boys' 5-2 win over Northern Ireland at Oldham, a game that was watched by United scout Bob Slater, and the following year won four more international caps for his appearances against Wales (twice), Scotland and Eire. Despite visiting Arsenal to see and hear what they had to offer, a personal visit from Matt Busby swayed him in United's direction and he was taken on at Old Trafford soon after leaving Doncaster Technical School.

Skipping the Juniors and Colts, he started the 1951/52 season in the 'A' team. By October 1951, with regular left-winger Roger Byrne repositioned at left full-back, Pegg had been pushed into Central League action for the first time in a 3-0 home win over Blackburn. Progress for his age was excellent, a fact evidenced by his participation in a dozen Reserve matches that season.

He had been on the Reds' books for over a year, and was already a professional, before making his initial Youth Cup appearance in October 1952 when scoring once from the inside-left position as United comfortably defeated Leeds. In the November of that year he trawled five goals against Nantwich prior to being given an early introduction to life in the First Division the following month. At just a little over two months past his 17th birthday, his senior debut came in a 3-2 home win over Middlesbrough.

He made 21 consecutive senior appearances in the 1952/53 campaign. Scoring on four occasions, as the proceedings drew to a close he registered one of the Reds' seven goals in the opening leg of the Youth Cup final. The 9-3 aggregate win over Wolves gave him a tangible reward for a season that had more than met all of the wildest expectations he may have held when it began.

On the road to winning the Youth Cup in 1954 he made a full complement of ten appearances. Firing one of the goals against Wrexham in the Second Round, that feat was easily surpassed when a hat-trick was plundered against Bradford Park Avenue at the next stage. Pegg totted up another two goals in the first leg of the semi-final at West Brom and was on the scoring list twice more in the Old Trafford half of the final. When the boys arrived at Molineux for the second leg, with the scores locked at 4-4 on aggregate, nerves were tested to the full when the Reds were awarded a penalty, however, his calmly executed spot kick proved the deciding goal that gave United a second Youth Cup triumph.

Following that early burst into the first-team picture, he made only fifteen senior appearances spread over the 1953/54 and 1954/55 terms. He kept plugging away, though, and a high level of consistency in the Central League side eventually paid off when, in September 1955, he won a recall for a 1-0 defeat at Sheffield United.

Two weeks later he scored in a 3-2 win over Preston at Old Trafford. The game against North End began an unbroken sequence of appearances in the first-team, the run lasting until the end of a marvellous campaign which finished with United winning the championship, and his contribution amounted to scoring nine times in 36 First Division and F.A. Cup fixtures.

During the course of the season, in February 1956, he also won an England under-23 cap through his involvement in a 3-1 win over Scotland at Hillsborough. A month later he again represented his country, this time for England 'B' against Switzerland when the home nation achieved a 4-1 success at Southampton.

The First Division championship was retained the following year, with him missing from only five games. His contribution of seven goals from 52 matches was rewarded with a gold medal courtesy of the divisional triumph and a silver one for his appearance in the 1957 F.A. Cup final.

His international credentials were also improved with games against Scotland at Ibrox Park (1-1) and Romania in Bucharest (1-0) for the under-23's. In May 1957, a week before travelling to Romania, he won a full England cap in a World Cup Qualifier against Eire when, featuring alongside United team-mates Roger Byrne, Tommy Taylor and Duncan Edwards, England achieved a 1-1 draw in Dublin.

The handsome Yorkshireman was still an automatic choice for the Reds when the 1957/58 term commenced. Pegg participated in another 26 consecutive fixtures until early December but, after United went three games without a win, he was dropped through suffering from what appeared to be a temporary loss of form and confidence.

biography

117

Taking up the fight to win his senior place back in the Central League over the next couple of months, in seven games he scored as many goals. His last performance was in a 4-3 home victory over Wolves Reserves, a match in which he managed a brace that included a penalty. A few days later he travelled as a non-playing squad member on the fateful trip to Belgrade and was one of the victims of the tragic return journey that also saw another seven of his United pals killed.

On both a club and country level, and at the age of only 22, his loss was a hideous waste of potential as most of his best years in football were seemingly still to come. His body was brought back from Munich shortly after the crash and he was buried close to the family home near Doncaster. Having now passed into that very special peace, the simple verse inscribed on his gravestone gave great comfort to a grieving mother and father, who would always remember him for his cheerful and down to earth disposition:

> Sleep on dear son your game is o'er
> Your Twinkling Feet will play no more
> God took your life He thought it best
> To grant to you Eternal Rest

His sister, Irene, decided not to donate items relating to her late brother's career to the United Museum because she felt it more appropriate that they should be seen in his home town. As such, some caps and medals are displayed in a glass case in Doncaster Museum. Every couple of weeks or so she tends to his grave where, more often than not, a single red rose or carnation lies next to her flowers. She is unaware of who places them, but they have been doing so for more than 50 years.

HAMILTON, Thomas Joseph (1952/53)

Born: Bray, County Wicklow, 22nd March 1935
Height: 5ft. 10ins., **Weight:** 11st.
Role: Centre-forward
Career: Dargle Rovers, Cualann Rovers, Shamrock Boys (all in the Bray Summer League)/ Johnville (Dublin)/ Eire Boys/ Eire Youth/ UNITED: Am. July 1952 Pro. August 1953/ **Shamrock Rovers** November 1955/ **Cork Hibernians** August 1962/ **Limerick** August 1965 to January 1969

As a young boy, Tommy Hamilton played much of his football in the Bray Summer League as he was a pupil at a school that participated in the traditional Gaelic code of football rather than soccer. While starring for one of his summer teams, Cualann Rovers, he was selected to represent Eire at under-15 level when they won at a canter by seven goals to one against their northern counterparts in Belfast.

After joining Johnville in the Dublin District Schoolboys' League, where he formed a lifelong friendship with Paddy Kennedy, the club spectacularly won the Irish equivalent of the F.A. Youth Cup, and he made a first football trip to England through his inclusion in the Eire Youth side that was beaten 3-1 by Liverpool County Youth at Goodison Park.

Recommended to United by Billy Behan, Joe Armstrong watched him perform in the 1952 Bray Summer League final on the Irish scout's tip-off. The Reds' talent spotter was actually on a 'busman's holiday' at the time and was so taken by the quality of what he saw in the youngster that he approached his parents immediately after the game. As a result, Hamilton travelled back to Manchester with Armstrong to sign amateur forms.

Making a start for the club in the August of that year, the Colts benefited from two of his goals in a 6-1 home win over Heywood St. James. Four days later he performed in a 3-1 victory at Roebuck Lane and then made a quick return to Bray because he still had to complete another year at school before obtaining his leaving certificate.

Assuming that there would be no more involvement with United until his education was over, one morning in February 1953 he was summoned to his headmaster's office to be informed that Jimmy Murphy was on the telephone advising that a place was waiting for him in the team which was due to face Everton in the Youth Cup at Old Trafford, should he be willing to make the trip over. Needless to say, Murphy didn't need to ask twice.

The reason for the unusual call-up came about because United's regular youth team centre-forward, Eddie Lewis, was needed for senior duty and the Irish lad was required to deputise. Even though he normally operated as an inside-forward, Murphy tasked him with leading the forward-line and he acquitted himself well as the Reds went through to the next round via a 1-0 margin over a formidable Everton eleven.

He left school in June 1953 and became a full-time footballer two months later. Registering five goals for the Colts on the opening day of the 1953/54 season in a 15-4 home success against Didsbury United, because of his age he was ineligible to play in the youth team after moving to England.

Over the next two years he rose up through the club ranks while making a huge impression, not least of which was amongst his fellow professionals, as a clever and highly skilled ball artist who forever had one eye on creating openings for his team-mates and the other on snapping up chances for himself.

Then, having made a few Manchester League appearances at the beginning of the 1955/56 campaign, the last of which was a 2-2 draw against Rochdale Reserves, he came face to face with a dilemma that was to have a radical bearing on his life and his career. In the October of that season he received conscription papers for National Service duty and, being a Republican Irishman, he was forced to choose whether to stay in England and serve two years in the military or return to his homeland. Unfortunately for United, he chose the latter. As he was only twenty at the time, the club was consigned to cancelling the contract of a superb prospect who carried the potential of rendering them many years of service.

Matt Busby was so loathe at losing him that terms were laid down specifying that if he subsequently signed for another English club, United would receive half of any transfer fee. The outright winner of this scenario was Shamrock Rovers, who obtained his services for nothing and were more than happy to accept the sell-on clause that Busby felt obliged to impose.

So, in November 1955, he simultaneously signed as a part-timer with the Dublin club and became an articled clerk with a firm of chartered accountants. Spending seven fabulous years with the Hoops, his time at Glenmalure Park was positively packed with glory. Shamrock Rovers were regarded as the most glamorous team in the Republic of Ireland just then and the addition of Hamilton to an already impressive list of players was seen as a major coup for them.

His career in Irish football got away to a magnificent start as, by the end of that season, Shamrock had finished as runner's-up in the League of Ireland and also lifted the FAI Cup in front of 35,000 spectators at Dalymount Park. With his main contribution being one of the goals, the trophy was won via a 3-2 victory over Cork Athletic and during the course of the campaign he also made his first appearance for the League of Ireland representative side.

The following term saw Rovers go one better in the league by taking the champion's crown while he headed the divisional scoring stakes with fifteen goals to his credit. The FAI Cup final was also reached again, but the Hoops couldn't complete the double when failing to beat Drumcondra without the injured Hamilton.

As league champions, Rovers qualified to compete in the European Cup in the 1957/58 season and, lo and behold, the draw for the Preliminary Round matched them with none other than Manchester United. Of course, that fortuitous turn of events gave him the opportunity to pit his skills against some of his old pals.

Because of the interest generated in the contest in Dublin, the opening leg was switched to the larger Dalymount Park where the Reds put the issue beyond all doubt with an emphatic 6-0 victory. To their eternal credit, Shamrock gave a gutsy display in the return in Manchester and despite his side going down 3-2, United's old boy had the Old Trafford crowd applauding when he scored with a wonderful strike that went under the body of Reds' goalkeeper Ray Wood. Two minutes later, he concocted what one of the press described as *'a glorious volley on the turn'* that was brilliantly saved by Wood to deny the part-timers a draw.

Nonetheless, Rovers' experience in Europe only served to consolidate what was another excellent campaign as they finished as league runner's-up and reached the FAI Cup final against Dundalk. History repeated itself when their ace forward was sidelined through injury for the second successive final, which Shamrock lost 1-0.

His Rovers team won the league title again in 1959 and, as the finishing post came in sight, he was afforded his highest honour in football when capped as a full international in a European Nations (now European Championships) Cup tie against Czechoslovakia in Dublin. The game went well for the Irish, who won 2-0, and a month later he claimed a second cap for his appearance in the return game in Bratislava.

The Hoops made it to yet another FAI Cup final in 1962 and, determined to make up for the two showcase matches missed previously, he whacked a couple of goals past league champions Shelbourne in a tremendous 4-1 win. Later that month Sunderland visited Dublin to take on Shamrock in a richly deserved benefit match for the player, which brought an end to a marvellous liaison that had benefited both he and the club in equal proportions. If further testimony were needed as to his popularity in the Emerald Isle, that same year he was voted as 'Irish Soccer Personality of the Year' by the Soccer Writers' of Ireland.

Outside of football, he had left the accountancy practice in September 1957 to work in the accounts department of an insurance company. Moving to another insurance firm in 1962, that job involved him relocating to Cork.

With a fee of £750 quoted, the Irish press reported that the striker was likely to sign for Limerick as he had recently taken part in some exhibition matches for them whereas later reports linked him with Cork Hibernians, who wanted him in exchange for their goalkeeper. Shamrock Rovers then signed future United 'keeper Pat Dunne from Everton, which blocked off that particular avenue of trade, and a deal was eventually struck when Cork Hibernians agreed to take him as a straight swap for another outfield player.

They were exciting times for the Cork outfit as, having just taken over a new ground which was rather romantically named the Flower Lodge, their star signing was captured in the week leading up to the club's first game in their new enclosure and he debuted for them that weekend.

Finding himself back on centre stage the following April with an appearance in the 1963 FAI Cup final, Cork were denied victory by a Shelbourne team containing Jackie Hennessy, himself a former United youth player. He gained further representative honours by his continued selection for the League XI, only stopping when reaching the grand total of 28 appearances.

Having been at the Flower Lodge for three years, in the close season of 1965 he guested for Limerick in a friendly against Leicester City. His appearance fuelled both local and national speculation that he was about to sign for the club and, as things transpired, that was exactly what happened.

Scoring in his first match for Limerick in August 1965, by the following April the side had reached the FAI Cup final only to lose the match by two goals to nil against one of his old clubs, Shamrock Rovers.

In December 1968, at the age 33, he played his last game and a month later announced his retirement from the sport. Limerick's secretary, Jack Tuohy, said that the club *'were proud to have a player of his calibre in the side for three seasons'* and that his decision to quit was accepted *'with regret'*. A magnificent sporting career had passed over the horizon and comments of that nature poured in from all corners of the world of football to emphasise the esteem in which he was held both at home and abroad.

By the 1990's, Tommy Hamilton had risen to the role of senior regional sales manager for the insurance company he commenced service with back in 1962. In recognition of his greatest days in football, he was elected to Shamrock Rovers' 'Hall of Fame' in May 1997.

Currently living south of Dublin, his son Tom has played Davis Cup tennis for Eire.

Just three Youth Cup appearances between a gifted pair of Irishmen; Billy Whelan (left) and Tommy Hamilton

WHELAN, William Augustine (1952/53)

Born: Dublin, 1st April 1935
Died: Munich, 6th February 1958
Height: 5ft. 9ins., **Weight:** 11st.
Role: Inside-forward
Career: St. Peter's School (Dublin)/ Home Farm (Dublin)/ Eire Boys/ Eire Youth/ UNITED: Am. April 1953 Pro. May 1953 to his death

A native of the Cabra area of Dublin, Liam Whelan was educated at a school that directly overlooked Dalymount Park, home of the Bohemians Football Club and the stadium which, for many years, was used to stage most of the major cup finals and international football matches in the Republic of Ireland.

He was active at sport from an early age and won his first medal, not at football but at hurling, when his school team captured the Johnston, Mooney & O'Brien Cup. Equally talented at Gaelic football and hurling, it is likely that he could have become just as well known at either of those sports had his fabulous soccer skills not overtaken them. As a boy he had the unusual honour to be selected for Dublin at both hurling and Gaelic football on the same day, and he chose the latter.

Made captain of a junior soccer side known as Red Rockets, they took part in games all over the city of Dublin, and from the age of thirteen he became associated with the famous Dublin junior football club, Home Farm. At its peak, the Whitehall outfit catered for up to seventeen youth and boys' teams and was once described by Matt Busby as *'the best organised amateur sporting organisation in the world.'* That accolade, coming from the great man himself, was as fine a testimony to the club's wonderful record in the development of young local talent as could possibly be paid.

While at Home Farm, Whelan blossomed into an incredibly creative individual who developed a loping style all of his own. Blessed with fantastic footwork, allied to quicksilver speed of thought and movement, he possessed the rare ability of being able to constantly spring the unexpected on the opposition. As well as fashioning openings for others, the youngster was also an exceptional finisher and a fabulous record in this facet of his play was constant throughout his career.

Honours came thick and fast during his time with Home Farm. In addition to being the recipient of many medals and trophies from domestic football, he was capped for his appearances in an Eire Boys team that also contained Paddy Kennedy and Noel McFarlane and later added youth caps to a growing list of soccer distinctions.

He initially came to United's attention when Matt Busby saw him, fate dictating that the initial viewing would take place in completely accidental circumstances and Billy Behan, the Reds' Republic of Ireland scout, recalled the events in a newspaper article some years later. Opening his story by revealing that United's manager was in Ireland to take a look at one of his recommendations, Jack Fitzgerald of Waterford, Behan continued, *'Busby decided to come over and have a look at Jack himself. Through a misunderstanding I did not know of Matt's arrival and he called to my house to find that I was out at Whitehall watching Home Farm Youths. Matt drove out to Whitehall to pick me up and he was the first from Old Trafford to see Liam Whelan (whom I had earmarked for a trial the following August) play that morning'.*

With Busby making a mental note of the teenager's skills, the tale then took another fateful twist. In April 1953, United were on the lookout for a replacement for the injury-jinxed John Doherty, who was ruled out of the Youth Cup final against Wolves the following month, and they particularly wanted someone who could deputise without unduly disrupting the team pattern.

Taking up the story again, Behan mentioned, *'Typically, United left no stone unturned in seeking an adequate replacement and their attention turned to Ireland, for the FAI Youths had just put up a very good performance in finishing sixth of sixteen in the Brussels Youth International Tournament. In fact, the Irish boys had lost 2-0 rather against the run of play to England in a play-off for fifth place. As a result, United sent over Bert Whalley in a bid to sign the Home Farm right-half Vinny Ryan, who in the youth tournament against Luxembourg at Malines had moved up to centre-forward to notch a hat-trick in Ireland's 3-2 win.*

However, soon after Bert Whalley's arrival, it became clear that prolonged negotiations would be necessary to obtain Ryan's signature. I had always thought that Ryan was a better defender than an attacker and I told Bert so, adding that I believed Ryan's Home Farm club-mate Liam Whelan, who had been at inside-right on the Irish Youths XI, was the player that United wanted in the prevailing circumstances.

We contacted Old Trafford and it was decided to bring Liam over straight away, and play him in a match on the Wednesday before the first leg of the Youth Cup final against Wolverhampton. We were unable to arrange boat travel and luckily for us Dr. Jerry Dempsey, then with Aer Lingus and an avid soccer supporter, came to our rescue and helped sort out Liam's transport arrangements.'

The first person to meet him in Manchester was United captain and fellow countryman, Johnny Carey. After the two said their hellos and shook hands, Carey inquired as to his first name and when the reply came back that it was normally shortened to Liam, the skipper jokingly advised him to hang on to it for as long as he could. The inference was that he was sure to attract a nickname sooner rather than later and, sure enough, Liam soon became 'Billy' to everyone who knew him on the English side of the Irish Sea.

The Dubliner had made his last appearance for Home Farm in a midweek fixture and, on what must have seemed like the entrance to a fairytale, exactly one week later he lined up against Wolves in the Youth Cup final at Old Trafford. His career in England got off to a dream start, as the Reds whacked the Wanderers by seven goals to one and he left his calling card by scoring once.

Repeating his goal feat in the second leg at Molineux, it took just those two games for the management to offer him a professional contract and the Manchester Evening Chronicle noted that United sent Home Farm a cheque *'as a gesture'* for obtaining his services.

After the cup success he was soon back in the Emerald Isle as a member of the Reds' youth squad which undertook two end of term fixtures there. When United faced the Athletic Union League representative side at Tolka Park in Dublin, he squared up to two of his former Home Farm team-mates, one of whom was none other than Vinny Ryan.

Appearing for the 'A' team for most of the 1953/54 season, the benefit of full-time training contributed greatly to his development in terms of both skill and stamina as he notched 29 goals in 19 matches between October and January, which included two four-goal hauls. On the penultimate day of January his exploits were deemed to merit a call up to the Central League eleven and he retained his place in the side thereafter while continuing his scoring exploits by thumping in a hat-trick at Derby.

At the completion of domestic commitments he was included to travel on the hugely successful youth tour of Switzerland, during the course of which some highly flattering attention was received from a totally unexpected source.

When United ran in four goals without reply past the Swiss national youth team in the Grasshoppers Stadium, watching was the whole entourage of the senior Brazilian squad. The South Americans were in Switzerland to participate in the 1954 World Cup finals and they looked on as the nineteen year-old chose to put on a mesmerising display, which included scoring a breathtaking solo goal. Picking up possession around the halfway line, he danced around practically the whole of the Swiss defence before side-stepping the goalkeeper and placing the ball in the net. The goal put the crowd, and in particular the Brazilians, into raptures.

At the final whistle, what appeared to be the whole of the Brazilian press ended up in United's dressing room. The media men had followed the president of the Brazilian F.A. into the changing area to take photographs of him, while pidgin-English enquiries were made as to how much it would cost to take him back to South America. The episode was ended firmly but politely by Busby, who informed the Brazilians that he wasn't available at any price.

The following season saw him assist the Central League team's cause by scoring sixteen times in 26 matches. Also given a gentle introduction to the senior side, it came in a friendly fixture at Lincoln City in March 1955.

Two weeks later, on the 26th of that month, he was in the first-team for real when appearing in a 2-0 win at Preston. Tom Jackson remarked in print that even *'a pitch inches deep in mud did not prevent young Whelan from making a valuable contribution'*. Including that victory at Deepdale, he made seven consecutive starts and got one goal, his first for the seniors, against Sheffield United on the 2nd April 1955, the day after his 20th birthday.

His development continued into the 1955/56 term as Busby utilised him even more. Four goals from thirteen games gained him a First Division championship medal and, having spent most of his time in the Reserves until early January, he also qualified for a similar Central League souvenir to make it a wonderful personal double.

Recognition of his growing stature came at the end of that memorable campaign when he won his first full international cap, wearing the green number ten jersey, against Holland in the Feyenoord Stadium in Rotterdam. Securing a great 4-1 victory over the Dutch, the Irish Independent claimed that his was a *'triumphant debut'*, while the Amsterdam newspaper Volkskrant echoed that view by proclaiming *'the virtuoso Whelan'*.

When United rolled up the shutters for the start of business in August 1956, the Dubliner was in the first-team from the off. Goals at Preston and West Brom in the opening month were simply a prelude for what was to come because he proceeded to slam goals in each of eight straight league matches during September and October and then made an appearance in the Charity Shield victory over Manchester City. Within that purple patch his full international home debut came against Denmark at Dalymount Park and, looking up from the pitch, he would have been able to see the classroom windows he used to peer out of just a few short years before. A 2-1 win against the Danes made it a thoroughly pleasant homecoming.

By the end of April 1957 he had completed 39 First Division games in a season that saw United at the top of the tree for the second successive time. Finishing in joint second place in the appearance stakes, his 26 league goals put him out of reach of anyone else in the scoring chart and he also registered four more in the F.A. Cup before the Reds eventually lost to Aston Villa in the final. Completing all six ties on the cup run, he won the Sporting Record's 'Man of the Match' award for his contribution to the Wembley showpiece.

Of all the goals the Irishman scored that term, undoubtedly the most vital one was actually seen by very few United fans at the time as it came in a European Cup game in northern Spain. After beating Anderlecht of Belgium in the opening round, during which he notched a brace in a record 10-0 score at Maine Road, the Reds were paired against Athletico Bilbao, with the away leg coming first. Performing in the most atrocious conditions imaginable, that of mud and driving snow, the team was staring down the barrel of a gun with a goal deficit of five to two against them. In the dying seconds, he collected the ball and ran 50 yards, ploughing through the slush while shaking off challenges along the way, before bulleting it past the Bilbao 'keeper.

The goal was not only one of tremendous skill, it also emphasised the bravery and determination in his make-up. It proved to be a lifeline to the club's aspirations in the competition and in the return at Maine Road, a classic contest of truly epic proportions finished at three-nil to United to earn them a place in the semi-final. Thankfully, a newsreel of events in Bilbao survives and, even by today's standards, his goal is stamped by the hallmark of sheer brilliance.

At the end of the campaign, in May 1957, two further international caps were won by virtue of appearances against England. The first of those matches was staged on the Wednesday following the F.A. Cup final defeat, Whelan making the return journey to London by train with Old Trafford's England contingent, Roger Byrne, Tommy Taylor, David Pegg and Duncan Edwards. England won 5-1 at Wembley but eleven days later at Dalymount Park, Eire acquitted themselves much better in a 1-1 draw and only a goal conceded in injury-time denied the home side a win they certainly deserved.

The 1957/58 football calendar started sensationally for him. Knocking in a hat-trick at Leicester on the opening day, by the time he sat out his first game of the term in late September, eight goals had been cracked home in just nine matches. That same month he returned to Dalymount Park once more as the Reds began their second attempt at the European Cup with a Preliminary Round tie against Shamrock Rovers.

A brace for him, out of United's six, made it *'mission impossible'* for the Hoops in the Manchester leg a few weeks later. The News Chronicle's Frank Taylor described his contribution in glowing terms when writing, *'He mastered the ball, he tamed the wind which threatened to make this match a game of blow football. He ignored the frightening roar of 46,000 Irish voices as he slapped in two magnificent goals in the 51st and 56th minutes which sank the good ship Shamrock without trace'*.

On the last day of November, the Reds lost a seven-goal thriller by the odd one to Spurs at Old Trafford, which was the first time they had conceded defeat to a London club in Manchester for nineteen years, and inevitably, he was one of the goalscorers. Two weeks later, United lost their second home game in nineteen years to a team from the capital when Chelsea secured a 1-0 win and, along with Ray Wood, David Pegg and Johnny Berry, he was dropped for the next match. His place went to the emerging Bobby Charlton and for the next two months he was required to content himself with a place in the Central League side.

In early February 1958, a United party flew to Belgrade where a draw would have been good enough to put them into the European Cup semi-final for the second time. Because of injury doubts to a number of the squad, the Irishman was required to travel to the Yugoslav capital.

The Reds got the draw they required but, along with seven of his colleagues and many others, he paid the ultimate cost when killed at Munich on the return journey. That terrible crash happened at four minutes past three on the 6th February 1958 and by ten o'clock that evening his family were told the news they had feared most. He was aged just 22.

His body was brought back to Dublin and after a service at the Church of Christ the King in Cabra he was laid to rest at the New Cemetery, Glasnevin, just a short distance from the family home. En route from the airport, former team-mates and friends from the Home Farm club stood in silence outside the Whitehall ground as the hearse passed by.

Those who were close to him speak highly of a charming person whose modesty, easygoing personality and quick smile endeared him to all he came into contact with, and so his memory lives on. Whenever or wherever football fans reminisce of the great players who have worn both the red of United and the green of Eire, his name is mentioned. Late in 2006, a delegation from Old Trafford attended a memorial ceremony in Dublin when the Connaught Street Bridge was renamed the Liam Whelan Bridge.

The last word is left to Billy Behan, one of the central characters in his meteoric rise to fame. Speaking about a Catholic service he attended shortly after the disaster at the King's Hall in Manchester, which drew 7,000 mourners with many others locked outside, he claimed, *'Liam's family were not at the service and I suppose I was one of the saddest there, especially as I recall Liam as a remarkably nice, unassuming, good living, thoughtful boy. But his qualities also made me one of the proudest.'*

YOUNG REDS GO ON IMPROVING

Chapter Three

REBIRTH & GLORY

1958-59

1) Trevor Powell
2) Phil Clay
3) David Brook
4) Brian Kelly
5) Jimmy Tucker
6) Alan Hockey
7) Trevor Hockey
8) Bruce Stowell
9) Allan Devanney
10) John Nussey
11) John Scott

1) David Gaskell
2) Barry Smith
3) Stan Ackerley
4) Nobby Stiles
5) Frank Haydock
6) Jimmy Nicholson
7) Phil Chisnall
8) Johnny Giles
9) Bernard Poole
10) Tommy Spratt
11) Jimmy Elms

OCTOBER 1958

BRADFORD CITY 1 v 3 MANCHESTER UNITED
Scott   Brook (o.g.), Chisnall, Stiles

Monday 13th
Kick-off 7.00 p.m.
Attendance 2,797

first round

Reds on Youth Cup trail again

By the autumn of 1958, things were slowly returning to normal at Old Trafford, with slowly being the operative word, following the traumatic events surrounding the club earlier in the year.

United's senior side had started their First Division campaign in a reasonable enough fashion, with four wins and four draws from the opening ten games, and they included encouraging and morale-boosting 5-2, 6-1 and 4-1 home wins over Chelsea, Blackburn and West Ham respectively. Some of the club's former Youth Cup winners were in decent form, as Bobby Charlton (ten), Albert Scanlon (five) and Alex Dawson (two) had been amongst the goals for the first-team.

Unfortunately, October wasn't proving too good for the seniors and so far that month they had been beaten 4-0 at Wolves and lost 2-0 at home to Preston, as well as drawing 1-1 with Arsenal at Old Trafford.

The second string, too, were slightly in credit, with six wins, two draws and five defeats the reward for their efforts so far. With those such as Barry Smith, Joe Carolan, Bobby Harrop, Harold Bratt, Ken Morgans, Johnny Giles, Shay Brennan and Mark Pearson appearing regularly in the Central League team, it seemed safe to assume that at least two or three of those formerly of the club's junior sides would soon break through into the senior ranks.

It was, of course, the last full season of the 1950's and the Reds found themselves in the unusual position of starting out on the Youth Cup road with no trophy to prove their virtual invincibility.

The line-up for the starting tie, away to Bradford City, saw introductions for two Manchester lads, Phil Chisnall and Stan Ackerley. The former came from Stretford

Like all of his fellow United defenders, new left full-back Stan Ackerley was never overstretched at Valley Parade

> "I kept my place in the side for the trip to Bradford, I think it was Matt Busby's first away trip with the team since Munich. Anyway, I was playing upfront again and their centre-forward bashed me on the head and then head-butted me. I was dazed and couldn't see more than three feet in front of me.
>
> The trainer came on with smelling salts but I was pretty much out of it for the rest of the match. I think Johnny Giles was just running the game that day."
>
> **BERNARD POOLE**

and had been a highly sought after England schoolboy prodigy prior to being engaged by United, while Ackerley, who hailed from the Wythenshawe district of the city, previously represented Manchester Boys as a defender.

Frank Haydock, an Eccles boy, took over the centre-half responsibility from Reg Holland and alongside him was Belfast-born Jimmy Nicholson, a former Northern Ireland Boys international of whom great things were already being predicted. Because of his all-action, power-packed performances, the wing-half would soon draw comparisons to the great Duncan Edwards.

Preparations for the opener included resting Giles on the weekend prior to the tie at Valley Parade, while the seven who were on duty that Saturday, namely Ackerley, Stiles, Haydock, Nicholson, Chisnall, Spratt and Elms, all took part in a 2-2 home draw with Rochdale Reserves.

The match proved to be a rather smooth introduction in United's quest to regain the Youth Cup and despite Bradford putting on a plucky display when using the age-old tactics of hard tackling and closing down space quickly, they were gradually worn down by their guests, who bossed the proceedings for long passages of the game. Rather encouragingly, United's middle trio clicked together almost from the off, and as well as consistently making positive use of the ball when in possession, their understanding of each other's play proved as solid as a brick wall and bolstered the team right through the match.

Any early nerves on the part of the newly-inducted Reds were soon settled when Bradford's left-back David Brook put past his own goalkeeper and they were dispelled almost entirely when Chisnall stamped his passport into the competition with a debut goal. Just to make things interesting, City's outside-left John Scott reduced the deficit just prior to the interval, which meant that the match retained something of a sustained edge.

The second half was a mainly United affair, and without ever reaching a level of complete superiority, their task was all but completed with a third goal courtesy of Nobby Stiles.

The Bradford Telegraph & Argus praised the efforts of some of the home side and also informed its readership that *'Nicholson was the outstanding player in the game'*.

The Manchester Evening Chronicle predicted *'United look well set for a good run'* in the tournament and added that they *'would have scored six or seven'* if it wasn't for a splendid performance by City goalkeeper Trevor Powell.

The Chronicle report also noted:

The first Youth Cup game, when the team are trying to find a new blend, is always the most worrying, but the United boys soon settled down. There are one or two problem positions but, by the later stages of the competition, the side should be really good.

It is based on an outstanding half-back line of Stiles, Haydock and Nicholson. The wing-halves are only fifteen and should be a grand foundation for the next year or two.

The defence was solid, and right-back Barry Smith showed signs of recapturing his best form.

122

1) David Gaskell
2) Barry Smith
3) Stan Ackerley
4) Nobby Stiles
5) Frank Haydock
6) Jimmy Nicholson
7) Phil Chisnall
8) Johnny Giles
9) Bernard Poole
10) Tommy Spratt
11) Jimmy Elms

1) Willie Mailey
2) Alan Bentham
3) Colin Green
4) Alan Jarvis
5) John Watson
6) John Connor
7) Andy Penman
8) Arthur Peat
9) Andy Gearie
10) David Boner
11) Phil Duffy

1958-59

MANCHESTER UNITED 2 v 2 EVERTON

Elms (2) Boner, Peat

NOVEMBER 1958

Monday 17th

Kick-off 7.30 p.m.

Attendance 15,566

second round

FOOTBALL
at Old Trafford
F.A. YOUTH CUP (2nd round)
UNITED Youth
(Winners five times)
v.
EVERTON Youth
(Old rivals and strong opponents)
on MONDAY, 17th November
Kick-off 7-30 p.m.
Admission: Grand Stands, 3/- & 2/-; Groundside and Covered Paddock, 1/-, Juniors 6d.

The evening after United's win at Valley Parade, an Everton side defeated opponents Leeds United 3-0 at Goodison Park. Their achievement brought the two Lancastrian clubs into Youth Cup conflict for the fifth time in just seven seasons, and for the third occasion at Old Trafford.

The Everton club were able to boast the fact that former England Boys' captain Alan Bentham was in their ranks, and the right full-back had already begun to make something of a reputation for himself with frequent appearances in their Central League side.

By the late 1950's, the Blues had established a big pull on young talent in the vicinity of North Wales and their starting formation included Colin Green, Alan Jarvis and John Watson, all of whom hailed from the Wrexham area. Jarvis and Watson had been capped for Wales as schoolboys and Everton's forward-line also showed two ex-internationals, with both Andy Penman and David Boner having starred for their native Scotland prior to joining the Merseysiders. Winger Penman carried the added experience of having already earned his senior spurs.

By rights, Everton should have fielded another schoolboy international against United but, while taking part in a Central League game at Huddersfield only two days before the Youth Cup tie, Welsh goalkeeper Graham Griffiths injured his ribs badly enough to be forced into leaving the field after only 23 minutes. On the day of the Youth Cup clash it was reported that Griffiths *'was much better this morning'* and that Blues' boss Johnny Carey was planning to include him against United. The goalie's condition later proved a little less healthy than was first thought and for the Old Trafford encounter his place was taken by a dependable deputy called Willie Mailey.

Despite Griffiths' absence, it was clear there were some very useful individuals in the Everton side and that the Reds would be required to fully concentrate themselves if they were to come out on top.

United were able to field an unchanged eleven from the match at Bradford, and the Review detailed their exploits with the following brief report:

In the tenth minute an unlucky clearance from Haydock struck an Everton player in the back and from the rebound Boner ran on to score an easy goal. This goal was a severe setback to United, but they were not disheartened and the Everton defence was put under heavy pressure before Elms scored a wonderful goal in the 35th minute.
Half-time 1-1.
After 68 minutes, a great pass from Giles found Elms standing unmarked on the left wing and, after moving ten yards, he hit a low, swerving shot into the far corner of the net. With United well on top it seemed that the game was settled but Everton had other ideas. Although their goal was under constant attack, they did break through occasionally and it was from one of these breakthroughs that they got their equaliser when Peat headed a centre past Gaskell in the 88th minute.

A hard game played in a very clean and sporting manner and we look forward to the replay at Goodison Park.

That spectacular late diving header from Arthur Peat, which levelled the tie, reciprocated a similar effort by United's Jimmy Elms in the opening half to set up an unwelcome replay on Merseyside.

The Reds hadn't got off to the most promising of starts, with what was identified as a *'self-inflicted'* goal scored by Toffees' inside-left David Boner, and for some time after they appeared unsettled. When United did get down to the task in hand, from then on it was practically one-way traffic towards Mailey until the break.

The Reds were helped by Johnny Giles stamping his influence all over the forward and midfield areas of the pitch, causing a reporter to claim *'if only a portion of the chances he created had been accepted United must have won this exhilarating game'*. That same article additionally identified the young Dubliner as the team's *'star performer'*.

It was a contest which really should have been sewn up with goals to spare for the Reds. They pounded incessantly at Everton's goal during the second period, a spell in which they saw efforts cannon back from both the bar and the post, and one observer even noted that the Blues were subjected to *'a ten-minute bombardment'* as United kept them firmly on the back foot.

Because Matt Busby's first-team were going through something of a lean stretch, which was sometimes attributed to chances created failing to be converted into goals, the Manchester Evening News felt that their *'hoodoo'* had now transferred to the youth side. Going on to mention that the under-18's *'peppered the Everton goal left, right and centre only to hit the goalposts or desperate defenders'*, their reporter pinpointed the requirement for a rematch when writing that United had *'shot very wildly and wasted good chances'* before adding that *'Everton rallied splendidly'*.

Now considered a Youth Cup 'veteran', Jimmy Elms' two crackers forced a replay with Everton

1958-59

1) Willie Mailey	9) Andy Gearie
2) Alan Bentham	10) David Boner
3) Colin Green	11) Ken Barton
4) Alan Jarvis	
5) John Watson	
6) John Connor	
7) Andy Penman	
8) Arthur Peat	

1) David Gaskell	9) Phil Chisnall
2) Barry Smith	10) Tommy Spratt
3) Stan Ackerley	11) Jimmy Elms
4) Nobby Stiles	
5) Frank Haydock	
6) Jimmy Nicholson	
7) Ian Moir	
8) Johnny Giles	

NOVEMBER 1958

EVERTON* 1 v 2 MANCHESTER UNITED

Penman — Chisnall, Spratt

Wednesday 26th

Kick-off 7.30 p.m.

Attendance 4,716

*Played at Anfield

second round replay

A letter sent to Goodison Park by Liverpool's secretary, which details the cost of using Anfield for Everton's Youth Cup replay against United

Liverpool Football Club & Athletic Grounds Co. Ltd.

TELEPHONES: ANFIELD 2361/2
MANAGER: P. H. TAYLOR
SECRETARY: J. S. McINNES

ANFIELD ROAD,
LIVERPOOL, 4.

10th December 1958.

W. Dickinson. Esq.
Everton Football Club Co. Ltd.
Goodison Park.
Liverpool 4.

Dear Mr Dickinson,

Thank you for your letter of the 5th inst., which was submitted to a meeting of Directors held last evening.

I have to inform you that my Board is pleased to accept your cheque for £ 53: 0: 0 in respect of the use of our Ground for your Youth Cup Replay v Manchester United on Wednesday, 26th November 1958.

Yours sincerely,

J.S. McInnes
Secretary.

The replay against Everton wasn't staged at the obvious place of their usual Goodison Park home but by the kind invitation of their Liverpool neighbours, at Anfield. The explanation for the switch in venue was down to the extremely poor condition of the Goodison Park pitch, which had lately come to resemble a sea of mud caused by severe drainage problems.

As the Blues were attempting to give their playing surface as much respite as possible for senior and Reserve matches, Liverpool came to the rescue by placing their ground at Everton's disposal for the Youth Cup game.

Both teams showed only one change each from the drawn game at Old Trafford, Everton replacing Phil Duffy with Ken Barton at outside-left, while United gave a first start to Ian Moir at outside-right. The Reds also took another forward to Anfield, an Altrincham boy by the name of Barry Jones, but Moir was given the nod ahead of him. Moir's introduction resulted in Phil Chisnall moving to centre-forward and Bernard Poole was resultantly omitted.

The Liverpool Echo made a record of the game which gave due notice of a United star in the making:

Managers John Carey, of Everton, and Matt Busby, of Manchester United, those colleagues of yesteryear from Old Trafford, sat together at Anfield last night to watch the F.A. Youth Cup Second Round replay between their clubs. Behind them was Jimmy Murphy, the United assistant manager, who had made a fast dash from Villa Park, where he had seen his Welsh team draw with England.

All three of them must have come away very satisfied that the future fortunes of their clubs are in good hands if the display they saw is any criterion. These lads look their age but play like men.

The crowd of 4,716 had enough thrills and enough good football to dispel the rigours of the cold and misty night.

Manchester United, who have monopolised this cup until Wolves took it from them last season, won 2-1 because of superior physical strength and the artistry of inside-right Giles.

This lad made both United goals and he took command of the second half when Everton were one up to turn the game his way. What a treasure he is from the United nursery!

If Giles was the outstanding player on the night, there were Everton boys not far behind him. I thought goalkeeper Mailey, smallish but very safe, full-backs Bentham and Green and wing-halves Jarvis and Connor excellent in their own right.

Inside-left Boner had a splendid first half but faded later and had the misfortune to shoot over the bar from only three yards out just before the end as Everton fought for the equaliser.

Outside-right Penman, who, of course, has appeared in floodlit games for the first-team this season, scored Everton's goal. He was often dangerous with his well placed crosses into the goalmouth but Everton made the mistake of pushing the ball over high into the penalty area where United centre-half Haydock, a tall, commanding figure, completely dominated the home inside-forwards.

Behind him was goalkeeper Gaskell, who has played in First Division football, and he performed like a player ready to continue in the top class.

Everton took the lead after 40 minutes when Penman and Peat beat an offside trap for the winger to score from a narrow angle. They held it until the 63rd minute when the genius of Giles – no farmer he – laid on a goal for inside-left Spratt.

United finally took the lead after strong pressure four minutes from time and again it was a Giles inspired goal. He slipped through a gem of a pass to centre-forward Chisnall and the United leader just beat Mailey to the ball to slam it high into the net.

The Everton boys need not be disappointed with the result for this strong, competent United side are favourites to win the cup. And Giles made all the difference between victory and defeat to them, for rarely have I seen any player dominate a game to the same extent as this brilliant Irish boy did in the second half.

The general skill and behaviour of both teams was a credit to the expert coaching they received. Here was the junior level of these famous clubs playing with all the confidence and composure which augurs so much for the future.

It was a very fine game enjoyed by everyone and a pat on the back, too, for referee J. Mitchell, of Prescot, who handled a fast, often slightly tough, game with firm control.

Deemed to be a particularly encouraging win for the Reds, as they were required to perform with only ten men for a lengthy section of the match, the player injured was left-back Stan Ackerley, who suffered a damaged right leg as early as the 20th minute.

Jimmy Murphy, who was present at Villa Park in his capacity as the Welsh team manager, had been forced to endure a frantic car journey to Anfield following his country's 2-2 draw with England in Birmingham earlier in the day. Murphy faced little option other than to utilise Ackerley simply for his nuisance value on the left flank for the remainder of the game.

Jimmy Elms, whose two goals brought United to the replay, was again hailed for his heroics as he had been redeployed, initially to left-half and then still deeper to left-back, and was to prove a vital element in the win.

The shuffle undoubtedly spurred the Everton lads, who sensed an opportunity to grasp the initiative. The junior Toffees subjected the Reds to unrelenting pressure from then until half-time and during that stage David Gaskell was a key figure in keeping United in the frame with numerous brave stops.

With Jimmy Murphy delivering his second interval pep-talk of the day whilst directing the necessary tactical adjustments, the later period was a completely different story. The new manoeuvres put in place allowed Giles the freedom to use the length and breadth of Anfield in order to display the full expanse of his blossoming talents, and Everton were punished with a late knock-out.

The Manchester Evening News passed judgement in one sentence by stating *'In an excellent game, with both sides showing outstanding ability, United were full value for victory'.*

Even so, the margin between the teams had been mighty fine. An aggrieved Everton could recall golden opportunities they scorned, particularly from Gearie in the first section of the tie, and with numerous Reds defensively packing their penalty area like soccer sardines, that late skied effort from Boner.

1958-59

1) Alan Guinn	9) Dave Shawcross	1) David Gaskell	9) Phil Chisnall
2) Arthur Harrison	10) Peter Richardson	2) Barry Smith	10) Tommy Spratt
3) John Woodward	11) Dave Wagstaffe	3) Stan Ackerley	11) Jimmy Elms
4) Tommy Hill		4) Nobby Stiles	
5) Sandy Wann		5) Frank Haydock	
6) Alan Oakes		6) Jimmy Nicholson	
7) Alan Fenner		7) Ian Moir	
8) Mike Pearson		8) Johnny Giles	

MANCHESTER CITY 0 v 4 MANCHESTER UNITED

Giles (2, 1 pen), Spratt (2)

DECEMBER 1958

Monday 15th

Kick-off 7.30 p.m.

Attendance 21,478

third round

The Third Round brought about a meeting with Manchester City which, to anyone connected to United, and at any level, is always considered highly serious business.

The 1958 Maine Road encounter was given a much higher profile in the Manchester newspapers than the only other Youth Cup clash between the two clubs which had taken place four years earlier. In order to satisfy the greater level of interest in the contest, the Evening News ran a full match preview, written by Eric Thornton, and it was accompanied by profiles of both sets of players and their photographs:

David Shawcross, a seventeen year-old youngster who was left-half for Manchester City against Arsenal at Highbury on September 20, and Barry Smith, eighteen year-old product of local schools' soccer, will captain the rival 'derby' line-ups when Manchester United visit Maine Road tonight in the Third Round of the F.A. Youth Cup.

Shawcross will be at centre-forward in a City team averaging sixteen years, five months, while Smith will be at right full-back in a United team averaging sixteen years, eight months.

Goalkeeper David Gaskell, now eighteen, will be United's last line of defence and their only player to have figured in the league team.

United will be unchanged. This means they will have Phil Chisnall, the sixteen year-old former England schoolboy wing-forward, leading the line with Ian Moir, a fifteen year-old Aberdeen recruit, at outside-right.

Sandy Wann is the City boy to note – apart from Shawcross – because at Maine Road they reckon he'll eventually become their regular first-team pivot.

Dave Ewing, present holder of that position, holds a high opinion of this youngster who comes from his home town – Luncarty.

One of the biggest crowds of the season is expected to watch this battle. United started favourites, having won the trophy five times in six years.

The pitch, churned up during Saturday's league game, was today nicely level, though hard in parts.

With no fog to contend with this time around, over 21,000 Mancunians turned out to see, depending on where their particular allegiances lay, whether City could turn the tables on the Reds following their earlier Youth Cup exit or, conversely, if United would prove good enough on the night to live up to their pre-match billing as favourites to beat the Maine Road teenagers.

City's programme editor made the following notes:

The youngsters who will provide you with your league football at Maine Road and Old Trafford in years to come, step out under the lights here tonight.

A number of them have already tasted soccer's big time by making league appearances before they were seventeen, but for the majority it will be their first big occasion.

And a very big occasion it could be – weather permitting. The loyalties of Manchester's soccer fans and their natural desire to get their own view of team building have brought the Central League attendances at Maine Road and Old Trafford in the last few months well into line with many league gates.

The same editor then went on to make comments on City's earlier Youth Cup ties of that season, which resulted in a 2-1 win at Southport and a 3-1 victory at Huddersfield.

United were undoubtedly the sharper in adapting to the sticky Maine Road surface and early raids threw up indications that the City rearguard was a little on the soft side. In the eighth minute it became apparently clear that those initial pointers were correct when the Reds clocked their opening goal. A combination between United's Irish pair, Johnny Giles and Jimmy Nicholson, gave Tommy Spratt a sight of goal from outside the area and with great aplomb he hammered the ball into City's net with Alan Guinn stretching for a shot there was no earthly chance of him stopping.

United kept up the pressure on City's defence and in the 25th minute they went 2-0 up from a penalty converted by the scheming Giles. The spot kick was awarded after a shot-cum-cross by Moir was met by Chisnall, whose accurate header seemed destined for the back of the goal until the ball was stopped by a City hand.

City showed a spark of life soon after, when a Mike Pearson drive was saved by a leap from the flamboyant Gaskell. The Maine Road youngsters were suffering through the burden of poor performances from some of their key players, particularly skipper Dave Shawcross, whose contribution was almost non-existent

and as the contest crossed into the second half, the Reds were still by far the most efficient entity.

The game went beyond City's grasp entirely in the 56th minute after Giles claimed his second goal. With the home defence infected by a dose of the dithers, a loose ball was collected by the midfielder and he unhesitatingly smashed it beyond Guinn from near to the eighteen-yard line.

The City goalkeeper was further busied for the remainder of the game as United ran the show with an increasing confidence. With the clock showing 80 minutes, Spratt made what was already a good night even better for the Reds when volleying in a fourth from a pass he had collected from the unstoppable Giles.

In searching for a consolation goal, City's best chance of the evening came about when Pearson powered in a shot from distance. Gaskell was equal to it and earned his clean sheet with a spectacular save, diving at full-length to finger-tip the ball past the upright.

Chronicle reporter Ray Wergan claimed *'there was a professional touch about everything that United did'*. Wergan also pinpointed the main reasons for the Reds' dominance by stating that *'above all, they played football, slipping the ball into the open spaces knowing that a team-mate would be in the right place to pick it up'* and added *'United's superiority can be judged by the fact that of the City youngsters only Wann and Oakes would come into the reckoning for a Combined XI selected from last night's sides'*.

In the United Review match report, comments such as *'our boys put on a dazzling display of top class soccer under difficult ground conditions'*, *'this had been a grand all-round show by our boys which a crowd of just under 22,000 was quick to applaud'* and *'our players are beginning to show more blend and rhythm'*, indicated that optimism was growing within Old Trafford about the side's prospects of further success. The report concluded with the writer's view that *'on this display (they) must have a fine chance of lifting the trophy which they lost last year for the first time in six years'*.

It was left to the Evening News' Manchester City correspondent to summarise the night's main events within the confines of a few paragraphs:

Speed + strength beat City boys

BY ERIC THORNTON

LET'S be truthful, without being harsh, and point out that there were three reasons why Manchester United beat Manchester City 4-0 in the third round of the Youth Cup at Maine Road—they were faster, stronger, and had in 18-year-old John Giles an inside-right of boundless energy and skill.

Already an Eire schools' international, Giles' long Central League experience stood him in good stead as he became the man of the match. With the backing he got from this team it's pretty obvious he'll always be a menace to any defence. He fully deserved his two goals even though the first was a penalty.

Tommy Spratt, 16-year-old ground staff boy, collected the other two with an excellent display at inside-left, while outstanding in a strong, good positioning United defence was 18-year-old Frank Haydock—just my cup of tea at centre half.

City's old fault was again apparent. They were weakest on the wings. And, in addition, 17-year-old David Shawcross was never as effective as a deep-lying centre as he is at wing-half.

Sandy Wann, a 17-year-old from Dave Ewing's home town of Luncarty, can look back with pleasure on a tireless display at centre half, and there must also be good marks for Alan Guinn, a 17-year-old who is a "natural" between the posts.

125

1958-59

1) Brian Chicken	9) Harry Clark
2) Cecil Irwin	10) Gordon Clayton
3) Gordon Lister	11) Norman Turner
4) Martin Harvey	
5) Alan Crudace	
6) Harry Grievson	
7) Tommy Carrick	
8) Stewart Buchanan	

1) David Gaskell	9) Phil Chisnall
2) Barry Smith	10) Tommy Spratt
3) Stan Ackerley	11) Jimmy Elms
4) Nobby Stiles	
5) Frank Haydock	
6) Jimmy Nicholson	
7) Ian Moir	
8) Johnny Giles	

JANUARY 1959

SUNDERLAND 1 v 2 MANCHESTER UNITED
Carrick *Spratt (2)*

Saturday 17th
Kick-off 3.00 p.m.

fourth round

The implications of the Fourth Round draw saw the Reds making the first of what would be many long treks to the North-East on Youth Cup operations with an engagement at Roker Park. Because Sunderland's senior side were away on league duty at Stoke, the game was timed for the prime Saturday p.m. slot.

As most northerly regions of the country had recently endured a severe blast of arctic weather, there were doubts over the match taking place on schedule. In view of the prevailing weather, referee Mr. T.S. Blenkinsopp of South Shields conducted a pitch inspection 24 hours before kick-off when he declared that the game would definitely go ahead pending no further deterioration in conditions.

Jimmy Murphy and the United squad were on their way up to Sunderland as soon as the result of the pitch inspection was known and following a good night's rest at the Seaburn Hotel, they spent a leisurely pre-match Saturday morning by taking in the bracing coastal air with a walk along the nearby seafront.

Just prior to kick-off, a slight wind coupled to a brief shower of rain made no significant change to the playing surface and the tie commenced with a crisp layer of snow covering the pitch. The Roker Park ground staff had worked hard in order to make the lines visible and the major disappointment caused by the weather was the small attendance, estimated at 2,000, which, under more favourable circumstances, would have been expected to have topped the five-figure mark.

Sunderland, who won the toss and elected to defend the Roker End, began promisingly and weren't far away from scoring with their initial probe. When Stewart Buchanan stole in behind the United defence he just had Gaskell to beat only to then lose his composure and put the ball into the side-netting.

Buchanan was central to another Sunderland thrust when he carried possession through the heart of the United defence, leaving defenders standing, before releasing the ball to Clark. The sequence was halted when Haydock stepped in to win a firm, well-timed tackle. Moir was United's liveliest forward and it was he who fired off the Reds' opening shot upon receiving a pass from Phil Chisnall. In keeping with United's lack of progress so far, his tame effort couldn't trouble Brian Chicken between the Sunderland sticks.

Sunderland were without question the pick of the two sides early on because, unlike the Reds, they appeared to make light of the snowy surface, which showed increasing signs of churning up as the game went along. Their progress continued when Clark moved the ball out to Clayton, who put over a dangerous high cross that Gaskell accepted responsibility for when leaving his line.

In their next offensive, Sunderland created a similarly dangerous situation and United's goal was left intact only because Haydock stopped Clark from making any further progress. It was only a temporary respite for the Reds as the Rokerites turned their dominance into a goal after 31 minutes of play.

Clark was again involved and after moving out wide to the right-hand side of the field, the Sunderland centre-forward delivered a through pass to Carrick. The winger rode a challenge from Stan Ackerley, who had been in the wars and was soldiering on despite taking a crack on the head, and he drilled a shot that passed the advancing Gaskell and hit a post before crossing the goal-line. For the second time in three games, the adaptable Jimmy Elms was required to fill the left-back role when Ackerley later moved out to the wing.

The home team were good value for their lead and they retained it until the break without any further pressure from United. Sunderland appeared the most cohesive of the two opposing units and their wing-halves and inside-forwards had worked like Trojans to win the ball and create space for the front men. The Reds could easily have been further behind, and as an attacking force they were miles short of the standard expected of them.

The early section of the second half represented the most sustained period of possession United could muster in the whole game and, fortunately, it encompassed an equaliser in the 53rd minute. The goal was a fairly simple affair and it developed when Moir raided down the right and screwed the ball back to Nobby Stiles from near the corner flag. Stiles intelligently chipped into the middle where Tommy Spratt sprang to beat Chicken from close range.

Probably caused by built-up frustration, an overspill of temper crept into the play of several of the United lads and Stiles was just one of a few young Reds who earned a lecture from the referee for overzealous actions.

During the 90 minutes of normal time, Sunderland would have a total of three 'goals' disallowed, all considered offside. It must have been quite galling, then, to lose a game that they always seemed to have within their grasp by a late strike which the Sunderland Echo correspondent considered to be *'palpably offside'*. With only six minutes remaining, Johnny Giles, himself hindered by a thigh knock sustained earlier, created an opening that was just wide enough for Spratt to ram home his, and United's, second.

Spratt's goals, both of which were expertly executed, acted as the key that bailed his team out of jail. In defence of their performance, the pitch certainly hadn't suited United's preference for passing but, even so, they could consider themselves extremely fortunate to have settled the issue without the necessity of a replay.

The referee came in for a large measure of criticism, particularly from the local press, as the contest had spiralled out of hand in terms of the behaviour of certain individuals. Mr. Blenkinsopp apparently allowed a number of unsavoury incidents to pass by without taking strong action and much blame was levelled at his lack of firmness.

David Gaskell leaps to punch clear from a Sunderland corner on a snow-laden Roker Park pitch

1958-59

1) Garry Brown	9) Tony Bridges
2) Jim Whitehouse	10) Brian Perry
3) Vic Cockcroft	11) Alan Hinton
4) John Kirkham	
5) Maurice Donaghy	
6) Graham Jones	
7) Dave Read	
8) Barry Clark	

1) David Gaskell	9) Phil Chisnall
2) Barry Smith	10) Tommy Spratt
3) Stan Ackerley	11) Jimmy Elms
4) Nobby Stiles	
5) Frank Haydock	
6) Jimmy Nicholson	
7) Ian Moir	
8) Johnny Giles	

WOLVERHAMPTON WANDERERS 0 v 3 MANCHESTER UNITED

Chisnall, Elms, Spratt

MARCH 1959

Monday 16th

Kick-off 7.15 p.m.

Attendance 15,879

fifth round

The satisfaction of squeezing through at the expense of Sunderland was soon tempered by the news that an equally tough prospect was waiting in the Fifth Round. Wolves at Molineux was the scene of United's only previous exit from the Youth Cup and the pairing of the two clubs offered a contrast in perspectives from both camps.

For United, a quick revenge would be all the motivation they required to put one over their old foes, while from the Wolverhampton angle, the Reds would once again be seen as the greatest obstacle remaining in their ambition to lift the Youth Cup for the second year running.

From their 1958 winning line-up, Wolves had the distinction of having both John Kirkham and Brian Perry reach the England Youth team along with newcomers Vic Cockcroft and Alan Hinton.

The United eleven was now in a self-selection state, with Jimmy Murphy seemingly content that he had found his best blend. Johnny Giles, the midfield maestro who provided almost boundless inspiration, was declared fit after overcoming a knee injury that had recently seen him sidelined from Central League duty and with the Irish lad in place, Murphy could look on in the faith that his most powerful formation was on the park.

Recorded by the Wolverhampton Express & Star, the outcome was every bit as good as Murphy could have hoped for:

> ONE of Wolves' six trophies that will not be on the club sideboard at the end of the season is the F.A Youth Cup. Their bid to retain it ended under the Molineux lights last night when their original twin-final rivals and five-year monopolisers of the trophy, Manchester United took their seventh successive semi-final place in the tournament with a 3–0 victory.
>
> It was a victory the right to which none could deny them (writes "Commentator"). After both teams had run out of the initial exuberance that kept the game going at breathtaking speed, without bringing any goal-reward, it was the United who settled down to the more deliberate and effective football.
>
> That is why the scoring was concentrated into a 14-minute spell between the 59th and 73rd minutes. By that time the Wolves forwards had made their big effort—they were particularly in the ascendant at the early part of the second half—but it was not good enough to get the better of a hefty, hard tackling and composed defence.
>
> It was in a break-out from a Wolves assault, powered by tremendous enthusiasm, that United took the lead.
>
> For the first time in the match the ball was swept inside Wolves highly efficient left back Cockcroft (their best performer) and right winger Moir lifted it across goal. It dropped at the feet of inside-left Spratt and as goalkeeper Brown hesitated the ball was lobbed back to inside-right Giles to head against the underside of the bar and into the net.
>
> **BRILLIANT GOAL**
>
> Just ten minutes later left winger Elms moved into the middle to drive through following a free kick but the goal of the match was yet to come—and it was a beauty.
>
> Moir made another of his rare escapes from Cockcroft, chased a fine through pass to the bye-line, and flashed it across goal for Spratt, following up at speed, to head a goal that deserved the rich applause it gained from the 15,879 crowd.
>
> That settled it but Wolves were still able to make dying kicks in the form of a left wing run by Perry—he moved there after an injury—and a header by the same player that passed only inches wide of a post to deny Wolves at least a consolation goal.
>
> **THE DIFFERENCE**
>
> Wolves, enthusiastic enough, never entirely rid themselves of an air of excitability which, with the notable exception of Cockcroft and left-half Jones, made them do things too hurriedly.
>
> United, by comparison, were calmer with Haydock an outstanding centre-half and Stiles a busy half-back in the Eddie Colman mould.
>
> Nor were the Wolves able entirely to overcome the absence of youth-experienced regulars like right-back Royle and centre-half Corbett. Their deputies, Whitehouse and Donaghy, were far from letting the side down, but United, by their more studied football and their better positional sense, made the most of their opportunities.
>
> **BUFFETED ABOUT**
>
> Some of the light-weight Wolves players were several times in the wars for this was about the heftiest United youth team I had seen.
>
> It will take a youth team of outstanding ability to prevent the 1959 Busby Babes taking the trophy to Old Trafford for the sixth time in seven seasons.

In true United fashion, the youngsters won their passage into another semi-final by keeping the ball on the carpet and sticking to a passing game. In contrast, Wolves, like Manchester City at the earlier stage, relied on a style fashionably called 'long ball' nowadays but which in 1959 parlance was known as 'kick and rush'. Whatever description is used, the result is usually the same, loss of possession too easily and too often.

Following a frenetic and bitty beginning, which wasn't helped by a wind which occasionally caused the ball to alter its course, the lads from Old Trafford settled when an understanding between the wing-halves and inside-forwards clicked at a point somewhere near to the break. Once United went into the lead from Chisnall's header, which was incorrectly attributed to Giles by the Wolverhampton press, it seemed only a matter of time before more goals would come for them.

Strangely, United chose to wear the same all-white strip at Molineux that they had sported at Roker Park in the last round, even though there was no colour clash with the Wanderers. But as one reporter noted in his after-match notes, he held a conversation with a home supporter who told him: *'You would have known they were Manchester United whatever colours they wore',* sentiments that succinctly summarised the evening's events.

Eleven days later, on Good Friday, 27th March, Keith Dewhurst's column in the United Review contained the following piece:

> *After seeing their convincing 3-0 victory at Wolverhampton I am not surprised that Manchester United are favourites to win the F.A Youth Cup once again.*
>
> *It was only the second time I had seen the youth team this season and I was amazed at the improvement in both team work and individual skill. It was positive proof of the success and devotion of United's coaching system.*
>
> *Fortunately the semi-final (and final if they reach it) is two-legged, so United supporters will get a chance to see their team. Five of their six Cup games so far have been away from home, although they did play one at Maine Road.*
>
> *Having to play so many games away is hard, but from another point of view it is excellent experience, and I am sure it has contributed in some measure to the team's great poise and confidence.*
>
> *It is always difficult to compare individuals in the youth team because some of the players have had two or even three years more experience than others.*
>
> *The young outside-right Ian Moir, for instance, had a tough time against a very good Wolves left-back. But he is only fifteen and a half, and the way in which he refused to be put off his own game and many little touches showed him to be a player of great potential.*
>
> *Johnny Giles and David Gaskell looked very mature and centre-half Frank Haydock was tremendous. The overall moral is that the star-making system is in full swing again.*
>
> *The game gave another clue to United's success. Practically the entire coaching staff travelled to watch it, as well as two directors and a large party of players, both first-team and juniors. I also saw members of the office staff.*
>
> *This is club spirit, for which there is no substitute.*

Johnny Giles' hugely influential performance at Molineux resulted in him being called an 'outstanding schemer' by the United Review

127

1958-59

1) Barry Griffiths	9) John Jervis	
2) David Wells	10) Paddy Daly	
3) Fred Pickering	11) Paddy Mulvey	
4) Mike England		
5) Trevor Rimmer		
6) Vinny Leech		
7) Barrie Ratcliffe		
8) Keith Newton		

1) David Gaskell	9) Phil Chisnall	
2) Barry Smith	10) Tommy Spratt	
3) Stan Ackerley	11) Jimmy Elms	
4) Nobby Stiles		
5) Frank Haydock		
6) Jimmy Nicholson		
7) Ian Moir		
8) Johnny Giles		

APRIL 1959

BLACKBURN ROVERS 1 v 1 MANCHESTER UNITED
Jervis — *Spratt*

semi-final 1st leg

Wednesday 8th
Kick-off 7.30 p.m.
Attendance 19,600

For the penultimate round of the tournament, Blackburn Rovers met United in an all-Lancashire semi-final.

Under the guidance of manager Dally Duncan, Rovers were spending their first campaign back in the top flight after languishing for ten years in the Second Division. Duncan had taken over at Ewood Park earlier in the season when former United captain Johnny Carey was tempted away to become the new boss at Everton. It was obvious that the Irishman's influence still permeated through the club and Carey's concerted efforts at youth level demonstrated just how much he had learned from the Matt Busby school of cultured thought.

Carey had set his stall on developing a productive youth system at Blackburn before leaving for Goodison Park and he managed to entice some wonderfully promising boys to the central Lancashire club. The Rovers' scouts seemingly spent much of their time in and around the Manchester conurbation as no fewer than four of the Blackburn side were plucked from right under Busby's nose.

Goalkeeper Barry Griffiths and forwards Paddy Daly, Paddy Mulvey and Keith Newton had all represented Manchester Boys and Mulvey actually signed for Blackburn despite United's intense efforts to capture him. It is said that imitation is the sincerest form of flattery and, for certain, Carey must have admired Busby immensely by replicating the youthful foundation he witnessed at Old Trafford over at Ewood Park.

The build-up to the first leg was somewhat soured by bad vibrations between the two clubs, a rift caused by a failure to agree on suitable dates for both matches. Busby, in an attempt to buy some time, called for the games to be played at dates later than those preferred by Blackburn as he wanted to ensure that Tommy Spratt and Nobby Stiles, who were both due to travel overseas with the England Youth party, would be available. Understandably, in trying to grasp the initiative, Dally Duncan initially demanded that the games be staged on the earlier dates that Rovers had suggested.

The tiff was resolved to a satisfactory conclusion as a result of a telephone conversation between the rival managers in which the Blackburn chief agreed to Busby's request of the later slots. There was some typical newspaper talk, which made mention of Busby and Duncan *'burying the hatchet'*, although the inference of a major rift was grossly exaggerated. Whether the Rovers' boss had a change of heart or was charmed by Busby's renowned smooth talking is debatable, but Duncan later told the Manchester Evening News that he *'gave way happily in the end'*.

Blackburn prepared for the clash by blooding some members of their youth side in the Central League while United's preparations included a light training session on the evening before the Ewood Park leg. Jimmy Murphy and coach John Aston had the team working out under floodlights in order to help them acclimatise to the conditions they would be exposed to.

Earlier that day, the youth squad were excused polio jabs until a later date while the remainder of United's playing staff were made to stand in line for their inoculations.

The game's considerable interest in the town could be gauged by an article which appeared in the Lancashire Evening Telegraph:

A 30,000 crowd is confidently anticipated at Ewood Park tomorrow night when Blackburn Rovers clash with Manchester United in the first leg of the F.A. Youth Cup semi-final – the return at Old Trafford will be the following Wednesday night.

The Rovers, writes 'CENTURION', will field the side that has taken them to the semi-final for the first time, with wins in previous games against Blackpool, Burnley, Bolton Wanderers, Newcastle United and Portsmouth.

Both clubs were able to name full-strength sides despite the feeling that each were prepared to take risks with the fitness of certain key players. Blackburn, whose confidence was sky-high after winning three of their previous Youth Cup games away from home, decided to include Southport-born centre-half Trevor Rimmer even though he was carrying a niggling injury.

Jimmy Murphy's major doubt centred on the fitness of Johnny Giles, whose continued troubles were caused through a recurring and painful knee problem, and such was the midfielder's influence on the side's style of play, the option to safeguard him for the return leg was bypassed. United's coach was gambling heavily on Giles being able to put on a performance in the knowledge that he wouldn't be able to function one hundred per cent effectively.

The fever pitch expectations felt amongst the football fraternity in Blackburn deemed that the local Evening Telegraph felt compelled to produce a pink 'Youth Cup Special' newspaper which contained articles on the competing players and prospects for the game.

In a tie that was brim-full of passion and sprinkled with a fine coating of controversy, honours were shared evenly at full-time.

A Blackburn Evening Telegraph reporter was in attendance:

Young Rovers made great fight

Referee caused storm

IGNORING the disallowed "goal" incident that will provide a talking point for many a day, Blackburn Rovers' under-18 side did enough at Ewood Park last night to have taken them to Old Trafford next Wednesday for the second leg of the FA Youth Cup semi-final with a substantial lead over Manchester United. But they had all the bad luck that was going, and they missed several good chances.

What a rousing game this was, writes "CENTURION." It kept a 19,600 crowd roaring to the end. Credit the young Rovers with a great fight after early signs of nerves had made it easier for United to look the classier side in attack—but still with few ideas of how to break the Rovers' grand defence barrier, in which every man was a real hero.

Turned tables

In the second half the Rovers turned the tables completely after they had been roused to fury by a refereeing decision by Mr Leslie Tirebuck, of Halifax, that seemed inexplicable at the time.

This is what happened: John Jervis was challenging for the ball down the middle when he was brought down by the United right-back. The ball went out to Ratcliffe, who cracked it into the net. War dance for a goal was stopped when Mr Tirebuck (who had been well behind the play) pointed for a free kick.

The ball was put on the six-yard line and there was the extraordinary spectacle of every United player on the goal-line to charge down Fred Pickering's free kick, get the ball away and add insult to injury by going down almost immediately to take a 38 minutes lead through inside-left Spratt.

At the interval Mr Tirebuck told me that before Barry Ratcliffe netted, he had twice blown for obstruction on Jervis, but the noise of the crowd had evidently prevented the players hearing the whistle.

The incident will not add to Mr Tirebuck's popularity with the Ewood crowd, who recall that he was the official who sent off Matt Woods after his clash with Dave Hickson of Everton on March 21.

For the second half, there was only one side in it. Jervis equalised in 51 minutes as he chased a cute Paddy Daly pass and shot from the left of goal, Gaskell making his one mistake by diving too soon, the ball going into the net over his body. Then the young Rovers hit United with everything except the trainer's bucket. But they were too impetuous near goal. Jervis missed two chances by shooting too soon when he had time to bring the ball under control. Newton headed over and Ratcliffe had wretched luck when a screaming shot hit the underside of the bar and bounced out.

If they play as well at Old Trafford, these young Rovers can still reach the Final for the first time ever. But they would be advised to vary their attack tactics more, instead of relying too much on the long ball down the middle for Jervis to chase. Jervis is a tremendous worker and a taker of chances, but his lack of inches put him at a disadvantage against the United centre-half when the ball was in the air. On the ground, Jervis worried him incessantly.

Tireless

Apart from Mulvey, who had a quiet game, the Rovers' attack was very good, with Daly in rare form as a tireless worker and making shrewd use of the ball.

Fred Pickering's cool class made him the outstanding defender, but wing-halves England and Leach were always well in the picture, and Wells improved tremendously in the second half. Rimmer played under difficulties with a thigh strain, but he was in command of the middle, and Griffiths had a good game in goal.

APRIL 1959

That chalked off goal was the cue to set tongues wagging in the Lancashire town and a week later it was the subject of a letter to the Blackburn Evening Telegraph's 'Cliff Graeme's Sports Quiz' column, in which a soccer poser appeared. 'Why was it', asks D.T. (Blackburn), 'that in the Blackburn Rovers v. Manchester United Youth Cup semi-final at Ewood Park last week, the whole of the United team were allowed on the goal-line - less than ten yards from the ball when the free kick was taken?'

The query gained a simple answer from Mr. Graeme, who replied, *'That's easy. The United team would have been off the field of play had they been ten yards away. The referee probably told them that they could stand either on the line or behind the ball'.*

The Evening Chronicle's Keith Dewhurst rated the Reds *'a shade lucky'* to come away from Ewood Park with a draw before going on to predict that *'United will win the second leg at Old Trafford, although it will be a stern affair'.*

Johnny Giles calls for Ian Moir to take his place on United's goal-line while Blackburn's John Jervis receives attention after the *'disallowed goal incident'*

Partly hidden behind a post, David Gaskell's error allowed Blackburn to equalise

semi-final 1st leg

1958-59

1) David Gaskell
2) Barry Smith
3) Stan Ackerley
4) Jimmy Nicholson
5) Frank Haydock
6) Willie Donaldson
7) Ian Moir
8) Nobby Stiles
9) Phil Chisnall
10) Tommy Spratt
11) Jimmy Elms

1) Barry Griffiths
2) David Wells
3) Fred Pickering
4) Mike England
5) Keith Newton
6) Vinny Leech
7) Barrie Ratcliffe
8) Alan Bradshaw
9) John Jervis
10) Paddy Daly
11) Paddy Mulvey

APRIL 1959

MANCHESTER UNITED 2 (3) v (4) 3 BLACKBURN ROVERS

Chisnall, Stiles — Daly, Jervis, Ratcliffe

semi-final 2nd leg

Wednesday 15th
Kick-off 7.30 p.m.
Attendance 35,949

Reds miss scheming of Giles

The risk of starting Johnny Giles at Ewood Park backfired with the direst of consequences as he had been a limping passenger throughout most of the game. Counted out of the return seven days later, his exclusion even then must have been a touch and go decision for Jimmy Murphy, with the cultured Irish ace given right up until the morning of the game to prove his fitness.

The management's solution to his loss was to move Nobby Stiles forward into Giles' position and bring in Willie Donaldson, a Northern Ireland schoolboy international from Belfast, at left-half.

The Rovers were also in for changes, because stopper Trevor Rimmer had broken down in training in the interim period and couldn't be considered. Keith Newton was installed in Rimmer's position with Alan Bradshaw introduced to their forward-line. Bradshaw, who attended the Queen Elizabeth Grammar School in Blackburn, had recently learned of his selection to play for an English Grammar Schools' XI against the Scottish Grammar Schools' team.

The delicacy of the tie, geared to the controversial events surrounding the build up to, and the events of, the game at Ewood Park, ensured a massive attendance that would remain as the record crowd for any Youth Cup match for almost 50 years. Boosting the huge gate was a large and expectant following from Blackburn.

It was another match of high drama, although the majority of the crowd went home acknowledging that their team were strictly second best on the night. Those same spectators were witness to the events which meant that at least another year would elapse before United could reclaim the 'kids' knock-out cup'.

MANCHESTER UNITED F. C. LTD.
STAND C   ROW M   SEAT 111
F.A. Youth Challenge Cup — Semi Final 2nd Leg
Manchester United v. Blackburn Rovers
AT OLD TRAFFORD   KICK-OFF 7-30 p.m.
WEDNESDAY, 15th APRIL, 1959
Admission 4/-   L. Olive, Secretary
NO MONEY RETURNED
Issued subject to the Rules, Regulations and Bye-Laws of the Football Association.
KEEP THIS PORTION

The Blackburn Evening Telegraph credited their heroes in a suitable way:

BLACKBURN ROVERS' under-18 side battled their way through to the Final of the FA Youth Cup by a grand 3-2 win over favourites Manchester United before a 35,949 crowd in an Old Trafford rainstorm last night.

And battled is the only word for it, writes "CENTURION." As at Blackburn the week before when they held the Rovers luckily to a 1-1 draw, United's youngsters were unnecessarily vigorous. Referee J. Powell of Rotherham had to handle them very firmly indeed.

Significant

Mark well the "gate." It was higher than at any of the nine League games last night—three in the First Division and two in the Second.

The Rovers, in the Final for the first time ever, will play either West Ham or Arsenal who have still to play their semi-final second leg after a 1-1 draw at West Ham in the first.

After disposing of United, who have won the Cup five times out of six possible, the young Rovers need fear no one —they must have a great chance of compensating manager Dally Duncan for the fact that he left Luton Town in the season they reached Wembley and the FA Cup Final for the first time.

Streets ahead

As United manager Matt Busby was the first to admit, the Rovers were by far the better side. They surprised the crowd— so used to seeing a succession of Busby babes' triumphs—by the quality of their football and the confident coolness with which they played under a great deal of provocation.

In fact, they looked very, very good—with not a weak link— emphasising Ewood's rich promise for the future.

Off to a tonic start, the Rovers were two goals up in 15 minutes. Paddy Daly, looking like young Alex James with his shirt sleeves flapping and his baggy pants— and, incidentally, colouring the game like the Scottish maestro did—made a chance for Bradshaw. Gaskell saved brilliantly, but the ball was only pushed out to JERVIS, who made no mistake.

That was after seven minutes; at the quarter hour Daly was again through like a flash, with Jervis with him. Jervis rounded the Manchester centre-half and hit the foot of the post with his angled shot, the ball rebounding for RATCLIFFE to tap it through.

Rare slip

The Rovers were so much on top that even a rare slip by Fred Pickering, who took a tumble on the greasy ground and let in Moir for a centre which STILES banged in to reduce the arrears in 26 minutes, had no effect on their composure.

A minute after the restart the Jervis - Daly double spearhead pierced the United defence for the vital third goal. Jervis bored through, defying two hard tackles, and Gaskell could only push his shot out to the waiting DALY.

Haydock, the United centre-half, whose limitations on the ground were cruelly exposed by Jervis, gave away a penalty by a crude tackle on the centre-forward.

But Pickering hit the ball wide from the spot in trying to place it.

It made no difference. United were reduced to tearaway tactics at different times Jervis, Daly and Mulvey were over the line for treatment, while Barry Ratcliffe was floored so many times by the desperate United left-back that he was scarcely recognisable through a layer of mud.

United's second goal came in injury time when Moir crossed for CHISNALL to head past Griffiths.

Full marks to every young Rover. It was a terrific all-round performance, proving a tremendous team spirit.

Newton, in his emergency role at centre-half, was a revelation. His height enabled him to command the middle, his speed was too much for Chisnall, and he tackled safely. The wing-halves, England and Leach, made a big contribution by their sure defence and accurate distribution.

Wells kicked surely and marked the United outside-left out of the game, while Pickering was coolly dominating, if rather too casual at times. Griffiths handled the greasy ball well.

Daly was the dominating forward, with Jervis little behind and Mulvey always dangerous in possession.

Alan Bradshaw fitted in well in his first game, using the ball beautifully, while Ratcliffe's strong running and go-ahead tactics made him a marked man in more ways than one—he was a mass of bruises after the game.

David Meek had no hesitation in giving his opinion on the main reason for the Reds' failure:

Manchester United sadly missed the scheming of Giles. Without a tactician their youth team were well beaten by Blackburn Rovers in the second leg of the F.A. Youth Cup semi-final – result 3-2 and on aggregate 4-3.

Wing-half Nicholson came nearest to dictating play for United but he could not match the bustling Rovers' attack, led in dashing style by Jarvis.

The Reds showed some brilliant touches but the Blackburn defence were rugged. Moir had a good game for United but he was up against Blackburn's best defender in team captain, Fred Pickering.

Rovers were two goals up in the first quarter-hour and they set the pace throughout the match. Full marks to both teams, though, for a superbly exciting game which earned the 35,949 crowd.

1958-59

APRIL 1959

Keith Dewhurst, Meek's opposite number over at the Chronicle, felt Blackburn fully deserved their passage into the final because they were by far the stronger and more cohesive unit and that their efforts put them *'well on top for all but the last twenty minutes of the first half'*. He went on to agree with his fellow reporter by stating *'without Johnny Giles, United never looked likely to break through the Blackburn defence'*.

Dewhurst wagged a finger in the direction of referee Mr. Powell by implying that the Rotherham official caused events to turn sour for United almost from the off. Specifically remarking on Blackburn's early breakthrough, the reporter wrote icily *'it seemed to me that (Jervis) and another forward were yards offside'*.

His article continued with an opinion that the clash *'was a disappointment after the Wolves game, but in the long view I suppose the team had too many under-sixteen year-old players in the key positions'* and it ended with the comment, *'it will be interesting to see how they develop next year'*.

Blackburn left Manchester with the spoils because they had produced 90 minutes of resourceful and adventurous football when it mattered. Without question the more accomplished of the sides over two legs, Rovers turned up the heat on United in their own kitchen and it proved uncomfortably hot as far as the hosts were concerned.

While not providing an adequate measure of compensation, for the second season in succession the Reds later learned that they were beaten by the team that went on to win the Youth Cup.

In the final, Blackburn met a West Ham team containing Bobby Moore and, returning from injury for the second leg, Geoff Hurst. In the opening game, the Hammers were contained to a 1-1 draw in front of an Upton Park faithful numbering 10,750.

The decisive action came at Ewood Park, where a crowd of over 28,000 flocked to see a 1-0 victory for the Rovers. Blackburn goalkeeper Barry Griffiths made himself a hero by saving a penalty with the score locked at 0-0, and the all-important goal came from Paddy Daly eleven minutes into extra-time.

semi-final 2nd leg

The United eleven who faced Blackburn Rovers in the 1958/59 semi-final second leg
Back row (l-r) Jimmy Nicholson, Frank Haydock, David Gaskell, Stan Ackerley, Barry Smith, Phil Chisnall
Front row (l-r) Ian Moir, Willie Donaldson, Nobby Stiles, Tommy Spratt, Jimmy Elms

131

1959-60

1) Ronnie Briggs	9) Phil Chsinall
2) Bobby Smith	10) Tommy Spratt
3) Stan Ackerley	11) Sammy McMillan
4) Jimmy Nicholson	
5) Alan Atherton	
6) Willlie Donaldson	
7) Ian Moir	
8) Nobby Stiles	

1) John Boardman	9) Mike Croft
2) Billy Wylie	10) Barry Palmer
3) Chris Wright	11) Trevor Webb
4) Tony Holt	
5) Alan Langridge	
6) Ken Armistead	
7) Frank Wilkinson	
8) Terry Ainsworth	

OCTOBER 1959

MANCHESTER UNITED **14 v 0** MORECAMBE

Chisnall (3), Langridge (o.g.), McMillan (2), Moir, Nicholson (2), Spratt (2), Stiles (3)

Monday 12th
Kick-off 7.30 p.m.
Attendance 10,882

first round

LOSE 14-0 BUT SHARE £634 'GATE'

If the people at United were looking for a cushy opener in their quest to bring the Youth Cup back to Old Trafford, they were counting their blessings with the news that a home draw against non-league Morecambe was to be their start to the 1959/60 season.

The composition of the Reds' under-18 side lately displayed a very definite 'emerald' tint as the previous season's Northern Ireland duo of Jimmy Nicholson and Willie Donaldson were now supplemented by Ronnie Briggs, the party nominated to take over David Gaskell's goalkeeping jersey, and outside-left Sammy McMillan, who was the chosen replacement for Jimmy Elms. The number of Ulster boys in the team clearly indicated that Bob Bishop, the club's chief scout in the province, had his finger on the pulse and his connections and astute eye for unearthing a gem or two was paying rich dividends.

Other changes meant debuts for two local boys, former Manchester and Lancashire Boys prodigy Alan Atherton at centre-half and Bobby Smith at right-back. Smith not only shared an identical surname with his immediate predecessor, he also held similarly high credentials as both had captained England Boys before signing for the Reds.

Morecambe's squad contained a group of players whose background in football was in almost complete contrast to United's stable of pedigrees. The majority of their team was composed of local talent and Tony Holt, a Blackpool lad, was the solitary professional in the side. Morecambe's youth team were normally found competing amongst the modest confines of the North Lancashire Junior League, although they were able to boast that three of their number had risen to Football League status in the recent past. They were Ray Charnley of Blackpool, Ron Mitchell of Leeds United and Jeff Slack of Stoke City, a trio of success stories which constituted an enviable record for an organisation of Morecambe's size and stature.

As would be expected, the tie was greeted with a certain amount of 'big game' fervour in the seaside town. When the team bus carrying the Morecambe players, plus 'reserves' Brian Holmes, Barry Greenwood, David Miller and David Kirkham along with trainer Maurice Vickers and various club officials, wound their way down to Manchester, they were followed by no less than five coaches crammed full of enthusiastic supporters.

Even though five of the Morecambe lads, Wylie, Langridge, Croft, Webb and Armistead, were involved in the Youth Cup home defeat to Bradford City during the previous season, their past participation counted for nothing as the Reds contemptuously brushed them aside to record their second highest victory margin in the competition to date.

The visitors' angle was covered in the Morecambe Guardian:

Though beaten 14-0 by Manchester United Juniors under the Old Trafford floodlights in the F.A. Youth Cup on Monday night, Morecambe Juniors had the consolation of sharing in a £634 "gate," they also received a sympathetic ovation from the Manchester crowd for their gallant display against a vastly superior side.

Morecambe Juniors' team of Saturday afternoon footballers had the rare distinction of playing under Old Trafford floodlights before a crowd of 11,000. They were given a tremendous ovation at the end of the game by a crowd who appreciated their sportsmanship and spirit.

The fact that they lost 14-0 is of little significance. The result could hardly be otherwise when it is considered that Manchester had in their ranks six players with Central League experience and at least three who will possibly make the international grade.

Morecambe were obviously outclassed by a team which included in its ranks some of the finest young players from all parts of Great Britain picked by scouts whose job it is to get boys interested in joining United's ground staff. These boys come from Ireland, Scotland and Wales – all of them schoolboy internationals in their own right.

Then they are trained and coached by great players. It is not surprising that they were yards faster, cleverer ball controllers and more expert in craftsmanship. Some of the goals scored on Monday would have been a credit to First Division players.

Yet for all that and the difference in class, the coach load of Morecambe supporters had reason to be proud of their team. They never gave up trying, even to the final whistle, and there wasn't a questionable tackle in the whole game.

When trainer Maurice Vickers lined the team up in continental fashion at the end of the game, the crowd rose to their feet and gave the Morecambe lads a tremendous ovation. It was a sight to be remembered.

In a Morecambe team that was outclassed in every department, Holt, who plays for the Reserves, was outstanding and Croft was also impressive at centre-forward. But Morecambe's goalkeeper Boardman deserved the highest praise. He made some tremendously good saves and was applauded time and time again. Only once did he make a mistake and that was when he failed to get his body behind a shot which spun out of his hands into the net.

For United, Nicholson impressed as the probable natural successor to Duncan Edwards.

One of the happiest features of the game was that Morecambe share the gate of £634. This helps to compensate for the first-team's early exit from the F.A. Cup.

The sequence of scoring was later recorded by the United Review:

Programme notes for this match expressed the hope that the game would provide a fair measure of good, lively football. Events proved that the measure was full to overflowing and 11,000 spectators rose to the teams as they left the field to show their appreciation.

The pattern of the game was set by goals in six and seven minutes from Stiles and Chisnall after two well conceived moves. These moves, particularly the ball through the middle, were to be repeated time and again as the game progressed to produce some excellent goals.

The non-leaguers had no answer to this approach or the skilful manner of its execution. They were unable to match the speed or the craft of the United youths and so were frequently out-manoeuvred.

The third goal came after seventeen minutes when Stiles evaded several challenges in carrying the ball along the goal-line before turning it into the area where Boardman fumbled. A hurried clearance off the goal-line by Langridge struck the 'keeper and rebounded into the net. Spratt quickly added a fourth with a close-range shot from a ball through the middle by Stiles then Moir took advantage of a mis-kick by Wright and after one of many spectacular runs crossed the ball to the far post for McMillan to crash it first time into the net.

A well placed pass by Nicholson sent Moir away and cutting in along the bye-line, the winger smashed the ball home from a very acute angle to complete the first half scoring.

Although mainly on the defensive in the first period, Morecambe had had their moments in attack. One good move left Croft well placed but his shot was well off-target whilst Ainsworth was only inches wide with a good header from a nicely placed free kick.

After half-time, Stiles, Chisnall and Spratt added further goals before Nicholson got what was probably the goal of the match. After good midfield work, Chisnall turned the ball inside to Stiles who cheekily gave it a back-heel flick for Nicholson to collect, take through the middle and smash home from 25 yards.

When Chisnall sent Stiles away, his speed easily took him through the defence to finally chip the ball home over the advancing Boardman. A speculative long-range effort by Nicholson deceived the 'keeper and spun out of his arms for number twelve and good work by Moir enabled Chisnall and McMillan to round off the scoring.

The mention of the gate money by the Morecambe newspaper was an interesting point because, following the deduction of expenses, both clubs were entitled to an equal share of the evening's gate takings. While it may have counted as small beer to United, what a financial godsend it would have been to the visiting club, the sum involved very probably representing the aggregated income from several of their senior fixtures.

And the reward for the members of Morecambe's youth team? Besides the indelible memory of performing in one of the most famous football arenas in the world, the only tangible remuneration they gained was to be treated to a fish and chip supper on the bus journey home.

IRISH FRIENDLY

HOME FARM

1959-60

OCTOBER 1959

Monday 26th

Kick-off 7.45 p.m.

Two weeks after the defeat of Morecambe, a party consisting mainly of current youth team members took the short hop over to Dublin to undertake a friendly match with Home Farm, a club United have enjoyed a cordial relationship with since the early 1950's. Pictured above, on the squad's return to Ringway Airport on Wednesday 28th October, trainer Arthur Powell is the first to disembark while immediately above him youth coach John Aston senior rests his hand on Jimmy Murphy's shoulder. Scout Joe Armstrong is at the top of the boarding stairs alongside two Irish Airlines stewardesses.

The players in the photograph are, in descending order, Nobby Lawton and Stan Ackerley (partly obscured), David Gaskell, Phil Chisnall (left), Frank Haydock, Bobby Smith, Ian Moir (in light overcoat), Nobby Stiles and Tommy Spratt.

United won the game 2-1, with both goals scored by Spratt.

irish friendly

133

1959-60

1) Ronnie Briggs
2) Bobby Smith
3) Stan Ackerley
4) Jimmy Nicholson
5) Alan Atherton
6) Willie Donaldson
7) Ian Moir
8) Nobby Stiles
9) Phil Chisnall
10) David Latham
11) Sammy McMillan

1) Gordon West
2) David Hartwell
3) Jack Fillingham
4) Eddie Webster
5) Glyn James
6) Neil Turner
7) Dave Demaine
8) Les Lea
9) Fred Hearne
10) Johnny Watt
11) Brian Tyrrell

NOVEMBER 1959

MANCHESTER UNITED 2 v 1 BLACKPOOL

McMillan, Nicholson (pen)

Demaine

Monday 16th

Kick-off 7.30 p.m.

Attendance 13,016

second round

Just over a month after Morecambe were shot out of town with their tails between their legs, Old Trafford was visited by a team representing another Lancashire coastal town, on this occasion Blackpool, and the young Reds had only recently taken on a Bristol City Youth XI at Ashton Gate as a warm-up for the Tangerines' visit. The Bristol club, whose aspirations for a prolonged run in the Youth Cup caused them to seek out what they felt was suitably stern opposition, were beaten by four goals to two.

With Tommy Spratt unavailable because of a damaged knee, ex-Manchester Boys star David Latham was brought in for his first Youth Cup game as a direct replacement. Nobby Stiles was deemed as okay to start, despite having been out of commission for three weeks, while Jimmy Nicholson still had praise ringing in his ears after putting in a fine performance for Northern Ireland's 'B' team against France the week before.

For the Seasiders, Les Lea from Stretford was named at number eight, although they had some bad news to contend with when Alan Burrows, normally the team's captain, was ruled unfit with a broken collarbone.

Memories of the Reds' comfortable 7-0 win at Bloomfield Road two years previously were still fresh in the minds of United's supporters and with the advantage of a home draw, it appeared as though a rather uncomplicated passage through to the Third Round might have been on offer.

Surprisingly, that wasn't exactly the way the pages turned, as the United Review recalled in its account of the night's main events:

This was a game in which Dame Fortune smiled and frowned in spasms. Happily for us she smiled in our direction in the late stages when it mattered most.

It certainly seemed that we would be very much out of favour for, after missing two easy chances early on, we lost the services of McMillan with slight concussion after 25 minutes. When, seven minutes later, Stiles left the field with a leg injury, our boys seemed to be fancying an uphill task. The visitors unaccountably failed to press home their attacks against our depleted side and thanks to some grand work by the defence we survived until the interval.

We resumed with eleven men although Stiles was obviously in difficulty and McMillan appeared bemused. Not too much so, however, to cause panic in the Blackpool defence with a lob which caused a scramble almost on the goal-line. He seemed even more himself when after 65 minutes he poached effectively to give us the lead from a good through ball from Chisnall. This was the signal for some strong attacks which kept West fully engaged, although good efforts by Chisnall and Latham had him beaten but were just off-target. Then a Moir lob appeared to enter the net but when the 'keeper scrambled the ball away, the referee ruled in his favour.

Just as our rearranged side seemed to be gaining command, the visitors levelled the scores with a rather fortunate goal. Some confusion over the taking of an offside kick ended with Briggs placing the kick at the feet of Demaine, whose half-hit shot trickled in off a post.

The final twist of fortune's wheel came five minutes from time when we were awarded a penalty, an award which puzzled most spectators but was given emphatically and without hesitation by referee Taylor. Despite an appreciable delay before the kick was taken, Nicholson remained unruffled and calmly placed his shot well out of the reach of West to settle the issue.

The injuries to Stiles and McMillan and the consequent reshuffle of the side gave our boys little chance to produce the rhythm hoped for.

Nevertheless, the win was fully deserved once they had survived the nine-man period. Blackpool had their bright spots but they missed their way in the twenty minutes before the interval.

So it transpired that rather than making the expected easy entry into the following stage, United were given to rely on a contentious penalty in order to progress to the next level of the competition. With the award of the spot kick as confusing to most of the players as it was to the majority of onlookers, the Blackpool Gazette informed its readership that a *'harsh penalty decision robbed Blackpool of a replay'* and then put the incident further under the microscope with a short description:

Ten minutes from time the ball bounced awkwardly as Webster went to head it and it hit him on the arm. It certainly was not a deliberate handling offence and the incident did not give Blackpool the advantage as there was no threat to their goal at the time.

But Wigan referee, M.Taylor, gave a penalty from which Nicholson scored the winner.

The claimant of seven goals in as many appearances for the Juniors already that season, David Latham's achievements merited a run-out in the Youth Cup team

The Manchester youths, stronger in the tackle and more direct and purposeful in attack, deserved their win, but until that penalty decision Blackpool's stonewall defence looked like earning a replay.

A week later, the Blackpool Gazette made further reference to the game and not for the first time the focus was on the marvellous attendances that United were attracting for Youth Cup games:

The Blackpool officials who accompanied the team to Old Trafford last Monday night for the F.A. Youth Cup Second Round tie frankly were staggered at the gate. On this wet and cold night 13,016 spectators turned up – and how they cheered Manchester United.

I am convinced that the highly partisan crowd had a lot to do with United's 2-1 win, for they never relaxed their vociferous support.

'I wish we could get them cheering like that at Bloomfield Road,' sighed one Blackpool player.

Manchester officials, including manager Matt Busby, openly admitted that they were impressed by the Blackpool team display and the form of one or two of the players in particular.

They also moaned about 'the disappointing gate.'

'If it had been a decent night we would have had 20,000 here,' said a director.

He was considerably cheered up, however, when it was pointed out to him that the attendance was only 2,654 less than the gate for Blackpool's First Division match against Newcastle United at Bloomfield Road last Saturday!

1) Ronnie Briggs	9) Phil Chisnall	
2) Bobby Smith	10) Tommy Spratt	
3) Stan Ackerley	11) Sammy McMillan	
4) Jimmy Nicholson		
5) Alan Atherton		
6) Willie Donaldson		
7) Ian Moir		
8) Nobby Stiles		

1) Jimmy Williamson	9) Nick Sharkey	
2) Jimmy Richardson	10) Willie McPheat	
3) Cecil Irwin	11) Gordon Clayton	
4) Martin Harvey		
5) Alan Crudace		
6) Ian Rodden		
7) Jimmy Davison		
8) Dave Lackenby		

1959-60

MANCHESTER UNITED 5 v 0 SUNDERLAND

Chisnall, Donaldson, McMillan (2), Nicholson (pen)

DECEMBER 1959

Monday 14th

Kick-off 7.30 p.m.

Attendance 17,409

third round

DONALDSON NOW READY TO STEP UP

The attendance for the Blackpool tie was surpassed by over 4,000 when Sunderland came to Old Trafford searching for their first Youth Cup win over the Reds in four attempts. Four was also the number of players that Sunderland had remaining from the Roker Park clash which United won narrowly earlier in the year. Because Tommy Spratt was back to fitness, the home team contained six personnel from that earlier game on Wearside.

With three of the Sunderland youth side, Cecil Irwin, Martin Harvey and Jimmy Davison, having already experienced some senior exposure, and the team also proving almost unbeatable in the Northern Intermediate League, there was a suggestion that United would have their work cut out to earn their passage to the next round. In addition, Sunderland's Harvey had earned representative honours with Northern Ireland's 'B' team and was, in fact, an international team-mate of Jimmy Nicholson.

If a lack of top form was displayed against Blackpool, the same couldn't be said of the contest against the Rokerites who, as the Sunderland Echo reported, came across a United combination which managed to hit a devastating peak on the night:

The part Willie Donaldson played in the win over Sunderland caused the Evening Chronicle to afford him a 'star-turn' tag

SUNDERLAND youth team, all-conquering in every other sphere, met their masters at Old Trafford last night when they were beaten 5—0 by Manchester United in the F.A. Youth Cup (Third Round).

United, playing the brisk, hard-hitting game in which all Old Trafford sides specialize, earned a clear advantage for themselves by their forceful tactics and a generous helping of high quality football.

It was not until the second half that Sunderland really warmed to their task. By then they were 3—0 down and fighting well, but their chances of staging a come-back disappeared when Syd Williamson was carried off unconscious on a stretcher.

Williamson left in the 50th minute, but the starting point of his troubles was half an hour earlier, when he was charged in the back as he held a right wing corner and crashed into the post as he fell. The concussion which he received then was aggravated when he fell heavily in a vain effort to stop the third goal. And the final blow came in the 50th minute when he dived out to save from Spratt and received the follow up shot from McMillan full in the face from only a few yards range.

Ian Rodden took over in goal to give a plucky display and earn a special ovation at the finish. Over the 90 minutes, too, this was a generous 17,409 (£1,024) crowd, enjoying the match-winning play of their favourites, but always ready to recognize and applaud merit in Sunderland's play. What a pity that they could not have seen something more representative of the Sunderland side's abilities.

There was educational value for every Sunderland youngster in last night's game. And those who took the lesson to heart in time to make use of it before the finish were Irwin, McPheat, and Harvey. They were "buzzing" with the same urgency and power in the last quarter as that which had shown in United's play from the start.

Yet McPheat was the only player who reached anything like average form. Twice in the first half he missed scoring chances which would have been snapped up easily enough in a less trying atmosphere.... chances which might have changed the course of the game. But he was in great form for the rest of the time and was just as successful when he took over at left half from Rodden, whose defensive play had not been at all impressive.

Sharkey was very much a marked man, particularly from set positions. When corner-kicks were taken he was effectively shut out by a two—sometimes three-man bodyguard. He did manage one break from a Clayton centre, and timed it nicely with tackles coming in from both sides, only to see his shot beat the goalkeeper and go behind from the foot of the post.

Lackenby fought and worked hard, without producing either the subtlety of finishing power needed in an inside forward, while neither Davison nor Clayton, though good in patches, managed to hit the right game for the occasion.

Sixteen-year-old Alan Crudace had a tough time of it, but there is plenty of spirit in this youngster and he stood up to it well, without quite managing to dominate the middle.

Richardson's tendency to stand off his man, particularly when the ball was in the air, ran him into a lot of trouble which tended to pull the rest of the defence out of position.

UNITED went ahead in the fourth minute, when McMillan went in to score from a pass by Stiles and in the 30th minute Stiles popped up again to resist a tackle by Rodden and stroke the ball through for Chisnall to score a second goal.

Donaldson made it three after 40 minutes when he hit a 25-yard shot on the volley. It could have gone anywhere but it crashed into the top right-hand corner of goal well out of Williamson's reach.

Breaking away to the right of goal, Chisnall hit a centre from which McMillan headed United's fourth goal from the far post in 55 minutes. Then, seven minutes from the end, came the crowning blow. A clearance struck the referee, who was only about 15 yards out, and rebounded to the feet of Chisnall, whose shot was on its way into the net when Irwin shouldered it away. The referee immediately awarded a penalty, which was converted by Nicholson.

Sunderland's unfortunate goalkeeper Williamson was detained overnight in the Manchester Royal Infirmary for observation with concussion and a suspected neck injury. The following day, he was transferred to the orthopaedic ward and underwent an X-ray and further tests before being discharged only a little the worse for wear.

There were plaudits aplenty for his stand-in, of whom the United Review felt *'looked anything but a deputy with some breathtaking saves'* and cited one in particular as *'a mid-air dive to save a Moir cross (that) even had the referee applauding'*.

Williamson's woes rather spoiled a spectacle in which the young Reds performed at a level reminiscent of years gone by. Nevertheless, the keeper's departure couldn't detract from the outcome of the game, which had been as good as decided prior to him leaving the action.

Sunderland's custodian wasn't the only one who was subjected to a measure of pain, because the following day it was revealed that Nobby Stiles had completed the match despite still suffering from a troublesome knee.

135

1959-60

1) Ronnie Briggs	9) Phil Chisnall	1) Morris Emmerson	9) Joe Livingstone
2) Bobby Smith	10) Tommy Spratt	2) John Kirk	10) Doug Cattermole
3) Stan Ackerley	11) Sammy McMillan	3) Gordon Jones	11) Norman Fisher
4) Jimmy Nicholson		4) Neville Chapman	
5) Alan Atherton		5) Gilbert Dunford	
6) Willie Donaldson		6) Johnny Walker	
7) Ian Moir		7) Bill Povey	
8) Nobby Stiles		8) Billy Horner	

JANUARY 1960

MANCHESTER UNITED 3 v 0 MIDDLESBROUGH

Chisnall, Moir, Nicholson

Wednesday 27th
Kick-off 7.30 p.m.
Attendance 23,007

fourth round

Just over three weeks into a new decade and more North-East opposition was to follow with the arrival of Middlesbrough at Old Trafford. The Boro' were the last remaining contenders from that neck of the woods because, while United were busy knocking out Sunderland in the Third Round, they were inflicting the same fate on Newcastle.

With interest in the Reds' youth games steadily increasing, special buses were laid on to the ground from points at All Saints and Piccadilly in the city centre, in addition to normal services, and spectators were again out in force to see an unchanged home eleven.

It was hardly surprising that crowds for United's Youth Cup matches were as large as they were in the late 1950's and early 1960's. Floodlit games were still something of a novelty back then and even for those soccer supporters fortunate enough to own a television, there was practically no football to be seen on the box in those days. Prices of admission for under-18 matches were pegged at the same as those for Central League fixtures, so the Youth Cup games represented superb value for the entertainment on offer.

Middlesbrough had performed marvels to progress into the Fourth Round as the average age of their team was only sixteen. Of the five professionals in the side, which included centre-forward Joe Livingstone, who had signed a full-time contract just days prior to travelling to Manchester, four had played at Reserve level. With the exception of Scot Johnny Walker, every member of the Middlesbrough side was locally born.

Boro' manager Bob Dennison was coy when interviewed about the chances of his charges in Manchester, preferring to say simply *'they are a useful side'*. In the same interview, Dennison was a little more revealing about one particular prospect in his squad when claming that he rated sixteen year-old Gordon Jones as *'one of the best propositions for his age'* that he had ever come across.

The United Review gave a concise report on another fine performance from the Reds:

In the fast opening spell Emmerson was well tested before United took the lead after fifteen minutes. A half-hit clearance as Stiles tried to force his way through gave Chisnall the chance to drive into the net from ten yards. As we piled on the pressure with some precise, slick football, a tight and confident Middlesbrough defence left few loopholes, with the diminutive but sprightly Emmerson making some smart saves.

The second half opened with the visitors the more methodical side but, despite some delightful approach work, they seldom troubled Briggs.

It was a goal by Moir after 65 minutes that put us once again in command and started a further onslaught on the visitors' defence. A corner by Spratt was neatly headed through by Nicholson for the winger to head in from close range. After more good work by Emmerson, Nicholson put the issue beyond doubt when he crashed the ball home from the edge of the box as it came loose following a Moir corner kick.

Whilst our boys have shown better all-round form than they did in this game, this was a sound win, gained by greater fluidity in attack with punch all along the line. To notch three goals – and a number of very near misses – against a defensive strategy so well executed was a highly creditable performance.

Middlesbrough had hit the canvass despite putting on a workmanlike performance that was often punctuated by them being required to display their best football in order to get out of trouble. They had certainly lacked any penetration from the wide areas and, also unable to match the power generated by United's engine room, particularly from Jimmy Nicholson and Willie Donaldson, they were eventually ground down by a greater authority.

There was much post-match praise for 'Boro goalkeeper Morris Emmerson, who crowned a superb personal display with a cat-like save to repel Nicholson's cannon shot late in the game.

The costliest 'keeper in the business, United's World Cup star Harry Gregg, claimed of Emmerson, *'He is the finest boy goalkeeper I have ever seen. Everything he did was top class and one save in the second half was easily the save of the season in my view.'*

Number seven Ian Moir wheels away after scoring United's second goal against gallant Middlesbrough goalkeeper Morris Emmerson

136

1) Ronnie Briggs	9) Phil Chisnall	1) Brian Sherratt	9) John Walters
2) Bobby Smith	10) Tommy Spratt	2) Terry Lowe	10) Alan McGrath
3) Stan Ackerley	11) Sammy McMillan	3) Ron Wilson	11) Keith Bebbington
4) Jimmy Nicholson		4) Barry Griffiths	
5) Alan Atherton		5) Alan Bloor	
6) Willie Donaldson		6) Alan Philpott	
7) Ian Moir		7) Trevor Jones	
8) Nobby Stiles		8) Bob Bassett	

1959-60

MANCHESTER UNITED 2 v 1 STOKE CITY

Spratt (2)   Bassett

MARCH 1960

Monday 14th

Kick-off 7.30 p.m.

Attendance 27,100

With the youths in such inspired form, and the club then discovering that the under-18's had received their fifth consecutive home draw of the season, a decision was made to sell match tickets in advance of the visit of Stoke City.

While the Potteries club didn't possess the best of track records in the Youth Cup, City's best effort coming when reaching the last four in 1955, their current squad had displayed an almost faultless defensive record on their way to the Fifth Round. Considered to be at least as talented as their predecessors of five years previously, all of the Stoke team bar Ron Wilson (Mussleburgh) and Keith Bebbington (Mid-Cheshire) actually hailed from in or around the Potteries.

The (Stoke-on-Trent) Evening Sentinel stimulated its readers' interest in the tie with the following match preview:

Exacting test for Stoke youth eleven

ACCENT this week at the Victoria Ground, Stoke, moves down the scale from the first team to the youth side, who face their most important and exacting game to date next week.

On Monday evening (kick-off 7.30), under the Old Trafford floodlights and before an audience confidently expected to be of First Division proportions, they will be playing Manchester United in a quarter-final of the F.A. Youth Cup.

At this end the game is creating something like the interest of a senior cup-tie, and in Manchester, where all the youth cup matches this season have averaged an attendance of 23,000, a crowd of about 30,000 is likely.

Some hundreds of stand tickets have been sold at Stoke and altogether, by train, bus and motor-car, over 1,000 supporters will be going from the Potteries.

Fine season

This is Stoke's best season in the Youth Cup since they were beaten 2-1 on aggregate in a semi-final by West Bromwich Albion several years ago.

One of the great League teams of the present generation, Manchester United have also a wonderful reputation in youth football and for the first few years after its inception won the cup.

They are bidding strongly this time to recapture it. In the past two years the cup has been won, in turn, by Wolves and Blackburn Rovers, both of whom were eliminated in earlier rounds this season.

● Stoke have been fortunate in the previous rounds to be drawn at home. All the same, their record is impressive, with 12 goals scored and only one conceded. They have beaten Shrewsbury Town 6-0, West Bromwich Albion 1-0, Sheffield United 2-0 and Notts County 3-1.

Even for a youth side, Stoke's is a very young team and considerably below, in nearly every instance, the under-18 limitation at the beginning of the season.

Bright prospects

In fact, all except one — full-back Ron Wilson — will be eligible to play in the competition next season, which gives Stoke a bright future prospect with every chance of being an even stronger formation in 1960-61.

Three of the City's youths have had considerable experience in the Reserve side: Ron Wilson, left-back, who has been in the team most of the season, Alan Bloor, centre-half and Alan Philpott left-half.

A large proportion of Stoke's team are former members of Stoke-on-Trent Schoolboys.

Both clubs are awaiting the outcome of to-day's games before naming their sides for Monday, but the choice is expected to be made from some 12 or 13 players in each case.

Stoke had, in fact, shifted 750 seat tickets up to the eve of the tie and special trains were in operation to ferry supporters from the Potteries to Manchester.

With City's previous two first-team home attendances falling to under the 10,000 mark, it appeared that the club's followers were pinning all of their hopes on the youth team to bring some glory back to the Victoria Ground. As it was, they did the Stoke fans proud with a great display which earned a tremendous ovation from the huge crowd and indeed, the performance of both teams was so exceptional that within seconds of blowing his whistle to conclude the game, referee Mr. F. Collinge of Rochdale joined in with the clapping.

It took a little time for the match to come to the boil, as all of the early moves were brought to an end by keen marking and swift, hard tackles, until Stoke made some initial progress with a hoisted punt which United's defence was forced to deal with.

The Reds' response was both fast and effective. In managing to squeeze a low ball behind the Potters' rearguard, it freed Tommy Spratt to gallop into an almost empty penalty box where left-half Philpott barged across him. Jimmy Nicholson made a mess of the spot kick by firing straight at Sherratt, who knocked the ball down, and the goalkeeper ensured the match remained goalless when making a clearance as United's number four darted in with a futile follow-up.

The pace of the game seemed to pick up considerably thereafter, although there were no more chances or significant incidents before the break.

The next talking point followed a rapid interchange of passing from the Reds in the 51st minute when Ian Moir hooked the ball over to Sammy McMillan. The outside-left headed it into the path of Tommy Spratt, who smacked it into the net while on the run.

Spratt's goal served to open up the game still further, and Ronnie Briggs made an unlikely ground save prior to Moir and McMillan scorning opportunities to double United's advantage. Briggs then misjudged a bouncing ball and was let off when Alan Atherton booted it off the goal-line.

Philpott volleyed a shot into the Reds' net seconds after a colleague was caught offside and then Phil Chisnall and Nobby Stiles got in on the act with forceful attacks which caused anxiety for Stoke.

The Potters levelled up the scores on the 66-minute mark. Using what the United Review rather harshly described as *'harassing tactics'*, their pay-off arrived when inside-right Bob Bassett stuck one past Briggs after team-mate John Walters rolled a perfect pass into his path.

The City lads tried for all they were worth to put themselves into the lead and their considerable efforts were matched every step of the way by United. The away side certainly had no problems in making their way towards Briggs' end of the pitch, although, apart from the skill and craft of number nine Walters, they were unable to fashion much in the final third of the pitch.

There were only fifteen minutes left when United scored their winner, a goal which answered a heck of a lot of prayers on the Old Trafford terraces. McMillan again acted as provider when he brought a long pass under control out on the left wing. Then cutting inside before appearing about to shoot, he instead acted with what the Evening Sentinel noted as *'remarkable coolness'* to square the ball for Spratt to smash past Sherratt.

Rather than resting on their lead, United drove ever forward in an attempt to produce a third goal which would have made the game safe while City's defence continued to defy them. There was just one last chance for the Reds before the end, when Stoke's goalie reacted with a superb save to prevent Stan Ackerley from penning his moniker on the score sheet.

Manchester Evening Chronicle correspondent Peter Slingsby felt the main difference between the two sides was that Stoke *'never moved with the same rhythm or understanding in attack as United had'*, whereas the Review observed that City's forward-line *'did not work with cohesion, relying on the speed of centre-forward Walters, who lacked support'*.

The win over Stoke capped a day to remember for Reds' full-back Bobby Smith, who had managed to celebrate his 16th birthday in a memorable way.

> *During my time in the youth team we seemed to come out of the hat against the same teams. Stoke were one and Sunderland were another, and we got huge attendances for all those games. Stoke were a very hard running side and quite physical, which was at odds with our purer football methods. As a goalkeeper, I knew I would be tested with plenty of crosses and challenges. Just how I liked it!*

RONNIE BRIGGS

fifth round

137

1959-60

semi-final 1st leg

1) John Barton	9) Peter Thompson
2) George Ross	10) Alan Spavin
3) Rodney Webb	11) Jimmy Humes
4) Ged Baldwin	
5) David Will	
6) John Hart	
7) Mike Smith	
8) Dave Wilson	

1) Ronnie Briggs	9) Phil Chisnall
2) Bobby Smith	10) Tommy Spratt
3) Stan Ackerley	11) Sammy McMillan
4) Jimmy Nicholson	
5) Alan Atherton	
6) Willie Donaldson	
7) Ian Moir	
8) Nobby Stiles	

APRIL 1960

PRESTON NORTH END 3 v 0 MANCHESTER UNITED

Humes, Thompson (2)

Monday 11th
Kick-off 7.15 p.m.
Attendance 18,430

NORTH END EXCEL IN YOUTH CUP
United three goals down

The opening leg of United's eighth semi-final had something of a ring of newness about it, as it was actually their first away game of that season's competition. The short journey over to Preston's Deepdale enclosure meant that another North v. South final was now inevitable because Bristol City and Chelsea were contesting the concluding instalment of their semi-final on the same evening in London.

Whereas United were relatively untroubled when notching up a victory on their only other Youth Cup visit to Deepdale in October 1955, everyone at Old Trafford was under no illusions that the current Preston side would present a vastly different threat.

North End had eliminated, in order, Wigan Athletic (4-0, home), Huddersfield (3-2, home) Liverpool (4-1, away), Durham City (4-2, away), Birmingham City (2-0, home) and Swansea (4-1, away) with dangerman Peter Thompson's goals record standing at ten. Besides the inclusion of the highly rated Thompson, Preston were strengthened by the presence of goalkeeper John Barton and outside-left Jimmy Humes, both of whom had already seen service in their First Division side.

With the two clubs able to field their regular and best available players, Alan Atherton passing a fitness test earlier in the day for United, the young Reds contrived to concurrently lose both their cool and any advantage they could have hoped to bring back to Manchester.

A Lancashire Evening Post correspondent saw it all:

FOLLOWING an exhilarating display against Manchester United's under-18 team at Deepdale last night, Preston North End are at least half way towards the club's first appearance in the F.A. Youth Cup Final. The home side won an exciting semi-final first leg by 3—0.

The eventual winners will meet Chelsea, who are in the final for the second time in three years.

Chelsea, in last night's second leg at Stamford Bridge, repeated their 3—0 win at Bristol. Mr. "Ted" Drake's youngsters have scored 41 goals and conceded only two in reaching the final stage.

The merit of North End's performance was enhanced by the fact that Manchester United had scored 26 goals to two in their five previous ties. That itself emphasises the measure of their achievement. United have a good team, strong and well knit, as was soon obvious to observant eyes in the crowd of 18,430. This excellent attendance proved the considerable interest being taken in North End's young players.

Too much vigour

The United might be better still if they stuck to playing football and cut out rough tactics. I cannot understand why any team possessing above the average footballing ability should resort to an excess of vigour, unless the idea is to intimidate opponents not as well endowed physically as themselves.

Irrespective of this regrettable aspect of a determined display, Manchester United clearly face a big task in having to score four goals without reply to win this tie, and more if Preston's forwards are again in scoring form.

The odds are against the Busby boys. I hope there is a different referee for the second encounter. The one in charge last night almost succeeded in ruining the game by indulging in a whistling solo for one foul after another.

My record of free kicks for fouls showed 19 against the visitors, seven against Preston. It is hard to imagine as many offences occurring in a showpiece put on by youthful players. I say without hesitation that any referee who allows the toll to mount in this way, especially when dealing with youngsters under 18 merits a reproof for not exercising firmer discipline.

Warning called for

There were three fouls against United in the first five minutes. That ought to have been enough to justify a general admonition and warning to both sides that the next bad foul, semi final or not, would mean marching orders. I could hardly credit seeing so many old-fashioned tricks perpetrated by such young players.

Instead of calling everyone to order, Mr. F. V. Stringer of Liverpool, a Football League official, merely went on observing the letter of the law, except when he thrice failed to apply the advantage rule or ignored linesman's signals for other fouls which the referee did not deem worthy of being penalised.

In a match of this sort spectators have every right to expect a higher standard of behaviour and to see it played in the true spirit of the game. So much "playing of the man" certainly was not an edifying spectacle.

In every other respect the game was thoroughly enjoyable, full of vitality, teeming with incident, and sufficiently fluctuating to hold everyone's interest.

Both sides played attractive and purposeful football in their varied styles. United moved rather more briskly than Preston, who offset their more deliberate methods by passing well and varying the point of attack.

Fine goalkeeping

Challenges for possession were fearless and they were met unflinchingly, decidedly so by the Preston goalkeeper, Barton. Three times he unhesitatingly dived at an oncoming forward's feet to avert a possible goal.

Barton's confidence was infectious and his touches of showmanship, which did not detract from his effectiveness, added to the crowd's enjoyment. He was in fine form, and the same must be said of his skilful opposite number, Briggs, who made one particularly fine save from Preston's dangerous spearhead, Peter Thompson.

Both these boys are big, weighty as well as tall, but neither was cumbersome. On the contrary their agility and smart anticipation frequently discomfited opposing raiders.

Preston were two goals ahead at half-time and worthy of this lead. In a more evenly contested second half they added a third, still without reply. In the excitement missed chances were inevitable. There were not many, but United were rather more remiss than Preston.

Two for Thompson

North End's scorers were Thompson (2) and Humes, which fact should please people in Carlisle from which city both hail. Thompson's brace made his share of North End's total of 24 a round dozen, and he has had the satisfaction of scoring at least once in every round.

Comparable satisfaction for the defence was their preventing United scoring for the first time in the series.

A free kick cost Manchester the first goal after 12 minutes. Hart drove the ball into the crowded goal area and Thompson, taking advantage of the momentary hesitation by defenders, promptly applied an intercepting foot to glance the ball out of the goalkeeper's reach, a chance very well taken.

After half an hour an accurately directed centre by Thompson would have yielded a second goal if Ackerley, standing on the goal line, had not pushed out Smith's shot with his goalkeeper beaten.

Nine minutes later the speedy, roving Thompson repeated this move on the other flank. Centring delightfully from Wilson's pass, he presented Humes with an opportunity which the tall left winger instantly accepted from about 10 yards' range.

Exciting escapes

Both sides had escapes in a rousing second half. I noticed with satisfaction how often and well the Preston inside forwards, Wilson and Spavin, who were both hard workers, fell back to help their defence. Briggs made fine saves from Thompson, and Spavin and Wilson narrowly missed. Barton capably dealt with a goalworthy drive from Stiles, but ought to have been beaten in the 39th minute, when Chisnall, having broken through, shot wide.

A minute later Thompson scored his second. Hart started a left wing move after breaking up an attack and Thompson, cutting in, scored with a fiery cross shot to prove again that it is dangerous to leave him the slightest loophole.

Preston's team effort was first class. One or two were not perhaps as conspicuous or as strong as others, but all made useful contributions to a splendid performance. North End had an advantage in possessing players who could hold and work the ball, a disparity which frequently told against the United. A well-balanced attack showed pluck as well as skill, and sterling support was provided by Wilson and Spavin.

Hart, the captain, had no superior and was an inspiration at left half. Will was commanding and quick-witted at centre half; Webb earned high praise for capably coping with United's most polished and dangerous forward, outside right Moir; and Ross, the other full back, also gave a sound exhibition against a winger who has been much to the fore in the Youth Cup as a marksman.

The following day, the Evening Chronicle's Peter Slingsby wrote sternly that *'United can say goodbye to their hopes of winning the F.A. Youth Cup'* and later compounded his forecast when adding *'they do not have an earthly chance of getting through to this season's final'*.

Reasoning the team had *'resorted to un-United-like tactics in a vain effort to upset the streamlined team-work of Preston,'* Slingsby described North End's performance as *'polished'* and felt that their win was fully deserved, by having *'played superb soccer at times'*.

1959-60

APRIL 1960

semi-final 1st leg

THE FIRST TO THOMPSON.—Briggs, the Manchester goalkeeper, here beaten by Thompson (head protruding behind Briggs) for North End's first goal, at Deepdale, in the Youth Cup semi-final, last night.

THE SECOND.—Humes, on the ground, gets in his shot in spite of United goalkeeper Briggs' advance, and the covering of right back Smith (R.) on the line, to score North End's second goal at Deepdale, last night.

1959-60

1) Ronnie Briggs	9) Phil Chisnall	1) John Barton	9) Peter Thompson
2) Bobby Smith	10) Tommy Spratt	2) George Ross	10) Alan Spavin
3) Stan Ackerley	11) Sammy McMillan	3) Rodney Webb	11) Jimmy Humes
4) Jimmy Nicholson		4) Ged Baldwin	
5) Alan Atherton		5) David Will	
6) Willie Donaldson		6) John Hart	
7) Ian Moir		7) Mike Smith	
8) Nobby Stiles		8) Dave Wilson	

APRIL 1960

MANCHESTER UNITED 2 (2) v (4) 1 PRESTON NORTH END

Moir (2)   Thompson

semi-final 2nd leg

Thursday 21st

Kick-off 7.30 p.m.

Attendance 29,122

FOOTBALL
at Old Trafford
F.A. Youth CHALLENGE CUP
SEMI-FINAL — 2nd LEG
UNITED
v.
PRESTON NORTH END
ON THURSDAY, 21st APRIL
Kick-off 7-30 p.m.
Although losing the First Leg 3-0 our boys are determined to make this game another "Bilbao."
Car Park arrangements as for First Team.

When the second leg rolled around ten days later, David Meek was typically upbeat in his pre-match preview:

United are not counting themselves out yet. They reckon they played badly at Deepdale and can do much better. With the advantage of playing at Old Trafford they believe they can pull back the deficit.

Contained in the match programme were notes penned by the editor, whose optimism was slightly more veiled than that of Meek's:

In the first leg Preston were worthy winners in a hard game and they have set the United boys a tremendous task in trying for their first ever final. Youthful exuberance and excitability tended to mar what could have been a grand game at Deepdale last week. If the boys can curb this tendency and concentrate on producing the brand of soccer we saw in flashes then this could be a game which could be remembered for a long time.

The referee who had been in charge of the Deepdale contest came in for widespread slating for his handling of the game and he and his two linesmen were replaced by three new officials.

With a goodly number of Preston fans having journeyed to Manchester, as well as some senior players and Reserve team members from Deepdale, anticipation of a much improved spectacle was definitely the order of the day. For those North End supporters unable to travel to Old Trafford, the Lancashire Evening Post office window in Preston's Fishergate carried a poster that promised a final result service by 9.10 p.m., a news display which would make happy reading for the local townsfolk by the nominated time.

On the following day, the Evening Post summarised a much more even contest:

Preston North End are in the F.A Youth Cup final for the first time. As I confidently expected, the 3-0 lead gained in the first leg of the semi-final with Manchester United proved to be too big a handicap even for this powerful young side in the return game at Old Trafford last night.

Although winning on their merits, United's margin of success was kept down to 2-1, so that Preston prevailed on the aggregate by 4-2.

They will meet Chelsea at Stamford Bridge on Tuesday (7.30) in the first leg of the final, with the return encounter at Deepdale the following Tuesday (7.15). The London side had won the toss for the right to play at home first.

If interest in the deciding tie is comparable with that shown in the clash at Manchester, there will be a big 'gate'. In spite of United having only a thin chance of winning, a crowd of 29,122 saw them play with the utmost determination in a great bid to pull back three goals.

They went down fighting and earned everyone's admiration by a mighty effort to revive Old Trafford glories in this competition.

It was a hard game for all who took part in it, and certainly a hard one to watch, in the sense that the excitement which inevitably affected the players swayed and caught the imagination of spectators.

The tension was sustained on and off the field almost to the finish. The circumstances were similar to those when Wolves returned from a European Cup drubbing at Barcelona with several goals to wipe out before they could claim even equality. In other words, the United boys were obliged to throw all their energies into attack, strive for the incentive of a quick goal and fervently hope there would be no setbacks at the other end.

The match was contested throughout with vim and vigour and fought at a fierce pace which never slackened. An endurance test, it left no doubt about one thing – that every player was supremely fit.

They expended energy with all the enthusiasm of youth and still seemed to have some to spare when the battling was over. While some of the exchanges were robust, vigour was not used to excess as in the previous meeting.

It was a better tempered match, with zeal and endeavour the over-riding factors. Both sides had the will to win, and it was this which appealed most to the crowd, which included a large contingent from Preston. The Old Trafford roar of encouragement for United drew plenty of cheering in response from the North End supporters.

Knocks and tumbles were frequent, without anything vicious intruding. The control by the referee (Mr. J.E. Carr, of Sheffield) was sound, firm and judicious. Any trend towards friction was promptly curbed, and, two or three times, boys whose keenness outweighed discretion were tactfully told to quieten down. There was not a great number of fouls and most of them were due to impetuosity rather than, as on the previous occasion, to a then all-too-prevalent tendency to play the man instead of the ball.

United duly gained the spur they sought when, in the third minute, Moir, who had wandered into the middle, profited from a defensive mix-up to take a chance with a fine left foot drive which left Barton helpless.

Their joy was soon extinguished. Preston, three minutes later produced one of their few flashes of rhythmic football, to open up a path for centre-forward Thompson.

North End's young leader, again showing the composure which has marked his play throughout the tournament and caused many people to remark upon and note his high promise, moved rapidly into the opening, slipped a would-be challenger and glided a low, perfectly-timed shot past the advancing goalkeeper.

It was his 13th goal out of 25 credited to North End and maintained his record of having scored in every tie.

A terrific onslaught developed, as United strove to regain the initiative and establish supremacy. Preston were not at their best in defence during this phase. An ominous wobble developed, chiefly through indecision by the backs and centre-half, plus excitability which caused two or three of these inexperienced players to become flustered and over-anxious.

Happily for North End, Barton was completely untroubled by nerves of any kind. He achieved three splendid saves, generally performed grandly with an unfailing certainty of touch, and his example produced the steadying influence his harassed colleagues badly needed. The United's long-sustained offensive spent itself, and confidence in Preston was restored.

Seven minutes from the interval, however, another stormy gust of attacking sent United's hopes soaring again. The elusive Moir repeated his successful move of the opening spell and appeared to take Barton slightly unaware by the swiftness of his execution in snapping up another opportunity.

As at Deepdale, Moir was the outstanding Manchester forward. Spratt was a fine worker and McMillan was also prominent, though wasteful.

In the second half United were well on top throughout. North End, no longer hesitant or confused, had a counter for everything they tried. The covering was whole-hearted and unselfish, and none did better than Ross, Baldwin, Will and Hart. With Barton unbeatable, all United's valiant, almost non-stop efforts were fruitless. They had to concede that North End are decidedly not a team of weaklings.

As Spavin and Wilson were mainly occupied in assisting the defence and Humes a 'passenger' in the last half hour, through a leg injury, Thompson and Smith were lone attackers. Nevertheless, Preston's forlorn spearhead was dangerous whenever it gained an opportunity and a sight of goal. It was as well for United that they, too, made few mistakes when under pressure.

We have seen how good the Preston attack can be. Now we observe the quality and fighting spirit of the side in a rearguard action from which everyone emerged with high credit.

1959-60

APRIL 1960

semi-final 2nd leg

Despite putting on an infinitely better display than they had managed at Deepdale, the task of overturning Preston's lead proved too steep a slope for the Reds to climb. To all intents and purposes, performing poorly in their only away game of the cup run was the team's undoing and ultimately denied them a spot in the final.

David Meek's match report appeared under a headline proclaiming 'NERVES BEAT UNITED', in which reference was made to the Reds' strikers, who were apparently *'trembling with anxiety and nervousness when they got into the Preston target area'*. The Evening News' scribe also observed United's forwards *'fell over themselves trying to pull back a three-goal deficit'*.

In a typically sporting observation, for which he became respected during his many years of covering United's fortunes, Meek concluded that *'Preston centre-forward Peter Thompson was the star in attack, while the Deepdale defence retreated into a near-impassable line'*.

The final itself seemed to be going Preston's way when they returned from Stamford Bridge with a 1-1 draw played in front of a crowd of just over 9,000. The Chelsea team, which included future famous names such as Peter Bonetti and Terry Venables, had other ideas and stormed into a two-goal lead at Deepdale, a goal for each side in the second half proving enough to take the Youth Cup down south for the very first time.

> *Preston's goal at Old Trafford was really due to a mix-up between me and our goalie, big Ronnie (Briggs). I suppose it was just down to a lack of communication. We left a ball to each other, I'd blame him whereas he'd probably have blamed me.*
>
> *Anyway, Peter Thompson nipped in-between us and put the ball in the net. It was that goal which probably cost us the tie and a place in the final.*

ALAN ATHERTON

The United eleven who were defeated on aggregate in the 1959/60 Youth Cup semi-final by Preston North End
Back row (l-r) Jimmy Nicholson, Bobby Smith, Ronnie Briggs, Alan Atherton, Willie Donaldson, Stan Ackerley
Front row (l-r) Ian Moir, Sammy McMillan, Nobby Stiles, Phil Chisnall, Tommy Spratt

1960-61

1) Ronnie Briggs	9) Ernie Ackerley
2) Bobby Smith	10) Barry Fry
3) Mike Lorimer	11) Dennis Walker
4) Jimmy Nicholson	
5) Wilf Tranter	
6) Willie Donaldson	
7) Ian Moir	
8) Phil Chisnall	

1) Vic Webster	9) Alf Arrowsmith
2) Jim McKenzie	10) Gordon Wallace
3) Stan Crombie	11) Frank Jevons
4) Bob Connelly	
5) Chris Lawler	
6) Phil Tinney	
7) Bobby Graham	
8) George Scott	

OCTOBER 1960

MANCHESTER UNITED 3 v 0 LIVERPOOL

Ackerley (2), Chisnall

first round

Saturday 8th
Kick-off 3.00 p.m.
Attendance 11,459

In the gradually darkening days of October 1960, United kicked off a new Youth Cup campaign against a Liverpool team that had already disposed of Wrexham by three goals to two in the Preliminary Round of the competition. All three of Liverpool's goals against Wrexham were registered by former Ashton United forward, Alf Arrowsmith.

Collectively at least, the United boys weren't short on experience when the Merseysiders arrived at Old Trafford, and for Willie Donaldson, Phil Chisnall, Jimmy Nicholson and Ian Moir it was a third, and last, chance to finish with a Youth Cup medal. The last two named were expected to make a big contribution to the cause as they were in the type of form that had seen them both introduced to the rigours of the First Division, Nicholson at Everton on the opening day of the season and Moir just a week before the Youth Cup got going at Bolton.

In goalkeeper Ronnie Briggs and full-back Bobby Smith, United fielded two players who were making their second excursion down the Youth Cup trail. Smith's new full-back partner was Mike Lorimer, a Dundee boy who was given the responsibility of taking over from Stan Ackerley, and United's number nine for the new campaign was a different Ackerley, Ernie, a cousin of the retiring Stan. Centre-half Alan Atherton was another who was in his second Youth Cup season but, for this First Round tie, Wilf Tranter, normally a wing-half, featured in the middle of the defence as the regular pivot was ruled out with a bout of tonsillitis.

United's composition was completed by England schoolboy international Barry Fry at inside-left and Dennis Walker on the left wing, the last named holding the distinction of being the very first black player to sign for the club.

Over half of the visiting Liverpool side, full-back Jim McKenzie (Stirlingshire), wing-halves Bob Connelly and Phil Tinney (both Dundee), and forwards Bobby Graham (Motherwell) and George Scott (Aberdeen), came from north of the border as did Glaswegian Gordon Wallace, who was the son of former Scottish centre-forward, Dougie Wallace.

With the United versus Nottingham Forest First Division game postponed because of international call-ups for a Northern Ireland against England fixture, the youth game was afforded a Saturday afternoon slot, the timing of which practically guaranteed it a reasonable attendance.

'It was a game of two halves' is an often quoted football phrase, but the meeting between United and Liverpool was almost like two games in the first half alone. United, starting sluggishly, were under threat several times during the opening twenty minutes when efforts from Scott and Arrowsmith, twice, tested Briggs' reflexes.

During that same period the home forwards made little headway against Liverpool's defence and goalkeeper Vic Webster was barely troubled, with just a tame effort from Chisnall to deal with.

After 25 minutes, United went into an undeserved lead with a goal which would infuse them with a greater all-round confidence and thereafter they never looked likely to lose their hold on the game. Ernie Ackerley, who was keen to provide a 'thank you' gesture for having been signed as a professional just hours prior to kick-off, spotted Webster a touch too far off his goal-line. Clipping an accurate 25-yard shot just above Webster's reach, it finished by bulging the back of the net.

United could, and should, have made the game safe before the break and only failed to do so by wasting a couple of clear-cut openings. Of that particular phase of the match, the Liverpool Echo noted that the visitors had *'lost a lot of their early fire and but for poor finishing by the home side would have gone further behind'.*

After returning down the tunnel at the expiry of the interval, United retained a firm grip on the initiative and with their feet pressed firmly on the accelerator pedal, rifled two more goals, one each for Chisnall and Ackerley, to produce a scoreline that was more than justified on the balance of possession and chances created.

United were described as a *'useful but not brilliant side'* by the Evening Chronicle's Peter Slingsby. Nevertheless, the Chronicle man reserved a few special words for a young chap who was seemingly on the verge of emulating one of the club's all-time greats:

The side also had good cause to thank Jimmy Nicholson, who played an inspiring captaincy role. The Irish boy 'made' two of the goals, began the third and overall gave a striking Duncan Edwards-style display of power play both in defence and attack.

Matt Busby had, in fact, contemplated leaving Nicholson out of the youth clash in order to save him for a prestigious first-team friendly against Real Madrid at Old Trafford on the following Thursday.

Eventually deciding to stick with the age-old principle of putting his best players out on the park, Busby's choice in sanctioning the Irish lad's inclusion was a major factor in helping to ease United up and into the next stage.

From Dundee, Mike Lorimer's Youth Cup bow was something of a cakewalk

Wilf Tranter deputised for the out of sorts Alan Atherton against Liverpool

1) Ronnie Briggs	9) Ernie Ackerley	1) Dick Terry	9) Brian Kelly
2) Bobby Smith	10) Phil Chisnall	2) Alan Newton	10) Trevor Hockey
3) Mike Lorimer	11) Dennis Walker	3) Tommy Hey	11) Barry Holmes
4) Jimmy Nicholson		4) Billy Walker	
5) Alan Atherton		5) Roy Ellam	
6) Willie Donaldson		6) Bert Padgett	
7) Ian Moir		7) Bob Dover	
8) Barry Fry		8) Ray Killick	

MANCHESTER UNITED 6 v 0 BRADFORD CITY

Chisnall (2), Fry, Moir (2), Walker

NOVEMBER 1960

Monday 14th

Kick-off 7.30 p.m.

Attendance 7,766

Youngsters give Busby a boost

By the time that Bradford City presented themselves in Lancashire five weeks after United had dumped Liverpool out of the national tournament, Jimmy Nicholson had been capped as a full international by way of his appearance for Northern Ireland against Scotland. Already with eighteen senior appearances to speak of, Nicholson also filled the left-half position in a 3-1 defeat at Birmingham City just two days prior to the Youth Cup tie.

He wasn't the only one of the under-18's on duty that Saturday either, because Ronnie Briggs, Mike Lorimer, Willie Donaldson and Ernie Ackerley were all caught up in Central League affairs while Dennis Walker took his favoured right-half position for the 'A' team and Bobby Smith, Alan Atherton and Barry Fry occupied places in the 'B' side. It looked at though there was still plenty of talent ready to come through from the bottom deck as well, because Platt, with nine, and Ray Hewitt, with ten, rifled in all bar two of the Juniors' goals in a 21-0 bludgeoning of sorry Sharston.

The conquerors of lowly New Brighton in the First Round, Bradford sent a woefully inexperienced side to Manchester. Apart from Trevor Hockey's senior experience, and the inclusion of professionals Roy Ellam and Brian Kelly, most of their team was comprised of complete novices while two of the Bantams' forwards, Bob Dover and Ray Killick, were actually still pupils at the Belle Vue Grammar School in Bradford.

Over in the United camp, there was only one change to the team that had defeated Liverpool. Because Atherton was now back in the pink of health, Wilf Tranter was the unfortunate victim of the selectorial axe.

There was a glimmer of hope for the Yorkshire youngsters as their first-team colleagues had registered a memorable, if highly unexpected, win over the Reds in the newly-initiated Football League Cup at Valley Parade just two weeks previously. Despite carrying aspirations of emulating the feat achieved by their seniors, it was a benchmark they would find impossible to emulate.

United soon took up where they left off against Liverpool and went a goal to the good, made by Nicholson and scored by Fry, in only the tenth minute. The United Review match reporter recorded that the strength of the home side lay *'in their individual talent – particularly in the half-back line, which took an early grip and never relaxed it'.*

Bradford excursions into the opposing half became a rarity and goals soon rained down on the Bantams. Chisnall, Moir and Walker added three more before Moir hit home his second, and the Reds' fifth, before the turnaround, causing the Review to call this period of unrelenting United pressure *'a procession'.* With their mission accomplished, the home side seemed to turn down the power supply during the remaining 45 minutes, apart from when Chisnall claimed another goal to leave Ackerley as the only United forward not to beat the visiting goalkeeper.

In truth, the City side looked far less hassled after the break and actually managed to put on something of a reasonable display. Centre-forward Kelly wasn't without courage and wingers Dover and Holmes produced a few deft touches which didn't go unappreciated by the 7,000-plus crowd.

As a more natural for the position, Ian Moir took the eye as United's better wing man and most of the danger posed by the Reds came from his side of the field. One thing was for sure, both he and Chisnall had undoubtedly benefited from a rest over the preceding weekend as the pair looked lively when claiming a brace apiece.

The Bradford Telegraph & Argus felt the Bantams *'were far from disgraced'* and additionally claimed that *'even though it soon became obvious they were fighting for a lost cause, they never gave in'.* The Bradford reporter also reckoned that in *'Moir and Chisnall, United have two future stars'* while the Manchester Evening News, in reference to the disastrous Football League Cup defeat, offered views that the youth team had *'convincingly restored club honour'* and *'were much superior'* than their cross-Pennine opponents.

The Evening News' summary ended by recording the young Reds had *'fought as if it was a cup final against continental opposition'.*

An imposing figure to opposition forwards, goalkeeper Ronnie Briggs was rarely troubled by Bradford City

second round

1960-61

1960-61

1) Dick Woan	9) Peter Thompson	1) Ronnie Briggs	9) Ernie Ackerley
2) George Ross	10) Joe Jacques	2) Bobby Smith	10) Phil Chisnall
3) Alan Lyons	11) Alan Shaw	3) Mike Lorimer	11) Dennis Walker
4) Bill Laing		4) Jimmy Nicholson	
5) David Will		5) Alan Atherton	
6) Colin Alty		6) Willie Donaldson	
7) Mike Smith		7) Ian Moir	
8) Dave Wilson		8) Barry Fry	

DECEMBER 1960

PRESTON NORTH END 1 v 2 MANCHESTER UNITED
Jacques — *Chisnall, Walker*

Monday 19th
Kick-off 7.15 p.m.
Attendance 5,391

third round

UNITED AVENGE YOUTH CUP DEFEAT

Notwithstanding their appearance in the Youth Cup semi-final earlier in the year, which of course needed to be staged on a home and away basis, the young Reds had enjoyed a lengthy run of home engagements which ended, coincidentally, with another visit to Preston's ground in the very last days of 1960. The pairing presented an unexpected opportunity for the United boys to redress the sound beating they were forced to endure there at the hands of the North End youngsters.

Preston's obvious intention was in attempting to reach the final once again and then to go one better than previously by actually lifting the trophy. They would have viewed United as something of a yardstick to their aspirations and with a line-up that included five of the side who saw duty against Chelsea in the final, the will to win certainly wouldn't have been missing from North End's make-up.

With Deepdale seemingly able to bring out the worst possible behaviour in the Reds, the outcome was infinitely better than on their last visit there:

Youth Cup finalists last season, when Chelsea won the trophy, Preston North End were knocked out at Deepdale last night in the Third Round of this popular F.A. sponsored tournament by Manchester United, who thus avenged their semi-final defeat by Preston in the previous tournament.

A 30-second snap goal by Chisnall unnerved the home side, who failed to make a real challenge until it was too late. Manchester United were then leading by 2-0, Walker having increased their lead after 70 minutes. All that North End could do was to reduce the arrears with a goal by Jacques.

In spite of the wintry weather the match attracted 5,391 spectators. The attendance would have been much larger but for thick fog patches during the afternoon, raising fears of a postponement.

Happily the fog lifted, although the ground was still shrouded with mist at the start. Subsequently it cleared entirely, but the damage had been done.

The return of frost glazed the surface and made it somewhat treacherous under its coating of sand. Indirectly this contributed to an early setback which put North End right off their normal game and gave the United youths the best kind of incentive in a cup tie.

Almost straight from the kick-off Manchester United sought a quick lead, and gained their chance in a breakaway through Alty slipping when he had intervened and had time to clear. He tried to hold the ball instead. As a result Chisnall had a clear sight of goal, and he promptly beat Woan with a fast, hard, low shot.

Indecision also cost North End the second goal. Ross found himself caught between the oncoming left-half and the outside-left.

Primarily he was not to blame, but had reason to regret an impulsive move forward when he might have staved off the threat by delaying tactics.

As a result Woan was left in a quandary, came out too soon and too far, and all Walker eventually had to do was shoot into the open net.

Between these reverses North End were guilty of bad misses from two of the few chances their ragged and much-harried attack had been able to create.

First a centre from Shaw left United's defence wide open with both Wilson and Smith in a position to score. Wilson let the ball pass on instead of trying to score, thereby surprising Smith who missed his kick.

Then a centre by Smith glanced off the goalkeeper to Peter Thompson, who was only two or three yards from the goal-line. He failed to get his foot to the spinning ball, when only a touch was needed to equalise.

United's second goal came midway through the second half. There was still time for North End to rally, but they made little headway owing to close marking and tackling which was far too keen.

Determination was carried to excess, and referee H. Hawksworth of Bolton failed in his duty by not calling a halt much earlier to administer a general 'dressing down'.

He spoke to United's right-half, Nicholson, three times, reprimanded Chisnall, and blew his whistle incessantly, but could have quietened this aggressive spirit by taking a firm stand when it became clear that the game was going to be spoiled by too much 'needle'.

It has come to something when nearly 30 free kicks for fouls are given in a youth match. There were four against Preston and 25 against Manchester United, eight of them involving Nicholson, already an Irish international and a first-teamer.

In addition there were frequent displays of tantrums and peevishness, together with petty actions, which ought to have no place in a match of this kind. In the 80th minute North End's efforts were rewarded when Peter Thompson beat Briggs with an oblique shot which rebounded off a goal-line defender to Jacques, who promptly slammed the ball through at short range.

The team fought hard to the end, but the awakening had come too late. United clung grimly to their lead through increasing pressure and never panicked.

North End fiddled and dribbled too much in attack to be effective against resolute tacklers. The forwards made the mistake of holding too long, instead of beating the opposition with the pass and going forward at speed. There was also a marked disinclination to shoot. In fact all the faults of the first-team forwards were seen in a disappointing display, and with familiar results.

There was not much wrong with the defence, in which Ross was an immaculate, polished back, with a mature grasp of his job. It was a pity his fine display was marred by one fatal moment of indecision.

Will also played well in curbing Ackerley, the leader of a crude, but bustling and forthright Manchester attack.

The United Review informed its readership that *'the game never reached the expected standard'* and that the Reds *'played with a tenseness which materially affected their performance, no doubt due to anxiety to avenge last season's defeat'.* Then going on to point out that the team *'never touched the form that has been seen in earlier rounds'*, some felt that particular comment and another observation about the match rarely rising *'above the mediocre'* could have been explained by the unfavourable condition of the pitch.

Despite not occupying his usual position, Dennis Walker hit the back of the net for the second time in three Youth Cup games at Deepdale

1) Ronnie Briggs
2) Bobby Smith
3) Mike Lorimer
4) Jimmy Nicholson
5) Alan Atherton
6) Willie Donaldson
7) Ian Moir
8) Barry Fry
9) Ernie Ackerley
10) Phil Chisnall
11) David Latham

1) Jim Montgomery
2) Mel Slack
3) Jimmy Richardson
4) Alan Sproates
5) Colin Rutherford
6) Joe Kiernan
7) Jimmy Davison
8) Tommy Mitchinson
9) Nick Sharkey
10) Mel Smith
11) Brian Usher

1960-61

MANCHESTER UNITED 1 v 1 SUNDERLAND
Moir   Smith

FEBRUARY 1961

Wednesday 8th

Kick-off 7.30 p.m.

Attendance 13,091

United Youths scramble to late draw

On the day when a fifth pairing in just six seasons brought familiar adversaries Sunderland to Stretford, David Meek spilled some news regarding two former members of United's Youth Cup sides.

Meek wrote that Wilf McGuinness had taken his *'first limping lap'* around Old Trafford in his *'brave come-back bid'* after badly breaking a leg over a year ago. The Evening News scribe told that a specialist had at last given the ex-under-18's skipper the green light to get down to some real training and that his *'bone-grafting operation has been a complete success'*. The article also contained the information that McGuinness' leg was now strong enough to stand the strain of running and kicking a ball, which was something he *'has itched to do for almost as long as he can remember'*.

Along with those words on McGuinness, there were also a few about Tommy Spratt, whose time at the club looked to be coming to an end. It was claimed that Spratt was wanted by Chester, a club whose manager was former United striker Stan Pearson. The Chester boss had apparently agreed the terms of a deal with Matt Busby and he was now in discussions with officials of the Sealand Road outfit in regards to the proposed transfer.

The Sunderland club was, of course, still looking for their first Youth Cup win over United. With the Rokerites' Jimmy Davison having been blooded in their senior side, and two or three others regularly appearing in the club's Reserve fixtures, most of the remainder of their squad were members of a Northern Intermediate League side that topped the listings by three points and held as many games in hand over their nearest rivals. Understandably, pre-match predictions pointed to a match that could be evenly balanced.

There was a recall to the United line-up for David Latham, a striker who hadn't featured in the youth set-up for over a year. Nominated to tackle the outside-left responsibility, a position for which the Reds were obviously lacking a 'natural' of the required standard, converted wing-half Dennis Walker could consider himself badly done by in having to vacate his place after scoring in both of his last two Youth Cup appearances.

All eyes were sure to be on United goalie Ronnie Briggs, who had recently been elevated into the first-team for three matches, which included a disastrous 6-0 defeat at Leicester and a 7-2 home F.A. Cup hammering at the hands of Sheffield Wednesday. There were bound to be some concerns over his confidence within the confines of Old Trafford and whether or not his unhappy experiences in the senior grade would continue against the North-East teenagers.

The referee for that evening's match was Mr. Ken Tuck of Chesterfield, an official who had recently received a certain amount of notoriety by abandoning an F.A. Cup tie at Luton, in which the five goals scored by Manchester City's Denis Law were ruled out. Typical of City's luck, they then infamously lost the rearranged game.

Tuck was again at the centre of attention, by adding on the stoppage time that proved to be United's salvation, and the Sunderland Echo printed the events of the Reds' close escape:

Sunderland youth team put on a fine show against Manchester United under the Old Trafford floodlights last night and it was only in the last half-minute of the three minutes allowed for injuries that United managed to snatch a goal which made it a 1-1 draw.

It was a fast-moving game in which a young Sunderland side – average age just under seventeen – showed both courage and skill against powerful opposition. And though they were naturally disappointed after looking set for a hard-earned win, it was still an excellent performance to bring United back to Roker Park for a replay.

They had to withstand a tremendous barrage for the first twenty minutes, with Slack and Montgomery in brilliant form, and when play levelled off they began to build up their attacks just as convincingly as United had done. Sharkey twice narrowly failed from openings created by the fine work of Davison and Mitchinson, but it was the left-wing pair who set the game rolling Sunderland's way.

Outside-left Usher stroked a brilliant pass through for Smith to close in under challenge and beat Briggs from an acute angle with a well-placed shot in the 60th minute.

Mitchinson nearly made it two with a shot which struck goalkeeper Briggs

Frequently on target himself, Phil Chisnall acted as a late provider for Ian Moir in the squared game against Sunderland

before United began to hit back powerfully in a storming finish. This was the point at which there was the greatest benefit from the generalship of Kiernan, who starred in the rearguard action.

Then, with the referee paying as much attention to his watch as he was to the game, Moir killed a long pass from Chisnall and moved inside of Richardson in the same action to go in and beat Montgomery with a low shot just inside the far post. This was a severe test for the sixteen year-olds – Slack, Sproates, Rutherford and Usher – but they came through it in fine style.

And a special word of praise for Mel Smith, whose task was to police Ireland 'B' international and United first-team wing-half, Jimmy Nicholson. He carried it out well and played a forceful, attacking game, too.

That Echo match report concentrated on the resilience of Sunderland's performance, although the Review comments that *'United youths will probably never be nearer defeat yet more worthy of victory'* and *'the Sunderland goal was apparently haunted by a team of gremlins'* emphasised the sway that the Reds held over the game.

In his report for the Manchester Evening News, David Meek hinted that a more clinical approach was required in and about their opponents' penalty area, when advising United's youngsters *'to steady down and remember their craft when they see the whites of Montgomery's eyes'* in the rematch.

fourth round

145

1960-61

1) Jim Montgomery	9) Nick Sharkey	1) Ronnie Briggs	9) Ernie Ackerley
2) Mel Slack	10) Mel Smith	2) Bobby Smith	10) Phil Chisnall
3) Jimmy Richardson	11) Brian Usher	3) Mike Lorimer	11) Dennis Walker
4) Alan Sproates		4) Jimmy Nicholson	
5) Colin Rutherford		5) Alan Atherton	
6) Joe Kiernan		6) Willie Donaldson	
7) Jimmy Davison		7) Ian Moir	
8) Tommy Mitchinson		8) Barry Fry	

FEBRUARY 1961

SUNDERLAND 1 v 1 MANCHESTER UNITED
Sharkey *a.e.t.* Ackerley

fourth round replay

Wednesday 15th

Kick-off 7.00 p.m.

Attendance 23,647

Seven days after United's near-exit from the competition, Roker Park was a cauldron of noise when they and Sunderland met up for a much-anticipated replay.

The Wearside club's prospects had showed a marked improvement over the recent past, which caused the local Echo newspaper to slate an upbeat review for the Youth Cup clash:

Great efforts in league and cup have made Sunderland a top-line attraction again and this is reflected in an average attendance of 43,537 in their last five games at Roker Park. Tomorrow night at Roker Park it is the turn of the unbeaten Sunderland youth team to put on the show game of the season at under-18 level.

And what bigger attraction could there be than the visit of Manchester United in the F.A. Youth Cup.

The Sunderland lads won the right to fight this Fourth Round tie over again tomorrow night by their great performance at Old Trafford last week when they held the powerful United combination to a 1-1 draw........and were, in fact, within 30 seconds of a surprise victory.

The stage is set for another helping of the Old Trafford thriller, with both clubs announcing unchanged sides.

Luck of the draw has kept Sunderland's home attractions down to a minimum in this competition. This season, after being drawn away in the first two rounds, they were given home advantage over North Shields before being drawn away to United.

It was a great effort to bring them back to Roker Park, and with the Sunderland crowd to help them on they can go all out to earn a place in the quarter-finals against either Aston Villa or Stoke City.

This great Sunderland youth side, used consistently to produce players rather than to win trophies, have played all but three of their 27 (Northern Intermediate League) games this season against Football League opposition and have come up with the astonishing record of 25 wins and two draws with a goal ratio of 128-25.

True, they have not been meeting sides of United's calibre every week, but the Old Trafford game showed exactly how they stood by comparison and tomorrow night they can set the seal on a great season before the biggest crowd they have ever attracted to Roker Park.

The long-standing criticism of the Sunderland club is that they have never seemed to get their fair share of the young talent which abounds in the North-East. Tomorrow night they will be served by a team which changes all that.

Apart from left-half and captain Joe Kiernan and centre-forward Dominic Sharkey, two of the brilliant quintet of Scots boys on the club's books, all the remaining players are drawn from within a few miles of Roker Park.

Like most Manchester United sides they are schooled to a mixture of skill and toughness, though there is much more emphasis upon skill in the current team.

It promises to be a great occasion and at Reserve team prices there should be a big turn out of Sunderland supporters.

Despite numerous fluffed chances from almost all of the Reds' half-backs and forwards in the clash at Old Trafford, David Latham's missing of a particular 'sitter' with his head probably contributed to his swift displacement. Dennis Walker gained a reinstatement at his expense, and the Wearside public did indeed show up in force in anticipation of seeing a rousing battle and ultimate victory for the local team.

With the Sunderland Echo again reporting, what the crowd actually got was only half of what they had bargained for:

Though at a disadvantage in terms of physical strength, the Sunderland youngsters put on a fine display before a 23,647 crowd at Roker Park last night in a 1-1 draw with Manchester United youth team in an F.A. Youth Cup (Fourth Round) replay.

With the scores level after 90 minutes, it seemed that United's strength must see them through in the extra-time. But the Sunderland lads rallied bravely and United were flagging, too, before the finish.

Mel Slack and Jimmy Montgomery, outstanding at Old Trafford last week, were again the players who wrecked United's hopes with brilliant work under extreme pressure.

Neither side was on top in more than snatches, but Sunderland had the bigger count in terms of clear-cut chances. After Sharkey had headed them into the lead with a great goal in 22 minutes, United came back through Moir, in the outside-left position, whose centre was cracked home in fine style by Ackerley for an equaliser in 37 minutes.

Split-second hesitation by Mitchinson lost a great chance just before the end of 90 minutes and then in extra-time Smith, scheming the opening brilliantly, hit a shot straight at Briggs and then sent the rebound behind.

Apart from his many fine saves on the line, Montgomery cut out two certain goals for United by racing out to dive at the feet of opponents.

Davison was the most successful Sunderland forward, though the best results were not obtained from his play because he consistently dropped his centres and corner kicks within easy reach of United's 6ft. 1in. goalkeeper, Ronnie Briggs.

United were without centre-half Atherton for a spell in the first half while he had stitches inserted in a cut under the eye and again in the second when the wound reopened.

For the record, the count of free kicks for fouls showed that Sunderland were awarded 31 over the 120 minutes while United received eleven.

The view that a draw was a fair result was shared by all neutral and even some of the most partisan onlookers. A few felt that Sunderland could have taken more advantage of the disruption caused to the Reds by the injury encountered by Alan Atherton, although it was noted in certain quarters that those around him in United's defence coped admirably in his absence.

While Mike Lorimer was hard-pressed to contain the livewire Davison, Bobby Smith managed to quash the ever-present threat of Brian Usher and the home midfield got precious little change out of workaholics Jimmy Nicholson and Willie Donaldson.

Ernie Ackerley, whose first half equaliser necessitated a third meeting with Sunderland's determined teenagers on the following weekend

1) Jim Montgomery
2) Mel Slack
3) Jimmy Richardson
4) Alan Sproates
5) Colin Rutherford
6) Joe Kiernan
7) Jimmy Davison
8) Tommy Mitchinson
9) Nick Sharkey
10) Mel Smith
11) Brian Usher

1) Ronnie Briggs
2) Bobby Smith
3) Mike Lorimer
4) Wilf Tranter
5) Jimmy Nicholson
6) Willie Donaldson
7) Ian Moir
8) Barry Fry
9) Ernie Ackerley
10) Phil Chisnall
11) Dennis Walker

1960-61

SUNDERLAND 1 v 2 MANCHESTER UNITED
Mitchinson — Ackerley, Walker

FEBRUARY 1961

Saturday 18th

Kick-off 3.00 p.m.

Attendance 16,585

fourth round 2nd replay

No Answer To Brisk, Bustling United
ROKER YOUTH HIT BY THE LOSS OF SHARKEY

Following on from the second drawn encounter, which the United Review chose to describe as *'a real thriller'*, Sunderland won the toss to stage the third meeting just three days after the second replay.

Because their first-team was away at Norwich on F.A. Cup duty, and Sunderland's Reserves were without a game, Roker Park was conveniently free for the youth match.

United's resolve to succeed in the tie was underlined when Jimmy Nicholson was withdrawn from senior duties so that he could continue captaining the youngsters.

One of the reasons that contributed towards Nicholson's inclusion in the youth team was Alan Atherton's injury, which was a wound held together by four stitches below his right eye that hadn't healed sufficiently for him to be considered for the clash.

Events conspired to make it third time lucky for United, even though it was an unfortunate knock to one of the Roker Park youngsters which finally helped to tip the scales in their favour.

For the third successive time, the Sunderland Echo supplied the match details:

SUNDERLAND youth team had their third crack at Manchester United youth in ten days this afternoon when they met at Roker Park this afternoon for the second replay in the F.A. Youth Cup (Fourth Round).

Sunderland kept the same team that had played in the other two games, but Manchester were forced to make changes. Irish international Jimmy Nicholson was left out of Manchester United's first team and came in at centre half in place of Atherton. His place at right half was taken by Tranter while Moir changed wings and Walker took his place at outside left.

Manchester soon showed they meant business and Sunderland were lucky not to find themselves a goal down in the first minute. From the kick-off Ackerley put Chisnall through and Montgomery was forced to dive at the inside left's feet to save.

Sunderland began to get the measure of the fast moving United attack but not before Montgomery had made a flying leap to keep out Chisnall's header. In the sixth minute Sharkey was unlucky when he ran through a packed defence only for Briggs to come out and block his shot. But Sharkey was not beaten. He fastened on to the loose ball and with Briggs well out of his goal the centre forward sent a snap shot just wide.

Manchester immediately came back and Ackerley again put Chisnall clear of the defence on the right wing but from his centre Walker headed against a post.

United soon gave Sunderland something to shout about when they gave away two fouls in quick succession. The mood soon changed to one of open hostility when Sharkey was taken off after a collision in the 15th minute.

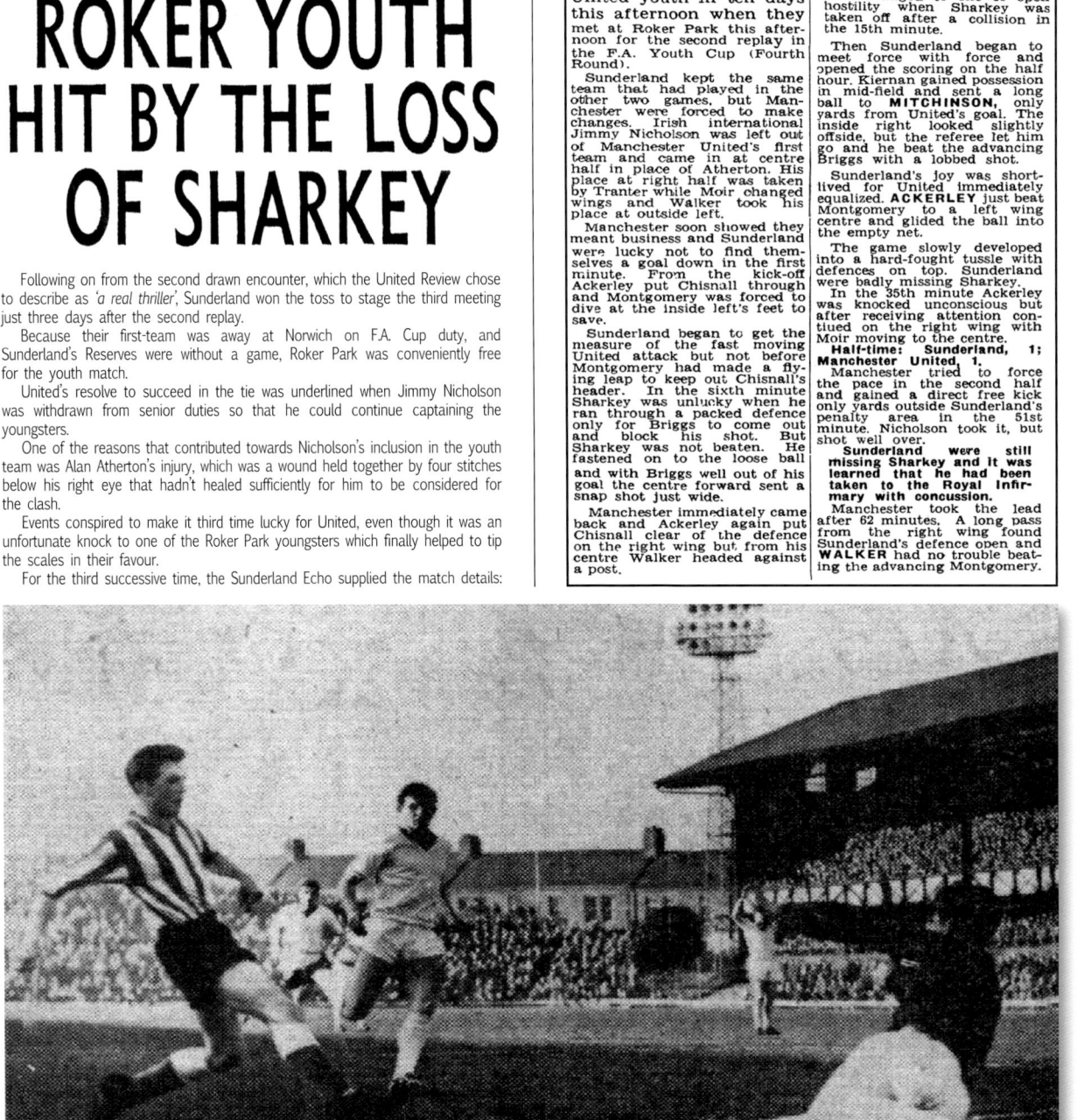

Then Sunderland began to meet force with force and opened the scoring on the half hour. Kiernan gained possession in mid-field and sent a long ball to **MITCHINSON**, only yards from United's goal. The inside right looked slightly offside, but the referee let him go and he beat the advancing Briggs with a lobbed shot.

Sunderland's joy was short-lived for United immediately equalized. **ACKERLEY** just beat Montgomery to a left wing centre and glided the ball into the empty net.

The game slowly developed into a hard-fought tussle with defences on top. Sunderland were badly missing Sharkey.

In the 35th minute Ackerley was knocked unconscious but after receiving attention continued on the right wing with Moir moving to the centre.

Half-time: Sunderland, 1; Manchester United, 1.

Manchester tried to force the pace in the second half and gained a direct free kick only yards outside Sunderland's penalty area in the 51st minute. Nicholson took it, but shot well over.

Sunderland were still missing Sharkey and it was learned that he had been taken to the Royal Infirmary with concussion.

Manchester took the lead after 62 minutes. A long pass from the right wing found Sunderland's defence open and **WALKER** had no trouble beating the advancing Montgomery.

Mitchinson opening the scoring for Sunderland in this afternoon's Youth Cup replay against Manchester United at Roker Park.

147

1960-61

1) Brian Sherratt	9) John Walters	1) Ronnie Briggs	9) Ernie Ackerley
2) Len Parton	10) Graham Matthews	2) Bobby Smith	10) Barry Fry
3) Alan Philpott	11) Keith Bebbington	3) Mike Lorimer	11) Dennis Walker
4) Bill Winder		4) Jimmy Nicholson	
5) Alan Bloor		5) Alan Atherton	
6) Barry Griffiths		6) Willie Donaldson	
7) Alan McGrath		7) Ian Moir	
8) Gerry Bridgwood		8) Phil Chisnall	

MARCH 1961

STOKE CITY 2 v 0 MANCHESTER UNITED
Matthews (pen), Walters

Wednesday 22nd
Kick-off 7.15 p.m.
Attendance 14,723

fifth round

Smith injury hits United

> *"It was a horrible night down at the Victoria Ground. It was a really rough game played on a bad pitch and it was also extremely cold and wet. Stoke were quite a physical side, there was a heck of a lot of barging, and that probably upset our ball-playing style more than it did them."*
>
> **ALAN ATHERTON**

A little over a month after finally crushing Sunderland's plucky attempts at ousting them from the Youth Cup, the Reds were forced into facing another difficult prospect with a tie at Stoke.

Of course, it was at the same stage a year previously that United had knocked the Staffordshire side out by a single goal margin and with the loss of home advantage, a major effort would be required from the Reds if further progress was to be made. Stoke were able to field as many as seven of the team who were defeated at Old Trafford and United's personnel exactly matched that number from the same game.

Both sides were clear of injuries, and the Reds' determination to reach the later stages of the tournament couldn't have been more clearly demonstrated. Jimmy Nicholson's continued inclusion in the side at the expense of his senior responsibilities, as well as that of Ian Moir, who one newspaper reporter felt *'is playing so well in United's First Division side'*, constituted a major investment from their standpoint.

Just as the Reds had progressed at Sunderland's expense up at Roker Park, where a crocked team member proved to be one of the telling factors, it was now their turn to suffer from a similar fate in Stoke.

At the end of an enthralling 90 minutes, the red and white half of the Potteries was rejoicing in a famous victory which no-one could dispute was fully merited given their performance on the night.

Sporting their change strip of all white with red trims, United's 1960/61 youth team came to grief at the Victoria Ground
Back row (l-r) Mike Lorimer, Phil Chisnall, Bobby Smith, Ronnie Briggs, Ernie Ackerley, Alan Atherton, Arthur Powell (trainer)
Front row (l-r) Ian Moir, Willie Donaldson, Jimmy Nicholson, Barry Fry, Dennis Walker

1960-61

MARCH 1961

fifth round

The (Stoke-on-Trent) Evening Sentinel noted the events which added up to United's downfall:

> Quicker to the ball and generally stronger in their all-round work, Stoke City won their fifth-round F.A. Youth Cup-tie at the Victoria Ground with Manchester United 2-0 last night, and entered the semi-final.
>
> They will now be at home in the first game of their two-leg meetings with Everton.
>
> United found more than their match and the result was sweet revenge for Stoke, who lost 2-1 away to Manchester at the same stage last season.
>
> **Nose fractured**
>
> Both goals were scored in the second half after an injury to right-back Smith, whose nose was fractured in a collision, had caused United to reorganise their side. Smith, with his broken and cut nose plastered up, played for the last 25 minutes in the forward line.
>
> That incident was the turning point for both sides.
>
> Before the United had become attuned to their upset, Stoke really gained the grip which they had previously suggested they might take.
>
> It was not until a penalty was awarded that they got their first goal. The second, excellently worked, came near the end, when Stoke were storming in to make the margin safe.
>
> Close-marking on both sides and a lively ball which neither team really satisfactorily controlled, were against sustained flow in the play, and the standard did not come up to expectations in the first half, although life and excitement developed in the second.
>
> **Nearly 15,000**
>
> Nearly 15,000 people, Stoke's best crowd, Cup-ties apart, of the season, gave the City lads rousing encouragement.
>
> The measure of Stoke's greater activity in attack was the amount of work that Briggs had to do in the United goal—three times as much as the Stoke goalkeeper. City's defence was sound, well directed by Bloor at centre-half, who was flanked by two commanding wing-halves in Winder and Griffiths. Parton was a cool full-back.
>
> Stoke's best player was inside-right Bridgwood, a constructive and assertive forward, and Matthews on the other inside position was not far behind.
>
> Early on Stoke made sharp thrusts through the agency of their inside forwards, with Walters a go-ahead centre-forward.
>
> For a long time the trends were strongly in favour of the City, but they had not much to offer on the wings and United's defence, with Atherton at centre-half, and Briggs, performing soundly, stood firm.
>
> Towards half-time Manchester had improved and their forwards were seen in a number of spritely raids, which once or twice nearly upset Stoke.
>
> While Smith was off the field having treatment, Bebbington missed a great chance for Stoke.
>
> Stoke began to hammer away for a goal, urged on by a roaring crowd.
>
> Smith came back after 10 minutes and moved into the attack. Stoke were still pressing and McGrath's shot crashed against the side of the post.
>
> It required a penalty to put Stoke ahead after 68 minutes. The decision seemed a bit harsh, as Walters appeared to be already on his way to a tumble as two defenders came across him. Matthews hit the spot kick well out of reach.
>
> Stoke missed a chance of going further ahead and Sherratt's brilliant save from Nicholson prevented a United equaliser before the City scored a second with four minutes to go.
>
> Walters took the ball and drove it through after Bridgwood had cleverly made the opening for him.

Peter Slingsby of the Evening Chronicle was more forthright about United's failures than the Sentinel, as the 'UNITED WERE LET OFF LIGHTLY' headline to his piece on the game indicated:

Manchester United gave a disappointing display in the quarter-final of the F.A. Youth Cup at Stoke, where a 2-0 scoreline did them no injustice. In fact, they were fortunate to escape so lightly.

Even allowing for the injury absence of Bobby Smith in the second half – he broke his nose and spent half-an-hour on the wing – Stoke were crisper, more assured and always more potent as they thundered through to a semi-final meeting with Everton.

Only three United players matched Stoke's top-class showing. Ron Briggs, whose handling was first-class, Alan Atherton, probably the best defender on view, and the hard-working Barry Fry. Biggest disappointments were Ian Moir and Jimmy Nicholson. This was the first time that United had failed to reach the last four of the competition in the nine years of its existence. For Stoke, victory was sweet revenge for their narrow defeat at the same stage last season.

Crowd note: This was the biggest ever at Stoke for a Youth Cup match. It was also TWICE as many as watched the first-team in an anti-relegation clash 48 hours earlier.

Stoke had entered the tie with a seemingly greater passion to succeed than United and even though the injury to Smith could have been considered as a contributing factor to their downfall, the plain truth was that the Reds were unable to trouble the Potters' defence sufficiently or consistently enough to earn the right to a semi-final placing.

The United Review philosophically summed up the disappointment:

In failing to reach the semi-final stage for the first time since the inception of the Youth Competition, our boys were deservedly beaten by a Stoke side which was stronger on the ball, livelier and much more purposeful in their work. A facial injury soon after the interval, which caused Smith to retire for a time before resuming in the forward-line, meant a reshuffle in defence but this does not detract from the merit of the home team's win. They had looked the better side in the first half and only several daring saves by Briggs prevented a score. Only in the ten minutes before the interval did our boys begin to move with any smoothness and offer any real threat to the Stoke defence. Oddly enough, we might have taken a lead in this period which could have proved the tonic which was needed. A fierce drive by Walker all but did the trick only to crash against the underside of the bar.

After the change round there was never a great deal in the game territorially but Stoke, always faster and stronger on the ball, looked more impressive yet when they did take the lead midway through the half, it seemed a little unjust. Matthews scored from the spot after Walters had been brought down but it did appear that he had fouled Atherton before the penalty offence. A spirited effort to get on terms by our boys had the home defence in difficulties for a time and only a superb save by Sherratt from a first time drive by Nicholson prevented them from doing the trick. With time running out, Stoke again took command and after good work by Bebbington, Walters had a simple task to settle the issue.

A hand for Stoke who won well and earned their first semi-final appearance. Our boys just failed to capture their best form when it mattered and we were never really firing on all cylinders with only Briggs, Atherton and Fry gaining full marks.

In the Stoke v. Rotherham programme dated 1st April 1961, mention was made of the monetary aspects of the Potters' victory over United:

Stoke City's needy finances will get a substantial fillip by reason of the club's Youth XI reaching the semi-finals of the F.A. Youth Cup for the first time. The semi-finals and final of the Youth Cup are on a home-and-away basis – a total of six games or more – and each of the semi-finalists receive a 12½ per cent share of the pooled receipts of all the matches. The finalists have an allocation of 25 per cent each of receipts.

If they could reach the final, Stoke might well net £2,000. The 14,700 'gate' for the quarter-finals youth game between Stoke and Manchester Utd yielded a total of £1,300.

Sadly for them, both the Potters' financial and football ambitions didn't quite come to fruition as, upon running into Everton in the semi-final, it was at that point where their progress was halted, with defending cup-holders Chelsea then defeating the Merseysiders on a 5-3 aggregate in the final.

> " *Jimmy Murphy was still very much in charge, giving team talks and geeing everyone up. Jimmy never made us work at tactics, if you were at United it meant that you could play and so we only focused on our strengths. He wanted us to do what we were good at and let us express ourselves.*
>
> *We played a 4-3-3 formation with Jimmy Nicholson, Barry Fry and myself working in a midfield-type role with Ernie Ackerley upfront and Dennis Walker and Ian Moir on the wings. They were real 'magic nights'. Running out in front of 20,000 people with great players around you, it was just fantastic.* "

PHIL CHISNALL

1961-62

1) Brian Wright	9) Ernie Ackerley	1) Andy Rankin	9) Wally Bennett
2) Joe Clayton	10) Barry Fry	2) Roy Parnell	10) George Morton
3) Mike Lorimer	11) Alan Duff	3) Wakes	11) Gerry Humphreys
4) Dennis Walker		4) Barrie Rees	
5) Wilf Tranter		5) Ken Griffiths	
6) Bobby Smith		6) Bernard Coupe	
7) David Latham		7) Colin Green	
8) Eamon Dunphy		8) Stuart Shaw	

SEPTEMBER 1961

MANCHESTER UNITED 3 v 2 EVERTON

Ackerley, Duff, Fry — *Bennett, Shaw*

preliminary round

Wednesday 13th

Kick-off 7.30 p.m.

Attendance 9,717

The opening tie of United's 1961/62 Youth Cup campaign took place rather earlier in the year than had been the case in the past, with a home game against Everton meaning that the club's under-18 team were required to hurdle the Preliminary Round of the competition. In short, increased entries meant that the young Reds needed to beat the Toffees for a right they had previously taken for granted, that of entering the First Round Proper.

Despite there being seven in the United side with experience of the tournament, it was noted that half a dozen of the now retired regulars from the previous term, Briggs, Nicholson, Moir, Donaldson, Chisnall and Atherton, had amassed 105 Youth Cup appearances between them. It was, therefore, quite obvious that any formation named would have to be considered something of a transitional one.

Those exiting the side brought about the usual annual changes to the team's composition, but the proposed new goalkeeper suffered an injury just prior to the beginning of the competition. After impressing at junior level, local Prestwich youngster Mervyn Maneely was earmarked to wear the goal-guardian's jersey before his misfortune forced United to move quickly in an attempt to fill the specialist role and so seventeen year-old Liverpudlian Brian Wright was hurriedly signed from Cheshire League club Winsford United and thrust into Youth Cup action against Everton with only one 'B' team appearance for the Reds under his belt. There were also tournament introductions for outside-left Alan Duff, defender Joe Clayton and ex-Eire schoolboy international Eamon Dunphy, while David Latham was nominated for his third start in the tournament in as many seasons.

Signing only five months before, Duff had made an extremely positive start to his time with the club and his six goals from three 'B' team appearances were supplemented with a couple of games for the 'A' side already that season.

Initially taken on as an amateur, Clayton had been with United since January 1958 and signed as a professional exactly two years later. He was still a fixture in the 'B' team and had been unable to dislodge a couple of Smiths, firstly Barry and then Bobby, in order to gain a place in the Youth Cup eleven, but with the latter resituated to accommodate him, Clayton's chance in the under-18's had now arrived.

On a night when approximately two dozen Football League Cup fixtures realised average gates of only around 7,500, the Old Trafford faithful ensured that the United v. Everton youth fixture would top that figure by a couple of thousand and more. Those in attendance saw a closely fought duel which represented eminently good value for their admission fee.

The United Review gave the following report:

A crowd of 10,000 saw another close game between these old rivals who, in six previous meetings, have drawn twice and been separated by the odd goal three times. Despite opening the scoring and looking the more dominant side for a spell after the interval in which they drew level, Everton again found United a stumbling block to their Youth Cup aspirations.

There could be no complaint about the result, however, for the United boys had been more forceful in attack and the visitors had Rankin to thank for the narrow interval margin. United played the more purposeful and attractive football and looked far more dangerous near goal. With their scoring chances limited to half a dozen, the visitors did well to keep the game alive and remain in with a chance. The Everton defence had many anxious moments in the first half hour but with one of their few scoring opportunities, the visitors went ahead in 32 minutes. The flight of a long lob deceived Wright and Bennett beat the 'keeper to the ball to hook in from an acute angle.

United fought back strongly against this reverse and after Rankin had tipped a Duff drive over the top, the latter headed home a Latham centre for the equaliser. Three minutes before the interval, United took an overdue lead when Ackerley rose above a crowded defence to head home a well-placed free kick by Walker.

The Merseysiders resumed in determined fashion to dominate the exchanges but showed little fire near goal. They were a trifle unlucky when Rees crashed the ball against the crossbar and Bennett, running in, headed the rebound over. Consolation came soon afterwards when their efforts were rewarded with an equaliser in the 65th minute. The scorer was Shaw, who beat off several challenges before shooting beyond the reach of Wright.

With Everton still holding slight territorial advantage, the Reds came through on the left and Smith slipped a neat pass forward for Fry to move in and pick his spot and restore the home lead. This proved the tonic required to restore much of the United first half rhythm and they were in command in the closing stages despite several dangerous looking Everton raids.

An interesting game ended with United deservedly earning the right to meet Wigan in the First Round of the competition. This game is due to be played at Wigan but no date has yet been fixed.

The Reds were spared with a let off when Everton's Barrie Rees dirtied the frame of the goal with a terrific 30-yard piledriver in the second half and the same player also saw his wicked shot pushed onto the angle of crossbar and post by Wright in the early part of the game.

The Liverpool Daily Post felt a *'lack of finishing was Everton's failing'* before balancing the criticism with a view that they had also *'put up a great fight'*.

The Manchester Evening News' David Meek reasoned that United were *'at a rebuilding stage with their youth team'*. Even so, Meek witnessed encouraging signs from the current crop, causing him to comment that *'Eamon Dunphy, a Dublin-born inside-right, looked thoroughly at home'* and that the Irish boy and David Latham *'formed an impressive right wing'*.

The Chronicle's Peter Slingsby agreed with him, predicting that the crowd saw *'at least three future first-team stars'* in Fry, Dunphy and the indefatigable Dennis Walker, who, he claimed *'outshone them all, even the bigger and more experienced Everton players'*. Slingsby thought it *'appropriate that a Dunphy-Fry link-up should provide the winning goal'* and he recorded how he had been *'impressed by the work of makeshift right-winger David Latham, who could so easily make the top grade'*.

An encouraging performance against the Toffees earned Eamon Dunphy special praise from both David Meek and Peter Slingsby

1) Trevor Darbyshire
2) John Dickenson
3) Don Moss
4) Ian Dale
5) Colin Blakemore
6) George Morris
7) Ernie Bowen
8) John White
9) Frank Picton
10) Graham Knowles
11) Howell Redrobe

1) Brian Wright
2) Joe Clayton
3) Mike Lorimer
4) Dennis Walker
5) Wilf Tranter
6) Bobby Smith
7) David Latham
8) Barry Fry
9) Ernie Ackerley
10) Eamon Dunphy
11) Alan Duff

1961-62

WIGAN ATHLETIC* 1 v 10 MANCHESTER UNITED

Knowles

Ackerley (3), Dunphy (2), Fry (3), Latham, Moss (o.g.)

OCTOBER 1961

Monday 9th

Kick-off 7.30 p.m.

Attendance 6,634

*Played at Old Trafford

first round

As the United Review noted at the tail-end of the Everton match report, the reward of victory was a First Round tie at Wigan. It was the fifth time the Reds had been drawn to meet a team from outside the boundaries of the Football League but, in a similar set of developments to those which preceded their match against Nantwich nine years earlier, Athletic forfeited their home advantage and allowed the fixture to be moved to Manchester.

An explanation for the choice of ground was given in the Wigan Observer:

Wigan have switched the F.A. Youth Cup tie with Manchester United Youth from Springfield Park to Old Trafford. Athletic would have liked the match to be played on a Saturday afternoon at Wigan but as this was not convenient to United, they agreed to a floodlight game at Old Trafford on Monday, 9th October to ensure a larger 'gate'.

The Latics were faced with little choice other than to suggest a Saturday kick-off as Springfield Park wasn't equipped with floodlights in 1961. Their decision to alter the match venue was fully vindicated by an attendance of over six and a half thousand spectators, who coughed up gate receipts of £423, although it did lead to a rather inevitable outcome in terms of the result.

The United Review provided an account of the match highlights:

Fry took a neat pass from Dunphy to open the scoring. He added a second with an easy chance after Darbyshire had mis-fielded a shot by Latham. A clever home move ended with Fry flicking the ball neatly through for Ackerley to score from close range. Playing delightfully crisp and punchy football, United continued

Full-back Joe Clayton encountered few problems against Wigan

to command and added further goals through Fry, Latham and Ackerley to lead 6-0 at the interval.

Wigan were soon in difficulty after the change-round and when Darbyshire punched out a Latham centre, Dunphy crashed the ball home from the edge of the penalty area. The visitors gained some consolation for several lively attacks when, after some scrimmaging in the home goal area, Orritt forced the ball into the net. Within a minute, Ackerley coolly picked his spot to head in number eight.

A hand injury caused Wright to retire and Ackerley took over in goal but this gave the visitors' defence little respite. Time and again the ball was scrambled off the line and shots charged down before Fry turned a ball neatly inside to Dunphy who jinked his way through to increase the lead. A nightmare occasion for Darbyshire was completed when he punched a corner from Walker into his own net.

A gallant 'backs-to-the-wall' display from Athletic defenders Colin Blakemore and John Dickenson, plus some neat footwork from inside-forward John White and a couple of surging runs from outside-right Ernie Bowen, was nothing like enough to disguise the massive gulf in class between the two contestants.

During a display crammed full of confidence and slick performances from the United lads, it was topped off nicely with a brace from Eamon Dunphy and hat-tricks for the more experienced Barry Fry and Ernie Ackerley. The Reds' final scoring effort was later credited as an own goal by defender Don Moss, the ball possibly cannoning off him before crossing the line. The Review correspondent was also unaware that John Orritt, who was noted as the Latics' inside-left in the match programme, had actually been replaced by Graham Knowles.

A goalscorer in the last tie against Everton, Alan Duff provided numerous chances for his colleagues in the huge win over Wigan

" I signed as a professional but my dad cancelled the contract almost immediately as he wanted me to get a trade. Instead of training with all the other lads during the day, I went to Old Trafford on a Tuesday and The Cliff on a Thursday, going through evening routines with all the amateurs. When I was called into the youth team I had never trained with them before. Luckily, I had played for Manchester Boys along with Wilf Tranter, Ernie Ackerley, Bobby Smith and especially David Latham, who always played in front of me down the right side, so we already had a good understanding. "

JOE CLAYTON

151

1961-62

1) Mervyn Maneely	9) Ernie Ackerley
2) Bobby Smith	10) Eamon Dunphy
3) Mike Lorimer	11) Alan Duff
4) Dennis Walker	
5) Wilf Tranter	
6) Jimmy Keogh	
7) David Latham	
8) Barry Fry	

1) David Downes	9) Glyn Pardoe
2) Mike Harold	10) Bobby Cunliffe
3) Peter Loftos	11) Neil Young
4) Fred Eyre	
5) Mike Batty	
6) Derek Floyd	
7) Vic Smith	
8) Ken Fletcher	

NOVEMBER 1961

MANCHESTER UNITED 3 v 0 MANCHESTER CITY

Ackerley, Fry, Walker

Monday 20th
Kick-off 7.30 p.m.
Attendance 13,043

second round

REDS WAIT FOR TRANTER TEST

A better quality of opposition by far was next on the menu, when United acted as guests to a Manchester City team that had already bundled Leeds and Burnley out of the competition. The pairing represented something of a minor sporting occasion in the locality as it was City's first Youth Cup visit to Old Trafford, although the Maine Road representatives wouldn't have needed reminding that they were still searching for a victory over the Reds in the tournament.

The hand bash sustained by goalkeeper Brian Wright that forced his early withdrawal against Wigan, allowed the now fit Mervyn Maneely to claim a place in United's side. Despite the match programme naming Mike Lorimer at number five and Denton-based Bill Hampson at number six, Wilf Tranter undertook a late fitness test and he was given the thumbs-up to start at centre-half.

Because Joe Clayton felt a little unwell in the lead up to the clash, Bobby Smith was able to revert to his familiar right full-back position and former Republic of Ireland Boys star Jimmy Keogh squeezed into the team ahead of Hampson at left half-back.

City displayed two teenagers who would become an integral part of the Maine Road success story later in the decade. Centre-forward Glyn Pardoe had registered twice against Burnley in the last round and to his far left was another who had also been amongst the goals, the tall and elegant Neil Young. Also the recent scorer of a brace, Young's strikes came in a Central League fixture at Blackburn just two days prior to the youth game.

Despite an apparent abundance of talent in City's ranks, and a plentiful amount of application, the game went according to tradition when the Blues collapsed in the face of a United onslaught.

The tie was reported on for the Chronicle by Bob Parkinson:

There were sixteen and seventeen year-old youngsters on parade at Old Trafford last night – when Manchester United beat Manchester City 3-0 in their Second Round Youth Cup clash – who would fetch £10,000 or more in this era of rising soccer values. They would be worth this simply because of the promise they showed in their spirited battle.

Top of the list comes United's dusky dynamo, right-half Dennis Walker, who showed astonishing stamina and ability. He set United on the winning trail with a finely headed goal – he's a converted centre-forward – and he deserved a second one late in the game when, showing typical alertness and anticipation, he ran half the length of the field and nearly hooked in a long cross.

Not far behind him in promise came City's left-winger, Neil Young. City, for so long lacking orthodox and powerful wing play, have now got two of the finest young wingers in the game in Wagstaffe and Young, and these two could hold down first-team places for years if City's plan to convert Young to the right-wing succeeds.

United inside men Fry and Dunphy showed up well, but City's wing-halves had an off day and it was Ernie Ackerley who really caught my eye. Up against strong and promising Mike Batty, he roamed intelligently and showed all the attributes of a good, orthodox centre-forward. David Latham was also an accomplished attacker for United.

Pardoe didn't get much change out of Tranter, so all the hard work on either side of him by Cunliffe and Fletcher came to nothing, but it was good to see light-blue shirted inside men covering so much ground.

One note of caution: The United lads already seem to be over-imbued with the habit of hugging each other violently after scoring and with making of dramatic gestures of disappointment when a decision goes against them. They should cut it out.

Preceded by a strapline proclaiming 'YOUNG REDS AND BLUES PLEASE', the Evening News also carried a few short paragraphs on the match:

Managers and fans alike must have found Manchester's F.A. Youth Cup derby a tonic. Manchester United's youngsters not only provided a fluency and confidence missing recently in the league side – they won, an experience Matt Busby has missed lately.

Manager Les McDowall did not have that satisfaction, but he can be well pleased with the youngsters George Poyser has brought to Maine Road.

There was nothing to choose between the two sides until the second half when Dennis Walker capped a great game with a smartly taken goal.

Five minutes later Barry Fry scored, and United finished in impressive style with Ernie Ackerley also scoring.

> *It was the morning of the match and Johnny Aston told me that Wilf Tranter would most likely miss the game and that I was playing. However, Wilf was passed fit and Johnny had to tell me I wasn't playing after all. I was very disappointed but I was still taken to have a meal with all the other players at Davyhulme Golf Club.*
>
> *Following the meal Joe Clayton suddenly took ill and as we got off the team bus Johnny Aston once again told me I was playing but wasn't sure in which position. In the end I started in my usual position in the half-back line. Early in the game I put Alan Duff through with a good ball and he went on to score. I thought 'that's a great start for us' but the referee disallowed the goal for offside.*
>
> *We won comfortably, so it all turned out well in the end.*

JIMMY KEOGH

1)	Mervyn Maneely	9)	Ernie Ackerley
2)	Bobby Smith	10)	Eamon Dunphy
3)	Mike Lorimer	11)	Alan Duff
4)	Dennis Walker		
5)	Wilf Tranter		
6)	Jimmy Keogh		
7)	David Latham		
8)	Barry Fry		

1)	Stan Day	9)	Bob Collins
2)	David Keighley	10)	Bob Swain
3)	Geoff Mitchell	11)	Rod Butler
4)	Terry Bolland		
5)	Alan Newton		
6)	Dick Garbutt		
7)	Danny Hazelgrave		
8)	Graham Keighley		

1961-62

MANCHESTER UNITED 9 v 0 BRADFORD CITY

Ackerley (2), Dunphy (2), Fry (3), Latham (2)

DECEMBER 1961

Monday 4th

Kick-off 7.30 p.m.

Attendance 7,265

third round

YOUNG REDS LASH NINE

By the time of Bradford City's arrival at Old Trafford just a fortnight after the youth team had disposed of Manchester City, the senior Reds were a long way down the list of a depressing run of results. They included two 5-1 defeats, at Everton and Arsenal, and a couple of 4-1 losses, away at Ipswich and at home to Burnley, the last two falling on consecutive Saturdays in November.

Sadly, their lack of form had yielded just two draws and as many as eight defeats from their last ten games. A lack of goals away from Old Trafford seemed to be developing into a major problem for the first-team, as they had managed just one in each of the last six matches on their travels.

Results were only marginally better for the Central League side. After getting off to a great start to the season, with seven wins and a draw and a goal record of 33 scored and fourteen conceded from their first nine games, they had gone off the boil.

In their last six matches the Reserves had won three and lost three, one of the latter including a 5-0 battering on a particularly bad day at Burnley. Of the youth team, Ernie Ackerley and David Latham had recently occupied places in the Central League team, although only Bobby Smith, with a full deck of twenty second string appearances, could consider himself a regular at that grade.

The 'A' team lads, too, were going through a tricky time of it, and of their thirteen games played so far only three had produced wins and an equal number yielded draws. Conceding goals was the third team's major problem, the total of 33 equating to a worrying average of nearly three per match.

The 'B' team weren't pulling up any trees, either. They began their campaign with a 5-0 win over Oldham and followed up with a 6-0 success against Tranmere, but their fortunes were waning and latterly they had gained just two wins and a draw from their last five outings.

There was, then, just a little more expectation than usual resting on the youth side because a win from them was seen as the perfect way to lift some of the gloom and despondency from around the ground. Such was the need for a morale-boosting result, it was decided to rest as many of the team as possible on the prior Saturday.

As such, Maneely, Lorimer, Walker, Tranter, Keogh, Fry, Dunphy and Duff found themselves with a completely free weekend and able to concentrate themselves on the knock-out task to come. United's management were obviously suitably impressed with the blend of the side that had convincingly beaten the Maine Road teenagers and accordingly a 'same eleven' team sheet was displayed on the club's notice board.

The Bantams had already defeated one Manchester team in the Youth Cup during the course of the season, through knocking out lowly Droylsden by six goals to three, and they followed that win with a 2-1 victory over Wrexham.

Only Alan Newton had featured for Bradford in their Second Round tie in Manchester just over a year ago. If he was expecting a better result for City than they achieved on their last visit to Old Trafford, there was a rude disappointment in store for him at the outcome, which the United Review again reported on:

Only a plucky display by Day in the Bradford goal and some very uncontrolled finishing by the United forwards - particularly in the first half – prevented the score from running well into double figures. Apart from a ten-minute spell in the second half – strangely enough when reduced down to ten men and already six goals down – the visitors never issued a serious threat to the United defence.

Despite attacking almost continuously and creating numerous scoring chances in the first half, our youths led by a solitary goal at the interval; a lovely header by Latham from a well-placed free kick by Walker.

Two goals by Fry within three minutes of the resumption put the game more in perspective. Bradford's first real shot came from inside-left Swain but his effort was easily smothered by Maneely to be quickly followed by United's fourth goal. This was a header by Dunphy from a Walker cross after good work by Ackerley. The centre-forward was rewarded three minutes later with a neat through ball from Fry to increase the home lead, his finishing shot giving Day no chance.

A grand run by Latham and an equally good left-foot shot put the visitors further in arrears and their troubles were increased when Mitchell was carried off with strained knee ligaments. Almost immediately United added a seventh. A clever run by Ackerley, a short ball to Latham was quickly returned for Ackerley to smash home a fierce drive.

Bradford had their brightest attacking spell at this stage to force three corners in succession but United soon regained command for Latham to turn a neat pass inside for Dunphy to smack home from close range. The scoring was completed when Fry nipped in smartly to take advantage of a weak back pass to shoot from close range.

Our boys were on top of their job from the start in this game, playing with purpose and enthusiasm to produce a blend which could carry them far in this season's competition, provided there is more composure in the finishing.

The loss of captain Geoff Mitchell on a stretcher in the 67th minute didn't help Bradford's cause, but by that point the Reds had already ran up a goals count equal to last season's equivalent encounter. To cap City's misery, a further three lashes dispensed by United's forwards sent them home distinctly sore and sorry.

David Meek expressed an opinion that *'early in the season, Manchester United's youth team was rated poor in comparison with previous ones'* and he went on to state *'after wins against Everton, Manchester City, and last night's 9-0 victory over Bradford City, the youngsters can claim top consideration'*. Remaining firmly in a positive zone, Meek noted the Reds had *'showed their ability'* by scoring a number of *'superb goals'* which underlined their clear superiority.

Stamping a fine impression in the Youth Cup team, Barry Fry blasted in another three goals at Bradford City's expense to take his total for the season to eight

153

1961-62

1) Mervyn Maneely	1) Stan Craig
2) Bobby Smith	2) David Craig
3) Mike Lorimer	3) Colin Clish
4) Dennis Walker	4) Clive Chapman
5) Wilf Tranter	5) John Markie
6) Jimmy Keogh	6) Dave Turner
7) David Latham	7) Alan Suddick
8) Barry Fry	8) Alan Wilkinson
9) Ernie Ackerley	9) George Watkin
10) Eamon Dunphy	10) Bobby Moncur
11) Alan Duff	11) Les O'Neill

JANUARY 1962

MANCHESTER UNITED 1 v 2 NEWCASTLE UNITED

Ackerley   *Moncur, Suddick*

Monday 22nd
Kick-off 7.30 p.m.
Attendance 11,188

fourth round

With United securing a home engagement once more, and no-one in the treatment room apart from long-term casualty Alan Atherton, the club's best available eleven were selected for the third consecutive time. Visitors Newcastle had carried a couple of heavy defeats away from Old Trafford through past Youth Cup encounters but, with a confidence boosting 3-1 win over local rivals Sunderland at Roker Park behind them in the Third Round, the latest batch of fledgling Magpies were banking on a better showing this time around.

The Newcastle team included seventeen year-old Alan Suddick, already with appearances in their Second Division side before a back problem had temporarily sidelined him, and team boss Norman Smith and club director Stan Seymour were at Old Trafford to check on the boy's current form with a view to recalling him for their first-team clash at Leeds on the forthcoming Saturday. Also in the stands was Charlie Mitten, former Old Trafford hero and latterly Newcastle manager. Mitten, who was credited by the press as having discovered Suddick, was now out of work and reportedly ready to relocate to the Manchester area.

The following short preview appeared in the Newcastle Evening Chronicle, and it gave an indication as to the geographical span covered by the St. James's Park club in search of suitable new blood:

Newcastle United's N's team show their paces at Old Trafford tonight when they oppose Manchester United Juniors in the F.A. Youth Cup. Team: Craig S. (ex-Wallsend Corinthian Juniors); Craig D. (Ireland), Clish (Easlington); Chapman (Belford), Markie (ex-Scotland Boys' skipper), Turner (Retford); Suddick (Chester-le-Street), Wilkinson (Bedlington), Watkin (Chopwell), Moncur (ex-Scotland Boys'), O'Neill (Blyth).

The United Review yet again provided a record of the twists and turns which ultimately spelt the end of the line for the Reds' exploits in the tournament for another season:

The youth team made their exit from the Youth Cup in a game which was so full of promise but failed to live up to expectations.

Despite commanding the game territorially for long periods, our youths were not really moving with their usual rhythm. Most of the goalmouth excitement was at the Newcastle end with the visitors' scoring chances restricted to the two which gave them victory. Time and again the ball was scrambled away or charged down when a goal was imminent and once when a cross from Fry beat Craig, the ball was kicked off the line. Newcastle opened the scoring after 25 minutes when a Moncur shot swerved within the reach of Maneely.

With numerous chances, we failed to get on terms before the interval. In the first minute of the second half, a high lob bounced almost on the goal-line only to be once more scrambled away and then a fierce shot by Ackerley was saved in grand style by Craig. The centre-forward put us on terms with a header just inside the post and the stage looked set for victory, so heavy was the pressure on the Newcastle goal.

But the breakthrough against a back defence never came despite many chances coming our way. Eight minutes from the end, Suddick clinched the game for Newcastle with a twenty-yard drive following some slack defensive play. Right on time yet another chance came our way to retrieve the situation when Walker burst into the penalty area but his half-hit shot went straight to Craig.

Suddick's rocket handed Newcastle victory in a game which was often blighted by an intruding and inconvenient wind. In keeping with the blowing weather, the home side were full of huff and puff but managed to cause only minor damage to their guests' defence. It was Newcastle who, despite being under the cosh for most of the time, kept faith with a progressive brand of football and converted their chances once they revealed themselves.

The Manchester Evening News delivered the verdict that United *'played below form'* prior to adding that they *'did enough to secure a replay'*. After making enough space to praise the efforts of Ernie Ackerley and Mike Lorimer, the Evening Chronicle countered that *'the rest of the team was distinctly off colour'*.

For Ackerley, United's consolation was his eighth Youth Cup goal of the season and despite an admirable record of scoring in every round of the truncated cup run, it wasn't enough to prolong the Reds' interest in the tournament.

If there was any solace for United, it was taken with the news that Newcastle then negotiated all further hurdles to claim their first Youth Cup triumph. In the final, the junior Magpies defeated Wolverhampton Wanderers on a slender aggregate of two goals to one.

Lively United centre-forward Ernie Ackerley heads home a terrific equaliser against Newcastle

1) Mervyn Maneely	9) Albert Kinsey
2) Eddie Harrop	10) Barry Fry
3) Bobby Noble	11) Ken Morton
4) Dennis Walker	
5) Wilf Tranter	
6) Eamon Dunphy	
7) Willie Anderson	
8) Barry Grayson	

1) Chris Lockwood	9) Mike Pamment
2) Malcolm Naylor	10) Pete Leetham
3) Jim Blacker	11) Graham Keighley
4) Rod Butler	
5) Ian Watson	
6) Keith Sykes	
7) John Shaw	
8) Steve Ingle	

1962-63

MANCHESTER UNITED 15 v 0 BRADFORD CITY

Anderson, Dunphy (2, 1 pen), Fry (5), Grayson (2), Kinsey (3), Morton, Walker (pen)

DECEMBER 1962

Monday 10th

Kick-off 7.30 p.m.

Attendance 7,836

second round

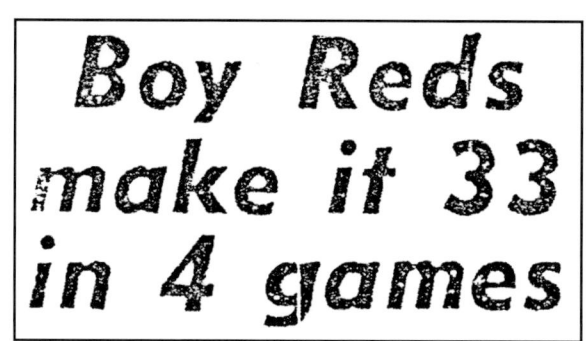

Boy Reds make it 33 in 4 games

The effect of yet another increase in the number of clubs participating in the Youth Cup, and the consequent restructuring of the early stages of the tournament, gave the Reds their soon-to-be customary start at the Second Round phase with Christmas 1962 a mere two weeks away.

For the third year on the run, Bradford City came out of the hat immediately after United and they took a team to Old Trafford which was made up of nine personnel who hadn't made the trip a year ago. The Bantams were unable to use their regular youth team 'keeper, David Roper, who had been crocked while representing the West Riding F.A. against the Lancashire F.A. on the preceding Saturday. Other than Roper's absence, City were at peak strength with Graham Keighley and Rod Butler, albeit now in different positions, the only two inclusions with experience of the game twelve months previously.

United blooded two new full-backs, one of whom was local boy Eddie Harrop and, Barry Fry apart, a whole new forward section. It included two Merseysiders, right-winger Willie Anderson and centre-forward Albert Kinsey, with Mancunian Barry Grayson at inside-right. Eamon Dunphy was moved back into the left-half role and at outside-left, Alan Duff was ousted in preference to Ken Morton.

There appeared to be no diminishment in the quality of teenage personnel that the club were able to attract just then as Harrop, Anderson, Kinsey and Morton all came with England schoolboy credentials whereas Grayson had represented Lancashire Boys. Making up the newcomers was Bobby Noble, formerly of Cheshire Boys, who had unsuccessfully undertaken England trials.

The tie proved to be an encouraging workout for the Reds. With deputising Bradford goalie Chris Lockwood needing to be by far the busiest player on the field, the score came the closest yet to beating United's elusive Youth Cup record of 23 goals in one game.

It meant that the United Review's columnist was barely able to cram all of the mainly one-way goal action into his match report:

Although they continued to try and play football and never gave up trying right to the end, Bradford City proved no match for our youths in a game watched by nearly 8,000 spectators.

The visitors' goal was under almost constant siege whilst our own defence had few anxious moments. Our boys were always playing strong, forceful and intelligent football, rounding off many classy moves with power packed finishing. But for the agility and anticipation of 'keeper Lockwood, and a number of inexplicable misses, the Bradford gloom would have been even deeper.

After surviving early attacks, the visitors ran into a real goal storm. United netted five times in the space of fourteen minutes, so setting the pattern to follow for the remainder of the 90 minutes. Anderson started the barrage in the 19th minute and a Dunphy penalty followed four minutes later. Two in as many minutes by Grayson and Fry, and another shortly after by Morton, gave the young Reds a commanding half-time lead. Just before the interval, United were almost caught napping but Maneely managed to finger-tip a good effort by Leetham against the bar.

A great header by Kinsey within a minute of the resumption and a goal cracked home by Fry from twenty yards six minutes later showed there was to be no respite for the overworked City defence. Bradford repeatedly failed to counter the clever through ball which always seemed to find a United attacker moving in for the kill. It was one of many such moves – this time by Grayson – which gave Kinsey goal number eight.

A penalty award when Anderson appeared to be brought down 'outside' the area seemed rather harsh but Walker duly converted. It was again the through ball *which gave Fry two in two minutes, with a flying save by Maneely from Pamment wedged in-between. Bradford's best move of the game gave Ingle a great chance but he shot straight at Maneely. There was no let up by United with wing-halves building up and joining in the pounding at the visitors' rearguard. Goals by Kinsey, Fry and Grayson were the result of slick and clever approach work and from one of many good centres by Anderson, Dunphy scored from close range to complete the rout.*

This was a heartening start to the competition by our youths, who gave a grand all-round performance which augurs well for their prospects. After making due allowance for the calibre of the opposition, there can be no denying the quality of the football and the excellence of the teamwork, much of which was reminiscent of the 1952-57 era.

Bradford City well earned the ovation they received at the end for their contribution to a game which had always been entertaining, despite the result, and in which there were noticeably few infringements.

The ball had hit the back of the Bradford net on average once every six minutes and with every home forward and both wing-halves getting in amongst the goals, various match reports made mention of the Reds' *'maturity'* and *'potential'*.

Not surprisingly, the Bradford Telegraph & Argus referred to United as the Bantams' *'bogey team'* as they had now slammed 33 goals past them in just four meetings spanning a period of just over as many years. The Bradford newspaper also stated City were rarely in the hunt and that *'they only had three worthwhile shots'* before going on to add the Valley Parade *'wing-halves never got in touch with the game and the Manchester inside-forward trio had a picnic'*. That comment applied to none more so than Barry Fry, whose personal haul of five goals was the best individual tally of a United player in the Youth Cup since Alex Dawson's identical number against Blackpool in November 1957.

David Meek offered the view that it *'will be interesting this season to see (the youth team) against stronger opposition'*. Meek added that the under-18's *'could go all the way'* because he sensed *'there seems to be a better balance about the side, with more forwards capable of hard-shooting'*.

Deciding for a change to add a note of caution, the Evening News man asked for his readers to *'remember that last year'* the youths *'slammed nine against Bradford, but still came unstuck in the quarter-finals.......'*

155

1962-63

1) Mervyn Maneely	9) Albert Kinsey	1) Derek Kirby	9) Gary Moore
2) Eddie Harrop	10) Barry Fry	2) Dick Moran	10) Barry Davison
3) Bobby Noble	11) Ken Morton	3) Jimmy Shoulder	11) Allan Gauden
4) Dennis Walker		4) Alan Purvis	
5) Wilf Tranter		5) Keith Stephenson	
6) Eamon Dunphy		6) Dave Elliott	
7) Willie Anderson		7) Keith Storey	
8) Barry Grayson		8) John O'Hare	

FEBRUARY 1963

MANCHESTER UNITED 1 v 1 SUNDERLAND
Walker (pen) — Davison

Wednesday 27th*

Kick-off 7.30 p.m.

Attendance 8,108

third round

After all the action of the Bradford contest, there then followed a void of over two and a half months prior to Sunderland's trip to Old Trafford to contest the Third Round. The original date for the tie was scheduled for the first Monday of January in 1963 which, until the onset of one of the worst and most prolonged winters in living memory, meant that the fixture list required rewriting on a number of occasions. Football was just one of the many casualties of the abominable weather when Britain found itself submerged under a freezing blanket of snow and ice.

The severity of the conditions meant that the game finally got the green light seven weeks after the initial date was set, and there was so much uncertainty as to when the tie would eventually be staged that the match programme was prepared in advance and printed dateless. As hardly any football at all was seen in England over the months of January and February that year, soccer's authorities eventually agreed to an extension of the season.

When the inevitable thaw began to take effect at last, the Rokerites' prospects were detailed in a Sunderland Echo match preview:

While doubt remains over the weekend game, Sunderland have been assured that Old Trafford will be in a playable condition for the F.A. Youth Cup (Third Round) tie between Manchester United and Sunderland youth teams tomorrow night.

The youngsters know well enough that they are tackling a difficult task and one which has most sides in trouble, for United's youth stream is famed for its products. But, having upset the odds by beating Manchester City 4-1 at Roker Park, the Sunderland players can go into this game with a good deal more confidence than at one time seemed possible.

One remarkable change in fortunes since that game against City concerns the centre-forward position in the England (Youth) side. At the time the holder was City's Pardoe, who has had First Division experience.

Since then, however, Moore has been winning warm praises all along the line and on the strength of a fine performance in an international trial game on the Nottm. Forest ground last week, he has now been named to lead the England line against an amateur side at Wimbledon a week today.

He celebrated his selection with a hat-trick against Grimsby Town Reserves in a North Regional League game at Roker Park on Saturday and will certainly prove a rare handful for United tomorrow night.

One major problem which required solving as a result of the big freeze was that football clubs needed to keep their playing staff at a peak of fitness for when the better weather eventually came. Matt Busby had the foresight to take his senior squad over to Ireland, where the weather was considerably milder than on this side of the Irish Sea, and during a friendly fixture against Bolton which was staged in Cork, the manager sent on Dennis Walker as a replacement for Bobby Charlton.

Walker was reinstalled in the youth team in his preferred wing-half position against Sunderland, although another prospect who would soon be a new alternative for the management to consider was temporarily unavailable. The development moved the Evening Chronicle to devote a few words to the subject matter:

David Sadler, the seventeen year-old England amateur international forward, who was signed as a professional last week, will not be playing on Wednesday. He is still working his notice as a bank clerk at Maidstone.

The Wearsiders proved a tough nut to crack for United, and their considerable efforts caused the Sunderland Echo to deliver the following match verdict:

Courage and a refusal to panic enabled Sunderland youth team to force the strongest, bravest result of the season at Old Trafford last night, when they held Manchester United to a 1-1 draw in the F.A. Youth Cup (Third Round).

I could have excused the Sunderland youngsters if they had surrendered after the first fifteen minutes, in which an impressive United side carved out so many chances that they might well have been five or six goals to the good.

Centre-forward Albert Kinsey alone had five chances. Inside of nine minutes he had shot against a post and headed against the bar with the goal wide open and then hesitated long enough for centre half Keith Stephenson to cover up another open-goal chance. Another two shots travelled wide after Barry Fry had seen a close-range shot rebound from a defender.

By then the storm had reached its peak and United's supporters – 8,108 of them paid £503 for admission – were rubbing their hands in expectation of a goal feast. But three great saves by Derek Kirby and tireless work by the Sunderland defenders, which forced United into making all their shots quickly, levelled the game for a spell.

When Fry was brought down eight yards from goal and the referee awarded a penalty in the 37th minute, Sunderland's hopes must have slumped badly. And even though Kirby, diving to his right, managed to reach Dennis Walker's spot kick, the ball was shaken from his grasp as he hit the frozen ground and it rolled over the line before he could recover.

Twelve seconds later, however, they were back in the game, when a move straight from the restart ended with Keith Storey stroking the ball through for Barry Davison to move in and make his scoring shot at such a pace that he was over halfway to the corner flag before he could turn to receive the congratulations of his colleagues. That was not the end of the ordeal by any means, for United still felt – and looked – as though they could pull out the winning goals. And as late as two minutes from the end, there were split-second saves by Stephenson, Moran, and Kirby, right on the line.

Top performances in a great-hearted defence came from Kirby, Stephenson and Elliott, while Moore's marathon effort in a roaming centre-forward role carried him into the thick of things without a great deal of reward.

It was a tired but happy party which arrived back in Sunderland at four o'clock this morning, after a six-hour battle against fog and ice. But they were sore, too, for there was scarcely a player who did not have huge patches of skin ripped from knee, thigh, and hip by the rock-hard ground, which carried a sprinkling of coarse sand.

So the Reds were forced into another replay up on Wearside despite monopolising the game almost from start to finish. The United Review rightly concurred with the majority of observers, offering the view that *'it seems incredible that a replay is necessary'*, and most match reports suggested that the only reason a second game was required was through the youthful over-eagerness of the home forwards in their desire to put the ball in the back of the net.

Local forward Barry Grayson's second appearance in the Youth Cup proved infinitely less fruitful than his first

*This game was originally scheduled for Monday, January 7th but was postponed due to a snowbound pitch

1) Derek Kirby
2) Dick Moran
3) Jimmy Shoulder
4) Alan Purvis
5) Keith Stephenson
6) Dave Elliott
7) Keith Storey
8) John O'Hare
9) Gary Moore
10) Barry Davison
11) Allan Gauden

1) John Pearson
2) Eddie Harrop
3) Bobby Noble
4) Dennis Walker
5) Wilf Tranter
6) Eamon Dunphy
7) Willie Anderson
8) Barry Grayson
9) Albert Kinsey
10) Barry Fry
11) Alan Duff

SUNDERLAND 2 v 3 MANCHESTER UNITED

Noble (o.g.), Storey — Anderson, Grayson, Walker

1962-63

MARCH 1963

third round replay

Tuesday 26th

Kick-off 7.15 p.m.

Attendance 3,185

Caused by a backlog of fixtures, the game up at Roker Park was set for a date when, under normal circumstances, the Fifth Round would already have been done and dusted. Sunderland had originally wanted to host the match on Saturday, 16th March until United responded by claiming commitments at minor levels on that date would have restricted their choice of personnel and consequently the match was scheduled for a week and a half later.

On the day that the Reds were due to travel to the North-East, a bombshell dropped on their preparations when goalkeeper Mervyn Maneely was ruled out of contention. Maneely had taken a nasty whack during a junior game on the previous weekend and a couple of cracked ribs, as well as other complications which were continuing to cause him pain, prevented his inclusion in the journeying party.

With no other Youth Cup qualified goalkeeper available at such short notice, former Wigan and England schoolboy striker John Pearson was pressed into action between the posts. One other change, Alan Duff earning a recall in place of Ken Morton on the left flank, was the only difference from the Old Trafford contest.

Prior to the game, the Sunderland Echo made note of the Roker Park boys' chances:

They made a brave fight of it at Old Trafford and after United had taken the lead from the penalty spot, they fought back well to claim a draw.

If Alan Gauden is fit, Sunderland will field the same side, but Middlemiss stands by to deputise. This is the youngest side Sunderland have ever fielded in this competition, but United are able to call upon several matured juniors who have considerable experience up to Central League level.

A day later, the Echo also recorded the conclusion to a rousing tie that went right down to the wire:

For the second time in 24 hours, Sunderland had the unhappy experience of having their cup hopes dashed only minutes from the end of a game which they appeared to have well won.

At Coventry on Monday the disastrous swing came eight minutes from the end. Last night, when the youth team met Manchester United in the F.A. Youth Cup (Third Round) Replay, they were leading 2-0 with fifteen minutes to go but went down 3-2, the winning goal being scored in the extra-time allowed for stoppages.

But what a fine performance it was by the youngest side Sunderland have ever fielded in this competition.

No fewer than five of the players were appearing in schools' football last season, but onlookers would not have guessed it from the way they stood up to a tough United side who played throughout in the manner we have come to expect from Old Trafford products.

Skipper Dave Elliott and England youth trialist Gary Moore were the experienced players whose all-round work played a big part in holding the game in Sunderland's favour for so long, while sixteen year-olds John O'Hare, Keith Stephenson and Jimmy Shoulder were in great form.

It was fine work between Purvis and Storey that sent Sunderland into the attack which produced a goal in the fifth minute. The ball was forced out to the left and from Gauden's header, Moore headed the ball on for Storey to force it home.

Two minutes before half-time O'Hare sent in a powerful header which a defender could only help into the net to put Sunderland two up.

United's hard, forceful play had a wearing effect in the second half, but the Sunderland youngsters held on well until fifteen minutes from the end when Grayson scored from a centre by Duff. Nine minutes later Anderson was left clear and unmarked from a left-wing pass to hit the equaliser. Then, with extra-time apparently on its way, right-half Walker burst through the middle to score the winning goal.

It was a mightily relieved United contingent which left Roker Park that evening, for the unanimous verdict was that the team never got anywhere near to hitting their best form. Nevertheless, at 2-0 down with only a quarter of an hour left to play, credit was paid to the side's never-say-die spirit, even though it was the slenderest of close calls that had finally seen them through.

The Review report was short, sharp and to the point:

Our youths' performance in this game was well below par and they all but paid the penalty for failing to press home their overwhelming territorial advantage in the first meeting. It could well be that the last minute withdrawal of Maneely

had an unsettling effect.

Pearson did an admirable job in the circumstances but the fact that he is not a recognised 'keeper could hardly have imbued the lads with confidence.

They have the chance to prove this form all wrong and an opportunity to gain revenge for last season's unexpected defeat when meeting Newcastle in the Fourth Round on a date still to be fixed.

" *I walked into The Cliff that morning for training and Joe Armstrong and Jimmy Murphy pulled me to one side to ask me if I would play in goal for the youth team at Sunderland that night. I would often play in goals during five-a-side matches in training and I suppose they thought I would cope okay. I was then taken straight to Old Trafford where Harry Gregg came out to give me some coaching. It was only about half an hour of tuition, but he worked on my positional play, taking crosses, corners and so on.*

Then it was straight on the bus up to Sunderland. I was told not to tell anyone and the other players thought that another 'keeper was going to meet us at the ground. As we got off the bus everyone was told that I was playing in nets and you could see the surprise on their faces. In the end I did okay, I made a few decent saves and one of their goals came about when Bobby Noble headed the ball into the net from a cross when I was going the other way. People seemed pleased with me and back in Manchester I was even asked if I fancied playing in goal full-time, but I was always a forward at heart. "

JOHN PEARSON

157

1962-63

1) David Ikin	9) David Sadler
2) Eddie Harrop	10) Barry Fry
3) Bobby Noble	11) George Best
4) Dennis Walker	
5) Wilf Tranter	
6) Eamon Dunphy	
7) Willie Anderson	
8) Albert Kinsey	

1) Alan Imrie	9) Barry King
2) John Markie	10) Geoff Allen
3) Billy Watson	11) Keith Webster
4) George Smith	
5) John Pickering	
6) Bobby Moncur	
7) Bryan Robson	
8) Alan Caldwell	

APRIL 1963

MANCHESTER UNITED 3 v 0 NEWCASTLE UNITED
Fry, Kinsey (2)

fourth round

Wednesday 24th

Kick-off 7.30 p.m.

Attendance 12,199

By the time that holders Newcastle United came seeking their second Youth Cup victory at Old Trafford, the Reds had been able to find a proper replacement for the still unavailable Mervyn Maneely. Captured from Macclesfield Town of the Cheshire League, David Ikin actually hailed from Newcastle, but his birthplace was Staffordshire's 'under-Lyme', rather than the North-East's 'upon-Tyne', version.

Free now from his working commitments, David Sadler came into the reckoning, as did another individual whose name was then largely unknown but will forever be linked to that of Manchester United, the mercurial, mesmerising and majestic George Best. Even though they were now members of the same youth team, and actually lived together at landlady Mrs. Fullaway's house, their journey to that point couldn't have been more different.

Sadler had enjoyed an extremely fine time as a schoolboy footballer and captained Kent Boys while still aged only fourteen prior to undertaking trials for England Boys. Then introduced to Maidstone United's first-team at the age of fifteen, Sadler was capped by his country at amateur and youth levels prior to signing for the Reds in November 1962. However, because of having to work his notice and complications surrounding the extreme weather, prior to the Youth Cup clash he had only resided in Manchester for six weeks and hadn't made much above a couple of appearances for the club.

Best's circumstances were nowhere near like those of his new colleague, as he wasn't blessed with the physique of Sadler as a young lad and consequently found himself completely overlooked for schoolboy honours. Despite only playing for his school and a youth club in Belfast at a young age, his skills didn't escape the keen eyes of Ulster scout Bob Bishop, who made sure he would eventually connect with United.

Best had already been at the club for eighteen months and for the vast majority of that time he was involved at 'B' team level. Having begun to build up some body strength, just recently he had gone on a goals' spree which landed him a more regular spot in the 'A' side, and with the benefit of seeing his talent develop on an almost daily basis, those behind the scenes at Old Trafford obviously felt the time was right for him to make his mark in the under-18 eleven.

Outgoing to make way for Sadler and Best respectively were Barry Grayson and, following the briefest of recalls, Alan Duff.

For former Reds' junior and now Newcastle half-back Bobby Moncur, the youth match was his second game in the space of 24 hours because he had been included in the Magpies' first-team that played at Charlton on the previous evening. Newcastle's seniors arrived back from The Valley in the early hours of the morning and soon after waking from a short sleep, Moncur was back on a coach heading towards Manchester.

David Sadler catches up with some cricket in his free time at Mrs. Fullaway's

Charged with the opportunity of making progress at the expense of the current keepers of the trophy and last season's nemesis, the boy Reds were well up for the fight and it was left to the United Review to summarise the action:

A crowd of just over 12,000 saw our youths convincingly avenge last year's defeat at the hands of Newcastle. Although clearly in command for most of the game, it was not until the late stages that we consolidated the winning position preconceived by a Fry goal midway through the first half.

Much more in command, showing an abundance of good football, United always looked the more dangerous but all too often were off target with their finishing. A 1-0 lead at the interval was scant reward for their efforts.

There was little variation to the pattern after the resumption and though for a brief period United appeared to lose their grip, the visitors failed to take advantage.

Six minutes from time a free kick on the edge of the penalty area caused the ultimate downfall of a dour Newcastle defence. Hit hard and low by Walker, the ball appeared to be travelling wide of the target but Kinsey nipped in smartly with a novel side-foot into the net. Any further doubt about the result was dispelled three minutes later when Kinsey chased a long, high ball down the middle from Best to beat Pickering and the advancing Imrie in the air and head into the untenanted net.

Sampling the youth team atmosphere for the first time were David Ikin, David Sadler and George Best. Each had a promising debut and to a varying degree made a fair contribution to an entertaining game.

It was a top rate showing from United, which had a lot to do with the industry and flair shown by their wing-half pairing. The Reds held a firm grip on the game for almost the entire 90 minutes and only wayward finishing, yet again, had prevented Newcastle from a severe hammering.

Peter Slingsby of the Evening Chronicle reckoned Sadler to be *'a fine prospect who will improve rapidly'* while also noting that *'Best and Kinsey were the pick of a lively Manchester attack'.*

Reaching the conclusion that the Reds' win was so *'convincing'* it now made them *'favourites to win a trophy that has spent more time at Old Trafford than anywhere else'*, Slingsby wrote that it *'was mainly due to gallant defence work by Newcastle goalkeeper Imrie and Moncur and Markie that the continual one-way traffic towards their own goal did not pay off until the last five minutes......'*

His piece ended with a statement that *'Dunphy and Walker were in great form, whether attacking or defending, Dunphy in particular'.*

Then practically unknown to most United supporters, George Best claimed the outside-left position from Alan Duff for the visit of Newcastle

1962-63

1) Phil Kennedy	9) Peter Slater	1) Neville Fletcher	9) David Sadler
2) Andy Burgin	10) David Ford	2) Eddie Harrop	10) Barry Fry
3) Frank Noble	11) Malcolm Barrowclough	3) Bobby Noble	11) Willie Anderson
4) Barry Denton		4) Dennis Walker	
5) John Hickton		5) Wilf Tranter	
6) Wilf Smith		6) Eamon Dunphy	
7) Tony Mee		7) George Best	
8) Mike Little		8) Albert Kinsey	

SHEFFIELD WEDNESDAY 2 v 0 MANCHESTER UNITED

Ford, Hickton

APRIL 1963

Tuesday 30th

Kick-off 7.00 p.m.

Tonight at Hillsborough!!
F.A. YOUTH CUP
Sheffield Wednesday versus
MANCHESTER UNITED
Kick-off 7.0 p.m.

Because of the impending close to the season, United were compelled to take on Sheffield Wednesday at the quarter-final stage just six days after defeating Newcastle, and with such a solid showing only just behind them, it could be safely assumed that those in charge of selection wouldn't have wanted to make any alterations to the team.

Alas, as David Meek reported in the Evening News, the Reds' old goalkeeping hoodoo chose just such a time to rear its ugly head once again:

Injury-hit Manchester United have had to call up fifteen year-old schoolboy Neville Fletcher to keep goal in their F.A. Youth Cup Fifth Round match at Hillsborough tonight. United have been hit hard with a goalkeeping problem for their youth team since Mervyn Maneely was taken ill. At short notice they had to play an inside-forward in goal in the tie against Sunderland. Then they recruited David Ikin from Macclesfield in their last round against Newcastle.

Ikin looked the answer but was hurt on Saturday playing for his Cheshire League club and he has failed to recover from a bruised shoulder. So, today a call went to Blackley Central Technical School for Fletcher, who was excused school and left with the team for Sheffield. Otherwise United are unchanged with the team that beat Newcastle 3-0 in the Fourth Round.

By the time of the youth team's engagement at Hillsborough, United's seniors were booked to appear in the F.A. Cup final, despite the fact that their form in the First Division had remained exceedingly poor almost throughout the season. The tremendous boost that reaching Wembley injected into the staff at Old Trafford was palpable, prompting a confident Jimmy Murphy to predict of the under-18's, *'We have a good side and I think that we shall win the Youth Cup as well as the F.A. Cup.'*

Wednesday's youth eleven had snuffed out Stoke's hopes in view of a gate consisting of barely a thousand spectators. That dismal attendance was commented on by Matt Busby in an interview with the Sheffield Telegraph, in which he said, *'If the match with Wednesday was played at Old Trafford there would be a 25,000 gate, especially now the first-team have reached the F.A. Cup final.'* Later sensing the need for a positive quote, Busby then claimed, *'My youngsters want to make it a cup double for the club.'*

In view of the game's interest in the steel city, the Sheffield Star went to the trouble of producing an informative match preview:

Hillsborough's First Division stars take a back seat tonight to make way for Sheffield Wednesday's youth side, whose hopes of F.A. Youth Cup glory may rest on the shoulders of a teenager who has no ambitions of stepping up into professional football.

He is eighteen year-old Peter Slater, who leads the Wednesday attack against Manchester United in the quarter-final of the trophy at Hillsborough tonight.

Slater, who has been with Wednesday since he was fifteen, has high academic hopes.......he has already been for an interview to enter St. John's College, Oxford.

So, for the robust, goalscoring attack leader, sciences come before soccer.

Wednesday, who have scored fourteen goals against two in their three matches in the competition so far this season, will field only two full-time professionals.

They are centre-half Hickton, and inside-left Ford, both of whom have had Central League experience.

Hickton, however, has played most of his football this term in the forward-line.

Slater, and left-back Frank Noble, a seventeen year-old joiner, are the side's two amateurs. The remainder are apprentice professionals.

Wednesday's Youth Cup progress so far has dismissed Wallsend Corinthians, Stoke City and Middlesbrough.........4-0 away, 5-1 at home, and 4-1 away, respectively.

But tonight's match is likely to be the Hillsborough side's toughest so far.

Meanwhile, team chief Vic Buckingham has to wait until match day before he can name his senior side to meet Manchester United at Old Trafford tomorrow.

For all of the pre-match expectations that were heaped upon them, the United lads finished as the losers in a game they should have had tied up in ribbons and bows by the break.

The Sheffield Telegraph reported on the Reds' sad and highly unexpected demise:

For the second time in 24 hours, a Sheffield Wednesday team was cheered off the field when a fighting second half show by the youth side produced one of the biggest shocks of the F.A. Youth Cup by toppling the glamour-ridden Matt Busby youngsters.

And if anyone has to be singled out of this great win at Hillsborough last night, it must be centre-half John Hickton, whose goal put Wednesday well on the road to the semi-finals.

After spending 65 minutes watching his forwards struggle under the iron grip of United's defence, the swashbuckling Hickton charged up field and blasted the ball in after Wilf Smith had shaken the bar with a rasping drive.

Then, with confidence oozing out as the minutes ticked away, David Ford rubbed it in and grabbed a bit of well-earned glory for himself with a second goal ten minutes from the end.

No wonder the Old Trafford youngsters – striving to make it a cup double for the club – looked downcast at the whistle......but they only had themselves to blame.

Slicing through a hesitant Wednesday defence time and time again during the first half, they failed miserably when it came to the all-important pay-off punch, and the Hillsborough team must have been relieved to hear the half-time whistle.

England Youth international David Sadler shot wide with only Kennedy to beat......Kinsey hooked over the top of an empty goal......chances and more of them like these went begging, while all Wednesday had to offer was a Ford drive that Fletcher did well to finger-tip to safety.

But then all the crowd will remember – and want to – is a storming second half that saw Wednesday grab the whip and lash United where it hurt most, with attack after attack.

After Hickton's moment of glory, United's Walker moved up into attack trying in vain to find a loophole in the Wednesday rearguard, but the only gap to be seen was the one he had left for Ford, who cashed in on his freedom with a smart goal to make the joy-night complete.

Wednesday youth coach Hugh Swift can be proud of his lads.......and how they deserved those end-of-the-match cheers.

Quite simply, United had shown both their Jekyll and Hyde faces during the course of the game, with the opening period seeing them hit the type of form that could cut defences to shreds while following the break they appeared to take the matter in hand a little too lightly and paid the cost accordingly. The match was effectively over from the moment when Wednesday registered their opener and from then on the Reds must have felt like a rain-soaked commuter who had missed the last bus home.

The Manchester Evening News reflected the teenagers' disappointment with the following match summary:

At half-time Manchester United Juniors looked set for a comfortable passage into the semi-finals of the F.A. Youth Cup at Hillsborough.

Though there was no score, they had been by far the better side.

But something went drastically wrong with Busby's new babes after the break and they lost 2-0. No longer were they able to break Wednesday's defensive grip. No longer was lanky David Sadler a threat in front of goal.

Wednesday gradually climbed on top though their forwards never got the consistent service that Dennis Walker provided for the United front-line.

The fight was drained out of United in the 66th minute when Wednesday centre-half Hickton moved up for a corner and scored after wing-half Smith's shot had rattled the bar. Wednesday's best forward, inside-left Ford, hit a second goal eight minutes from the end. By that time United were a well spent force.

A fortnight after beating the Reds, Sheffield Wednesday met Liverpool in the Youth Cup semi-final. Because the month of May was already half-way through, the semi was staged on a 'one-off' basis, with Liverpool gaining home advantage. The boys from Anfield exploited their good fortune, by nudging Wednesday out of the competition and thereby booking their place in the final for the first time.

At the last stage, Liverpool were defeated after a titanic tussle with West Ham, eventually going down by an aggregate of six goals to five.

fifth round

159

1963-64

1) Jimmy Rimmer	9) Frank McEwen
2) Alan Duff	10) Albert Kinsey
3) Bobby Noble	11) Ken Morton
4) Peter McBride	
5) David Farrar	
6) John Fitzpatrick	
7) Willie Anderson	
8) George Best	

1) Ray McGuire	9) Alan Lappin
2) Roger Lappin	10) Billy Pritchard
3) Billy Russell	11) Mike Knox
4) Emlyn Hughes	
5) Adrian Slowey	
6) Frank McKechnie	
7) Bob Knox	
8) Peter Marshall	

DECEMBER 1963

MANCHESTER UNITED **14 v 1** BARROW
Anderson, Best (3), Kinsey, McEwen (4), Morton (5)   Knox M. (pen)

Wednesday 18th
Kick-off 7.30 p.m.
Attendance 5,487

second round

One-goal Bert is man-of-match!

With the seniors' superb F.A. Cup final success at Wembley against Leicester belatedly kick-starting United's entry into the 'swinging sixties', there followed a genuine belief that the current intake of youth starlets, alongside those with prior participation, were now capable of mounting a serious challenge to bring the Youth Cup back to its spiritual home.

By the time Barrow arrived at Old Trafford in December to contest the Second Round and taste a sample of big time soccer, Matt Busby had introduced both George Best and David Sadler to the first-team. Sadler went straight into the senior side on the opening day of the season and was present for a run of twelve consecutive games, whereas Best was required to wait until mid-September to be handed his chance in a 1-0 win over West Brom at Old Trafford. Because his bodily profile wasn't quite up to that of regular first-team football, the waif-like Best was then put back in cotton wool for a little while longer.

The goalkeeping merry-go-round that United's youth side had endured over the last couple of seasons looked to have been resolved as a very fine prospect had been secured in the agile and quick-reflexed Southport-born custodian Jimmy Rimmer. The middle-line was entirely new and subsequently, if there were any doubts about any particular section of the team, they centred on the largely unknown effectiveness of Peter McBride, David Farrar and John Fitzpatrick. Previously of England Boys, Farrar was flanked by two promising lads who seemed to share both the attacking and defensive qualities required to make a living out of the game.

Two goals in the first half and three in the second saw Ken Morton become the seventh Red to register five times in a Youth Cup match

All five forwards were more than capable of scoring goals, including newcomer Frank McEwen, a proven sharpshooter with Republic of Ireland schoolboy international experience, and it said much about the confidence held in the squad that the management felt able to exclude Sadler entirely from their plans for Barrow's visit.

A week and a half prior to the Youth Cup opener, United's 'B' side was fortuitously left with a blank Saturday, the open slot providing an opportunity for most of those who were expected to feature against Barrow to come together in the 'A' team. Youth Cup novices McBride, Farrar, Fitzpatrick and John Aston blended well with some of their slightly older club associates, such as Barry Fry, when helping to bring Tranmere Rovers 'A' to their knees at The Cliff with a resounding 10-1 win. Albert Kinsey took the laurels with four of the total, and with Best and Aston contributing two goals each, the other scorers were John Pearson and Glendon Andrews.

The two extremes of football club resources were brought into sharp focus with Barrow's visit. While the away team was culled exclusively from Barrow and the surrounding districts, United paraded seven Englishmen, Rimmer, Kinsey, Farrar, Ken Morton, Willie Anderson, Alan Duff and Bobby Noble, two Scots, McBride and Fitzpatrick, and one representative each from the north and south of Ireland, Best and McEwen.

Of those named besides Best for the Reds, Rimmer, Morton and Anderson had been utilised in the Central League side already that season whereas Duff and Noble were almost ever-present in the 'A' team. With Fitzpatrick and Kinsey also usually found at 'A' grade, only McEwen, Farrar and McBride were mainly deployed in the 'B' eleven.

Every member of the visiting side had been involved with Barrow-in-Furness Boys at one time or another and were therefore truly representative not only of the football club but also of the town. A most unusual feature of the team's make-up was that it contained not just one pair of twins but two. Roger and Alan Lappin were at right-back and centre-forward respectively, while stationed on opposite wings were Bob and Mike Knox.

At right-half for Barrow was Emlyn Hughes, a young man whose father played as a professional for Barrow RLFC and who was himself destined to hit the heights in the future as a Liverpool and England soccer star. Strictly speaking, Hughes didn't actually form part of Barrow's youth set-up as he was merely guesting for the club.

The headline "IT WILL BE TOUGH' SAYS STANIFORTH', which appeared in the North-West Evening Mail, gave a stark pointer to the final outcome of the game for the Cumbrians:

The Barrow AFC under-18 side face a stiff test at Old Trafford tomorrow night when they meet Manchester United in the F.A. Youth Cup competition's Second Round.

'It couldn't be tougher,' says manager Mr. Ron Staniforth, 'but the players stand to learn a lot.'

The side is made up of the players who played in the two meetings with Chester in the First Round, which Barrow won 4-2 after a 1-1 draw at Sealand Road.

In the half-back line, McKechnie is recalled and takes over from Pritchard who joins the forwards.

There are positional changes in the attack and Mike Knox is included after missing the First Round replay.

The Reds took a little while to get a head of steam going, but the wait was soon over when Best not only found the keys to unlock Barrow's defence, he also helped himself to his first Youth Cup goal in the 12th minute. With over a quarter of the game gone, and the goal deficit apart, Barrow seemed to be coping reasonably comfortably until the growing rumblings in the distance announced an advancing tidal wave which would soon engulf them.

From the time of Best's second goal in the 28th minute, the Reds then hit five more before the break, with McEwen laying claim to a hat-trick. All three of McEwen's goals came between the 39th and the 44th minutes and they followed on the heels of two successful strikes by Ken Morton.

As the second period got underway, it soon became obvious that United's thirst for goals hadn't entirely been quenched and with seven already on the scoreboard, the Barrow players must have been extremely apprehensive about the final outcome. As it so happened, it was they who scored next. With the clock showing 52 minutes gone, an incident in the home penalty area, when United's McBride was adjudged to have handled the ball, resulted in Barrow being awarded a penalty which was subsequently converted.

The Reds hit back again in the 58th minute with a goal from Albert Kinsey, and in a following Barrow raid, number eight Peter Marshall gasped as his seemingly goal-bound header thudded against the post with Rimmer stationary.

It was to be Barrow's last worthwhile attack as United buckled down to the task of plundering further goals. Morton scored in the next foray, and after the Reds struck the post twice in quick succession, McEwen then got his fourth of the night.

With fifteen minutes to go, the worst period of the game was still to come for the visitors. Willie Anderson finally got on the scoring list to make it a full complement of forwards to register and then Best, to complete his hat-trick, and two more from Morton, made the goals against column look a sorry sight for poor Barrow.

Bob Knox recalled his Old Trafford experience in an interview with the North-West Evening Mail many years later, the Barrow skipper vividly recalling the impression that one person in particular had made on him. Knox said, 'The thing that sticks in my mind the most is how slightly built he (Best) was, and thinking that he must have been a fabulous player to have achieved so much with nothing on him.

No-one really stood out on the night for them, they were such a good team. It was a marvellous experience for us, an incredible night all round. You don't get many chances to play at a ground like Old Trafford.

There were five or six thousand supporting United, all stood behind our goal, and although they thrashed us 14-1, it could have been 50 if it wasn't for our goalkeeper, the woodwork and missed chances.

Before the match our manager, Ron Staniforth, had told me to play at outside-right and our Mike to play outside-left, but within minutes we were both playing centre-half as were the rest of the team.

I was captain on the night and I said to the lads before the game that if we get a penalty 'I'm taking it' and nobody disagreed. But when the ref gave the penalty, when we were already seven or eight down, our Mike said 'I'm taking it'.

Jimmy Rimmer, the United 'keeper, was playing hell that the penalty should never have been given, and then something happened that I have never witnessed before or after in 30 years of being involved in football. Mike took about a twenty-yard run-up to the ball and blasted it so hard that it came straight back off the stanchion in the back of the goal, over his head, and flew out of the penalty box!

All the United supporters who were about 110 yards away at the other end of the ground thought it had hit the crossbar and had come back out. Our Mike had hit it so hard no-one had seen it!'

There was plenty of sympathy for the losers in various match reports following the one-sided affair. Not so in their own backyard, though, because the North-West Evening News rather harshly noted Barrow were 'out-plotted, outplayed and outgunned' before going on to record the team had been 'humiliated'.

The Manchester Evening News could afford to be more upbeat and was keen to point the most influential individual nomination straight at Albert Kinsey, despite his contribution of only the one goal. The Evening News also described the approach play of Best and Kinsey as 'devastating'.

All things taken into consideration, it was exactly the confidence-building start to the tournament that United would have wanted.

George Best slides in for the ball, diverting it away from advancing Barrow 'keeper Ray McGuire and over the line to record United's opener

1963-64

1) Jimmy Rimmer	9) Frank McEwen
2) Alan Duff	10) Albert Kinsey
3) Bobby Noble	11) Ken Morton
4) John Fitzpatrick	
5) David Farrar	
6) John Aston	
7) Willie Anderson	
8) David Sadler	

1) Alan Jones	9) David Gregory
2) Peter Davidson	10) Harry Robinson
3) Jimmy Shelliker	11) Barry Dugdale
4) John Strachan	
5) Graham Rowe	
6) Ken Morris	
7) John Hobson	
8) Eddie Loyden	

JANUARY 1964

MANCHESTER UNITED 3 v 2 BLACKPOOL

Anderson, Kinsey (2) — Loyden (2, 1 pen)

Wednesday 22nd
Kick-off 7.30 p.m.
Attendance 8,106

third round

Aston debut in young Reds side

There were more rewards in store for one particular member of the youth team and they came in the weeks prior to Blackpool's appearance at Old Trafford when winger Willie Anderson made his debut in both the First Division and the F.A. Cup.

Assisting the senior side was now also figuring more prominently in George Best's workload. After scoring twice in the last four first-team matches, Matt Busby withdrew him from the Youth Cup tie in view of United's impending F.A. Cup clash against Bristol Rovers, which was set to take place at Old Trafford on the forthcoming weekend.

Best's place was given to David Sadler, and with Peter McBride dropped from the side, John Fitzpatrick switched half-back places to give an opening appearance to John Aston junior, son of the Reds' former playing legend and current club coach. Despite previously performing for both Manchester and Lancashire Boys as an outside-left, young Aston had been utilised in an experimental role at left-half for the 'B' team and the trial run now extended to his involvement with the youth side.

Programme notes for the game contained the following observations:

Our youths opened the season's campaign with a visit from Barrow Youth and despite making a slow start coasted to a comfortable victory.

All the forwards shared in the goal spree with Ken Morton going 'nap'. Frank McEwen celebrated his introduction to the youth team with four well-taken goals. Dame Fortune frowned on him a few days later, however, when he chipped a bone in his arm in a 'B' team game. Happily there were no complications and he is now back in training.

Besides striving to remain part of the first-team picture, there was also another little extra incentive for Anderson to put in a good performance as he was due to celebrate his 17th birthday on the day after the Blackpool tie. As it transpired, the Scouser scored with a scorching shot and set up another as United dragged themselves back from being twice behind.

The Blackpool Gazette laid bare the main details of the game:

Blackpool have only themselves to blame for being out of the Youth Cup.

Manager Ron Suart should tell his youngsters that physical strength is no substitute for soccer skill.

After twice holding the lead in the away game last night, Blackpool surrendered the initiative by conceding a string of free kicks, which culminated with Blackpool inside-right Eddie Loyden having his name taken by the referee.

The smaller United boys refused to be rattled and kept on playing football, and although their winning margin was slender Blackpool could not quibble, for after a promising first half their defence took a hammering in the second period.

If the players had taken an example from their skipper and centre-half, Graham Rowe, Blackpool might still have had an interest in the trophy.

At 6ft. 2½" Rowe towered above everybody else on the field, yet his tackling was clean and effective and he gave United centre-forward Frank McEwen little scope. United's danger men were outside-right Willie Anderson and inside-left Bert Kinsey. Jimmy Shelliker found Anderson, who had twice played for United's first-team, a rare handful, and Kinsey's roaming tactics proved puzzling for right-half John Strachan.

Frank McEwen's spectacular diving header flashes inches over Blackpool's crossbar

1963-64

JANUARY 1964

Blackpool had the inspiration of a ninth minute lead when John Hobson stroked a long pass into the United penalty area for Loyden to stab home.

United equalised with a 30-yard drive by Anderson, but Loyden put his side ahead again two minutes before the interval when he converted a penalty after Barry Dugdale had been brought down.

The second half belonged to the home side. Kinsey put them level three minutes after the changeover. Then the same player hit the winner in the 63rd minute.

Aside from the many plaudits that were showered upon the rapidly developing Anderson, the match was also notable for Albert Kinsey, who managed to bang in a couple of goals following a display against Barrow that saw him pitched into more of a providing role. His first, which squared the scores at 2-2, saw him glide into the middle in order to place Anderson's low cross home.

The Daily Mail described that passage of play by claiming Kinsey was 'able to walk the ball in the net after an astonishing run by the right winger'. The Mail also proclaimed Blackpool 'knocked United out of their stride' prior to pinpointing the reason for the Reds' win when noting they had 'remembered the golden rule of soccer' by 'keep playing football and the goals will come'.

Kinsey's second goal gave United the decisive edge and a passage through to the next round with a move that Houdini would have been proud to put his name to. In performing a now-you-see-me, now-you-don't illusion trick when slipping his way into position, and with space at a premium, the inside-forward then managed to blast a rasping shot beyond the Blackpool goalie.

Another match summary read that Anderson 'was certainly the top of United's parade' and accorded an 'outstanding' tag to Bobby Noble, as well as claiming Fitzpatrick was 'a forceful right-half' against a 'hard and lively Blackpool side'.

The Review added a few facts about the Reds' victory:

Territorially on top, we missed a number of scoring chances. Blackpool, by contrast, made good use of their limited chances and always looked dangerous when on the attack. They opened the scoring against the run of play after ten minutes, a cross from Hobson beating the defence to give Loyden an easy chance. A United equaliser always looked 'on' but was delayed until the 40th minute. It was a cracking shot from Anderson and was worthy of the waiting.

Within three minutes the visitors were back in the lead, Loyden netting from the spot after Duff had tripped Dugdale. The second half was barely two minutes old when we got on terms. Anderson made the goal when he moved smartly down the wing then hit a hard, low centre for Kinsey to shoot first time from close range. This was a bright start and gave our boys the required initiative. After Jones had turned a fierce Fitzpatrick drive round the post and Anderson had hit the woodwork, they went ahead for the first time. Kinsey was the scorer, cleverly beating two men before firing in a shot from twenty yards.

MANCHESTER UNITED YOUTH XI 1963-64

Photo-cards of the under 18's were available for purchase, probably through the Supporters' Club
Back row (l-r) John Fitzpatrick, Peter McBride, David Farrar, Jimmy Rimmer, Alan Duff, Bobby Noble
Front row (l-r) Willie Anderson, George Best, David Sadler, Albert Kinsey, John Aston

third round

1963-64

Manchester United	Manchester City
1) Jimmy Rimmer 9) David Sadler	1) Alan Ogley 9) Chris Jones
2) Alan Duff 10) Albert Kinsey	2) Mike Doyle 10) Bobby McAlinden
3) Bobby Noble 11) John Aston	3) Dave Wild 11) Dave Connor
4) Peter McBride	4) John Clay
5) David Farrar	5) Alf Wood
6) John Fitzpatrick	6) Phil Burrows
7) Willie Anderson	7) Ronnie Frost
8) George Best	8) Glyn Pardoe

APRIL 1964

MANCHESTER UNITED 4 v 1 MANCHESTER CITY

Kinsey (3), Sadler   Pardoe

Wednesday 8th

Kick-off 7.30 p.m.

Attendance 29,706

semi-final 1st leg

Derby 'edge' creeps into Youth Cup

Down in the more southerly regions of the country, Swindon Town were waiting to meet the winners of the Luton v. Queen's Park Rangers clash for a place in the Youth Cup final. Whichever one of those clubs made it through were absolutely certain of a trip to Manchester, as a City against United clash ensured that one of the metropolis' representatives were sure to contest the final stage of the tournament.

While the Reds took just four games to reach the semi-final, City were made to travel a much longer route to the same spot. A total of seven ties constituted their efforts so far, and successive 4-1 defeats of Oldham and Burnley at Maine Road were followed by a mammoth battle against Preston. A 0-0 draw, again in Moss Side, meant that City were compelled to visit Deepdale, and they were actually losing 3-2 when the game was abandoned. In the third duel, City made their good fortune count for something by winning to the tune of three goals to one. An emphatic 6-1 victory over Middlesbrough in Manchester then preceded a terrific quarter-final tie with Leeds at Elland Road, where a fabulous bare-knuckle joust ended four goals to three in City's favour.

Built around Macclesfield-born centre-half and captain Alf Wood, almost all of the Light Blue contingent were from the vicinity of Manchester, and in that respect the composition of their ensemble was similar to past City sides that had faced United in the Youth Cup. One exception was England Youth cap Alan Ogley, an outstanding goalkeeping prospect from Barnsley who had already tasted first-team experience. Winsford boy Glyn Pardoe was another with England Youth honours and he, too, had gained senior recognition by that time. Pardoe, a fantastic footballer and an exemplary sportsman would go on to serve the Maine Road club with great distinction in both playing and coaching capacities over a period of very many years.

Having already made 21 appearances for the season, George Best was by now a regular in United's senior side and he was brought back for the City tie at the expense of the unfortunate John Pearson.

With the anticipation in the air that the winners of this particular semi-final would almost certainly progress to claim the Youth Cup trophy as their own, nearly 30,000 Manchester football enthusiasts rolled up at Old Trafford to see the shape of things to come. Significantly, the crowd topped the attendance of the seniors' last home appearance against Aston Villa by nearly 4,000.

City opened confidently enough, stroking the ball around and showing flashes of good movement in all areas while United searched for possession. Even so, it was a false start and their prospects were subjected to a raking thrust of the dagger when the Reds scored with their opening attack as early as the fourth minute. At the conclusion of a persistent run down the left by Willie Anderson, his cross was met by Albert Kinsey. The lurking Kinsey reacted by crashing the ball past Ogley, who was deemed by some as reacting too slowly to the danger.

Far from caving in to the early blow, City persisted with an attractive brand of football and it was they rather than the Reds who proceeded to hold the upper hand for the majority of the opening period. Only wayward shooting halted their progress, and with by far the bulk of possession to call upon, they were unable to exploit any holes found in United's defence. The sum total of City's attacking exploits were a tame effort by Pardoe, which was held with ease by Rimmer, and a rather better header from the same player that flew inches over the crossbar and landed on the roof of the goal-net.

With the twin incentives of a final spot and a great deal of local pride at stake, the play slowly started to become fraught. Several personal battles began to flare up and the referee was required to tackle the problem by ticking off a few of the contestants for overzealous tackling. The physical aspect was a factor that City possibly hadn't legislated for and their sophisticated style of soccer slowly started suffering as a result.

On 37 minutes, United went two-up. In a not-so-dissimilar set of circumstances to the previous goal, Anderson was the perpetrator of City's undoing and after gliding unchecked down the left flank, the winger whipped over a hanging cross while Kinsey, reacting with predatory instinct once again, sprinted into position. As the ball dropped, Kinsey flick-headed it unstoppably past Ogley, causing even the most partisan of City supporters to admit that the effort was a real beauty queen.

The United Review was later moved to comment about the half-time lead being *'against the run of play, perhaps, but a just reward for better finishing'.*

In true 'game of two halves' fashion, the Reds began the second instalment of the match with the majority of the territorial advantage. By then, Ogley was receiving less and less assistance from his defenders and he needed to be quick to react from shots by Sadler and Anderson which were turned away for successive corners. Ogley was then forced to smother the ball at the feet of Best and he later performed a similar feat with Aston bearing down on him.

In the 65th minute, United punished City for the third time. Awarded a direct free kick just beyond the perimeter of the penalty area, Kinsey smashed the ball home to complete a highly laudable hat-trick.

Just when an unassailable outcome was looking likely for United, City bounced back into the picture just two minutes later with an absolute peach of a goal. On a direct run at the home defence, Pardoe struck a wonderful shot that positively sizzled past Rimmer, the ball rattling United's bar before bouncing down and spinning back out of the netted enclosure. All eyes were directed at Ken Dagnall and the Bolton referee indicated that the ball had crossed the line by immediately pointing to the centre circle.

A little more 'aggro' crept back into the proceedings soon after, and United were adjudged as being by far the greater of the culprits. John Aston and David Sadler were both lectured by Dagnall on two occasions and the tension felt inside the stadium was further exacerbated when mindless idiots in the crowd began tossing coins at City's goalkeeper. Ogley handed some of the coins to the referee and from then on the police began to patrol the back of his net.

Just as the game entered its later stages, a Best shot cannoned against a City post and the Reds then scored their fourth and final goal in the 82nd minute following an Aston corner which was cleared only as far as Sadler. Instantly striking a venomous volley into a ruck of players, Sadler watched as his drive dissected them and passed the unsighted Ogley.

If only to complete a miserable night for City, outside-right Ronnie Frost was taken off two minutes from the end with a serious leg injury.

Even if the performance was far from vintage, the Reds could feel pleased that they had built up a tidy advantage which was forged on a platform of hard work, rugged endeavour and finishing of a particularly high standard. Fifteen fouls given against United, with City penalised only six times, reflected another side of the proceedings entirely.

The Daily Mail's Ronald Crowther reckoned the game had been a *'bruising battle'* which *'left an aftertaste of bitterness'* and he also felt that United's tactics effectively *'softened up the more elegant City for the kill'.*

Over at the Manchester Evening News, David Meek delivered his match report under a headline that requested the teams to 'PLAY IT COOLER, BOYS!'

Noting that an *'edge'* had crept into the match, he expressed a desire that the friction between the two sides wouldn't be carried over into the second leg.

Meek's colleague, Eric Thornton, penned a match report from a City perspective which was headlined 'CITY WILL MAKE A BONNY FIGHT OF IT' and it began with a warning for the Reds:

Despite Manchester United taking a 4-1 lead in the first leg of the F.A Youth Cup semi-final against Manchester City at Old Trafford, I think they have got a bonny fight on their hands in the return at Maine Road. I think City should have been ahead at half-time and possibly at full-time as they had the better scoring chances. But United came off best from close range and so go into the return game with a three-goal lead, which might look formidable at first glance......but really is not.

It seemed to me that Alan Ogley was slightly faulted when United opened the scoring in their first attack, and they were given too much space to notch their second.

But generally the Blues' defence was on its toes, with wing-halves John Clay and Phil Burrows playing particularly well.

For Alf Wood it was a mixed rough-and-tumble affair. He was on his back one minute and heading the ball away the next.

It was also a slow start for Glyn Pardoe, who grabbed City's only goal. But he showed his class later, especially when linking up with David Connor.

Similarly, the United Review match summary ended on a cautionary note when reasoning that even though the Reds held most of the aces, *'City played well enough to suggest that better finishing could still swing the tie in their favour'.*

Clearly, there was still much for United to do at Maine Road.

1963-64

APRIL 1964

Manchester City goalkeeper Alan Ogley leaps above George Best (partly hidden) and Albert Kinsey while David Sadler (left) watches for an opportunity

Albert Kinsey (far left) heads home the second goal of his hat-trick past Ogley as George Best (extreme right) surveys the scene

semi-final 1st leg

1963-64

1) Alan Ogley 9) Chris Jones 2) Mike Doyle 10) Bobby McAlinden 3) Dave Wild 11) Dave Connor 4) John Clay 5) Alf Wood 6) Phil Burrows 7) Max Brown 8) Glyn Pardoe	1) Jimmy Rimmer 9) David Sadler 2) Alan Duff 10) Albert Kinsey 3) Bobby Noble 11) John Aston 4) Peter McBride 5) David Farrar 6) John Fitzpatrick 7) Willie Anderson 8) George Best

APRIL 1964

MANCHESTER CITY 3 (4) v (8) 4 **MANCHESTER UNITED**

McAlinden, Pardoe (2) — Best, Doyle (o.g.), Sadler (2)

semi-final 2nd leg

Monday 20th
Kick-off 7.30 p.m.
Attendance 21,378

Because Ronnie Frost was ruled out through the injury he sustained at Old Trafford, City brought in Max Brown as a replacement at outside-right for the Maine Road showdown. Brown was actually City's normal under-18 left-winger, but he himself was crocked at the time of the first leg. His deputy at Old Trafford, Dave Connor, retained the number eleven shirt, which meant that Brown needed to be switched over to the other flank, and that one change was the only difference in personnel made by either side from the opening tie, City skipper Alf Wood surviving a scare with a knee problem to be declared fit for purpose.

There had been glad tidings for one member of the United camp since the game at Old Trafford. West Gorton-based centre-half David Farrar had passed his 17th birthday and the management chose to present him with a professional contract to mark the occasion.

There had also been a leg up the ladder for City half-backs John Clay and Phil Burrows. So impressed was Maine Road supremo George Poyser with their performances at Old Trafford that they were instantly promoted into City's Central League side.

There were high expectations at Maine Road that forwards Glyn Pardoe, Bobby McAlinden and Chris Jones could add to their total of eighteen out of City's 22 Youth Cup goals for the season, and the overwhelming consensus was that they would indeed require a rapid goal or two if they were to stand any chance of making it past United and into the final.

Those of a red persuasion were similarly optimistic that the improving pair of George Best and David Sadler could pose some searching questions of the home defence and also that Albert Kinsey would be up to duplicating his first leg scoring feat on the other side of town.

On a night of steadily falling rain, over 21,000 spectators took the aggregate crowd for the two matches past the 50,000 mark, which was a splendid reflection of Manchester's soccer tradition of supporting young talent.

The game pattern became obvious quite quickly when City, whose need for goals was more desperate, began as they had at Old Trafford, with the greater control. The Reds, on the other hand, were satisfied to soak up pressure and look for their chances when countering quickly on the break. City's forwards started with great spirit and energy, but United wing-halves Peter McBride and John Fitzpatrick were clearly following strict instructions in that their primary task was to provide an initial obstacle to any probings.

Just after the quarter hour point, United went ahead with a rather fortunate goal. When Sadler and Willie Anderson linked up to give Best an opening to shoot, the Irishman frowned as his effort was blocked by Ogley, the stray ball then squirming into the path of Wood. City's centre-half hacked at it wildly, only in doing so he managed to hit the ball against colleague Mike Doyle, and in a moment of great embarrassment to the two of them, the full-back fell on his backside in a failed attempt to prevent it trickling over the line.

The goal enhanced what was already shaping up to be a much more agreeable spectacle than that which had taken place at Old Trafford, and a pleasing aspect from the crowd's perspective was that both sets of forwards were seeing plenty of the ball. The 'niggle' which had been an unwanted undercurrent of the opening leg was largely gone and the entertainment factor benefited accordingly. Goalkeepers Ogley and Rimmer were in action on several occasions and it was obvious that the score couldn't remain as it was for long.

For the Reds, the movement of Best became a feature of their play, as did the continuing work undertaken by Fitzpatrick and McBride. As far as City were concerned, Pardoe was seemingly their greatest prospect of turning the scoreline around.

With barely two minutes to go to the interval, a spell of concerted City pressure at last paid dividends for them when a corner was won that United's defence initially cleared for another flag kick. In attempting to stand his ground in a six-yard area packed tightly with both light blue and red shirts, Rimmer was unable to grasp the flighted ball and he was stranded as Pardoe turned it home to give City a lifeline.

United's second half reply was both fast and furious, even though it was City's tendency to fall asleep at various times that would prove to be their ultimate undoing.

It was again the Reds' most constructive individual who was to give them a goal. Best, on the mazy type of dribble that would become one of his most famous trademarks in the years to come, mesmerised the City defence into a trance. Just when the time was right, he intelligently picked out the unmarked

Defenders Mike Doyle (on ground) and Alf Wood get in a muddle for the Reds' opener at Maine Road.......

168

1963-64

APRIL 1964

semi-final 2nd leg

.......and City's skipper collects the ball from the back of the net while Best turns to celebrate

Sadler, the lanky leader finishing the job off with a neatly placed shot into the net.

United soon scored again with a goal that crowned a great virtuoso performance by the lively Best. Picking up possession just inside City's half of the field, Best body-swerved and jinked his way past opponent after opponent before confidently planting the ball past Ogley to earn himself a tremendous ovation from both sets of supporters.

The Reds were now five goals ahead on aggregate, but brave City then stormed back to produce their best football of the entire tie. In a twenty-minute bombardment, they stormed the United barricades and with cracks finally appearing in the fortress, Pardoe scored his, and City's, second. In causing defenders to look innocently at each other while wondering where he had appeared from, Pardoe ghosted into the middle and netted with only Rimmer to beat.

City's all-out attacking policy left acres of space at the back for United's forwards and Aston contrived to hit a post following yet another Best dribble. Moments later, City inched nearer to the Reds' total when McAlinden forced over a third while United's defence showed a lapse in concentration.

With twenty minutes remaining, City were still required to score three times more in order to draw level and it was at that juncture when their dreams instantly evaporated after Kinsey cut a path through their back-line. Waiting to pounce was the stealthy Sadler, who stroked in a fourth Reds' goal of the evening which conclusively rubber-stamped their entry into the final.

There was much more good football to enjoy at Maine Road than had been the case in Stretford and with seven goals on the menu, David Meek described the dish on offer as *'thrilling'*.

The Daily Mail's Ronald Crowther summarised the events by proclaiming that the game *'produced dazzling goals by both sides and a stirring second half rally by City'*. Airing the view that United had *'confirmed their superiority'* over the 90 minutes and that the *'City defence had no answer'* to the *'surprisingly mature'* Best, Crowther also described the number eight's goal as *'his most brilliant movement of the night'*.

The United Review claimed the contest *'never lacked interest or excitement'* and congratulated both teams *'on an entertaining game played in a sporting spirit with fouls the result of youthful exuberance rather than malice'*.

It was then left to Manchester Evening News columnist Eric Thornton to take the widest possible view:

Let us breathe the clean air and rejoice, because Manchester's soccer future has never looked brighter.

I cannot recall a time when City and United had so many fine youngsters to call on. So many are coming off the production lines at Maine Road and Old Trafford now there is a distinct possibility of both clubs' line-ups being almost entirely home-grown within a few more years.

The signs were there for everyone to read when the clubs met in the first leg of the F.A. Youth Cup semi-final at Old Trafford earlier this month when United won 4-1.

They were there at Maine Road again last night, when a final score of 4-3 gave United a deserved 8-4 aggregate passage into the final.

The first, tough meeting gave United the goals but saw City playing the better football. The second meeting – a more pleasant affair altogether – saw United's defence take the honours, but George Best the top marks of the night for a personal display. Best, a full Irish international though still only seventeen, had a great time as a roaming inside-right and was a scorer.

Glyn Pardoe, who, like Best, is now a first-team regular, and was also scheming well for the Blues, equalised just before half-time, but then City went out of the competition 40 minutes before the end because of defensive errors, though they played some grand football – very cultured stuff at times.

They gave Sadler too much room right in front of goal and he was home high and dry on the 48th minute. Within two minutes Best had scored United's third, which gave them an aggregate of 7-2.

I wondered how City would react. They gave the quick answer. They fought harder and returned the arrears with fine goals by Pardoe and Bobby McAlinden, but another goal from Sadler gave United their 4-3 win.

169

1963-64

Swindon Town	Manchester United
1) Tony Hicks	1) Jimmy Rimmer
2) Brian Foscolo	2) Alan Duff
3) Terry Ling	3) Bobby Noble
4) Bernard Griffin	4) Peter McBride
5) Roger Brown	5) David Farrar
6) Dennis Prosser	6) John Fitzpatrick
7) Don Rogers	7) Willie Anderson
8) Dennis Peapell	8) George Best
9) Dick Plumb	9) David Sadler
10) Ricky Tabor	10) Albert Kinsey
11) Bruce Walker	11) John Aston

APRIL 1964

SWINDON TOWN 1 v 1 MANCHESTER UNITED

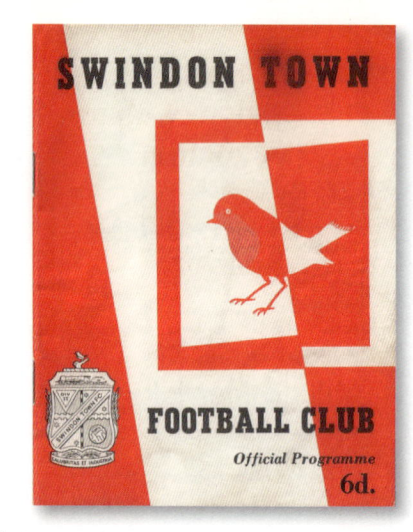

Rogers — Best

final 1st leg

Monday 27th
Kick-off 7.30 p.m.
Attendance 17,000

United's first Youth Cup final appearance for seven years had them pitched up against Swindon Town, one of football's perennially less fashionable clubs.

Matt Busby had taken a short break in Ireland prior to the opening leg at the County Ground and he was realistic about the Reds' chances of recapturing the trophy when spelling out his feelings to the Manchester Evening News. 'Obviously it will be hard,' he said before admitting, 'We know we have got to hit top form because Swindon have knocked out a string of southern First Division clubs. But we feel after Manchester City we should be capable of going all the way.'

The Wiltshire outfit had indeed enjoyed a fine run, and following a First Round bye they took part in a festival of goals at Fratton Park at the next stage when beating Portsmouth by five goals to four. They never came close to losing following that excellent victory, as they then proceeded to beat Brighton, 4-2, and Plymouth, 4-1, both at the County Ground in Rounds Three and Four respectively.

However, it was a superb 2-0 home win over Arsenal in the quarter-final that really made all the doubters finally sit up and take Swindon's progress seriously. Queen's Park Rangers were then duly beaten home and away at the penultimate stage, 2-0 in west London and 4-1 at the County Ground, to give the Robins a richly merited place in the final.

The Swindon side contained a degree of talent in all positions, with the undoubted star of the team formed by the shape of wing wizard Don Rogers, already a fixture in the Town's senior eleven. Much of Swindon's chances of capturing the silverware rested on Rogers' shoulders, and with home advantage in the first leg, the Wiltshire club were mindful that taking a lead to Old Trafford would be desirable, if not essential.

Of course, the United side contained a little wizard of their own, and in George Best they possessed a forward who was optimistically facing a busy end of season spell. The only member of the Reds' youth team who had been called upon to play over the previous weekend, Best assisted the seniors to a 3-1 win over Nottingham Forest at Old Trafford, the victory ensuring their campaign ended in splendid fashion by taking second spot in the First Division.

The following preview to the action, headed 'SUPREME TEST FOR TOWN'S YOUTH POLICY', was provided by the Swindon Advertiser:

Swindon Town's 'youth policy', brought into being by manager Bert Head, faces its greatest test tonight when Donald Rogers and his colleagues take on Manchester United at the County Ground in the first leg of the F.A. Youth Cup final.

Until this season, Swindon have never advanced beyond the Fifth Round. That was achieved in the days of Ernie Hunt, Mike Summerbee, Terry Woollen and John Trollope. The present side relies more on strength of teamwork with England Youth international Rogers the one outstanding player, but if Mr. Head is to achieve his dream of winning the national cup, his youngsters must triumph against one of the competition's most successful clubs.

Manchester United won the trophy in the first five years of existence and, although they have never won it since, they have gone extremely close during the last few years.

United's early success came during the period when Bobby Charlton, Duncan Edwards, Eddie Colman, Billy Whelan and David Pegg made the Busby Babes world famous.

The present side contains England Youth international centre-forward David Sadler and full Irish international George Best.

Best, normally a winger, played at inside-forward in United's semi-final team but for the Division One side and Ireland he plays on the wing. His success this season, however, is likely to rebound on his club, for next Wednesday Best plays for Ireland against Uruguay and may miss Thursday's second leg at Old Trafford.

Sadler, of course, was England's leading scorer in the Junior World Cup tournament in Holland over Easter, when England retained the trophy.

Rogers, too, was well up in the list of scorers and, like his international colleague, leads his club's cup marksmen.

The key player in United's defence is seventeen year-old left-back Bobby Noble, who also played in Holland, while wing-halves John Fitzpatrick and Peter McBride are the most improved players in the team.

Like Swindon, United made a rather shaky start in this year's competition. Although Barrow proved no match for them in the Second Round, Manchester found the going much harder against Blackpool.

Their luck in the draw continued, however, with home ties against Sheffield United and Wolverhampton Wanderers and not until the semi-final did they play away from Old Trafford. And then the journey was only across the city to Maine Road for the second leg clash with Manchester City.

In his youngsters, Matt Busby sees a chance for the club to atone for its near misses in senior football this season, for the first-team faltered at the last stages of the league championship, F.A. Cup and the European Cup Winners' Cup.

Manager Head returned unimpressed from watching the game at Maine Road and his team, bolstered by recent Wessex Youth League victories and encouraged by a crowd of anything up to 20,000, may establish the two or three-goal lead they will undoubtedly need from the first leg.

At Old Trafford they are likely to play before a crowd of more than 30,000 and in that sort of atmosphere Swindon may well find themselves restricted to desperate defence.

Since they will be up against what must be the most dangerous youth forward-line in the country, it is as well that Swindon's defensive play has improved immeasurably since the start of the season.

Tony Hicks, with a series of superb performances, has shown himself to be a 'keeper of the highest merit and in the semi-final against Queen's Park Rangers, he looked more polished than Peter Springett, regular in the England Youth team.

Brian Foscolo, from his early season clumsiness, has developed into a powerful and accomplished right-back and captain, while right-half Bernard Griffin is easily the most improved member of the team.

Both attracted the interest of Welsh selectors during the season and if they continue their development may well help to realise Mr. Head's hope of acquiring four or five first-team players from the youth squad.

Now that Richard Tabor has moved up to the forward-line, the attack has far more power but the best chance of breaking down United's defence, of course, lies in Rogers.

And if they can win against Manchester United they will have the satisfaction of bringing home a trophy held by West Ham United, the Division One club responsible for Swindon's exit from both the F.A. Cup and Football League Cup this season.

Victory will also mean a cup and league double, for despite the last minute rush of fixtures, Swindon are certainties for the Wessex Youth League title.

Town manager Bert Head appeared to be fighting a psychological war years before they became fashionable, by making uncomplimentary remarks about the United lads prior to the game. Specifically regarding the semi-final second leg at Maine Road, Swindon's boss said that he had 'expected more from a game between two first-class teams'. He went on to say that the Reds 'had the skill, but I would have thought there would have been more endeavour and effort from more players.'

Head then predicted, 'I think we shall have the edge in the amount of effort the (Swindon) players are prepared to put into the game. We certainly have bigger players and I look forward to two interesting matches. You can certainly say we are quietly confident.'

With the priority of both sides in being able to gain a firm foothold for the second leg, United were the more pleased of the two parties at the end of 90 minutes of football which was recorded by the Swindon Advertiser:

170

1963-64

APRIL 1964

United Youths miss a bagful of goals

ONLY the courageous Tony Hicks stood between Swindon Town and heavy defeat at the County Ground last night. Due to his efforts, Swindon escaped from the FA Youth Cup final first leg on terms with a powerful Manchester United side.

Swindon now go to Old Trafford for the second leg on Thursday, but if they are to survive the ordeal before something like 30,000 United fans, they must give their gallant goalkeeper far more support.

England youth international Donald Rogers was the only Swindon forward to find his way through United's defence, although even his performance was for once overshadowed by Hicks.

As in the first leg of the semi-final against Queen's Park Rangers, Hicks made scarcely a mistake as, time after time, he defied Manchester's finely-poised attack.

His one consolation is that the man behind the visitors' major threats, Northern Ireland international George Best, may miss Thursday's game.

For Best, a frail but brilliant footballer, gains his second full cap against Uruguay tomorrow, and may find four games in six days too much for him.

Best it was who schemed nearly every dangerous United movement, and more than once his fierce flashing shots brought fine diving saves from Hicks.

SKILFUL PROMPTING

Manchester, who won the trophy during the first five years of existence, showed glimpses of their promise from the first whistle, with Best's skilful prompting keeping Swindon's defence at full stretch, but the early flurry ended with Aston shooting wide of an open goal.

Rogers caused a couple of moments of near panic in the Manchester goal area before Hicks began a busy evening by saving shots from Best and centre forward David Sadler.

For half an hour chances were made and missed without bias but it was Swindon who slipped ahead after 31 minutes.

Left winger Bruce Walker slung a high cross-field pass to Rogers' foot, the outside right accelerated round Duff, swayed inside and hammered a ground shot past Rimmer.

The last few moments of the half saw three grand saves by Hicks—first from a Kinsey drive, then a Best header and finally at the feet of Sadler.

Hicks, fresh from the applause of the crowd, was back in action within seconds of the restart but even he was helpless when a magnificent attempt by Sadler slammed against the underside of the bar.

THE EQUALISER

He defied United until the 70th minute when Best scored the elusive goal.

McBride pushed a pass through an opening in Swindon's defence and Best took the ball to the advancing Hicks before flicking it towards the net. The goalkeeper could do no more than help the ball on its way.

Thereafter, Swindon fell back in desperate defence, with Hicks keeping well in trim for the second leg with yet more leaping saves.

Fortunately for Swindon, United were guilty of inaccurate shooting at the most vital moments. Even when they really established control in the second half, their play was a little over-eager and lacked the steadiness that brings goals.

CHIEF WEAKNESS

Swindon's main weakness was at inside forward where Plumb too often found his thrusts down the middle virtually unsupported. Although the defence took tremendous punishment without cracking, far more mistakes than usual left Hicks at Manchester's mercy.

final 1st leg

David Meek kicked off his piece on the match from a gambler's angle:

It's odds on Manchester United having a trophy to put on show at Old Trafford next season.

A team that misses chances in front of goal cannot expect to win, of course – and United missed a bagful in last night's first leg of the Youth Cup final at Swindon.

They deserved no more than the 1-1 result. But at the same time I simply cannot see them fluffing quite so many opportunities in the return match as they did at Swindon. They are also not the kind of team to take anything for granted.

Right-half Peter McBride, with his red hair and blend of determination and skill, is looking more like a pocket edition of Tony Kay every game. It was this young Scot from Motherwell who lobbed through the pinpoint pass that led to United's goal in the 71st minute.

He found Best, who took the ball in his stride before beating goalkeeper Tony Hicks, who overall had a great game. This was the equaliser for Swindon's brilliant 31st-minute goal by Don Rogers, the England Youth winger.

Full-back Alan Duff had the hardest job of any United player trying to hold Rogers, but he settled down and finished with a much firmer grip on his tricky opponent.

The Swindon ground was hard, which did not suit United's players, who had the ball in the air far more than usual. Old Trafford will be softer, and although Swindon have a strong, well-built side with Rogers particularly dangerous, I will take United to clinch a cup at last!

1963-64

APRIL 1964

final 2nd leg

United goalie Jimmy Rimmer arches backwards as a Swindon effort is skied at Old Trafford

David Sadler is on hand to plant the ball past gallant Town 'keeper Tony Hicks

1963-64

APRIL 1964

Ironically, at the beginning of the competition, the current youth team were not rated outstanding by previous standards.

Uncertain they may have been in early rounds, but there was no mistaking the force and finesse of their football against Swindon.

The 25,563 crowd – a fine one considering the rain – chose two heroes.

'Georgie Best, Georgie Best' they chanted during the cup presentation at the end. And who would not have joined them after watching this slender dark-haired youth tease and tantalise the opposition with uncanny ball control.

It was also a great night for John Fitzpatrick, the boy from Aberdeen. His pants were thick with mud after the first few minutes as he stormed into action. Then he matched his devastating tackling with beautiful distribution.

David Sadler took the scoring honours with a hat-trick from chances created mostly by Best. John Aston scored the other goal in the 4-1 win in this second leg to make an aggregate 5-2 victory.

Even though the crowd had its heroes, success was basically a team effort in which there were no disappointments.

Adorned with red and white ribbons, the Youth Cup is lifted above skipper Bobby Noble's head in the Old Trafford tunnel

final 2nd leg

1964-65

1) Geoff Barnett
2) Dave Pearson
3) Frank D'Arcy
4) John Hurst
5) Eric Curwen
6) Dennis Yaager
7) Alec Wallace
8) Gerry Glover
9) Tony McLoughlin
10) Jimmy Husband
11) Aiden Maher

1) Jimmy Rimmer
2) Eddie Harrop
3) Bernard Marshall
4) Peter McBride
5) David Farrar
6) Francis Burns
7) Willie Anderson
8) John Pearson
9) Frank McEwen
10) John Aston
11) Ken Morton

DECEMBER 1964

EVERTON 5 v 0 MANCHESTER UNITED

Husband (2), McLoughlin (2), Wallace

Tuesday 8th
Kick-off 7.30 p.m.
Attendance 5,676

second round

Manchester United Football Club Ltd.

M. BUSBY, C.B.E., Manager
L. OLIVE, Secretary

TELEGRAPHIC ADDRESS:
STADIUM, MANCHESTER
TELEPHONE TRAFFORD PARK
1661 & 1662

Old Trafford,
Manchester, 16.

26th November, 1964.

LO/AG

W. Dickinson, Esq.,
Secretary,
Everton Football Club,
Goodison Park,
LIVERPOOL 4.

Dear Mr. Dickinson,

F.A. YOUTH CUP - SECOND ROUND

We confirm telephone conversation arranging to play the above match at Goodison Park on Tuesday, 8th December, kick-off 7-30 p.m.

Pen pictures of our probable team are shown in the enclosed programme.

If you require any further information please let us know.

Yours sincerely,

L. Olive
Secretary.

Alan Duff, Bobby Noble, Albert Kinsey, George Best, David Sadler and John Fitzpatrick were names that had been consigned to the Youth Cup archives by the time the Reds learned that their defence of the trophy would begin, just as it had in 1953, at Everton's Goodison Park stadium.

The backbone of United's team for the 1964/65 season was made up of goalkeeper Jimmy Rimmer, half-backs Peter McBride and David Farrar, along with forwards John Aston and Willie Anderson, though some of the remainder of the side had seen Youth Cup action previously.

Eddie Harrop won a recall at right-back after not featuring at all during last season's winning streak and he lined up alongside newcomer Bernard Marshall, a Liverpudlian who was faced with a particularly hard act to follow by taking the left-back berth vacated by former captain Noble. Francis Burns, a Scottish lad with international schoolboy exposure, came in at number six, while the team was consolidated by forwards John Pearson, Frank McEwen and Ken Morton. All three of those front men had something to prove, having taken part in the earlier rounds of the previous term's tournament before finding themselves overlooked for the later stages.

Everton's side was built on eight apprentice professionals, and the three amateurs in the team were left-half Dennis Yaager, a trialist over from Australia, outside-right Alec Wallace and centre-forward Tony McLoughlin. Both Wallace and McLoughlin were local boys, with the last named a capture from South Liverpool Football Club.

Goalie Geoff Barnett represented Cheshire Boys prior to winning four England caps and was taken on at Goodison Park straight from school. Left-back Frank D'Arcy was another local prospect, while his defensive partner, Dave Pearson, came from Flint and had achieved Welsh international schoolboy honours.

The remainder of the Everton side were all ex-England Boys players. Centre-half Eric Curwen and right-half John Hurst had both starred for Blackpool and England, with the number five honoured with the captaincy of his country, and at inside-left, outside-left and inside-right respectively, Jimmy Husband, Aiden Maher and Gerry Glover had all also been capped. Maher and Glover were spotted by Everton scouts while on duty for Liverpool Boys, whereas Husband was recruited from Newcastle.

In total, there were thirteen participants with schoolboy caps on show, with the Reds for once being slightly outnumbered by their six internationals to Everton's seven.

In those days, the normal transport arrangement for United's youth team away fixtures of a reasonably close destination was coach travel, and because Goodison Park is only approximately 40 miles away from Old Trafford, the usual company was engaged to ferry the party to Liverpool. As the coach made its way along the East Lancs Road, and with some distance to go to reach its intended destination, it suddenly broke down. Several minutes then passed, when numerous attempts at repairs took place, but it eventually became clear there was nothing that could be done within an acceptable timescale to get the coach to restart.

In order for the players and support staff to reach Liverpool in time for the kick-off, they were faced with the choice of either waiting for alternative transport to arrive or thumbing a ride for the remainder of the journey. It was agreed to take the latter course of action, and it was only the kindness of passing motorists which allowed the United contingent to arrive at Goodison Park, although even then it was with precious few minutes to spare. Some of them were even transported in a lorry.

The Reds' coach wasn't the only thing that came to a shuddering full stop that day because, at the end of play, so did their short participation in the competition.

The Liverpool Echo told of United's misery:

FINE DISPLAY BY YOUNG EVERTON

Everton gave one of their best displays in under-18 football for many years when they beat a strong Manchester United side 5-0 in the second round of the F.A. Youth Cup, at Goodison Park last night.

United, with five members of the team which won the Trophy last year still eligible to play, fielded a side which contained eight former schools internationals, and they opened as if they were going to crush Everton.

The match turned dramatically in the 13th minute when Barnett, the Everton goalkeeper, made a fine save from United's inside left. Aston, and sent his side quickly onto the attack with a good clearance.

United, caught off balance, never recovered from this quick break by Everton and when Maher centred from the left wing, goalkeeper Rimmer could only push the ball down to the foot of Husband, who volleyed it into the net.

INTERNATIONAL CLASS

Husband, who looked youth international class during the first half, laid on goal number two for centre forward McLoughlin with a clever header four minutes later, and a D'Arcy free kick was headed home by Husband at the 22nd minute for Everton's third.

The ball ran kindly for Everton at this stage, but they took their chances well. United never deserved to go in at the interval three goals behind, but had only themselves to blame.

They created as many chances as Everton, but only went near to scoring on one occasion, when a good shot by John Pearson beat Barnett and just missed the upright.

There was a touch of luck about all Everton's first half goals, but this could not be said of the two they added after the interval.

A superb dummy by Maher sent the whole United defence the wrong way nine minutes after the interval and the winger was able to cross the ball for right winger Wallace to head a fine goal.

FINE HEADER

Everton's final scoring effort came 26 minutes from time when McLoughlin made a very fine header from a Wallace centre.

Husband and Maher were in tremendous form for Everton and gave United's right defensive flank of Harrop and McBride a match they will quickly want to forget. Centre forward McLoughlin took his chances well, while outside right Wallace had a good second half. Glover worked hard in the link position of inside right.

Local boy Frank D'Arcy, Everton's left back, was the game's outstanding defender, while Barnett gave a display of confident goalkeeping which suggested that Gordon West, and perhaps Andy Rankin, will have to work hard to deny him promotion.

At centre half Curwen did his job coolly and well, as did Hurst, Yaager and David Pearson, after they had come through the lively United opening spell.

1964-65

DECEMBER 1964

The United Review countered with some observations of its own:

Having failed to profit from some enterprising football in the early stages, United let the initiative slip when defensive lapses let in Everton for three goals in the 15th, 17th and 23rd minutes. Territorially, the game continued to be fairly even, but the guile and strength of the home team always carried the greater menace. Although perhaps flattered by the final score, there was no doubt that Everton were worthy winners.

The opening goal came when Rimmer palmed a centre from Maher to the feet of the unmarked Husband. Two minutes later, a free kick from the touchline drifted through the defence for McLoughlin to scramble the ball over the line. Maher, who had been the spearhead of most Everton attacks, provided the centre for the well-positioned Husband to beat Rimmer in the air to head goal number three.

Full-length saves by Barnett from Aston and Pearson prevented our youths fighting back into the game before the interval. Any remaining hopes faded nine minutes after the resumption when Wallace headed home another good cross from Maher.

Two excellent saves from Rimmer prevented a quick increase in the home lead, but he was well beaten when McLoughlin headed the best goal of the match.

In the aftermath of a crushing defeat, the Manchester Evening News delivered some rather forthright views, which included comments such as *'right-back Eddie Harrop had a nightmare match'* and *'Peter McBride had little more success in his efforts to stop inside-left Jimmy Husband'*. The newspaper concluded the sorry tale with a view that the Reds *'were soundly beaten.......by a very good Everton side'*.

Many years later, United's goalkeeper Jimmy Rimmer claimed the defeat was all down to him, totally discounting the long held view that the team's poor performance was caused by their broken bus and consequential late arrival.

Rimmer further pointed out that he and his team-mates were calm and collected, even enjoying a few laughs about the whole affair in the dressing room prior to kick-off.

In an astonishingly frank and honest admission, the custodian went on to give the opinion that every Everton goal resulted from his mistakes. While he certainly didn't put in one of the better performances of his long and distinguished career, it seems something of an exaggeration for him to try to shoulder all of the responsibility. The finger of blame would definitely be pointed in his direction for Everton's opener, and he probably could have done more to prevent the second and third goals. The outcome was as good as over by then, and he certainly had no chance with the two strikes which registered against him after the break.

Whatever the reasons for United's defeat, Everton went on to become the latest team to use a victory against them as a step on the ladder towards winning the competition. With the Blues positively ripping through the various stages of the tournament before defeating Arsenal in the final the following spring, their success meant that of the thirteen seasons the Youth Cup had been in existence, and excluding the six occasions that the Reds had won it, four of the clubs that captured the trophy were required to defeat United along the way.

The loss at Goodison Park proved to be much more than just a heavy defeat and the game is now acknowledged as something of a watershed, because in all of their previous adventures in the Youth Cup, the Reds were always there or thereabouts, only once failing to reach at least the quarter-finals.

Following the debacle at Everton in December 1964, United's young representatives would still enjoy some fine runs in the competition. However, they would have to wait many long years to instil the fear in their opponents as they had previously and it would also take a couple of decades or more for them to finally regain the lofty prestige they once held in the most important youth tournament in the country.

second round

Seen on the far right, coach Johnny Aston shares some of his vast football knowledge with the club's young prospects
Back row (l-r) Player unknown, John Fitzpatrick, Dave Farrar, Bernard Marshall, Jimmy Rimmer, Ian Brough, Ken Morton, John Connaughton, John Pearson, Eddie Harrop
Middle row (l-r) John Aston Jr., Billy Beswick (partly obscured), J. Whittingham, Peter Woods, N. Kirk
Front row (l-r) Peter McBride, Willie Anderson (partly obscured), Frank Kopel (holding ball), John Cooke, Steve Lang

177

1965-66

1) Peter Mellor	9) Steve Walker	1) Jimmy Rimmer	9) Wayne Emmerson
2) Don Smeaton	10) Chris Glennon	2) Frank Kopel	10) Frank McEwen
3) John Lutley	11) Stan Bowles	3) David Weir	11) Brian Kidd
4) Keith Mason		4) Willie Watson	
5) Jeff Street		5) Paul Edwards	
6) Jim Barton		6) Francis Burns	
7) Malcolm Ryan		7) John Cooke	
8) Ian Mills		8) Carlo Sartori	

DECEMBER 1965

MANCHESTER CITY 0 v 5 MANCHESTER UNITED

Cooke, Emmerson, Kidd, McEwen (2)

Monday 13th
Kick-off 7.30 p.m.
Attendance 6,019

second round

REDS RELY ON FOREIGNERS

More than a year had passed before the Reds were able to resume Youth Cup duties following their comprehensive defeat by Everton. If there was any benefit at all to be derived from the game at Goodison Park twelve months ago, it was that the weight of expectancy on United's youngsters was now considerably less than in seasons gone by.

Another game at Maine Road gave an airing to a new influx of hopefuls that consisted of no less than eight new faces, and the Manchester Evening News made notes about a United forward-line which sported a distinctly international look about it:

> **MANCHESTER UNITED** will spearhead their FA Youth Cup bid at Maine Road tonight with an Italian, a Canadian, and a Republic of Ireland man, writes DAVID MEEK.
>
> Wayne Emmerson, who was born in Ottawa, will be at centre forward. Carlos Sartori, who comes from Milan, at inside-right, and Frank McEwen, from Eire, at inside left.
>
> But like Manchester City their opponents in this second round tie, the Reds are something of an unknown quantity.
>
> Only five of the team played in last season's side, and they are young with seven eligible for next season's competition.
>
> But they do have the confidence of a heavy win when they represented the B team last month in the Lancashire League Second Division Supplementary Cup final. They combined well to beat Blackburn Rovers B team 7-2 at Old Trafford.
>
> They have only one change from that side, Colin Curran is ineligible to bring in David Weir at full back as partner for the versatile Frank Kopel, who has played four Central League games as a forward.
>
> **THE LOCALS**
>
> City will not select their side until shortly before the kick-off. Terry Wood, their full back, has not yet recovered from a recent ankle injury and is definitely out, while there are other doubts, including goalkeeper Peter Mellor with an injured finger. Seventeen-year-old Derek Barber stands by.
>
> The Blues have named 15 players, all locals, with the exception of David Hoare, a 16-year-old inside forward from Liverpool.

Placed on the right side of the Reds' attack was a gifted Sheffield boy, John Cooke, while positioned on the opposite flank was Brian Kidd, a slender yet powerful and determined Collyhurst lad who was in the early stages of a long love affair with the club.

Other newcomers were full-backs Frank Kopel and David Weir, as well as centre-half and right-half respectively, Paul Edwards and Willie Watson. Edwards came from near Oldham while Kopel, Weir and Watson were all former Scotland schoolboy prospects.

The Maine Road pitch that greeted the players could only be described as an absolute quagmire. The ability to function on a surface that resembled a World War One battle scene was central to the tactics of both sides and would become a major contributory factor in deciding which one of them would make it into the next round.

There was no display of stage fright from the Reds, who got off to the perfect start with a goal within a minute from old hand McEwen, the early reverse meaning that City were immediately put under some pressure to go in search of an equaliser.

Sadly for them, any artistry they possessed tended to be halted either by the clinging mud or United's defensive capabilities. The Reds, on the other hand, applied themselves to the conditions as best they could and were rather uncharacteristically content to bulldoze after long balls which were repetitively launched straight down the centre of the field.

United's methods were far from refined or pretty to watch but, nevertheless, proved effective enough, and after near misses by Sartori and Emmerson, they went 2-0 to the good with just nineteen minutes gone. In the moments leading up to the goal, City's Mellor made a fine save from Burns, but the young Scot soon put the scorned chance behind him when furnishing Cooke with possession. An accurate centre from Cooke gave the poaching Kidd enough ammunition to fire home within handgun range.

The slippery winger then provided another easy chance for McEwen to gobble up barely 60 seconds later, and the roles were reversed three minutes before half-time when Cooke glanced in an accurate header from the number ten's superb cross.

At 4-0 down, the home team's prospects of progress were blacker than the puddles on the pitch when the restart was sounded. The game was something of an anticlimax during the second period and it was down to Emmerson to round off the scoring in the 62nd minute when he beat Mellor to the ball and knocked in United's fifth.

City put in a late rally in their search for some type of a consolation. A long-range free kick was coolly held by Rimmer and the Reds' goalkeeper was then on hand to make a much more demanding stop from Mills' header. City's night was summed up to a tee in the last minute of the game when they were awarded a penalty, Lutley tamely placing the spot kick within reach of Rimmer, who made a simple save look just that.

Despite conceding five times, Mellor was fêted as a hero by the Maine Road crowd. A busy display from the goalie helped to keep the score under the embarrassment line and through his considerable exertions he left the field quite literally covered from head to toe in mud.

The Reds' under-18 centre-forward for the 1965/66 season, Wayne Emmerson wrote his name on the score sheet with the fifth goal against Manchester City

1965-66

1) William Conlan	9) Doug Livermore	
2) George Bolland	10) Ken Walker	
3) Peter Carroll	11) Bob Roach	
4) Tom Stanton		
5) Kevin Marsh		
6) Roy Evans		
7) Steve Peplow		
8) Malcolm Bland		

1) Jimmy Rimmer	9) Wayne Emmerson	
2) Frank Kopel	10) Frank McEwen	
3) David Weir	11) Brian Kidd	
4) Willie Watson		
5) Paul Edwards		
6) Francis Burns		
7) John Cooke		
8) Carlo Sartori		

LIVERPOOL 3 v 0 MANCHESTER UNITED
Kopel (o.g.), Livermore, Roach

JANUARY 1966

Monday 17th

Kick-off 7.00 p.m.

Attendance 5,658

While United were in the process of eliminating their nearest neighbours, next opponents Liverpool were also putting the Youth Cup skids under a club within close proximity, as they defeated Tranmere Rovers by a 4-3 margin to earn the right to entertain United.

The Old Trafford management ensured that the team arrived at Anfield in a more reliable coach than had been the case at Everton in the previous campaign and it contained exactly the same eleven players who had performed so well at Maine Road. In front of a crowd that was almost identical in number to the one which was present at Goodison Park just over a year before, United started well, just like they had against Everton. Then faltering badly, it added up to a case of capitulation on Merseyside for the youths for the second successive season.

The opening two sentences of the Liverpool Echo match summary, which went under the title 'ANFIELD LESSON FOR UNITED', perfectly captioned a punchless performance from the away side:

Goals win matches and hard luck doesn't count at all. That was the tough lesson that Manchester United learned when they went out of the F.A. Youth Cup last night, beaten 3-0 by Liverpool in a Third Round match at Anfield.

Sporting a strip consisting of dark blue shirts and white shorts, United only had themselves to blame, because in the opening half they were in so much control that Sartori, McEwen and Burns frequently supplemented strikers Cooke, Emmerson and Kidd to make up a six-man forward-line.

Liverpool rode out the early storm to get off the mark in the eleventh minute completely against the run of play, and the goal came about as a result of their rather crude early method of belting the ball up the middle on the hard and slippery surface. Left-back Carroll hoovered up a sloppy United clearance near to the half-way line and whacked a long ball into the penalty box. Walker and Livermore conspired to bamboozle their markers, the latter finishing with a terrific shot which was only one of two worthwhile efforts on goal the home team could muster before the break.

United continued to adjust themselves better to the unyielding surface and high bouncing ball, and by fashioning a number of clear-cut chances it seemed only a matter of time before they would level up the score. Sartori brought a good save out of Conlan and Emmerson then knocked the ball across a temporarily unmanned Liverpool goalmouth. With winger John Cooke instigating most of United's most promising moves, Liverpool's Carroll bravely threw himself in front of an on-target McEwen shot when a goal seemed the most obvious outcome.

The Anfield team changed tactics following the restart and by keeping the ball down their passing increased in quality while their possession ballooned in quantity. Also, while never entirely subduing their opponents, Carroll quietened Cooke down a little and Evans and Stanton dealt likewise with Sartori and McEwen.

In the 51st minute, a Peplow cross was headed away by Paul Edwards, a clearance which only went as far as Roach who stood about six feet outside the eighteen-yard box. Hitting an instinctive first time volley, the outside-left's attempt struck a startled Edwards and diverted past Rimmer into the net.

United continued to produce some neat approach work, although Liverpool's sharp breaks out of defence were now causing them problems they hadn't encountered earlier in the game. Sartori's fifteen-yard shot was tipped over the bar by Conlan and minutes later McEwen blasted an attempt against an upright which bounced clear. Frank Kopel was involved in the next incident of note, in the 68th minute, when he appeared about to be challenged by Walker while attempting to guide the ball back to Rimmer. Walker's presence proved enough to unsettle the full-back, whose pass went way off its intended course and flew into the top corner of the net.

Liverpool almost scored again in the dying minutes when the impressive Peplow went on a terrific run prior to driving in a scorching shot which brought a magnificent save out of Rimmer.

In analysing the match, it could fairly be said that for all of United's efforts, no-one had been able to capitalise on their territorial superiority in the first half nor their opportunities in front of goal during the second. There was also some flack flying in regards to United's change of tactics midway through the second period when Sartori, easily the team's most influential individual, was asked to occupy a deeper role while Frank Kopel found himself operating in a more advanced position. One report specified that Sartori was *'the cleverest forward on view and the most likely to spark off any United rally'*.

The Liverpool Echo report concluded on the events with the following views:

The Anfield team may not be as skilful as the Everton side which won the Youth Cup last season, but they possess those fighting qualities so necessary in a knock-out competition, and preventing this United side from scoring must have boosted the confidence of their defence.

Another report claimed *'the scoreline gives little indication of the course of the game'* and went on to state that *'United will be trying to puzzle out how they failed to score, for had their finishing been anything like their approach work, especially in the first half, the result might have been different'.*

The Merseysiders were accorded their due, however. One reporter offered the opinion that it was *'the all-round team work and team spirit'* which allowed them to account for a more talented combination, as well as the effort put in by a forward-line that *'worked hard and often fell back to help in defence'.*

There was a great deal of grief within Old Trafford at the early exit simply because Liverpool hadn't been expected to provide too great a barrier to United's ambition of furtherance in the competition.

In the Review, Jack Pauline penned the last words on the loss:

The defeat of the youth team at Liverpool came as a bitter disappointment after our grand show at Maine Road in the previous round. It was the more unpalatable because we had so much the better of the first half exchanges and would not have been flattered by a three or four-goal lead at the interval. Unfortunately, the ball was never running kindly for us, especially near goal, whilst in one of their rare visits to our penalty area, the home team grabbed the lead.

They had another slice of fortune six minutes after the change round when a shot from Roach was deflected wide of Rimmer to put them two up. This was just the incentive required to set the Anfield boys alight and for long periods our defence was under heavy pressure. Even so we still had our moments - notably when a McEwen shot hit the woodwork and a good effort by Sartori was saved in great style by Conlan - when a goal was badly needed. An own goal by Kopel when under no great pressure was typical of the ill-luck which had attended our efforts throughout. With it our chances of saving the game finally evaporated.

Despite being United's best individual against Liverpool, all of Carlo Sartori's good work went to waste at Anfield

third round

179

1966-67

1) Alex Clarke
2) Dave Turner
3) Archie Styles
4) Billy Brindle
5) Roger Kenyon
6) Chris Dunleavy
7) Terry Owen
8) Alan Whittle
9) Joe Royle
10) Alan Tarbuck
11) Frank Thornton
12) Unknown

1) John Connaughton
2) Frank Kopel
3) David Weir
4) Willie Watson
5) Steve James
6) Francis Burns
7) Ian Brough
8) John Cooke
9) Don Givens
10) Brian Kidd
11) Frank Gill
12) Alan Gowling

DECEMBER 1966

EVERTON 0 v 0 MANCHESTER UNITED

Tuesday 6th
Kick-off 7.30 p.m.
Attendance 5,298

second round

'Solid' Steve James did much to prevent Everton from scoring

With the club's Youth Cup reputation having taken something of a battering over the last couple of years, to their utter dismay, United's under-18's discovered that they had been drawn to play a tie on Merseyside for the third consecutive term. In view of the Reds' recent results within a short walking distance of Stanley Park, it would undoubtedly have been with a great deal of trepidation when learning that they were due to face Everton at Goodison Park in their opening game.

United brought in a new goalkeeper, Billinge-born John Connaughton, and fresh centre-half Steve James, who hailed from near Wolverhampton, while the full-back pairing and two half-backs remained unchanged from the previous season.

Also drafted in were three Youth Cup rookies, ex-England Boys' starlet Ian Brough, Manchester lad Frank Gill and Republic of Ireland schoolboy prodigy Don Givens, while Alan Gowling, a teenager from Stockport who possessed the physique of a beanpole, was named as the club's very first substitute in the competition. Brian Kidd and John Cooke were on hand to lend some tournament experience upfront, although only new skipper Francis Burns remained from that embarrassing dismissal on the same ground almost two years ago to the day.

Six of the United team, Kopel, Burns, Brough, Cooke, Kidd and Gill, had already been with the club for at least a couple of years and all of them were charged with at least some experience in the Central League. Gill had recently wrested the outside-left slot from John Aston in the Reserves and Kidd was already into double figures in the goal stakes at that standard. Kopel's worth to the second string was evidenced by the fact that he had occupied four positions for them that season while Burns, who had spent about half of his time in the Central League side, was usually found at left-half but had also lent them his assistance at left full-back.

Connaughton, Weir, Watson, James, Brough, Cooke and Givens usually made up the bulk of an 'A' team that had suffered only one loss during the campaign, ironically to Everton 'A' in a Supplementary Cup tie. Of their sixteen matches completed, United's 'A' side had conceded one goal or less in twelve of them and could boast of scoring three or more in nine of those games.

During a poor Youth Cup tie, in which too many of the participants consistently cavorted around the centre circle, the redeeming feature from the Reds' standpoint was that they showed a marked improvement than on their last visit to Everton's enclosure. When the ball was found at the danger ends of the pitch, both sets of strikers were restricted to infrequent opportunities as their markers threw a blanket over any scoring intentions they harboured.

The Liverpool Daily Post divulged the dreary details on a dismally drab duel:

FEW SHOTS IN YOUTH CUP DEFENSIVE TUSSLE

A draw was a fair result to an F.A. Youth Cup second round match at Goodison Park last night in which the outstanding feature was the small number of direct shots the goalkeepers had to save.

It was a defensive tussle with the forward lines given little chance to show their talents.

Former Liverpool schoolboy Alan Whittle worked hard trying to break down the United defensive wall only to see his colleagues failing to make the best of the openings he was able to create.

Everton claimed a penalty five minutes from time when the fair haired inside right was brought down as he weaved his way into the area, and they appeared to have a strong case when all they got was a throw in.

On the other hand Everton had two narrow escapes during the second half. After 64 minutes only a great save by Clarke foiled Givens, the United centre forward after he had cleverly rounded Kenyon and Turner.

Then Styles, the Everton left back, timed his header perfectly to put the ball over the bar after Clarke had punched clear and United left winger Gill had headed the ball goalwards.

Referee V. J. Batty, of Helsby, was forced to have a word with four or five players during the match and one United defender was fortunate to escape a booking.

The first 45 minutes are best forgotten and although the game improved afterwards spectators are drawn to this type of football mainly by the fine goals it often produces so in this respect soccer took a step backwards last night.

Kenyon also did well at centre half and the whole defence did as much as could be expected of it. In attack however only Tarbuck showed signs of being able to appreciate Whittle's clever approach work.

An alternative report made a note about neither team being *'able to break quickly enough to cause the other any undue anxiety'* and then mentioned *'particularly in the first half, we had much of the pushing, tripping and over-enthusiastic tackling which seem part of the modern defensive plan'.*

As far as favourable comments were concerned, they were laid at the feet of one of the Reds' debutants, as well as an individual who was looking to improve on a Youth Cup record of two defeats in three appearances. In claiming *'many defenders came out of the game with great credit, and none more than United's solid centre-half, James'*, it was also said in the same report that *'there was no stronger tackler on view than United's left-half Burns'.*

Apart from a couple of rare chances at either end, the stalemate was almost instantly forgettable from a viewing perspective. The most notable openings for the host side came from a long free kick by winger Terry Owen and, later, when a great recovery save by Connaughton denied Joe Royle after the Reds' goalie invitingly spilled a cross into the path of the big Everton centre-forward.

1) Terry Poole	9) Don Givens	1) Alex Clarke	9) Joe Royle
2) Frank Kopel	10) Brian Kidd	2) Dave Turner	10) Alan Tarbuck
3) David Weir	11) Frank Gill	3) Archie Styles	11) Frank Thornton
4) Willie Watson	*12) Peter O'Sullivan*	4) Billy Brindle	*12) Charlie Fraser ◊*
5) Steve James		5) Roger Kenyon	
6) Francis Burns		6) Chris Dunleavy	
7) Ian Brough		7) Terry Owen	
8) John Cooke		8) Alan Whittle	

MANCHESTER UNITED 3 v 2 EVERTON

Cooke, Givens, Kidd — Royle, Thornton

DECEMBER 1966

Monday 12th

Kick-off 7.30 p.m.

Attendance 6,276

Because the 'A' side were without a game on the intervening Saturday, over half of the youth team were rested for the replay at Old Trafford six days after contesting a poor excuse for a match at Goodison Park. The Blues named an unchanged team whereas United, for what seemed like the umpteenth time, were forced into making a last minute move to replace an injured goalkeeper.

With John Connaughton sustaining a heavy bang on the arm during the game on Merseyside, and through him being nowhere near back to regaining fitness when the rematch rolled around, his absence created an opening for an able understudy in Chesterfield schoolboy Terry Poole.

There was a terrific boost for Brian Kidd on the day of the second instalment when it was announced that he had been chosen to play for an England Youth team who were due to face a Sunderland XI at Roker Park the following week.

In complete contrast to the initial dour encounter between United and Everton, the two sides showed their entertaining face at Old Trafford and those present were left well satisfied by a cracking hour and a half of football which was studded with five goals and plenty of talking points.

A day later, the Liverpool Daily Post remarked on a satisfactory conclusion for the Reds:

In an incident-packed F.A. Youth Cup Second Round Replay at Old Trafford last night, United gained a thrilling 3-2 victory over Everton, who played a handsome part in a fine match.

United just deserved their win, if only for their magnificent first half display, during which they were constantly on the move, scored three goals and might easily have doubled their tally.

Everton fought back with great skill and spirit and had much the better of a more rugged and ragged second half.

Kopel, an outstanding right-back, fashioned the opening for United's first two goals.

In the third minute, his long centre from the right dropped at the feet of Kidd, who slammed the ball home from ten yards.

Seven minutes later, Kopel sent Burns and Gill away and Cooke hammered home another centre, this time from the left.

Everton, inspired by the stylish Whittle at inside-right, and Brindle, an industrious right-half, reduced the lead after 23 minutes through Thornton following a flowing three-man move.

Givens regained United's advantage by stabbing the ball home from close range after neat work by Brough, a constant menace on the right wing, and Gill, on the half-hour.

Some of the sparkle disappeared as the second half progressed and the sides tired in the mud.

Another great goal came eight minutes after the resumption as Everton hit back strongly. Brindle swept through with a superb dribble and left Royle to finish off a splendid move with a fierce drive.

In a match in which the fortunes of both sides ebbed and flowed, the task proved an uphill one for the visitors from the time when the Reds capitalised on their early endeavour.

Kidd twice failed to increase United's lead when the scores stood at 2-1. Firstly, his goal-bound header brought a fine save out of Clarke, and Everton's defence later frustrated Kidd again when another of the striker's attempts was cleared off the line. The Reds' best second half openings ended when Clarke repelled a powerful shot from Givens and later, after Gill found himself dispossessed at the last moment just as a goal appeared the most likely outcome.

Everton were much aggrieved at the final outcome, and they could point to two disallowed goals, both marginal offside decisions, as well as a match-winning save from rookie Poole to deny Joe Royle with just three minutes remaining, as crucial incidents.

Johnny Aston (left) supervises a training session at The Cliff while the club's new indoor facility takes shape in the background

second round replay

1966-67

1966-67

1) Terry Poole	9) Don Givens	1) Ian Bertram	9) David Shaw
2) Frank Kopel	10) Brian Kidd	2) Steve Dunn	10) Frank Worthington
3) David Weir	11) Frank Gill	3) Geoff Spencer	11) Derek Stewart
4) Willie Watson	*12) Mike Fleming*	4) Geoff Hutt	*12) Angus Ferguson ◊*
5) Steve James		5) Ian Halfpenny	
6) Francis Burns		6) Steve Gibson	
7) Ian Brough		7) Bobby Hoy	
8) John Cooke		8) Brendan McGrath	

JANUARY 1967

MANCHESTER UNITED 3 v 0 HUDDERSFIELD TOWN

Burns, Givens (2)

Monday 16th*
Kick-off 7.30 p.m.
Attendance 8,138

third round

UNITED KEEP POOLE IN

It had been a little over ten years since United last met Huddersfield Town in the Youth Cup and on that most uncomfortable of cold and damp nights at Heckmondwike, the Terriers included a skinny forward called Denis Law in their formation. 'King' Denis was, by the early part of 1967, already well on his way to becoming a legend in the eyes of the Old Trafford legions as a direct result of his supreme goalscoring ability and showmanship style of play.

A rather inexperienced Town team arrived in Manchester and there were, no doubt, some United followers in the crowd wondering whether another amongst the visitors' ranks would one day come close to Law's crowd-pleasing flamboyancy and deadly accuracy in front of goal.

With John Connaughton still under treatment, the Reds' line-up remained unchanged from the last round.

There were no frights from Huddersfield à la 1956, United enjoying what was arguably their smoothest ride in the tournament for some years. Just like in the previous game against Everton, they began brightly and, although not enjoying a complete stranglehold in terms of possession, were never at any time faced with the threat of defeat. Neat footwork, excellent passing, intelligent movement and a determined attitude from the United boys kept the Town persistently baffled, bothered and bewildered from the opening whistle to the last.

The gulf in class between the two sides was apparent almost immediately and within the time the Reds took to piece together a few moves, it always looked like a question of just how many goals they would score. At the conclusion of the match, that number appeared quite meagre.

Terriers' goalkeeper Ian Bertram was the busiest boy on view and only the dogged determination of wing-half Geoff Hutt allied to the skill and invention of right-winger Bobby Hoy gave Huddersfield something to cling to.

As soon as the 12th minute, United breached Bertram's goal when Francis Burns neatly controlled a Brian Kidd centre to shoot home powerfully and accurately from a distance of twenty yards.

The Reds then laid siege to Huddersfield's penalty area in search of a two-goal cushion and following numerous near misses the score did eventually enlarge when Don Givens registered after 36 minutes. The goal came about when Frank Gill aimed a corner into the six-yard box and Givens was adjudged to have made the last contact with the ball before it crossed the line. As is usual, there were numerous bodies in and around the goalmouth for the flag kick and one report even suggested that Bertram had been bowled over in mid-air as he attempted to clear the danger.

With their passage now practically assured, the United lads appeared inclined to do only as little as was required and the crowd had to wait until six minutes from the end for the score to change once more. An alert Givens was again the marksman when reacting quickest to another Gill corner in order to register a far less questionable effort than his first. Throughout the whole game, Terry Poole had only needed to deal with one direct shot, by Hoy from quite a distance, and it was with some considerable comfort that the Reds passed into the Fourth Round.

A short match report appeared in the Huddersfield Examiner, part of which read:

Huddersfield Town Juniors were beaten but not disgraced in the Third Round of the F.A. Youth Cup at Old Trafford last evening.

Manchester United, six times winners of the trophy, fielded half a dozen players with Central League experience and their maturity was too big a handicap for the Town youngsters to overcome.

There was also much to admire in the industry of wing-half Geoff Hutt, who had the task of marking the rising United youngster inside-left Brian Kidd.

Ian Bertram in the Huddersfield goal was under constant siege and accomplished many fine saves.

*This game was originally scheduled for Monday, January 9th but was postponed due to a frostbound pitch

Skipper Francis Burns opened the scoring against Huddersfield ....

.... and Don Givens' brace took the score up to 3-0

1) Joe Corrigan	9) Chris Glennon	1) Terry Poole	9) Mike Fleming
2) Tommy Booth	10) Keith Mason	2) Frank Kopel	10) Peter O'Sullivan
3) Ray Hatton	11) Alfie Moss	3) David Weir	11) Brian Kidd
4) Brian Woods	*12) Steve Walker ◊*	4) Willie Watson	*12) Peter Woods*
5) Derek Jeffries		5) Steve James	
6) Stan Bowles		6) Francis Burns	
7) Dave Hoare		7) Don Givens	
8) Bobby Cunliffe		8) John Cooke	

1966-67

MANCHESTER CITY 0 v 3 MANCHESTER UNITED

Cooke, Kidd (2)

FEBRUARY 1967

Wednesday 8th

Kick-off 7.30 p.m.

Attendance 19,111

fourth round

Wedged in-between the Huddersfield tie and yet another Youth Cup visit to Maine Road, a United Youth XI including a couple of over-age additions took on England Youth at Old Trafford. In the Review, Jack Pauline noted the national side approached the game *'in preparation for their forthcoming continental tours'* whereas the Reds used the meeting *'very much with an eye'* on the City clash.

Even though United lost the match 1-0 to a late goal by Everton's Joe Royle, it was significant that the front-line was reshaped at half-time, the initial Reds' line-up consisting of Jimmy Rimmer, Frank Kopel, David Weir, Willie Watson, Steve James, Francis Burns, Don Givens, John Cooke, Mike Fleming, Carlo Sartori and Peter Woods. For the second period Cooke was moved to outside-right, Alan Gowling took over the inside-right shirt and Peter O'Sullivan deputised for Sartori. It was probably due to the performance of the re-jigged offensive formation, allied to the expectation that the Light Blues would provide a much tougher obstacle than Huddersfield, which led to the dropping of Frank Gill and Ian Brough in preference to the incoming Fleming and O'Sullivan for the City Youth Cup clash.

Brian Kidd and Don Givens were placed in the slots vacated by Brough and Gill, while Fleming and O'Sullivan took up the spaces left by the former pair, and those alterations meant that the only person left in the same shirt from the forward-line formation against the Terriers was consistently effective inside-right John Cooke.

On this occasion written by Peter Gardner, the City v. United contest received its normal back page preview in the Manchester Evening News and the periodical made note of the Reds' Lancashire League Division One and Two defeats of 1-0 and 4-1 respectively over the previous weekend:

Manchester City hope to chalk up their first ever F.A. Youth Cup victory over neighbours United in tonight's Fourth Round clash at Maine Road.

Confidence in the City camp could not be higher after last Saturday's double victory when they had wins at 'A' and 'B' level over their more experienced rivals.

Says chief scout Harry Godwin, 'This is a real tonic for our boys and they are convinced they can win tonight. But no matter what happens we know that we have at least got some good young players on our staff.'

United possess more individual stars, but it has been 100 per cent effort and determination that has got City so far in the competition this season – their longest run since reaching the semi-final when they lost a two-legged tie to the Reds who went on to beat Swindon in the final.

The individual ability, plus extra experience of United, can be cancelled out with City having ground advantage, though the big danger man is lanky Brian Kidd, one of the most promising youngsters at Old Trafford at the present time.

It should all add up to a feast of good football for a crowd that is expected to be near the 15,000 mark – weather permitting.

That same reporter was leading with the headline 'WHAT A LET-DOWN CITY!' 24 hours later when the lads from Maine Road again failed to exorcise their United jinx in the Youth Cup. As well as recording that City had *'slipped ingloriously'* out of the tournament, Gardner appeared rather unsporting by claiming *'Manchester United did not have much to crow about either, despite the seemingly overwhelming superiority that a 3-0 score might indicate'.*

Putting aside his usual blue-tinted opinions for a time, Gardner did manage to concede the Reds some praise when stating they *'were a class higher than their neighbours, whose experience, of course, is inferior'* and adding that United *'made intelligent use of the ball while City's stereotyped long ball down the middle rarely troubled the Old Trafford defence'.* He concluded his report by claiming *'When City got a grip in the second half, Terry Poole proved himself a capable goalkeeper while Cooke and hardworking skipper Francis Burns also shone in the better balanced United side'.*

Jack Pauline treated the United Review readers to his usual excellent match summary:

First half chances were strictly limited for both sides but the City defence was split wide open when United went ahead in nineteen minutes. A through ball from Burns was neatly squared by O'Sullivan to find Kidd in the inside-right position with a clear way to goal.

When Corrigan fumbled a cross by Watson, Fleming took the half-chance but shot wide and was then only just off-target with a good header. City looked dangerous with two breakaways, which might have produced the equaliser, but Moss was slow to take a gilt-edged chance and, when equally well-placed, Glennon shot tamely wide.

Just after the interval, a defensive slip let in Cooke, but his shot was saved in great style by Corrigan. The 'keeper also did well to cover a shot from Kidd but must have been relieved to see Fleming hook the ball wide from a good position. The United defence were lucky when Moss hit the ball across the face of goal but failed to find a forward on hand to provide the final touch. A hesitant United defence then let in Mason for what looked the equaliser but Poole made the first of several good saves by diving at the inside-left's feet.

The Reds increased their lead when Cooke beat the offside tactics to race clear and hit a well taken goal. A spell of enthusiastic home pressure gave the United defence some hectic and anxious moments in which Poole was very active. The best of several good saves was when he turned a shot from five yards by Glennon round the post. Playing it cool, the United defence came through this period of sustained attack to take control again in midfield.

The City offside trap repeatedly held up some promising moves but paid the penalty when a through ball from Watson found Kidd unmarked and he had no difficulty in adding a third.

Terry Poole proved an accomplished deputy for John Connaughton, keeping two clean sheets in his three Youth Cup appearances

183

1966-67

1) Derek Forster	9) Billy Hughes	
2) Peter Robinson	10) Albert Brown	
3) Eamon McLaughlan	11) Dennis Tueart	
4) Brian Chambers	12) Unknown	
5) Dick Huntley		
6) Keith Felton		
7) Bernard Fagan		
8) Colin Suggett		

1) John Connaughton	9) Mike Fleming
2) Frank Kopel	10) Peter O'Sullivan
3) David Weir	11) Brian Kidd
4) Willie Watson	12) Ian Brough
5) Steve James	
6) Francis Burns	
7) Don Givens	
8) John Cooke	

MARCH 1967

Wednesday 8th
Kick-off 7.30 p.m.
Attendance 11,011

SUNDERLAND 2 v 1 MANCHESTER UNITED
Brown, Tueart — Watson

fifth round

REDS FADE AT HAPPY HUNTING GROUND...

A semi-final place now beckoned United and barring their way to that treasured spot was a 90-minute liaison with Sunderland at Roker Park. By then, the management seemed much happier in relation to individual performances and the overall composition of the team and so the only change they deemed necessary came about in the goalkeeping position.

Now that John Connaughton was back to full fitness, Terry Poole was forced to give up the gloves despite creating a hugely favourable impression during his three appearances in the tournament. It seemed that a combination of Connaughton's greater know-how, and the tough proposition that the Sunderland fixture seemed to pose, contributed to Poole's enforced stand-down.

Having lost 5-3 on aggregate to Arsenal less than a year ago, the Rokerites' held recent experience of a Youth Cup final in their memory bank, and in conceding home advantage, the visiting Manchester contingent knew full well that nothing except an all-out effort was needed if they were to progress into the last four stage.

The opportunity was there for the Reds to be the first side to book their place in the semi-finals as all of the other quarter-finals had already taken place, every one of them resulting in draws.

A measure of the Reds' task was gauged in the knowledge that Sunderland's Youths topped the Northern Intermediate League by a huge ten-point lead over their nearest rivals. With only seven games remaining in order to fulfil their divisional programme, Sunderland had lost only twice during the entire calendar while scoring 62 goals and conceding only twenty. Top scorers for the Wearsiders in the NIL were Dennis Tueart and Albert Brown, on nine goals apiece, while Colin Suggett could claim eight.

Clearly, United would have their hands full.

On a week of great cup excitement at Roker Park, in which the club's first-team were ready to take on the might of Leeds in the Fifth Round of the F.A. Cup just three days later, the Sunderland Echo gave their readers an insight to the junior contest:

Cup fever continues to mount on Wearside, but, with the intervention of the F.A., the waiting strain has been relieved for Sunderland supporters by the addition of another crowd-pulling cup-tie to the Roker programme.

Relief comes with the staging of the F.A. Youth Cup quarter-final with Manchester United tomorrow night and it is a chance for Roker enthusiasts to let off a little steam.

It is a month since Sunderland and Manchester United qualified for this stage of the competition by beating Preston N.E. and Manchester City respectively. On February 8th, United were unable to agree to the dates suggested by Sunderland so the F.A. stepped in yesterday with a telephoned directive to the Roker club that the game should be played tomorrow night.

The short notice would normally be a greater inconvenience to the visiting side, but it landed Sunderland manager Mr. Ian McColl with a problem, too, for instead of the 'same team' announcement which he had confidently expected to make, he has to reshuffle his attack through injury.

The unlucky player is centre-forward Malcolm Moore, who was on the receiving end of a foul tackle against Newcastle United in a Northern Intermediate League game on Saturday. He has a knee injury which rules out any chance of him playing tomorrow night.

Mr. McColl meets the situation by switching outside-left Billy Hughes into the middle and bringing in sixteen year-old Dennis Tueart for a Youth Cup debut on the left wing.

From outside-left to centre-forward is no new experience in the Hughes family. Big brother John, of Celtic and Scotland fame, has been an outstanding success in both positions at representative level and young Billy will probably welcome the chance to prove that, with his flair for goalscoring, he can be just as effective in the middle.

Otherwise, the side will be unchanged from that which accounted for Preston N.E. and Hartlepool United in the previous rounds.

Colin Todd, who played in the 4-0 win over Newcastle United in the Second Round, is still eligible, of course, but is now an established first-team player and his replacement, Brian Chambers, who was one of the big successes in the win over Preston, will continue at right-half.

At the conclusion of the evening's play, Sunderland were celebrating both a place in the semi-final in addition to ending United's lengthy superiority over them in the competition, a run which consisted of nine previous contests and stretched way back to December 1955.

The Sunderland Echo provided graphic details of United's downfall:

Sunderland Claim First Youth Cup Win Over United

SUNDERLAND qualified for the semi-final of the F.A. Youth Cup for the third successive year by beating Manchester United 2—1 at Roker Park last night. This was their first-ever win over United's juniors, whom they were meeting for the eighth time in this competition.

It was a hard game all the way, with the more attractive flow of football reserved for the second half after a first half in which courage was the vital quality.

Errors and uncertainty in defence, which often had Sunderland players impeding each other, enabled United to look the more dangerous in the early stages. Forster made two excellent saves and determined work by Robinson, well supported by Fagan, imposed a brake upon outside left Kidd, who has been United's match-winner in the competition so far.

Kidd lost much of his power after being injured in a tackle by Robinson and then, in the bounce up which followed, another tackle by Fagan.

Hughes was already limping when Brown was injured in blocking a drive by Cooke two minutes before half-time and the goal-less half ended without Sunderland having shaped like winners.

INSPIRATION

Just five minutes into the second half, however, Sunderland gained inspiration from a great goal and stepped up their game immediately.

Quick-thinking Suggett forced the break after being fouled by James on the left wing. The referee was still signalling the free-kick when Suggett pushed a square pass just outside the penalty area and had to give Tueart a shout to let him know the ball was there. The 16 year-old winger moved on to it ahead of two defenders to hit a right foot drive which curled just inside the far post.

United came back in the 63rd minute when O'Sullivan, taking a right wing corner, hit the ball hard and low out to the edge of the penalty area, where Watson placed it through the crowded goalmouth to leave unsighted Forster helpless.

Two minutes later Sunderland were claiming the match-winning goal. Suggett floated over a long centre from the right wing and Tueart, making a lot of ground to reach the ball outside the far post, could only head it up. But Brown performed the astonishing feat of breasting it down quickly on the run and slamming a right-foot shot which flashed just under the bar.

Tueart, who is still at school in Newcastle, made an exciting debut in Youth Cup football, but the player who came through this exhausting battle with the greatest credit was centre half Huntley, who was particularly strong in the air.

Suggett, an inspiring skipper, was well supported by Brown in keeping the attack moving smoothly, while Felton's midfield work was of a high standard.

184

1966-67

MARCH 1967

Reflecting on the team's performance in the Review, Jack Pauline felt that *'failure to take chances and defensive slackness'* were the Reds' major shortcomings. The astute Mr. Pauline nominated the swiftly executed set piece which led to Sunderland's winner with the description of *'the oldest trick in the book'*, and he went on to pencil his version of the team's exit thus:

The home 'keeper was soon in action in this game, making a tremendous save in the first minute when a high cross beat the defence to leave Kidd with the goal at his mercy, then smartly collecting a header by Givens. The latter then headed over from a well-placed Weir free kick. The United defence had a let-off in the opening period when a loose ball broke for Brown but, with an open goal, he shot past the post.

Sunderland had an even larger slice of luck when Forster dropped the ball on the edge of the penalty area, but Fleming and Kidd failed to connect properly in a shot at the untenanted goal.

Whilst the home side had only one scoring effort in the remainder of the first half – a long range shot from Hughes following a particularly good move – United had two easier chances which might have produced the all-important first goal. Both fell to Cooke. First, when he surprised Forster with a first-time shot which the latter just turned round the post, then after a good run he sliced his shot wide of the post.

A quickly taken free kick five minutes after the interval caught the United defence flat-footed and Tueart beat Connaughton with a shot from the edge of the box. This gave Sunderland the initiative for a time, although they still produced little in the way of finishing effort. Back in the game United had two further chances, Kidd just failing to connect with a Fleming centre and Cooke with only the 'keeper to beat fired wildly over the bar. The equaliser came after 63 minutes when an O'Sullivan corner was allowed to run through for Watson to shoot through a crowd of players into the corner of the net.

The tonic effect of this overdue goal was not allowed to materialise by the home side who restored their advantage within two minutes when Brown gained possession after some very casual defensive play. Despite narrow escapes when the ball was twice scrambled off their goal-line, United did most of the attacking in the later stages but met a resolute and tight defence which had the semi-final in its sights. Givens had a great chance to force a replay, but he headed wide from a good centre by Cooke and, in the last minute, Watson moved in for what could have been a replica of his earlier goal but his half-hit shot went straight to the 'keeper.

It was the end of the road for United, even though there was still some distance yet to travel for their conquerors. In making up for the disappointment of the previous year, the Wearsiders eased into the final where they met Birmingham City and on a 2-0 aggregate they deservedly took the Youth Cup to Roker Park at last.

fifth round

Seen on the far right, coach Johnny Aston lines up alongside United's 1966/67 youth squad
Back row (l-r) Brian Kidd, Steve James, Bob Loftus, Jimmy Rimmer, Steve Lang, Don Givens, Ian Brough, John Connaughton, Ken Goodeve, Willie Watson, Johnny Aston jnr., Wayne Emmerson
Front row (l-r) Francis Burns, John Cooke, David Weir, Frank Gill, Frank Kopel, Peter O'Sullivan, Peter Woods, Mike Fleming, Carlo Sartori

1967-68

1) John Connaughton
2) Ken Goodeve
3) David Weir
4) Willie Watson
5) Steve James
6) Bob Loftus
7) Ian McMurdo
8) Peter O'Sullivan
9) Jimmy Hall
10) Peter Woods
11) Mike Kelly
12) Laurie Millerchip

1) Ian Bertram
2) Alan Jones
3) David Brown
4) Terry Larkin
5) Geoff Hutt
6) Garry Tolson
7) Ray McHale
8) Bobby Hoy
9) Brian Mahoney
10) Paul Maloney
11) Graham Mowbray
12) Geoff Hall (for 9)

DECEMBER 1967

MANCHESTER UNITED 2 v 0 HUDDERSFIELD TOWN

Hall, James

Monday 4th

Kick-off 7.30 p.m.

Attendance 4,889

second round

As had become tradition over the past fifteen years, a new Youth Cup campaign seemed an apt time to take stock of the progress achieved by those of United's club staff who had recently taken part in the competition. In late 1967, an Englishman, Steve James, a Welshman, Peter O'Sullivan, and two Scots, David Weir and Willie Watson, were making at least some inroads onto the Central League scene while a few of the others saw their credentials revealed in an Evening News article:

Manchester United have five newcomers in their team to play Huddersfield Town in the Second Round of the F.A. Youth Cup at Old Trafford tonight.

They include three youngsters who played for Manchester and Lancashire schoolboys, full-back Ken Goodeve, left-half Bob Loftus and outside-right Ian McMurdo.

Also new to Youth Cup football is centre-forward Jimmy Hall, a former Irish international schoolboy, and Mike Kelly, an eighteen year-old left-winger signed after playing with rugby-minded Blackrock College in Dublin.

An ex-starlet of Cheshire Boys who hailed from just down the road in Sale, Peter Woods was also brought into the side after featuring as an unused substitute against Manchester City during the previous season while nominated for bench duty for the Terriers' visit was Laurie Millerchip, a defender recently of Nuneaton Boys whose honours included five international caps. Woods was by then a regular in United's Lancashire League Division One affairs whereas Millerchip began the season in the 'B' team only to gain promotion to the 'A' side on three occasions alongside his more experienced colleague.

United inside-left Peter Woods, who could consider himself unlucky not to score against Huddersfield

The newly-introduced personnel were mainly in the forward-line, their inclusion meaning that only O'Sullivan was equipped with prior Youth Cup knowledge. However, the side still contained four others whose experience was likely to be a key factor in their search for progress and it was generally expected that the Reds would be presented with fewer problems at the back and in the midfield area rather than with their offensive capabilities.

Watson, whose 18th birthday coincided with the Youth Cup match, had only recently recovered from a broken leg suffered during a close season fixture in the Blue Stars youth tournament and United's right-half ended the Huddersfield game in some obvious discomfort through a knock sustained late in the game. Despite the Reds winning, fortunately with no other significant injury worries, observers weren't slow to point out that the success didn't come quite so easily as their victory over the Terriers back in January.

The United Review chronicled the match highlights, which included a first goal in the 17th minute:

Always looking the more dangerous in attack, United twice hit the woodwork before a well headed goal by James from a Goodeve cross put them ahead. This was followed eight minutes later by a similar effort from Hall, who timed a Watson centre perfectly.

Despite some neat methodical midfield football, Huddersfield carried little threat near goal. Apart from a good shot by Hoy which was calmly collected by Connaughton, their best scoring chance came when a free kick caused a scramble in the United goal area. Connaughton finally dived on the loose ball to avert the danger.

The visitors opened the second half in more determined fashion and after Mahoney had fluffed an easy chance from close range, a good shot from Larkin brought out the best in Connaughton. With United regaining command, a neat hook by Woods from a McMurdo centre was cleverly taken by Bertram to be followed by an equally good save from another Woods effort.

The 'keeper was beaten by a Watson short centre but quickly recovered to save from Hall at three-yards range. He was lucky to see a shot from Woods which had him well beaten crash against the post.

The local newspaper also produced a brief summary of the evening's events and it contained a few words of advice:

> MANCHESTER UNITED accounted for Huddersfield Town comfortably enough in the FA Youth Cup second round at Old Trafford.
>
> But the young Reds will have to find more poise and care if they are to recapture the trophy last won for the club by Bobby Noble's team in 1964.
>
> Perhaps it will come when the five newcomers in the side, including the promising inside-forward Peter O'Sullivan, have blended better with the more experienced players like Willie Watson, who finished this match limping.
>
> First-half goals by Steve James, the centre half, and centre forward Jimmy Hall, gave United a 2-0 win and set them on the way to a repeat of last season's Youth Cup win over Huddersfield.

1) John Connaughton
2) Ken Goodeve
3) David Weir
4) Willie Watson
5) Steve James
6) Bob Loftus
7) Ian McMurdo
8) Peter O'Sullivan
9) Jimmy Hall
10) Peter Woods
11) Mike Kelly
12) Mel Simmonds (for 10)

1) David Johnson
2) Paul Brown
3) Billy Kay
4) Alan Fish
5) John McNicholas
6) Gordon Masson
7) Gordon Fisher
8) Martin Dunkerley
9) John Hughes
10) Dennis Wann
11) Eric Potts
12) Steve Wojciechowicz (for 6)

MANCHESTER UNITED 4 v 0 BLACKPOOL

Hall, McMurdo, Woods (2)

JANUARY 1968

Monday 8th

Kick-off 7.30 p.m.

Attendance 4,795

YOUNG REDS POINT WAY TO FUTURE

Defeating Huddersfield was a useful starting point in United's latest attempt to recapture the Youth Cup, especially for the newer lads, and it resulted in them being drawn at home to the under-18 side of Second Division Blackpool at the next stage, a game previewed by the Blackpool Evening Gazette:

Blackpool's youngsters, who have created quite a reputation for themselves in the F.A. Youth Cup this season with emphatic victories over Gleneagles and Blackburn Rovers, face their toughest test in the competition so far when they line up against Manchester United in the Third Round at Old Trafford tonight.

For United, one of England's wealthiest clubs, have always had a large pool of talented youngsters and will field a strong side which will test the Blackpool boys to the utmost in their first away tie in the competition so far.

But the Blackpool boys, who convincingly beat a Blackburn side which looked strong, will go into tonight's game without any feeling of inferiority.

One of them said, 'We are looking forward immensely to playing on Old Trafford. In fact, it is a very good draw for us.'

Blackpool will be unchanged from the Second Round, fielding a side comprised of two apprentice professionals, strong-tackling right-back Paul Brown and clever inside-left Dennis Wann, and nine amateurs.

The strength and finishing power in the middle of the attack is supplied by Welsh teenager John Hughes, who has scored in both previous rounds. Skill and speed is provided on the wing by Gordon Fisher and Eric Potts. Blackpool also have a solid half-back line.

Manchester United, who have won the trophy six times since the competition began in 1953, field an unchanged team.

Youngest member of the side is Jimmy Hall, from Northern Ireland, who is sixteen.

The gulf in resources between Blackpool and their hosts was epitomised by United's choice of substitute because, for the second time in a row, the Reds were afforded the luxury of holding an international on the sidelines. Even though he had been capped six times for England Boys, Reading youngster Mel Simmonds, an accomplished half-back whose progress extended to him already making a couple of appearances for the 'A' team, could nevertheless only make the bench.

On paper at least, it appeared that the Seasiders held little hope of securing any positive type of result, and with just their custodian and some wayward shooting standing between them and a cricket score, Jack Pauline was on hand to record the salient events for the Review:

It took United 38 minutes to open their account but for most of this time they were buzzing around the Blackpool goal. Too often the finishing shot went straight to Johnson in the visitors' goal, although the 'keeper on occasion found the hard ground a useful ally.

He could have known little about a header from James into the top angle which he managed to turn round the post, then was lucky to see the ball scrambled off the line from the resulting corner.

Blackpool's first serious attack came on the half hour but it offered little threat and with the resumption of the United pressure, Johnson made great saves from Hall and James, then saw the ball again kicked off the line. When the visitors forced only their second corner it led indirectly to United taking the lead. Gaining possession from the clearance, Hall cleverly pushed the ball inside the back for McMurdo to move in and hit a great goal.

Blackpool went straight to the attack with a chance to draw level but only a weak shot straight at Connaughton by Potts came from a free kick on the edge of the box and a corner. Right on the interval Woods was put through by Watson to hit a good shot in off the foot of the post.

There was no let up in the United pressure on the resumption and after 59 minutes Woods hit a well taken goal then had a great chance to make it a hat-trick when he burst clear of the defence only to slice his shot past the post.

It was all United from this point and Johnson dealt capably with shots from Hall, Watson and Kelly but he was well beaten by a shot from the latter which crashed against the post. Twelve minutes from time, Hall rounded off the scoring when he had a good header stopped on the line but recovered quickly to force the ball home.

On a pitch which was partially frozen, a little bumpy and proved a nuisance for both sides, the away team escaped further punishment on numerous occasions because the Reds were wasteful in front of goal time and again. The Blackpool Gazette was realistic in its assessment when remarking 'the Seasiders were outclassed in every department and it was only poor finishing by the United forwards which prevented a rout'.

The Gazette's reporter also noted that *'with one minute left in this F.A. Youth Cup Third Round match, Manchester-born Martin Dunkerley almost got a goal for Blackpool with a low drive from close range, which went just wide of a United post. The effort brought an ironic cheer from the 4,795 spectators because it was the nearest that Blackpool had been to scoring. It just about summed up this one-sided tie'.*

In his report for the Evening News, David Meek expressed a view that *'United's current crop of youngsters are not rated quite as highly as some of the elite youth teams produced over the years at Old Trafford'.* Also dropping a hint that the youths might be able to mount a serious challenge to reclaim the coveted silverware, Meek expressed an opinion about the side *'knitting together with much improved team work and a thrust for goals'* before ending his piece by claiming they *'could finish up surprising us'.*

Seen here in one of his England caps and shirt, Mel Simmonds became United's first ever used substitute in the Youth Cup when going on for two-goal Peter Woods in the last half-hour of the win over Blackpool

third round

1967-68

1967-68

1) John Connaughton	9) Jimmy Hall	1) Gerry McEvoy	9) Willie Brown
2) Ken Goodeve	10) Peter Woods	2) Peter Jones	10) Dave Thomas
3) David Weir	11) Mike Kelly	3) John Heath	11) Steve Kindon
4) Willie Watson	*12) Laurie Millerchip*	4) Mick Docherty	*12) Eddie Cliff*
5) Steve James		5) Wilf Wrigley	
6) Bob Loftus		6) Alan West	
7) Ian McMurdo		7) David Hartley	
8) Peter O'Sullivan		8) Eric Probert	

FEBRUARY 1968

MANCHESTER UNITED 0 v 0 BURNLEY

Monday 12th*
Kick-off 7.30 p.m.
Attendance 5,965

fourth round

IT LOOKS TOUGH FOR THE YOUNG REDS NOW

A continued spell of wintry weather around the UK coincided with a draw which gave the Reds their third home tie of the season, on this occasion against Burnley and as so frequently happens in football, it corresponded with both of United's junior sides facing the Clarets over the weekend just gone. Because most of the youth squad were rested for the Monday night clash, the reinforcements showed their mettle when the 'A' team fought out a creditable 3-3 draw while the 'B' side proved too strong in their match at Padiham and ran riot to record a 6-0 victory.

The Clarets were, of course, making their first trip to Old Trafford for a Youth Cup game, although the two clubs did meet at The Cliff way back in 1956 and at Turf Moor a year later.

The original date for the 1968 clash was delayed by a week, the reasons for which were detailed in the Burnley Express & News:

Burnley youth team arrived at Old Trafford last night for their F.A. Youth Cup Fourth Round tie against Manchester United - and found that the game had been postponed because the pitch was unfit for play.

It was thought to be playable when Burnley's youngsters left Turf Moor but Manchester's first snow for several days left the surface treacherous as the snow was thawing as it fell and there were pools of water down the centre of the field, and also patches of ice underneath.

Match referee Roy Harper travelled from Sheffield and inspected the pitch with Manchester United manager, Mr. Matt Busby.

Mr. Harper said, 'Unfortunately the pitch is not playable. The snow which has fallen in the last couple of hours has made it too dangerous and I have had to call it off. Apparently, when a local referee inspected it earlier in the day, prospects seemed fairly good and that is why Burnley made the journey.'

That spell of bad weather not only resulted in the Youth Cup match being delayed, it also cost Burnley winger Steve Kindon an international cap. Soon after the Old Trafford postponement, Kindon made his way home to Warrington having received a late call-up for England's Youth team, who were due to meet Eire Youth 48 hours later. Unfortunately, the following day's heavy snowfall meant that his train back to Manchester was delayed, and he subsequently missed a connection to London from where he was due to catch a flight to Dublin. Utterly disconsolate, Kindon was left with no choice other than to track back to base.

United's Mike Kelly was infinitely luckier as he managed to make the plane over to Dublin and it allowed him to put in an appearance for Eire Youth in a 0-0 draw with their English opponents at Dalymount Park.

There was a reprieve for United full-back Ken Goodeve due to the postponement because he had been suspended for seven days for striking an opponent in a junior game against Blackburn, a contest in which one of the Rovers' team was dismissed as a result of the same incident. Laurie Millerchip gained the nod to replace him for the original game, but by the time the tie was rearranged Goodeve's ban was spent.

It seemed likely that Goodeve would be in for a busy night on United's right flank because, not only was he directly up against the flying Kindon, just inside the Burnley left winger was Dave Thomas, a highly rated England Youth international who had already made three appearances in the club's senior side.

The Burnley Express & News had much to say about a perfectly palatable performance from both participants:

Led by an inspirational skipper in seventeen year-old Mick Docherty, Burnley played superbly and with great spirit at Old Trafford last night to earn a draw deservedly in the Fourth Round of the F.A. Youth Cup against Manchester United, six times winners of the competition.

The stocky, go-ahead Docherty was the king-pin of an impressive, hard-working Burnley side although this draw, which means a Turf Moor replay, was a triumph of team enterprise and effort.

It is rather unfair to single out individually but special mention must be made of a faultless display by Gerry McEvoy, one of only two amateurs in the Burnley side, and Burnley had another key man in Dave Thomas, whose skill in midfield and in prompting attacks was an important ingredient in the result.

Although McEvoy made two fabulous saves in the opening minutes, Burnley more than held their own in a keenly contested first half which kept the crowd on its toes.

McEvoy dived at the feet of Hall to cover a goal chance and a minute later amazed onlookers by hurling himself across goal to make an incredible save from a 25-yard piledriver by right-half Watson.

United have a tremendous record in the Youth Cup but if they thought they were going to have things all their own way they were soon proved wrong. If anything Burnley were the more dangerous looking outfit in the first 45 minutes with skipper Docherty a general and an inspiration and with the left-wing pair of Thomas and Kindon a real menace to United.

The nearest Burnley came to scoring before the interval was in the 43rd minute when after a through pass from Probert, Kindon used his speed to squeeze between two defenders in the penalty area and was only thwarted by a desperate dive from the goalkeeper. A minute later, after a brilliant link up between Kindon and Thomas, Probert sent in a header which goalkeeper Connaughton did well to save.

The interval arrived with no goals but it had been an exciting first half and every credit was due to young Docherty (watched by his famous father) and his team.

Early in the second half of this enthralling match, Burnley seemed certain to score what would have been a deserved goal. Centre-forward Brown accelerated past three defenders and hit the advancing goalkeeper with a hard, low drive.

Both defences were well organised and Docherty continued to be an inspiration for the lively young Clarets. He did well to stop Hall as the centre-forward moved into the danger area and then McEvoy produced another terrific one-handed save from a free-kick by O'Sullivan.

These teams were fairly matched and after surviving a spell of United pressure, Burnley zipped into attack down the left with Kindon, like Hartley, a smart winger, rounding two defenders and moving in only to finish off the move without his usual sting. His opposite number, Kelly, was easily the most menacing United forward and after he had twice put Burnley's defence in difficulty, Kindon struck again with a low cross which Brown very nearly diverted into the net.

But undoubtedly a draw was the fairest possible outcome to a splendid tie and now the teams must meet again to decide which one visits Sheffield United in the quarter-final.

The result caused the Reds' regular correspondent David Meek to cast a doubt over their chances for the rematch:

Burnley must start favourites when the F.A. Youth Cup Fourth Round with Manchester United is replayed at Turf Moor. Ground advantage will point their way after forcing a goalless draw at Old Trafford.

But it seemed to me there was very little difference between these two teams and the result could still go either way.

In fact, victory could hang on which goalkeeper makes the first mistake, so well matched are two dominant defences. John Connaughton for United and Gerry McEvoy for Burnley both made a series of excellent saves with winger Mike Kelly the Reds' hardest-shooting forward and inside-left David Thomas the visitors' outstanding player.

Both teams showed skilful touches, but fierce tackling and tremendous endeavour prevented either side taking a real grip on the game.

United came strongly in the last quarter of an hour to raise Red hopes that they might yet upset the odds at Turf Moor.

*This game was originally scheduled for Monday, February 5th but was postponed due to ice and water on the pitch

188

1967-68

1) Gerry McEvoy	9) Willie Brown	1) John Connaughton	9) Jimmy Hall
2) Peter Jones	10) Dave Thomas	2) Ken Goodeve	10) Peter Woods
3) Eddie Cliff	11) Steve Kindon	3) David Weir	11) Mike Kelly
4) Mick Docherty	*12) Pat Dooney*	4) Willie Watson	*12) Laurie Millerchip*
5) Wilf Wrigley		5) Steve James	
6) Alan West		6) Bob Loftus	
7) David Hartley		7) Ian McMurdo	
8) Eric Probert		8) Peter O'Sullivan	

BURNLEY 2 v 1 MANCHESTER UNITED

Brown, Hartley — Hall

FEBRUARY 1968

fourth round replay

Tuesday 20th

Kick-off 7.30 p.m.

Attendance 5,126

Sandwiched between the Old Trafford stalemate and the replay, Burnley's senior side took two points from United at Turf Moor, an outcome which caused the local newspaper to pose the question 'CAN YOUNG CLARETS WIN AND MAKE IT A UNIQUE DOUBLE?' as an introductory headline to their Youth Cup match preview:

Following Saturday's great win, Burnley can complete a unique double tonight by defeating Manchester United again, this time in an F.A. Youth Cup Fourth Round replay at Turf Moor. The teams played a goalless draw at Old Trafford last week and the young Clarets have a splendid chance of reaching the quarter-final for the first time.

Manager Harry Potts, jubilant yesterday about the performance of the seniors against the champions, said that the team for tonight's match would be chosen from the same twelve which were on duty at Old Trafford.

United will also have a similar team on duty to that which played in the enthralling first meeting and these sides are so well matched that a tense, tight game is expected. The Burnley youngsters played so well together last week under the captaincy of Mick Docherty that they deserve a good turn out of support tonight and those going to the game are reminded that Central League prices and admittance arrangements will apply.

The conclusion in North-East Lancashire didn't go according to plan from United's perspective and their aspirations of reaching the quarter-finals weren't aided by a moment of indiscipline from Mike Kelly, Burnley's chief tormentor at Old Trafford. Despite losing Kelly when he was ordered off for an early bath, the Reds performed heroically for over an hour of normal time before tumbling out of the cup in the minutes added on for stoppages.

The Burnley Express & News gave its views on the evening's events:

Burnley's first-team have no chance of honours this season. It's all rather sad. But the Turf Moor juniors can salvage some glory for the club by continuing to do well, and perhaps even winning, the F.A. Youth Cup.

They must be fancied to make further progress. The way they won a Fourth Round replay, to add the scalp of six-time winners Manchester United to that of Manchester City, was most impressive and the young Clarets now travel to Sheffield United in the quarter-final.

The quarter-final draw is Sheffield United v. Burnley, Everton v. Sunderland, Chelsea v. Crystal Palace or Charlton, Aldershot or Cardiff v. Coventry or Oxford.

Few of the 5,126 crowd who saw Tuesday's exciting game will dispute that Burnley must have as good a chance as any other team, although Everton, Sheffield United and Charlton are also said to have very strong youth squads.

No doubt about it – the Clarets have never had a better all-round Youth Cup side. They showed again, in defeating United 2-1, that they have a real captain in Mick Docherty, another strong wing-half in Alan West, from Stalybridge, and a superb left-wing pair in David Thomas and the phenomenally fast Stephen Kindon. If these boys don't make the grade, who can we expect will do?

Tuesday's win, though, was, like the success of the seniors by the same score three days earlier, a triumph of team effort. And while Burnley's defence had a fairly quiet night, it must not be forgotten that lads like goalkeeper Gerry McEvoy, right-back Peter Jones and centre-half Wilf Wrigley played key roles in earning the replay at Old Trafford last week.

Tuesday's second meeting was one-sided after an unfortunate incident in the 23rd minute. Mike Kelly, United's best forward in the first match, was sent off for throwing a punch at Jones. True enough, United took the lead nine minutes later with a smart header from Hall, but after that, and particularly in the second half, it was one-way traffic towards the Manchester goal.

For a long time it looked as though United might hold on. Despite Burnley's terrific enthusiasm United's powerful, packed defence kept throwing back raids and whenever the Clarets found a gap in the nine-man wall, goalkeeper Connaughton kept his goal intact. He made one great save from Docherty and, like the rest of the United defence, was especially sound in the air.

But the speed, power and determination of this fine prospect, Kindon, finally prised a way through. In the 77th minute the Warrington lad produced an amazing burst of speed to stop a ball that seemed to be running out and in the same movement swept over a centre which Brown headed in. Then, after Brown and Cliff had both gone near, and with only seconds remaining, Kindon struck again.

In a swerving run which had the crowd, as well as United, spellbound, he beat three defenders for Brown to take the ball on and it fell nicely for Hartley to score from close in.

Jack Pauline sounded sore when writing that United '*did not meet with the best of fortune*', and he went on to complain about '*a couple of late scoring chances at Old Trafford in the first meeting*' which '*could have made the journey to Turf Moor unnecessary*'.

A short Manchester Evening News article summarised the Reds' fate:

Manchester United youth team paid dearly for one rash action from winger Mike Kelly, who was sent off after 23 minutes in the Fourth Round Youth Cup replay at Burnley.

For almost three-quarters of the game, United had to struggle against the disadvantage of having a man short. But they never threw in the towel and even took the lead through centre-forward Jim Hall.

Burnley battered them non-stop, but United held out for 45 minutes until Brown equalised, and in injury-time Hartley got the winner. Had United not missed chances early on when they looked every bit as good as Burnley, things would certainly have been very different.

Goalkeeper Connaughton and half-backs Watson and James played magnificently in United's hard-pressed defence and, indeed, the whole side were to be praised for the way they played against the odds.

There was certainly no disgrace in losing at Turf Moor as the multi-talented Burnley side continued to blossom all the way to a Youth Cup final in which they defeated Coventry by three goals to two on aggregate.

At the end of an historic season for the club, Manchester United became the first English representatives to win the European Cup by defeating Benfica 4-1 at Wembley Stadium. Ten years after the Munich air crash, Matt Busby had reassembled a team good enough to beat the best that Europe could offer.

Included in United's side were no less than eight players, Shay Brennan, Nobby Stiles, Bill Foulkes, George Best, Brian Kidd, Bobby Charlton, David Sadler and John Aston, all of whom were graduates of the Old Trafford production system, as was substitute goalkeeper Jimmy Rimmer. Of the nine mentioned, all except Bill Foulkes had participated in the Youth Cup on the Reds' behalf.

It was a fantastic testament to Busby's continued belief that an efficient and vibrant youth set-up was central to the club's well-being. The defeat of the Portuguese giants wasn't only the pinnacle of the great man's career, it also stands as the high watermark of Manchester United's success during a memorable phase of their history.

Mike Kelly's dismissal severely compromised United's chances at Turf Moor

189

SARTORI, Carlo Domenico (1965/66)

Born: Caderzone, Italy, 10th February 1948
Height: 5ft. 7ins., **Weight:** 10st. 5lbs.
Role: Inside-right
Career: St. Malachy's School (Collyhurst)/ Manchester Boys/ Lancashire Boys/ UNITED: Am. July 1963 Pro. February 1965/ **Bologna** (It) February 1973/ **Spal** (It) July 1974 to June 1976/ **Benevento** (It) (L) December 1975 to May 1976/ **Calcio Lecce 1912** (It) July 1976/ **Rimini** (It) July 1979/ **Trento** (It) July 1982 to June 1984

With a population of less than 500 people, job prospects after the Second World War were limited in the small Italian valley town of Caderzone, 30 miles north of Trento, where nearly everyone was employed on the land. Many of the locals held visions of a better life elsewhere, leaving the area for the lure of America, Australia or Great Britain, and when Carlo and his twin sister were born in the winter of 1948, their parents had already considered moving away from the region. Tragically, the baby girl died at birth, so it was with a total of three boys and one girl that Mr. and Mrs. Sartori emigrated to England ten months later.

The family set up home at Blossom Street in Ancoats, an area which was known locally as the 'Italian Ghetto'. Luckily, the respectable and hard working family weren't there too long as, by the time Carlo was two, they were living on a newly developed council estate in Collyhurst where their experience was put to good use by establishing a thriving knife sharpening business.

There was obviously something in the air in that part of Manchester as far as the development of footballers was concerned, because Nobby Stiles and Brian Kidd attended St. Patrick's School in Livesey Street while the young Sartori went to St. Malachy's in Eggington Street, just half a mile up the road. He played for his school side from the age of eight and assisted them to victory in various local competitions.

Sometime in the 1961/62 season he attended trials for North Manchester and was also selected for the Manchester Boys under-14 team only to come under the watchful eye of a Mr. Whetton. Conspicuous by his short red hair, he was as enthusiastic as a Jack Russell on rabbit duty, seemingly full of restless energy and attacking instincts. He excelled as an inside-forward for the Manchester under-15's during their 1962/63 campaign and was then selected for Lancashire Boys in the same term.

Heavyweights such as Everton, Burnley and West Brom had noted his name, and following a trial with the latter he was invited to take a look around Manchester City's facilities. His older brothers were both City fans and they had taken him to Maine Road many times, therefore it was highly tempting to commit to a club that his boyhood idol Denis Law had once starred for.

He revealed, 'On my last day at school, a teacher informed me that 'Mr. Joe Armstrong from Manchester United is coming to your house to see you' and he arrived on the number 112 bus from Old Trafford. He had a cup of tea with my mum and we then took the bus back to the ground where I was introduced to some of the players, including Denis.' After experiencing what he called 'the Manchester United way', Sartori felt that 'it was the place to be' but, because he was helping out in the family firm at the same time, he didn't take up an apprenticeship and instead penned amateur forms.

Missing from the opening weeks of the 1963/64 season, his debut for the 'B' team on the 14th September concluded in a 2-0 defeat at Rochdale. He then started to suffer severe discomfort with muscle spasms in his back and as a consequence was required to sit out the next three months. His return was marked by scoring half a dozen goals in as many games, including a hat-trick in a 9-0 home thrashing of Manchester City. Supporting the Light Blues didn't prevent him from turning in a superb performance against them and he continued his progress by featuring in the 'B' side for the remainder of the term.

His journey through the following campaign was similar to the previous one as he missed the first few games before becoming prevalent in the 'B' team again, finding the net with some regularity from either of the inside-forward positions, and by the halfway mark of the season he had scored seven goals in ten starts. Signing as a professional on his 17th birthday in February 1965, over the second half of the term he turned out on half a dozen occasions for the 'A' team. As activities drew to a close, the coaching staff moved him into the half-back line, a role he would later assume for the first-team.

After the 'B' side helped themselves to the Lancashire League title, he was selected as one of the youth squad who travelled to Zurich for the Blue Stars tournament in late May. Despite sitting out the final, nevertheless he was delighted to see the Reds record a 2-1 victory over Bologna of Italy. Little did he know that in eight years time he would be swapping the red shirt of United for the red and blue stripes of their continental opponents.

Pleasantly surprised to find himself involved with the Reserves for the opening day fixture of the 1965/66 campaign at Wolves, he kept his place in the side for the following home match against West Brom before dropping back down a grade.

In amongst the goals as United defeated Blackburn 7-2 to win the home leg of the Supplementary Cup in November, the following month finally saw him involved in the Youth Cup. Sartori had missed out a year previously because he was considered small in comparison with his peers, but he relished his chance when it came as the Reds hammered Manchester City 5-0. It was a significant event in the club's history as, along with Wayne Emmerson in the same match, they became the first overseas born players to feature for United in the competition. The Reds were then eliminated by Liverpool in the following round, an unwanted development that ended his brief association with the tournament.

By February 1966 he had started to appear in the Reserves once again and following his hat-trick for the 'A' team in a 4-2 win at Bury in mid-March, he was given a decent run in the second string. Maintaining a place in the side throughout the 1966/67 season when appearing either at inside-forward or half-back, with David Herd and Denis Law firing on all cylinders as United raced towards the First Division title, it was accepted that he still had some distance to go to reach first-team standard.

The 1967/68 term was a virtual replica of the previous one as he was a mainstay of the Reserves when they ended in second place in the Central League. With nine goals in nineteen games to his name, Sartori was delighted to be named as substitute for a senior match at Newcastle in December. He wasn't needed, although the experience of travelling with the squad and the realisation that he was in Matt Busby's thoughts buoyed him.

After five years spent learning his trade, the beginning of 1968/69 season saw him in an optimistic frame of mind. Having matured significantly and now much stronger physically, which meant that he was better equipped to deal with the demands of top-flight football, in early October he put on a dazzling display and scored twice in a 5-0 Lancashire Senior Cup home victory over Netherfield in front of the ever watchful Busby.

Two days later he was entrusted with the number twelve jersey for the seniors' trip to Spurs. When Francis Burns left the field with a cartilage problem he was introduced to the rigours of the Football League in a 2-2 draw and on the following Saturday his first full start at Liverpool was as a replacement for George Best.

Some of the playing personnel were withdrawn from the game at Anfield in preparation for the forthcoming midweek return match with Estudiantes in the World Club Championship and he was gobsmacked to discover that he had been named as the substitute for the crucial home clash. Just before half-time, Denis Law picked up an injury and he was thrown into the action, accounting for himself admirably in a 1-1 draw which saw the Argentinians head off with the trophy. He was then involved in most senior activities through to February, featuring in a further fourteen games, and also came by a Lancashire Senior Cup medal when Liverpool were defeated 1-0 in the final.

Following those marvellous experiences he was keen to push for a regular first-team place in the 1969/70 season, although with the Reds struggling in the league he was never able to ratchet down a spot in the side. Law was on the treatment table for much of the time and manager Wilf McGuinness experimented with the likes of Don Givens, Alan Gowling and Sartori on occasions but usually preferred to rely on experience. Nevertheless, he still turned out in seventeen league games and most of the knock-out matches as United reached the F.A. Cup and League Cup semi-finals, and at the end of the proceedings he was taken on a senior tour for the first time when the Reds visited Bermuda and North America.

With United again displaying dismal league form during the 1970/71 campaign he featured in only eight games, five of them from the bench. It was now obvious that he wasn't going to be given a decent run in the team, although when Frank O'Farrell was appointed as manager in 1971 he thought that it was worth at least giving it one last shot.

Not involved at all until early January, it was then when he decided to leave. A number of clubs wanted him, including Southampton, Ipswich and Oldham, and Brighton's manager pestered him with repeated telephone calls in an attempt to convince him to join the south coast outfit. At that point Gigi Peronace, the Italian football agent who had been instrumental in bringing Denis Law to United ten years earlier, intervened by holding discussions regarding a possible move to Italy. With only two substitute appearances under his belt all term, moving on was now a necessity to him.

He continued with the Reserves for the opening three months of the next season and then took trials at Fiorentina and Bologna in November 1972 after Peronace had brokered opportunities with both clubs. Sartori participated in a practice match with the former only to be put off by their style of football, while in contrast he fitted in almost immediately at Bologna and a transfer fee of £50,000 was soon agreed.

He again represented United in the Central League while the formalities were being resolved and his personal arrangements could be concluded. His last game fell on the 23rd December in the Reserves' 3-0 defeat at Everton and his liaison with the Reds, which had lasted for just shy of ten years, ended with him having made just over 50 senior starts in all competitions. Under four different managers he had simply been unable to retain a place in the first-team for any length of time.

Upon landing in Italy, the 25 year-old was faced with the strangest of situations as, being a native of the country, it was a requirement for him to undertake National Service. Officially not regarded as an Italian citizen and as such initially barred from playing for his club in league games, ironically he was eligible to represent the Italian Army and could also take part in Bologna's Anglo-Italian Cup ties. Weirder still, his debut was in the latter competition at the unlikely venue of St. James's Park in Newcastle.

While Bologna took their grievances to court in an attempt to get the rules changed, their new signing was selected to represent Italy in the World Military Cup in Brazzaville, Congo. The Italians had successfully seen off Algeria and Belgium in the group stage leading up to the finals with a team containing a number of future full internationals, including Francesco Graziani, Gabriele Oriali and Ivano Bordon. During the finals, which were based on a league format, Italy drew with Kuwait and defeated the host nation, Iraq and the Ivory Coast, and he and his colleagues' efforts were rewarded when they walked off with the trophy. He continued in the Italian Army team, meeting up in Rome on Tuesdays for training and then tackling Serie B and C teams in friendly matches on Thursday evenings.

Back at Bologna, the club finally convinced the authorities to alter their rulebook and Sartori was officially registered with them on the 1st July 1973. During the following campaign he finally got his chance to feature in Serie A and, even though not included in the final, he won an Italian Cup medal when the Rossoblu defeated Palermo. Staying only the one term at the Stadio Comunale before moving on to join Spal in Serie B, he spent two years with the Ferrara-based club before going on loan to Serie C team Benevento.

With his contract due to expire at the end of that season, his sparkling form ensured that he was linked to a number of clubs, including giants Juventus and Napoli, but even so, he preferred the set-up at Lecce and instead transferred to them. For the next three years he was integral to a squad that consistently pushed for promotion to Serie A, falling just short each time, though he did collect an Anglo-Italian Cup medal when Lecce defeated Scarborough in June 1977.

He moved to Rimini in 1979 and captained the team to promotion from Serie C at his first attempt. The midfielder remained at the Stadio Romeo Neri for a couple of years longer prior to docking at Trento, his last port of call, and a final game for the club was actually at Bologna, the very club that had lured him over to Italy. It seemed that events had now gone full circle, as he was also back in the area where he was born in South Tyrol.

Wearing the distinctive blue and yellow hoops of Trento, he spent almost two years at the Stadio Briamasco and over the latter part of that period undertook his coaching exams in preparation for a job as a football manager. He was extremely happy in Italy with his Mancunian wife and two children but, because one of his brothers had passed away and the other was finding it difficult to cope with the family business, he returned to England in September 1984. The decision to bid 'arrivederci' was made after he declined the offer of the player/manager job at Serie C club, Merano.

Carlo Sartori's most vivid memories of representing Manchester United are scoring the aggregate winning goal at Anderlecht in November 1968, taking part in three gruelling F.A. Cup battles with Leeds in 1970, as well as helping to win the Daily Express five-a-side tournament that same year.

He continues to work for the family knife sharpening firm to this day.

TRANTER, Wilfred (1960/61, 1961/62, 1962/63)

Born: Manchester, 5th March 1945
Height: 5ft. 9ins., Weight: 12st.
Role: Centre-half or left-half
Career: St. Mark's Primary School (Pendlebury)/ St. Gregory's Technical High School (Ardwick)/ Manchester Boys/ Lancashire Boys/ UNITED: Am. June 1960 Pro. April 1962/ Brighton & Hove Albion May 1966 to January 1969/ Baltimore Bays (USA) (L) April to August 1968/ Fulham January 1969/ St. Louis Stars (USA) May to August 1972/ Dover October 1972 to May 1974

When 'Alo' Gallagher arrived in Lancashire to work in the local coal mine, the Irishman stayed with the Tranter family. Mr. Tranter was a fellow miner and quite partial to watching Swinton RLFC on Saturdays, his wife even washed the team's kit. Their lodger wasn't so keen on rugby, though, and, deciding to find a football match instead, he picked a game which involved Bolton and Leicester at Burnden Park.

At that point he asked his landlords if their son, Wilf, would like to accompany him. Having only ever experienced rugby in the flesh, not surprisingly Swinton usually being involved, the eight year-old jumped at the chance and he fell in the love with the round ball game, and specifically Bolton Wanderers, that very day.

Tranter was born at St. Mary's Hospital in Manchester and grew up over the divide in the Salford rugby league stronghold of Pendlebury. Following Gallagher's intervention he would often skip Wednesday afternoon lessons in order to take in a football match, preferably at Bolton, although he could just as easily be found at Old Trafford or Maine Road. After commencing secondary school education, his participation in the sport was influenced by the guidance of headmaster Joseph Rocca, a relative of legendary United scout, Louis Rocca. Operating anywhere across the half-back line, he was a member of the same school eleven as Terry Brennan, Shay's younger brother, who was also captain of the team.

At the age of thirteen he obtained a ticket for the 1958 F.A. Cup final at Wembley, where he cheered his Bolton heroes to a 2-0 victory over a Munich-ravaged United, and later skippered Manchester Boys right through a 1959/60 campaign that proved to be one of the most successful in their history. Alongside Ray Hewitt and Barry Grayson, two youngsters who were also destined to join the ground staff at Old Trafford, the side gained victory in the Lancashire Trophy final over a Liverpool team captained by Tommy Smith. Manchester also captured the Inter-City Challenge Trophy, in which they came out on top of a combined London Boys side led by Ron Harris, as well as claiming joint ownership of the Manchester County Trophy with Stockport.

Manchester Boys were also triumphant in the prestigious English Schools Trophy, defeating East London Boys in the final, and with a 2-0 victory at Maine Road already in the bag, Tranter, Grayson and Hewitt got amongst the goals in a 5-1 second leg win at Millwall.

It was during the Trophy run when he was chosen for England Boys trials. With Manchester Boys having played eight of their nine ties away from their home patch of Maine Road, the selectors requested him to attend trials in Yorkshire the day after a match against Grimsby Boys. Feeling shattered after a particularly hard game, he was given a brief run out lasting barely twenty minutes and missed out on final selection. It was a bitter blow and, despite later making two appearances for Lancashire Boys, circumstances seemed to have conspired to deny him the international recognition he was certainly worthy of.

Explaining how the story unfolded from then on, he revealed, *'As well as United, quite a few clubs wanted to sign me and Blackburn and Wolves made approaches to my parents, who were quite happy for me to take up a career in football. I was working at the Pilkington tile factory in my summer holidays in 1960 when little Joe Armstrong arrived in a taxi and I went with him to Old Trafford where I signed an amateur contract. I had actually been studying economics and history at Salford Technical College and I turned down the chance of a place at Loughborough Training College in order to join United.'*

His first game for the club was in the Juniors' win at Cheadle Boys in September 1960. Remaining in that side for a few months before starting to feature for the 'A' and 'B' teams, in the October he deputised for the injured Alan Atherton when the Reds defeated Liverpool 3-0 in the Youth Cup. It wasn't normal practice to be called upon with so few matches under his belt and the development indicated just how much faith the coaching staff held in him.

Over the January and February period of 1961 he took up residence in the 'A' team and in the latter month was again recalled to understudy Atherton for another Youth Cup tie, this time at Sunderland. Reflecting on the strides made through the season, there had been a rise through the ranks and he also secured himself some glory as the Juniors captured their league title together with the Whitaker Cup when defeating Crossford in the final.

During the 1961/62 fixture list, Tranter was predominantly utilised in either the 'A' or 'B' teams at right-half or centre-half and, despite not being a natural in the pivot role, he quickly learned how to defend from that position. Present for all five Youth Cup matches as United were elbowed out by Newcastle in a surprising upset, he was soon called up for his Central League debut at home to Manchester City.

'I was so excited that I didn't notice the additional message on the team sheet advising all the players to meet at Davyhulme Golf Club,' he admitted. *'The first-team were also due to face City, at Maine Road, and both they and the Reserves were due to lunch together. I got a message just in time, and it saved me from the embarrassment that would have been caused by my absence.'*

In the event the Reserves lost 3-2, but he hung onto his place for the following game at Leeds and was able to count on nine appearances in the

Central League by the end of the of the campaign.

The 1962/63 season turned out to be one of consolidation rather than advancement as he found himself largely confined to the 'A' team and in his least favourite role of centre-half. He made a total of only three starts for the second string as Frank Haydock held the number five jersey at that level, although the honour of captaining the Youth Cup side was a pleasing consolation.

High hopes were held in that respect because the Reds had what appeared to be a decent team, only serious problems in the goalkeeping department proved unsettling and they were eventually knocked out of the national tournament at Sheffield Wednesday.

Drafted back into the Reserves for the opening Central League match of the 1963/64 term, he missed only two games for them in the whole campaign. The first was when he was injured in October and the second in early March fell just after his 19th birthday, an event that prompted a belated and unexpected present.

'A telegram arrived one Thursday morning at our house at 16, Heron Street, Pendlebury,' he noted. 'It read 'Report ground 10.00 a.m. Prepare to travel to London. Matt Busby'. We didn't have a telephone in the house and so I couldn't contact the manager to confirm any more details. I packed my kit as quick as I could and made my way to the ground where I was told that I would be deputising for Bill Foulkes at West Ham. Busby had decided to rest most of the senior team due to the F.A. Cup semi-final tie against the Hammers the following week.'

In a game in which Pat Crerand captained United for the one and only time, future World Cup hero Geoff Hurst got no change out of the debutant as the Reds ran out 2-0 winners. By the close season Tranter could look back over 40 Central League games as well as his bow in the Football League and, understandably, he was generally quite pleased with the way things were going.

Continuing in the Reserves through the first section of the 1964/65 term, changes were taking place which would see him relegated back to 'A' standard for the last few weeks of the campaign as many of those who had been part of the successful 1964 Youth Cup team were now starting to seek places in the second string. Bobby Noble made the left full-back position his own and, with Noel Cantwell switched to centre-half, Tranter became a victim of the developments.

In his final season with the club, his time was spent bouncing between 'A' team and Central League duties. He asked Jimmy Murphy if he could take up either a left-half or right-half berth as opposed to being stationed in the centre of the defence but, with John Fitzpatrick and Peter McBride holding down those very same spots for the Reserves, opportunities were limited. With 91 appearances at Central League level, and over 200 starts in total during his six years at Old Trafford, the plain fact was that younger men had overtaken him and forced him into looking for pastures new.

There were a few enquiries regarding his availability, with Middlesbrough and Brighton making firm offers. After considering the merits of both he eventually chose the south coast option, joining the Third Division club in the spring of 1966 while simultaneously bringing forward his plans to marry. In his early days at the Goldstone Ground he found it difficult to break into the senior side, but during the 1967/68 term upped his appearance level to 29.

As the campaign was drawing to a close he received a telephone call from Dennis Viollet, who was then starring for Baltimore Bays in America, and his former Old Trafford colleague recommended that he should talk to manager Gordon Jago about the possibility of a loan there. Following a positive conversation with Jago, Tranter signed for Baltimore and scored twice in twelve starts for them in their 1968 season. With only five English-speaking players in the side, learning Spanish was required in order that he could converse with a number of his new team-mates.

Upon returning to the UK, he was approached by Fulham boss Bobby Robson, who was aware that his contract at Brighton was due to expire. Having agreed to a trial with the Cottagers, Robson was sacked in the December of 1968 when Bill Dodgin took over the reigns. Fortuitously, Dodgin was happy to honour the offer and got his man just a few weeks later.

Tranter made nine starts from then until the end of the 1968/69 term as Fulham were relegated to the Third Division and in the following campaign he featured in only seven senior games. Over the next two years the situation worsened as he appeared just four times for the first-team.

As the 1972 close season approached, he was sounded out regarding opportunities in the States and, with very little interest from English clubs, decided to return there. By now with three children, he uprooted to Missouri to join the St. Louis Stars and in a successful spell he took part in fourteen games as they reached the national final. That game ended in a 2-1 defeat by New York Cosmos, although recognition to the team's effort came his way when he was selected for the NASL All Stars Second XI.

He received a decent salary in the States, particularly in comparison with the wages in England, and seriously considered taking a coaching role there before his wife made it known that she wanted to return home. His coaching badges had been achieved while at United and, at only 23 years of age at the time, he was one of the youngest ever to attain them.

In October 1972, he joined a Dover side that went on to finish third in the Southern League, just two points behind Ron Atkinson's champions Kettering Town. Returning to Manchester in 1974, at which point he joined Chloride of the South-East Lancashire League, about then he also started his own property development business.

Ex-United pal Bobby Smith installed him as his assistant at Swindon Town in 1978 and during a span of two and a half years the Wiltshire club reached the semi-final of the Football League Cup.

Joining Witney Town in November 1980, in his first full year in charge they won an Oxon Benevolent Cup and Oxfordshire Professional Cup double. The club went up to the re-established Southern League Premier Division in 1982 and also retained the Benevolent Cup. He made a substitute appearance for Witney in April 1983 and that same year led them to a third consecutive Benevolent Cup victory prior to tendering his resignation a few weeks later simply because he wanted a break from the game.

After returning to football in the late 1980's he spent some time as assistant manager of Isthmian League Division One members Hungerford Town and in 1992 was promoted to the position of manager. Following a dismal opening half to the following term he departed the club although, with his property business now requiring more and more of his time, the decision to exit from football management was an easy one.

Having retired in 2003, Wilf Tranter nowadays lives in Cyprus and much of his time is spent engrossed with golf, he being the former captain of Carswell Golf and Country Club in Wiltshire. He has a son, Andy, who notched up well over 500 appearances for Faringdon Town and is now involved with Shrivenham Football Club.

NOBLE, Robert (1962/63, 1963/64)

Born: Manchester, 18th December 1945
Height: 5ft. 7ins., Weight: 9st. 9lbs.
Role: Left full-back
Career: Cheadle Primary School/ Broadway Secondary School (Cheadle)/ Cheadle Boys/ Stockport Boys/ Cheshire Boys/ UNITED: Am. June 1961 App. Pro. June 1961 Pro. December 1962 to March 1969/ Mossley July and August 1971

It should have been the greatest night of his career but, as Bobby Noble watched the celebrations going on all around, it turned into one of the most heart-wrenching experiences of his life. The date was the 29th May 1968 and Manchester United had just clinched the European Cup by defeating Benfica on a balmy night at Wembley.

As the festivities carried on into the early hours at the Russell Hotel in London, Noble, who was still taking medication because of the injuries he sustained in a car accident thirteen months earlier, was under strict instructions not to drink alcohol. Happy and relieved at the outcome of the game, he still couldn't help feeling that he should have had his hands on the trophy and a share in the glory. Regretably, less than a year later he was forced to quit the game when a brave and painful attempted comeback failed.

Hailing from a family with strong football traditions, his father, John, was once a part-time professional with Stockport County and also operated on the local semi-professional scene. In November 1945, John Noble scored what could be claimed as one of the strangest goals ever when his shot was deflected into Droylsden's net by a stray dog while playing for Mossley.

The Nobles moved to Cheadle when young Bobby was only five and, learning to be competitive while kicking a ball about with his dad in a local park, after shining for his junior school team he was selected as inside-forward for Cheadle Boys when aged about ten or eleven. As captain of the Broadway Secondary School team he demonstrated the way of a winner and natural leader, not only with his ferocious tackling, but also because he was a shouter and an organiser.

Regularly watching Cheadle Rovers with his father by then, at the age of twelve he signed for Westbourne Rangers and they went on to win league and cup honours from their home base at Houldsworth Park. Westbourne's manager ran three different junior teams in the Stockport area and he was responsible for ensuring that his best prodigies had trials with Manchester City.

Selected at inside-forward in his first year with Stockport Boys before being pushed back to wing-half the following season, by then he had developed a reputation for being a tough cookie on both the physical and vocal fronts and was subsequently installed as captain of both Stockport Boys and Cheshire Boys.

During his time with Stockport Boys they reached the final of the Manchester County Cup, won the Cheshire Cup by beating Birkenhead Boys, and also defeated Manchester Boys for the first time in a game staged at Edgeley Park. He represented Cheshire in a number of games throughout the 1960/61 campaign, one of which was a 3-2 victory over Lancashire at Gresty Road, Crewe. Future United club-mate Albert Kinsey was a reserve for Lancashire that day and both lads were selected for England Boys trials in early 1961. In one of the trial games at Billingham, his ankle was fractured in a bad tackle with Howard Kendall and not only did it cause him to miss the opportunity of representing his country, he was also required to sit out the remainder of the schools' season.

He took trials with a clutch of clubs within a short travelling distance of his home, including Bolton and Preston, and was offered terms by both United and City. Even though the package City came up with was significantly better, the option to embark on a career at Old Trafford was made on the gut instinct that the Reds were much more capable of *'going places'* in relation to their rivals from Maine Road.

Making his club debut in August 1961, over the first part of the campaign he was a mainstay for the 'B' eleven at half-back. By December, Jimmy Murphy had switched him to full-back where he featured in both junior teams for the remainder of the term, operating on opposite sides of the defence. Although strictly speaking right-footed, he felt equally at home on the other side of the park and it was in the left full-back berth where he would soon make his name in higher spheres.

In October 1962 he was promoted into the Central League side for a 0-0 home draw against Aston Villa and, despite gaining only one further start for the Reserves during the season, even then his potential was as clear as daylight. Participating in a full complement of five Youth Cup games as the young Reds were derailed by Sheffield Wednesday the following April, that term he was also called up for England Youth trials.

With leadership qualities that were evident to all, he skippered the 'A' side whenever Bobby Smith was unavailable and also found himself bestowed with the captaincy of the under-18 team right at the start of the 1963/64 Youth Cup trail. Up to that point he had been biding his time for chances in the Reserves and, with Shay Brennan and Mike Lorimer holding down the full-back posts in the Central League side, it wasn't until December when he was elevated into the second string again.

Having now been in full-time training for a couple of years, as a consequence he was lightning quick, could read the game like an open book and his tackling combined granite-hardness with timing that a Swiss watchmaker would have been proud of. Unsurprisingly, his reputation as a difficult opponent began to gather pace and few wingers fancied spending an hour and a half up against him. Even though the likes of George Best, David Sadler and John Fitzpatrick were the subject of rave reviews, it was becoming more and more obvious that he would also make a name for himself before much longer.

He also caught the eyes of the international selectors and, following the award of a first England Youth cap in a 2-1 victory over Spain in Murcia in February 1964, his name was added to the squad which successfully retained the European Youth Tournament in Holland that Easter. Playing in a full quota of five matches, England won three and drew one to reach a final in which they faced Spain in Amsterdam. After the previous close encounter with the Spaniards, England expected a tight contest, but superior form on the day resulted in a comfortable 4-0 victory. During the competition Chelsea starlet John Hollins confided to Noble that his manager, Tommy Docherty, wanted to take him to Stamford Bridge.

Back on the domestic scene, he led the Youth Cup team to further successes in the competition, notably over Manchester City in a semi-final in which he came up against a few of the former Stockport Boys team, and then at the last stage against Swindon. Following the 5-2 aggregate final victory he became the sixth United captain to hoist the silver cup.

While the seniors began their chase for the 1964/65 First Division title, Noble contested a place in the Reserves. In March 1965 he was called into the senior squad for the first time, when named as 12th man for the F.A. Cup semi-final against Leeds, and it proved to be both a valuable experience as well as an indication of how close the major breakthrough was.

Having completed only three matches for the 'A' team at the start of the 1965/66 term, a cartilage operation caused him to miss the next three months. He was back in the Reserves by December, but was unable to force Brennan or Tony Dunne out of their senior berths. When Noel Cantwell was recalled to the First Division side he requested a meeting with Matt Busby at which he demanded a transfer, while also informing the manager of Chelsea's interest. The canny Busby was smart enough to sense that the real reason for the meeting was the defender's desire for first-team football and convinced him to bide his time.

In early April 1966, his fortune suddenly took a massive upswing. Recalling the events that led to his First Division entrance, he remarked, *'I was still a bit fed up when our trainer, Jack Crompton, confided that I would get my chance in the next home match against Leicester. I wasn't sure whether to believe him, but sure enough, when the side was named I was in it. We lost the game 2-1, and I then played in a 1-1 draw with Leeds on the last day of the season.'*

For the first few weeks of the 1966/67 fixture list he was with the Reserves, gaining a recall to first-team duty in early October for a trip to Blackpool. A few days later he was off to Italy, where the Reds took on Fiorentina in a friendly match to celebrate British Fairs Week, and following a 2-1 victory he became an ever-present in the side that challenged for the First Division title.

By the spring of 1967 many thought he was the most accomplished number three in the country and, while being widely tipped for England honours, a majority of the Old Trafford faithful assumed that he would become the club's future captain and lead the team for years to come.

Then disaster struck.

Following United's 0-0 draw at Sunderland in April 1967, the players arrived back in Manchester and most of them headed off for a quiet drink. Only recently married on Valentines Day, the Reds' defender chose instead to make his way home and was driving down Washway Road in Sale when he was involved in a car accident. Suffering severe chest, leg and head injuries, his chances of surviving were said to be only 50-50 and he lay in a coma in Altrincham General Hospital before finally regaining consciousness a few days later.

During one visit, Busby asked him who he played for and when the patient replied *'Scunthorpe United'*, it was quite obvious that he faced a long and tortuous road to recovery. With only three games to go to complete their fixture commitments, the Reds required just two wins to be sure of the title and, even though he collected a championship medal when the points were secured, it was scant consolation considering his predicament.

Noble's determination and supreme physical fitness were always in abundance, but he still staggered everyone at the club who witnessed his return to football barely eight months after the crash. Making his comeback in a 'B' team game against Everton in early December 1967, before Christmas arrived he had taken part in two further matches. After not featuring at all for a time, he was back in action again in March, making a further six 'A' team appearances and one start for the 'B', but there was little or no improvement in his condition as he was still unable to read the flight of the ball properly.

Commenting on his situation many years later, he revealed, *'Numerous problems surfaced because of my injuries. My knee kept swelling, which affected my speed, and I had muscle damage in my eye. It meant that I was mistiming tackles and my decision-making in matches was hampered because my vision was blurred. I visited a specialist in Manchester and he then referred me to a leading Harley Street surgeon.'*

Continuing to train with the seniors, whereas previously he was always one of the first to be chosen for five-a-side matches, he now found himself as the last. So, in May 1968, with the European Cup glistening in the Old Trafford trophy cabinet, he prepared himself for another operation to correct his sight. Including two F.A. Cup ties he had figured in 33 competitive matches for the first-team, though deep down he knew his days as a professional footballer were pretty much over.

Courageously returning for the third and last time in September 1968, he managed around a dozen more 'A' team matches before admitting that the demands of the game were now beyond him. At the age of 23, his last appearance on the 25th January 1969 ended in a 2-0 defeat at Crewe.

He then planned to take a coaching course and was even offered a position by Liverpool University to coach their football team, but their gesture was inexplicably turned down. In June 1969, former Reds' winger Harry McShane helped to secure him a job as a clerk at the Massey Ferguson engineering company. Now suffering from depression, he was unable to hold it down for very long.

In the December of that year he was awarded £25,000 plus costs for his accident at Manchester Assizes. United's management then blocked an appeal for a testimonial, citing that he had already been financially compensated, although they generously assisted him to buy his club house.

A year and a half later he attempted to reignite his career by appearing in a couple of pre-season warm-up matches for Mossley, the first one being at Blackpool Mechanics and the second at home to Barnsley Reserves, and a few days later a club spokesman informed the press that, *'Clearly, it is too soon to say how Bobby will shape up, but we're hoping for the best'*. Sadly, the player himself felt that he wasn't up to the standard required and his only other involvement with football from then on was a few training sessions with some friends at Buxton.

Over the ensuing years he held numerous jobs, ranging from labouring on a building site, as a security guard, and working in a bakery amongst others. Following a series of personal tragedies within his family, he was forced to sell his prized 1967 First Division championship medal at auction. Purchased by United, it is displayed in the club museum for all to see.

Bobby Noble is now semi-retired and still lives in the same former club house in Sale.

NICHOLSON, James Joseph
(1958/59, 1959/60, 1960/61)

Born: Belfast, 27th February 1943
Height: 5ft. 9ins., Weight: 11st.
Role: Half-back
Career: **Belmont Primary School (Belfast)/ Methody College (Belfast)/ Northern Ireland Boys/ All-Ireland Boys/ UNITED**: Am. May 1958 Pro. February 1960/ **Huddersfield Town** December 1964/ **Bury** December 1973/ **Mossley** June 1976/ **Stalybridge Celtic** December 1976 to May 1977

A local of Standtown in West Belfast, Jimmy Nicholson attended a rugby school and participated far more in that particular sport rather than football in his early days. His involvement in rugby gave him a strong physique and a powerful tackling style, attributes which contributed greatly to his success when he eventually became a footballer.

As and when his rugby commitments allowed, he took up soccer on a casual basis with the Boyland Youth Club, then under the auspice of the National Association of Boys Clubs in Belfast and managed by Bob Bishop. As the ad hoc games became more formalised, Nicholson's appearances for Boyland began increasing when he was about ten years-old. Under the watchful gaze of Bishop and fellow Boyland associate Bob Harpur, it was quickly identified that the boy possessed great potential and he was earmarked for trials with United at an early stage.

Because there were no Belfast Boys games at the time, he took part in a 'Probables versus Possibles' fixture which earned him a call up for Northern Ireland Boys in the 1957/58 term. Then captaining the All-Ireland Boys side, in the spring of 1958 he signed for the Reds.

'The club still bore the scars of the Munich tragedy when I joined,' he reflected. 'When I got to Manchester I moved into digs with Bobby Charlton in Stretford, quite near to the ground.'

In those days the usual custom was for the rookies to establish themselves in the Altrincham Junior League, but he wasn't required at that level during his first year. Following his appearance in the Lancashire League Division Two home defeat by Manchester City that August, he went on to straddle the 'A' and 'B' teams.

Clearly singled out to be 'fast-tracked' through the system, while still aged only fifteen and having completed only eight games in United's colours, in October he was used in a 3-1 Youth Cup win at Bradford City. Situated in one or other of the half-back berths on each step of that campaign's Youth Cup run, it was ended by Blackburn, the eventual winners of the trophy.

He had made only two starts in his second season before being drafted into the Central League side for a 5-0 home win against Barnsley and held his place at that level for the next three games. Six weeks later he scored twice in the Youth Cup, when the Reds had a field day against Morecambe at Old Trafford.

In the later part of November he represented Lancashire Youth in a game against Manchester County Youth. Lining up alongside Alan Atherton and Ian Moir, it was slightly strange to see fellow United team-mates, Ron Briggs, Willie Donaldson and Stan Ackerley, who were all on the Manchester side.

Again present for every round of the Youth Cup until the Reds were eliminated at the penultimate stage by Preston, his growing appearance count at Central League level earned him a championship medal when the title was won by a six-point margin over second-placed Liverpool.

He had certainly made great strides during his two years at the club and it was commonplace to hear or read of him being compared to Duncan Edwards. Of those comments he said, 'I heard them, but I took no notice because I just wanted to concentrate on my football.'

In August 1960 he made the first-team squad for their pre-season practice match, although the occasion almost turned sour when he was injured and needed to be carried off the field. Luckily, the knock wasn't too serious and after playing in the Central League on the opening day of the season, the Belfast lad was chanced in the First Division at Goodison Park on the 24th of that month. The start to his senior career wouldn't have been what he wanted, though, because United were convincingly trounced 4-0. Nevertheless, the chance of retribution came in the return match a week later and he exercised it by recording his first league goal as the Reds returned the compliment over Everton by scoring four times without reply.

He cemented his place in the side by making 33 consecutive first-team appearances in league and cup as the term moved into February. Over that same period he was nominated for Youth Cup duty for the third season in succession and, as such, joined a group of Reds who have played in the Football League while still participating in the tournament.

During that same campaign he gained further experience in the newly inaugurated League Cup competition. Together with Nobby Stiles, he formed one of the youngest pair of wing-halves in the First Division until a dip in form resulted in him being returned to the Reserves that March. Good news was at hand, however, as he was honoured with a full Northern Ireland cap for his appearance against Sweden the very next month and a few more starts were made for the seniors before the football calendar was concluded.

It had been a great year for him so far and he anticipated even more first-team exposure during the 1961/62 fixture list, only his sunshine soon turned to rain due to the fine form of Stiles and Maurice Setters as he spent the opening half of the season in the Reserves. Along with Ronnie Briggs, in February 1962 he appeared in Northern Ireland's first ever under-23 game against Wales in Belfast, while back at Old Trafford he then had to make do with the odd few starts here and there.

A similar pattern emerged over the following campaign, as he was given a run of five first-team matches in August and September 1962 and then got only the same number of games before the end of the term.

'It was about then that I started having a problem with my back,' he complained. 'It was so severe that I sometimes found it difficult to walk. I don't know whether it was due to the new weight training methods that Jack Crompton had brought in or if I had picked up a virus.' Whatever the cause was, it had a marked impact on his performances. Struggling to regain his place as a result, when Matt Busby bought Pat Crerand from Glasgow Celtic the situation became profoundly more difficult and it was then that he began to wonder if there was a future for him at the club.

Over the next 22 months he was confined to Central League football, totally unable to force his way back into Busby's thoughts. So, when Ian Greaves, his former club-mate who was coaching at Huddersfield, suggested that a transfer was worth considering, the young Irishman spoke with the Town's manager. After gaining Busby's agreement he moved to Leeds Road on the 8th December 1964 for a bargain fee of £8,000, having played his last Central League game for United three days previously at Villa Park. Even though he had shown so much promise as a junior, and was a fixture in the Northern Ireland side, he flew the coop in order to secure the regular first-team football he craved.

Despite the embarrassment of conceding an own goal on his first 90-minute shift for Huddersfield, Nicholson accumulated over 300 league and cup appearances for the Terriers and captained the side to the Second Division championship in 1970. Along with ex-United junior Terry Poole, he then got the chance to return to Old Trafford later that year when Huddersfield met the Reds in a First Division clash.

While at Leeds Road, a serious knee injury required an operation to remove most of his cartilage. The surgery left him with very little lateral movement, which in turn inhibited both his tackling and passing, two of his main strengths. Huddersfield were relegated from the Second Division in 1973 and he was soon offered the chance to join another ex-Red, Bobby Smith, at Bury.

With first-team opportunities at Leeds Road limited, he moved to Gigg Lane in the December of that year and spent two and a half years at Bury, during which he helped them to win promotion from the Fourth Division. Realising that his playing days were coming to an end, and still suffering from knee problems, he inhabited the non-league scene with Mossley and Stalybridge for another year before giving up in 1977.

Having gained numerous honours, the midfielder was fortunate to enjoy a lengthy spell as a sportsman and his collection of 41 full caps for Northern Ireland, on top of 58 starts in the First Division for United, are reminders of some of the most memorable moments.

While with Mossley he enrolled at the Abraham Moss College in Crumpsall in order to study for a leisure management and business studies degree and graduated at the same time he retired from football. After unsuccessfully applying for managerial vacancies at Rochdale and a couple of non-league clubs, he took up a role as a supervisor of Walton Park Leisure Centre in Sale. Originally an old warehouse, with his help the facility was transformed into a modern sports complex that boasts a gymnastic area, rowing facility, weight training room, indoor five-a-side pitches and a model railway club.

ACKERLEY, Stanley (1958/59, 1959/60)

Born: Wythenshawe, Manchester, 12th July 1942
Height: 5ft. 9ins., Weight: 11st.
Role: Left full-back
Career: **Baguley Hall Primary School (Wythenshawe)/ Baguley Hall High School (Wythenshawe)/ Manchester Boys/ Lancashire Boys/ UNITED**: Am. July 1957 Pro. November 1959/ **Oldham Athletic** June 1961/ **Kidderminster Harriers** July 1962/ **Altrincham** February 1963/ **Slavia** (Aus) May 1963/ **Apia Leichhardt** (Aus) March 1964 to October 1965/ **Plymouth Argyle** January 1966/ **Witton Albion** March 1966/ **Apia Leichhardt** (Aus) April 1966 to October 1973/ **Sydney Croatia** (Aus) 1973 and 1974/ **Toongabbie** (Aus) 1974 to 1983

Stan Ackerley's career in English football could, at best, be described as modest as he failed to progress beyond second string status with United and appeared in just two Football League games before taking up with a couple of non-league outfits. Following emigration to Australia in 1963 his fortunes changed dramatically by joining the biggest club on the continent for a period of nine years. Success flowed from then on as he made three representative international appearances while also winning caps at full international level on another 25 occasions.

His stature in the game in that country grew to such an extent that in a survey of players and managers he was nominated for a position in the best Australian team of the 20th century. In 2003, Ackerley was also honoured by induction into the Australian Soccer 'Hall of Fame' for his valued and continuing contribution to the national game.

The youngest of seven children, his early idea of Saturday recreation was to play for Baguley Boys Club, a team that was managed by his father. Before long he was attending trials for South Manchester Boys and later progressed into a full Manchester Boys eleven who reached the last eight of the national schools' competition in 1956 when they encountered London Boys at White Hart Lane. Later elevated into a Lancashire Boys side that contained Nobby Stiles, the two youngsters soon formed a lasting friendship. He also attended trials for England Boys and was pitched in for both 'North against South' and 'Probables versus Possibles' matches only to lose out on international recognition at the last stage.

It was while with Manchester Boys when he came under the watchful eyes of Joe Armstrong and Bert Whalley prior to being given an invite to attend trials for United. Even though he supported Manchester City, and both they and Wolves also offered him a similar examination, the Reds' youth policy had such a big pull that he agreed to sign amateur forms only days past his 15th birthday.

Making his club bow in September 1957 with the Juniors, after remaining at half-back with them until the following February, the ramifications of the Munich disaster triggered a call up to the 'B' team. Because the defender was a member of the ground staff he was required to train during the day and then take part in friendly matches in the evening while boys flocked from all over the country in order to assist United in their hour of need. Despite not being with the club very long when the tragedy struck, he cites Bert Whalley as being an enormous influence and the emotion felt over the death of the popular coach and other members of the club's personnel had taken its toll on all of the staff by the end of that mournful season.

Starting the 1958/59 term in the 'B' team, in October he gained a temporary peg up to the 'A' side and at that juncture was also moved from half-back to full-back. He was used in a Youth Cup tie at Bradford that same month and kept hold of his place for all eight games during the cup run. Unable to sustain 'A' status on a regular basis, at the end of the campaign he was selected for the Blue Stars tournament when United won the trophy with a final victory over Verona.

At a time when a full-back's job was three-fold; defend properly, win possession and give the ball to the half-backs or inside-forwards, the Wythenshawe lad's game was underpinned by honesty and hard work. Unyielding in the tackle, he didn't lack pace and carried a mean streak which was fused with an engrained hatred of losing.

During the 1959/60 season, his third at the club, he again started out in the 'B' side and was additionally selected for Youth Cup duty as United reached the semi-finals once more. Again elevated up to the 'A' team towards the end of the fixture list, his efforts weren't enough to force Tommy Heron out of the Reserves. After then travelling over to Zurich for the Blue Stars tournament, for the second successive year he returned home with a gold medallion as the young Reds beat Grenchen in the final.

Having just attained voting age, there was hope of greater things from him during the following campaign and, with his form encouraging, Ackerley started seven consecutive games in the 'A' side. Selected for the Reserves in the annual Central League 'Champions versus the Rest of the League' match in October 1960, which ended in a prestigious 1-0 victory to the Reds, by the middle of December he had finally bore into the Central League side for a 3-0 home defeat by Blackburn.

Despite appearing regularly in the Reserves from then on, the sand was running out in his hourglass. With a newly-introduced wage deal which forced clubs into releasing staff in order pay their top men more money, United let him go in a batch of seven following the Reserves' 3-3 draw at Chesterfield on the 12th April 1961.

Ackerley then shook hands on a one-year deal at Oldham, the fee costing the Latics £250, and he was required to mature quickly at Boundary Park as life was much harsher there than at Old Trafford. Still only nineteen, it took him time to settle but, although gaining first-team selection at Tranmere in April 1962, for the most part he was confined to their Lancashire Combination side. His second start in the Fourth Division came just 24 hours after his first, in a home game against Chesterfield.

With his prospects having dimmed at Boundary Park, in July 1962 he joined West Midlands Regional League members Kidderminster Harriers. Frequently partnered in defence by another ex-United junior, Alan Dunn, a splendid 4-0 win at Stratford Town on the opening day of the campaign preceded a stay at Aggborough which lasted only until the following February when he signed for Altrincham.

Marriage was now in the air and following discussions with some friends about his future, he elected to try things out in Australia, originally for a twelve-month trial period. In May 1963, he agreed terms with the Slavia club of Melbourne and moved to a new life 12,000 miles away. Fortunately, Slavia were caring employers and they helped him to settle quickly by finding him a house and a job. Just five months after landing he was present for Slavia in an Australian Cup game against Sydney-based Apia Leichhardt and was soon contacted with a view to joining the Italian-influenced club.

Because his daughter was about to be born, he delayed until March 1964 before making the 800-mile journey to Sydney, but the wait was worth it as his association with them was both long and satisfying. During his time with Apia he played representative football for, firstly, New South Wales and then for the full Australian side in their November 1965 World Cup Qualifiers.

His international debut was made during a 6-1 defeat by North Korea in what was a two-legged tie in neutral Cambodia. Because the Australian Soccer Federation was aware that he still held a British passport, they pushed his naturalisation papers through so that he could compete against the North Koreans. After training in the heat of the Queensland sun in preparation for the match in Asia, an exhausted team were well beaten by a crack Korean outfit. The Mancunian wasn't selected for the second tie in Phnom-Penh, but did win a place in the side that took on Cambodia in a friendly during the visit.

Towards the end of 1965 his wife was feeling a little homesick. Plans were put in place for a return to England and after contacting Plymouth Argyle manager Malcolm Allison, it was agreed that he could join the Home Park club. It was then in the Australian off-season and being out of contract meant that he could sign for the Pilgrims without the requirement for international clearance. However, by the time he landed in early 1966, Allison had moved on and, staying only a few weeks in Devon, he came to realise that life 'down under' wasn't so bad after all.

Within his short stopover, during which he was unable to edge into the Argyle senior side but did manage to squeeze in four games for Witton Albion of the Cheshire League, Ackerley wrote a number of articles for the Daily Express in relation to the forthcoming World Cup finals. His knowledge was sought primarily about North Korea, who were practically an unknown quantity as far as the Europeans and South Americans were concerned.

With first-hand experience of the subject matter, his opinion was that they shouldn't be underestimated and his prediction was fully borne out as the Koreans produced some dazzling displays to reach the last eight.

Returning to Sydney to rejoin Apia, a huge disappointment was in store when discovering that he had been dropped from the New South Wales side that met United on their 1967 Australian close season tour.

With fourteen international caps already to his credit, in March 1968 he was honoured with the captaincy of his adopted country in a 3-1 victory over Japan in Melbourne and he retained the armband for the third of a three-match series in Adelaide in early April.

His international career reached its pinnacle in 1969 when he was chosen for eleven matches. Following three games against Greece as part of their World Cup preparations in July, the Australians flew to Seoul for a round of eliminating matches. He featured in all four games as the 'Socceroos' topped the group to progress to the next phase and then played twice against Rhodesia before coming up against an excellent Israel side in the final deciding stage. Victory would have sent the Aussies to Mexico, only they lost by an odd goal and, following the appointment of a new coach, his days on the international stage were over.

All through that time he had worked for a construction company owned by one of Apia's directors and in 1972 he began employment with the local council by driving large machinery. His time at Apia was coming to an end and he was asked to set up a new club, Toongabbie, on the west side of Sydney. As the new venture was developing he joined Sydney Croatia for twelve months and finally assumed the office of player/coach of Toongabbie in 1974, succeeding in taking them up to the First Division in his nine years there.

The role of assistant manager at new National League side Penrith City beckoned in 1983 and from 1986 he managed a few local sides. His son, Chris, journeyed to England for trials in 1986 and took part in two 'B' team matches for Manchester United but wasn't offered a contract.

He was the boss at Penrith Soccer Club by 1990 and took them all the way to the Premier League before guiding Schofield Scorpions from the Fourth to the First Division from 2001 onwards. The success of the Scorpions was largely based on a youth policy he was a part of over half a century earlier at Old Trafford.

Currently living in the Penrith area of Sydney's western suburbs with his Manchester-born wife, Stan Ackerley has also coached at Bonnyrigg White Eagles, Penrith Panthers and Canterbury Marrickvale. Now the director of coaching for Penrith Nepean United and first-grade coach for their women's team, a family connection exists in the sport as his son-in-law, Mike Gibson, represented Australia at football in the 2000 Olympic games.

McEWEN, Francis Kevin
(1963/64, 1964/65, 1965/66)

Born: Dublin, 15th February 1948
Height: 5ft. 8ins., Weight: 10st. 8lbs.
Role: Inside-left or centre-forward
Career: St. Theresa's Primary School (Dublin)/ Clogher Road Technical College (Dublin)/ Dublin Boys/ Eire Boys/ UNITED: Am. July 1963 Pro. May 1965/ Rochdale November 1966/ Drogheda United (Ire) January 1968 to November 1971/ Hakoah Eastern Suburbs (Aus) 1972/ Shamrock Rovers (Ire) January 1973/ Boyne Rovers (Ire) August 1975/ St. Patrick's Athletic (Ire) November 1975/ Boyne Rovers (Ire) October 1976/ Aer Lingus (Ire) 1977/ Drogheda United (Ire) February to August 1978

When asked about one of the most important moments in his life, Frank McEwen reminisced, *'I suppose my date with destiny occurred sometime around the spring of 1963 when an elderly man wearing a bowler hat and smoking a pipe showed up at Ringsend Park in Dublin after I had just finished a game of football there. He introduced himself as Bob Bishop and asked me if I fancied a trial with Manchester United! No other professional clubs had shown any interest in me at that stage and, with the incentive of being able to meet my boyhood hero, Denis Law, I and another lad called Johnny Foran caught the boat over to England for trials.'*

Hailing from the south Dublin suburb of Kimmage, many of his younger days were spent playing Gaelic football because his school sides had no involvement in the association code, although he later joined Dublin District Schoolboy League members Bolton Athletic who staged their home games at the Ringsend fields. Quite tall for his age and incredibly fast over short distances, that speed came in useful as he won two consecutive league titles with the Athletic while also gaining a reputation as a free-scoring centre-forward.

Having already secured representative honours for Dublin, around the time of his meeting with Bob Bishop he was introduced to the international arena when Eire Boys were humiliated in a 9-0 defeat by Wales at Newport. Despite that unfortunate start, Eire made amends in their following match by registering a 2-2 draw against the might of England at Leicester, where McEwen grabbed their equaliser.

Upon his arrival at Old Trafford in April 1963, the raw youngster clocked his first United goal in the 'B' team's 3-1 home win over Burnley and netted another five days later against Tranmere before heading home to Dublin. Due to rules in force at the time, young prospects from outside of England couldn't be offered an apprenticeship but, through displaying the necessary quality during his trial, he was asked to return a little while later when he would be taken on as an amateur.

He scored for the 'A' side on the opening day of the 1963/64 season and then bedded down into the 'B' team for most of the campaign. Featuring predominantly at number nine, McEwen found the net at regular intervals and it was no surprise when he was chosen for the Youth Cup opener against Barrow.

Marking his Old Trafford baptism in some style, by notching four times in the 14-1 victory, he recalled, *'Three days after the Barrow game I chipped a bone in my arm in a collision with an opponent and I was out of action for four weeks. In that time Dave Sadler was signed from Maidstone and even though I retained my place in the Youth Cup team for the following round, I eventually lost it to him.'*

He concluded that season with the splendid scoring average of a goal every second match and then exploded into action at the commencement of the 1964/65 campaign by knocking in a hat-trick for the 'B' side in their opening fixture against Rochdale. Even so, he still had to bide his time while waiting for openings in the grade above, because Sadler held the number nine jersey in the Reserves while Albert Kinsey remained in prime position for the 'A' team. Collecting his first club honour in October 1964 when nicking the winner in a 1-0 victory over Everton in the Supplementary Cup final, he plundered a further sixteen goals as the 'B' side won the Lancashire League Division Two title by overtaking the Toffees in the final weeks.

After two years of learning his trade in the juniors, the 1965/66 term offered him the chance to make a breakthrough. With a one-year extension to his contract signed in the summer, he discovered his name on the team sheet for the first Reserves' fixture of the campaign at Wolves and was keen to repay the club's vote of confidence in him. Despite being asked to take up an unfamiliar role at outside-right, McEwen was pleased to finally make the step up regardless of the fact that the Reds came away from Molineux after being subjected to a 2-0 reverse.

The Dubliner returned to the 'A' team, scoring eight goals in eleven starts over the months of September and October, and was then recalled to the Reserves for the rest of the season. A few days after returning to Central League duties he blasted another hat-trick, on this occasion against Blackburn in the first leg of the Supplementary Cup final, as the Reds ran out comfortable 7-2 winners. Then given the honour of captaining the Youth Cup team from the inside-left position, even though United exited the national knock-out competition as early as the Third Round stage, it hardly dampened his delight at the recognition it bestowed.

By now an Irish Youth and under-21 international, he resumed the 1966/67 term in the Reserves only to be discarded after just one appearance as Jimmy Ryan and Wayne Emmerson gained preference in the forward-line. Having only just agreed to another one-year deal and holding the expectation of better and greater things to come, he then became increasingly despondent.

On the 12th November 1966, he scored for the 'A' team in a 2-2 draw at Rochdale, where his performance attracted the attention of Tony Collins. The 'Dale manager and future United chief scout later approached him with the promise of increased wages and a £500 signing on fee and just two weeks later he joined the Fourth Division outfit with the extended security of a two-year contract.

His time at Spotland was one of disappointment, however, as he found great difficulty in adapting to life in the lower reaches of the Football League. Scoring just twice in seventeen league appearances while struggling in his bid to get regular first-team football, the nineteen year-old ended a thoroughly unhappy period by returning to Ireland in January 1968.

With a number of League of Ireland clubs chasing his signature, including Waterford and Shelbourne, it was Drogheda who showed the most persistency. Based 30 miles from Dublin, in almost four years at the Lourdes Stadium he operated either in midfield or on the right wing. One of his greatest achievements in football came in March 1971, when scoring a last-minute extra-time winner in a semi-final replay against Cork Hibernians to put Drogheda into the FAI Cup final for the first time in their history.

Part way through the 1971/72 term he was contacted by Ray Baartz, an ex-United colleague who was playing for Hakoah Eastern Suburbs, a Jewish club based in Sydney. Suggesting the New South Wales State League outfit as a career option, the recently married Irishman agreed to move to Australia and he and his wife settled in the Waverley area. In spite of all the obvious attractions of life in the southern hemisphere, the newly-weds decided there was no place like home and McEwen became a Shamrock Rovers capture in January 1973.

Several months later he faced some of his former team-mates when taking part in a friendly game against a full-strength Manchester United side at Glenmalure Park. The Rovers lost 2-1, nevertheless the match provided a nostalgic reminder of what could have been as he came up against former youth colleagues George Best, David Sadler and Brian Kidd.

Resident at the famous Milltown club for two and a half years, his association with them ended when he joined Boyne Rovers, a team based in Drogheda. He then spent fairly brief spells at St. Patrick's, Boyne Rovers again, and Aer Lingus before playing for, as well as coaching, Drogheda's Reserves.

Then working as a sales representative for a cleaning company, McEwen resigned his post in August 1978 because, as the local newspaper reported, he had *'set up a business in the last six weeks'* in the same industry.

Living in Drogheda still, his overriding memory of his time at Old Trafford is of the incredible skills of George Best and he spoke of the incomparable one, *'We used to wear these black pumps for training. They were good for running but had no grip and were terrible on the slippery surface at The Cliff, so ball work was always difficult and everyone fell over. That was, everyone except George.*

Other players tried to kick him to make him fall over but they just couldn't get the ball off him and he would just look at the kicker with a blank face. I used to go home and tell all my friends about him. He had such an incredible temperament and it was no surprise when he made it because everyone knew he would.'

STILES, Norbert Peter (1957/58, 1958/59, 1959/60)

Born: Collyhurst, Manchester, 18th May 1942
Height: 5ft. 7ins., Weight: 10st.
Role: Right half-back or inside-right
Career: St. Patrick's School (Collyhurst)/ Manchester Boys/ Lancashire Boys/ England Boys/ UNITED: Am. July 1957 Pro. May 1959/ Middlesbrough May 1971/ Preston North End August 1973 to May 1975

One of the most iconic sporting images of the 20th century occurred one July day in 1966, in the minutes following England's World Cup final defeat of West Germany. With viewers all around the globe glued to their television sets, the sight of one Norbert Peter Stiles dancing a jig of joy on the Wembley pitch as Englishmen everywhere celebrated the moment was a sight many will never forget.

Returning to the Empire Stadium two years later for a date with destiny, Manchester United won the European Cup by beating Benfica. Just as victory against the Germans crowned his time as an international, defeating the Portuguese signified the pinnacle of an outstanding club career.

Many now only remember his supreme defensive qualities, but there are those who recall him starting out as a skilful inside-forward who was often amongst the goals. It is certain that the experience gained upfront in those early days helped immensely in his later development as a defender, because he was well aware of a forward's way of thinking and therefore found himself better equipped than most to know how best to combat their threat.

There were other footballers in his family. His father, an undertaker, had been more than useful while his elder brother Charlie was a great influence and actually played alongside him in a number of matches during his first season at Old Trafford.

Spending many hours kicking a football around the Red Rec(reation) pitch at Monsall or the Loco(motive) Ground in Newton Heath, close to where Manchester United began their existence, competing amongst those who were three or four years older had a beneficial 'toughening up' effect on the boy. An avid Red even then, Nobby, as he was known, had cheered on to the radio commentary when United won the 1948 F.A. Cup final.

A teacher by the name of John Mulligan picked him for the school under-12 side and, with unquestionable self-belief, he exuded maturity from an early age, demanding the ball at every opportunity while displaying a will to win that was second to none.

He captained Manchester Boys to the quarter-finals of the national schools' competition in the 1956/57 season and later earned the ultimate accolade for a young footballer by appearing five times for England Boys. His caps covered home games against Eire, Wales and Scotland, as well as matches in West Germany and Northern Ireland.

It wasn't long before scouts from all over the country started circling and his father met with representatives from Wolves, Burnley and Bolton, amongst others. Despite their attentions the budding prospect only ever wanted to join United, where he could be near his hero, Eddie Colman, and he was taken on the ground staff at a weekly wage of £3.

His debut for the Juniors in September 1957 was as an inside-forward and it concluded with him scoring a hat-trick in a 25-0 away annihilation of Knutsford Lads. The standard was clearly too easy for him and in eight games for the Juniors he managed to find the back of the net no less than eleven times. By the November of that year he had graduated to the Colts at wing-half and only remained in that side until the end of January when elevated into the 'A' team.

The club's teenage hopefuls would often have to wait a year or more before being considered for Youth Cup duty but, on the merit of advanced progress, his selection for a tie at Leeds was justified with a sound performance and a 4-1 win. For sure, it was a fairly rapid rise for one who was in the company of some of the country's top young talent.

The youth team bettered their cup win in Yorkshire by dismantling Newcastle in early January and all seemed rosy in the United garden. The following month, while showering at Old Trafford after completing his chores and a spot of training, Bill Inglis and Arthur Powell broke the devastating news that United's plane had crashed at Munich. Reading a newspaper on his way home, reports revealed the extent of the tragedy, which hit him especially hard when discovering that Eddie Colman was one of the dead.

Even though he was as distraught as anyone at the time, the event filled him with a desire to succeed in memory of his lost colleagues. Whereas others were pushed into the void, perhaps to the detriment of their future progress, his career continued in the 'A' side while the Youth Cup finally left Old Trafford following the Reds' defeat at Wolves.

In October 1958, Stan Crowther was required for the first-team, a development which enabled the sixteen year-old to break through the Central League threshold in a 3-2 home defeat by Aston Villa. Just over a week later he scored one of the goals in a 3-1 Youth Cup win at Bradford City and, taking over the captaincy somewhere along the cup run, it ended at the hands of Blackburn.

Stiles continued to make the right type of progress and began the 1959/60 campaign in the Reserves. United recommenced in the Youth Cup by running riot against Morecambe with the help of his hat-trick, although it wasn't third time lucky for him in the competition as the Reds were ousted in the semi-finals once again.

The 1960/61 season was key in terms of his future and he started the opening nine games with the Reserves, initially at half-back and then at inside-right, before being called up for a Football League encounter away to Bolton at number four. He kept his place throughout most of that and the following month, and his opening First Division goal against Newcastle was immediately dedicated to the memory of Eddie Colman. Getting in several games or so at a stretch before Matt Busby would 'rest' him in the Reserves, the process continued until he was eventually regarded as a fully-fledged first-teamer.

August 1961 saw his participation in pre-season tour games in Germany and Austria and on returning home he settled down into life as a senior. Apart from a period in the Central League around Christmas, for most of the time he was situated in his usual half-back position, with a few appearances in the number eight and ten shirts. It was around the end of that campaign when Johnny Giles moved in with his family and when Stiles later accompanied the lodger over to Ireland for a break, he met Giles' sister Kay and eventually the two got engaged.

Again involved with the first-team as the 1962/63 term got underway, and with the side languishing at the bottom end of the table, in February 1963 Busby bought Pat Crerand from Celtic. Crerand immediately took over his right-half role and from then on he was reliant on injuries in order to get back into the side. As United finally clicked into some sort of form he took part in two critical matches, an F.A. Cup semi-final success over Southampton and a relegation dogfight win over Manchester City.

Tweaking a hamstring caused him to miss the penultimate league game against Orient, only for him to reappear in the last match against Nottingham Forest whereby the injury flared up again and resulted in him being ruled out of the F.A. Cup final. It was a terrible blow, especially as he was due to marry Kay just a few weeks later.

With Crerand making the right-half position his own, at the start of the following season he was in and out of the first-team. About then he was finding particular difficulty in seeing the ball clearly and after Harry Gregg alerted Busby to the situation, a specialist prescribed contact lenses. Following a period of adjustment his form improved to the extent that he was soon pushing hard for a recall to the senior side.

Arguably the most significant turning point in his career came in March 1964, when Busby asked him to take up a defensive wing-half role in the immediate aftermath of a crushing 5-0 loss to Sporting Lisbon in the Cup Winners' Cup. Having been situated in the position on many occasions, previously he had always displayed an attacking bent. The experiment was tried out at White Hart Lane, where he practically snuffed the prolific Jimmy

Greaves out of the match.

Finally finding his niche, from that moment on his major talents, those of anticipating and breaking down attacks, developed rapidly and the major benefit of his ball-winning skills was that the most technically gifted in the team were able to spend more time in possession. He appeared in ten out of the last eleven league fixtures and after benefiting from a break in Ireland he couldn't wait to get back to work.

Undertaking extra training during the summer, he arrived back at Old Trafford fitter than ever and his vision was such that tackles were now extremely well timed. After losing twice in the first five matches, United's defence then conceded relatively few goals throughout the campaign.

In February 1965, he was selected for England's under-23 side against Scotland at Pittodrie, which called for a big decision because the Reds were due to face Sunderland at Roker Park that same day.

In the end, it was felt that the honour of representing his country provided him with the possibility of even greater success, so John Fitzpatrick was drafted in as his replacement for what proved to be the only game he missed that term.

Then chosen to represent the Football League against the Scottish League at Newcastle, an excellent performance was rewarded by selection for his full England debut against Scotland at Wembley. Forming a fine defensive barrier alongside the giant Jack Charlton, the impression they made didn't go unnoticed by manager Alf Ramsey.

As the season headed towards its later stages, the Reds were fighting on three fronts as they had reached the last four of the F.A. Cup, the quarter-final of a European competition and were challenging for the First Division title. At the end of March, Leeds knocked them out of the F.A. Cup prior to the Reds clinching the league title on goal difference by bouncing back to win seven games in a row. Then coming up against Ferencvaros in the semi-final of the Inter-Cities' Fairs Cup, they lost a play-off match in mid-June. On a personal level it had been a long campaign, nevertheless it was quite a successful one.

The 1965/66 term was one of a few lows and a huge high. By now an England regular, Stiles looked forward to appearing in the World Cup finals. United started slowly in the championship race and dropped too many silly points along the way, conversely performing well in the F.A. and European Cups, with the gritty defender putting in consistent displays in an unsettled defence. Having reached the last four of those competitions, and even though the Reds were highly fancied to win their semi-final games, they lost them both. While the defeats disappointed, there was still the World Cup to think about.

England drew their opening game with Uruguay and then defeated Mexico and France to achieve a quarter-final pairing with Argentina. It was at that stage when he faced one of his greatest challenges, as a badly mistimed tackle on Jacques Simon in the previous match left the French midfielder sprawled out on the pitch. The referee took no action, although the ensuing media frenzy jeopardised both his immediate place and international future. Ramsey held firm when put under intense pressure to drop him and was rewarded with a solid performance from the little dynamo when England won 1-0 to march into a semi-final tie with Portugal.

Not for the first time, his job was to mark the fabulous Eusebio and another controlled display crucially assisted England into the final with a 2-1 win. So, at the age of 24, the proud Mancunian took part in the most important game of his life and the post-match celebrations were capped with that famous victory jig, making his face known around the world.

Back at Old Trafford, Busby decided to strengthen the team soon after. The manager bought Alex Stepney, while Bobby Noble was promoted into the side and David Sadler appeared on a number of occasions.

Beginning the league calendar in good form, by December 1966 United were maintaining a challenge at the top of the table. An early exit from the F.A. Cup meant they were able to concentrate on the league and their efforts culminated in a 6-1 win over West Ham in the last away fixture, with the championship success it brought meaning that the Reds were back in the European Cup.

Taking time to find their rhythm in the 1967/68 season, the Reds were soon staking a claim to retain the First Division title. It was at this juncture when he experienced his first major injury problem as, in October, a twisted knee caused him to suffer a bad reaction and he eventually underwent a cartilage operation which caused his absence until the December. Then, in only his second game back from injury, his knee broke down again and further treatment was required. Returning once more in an 'A' team game in late January, he came through with no ill effects.

After an absence of over three months, in which he missed more than a dozen league games, his return to the first-team ended in a 2-1 defeat at Burnley. It was a worrying time for him as he had previously missed an F.A. Cup final due to injury and there was a definite concern about rushing back too soon.

Quickly re-establishing himself, the Reds then overcame Gornik of Poland and Real Madrid to reach the European Cup final and, on the 29th May 1968 at Wembley, Benfica provided their final barrier. Again given the task of shadowing Eusebio, United famously came out on top to win 4-1.

In the 1968/69 campaign, the Reds were a changing team as new men were introduced while injuries took their toll on others. As a consequence, they were never able to challenge for domestic honours and AC Milan ended their aspirations of retaining the European Cup in the semi-final.

It was also during this term when United contested the World Club Championship, in which the champions of Europe faced their counterparts from South America. The first leg against Estudiantes took place in Buenos Aires in September 1968 and Stiles, who undertook incredible provocation throughout, was sent off for arguing over an offside decision. United lost 1-0 and he was forced to sit out the return at Old Trafford the following month, when a 1-1 result ensured the trophy went to the cynical Argentineans. By the end of the season, a recurrence of his cartilage problems merited another operation.

Missing the majority of the 1969/70 campaign through injury, another comeback came just prior to the second of three F.A. Cup semi-final clashes with Leeds, which the Reds eventually lost at Burnden Park, and following his absences he was then unable to hold down a permanent place. However, having made only a few league appearances, he received a massive boost when called back into Ramsey's squad for the 1970 World Cup finals. Despite travelling to Mexico, his services weren't required as the holders were knocked out in the quarter-finals and he never again added to his 28 full England caps.

He was used off the bench for two of United's three Watney Cup ties in August 1970 and managed only seventeen further games in the First Division before concluding that a move was required in order to prolong his career. Not wanting to simply hang around in the Reserves or wait for a testimonial, in May 1971 a £20,000 fee made him the property of Second Division Middlesbrough.

Despite Middlesbrough challenging hard for promotion in the second of his campaigns there, he never really enjoyed his two years at Ayresome Park and so when Bobby Charlton offered him the chance to join Preston in 1973, the opportunity was welcomed. Despite still struggling for fitness, he managed to last another 46 league matches at Deepdale while also achieving some coaching qualifications.

When Charlton left North End, Harry Catterick took over and Stiles acted as his number two. By then he had ceased playing and, following two unsuccessful years, Catterick was fired and his assistant stepped up to replace him.

In his first term in charge Preston climbed into the Second Division, but a couple of years later they were relegated back from whence they came and he paid the price with the sack.

A coaching job in Canada with Vancouver Whitecaps became the next entry on his C.V. and, working alongside brother-in-law Johnny Giles for two years, he returned to England as a coach when the Irishman was installed as West Brom's manager. Remaining there until 1989, when he felt that it was time for a change, within a few days of his exit from The Hawthorns, Alex Ferguson offered him a job at Old Trafford. He had been away for all of eighteen years and there was great delight all round at his homecoming.

The former defender worked alongside Eric Harrison at the School of Excellence, assisting the under-10's, under-11's and under-12's, and also shared coaching duties with Brian Kidd. Starting by guiding the youth team to the final of the 1989 Northern Ireland Milk Cup, he was later entrusted with more control and moved up the managerial ladder. Subject of the television show 'This Is Your Life' in 1991, some of his fondest memories were relived for the viewing millions.

He was later offered Kidd's old job and a number of United's star performers of the 1990's benefited from his coaching and guidance, as well as his endless store of enthusiasm. Totally fed up with the increasing amount of paperwork involved, in 1993 he astonished many by suddenly tendering his notice.

Since then he has spent time as an after-dinner speaker, recalling his memories of the Busby Babes and winning the World and European Cups while working with Alex Ferguson, Matt Busby and Alf Ramsey, three of the best managers the game has ever known. Awarded the MBE for his services to the game in 2000, seven years on he was inducted into the English Football Hall of Fame.

A genuine United legend, Nobby Stiles has, for many years, lived in the same former club house in Stretford, just around the corner from Old Trafford.

When looking back over his incredible achievements in the game, in June 2010 he informed the Manchester Evening News that he was originally taught how to play football by a nun. In the October of that year a quantity of his football memorabilia was auctioned in Edinburgh, including his World Cup and European Cup medals, and he was reported to have raised over £400,000 from the sale.

BURNS, Francis (1964/65, 1965/66, 1966/67)

Born: Glenboig, near Coatbridge, 17th October 1948
Height: 5ft. 9ins., Weight: 10st. 10lbs.
Role: Left half-back
Career: **Our Lady & St. Joseph's Primary School (Glenboig)/ St. Augustine's High School (Coatbridge)/ Coatbridge Boys/ Coatbridge & Airdrie Boys/ Scotland Boys/ UNITED:** Am. June 1964 Pro. October 1965/ **Southampton** June 1972/ **Preston North End** August 1973/ **Shamrock Rovers** October 1981 to March 1982

'I supported Celtic when I was a young boy,' revealed Francis Burns, who went on to say, *'I played football for my school and when I was thirteen I also had some involvement with the Parish Boys' Guild side. I was one of Jim Mathie's discoveries.*

I was playing for Coatbridge Boys in a game against Airdrie Boys at Broomfield Park, Airdrie in October 1963 and even though I was at left full-back, I scored a hat-trick as we won 7-1.

At one point I had over twenty clubs from England and Scotland asking about me. In the November of that year I visited Celtic's ground in order to look over their facilities and exactly a week later I was a guest at Old Trafford to watch United beat Spurs 4-1.

Even though I was still too young to sign, I was quite happy with what I saw in Manchester and I made it my ambition to join (the Reds) as Pat Crerand and Denis Law were both idols of mine.'

Chosen for trials for Scotland Boys in February 1964, and despite the feeling that he *'hadn't done too well'*, Burns was honoured not only by selection but also the captaincy of the side that met Wales Boys at Ninian Park.

Later involved in a 4-2 defeat by England Boys at Dundee, as well as a 5-1 win over Northern Ireland Boys in Belfast, Jimmy Murphy was a spectator at the second of those games and United's assistant manager saw enough quality in the boy to agree with Mathie's assessment that he could be an asset to the club.

He signed as an amateur that June and his first contribution for the club was in a 10-1 home Lancashire League Supplementary Cup win over Rochdale.

Then appearing mainly for the 'B' side while making a barely noticeable gear change up to 'A' level, success came early as he was one of the eleven who won the Supplementary Cup in October by defeating Everton 1-0 on Merseyside. By early December he had seen the other side of the coin when, against the same opposition, his Youth Cup entrance was ruined by a 5-0 defeat at Goodison Park.

Utilised in the second of the Reserves' 1965/66 fixtures, three months later he was party to a second Lancashire League Supplementary Cup triumph when Blackburn were defeated 9-3 on aggregate in the final. By the end of the season the 'A' team had finished in the top three and the Reserves around mid-table, though Burns found his way to the latter status temporarily blocked by those such as John Fitzpatrick and Wilf Tranter.

Holding aspirations of continuing his early progress, the Scot was again with the Reserves as the 1966/67 term dawned and in November, with Bobby Noble already elevated to the first-team, the coaching staff moved him from his customary half-back role to left full-back. He had already taken part in a third Supplementary Cup final win in October as the Reds defeated Liverpool 3-2 and when the Youth Cup came around in early December he was chosen to lead the side.

With creditable wins over Everton, Huddersfield and Manchester City, the youth team held what he called *'real expectations of going all the way'* until a narrow reverse in the Fifth Round at Roker Park put paid to their involvement in the competition.

Commonly known as 'Frannie', he continued in the Reserves and numerous sterling displays at that level were acknowledged when he was asked to skipper Scotland Youth. With the Reds pushing towards the First Division Championship, at Eastertide in 1967 he was also included in the senior squad for games against Liverpool and Fulham.

Towards the end of the campaign there was some great news in store for him when hearing he had been nominated to travel with the seniors on their tour to the USA, New Zealand and Australia over the months of May and June.

Not used for either of the games in the States versus Benfica and Dundee, when United reached New Zealand he lined up at full-back for an 8-1 win over Auckland Association. *'I only got the one game,'* he said regretfully, *'as I got a knee injury and had to fly home unaccompanied to have an immediate cartilage operation.'*

Following a summer of recuperation he then participated in the opening four Central League games before being beckoned into the First Division as Shay Brennan's stand-in for a 3-1 win at West Ham on the 2nd September 1967. Establishing himself further by making his European Cup bow against Hibernians of Malta later that month, he went on to enjoy a great run as the Reds challenged for both league and European titles.

Sadly, his delight turned to heartbreak when, with the finishing line in sight, a crocked ankle caused him to miss a home game with Sheffield United.

Brennan was recalled to the side and, even though Burns regained his fitness, Matt Busby kept faith with the older man and as a result the twenty year-old missed both the European Cup semi-final second leg in Madrid and the final itself. He had featured in all of the earlier rounds and, quite understandably, his omission came as a devastating blow.

The despair felt at the latter part of the 1967/68 season was soon replaced by an extra incentive for him to re-establish his position in the senior side. His contributions towards United's cause hadn't escaped the notice of the international selectors and, having already been capped for his country at under-21 level, that year he was chosen for Scotland's under-23 team against England.

The 1968/69 term was very much a mixed bag for him and, commencing in the Reserves again, during August he was on the first-team's substitute bench. He then started half a dozen senior games and continued to fade in and out of the frame while contesting the full-back positions with Fitzpatrick and Tony Dunne.

A relatively stale twelve months came to an end when he reclaimed his place at the outset of 1969/70 campaign as Wilf McGuinness took over from Busby. Because McGuinness was prepared to use the younger players at his disposal, Burns was given the nod over some of the club's more established stars. However, the highlight of that period wasn't anything to do with United's affairs, as it came in November 1969 when he proudly made his one and only full Scotland appearance against Austria in Vienna.

The 1970/71 season saw him once more viewed as second choice to Dunne. He described it as his most frustrating time and also commented that, *'I seemed unable to regain a place regardless of how well I played.'*

When Frank O'Farrell joined as the manager in 1971 there was the hope of a fresh start but, even though he got in twenty consecutive first-team appearances from November to the following February, the acquisition of Martin Buchan from Aberdeen meant that from early March onwards he couldn't force his way back into contention. His eight-year United adventure ended with a 2-0 Central League home defeat by Stoke in April 1972 and two months later O'Farrell sold him to Southampton for £50,000.

Remembered as a highly dependable character, both in respect of on-field and personality contexts, the defender possessed a creative streak and was always a precise passer, particularly over long distances. Never a showy type and a valued and universally liked member of staff, he could consider himself unlucky to be around at a period of significant upheaval during which it was difficult for anyone other than the high-profile names to get a decent run in the side.

His sojourn at The Dell wasn't a memorable one. Injuring his knee again, which required a fourth cartilage operation in October 1972, his time at Southampton terminated when he became Bobby Charlton's first signing for Preston in August 1973.

Named as the club's 'Player of the Year' in his maiden season, Burns went on to serve North End for the next eight years, totalling over 270 League appearances and helping to earn them a promotion during Nobby Stiles' one term in charge. Still plagued with a troublesome knee, he left Deepdale, and the Football League, in the autumn of 1981.

Shamrock Rovers then fixed him up with a match-by-match contract for four or five months before the financial implications of getting him over to Dublin every weekend caused them to terminate the arrangement in March 1982.

He later spent some time coaching at West Bromwich Albion, again under Stiles, and helped to set up the first Academy system at The Hawthorns while also utilised on some scouting activities for the club.

In 1986, he emigrated to the Australian city of Perth and found work there in a sales capacity. Employed by an American appliance firm until 1995, at that point he branched out to set up his own cleaning company which he operated for four to five years.

Within that period he was connected to a number of local football teams. Initially managing Perth Italia for a period of twelve months, that spell was followed by a two-year stay in charge of Kingsway Olympic. He later took over at Kelmscott, an outfit with a broad English base, before finishing his managerial career with Bayswater Inter, a club which boasts a strong Italian following.

Francis Burns still lives on the west coast of Australia and spends some of his free time commentating on soccer for a local radio station, with the programmes he is involved in aimed at an audience mainly consisting of British ex-pats.

BRENNAN, James (1954/55)

Born: Withington, Manchester, 6th May 1937
Died: Tramore, Co. Waterford, Ireland, 9th June 2000
Height: 5ft. 9ins., Weight: 10st. 10lbs.
Role: Inside or centre-forward
Career: St. John's School (Wythenshawe)/ UNITED: Am. December 1953 Pro. April 1955 to June 1970/ Waterford player/manager August 1970 to c/s 1974

When Shay Brennan struck two goals in a 3-0 F.A. Cup win over Sheffield Wednesday on the 19th February 1958, his name became inextricably woven into the very fabric of Manchester United folklore. The game was staged in the saddest of circumstances, coming as it did less than two weeks after the Munich air crash.

Considering the heavy weight of expectancy inside Old Trafford on that most emotional of evenings, and the fact that the game also represented his senior debut, his brace against the Owls would by itself have been enough to ensure his future popularity among Reds' followers. As it transpired, he would additionally be remembered as a loyal and dedicated servant over a period of many years, becoming an integral part of some of the club's finest moments during a dazzlingly colourful period in its history.

His roots were in the Benchill district, on the southern fringe of Manchester, although both of his parents originated from the Republic of Ireland. He didn't share the same high football pedigree of many youngsters who were captured by United in the early to mid-1950's and, indeed, after playing for his school team, his budding talents were only ever displayed for St. John's Youth Club in Wythenshawe.

Despite performing in fairly modest confines, the rave reviews he earned as a raiding forward attracted attention from Bolton and Manchester City, as well as United. His preference led him in the direction of Old Trafford even though, as a comparatively late developer, at the time of signing amateur forms he was already sixteen and a half years-old.

His name was initially noted in the United Review when he scored twice for the Juniors from the inside-left position in a 10-2 win over Sale Albion in February 1954, and his reputation increased by way of him registering numerous goals throughout the remainder of the campaign.

Besides his undoubted soccer skills he was equally blessed with an extremely easygoing and friendly nature, and consequently was very popular both with his playing colleagues and the various members of the club's backroom staff.

Commencing the 1954/55 season in the Juniors once again, a nine-goal haul in the opening three games pushed him into the Colts within six weeks. A hat-trick against Oldham preceded his Youth Cup entrance at Liverpool, where his brace edged the Reds to an encouraging 4-1 win, but after appearing at the next stage against Manchester City his place went to Terry Beckett. He then enjoyed a scoring recall against Sheffield Wednesday and in March 1955 a hat-trick in the Fifth Round against Plymouth at Old Trafford consolidated his spot in the side.

When the Reds were drawn against a highly-fancied Chelsea outfit at Stamford Bridge in the opening leg of the Youth Cup semi-final, even the normally unflappable Mancunian was afflicted with a dose of pre-match tension and he later claimed it was the only occasion during his time in football when he was ever affected by nerves. It was an understandable reaction as, because of his age, it would be the only opportunity open to him to taste success in the national competition and, on the day, he was asked to fulfil an unfamiliar centre-forward role.

With the considerable threat from Chelsea over, United then went on to put West Brom to the sword in the final and at that point he was able to crown his short and sweet association with the Youth Cup by scoring two of the Reds' goals in the second leg at The Hawthorns.

Progressing to become a regular for the 'A' team in the 1955/56 term, at its conclusion he was present when the young Reds defeated Swiss-based

Manchester United's triumphant 1968 European Cup winning squad, the majority of whom had graduated through the club's ranks
Back row (l-r) Bill Foulkes, John Aston jnr., Jimmy Rimmer (all three former juniors), Alex Stepney, Alan Gowling (former junior), David Herd
Middle row (l-r) David Sadler (former junior), Tony Dunne, Shay Brennan (former junior), Pat Crerand, George Best, Francis Burns, trainer Jack Crompton (the latter three former juniors)
Front row (l-r) Jimmy Ryan, Nobby Stiles (both former juniors), Denis Law, manager Matt Busby, Bobby Charlton, Brian Kidd, John Fitzpatrick (the latter three former juniors)

side Concordia 3-0 in the Blue Stars final.

His development continued at a steady pace and in December 1956 he was called up for his Central League debut as a late replacement for Alex Dawson, who had failed a fitness test. Giving a good account of himself in a 1-0 home victory over Stoke, it was hardly surprising that he felt a little jaded at its conclusion because he had already been on 'A' team duty at Bury earlier that day.

By the end of the campaign he had amassed four goals in twelve appearances for the Reserves and, while not especially looking out of place, competition for places was intense and so he returned to the 'A' team to plunder a few more goals until oncoming events threw the club into turmoil.

In the immediate aftermath of Munich he was occasionally called upon for first-team duties and by the close of the 1957/58 season could count up five league appearances. His affinity with the F.A. Cup continued in the semi-final replay against Fulham at Highbury, where he distinguished himself by scoring one of the five goals that propelled the Reds to their second successive Wembley showpiece, although he was overlooked for the final itself.

A mainstay of the Central League side for the opening half of the 1958/59 term, mainly at centre-forward, just after Christmas he was moved to right half-back prior to being recalled into the first-team at number six on the last day of the campaign at Leicester. The move to a half-back role evidently suited his style and reading of the game, and he retained that responsibility for the seniors throughout the August and September of 1959.

It was as a result of the terrible injury suffered by his close friend Wilf McGuinness that he was finally able to establish himself at the higher level, and from December to the end of that campaign Brennan made 26 consecutive league and cup appearances as United finished in the top third of the division. All things considered, it was viewed as a modest success.

Again given a wing-half role for a 3-1 home defeat by Blackburn on the opening day of the following season, he was immediately moved still deeper in order to fill a full-back position. From then on it was felt that he was fully able to display his true potential and he went on to miss only one game of that term's fixture list.

Over the next three years he made over 100 first-team appearances as the Reds strove to re-establish themselves as a major power in the English game and his form was such that he was named as one of the 40 chosen for England's 1962 World Cup squad. While overlooked for the trip to Chile when the smaller travelling party was named, his inclusion in the initial group was recognition of his growing reputation as a skilful defender who was unfailingly consistent. The major black spot of that period was his exclusion from the F.A. Cup final team in 1963, when Noel Cantwell and Tony Dunne were the preferred full-backs.

His endeavours at club level were finally rewarded in a tangible way in 1964, a year in which he collected a First Division runners-up medal. Heady success as that was, it provided only a foretaste of what was to follow.

Forging a fabulous three-way defensive partnership with fellow full-back Dunne and centre-half Bill Foulkes all through the 1964/65 campaign, when United snatched the First Division title by a hair's breadth from Leeds, the threesome made up a solid cornerstone of the triumph, each contributing a full complement of 49 league and cup appearances.

Seven days after the close of the domestic season he was capped as a full international for the Republic of Ireland, a surprising turn of events considering his earlier involvement in the England set-up, and the opportunity came about because he had decided to take advantage of the newly-introduced rule allowing players to represent the country of birth of either of their parents. Featuring in a 1-0 victory over Spain in Dublin, he was joined by three others from Old Trafford; his trusty full-back partner Dunne, goalkeeper Pat Dunne and, starring at centre-forward, Noel Cantwell.

Two years later, and by now the proud recipient of seven Irish caps, he assisted the Reds to the First Division title again. His number of appearances for the first-team was reduced to sixteen due to the emergence of the exciting Bobby Noble and it was as a consequence of the newcomer's career-ending car crash that Brennan was able to re-establish himself towards the latter part of the term.

In the 1967/68 campaign his spot was again put under pressure by another up-and-coming teenager, Francis Burns, though he had regained his place in the senior side by the later stages of the season. His re-emergence couldn't have been timed any better as he was the favoured right full-back when United took on Benfica at Wembley in May 1968 to clinch their first European Cup final success. That historic victory over the crack Portuguese side undoubtedly represented his greatest day in football.

During his final term at Old Trafford, youngsters such as Paul Edwards and John Fitzpatrick were utilised in the right-back position and as such he made only nine First Division appearances. Wearing the number two jersey, and now aged nearly 33, his last game was a Central League fixture at Blackburn in April 1970.

Due to his length of service, he was entitled to a benefit match but, with Bill Foulkes already ahead of him in the queue for a testimonial, the logistics of arranging another such game were out of the question. Instead choosing the option of receiving an income for life, he became the very first United recipient of that type of financial benefit. His pension was set at £15 per week and was payable upon reaching the age of 35.

Two months after cutting his ties at Old Trafford he rebuffed interest from Preston, who wanted him to take over the reigns at Deepdale, and instead took up a position with Waterford, the relocation to Ireland made as a direct result of advice received by Matt Busby. Waterford were undisputedly top dogs in the League of Ireland at that time and when Brennan took over the reigns at Kilcohan Park they had already won the championship three years in succession. The Munster Express, dated 14th August 1970, noted that he was to be the club's player/manager and had secured a three-year contract. His first start that same month resulted in a 3-2 win at Cork Celtic.

In his early days at Waterford he made three further international appearances, the last of which was in a 3-0 reverse against Italy, and it increased his total number of caps to nineteen. The game in Florence took place in November 1970 and within days he had signed former United team-mate David Herd for Waterford.

By the following April some silverware was stashed in the club's trophy cabinet following a 4-2 win over Bohemians in the Independent Cup final, and the campaign was also memorable for Waterford's involvement in the European Cup, which ended at the hands of Glasgow Celtic.

In his second season in charge he successfully guided the Blues to the League of Ireland championship, the team only failing to make it a double by losing to Cork Hibernians in the 1972 Irish Cup final. Things seemed to be going along splendidly for all concerned at the club when, in August 1972 and without any prior warning signs, the local newspaper ran a story about him being dismissed. Apparently, internal politics had split the board, one of whom called the sacking *a disgrace*. It was an unsavoury incident in which the manager was an unwilling pawn but, when the dust settled, he was allowed to carry on his duties and remained at the helm for a further two years.

Waterford finished the 1973/74 term in fifth position in the league and in the May of that season one of his last acts as their manager was to arrange a celebrity five-a-side competition. The tournament was staged in order to raise much needed funds and included such soccer luminaries as Bobby Charlton, Johnny Giles, Roger Hunt, Nobby Stiles and Peter Osgood.

After vacating his position at Kilcohan Park, Brennan severed his day-to-day involvement with football entirely. Having settled happily in the area and electing not to return to England, he instead set up a transport company specialising in parcel deliveries. Later, following a heart bypass operation, he went into semi-retirement and substantially increased the number of hours spent on his other sporting passion, golf.

In August 1986, after suffering a heart attack, the testimonial denied to him sixteen years previously took place when Ron Atkinson's Manchester United were guests of Shamrock Rovers in Dublin. The game was played at Glenmalure Park and attracted a five-figure crowd who were only too willing to pay homage to a fine and likeable sportsman. Becoming a frequent visitor back to Manchester in order to attend various reunions, his liking for socialising proved to be undiminished and on one occasion he entertained a small crowd in a city centre pub with one of his lesser known talents, that of singing.

Sadly, in June 2000 at the age of 63, Shay Brennan died on a golf course close to his home at Tramore. Even though his life has passed, his exploits and achievements as a footballer, particularly for Manchester United and Eire, will forever shine in the record books, while his personality and charm will never be forgotten by his many friends and legions of admirers.

CHARLTON, Robert (1953/54, 1954/55, 1955/56)

Born: Ashington, 11th October 1937
Height: 5ft. 8ins., Weight: 10st. 4lbs.
Role: Forward
Career: **Hirst North Junior School (Ashington)/ Bedlington Grammar School/ East Northumberland Boys/ Northumberland Boys/ England Boys/ UNITED**: Am. June 1953 Pro. October 1954/ **Preston North End** manager June 1973, then as player/manager from May 1974 to August 1975/ **Waterford** (Ire) January and February 1976/ **Arcadia Shepherds** (SA)/ **Bangor City** March 1978/ **Newcastle KB United** (Aus) August 1978/ **Blacktown City** (Aus) March 1980

An avid supporter of Newcastle United as a boy, and a regular standing patron at the Gallowgate end of St. James's Park, Bobby Charlton was born at Laburnum Terrace in the tough Northumberland pit town of Ashington. His affection for the Magpies was perfectly understandable as they were his local team but, more importantly, the great goalscoring legend who acted as Newcastle's centre-forward at the time, Jackie Milburn, was his mother's cousin. If he ever dreamt of emulating his 'Uncle' Jackie's soccer fame during his schooldays, little could he have imagined they would all come true and that his destiny was to become nothing less than a football icon from the late 1950's right through to the 1970's.

Coming from such a humble working-class background, his road to the top began in typically modest circumstances, as he was appointed captain of his junior school team at the age of ten before playing at secondary school, district and county levels.

Having received a tip-off about the youngster's outstanding ability from a local headmaster, a Mr. Hemmingway, United scout Joe Armstrong stalked him almost from the moment he was chosen for East Northumberland Boys. By the time he had won the last of his four caps for England Boys in 1953, an agreement was reached that he would go to Manchester upon leaving school that spring.

Because of his connections with Newcastle, and the fact his older brother Jack had joined Leeds sometime earlier, it was perhaps rather surprising that he ended up at Old Trafford. However, a combination of Armstrong's persuasive powers and United's growing reputation of developing a stable of quality prospects appeared to win the day. The decision of who to join was not borne out of any financial considerations, which may have been the case if it were made nowadays, as he would have received exactly the same £10 signing-on fee from whichever of the eighteen clubs that were reputed to have made overtures to him.

But what a fabulous acquisition he was. Possessing practically every attribute a forward could have wished for, he had superb balance, pace in abundance, a devastating body swerve and two feet so good that it was impossible to distinguish which of them was the better. His other credentials were a passing technique that often saw the ball swept from one side of the pitch to the other with unfailing accuracy and a scintillating shot which frequently ended with net-bulging consequences.

Welded to a mild and sporting manner that would soon endear him to a generation of football followers across the globe, it was as predictable as night following day that he was destined to rise right to the very pinnacle of his profession.

In time-honoured fashion, his soccer apprenticeship commenced on the bottom rung at Old Trafford. Beginning for the Blues in the customary Reds v. Blues pre-season trial game in August 1953, a four-goal salvo for the Juniors in an 11-1 crushing of Lancashire Dynamo a little while later saw him earn an early sample of adventure in the Youth XI, when taking part in a Tomlinson Trophy game against Sheffield & Hallamshire.

Starting in mid-September, over the next five matches he smashed in eighteen goals for the Juniors, a feat which justified his promotion into the Colts for most of the remainder of the campaign. Whenever he did drop back down to the Juniors, goals simply flowed from him and his contribution assisted them to the Altrincham Junior League championship, as well as three cup finals.

Having deputised for David Pegg against Sheffield & Hallamshire, a month later he played in his first Youth Cup game alongside Pegg at Everton. He scored twice against Wrexham in the Second Round and appeared in every subsequent tie, taking up various offensive positions, as United marched unerringly through the tournament to beat Wolves in the final. Within a fortnight he had won his only youth cap against Northern Ireland at Newtownards where, scoring once in a 2-2 draw, the result secured England the Home International Youth Championship.

There was another late season achievement for him in the Petit Cup final, when a 2-0 deficit to Hulme Lads Club with twenty minutes remaining was turned into a 6-2 victory for the Colts, his contribution amounting to four of the goals.

He starred regularly for the Colts in the 1954/55 term and was ever-present for all nine Youth Cup ties. The Geordie normally took up an inside-forward position for the Colts, but in January he was placed at outside-left, and it was in that same role from which he grabbed a Youth Cup Fourth Round brace against Sheffield Wednesday and a hat-trick against Plymouth at the next stage.

Once again wearing the number eleven jersey, in March 1955 he celebrated his call-up to the 'A' team by hitting a hat-trick against Prescot Cables Reserves and over a nineteen-match spell totalled no less than 37 goals, which included two in the Supplementary Cup final against Preston in April. With his star firmly in the ascendancy, on the ninth of that month his inclusion at outside-right in the Reserves' 1-0 home defeat by Burnley was certainly well merited.

A few weeks later he moved to inside-left for the Youth Cup final matches against West Brom in order to accommodate left-winger Dennis Fidler, scoring in the first leg at Old Trafford where the Reds set up a 4-1 lead they added to at The Hawthorns.

An opening day hat-trick in a 9-2 'A' team blitzing of Bury in August 1955

levered him back into the Central League side, for whom he went on to notch 37 goals in as many games, which included a stupendous six at West Brom's expense late in the term.

His Youth Cup exploits also began in superb fashion that season, with a hat-trick at Preston. Three weeks prior to the Deepdale trip he had been given a first-team blooding in a floodlit friendly, clocking the third United goal in a 5-1 win before a crowd of 8,817 at Bury. Then returning to the youth team to hit a personal best of five goals against Bexleyheath & Welling at the last eight stage, with the defeat of Chesterfield in the final he could look back over a record 27 consecutive Youth Cup contests which had yielded 23 goals and a maximum number of winners' plaques.

He made nine consecutive starts in the Central League at the beginning of the 1956/57 campaign, notching six goals, at which point Matt Busby called him up for his competitive debut at senior level.

That First Division entrance came in October 1956 when, as deputy for Tommy Taylor and despite feeling some discomfort from an ankle injury, he scored twice from the centre-forward position against his namesake club, Charlton Athletic, in a 4-2 home win.

Grabbing another three goals against the Addicks in the return fixture at The Valley, and finishing the campaign with totals of ten goals in fourteen starts for the first-team, those appearance figures were sufficient to give him a championship medal. He also put in an appearance against Aston Villa in the 1957 F.A. Cup final, as well as gaining further valuable experience along the way by appearing in the European Cup.

He took part in another seventeen Central League fixtures from August to December 1957 and at that point again forced his way into the first-team. Charlton then added eleven senior appearances when, after scoring twice in the away leg of the European Cup quarter-final against Red Star Belgrade in February 1958, he mercifully survived the plane crash which killed eight of his team-mates on the return journey. Despite the terrible scenes he must have witnessed, the twenty year-old was left almost unscathed and resumed his career within a month of the disaster.

As Jimmy Murphy strove to put the club back on an even keel, and following only a brief period of recuperation back home in Ashington, he contributed towards taking United back to Wembley, where he again finished with an F.A. Cup finalist's medal. By the close of the term he was able to count thirteen goals from 28 First Division and F.A. Cup appearances.

Within a couple of months of escaping from the wreckage of the smashed aircraft at Munich he had been awarded a full England cap. It was a scoring start for him, as he registered a goal when assisting the visitors to defeat Scotland by 4-0 at Hampden Park, and in England's next game he grabbed both goals as Portugal were beaten 2-1 at Wembley.

Even though the honour of representing his country filled him with pride, it also put him in something of a quandary because he knew full well his absence from club football only helped to deplete United's playing staff still further at a time when they needed him most. Nevertheless, in a rather thoughtless act, England's management team saw fit to call him up and it resulted in him being unable to assist the Reds in their European Cup semi-final clashes with AC Milan in May 1958.

Back at Old Trafford, during the 1958/59 season he top scored in the league with 29 goals from 38 appearances, following up by finding the net eighteen times from 37 starts in the next campaign. By that time his full England cap collection had already ballooned to seventeen.

During the latter part of the 1950's he was deployed in a wide left position in the England forward-line, where his speed, allied to an ability to cut inside from the wing and unleash ferocious right-foot shots on goal, unhinged many a defence. Starting in the spring of 1960, Busby also favoured using him in that position for a number of years, having initially nominated him as an inside-forward.

The 1960's really were Charlton's heyday and, as his goals and appearances totals clocked up week by week, the trophies and accolades began to be drawn to him like a magnet. At club level, the Reds won the F.A. Cup in 1963 by defeating Leicester, a development that meant he had at last secured a victory medal from the competition at the third time of asking, and two years later the First Division championship came to Old Trafford, by which time he had been moved from his wing berth into a deep-lying forward responsibility for United.

Soon after, England manager Alf Ramsey also recognised the effect his shooting and passing ability had when following in behind the recognised strikers. With either of those skills he was frequently able to break down even the best organised of defensive strategies.

His finest hour in an international shirt arrived in the summer of 1966, when England won the eighth World Cup final with a 4-2 victory against West Germany, and his personal contribution to that proudest of times for the national side was simply immense.

A dismal 0-0 draw against Uruguay was the result of the home nation's opening World Cup match, and England then looked to be stuttering in the following game against Mexico when, courtesy of television screens all over the world, millions of viewers were able to witness a genuine Ashington thunderbolt. Picking up possession just inside his own half while running at the Mexican defence, he feinted to go to the left before dropping a shoulder when veering to the right, and from all of 25 yards, he then struck a shot that zoomed like a missile past the flailing Mexican 'keeper to put England one up. Club and country colleague Nobby Stiles later claimed that it was the best goal he ever saw and, standing directly behind the scorer when the unstoppable drive was launched, the little defender was in the perfect place to pass judgement.

That magnificent moment undeniably set England on their way. The Mexicans conceded again to give England a 2-0 win and victories over France and Argentina followed, by which time it appeared that every man, woman and child in the country was gripped by football frenzy.

The United man then claimed both of England goals in a 2-1 win over Portugal, the effect of which was to ease the home nation into the final where the ultimate prize in world football was achieved. Operating behind Bobby at centre-half was his big brother, Jack, and between the posts for England was Gordon Banks, the goalkeeper who had made such a good impression against the Reds in the Youth Cup final for Chesterfield ten years earlier.

For those monumental efforts towards England's success in the 1966 World Cup, he was recognised with two of the most prestigious awards in world football. Voted 'Footballer of the Year' in England as well as claiming the crown of 'European Footballer of the Year', his fame just then was such that it was claimed there was nowhere in the world that the name of Bobby Charlton wasn't known.

In May 1967, United regained the First Division crown, the outcome of which meant that the club was back on the European scene once more. A year later, the prize he craved most of all was secured when the Reds defeated Benfica in the European Cup final at Wembley, where he scored the first and fourth goals in a 4-1 victory that will forever live in the hearts and memories of Manchester United fans.

He won his 100th full international cap when skippering and scoring in a 3-1 win over Northern Ireland at Wembley in April 1970 and two months later he travelled to Mexico in order to assist England's efforts to try to retain the World Cup. Included in a side many rated as better than the one which had triumphed at Wembley four years earlier, England lost 3-2 to West Germany at the last eight stage in the glaring heat of Leon.

With the holders surrendering a 2-0 lead, the Germans got a goal back as England were preparing to substitute Charlton who, at almost 33 years of age and having played his fourth game in the space of twelve days, was felt in need of a rest. Manager Alf Ramsey was later crucified by the press for the switch as England capitulated without the presence of their star orchestrator.

That game in Leon was his 106th and last appearance as a full international, a record at that time. Since April 1960, when England played their first game of the decade in a 1-1 draw with Scotland in Glasgow, to his departure against West Germany in Mexico, he had missed only nineteen from a possible total of 111 England fixtures.

It was a fabulous record which, including his six appearances for the under-23's made between September 1958 and November 1960 and various youth and schoolboy honours, meant that his haul of caps embroidered with the three lions amounted to 117, while he had additionally represented the Football League on eight occasions.

His total of goals scored as a full international finally settled at 49, a number which is as yet unsurpassed by an Englishman. Some of the milestones in that record tally included hat-tricks against the USA in May 1959, Luxembourg in October 1960, Mexico in May 1961, and Switzerland in June 1963.

For the next three years he was able to concentrate his football efforts solely on United duties. In seasons 1970/71 and 1971/72 a position of eighth in the First Division table was achieved, and in the 1972/73 campaign, following a dismal start, the Reds ended up in 18th place. Now aged 35, and with the season nearing to a close, he announced his retirement.

On the 28th April 1973, he made the last of his 606 league appearances for the Reds against Chelsea at Stamford Bridge and a few days later scored twice during a 4-1 away victory in an Anglo-Italian Cup-tie against Verona to finally close the book on his Old Trafford playing career.

Even though the number of games he had played for United was surpassed by Ryan Giggs in 2008, his club record of 199 league goals still stands. Besides his massive contributions in the bread and butter of the First Division, he also featured in a further 153 F.A. Cup, Charity Shield, Football League Cup and European Cup games, scoring 50 times.

Soon after returning from Italy he became the manager of Preston and a difficult maiden baptism at the helm ended with North End's relegation to the Third Division in 1974. For the start of the following term he took the precaution of re-registering as a player and, donning his boots again, in August 1974 he made his first appearance for Preston in a 1-0 home win over Plymouth wearing the number four jersey.

Accumulating 38 league (eight goals), four F.A. Cup (one goal) and three Football League Cup (one goal) appearances for the season, his final match was a 2-1 defeat at Port Vale in March 1975 as Preston finished eighth in the order of merit. Then, in August 1975, he abruptly resigned his post over a dispute with a Preston board who were reputedly selling playing staff over his head.

In January 1976, he signed on an open-ended contract for League of Ireland side Waterford and, now playing more or less for the fun of it, the attendance for his debut was the biggest the club had enjoyed for a number of years. Nevertheless, his association with the Kilcohan Park outfit lasted for just four games and later that year he made a solitary appearance for Arcadia Shepherds in South Africa.

A little later still he became an executive director at Bangor City. The progressive Farrar Road club actually managed to press him into action on one occasion and in March 1978, a goal from the 40 year-old veteran helped Bangor to a 2-1 win over Treviso in the Anglo-Italian Cup.

Outside of football he occupied his time by opening a travel company and in March 1980 also became a director at Wigan. Opted onto the Athletic board by chairman Freddie Pye, that same month he began a short stay in Australia with New South Wales State League First Division outfit, Blacktown City.

He registered a goal on his only appearance for them against St. George Budapest and a picture of it is still on display at the club to this day. It was actually their first game in the National League and they went on to win 4-2. At that time Blacktown operated a School of Excellence for youth players whereby they could train and develop their skills in a non-competitive environment, and it is said he was sufficiently taken with the idea that it would be incorporated into his own soccer schools sometime later.

At the end of the 1979/80 campaign he played as a guest in a friendly fixture for Maltese side Floriana, while almost two years later he turned out for Wigan in another friendly against Norwegian club, Bodo Grand. Over the years he has also appeared in countless other charity and non-competitive matches.

He took temporary charge of team affairs at Springfield Park following the dismissal of manager Larry Lloyd in April 1983 and in his first game at the reigns, Wigan, who were in a perilous position, defeated Wrexham. With Athletic eventually managing to avoid relegation by one point, at the end of the season he handed over responsibility to the club's assistant manager and also resigned as a director, along with his chairman, as a new board took over the club.

During the 1980's he launched the aforementioned 'Bobby Charlton Soccer Schools', an initiative conceived with the development of junior footballers in mind. Easily the most famous discovery of the immensely popular and successful coaching classes was future soccer superstar, David Beckham.

To the great acclaim of all Manchester United supporters, in the 1984 close season he was brought back to Old Trafford as a director. For the greater part of 30 years he has devoted a similar level of commitment and diplomacy to the Reds' cause in the boardroom as that which he displayed in the world's football stadiums throughout his long and illustrious playing career.

Having already received an OBE in July 1969, in June 1994, ten years to the month after returning to United, he was knighted for his services to football, since when the club has undoubtedly enjoyed the most successful period in its history. Another honour followed when it was announced in December 2008 that he was to be made a Freeman of the City of Manchester.

Nowadays, Sir Bobby Charlton divides his United responsibilities with travelling the world as a football ambassador.

FARRAR, David (1963/64, 1964/65)

Born: Manchester, 7th April 1947
Height: 5ft. 8ins., Weight: 12st. 6lbs.
Role: Centre-half
Career: Thomas Street Primary School (West Gorton)/Nicholls Secondary School for Boys (Ardwick)/ Manchester Boys/ Lancashire Boys/ England Boys/ UNITED: Am. May 1962 App. Pro. December 1962 Pro. April 1964/ Southport June 1966/ Winsford United July 1967 to November 1969

It is a fact of modern day soccer that Academy systems actively try to prevent the juniors under their care from playing too much football in order to cut down on the risk of them going stale. United's staff at Carrington are very specific about the amount of time young boys can spend out on the pitch and 'encourage' them not to turn out for their school or local representative sides. 'Burnout' isn't a recent phenomenon in the sport, though, and by the age of fourteen David Farrar had already decided that he wasn't too interested in football any longer.

Clearly very active at that period, the Mancunian said of his younger days, 'I really liked sports at school and was lucky in that I was naturally quite good at most things. I was captain of Thomas Street cricket team and was a decent all-rounder. In fact, I was better at cricket than football at primary school. During the week my mates would throw stones against my window to get me up and we would kick a ball about all day as we used to play on the shale pitch behind the flats where I lived.

I also used to play indoor five-a-side at Openshaw Lads Club and I was soon asked to have a try out in the East Manchester Area team for Manchester Boys trials. I was only thirteen and remember going down to London for the first time to play London Boys at White Hart Lane. Anyway, by the time I turned fourteen I had already featured in the Manchester Boys team for two years and I was a regular for Lancashire Boys. I was in my final year at school and I couldn't wait to leave, get a job, be with my mates and try different things.'

He then went on to detail the next crucial event in his life by stating, 'In February 1962 (Nicholls School headmaster) Mr. Roberts told me that I had been selected for the North versus South England trials at Shrewsbury. It was around then that I just felt I had had enough and really didn't fancy it.

Mr. Roberts explained it was a big honour for the school and that I should at least go for the trials. I was really shy as a kid and I didn't even want my name to be read out at assembly, but he convinced me to try out and the next thing I knew I was picked for England Boys. It was too late to say no by then.'

An only child who lost his father to cancer when he was eight, despite having failed the eleven-plus exam, at that point he wasn't overly concerned because he was fully prepared to learn a trade in order to earn a living. With a new avenue of opportunity opening up before him, it now appeared that football could provide a way of getting out of a school system he hated.

The first of his five England Boys caps came against Wales at Newcastle and two weeks later he was pitched in against Northern Ireland at Burnden Park. Also present when England suffered a reverse at the hands of West Germany at Wembley, his appearance total was completed against Scotland in Glasgow and in the Republic of Ireland.

Expanding on those crazy couple of months in the spring of 1962, he said, 'It was all a bit of a whirlwind really. There were loads of scouts knocking at the door, and given that my dad wasn't around, I was used to making most of my own decisions. I remember Joe Armstrong being one of the first to show an interest and my mother really liked him. Bolton and Burnley wanted me to sign and (Oldham manager) Jack Rowley also came to see me.

Even though I had been to London before with Manchester Boys, to play at Wembley was fantastic. After the game we were shown around the Houses of Parliament, which was agony as my feet were killing me from playing. We had a big posh banquet with all the German team, it was a real experience. Then for the last game Joe Armstrong flew my mother over to watch me in Dublin. I'm not sure if that sort of thing was allowed, but it was certainly a nice touch.

Then (Manchester) City came in right at the end asking me to join them. I was a City fan as a boy, and my father often took me to Maine Road, but I liked United and Joe Armstrong.'

Mature beyond his years, Farrar agreed to join United subject to them obtaining him an apprenticeship and so the club arranged for him to join Salford builders Matthew Cowans as an indentured plumber. Leaving school at the Easter break, from then on he trained at The Cliff a couple of times a week and over the summer months.

A 5-2 defeat for the 'B' team at Burnley marked his start for the Reds and he remained at that grade, either at centre-half or right-half, throughout the 1962/63 campaign. Despite his strength, aerial prowess and hard-tackling assets, with Christmas in sight it had become clear that if further progress was to be made he needed to give up his plumbing job and concentrate on being a footballer. As a consequence of terminating his employment with Cowans and signing as a club apprentice in the December, there was an immediately noticeable improvement in his game.

'I remember at the end of my first year thinking I'm going to have to work really hard here,' he admitted. 'What was interesting, though, was that both George Best and Willie Anderson were then just okay, they didn't particularly stand out.'

While his physique and tenacity allowed him to compete alongside more technically gifted team-mates, it was during his second season when he made greater strides than previously. While sharing the centre-half position in the 'B' team with Paul Edwards, he began to break through to the 'A' side on a more sustained basis and in October 1963 was unexpectedly thrust into the Central League team as a late replacement for Wilf Tranter.

Experiencing a relatively untroubled game alongside Jimmy Nicholson and Nobby Stiles as United thrashed Barnsley 8-0 at Old Trafford, he later recalled just how much his progress and achievements meant when mentioning, 'I was dead chuffed about playing in the Reserves but also quite nervous. During the game every time I looked up there was Nobby or Jimmy either telling me what to do or asking for the ball, so they really helped me through what turned out to be an easy 90 minutes.'

From his perspective, that period was easily most notable for a Youth Cup run in which he was integral to each and every one of the eight ties. Taking up the story, he proudly claimed, 'I was named in the youth team and after a comfortable win over Barrow we faced Blackpool. I remember the match distinctly because I played really well and a few of the first-team congratulated me afterwards. We had a marvellous run, I was really enjoying my football, playing in front of big crowds, it gave me a lot of confidence. Then to win the Youth Cup was just fantastic.'

At the end of the campaign he was selected to participate in the Blue Stars tournament and while on tour he, Eddie Harrop and at least two others decided to sample a couple of beers. While such an excess would certainly have been frowned upon by Matt Busby and Jimmy Murphy, the manager and his assistant knew that the two Manchester lads had been drinking alcohol for some time and the boys' actions weren't considered wildly excessive in the context of the times. In his autobiography, George Best recalled that for him and John Fitzpatrick it was their first drinking session, and the Irishman also remembered the experience leaving them both the worse for wear.

Farrar made it his aim to claim a place in the second string during the 1964/65 season but, with Tranter and Noel Cantwell sharing the centre-half position, he was only able to squeeze in two Central League appearances.

In the December he captained the youth side in a crushing 5-0 defeat at Everton from the centre-half position, but by the following March he had been moved to a half-back role as he was finding life difficult in the middle of the defence. The reason for the switch came about because he was now eighteen and hadn't grown since leaving school. Resultantly, most of the other juniors had caught up with him physically and he wasn't tall enough to deal with the aerial battles that often took place between centre-backs and big, powerful centre-forwards.

Also, because David Sadler had impressed with a number of eye-catching displays over in Zurich, Farrar consequently faced even more competition for a place in the second team.

As he explained, it was then that his indifference to football surfaced for the second time, 'I suppose I never loved the game in the same way as other lads as I always had other things that competed for my attention. I was mad about cars, so Wilf (Tranter) helped me get a part-time job in a garage in Sale. After we lost the Youth Cup tie at Everton there wasn't really much to play for and I wasn't getting a game in the Reserves, so football started to come second to my mates and my other job. Don't get me wrong, I was still giving 100% on the park, but I had just had enough.'

He started the 1965/66 campaign once again in the 'A' side before taking advantage of some poor form by Peter McBride when getting in a run of eleven consecutive Reserve games through September and October. With him stationed at right-half, the Reds managed only two wins and he returned to the 'A' team for the remainder of the term.

Although outstanding at junior level, it wouldn't be unkind to suggest that he simply stopped developing as a footballer during his last two years at the club and, added to his fading appetite for the game, it led to an inevitable parting of the ways.

Along with McBride, in June 1966 he joined Southport as a part-time professional. From his angle the arrangement was ideal as it meant that he could continue with football, hold down a job as a mechanic and also spend some time socialising.

A kick in the groin scuppered any immediate thoughts of getting a game in Southport's senior side and following a hernia operation in Ancoats Hospital he was ruled out for the rest of the season. With the Sandgrounders ending it by winning promotion to the Third Division, his release came as a result of the club choosing to go fully professional. Far from being disillusioned at the development, he was pleased that he could now devote more of his energy towards working on cars.

After departing Southport he was attached to Winsford United for a couple of years, with the highlight of that period being an appearance in the Cheshire Cup final. By now employed in the heavy plant industry, and because he was required to put in long hours, the 22 year-old felt it was an appropriate time to leave the game.

In 1970, he was offered an opening as a long distance lorry driver for an exhibition company, a job which entailed him travelling all over Europe for most of the decade. Having changed jobs since, he has remained in the same industry and still drives for a living at home and abroad.

David Farrar started watching football again in the late 1970's and now gets to Old Trafford whenever he can. As someone who has always tried to maintain his fitness, he undertook a couple of marathons in his late 30's. Possibly one of the first to suffer from the syndrome of playing too much football at an early age, the Altrincham resident understands only too well the importance of taking it easy with the juniors of today.

SMITH, Barry (1956/57, 1957/58, 1958/59)

Born: Dawley, Shropshire, 3rd September 1940
Height: 5ft. 10ins., Weight: 11st. 7lbs.
Role: Right full-back
Career: Peacock Street Junior School (Gorton)/ Spurley Hey Secondary School (Gorton)/ Manchester Boys/ Lancashire Boys/ England Boys/ UNITED: Am. July 1956 Pro. April 1958/ Buxton August 1961/ Cambridge City November 1961/ Cambridge United July 1963/ Hastings United September 1963 to May 1964/ Ely City September 1964/ Buxton November 1964 to May 1965/ Droylsden August to November 1966

Barry Smith was associated with United for five years and, initially at least, it seemed that only time and experience stood between him and a senior call-up. He gained plenty of international knowledge while on schoolboy and youth duties, on top of figuring regularly for the Reds at second and third team grades over a period of four seasons, but it was as a result of failing to properly establish himself in the Central League side that he was allowed to leave.

Effectively becoming both a victim and a beneficiary of the lifting of the maximum wage for footballers when United's directors trimmed the playing staff in 1961, the decision to off-load a number of personnel was made in order that the wages of the club's top stars could be increased, only without the commitment of a significant jump in outgoings.

As the Old Trafford door closed behind him, so another opened at Southern League Cambridge City. In those days City were bankrolled by a wealthy chairman, who also happened to be the owner of a local building company, and Smith joined them after being offered a substantially better financial package than he could have hoped to secure from the majority of Football League clubs.

For a short duration prior to moving south, he engaged in a weekly contract with Buxton. The stopover at Silverlands was arranged in order to help keep up his fitness level, and on the day of the penultimate game for the Derbyshire club he was married in the morning and helped to see off Chester Reserves in the afternoon.

Once the move to Cambridge was completed he went on to accumulate over 30 appearances in his opening term. Crowds at Milton Road were usually between three and four thousand strong, with over 8,500 viewing the local derby against Cambridge United.

Pocketing a Playing Fields Cup winners' medal following victory over Wisbech Town, that achievement was surpassed in February 1962 when City defeated Cambridge United over two legs to win the Cambridgeshire Professional Cup. During a hugely enjoyable first year he also played in prestige home floodlit friendly games against Chelsea, Ipswich, Coventry and Huddersfield.

If the 1961/62 campaign had been good for him, the following one was in almost total contrast as he made only three appearances in their senior side up until November and was then consigned to Reserve football in the Eastern Counties League for the remainder of his spell with the club.

Making the short journey across the River Cam in order to join their arch rivals, the local newspaper revealed that he had been unable to regain his place in the City first-team since breaking his nose in a friendly against Doncaster. In an uneventful stay he made only three starts for Cambridge United prior to signing for Hastings, who were also members of the Southern League.

He performed around sixteen times in senior league and cup games for the Pilot Field outfit, although his time at Hastings involved a lot of travelling and consequently it lasted less than a season. A much more convenient move came about shortly into the 1964/65 term when he agreed a contract with Ely City. By that time he had decided to return to the North-West and, resultantly, his stay at Ely involved just above half a dozen matches.

Quickly re-engaged by Buxton on his return to the Manchester area, his second 'debut' for them was against Wigan Athletic at Silverlands in November 1964. He increased his Buxton appearance totals by making 23 Cheshire League and three Derbyshire Senior Cup starts for them before the campaign ended.

Over a year after leaving Buxton he was tempted out of retirement by Lancashire Combination members Droylsden and twelve matches for them proved to be his last as a paid footballer.

Twenty-six years earlier, he came into the world in the county of Salop, after which his family set up home in Manchester's Gorton suburb when he was six.

Keen on numerous sports as a boy, he was an excellent swimmer, and a more than useful competitor at athletics, but it was out on a football pitch where, from an early stage, it was obvious that he possessed a natural flair. After representing both his junior and senior schools he was chosen for Manchester Boys, and from that point onwards United had designs on him, with Joe Armstrong becoming a regular observer of matches he played in.

He then won county honours before making five appearances for England Boys in the spring of 1956, one of which was as captain. With Wales defeated 3-2 at Ashton Gate in Bristol and West Germany thumped 5-1 at Portsmouth's Fratton Park, a slender 1-0 win over Eire at Tolka Park in Dublin made for an impressive hat-trick of victories. Scotland, though, proved to be England Boys' bogey side that season, inflicting losses of 3-1 in Dundee and 2-1 at a near-capacity Wembley on them.

Within a few weeks of those games he became a United player following a visit to his parents by Bert Whalley. The club was hard pushed to obtain his signature because they were required to deflect strong interest from both Chelsea and Bolton to get it.

Equally adept with both feet, the local prospect was principally an aggressive defender. His powerful aerial strength, allied to a robust tackling style, meant that he was comfortable at centre-half or full-back and he provided a stubborn obstacle for opposing forwards in either of those positions.

As the club's coaches felt that he was already above playing for the Juniors, on the day the curtain was lifted on the 1956/57 term he took up the centre-half role for the 'B' team. Used as a pivot for ten out of the opening eleven matches before being switched to right-back in October, that same month he also took up the number two jersey when the Reds knocked Burnley out of the Youth Cup at The Cliff.

He bounced between the 'A' and 'B' teams from November onwards and remained a defensive force for all further nine Youth Cup ties as United went on to beat West Ham in the final. His principal task as a full-back would have been to tightly mark the opposition's left winger and he boasted an unblemished record in that respect as not one outside-left managed a goal against the Reds along the cup trail.

Also utilised for a post-season triumph, when the youngsters swept Augsburg aside 2-0 to win the Blue Stars final in Zurich, those two successes represented a fantastic start to his career at Old Trafford.

He replaced Ian Greaves for a resounding 6-1 home Central League victory over Aston Villa in September 1957, keeping his place in the Reserves for the following fixtures at Derby and at home to Sheffield Wednesday. Burnley were again the victims when the Reds started that term's Youth Cup run which, following convincing wins over Blackpool, Leeds, Newcastle and Doncaster, ended in defeat at the hands of Wolves. Reinstated for the Reserves' last fourteen matches after the Munich tragedy, at the end of the campaign he was handed a professional contract.

He was involved in twelve of the first sixteen Central League games of the 1958/59 season and then entered into a second stretch at that level from January through to the middle of March. Also captaining the under-18's for a spell that term, when defeat came at the hands of Blackburn in the semi-final it brought his Youth Cup days to a conclusion. In all, he had accumulated 25 consecutive appearances in the competition.

While making strides through the junior and Reserve teams, he also won youth caps for England. Some of the England Youth games were televised and consequently he and his international colleagues became well-known soccer names for a time. The pinnacle of his England Youth period came in a contest against the Spanish under-20 side in Madrid's magnificent Bernabeu Stadium. Despite giving away a two-year age advantage, as England were an under-18 XI, a superb 4-0 win over the Spaniards, in front of 65,000 spectators, made it a memorable occasion for Smith who was operating alongside future England skipper, Bobby Moore.

He started the 1959/60 campaign by taking part in all bar three of the opening fourteen Central League fixtures before losing his central defence spot to Frank Haydock. With Reg Holland and Tommy Heron pinning down the full-back places, from then on he was only able to get an odd game at that level, such as when injuries allowed.

In the following season he, Haydock and Ronnie Cope battled for the centre-half position in the Reserves while Heron, Tony Dunne and Joe Carolan shared the full-back responsibilities. In and out of the side for much of the time, his best run was achieved by taking part in their final five matches, of which the last was a 4-3 defeat at Turf Moor. Within weeks he became a victim of the club's fiscal pruning shears.

Outside the game, Barry Smith was employed in the transport business and spent periods as both a heavy goods driver and a transport manager. His love of the game never diminished, though, and he was later involved with Martley of the Hyde & District League for a number of years. Variously a player, coach and manager of the club, his on-field contributions only stopped when he reached the age of 50.

JAMES, Steven Robert (1966/67, 1967/68)

Born: Coseley, West Midlands, 29th November 1949
Height: 6ft., **Weight:** 12st. 7lbs.
Role: Centre-half
Career: Manor School (Woodcross, Coseley)/ Brierley Hill, Sedgley & Tipton Boys/ Staffordshire Boys/ Birmingham County Boys/ UNITED: App. Pro. July 1965 Pro. December 1966/ **York City** January 1976/ **Kidderminster Harriers** July 1980 to May 1982

In April 1966, Bill Foulkes was going through a wretched time as United were knocked out of the European and F.A. Cups within the space of three days, both at the semi-final stage. The experienced campaigner was dropped for the last seven games, with the versatile Noel Cantwell taking over at pivot. During the following term, as Old Father Time crept up on the loyal Foulkes, supporters and pundits pondered over who Matt Busby might target as a potential replacement.

The F.A. News magazine analysed United's tactics in an article in their March 1967 issue and suggested Tottenham's Mike England as the number one option while also predicting that David Sadler could make the position his own. In the 1967/68 season, Sadler and Foulkes actually shared the centre-half role, though Busby remained loyal to the latter in the big matches because the flint-hard veteran rarely let him down on such occasions.

Even so, the club was about to enter a transitional period and early in the following campaign, with David Herd transferred to Stoke and Denis Law, Francis Burns, Nobby Stiles and John Aston all on the casualty list, Sadler was switched to centre-forward, a position he had occupied in the past. So, when Foulkes picked up a knock, Busby resisted the temptation of the transfer market and dipped into the defensive depth already at his disposal. Of his younger options, Paul Edwards was struggling with an injury and so the manager instead chose to elevate an inexperienced rookie for a tough encounter at Liverpool in October.

The newcomer later found his performance assessed in the United Review:

It was probably Steve James who had the greater testing. Still only eighteen, he had to bear a lot of pressure as centre-half stand-in for Foulkes. Curiously enough he found himself lined up against an old team-mate from his school days in Alun Evans.

The two of them played together for Staffordshire Schoolboys and were also together in last season's England Youth team. Perhaps this gave the United man confidence, for he certainly acquitted himself well. Here perhaps is United's home grown answer to the problem of who follows Bill Foulkes.

The Review again commented on his progress the following February:

The cup tie could well prove important in the general development of the club. For instance Steve James, the young centre-half, responded to the tension and pressure with a very elegant game to complete a dozen cup and league games since making his debut at Liverpool in October.

Bill Foulkes, one of the most experienced centre-halves in the business, saw the game and agreed that the future at number five is in good hands. 'Steve's greatest asset is that he wants to learn,' says Bill. 'We have had quite a few chats and all he is lacking now is experience. This of course is coming with every game. He has two cup ties behind him now and is coming along nicely.'

Seemingly popping up from nowhere to make a name for himself, by the end of the 1968/69 term he had notched up an impressive 29 starts in all competitions, a huge leap for the relatively unknown teenager whose father, Ron, had been a half-back with Birmingham City and Northampton Town immediately after the war.

Earlier in the decade, specifically in January 1964, the younger James was selected for Staffordshire Boys against Cheshire Boys at Gresty Road despite most of his colleagues being a year older. During the following school year he was an automatic pick for both his town and county teams and also represented Birmingham County in their annual challenge match against London in March.

Featuring in the final of the Birmingham Schools Senior Shield against South-East Staffordshire the following month, in early May he helped Brierley Hill, Sedgley & Tipton Boys to claim the Birmingham Shield following a 2-1 final victory over South Staffordshire Boys. With the Staffordshire Leckie Shield already secured, it proved a productive campaign for the unfancied town team and they followed their domestic accomplishments with a five-game tour of Germany.

Named as a reserve for England Boys during the 1964/65 Victory Shield calendar, as such he became hot property. Eventually deciding on a move north to join the Reds, he was a rock at the heart of the 'B' team's defence for all except three games of their 1965/66 season. In the early stages of the following term he was tried in a number of positions, including full-back and outside right, when facing competition from Edwards for the stopper role.

Soon after, when Edwards moved to full-back, James settled into his more familiar role of centre-half with the 'A' team and was called into a Youth Cup side that was knocked out at Sunderland in March. Later that month his fortunes took a sudden upswing when an injury to Alan Duff resulted in him being called up into the Reserves for a 1-0 win at Bury.

Over the course of the Reds' European Cup winning campaign he flitted between both of the club's junior teams and was occasionally involved with the Reserves. Creditably marking his captaincy of the Youth Cup team with a goal in the opening tie against Huddersfield, sadly the side's progress was halted in the Fourth Round.

Early in the New Year, he was chosen for an England Youth team that faced France in Paris and retained his place for a couple of International Youth Tournament Qualifiers against Eire. After taking part in a 0-0 draw in Dublin in early February, England defeated the Irish 4-1 at Portsmouth three weeks later, and he was then named in the squad that travelled to France for the tournament finals only to feature in one match, a 0-0 draw with Bulgaria in Nimes. Nevertheless, the season ended in glory when collecting his first club medal by virtue of the youth side defeating West Ham in the final of the Blue Stars Tournament.

His name was pencilled in at number five for the Reserves' maiden fixture of the 1968/69 term and he proceeded to see service in their opening twelve matches. Then stepping into the senior limelight for the first time at Anfield with less than 20 Central League starts behind him, he was recalled to the First Division in November, impressing in 0-0 draws with Ipswich and Stoke, and found himself elevated for the third time in mid-December to chalk up a further 26 appearances. It was a fine record, and even the hurt of being excluded in favour of Foulkes for both European Cup semi-final ties with AC Milan couldn't detract from his splendid achievements.

Because Foulkes' career crashed unceremoniously only three games into the 1969/70 campaign, new manager Wilf McGuinness suddenly found Ian Ure at his disposal. With the £100,000 capture partnering either Sadler or Nobby Stiles at the back, the youngster saw first-team action only three times that season.

A quiet, reserved lad off the pitch, the United Fan Club interviewed the gangly twenty year-old in January 1970 when he gave an insight into his personal preferences by answering a range of questions in a 'Shoot Magazine' type questionnaire:

Car: *Wolseley 1300*
Favourite Players: *Brian Labone and Billy McNeill*
Favourite Other Team: *West Ham United*
Most Difficult Opponent: *Ron Davies (Southampton)*
Most Memorable Match: *My debut versus Liverpool*

Biggest Thrill: *Scoring my first league goal versus Chelsea*
Biggest Disappointment: *Not playing against AC Milan*
Best Country Visited: *Switzerland*
Favourite Food: *Steak or Scampi*
Favourite Drink: *Coffee or Milk*
Miscellaneous Likes: *Driving, Travelling*
Miscellaneous Dislikes: *None*
Favourite TV Show: *Till Death Us Do Part*
Favourite Singer: *Frank Sinatra*
Best Friend: *Don Givens*
Biggest Drag In Soccer: *I've not found one yet*
Biggest Influence On Career: *My father*
If You Weren't A Footballer: *Something connected with sport. A PE teacher, maybe*
Personal Ambition: *To stay with Manchester United for the rest of my playing career*
Professional Ambition: *To help them to even more success*

He began the 1970/71 term with the Reserves until McGuinness dropped Ure in the October and recalled him to the team. Entering into a run of eleven consecutive matches, which included the first leg of an unproductive League Cup semi-final against Aston Villa, things changed quickly when McGuinness was relieved of his duties and replaced by Matt Busby. In a bid to shore up a suspect rearguard, Busby promoted Edwards and James was one of several casualties. His future at the club was now uncertain, fans questioned whether or not he was good enough and many suggested that United needed to buy a quality centre-half, with Luton's Chris Nicholl being widely tipped to join the Reds.

When Frank O'Farrell took over in July 1971, the new boss decided that Ure and Edwards would form the Reserves' central defensive partnership while James and Sadler were to fill those same roles for the first-team. It was a massive vote of confidence, and under O'Farrell's leadership the Reds won fourteen of their first twenty league games and lost only twice to lead the First Division while displaying some of their finest football for years. Unfortunately, the wheels fell off the bandwagon after Christmas and United staggered across the finishing line in eighth place. While disappointing from a team perspective, particularly after such a superb start, it was a tremendous campaign for him on a personal level as he missed only seven games in total, all through minor knocks.

Because United lost their opening three games and won only one match of their first twelve to put them deep in the relegation mire, O'Farrell came under increasing pressure in the early weeks of the 1972/73 season. As a consequence, and not for the first time, James was dropped while the manager tried to find a winning formula.

Remaining in the second string over the next few months, and witnessing the axe fall on O'Farrell, the arrival of the more confident Tommy Docherty in December represented his fourth manager in as many years. Results didn't improve immediately under Docherty, with only one win in his first nine games, and in early March James was back on first-team duty for a 2-1 home win over West Brom. The Reds then went on a run of five wins from the next eight games to help stave off relegation, although the recalled centre-back missed the last two matches of the term through injury, both of which were lost.

The Reds' relegation campaign proved a terrible experience for him, as well as everyone else connected with the club, and after only two league games he picked up a knock that put him out of action for a few weeks. It prompted a sequence of recovery and repair, and like a broken engine, he found it difficult to change up and down the gears, missing much of the action.

United's first season in the lower division for over 35 years saw Jim Holton partner Martin Buchan in central defence and when the former fractured a leg at Sheffield Wednesday in early December, it was Arnie Sidebottom who was given a run of six games in the side. Significantly, the Reds dropped three valuable promotion points and were knocked out of the F.A. Cup at the first hurdle, events which forced Docherty to elevate James into the senior eleven. Even though the Coseley kid retained his place throughout United's eventful push for the championship apart from injury, the writing was on the wall, for during one of his spells out of action the manager had experimented with a Greenhoff/Buchan defensive duo. It was a resounding success and a delighted Docherty concluded that another part of his team-building puzzle had now fallen into place.

James' last term at the club followed an all-too-familiar pattern as he was present for the first four Central League games before picking up another injury that sidelined him until mid-October. This time there was no coming back, because Greenhoff and Buchan were a rearguard revelation as the Reds took the First Division by storm and he was present for only three further Central League fixtures before being transfer listed.

Eventually bowing out in the Reserves' 6-1 home thrashing of Huddersfield in December, he left the club without any fanfare, his exit matching his personality in that respect. While his methods were broadly similar to that of an old-fashioned centre-half, the modern trend demanded more creative and cultured contributions, attributes that Buchan and Greenhoff offered and Docherty seemingly felt he didn't.

Fortunately, York City manager Wilf McGuinness had been monitoring him for some months and suggested that he watch their F.A. Cup tie against Hereford on the first Saturday of 1976. The Minstermen put in a solid performance and so McGuinness' target agreed to join the Bootham Crescent club in mid-January. He was immediately thrown into York's relegation dogfight but, despite his best efforts, they slid into the Third Division. A mainstay of the team over the next two campaigns, he then experienced his third relegation in four years as the club plummeted to the bottom rung of the league ladder. A serious injury kept him out of action for all of the 1978/79 season before he added eighteen further starts to his career total in his final year of league football.

With over a century of appearances in York's colours to his name, Kidderminster Harriers gave him the opportunity to return closer to his roots in 1980 and he repaid them by assisting in their commitments over the next two years. During that period they captured the Staffordshire Senior Cup and he missed only one of their 61 fixtures in his last term.

Contrary to information given by some sources, he gave up football entirely after leaving Aggborough to become the licensee of a public house. Known to have managed at least two hostelries, one of them was the Saracen's Head in Dudley town centre.

Steve James was a hard working, conscientious player, strong in the tackle and not easily beaten in the air, competences usually expected in a centre-half. While never quite managing to forge a lasting place in the side at Old Trafford, he still managed to clock up over 160 senior appearances for Manchester United through a time of some turbulence at the club.

SMITH, Robert William
(1959/60, 1960/61, 1961/62)

Born: Prestbury, Cheshire, 14th March 1944
Height: 5ft. 7ins., **Weight:** 10st. 12lbs.
Role: Right full-back or left-half
Career: Moston Lane Primary School/ Ducie Avenue Technical High School (Moss Side)/ Manchester Boys/ Lancashire Boys/ England Boys/ UNITED: Am. July 1959 Pro. April 1961/ Scunthorpe United March 1965/ Grimsby Town January 1967/ Brighton & Hove Albion June 1968/ Chester June 1971/ Hartlepool United October 1971 to May 1973/ Bury July 1973 to May 1974

With Hitler's bombs dropping with some regularity in and around Manchester during the early part of 1944, a lady by the name of Mrs. Smith entered St. Mary's Hospital in Prestbury to give birth to her second son, Robert. It wasn't on the leafy lanes of the Cheshire village that Bobby, as he came to be known, grew up but on the somewhat tougher streets of Moston in north Manchester. His family lived on Moston Lane, and Bobby developed a love for the game of football on the wide expanse called Boggart Hole Clough. In his younger days he had seen future Bolton, Carlisle and Barrow goalkeeper Joe Dean and soon-to-be United starlet Wilf McGuinness demonstrate their capabilities on the same patch of grass and it filled him with a passion to emulate the feats of the two local boys.

Saturday afternoons were often spent at the Newton Heath Loco Ground, where he would clamber over the perimeter wall to watch various amateur teams, or perhaps he might catch a game in which budding youngsters such as Nobby Lawton would parade their skills for Manchester Boys.

When he was on the verge of moving up to secondary school, Smith required an operation at Booth Hall Hospital in order to remove a cyst from his ear and he missed the first four months of the curriculum, as well as initial selection for the school football side. Eventually chosen to keep goal for a while, before properly establishing himself in the team he was also tried at centre-half. And what an ace combination they were. Just then Ducie Avenue were the city's school football kings, plundering league and cup honours for four consecutive years while amazingly remaining undefeated throughout that whole period.

During the 1958/59 school campaign it seemed that he was hardly ever in class because of the amount of time spent on football duties. He again missed the opening of the term due to illness and was overlooked for West Manchester Boys until Fred Eyre, a prodigy who was destined for Manchester City, convinced the selectors that his friend should be in the full Manchester Boys team.

With Lancashire Boys experience to call on, he was then nominated as a possible for England. Initially taking part in the northern trials, on top of a 'North versus South' match, in March 1959 he represented England against 'The Rest' at Ipswich and was delighted to make the squad for the forthcoming international programme. By then Blackburn, Manchester City, West Ham and Aston Villa counted among a clutch of suitors who had made him offers.

He went on to win six England Boys caps, half of which were for Victory Shield appearances against Scotland, Wales and Northern Ireland. The main event of that period was a 2-0 win over West Germany at Wembley in front of 95,000 fans and, in his final two games, England also played Eire in Dublin and West Germany in Essen. By the end of the school year, Ducie Avenue held both the Technical Schools Trophy and the First Division Shield.

'There had been a whisper about me signing for United before Joe Armstrong convinced my mum that they would be a good option for me,' he explained. *'Even while Joe was charming mum I wasn't averse to the proposition as I'd held a bit of a soft spot for the club since the Munich tragedy.'* He jokingly added, *'The thing that really swung it was that the 112 bus from Moston Lane stopped right next to Warwick Road.'*

He became a member of the ground staff in July 1959, and later playing in the Juniors was obviously no test for him because after just five games he was elevated into the 'B' side. At Youth Cup time, which started in October, Smith was selected at right full-back.

The following term unfolded much as the previous one. Predominantly in the 'B' team for most of the season, he also gained an occasional appearance for the 'A' side and in February 1961 there was a first start for him in the Central League due to an injury to Tony Dunne.

A month later he earned his first England Youth cap in Utrecht and, even though the Dutch won, he did enough to retain his place against West Germany 72 hours later. The young Lions were defeated again in Flensburg, but the defender was later presented with an England blazer and informed that he was in the squad which would contest the European Youth Championships staged in the Canary Islands that summer.

Involved in all seven of the 1960/61 campaign's Youth Cup ties for United, which ended in defeat at Stoke in the Fifth Round, as he recalled, the match was something of a double blow, *'Not only did we get knocked out, I also broke my nose in a collision with Barry Fry. Because my place in the England Youth team was at stake I was prepared to delay an operation. The club wouldn't wear it, and I was sent to Stockport Infirmary for surgery.'*

In August 1961, he was drafted back into the Reserves and retained his place right through to January. Also chosen to skipper the Youth Cup team, when United faced City at Old Trafford in a night match, the Blues' captain was none other than Fred Eyre, an event he recounted with some amusement, *'Just before we kicked off Fred and I began discussing where we were going in town after the match. Because we won, he disappeared as soon as the game finished!'*

Events soon turned more serious, as he later noted, *'I had received a 'dead leg' and I was playing through the pain barrier. Like a lot of clubs then, United only employed a part-time physiotherapist (Ted Dalton) and he dealt with all the injuries he could in the morning before attending his private practice in Manchester in the afternoon.*

Ted often only had time to deal with the first-team's problems while the Reserves and the kids had to wait their turn. It was actually fairly common practice for a lot of the younger staff to get private treatment, which they paid for out of their own pockets. While I was waiting, my injury calcified and anyone could see that I was in a lot of pain. I had an X-ray, which showed I had a blood clot, and I then spent a few months in hospital with a haematoma.'

A strong wing-half with great stamina rather than blistering speed, he was back for the beginning of the 1962/63 season, playing three times for the 'A' team before being selected once again for the Reserves. However, rather than taking up his normal right full-back role, the Mostonian was selected in the half-back line, a position he was most comfortable with.

After twenty matches for the Reserves from September through to early March, on the 18th of that month he accompanied the first-team for their game at West Ham. Named as 12th man for the trip to Upton Park, he was chosen in that capacity on a handful of occasions thereafter.

His career began to stagnate over the late 1963 and early 1964 period as he accumulated only thirteen more Central League appearances while operating in the 'A' team for most of the time.

Smith did slightly better in the 1964/65 term by chalking up twenty appearances for the Reserves but, with fresh competition from John Fitzpatrick and Peter McBride, it seemed sensible to move on. Following a meeting with Matt Busby he agreed to transfer to Scunthorpe for the promise of first-team games and after almost six years at the club his exit came in a 4-0 home win over Chesterfield Reserves on the 24th February 1965.

Making his Football League debut for the Irons ten days later at Carlisle, he notched over 80 matches during a 22-month tenure at the Old Show Ground. As his contract was nearing its end, overtures from Aston Villa and Brighton were ignored in favour of taking an improved deal from Grimsby.

Commencing in January 1967, his time at Blundell Park was disrupted by managerial changes and less than a year and a half into his contract he moved to Brighton. He added over 70 games to his experience in three years at the Goldstone Ground while never really hammering down a place in their senior side.

At the commencement of the 1971/72 campaign he spent a short spell with Chester, for whom he played just twice prior to signing for Fourth Division Hartlepool. It was touch and go for Hartlepool as they nearly lost him to Northwich Victoria, with the newspaper in that area claiming he was on the verge of taking over as their manager and had already *'coached Chester's younger players'*. He turned out another 70-odd times for the Victoria Park club over a couple of seasons before deciding to apply for the player/assistant manager vacancy at Bury.

Having taken his coaching badges while only in his mid-20's, the job was just the challenge he had been looking for. Suddenly, when Allan Brown departed to take over at Nottingham Forest in November 1973, he was unexpectedly promoted and the appointment made him the youngest manager to that point in the Shakers' history, just four months short of his 30th birthday.

Despite steering Bury out of the Fourth Division in 1974, further progress eluded him and his reign at Gigg Lane ended with the sack in October 1977. He wasn't out of work long, though, and by the following day he had joined struggling Port Vale as their new boss, remaining until the end of that term when they were relegated to the basement division.

At the conclusion of his short and strained spell at Vale Park, in May 1978 he was quickly appointed manager of Swindon, the Town needing to compensate Port Vale to the tune of £10,000 for his services. Despite still being a relatively young manager, during his first campaign in charge they missed promotion by only three points when agonisingly losing their last two games.

His major achievement at the club came the following year, when Swindon beat Arsenal to reach the last four of the League Cup, and they only narrowly missed going to Wembley through Wolves scoring the winner five minutes from the end of the semi-final second leg. A huge amount had been invested in the transfer market by Swindon's standards, including £250,000 on just two players, and when they lost their first five matches of the 1980/81 term the board relieved him of his duties.

He then acted as assistant boss at Blackpool for a couple of years prior to joining Newport County in a similar capacity. Following four years at Newport he became the number two at Cardiff City, remaining there for a further four seasons. A spell as assistant at Hereford preceded a return to management with Swansea, his tenure there lasting only 80 days. Jimmy Rimmer was then handed the job of caretaker manager and Smith supported the ex-United 'keeper until the end of the 1995/96 fixture list prior to becoming Sheffield Wednesday's chief scout.

He ran his own football agency in 2000 before joining Sven-Göran Eriksson's England set-up as a senior scout. Responsible for watching many of England's opponents, after taking in the Finland v. Germany game in 2001 he pinpointed the Germans' defensive frailties to the coaching staff. His comments and recommendations were noted, particularly regarding their lack of pace in defence, with the result being that England recorded an historic 5-1 victory in Munich in the September of that year.

Now retired, Bobby Smith and his second wife live near Swansea.

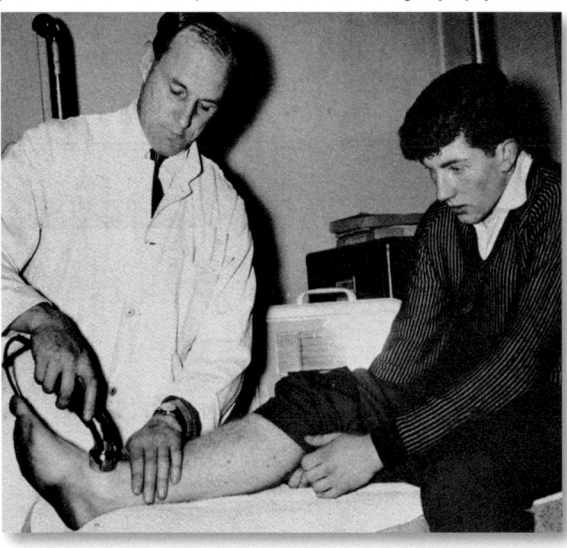

An injured Bobby Smith receives some in-house treatment for his ailment from trainer Jack Crompton

Another let-down for Reds

Chapter Four

DARK DAYS

1968-69

1) Malcolm Crozier	9) Gordon Masson	1) John McInally	9) Jimmy Hall
2) Dean Hill	10) Dennis Wann	2) Laurie Millerchip	10) Peter O'Sullivan
3) Alan Tuson	11) Jeff Hesketh	3) Kevin Lewis	11) Damien Ferguson
4) Paul Brown	*12) Ken Boardman (for 4)*	4) Brian Greenhoff	*12) Tony Young*
5) Malcolm Howard		5) Ken Goodeve	
6) Colin Monks		6) Eric Young	
7) Wyn Jones		7) Barney Daniels	
8) Joe Auguste		8) Ian McMurdo	

DECEMBER 1968

BLACKPOOL 0 v 0 MANCHESTER UNITED

Monday 2nd

Kick-off 7.30 p.m.

Attendance 1,073

second round

The Reds approached their 17th crack at the Youth Cup with a substantially different side to the one upended from the tournament earlier in the year, which in itself wasn't the best of omens for their chances of actually lifting the trophy once again.

United displayed a completely new defence save for Ken Goodeve. He found himself switched from right full-back to centre-half while Laurie Millerchip, who was named as a substitute three times during the previous season without taking part in any of the action, went in at number two.

New to the club was Brian Greenhoff, a versatile individual from the Barnsley area whose older brother Jimmy was a professional at Birmingham City. Greenhoff slipped into the right-half berth, the position he currently occupied in the 'B' team.

The rest of the Reds' defensive formation was made up of former schoolboy internationals and they included John McInally from Gatehouse of Fleet in the south of Scotland, a goalkeeper who was already well into his second term with the club. By then McInally was making some headway into the 'A' side, the kind of progress which fairly represented what would have been expected of someone with his quality.

Just in front of him was Kevin Lewis, a powerful and determined lad from Hull who had captained England on his way to winning five caps. Despite only being with the club since the summer, an excellent start to his career at Old Trafford was evidenced by him already spending more time in the 'A' team than with the 'B'.

Making up the last of the middle section was Stockton-on-Tees born Eric Young, a midfielder whose England experience ran to half a dozen appearances. Eric was no relation to United substitute and true Mancunian Tony Young, even though the father of the former originally hailed from Fallowfield. An intelligent forward, Tony had represented both Manchester and Lancashire Boys over the last couple of seasons.

The front-line included Youth Cup experienced Jimmy Hall, Ian McMurdo and Peter O'Sullivan, and they were supplemented at outside-left by Dubliner Damien Ferguson, an Eire Boys international, as well as local lad Barney Daniels.

An explosive winger whose goals tended to come in bunches, Daniels had already scored a hat-trick in his only appearance for the 'B' team that season, an achievement which came on top of nine goals in thirteen starts for the 'A' eleven. Manchester lad McMurdo had worn the number seven jersey for all four Youth Cup games in the previous season, scoring once, and his progress was marked with a couple of appearances for the Reserves.

As for the Reds' destination at the opening stage, the thought of Blackpool in December invariably conjures up mental images of dark clouds, a windswept promenade and lines of amusement arcades with the shutters closed and locked, which was precisely the scene along the seafront as United prepared to do battle.

The draw historically favoured the Reds who, in four past meetings with Blackpool had won every time, and on two of those occasions with plenty of leeway to spare.

Over the preceding weekend, the News of the World's Peter Slingsby made reference to the game:

This week has seen the launching of this season's F.A Youth Cup competition – Liverpool, Everton and Manchester City, among others, were in action – and on Monday the youngsters from Old Trafford begin their campaign at Blackpool.

And the emphasis in the United team will quite definitely be on youngsters, with a host of new names appearing on the team sheet at Bloomfield Road.

I gather from club officials that the team this winter will be an extremely young one, but on looking over the pedigree of candidates there's little doubt that Joe Armstrong and his scouts have again been highly successful in their recruiting 'sorties'.

Obviously – writing as I do well before the event – the team has not been selected, but in a truly competitive field Mr. Armstrong and his aids have done their work well once again and they will follow the careers of the newest crop of 'Busby Babes' with considerable interest.

No one needs reminding that United's youth policy is admired all over Britain; in its way, the success of so many home grown players at senior level must be almost irresistible for parents planning a football career for their talented off-spring.

Most recent case in point is Steve James, who has made his First Division debut this season at centre-half.

Only a year ago this son of a former Birmingham player was in the Youth Cup side that played against Huddersfield, Blackpool and Burnley.

Men like Nobby Stiles, George Best, Bobby Charlton, Brian Kidd, David Sadler, Carlo Sartori, Francis Burns, John Fitzpatrick and many others began their climb

to the top sphere via the competition, and hopes are high for the newest starlets who will wear the same colours at Blackpool.

A snapshot of the hosts' angle was given a viewing via the local Gazette newspaper:

Blackpool youngsters face a tough task in the Second Round of the F.A. Youth Cup when they meet Manchester United at Bloomfield Road tonight.

Blackpool had a bye in the First Round but tonight will come up against the cream of United's young talent.

All the players on show tonight had to be under eighteen before September 1.

In addition to players seen by Blackpool supporters before, the Blackpool side will include some youngsters as yet unknown to the fans.

These include goalkeeper Malcolm Crozier, a seventeen year-old from Manchester, recently signed on amateur forms. He has made a few appearances in the 'A' team.

At right-back will be another Manchester lad, sixteen year-old Dean Hill.

John Hughes is included in seven players from whom the attack will be chosen but it seems unlikely that the young Welshman, who cracked two ribs earlier this month, will play.

The pitifully small number of folk in attendance viewed a contest in which both goalkeepers were kept busy yet ultimately remained unbeaten.

A Blackpool Gazette reporter was on hand to record just a few of the game's main events:

> BLACKPOOL live to fight another day after a tense second round FA Youth Cup tussle with Manchester United at Bloomfield-road last night, writes Philip McEntee.
>
> A draw was just about the right result for two sides who produced a lively and entertaining game, although United, with a replay on their own territory, must be favourites to get through to the next round.
>
> Blackpool were the better side in the first half but United went flat out in the second and might have snatched victory. But their attacking game almost back-fired on them in the last minute.
>
> Then Wann, Blackpool's most enterprising player, ran beautifully on to a pass from Boardman but, with goal-keeper McInally coming out, he pushed his effort outside the post to miss a late chance to win the game.
>
> **Brown injured**
>
> During the United pressure young Blackpool 'keeper Malcolm Crozier showed what a fine prospect he is with some great goalkeeping.
>
> He made fine saves from Hall and McMurdo and always cleared his lines intelligently.
>
> Another outstanding Blackpool performer was wing half Paul Brown, who fights like a terrier for every ball.
>
> Unfortunately, he was injured soon after the interval.
>
> Blackpool moved Gordon Masson back to wing half and brought on Boardman to lead the attack but they missed Brown's fire and the attack generally did not have a happy night.

To which Jack Pauline added a few comments in the Review:

In the first minute a loose ball screwed out of McInally's hands but he quickly recovered to prevent the ball crossing the line to give the home side an early lead.

From this point neither side looked dangerous near goal in an evenly contested first half, although McInally was prominent with a save from Wann and McMurdo was unlucky to see a good centre go across the face of goal with no forward managing to get a touch.

Having much the better of the second half, United always threatened to take the lead but weak shooting and good work by Crozier proved a barrier.

Two notable saves by the 'keeper just about broke the United pressure, one a full-length effort from McMurdo and another from a shot by Daniels on the half turn.

1) John McInally	9) Jimmy Hall
2) Laurie Millerchip	10) Peter O'Sullivan
3) Kevin Lewis	11) Damien Ferguson
4) Brian Greenhoff	*12) Tony Young*
5) Ken Goodeve	
6) Eric Young	
7) Barney Daniels	
8) Ian McMurdo	

1) Malcolm Crozier	9) John Hughes
2) Dean Hill	10) Dennis Wann
3) Alan Tuson	11) Jeff Hesketh
4) Paul Brown	*12) Joe Auguste (for 2)*
5) Malcolm Howard	
6) Gordon Masson	
7) Wyn Jones	
8) Ken Boardman	

MANCHESTER UNITED 7 v 2 BLACKPOOL

Daniels (2), Hall (3, 1 pen), McMurdo, O'Sullivan   Boardman, Hughes

1968-69

DECEMBER 1968

Monday 16th

Kick-off 7.30 p.m.

Attendance 4,203

second round replay

Officials of the two clubs weren't able to agree on a quick date to settle which of the teams would go through to the Third Round so the replay was staged exactly a fortnight after the initial conflict and it made up in no short measure for the previous absence of goals at Bloomfield Road.

The visitors brought what they felt was an improved combination to Old Trafford and fit-again John Hughes was able to spearhead their attack while Gordon Masson resumed at left-half. Ken Boardman continued, and out went Colin Monks and Joe Auguste, the latter to occupy the substitute's bench.

Because neither of United's Lancashire League sides were in action over the previous weekend, most of the under-18 team were rested. Their pent-up energy was expended on the Seasiders, who missed a couple of chances early on and then offered little resistance until the result was way beyond them.

The Reds opened the scoring in the 24th minute, taking up a 3-0 lead by half time, and a much improved performance was crowned with a trio of goals from a member of the home side whose reputation seemed to grow every time he found the back of the net.

David Meek was in attendance:

Manchester United's youngsters found their feet in their F.A. Youth Cup Second Round replay against Blackpool at Old Trafford.

They failed to score in the first game at Bloomfield Road but ran amok amongst the goals against a plucky but outplayed side.

The Reds were much more powerful down the middle where, with the help of a penalty, centre-forward Jimmy Hall hit a hat-trick. Inside-forwards Peter O'Sullivan and Ian McMurdo pulled the Blackpool defence to pieces at times and had a goal apiece.

United were also speedy on the wings with amateur outside-right Bernard Daniels scoring two goals.

With one of the youngest teams they have had for several years, the Reds have four first-year boys in the side and all but three of the team will be eligible for next season's competition.

Only O'Sullivan and Ken Goodeve are full professionals.

Blackpool fought right to the end and grabbed a couple of goals through John Hughes and Ken Boardman but United's defence gave little else away, other than a booking for Laurie Millerchip, who yanked an opponent back by the jersey.

It had been over four and a half years since David Sadler last bagged a Youth Cup hat-trick for the Reds, and the deadly Jimmy Hall's identical accomplishment was entirely in keeping with the goalscoring feats he often achieved for the club's third team.

In defence of the defeated side, goalkeeper Malcolm Crozier was handicapped by an injured hand in the second period, although it could be argued that his side's fate was already sealed by then.

The Blackpool Gazette noted he and centre-half Malcolm Howard *'who had played such great parts'* in keeping their team in the competition, *'were sadly out of touch in this game and allowed United's rampaging forwards to run riot'.*

Scout Joe Armstrong (left) and trainer Joe Travis bookend the Reds' 1968/69 youth squad
Back row (l-r) Brian Greenhoff, Barney Daniels, Kevin Lewis, Ken Goodeve, Damien Ferguson, Jimmy Hall, Ronnie Miller
Front row (l-r) Tony Young, Tommy O'Neil, Ian McMurdo, John McInally, Eric Young, Laurie Millerchip

1968-69

1) John McInally	9) Jimmy Hall	1) Keith Williams	9) Mike Lyons
2) Laurie Millerchip	10) Peter O'Sullivan	2) Tommy Hughes	10) Terry Darracott
3) Kevin Lewis	11) Damien Ferguson	3) Les Ormrod	11) Gary Jones
4) Tommy O'Neil	*12) Tony Young (for 8)*	4) Peter Scott	*12) Alan Wilson*
5) Ken Goodeve		5) Steve Seargeant	
6) Eric Young		6) Bryn Jones	
7) Barney Daniels		7) Bill Kenny	
8) Ian McMurdo		8) David Johnson	

MARCH 1969

MANCHESTER UNITED 0 v 0 EVERTON

fifth round

Monday 3rd
Kick-off 7.30 p.m.
Attendance 8,001

Young Reds lose that goal flair

Two days before Everton's under-18's came to Manchester in search of a Youth Cup semi-final spot at United's expense, the club had encountered a mixed day against their esteemed Liverpudlian rivals.

From the Reds' point of view, the big talking point over the last 48 hours was the Toffees' 1-0 F.A. Cup Sixth Round success over United at Old Trafford, a devastating result which ensured that the seniors would have no domestic silverware to show off for the season.

That disappointment was counterbalanced only slightly when both of the Reds' Lancashire League sides registered wins over Everton, the 'B' gaining a 2-1 away victory while the 'A' managed to score two goals without reply at The Cliff. On the face of it at least, there seemed no way that the Reds could do anything but win their Youth Cup tie.

However, all wasn't quite as it seemed.

Because United's Central League fixture had been postponed over that weekend through the ground being required for the F.A. Cup clash, ironically when the second string were due to meet Everton Reserves, the club's management elected to rest all of the youth team's starting eleven and instead pitted the Reserves against Everton 'A'.

In a Youth Cup match that the Reds could have won in the final moments, particularly when Damien Ferguson beat three Everton defenders in a mesmerising run only to see his goal-bound shot strike the back of a defender's head and divert to safety, witnesses saw a particularly untidy affair which rarely set their pulses racing.

The Liverpool Echo noted:

After the excitement of the previous week, there was something of an anticlimax at Old Trafford last night where Manchester United and Everton fought a goalless draw in the quarter-final of the F.A. Youth Cup.

Neither side mastered the light ball and tricky breeze, with the result that although there was a great deal of effort, not very much good football accompanied it.

Everton centre-forward Mick Lyons, playing back and leaving inside-right Dave Johnson to occupy the mind of United's smart centre-half Goodeve, went close several times to snatching victory for the Goodison boys, but far more of the action was at the other end.

Several Everton defenders have to thank the alert goalkeeping of Keith Williams for covering up their mistakes. But the goalkeeper himself was probably pleased to see Tommy Hughes and Steve Seargeant doing so well in front of him.

Both sides looked short of match practice and a higher standard is expected when they meet again at Goodison Park. Certainly Everton will have to watch clever inside-left O'Sullivan and driving wing-halves O'Neil and Young, but they must also find a way of giving their own forwards, especially left-winger Gary Jones, a better service.

Just over 8,000 watched the game but I feel that Everton fans will manage to top this figure at the replay.

Matt D'Arcy's summary for the Evening News contained an observation about United having *'lost their sparkle'* in a game they *'were favourites to win'*. D'Arcy added *'the same fluency they have showed so far in the competition was missing'* and he also shared the view that *'Everton dominated the first half hour when Ken Goodeve emerged as a fine prospect'*.

Scot John McInally, who was happy to keep his second Youth Cup clean sheet against Everton

United captain Ken Goodeve was cool, calm and collected when the Reds were most under pressure in the opening third of the match

1) Keith Williams	9) Mike Lyons	1) John McInally	9) Jimmy Hall
2) Tommy Hughes	10) Terry Darracott	2) Laurie Millerchip	10) Peter O'Sullivan
3) Les Ormrod	11) Gary Jones	3) Kevin Lewis	11) Damien Ferguson
4) Peter Scott	*12) Alan Wilson (for 7)*	4) Tommy O'Neil	*12) Tony Young (for 8)*
5) Steve Seargeant		5) Ken Goodeve	
6) Bryn Jones		6) Eric Young	
7) Bill Kenny		7) Barney Daniels	
8) David Johnson		8) Ian McMurdo	

1968-69

EVERTON 1 v 3 MANCHESTER UNITED
Johnson *a.e.t.* Daniels (2), Hall

MARCH 1969

Tactical switch wins it for United

What seemed like an ongoing soap opera between Everton and United continued when the respective seniors battled out a 0-0 draw at Goodison Park on the prior Monday.

Without any changes of personnel or shuffling of packs to either side for part two of the under-18 saga, the concluding match had been pre-arranged for the following Saturday until being hastily changed due to United's Central League commitments.

On a wintry night, which undoubtedly kept a goodly number of supporters by their firesides, the young Reds soon got back their scoring habit, the Liverpool Echo recording the events that propelled them into the last four:

A successful tactical switch by Manchester United midway through the second half of the quarter-final replay at Goodison Park last night ended Everton's F.A. Youth Cup hopes for this season.

United were then trailing by 1-0 to a goal scored by Everton inside-right Dave Johnson after 53 minutes, but they levelled the scores and then went on to get two more in the first period of extra-time to win 3-1.

In the United switch, outside-right Bernard Daniels and inside-left Peter O'Sullivan changed places and this, coupled with the substitution of Tony Young after 66 minutes for inside-right Ian McMurdo, brought out the best in their attack.

At 78 minutes, Daniels cut through a hesitant Everton defence in superb style, before running onto a return pass from Young to score a fine goal.

In the fifth minute of extra-time, it was O'Sullivan who crossed the ball from the right to enable centre-forward Jimmy Hall to head the second, and six minutes later left-winger Damien Ferguson sent Daniels through to put the issue beyond doubt.

Wednesday 12th*

Kick-off 7.30 p.m.

Attendance 2,940

Jimmy Hall scored a ninth goal in his tenth consecutive Youth Cup appearance

On a heavy pitch, with snow and sleet falling throughout, both sides did well to provide so much entertainment for the 2,940 spectators.

It was a hard game, with more than the average number of free kicks, and the names of United right-back, Laurie Millerchip, and Everton's outside-left, Gary Jones, appeared to go into referee Dennis Corbett's book.

Had Everton managed to produce a second goal during the only period that they really took command – at the start of the second half – then it would be they who were going forward to the semi-final, but in the end United, who had more skill in midfield and attack, deserved their success.

Both defences played well considering the difficulties, with the centre-halves, Steve Seargeant (Everton) and Ken Goodeve (United) impressing.

But with Gary Jones appearing to feel the effect of some rough treatment early in the game, centre-forward Mick Lyons being tightly marked by Goodeve, and outside-right Bill Kenny never finding his touch – substitute Alan Wilson replaced him in the second half of extra-time – Everton lacked that skill and enterprise in attack which decided the game in United's favour.

The Reds had undoubtedly pulled off a fabulous win, and an alternative view on why they went through was aired in the first paragraph of a match summary prepared over in Manchester.

An Evening News reporter claimed United *'had the edge in pace and fitness in gruelling conditions'* and that they *'powered'* their way to victory. Later adding the home team were tipped by many for a final spot, the piece also included an observation that the Reds *'ran the Everton defence weary'.*

Damien Ferguson (number eleven) looks uncomfortable in Mike Lyons' den

fifth round replay

*This game was originally scheduled for Saturday, March 8th but was postponed due to United's involvement in the Manchester Reserves' 'derby' played at Maine Road on Friday, March 7th

215

1968-69

1) Gordon Nisbet	9) Keith Morton	1) John McInally	9) Jimmy Hall
2) Lyndon Hughes	10) Len Cantello	2) Laurie Millerchip	10) Peter O'Sullivan
3) Syd Bell	11) Hughie MacLean	3) Kevin Lewis	11) Damien Ferguson
4) Stewart Woolgar	*12) Doug Findlater (for 11)*	4) Tommy O'Neil	*12) Ian McMurdo*
5) Jim Holton		5) Ken Goodeve	
6) Alistair Robertson		6) Eric Young	
7) David Butler		7) Barney Daniels	
8) Asa Hartford		8) Tony Young	

MARCH 1969

WEST BROMWICH ALBION 3 v 2 MANCHESTER UNITED

Bell, Hartford, Morton   Ferguson, O'Sullivan

semi-final 1st leg

Monday 31st
Kick-off 7.00 p.m.
Attendance 9,200

West Brom provided the opposition and The Hawthorns was the venue for the initial leg of United's 1969 Youth Cup semi-final. It was, of course, a stadium where the Reds had secured a victory at the same round in 1954 and in the final one year later.

Tony Young's contribution at Goodison Park earned him a place in the side, with the player he substituted for, Ian McMurdo, reversing roles. West Brom included, with first-team experience, ex-Manchester and England Boys midfielder Len Cantello and alongside him was an emerging star in Scot Asa Hartford.

The referee at The Hawthorns was the humorously named Mr. Fussey who, curiously, was also due to officiate at Old Trafford two days later when United and West Brom were down to meet in a First Division encounter. A larger than usual number of injuries at Old Trafford, allied to the preparations required for the Youth Cup tie, caused United to pull out of a Central League fixture at Blackburn. Fortunately, none of the youth team were carrying knocks and their preparations for the journey to the Midlands went more or less as they should.

Still clearly buoyed by their splendid result against Everton, the United lads started by looking purposeful and confident until the Albion eventually began to get into the tempo of the game. Raids on United's goal were repelled by a determined defence in which Ken Goodeve was again a rock, the full-backs Millerchip and Lewis were sound, and half-backs Eric Young and Tommy O'Neil worked their socks off.

An increasing lack of possession meant that United's forwards were soon severely underemployed in attacking responsibilities and their main contribution towards the cause just then was to undertake tackling back duties in order to cover potential danger as and when required.

With Hartford developing a prominence for the Albion as the game unfolded, the home side gained a crucial edge right on the stroke of half-time when a speculative shot from a distance of 30 yards by Baggies' full-back Syd Bell initially appeared to be covered by McInally. The goalkeeper inexplicably allowed the ball to pass him and it squirmed just inside a post, the goal bringing agony to McInally and his team-mates and ecstasy to the Albion players and supporters.

Seven minutes after the interval, West Brom went two-nil up with a superbly engineered strike which was practically text book in execution. When Lyndon Hughes drove a free kick into United's area, it was neatly flicked on by centre-half Jim Holton. The ball came across to Hughie MacLean, who headed it back into the middle where Hartford darted in to score.

By the 77th minute, the Albion seemed to have completed the Reds' destruction with a third goal in which Hartford was also involved. The midfielder picked out winger MacLean with a beautiful 40-yard pass that sailed accurately over United's defence. MacLean carried possession for a while, until delivering a pinpoint centre which was glanced past a stranded McInally by number nine Keith Morton.

While the tie now looked a lost cause for United, the game's storyline was still incomplete by a couple of chapters. There were just seven minutes left on the clock and with the minds of the Albion players seemingly full of cup final dreams, the Reds pulled back what appeared to be a mere consolation goal. A corner was swung into the West Brom goalmouth, where 'keeper Nisbet seemed to have the situation under control, and he followed McInally's earlier boob by dropping the ball like a hot potato only for Damien Ferguson to gratefully bang it over the line from close quarters.

With the earlier composure displayed by the Albion now significantly less than it was, United went full throttle for another goal and with just two minutes to go they got it. The Baggies' Nisbet was again deemed to be the guilty party when failing to cut out a cross and the ball soon fell at the feet of the consistently impressive O'Sullivan, who fired it past the bumbling 'keeper from the outskirts of the box to edge the Reds further back into contention.

Whether West Brom allowed complacency to creep into their game was a question only they could answer, but the United boys demonstrated that whatever failings they may have had, a lack of fight wasn't one of them. The Albion were disconsolate at allowing their guests to re-enter a game they were completely locked out of with only thirteen minutes remaining and the burning questions now were; how would it affect them at Old Trafford and, more importantly, would one goal provide them with enough of a safety margin?

CLEARING HIS LINES... Laurie Millerchip (right) repels a West Bromwich Albion attack during Manchester United's FA Youth Cup semi-final clash

1) John McInally
2) Laurie Millerchip
3) Kevin Lewis
4) Tommy O'Neil
5) Ken Goodeve
6) Eric Young
7) Barney Daniels
8) Tony Young
9) Jimmy Hall
10) Peter O'Sullivan
11) Tony Whelan
12) Brian Greenhoff

1) Gordon Nisbet
2) Roger Minton
3) Syd Bell
4) Lyndon Hughes
5) Jim Holton
6) Alistair Robertson
7) Stewart Woolgar
8) Asa Hartford
9) Keith Morton
10) Len Cantello
11) Hughie MacLean
12) David Butler (for 9)

1968-69

MANCHESTER UNITED 1 (3) v (5) 2 WEST BROMWICH ALBION

O'Sullivan

Bell, Woolgar

APRIL 1969

semi-final 2nd leg

Monday 14th

Kick-off 7.30 p.m.

Attendance 11,441

The seriousness of Albion's intentions for the second leg two weeks later were spelled out as plain as could be by the Evening News:

West Bromwich have pulled Asa Hartford out of their First Division match tonight to play against Manchester United in the F.A. Youth Cup semi-final second leg.

Hartford will line up at inside-forward with Len Cantello, the Manchester youngster who got through the local scouting net.

Albion are taking no chances in their efforts to hang on to the one-goal lead from their first-leg 3-2 win.

Albion also have their defence back to full strength with right-back Roger Minton passing a test this morning.

But United are still wrestling with the problem of how to replace outside-left Damien Ferguson, who broke his arm in a friendly kick-about game at home in Ireland.

The Reds have three players standing by – Ian McMurdo, who is still displaced at inside-forward by Tony Young, Brian Greenhoff, the brother of Birmingham City's Jimmy, and Tony Whelan.

Old Trafford expect a crowd of over 10,000.

Said assistant manager Jimmy Murphy, 'We had a 10,000 crowd at The Hawthorns and they saw a very good game. Our fans have always given us good support in the past and I would like to see them rally round and top that figure tonight.'

Unfortunately, United's spirited recovery at The Hawthorns went completely to waste when the Albion stretched their lead early on at Old Trafford and pulled even further ahead a minute after the resumption of the second period. Despite O'Sullivan responding for the Reds with a little over twenty minutes remaining, it was too late to salvage a place in the final.

David Meek attempted to accentuate the better aspects of United's performance in his report:

Manchester United's youngsters are probably downhearted and disappointed after their F.A. Youth Cup knockout.

They shouldn't be.

Certainly West Bromwich saw them out of the semi-finals in convincing style, winning 2-1 at Old Trafford to make it an aggregate 5-3 victory.

But the Reds went down with colours flying, a most spirited performance that combined guts and skill to the high degree that we have come now to expect from this youth competition.

The young Reds – and they are young this season – went much further than anticipated, and though semi-final defeat is always the most bitter, they did extraordinarily well to reach this stage.

Peter O'Sullivan, the most experienced of United's forwards, pulled everything out against a team that, led by England Youth skipper Lyndon Hughes, was just that little bit stronger.

United did not help themselves with a sloppy opening in each half. Albion scored from a long-range free kick in only the second minute and they were just as quick off the mark after the interval with a goal from Stuart Woolgar.

O'Sullivan scored for United, ramming home a penalty rebound, and the Reds certainly piled on the pressure in the last twenty minutes when Tony Whelan fully justified his promotion at outside-left.

Most of the United team are eligible next season. They can look forward to the next go with every confidence.

The West Bromwich Midland Chronicle heaped as much of the wholly deserved praise as possible on the Baggies' youngsters in its match summary:

Albion's youth team were the toast of the town when they battled their way into the F.A. Youth Cup final.

They hit United hard and fast at the beginning of each half and then withstood a tremendous second half barrage as the Reds surged forward, especially after they had reduced Albion's lead, but the entire team stood as solid as the Rock of Gibraltar and never once did United penetrate to any depth.

The heroes were left-back Syd Bell, who scored with a 40-yard free kick, and Stuart Woolgar, a lad with an extremely bright future, who scored the second with an opportunist goal.

The experience of Len Cantello, Lyndon Hughes and Asa Hartford kept their team-mates cool with all three stamping their mark in the respective positions.

Gordon Nesbit had cruel ill-fortune with the United penalty goal. He saved the first attempt and was more than equal to the long range shots United were restricted to trying. Jim Holton effectively blocked up the middle.

At the last stage, West Brom were defeated on aggregate by six goals to three by Sunderland, and it represented the second such triumph in just three years for the Roker Park outfit.

"The match against West Brom was the biggest game of my career up to that point and I desperately wanted to get a win to get to the final. I had played against many of their side before when I was in the Wales schoolboy team and although they beat us in the first leg we still felt we had a chance.

When they scored our heads dropped a little. I pulled one back and we still had a chance, but it wasn't to be. It was a horrible night at Old Trafford and I came off the pitch soaking wet and full of mud just feeling absolutely gutted."

PETER O'SULLIVAN

217

1969-70

1) Chris Ogden	9) Steve Bamborough	1) Willie Carrick	9) Jimmy Hall
2) John Cook	10) Ian Robins	2) Laurie Millerchip	10) Eric Young
3) Bob Sykes	11) Ian Buckley	3) Kevin Lewis	11) Damien Ferguson
4) Kevin Crumblehulme	*12) Ian Holmes (for 9)*	4) Tommy O'Neil	*12) Tony Whelan*
5) Steve Hoolickin		5) Bill Fairhurst	
6) Mike Romanienko		6) Ian Donald	
7) David Henry		7) Tony Young	
8) David Warley		8) Ronnie Miller	

NOVEMBER 1969

OLDHAM ATHLETIC 0 v 1 MANCHESTER UNITED
Ferguson

Tuesday 25th
Kick-off 7.30 p.m.

second round

United began their 1969/70 Youth Cup expedition on unfamiliar territory when they were paired to tackle new opposition in the competition, in the shape of local Lancashire rivals Oldham Athletic.

Gone now were John McInally, Ken Goodeve and Peter O'Sullivan from last season's creditable run and into the vacated places went Willie Carrick, Bill Fairhurst and Ronnie Miller. Because Barney Daniels was also gone, Eric Young was repositioned while new recruit Ian Donald took over the latter's former number six jersey. On the face of it, there appeared to be no lessening in the club's exhaustive search for future stars as Donald and Miller were formerly of Scotland Boys while Carrick had similarly represented the Republic of Ireland.

Jim Williams of the Oldham Chronicle gave Latics' followers a match taster:

Ian Robins, Athletic's England Youth trialist, has been passed fit for tonight's opening F.A. Youth Cup clash with Manchester United at Boundary Park. Robins, out of action at the weekend because of a bout of tonsillitis, plays at inside-left in a match that should give a fair indication as to how well Athletic's youth policy has progressed.

United, who have a really impressive record in this competition, have a new batch of youngsters on show. The youth team that once produced the fabulous Busby Babes, and then the players of the quality of George Best and Brian Kidd, will give Athletic a really tough test.

A slender 1-0 win was sufficient to put United through against a battling Oldham, whose defence in one report was curiously described as *'oyster tight'*.

United could have doubled their score in the last couple of minutes, when Eric Young rattled the bar, although an open invitation scorned by the Latics in the second half provided the main after-match talking point.

Jim Williams put his pen to work once again:

Every game has a turning point, a crucial contribution or a mistake from one player that turns a game. For Athletic, in their bid for Youth Cup glory last night, it came in the 58th minute. Athletic's teenage talent had been pressured to the point of total collapse in a first half dominated by the physical might of Manchester.

But after a half-time lecture, they came out full of fight and fire and had United on the run and heading towards defeat.

In the 48th minute a sudden surge of pace and control took Steve Bamborough clear down the right wing and into the penalty box. He beat Lewis and drew Carrick off his line but no-one moved into the middle to take the pass.

A minute later, Ian Robins, out-jumping O'Neil, flashed a header fractionally wide of the far post with Carrick beaten. In the 54th minute, Robins, producing a glimpse of his very real talent, controlled and passed on the volley to send Warley thrusting into the penalty box. Warley fired in a fierce shot, which deceived Carrick, and the ball hit the goalkeeper's leg and flew over the bar.

The pace and precision being shown by Athletic during this spell had United in such a state that Fairhurst had to handle to prevent a Bamborough cross from reaching Robins. And here comes the turning point, the crucial moment when the match was virtually decided. Robins stroked the penalty kick goalwards but Carrick blocked it. The ball ran straight back to Robins and from four yards, he again shot straight at the prostrate goalkeeper.

No team that misses a penalty deserves to win and, taking the game as a whole, Athletic did not deserve to win last night. They had gone behind in the 12th minute to a goal that United had threatened to score from the start.

United's centre-forward Jimmy Hall – one of the best forward prospects I have seen for some time – controlled a superbly flighted pass from Ferguson and spun round Hoolickin. Spotting a big gap to his left, he slid a perfect pass through and Ferguson zipped in to beat Ogden with a powerful blast. For the rest of the first half, United powered their way forward and ran Athletic's defence ragged. Only Chris Ogden, in inspired form, really kept Athletic in the match.

After the break they had that tremendous spell of pressure and it is possible that if Robins had converted the penalty, Athletic might have romped on to a victory or at least a draw.

In his column in the Review, Jack Pauline revealed the Boundary Park pitch was *'hard and slippery'* and that some of the players experienced problems in adapting their game accordingly. Pauline ended his account pointedly, by warning *'improved finishing is a must'* if the Reds were to make further progress.

The referee blows for an infringement as Ronnie Miller (right) stabs an attempt over the bar and Tony Young (far left) waits to provide support

218

1969-70

1) Keith Williams	9) Mike Lyons	
2) Tommy Hughes	10) John Smith	
3) Les Ormrod	11) Ronnie Goodlass	
4) Bill Kenny	*12) David Graham*	
5) Peter Scott		
6) Bryn Jones		
7) David Johnson		
8) Alan Wilson		

1) Willie Carrick	9) Jimmy Hall	
2) Laurie Millerchip	10) Eric Young	
3) Kevin Lewis	11) Tony Whelan	
4) Tommy O'Neil	*12) Ian McMurdo*	
5) Bill Fairhurst		
6) Ian Donald		
7) Tony Young		
8) Brian Greenhoff		

EVERTON 1 v 2 MANCHESTER UNITED

Johnson — Hall, Young E.

DECEMBER 1969

Tuesday 30th

Kick-off 7.30 p.m.

Attendance 4,451

third round

For the sixth time since 1953, Goodison Park was again United's destination as John Aston named a squad of fourteen teenagers to take on Everton. The club's youth coach made optimistic noises in the Evening News about the Reds' chances of regaining the coveted trophy, and his views were based on him being in charge of a pool of players which was just deep enough to hopefully breed some healthy competition for places.

Later going on to make a statement that was more accurate than not, Aston claimed, 'This is a competition we always do well in' and he then proceeded to implement two changes to the forward-line by bringing in Brian Greenhoff and Tony Whelan. Out of the starting eleven went Damien Ferguson and Ronnie Miller, a rather drastic fate for the former, whose goal had registered as a Second Round winner at Boundary Park just over a month before.

On duty for Everton were the majority of the team whom the Reds had defeated at the second attempt nine months earlier, and with their average age and experience allied to the advantage of a home tie, the Toffees just about shaded the odds to become the pre-match favourites.

Down at the western end of the East Lancs Road, the Liverpool Echo was required to mention two games:

After Saturday's blank, Liverpool springs back to life tomorrow with a double bill of youth football. At Goodison Park, Everton are hosts to Manchester United while at Anfield, Liverpool entertain Leeds. Both are F.A. Youth Cup Third Round matches.

Everton have a score to settle with the Old Trafford club, who beat them 3-1 in the quarter-finals of last season's competition after a 0-0 draw at Old Trafford.

The Goodison under-18's must fancy their chance, for in this year's youth squad are no fewer than eight players who took part in that match last season – goalkeeper Keith Williams, full-backs Tommy Hughes and Les Ormrod, half-backs Peter Scott, Bryn Jones and Bill Kenny, and forwards Dave Johnson and Mick Lyons. In fact, Hughes, Johnson and Kenny all played against Burnley in 1967/68 when Everton were defeated in the semi-finals.

This year, Everton beat Blackburn 5-0 at Goodison Park, after having been held to a 3-3 draw at Ewood Park, while Manchester United got through by 1-0 at Oldham on a difficult pitch.

Much to the Reds' displeasure, the game got off to a crackerjack of a start, but with resilience and determination, they soon turned the tide in their favour and went on to complete a wonderful win.

The Liverpool Echo gave an account of the game, which attracted an attendance almost double in size to the Youth Cup counter attraction that simultaneously took place just across Stanley Park at Anfield:

For the second successive season Everton's F.A. Youth Cup hopes were ended at Goodison Park last night by Manchester United, yet Everton got off to a flying start in this Third Round match with a goal in the opening seconds.

From the kick-off, the ball was played to Everton's left-half Bryn Jones who pushed it up the centre of the field where outside-right Johnson had raced to the edge of the penalty area. Before a United player could touch the ball, Johnson turned it past goalkeeper Carrick's left hand and into the net.

Inside-left Eric Young hit the Everton upright with a shot from eighteen yards after eleven minutes for United's best effort in a first half played mainly in midfield between two very evenly matched sides.

The second half was only seven minutes old when United inside-right Greenhoff broke down the wing and from his perfect centre, Eric Young rose above the Everton defence to head the ball into the corner.

There was a further setback for Everton at the 67th minute when winger Tony Young collected the ball by the half-way line, cut in from the right and made towards goal. His shot from just outside the penalty area did not find the target but it was deflected through the mass of legs in the penalty area to centre-forward Hall, who made no mistake from close in.

Everton tried desperately to get an equaliser but the ball did not run for them against a solid Manchester defence in which full-backs Millerchip and Lewis, with centre-half Fairhurst, were outstanding. Smith (inside-left) and Lyons (centre-forward) worked hard in the Everton attack and carved out several openings for wingers Johnson and Goodlass in the closing stages but after that early goal there was no real finishing power in the Everton attack.

There was much crowing about the result nearer to home, with a sentence in Matt D'Arcy's Evening News piece reading *'United showed they had class and skill as they commanded this game against a talented Everton side',* and of the Merseysiders' early opener he felt *'it was the only real chance they were able to carve out of this determined United defence who tackled fast and hard'.*

D'Arcy then stated *'the game came perilously close to exploding and in fact referee Keith Styles, a Barnsley schoolmaster, booked United centre-half Bill Fairhurst after 73 minutes for a foul on the Everton left winger. It was the only black spot to mar a grand game by Fairhurst, who blocked every avenue down the centre of the field to Everton after the initial goal'.*

The reporter also wrote *'it was only a matter of time before United got the goals to take them through, so dominant were they in midfield and attack'* prior to adding Eric Young, *'brilliantly making space for himself,'* nodded the Reds' equaliser into the bottom corner of Keith Williams' net.

The triumph at Everton, allied to Matt Busby's recent statement about United now boasting their best batch of prospects for some years, brought a decade fondly remembered by the Old Trafford masses to a sweet conclusion in Youth Cup terms.

The matter of the Blues' goal continued to be the subject of much chat, and an article devoted to it in a Toffees' first-team programme a couple of weeks later began and ended with a couple of posers:

Just how quickly is it possible to score a goal from the kick-off? It is an age-old query that has inspired all kinds of research with stop watches in training matches and the general opinion seems to be that FIVE OR SIX SECONDS is the answer unless the ball is actually kicked home from within the centre circle.

And six seconds just happens to be the time on our stop watch when Everton junior David Johnson scored the opening goal in the F.A. Youth Cup tie against Manchester United on 30 December.

United general manager Matt Busby saw the goal and said it was 'one of the quickest I have seen'.

The ball, kicked off by Mike Lyons, was switched by Alan Wilson, played back to Bryn Jones, and then hit down the centre for Johnson to touch past the 'keeper.

One reporter actually clocked the goal in five seconds, but the general opinion was six seconds.

But of course all these claims and records have no exact confirmation, simply because there is not an official timekeeper in soccer. Johnson's goal for the youth team may well be the quickest seen at Goodison.......BUT WHO KNOWS FOR SURE?

Willie Carrick conceded within record time at Everton

1969-70

fourth round

FEBRUARY 1970

Monday 2nd

Kick-off 7.30 p.m.

Attendance 7,123

MANCHESTER UNITED 4 v 1 **SHEFFIELD UNITED**

Hall (3), Whelan — Ogden

Manchester United:
1) Willie Carrick
2) Laurie Millerchip
3) Kevin Lewis
4) Tommy O'Neil
5) Bill Fairhurst
6) Ian Donald
7) Tony Young
8) Ronnie Miller
9) Jimmy Hall
10) Eric Young
11) Tony Whelan
12) *Damien Ferguson*

Sheffield United:
1) Tom McAlister
2) Mick Bradshaw
3) Alan Foster
4) Mick Speight
5) Roger Higginbottom
6) Phil Archer
7) Graham Oliver
8) Paul Armitage
9) Malcolm Edge
10) Jimmy House
11) Alan Ogden
12) *Steve Golding (for 7)*

In the early part of February 1970, the Reds' former youth team skipper Wilf McGuinness was probably feeling fairly happy with his lot as United's manager. Despite the seniors going through a rather erratic opening half of his first season at the helm, a development which was somewhat understandable considering how long and successfully Matt Busby had been in charge, and an unlucky aggregate League Cup semi-final defeat to a certain side from Maine Road, the first-team hadn't experienced a defeat for two months.

In respect of their last ten matches, McGuinness' men had won five, which included home F.A. Cup triumphs over Ipswich and Manchester City. The seniors were drawn away to Northampton on the upcoming Saturday, when George Best was due to return from a lengthy ban, so it was widely expected that their knock-out escapades would last at least a little while longer.

At Central League level, the Reserves usually consisted of an eleven comprising entirely of home grown staff. They were more than holding their own in the division, with twelve wins and ten draws from 30 games played, and of the matches lost, six of them were by a single-goal margin.

Everyone at the club was aware of what a sterling job coach John Aston was doing with the junior talent at his disposal. Having lost only twice in 21 fixtures, the 'A' team were riding high, while the 'B' side's achievements were similar as they had tasted defeat only three times since the start of the season.

All in all, confidence wasn't such a scarce commodity at Old Trafford just then.

The luck of the Youth Cup draw meant that the task of facing the Reds' buoyant under-18's was a Sheffield United outfit whose serious approach to the tie included receiving a motivational talk from manager John Harris before setting off over the Pennines.

Prior to departure Harris informed the Sheffield Star newspaper, 'Manchester United are among the favourites to win the cup and we have a very young side this year, but our boys have done remarkably well in the competition and they are itching to get to grips with the Manchester lads. I am confident we have the ability to give United a good game.'

Ronnie Miller was recalled at the expense of Brian Greenhoff in the forward-line, and on a pitch which was liberally coated with energy-sapping mud, the Reds controlled possession for a large part of the first half without posing so much as a sniff of danger to the Bramall Lane brigade. Over half an hour passed before Ian Donald chanced his arm with a powerful shot and it brought about a terrific save from McAlister, who got down to save just inside an upright. Luckily for United, the Blades were almost equally as impotent over the same period, with their greatest threat posed by a number of much-practiced corners which Carrick dealt with efficiently.

That was, until the 43rd minute. It was at that point when the usually steady 'keeper messed up in attempting to catch a flag kick, instead giving possession to Sheffield's Malcolm Edge, who was able to drill in a shot from short range. The ball somehow ended up at the feet of winger Alan Ogden and a prod from him took it into the net to put the Reds behind.

Thankfully, it took less than two minutes for United to draw level following a short corner taken by Tony Young. He knocked a pass to Whelan and from the dead-ball line the winger crossed for Jimmy Hall to head home.

The Blades hit back early in the second half, a response which caused the Review to note that an 'early Sheffield flourish on the resumption had the United defence in slight difficulty'. However, it was a mistake by McAlister barely four minutes into the concluding period that resulted in the Blades going behind. Dropping a clanger which fairly equalled that of Carrick's earlier misdemeanour, McAlister spilled a Kevin Lewis centre straight in front of the lurking Hall, who carried out the simplest of tasks in scoring again.

Obviously rattled by his error, the visiting goalie was at fault for the second time just six minutes later when finding a shot from Miller too hot to handle, the ball having been worked into the feet of the blond-haired striker by the industrious O'Neil. Hall was again in the right place, converting what was an open invitation to complete his hat-trick.

McAlister managed to slow the Reds' scoring rate down in the 70th minute by brilliantly saving an Eric Young penalty. The spot kick was awarded when Blades' defender Mick Speight brought down Tony Young just inside the area.

The Reds continued to press their advantage and scored a fourth just three minutes from time with what Jack Pauline described as 'the goal of the match'. Having temporarily switched wings, Tony Whelan cut inside to twist past a couple of bemused Sheffield defenders before rattling in a blistering right-footed drive from the eighteen-yard line. A few seconds later, celebrations in the home camp died down when it was noticed that a linesman had raised his flag to signal an offside. Following a short consultation with his assistant, referee Mr. Lyden of Birmingham ruled that none of the home team were interfering with play prior to Whelan's shot bulging the net and indicated that the goal should stand.

Now in his third and final term in the youth team, the form and consistency of Jimmy Hall was a major plus factor for the Reds. The Irish marksman's Youth Cup goal tally was now up to twelve, although it was a defensive colleague who found a few paragraphs comparing him to one of the club's most admired post-war stalwarts in the next day's Evening News:

Shades of Bill Foulkes....Manchester United has a repeat model in the pipeline.

Built on the same lines as Foulkes, seventeen year-old Bill Fairhurst also comes from the St. Helens area and has a similar rugby background.

Fairhurst played for Lancashire schoolboys at RL and he must have been a mighty forward in schoolboy rugby.

Now he is an equally likely centre-half and was much too skilful as well as powerful for the forwards of Sheffield United in their F.A. Youth Cup tie at Old Trafford. United also proved too strong upfront for Sheffield and won through to the quarter-finals - and a home tie against Rotherham - with a 4-1 win.

Jimmy Hall, ex-Irish schoolboy international, scored a hat-trick. Two were headed goals and he won nearly every challenge in the air.

This, his third season in the Youth Cup competition, and his experience showed through. With nice touches from players like Eric Young, Tony Young and Tony Whelan, who hit a scorching shot for the fourth goal, the young Reds won at a canter.

Sheffield, with a goal from winger Ogden, opened the scoring and it was 1-1 at the interval.

United got ahead with a goal that looked a foul on the Sheffield goalkeeper but it was a lead they had threatened from the start and they justified the high rating this season's youngsters are being given by the club.

Eric Young was foiled in his attempt to register a spot kick by 'keeper McAlister

1) Willie Carrick	9) Jimmy Hall	1) Jim McDonagh	9) Trevor Phillips
2) Laurie Millerchip	10) Eric Young	2) David Abrahams	10) Kevin Ball
3) Kevin Lewis	11) Tony Whelan	3) Doug Hemmingway	11) Steven Kulic
4) Tommy O'Neil	*12) Ian McMurdo*	4) Mick Leng	*12) Les Saxton*
5) Bill Fairhurst		5) Alan Epton	
6) Ian Donald		6) John Breckin	
7) Tony Young		7) Paul Short	
8) Damien Ferguson		8) Bernard Coop	

1969-70

MANCHESTER UNITED 2 v 2 ROTHERHAM UNITED

Ferguson, Young T. *Breckin, Phillips*

FEBRUARY 1970

SCARE FOR RED BABES

Next up to try to topple the junior Reds were Rotherham, an outfit then managed by the confident and charismatic Tommy Docherty.

Even though he was unable to dislodge Tony Whelan from the outside-left position, Damien Ferguson returned to the side at inside-right while Ronnie Miller once again found himself totally excluded.

It was a week when the club's supporters were on full cup alert, with the first-team due to take on Middlesbrough at Ayresome Park in the senior F.A. version on the following Saturday. An exciting time for the fans, the situation caused youth coach Aston to comment, 'We hope to lead the way by being the first to a semi-final.'

Over in Yorkshire, the Millers' recent track record and prospects were revealed in the local Advertiser newspaper:

Rotherham United's F.A. Youth Cup tie with Manchester United will be played at Old Trafford next Monday, February 16th.

The Rotherham youngsters, having taken the club into the quarter-finals for the first time since the competition started in 1953, are not having an outstanding season in the Northern Intermediate League, but have risen to the occasion in their cup encounters.

Mansfield, Scunthorpe, Hull City and Bolton have all been beaten while the youngsters have been accumulating an impressive record of fourteen goals scored and one against, and now comes the supreme test against this formidable side christened the 'McGuinness Mites'.

United will not travel overawed by the situation. 'Myself and chief coach Clive Baker went to see United defeat Sheffield United in the last round and saw nothing to be frightened about,' said Millmoor boss Jimmy McAnearney.

The record of the Old Trafford youngsters over the years is one of which the club is justifiably proud, winning the trophy in the first five years of its inception, again in 1964, and reaching the semi-final last season when they went out to West Bromwich Albion on a 5-3 aggregate.

Monday's clash will bring back memories for older Millmoor supporters who remember 1954 when the two sides clashed in the Fourth Round. The game at Millmoor – before 7,200 spectators – ended in a 0-0 draw and included in the Old Trafford side then were Wilf McGuinness, present United manager, Bobby Charlton, David Pegg and Eddie Colman. Rotherham lost the replay 3-1, Duncan Edwards returning to the side and scoring a hat-trick.

Incidentally, there should be a rather large attendance for Monday night's game as the Manchester public are not slow to respond to good performances from their junior sides, and with the first-team enjoying their best run of the season interest is obviously very high.

The Reds had been on the receiving end of a startlingly early goal at Everton in the Third Round but it was a scoring feat at the exact opposite end of the match against Rotherham which managed to save their bacon, the late strike setting up a Millmoor replay nobody in the Manchester camp either wanted or expected.

The evening's events went better than the away side could have hoped for and caused the Rotherham Advertiser to record:

The band of Rotherham supporters at Old Trafford yesterday week will long remember the fine display, particularly that excellent rearguard action in the second half when Manchester threw everything except the Stretford End at the gallant Rotherham defence, only to be repelled time and again before snatching an equaliser in the fourth minute of injury-time.

No-one could really deny the 'McGuinness Mites' a replay chance, for they fought desperately hard in the second half to get on terms, but neither could anyone have grumbled if the Rotherham lads had hung on for a victory for which they had fought so hard.

Manchester took the lead when winger Tony Whelan left Abrahams trailing and crossed perfectly for Ferguson to clip easily past McDonagh, and with only two minutes showing on the clock, things looked black for Rotherham.

The young Millers gritted their teeth and were level within five minutes with a gem of a goal.

Phillips collected the ball in his own half, supplied Coop when his fellow front man asked for it, and the number eight shrugged off a challenge from Donald and then slipped a tackle from goalkeeper Carrick who had come out of his area. Coop steadied himself, crossed, and there was Phillips running in to head firmly into the net.

Then, after 49 minutes, Rotherham dreams almost came true when Breckin met Kulic's corner perfectly with his head to put his side in front. That was the signal for the home side to mount up pressure and the onslaught reached its peak fifteen minutes from time when inside 60 seconds Ferguson headed just over, Tony Young shot just wide, and then full-back Lewis hit the post only for Ferguson to slip and put the rebound wide when he looked a certain scorer.

United almost threw away their lead after 88 minutes when a back pass was intercepted by winger Tony Young, and although he went wide of McDonagh, he shot into the side netting.

That looked to be the Reds' last chance, but up popped winger Young in the dying seconds, diving courageously to head in a free kick and save the tie for his side.

Jack Pauline felt that the Millmoor side *'defended dourly, at times desperately, against almost continual United pressure in the second half'* and he went on to opine that it *'was no less than the young Reds deserved, however, for they did not have the best of fortune around the visitors' penalty area'*. Pauline concluded with the view that an *'earlier equaliser might well have turned the game in their favour and this all but came about when a fine effort by Lewis hit the inside of a post to rebound to safety'*.

Matt D'Arcy charted the game's main points in his Evening News summary. Claiming that Willie Carrick was too slow off his line in the build-up to Rotherham's first goal, a few of his other comments read:

The mature poise and confidence of Manchester United's youngsters deserted them twice in the quarter-final against Rotherham at Old Trafford - and almost cost them the chance of winning the F.A. Youth Cup.

United had to be content with a 2-2 draw and a replay next week after giving away two goals through slack defensive work.

United, who won the trophy for the first five years it was held, have not won it since 1964, but this current crop of youngsters is thought to contain enough talent to romp it easily this season.

But sloppy defensive covering of the kind they displayed against Rotherham will not win anything.

" *We had a very strong team that year and fancied our chances of going all the way.*

United always had talent in the youth team, players like Eric Young, Jimmy Hall and Tony Young could all score goals but sometimes it took time for our forwards to click.

If they did then the floodgates would often open, but if they struggled a little then we needed to make sure defensively we were strong.

I remember playing the old 2-3-5 at school, but when I arrived at United they operated with two centre-halves so I had to get used to playing alongside another defender like Ian Donald. We also had Kevin Lewis who was a very strong defender.

As for those games against Rotherham, they turned into a right marathon……. "

BILL FAIRHURST

Thursday 19th*
Kick-off 7.30 p.m.
Attendance 5,680

fifth round

*This game was originally scheduled for Monday, February 16th but was postponed due to a snowbound pitch

221

1969-70

1) Jim McDonagh	9) Trevor Phillips	
2) David Abrahams	10) Kevin Ball	
3) Doug Hemmingway	11) Steven Kulic	
4) Mick Leng	*12) John Ryder (for 7)*	
5) Alan Epton		
6) John Breckin		
7) Paul Short		
8) Bernard Coop		

1) Willie Carrick	9) Jimmy Hall
2) Laurie Millerchip	10) Eric Young
3) Kevin Lewis	11) Tony Whelan
4) Tommy O'Neil	*12) Brian Greenhoff*
5) Bill Fairhurst	
6) Ian Donald	
7) Tony Young	
8) Damien Ferguson	

FEBRUARY 1970

ROTHERHAM UNITED 0 v 0 MANCHESTER UNITED
a.e.t.

fifth round replay

Tuesday 24th
Kick-off 7.15 p.m.
Attendance 8,633

SIR MATT WATCHES YOUNGSTERS' BATTLE AT MILLMOOR

Because of the delay in staging the earlier match at Old Trafford, a replay date needed to be quickly agreed on by the two United's and so only five days separated the drawn tie at Old Trafford and a meeting in South Yorkshire. With most of the Rotherham public seemingly taking an interest in the outcome, another couple of hours of fully committed football from the two sets of opponents still failed to separate them.

The Rotherham Advertiser gave a full account of the second instalment:

Sitting in the directors' box at Millmoor on Tuesday night, the greatest man in football management, Sir Matt Busby, can have had no doubts about the future good health of the game.

He saw his own juniors from Old Trafford in a game of thrills and high skills in which the Rotherham United youngsters matched everything that Bill Foulkes has been able to teach the Manchester United youth side.

The battle went on for 120 minutes without a goal but it never lost interest. In this replayed quarter-final of the F.A. Youth Cup, Rotherham started in majestic form, defended stubbornly when Manchester took the initiative, and in the period of extra-time demonstrated that their staying power was equal to that of the young men from the First Division club.

Now there will be a second replay, and it will be held at Millmoor next Thursday night.

Apart from the high standard of play produced, the most encouraging factor to emerge was the record attendance of 8,633. Who would have thought a few months ago that there would be such support from the Rotherham public for a first-team fixture, let alone a juniors' game?

Trevor Phillips was clearly the 'Man of the Match'. In the class from which he has recently emerged to Rotherham's Third Division side, his speed and intelligent use of the ball stood out very sharply. Sir Matt must have been tremendously impressed, though Phillips' promise would certainly not be news to him.

On the other hand, the distinguished manager who for years has specialised in bringing young players to the fore, must have been highly satisfied with the performance of some of his own youth team lads, in particular the right-winger, Tony Young. This youngster already plays with the assurance and craft of the above-average League player, and it was a tribute to the resource and energy of Rotherham's left-back, Douglas Hemmingway, that he was contained as well as he was.

Had Rotherham taken their two clear-cut chances – one in each half – they may not have needed the courageous defence they put up when Manchester staged their second half offensive. McDonagh, a goalkeeper of rich promise, made several daring saves when the pressure was at its height, and Michael Leng saved his side when he kicked off the line after a goalmouth mêlée three minutes from the end of extra-time.

It is a satisfying reflection that nine of the Rotherham youngsters – including Trevor Phillips – will be eligible for the competition next season.

Trevor Phillips had obviously been earmarked as the potential danger to the visitors' supposed supremacy and he received a great deal of rough treatment from the Mancunian defenders, this being emphasised as early as the 23rd minute when the Manchester skipper, O'Neil, was booked by referee Lyden for a foul on the Rotherham leader.

Bernard Coop – whose striking partnership with Phillips has been one of the success stories of this cup campaign – missed a great opportunity of giving Rotherham the psychological advantage of a goal just before half-time, when he missed a perfect centre from Phillips, when all that was needed was the smallest of touches.

However, the linesman had raised his flag, so it might have been a disputed decision if Coop had managed to connect.

It was noticeable that Rotherham's other clear-cut chance of clinching the issue was six minutes before the end of the 90 minutes, when Kulic fed Coop, who took the ball to the line before hitting a low cross from the left. Kevin Ball failed to connect properly and his effort went wide of the post.

After the interval, the Manchester youngsters found something of their true rhythm when they started to move the ball around with conviction and create more space for themselves.

McDonagh was called upon twice in the opening minutes of this half when he dealt competently with a header from Eric Young, and then flung himself to bring off a brilliant full-length save to keep out a shot from Whelan.

In a newspaper printed to the west of the Pennines, it was felt that a *'pair of quick covering, strong tackling defences were the reason for Rotherham United and Manchester United battling for 120 minutes without a goal in their bruising, but entertaining F.A. Youth Cup quarter-final tie at Millmoor'.* Further noting the Reds had enjoyed long stretches of possession, particularly in the second half of normal time, the same reporter claimed they were *'inspired by intelligent work by Damien Ferguson and Eric Young, and fine wing play from Tony Young'* yet *'lacked the necessary power in the penalty area'.*

Matt Busby points the way for some of United's juniors at Manchester Airport. They are (l-r) Eric Young, Ian Donald (hidden), Kevin Lewis, Damien Ferguson, Ronnie Miller (top), Laurie Millerchip, Brian Greenhoff and Tommy O'Neil

1969-70

1) Jim McDonagh	9) Trevor Phillips	1) Willie Carrick	9) Jimmy Hall
2) David Abrahams	10) Kevin Ball	2) Laurie Millerchip	10) Damien Ferguson
3) Doug Hemmingway	11) Steven Kulic	3) Kevin Lewis	11) Tony Whelan
4) Mick Leng	*12) Alan Crawford ◊*	4) Tommy O'Neil	*12) Brian Greenhoff*
5) Alan Epton		5) Bill Fairhurst	
6) John Breckin		6) Ian Donald	
7) Phil Bendig		7) Tony Young	
8) Bernard Coop		8) Eric Young	

ROTHERHAM UNITED 1 v 4 **MANCHESTER UNITED**
Coop (pen) *a.e.t.* Ferguson, Hall, Lewis, Young T.

MARCH 1970

Wednesday 11th*

Kick-off 7.15 p.m.

Attendance 5,156

fifth round 2nd replay

REDS' CLASS TELLS IN EXTRA TIME

After winning the toss and thereby gaining the right to stage a second replay at Millmoor, Rotherham made arrangements for all of the gatemen who normally functioned at first-team games to report for duty. There had been complaints of long queues prior to the earlier replay, a problem which was directly caused by the small number of turnstiles in operation on the night, and in order to avoid the situation recurring, Rotherham sold tickets in advance to season ticket holders for what promised to be a close encounter of the third kind.

Jack Pauline commented on the proceedings as they had occurred so far, a few of his views reading thus:

The youth team had a rare tussle with Rotherham in the quarter-final of the F.A. Youth Cup, the marathon clash being reminiscent of United's meeting with Sunderland in 1960/61. Both sides could claim, with some justification, that the issue should have been settled in their favour at the first time of asking – at Old Trafford.

The (first) game at Rotherham was more evenly contested with United failing to find forward punch when having much the better of the extra-time. The defences rarely allowed time for manoeuvre and, although there were plenty of incidents around the areas, the 'keepers had few direct shots carrying any threat or danger. United might once again have snatched a goal in the last minute – of extra-time – to decide the issue. In a hectic scrimmage a yard or so from the Rotherham goal-line, several players tried unsuccessfully to force the ball home before a shot from Ferguson was kicked off the line for a fruitless corner.

Another postponement and a further period of added play delayed the final outcome until the Reds at last derailed the boys from Millmoor.

The Rotherham Advertiser was once more in attendance:

After 330 minutes of battling for a semi-final place in the F.A. Youth Cup, Rotherham United Juniors had to bow to the knee at Millmoor on Wednesday night to Manchester United Juniors. The score was 4-1 against the Rotherham lads, but it was a score that could be disregarded as representing the merits of the sides. The outcome of this further replay really hinged on Manchester's second goal, which came in the first minute of extra-time. It was a highly controversial affair, to say the least.

The Rotherham skipper, Breckin, who had played an outstanding part in the Millmoor side's courageous show against the youngsters from mighty Manchester, had a threatening situation well in hand when he was tackled and appeared to be charged in the back. The ball was dispatched by Hall into the Rotherham goal, and at the sound of the referee's whistle there were general expectations of a free kick in Rotherham's favour. There was, in fact, every appearance that the Manchester players, too, shared those expectations, and they were overjoyed when referee K. Howley made it plain that he had awarded a goal, making quite a show of pointing to his own shoulder, presumably to indicate a fair charge.

This goal was a sad blow to Rotherham, though they would be the first to acknowledge the Manchester skills. The trouble from the Rotherham point of view was that Manchester skill was accompanied by excessive vigour and belligerence. Phillips, never mastered by the Old Trafford defenders, was floored by Fairhurst in the penalty area in fifteen minutes, and Coop scored from the kick.

That was only the start of a series of offences against Phillips and Coop, in particular. The present wearer of the number nine shirt in Rotherham's Third Division side revelled in the mud, showing a rate of acceleration which once again bewildered the Manchester lads, well-drilled though they are. Manchester, however, drew level in 32 minutes through Tony Young.

Unfortunately, the Manchester reaction boiled over before half-time into one or two unsavoury spectacles. Fairhurst, already penalised for fouls, had his name taken in a mêlée of players, and the game was held up for a few minutes in a consequent mix-up, during which Mr. Howley's linesmen came to his assistance during preparations for a free kick against Manchester.

Their help looked necessary, because by that time a lot of bad temper was making itself visible, and two more Manchester names went into the referee's book. The incidents seemed to call for more severe action.

Fortunately, the heat was taken off in the second half, during which the two Youngs, both of them surely top-class players of the future, demonstrated their menace to Rotherham's hopes of meeting Coventry in the semi-final.

At 90 minutes, however, the score remained 1-1, and extra-time was needed, as it was needed when the teams met at Millmoor in the first replay. It was at the very start of that extra period that Manchester got their second, highly debatable goal.

That took the heart out of Rotherham, and further goals were added by Lewis and Ferguson before the extra half-hour was up.

Altogether it was a match to remember, in spite of the regrettable incidents of the first half.

Given that the outcome was finally decided in an overly physical battle by United's superior know-how and a favourable rub of the green, it was difficult not to feel a little sympathy for the young Millers.

The Evening News recounted the Manchester take on events, a summary which identified the Reds' good and bad sides:

It took another two hours of their F.A. Youth Cup quarter-final before Manchester United finally broke the resistance of brave Rotherham United with a 4-1 win in the second replay. Power and class finally told with three goals in extra-time, but despite the scoreline United still had to work desperately hard against dour, never-say-die opponents. Danger man Trevor Phillips soon had United in trouble and in only fifteen minutes Fairhurst floored the Rotherham leader inside the area, Coop scored from the spot.

United, with Ferguson, Whelan and Eric Young impressive upfront, struck back quickly and winger Tony Young fired in the equaliser on the half-hour. The strength of the United side began to show in the second half, and only some courageous and determined defending by the Rotherham side kept the scores level.

In the first minute of extra-time Hall, fortunate that a pushing offence went unnoticed, shot United into the lead, and further goals from Lewis and Ferguson emphasised United's superiority in the later stages of the game.

A fine match was marred by the bookings of Fairhurst, Millerchip and Lewis, and Fairhurst in particular was lucky not to be sent off.

> Because Tommy O'Neil and myself lived in St. Helens we didn't go into digs but lived at home instead. For Youth Cup matches we would get the train into Manchester and then a bus to The Cliff or Old Trafford. The team bus would then take us to the golf club for a meal or sometimes straight to the away ground.
>
> I remember the Rotherham centre-forward, Trevor Phillips, having a good reputation and although he wasn't tall, he was quick and skilful. I preferred to play against big, strong forwards so he really made it hard for me. Luckily our forwards clicked on the night and we came away with the win.
>
> When the bus arrived back in Manchester it was too late to get home so I stayed in digs with Jimmy Hall, and with the landlady asleep, he showed me Duncan Edwards' old room with some of his old memorabilia still on the wall.
>
> That was really something.

BILL FAIRHURST

*This game was originally scheduled for Thursday, March 5th but was postponed due to ice on the pitch

223

1969-70

1) David Icke	9) Colin Randell	1) Willie Carrick	9) Jimmy Hall
2) Ivan Crossley	10) Mick McGuire	2) Laurie Millerchip	10) Eric Young
3) Jimmy Holmes	11) Trevor Smith	3) Kevin Lewis	11) Tony Whelan
4) Dennis Mortimer	*12) John Stevenson*	4) Tommy O'Neil	*12) Brian Greenhoff (for 3)*
5) Alan Dugdale		5) Bill Fairhurst	
6) Bob Parker		6) Ian Donald	
7) Les Cartwright		7) Tony Young	
8) Alan Green		8) Damien Ferguson	

MARCH 1970

COVENTRY CITY 3 v 1 MANCHESTER UNITED

Cartwright, Mortimer, Smith — Whelan

semi-final 1st leg

Thursday 26th
Kick-off 7.30 p.m.
Attendance 2,403

A second successive semi-final had the Reds paired against Coventry City, with the venue for the opening leg down in the Midlands. Because United's seniors were meeting Leeds in an F.A. Cup semi-final second replay at Bolton on the same evening, there was plenty of expectancy around the vicinity of Old Trafford that two cup final appearances might be in the offing for the club.

The Coventry Evening Telegraph gave an appropriate profile to the under-18 game:

Coventry City's youngsters face their most important occasion of the season at Highfield Road tomorrow evening when they go for a first leg lead in the semi-final of the F.A. Youth Cup against Manchester United.

City's task against the most successful side in the history of the competition is formidable, but with England international Dennis Mortimer skippering them, they have high hopes of tackling the second leg at Old Trafford a week today with an advantage.

The Sky Blues put their strongest side into action against United, who have won the trophy six times and on their last triumph in 1964 fielded such names as George Best, John Fitzpatrick, David Sadler and John Aston.

Welsh youth internationals Colin Randell and Les Cartwright figure in attack, where Colin Green's incisiveness will be vital in City's cause.

There are two former rugby league stars in the United line-up. Centre-half Bill Fairhurst played for the St. Helens town team, while right-half Tommy O'Neil was a double international at soccer and rugby league for England schoolboys.

United, like City, are a young side with eight of the team eligible to play in next season's competition and everything points to a splendid tie.

It was a night of double disappointment for United supporters. The seniors bowed out of the F.A. Cup at Burnden Park, while the youngsters gave themselves a formidable task in the second leg by turning in an indifferent display.

The Coventry Evening Telegraph headline 'YOUNG SKY BLUES HEAD FOR FINAL' gave a strong pointer to the ultimate outcome:

City's youngsters brilliantly carved out a lead over Manchester United last night that should prove sufficient to carry them into the final of the F.A. Youth Cup for the second time in three seasons.

The display from the young Sky Blues after the break was the finest 45 minutes' football I have seen from a City under-18 side. And they must be favourites to emerge from next Wednesday's second leg at Old Trafford and qualify to meet either Tottenham or Bristol City in the two-leg final.

Yet, for twenty minutes up to the interval, there were doubts whether City would be able to overcome a stubborn defence.

City dominated play in the opening stages and, with goalkeeper Carrick often coming wildly off his line and losing control of his six-yard area, the home lads could have been two or three up instead of one after seventeen minutes.

Dennis Mortimer, the City captain, again showing the example with superb poise and intelligent play, hit a tremendous shot from an acute angle following a Green cross-shot.

A few moments earlier, a Green header had struck Fairhurst, United's huge centre-half, on its way to the net, and the visitors escaped.

It was a shock when United equalised after 35 minutes through Whelan after Les Cartwright had failed to get in a worthwhile challenge on another United player on the edge of his own box.

This saw City lose their composure and it was anybody's game as the teams went in at half-time. But City took charge afterwards, and top referee Bernard Homewood (Sudbury) had to pull up a desperate United over a dozen times as they tried to counter some great attacking with physical marking.

But the City boys picked themselves up off the deck, shrugged off the rough tackles, and hit two good goals in the space of six minutes.

First, Smith came in from the left to send a looping header over Carrick's outstretched arms from Crossley's long cross in the 62nd minute. Then, when United rashly allowed Mortimer's corner to run across the face of the goal, Cartwright hit a 'screamer' back into the far corner.

If Green had not got his toe under a Smith centre thirteen minutes from time, United would have been further punished.

Bob Parker did a great job of sweeping up alongside Alan Dugdale, and once Mick McGuire had got working, he found some awesome gaps in United's suspect defence which City – with some exciting wing play – fully exploited.

Jack Pauline reckoned the 'second half belonged almost entirely to the home side. They were quicker to the ball and always creating danger', and he also conceded the Reds 'were perhaps a little fortunate to stem the Coventry raids and keep within reasonably striking distance for the second leg'.

From a Coventry corner, Willie Carrick catches confidently while Bill Fairhurst (far left) and Tony Whelan (number eleven) appear alert to the danger

1) Willie Carrick	9) Ronnie Miller	1) David Icke	9) Colin Randell
2) Laurie Millerchip	10) Damien Ferguson	2) Ivan Crossley	10) Mick McGuire
3) Kevin Lewis	11) Tony Whelan	3) Jimmy Holmes	11) Trevor Smith
4) Tommy O'Neil	*12) Ian McMurdo (for 9)*	4) Dennis Mortimer	*12) John Stevenson*
5) Bill Fairhurst		5) Alan Dugdale	
6) Ian Donald		6) Bob Parker	
7) Tony Young		7) Les Cartwright	
8) Eric Young		8) Alan Green	

1969-70

MANCHESTER UNITED 0 (1) v (4) 1 COVENTRY CITY

Smith

APRIL 1970

Wednesday 1st

Kick-off 7.30 p.m.

Attendance 5,037

semi-final 2nd leg

YOUTH CUP DEFEAT IS TRIPLE BLOW FOR REDS

There was more grief in store for United on the injury front as the second leg approached because question marks over the availability of one of their regular defenders and main striker lingered right up until the day of the return fixture, a situation which was commented on in the Evening News:

Manchester United will probably be without Jimmy Hall, one of their leading scorers, for tonight's second leg F.A. Youth Cup semi-final against Coventry City at Old Trafford.
The Irish centre-forward twisted his ankle and is doubtful for the match which the young Reds have a two-goal deficit to pull back from the first leg at Coventry.
Ronnie Miller, Scottish schools' international, is standing by in a party of fourteen players from which the side will be named this evening.
Full-back Kevin Lewis, who has been doubtful with a leg strain, is expected to be fit. Coventry will be at full strength.
United lost 3-1 at Coventry but are confident they can pull back.
Said chief coach Wilf McGuinness today, 'I'm looking for the youngsters to show what they are made of and fight back for those two goals, which I know they are capable of doing.'

The Sky Blues remained unchanged, despite skipper Dennis Mortimer injuring an ankle in a first-team fixture against Burnley on the preceding Saturday, and 48 hours later left-half Bob Parker got an injection of added experience by making his First Division debut in a 1-1 draw at Old Trafford.

The Youth Cup story ended in sorrow for United when Coventry extended their aggregate to gain the place in the final which their performance fully merited. It was a crushing blow to all connected to the youth team, their defeat only serving to compound the seniors' losses in the semi-finals of both major domestic cup competitions.

The Coventry Evening Telegraph featured a report which detailed the alighting stop for United:

Coventry's triumphant youngsters left Old Trafford last night with praise ringing in their ears from Sir Matt Busby.
City confidently held their advantage from the first leg then sank United with a 62nd minute goal from diminutive Trevor Smith.
And Sir Matt said, 'A great performance. They were certainly the better and more skilful side.'
So, for the second time in three days, Old Trafford proved a happy hunting ground for the Sky Blues. And the way the City lads assuredly took all United had to offer and then outplayed them in the last half-hour suggests they have a great chance of winning the cup for the first time.
Now they await the winners of the other semi-final between Tottenham and Bristol City but must feel confident about tackling either club in the two-leg final.
United's ploy was only too clear; they had to put early pressure on City's goal to stand a chance of making a real fight of it. They got the ball into the City net after half an hour but fouled goalkeeper David Icke in the process. This was the nearest they got to piercing a stubborn defence in which every lad played a heroic part.
The longer it went, the more obvious it became that City had the game under control, dictating it their way, forcing United into errors, and gradually breaking out with more menace. Alan Green, in fact, hit a post after 23 minutes and, even at that early stage, United got a glimpse of the visitors' striking power.
United 'keeper Carrick had to tip over a cross-shot from Jim Holmes, who must hit the ball with his left-foot more powerfully and cleanly than anyone in the club with the exception of Dave Clements.
The first part of the second half was played in an incredible snow blizzard and it had just subsided when City scored the goal that put United's task out of reach.
Colin Randell took a throw on the right, Ivan Crossley swung the ball over, and, as right-back Millerchip failed to intercept, Smith was in swiftly with a low shot.
Tony Young missed an 85th minute penalty after being floored by Alan Dugdale, shooting high over the top.
It was the dying gesture of a well-beaten side.

Jack Pauline made reference to a couple of early chances for United in the Review, the first a free kick in the opening minute that O'Neil planted just wide of the mark. The second was as a result of a high ball dropping into Coventry's penalty box and causing a wave of pandemonium before being cleared.

Pauline viewed City to be *'the sharper team'* and he went on to admit Smith's goal *'virtually settled'* the issue, even though there was still almost half an hour to go.

David Meek penned the understatement of the season when writing that United *'probably missed the injured Jimmy Hall in attack'.* Also claiming the teenage Reds *'made little impression',* Meek pointed out that the two Youngs *'showed up well'* despite not having *'much support from behind, where the United defence always looked vulnerable'.*

Coventry met Spurs in the final and for the second time in three attempts, the Sky Blues fell at the last hurdle, on this occasion by a 4-3 aggregate.

Two of the club's brightest prospects, Tony Whelan (left) and Tony Young couldn't find a way past Coventry at Old Trafford

225

1970-71

1) Neil Shepherd	9) Graham Futcher	1) Willie Carrick	9) Tony Whelan
2) Mike Worrall	10) Jeff Moody	2) Tommy O'Neil	10) Peter Fletcher
3) Paul Beckett	11) Ifan Williams	3) Kevin Lewis	11) Eric Young
4) Colin Rowlands	*12) Glyn Roberts ◊*	4) Brian Greenhoff	*12) Paul Jones*
5) Gary Stephan		5) Bill Fairhurst	
6) John Relish		6) Clive Griffiths	
7) Graham Vile		7) Sammy McIlroy	
8) Kelvin Arthur		8) Tony Young	

DECEMBER 1970

CHESTER 0 v 4 MANCHESTER UNITED

Fletcher, Whelan, Young T. (2)

Thursday 3rd
Kick-off 7.15 p.m.
Attendance 1,103

second round

Four goal margin flatters United

With senior star Pat Crerand, manager Wilf McGuinness and Sir Matt Busby in accompaniment, the club's requirement for the opening sortie of the 1970/71 season was an excursion to the picturesque county town of Chester, which represented a new Youth Cup venue as far as the Reds were concerned.

The Reds' starting line-up at Sealand Road revealed only three new faces from the last campaign, as Pontypridd-born defender Clive Griffiths wore the number six shirt, Northern Ireland prodigy Sammy McIlroy was placed at outside-right and Mancunian Peter Fletcher at inside-left while Paul Jones, from Stockport, found himself assigned the substitute's job.

For four of the established members of the youth team, Tommy O'Neil, Kevin Lewis and the two Youngs, it was their third and final chance to win the trophy, and the same applied to Brian Greenhoff, who had made three starts, one substitute appearance and warmed the bench on another three occasions in the competition over the past couple of years.

When their combined knowledge was added to that of Tony Whelan, Willie Carrick and Bill Fairhurst, who shared 24 Youth Cup starts equally between them, and the fact that the scoring tally of fresh face Fletcher already stood at ten for the junior sides that season, the hopes of an extended run were viewed as reasonable.

Additionally, Eric Young was by then more or less a fixture at number ten in the Reserves, as was Kevin Lewis at left full-back. While featuring in seventeen out of twenty of that season's Central League matches, Tony Young had occupied three different positions, and Whelan, Fairhurst and O'Neil were all beneficiaries from some experience of life at that standard.

It is certain that Crerand, McGuinness and Busby would have been wholly satisfied with the outcome of the tie, and certain parts of the showing, even though there were a few negatives to be drawn from the performance along with the many positives.

In his notes, Jack Pauline felt the game provided *'a fair start for our youths, leaving them plenty of lessons to be learnt before meeting even more testing opposition (which is) likely to come from the First Division clubs'.*

A blast of goals in the final seven minutes painted a rather pretty picture as far as the Reds were concerned. In a game in which the two combatants had not only each other to contend with, but also a downpour of almost monsoon proportions, the visitors unquestionably looked the livelier in the opening exchanges and their dominance culminated when Tony Whelan missed an inviting chance to open the scoring after a quarter of an hour.

Chester then got into a rhythm of sorts, by bouncing back to create a couple of skirmishes in the United goalmouth. Just after, with little to choose between the sides in terms of their possession and quality of play, the Reds forged into the lead when a lightning break by Eric Young down the left wing gave rise to a pass which slashed across the outside of Chester's penalty area.

Whelan appeared to be the recipient of Young's skilful intention until instead electing to cleverly dummy over the ball. It ran on to Fletcher, whose anticipation allowed him both the time and space to hammer his shot past a static Neil Shepherd.

Undeterred, Chester continued to contribute to what was developing into an entertaining spectacle and they were extremely unfortunate not to get back on level terms when Carrick pulled off a terrific save from a free kick. Seconds before the break, United scorned a great chance to increase their advantage when Whelan was put in possession from a set-piece, his shot rebounding to safety from the advancing home goalie.

Two soggy sets of players trooped off for a half-time cuppa, and immediately upon the restart the Reds were subjected to a major assault by their hosts. The liveliest of the home forwards was centre-forward Graham Futcher, one of a famous family of footballers, and at the 56-minute mark he was desperately unfortunate not to equalise.

The opportunity presented itself when Chester half-back John Relish floated a free kick into United's area, Futcher rising tallest to thud an expertly-timed header against a post with Carrick well beaten.

Shepherd was later alert to several dangerous United attacks, which became increasingly frequent as the seconds ticked by. In the 83rd minute, the Reds grabbed their second goal and with it they effectively killed the game as a contest. Intelligent running and a clinical finish from an acute angle along the bye-line brought Whelan the credit he deserved, despite an exposed Shepherd making a desperate attempt at keeping the ball out of the net only to inadvertently help it over the line.

In the 87th and 89th minutes, Tony Young twice put his name on the score sheet. His first goal came about when he was the sharpest to react in the six-yard area and shot home from among a ruck of players.

His next was much more pleasing to the eye. Neatly controlling a pass from Brian Greenhoff, which had sliced open a tiring defence, Young guided the ball home past an advancing Shepherd, who was left unprotected by an absence of cover.

Reports claiming that the Reds were *'a little fortunate'* and *'a shade lucky'* to defeat the plucky Sealand Road youngsters by such a wide margin seemed well off the mark because, apart from a concerted spell at the beginning of the second period and a couple of isolated chances, the Old Trafford kids were always in control.

Jack Pauline's shared thoughts about Chester *'playing nice football in midfield'* without getting *'within striking distance as the game went on'* were properly balanced with a statement about the Reds, who he felt *'always seemed likely to extend their slender lead'.*

Prolific inside-left Peter Fletcher got the Reds underway against Chester with a terrific shot from a distance of approximately twenty yards

1) Willie Carrick
2) Tommy O'Neil
3) Kevin Lewis
4) Brian Greenhoff
5) Clive Griffiths
6) Drew Harris
7) Sammy McIlroy
8) Tony Young
9) Tony Whelan
10) Eric Young
11) Peter Fletcher
12) Paul Jones

1) Jimmy Bell
2) Peter Lucas
3) Don McAllister
4) Jimmy McGill
5) Paul Jones
6) Stuart Bourne
7) Jeff Hindle
8) Stuart Lee
9) Roger Denton
10) Joe Welsh
11) Peter Olinyk
12) David Height (for 7)

1970-71

MANCHESTER UNITED 2 v 0 BOLTON WANDERERS

Fletcher, Whelan

DECEMBER 1970

Wednesday 23rd

Kick-off 7.30 p.m.

Attendance 1,323

third round

A Bolton team that had already edged Tranmere out of the Youth Cup prior to visiting Old Trafford for the Third Round seemed to provide the very type of opposition Jack Pauline alluded to in his Chester match report.

Bolton's youth team manager George Taylor was faced with no choice other than to leave two of his regulars out for the short hop over to Manchester, as giant centre-half Sam Allardyce and Scottish winger Willie Graham were both suffering from heavy colds.

Bill Foulkes was pressed into making just one personnel change from the win over Chester, with Clive Griffiths switching into the number five shirt normally occupied by Bill Fairhurst, who had been injured in an 'A' team match against Rochdale Reserves a few days before. To fill Griffiths' place Foulkes chose the adaptable Drew Harris, a Belfast boy who was a mainstay of the Lancashire League Division One side, albeit in a variety of positions.

The Bolton club invariably provide stern tests for the Reds, whether at home or away and at any level, and the Youth Cup contest fully lived up to that long-standing tradition. Herculean efforts from both sets of players produced an almost total cancelling out of any measure of skill prior to the break and so a stalemate existed at half-time. By far the best chance of the first half was when the Wanderers' Hindle completely and inexplicably missed the target despite being in a most advantageous position.

While there were fine individual performances from Bolton defenders Jones and McAllister, as well as Manchester's meandering menace Tony Whelan, the opening 45 minutes contained a monumental amount of the physical, prompting the Bolton Evening News to print a few words on that aspect of the match in its report:

The game was not helped by some indifferent refereeing, with players failing to get the protection they needed. And the lesson for the young Wanderers was that there is more to professional football than just looking clever on the ball.

It is necessary to combat all sorts of 'niggles', take all kinds of knocks and rise above them. Some of the more experienced Bolton boys had this message already, but the game must have been an eye-opener for the others.

Whelan continued to hog the spotlight for almost the entire second period, whereas his forward team-mate Fletcher provided a mere supporting role. The Reds' number nine resumed his contribution by smashing a rising drive over Bolton's bar and he later stuck the ball in the net twice only to be ruled offside on both occasions. With space denied to most of United's forwards, and virtuosity at a premium, the Reds were forced into relying predominantly on Whelan's pace to prize open some gaps in the Wanderers' ranks.

Bolton's Denton, whose tussle with Clive Griffiths developed into something of a battle royale, was sent on his way with a measured pass from centre-half Jones. Denton pulled the ball back across the penalty area to no-one in particular when, with the benefit of hindsight, a wiser choice would have been to attempt a shot at the target.

There were only a little over ten minutes remaining when United got the all-important opening goal which came, predictably, from the impressive Whelan. Released by a raking through-ball from Fletcher, and with shouts for offside on this occasion ignored by a linesman, he raced away from Lucas and veered to the left of the Wanderers' box before unleashing an unstoppable left-foot shot beyond 'keeper Jimmy Bell.

Time was now in short supply, so Bolton undertook a radical change of tactics by committing themselves to an all-out attacking policy, which subjected United to a severe battering in the later stages. Willie Carrick took a hard knock in one particular offence, but with time almost out, he chose to soldier on through the pain. Bolton were now making the Reds sweat somewhat, and with waves of constant pressure, they forced four corners in quick succession.

The allotted time was almost exhausted before United obtained blessed relief when Harris, whose performance proved more and more telling as the game went on, moved the ball out to the right. From over on the wing, Tony Young swept a grass-skimming pass into Bolton's goalmouth, where namesake Eric and Peter Fletcher were both nicely placed. Fletcher made the final contact, and with the ball barely crossing the decisive strip of white paint, the end result finished 2-0 to United.

The win over the Burnden Park side was a welcome aside on what proved to be an otherwise horrible day for the club. At exactly the same time when the youths were making cup progress at the expense of Bolton, the seniors were embarrassingly losing a Football League Cup semi-final second leg to Aston Villa, a club then ensconced in the Third Division. The Reds' aggregate defeat ultimately cost club manager Wilf McGuinness his job and resulted in Matt Busby taking over the Old Trafford reigns once again.

Snapped in action at Bolton in the newly-inaugurated Lancashire F.A. Youth Cup, Clive Griffiths (left) deputised capably for Bill Fairhurst at home to the young Trotters

1970-71

1) Jeff Parton	9) Ian Brennan	1) Mike Wylie	9) Tony Whelan
2) Peter Harris	10) Harry Falconer	2) Clive Griffiths	10) Eric Young
3) Harry Wilson	11) Leighton James	3) Kevin Lewis	11) Sammy McIlroy
4) Ronnie Welch	*12) Colin Morris*	4) Brian Greenhoff	*12) Peter Abbott (for 8)*
5) Duncan McMahon		5) Bill Fairhurst	
6) Joey McNamara		6) Tommy O'Neil	
7) Paul Bradshaw		7) Tony Young	
8) Billy Ingham		8) Peter Fletcher	

FEBRUARY 1971

BURNLEY 2 v 0 MANCHESTER UNITED

Bradshaw, Brennan

Tuesday 2nd
Kick-off 7.30 p.m.
Attendance 2,972

fourth round

Red 'babes' got stuck in the mud

There were good and bad tidings on the injury front while the young Reds reorganised themselves for a visit to Turf Moor, a venue where they had fallen out of the Youth Cup three years earlier.

Bill Fairhurst was now recovered and able to take his usual place at centre-half, but that ray of sunshine from the treatment room was completely blotted out with the inevitable absence of Willie Carrick, who had recently broken an arm. It was a terrible turn of luck for the likeable and talented 'keeper, although his absence provided an opening for Mike Wylie, a Boltonian who was the normal 'B' team goalie.

The Reds' back, middle and forward-lines were all in for a re-jig. There was an altering of the half-back line as a result of Fairhurst's return, and the repositioning of Clive Griffiths was a move felt necessary in order to counter the threat of Burnley's flying winger, Leighton James. Upfront, Sammy McIlroy swapped wing berths while Peter Fletcher moved to inside-right and Tony Young slipped into McIlroy's former position.

The ill-feeling between United and Burnley had persisted in the respective junior camps ever since the Reds' Youth Cup defeat in January 1968 and an over-familiarity at under-18 level wasn't an ideal scenario going into the latest clash, as it was now the third meeting between them in just a matter of weeks.

A washed out game at Turf Moor in the November just passed saw the two clubs partly contesting their first ever Lancashire Youth Cup tie and then, on a couple of Saturdays prior to the national cup meeting, a United 'A' side containing Fairhurst, Griffiths, Fletcher and Peter Abbott claimed a morale-boosting 3-0 victory over Burnley 'A' at The Cliff. The win completed a Lancashire League double over the Clarets, the Reds having defeated Burnley by five goals to one on their home patch earlier in the campaign.

On the eve of the game, the Burnley Express & News had its pre-match say:

Burnley, the 1968 winners, will be at full strength tonight when they attempt to reach the quarter-final of the F.A. Youth Cup by beating Manchester United at Turf Moor. Jimmy Adamson will not be naming his side for the Fourth Round game until today.

When all was settled bar the shouting, it was a case of same round, same opposition, same venue and same outcome as three years previously for United. With the young Reds' expectations soaring after their relative successes in the tournament over the past two seasons, they were again thrown out of their stride by the boys from Turf Moor, an unwelcome outcome which was relayed by the Manchester Evening News:

Manchester United's great hopes of seeing their talented youngsters make their mark in this season's F.A. Youth Cup got stuck in the mud of Burnley.

The Reds lost their Fourth Round tie 2-0 in gruelling conditions and driving rain that lasted throughout the game.

United, with practically the team that reached the semi-finals last season, might have edged ahead but for the goalkeeping of Jeff Parton, who made three tremendous saves from Eric Young, Tommy O'Neil and Tony Whelan.

Burnley were strong in midfield, but their match-winners were wingers Paul Bradshaw and Welsh Youth international Leighton James.

Bradshaw scored Burnley's first goal in the 16th minute and Ian Brennan, a lively centre-forward, shot the second early in the second half after James had opened up the way to goal.

United's night of disappointment was completed when they had left-back Kevin Lewis and outside-left Sammy McIlroy booked, both for fouls on Bradshaw.

An exasperated Jack Pauline was unable to conceal his despair:

Results in recent junior games have not been particularly favourable and the defeat of the Youth Cup team at Burnley was a disappointment. With so many players experienced in the competition and at Central League level there was no disguising our optimism for a repeat of the 1963/64 season.

Burnley were our masters on the night and worthily passed into Round Five. By the time these notes appear we should have a chance to prove the result all wrong, for we were due to meet the Turf Moor youths in a replay of the Lancashire F.A. Floodlit Youth competition, previously cancelled at half-time because of heavy rain.

Pauline later delivered his match notes in the same edition of the Review:

Some competent 'keeping by Parton in the home goal prevented an early breakthrough. Good understanding between Wilson and James, with the latter putting across the face of the exposed United goal, gave a foretaste of the danger to come.

James was the architect when Falconer was left with an open goal, only to hit the woodwork, and again in the 17th minute Bradshaw opened the score during a scrimmage in the United area. A couple of good saves by Wylie prevented Burnley from deservedly increasing their lead before the interval.

United again opened promisingly on the resumption but, forcing three corners in quick succession, the home side showed they were still in the game. They proved the point when breaking from a United attack midway through the second half to increase their lead, Brennan running nearly half the length of the field without serious challenge before slotting the ball past Wylie.

Sammy McIlroy, whose caution for fouling Burnley's Paul Bradshaw was another sorry event from United's perspective

FEBRUARY 1971

The introduction of Abbott for Fletcher twenty minutes from time sparked off a late United rally, though nothing much went for them in the penalty area when a goal might have put them back in the game. Abbott was twice only just off-target with good efforts and several good saves from Parton ensured his side of a merited victory.

An article about the Reds' fate also appeared in the Burnley Express & News, a few lines of which read:

Burnley are to be complimented on their scientific football throughout in atrocious conditions of mud and driving rain.

One wondered what Sir Matt Busby and Bobby Charlton, who watched from the directors' box, thought about it all.

United expected another good run in the competition, but it was not to be, and they could not grumble about a result that gave success-starved Burnley fans something to cheer about at last.

A fortnight after their exit from the Youth Cup, the Reds went some way towards avenging their defeat by beating Burnley 3-1 in the rearranged Lancashire Youth Cup game at Turf Moor, a couple of goals from Sammy McIlroy and one from Tony Young doing the trick for United.

> *It was exciting playing in those cup ties as they added a bit more spice than the usual 'A' team game on a Saturday. We used to look forward to them, to pit ourselves against other good teams in the country. The 'edge' was always with you at United so teams like Burnley always wanted to prove that they were just as good, that we weren't better than them even though United had the pick of international schoolboys.*
>
> *Then when you get two young seventeen year-old teams with loads of keenness and enthusiasm, well. I wouldn't necessarily say that Burnley were more physical than us that day, you tended to learn that stuff when you were a little older, but they clearly wanted to do one over us and perhaps showed more effort.*

PETER FLETCHER

Circa early 1970, pictured in the indoor training facility at The Cliff are seventeen of the club's younger staff
Back row (l-r) Eric Young, Bill Fairhurst, Peter Fletcher, Damien Ferguson, Willie Carrick, Ian Donald, Peter Abbott, Tony Whelan, Brian Greenhoff
Front row (l-r) Clive Griffiths, Paul Jones, Kevin Lewis, Frank McGivern, Tommy O'Neil, Tony Young, Drew Harris, Danny Healey

1971-72

1) Mike Wylie	9) Peter Fletcher
2) Alan Clarkson	10) Ken Ayres
3) Mike Wardrop	11) Danny Healey
4) Roy Morton	*12) Victor Hooks*
5) Clive Griffiths	
6) Paul Jones	
7) Frank McGivern	
8) Sammy McIlroy	

1) Brian Parkinson	9) George Telfer
2) Paul McEwan	10) Ray Pritchard
3) Alan Kenny	11) Ronnie Goodlass
4) Mick Buckley	*12) Tony Hogan*
5) Ken McNaught	
6) Don Tobin	
7) Cliff Marshall	
8) Ian Bacon	

DECEMBER 1971

MANCHESTER UNITED 1 v 1 EVERTON

McGivern — *Goodlass*

Wednesday 1st

Kick-off 7.30 p.m.

Attendance 4,263

second round

Because most of the team members who lost at Burnley earlier in the year had become victims of birth certificate exclusion, the process of rebuilding a competent youth side was required to begin all over again for the Old Trafford backroom staff.

For Tommy O'Neil and Kevin Lewis in the full-back roles now read Altrincham-born Alan Clarkson and Salford resident Mike Wardrop, while along the half-back line Brummie Roy Morton and Paul Jones were named in the spaces left by the retiring Brian Greenhoff and Bill Fairhurst. In the goal-getting department of the team, Ken Ayres, whose experience extended to winning five caps for England Boys, Mancunian Danny Healey, and Frank McGivern, formerly of Yorkshire Boys, came into the side for the two Youngs and Tony Whelan.

The influx of so many new lads meant that there were only four 'old hands' remaining, goalkeeper Mike Wylie, centre-back Clive Griffiths, and Sammy McIlroy and Peter Fletcher in the striking section. Victor Hooks who, like McIlroy, was from Belfast, found himself tagged as twelfth man.

United enjoyed the luck of the draw in one respect, through being handed home advantage, while in another, the prospect of a strong Everton team travelling to Stretford meant that any gradual 'easing' into the competition wasn't a given option.

The task facing an extremely immature United eleven was underlined when Everton named five former schoolboy internationals for the contest, midfielder Mick Buckley, central defender Ken McNaught, forward Ray Pritchard, and wingers Cliff Marshall and Ronnie Goodlass.

A number of openings that went begging, particularly in the later stages of the dual, and more specifically two shots from United players which rebounded off the crossbar, were the principle reasons that a replay was required.

Reporting on the game for the Manchester Evening News was Joe Lancaster, himself a future United Review contributor:

Manchester United's young sharp-shooter Sammy McIlroy ran himself to exhaustion trying to snatch victory against Everton in the Second Round of the F.A. Youth Cup at Old Trafford last night.

His efforts should not have been needed, for United ought to have coasted home. Instead they had to be satisfied with a 1-1 draw.

United took the lead in sixteen minutes when Frank McGivern deflected a McIlroy free kick, but Everton had hit back after 37 minutes. Schemer Mick Buckley, formerly of Manchester Boys, waltzed from the half-way line and laid on a perfect pass for Ron Goodlass to lash the ball home.

On the stroke of half-time, United missed a great chance of going ahead, when Fletcher and Ayres kept returning each other's passes in front of an Everton open goal.

After the interval, United turned on the pressure. Two drives from Ayres were blocked on the line, Healey hit the bar and McIlroy wrung his hands in desperation when Parkinson tipped a shot round the post.

The bombardment continued but United just couldn't score.

There was much amazement about the Reds being unable to win a match they dominated almost totally, and even the Liverpool Echo was moved to report that the junior Toffees 'wilted' under wave upon wave of pressure in the second half. If there was any comfort at all to be gained from the draw, it was that a confident United would travel to Merseyside fully expecting to complete the job in hand in Everton's own backyard.

Chief scout Johnny Aston advises Old Trafford's new recruits of 1971 to aim high
Back row (l-r) Geoff Smith, Alan Clarkson, Ken Ayres, Roy Morton
Front row (l-r) Willie Conroy, Mike Wardrop, David Brooks, Brendan McKelvey

1) Brian Parkinson	9) George Telfer	1) Mike Wylie	9) Ken Ayres
2) Paul McEwan	10) Ray Pritchard	2) Paul Jones	10) Peter Fletcher
3) Alan Kenny	11) Ronnie Goodlass	3) Mike Wardrop	11) Danny Healey
4) Mick Buckley	*12) Tony Hogan*	4) Roy Morton	*12) Victor Hooks*
5) Ken McNaught		5) Clive Griffiths	
6) Don Tobin		6) Paul Prophet	
7) Cliff Marshall		7) Frank McGivern	
8) Ian Bacon		8) Sammy McIlroy	

1971-72

EVERTON 2 v 1 MANCHESTER UNITED

Bacon, Telfer — McIlroy

DECEMBER 1971

Tuesday 7th

Kick-off 7.30 p.m.

Attendance 7,051

second round replay

McIlroy's stormer in vain

Less than a week later, the rematch took place at Goodison Park. United defender Alan Clarkson was ruled out with a knock, an unfortunate development which signalled a debut for Paul Prophet, a sixteen year-old apprentice. The Wythenshawe teenager was blooded at left-half and captain Paul Jones transferred into the place vacated by Clarkson.

Everton were luckier in terms of injury, so they elected to field exactly the same personnel who had escaped from Old Trafford with their cup hopes still intact.

The next day's Liverpool Echo delivered the details of United's demise:

> **What a difference an hour can make.** At ten past eight last night at Goodison Park, Everton looked like a group of individuals destined to make an early exit from this year's F.A. Youth Cup at the hands of Manchester United.
>
> By ten past nine, it was a leg weary United who staggered off the pitch, beaten 2-1 in this second round replay by a transformed Everton team that looked capable of going a very long way in the competition.
>
> In the first half Everton, apart from some fine play by Mike Buckley, had left midfield to United, with the result that Old Trafford's latest star, Sammy McIlroy, did pretty much as he pleased.
>
> **25-yards goal**
>
> The ease with which McIlroy put United in front after nine minutes illustrated this, for no one in a blue shirt challenged when the inside right collected the ball 25 yards from the Everton goal.
>
> McIlroy put the ball on his left foot, transferred it to his right, and then placed it coolly into the far top corner of the net, giving Brian Parkinson, in the Everton goal, little or no chance.
>
> One of Everton's best moves in the first half saw Buckley split the United defence with a long pass. Outside left Ron Goodlass raced on to the ball and beat Mike Wylie, the United goalkeeper, with a tremendous shot, but left back Mike Wardrop hooked the ball to safety.
>
> Everton were decidedly unlucky not to get a penalty just before half time when Roy Morton handled, but the first half belonged to United, and particularly McIlroy, who saw another of his shots strike the crossbar.
>
> How different things were after that. In Buckley and Ian Bacon, Everton had two players working with the enthusiasm of Alan Ball. Ray Pritchard, always a tower of strength, received full support from Ken McNaught in closing up the middle of the defence, and George Telfer found some of his enthusiasm rubbing off on his co-forwards.
>
> It was centre forward Telfer who got Everton's equaliser at the 50th minute—McIlroy appearing to be booked for something he said to the referee as the build-up was going on—and Bacon settled the issue with a second goal at the 63rd minute.
>
> **Inspiration**
>
> There were flashes of inspiration for United from McIlroy after this, but it was always Everton who looked the more likely to score.
>
> After a game that exceeded all expectations, both in standard of play and entertainment, the teams received a standing ovation from the 7,051 spectators.
>
> And Everton formed up in two lines to clap the exhausted United side off the pitch, surely knowing that there will be another big crowd behind them when they tackle Sheffield Wednesday at home in round three.

The pain of losing was excruciatingly hurtful because the Reds had dominated the game in Manchester and were easily on top in the replay until Everton's second goal. Taking the two games as a whole, United had monopolised the proceedings for the vast majority of the time and were streets ahead in respect of goalscoring opportunities.

Sammy McIlroy's efforts over the two matches went completely to waste, and there was no mention in the Echo's report about him smashing a terrific attempt against an upright at the end of one move and then firing a shot into the side-netting of Parkinson's goal at the conclusion of another.

For the Manchester Evening News, Matt D'Arcy brought the matter to a conclusion with his views:

Sammy McIlroy lorded it over Goodison Park last night – and finished on the losing side as Manchester United were unluckily shot out of the F.A. Youth Cup by Everton.

McIlroy scored United's goal – a sizzling 25-yarder after nine minutes – hit the post, caused general panic in the Everton ranks.......and was booked as Everton equalised in 50 minutes. It happened after he lost possession in the centre circle. The ball struck the referee, but it bounced right for Everton, who went on to score. McIlroy gave vent to his feelings – and was booked.

Pat Crerand, coach to the young Reds, has created a sound, tactically aware side – but it's now up to the players to learn they must fight back rather than capitulate when the pressure is on them.

United collapsed when Everton went ahead through Ian Bacon after 63 minutes, even though left-back Mike Wardrop, right-half Roy Morton, big defenders Clive Griffiths and Paul Prophet, and right-winger Frank McGivern all look good prospects.

Paul Prophet, whose association with the Youth Cup lasted just 90 minutes

1972-73

1) Dave Ryan	9) Robin Clarke	1) Gary Plumley	9) Mick King
2) Alan Clarkson	10) Ken Ayres	2) Martyn Capewell	10) Graham French
3) Paul Bielby	11) Brendan McKelvey	3) Graham Capewell	11) Graham Hunt
4) Mike Wardrop	*12) David Brooks (for 11)*	4) Tom Kilkelly	*12) Rod Wood*
5) Clive Griffiths		5) John Lane	
6) Jimmy Nicholl		6) Jim Blacklaw	
7) Pat Olney		7) John Bowtell	
8) Roy Morton		8) Peter Hearne	

DECEMBER 1972

MANCHESTER UNITED 2 v 1 LEICESTER CITY
Ayres, McKelvey — *Hearne*

second round

Monday 11th*

Kick-off 7.30 p.m.

Attendance 1,316

Goal jolt wakes up young Reds

By December 1972, Frank O'Farrell had been in charge at Old Trafford for about a year and a half. The contrast between twelve months before, a period in which the Reds sat proudly at the top of the First Division, and the present, a time when the club was wallowing in the depths at the foot of the table, couldn't have been more different.

Along with the legions of United supporters and his staff, O'Farrell had certainly suffered during the second half of the 1971/72 season, mainly as a result of the expectation caused by what went on in the months immediately before. Consequently, a final position of eighth, exactly the same place the team had finished in both of the previous two years, was viewed as a major disappointment by all of those with the club's interests at heart.

Results continued to cause O'Farrell headaches in his second term, with home defeats by the likes of Ipswich, Coventry, Stoke and, most embarrassingly, Bristol Rovers in the League Cup, heaping untold misery on a man who was under immense pressure to turn things around, and quickly.

It was against that sombre backdrop when a twice-delayed Second Round home tie against Leicester City began a fresh assault on the Youth Cup for the young Reds, the time gap between the original date and the staging of the game allowing the Foxes to include Graham French. The striker had served out a suspension in the interim period and his appearance meant both sides started at full strength.

For United, a new goalie was introduced in the form of Dave Ryan and there were also competition debuts for defenders Paul Bielby and Jimmy Nicholl, the latter a Belfast native who had represented Northern Ireland as a schoolboy. With the exception of Ken Ayres, who demonstrated some sharp current form by scoring six goals in his last two 'B' team appearances, four of which came in a Supplementary Cup victory over Bury, the forward-line was lacking in any tournament experience.

Ayres was accompanied upfront by Robin Clarke who, like Nicholl, had won caps for Northern Ireland Boys, while Pat Olney occupied a position on the right flank. That left Edinburgh-born Brendan McKelvey to claim the outside-left spot and David Brooks, a prospect from the Altrincham area, to gain the nod for the substitute role.

Even though the opening half was barren of goals, United could lay claim to producing the two best chances of breaking the deadlock. Firstly, when Ayres connected with an accurate Clarkson free kick, the resultant header was booted off the line, and that effort was followed by an Olney piledriver which grazed Leicester's bar. Those fleeting moments of excitement apart, it was a 45 minutes consisting mostly of drab entertainment and poor quality soccer from both sides.

Just two minutes after the interval, the game finally bloomed into life when Leicester took both the initiative and the lead after French hit a powerful shot from distance which Ryan could only parry. The ball ran loose, and kindly, to Peter Hearne and the former England schoolboy starlet kept his head to score with a shot which found the left-hand corner of Ryan's net.

Undeterred, the Reds pressed on and were able to draw level just ten minutes later with a terrific goal.

The lion's share of the credit for the equaliser went to Cardiff-born Olney, the Welsh winger making an incisive run through Leicester's defence before playing Ayres in with an exquisite pass. The number ten was totally unmarked, and in a position where he could hardly fail to beat Plumley in the Foxes' goal.

In the 65th minute, United forged ahead. A probing assault from Clarke resulted in the Ulster boy planting possession to the unmarked McKelvey, the winger closing in on goal before gleefully sinking the ball into the back of City's net.

The point at which the home side went in front signalled the beginning of the best period of the contest as far as they were concerned. New boys and old at last blended into a harmonious synchronicity and their football leapt to a level which was infinitely more polished than anything seen previously.

The Reds' performance in the later stages of the game gave rise to the prospect that there was more to come from them in terms of further development, causing the Manchester Evening News to mention that *'for twenty minutes the youngsters hit vintage youth team standard with fast, flowing football'* before adding *'United were well on top and amply compensating for their indifferent first half'*.

The tie had been somewhat boisterous from the opening whistle, with United's Griffiths and City's Martyn Capewell already cautioned for misdemeanours. Then, after Leicester missed two decent opportunities to draw level, initially when Blacklaw sent a free kick just over and later through Bowtell putting a shot inches past a United post, the tail-end fireworks started.

With only seven minutes remaining, Roy Morton had the ball at his feet in Leicester's eighteen-yard area when his legs were taken from under him. The victim of a certain foul, Morton was sprawled out on the deck and so referee Ron Boyles of Derby awarded a penalty which appeared obvious and quite incontestable. It was then that Martyn Capewell's twin brother, Graham, unaccountably proceeded to remonstrate with a linesman. Finally dismissed by Mr. Boyles for using abusive language, it proved a wholly unnecessary sending-off as Plumley kept his team in with a slender chance of saving the game by brilliantly parrying Mike Wardrop's spot kick.

That slim hope came to nothing, because the match petered out with the Reds unwilling to surrender anything more than brief snatches of possession to their depleted opponents.

Blackley-born Dave Ryan had made only one 'A' and nine 'B' team appearances prior to being chosen for Youth Cup duty

This game was originally scheduled for Monday, November 27th but was postponed due to a 'flu epidemic at Filbert Street. The game was rearranged for Monday, December 4th but was postponed again due to a waterlogged Old Trafford pitch

232

1) Tony Bell	9) David Brown	1) Dave Ryan	9) Robin Clarke
2) Ray Blackhall	10) Alan Barker	2) Alan Clarkson	10) Ken Ayres
3) David Dodds	11) Colin Ayre	3) Paul Bielby	11) Brendan McKelvey
4) Trevor Todd	*12) Keith MacDonald (for 7)*	4) Mike Wardrop	*12) David Brooks*
5) John Thomson		5) Clive Griffiths	
6) Bobby Chilton		6) Jimmy Nicholl	
7) David Norton		7) Pat Olney	
8) Joe Pooley		8) Roy Morton	

NEWCASTLE UNITED 1 v 1 MANCHESTER UNITED

Brown — Clarke

1972-73

DECEMBER 1972

Monday 18th

Kick-off 7.30 p.m.

Due to the delay in completing the Second Round game, United resumed Youth Cup duty just a week after defeating Leicester with a long trek up to Tyneside.

Quite a lot had happened over the last few days as, on the prior Saturday, the senior Reds were on the sticky side of a 5-0 scoreline at Crystal Palace. That crushing loss, in which United looked despondent, disorganised and lacking any fight, represented the final straw as far as the club's directors were concerned. Frank O'Farrell paid the price by losing his job, and following him out of the door was his assistant, Malcolm Musgrove.

United's First Division fortunes were certainly in a perilous state and so a call went out to Tommy Docherty, who was tasked with hauling the club out of its present predicament. Of course, changes were needed, although one of the saddest aspects of O'Farrell's sacking was caused by the incoming man wanting as clean a sweep as possible. That, unfortunately, meant the long-serving Johnny Aston senior, a respected member of the backroom staff who had achieved so much as a player and coach at Old Trafford, also found himself out of work. Aston's sacking broke a link which, apart from the period spent on active duty as a Royal Marine Commando in the Second World War, stretched all the way back to his time with the MUJACs commencing in 1938.

Containing comments from a former St. James's Park hopeful, who personally came across the Reds in the national under-18's knock-out tournament in 1963, the Newcastle Evening Chronicle provided a preview to the Youth Cup action:

Newcastle N's take on the starlets of Manchester United in the Third Round of the Youth Cup at Gallowgate tonight with a massive boost from coach Geoff Allen.

'I'm certain we'll win tonight and have a good run in the competition. I've got a good squad here – we've only lost one game all season. We beat Leeds United away in the last round and I think that was a more difficult draw than this one at home.'

The N's, perched proudly at the top of the Northern Intermediate League, are also boosted by the return of two key players who missed the 1-0 (Youth Cup) win at Elland Road.

Skipper Bobby Chilton is back after recovering from a broken nose and left-back David Dodds also resumes duty to give the defence a more stable look.

Allen has named a squad of fourteen players because of a fitness doubt over Colin Ayre, who missed Saturday's 2-0 league win against Barnsley with an ankle injury.

Manchester United Juniors, coached by Paddy Crerand, bring a squad littered with schoolboy internationals.

Following a determined display, the Reds would have been much the more pleased at an outcome which meant that the junior Magpies needed to secure a positive result in Manchester if they were to live up to their coach's confident predictions.

The Newcastle Journal published the following concise match report:

David Brown, a full-back converted into a centre-forward, earned Newcastle a replay at Old Trafford against Manchester United when he hit a late equaliser in this F.A. Youth Cup Third Round tie at St. James's Park last night.

Brown, who scored the goal which knocked the talented youngsters of Leeds out of the competition in the last round, broke through the Manchester defence when it looked as if Newcastle's youngsters were never going to score.

With only eighteen minutes left, he worked a neat one-two with fellow striker Alan Barker before slotting the ball past Manchester 'keeper David Ryan.

Manchester had taken the lead in the 28th minute through their centre-forward Robin Clarke.

The chance was created for him by Ken Ayres, who won a battle for possession with Newcastle sweeper Bobby Chilton, before squaring the ball to Clarke.

Newcastle made a desperate attempt to snatch a winner in the dying stages but Manchester's solid defence stood firm.

A tracksuited Pat Crerand conducts a coaching session for his youthful charges at The Cliff
The players seen are (from l-r) Clive Griffiths, Robin Clarke, Mike Wardrop, Paul Bielby, Ken Ayres, Willie Conroy, David Brooks, Brendan McKelvey

third round

1972-73

1) Dave Ryan
2) Alan Clarkson
3) Paul Bielby
4) Mike Wardrop
5) Clive Griffiths
6) Jimmy Nicholl
7) Pat Olney
8) Roy Morton
9) Robin Clarke
10) Ken Ayres
11) Brendan McKelvey
12) David Brooks (for 7)

1) Tony Bell
2) Ray Blackhall
3) Trevor Todd
4) Bobby Chilton
5) John Thomson
6) Keith MacDonald
7) David Brown
8) David Dodds
9) Alan Barker
10) Clive Swindle
11) Colin Ayre
12) David Norton (for 7)

JANUARY 1973

MANCHESTER UNITED 4 v 1 NEWCASTLE UNITED

Ayres, Clarke (2), Griffiths — Barker

Wednesday 10th
Kick-off 7.30 p.m.
Attendance 2,379

third round replay

Newcastle's challenge was swept aside in the replay by a United side employing an attacking style which wasn't much in evidence at St. James's Park. The Reds went ahead in the eighth minute and the goal simultaneously opened up the scoring and the game as a spectacle.

Jack Pauline filled a few lines on the matter for the Review:

United opened briskly and took an early lead when Griffiths headed in from close range a well-placed Olney corner but for a time the visitors looked the more dangerous in the penalty area. In this period Ryan did well with several high centres, one just under the bar, to keep the lead intact. Olney went near to increasing the advantage when he rounded one of our best moves with a left-foot shot which went just past the post.

A long free kick to Newcastle caught our defence strangely square but with a great chance to equalise, Swindle headed over. There was little to choose between the teams at this stage but the Newcastle attacks carried the greater threat. It was no more than they deserved when a Brown header from the second of two corners put them on terms.

This proved to be the visitors last spell of sustained pressure for once Ayres had restored the lead nine minutes before half-time, United remained in command. The goal came from a Clarkson centre when Morton resisted the temptation of a difficult header to gently back-head the ball to the feet of Ayres who took an easy chance.

Newcastle hopes faded twelve minutes after the interval when McKelvey powered his way down the left wing then turned in a good centre for Clarke to add number three after 57 minutes.

Brooks for the injured Olney at this point did little to halt the United momentum and, playing some of their best football, they coasted to a Fourth Round appearance. Newcastle broke the pattern with several good moves but they rarely produced a finish to their attacks. In this form our youths are going to prove difficult to beat and we can anticipate the meeting with Arsenal with quiet confidence.

With Clive Griffiths alongside him in central defence, Jimmy Nicholl withstood numerous Newcastle assaults until the Reds made the game safe

Substituted due to a knock in the second period, Pat Olney's accurate flag kick led to United inflicting a quick early blow on Newcastle

There was a measure of agreement with Pauline's comments in the Newcastle Journal, the newspaper claiming that the Magpies, after drawing level, *'lost their competitive bite'*. In describing the Reds' fourth goal, a real gem, the Journal noted:

Thomson and Blackhall tried to hold (Newcastle) together but there was no stopping Manchester's Clarke in the 81st minute. He made a 35-yard run and finished off with a twenty-yard drive.

David Meek wrote about the incidents which sealed the Magpies' fate and also correctly identified their goalscorer:

Manchester United's youngsters have set the right cup mood for the big F.A. Cup clash at Wolves on Saturday. The young Reds stormed to the attack to dispose of Newcastle United in their Third Round Youth Cup replay at Old Trafford. And after the 1-1 draw at St. James's Park, this was a decisive 4-1 win.

Now United will play Arsenal at Old Trafford in the next round, and though a very young side they are clearly going to give the Gunners a testing time.

Centre-half Clive Griffiths put United in front, with the help of a deflection, after nine minutes, then Newcastle proved their worth with a great equaliser from Alan Barker in the 32nd minute. Robin Clarke restored United's lead six minutes later. The Reds' England Youth international Roy Morton played a part in both goals, and was outstanding in midfield.

In the second half, the men in front of him came into their own. Ken Ayres scored after a splendid run by Brendan McKelvey (57 mins), then Clarke, only fifteen and in his first year as a striker, scored his second with a powerful run.

United's plight in the First Division may be a little worrying, but their future certainly looks to be in good hands.

1) Dave Ryan
2) Alan Clarkson
3) Paul Bielby
4) Mike Wardrop
5) Clive Griffiths
6) Jimmy Nicholl
7) Pat Olney
8) Roy Morton
9) David Brooks
10) Ken Ayres
11) Brendan McKelvey
12) Willie Conroy (for 9)

1) Gareth Williams
2) Peter Rixon
3) Dave Donaldson
4) Richie Powling
5) David Price
6) Liam Brady
7) Wilf Rostron
8) Barrie Vassallo
9) Frank Stapleton
10) Brian Hornsby
11) John Matthews
12) Tony Winston

1972-73

MANCHESTER UNITED 2 v 2 ARSENAL

McKelvey (2, 1 pen)   Rostron, Vassallo

JANUARY 1973

Wednesday 31st

Kick-off 7.30 p.m.

Attendance 3,721

Arsenal made the journey north on the last day of January with a stand-in 'keeper who would be recognised as one of their main successes before the night was out. Welsh-born Gareth Williams was pencilled in to play his very first game at any level for the Gunners as a result of an injury to Neil Freeman, Arsenal's regular youth team number one.

With Robin Clarke recovering back home in Northern Ireland, having already spent a short spell in hospital with appendicitis, David Brooks was installed at centre-forward for United and Harrogate-based Willie Conroy occupied the bench.

The Review came up with the following observations:

Each goal had a narrow escape in the opening minutes but playing with more flair, Arsenal looked the more dangerous to deservedly go ahead in sixteen minutes, Vassallo shooting just inside the upright from a move on the left.

Having twice survived when defensive mistakes let in Arsenal for scoring chances, we moved to the attack to level the scores. Bielby supported down the left to return a cross from the right and, as the ball ran loose, McKelvey hit a fine shot from just inside the penalty area (33 mins).

We were lucky not to go in arrears again soon afterwards when Stapleton was well clear only to shoot weakly at Ryan near a post from a couple of yards out. One each at the interval was a pleasant but surprising position for us after a first half in which the visitors had looked much the livelier in attack and held command in midfield.

We were soon in difficulties on the resumption but weathered the pressure to start a short spell on the attack. We had a chance to take a surprise lead when Ayres broke clear of the defence but his effort faded out when a Morton shot was charged down. McKelvey's shot from the rebound was saved in good style by the 'keeper. He gained consolation a few minutes later with a 'spot' kick after Wardrop had been brought down.

We kept up the pressure for a time but had a let off when Hornsby fired wildly over after a free kick on the edge of the box had been neatly returned from the far post. We had done better in this half but Arsenal fought back in the later stages to again take control and drew level with nine minutes left.

It was another set piece, similar to the one in which Hornsby had failed, but this time Rostron made no mistake, taking advantage of a slight uncertainty between Nicholl and Ryan.

The closing minutes were hectic with each side having the chance of a late winner.

The clash hinged on two major penalty area incidents, both of which went in the Reds' favour. When the Gunners' Wilf Rostron was unceremoniously decked in United's eighteen-yard area moments before half-time, referee Mr. Wallace of Crewe chose to wave play on. The man in black appeared to get it wrong for the second time with the award of McKelvey's 66th minute spot kick, which was described by the Islington Gazette as *'harsh'* and the Daily Mail as *'dubious'*.

The Manchester Evening News also carried a summary, the opening sentence of which spelled impending danger:

The young Reds, outplayed for long spells at Old Trafford last night, will find the odds stacked against them in London, facing a team who could well win the competition.

But for all that, United were within ten minutes of pulling off a victory as they matched their opponents' strength and skill with tremendous spirit before a 3,721 crowd. But a defensive mix-up ten minutes from the end let in Wilf Rostron to give Arsenal an equaliser.

It was disappointing for the United youngsters, who had played themselves to a standstill on a heavy pitch.

United are capable of improved form, even against a big side.

Said trainer Gordon Clayton, 'Arsenal were good but we can be better than last night. Perhaps away from home we will be more relaxed and surprise them at Highbury.'

fourth round

Not destined to achieve very much as a collective unit, the majority of the Reds' 1972/73 youth squad are all smiles at The Cliff
Back row (l-r) Roy Morton, Arthur Albiston, Alan Clarkson, Roy Walsh, Victor Hooks, Mike Wardrop, Noel Mitten, Ken Ayres
Front row (l-r) Brendan McKelvey, Jimmy Kelly, Willie Conroy, David Brooks, Brandon Davies

235

1972-73

1)	Gareth Williams	9)	Brian Hornsby	1)	Dave Ryan	9)	Ken Ayres
2)	Dave Donaldson	10)	Frank Stapleton	2)	Alan Clarkson	10)	Jimmy Kelly
3)	Richie Powling	11)	Wilf Rostron	3)	Paul Bielby	11)	Brendan McKelvey
4)	David Price	*12) Tony Winston*		4)	Mike Wardrop	*12) Arthur Albiston (for 10)*
5)	Peter Rixon			5)	Clive Griffiths		
6)	Barrie Vassallo			6)	Jimmy Nicholl		
7)	John Matthews			7)	Pat Olney		
8)	Liam Brady			8)	Roy Morton		

FEBRUARY 1973

ARSENAL 2 v 0 MANCHESTER UNITED
Hornsby, Matthews

Tuesday 6th
Kick-off 7.00 p.m.

fourth round replay

It had been almost sixteen years since United were required to play a Youth Cup tie in the capital and they arrived there with a third centre-forward in as many matches. Because David Brooks had cut a mere peripheral figure against the Gunners in Manchester, Jimmy Kelly, a recruit from the Carlisle area, was selected at number ten while Ken Ayres figured in the number nine jersey.

The result on this occasion was not nearly so pleasant as the last time, Arsenal proving United's masters at Highbury. After a competent initial 45 minutes, in which the whole team knuckled down to unselfish running and the well-worn tactic of closing down space, the Reds were unable to move up the gear or two necessary to get back on terms once the home side went in front.

The Islington Gazette was on hand to record United's defeat:

Arsenal's young brilliants made themselves favourites for the F.A. Youth Cup with this power-packed performance that clinched a Fourth Round replay victory over Manchester United at Highbury on Tuesday.

Ian Crawford's young Gunners are now away to Bristol City in the quarter-finals on February 21st but I cannot see anybody living with his side in the remaining rounds. Arsenal's strength is built on the solid foundation of David Price and Richie Powling at the back - and is boosted by the skill in midfield of Irish Imp Liam Brady.

With the shooting power of leading scorer Frank Stapleton and the cheeky wing running of schoolboy Wilf Rostron - what a find - it will take a very good team to stop them this season. Ironically, Arsenal beat Manchester United for the signatures of Price, Brady and Stapleton.

Arsenal had to fight hard before breaking down United. Their task was made difficult in the first half when they had to contend with a swirling wind but there was no stopping them in the second session.

Former Highbury schoolboy John Matthews broke the deadlock in the 51st minute when he charged past two tackles before shooting powerfully home from the edge of the box. Arsenal's second in the 75th minute brought the 3,000 plus fans to their feet. Brian Hornsby played a neat one-two with Brady before picking his spot.

Coach Crawford commented, 'Over both games we proved the superior side. We should have won at Old Trafford but there was no doubts this time. I thought our back four played magnificently in both games.'

Matthews' goal by itself was worthy of winning the game. Staving off the attention of a couple of United defenders who had moved up almost to the centre circle, he pushed the ball downfield and set off in chase. Dave Ryan, who the Manchester Evening News noted had impressed with his *'safe handling and dominance'* was for once seemingly unsure as to whether to come off his line or not and he was left completely stranded in no-man's land as Matthews powered the ball past him. With little option other than to pitch forward in search of a leveller, United were left short in defence at the time Hornsby sealed their fate.

It was a major shock when the young Gunners were eliminated by Bristol City in the next round, as several members of their exceptionally talented side went on to total 729 appearances in Arsenal's First Division games and take part in another 1,975 Football League matches between them.

Along with fellow midfielders Mike Wardrop and Roy Morton, Jimmy Kelly was never able to fully get to grips with a powerful Arsenal side

The Gunners' Matthews beats an exposed Dave Ryan to break the deadlock at Highbury

TOUR OF JAMAICA

1973

KINGSTON COLLEGE, VERE TECHNICAL SCHOOL, JAMAICA YOUTH XI

NOVEMBER/ DECEMBER 1973

Saturday 24th
to
Monday 3rd

jamaican tour

A schedule booklet issued by the club to everyone who travelled on the tour

With the seniors struggling for points and about to embark on a mini-break to Majorca, where it was hoped they would discover some fresh impetus in their quest for First Division survival, in late November 1973 it was decided to send a youth squad on a Caribbean tour.

The juniors had been participating in tours to Ireland and other parts of Europe since the early 1950's, but this was yet another groundbreaking trip as it was the first time that any of the club's teenagers had journeyed to the Americas for football purposes. The Reds' first Youth Cup tie of the campaign was timetabled for the 5th December at Oldham, so arrangements were made to depart for Kingston in Jamaica a week after the 'A' team's fixture at Liverpool on the 17th November.

The youngsters were scheduled to take part in three games, against Kingston College, Vere Technical College and the Jamaican under-20 youth team. For many years, Vere Technical and Kingston Colleges had been battling for local bragging rights in the Manning Cup, Walker Cup, DaCosta Cup and Oliver Shield, and now it was their chance to test themselves against the famous Manchester United.

Frank Blunstone selected a party of fifteen players, who were: Dave Ryan, Tom Cavanagh, Alan Clarkson, Lindsay McKeown, Alan Kirkup, Jimmy Nicholl, Arthur Albiston, Mike Wardrop, Peter Sutcliffe, Albert Hannon, Ken Fitzpatrick, Pat Olney, Brendan McKelvey, Jimmy Kelly and Paul Bielby.

The son of United coach Tommy Cavanagh, Tom jnr. was showing promise as a 'keeper, although his university studies forced him to sign for the club on an amateur basis. Meanwhile, another amateur, Albert Hannon, was a capture from Ireland in the summer just gone.

With Robin Clarke not offered professional terms and deciding to return to his native Belfast, the only other notable absentee was Ossie Smith, who was unable to make the trip due to school commitments. It was a particular shame for Smith, because passing up on the opportunity denied him the chance of playing in the city of his birth.

Prior to leaving for the Caribbean, both Paul Bielby and Alan Kirkup signed as full professionals, so there was a mix of experience within the squad.

The Reds' first match saw them paired with Kingston College in the school grounds on the evening of Monday, 26th November. Kingston College was formed in 1925 next to the famous home of West Indies cricket, Sabina Park, but it was only after World War Two when their football team started to become a force within local competitions.

The playing conditions were in stark contrast to those of Manchester for that time of year. The pitch comprised of an almost grass-less, sun-baked, uneven surface and, despite the campus being situated close to the sea, the temperature gauge hovered well over the 80 degrees Fahrenheit mark.

Alan Kirkup and Jimmy Nicholl featured in central defence, while Jimmy Kelly pulled the strings in midfield to enable the boys to open their account with a 2-0 victory. Goals from Sutcliffe and substitute McKelvey made it a comfortable win, with the result not accurately reflecting the Reds' superiority in both teamwork and technical ability.

Kingston College 0 Manchester United 2
Team: Ryan, Clarkson, Kirkup, Nicholl, Albiston, Wardrop, Sutcliffe, Hannon, Olney, Kelly, Bielby. Subs: McKelvey (for Sutcliffe), Fitzpatrick (for Bielby), McKeown, Cavanagh.

Two days later, the Reds journeyed a couple of miles inland to face Vere Technical College. Vere represented a considerably sterner test for the Old Trafford youngsters because they had won the DaCosta Cup, the island's major schools' competition, on the previous six occasions.

Frank Blunstone made four changes to the side, with Cavanagh, McKeown, Fitzpatrick and McKelvey all getting a start. United once again faced older boys and, while the College eleven contained a few with some decent individual skill, a collective ability within the touring team was enough to give them another 2-0 win with goals by Kelly and Kirkup.

Vere Technical College 0 Manchester United 2
Team: Cavanagh, McKeown, Kirkup, Nicholl, Albiston, Wardrop, Sutcliffe, Fitzpatrick, McKelvey, Kelly, Bielby. Subs: Olney (for McKelvey), Hannon, Clarkson, Ryan.

The final tour match took place on the evening of Saturday, 1st December at the National Stadium. Boosted by the inclusion of two full internationals, the local team were regarded to be at the same level as the England under-23 side. The quality of opposition was, therefore, a considerable step-up for 'Blunstone's Boys'.

With extra coaching duties, Frank Blunstone had a busy time of it in Jamaica

1973

NOVEMBER/ DECEMBER 1973

jamaican tour

United's coach once again made changes to the team, with the same eleven who faced Kingston College five days earlier gaining starting berths. The only other difference was the absence of Brendan McKelvey, who wasn't able to fill a place on the bench given that he was suffering from sunburn and sunstroke.

The young Reds acquitted themselves well and a Pat Olney strike was enough to earn the lads a creditable 1-1 draw. The only other incident of note was a half-hour delay due to floodlight problems.

Jamaica Youth XI 1 Manchester United 1
Team: Ryan, Clarkson, Kirkup, Nicholl, Albiston, Wardrop, Sutcliffe, Hannon, Olney, Kelly, Bielby. Subs: Fitzpatrick, McKeown, Cavanagh.

While the players were able to take time out during the trip for sightseeing and relaxing by the pool, Frank Blunstone was kept busy as, apart from seeing to the needs of his charges, he also delivered two coaching clinics to some of the football crazy locals.

It was regarded as a worthwhile tour and provided a unique experience for most of the United boys, many of whom have never been back to the West Indies.

Arthur Albiston's experience in the Caribbean left him in the dark

"We went to the National Stadium the day before our last game to train on the pitch and the authorities were moving lots of people out of the ground. I couldn't believe it, but these people were living under the stands as they had nowhere else to go.

It was a real eye-opener.

The match itself wasn't a memorable one, but the floodlights failed during the first half and it went pitch black. Arthur Albiston was shouting at me, 'Dave, Dave, where are you Dave?'

Looking back it was quite funny."

DAVE RYAN

Property of Dave Ryan, a postcard of Jamaica's National Stadium in 1973, the venue in which United completed their final tour commitments against a Jamaican Youth XI

1) Malcolm Bowring	9) Phil Mullington	1) Dave Ryan	9) Brendan McKelvey
2) Eric Greatrex	10) Geoff Harris	2) Alan Clarkson	10) Mike Wardrop
3) Dave Prince	11) Mel Jones	3) Alan Kirkup	11) Paul Bielby
4) Dave Ryan	12) *Steve Wilkinson*	4) Jimmy Nicholl	*12) Lindsay McKeown (for 3)*
5) Steve Cox		5) Arthur Albiston	
6) Andy Clough		6) Ken Fitzpatrick	
7) Kevin Taylor		7) Peter Sutcliffe	
8) John Duddy		8) Jimmy Kelly	

1973-74

OLDHAM ATHLETIC 1 v 2 MANCHESTER UNITED

Harris *Bielby, Sutcliffe*

DECEMBER 1973

Wednesday 5th

Kick-off 2.00 p.m.

Just two days after returning from Jamaica, the destination of Sheepfoot Lane in Oldham provided a potentially testing start to the Reds' aspirations of becoming Youth Cup kings of the realm once more.

In a bid to improve standards at junior level, some strategic changes had been implemented at Old Trafford several months previously and, as well as Frank Blunstone being tasked with the responsibility of looking after the under-18's affairs, ex-United trainee Jimmy Curran accepted an invitation to rejoin the club in order to take over the 'B' team. A little higher up the scale, two more of the club's former players, Pat Crerand and Jack Crompton, were now in charge of the second string.

In those days not particularly noted for producing much in the way of first-team material from their junior ranks, under the astute guidance of manager Jimmy Frizzell, the Latics were in the process of trying to reverse that trend.

With some successes in league and cup to boast about for the club's aspiring stars, the Oldham Chronicle's Jim Williams provided an appropriate background to the contest:

Athletic hit the F.A. Youth Cup trail at Boundary Park tomorrow with the squad of players which has carried them to tremendous victories over Blackpool, Barrow and Preston in recent weeks.

But tomorrow's game against Manchester United is the big one for Athletic's youngsters as the F.A. Youth Cup is the leading youth soccer tournament in the land. And the visitors will provide Athletic with their toughest task to date.

Over the years, United have a remarkable record in F.A. Youth Cup football and have won the trophy on several occasions. They have been tuning up for the start of the tournament with a short stay in the West Indies where they played several friendly games.

Athletic's preparations have not been so grand. The chief part of their build-up programme was a Lancashire Youth Cup tie against Preston at Deepdale.

The Athletic youngsters scored a most impressive 3-0 win over Preston and will be hoping to repeat that success tomorrow.

The United squad includes six players who have gained international honours at schoolboy level. They are Alan Clarkson and Mike Wardrop, who have represented England, Jimmy Nicholl and Lindsay McKeown (Ireland) and Brendan McKelvey and Arthur Albiston (Scotland).

The match starts at 2.00 p.m. and only three parts of the ground – the Main Stand, the Main Stand paddock and the Chadderton Road end – will be open.

Admission will cost 5p for boys and pensioners and 15p for adults.

The explanation for an early kick off slot was down to the prevailing political scenario in Great Britain at that time. The infamous 'three-day (working) week' came about because of a protracted strike by the nation's coal workers, their withdrawal of labour giving rise to the government imposing power restrictions. As far as football was concerned, the major consequence of this unusual situation was the curtailing of the use of floodlights.

The afternoon starts became a feature of all of United's Youth Cup ties for the season and it meant that very few of the club's followers actually got to see the contests.

Jim Williams told the tale of Latics' last minute heartbreak:

A split second of indecision at the end of a brave and often brilliant fight by Athletic's youngsters gave Manchester United an undeserved passport into the Third Round of the F.A. Youth Cup at Boundary Park yesterday.

With just a minute to go, both teams were locked in a tense, absorbing stalemate that had seen the balance of power switch backwards and forwards with all the frantic excitement of a roller-coaster ride. And then Bielby, straying wide on the left, looped over a centre-cum-shot more in hope than hostility. But Athletic's defence allowed the ball to flash through their ranks and, with goalkeeper Malcolm Bowring hopelessly out of position, it struck the far post and crossed the line.

It was a disastrous climax to a highly skilled and enterprising game of football that should have been sewn up in the first 45 minutes by Athletic's youngsters.

For in a first half where their poise overcame United's power, Athletic should have scored four times.

Driven on by the relentless energy of John Duddy in midfield and inspired by the pace of Geoff Harris and the determination of Phil Mullington, Athletic were in complete command.

They attacked – generally with five forwards – from the first whistle and really shook United rigid with the quality and aggression of their play.

They even recovered from a devastating blow when United scored with their first attack of the game after only ten minutes. A centre from the left caught Athletic's defence with their attention diverted by a cluster of big men at the edge of the area, and the tiny Sutcliffe blasted a header into the roof of the net.

Athletic should have been level in the 15th minute when Harris, breaking swiftly for the open spaces, worked his way into the United area, but then shot narrowly wide.

But in the 28th minute, justice was done. A corner from Jones was headed first by Cox and then Mullington before Harris flashed in to head crisply over Ryan.

For the remainder of the first half Athletic, knocking the ball about with a smooth efficiency, looked a couple of classes higher than United, whose only answer was to adopt strong-arm tactics.

But Athletic could not find the net again. On the stroke of half time they had an excellent chance when Taylor crossed from the right and Jones brought the ball down superbly on his chest. But the shot from six yards was well wide.

Early in the second half, Harris had another chance, but squandered it, and then United drafted substitute McKeown into midfield in place of the injured Kirkup.

The added power that McKeown injected into United sapped Athletic's control until finally it was United, thrusting forward from the depths of defence, who were in command. By sheer physical might, United wore down Athletic and the home side became disjointed and disorganised, with too many players trying to do too much on the ball and not enough off it.

But still, with Cox and Clough in impressive form at the heart of Athletic's defence, United had precious few scoring opportunities.

United, like Athletic, had settled for an honourable draw until that last minute winner undermined the effort, skill and industry that the home team's youngsters had poured so liberally into a most entertaining match.

Centre-back Alan Kirkup and his defensive colleagues were made to endure a prolonged onslaught at Boundary Park and could consider themselves fortunate to defeat a highly-charged Oldham

second round

239

1973-74

1) Dave Ryan	9) Brendan McKelvey	1) Andy Nelson	9) Brian Williams
2) Alan Clarkson	10) Jimmy Kelly	2) Martin Shaw	10) John Coleman
3) Ken Fitzpatrick	11) Paul Bielby	3) Ken Bellis	11) Martin Farnworth
4) Jimmy Nicholl	*12) Ossie Smith*	4) Barry Beesley	*12) Burr (for 7)*
5) Arthur Albiston		5) John Yates	
6) Lindsay KcKeown		6) Alan Whitehead	
7) Peter Sutcliffe		7) Peter Locke	
8) Mike Wardrop		8) Malcolm Brown	

DECEMBER 1973

MANCHESTER UNITED **1 v 1** BURY

Wardrop — Farnworth

Wednesday 19th

Kick-off 2.00 p.m.

Attendance 214

third round

Keeper played with dislocated finger

BURY'S youth team goalkeeper Andy Nelson played the whole of Wednesday's match at Old Trafford with a dislocated finger.

His injury was sustained in a 'B' team game and although his finger was heavily strapped for the Old Trafford tie it was a touch and go decision whether he played or not.

Instructions were given to centre halves Yates and Whitehead to give him as much protection as possible on crosses and the pair of them played superbly to help keep United at bay.

In the second half Nelson dived to save a low cross shot and the finger was knocked back again and from then on he was playing with virtually one hand.

It was this handicap which helped United to equalise and force a replay for when the Bury defence was beaten by a cross Nelson stayed on his line and Wardrop nodded the ball home.

Farnworth, arrowed, watches his shot from 30 yards flash into the net with 'keeper Ryan well beaten.

The Third Round also provided local opposition for the Reds, with a tie which would extend to two instalments. Alan Kirkup failed to recover from the ankle injury he sustained at Boundary Park, so Lindsay McKeown made the starting gate against Bury and talented Stretford resident Ossie Smith was given the substitute role.

Away wins over Chester, 2-0, and Gateshead, 4-0, brought the Shakers on Youth Cup duty to Old Trafford after a gap of over 21 years. A combination of cold weather, a daytime kick-off for the midweek game, and the Christmas period just a few days away, meant that only a meagre number of supporters were in attendance and the tie actually signifies the lowest ever recorded gate for any Youth Cup match involving United. Club officials anticipated a small crowd and chose to open only blocks 'B' and 'C', which constituted just half of the Main Stand.

There was a special incentive for Shakers' manager Bobby Smith to obtain a result as he was making a nostalgic return to the ground where his full-time career in the game began. Smith was, of course, United's recognised Youth Cup right-back for most of the period between October 1959 and January 1962, a spell in which the Reds reached a quarter-final and a semi-final.

Smith could feel reasonably confident of his charges' chances at Old Trafford. Their preparation couldn't have been much better as, on the previous weekend, they crushed Tranmere 5-0 in a Lancashire League fixture, Brian Williams recording a fine hat-trick during that encounter. The game against United gave Williams' colleague Alan Whitehead the chance to emulate his father Bill, who had been on duty for the Shakers in only the second ever Youth Cup tie at Old Trafford in November 1952.

The match also represented a quick resumption with Bury for Alan Clarkson, Arthur Albiston, Mike Wardrop and Jimmy Kelly, all of whom had taken part in a dreadful 5-1 Central League defeat at Gigg Lane just a few days before.

A Bury Times reporter made notes on the key moments in the under-18's game:

It wasn't exactly a giant-killing act because the teams have to meet again to decide which of them goes through to the Fourth Round of the F.A. Youth Cup but Bury deserve a second chance.

They may even have felt they were a little unfortunate to have to play again for in the second half United survived by courtesy of goal-line clearances, although they themselves can claim a near miss after the ball had struck the inside of an upright.

The early stages of the game saw Bury as the more dangerous side for they settled down the quicker and some tigerish tackling gave United precious little time in which to control the ball and use it with any real degree of accuracy.

They were stunned, too, when Bury took a 15th minute lead and it was a goal conjured out of nothing.

Shaw won the ball on the right and a pass up the wing found Farnworth. He cut inside his man and from all of 30 yards a swerving shot flashed over goalkeeper Ryan and into the far corner.

With twin centre-halves Yates and Whitehead superb in the air, Bury looked capable of holding the United forwards but there was a lucky escape in the 38th minute when a cross shot from Wardrop was touched onto the inside of an upright by Nelson, who pounced on the rebound as it was about to cross the line.

Williams, who was to play an increasingly lone role at the front, was booked for a foul five minutes before the interval and there were ominous signs that United were gaining the greater share of possession, a situation which continued after the break when some of the Bury side seemed to lose concentration.

McKeown and McKelvey both went close for the home side without bringing Nelson into action and then, following a brilliant short run by Williams, there was a mis-cue from Coleman when it seemed Bury might increase their lead.

It was a pity that Coleman should be the guilty party for throughout the game he was in fine form as he repeatedly held up and broke up raids in midfield, although with United concentrating more on wing play in the second half it was only on the break that Bury were dangerous.

Brown saw a header cleared off the line by Albiston and United went close on a couple of occasions before they produced the equaliser in the 70th minute.

For the first time in the game, Bury's defence was asleep and opposition players were unmarked when Bielby swung the ball across from the left to give Wardrop the opportunity of moving in at the far post to beat Nelson with a close-range header.

Two minutes later Burr replaced Locke as Bury tried to save the game and once again there was a sense of urgency about their play with Williams bringing Ryan to a full stretch save with a low drive.

With ten minutes remaining, Williams again disrupted the United rearguard to force a corner and when Ryan had half-punched the cross, Coleman volleyed a first time shot over a posse of players only for Albiston to make his second goal-line clearance of the game and take the tie to a replay.

1) Graham Forrest
2) Martin Shaw
3) Ken Bellis
4) Barry Beesley
5) John Yates
6) Alan Whitehead
7) Peter Locke
8) Malcolm Brown
9) Brian Williams
10) John Coleman
11) Martin Farnworth
12) Alan Whitmore (for 4)

1) Dave Ryan
2) Lindsay McKeown
3) Ken Fitzpatrick
4) Jimmy Nicholl
5) Arthur Albiston
6) Mike Wardrop
7) Jimmy Kelly
8) Peter Sutcliffe
9) Brendan McKelvey
10) Ossie Smith
11) Paul Bielby
12) David McCreery

1973-74

BURY 1 v 3 MANCHESTER UNITED
Locke — Kelly, Smith, Sutcliffe

JANUARY 1974

Saturday 5th

Kick-off 1.30 p.m.

Attendance 670

Bury goalie Andy Nelson was still in recovery by the time the replay came around in early January and he was replaced by Graham Forrest, younger brother of John, then the club's current senior custodian. The Gigg Lane rematch was pencilled in for a slightly earlier start time than the game at Old Trafford in order to allow for the possibility of extra-time and it was staged on the same afternoon when the senior Reds were engaged in a home F.A. Cup clash with Plymouth Argyle.

Having gained the measure of their opponents, the young Reds were in highly acceptable form and their triumph was recorded by the Bury Times:

Bury's youngsters saved face if not the match with a spirited second half fightback in Saturday's F.A. Youth Cup Third Round replay at Gigg Lane.

They trailed by 3-0 at half-time against a slicker moving side who made better use of the wings but the second period belonged almost entirely to the Bury lads, who might have forced extra-time had they accepted their chances.

As it was they went very close with goalkeeper Ryan making a great save in the closing minutes after Bury failed to win a strong appeal for a penalty as the United defence struggled under severe pressure.

It could have been a far different story had Bury been able to maintain their early form for in the first ten minutes they dominated the game without forcing the early breakthrough and then, as torrential rain swept down into their faces, they found themselves two goals behind in the space of three minutes.

In the 12th minute, Kelly made ground on the right and after cutting inside Brown he unleashed a left-foot shot from 25 yards which flashed over the diminutive Forrest in the Bury goal.

A clever run by Coleman might have produced the equaliser but he pulled his shot wide and before Bury knew what had happened, United added a second.

McKelvey chased a long through pass and when Forrest dived at his feet, the ball spun off the 'keeper's body for the centre-forward to have another opportunity. His shot would have gone wide but with defenders sliding in the goalmouth morass, Sutcliffe was able to steer the ball into the net.

Williams, Brown, Farnworth and Beesley all had the United defence in trouble despite Bury not clicking into top gear and the more determined United increased their lead in the 36th minute when Forrest could only half stop a low, driven cross from Bielby and Smith was on hand to poke home the loose ball.

Three minutes later Whitmore substituted for Beesley and went close to scoring on the stroke of half-time but after the break Bury were left with a lot of ground to make up if they were to save the game.

Forrest made a fine save from a low shot by McKelvey while Bury left-back Bellis raised Bury's morale with a 25-yarder which dropped over the crossbar.

From then on it became one-way traffic towards the United goal as Bury opened up the game down the wings, and Williams at last burst into the form of which he is capable and began to lead the United defence a merry dance.

He brought Ryan to a very good save after bursting through and lashing the ball at goal and he was involved in the slick move which produced Bury's goal in the 61st minute, Locke forcing the ball over the line at the second attempt after Whitmore's low centre had evaded the visitors' defence.

With the crowd urging them on, Bury responded to the challenge with Farnworth hammering the ball over the top from a Williams cross and then Brown was unable to control the ball when it dropped at his feet in front of goal.

Williams it was who again had the United defence reeling with a superb run on the right. A low centre gave Locke the chance to shoot but the effort was blocked. The ball ran to Farnworth whose volley was almost certainly handled by a defender but United rode their luck and the referee ignored Bury's appeals for a penalty.

Another break by Williams, this time a 60-yards dash down the right, ended with a poor cross but when Locke and Whitmore cleverly created an opening for Coleman it took a brilliant save from Ryan to prevent a goal.

Nicholl almost turned the ball into his own goal as Bury pressed forward while United would almost certainly have scored their fourth in the closing minutes had Forrest not raced off his line to block a shot from McKelvey.

At the final whistle Bury deserved the applause of the crowd for their second half efforts and none more than Williams and Bellis.

third round replay

Paul Bielby (left), Jimmy Nicholl, Dave Ryan and Arthur Albiston can only watch as Peter Locke registers a consolation goal for Bury while one of the 670 crowd gets excited

1973-74

1) Dave Ryan
2) Lindsay McKeown
3) Alan Kirkup
4) Jimmy Nicholl
5) Arthur Albiston
6) Ken Fitzpatrick
7) Peter Sutcliffe
8) Mike Wardrop
9) Brendan McKelvey
10) Ossie Smith
11) Paul Bielby
12) David McCreery (for 10)

1) John Brighton
2) Malcolm Rafferty
3) Colin Griffin
4) Trevor Thompson
5) Don O'Riordan
6) David Langan
7) Steve Boseley
8) Derek Bell
9) Mark Bradley
10) Donato Zaccaria
11) Eddie Hogan
12) Tony Buckley

JANUARY 1974

MANCHESTER UNITED 3 v 2 DERBY COUNTY

McKelvey, Nicholl, Wardrop — Bell (2)

fourth round

Wednesday 30th
Kick-off 2.30 p.m.
Attendance 416

Young Reds keep Cup flag flying

The plight of Manchester United was becoming more and more desperate by the week, as the senior side languished around the bottom of the First Division table, and Derby County's youth team stopped by at Old Trafford with the intention of inflicting more misery on the club by gaining a Youth Cup quarter-final place at the Reds' expense.

United were without the services of Jimmy Kelly, who had undergone a cartilage operation, and so recently signed amateurs Alan Gresty, a forward, and midfielder Ian Meek were named in a party of fifteen. Possibly as a consequence of the Old Trafford management choosing not to run a 'B' team for this season, Gresty and Meek were included in the squad despite never previously kicking a ball in anger for the club.

Derby also lacked a squad of sufficient depth, if not quality, and the Rams' youth team coach was forced into nominating a crocked goalkeeper as their 12th man. Committing a couple of grave errors before any early nerves had subsided, it was his replacement who practically gifted United a spot in the next round.

Ray Yeomans of the Derby Evening Telegraph told the tale of County's woes:

Twenty-two youngsters lifted some of the gloom hanging over Old Trafford with a great F.A. Youth Challenge Cup (Fourth Round) tie yesterday.

The football was simple, uninhibited, classy and a delight to watch.

Derby, although in control for much of the game, never recovered from the blow of giving away two soft goals in the first ten minutes.

Young John Brighton, replacing the injured Tony Buckley in goal had a nightmare start.

After only six minutes he misjudged a corner from Sutcliffe and Nicholl scored easily from close range. Four minutes later he missed a free-kick from McKeown and Brendan McKelvey headed a fine goal.

United, looking sharp and full of confidence, piled on the pressure and Brighton did well to turn a fierce shot from Albiston over the bar.

The goalkeeper made a good stop from McKelvey as he broke away from Donald O'Riordan, who did not look happy at centre-half, but almost gave United a third goal when he made a hash of the resulting corner. Luckily Nicholl's shot was blocked on the line.

Ossie Smith missed two good chances as United continued to dominate the game.

But gradually Derby began to pull themselves together. Brighton looked more composed and the Rams began to play with confidence and authority. Donato Zaccaria shot over and then forced a good diving save from Ryan with a twenty-yard shot.

Steve Bosley dropped a corner on to the crossbar and Derek Bell, who was beginning to show up well, forced Ryan into another good save with an angled shot. United looked capable and dangerous in attack, but slowly Derby began to take command.

In the second half United were completely outplayed. Derby pulled Zaccaria back to full-back and pushed O'Riordan into midfield. Eddie Hogan, finding a little more room, began to cause problems with his excellent ball control and delicately flighted balls along the touchline for Bell.

Thompson and Griffin were playing well at the back and it was no surprise when Derby scored after 49 minutes.

Hogan began the move with a cheeky back-heel. David Langan's shot hit the goalkeeper's legs and Bell stroked the ball into the empty net.

But United restored their two-goal lead against the run of play in the 71st minute.

Bielby lobbed the ball over Thompson's head to McKelvey. Thompson and Rafferty both failed to get in a challenge and the centre-forward clipped the ball over Brighton's head into the net.

But three minutes later the Rams, showing great determination and courage again put the game within their grasp with another goal from Bell.

Bradley had a shot blocked from Hogan's pass, but the ball ran to Bell who took his chance well.

Smith missed two headed chances for United before limping off with four minutes to go.

Bielby and Sutcliffe began to cause a few problems towards the end, but Bielby was slowed by a tremendous tackle from Griffin which propelled him ten yards into touch.

Derby, fighting for an equaliser, almost forced a replay with the last kick of the game, but Bradley failed to connect with Hogan's low cross about eight yards out.

Coach Alan Hill said Derby were unlucky to lose and thought they were the better side. Certainly, United faded after the first twenty minutes, but they took the chances Derby presented them with extremely well.

Jack Pauline conveyed the message that victory over the Rams was *'hard earned'*, and he went on to correctly remind his readers about the win marking *'our best progress in the competition since losing to Coventry in season 1969/70'*. Pauline admitted that towards the end of the game the boys *'were hanging on grimly to our narrow advantage'* because, *'having recovered from the early set-back'*, Derby then *'looked the smarter side'* for the majority of the second period.

He and the Manchester Evening News also correctly identified Mike Wardrop and not Brendan McKelvey as the scorer of United's second goal.

When the dust finally settled and the inquests were concluded, it was a match all at Old Trafford were relieved to have come through with future hopes of progress still intact.

Undoubtedly relishing the change from defence to attack in the under-18 side, Paul Bielby posed Derby a few questions

242

1973-74

JANUARY 1974

Fifteen members of Manchester United's youth squad for the 1973/74 season
Back row (l-r) Lindsay McKeown, Ken Fitzpatrick, Alan Kirkup, Dave Ryan, Jimmy Nicholl, David Bradley, Ossie Smith, Arthur Albiston
Front row (l-r) David McCreery, Ray Storey, Peter Sutcliffe, Jimmy Kelly, Brendan McKelvey, Ray Botham, David Morris

fourth round

> The first thing I did was to bring Joe Armstrong and Johnny Carey back as scouts because I wanted to re-establish the youth policy which had gone to the dogs. With names such as Carey and Armstrong knocking on doors we had a chance and I then convinced Frank Blunstone to join us. He had just been in a car accident but I went to see him in hospital in Crewe and offered him the job. He immediately said 'yes' and we got the best youth coach in Britain. He had already done it at Brentford and Chelsea and I knew he could do it at United.
>
> We then brought Jimmy Curran in as Frank's assistant. Norman Scholes and Gordon Clayton were already there so I felt comfortable that they would sort it all out. I went to see both of them in action and they were terrific professionals.
>
> On the scouting side we also had Jimmy Murphy. I once asked him to fill in a team sheet identifying all the positives and negatives of players and Jim responded by saying that by the time he had completed all the forms some other club would have signed the lad. After that I just gave Jimmy 'carte blanche' to sign schoolboys.
>
> Then, either Frank or Jimmy would ask me to visit boys' houses and meet the parents. We would show them pictures of all the past youth teams and the current side with all the youth players to come through the system, saying that we would give them a chance at United.
>
> We had Billy Behan in Ireland and things were tied up in Belfast with Bob Bishop, the 'Pathfinder' I used to call him. He could always find his way to talent and had kids following him everywhere like a 'pied piper'. We used to bring the Irish boys over to stay in the Halls of Residence in Salford when they were twelve years-old at Christmas and Easter breaks. We had Kevin Moran, Paul McGrath and Norman Whiteside already lined up.
>
> During pre-season and post-season tours we would regularly take two or three kids with us, to give them the experience but also to see if they could handle being a first-team player. I was trying to get to a place where the whole first-team had come through the youth ranks and by the time I left I felt we had the best set-up in the country without a shadow of a doubt.

TOMMY DOCHERTY

1973-74

1) Dick Taylor	9) Bob Newton	1) Dave Ryan	9) Brendan McKelvey
2) Alan Sweeney	10) Dave Nichols	2) Lindsay McKeown	10) Ken Fitzpatrick
3) Paul Cooper	11) Franny Firth	3) Alan Kirkup	11) Paul Bielby
4) Steve Barrett	*12) Paul Holmes ◊*	4) Jimmy Nicholl	*12) David McCreery*
5) Peter Hart		5) Arthur Albiston	
6) Martin Fowler		6) Mike Wardrop	
7) Lloyd Maitland		7) Peter Sutcliffe	
8) Bob Mountain		8) Ossie Smith	

MARCH 1974

HUDDERSFIELD TOWN 2 v 0 MANCHESTER UNITED

Firth, Mountain

fifth round

Wednesday 6th

Kick-off 3.00 p.m.

A First Round win at Doncaster Rovers by a 5-0 margin sparked Huddersfield's Youth Cup flame, and Town's torch continued to burn brightly with a 2-0 victory at Bradford City and a 2-1 success at Turf Moor over Burnley following a 1-1 draw at Leeds Road. Charlton then failed to douse the Huddersfield fire, despite the advantage of a home tie. Two goals all at The Valley was the best the Addicks could manage, so they were duly scorched out of the tournament following a 1-0 replay defeat in the West Riding.

Town's youth side were bolstered by the experience of Franny Firth, their most recently promoted first-team player, and the Terriers even enjoyed the luxury of being able to leave out another senior, Paul Garner, who hadn't participated in a single junior game all season because of his Second Division commitments. Despite the great desire Huddersfield undoubtedly held of ending United's Youth Cup run, Garner wasn't considered for the tie due to the slim mathematical chance of promotion which the club still harboured.

Former Reds' defender and current Town manager Ian Greaves named a squad of thirteen and of that number, seven of those selected were forwards. One of the strikers Greaves chose to start was Bob Mountain, the burly front man having scored six of Huddersfield's total of thirteen Youth Cup goals that season.

United kept faith with exactly the same twelve who had seen to the defeat of Derby, though there was a juggling around of positions in the hope of fine-tuning the performance. Jimmy Nicholl signed professional forms in the preparation period, but the end result at Leeds Road put a big black mark on his week.

The Huddersfield Daily Examiner gave its printed verdict:

> **TOWN JUNIORS** are through to the semi-finals of the FA Youth Cup.
>
> An enthusiastic audience of almost 1,000 people watched the young hopefuls beat Manchester United to reach the semi-final . . . and the club's history books.
>
> It is the first time that Town have reached this stage of the competition. And they climbed there with style, conviction, determination, a pinch of luck and eventually sheer hard work.
>
> Nippy striker Bob Mountain and winger Francis Firth scored the goals but the man who wore the laurels at the end of this riveting clash was goalkeeper Dick Taylor.
>
> Taylor clawed and twisted his way across his line to make a series of heart-shaking saves which shocked United's gallant and never tiring youths.
>
> If this Farnley Tyas seventeen-year-old is only good enough to be the England youth second choice then Blackburn's Bradshaw, the player who keeps him out of the national side, must be one hell of a goalkeeper.
>
> United fielded a side gathered from all parts of the United Kingdom. There were three Scots, two Irishmen, and six Englishmen. It might sound like a mixture of music-hall jokes. Nobody laughed. Everybody admired their drive and spirit.
>
> Town fielded a side without the two most experienced players — Stephen Spriggs and Paul Garner. The loss was theirs. It was cruel luck that anybody with the qualifications to play in this team should miss out on such a memorable display.
>
> Town started with a flurry, a confident air and a goal. Fowler, a defensive wing-half with a sense of timing and skill which must force him to senior standard before he is twenty, drilled a low ball through the United defence. Goalkeeper David Ryan was a shade slow leaving his line, centre-half Arthur Albiston fell on the softest part of his anatomy, and Mountain breezed in to clip the ball into the net.
>
> With only eight minutes gone Town could not have asked for a better opening. Ten minutes later Firth missed out on a 50—50 chance, but with half an hour gone he didn't fail to score the decisive second.
>
> About fourteen players were clustered to the left of the United area when Mountain emerged from the crowd to sweep the ball thirty yards on to Lloyd Maitland's instep.
>
> United scurried to cover but they were a yard late. Maitland dragged the ball across, chipped it forward and Firth's head did the rest.
>
> But if Town thought they were through to the semi-final United were intent on making sure they had to sweat.
>
> The man who opened the pores was right-winger Peter Sutcliffe. He looked frail and tiny compared with the number of beefy six-footers around him. He finished the biggest of them all.
>
> How unfortunate that it was to be this skilful and fast performer who should contribute to his side's loss of interest in the competition!
>
> For once Taylor was beaten. Brendan McKelvey's powerful shot left the goalkeeper stranded, but just as the United striker turned to celebrate a goal the ball struck Sutcliffe on the back and sailed harmlessly over the bar.
>
> It was another stroke of misfortune that United could have done without for ten minutes earlier Ossie Smith somehow blasted wide from four yards.
>
> Taylor made sure their luck did not turn
>
> Referee Perkin handled the potential volcano with commendable certainty and had no alternative but to book Town's Dave Nichols and United's Lindsay McKeoun for what was a stupid and needless touchline incident.
>
> But none of the twenty-two players left the field without giving everything. If some stood above others it was not because they had tried any harder. The match was worthy of a final. On this performance, and particularly that of the first half, Town can get there.

Backed up by Jimmy Nicholl, Arthur Albiston contests a high ball

It was, by all published accounts, an exhilarating duel with the outcome decided, as most games must be, on the taking or squandering of the opportunities on offer.

The last words on the subject were given by Jack Pauline, who felt that *'our second half assault on the home goal deserved a kinder run of the ball'*. Recalling the half-hour spell immediately after the break, Pauline reckoned United *'were in complete command for this period but the goal we badly needed never came'*.

Not only did Huddersfield write a new chapter in their history by reaching the last four, they then went on to make the final, a 1-0 home win and a 1-1 draw at The Hawthorns against West Bromwich Albion proudly installing them as the first Yorkshire club to reach the last stage.

They couldn't breast the winning tape, though, and Spurs lifted the trophy on a 2-1 aggregate.

Any disappointment felt by United's supporters at the Youth Cup exit was positively dwarfed by the grief which engulfed them at the end of the campaign, when the diminishing points tally the Reds had accumulated season-on-season since the 1968 European Cup final eventually fell below the level required to keep them in the First Division.

Tommy Docherty had overseen a major clear-out of the playing staff he inherited in his time as manager, but he was unable to bring in enough quality personnel to stave off an event which would have seemed inconceivable during the glory years of the previous three decades.

The summer of 1974 was a time for Docherty and the board of directors to do some hard thinking, to take stock of the catastrophe, and to plan properly for a rapid return for the Reds.

1973-74

MARCH 1974

fifth round

Jimmy Nicholl puts in a sliding tackle on Huddersfield winger Franny Firth at Leeds Road

Reds' 'keeper Dave Ryan is left on the grass as Town's Mountain (arm raised) scores, with Jimmy Nicholl (left of Mountain) and Lindsay McKeown (number two) arriving too late to avert the danger

1974-75

1) Glyn Cross	9) Mike Smith
2) Tommy Cooper	10) Brian Thompson
3) Steve Lindop	11) John Shankland
4) Steve Moran	*12) Colin Sidley (for 11)*
5) Graham Howson	
6) Steve Howson	
7) Russell Pointon	
8) Kenny Beech	

1) Dave Ryan	9) Ray Botham
2) Lindsay McKeown	10) Jimmy Kelly
3) David Bradley	11) Paul Bielby
4) Jimmy Nicholl	*12) John Lowey (for 9)*
5) Arthur Albiston	
6) Ken Fitzpatrick	
7) Peter Sutcliffe	
8) David McCreery	

DECEMBER 1974

PORT VALE 0 v 0 MANCHESTER UNITED

second round

Tuesday 3rd
Kick-off 7.00 p.m.
Attendance 1,463

The status of United was such that they were now no longer a top-flight club for the first time since prior to the Second World War. While the lower grade of football being performed by the seniors might not have immediately affected the youth team's fortunes, the dual effect of trying to attract the cream of Britain's soccer starlets to a Second Division organisation, and the resources required into propelling the club back into the elite league, would inevitably be felt some time later in the decade.

The personnel who locked horns with Port Vale in the Potteries for the beginning of a new assault on the Youth Cup wasn't significantly different to those of last season as the goalkeeper, both full-backs, one central defender and a few of the midfielders and forwards remained from the previous campaign. After being nominated as substitute three times earlier in the year and getting on only once, David McCreery was finally promoted to the starting eleven.

With Alan Kirkup unavailable, Salford-born ex-England Boys' defender David Bradley took up a position in the middle of the defence while Ray Botham, a local boy who was another former England schoolboy prodigy, went into the attack for the over-age Brendan McKelvey.

The (Stoke-on-Trent) Evening Sentinel provided an appropriate taster for the action:

Full-strength Manchester United will field five internationals in the F.A. Youth Cup team to meet Port Vale at Vale Park tonight.

Capped players from Old Trafford are defenders Lindsay McKeown and Jim Nicholl, and striker Dave McCreery, of Northern Ireland, and Scots Jim Kelly and Arthur Albiston.

Also included in the United line-up is winger Paul Bielby, who had two games in the First Division last season when United were relegated and was also twice substitute.

United have a team comprised entirely of apprentice or full professionals but do not play striker Peter Coyne, who scored a hat-trick for England Schoolboys against West Germany at Wembley last season.

In contrast, Vale have a home grown team of mainly amateur players who will be aiming to raise their game in order to give a good account of themselves.

Vale beat Chester 5-1 away in the First Round but realise that United will be a much different proposition, although some of the local players have gained experience in the Northern Floodlit League.

It will be a good test for apprentices Brian Thompson, Ken Beech and Russell Pointon while Vale will also be looking to F.A. professionals Steve Moran and Steve Howson to provide United with a challenge.

Says Vale Youth coach Peter Drummond, 'Obviously we will be underdogs and it is up to us to play hard, first-time football to deny United any space. It will be a game of run, chase and tackle for us because we have to stop them. Otherwise we will be in trouble.'

The Vale youngsters have had a few games together recently to formulate some understanding and expect to play in front of a large crowd.

United are expected to have a good following and the attendance could exceed 2,000. The pitch will be heavy but perfectly playable and turnstiles will be open on the Railway Paddock stand and Bycars End of the ground.

In a game of precious few chances, the Vale achieved an encouraging moral victory by preventing an expected United success, the (Stoke-on-Trent) Evening Sentinel supplying the following snapshot of the main events:

Port Vale's youngsters exceeded expectations last night when they held Manchester United to an honourable goalless draw in the Second Round of the F.A. Youth Cup at Vale Park.

For many of the Vale team a visit to Old Trafford for the replay next Monday will be sufficient memory from the competition, yet with better finishing Vale could have pulled United asunder.

Apprentice professional Brian Thompson hung his head amid the celebrations in the Vale dressing room, knowing he might have emerged the hero.

Twice Thompson had chances to convert Vale's admirable spirit into goals in a match which was not notable for scoring opportunities.

For all United's finesse, pace and superior strength, the end product was surprisingly short of requirements and it was Vale who had the better chances, particularly in the 70th minute after Beech had been fouled outside the United penalty area.

From the free kick, the ball looped into the air and dropped nicely for the unguarded Thompson, who sliced his intended volley wide of the near post from close range.

It was also Thompson who fired just over the bar immediately on the resumption, after Pointon's cross from the right had been knocked into his path by Shankland.

The visitors, coached full-time by the likes of Frank Blunstone and Pat Crerand, included five youth internationals and a winger, Bielby, who has already sampled First Division football.

Yet they offered little threat against a well-marshalled Vale defence, in which every player raised his game.

Mr. Blunstone said, 'We played badly and earned a draw, so we are satisfied.'

Vale coach Peter Drummond, a local schoolteacher, said, 'I am over the moon. The lads did everything that could be asked of them.'

Vale's collection of local amateurs and apprentices were warmly applauded by the 1,463 crowd almost every time they ventured into United territory.

United had the ball in the net for the only time in the match after 24 minutes through Nicholl, but no goal was awarded.

Cross, a rugby player from St. Joseph's College, Trent Vale, served Vale well in goal, once pushing a header from Sutcliffe onto the crossbar when United looked to be gaining a grip.

Jack Pauline made reference to the Reds' visit to Vale Park as proving *'a little disappointing'*, with *'too few of our efforts carrying any real threat'* to a largely untroubled home defence. Also noting a couple of decent pops on goal by McCreery, as well as worthwhile attempts by Botham, Sutcliffe and Fitzpatrick, the latter seeing his lob tipped onto the bar, Pauline concluded realistically *'with Thompson missing the easiest chance of the match ten minutes from time, we must be satisfied to still have an interest'.*

A former skipper of Lancashire Boys and capped eight times for England as a schoolboy, David Bradley provided proof that, at least for the time being, United's quest for teenage quality was as relentless as in years gone by

1) Dave Ryan	9) Ray Botham	1) Glyn Cross	9) Mike Smith
2) Lindsay McKeown	10) David McCreery	2) Tommy Cooper	10) Brian Thompson
3) David Bradley	11) Paul Bielby	3) Steve Lindop	11) John Shankland
4) Jimmy Nicholl	*12) John Lowey (for 9)*	4) Steve Moran	*12) Colin Sidley (for 9)*
5) Arthur Albiston		5) Graham Howson	
6) Tony Grimshaw		6) Steve Howson	
7) Ken Fitzpatrick		7) Russell Pointon	
8) Peter Sutcliffe		8) Kenny Beech	

1974-75

MANCHESTER UNITED 3 v 0 PORT VALE
Fitzpatrick, Moran (o.g.), Sutcliffe

DECEMBER 1974

Monday 9th

Kick-off 7.30 p.m.

Attendance 1,862

A late fitness test for Jimmy Kelly prior to the replay resulted in his omission from the team and into the void appeared a new face, that of Tony Grimshaw, a former midfielder of Manchester and Lancashire Boys, while otherwise the personnel were the same as those in north Staffordshire.

After travelling to Old Trafford with a party of sixteen to choose from, Port Vale displayed exactly the same twelve who had performed so admirably six days beforehand.

The (Stoke-on-Trent) Evening Sentinel delivered their version of the evening's action:

Port Vale gave another creditable account of themselves in their F.A. Youth Cup Second Round replay at Old Trafford last night.

After last week's goalless encounter at home, Vale at least had the satisfaction of keeping United's anticipated victory within reasonable limits on their own ground.

Vale hardly appeared overawed by their visit to the famous stadium.

In fact, it took an unfortunate own goal to put United ahead in the first half and it was not until the closing minutes that they rammed home their undoubted superiority.

Nevertheless, the majority of the action took place in Vale territory and Graham Howson and his fellow defenders had a busy match.

Lacking real pace and strength in attack, Vale's replies were not surprisingly few, but they conjured one notable move after 26 minutes which might have brought them a goal.

Skipper Steve Howson and Cooper, who both had good games, linked smartly to find Thompson just outside the United penalty area, and Thompson dummied beautifully to create the space for a clear shot at goal. The effort was struck well, but Thompson's drive climbed just over the bar and United 'keeper Ryan was untroubled thereafter.

United had taken the lead five minutes earlier. Lindop presented the ball to Sutcliffe, whose soft cross carried little danger until Moran, in attempting to bring the ball under control, toe-ended it into his own net.

Despite the constant wing raids of Bielby and Sutcliffe, United's finishing powers were found to be inadequate against some well organised defensive work by Vale, although Graham Howson was fortunate to run an inswinging corner kick from Bielby against a post before the interval.

Vale retired at half-time having done rather better than expected, but they were unable to alter the match pattern on the resumption.

Cooper twice headed off the line, once from a header from Botham and then after Cross had half-saved an angled drive from McKeown, before Vale had the ball in the net.

A centre from Shankland on the left put Steve Howson clear of the United defence, but he was clearly offside, although nothing was going to stop him putting the ball in the net at Old Trafford.

The United Review pieced together the ending stages of the action:

Making a late bid to save the game, Port Vale produced only a few long-range efforts which gave Ryan no trouble and in 70 minutes we replaced Botham with Lowey.

The move seemingly paid off three minutes later when he ran well on the left and from his centre beyond the far post Sutcliffe fired the ball home after his first shot had rebounded from the 'keeper.

A minute later a neat bout of inter-passing between Sutcliffe and McCreery laid on an easy chance for Fitzpatrick to push the ball home from four yards to put the issue beyond doubt.

second round replay

Having recently turned down the opportunity to manage Chelsea in preference to remaining in his position as United's youth coach, Frank Blunstone looks entirely satisfied as he puts the club's youngsters through their paces

247

1974-75

1) Eddie Edgar	9) Steve Newstead	1) Dave Ryan	9) John Lowey
2) Peter Kelly	10) Kenny Mitchell	2) Jonathan Clark	10) Jimmy Kelly
3) Ray Blackhall	11) Colin Chambers	3) David Bradley	11) Paul Bielby
4) David Norton	*12) Richard Graham ◊*	4) Jimmy Nicholl	*12) Ray Botham*
5) Aidan McCaffery		5) Arthur Albiston	
6) Tony Smith		6) Ken Fitzpatrick	
7) Dave McLean		7) Peter Sutcliffe	
8) Alan Guy		8) David McCreery	

JANUARY 1975

NEWCASTLE UNITED 0 v 0 MANCHESTER UNITED

Monday 6th
Kick-off 7.30 p.m.

third round

United we draw!

Early into the New Year, United were required to fulfil a tie at Newcastle which, similarly to the previous round, was a task left undecided at the initial attempt.

There was mixed news on the injury front as Jimmy Kelly was able to reclaim a place in the side, although with Lindsay McKeown sidelined with a knock, Frank Blunstone decided to pitch the highly regarded Jonathan Clark into the team at right full-back. Originating from Swansea, Clark had made a hugely favourable impression on the club's scouts when earning representative honours at schoolboy level for Wales.

Blunstone said of the changes, 'We still have a lot of experience in the side and, while it is disappointing to lose McKeown, I have no qualms about bringing Clark into the team in his place. With Kelly coming back we also have some extra punch upfront and I expect our forwards to provide (Newcastle) some problems.'

When previewing the event, the Newcastle Evening Chronicle also made mention of a forthcoming League Cup clash at Old Trafford:

Newcastle's Juniors take on Manchester United Juniors in the Third Round of the Youth Cup at Gallowgate tonight - as a preview to a possible much greater clash between the two clubs later this month.

And there will be no fewer than four players on view with senior experience which, considering the eighteen age limit on the competition, is quite something.

Newcastle's biggest starlet is seventeen year-old Scottish right-back Peter Kelly, who played in the 0-0 League Cup draw with Chester at Gallowgate.

Currently hovering on the fringes of the first-team, David McCreery came close to breaking the deadlock at St. James's Park

But Manchester United have three players with League experience - left-back Arthur Albiston, who played at Oldham a fortnight ago; Belfast-born striker David McCreery, who has turned out twice as sub., and fellow striker Paul Bielby, who played two First Division games last season.

Newcastle, who include Aidan McCaffery, a regular in the Central League side, pick from the following thirteen: Edgar, Kelly, Blackhall, Morton, McCaffery, Smith, McLean, Guy, Newstead, Mitchell, Chambers, Graham, Gibson.

Manchester United's coach Frank Blunstone hopes to field the same side which hammered Preston Juniors 4-0 away on Saturday thanks to a hat-trick from sixteen year-old local boy John Lowey.

In a 4-2-4 formation it is: Ryan, McKeown, Bradley, Nicholl, Albiston, Fitzpatrick, Kelly, Sutcliffe, McCreery, Lowey, Bielby.

Botham and Clark make up the travelling squad.

Post-match, a Newcastle Journal reporter complained there 'was plenty of work by both sides in midfield, but that is where the game stayed'. Additionally noting there 'were no goalmouth incidents until the last twenty minutes, and then there were only two', the scribe also mentioned 'the first came after 76 minutes' when 'Bradley had a superb header cleared off the line by his opposite number Blackhall'. Jack Pauline managed to spot a little more action in the match, even though by all accounts it was a resoundingly drab affair:

United always looked the more cultured side with Newcastle playing the long ball in a difficult wind. There were few direct shots from either side to really trouble the 'keepers yet the home side might have won the game with the best eight minutes from time.

It was a fierce twenty-yarder from Mitchell which went much too close for comfort. This apart, only Newstead had the chance to open the Newcastle account but failed in the first half thanks to great recovery work by Albiston and in the second half was well placed when firing wildly over the bar.

The home 'keeper had several slices of good fortune, which enabled him to keep a clean sheet, and none more so than when his outstretched leg prevented a good effort from McCreery crossing the line in the first fifteen minutes. He was well beaten in the second half when headers by Lowey and Bradley were kicked off the line with United having their best attacking spell.

Frank Blunstone told one source that the young Reds 'were well worthy of the result' and he also said, 'I realise there wasn't a lot of entertainment value in the match because the two sides largely cancelled each other out. On the day we were quite evenly matched.

We set our stall out to attack them and I felt that we had more of the better chances. With a little more luck we could have won here tonight. We don't have any problems with injuries, so hopefully we can complete the job at our place.'

> *I was still at school at that time and had only played a handful of games for the junior sides when I was told I was going to replace Lindsay McKeown at St. James's Park.*
>
> *He was an experienced professional so it was a big thrill for me to play alongside Arthur Albiston and Jimmy Nicholl who had been knocking on the first-team door. I remember Frank Blunstone calling us in the day before and practicing set-pieces.*
>
> *I felt a lot of pressure to perform well and not let the team down. I must have done okay as Jim Harvey, the Newcastle United manager, offered United a blank cheque to sign me after the game, but United weren't having any of that.*
>
> **JONATHAN CLARK**

1) Dave Ryan	9) John Lowey
2) Jonathan Clark	10) Jimmy Kelly
3) David Bradley	11) Paul Bielby
4) Jimmy Nicholl	*12) Ray Botham*
5) Arthur Albiston	
6) Ken Fitzpatrick	
7) Peter Sutcliffe	
8) David McCreery	

1) Eddie Edgar	9) Steve Newstead
2) Peter Kelly	10) Kenny Mitchell
3) Ray Blackhall	11) Richard Graham
4) Ernie Kirby	*12) David Norton (for 7)*
5) Aidan McCaffery	
6) Tony Smith	
7) Alan Gibson	
8) Alan Guy	

1974-75

MANCHESTER UNITED 2 v 0 NEWCASTLE UNITED

Albiston, Sutcliffe

JANUARY 1975

Wednesday 8th
Kick-off 7.30 p.m.

third round replay

The stalemate on Tyneside resulted in the two United's being forced into a quick rematch, a game for which the Geordies made three changes to their starting eleven. Newcastle-born midfielder Ernie Kirby was drafted into a position near to the centre of the park in place of David Norton, who was forced to settle for a place on the bench, and Dave McLean was also ousted from the midfield, by Alan Gibson, while Richard Graham was promoted from substitute to take the number eleven jersey previously worn by Colin Chambers.

The game in Manchester proved an infinitely better spectacle than the one at St. James's Park, a fact confirmed by Jack Pauline in his condensed match jottings:

In the first quarter of an hour United looked likely to settle the issue fairly quickly with good efforts from Kelly, McCreery and Nicholl rounding off good moves but Newcastle were soon in the game.

Ryan did well with a header from Newstead and a centre-cum-shot from Mitchell who had gone so near to creating a late shock at Newcastle. United went nearest to scoring in this half when McCreery was well-placed from a Bielby centre but only half-hit his shot and a long-range effort from Kelly produced a full-length dive from Edgar. Right on the interval came the save of the match from Ryan from a fiercely hit shot by Kirby.

United were again quickly on the attack after the interval and were rewarded with a goal from Sutcliffe. Bielby ran well on the left and his cross from a difficult position was helped on by McCreery and Lowey to leave 'Sutty' with an open goal four yards away.

Within 45 seconds came the second great save by Ryan to foil an equaliser. There were few goal-worthy efforts after this. A free kick by Gibson was well taken in the upright-crossbar angle by Ryan and Edgar had to be sharp when Kelly flicked in a cross from Bielby.

In a quick break from defence a good run by McCreery had the visiting defence in difficulty and when the ball was scrambled clear, Albiston hit a fine shot from just inside the area.

The Newcastle Journal found just enough space to feature a short summary of the Magpies' downfall on its sports page:

After a goalless draw at St. James's Park, two second half goals put Manchester United Youth through to the Fourth Round of the F.A. Youth Cup.

Although United had more of the game, Newcastle always looked more dangerous. Newstead was a constant nuisance to the Manchester defence and went close in the 20th minute when he saw a shot go inches wide.

Gibson had his name taken for a foul on Bielby but this was his only blemish in an otherwise useful performance. When Manchester went into the lead two minutes after the interval, it was a centre from Kelly, a back-heel from Lowey, and winger Sutcliffe, always a worrier, was presented with an easy task from six yards.

Unusually lacking any Irish inclusions, this snap of some of United's youngsters comprised of three Scots, a couple of Welsh lads and thirteen English prospects
Back row (l-r) Ken Fitzpatrick, Jonathan Clark, Jimmy Kelly, Peter Coyne, Tony Grimshaw, Peter Loughnane
Middle row (l-r) Alan Kirkup, John Lowey, Ray Mountford, Dave Ryan, David Bradley, Paul Bielby
Front row (l-r) David Morris, Arthur Albiston, Peter Sutcliffe, Tommy Gilmour, Ray Botham, Ray Storey

249

1974-75

1) Dave Ryan	9) David McCreery
2) Lindsay McKeown	10) John Lowey
3) Alan Kirkup	11) Paul Bielby
4) Jimmy Nicholl	*12) Jonathan Clark*
5) David Bradley	
6) Ray Storey	
7) Jimmy Kelly	
8) Peter Sutcliffe	

1) Drew Brand	9) Barry Wellings
2) John Brogan	10) Mark Higgins
3) Neil Robinson	11) Dave Esser
4) Martin Mowat	*12) Unknown*
5) Tommy Sharp	
6) Jonathan Balm	
7) Nigel Groome	
8) Mike O'Halloran	

FEBRUARY 1975

MANCHESTER UNITED 0 v 1 EVERTON
Sharp

Tuesday 11th

Kick-off 7.30 p.m.

fourth round

Soon after the Youth Cup victory over Newcastle, coach Frank Blunstone told the Manchester Evening News that he felt the Old Trafford youths would now *'take some beating'*, only his view of things didn't quite work out as planned. Blunstone was pleased that the Reds had received a home draw at the next stage, against Everton, although his joy was tempered by the fact that both of the Toffees' junior sides sat proudly at the top of their respective leagues. In conceding only thirteen goals in 23 matches, Everton 'A' led the Lancashire League Division One by five points while their 'B' eleven headed Division Two by the same margin.

The Reds carried a big incentive going into the Everton clash as their opponents in the Fifth Round would have been Huddersfield Town, the team that had eliminated them from the competition less than twelve months earlier.

David Meek reported in the Manchester Evening News about a feeling among the young Reds that Huddersfield's win had been somewhat lucky and the implication was that the United boys were hungry for revenge and fancied their chances to extract it if they were allowed another crack at the Yorkshire side.

Sadly, they never got the chance, the wheels coming off for Blunstone's boys simply because they couldn't make their superiority in terms of possession count on the scoreboard. With the Reds buoyed by the return of Alan Kirkup, an almost fully endowed side spurned enough chances to have completely slaughtered their opponents prior to falling to a classic sucker punch.

Jack Pauline gave a report which documented Everton's tactical success, as well as the absence of the home team's shooting substance:

The keenly awaited F.A. Youth Cup tie with Everton proved to be a most disappointing affair from our viewpoint. Having much the better of the game and being in command for long periods we failed to turn our advantage into goals, then, as so often happens in these situations, conceded a rather sloppy goal seven minutes from time. Our boys played some great football but just lacked that final thrust near goal, although a slight element of luck would have been welcome on several occasions. The result seemed to be one of those travesties of justice which makes football the uncertain game it is and which our disappointed youths must learn to accept and take in their stride.

An abundance of good football enabled us to hold territorial advantage for long periods in this much delayed meeting but too often near excellent moves failed to produce a finishing shot, more especially in the first half. The nearest efforts were a Nicholl header which lacked power and a half-hit shot from a good position by McCreery which was kicked off the line. We did find the net just before the interval, a header from Sutcliffe, but it was disallowed for what must have been a hairline offside decision. Everton had produced only a few dangerous raids in this half but had failed to trouble Ryan.

We were unlucky in the first minute after the interval when, after a good run by McCreery, Kelly was only inches short of connecting with the centre. Continuing to hold command in this half also, United carried a deal more threat but the Everton 'keeper, Brand, was proving a rare obstacle. He smothered a McCreery effort when a goal seemed certain then tipped a fine drive from Bielby over the bar.

He had the luck all 'keepers need from a Bielby corner. A Kirkup back-header bounced off his chest, hit his arm, then went inches over the top. He knew little of that one but later made great saves from McCreery and Nicholl. Despite being generally overplayed, Everton had perhaps the easiest chance of the match. With United mounting an all-out attack, a sudden break left McKeown to deal with two forwards well clear. He covered the situation cleverly and the danger was cleared.

The deciding goal came seven minutes from time when an ill-judged pass back beat Ryan and from the resultant corner, Sharp forced the ball home from close range. In fairness to Ryan he was probably surprised by the back pass, having just hit the ball into touch anticipating a stoppage for a severe eye injury to Kirkup. Play was allowed to continue with Ryan probably still having the injury in mind. In a final, desperate rally Bradley was unlucky to see a fierce drive hit the top of the crossbar.

David Meek wrote that the Reds *'were confidently expected to put a shine back on the club fortunes after the (seniors') League Cup semi-final defeat and recent wobble at the top of the table'* and he then pointed out that it *'was a familiar pattern, too, with the United youngsters playing much more skilfully and dominating most of the game – yet failing to score.'*

The first-team's woes noted in Meek's report proved to be mere blips in a season of sweet success for Tommy Docherty's men. Promotion back to the heady heights of the First Division seemed inevitable from the early weeks of the campaign and was achieved the Manchester United way, before sell-out crowds, and in a style which harked back to the glory years under Matt Busby.

On 7th March 1975, just less than a month after the under-18's defeat by Everton, the club was rocked by the death of Joe Armstrong at Cranford Lodge Hospital in Knutsford. Along with Jimmy Murphy and Bert Whalley, United's former scout was one of the key figures during the club's halcyon Youth Cup period of the 1950's and 1960's.

A man possessed with almost infinite charm, he was charged with the responsibility of providing the coaches with a quality of raw material they could then attempt to mould into top-notch footballers and in that respect, Armstrong was arguably at the top of his class as he was either partly or fully responsible for the recruitment of many of United's junior aquisitions from the 1940's right through to the early 1970's.

Armstrong's father was a Lincoln baker who moved to Southport and wed a local lass in the later stages of the 19th century. The couple then relocated to Gorton in Manchester where the marriage produced a son, Joseph, on the 28th March 1894. The lad was educated at St. Francis' Roman Catholic School after which he entered into employment as a telegraph boy with the Post Office.

Involved with music from an early age, he blew a mean cornet in St. Joseph's Band and later, upon leaving school, with the Post Office Band. He was also proficient on the piano and a love of music extended to amateur dramatics, which was also a big part of his social activities in his formative years.

Despite a lack of height, Armstrong never rising above five foot five inches, he was quite agile and took up goalkeeping while still at school. Sometime later he got involved on the organisational side of Cleveland Football Club, an amateur outfit whose roots were very likely based at Cleveland Avenue in nearby Levenshulme. The team won some silverware and upon his recommendation, one of their star players, Charlie Needham, was signed by Aston Villa for £35.

After he and Hazel Grove girl Sarah Walsh married around the end of the First World War, the couple settled at 18, Ferndale Gardens in Burnage and were blessed with a son, Joseph junior, and a daughter they named Frances. The younger Joe also developed a love of football and actually beat his father to Old Trafford as he was attached to the club on junior forms in the 1940's.

The details of how Joe senior found his way into professional football are foggy, though it was almost certainly through being asked to do some part-time work for Manchester City manager Peter Hodge around the period of 1926 or 1927. It was while scouting for the Maine Road club that he developed relationships with City stars Matt Busby and Jimmy McMullan.

Former Scottish international McMullan later tasked Armstrong to scout for him prior to the Second World War after leaving Manchester to manage, amongst others, Sheffield Wednesday, Aston Villa and Notts County, and the two remained friends for many years. A man of high principles who was much admired within the game, none more so than by Busby, McMullan's style, vision and beliefs were profoundly influential on United's future boss and the older man became something of a mentor to his fellow Scot.

When discussing his father in 2009, Joe junior claimed, *'My dad was at Old Trafford before Busby arrived in 1945 and the youth system was already in place. There were never more than a dozen scouts in my dad's time with United.'*

Eventually moving his family out to Heaton Chapel and taking up the role of technician within the Post Office, the switch of responsibilities was to prove a massive bonus in respect of his football activities because, at a time when the vast majority of the British population didn't possess a telephone, he not only became proficient in their use but was also able to build up a network of useful contacts.

This was particularly so with schools' associations, headmasters and teachers, the very points of reference he needed in his quest for budding talent. By using a telephone, facts were established about his soccer requirements, such as kick-off times and venues, which are considered simple by modern means yet could prove exacting to find in the early post-war years.

Often working incognito, and meticulous about his scouting responsibilities, he would try to watch a target as many times as possible before making a recommendation about them. He remained in that capacity until 1954 when accepting United's offer to go full-time, an opportunity which his family encouraged him to take. It was little wonder that the club wanted to make more use of him as he had already been responsible for the signing of numerous talented prospects, including Mark Jones, Jeff Whitefoot, Dennis Viollet and Bobby Charlton.

Offically retiring from United in 1971, his work on behalf of the club continued until shortly before his death, despite the fact that he was afflicted with some health problems in the later years of his life. A huge contingent of current and former members of the club's staff attended his funeral, including manager Tommy Docherty, and many of those present had reasons to be grateful for the part that little Joe Armstrong played at the beginning of their career.

1) Ray Mountford
2) Jonathan Clark
3) David Bradley
4) Steve Paterson
5) Martyn Rogers
6) Ray Storey
7) Peter Loughnane
8) Ray Botham
9) John Lowey
10) Tony Grimshaw
11) David Morris
12) *George Bailey (for 2)*

1) Nigel Batch
2) Paul Fox
3) Bob Corish
4) Graham Fearn
5) Michael Webb
6) Mark Johnson
7) Peter Falconer
8) Steve Woods
9) Lee Adam
10) Paul Bowley
11) Clive Arthur
12) *David Hunt*

MANCHESTER UNITED 4 v 0 DERBY COUNTY

Botham, Loughnane, Morris (pen), Paterson

NOVEMBER 1975

Wednesday 19th

Kick-off 7.30 p.m.

Attendance 1,838

United's Youth Cup 'goals for' column saw its very first addition just 35 seconds into the 1975/76 campaign and it came by way of a Steve Paterson goal against Derby at Old Trafford which set them on the way to a cracking 4-0 win.

Paterson, from Mosstodloch near Elgin, was one of a fresh class of newcomers and he claimed the distinction of beating Nigel Batch, the current England Youth goalkeeper, to put the Reds in front. Batch went on to perform admirably for the Rams, even though his efforts were mainly confined to keeping the score down to shallow numbers as United made it an opening tie cakewalk.

Writing in the Derby Evening Telegraph, Joe Lovejoy shared his considered opinions regarding the reasons for the home side's triumph:

Dave Mackay, searching for a winger to complete the best first-team squad in the country, must have been jealous as Manchester United used two fliers to sweep the Rams out of the F.A. Youth Cup in the Second Round last night.

The pace and skill of Dai Morris and Peter Loughnane left the Derby defence wide open to United's quick breaks with full-backs Paul Fox and Bob Corish beaten time and again.

In fact United, who fielded six players with international experience, were sharper in every department.

Rocked back on their heels by a goal in the very first minute, the Rams did their share of attacking but never looked like getting to grips with the game.

The Reds got off to a dream start when Bowley fouled Loughnane on the right. Clark's free kick was aimed for the near post but beat everybody before falling to the unmarked Paterson, who slammed the ball past Batch from point-blank range at the far post.

Botham should have made it 2-0 with the game only six minutes old, shooting wide of an open goal after Loughnane had created the chance.

He made amends in the 24th minute, smashing the ball home at the far post after Grimshaw had flicked on a corner by Morris.

The Rams fought back bravely and Bowley and Fearn both had chances, while in the 29th minute United had to scramble the ball clear when Mountford dropped Falconer's corner.

But in the 31st minute Woods gave the ball away on the edge of United's area and a quick through pass from Storey set up the best goal of the game from Loughnane.

The speedy winger began his run inside his own half, finally beating Johnson on the edge of the area before angling his shot out of Batch's reach and into the far corner.

In the second half the Rams had more than their fair share of possession but were still ineffective in and around the box.

At the other end a goal looked on every time United attacked. Batch saved at Botham's feet and did well to knock away a shot from Clark.

But when the tricky Loughnane went past Corish again in the 72nd minute, the full-back brought him down from behind and Morris placed the penalty perfectly into the corner of the net.

Fifteen year-old Nottingham schoolboy Martyn Rogers had never played on the Old Trafford pitch prior to making his Youth Cup debut, but he was awarded a five-star rating by knowledgeable observers. It was he, along with gifted former Shrewsbury and Shropshire Boys' wide man Peter Loughnane and ex-Swansea and Wales Boys' star David Morris, who stole the honours.

The Manchester Evening News reckoned Rogers *'slotted magnificently into the back four and linked well with Tony Grimshaw'* while also emphasising that *'Derby could not cope with United's wingers'*.

Goalkeeper Ray Mountford's main contribution was in making two great saves from County's Adam and Woods in order to keep an unmarked sheet on his Youth Cup entrance, and the Reds' overall performance caused Jack Pauline to jot down a remark about the win representing a *'highly successful start'*.

Manager Tommy Docherty looks a happy man as Martyn Rogers, flanked by his mum and dad, signs for United

1975-76 — second round

251

1975-76

1) Mark Grew	9) John Trenter
2) Tony Cooper	10) Wayne Hughes
3) Derek Statham	11) Kevin Summerfield
4) John Loveridge	*12) Derek Hood*
5) Brian Clarke	
6) Martyn Davies	
7) Steve Lynex	
8) Colin Gregson	

1) Ray Mountford	9) John Lowey
2) Jonathan Clark	10) Tommy Gilmour
3) Steve Paterson	11) David Morris
4) David Bradley	*12) Ray Botham (for 7)*
5) Martyn Rogers	
6) Ray Storey	
7) Peter Loughnane	
8) David McCreery	

MARCH 1976

WEST BROMWICH ALBION 2 v 2 MANCHESTER UNITED
Hughes, Summerfield | Lowey (2)

Tuesday 9th
Kick-off 7.30 p.m.
Attendance 3,166

fifth round

'Super Kids' set ground alight

At the last eight stage, United were drawn to travel to The Hawthorns in order to face a West Brom side that had already conquered current Youth Cup holders Ipswich by two goals to one in a replay at Portman Road.

In-form Baggies' striker Mark Trenter and defender Derek Hood shook off ankle injuries and were able to take part in a light training session on the morning of the Reds' visit. Of the group of fourteen Albion teenagers who were present at the workout, eight had already been credited with Central League appearances.

The youth team weren't the only United presence in the West Midlands that evening, as the seniors had drawn a thrilling F.A. Cup tie with Wolves on the Saturday beforehand and the replay at Molineux was contested simultaneously with events over at The Hawthorns.

With David McCreery a passenger on the coach headed towards West Bromwich rather than nearby Wolverhampton, the youth side showed only one change, Tommy Gilmour coming in for Tony Grimshaw.

Both of the Reds' youth and senior teams endured similar setbacks, by going behind prior to reviving their fortunes, and a newspaper local to the West Midlands carried a summary on the under-18 game:

West Bromwich Albion were punished by Manchester United for two moments of defensive indecision in the F.A. Youth Cup Fifth Round tie at The Hawthorns.

And they were lucky to force a 2-2 draw for a trip to Old Trafford on Monday.

In the fourth minute Albion were taken by surprise when Bradley lashed in a long shot which looked to be swinging wide.

But the ball hit the underside of the bar and appeared to drop behind the line. The referee allowed play to continue and Albion breathed again.

Albion looked good in the midfield for long spells with Clarke breaking up a number of United attacks and Loveridge and Gregson sparking a series of well thought out attacks.

A Gregson-inspired move in 26 minutes was stylishly finished when Hughes headed in from a Lynex centre, but United made two set pieces pay off.

Grew, credited with a couple of good stops, failed to intercept the ball from a left wing corner and was stranded at the near post when Lowey nodded the ball in for the equaliser in 40 minutes. Three minutes later Lowey smacked the ball in from a right wing flag kick with the Albion defence static.

The non-stop Gregson sent Lynex away and he centred low for Summerfield to tap in the equaliser after 63 minutes.

Albion's late pressure was not made to pay off because of weak finishing.

On a chilly night, spectators at The Hawthorns were warmed by the quality of the youngsters' skills. The heat wasn't just confined to the playing area, as the local Fire Brigade was called to put out a small blaze in the Rainbow Stand during the second half and while both teams searched for a winner, flames rose skywards. Fortunately, there weren't any casualties and the Fire Brigade later reported the stand hadn't sustained any serious damage either.

It was a similar scenario on the pitch, where sparks flew for a time but, with both sides unable to inflict sufficient suffering on their opponents, each had to be satisfied in the knowledge that the issue would have to be settled on another day.

Frank Blunstone told a reporter that he reckoned the tie *'could have gone either way'* before adding a comment which indicated he felt David Bradley's early long-range drive should have been awarded as a goal. Blunstone also praised both sides, whom he felt gave *'good value'* and *'would enjoy meeting up again'* in Manchester.

The coach ended his interview by claiming, *'My lads really want to reach the semi-final at least, and they now know the size of the task that lies ahead of them. If they can repeat what they have done here tonight, I believe they have every chance.'*

Martyn Rogers (centre) and Jonathan Clark (number two) are unable to halt Wayne Hughes opening the score for the Albion

1) Ray Mountford
2) Jonathan Clark
3) Steve Paterson
4) David Bradley
5) Martyn Rogers
6) Ray Storey
7) Ray Botham
8) David McCreery
9) John Lowey
10) Tommy Gilmour
11) David Morris
12) George Bailey (for 7)

1) Mark Grew
2) Tony Cooper
3) Derek Statham
4) John Loveridge
5) Brian Clarke
6) Martyn Davies
7) Steve Lynex
8) Colin Gregson
9) John Trenter
10) Wayne Hughes
11) Kevin Summerfield
12) Derek Hood (for 7)

1975-76

MANCHESTER UNITED 1 v 4 WEST BROMWICH ALBION
Gilmour   Summerfield (3), Trenter

MARCH 1976

Monday 15th
Kick-off 7.30 p.m.
Attendance 10,063

Cup KO for boy Reds

United couldn't hold Colin Gregson in midfield and after half an hour, Kevin Summerfield beat Steve Paterson to increase Albion's lead.

United pushed David McCreery onto the right wing and brought Ray Botham into the middle for the second half. For the first time in the game they settled into the kind of form that in three earlier rounds saw them score seventeen goals without reply.

United hit back hard and in the 63rd minute Tommy Gilmour, a former Scottish schools' captain and a new boy in the team, zipped through the middle to pull a goal back.

United had the visitors on the run for a spell, but Albion's strong, skilful side, which has already knocked out Ipswich, the holders, were too good for the Reds. Summerfield scored twice in the closing stages to complete a fine hat-trick and give Albion a 4-1 win.

Post-match comments were forthcoming from the victorious camp, with an elated Albion manager Johnny Giles claiming, 'I am delighted. We have a good youth side and they played really well against United. The game was an all-round team effort but there are still two nights of hard work to be done before reaching the final.'

West Brom defeated an emerging Selhurst Park side in the semi-final to set up an all-Midlands affair against Wolverhampton Wanderers. After twice failing in previous Youth Cup finals, the Albion made absolutely certain the trophy would spend at least a year at The Hawthorns by convincingly defeating their near neighbours 5-0 on aggregate.

Ray Mountford couldn't be faulted for any of West Brom's goals

One significant hangover from the game at The Hawthorns was the injury to Peter Loughnane, whose substitution by Ray Botham took place with only five minutes of the first half remaining. The winger's problem hadn't righted itself in time for the replay, so Botham simply claimed the vacant number seven jersey. Loughnane's absence meant that McCreery would shoulder much of United's attacking responsibilities, despite knowing he was on stand-by for the first-team on the forthcoming Saturday.

While many may have felt United had seemingly done the difficult deed by bringing the Baggies back to Old Trafford, the Reds were unable to pull off a place in the last four of the tournament because a tremendous hat-trick by Kevin Summerfield, whose strikes came in the 30th, 81st and 89th minutes, was far better than anything they could muster, either individually or collectively.

The Manchester Evening News carried a few paragraphs on the fate of the crestfallen hopefuls:

Manchester United's hopes of a cup semi-final double crashed against West Bromwich at Old Trafford last night.

The young Reds failed to follow the example of their senior side and lost a replay that could have meant an F.A. Youth Cup semi-final against Crystal Palace.

A 10,063 crowd came to watch the promising youngsters at Old Trafford but they saw them beaten 4-1 by a fine West Bromwich team.

Albion struck early with a right wing burst from Steve Lynex, whose centre was headed home by John Trenter.

John Lowey was unable to add to his goals' total at Old Trafford

fifth round replay

255

1976-77

1) Andy Slack	9) Mike Carter
2) Mike Graham	10) Alan Froggatt
3) David Burke	11) Jan Novacki
4) Colin Salmon	*12) Bruce Bott ‡*
5) Brian Hart	
6) Craig Lyle	
7) Duncan Laing	
8) Chris Thompson	

1) Paul Field	9) Peter Coyne
2) George Bailey	10) Tommy Gilmour
3) Kevan Poppett	11) Ian Ashworth
4) Mike Duxbury	*12) John McDermott (for 9)*
5) Martyn Rogers	
6) Stuart Griffiths	
7) Jonathan Clark	
8) David Jackson	

NOVEMBER 1976

BOLTON WANDERERS 3 v 0 MANCHESTER UNITED
Bott, Carter, Graham (pen)

Monday 29th
Kick-off 7.30 p.m.

second round

Frank Blunstone took the wraps off a fresh goalkeeper and no less than six new outfield players for the outing to Burnden Park in November 1976. The fine form shown by Longsight-based former England schoolboy scoring sensation Peter Coyne, with four goals in his last two outings, guaranteed his inclusion while only Jonathan Clark, George Bailey, Martyn Rogers and Tommy Gilmour held prior experience of Youth Cup football, with most of the side named then mainly participating at 'B' team standard.

It was patently obvious that hosts Bolton Wanderers were overall better placed from previous knowledge in the tournament as several of the Trotters' squad were already familiar with the rigours of the Central League.

Up against his former club was one Jan Novacki. The Bolton number eleven accumulated seven appearances for United's 'B' team in the 1974/75 season and had signed as an apprentice for the Wanderers in the interim period.

The resulting contest was a mismatch of quality, the performance and outcome giving rise to an early exit for the Reds in a game which was best forgotten quickly.

The mini-whites of Bolton survived a couple of early frights prior to finding their feet, with Stuart Griffiths and Tommy Gilmour getting in competent shots which were ably saved by Andy Slack. From then on it was Wanderers all the way as the more direct approach employed by the home side saw United tormented, twisted and tortured into a terrible tangle.

At the top of the bill for Bolton was sixteen year-old Mike Carter, who continually wreaked havoc on United's defence. In producing numerous piercing runs, often beginning way inside his own half, the young centre-forward displayed skill, composure and determination in liberal proportions.

It was Carter who opened the scoring in the 41st minute when a long clearance from Slack was headed on by Brian Hart to put him in possession. The Warrington teenager found enough time and space to crash the ball beyond Field and give the Reds headaches during the down-time.

With Field becoming increasingly overworked as the second period got going, the Trotters unsurprisingly went two-up in the 55th minute after Alan Froggatt was upended by the fraught ex-England Boys' goalkeeper and Mike Graham planted the resulting penalty home. Graham punished the guilty Field with a hard shot, which was perfectly placed into the bottom corner of the net, the goal completely obliterating all hopes the Reds held of any further progress in the competition.

United's main problem was that they appeared to lack any form of leadership or direction and resultantly they were unable to hold onto the ball long enough to relieve the unyielding pressure exerted by the Wanderers. The impression was that Bolton players were everywhere and consequently the Reds were largely held as prisoners in their own area.

With twenty minutes remaining in order to try to salvage a little pride, United sent on John McDermott for Coyne, but the change proved futile and the incessant Bolton tide continued to lap against the visiting defence.

The Trotters' elation was heightened ten minutes from the end following a move that spelt danger when Carter jinked his way through a porous defence to the bye-line. A low centre resulted from the space Carter created for himself and substitute Bruce Bott claimed the honour of completing the scoring, making it look all too easy with a glancing shot which blurred past Field.

The later moments were ones of purgatory for United's defence, whose only wishes by then were centred on the sounding of the final whistle. Carter continued to tease by twice bringing more good work out of Field before the game ended and the away side looked miserable as they trooped off the pitch at the close of play.

In the aftermath of a sound beating, there was no disputing the validity or margin of Bolton's win.

For six of the United side, Paul Field, Kevan Poppett, Stuart Griffiths, David Jackson, Peter Coyne and Ian Ashworth, the defeat at Burnden Park proved to be their one and only appearance in a Youth Cup game.

Taken in 1976, the above photograph includes nine of United's twelve Youth Cup participants who were crushed at Bolton in the November of that year
Back row (l-r) Martyn Rogers, Jonathan Clark, David Bradley, Ray Mountford, Stuart Griffiths, John McDermott, David Haggett
Front row (l-r) David Cork, Mike Duxbury, Geoff Hunter, Tommy Gilmour, David Jackson, George Bailey, Ian Ashworth

1977-78

1) Paul Gregory
2) Pat Pearcey
3) Steve Searle
4) Andy Higgins
5) Gary Bellamy
6) Howard Millington
7) Gary Pollard
8) Ray Hill
9) Geoff Wragg
10) John Deacey
11) Andy Fantom
12) Dave Campbell

1) Stuart Plunkett
2) David Cork
3) Martyn Rogers
4) Mike Duxbury
5) David Haggett
6) Gary Micklewhite
7) Geoff Hunter
8) Steve Jones
9) John McDermott
10) Andy Ritchie
11) John Lucas
12) Paul Smith

CHESTERFIELD 0 v 4 MANCHESTER UNITED
Ritchie (4)

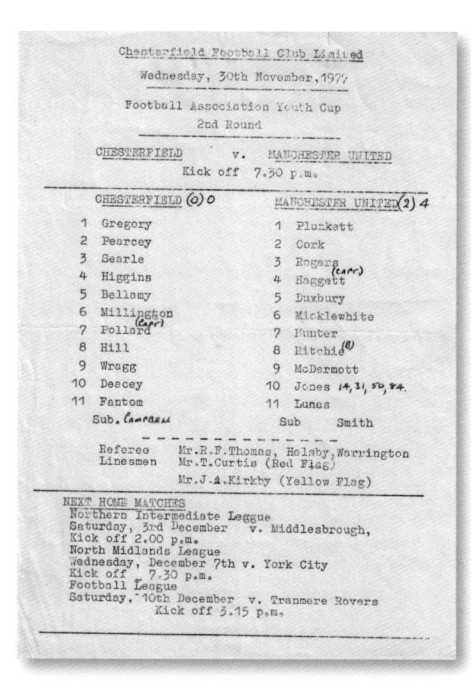

NOVEMBER 1977

Wednesday 30th

Kick-off 7.30 p.m.

Attendance 800

A year and a day after the nightmare capitulation at Burnden Park, a new generation of Reds wiped away some of the memory of that dreadful night when they made a good impression at the Recreation Ground home of Chesterfield Football Club.

A morale boosting win of four goals to nil was the outcome and as all of them were credited to local lad Andy Ritchie, it seemed that United might even have stumbled across a new star in the making.

Through being incorrectly noted at number eight on the match teamsheet, Ritchie might not have been credited for his feat by the Derbyshire Times and it took a knowledgeable United fan to point out to their reporter that the striker had, in fact, switched jerseys with Steve Jones.

The junior Reds were in decent form leading up to the tie, with welcome victories over Burnley and Manchester City in the Lancashire Youth Cup. Earlier that month they had also taken part in a friendly match against Staffordshire-based Madeley College as part of their preparations, when exactly the same outfield players who would face Chesterfield were on duty. The students found themselves on the end of a lesson in finishing and an in-form Ritchie much too difficult to stop as he punished any errors by banging five goals into their net while Geoff Hunter weighed in with a hat-trick.

Ritchie was assisted in offensive duties at Chesterfield by another Mancunian, John McDermott, who was a survivor from Burnden Park. The Reds fielded a fourth goalkeeper in as many seasons in Stuart Plunkett, a Shropshire-born boy, while Martyn Rogers, who was starting his third Youth Cup campaign, was numbered next to David Cork, a native of Doncaster.

There were further debuts for Welsh schoolboy caps David Haggett and John Lucas, Londoner Gary Micklewhite, former Hull schoolboy prospect Hunter, and Steve Jones, who came from Bootle, as well as Ritchie. Sat on the bench was Paul Smith, a 'B' team forward or midfielder who had already made some progress with three appearances in the 'A' side.

The signs looked encouraging right from the start, when the old boys and the novices appeared to slot almost effortlessly into the pace of the game, and one of the consequences of that bright beginning was shown by the United eleven continuing to hallmark the contest by producing a pleasing display of power, skill, effort and teamwork.

The Reds were certainly lifted by opening the score after just fourteen minutes, when a forward pass from Jones was followed by a tidy one-two between Ritchie and McDermott and rifled home by the former.

Less than twenty minutes passed before United were able to rack up their second. It came about when a corner from Lucas was flicked on by McDermott and Ritchie again obliged his striking partner by polishing off the move.

At the opposite end, Plunkett was required to handle the ball only infrequently during the opening 45 minutes, Chesterfield's only chance of the half falling to Wragg, whose shot went narrowly wide.

Shortly into the second period, the Reds practically guaranteed their place in the next round through Ritchie's achievement in completing a wonderful hat-trick. Jones acted as a direct supply line on this occasion after his long throw-in connected with the alert number ten just inside Chesterfield's penalty area. Following a deft turn, Ritchie temporarily lost his marker to make it number three by lashing the ball into the top corner of the Spireites' goal.

It took an hour for the Saltergate team to win their first corner, and soon after there was a crowd scene in and around Plunkett's six-yard area which almost resulted in them scoring.

There were far more chances to follow at the other end of the pitch, with Hunter, Ritchie, McDermott and Jones all spurning opportunities that presented differing degrees of difficulty. With time running out, Ritchie claimed another goal to complete his, and the Reds', scoring for the evening.

Chesterfield manager Arthur Cox was typically blunt and to the point when saying, *'We were outplayed and outclassed. United were tougher opponents than the first-team played on Saturday.'*

> *As I looked around the ground at Chesterfield before our Youth Cup match, all of the stands were wooden and they appeared very old-fashioned. I thought to myself that it wasn't anything like Old Trafford.*
>
> **ANDY RITCHIE**

second round

1977-78

1) Stuart Plunkett	9) John McDermott	
2) David Cork	10) Steve Jones	
3) Martyn Rogers	11) John Lucas	
4) Mike Duxbury	*12) Nigel Keen*	
5) David Haggett		
6) Gary Micklewhite		
7) Geoff Hunter		
8) Andy Ritchie		

1) Chris Woods	9) Darren Avis	
2) Paul Turner	10) Steve Kendal	
3) Simon Worthington	11) Steve Burke	
4) Kevin Collins	*12) Gary Rose (for 9)*	
5) Don McLeod		
6) Dale Smart		
7) Gary Mills		
8) Albert Briscoe		

JANUARY 1978

MANCHESTER UNITED 2 v 1 NOTTINGHAM FOREST

Hunter, Jones — *Kendal*

Saturday 7th

Kick-off 2.30 p.m.

third round

The only personnel change for the early New Year visit of Nottingham Forest was the inclusion as substitute of Barrow-in Furness teenager Nigel Keen in place of Paul Smith. Meanwhile, in a positional crossover, Andy Ritchie and Steve Jones swapped inside-forward berths.

With the seniors undertaking the long trek up to Carlisle in order to defend the F.A. Cup they had won the previous May, Old Trafford was vacant for a Saturday and Forest's visit offered the chance for those United followers not venturing up to Cumbria to see a knock-out game staged locally.

The Nottingham club were about to enter a glittering period in their history, soon to be crowned First Division champions and with European Cup glories only just over the horizon. However, the question to be posed on this particular day and at this specific venue was; how would Brian Clough's kids measure up to Dave Sexton's?

During the early stages of the game, Forest undeniably looked the better of the two sides until they were punished by United for a couple of silly and unforced errors. At the interval, the Forest boys were rather cruelly down by two goals to nil and fighting for all their lives to stay in contention. The Reds unhinged their guests with a beautiful opening goal in the 18th minute as, when MacLeod was robbed some 35 yards out, livewire midfielder Geoff Hunter carried possession a short distance prior to driving an unstoppable shot that crashed into the helpless Chris Woods' net just a split second after the ball connected with his left boot.

Nottingham came back strongly and for a time were camped around the home goalmouth, but with an equaliser appearing to look the most likely outcome, United countered by increasing their advantage. Only six minutes remained before the change of ends when Forest were found guilty of defending like a troupe of Morris dancers, the Reds concurrently building up a neat move which came to fruition when Jones hit a shot from the eighteen-yard line. The ball again whistled past Woods, clipped the bottom of the left-hand post and nestled inside his net to give United a handy cushion.

Shortly into the second half, Nottingham's Burke tried his luck with a drive that Plunkett grabbed at the foot of an upright. Burke's attempt was the prelude to a deserved Forest goal because, just minutes later, United's margin was halved after a short corner on the left found Mills. The winger proceeded to evade three home defenders along the touchline before guiding an accurate pass to Steve Kendal, who easily beat Plunkett.

The impressive Burke then saw a goal ruled out for offside as Forest fixed their immediate sights on taking the Reds back to the City Ground. Ultimately, and try as they might, the task of forcing an equaliser was beyond them.

While Manchester United might not have enjoyed much in the way of tangible success in the Youth Cup for some years, the competition continued to be taken very seriously by the club's officials. A look at the 1978 contract of one of the young hopefuls at Old Trafford reveals that his basic wage was £75 per week, a tidy sum which equates to approximately seven times that amount in today's terms, and the table below shows that an appearance in every match on a Youth Cup run to the final would have earned the teenager an extra £208:

Second Round = £3	Fifth Round = £20
Third Round = £5	Semi-final = £70 (2 x £35)
Fourth Round = £10	Final = £100 (2 x £50)

It should be noted that the amounts shown are for games played and not wins. However, a victory would have presented the opportunity of another appearance at the next stage.

There were other financial incentives put in place. A Central League draw earned £2, a figure which was doubled for a win, and a first-team game was worth a whopping £50. Additionally, there were also other, unspecified, *'success bonuses'*.

As far as the Youth Cup was concerned, the amounts involved signal a clear indication of just how highly the tournament was still perceived by the club's policymakers during a period of numerous changes under manager Dave Sexton, a time in which there were limited opportunities for players from the lower ranks. It appears that the young Reds' relatively indifferent achievements at that time could have had more to do with the talent available, the scouting network in place, or even coaching and tactics, as opposed to any absence of focus or monetary reward.

Another interesting fact about the life of a junior just then was their six-monthly progress reports. These were initially suggested by club scout Norman Scholes, a school headmaster who was familiar with the medium as he was used to preparing such assessments for the many children in his care.

Taken on board by Frank Blunstone, they were formed into nine sections, which included Shooting Power, Passing Technique, Defensive Qualities, Tactical Awareness and Ball Control. A section on Speed was divided into three sub-parts; Speed of Running, Speed of Thought and Speed of Control.

In regards to a section on Temperament, Blunstone wrote of Martyn Rogers:

Excellent. Does not allow opponents to disturb his concentration. Accepts officials' decisions whether for or against.

Under Heading Ability, it was penned:

Needs to get in line with the flight of the ball earlier, jumping and attacking the ball better when challenging opponents for possession in the air. Will have to get more height and distance when making defensive headers.

The report was concluded with a Personal Notes section, and of the same player Blunstone noted:

Martyn has worked hard, both on and off the field. An excellent timekeeper and a quiet, reserved personality. Always well behaved and keen to improve himself by listening and acting on advice given to him. Should continue to improve.

It could safely be assumed that the exercise was intended to inform not only the individual concerned in relation to his progress, but it also enabled his parents to be kept up-to-date on how things were going in their son's career.

With Frank Blunstone having left the club in October 1977 to link up once more with Tommy Docherty at Derby, Joe Brown took up the role of youth team coach at Old Trafford and it is highly likely that the practice of issuing such documents was continued, at least for a little while longer.

Having already been at the club since May 1975, the adaptable and dependable Mike Duxbury would remain at Old Trafford for another twelve years

1977-78

1) John Simon
2) Andy Johns
3) Jeff Peters
4) Mark Proctor
5) Mike Angus
6) Keith Nobbs
7) Colin Blackburn
8) Craig Johnston
9) David Hodgson
10) Tony Muthana
11) Billy Askew
12) Ray Pirie ◊

1) Stuart Plunkett
2) David Cork
3) Martyn Rogers
4) Mike Duxbury
5) David Haggett
6) Gary Micklewhite
7) Geoff Hunter
8) Steve Jones
9) Andy Ritchie
10) John McDermott
11) John Lucas
12) Nigel Keen (for 7)

MIDDLESBROUGH 1 v 0 MANCHESTER UNITED
Blackburn

MARCH 1978

Monday 6th*

Kick-off 7.00 p.m.

Attendance 1,460

Boro Juniors tame United

Due to a cold snap in the North-East through the early part of 1978, and a subsequent postponement of a previously scheduled meeting, two months passed between the win over Nottingham Forest and United's trip to Ayresome Park, where Middlesbrough awaited their arrival.

It proved to be a desperately disappointing display by the Reds and there could be no valid argument against their elimination.

United were made to wait until ten minutes into the second half before forcing their first flag kick and for the bulk of the game they were almost completely overrun and outplayed. The inescapable impression was that they had come up against a team which allied a greater desire to win with better organisation and more imposing football.

The main reason that the Boro' were unable to put the game beyond United's reach much earlier than they did was down to an inventory of glaring misses by inside-left Tony Muthana, who was particularly wasteful in regards to a number of aerial opportunities.

For the benefit of the readers of the Review, Jack Pauline was up on Teeside to record the match details:

The home side had much the better of the opening half but, although having the United defence in difficulty, failed to produce a worthwhile shot on target. A weak effort straight at Plunkett by Muthana was the 'keeper's only real call to duty, although often under pressure from centres which created danger without materialising.

United's only useful effort this half came from Ritchie but he was wide with his shot.

In the first minutes of the second half Duxbury did his second rescue act with Muthana clean through but the latter had several more easy chances to head Middlesbrough into a lead but failed. Two fine saves by Plunkett and a good interception by Jones kept our replay hopes alive until good work by Askew then a centre which gave Blackburn a close range chance to settle the issue.

Middlesbrough continued to look and play like a superior side but United did produce a number of late rallies which set up half chances to save the game, but it would have been a travesty of justice.

With the Daily Mail calling it *'an exciting match'* prior to recording that the result *'was just reward for a faster moving Middlesbrough'*, David Meek also chipped in with a number of observations of his own, several of which read:

United knocked the ball about confidently but lacked the final penetration to cause problems.

Twin strikers Andy Ritchie and John McDermott were always dangerous but lacked support. In defence Stuart Plunkett could do little about the goal and in the 62nd minute saved United as he raced out to clear from the advancing Dave Hodgson.

Dave Haggett, Martyn Rogers and Mike Duxbury came through with credit.

Meek also opined that *'United could have few complaints'* about their elimination, and on the same day his report went out, the Middlesbrough Evening Gazette gave due praise to their local teenagers:

Boro Juniors reached the quarter-finals of the F.A. Youth Cup when they sent Manchester United Juniors crashing to a 1-0 defeat in the Fourth Round tie at Ayresome Park last night.

The winners were always the more skilful and direct team and fully deserved their victory. Only poor finishing robbed them of a bigger victory, the winner coming from the seventeen year-old Richmond schoolboy, Colin Blackburn in the 68th minute.

Boro, the only remaining North-East side in the national competition, were well served by their midfield trio of Craig Johnston, Billy Askew and Mark Proctor, while Dave Hodgson was always a skilful and lively leader.

In defence, Andy Johns enjoyed a sound game and Mike Angus celebrated signing his apprentice forms only hours before kick-off with a splendid performance.

After a heavy tackle on Peters in the 22nd minute, United's David Cork received the yellow card. Only minutes before half-time Proctor beat United's offside trap with a fine, chipped ball but Askew's shot was wide.

On the resumption United were much more lively. They also brought on Keen for Hunter and enjoyed their best spell as Micklewhite and McDermott set up a promising move in the 55th minute, but Lucas shot behind.

In the 68th minute, however, Johnston and Askew engineered the move which gave Boro their all-important goal. Johnston laid out an intelligent ball to Askew who cut in deep, sweeping past four defenders before crossing an accurate pass to Blackburn. The Richmond schoolboy coolly left-footed a crashing volley which gave Plunkett no chance.

United hit back with a final onslaught as McDermott tried a clever overhead kick which flew just over the bar - but there was no denying Boro's worthy victory and they now visit Burnley.

Coach Joe Brown was short and sharp in summarising the outcome when stating, *'It was a game that looked as though it would be settled by the odd goal and Boro' got it. We were not at our best.'*

" *We all knew we had let the club down and there was a deathly silence on the coach all the way back to Manchester. No-one wanted to make eye contact with anyone else, we just wanted to get home, get to bed and forget all about it.* "

JOHN McDERMOTT

An obviously unimpressed Joe Brown was critical of United's feeble performance at Ayresome Park

fourth round

*This game was originally scheduled for Monday, February 13th but was postponed due to a snowbound pitch

1978-79

1) Stephen Pears	9) Andy Wray	1) Paul Leeming	9) Paul Maguire
2) Gary Micklewhite	10) Andy Ritchie	2) Norman Roberts	10) John Heywood
3) Nigel Keen	11) Chris Lynam	3) Brian Morley	11) Andy Stafford
4) Alan Davies	*12) Andy Reynolds*	4) Martin Hickson	*12) Ian Dunne (for 11)*
5) Chris Roberts		5) Neil Wilson	
6) Danny Keough		6) Brian Moran	
7) David Haggett		7) Kevin Pritchard	
8) Garry Worrall		8) Ian Aitchinson	

DECEMBER 1978

MANCHESTER UNITED 6 v 2 BLACKBURN ROVERS

Lynam, Ritchie (4), Wray   Dunne (2)

Monday 4th

Kick-off 7.30 p.m.

Attendance 5,329

second round

There wouldn't have been a single complaint from anyone connected with United at the draw for the opening Youth Cup tie of the 1978/79 season. Lancashire rivals Blackburn Rovers were certainly expected to improve on a 5-1 drubbing they had suffered at Old Trafford in a Lancashire Youth Cup tie only seven weeks prior to the game in the national tournament, though few people would have wagered much on them making any progress at the Reds' expense. In addition, United's 'B' team had already completed twelve out of their commitment of sixteen Lancashire League Supplementary Cup fixtures, and home and away single goal defeats of the Rovers were included amongst them.

The Reds fielded Andy Ritchie, Nigel Keen, David Haggett and Gary Micklewhite from last season's competition, but yet another new goalkeeper, Stephen Pears, and six debuting outfield players, Alan Davies, Chris Roberts, Danny Keough, Garry Worrall, Andy Wray and Chris Lynam, made for plenty of doubts, question marks and concerns regarding the distance that the new-look team would be equipped to go this time around. Of the seven freshly-introduced individuals, six were apprentices in their first year at the club.

There were a few optimistic signs, though, as Haggett, Worrall and Wray had managed to bag a few goals between them at junior level, while Chris Lynam, following a sluggish start to his campaign, could lay claim to five successful strikes in as many of his last 'A' team matches.

The record books have shown on countless occasions that it is far more improbable for a side to make much progress through the rounds with so many new faces at one time and, as a general rule, integrating three of four rookies into a principally established team is almost always the preferred option.

As in numerous years previously, it simply wasn't possible to apply such an obviously common sense principle at that precise moment in time and coach Joe Brown was forced to go with what he considered to be the best side available to him.

Despite the obvious lack of experience, and as was widely expected, the Reds saw off Blackburn convincingly enough, mainly because Ritchie was able to repeat his achievement of twelve months previously at Chesterfield with a superb individual display. The Stockport-based striker's haul continued a smashing personal run, as he had managed to find the back of the net in each of his first five appearances for the Reserves that season while also slamming another six goals in his last seven Central League outings.

The club gave advance notice that a token would be printed on the match team sheet, a move which undoubtedly helped to contribute to yet another splendid gate.

The Manchester Evening News' Brian Brett supplied the following concise details:

Andy Ritchie gave Manchester United manager Dave Sexton a reminder of his scoring potential when he hit four goals in the young Reds' 6-2 demolition of Blackburn in the F.A. Youth Cup Second Round at Old Trafford last night.

The eighteen year-old striker, who had four first-team games last season, gave warning of his shooting power with a 25-yarder for his first, just before the interval, and then cut loose in the second half.

He strolled through two tackles for his second, reached a hat-trick with a looping header and then slotted in a fourth as his experience exposed a poor Blackburn defence.

Andy Wray had given United a ninth minute lead with a first-time shot from the edge of the box after good work by Garry Worrall and Chris Roberts. Chris Lynam scorched a shot into the net after Ritchie had set up a 44th minute chance to give the Reds a 3-0 interval lead.

Clever approach work, usually inspired by the skilful Worrall, delighted a crowd of 5,329, who saw plenty of promise from this latest crop of United babes.

Danny Keough and Dave Haggett made significant contributions from midfield while Nigel Keen came forward from the back four to rap a shot against the bar.

The game was over as a contest by the interval and two goals by substitute Ian Dunne gave Blackburn a flattering scoreline.

Goals: Wray (9), Ritchie (40, 55, 62 and 67), Lynam (44) for United: Dunne (68, 80 for Blackburn).

Including some overage players, most of the personnel available for Youth Cup duty in the 1978/79 season line up next to the club's indoor facility at The Cliff
Back row (l-r) Mike Duxbury, Chris Roberts, Tom Sloan, Gary Micklewhite, Steve Jones, Steve Pears, David Haggett, Martyn Rogers, Alan Davies, Andy Wray, Andy Reynolds
Front row (l-r) Nigel Keen, Andy Ritchie, John McDermott, Garry Worrall, David Jeffrey, Phil McCandless, Chris Lynam

260

1) Stephen Pears
2) Gary Micklewhite
3) Nigel Keen
4) Alan Davies
5) Chris Roberts
6) Steve Jones
7) David Haggett
8) Garry Worrall
9) Andy Wray
10) Danny Keough
11) Chris Lynam
12) Andy Reynolds

1) Steve Cherry
2) John Lovatt
3) Wayne Richards
4) Keith Falconer
5) David Tarry
6) Nigel Steele
7) Trevor Morley
8) Steve Spooner
9) Kevin Murray
10) Steve Blades
11) John Clayton
12) Mike Quinn (for 2)

1978-79

MANCHESTER UNITED 0 v 3 DERBY COUNTY

Morley, Murray, Quinn

FEBRUARY 1979

Young Reds get jitters

Two factors contributed to the Third Round contest against Derby County commencing with an afternoon start. Firstly, coming as it did during a spell of wintry weather, it was thought that by bringing the game forward to an earlier slot, any possibility of the pitch freezing over would be greatly reduced. The conditions were such that the 'B' team hadn't fulfilled a fixture since the middle of December whereas the 'A' side's 9-0 home win over Morecambe Reserves represented their only game so far in 1979.

Secondly, it also avoided the match clashing with an England v. Northern Ireland European Championship Qualifier, which was being transmitted live on television later that evening. Because only a small attendance was anticipated, club officials getting it spot on in that respect, no token was printed on the match team sheet.

The absence of Andy Ritchie, who was on standby for possible senior requirements against Manchester City at Maine Road on the forthcoming Saturday, exposed still further a group of individuals who were collectively lacking in the required know-how. With the squad also containing little in the way of depth, the club was forced into obtaining special leave of absence from Danny Keough's school in Bacup in order for him to start the match as Ritchie's deputy.

While Keough might have demonstrated plenty of potential during his sporadic appearances in the Reds' junior sides, his season's record of a solitary goal in one and two starts for the 'A' and 'B' teams respectively, plus a game in midfield in the previous round of the Youth Cup, hardly came near to making up for a loss of firepower that the deadly Ritchie could have provided.

If any special ingredient was needed to add further flavour to the proceedings, it came via the former United connections still in employment at the Baseball Ground, as Rams' manager Tommy Docherty, coach Frank Blunstone and chief scout Gordon Clayton had now been at Derby for approximately a year and a half. While the departure of Blunstone and Clayton from Old Trafford might not have attracted too much attention, the popular Docherty's exit came about in widely publicised and acrimonious circumstances and they were still vividly fresh in the memory of the United faithful. Even so, upon Blunstone and Clayton's acceptance to form part of Docherty's new backroom set-up, Manchester United undoubtedly lost two hard working, highly respected and capable members of their staff.

The occasion turned into a joyful return for the former Reds' contingent because County paralysed the home side and in doing so they inflicted one of United's heaviest ever home defeats in the Youth Cup.

The Derby Evening Telegraph encapsulated the match highlights:

> **DERBY COUNTY had the edge in every phase of the game over Manchester United and came through the FA Youth Cup, 3-0 winners at Old Trafford yesterday.**
>
> They now travel again for the quarter-final meeting at Coventry.
>
> Tommy Docherty's youngsters struck the first blow in the 42nd minute through a cleverly taken chance by Trevor Morley.
>
> In boxing parlance Manchester United would have been counted out on their feet as Derby, with balance on the slippery surface that would have done justice to ice skater John Curry, sprayed long balls and one touch-passes.
>
> United had no answer nor anybody to match skipper Keith Falconer. He was magnificent and won more accolades when he moved to right-back after the interval replacing injured John Lovatt.
>
> **Justice**
>
> Subsitute Mike Quinn got Derby's second goal in the 61st minute rising to a cross from Steve Spooner and nodding it in.
>
> In the last minute, Kevin Murray did justice to the result with a coolly taken drive from 12 yards that skimmed low into the corner of the net.
>
> United winners of the trophy more times than any other club, squandered three golden chances in the space of five minutes.
>
> The possible hat-trick was missed by Steven Jones. He picked up a long ball on the halfway line in the 23rd minute with all Derby's defenders behind him and he raced into the box.
>
> Youth international Steve Cherry advanced at Jones whose weak shot hit the post. Minutes later he failed to beat the 'keeper again within seconds Cherry smothered a 12-yard drive from the helpless Jones.

There were also some words written about the game in the Manchester Evening News, a few of which read:

The jitters which have sent Manchester United tumbling down the First Division recently extended to the Reds' youngsters at Old Trafford last night, when they were beaten 3-0 by Tommy Docherty's Derby County in the Third Round of the F.A. Youth Cup.

The United boys started brightly, and it took a string of fine saves from Derby's England Youth 'keeper, Steve Cherry, to keep his side in the game.

The Reds' new youth coach, Syd Owen, attends to some essential administrative tasks behind the scenes

third round

Wednesday 7th*

Kick-off 2.30 p.m.

Attendance 654

*This game was originally scheduled for Tuesday, January 23rd but was postponed due to a snowbound pitch

261

1979-80

second round

DECEMBER 1979

Monday 10th*

Kick-off 7.30 p.m.

Attendance 600

*This game was originally scheduled for Wednesday, December 5th but was rearranged due to a waterlogged pitch

CHESTER CITY 3 v 5 MANCHESTER UNITED

Cooke, Rush (2, 1 pen) — Jeffrey, Lynam (2), Wynn (2)

Chester City:
1) Mike Keen
2) David Rowlands
3) Peter Mooney
4) Ian Edwards
5) Peter Zelem
6) Paul Blackwell
7) Colin Jones
8) Stuart Minten
9) Ian Rush
10) Kevin Jones
11) Terry Cooke
12) Paul Murray ◊

Manchester United:
1) Stephen Pears
2) Alan Stevenson
3) David Jeffrey
4) Nigel Keen
5) Chris Roberts
6) David Wynn
7) Danny Keough
8) Scott McGarvey
9) Chris Lynam
10) Alan Davies
11) Garry Worrall
12) Andy Reynolds (for 6)

Rush beats the flu to rock Reds

As the decade that is now synonymous with flared trousers, disco music and industrial disharmony neared its conclusion, the young Reds made a return to Sealand Road to face Chester, who by now had added City to their title, following a lapse of nine years since their last encounter at the same venue.

United coach Syd Owen decided to break in Rotherham boy Alan Stevenson and Belfast native David Jeffrey at numbers two and three respectively. Up to that point, Jeffrey could most often be found in one of the 'A' team's full-back spots, although he had been tried at centre-back in the 'B' side, while Stevenson, with just two starts on the lower rung, had gained appearances at numbers two, six and eight in the Lancashire League Division One team.

Ormskirk-born David Wynn also made his competition debut along with Scott McGarvey, who hailed from north of the border. The latter appeared a genuine gold-plated prospect, as his eight early season goals for the 'A' team saw him promoted into the Reserves, for whom he had already knocked in a couple of hat-tricks.

In what was practically a dress rehearsal for the knock-out showdown between the two sides, the Reds warmed to the task by defeating Chester in a league fixture just two weeks previously, an event the Chester Chronicle duly noted:

Chester took a psychological F.A. Youth Cup blow with their 3-0 defeat by next Wednesday's Second Round opponents Manchester United in their Lancashire League rehearsal last Saturday.

But even though assistant manager Cliff Sear, who is in charge of the team, concedes that United must be favourites to prevent Chester reaching the Third Round for the second successive season next week, he adds, 'It is what happens on the night that counts. United may be the favourites, but if we hit it off and they don't we could win.'

Sear's biggest problem is in midfield, where United could have the edge. He will experiment on Sunday in a specially arranged match against the Cheshire Association of Boys Clubs at Handbridge but is unlikely to make his final decision until the day before the game.

Even striker Ian Rush is not yet a certainty to play. With Chester due to play at Southend next Friday in a Third Division fixture, Alan Oakes had a doubt about the wisdom of risking Rush in the youth game but chances are he will be asked to play two matches in 48 hours.

Sear added, 'I would be happier if I could play the team we had available last year but some of these players are now over age. We will have to work hard to make up for our lack of experience.'

With the minor irritation of a postponement sandwiched between Sear's assessment of Chester's prospects and the game actually taking place, the few hundred throng present at Sealand Road were treated to a festival of goals, with the contest tentatively hinged at 3-3 midway through the second period. Two of those Seals' goals came from a talented Deeside teenager who had risen from his sick bed to play and would soon make a name for himself as one of the greatest soccer marksmen of all time.

The Chester Chronicle delivered the following commentary on what turned out to be a keen tussle:

Ian Rush shook off 'flu symptoms to go within inches of scoring an F.A. Youth Cup hat-trick against Manchester United on Monday night.

Rush defied the 'flu bug which struck down manager Alan Oakes a fortnight ago and ploughed through the Sealand Road mud to lead City in a stirring fight-back which scared the life out of mighty United.

Oakes paid tribute to his new goalscoring discovery after a match played for much of the time in torrential rain: 'Ian wasn't feeling well, but he did his stuff. He was very unlucky not to hit a hat-trick.'

Oakes' assistant Cliff Sear, who looks after the youth team, added, 'I was delighted with the team. I did not think they would come back after trailing 3-1 but they did and they were desperately unlucky not to score two or three more goals. I think it was United's greater strength which took them through.'

It looked all over for Chester at half-time as United enjoyed a 3-1 lead. David Wynn had scored off the post in the eighth minute to put the visitors in front and Chris Lynam added a second in the 27th minute when goalkeeper Mike Keen had done well to block his first attempt.

When Kevin Jones was pulled down in the 32nd minute, Rush stepped up to score from the penalty spot but United hit back in the 38th minute with a David Jeffrey header.

City had been unlucky when Colin Jones put an overhead kick onto the bar and Rush had a shot kicked off the line after rounding goalkeeper Stephen Pears.

Chester's fighting spirit showed through when Rush scrambled the ball home following a 56th minute corner and moments later he almost completed a hat-trick with a header after Terry Cooke had hit the woodwork.

But Cooke scored the goal of the match in the 67th minute with a spectacular 30-yarder only for Wynn to hit back two minutes later for United.

The clinging pitch was sapping Chester's strength and Lynam ran on strongly through a tired defence in the 75th minute to make sure a relieved United went through.

Chester were still battling at the end and another Rush shot was deflected over the bar when his hat-trick looked certain.

A rare sight at The Stadium (above) as heavy overnight rain left Chester F.C.'s pitch waterlogged on Wednesday, causing the F.A. Youth Cup tie against Manchester United to be postponed until next Monday.

1979-80

1) Paul Garner
2) Phil Ratcliffe
3) Steve McMahon
4) Derek Goulding
5) Mike Imlach
6) Kevin Richardson
7) Phil Gardner
8) David Barton
9) Mark Ward
10) Dean Kelly
11) Gary Stevens
12) Steve Fazakerley (for 9)

1) Stephen Pears
2) Shaun Lowther
3) Nigel Keen
4) Alan Davies
5) Chris Roberts
6) Garry Worrall
7) Danny Keough
8) Scott McGarvey
9) Andy Wray
10) Chris Lynam
11) Andy Reynolds
12) David Wynn

EVERTON 0 v 1 MANCHESTER UNITED

Wray

JANUARY 1980

Tuesday 8th

Kick-off 7.00 p.m.

Attendance 1,720

Sting Wray ko's Blues

Alan Stevenson and David Jeffrey, the latter through injury, were left out for the away test at Everton that followed the Reds' victory over Chester. Andy Reynolds, who replaced David Wynn late on in the tie at Sealand Road, was thrust into the starting eleven with Andy Wray and Shaun Lowther also included.

The Goodison Park outfit found themselves in a position which every club that has ever enjoyed any Youth Cup success must go through sooner or later, a time of rebuilding. The Toffees had gone as far as reaching the semi-final of the tournament in 1979 but were left almost threadbare in terms of experience for the current season. From that excellent run to the last four stage only Steve McMahon and Phil Garner were still available to play against United, although the Mersey Blues were buoyed by a confidence boosting win over near neighbours in their last Youth Cup tie.

With the Liverpool Echo even noting that the visitors *'looked the better all-round team'*, the issue was decided in the 65th minute by someone who had once taken trials at Goodison Park.

The goal developed when United's enterprising left-back Nigel Keen delivered the ball to Andy Reynolds in a dangerous and advanced position and from there the Welsh winger put over a tantalising cross, which was volleyed into the back of Everton's net by midfielder Wray.

Goalkeeper Paul Garner was the home team's stand-out performer in the first period. As early as the fourth minute he found himself called upon to make a brave low stop as Reynolds bore down on him and was then quickly back on his feet to parry Chris Lynam's follow-up attempt. Scott McGarvey proved a particular problem to the Blues, shooting over when well positioned on two occasions, and he felt further despair when Garner made a fine diving save from his drive just before the break.

The Manchester Evening News made a note that *'United were helped generally by erratic passing and unforced errors by Everton, who did not look the team which knocked Liverpool out of the competition in the previous round'*.

Toffees' striker Mark Ward was substituted at the break because of a knock, an occurence which caused the team to be subjected to a minor shuffle as Steve McMahon was pushed into midfield from the back four and Phil Gardner stepped up to the attack. The reorganisation inspired their best spell of the match, with McMahon soon finding Kevin Richardson with a beautifully weighted pass from which he forced a courageous save out of Stephen Pears.

The Blues' massive centre-half Derek Goulding then saw his powerful header stopped by United's 'keeper and McMahon got in on the act once again when hitting a nicely struck shot which missed its intended target by not much more than the width of a cigarette packet.

The Reds' goal arrived just after Everton's sustained period of pressure had finally relented and there was then a little relief for Syd Owen's lads before the Merseysiders again picked up the pace as the final whistle approached. The coach was relieved that the home team were wasteful during that period, and it was something the Liverpool Echo scribe felt compelled to end his report on:

The Blues youngsters tried hard to save the game in a spirited finale, but they spoiled a number of promising moves by blazing away from outside the penalty area.

Everton's Gary Stevens beats a challenge from Manchester United defender Lowther to get in a header during last night's Youth Cup game at Goodison.

third round

263

1979-80

1) Stephen Pears
2) Nigel Keen
3) David Jeffrey
4) Alan Davies
5) Shaun Lowther
6) David Wynn
7) Danny Keough
8) Scott McGarvey
9) Andy Wray
10) Chris Lynam
11) Garry Worrall
12) *Andy Reynolds (for 6)*

1) Chris Broadhurst
2) Martin Dale
3) Gary Pearce
4) Steve Bould
5) David McAughtrie
6) Steve Austin
7) Roy Mitchell
8) Paul Bracewell
9) Neil Proctor
10) Simon Bullock
11) Andy Shankland
12) *Martin Hanchard*

JANUARY 1980

MANCHESTER UNITED 2 v 1 STOKE CITY

Reynolds, Worrall — Bullock

Tuesday 29th
Kick-off 7.30 p.m.
Attendance 2,295

fourth round

Andy rescues United

The return to full fitness of David Jeffrey instigated yet another shake-up of United's 4-3-3 formation for the visit of Stoke City's under-18's as David Wynn, an unused substitute at Goodison Park, came back into the reckoning while Andy Reynolds revisited his place on the bench.

The Potters' new youth coach Graham Hawkins, who took part in a Youth Cup tie against United for Wolverhampton Wanderers way back in March 1964, was without a couple of regular defenders and because of Stoke's injury situation, he was forced into travelling to Manchester with four schoolboys in tow. As a result, lanky midfielder Steve Bould found himself switched into a defensive role while one of those still in full-time education, Liverpudlian Roy Mitchell, was given his maiden outing for the club in the middle of the park.

Despite their apparent problems, City sorely tested the Reds until the very dying moments of the contest, causing the (Stoke-on-Trent) Evening Sentinel to offer the following observations:

Livewire substitute Andy Reynolds ended Stoke City's gallant F.A. Youth Cup run with a last-gasp shot in the fourth minute of injury-time at Old Trafford last night.

Stoke's spirited teamwork appeared to have earned a Fourth Round replay as they held out confidently. Then what appeared to be a clear handling offence by a United player was ignored by referee Hough.

The ball was whipped out to the left, where Reynolds, whose inclusion from the 55th minute had pepped up United, streaked inside and delivered a cracking drive that hit the inside of the far post and rebounded home. It was almost the last kick of the game.

Stoke, forced to play three schoolboys in midfield, deserved a better fate. They took a grip on the game in the first half, never allowing United to settle, then led with a fine 37th minute goal from Bullock.

Bullock's fine control enabled him to carry on a neat one-two move with talented skipper Bracewell before coolly slotting the ball home to give Stoke an interval lead.

Stoke's reshuffled defence, following cartilage operations for Eccleston and Windsor, kept a tight hold on United's strikers.

Bullock might have added a second, but shot too hurriedly after being put through by Proctor.

The arrival of Reynolds gave United an extra attacking spark and he quickly had a shot superbly tipped round by Broadhurst, who has matured during the competition.

Stoke were forced gradually deeper into defence and a blistering shot from Worrall was deflected into the net for the equaliser after 65 minutes.

Bracewell's thrust put Stoke back in the driving seat, with Mitchell showing some neat touches on his first full appearance and McAughtrie calm and unruffled in defence.

Over-forceful challenges earned bookings for Reynolds and Proctor near the end, when Stoke hit back strongly.

Pears managed to tip out a cross from Shankland, was hurt in the attempt, and the extra time added on during his treatment was enough for United to storm to their dramatic winner.

It was rough justice in view of Stoke's spirited efforts, which deserved a better fate, but several members of the squad have at least shaped their careers promisingly during this five-match run.

David Meek countered with numerous views of his own:

Welsh winger Andy Reynolds finished a day of mixed fortunes as a winner for Manchester United's youth team against Stoke City at Old Trafford.

Early on, Reynolds got the boost of his first international call-up for the Welsh Youth squad preparing to play Northern Ireland in the European Championships next month.

Then a few hours later United dropped him from their side playing in the Fourth Round of the F.A. Youth Cup last night.

But the night finished happily for the lad from South Wales after he went on as second half substitute to give the Reds a 2-1 victory in the nick of time.

Reynolds, who lost his place despite helping to win at Everton in the last round, rescued the Reds in the last few seconds just when it looked as if they were going to pay the penalty for a nervous, inaccurate first half.

United had early chances and could easily have been awarded a penalty when Andy Wray was pulled down after cutting into the penalty area following a pass from Danny Keough.

Wray also missed a good chance when he headed wide from Scott McGarvey's cross. But it was Stoke, who came to Old Trafford after knocking out league clubs Blackburn and Leicester in the earlier rounds, who showed the way to go.

They were big and strong upfront and Simon Bullock, the latest from that well-known footballing family, slid Stoke into the lead in the 37th minute after a neat exchange of passes with Paul Bracewell.

It took United a long time to settle, despite stepping up the pressure after falling behind. Garry Worrall settled them down with a deserved equaliser and, as Stoke tired on the heavy ground, substitute Reynolds snatched the late winner to put United into the Fifth Round.

Following a cracking left-footed effort which was diverted before registering as a goal, Garry Worrall receives the congratulations of his team-mates

264

1979-80

1) Stephen Pears
2) Chris Roberts
3) David Jeffrey
4) Nigel Keen
5) David Wynn
6) Garry Worrall
7) Danny Keough
8) Scott McGarvey
9) Andy Wray
10) Chris Lynam
11) Andy Reynolds
12) Kel McDermott

1) Tony Parks
2) Terry Emms
3) Kevin Dickenson
4) John Cooper
5) Pat Corbett
6) Mark Bowen
7) Chris Harvey
8) Ian Crook
9) Terry Gibson
10) Jimmy Bolton
11) Alex Hamill
12) Steven Cox (for 6)

MANCHESTER UNITED 1 v 0 TOTTENHAM HOTSPUR

Reynolds

MARCH 1980

Wednesday 5th

Kick-off 7.30 p.m.

Attendance 3,387

The rarefied air of the quarter-final was an experience United hadn't been exposed to for four years and the splendid progress made over the present campaign certainly reflected well on the current crop of talent. A home engagement with Spurs, twice winners of the Youth Cup in the 1970's and a club well versed in producing first-team material from their junior ranks, was envisaged to be a severe test of the Reds' mettle.

That was precisely the way it proved to be, with the biggest surprise, bearing in mind the seniors' current position of second place in the First Division table, being the rather poor attendance. Those who took the trouble to make their way down Warwick Road were witness to the best performance, and yet another narrow winning margin, from United's youngsters.

Their considerable efforts caused the Review to report on the clash in the following way:

United overcame Tottenham Hotspur in front of a 3,387 crowd at Old Trafford to clinch their inclusion in the last four.

It was a fine victory which was achieved with some of the most skilful and attractive football to be played by a United Youth side for many years.

Led by an almost faultless display from skipper Nigel Keen, they were in command from the off and within seconds Andy Reynolds had put the Spurs goal under fire.

In the ninth minute Chris Lynam, who had a sparkling match, was unlucky not to get the Reds off the mark when his shot from close in was held by Tony Parks, the Spurs goalkeeper. Reynolds, the hero of the previous round, again used his orthodox wing play to good effect as time and again he put the Spurs defence under pressure with a selection of well measured crosses. David Jeffrey, Keen's partner at the centre of the defence, joined the attack frequently as the Reds searched for the vital opening.

Spurs included in their line-up the pint-sized striker Terry Gibson, who played in both of the senior F.A. Cup ties between the clubs in January and it was he and centre-half Patrick Corbett who were the pick of the visitors. Corbett, apart from being a sturdy defender, was a danger from set pieces and he shocked the Reds when he rattled their crossbar with a header as Spurs enjoyed their best period of the match just before the interval.

Following the break United continued to dictate the play with Garry Worrall firing a couple of shots over the bar and then, in the 53rd minute, United went in front and it was Worrall who set the move up. He won the ball some ten yards inside his own half and wasted no time in slipping it to Scott McGarvey. The young Glaswegian then picked out Chris Lynam with a pin-point pass and Lynam set off on a run that saw him sweep past Spurs full-back Kevin Dickenson. Then, just before he reached the dead-ball line, he clipped over a low cross and Andy Reynolds was there to push it past Parks.

Soon afterwards, Spurs' Jimmy Bolton followed his team-mate Corbett – earlier cautioned for a foul on McGarvey – into the referee's book after a heavy tackle on Danny Keough.

In the dying minutes, Bolton was foiled from levelling the scores when Stephen Pears dived to save his shot from point-blank range. That was the nearest, together with that header that struck the bar, that Spurs had gone to scoring all evening but it came too late to inspire them to greater deeds and when the referee sounded the final whistle, it signalled United's arrival at the semi-final stage for the first time since 1970.

The Manchester Evening News reckoned Reynolds was *'a man in a scoring hurry ever since he was dropped from the youth team'* and that his *'crashing shot into the roof of the net'* represented a *'thank you'* for his recall to the side. The report ended with a comment about the victory being *'sweet revenge for the club after being knocked out by Spurs in the senior F.A. Cup Third Round'* earlier in the season.

fifth round

Numerous of the club's younger element are seen at The Cliff with Syd Owen (back row, far right)
Back row (l-r) David Wynn, Garry Worrall, Alan Davies, David Jeffrey, Stephen Pears, Scott McGarvey, Shaun Lowther, Andy Reynolds
Front row (l-r) Chris Lynam, Alan Stevenson, Andy Wray, Nigel Keen, Chris Roberts, Danny Keough, Kel McDermott, Gareth Orritt

1979-80

Manchester United
1) Stephen Pears
2) David Wynn
3) David Jeffrey
4) Nigel Keen
5) Chris Roberts
6) Garry Worrall
7) Danny Keough
8) Scott McGarvey
9) Alan Davies
10) Chris Lynam
11) Andy Reynolds
12) Kel McDermott

Manchester City
1) Alex Williams
2) Gary Fitzgerald
3) Richard Cunningham
4) Steve Mackenzie
5) Gary Bennett
6) Ross McGinn
7) Andy May
8) Keith Parkinson
9) Gareth Bees
10) Steve Kinsey
11) Clive Wilson
12) Ged Elliott (for 2)

MARCH 1980

MANCHESTER UNITED 0 v 0 MANCHESTER CITY

Monday 31st
Kick-off 7.30 p.m.
Attendance 5,119

semi-final 1st leg

A super show by Babes

The Reds' achievement in edging Tottenham out of the tournament provided a great fillip for Manchester football fans as the penultimate stage brought United and City together for a re-run of the 1964 semi-final.

The sorry story from the Old Trafford perspective was that from the late 1970's and throughout much of the 1980's, City overtook the Reds as far as the recruitment and development of youth footballers was concerned.

Their appearance in the Youth Cup final only twelve months before was testament to the belief that they were heading along the right lines and the Light Blues were even in the enviable position of being able to leave out their centre-half Tommy Caton, whose main responsibilities lay in assisting with their First Division efforts.

Maine Road youth coach Steve Fleet, who was on the receiving end when the Reds nabbed a 2-1 win over City in the same competition in November 1954, shared his views on Caton's absence with the Manchester Evening News when saying, 'The first-team take priority, and so we will be without Tommy, but we shall be all right. Actually, he has played only one game for us in this season's competition, when we went to Sheffield Wednesday. He also played for us in the Lancashire Youth Cup when we knocked out United.

We have a well-balanced team which is probably better than the side that reached the final last season. We are hoping for a good game of football tonight.

At youth level I don't think the two-leg set-up will make much difference, like a European tie in senior football. What it does, basically, is to ensure that the better team comes out on top.'

Fleet's opposite number, Syd Owen, shouldered some concerns relating to injuries to a couple of his key players and caused him to put Kel McDermott and Gareth Orritt on standby while waiting to finalise his line-up. Goalkeeper Stephen Pears had featured for the Reserves two days earlier, seemingly without aggravating an ankle injury, but skipper Nigel Keen was a different proposition entirely. Keen had gone over on his ankle in an 'A' team fixture against Port Vale Reserves, was consequently taken off and then spent the whole of the second half with his foot in a bucket of ice cold water. However, his temporary discomfort paid dividends when Owen was able to name him in a full-strength United side that saw Alan Davies returning at the expense of Andy Wray.

A barren opening leg in terms of the scoreline was later covered by both the United Review and Manchester City's match magazine:

United Review: United's youth team make the short journey across town to Maine Road on Monday night for the F.A. Youth Cup semi-final second leg match against Manchester City with the knowledge that they have to improve on their last visit to 'enemy territory' if they are to reach the F.A. Youth Cup final.

Back in November, United were the Blues' guests in the Second Round of the Lancashire Youth Cup. The Reds appeared to have done enough to earn a replay with the score standing at 2-2 and the seconds ticking away, but Blues' winger Andy May changed all that with a last ditch effort to take his side through to what was eventual success in the competition when City lifted the trophy a few weeks ago.

So the Reds know the size of the task that awaits them after failing to gain any advantage from the home leg of the semi-final a fortnight ago.

Not that they played badly. On the contrary, it was another exciting display, particularly in the opening 25 minutes and a similar period towards the end.

The game was only seconds old when Chris Lynam set off on a run that was halted as he was about to shoot and then after three minutes the Reds went within an ace of taking the lead when Garry Worrall's shot hit the post after Danny Keough had opened up the Blues' defence. City had to reshuffle their ranks in the eighth minute when full-back Gary Fitzgerald was injured and had to leave the field. He took no further part in the game and his place was taken by substitute Ged Elliott.

Lynam had the crowd cheering in the 21st minute when he tried to switch play with an acrobatic scissors-kick and then four minutes later City had their first serious raid on the United goal. Keith Parkinson and Steve Kinsey both had shots blocked and on the half-hour Steve Mackenzie, easily City's outstanding outfield player on the night, had two 'certs' saved brilliantly by United 'keeper Stephen Pears. It was a great night for goalkeepers with Pears' opposite number, Alex Williams, also pulling off a string of vital saves.

Scott McGarvey and Alan Davies both tested the City 'keeper but it was the Blues who had the best scoring opportunity of the second half. That came in the 53rd minute when Gareth Bees, City's top scorer in the Youth Cup, headed against the bar from a Ross McGinn corner.

Andy Reynolds, whose goals pulled United through the earlier rounds with Stoke City and Tottenham Hotspur, did his best to lift the Reds again as the action intensified in the last quarter of the match. Mackenzie hit a shot that almost took a coat of paint off Pears' left-hand post and United's two Davids, Wynn and Jeffrey, both joined in the activity in the Blues' penalty area as United attempted to break the deadlock.

City will have, understandably, claimed the draw as a morale boosting victory but that will count for nothing at Maine Road where coach Syd Owen will look to his boys to produce the form that can put United into the F.A. Youth Cup final for the seventh time.

So if you have a spare evening next Monday, make your way down to Maine Road and give the youngsters the support that means so much.

Manchester City Magazine: In an entertaining, all-out attacking encounter, the game's top honours were shared by both goalkeepers. It could have ended with a torrent of goals had it not been for the agility and heroics of Alex Williams and his United counterpart, Stephen Pears. The 5,119 crowd really showed their appreciation of the standards.

The only time either was beaten, the woodwork came to their assistance. Garry Worrall rattled the City upright in the third minute with a rasping shot and a Gareth Bees header hit the United crossbar in the 54th minute.

In between, Steve Mackenzie was thwarted on three occasions by superb saves from Pears and Ross McGinn and Ged Elliott suffered a similar fate in a hectic first half.

It wasn't all City by any means. Not to be outdone, Williams made magnificent saves from Chris Lynam, Scott McGarvey and Andy Reynolds to keep the rampant Reds at bay.

City grabbed the initiative after a worrying opening 25 minutes and created far more openings as the game progressed.

The Blues were unlucky to lose Gary Fitzgerald after only three minutes with a damaged knee but Elliott filled in with credit.

Now City are firmly in the driving seat for the second leg at Maine Road. If the 'keepers carry on where they left off it could provide a marathon.

A few of David Meek's remarks summarised the 'feel good' factor generated by the game 24 hours later:

After the derby of despair came a derby of delight. The youngsters of Manchester United and Manchester City showed their seniors a much more pleasurable face of soccer in the first leg of their F.A. Youth Cup semi-final at Old Trafford last night.

The First Division derby of ten days ago was a tense, tortuous tussle, but the unspoiled Babes created a classic of expressive, entertaining football.

Now the stage is set for a cracking return.

The game was watched by 5,119 and I am sure all of them would vote it one of the best games of football they have seen for a long time.

> *"This clearly was the biggest game any of us had played in. We were confident of getting a good result going into the game despite the fact that City fielded a strong team. The first leg was tight, competitive, with no goals to show for what was a good display by the boys."*
>
> **NIGEL KEEN**

1979-80

semi-final 2nd leg

1) Alex Williams	9) Gareth Bees	1) Stephen Pears	9) Alan Davies
2) Andy May	10) Steve Kinsey	2) David Wynn	10) Chris Lynam
3) Richard Cunningham	11) Clive Wilson	3) David Jeffrey	11) Andy Reynolds
4) Gary Bennett	*12) Ged Elliott*	4) Nigel Keen	*12) Gareth Orritt (for 7)*
5) Tommy Caton		5) Chris Roberts	
6) Ross McGinn		6) Garry Worrall	
7) Keith Parkinson		7) Andy Wray	
8) Steve Mackenzie		8) Scott McGarvey	

MANCHESTER CITY 3 (3) v (1) 1 MANCHESTER UNITED

Kinsey, Mackenzie, Wilson — *Worrall*

APRIL 1980

Monday 14th

Kick-off 7.30 p.m.

Attendance 8,503

> *We have played City four times this season so far and honours are absolutely even. We have won one, City have won one and there have been two goalless draws.*
>
> *The first leg at Old Trafford was goalless and neither side scored when we met City later in the week. But they weren't dour, defensive games. It was open football, real end-to-end stuff and I think we shall see another entertaining game tonight.*

SYD OWEN

Two weeks later, United were welcomed to Maine Road for the concluding semi-final tie and the Manchester Evening News reported on the home team's election to use what was commonly viewed as their trump card:

Manchester City will have first-team starlet Tommy Caton in their team against Manchester United for tonight's second leg in the F.A Youth Cup semi-final.

The Blues pull seventeen year-old Caton out of their senior squad to help their youngsters in a match finely poised after a goalless draw in the first leg at Old Trafford.

Caton takes over at centre-half in a defence that will be missing Gary Fitzgerald at right-back. Fitzgerald damaged a knee in the first leg and has since had a cartilage operation.

United will be without Danny Keough who has torn ankle ligaments that could keep him out for two or three weeks. Kel McDermott will take his midfield place.

But coach Syd Owen cannot finalise his team until tests later on Chris Roberts, who has a knee injury, and Andy Reynolds, who was also hurt on Saturday in a tough test against Bradford City Reserves.

Andy Wray and Gareth Orritt stand by in the squad.

Says Owen, 'City will be stronger tonight with Tommy Caton who has a lot of league experience now in their defence. But we shall do our best and I am sure there won't be much in it.'

When the 90 minutes were up, City had finally broken free of the Youth Cup arm-lock that United had held them in for over 26 years.

With goals from three boys who would all go on to make their mark at senior level for the Maine Road outfit, the majority of the crowd were in raptures at the outcome.

The Manchester City match magazine summed up the Maine Road view:

City's skilful and exciting youngsters reached the F.A. Youth Cup final for the second successive year with a 3-1 aggregate win over a talented Manchester United team in a cracking second leg game at Maine Road that contained all the goals of the semi-final tie last Monday night. And it was the first time a City youth team had beaten United in the F.A Youth Cup in seven previous meetings – well worth the wait.

While 5,119 fans had thrilled to the goalless first meeting at Old Trafford on Monday, March 31st, a turn-out of 8,503 were treated to another exhibition of exhilarating youth soccer that contained commitment, artistry in abundance, goalmouth excitement as well as a fair share of mistakes.

The prize for the young City slickers is a two-legged final meeting with Aston Villa, who were the conquerors of Millwall, the cup holders, in the other semi-final. Millwall, you may remember, pipped City in last year's final.

There was so much that was splendid in the game that it would be difficult to catalogue the incidents. Inspired throughout by a controlled midfield performance by Steve Mackenzie, bolstered at the back by the first-team experience of Tommy Caton and the cool eye-catching defensive work of Gary Bennett, the Blues set the early pace.

The breakthrough came in the 18th minute when Steve Kinsey, who frequently flashed into the game with brilliance allied to pace, made a spurt through United's ranks on the right wing. His darting runs prized open the Reds and he got a kind run of the ball when his shot was blocked but bounced back into his path. The quick-witted youngster veered across the United penalty area and prodded a chance into the path of Clive Wilson, who had taken advantage of the disarrayed visitors' defence by working himself free.

Wilson, almost mid-goal and fifteen yards out, curved a low shot just inside the post past the outstretched arms of 'keeper Pears reaching to his left.

United were always active on the break and kept the game open and flowing, though they had no answer to City's second goal, a stunning shot from Mackenzie which zipped high into the net from the edge of the area.

The build-up skill was rapier-like and remarkable. Keith Parkinson crisply turned the ball into Gareth Bees, who cutely back-heeled at height a short pass to Mackenzie. And his first-time volley was unstoppable. That was almost on the stroke of half-time.

But United were never out of contention. Relying on the efforts of midfielder Worrall, they smashed open City's hold on the tie in the 68th minute. It was Worrall who floated an accurate shot from way out on the left which swept over the defence and 'keeper Alex Williams into the far corner of the net.

Now United had the bit between their teeth and their reorganisation due to a substitution created City more problems. The danger man was Wynn, who had looked a very accomplished full-back before his switch to an adventurous role in which he was even more effective.

For a spell it was City relying on the breaks and the crowd lost count of the thrills. They obviously admired much about City's work, the industry of Ross McGinn, a fierce competitor in midfield, and the promise of Richard Cunningham supporting the excellence of Mackenzie.

Fittingly, it was Mackenzie who squashed United's fervour later in the half. He bored through the visitors' defence and provided the clever whippet Kinsey with a scoring opportunity he smartly snapped up.

In this mood, with this commitment and show of skill, City will take some stopping in the two-legged final that is due to start with the first leg at Maine Road. A game that will be well worth the trouble of attending.

Peter Gardner, the Manchester Evening News' City correspondent, also had a say:

Manchester City are in the F.A. Youth Cup final for the second successive year.....and in their current mood they will clinch soccer's most prestigious junior trophy for the first time in history.

Even having to play the first leg at home to Aston Villa does not daunt the boy Blues, who maintained as one man after last night's semi-final victory over Manchester United: 'This is our year'.

No matter what problems Malcolm Allison may have at First Division level, youth coach Steve Fleet and his assistants have done a magnificent job with a bunch of kids who play the game as it should be played – simply, intelligently and, above all, entertainingly.

No-one in the magnificent 8,500 Maine Road crowd can have left displeased after a scintillating performance by two fine sides of whom the whole of Manchester can feel proud.

The future of both clubs is indeed in good hands if this is the standard we are soon to see at top level.

The Blues romped to a convincing 3-1 victory following the equally impressive goalless first leg at Old Trafford. But full marks must also go to United for making it a titanic struggle before bowing to their more convincing and impressive neighbours.

Said Fleet, 'These boys did the club proud. Now I am just hoping we can finish off the job by beating Villa. It won't be easy. They must be a good side if they can beat Millwall, who pipped us in last season's final. However, all we need is that bit of luck and we'll have the trophy at Maine Road for the first time.'

There was no doubting that City were the better side over last night's 90 minutes. The only time the Blues looked in any difficulty was when the commanding Garry Worrall pulled a clever goal back for United in the 68th minute.

But the Reds' rally was quickly snuffed out as the clever Steve Kinsey restored City's two-goal advantage following a great run by Steve Mackenzie.

It was the City skipper who had really set the game alight seconds before half-time when he clipped in a glorious goal, the likes of which has rarely been seen since the Summerbee-Lee-Bell-Young era.

Tommy Caton and the impressive Gary Bennett were City's heroes at the back, while Ross McGinn was a midfield motivator.

Apart from Worrall, Nigel Keen, Scott McGarvey and Alan Davies did well for United, but on this occasion it was City who stole the glory.

Sadly for the Maine Road teenagers, their Youth Cup hopes were blanked for the second time in a row when they were defeated at the final stage by the Villa, on aggregate, by three goals to two.

267

1980-81

1) Dave Redfern	9) John Pearson	1) John Armfield	9) Mark Hughes
2) Gavin Oliver	10) Seamus Ferguson	2) Gareth Orritt	10) Scott McGarvey
3) David Mossman	11) Tony Simmons	3) David Jeffrey	11) Andy Reynolds
4) Richard Beaumont	*12) Chris Riley (for 10)*	4) Graeme Hogg	*12) Kel McDermott (for 11)*
5) Trevor Matthewson		5) Sean Williams	
6) Paul Shirtliff		6) David Wynn	
7) Simon Mills		7) Alan Stevenson	
8) Mick Bentley		8) Danny Keough	

DECEMBER 1980

SHEFFIELD WEDNESDAY 1 v 2 MANCHESTER UNITED
Simmons — Hughes, McDermott

second round

Tuesday 2nd
Kick-off 7.00 p.m.
Attendance 724

Wednesday striker John Pearson shoots past Manchester United defender Jeffrey in last night's FA Youth Cup match at Hillsborough.

With the disappointment of failing at the penultimate stage of last season's competition slowly fading into the distance, there came a dawning realisation that coach Syd Owen had quite an experienced squad at his disposal as Danny Keough, Gareth Orritt, Andy Reynolds, David Jeffrey, Scott McGarvey, David Wynn and Alan Stevenson were all still available for the new campaign.

The main hope in United's camp centred around McGarvey's ability to continue for the youth team what was proving to be a solid sequence of scoring for the Reserves. His Central League goal record for the season stood at eight from fifteen appearances, a total which was boosted by five from his last six outings at that level.

Into the starting eleven for the opening task, a visit to the palatial home of Sheffield Wednesday, came a couple of faces that would soon become familiar to the Old Trafford faithful, a Scot by the name of Graeme Hogg and a fiery Welsh lad from Ruabon called Mark Hughes. Keeping goal for United was one John Armfield, a young man from Blackpool with more than a little football tradition running in his family.

Tasked with helping out at the back was another from Wales, Sean Williams, whose experience with the 'A' and 'B' teams was almost equal and extended to him donning the number two and five shirts for both sides.

The trip over the Pennines certainly wouldn't have been viewed as a jaunt by either United's management or playing staff and the hot pre-match news, as told by Ian Vickers of the Sheffield Star, was that the Wednesday side was to be bolstered by a couple of ringers:

Scoring sensation John Pearson spearheads Sheffield Wednesday's Youth Cup challenge against Manchester United at Hillsborough tonight. Pearson goes into the game with a first-team pedigree which must be unmatched by any other player in the competition. This season he made his debut in the Second Division and his four full games netted him four goals.

It doesn't necessarily follow that Pearson will automatically shine in tonight's setting but his presence and brief first-team experience should provide the team with added confidence. Wednesday's squad also includes another player with first-team experience, Gavin Oliver, who has made three appearances when coming on as sub this season.

It's a Second Round match tonight – Wednesday had a bye in the First Round – and last season's results of the two sides makes interesting comparison. Manchester City ended Wednesday's interest, in the quarter-final, and they then defeated United in the semi before losing to Aston Villa.

The present Wednesday side contains players, including Pearson and Oliver, who helped the club do so well last time out, and manager Jack Charlton said this afternoon, 'I think our side are quite capable of taking anybody on.'

One problem, he says, is the number of young players at the club, compared with the likes of Manchester United, but he adds, 'I think it will be a terrific game and hope the public come along – they are well worth watching.'

During a tie in which United looked positively anaemic throughout most of the first period against a generally taller and much more physical side, everything came up smelling of roses for Owen's boys when a substitute who only joined the action eleven minutes from time pencilled in some late drama near to the end of the story.

A Sheffield Star scribe divulged the match's main incidents:

A goal by Manchester United substitute McDermott a minute into injury-time knocked Sheffield Wednesday, quarter-finalists in last season's competition, out of the F.A. Youth Cup. Bitter disappointment was mirrored in the faces of the Wednesday players as they left the field, and it could be said that the better team on the night fell victim to individual skills.

After an opening burst by United which included a fine save by Redfern, Wednesday took a solid grip on the match. Young Paul Shirtliff rallied his midfield, while upfront Mossman and Pearson combined well. By the time Simmons headed in the opening goal after good work and a cross by Mossman on the half hour, the home side had already seen two good chances go wide.

United had only one chance before half-time, while Wednesday pressed forward and set up a string of opportunities, the most obvious just on half-time when Oliver was presented with the ball in the six-yard box, only for Armfield to scramble down and collect the ball. However, with 58 minutes gone defender Orritt, who shrugged off a knee injury suffered in the first half, came through on a fine run and Wednesday failed to snuff out the danger. Redfern blocked Orritt's shot but Hughes was on hand to level the score.

United's confidence grew as the match wore on and with over 90 minutes gone, Wednesday again made the mistake of allowing a man to run through unchallenged when Stevenson set up the goal for McDermott.

The Hillsborough decider certainly couldn't have come at a better time as, after Stevenson's oblique shot was palmed away by the Wednesday 'keeper, McDermott reacted quickest and rammed home the winner. To Syd Owen's great relief, there was only enough time left for the ball to be 'spotted' before the referee called a halt to the evening's entertainment.

268

1) Simon Farnworth	9) Kevin Gratton	1) Richard Howe	9) Mark Hughes
2) Chris Conway	10) Mike Bennett	2) Gareth Orritt	10) Scott McGarvey
3) David Fitzharris	11) George Mulligan	3) David Jeffrey	11) Andy Reynolds
4) Barry Atherton	*12) Simon Rudge (for 11)*	4) Graeme Hogg	*12) Kel McDermott*
5) Neil Berry		5) Sean Williams	
6) David Kay		6) David Wynn	
7) Barry Taylor		7) Alan Stevenson	
8) Wayne Foster		8) Danny Keough	

BOLTON WANDERERS 2 v 4 MANCHESTER UNITED

Foster, Taylor Hughes (3), Reynolds

1980-81

DECEMBER 1980

Tuesday 30th

Kick-off 7.00 p.m.

Hughes young Reds' hero

With the New Year looming large on the horizon, the next task for the young Reds was to be pitted up against Bolton Wanderers and the only team change at Burnden Park came with former Sheffield and England Boys' goalkeeper Richard Howe claiming the green jersey worn just the once by an unavailable John Armfield.

The home eleven included the promising Mike Bennett, who had occupied a first-team place just days before. Bennett also held the responsibility of captaining the under-18 Wanderers' eleven and he and his team-mates approached the clash with United in a confident mood because they were already assured of a place in the Lancashire Youth Cup semi-final.

Similarly to the earlier match at Hillsborough, it was the home eleven who enjoyed the better of the exchanges during the opening period and the Reds were thankful to centre-backs Hogg and Jeffrey that Bolton weren't already home and dry by the break. With the clock just about to tick off a full 45 minutes, and the United lads prematurely assuming they had escaped the punishment which was probably due to them, the Trotters' Wayne Foster headed his side into the lead. Coming as it did so near to the interval, the goal could have been viewed as a tough break for the Reds, though many would say it more fairly represented some justice for Bolton's energetic performance up to that point.

Whatever words of wisdom were imparted on the United lads by Syd Owen during their breather, which might just have included a reminder that manager Dave Sexton was watching from the stands, they most definitely did the trick, for within just five minutes of the restart his charges were back on level terms.

An ill-judged back pass by Trotters' winger George Mulligan started the rot from Bolton's perspective, and when the loose ball was slotted home by Andy Reynolds, all of a sudden the visitors looked a totally revitalised proposition. The main difference between United's performance in the second period to that of the first was due to them pressurising the previously reliable Bolton defence into a series of damaging errors.

Bang on the hour, Mark Hughes started a personal goal spree when he was conveniently placed to fire home from ten yards following a goalmouth scramble. Just four minutes later he extended his tally still further when banging in a simple chance which was the culmination of a brilliant move down United's left and Reynolds' pinpoint delivery into Bolton's penalty box.

In the 79th minute, Hughes wrapped up his hat-trick with a headed goal when Reynolds supplied him with another superb cross.

The Wanderers' fire hadn't been completely extinguished and with seven minutes of normal time remaining, Barry Taylor floated home a measured free kick to make the final score 4-2 in United's favour.

There was a post-match view from Syd Owen about wins seldom coming easy at Burnden Park, and the only sour note of an otherwise excellent exercise for the Reds was the late dismissal of David Wynn.

Mark Hughes scores his second goal to put United 3-1 up and edge them closer to securing a fine win over Bolton Wanderers

third round

1980-81

1) Ian Pass	9) Mark Shackleton	1) Richard Howe	9) Mark Hughes
2) Colin Murphy	10) Paul Halford	2) Gareth Orritt	10) Scott McGarvey
3) Graham Harbey	11) Aidan Gibson	3) David Jeffrey	11) Andy Reynolds
4) Tony Reid	*12) Colin Doyle*	4) Graeme Hogg	*12) Kel McDermott*
5) Paul Blades		5) Sean Williams	
6) Ian Dalziel		6) Danny Keough	
7) Dave King		7) Alan Stevenson	
8) Kevin Bird		8) Norman Whiteside	

JANUARY 1981

DERBY COUNTY 1 v 1 MANCHESTER UNITED
Reid — Reynolds

Monday 26th*

Kick-off 7.00 p.m.

Attendance 1,442

fourth round

Reynolds keeps Reds babes on the boil

United continued their dual misfortunes of the current Youth Cup campaign when drawn away from home, this time to the under-18 side of Second Division Derby County, while also again going a goal in arrears. Because David Wynn was serving a suspension caused by his sending off at Bolton, it was seen fit for Danny Keough to move into his place. Keough's usual number eight jersey was filled by a big, bustling but nonetheless highly perceptive and skilful youngster from Belfast who went by the, then largely unknown, name of Norman Whiteside.

The Baseball Ground affair promised to be a cracker when two goals were registered in the opening quarter of an hour. However, despite being a keenly contested tie overall, it failed to yield any further scoring and both camps had to be satisfied with honours divided.

The esteemed Gerald Mortimer, a long-time scribe on the often varied fortunes of the Rams, made his view about their main failing known in the Derby Evening Telegraph:

Derby County could not find the finishing power to beat Manchester United in the F.A. Youth Cup at the Baseball Ground last night and now face a Fourth Round replay at Old Trafford.

The hurdles become higher for the Rams but, after their spirited display in a thoroughly entertaining match, they certainly cannot be written off yet.

It was a dogged display by Ron Webster's youngsters, full of guts and honest endeavour. If some players made a less effective contribution than others, all eleven could hold up their heads in the knowledge that they had given everything.

United, as had been expected, were physically stronger, with more players near the top of the Youth Cup age limit. That advantage becomes more telling as the game wears on but there were two or three occasions in the second half when the Rams might have snatched victory.

They got off on the right foot with a glorious goal from Tony Reid after only six minutes.

When Aidan Gibson pushed the ball inside, Reid swayed past one man and beat a second before hitting a good, low shot into the corner of Howe's net.

Paul Halford, who followed up Saturday's two Central League goals with another impressive performance, was not much wide with a shot on the turn before United drew level in the 13th minute.

Reynolds, always dangerous, took a good return pass from Hughes and beat Ian Pass as he ran in. Pass, though, became one of Derby's heroes with some fine second half saves, turning round a shot from Reynolds and hanging on to a fierce free kick from McGarvey.

The goalkeeper has been recruited from the Sheffield area and handles the ball cleanly.

He also has a fair kick on him and one huge clearance two minutes after the interval sent Halford running clear. Halford knew what he wanted to do but a slight loss of poise allowed Howe to nudge the ball away as he came out.

Even so, Halford, a compact and alert player, has good control, uses the ball intelligently and has the instincts of a goalscorer. 'He has come on a lot in the last month,' said Webster.

United spread the play more in the second half, making particularly good use of Reynolds on the left. At the back, Hogg won a lot in the air but there were still chances which the Rams could not convert.

Although Reid drifted out of the game, Kevin Bird worked tremendously hard in midfield and, in the end, United were happy enough with the draw.

Whichever way the replay goes, the Rams have already shown that they are making encouraging progress at this level.

The impression made by the Reds at the Baseball Ground earned fulsome praise from County's youth coach, who said, *'You always expect United to have a few really outstanding kids but this team does not have a single weak link. Half a dozen of them are so exceptional that they are bound to make the grade with proper development.'*

Webster was almost certainly thinking of the likes of Scott McGarvey, a frequent menace to the home defence, Mark Hughes, whose combative style was always in evidence, and the raiding Andy Reynolds, who was a persistent thorn in Derby's side.

The match, which was deemed as being *'a marvellous, entertaining display'* by the Evening News, saw the away side *'gradually begin to command midfield'*. It was also noted that United were *'almost punished for missing their chances when Reid and Paul Halford went close in a late Derby rally'*.

> *I am not unhappy with either the result or our performance. We have created the majority of the chances and we might well have won it here tonight.*
>
> *I suppose that a replay gives the lads an opportunity to play at Old Trafford, and it would be nice to think that there will be a decent crowd to give them the support they deserve.*

SYD OWEN

Yet to get off the mark in this season's Youth Cup campaign, Scott McGarvey seriously threatened Derby's goal on at least four occasions

This game was originally scheduled for Saturday, January 24th but was put back due to Derby County's rearrangement of a first-team game

1) John Armfield	9) Mark Hughes	1) Ian Pass	9) Mark Shackleton
2) Gareth Orritt	10) Norman Whiteside	2) Colin Murphy	10) Paul Halford
3) David Jeffrey	11) Andy Reynolds	3) Graham Harbey	11) Aidan Gibson
4) Graeme Hogg	*12) Alan Stevenson*	4) Tony Reid	*12) Colin Doyle (for 11)*
5) Sean Williams		5) Paul Blades	
6) David Wynn		6) Ian Dalziel	
7) Danny Keough		7) Dave King	
8) Scott McGarvey		8) Kevin Bird	

MANCHESTER UNITED 2 v 1 DERBY COUNTY

Dalziel (o.g.), Reynolds (pen) — Halford

FEBRUARY 1981

Monday 2nd

Kick-off 7.30 p.m.

Attendance 1,569

Now that David Wynn's ban was over, Syd Owen took the opportunity to bring him straight back in for the replay along with John Armfield. Norman Whiteside remained upfront, those management decisions signalling a demotion to the substitute's bench for Alan Stevenson, whereas visitors Derby named exactly the same twelve who had performed so admirably at the Baseball Ground.

On a cold, damp night, when the wind blew and the heavens opened over Old Trafford, the United kids were just able to edge past the Rams, whose fate was sealed by an own goal inflicted on them by their skipper.

Joe Lancaster conjured up a typically witty report for the United Review:

Everybody stood up to be counted at the end of Manchester United's F.A. Youth Cup Fourth Round replay victory over Derby County.

The total was 1,563, only half a dozen short of the official count and, except for the six early deserters, the others seemed intent to make Old Trafford their home. It was the best place for this great crowd on a dirty Manchester night with rain persisting down.

As the fans cheered both teams off, a Derby supporter turned to the gang of three in the empty press box and quipped, 'What marvellous supporters'. 'Yes, and what a marvellous game' was the chorus from the lonely trio.

The 22 youngsters provided a treat. What better variety could you ask for at a match that included a penalty, an own goal and a cracking header that pulled back a goal for Derby to make the score 2-1. That is how it remained, with United reaching the quarter-finals.

That nodding touch from Paul Halford whipped past 'keeper John Armfield inside two minutes after the break. United went two up 30 seconds earlier when an Andy Reynolds cross struck the outstretched boot of County's captain Ian Dalziel. It cannoned off like an Alex Higgins shot right into a corner pocket of the net.

The score remained intact through the acrobatic saves of Derby's Ian Pass who earned medals with bars for bravery. Both defences were competitive from the start and none of the front runners were sluggish.

Derby's Aidan Gibson, after seven minutes, curled a shot that went inches wide of the woodwork and immediately Pass blocked a Mark Hughes drive. In the tenth minute he brought down Norman Whiteside and Reynolds hammered it from the spot for the opening goal.

From the 26th to the 42nd minutes, United rained blows at Pass. Reynolds tried a fancy overhead kick. Whiteside broke through but stubbed his toe when only ten yards out, a Scott McGarvey header was tipped clear and Reynolds latched onto a Whiteside through pass, turned and beat two men but had his blast smothered by the Derby 'keeper.

With a place in the trophy's last eight at stake, Derby rallied well. Tony Reid, who has had a run in their first-team, sent a rising drive that skimmed the bar. David King matched United's David Wynn for trickery on the ball but Syd Owen's young Reds had the edge at the back with Gareth 'Curly' Orritt, David Jeffrey and Graeme Hogg cool, firm and classy.

With United's seniors already eliminated from the F.A., League and UEFA Cups, David Meek, commenting on the win over Derby, reasoned that the youths were *'keeping cup football alive at Old Trafford'.*

Meek also mentioned that the under-18's *'have improved steadily as a team as the competition has progressed'.*

Seen here in action against Derby, Norman Whiteside was felled by the Rams' goalie to earn United a penalty which was converted by Andy Reynolds

1980-81

1) Tony Parks	9) Paul Wilkins
2) Mark Entwistle	10) Ian Crook
3) Kenny Dixon	11) Jimmy Bolton
4) John Cooper	*12) Unknown*
5) Simon Webster	
6) Mark Bowen	
7) Chris Harvey	
8) Terry Gibson	

1) John Armfield	9) Mark Hughes
2) Gareth Orritt	10) Scott McGarvey
3) David Jeffrey	11) Norman Whiteside
4) Graeme Hogg	*12) Kel McDermott (for 7)*
5) Sean Williams	
6) David Wynn	
7) Alan Stevenson	
8) Danny Keough	

MARCH 1981

TOTTENHAM HOTSPUR 3 v 0 MANCHESTER UNITED

Bolton, Gibson, Harvey

semi-final 1st leg

Monday 23rd
Kick-off 7.30 p.m.
Attendance 2,467

United 'babes' in Cup slump

With the smell of another Youth Cup final now wafting around Old Trafford, United discovered that their foes at the last four hurdle would be Spurs. In the other semi-final, Manchester City were given the job of defeating West Ham and the mechanics of the draw meant that there was the possibility of either an all-Manchester or all-London final.

Tottenham had, of course, fell to the Reds in the Fifth Round a year earlier and their side contained a selection of that vanquished eleven. The pairing allowed Syd Owen to obtain some practical information about the size of the task ahead and he divulged some of his findings to the Manchester Evening News when saying, 'Spurs won 3-1 at Elland Road in the last round so I talked to my former Leeds colleague Maurice Lindley and also to their manager, Allan Clarke.

Leeds were winning 1-0 but Spurs scored three times in the last fifteen minutes. They are a mature, strong side with nine players who were in last season's team. So we are going to have a hard battle, though after being drawn away in every round we should be fairly used to that by now.'

A party of fifteen United players travelled to London, with the outcome of fitness checks on two of that number bringing coach Owen rather mixed news. The consistent Andy Reynolds was given the thumbs down as a result of a strain whereas Gareth Orritt was passed as fit for duty through recovering from an infected toe.

After receiving permission from various authorities, United were given the green light to include schoolboys Whiteside and Armfield, their availability subject to the strict understanding that both were to be back at their desks the following morning. For Armfield, the condition imposed constituted a long motorway journey after the final whistle while Whiteside was required to be flown immediately back to Belfast.

The Evening News detailed the developments of a dreadfully disappointing display:

Manchester United's youngsters made a mess of the club's last cup hopes of the season at Tottenham last night.

The young Reds crashed to a 3-0 defeat in the first leg of the F.A. Youth Cup semi-final and it is difficult to give them a chance of rescuing the tie when they play the second leg at Old Trafford next Monday.

Spurs, winners of the competition in 1970 and 1974, are a strong, skilful side and thoroughly deserved their handsome victory.

The only hope of a United recovery lies in the fact that the youngsters who exceeded expectations in reaching the semi-finals can play a lot better.

As coach Syd Owen put it, 'It was the worst performance by our youth side this season. It was 40 minutes before we strung three passes together. Even our quality players didn't show. Spurs are a mature team but I know we can do a lot better as I hope we shall show at Old Trafford.'

United missed the raiding pace of the absent Andy Reynolds, out with a thigh injury, but their problems really started in defence.

Although schoolboy goalkeeper John Armfield was shaken after an early shoulder injury, the men in front of him exposed him dreadfully.

Central defenders David Jeffrey and Graeme Hogg fought bravely but were generally overwhelmed. Indeed, the Tottenham goals all came from defensive errors conceded under pressure.

The opening goal in the 24th minute followed a pass back and was well taken from a narrow angle by the lively Jimmy Bolton.

Terry Gibson, a dynamic little striker and man of the match, broke through the middle from a high bouncing goal clearance to score the second after 52 minutes.

Chris Harvey shot the third (72 minutes) which could well prove the winner when the semi-final is completed next Monday.

It was a sad and sore United team travelling home from London today. Nearly half of them will be under treatment for injury and one or two may be lucky to recover for the second leg.

In addition to the already injured Reynolds and Armfield, who was driven straight back to Blackpool after the match in order to be back at school today, United have Sean Williams with a bad groin strain, Norman Whiteside a bruised calf, and David Wynn a damaged ankle.

Joe Lancaster bemoaned what he felt was United's lack of breaks to the readers of the Review:

.......John Armfield was not given a chance to blow out the candles on his 18th birthday cake. Spurs did all the huffing and puffing and beat the United 'keeper three times without reply.

Referee Tom Bune of Cranleigh, Surrey, was also not in the mood for giving away presents. He closed his eyes or perhaps had them shut when Alan Stevenson was brought down in the box by Spurs' Kenny Dixon. In the second half there were more unheeded appeals when Norman Whiteside was pushed from behind in a goalmouth scramble.

Everything might have been different had Whiteside's early blast gone in instead of hitting the 'keeper's legs and cannoning for a corner.

" I travelled to the game at Tottenham with my dad, it was one of only about four games he ever saw me play. I got injured early on when one of their players sat on my shoulder. It was very painful and I struggled with anything over head height. Of course, there were no substitute goalkeepers in those days so I just had to get on with it.

Graeme Hogg did really well, he dealt with a lot of balls I would normally have gone for. At half-time, Syd Owen told me not to feel sorry for myself. It was a bad injury, though, as I was out for about four weeks afterwards. "

JOHN ARMFIELD

1) Richard Howe	9) Mark Hughes	1) Tony Parks	9) Terry Gibson
2) Gareth Orritt	10) Scott McGarvey	2) Mark Entwistle	10) Ian Crook
3) David Jeffrey	11) Andy Reynolds	3) Kenny Dixon	11) Paul Wilkins
4) Graeme Hogg	*12) Alan Stevenson*	4) John Cooper	*12) Pat Corbett (for 2)*
5) Clayton Blackmore		5) Simon Webster	
6) Kel McDermott		6) Mark Bowen	
7) Norman Whiteside		7) Chris Harvey	
8) Danny Keough		8) Jimmy Bolton	

MANCHESTER UNITED 1 (1) v (3) 0 TOTTENHAM HOTSPUR

Hughes

1980-81 — semi-final 2nd leg

MARCH 1981

Monday 30th

Kick-off 7.30 p.m.

Attendance 2,107

Seven days after the Reds' demoralising defeat in London, Spurs appeared at Old Trafford with an identical line-up to the one which had set up such a commanding lead at White Hart Lane.

With goals being their main priority, United were boosted by the return of Andy Reynolds, who passed a fitness test on the afternoon of the match, although there were other injury problems in the form of legacies carried over from the game in the capital. Neither John Armfield nor David Wynn were sufficiently recovered from their knocks and so Richard Howe resumed in goal and Kel McDermott was also included, his promotion serving to relegate Alan Stevenson to the bench once more. Sean Williams was omitted from the side, so Neath-born Clayton Blackmore was summoned up for a Youth Cup introduction at left-back.

The Reds recouped some of their lost pride by giving Spurs what Joe Lancaster called a *'pounding'*. Lancaster also commented that the home goalkeeper *'could have been given redundancy pay in the second half'* due to Tottenham's lack of forward activity and he also made a veiled reference to the visitors' tactics when mentioning *'good boys are not always winners'*.

That very subject was further expanded upon in the Manchester Evening News' match report:

Manchester United fans angrily rounded on Spurs' manager Keith Burkinshaw during the second leg of the F.A. Youth Cup semi-final at Old Trafford.

The London team cut up rough as they held the Reds at bay to go through to the final 3-1 on aggregate. They had five players booked as United piled on the pressure to win the match 1-0 but failed to recover from the three-goal deficit they suffered at White Hart Lane.

A group of home supporters waved fists and shouted at Burkinshaw, who was sitting in the directors' box watching his team.

They objected strongly to Tottenham's tough-tackling tactics.

Burkinshaw sat stonily through the demonstration and said afterwards, 'You expect that kind of thing don't you?' The answer to that, of course, is that you probably do if your team make a habit of using desperate defensive tactics.

The alarm bells rang for Spurs in the 35th minute when Scott McGarvey headed down Danny Keough's free kick for Mark Hughes to hook into the roof of the net.

From then on the bookings came steadily with Terry Gibson, Ian Crook, Mark Bowen, John Cooper and substitute Patrick Corbett all going into the referee's book.

Andy Reynolds was dangerous for United early on but United could never afford to commit themselves completely to attack as Spurs were skilful and dangerous on the break.

West Ham duly disposed of Manchester City in the other semi-final and the Hammers then claimed the trophy as their own by defeating Spurs by a couple of goals to one over the two legs of the final.

> *I came off the bench at White Hart Lane and missed a chance to score but played quite well. We were all looking forward to the return thinking we were still in the game. I thought with a bit more luck we could have turned it around, they certainly weren't that much better than us.*
>
> *At the end of the game I had mixed feelings. Although I was disappointed about the result and for the team, I thought I had done okay. Your ultimate objective was to get near to the first-team, so you tended to be a little selfish and look at things from an individual perspective.*

KEL McDERMOTT

Despite being eliminated at the semi-final stage of the F.A. Youth Cup, the youngsters experienced glory in the 1981 Lancashire F.A. Youth Cup final
(l-r) Syd Owen (Coach), Alan Jones (Trainer), Andy Reynolds, Richard Howe, Norman Whiteside, Gareth Orritt, David Jeffrey (back), Kel McDermott (front), Alan Stevenson (partly hidden), Mark Hughes, Graeme Hogg, Scott McGarvey, Danny Keough

275

GOODEVE, Kenneth George Alfred (1967/68, 1968/69)

Born: Wythenshawe, Manchester, 3rd September 1950
Height: 5ft. 10ins., **Weight:** 10st. 10lbs.
Role: Right full-back or central defender
Career: Benchill Primary School (Wythenshawe)/ Baguley Hall Secondary Modern School (Wythenshawe)/ Manchester Boys/ **UNITED**: App. September 1966 Pro. September 1967/ **Luton Town** April 1970/ **Brighton & Hove Albion** December 1973/ **Watford** June 1974 to June 1976/ **Bedford Town** August 1977/ **Hitchin Town** July 1982/ **Kidderminster Harriers** December 1982/ **Buckingham Town** June 1983/ **Barton Rovers** December 1984 to March 1985/ **Wootton Blue Cross** March 1986/ **Kempston Rovers** August 1986 to September 1987/ **Wootton Blue Cross** August 1990 to April 1997

Ken Goodeve joined the Reds in the month of his 16th birthday, just after Matt Busby's squad had embarked on what would be the club's last First Division title-winning term. Over 30 years later, at the same time when Alex Ferguson's men were heading towards their fourth Premier League championship, his links were due to be severed with Wootton Blue Cross in the aptly-named United Counties League (UCL). It had certainly been a long, varied and mostly enjoyable journey, with the once wide-eyed Old Trafford apprentice by then an experienced campaigner aged 46.

'I grew up in Benchill, and I really learned about football on the local 'rec',' he explained. 'I was playing for Manchester South against Manchester East in the 1965/66 schools' season when Joe Armstrong saw me and from then on I trained at The Cliff. Everton came in for me, but by then United already had my commitment.'

Despite being utilised as a full-back for Manchester Boys, his entry point for the Reds in August 1966 was at centre-forward, and he remained in the 'B' team's attack throughout the term. Registering a hat-trick in a 4-0 thumping of Blackpool in November, his name cropped up on the score sheet on quite a few occasions as the weeks went by.

Goodeve was surprised to find himself stationed at centre-half for the 'B' side at the outset of the following season. Of that development he commented, 'It wasn't my best position, but I accepted the role without complaint because I wanted to show willing.'

With something like fifteen months service under his belt, and just prior to the halfway stage of the 1967/68 term, he was finally able to take up his preferred position when moved to right full-back, the switch coinciding with the beginning of a four-game run in the Youth Cup which ended in elimination at Turf Moor. 'I remember the second game against Burnley most clearly,' he recalled 'as I was given a roasting by their winger, Steve Kindon.'

Keeping hold of the number two jersey throughout December and January before returning to central defence, in late April he was back upfront and notched a second career hat-trick a couple of weeks later when the Reds shared six goals with Oldham.

He described his economic style of defending by saying, 'I wasn't the quickest thing on two legs, but I had the knack of positioning myself in the right place because I could read the game well. I preferred to think of myself as a cultured full-back, as I was seldom rushed and liked to make the ball do the work. I was good at tackling and I preferred to play as a sweeper in the days before the role became popular.'

A month into the 1968/69 campaign he was utilised in a 2-0 Central League defeat at Newcastle. Thrilled to learn that he was to captain the Youth Cup team that season, he partnered Tommy O'Neil in the middle of the back four while Laurie Millerchip and Kevin Lewis were placed in their best positions at right and left full-back respectively. He appeared in all eight ties, the Reds reaching the semi-final only to lose both legs to a potent West Brom ensemble, and he had made upwards of a dozen second string appearances by the end of the term without really fastening down a place in the side.

In early May he played in both legs of the Knock-out Cup final when United defeated Blackpool 1-0 on aggregate. In keeping with his constant shuttling between roles, he wore the number nine jersey for the away tie prior to finding himself moved back into central defence for the return match.

Unfortunately, his once half-full glass soon turned half-empty through missing nearly five months of the 1969/70 campaign with a groin problem. At a time when he should logically have been holding a spot in the Reserves, the progress made in the previous season went out of the window. With his contract coming to an end, Wilf McGuinness informed him that he wouldn't be offered a new one.

The nineteen year-old was soon on his way to talk over a move to Cardiff City before immediately driving to Luton for the same purpose. Accepting the better terms offered by the latter, in April 1970 he left his Manchester home and moved in with Peter Woods, Don Givens and Jimmy Ryan, all of whom had joined Luton at a point when the club was on the verge of winning promotion.

It took him over a year to crack through to Luton's senior side for a Second Division game and most of his time at Kenilworth Road was spent captaining their Reserves. Goodeve made only fifteen senior appearances in total, six of which were from the substitute's bench, and the lack of opportunity caused him to slap in a transfer request while the Bedfordshire outfit were in pursuit of what would turn out to be another successful promotion push, this time to the First Division.

In December 1973, a £30,000 fee took him to Brighton where he came under the wing of one of football's most famous double acts, Brian Clough and Peter Taylor. However, it quickly became apparent that their management style was at odds with the principles he had been taught at Old Trafford and with only six Third Division matches to his name, it was mutually agreed that he should move on.

He was put out of his Goldstone Ground gloom when Mike Keen, a former Luton team-mate who had since taken over as manager of Watford, arranged for him to transfer to Vicarage Road. A regular for the Hornets over the next eighteen months with 67 league appearances, ripped groin tendons sidelined him for a considerable period. With his contract at an end, a new manager in place and his injury still not yet cleared, those three factors flagged up the end of his days in the Football League.

Accepting his fate by starting work at a brewery, a former Gillingham winger by the name of Bob Folds who lived in the same village suggested that Goodeve join him at Bedford. He agreed to sign for the Southern League Premier Division side for the start of a term which ended with their relegation, with the club then benefiting from his accomplished defensive contributions for another four years. They finished fourth in the league in 1979, third in 1980 and second in 1981, when they lost the title only on goal difference. Twelve months later, the leaseholders of the club's ground called time on the tenancy and, unable to find a new home, the once esteemed Bedford club was forced to disband.

Following a spell in the Isthmian Premier League with Hitchin, he made 33 appearances for Kidderminster Harriers during the 1982/83 campaign, which they ended by climbing into the division now known as the Conference, as well as winning both the Staffordshire and Worcestershire Senior Cups. The local newspaper commented that it had been 'the most successful season in the Harriers' history in the Southern League'.

A few weeks after leaving Aggborough, Goodeve transferred to Buckingham Town, where he enjoyed a similarly productive spell. Noted as one of the finest sides to grace the UCL in modern times, Buckingham won a Berkshire & Buckinghamshire Senior Cup, League Cup and divisional treble in 1984 and, later that year, for the first time in the club's history, they went as far as reaching the First Round Proper of the F.A. Cup before bowing out to Orient.

From then on he appeared only occasionally for his village team, Wootton Blue Cross, as well as Barton Rovers and Kempston Rovers, all of whom were members of the UCL, and he assumed the reigns at the former in the summer of 1993.

Simultaneously quitting as Wootton's manager and his post at the brewery in 1997, Ken Goodeve works as a customer care manager for a property development company in London.

BRADLEY, David (1974/75, 1975/76)

Born: Salford, 16th January 1958
Height: 6ft., **Weight:** 13st.
Role: Central defender
Career: Moston Fields Primary School (Moston)/ North Manchester High School/ Manchester Boys/ Lancashire Boys/ England Boys/ **UNITED**: App. April 1974 Pro. January 1975 to August 1978/ **Wimbledon** (L) March and April 1978/ **Doncaster Rovers** August 1978/ **Bury** August 1980/ **Northwich Victoria** August 1981/ **Dunedin City** (NZ) April 1984/ **Northwich Victoria** November 1984 to January 1985/ **Cape Town Hellenic** (SA) March 1985/ **Wits University** (SA) June 1985/ **Caernarvon Town** December 1985/ **Manurewa** (NZ) April 1986/ **North Shore United** (NZ) June 1987 to October 1988

Built in the correct proportions for the defensive tasks asked of him, the David Bradley package comprised of a hard, physical presence. Primarily a ball winner who could distribute efficiently, allowing the team's more creative individuals the possession required to influence the game, he was considered a rugged competitor both aerially and on the floor. Additionally instilled with a winning attitude, opponents weren't allowed to get behind him very often.

His star was on the rise in the days of Tommy Docherty, though he soon fell out of favour when Dave Sexton was appointed as manager at Old Trafford. Sexton's signing of Gordon McQueen in February 1978 had a major bearing on his departure as he was farmed out to a lower league club within weeks and transferred away permanently six months later.

Bradley was schooled in north Manchester and at the age of eleven he joined the Junior Clarets, who, as the name implied, were a feeder club for Burnley. Within a year he had switched to Junior United, who played on Sundays at Broadhurst Park in Moston. Ray Botham, John Lowey and Dave Ryan were all attached to the club that later became known as Mancunians and a number of future United starlets honed their skills there under the astute guidance of Jimmy Curran and Eric Walker.

He represented Manchester at under-11 level and began training at The Cliff in his school holidays. Moving up to under-14 and under-15 age groups with Manchester Boys, his football education expanded under the tutelage of former United striker Laurie Cassidy while attached to the city side and he was later named as captain of Lancashire Boys.

Continuing to collect honours via selection for England Boys, his international debut resulted in a sparkling 4-0 home win over Northern Ireland in March 1973 and England continued their good form with a 3-1 victory over Holland at Wembley in April. His side later triumphed over Wales at Rhyl and then won the Victory Shield outright following a defeat of Scotland at Chesterfield. He also played in a 5-0 victory over France in Paris, as well as two games in West Germany in May, and his eighth and last game at that level came against Scotland in June as the Auld Enemy defeated the home nation by four goals to two at Wembley.

Choosing to leave North Manchester High School in April 1974, that same month he was drafted into the Lancashire Youth Cup team which lost 2-0 at Everton. In joining United he followed in his father's footsteps as, in the early 1950's, dad Graham had been a member of the club's Colts team.

There were signs of rapid progress from him in the 1974/75 campaign. He was swiftly elevated from 'B' grade into the 'A' side, staying with them throughout August and September, and in October, while still only sixteen, an early Central League start came in a 2-2 home draw with Manchester City.

The Mostonian continued predominantly in the 'A' team up to Christmas and made a full appearance quota of five Youth Cup ties in a season that saw the under-18's exit the competition despite conceding only one goal. From January 1975 onwards he staked a much firmer place in the Reserves at right full-back, remaining at that standard right up to the campaign's conclusion, and then visited Zurich in May as United defeated Spurs in the Blue Stars final.

Bradley recommenced with the 'A' team from the starting bell of the 1975/76 term until the October, when he had a spell in the 'B' side for a few weeks. He was restored to the Reserves in November, remaining with them until the next February, and also captained the Youth Cup team, who were unexpectedly eliminated by West Brom in their fifth tie of the competition.

International recognition returned in March 1976, when the teenager was named as an unused substitute for an England Youth clash against Wales at Maine Road. Later skippering the Reds to a 4-1 aggregate victory over Everton in the Lancashire Youth Cup final in late April, a few weeks further on he was party to a second success in the Blue Stars tournament when Middlesbrough were defeated 1-0 in the last game.

Over the first half of the 1976/77 season he divided his time between the 'A' team and Reserves prior to again cementing his place in the latter during January. A couple of months later he was included in the first-team squad for the Glyn Pardoe testimonial match against Manchester City at Maine Road, where he made a substitute appearance by replacing Martin Buchan.

On 11th April 1977, he was named as 13th man for the Reds' First Division game at Sunderland and, in competitive terms, it would be as near as he ever came to an elusive senior spot with United. Finishing the campaign with the Reserves, Docherty's sacking soon after represented the first step of his walk out of the Old Trafford exit door.

Despite being practically ever-present in the Central League side from August 1977 to March 1978, it soon became apparent that Dave Sexton didn't rate him as highly as his predecessor. Whether that was because of his only major fault, a lack of pace, is debatable, and with McQueen on board he instinctively knew that he would never get another chance in the first-team.

Sexton was on good terms with Dario Gradi, then manager at Wimbledon, and arranged for him to go there on loan for a while. In a most historic season for the Dons, their opener in the Football League, the tough defender made the first of seven appearances for them on 8th March 1978 in a 3-1 defeat at Aldershot. His final game for the south London club came in late April at Barnsley and in between he took part in matches at Newport County, Southend and Doncaster, as well as a couple of games at Plough Lane.

His final au revoir turned out to be in the Blue Stars tournament, and he ended his four and a half years with United on a high note. After stroking in a penalty in the semi-final, he made it a hat-trick of gold medals when Leeds were licked 1-0 in the concluding match. Curiously, the Reds had beaten English opponents in each of the three Blue Stars finals he was involved in.

After contemplating his future throughout that summer, an initial offer from manager Stan Anderson to join Doncaster was rejected. Anderson then made a second approach a little while later and on this occasion he succeeded in getting his man. Beginning in August 1978, Bradley spent two years with the Yorkshire club and while there he was installed as the youngest skipper in the Football League at just 21 years-old by new manager Billy Bremner. Within that period he scored five times in 67 Fourth Division appearances for the Belle Vue outfit.

In August 1980, Bury offered him a one-year contract. His first game for the Shakers was in a League Cup tie against Newcastle, when he plundered the only goal in extra-time to register a major shock. Other than that, his stay at Gigg Lane wasn't especially productive and after just eight games in the Fourth Division for them he moved to Northwich Victoria, teaming up at the Drill Field with former Red Dave Ryan.

Following a bright opening term with the Vics, Bradley broke his leg twice in his second campaign and missed out on their 1983 F.A. Trophy final defeat by Telford at Wembley. Upon regaining fitness, a number of offers came in for him from the southern hemisphere. Turning down the chance to link up with ex-boss Docherty at Sydney Olympic, life across the Tasman Sea seemed much more appealing and so he instead joined Dunedin City as player/coach in April 1984. The appointment meant that he missed another opportunity of performing at Wembley because he had assisted Northwich to qualify for a second consecutive F.A. Trophy final just before jetting south.

Returning to Northwich that November, in March 1985 he moved to South Africa in order to spend a brief time with Cape Town Hellenic. He then transferred to Wits University and participated in their victory in the John Player Knock-Out Cup final, when Kaiser Chiefs were defeated 2-1 in a replay in front of 80,000 fans at Ellis Park in Johannesburg.

Upon arriving back in the UK, Caernarvon Town provided an extremely brief stopover during the 1985 Christmas period before he returned to New Zealand, and specifically Manurewa. Appointed as their player/manager a year later, he was sacked after barely two months in the job and so chose to sign for another Auckland club, North Shore United.

From an October 1988 starting point, David Bradley began working in the insurance industry for a time before starting up a company that sold consumer products through a network distribution business, an incredibly profitable venture which enabled him to build up an income stream through royalties. Since then he has continued in business by travelling the world in order to deliver motivational talks, and it hasn't been unknown for him to speak in front of as many as 25,000 people at one time.

Now living in Ohio, he continues to visit many points of the globe for business purposes and frequently stops over in England.

KEOUGH, Daniel Peter
(1978/79, 1979/80, 1980/81)

Born: Stacksteads, Bacup, 31st January 1963
Height: 5ft. 7ins., **Weight:** 9st. 5lbs.
Role: Midfielder or forward
Career: St. Joseph's R.C. Primary School (Stacksteads)/ St. Mary's College (Blackburn)/ Blackburn Boys/ Lancashire Boys/ UNITED: Ass. Schoolboy August 1978 App. July 1979 Pro. January 1980 to June 1984/ **Tornio Tops** (Fin) 1985/ **Exeter City** October 1985 to May 1987/ **KSV Baunatal** (Ger) late 1980's/ **Eintracht Haiger** (Ger) late 1980's and early 1990's/ **FC Herborn** (Ger) early 1990's/ **SSV Langenaubach** (Ger) mid-to-late 1990's/ **Haslingden** late 1990's/ **Mossley** late 1990's

Principally a midfielder, Danny Keough was known for his biting tackles and willingness to work from sun up to lights out in order to gain or keep possession. Once the ball was at his feet, his preference was to build attacks with short, effective passes. Injury setbacks derailed his progress with United, and following his release by Ron Atkinson he eventually joined up with two of his former youth team colleagues, Alan Stevenson and Andy Reynolds, in Germany.

Representing four clubs over a nine-year period in that country, his playing career effectively ended at SSV Langenaubach, where he also held some coaching responsibilities before returning to his homeland in the 1990's.

Like most others before and since, his involvement in the sport began at primary school. While also turning out for a local team, Marauders JFC, his first notable achievement was in scoring the winning goal for St. Joseph's in the 1974 Dorian (Lancashire Primary Schools') Cup final against St. Mary's of Burnley. It was an amazing achievement for such a small school, and further honours followed when he was selected for his town and county.

Only thirteen when Norman Scholes watched him performing for Blackburn Boys, Keough explained, *'I trained at Blackburn Rovers over the summer holidays and a number of other clubs invited me to do likewise, including Queen's Park Rangers, Leeds and Spurs, as well as United. I was very tempted by the offer I received from QPR, until (Reds' youth coach) Syd Owen swayed me by explaining just what and how much I could learn at Old Trafford.'*

Prior to signing as an associate schoolboy, he was invited to Zurich as a guest of the club for the Blue Stars tournament. There was even a substitute appearance in a tour friendly game in Switzerland, against FC Stafa, which provided a big thrill for the impressionable teenager.

Starting with a goal for the 'B' team in a 2-2 home draw with Tranmere in August 1978, he made only sporadic appearances for United that season as he hadn't yet finalised his education. Following just two more 'B' team games and one match for the 'A' side leading into December, Keough was selected to partner Andy Ritchie in attack when the Reds were drawn against Blackburn in the Youth Cup. Describing the match circumstances as *'slightly unreal'*, because he was required to compete against many of his former Blackburn training pals, he became one of the Reds' youngest ever participants in the competition as his 16th birthday was still two months away.

Following victory over the Rovers, he was then included in the team that was defeated by Derby in the Youth Cup, but thereafter was limited to just a couple of matches before rejoining the 'A' team in April once his studies were finished. He was a member of the side that conquered Tranmere in the final of the Lancashire Youth Cup in May 1979 and within a couple of months he had signed as an apprentice.

The 1979/80 campaign panned out with him taking up residency in the 'A' team, for whom he held a virtually ever-present record, and he was also selected for the first five Youth Cup ties as the Reds eventually came up against Manchester City. After being unveiled in the Central League for a 3-0 home win over Stoke on the opening day of March 1980, he then lined up against the Light Blues for the initial leg of the Youth Cup semi-final on the last day of the month.

A bizarre accident caused his absence from the return contest in Moss Side, as he later sheepishly admitted, *'I couldn't be considered for that game because I had damaged my ankle ligaments while showing off in front of my girlfriend by performing a cartwheel.'* Needless to say, while the feat might have impressed his beau, the incident didn't have quite the same effect on the coaching staff.

Then spending almost the entire 1980/81 term with the 'A' side while patiently waiting for opportunities in the second string, when the Youth Cup got going again in early December he was honoured with the captaincy of the team. Keough was present in that capacity for all seven ties, scoring once against Everton, and led United as they marched into the penultimate stage for the second year running. Two weeks after the Youth Cup defeat by Spurs, he skippered the side to victory in the final of the Lancashire Youth Cup and later participated in all four games in the Blue Stars tournament when the Reds beat Slovan Bratislava 3-0 to lift the trophy.

After honing his trade in the 'A' team for a couple of years, when the 1981/82 campaign commenced he was on the bench for the Reserves. He was back in the side in mid-September and a total of 27 appearances was built up steadily as ninth place was achieved in the Central League. At that time Remi Moses, Bryan Robson, Lou Macari, Sammy McIlroy, Steve Coppell and Ray Wilkins were all fighting for midfield places in the first-team, and he also needed to contend with Mike Duxbury and Alan Davies for a place in the Reserves.

His career up to then had been going just about right, with noticeable progress year on year, and the next campaign began with him seen in nine out of the first ten Central League fixtures. Then, in a home engagement against Leeds Reserves on the 18th December 1982, a bad tackle from behind resulted in a severe back injury that put him out for the next eight months.

Nominated as the Reserves' substitute for the opening game of the 1983/84 season, he wasn't called on and needed to wait to make his return in an 'A' team game. Soon restored to the second string as ten starts were accumulated up to the end of November, he was almost back into his rhythm when a bout of glandular fever left him bed-ridden and forced him to miss another four months. By now having lost significant impetus, the considerable amount of time forfeited couldn't be reclaimed and, with his contract approaching its end, he was told it wouldn't be renewed. Following his appearance in a 2-0 win at Burnley Reserves in April, a free transfer was a really disappointing conclusion to his six-year on-field association with the club.

Manager Atkinson offered him as much assistance as he could under the circumstances and salvation seemed to be at hand when Keough was offered a six-week trial at Doncaster. When a contract offer wasn't forthcoming he attended further trials at Bury, Preston and Burnley and, as no deal materialised from any of them either, Finnish outfit Tornio Tops seemed to provide the suitable home required to fully rebuild his fitness. The move was based on sensible thinking and it not only gave him back the main thrust of his game, while in Scandinavia he also felt a considerable confidence boost.

In the autumn of 1985, Exeter City made contact and, now badly wanting a return to England, their offer of a two-year contract sounded like a choir of angels to him. Going on to tot up 72 Fourth Division appearances for the Grecians, his extended stay in Germany commenced soon after.

Once back in the UK in 1996, he found employment outside of the game and also became assistant manager at Mossley following a spell at Haslingden. He played a solitary game for the North-West Counties League club, and also warmed the bench on several occasions, but predominantly helped out in a coaching capacity. During his time at Seel Park, the club came second in their division in 1999 and reached the final of the Premier Cup in their next campaign. When Mossley's manager left to take charge of Witton Albion in November 2001, Keough followed him.

Living in the Manchester vicinity, the day job entails working for former Red Garry Worrall in the supply of sports equipment and he also coaches United's under-16 Academy squad. All these years later, the UEFA 'A' coaching license holder still considers winning the Dorian Cup with his primary school to be his greatest honour, as it is a feat they have never repeated since.

CLARK, Jonathan (1974/75, 1975/76, 1976/77)

Born: Swansea, 12th November 1958
Height: 5ft. 9ins., **Weight:** 10st. 11lbs.
Role: Right full-back or midfielder
Career: Brynhyfryd Primary School (Swansea)/ Dynevor Comprehensive School (Swansea)/ Swansea Boys/ Glamorgan Boys/ Wales Boys/ Lostock High School (Stretford)/ UNITED: Ass. Schoolboy November 1973 App. Pro. March 1975 Pro. November 1975/ **Derby County** September 1978/ **Preston North End** August 1981/ **Bury** December 1986/ **Carlisle United** March 1987/ **Morecambe** February 1989/ **Southport** August 1989 to February 1990

Jonathan Clark was attached to the Reds for almost five years and made the kind of steady progress expected of someone with his talent. He briefly viewed life inside the senior circle prior to linking up at Derby with his mentor,

Tommy Docherty, and it is fair to suggest that had the Scot not lost his job at Old Trafford there would almost certainly have been further opportunities in United's first-team for him.

A skilful ball artist who was blessed with considerable flair, he was quick with both feet and renowned for his scoring ability, either from free kicks or when driving forward from midfield. Highly rated by the Reds' coaches and amongst his peers, after leaving United he gave value for money to four Football League clubs while never quite scaling the dizzy heights expected of him as a schoolboy and youth international.

Scout Walter Robbins' early reading of his promise was entirely accurate, with the result that the teenager was hunted by a posse of clubs, including Spurs, Crystal Palace, Ipswich, Arsenal, Liverpool, Chelsea and Manchester City. *'I only had trials with two clubs, Everton and United, and I was offered contracts by both of them,'* he recounted. *'When I moved up to Manchester I went to Lostock High School and the headmaster there was Warren Bradley, a former player at Old Trafford, and he allowed me day release in order that I could attend training.'*

Growing up in Swansea, there was a tradition of soccer in the family as his father was at Leeds when an injury curtailed his ambitions of becoming a professional footballer. Clark was attached to Cwm Albion of the Swansea Junior League from the age of ten and it was about then that Robbins first saw him in action. Sensing that other invites would soon land at the lad's door, the scout felt compelled to act with some haste and it was soon agreed that he would take a trial in Manchester after turning the age of twelve.

His schoolboy international entrance came as a substitute in the concluding game of the 1972/73 Victory Shield tournament against Northern Ireland at Ebbw Vale. In the following schools' season he was a member of the Welsh team that was subjected to a 2-1 defeat by England at Goodison Park and was also capped for his appearances against Scotland, Ireland and West Germany.

He holds the distinction of a double debut day for United as, on the morning of the 17th August 1974, he was included in the 'B' team that lost 4-0 at home to Everton, but the weekend improved considerably thereafter as he then featured for a 3-1 win with the 'A' side at South Liverpool Reserves. After proving his capabilities in the junior teams he was chosen at full-back for that campaign's two Youth Cup ties against Newcastle in place of the injured Lindsay McKeown, and only a month passed before he found himself facing Aston Villa in a 3-0 Central League home win. Three days later, with the under-18's regular number two having regained fitness, Clark was handed the substitute's shirt for the home Youth Cup tie that ended in defeat to Everton.

Training on a regular basis with the senior squad was the next step along his progress path and in April 1975 he was named as 13th man for the first-team's trip to Southampton. He mentioned of that experience, *'I sat beside Tommy Docherty while he talked me through the intricacies of the match in order to assist my development in reading the game.'* Two weeks later he scored his first hat-trick in United's colours as the 'B' side defeated Oldham 4-2.

He began the 1975/76 term in his usual midfield place for the 'A' team, but throughout that season's Youth Cup operation he was again utilised in the right-back position. Over the February and March of 1976 he was capped by Wales at youth level, featuring in both Qualifiers against England for the UEFA under-18 Youth Tournament.

He was involved in nine games for the Reserves leading up to November 1976, after which Docherty named him as the substitute for a First Division home engagement against Sunderland, and soon into the second half he replaced Colin Waldron before 42,685 fans in an exciting 3-3 draw.

Later that month events went bumpy on him as he captained the side that was defeated by Bolton in the opening round of the Youth Cup. Despite that black spot he finished the campaign with 34 appearances for the Reserves and, while another chance at senior level failed to materialise, at that stage the eighteen year-old felt confident and satisfied with both his performances and future prospects.

In September 1977, with Dave Sexton having replaced Docherty, Clark put the gloss on some sterling shows in the Central League by recording another hat-trick in a 5-0 victory at Sheffield United. The following month he was rewarded with inclusion in the first-team squad that travelled to Tehran for a game which was organised as part of the British Trade Week and while there he replaced Stuart Pearson in a 2-0 victory over the Iranian national 'B' side.

Early December saw him recalled to the seniors again, this time for a friendly with St. Etienne, and over in Paris he was utilised from the bench once more, on this occasion for Sammy McIlroy. Finishing the term with the most appearances for the Reserves while also winning the first of two under-21 caps for Wales against Scotland, his eye-catching form was rewarded when he was asked to join the first-team squad on their close season trip to Norway and the United States. Used as a substitute in all four of the tour matches, against Ajax and Brann in Norway and Tampa Bay and Tulsa Roughnecks in America, a new two-year contract was accepted around the same time.

When he reported back for training following the 1978 summer break, the scenery had begun to shift as there was much speculation about Sexton's intention to bring Ray Wilkins and Mickey Thomas to the club. Expanding on the events which would alter the course of his immediate future, he revealed, *'I knew that if those signings were made I would have less first-team opportunities, so I sought a meeting with the manager. Sexton confirmed his plans to me face to face and I knew then that I would have to look for pastures new.'*

Docherty wasn't slow to make enquiries about his availability to transfer to Derby and, now married to a lass who had worked at Old Trafford in administrative duties, senior football was a matter of urgency. The midfielder penned a three-year deal with the Rams while also costing them a fee of £50,000. The Reserves' home fixture against Burnley on 23rd September 1978 which ended 1-1 represented his last game for United and five days later he was gone.

Fortunes fluctuated during his spell at the Baseball Ground as Derby inhabited the top-flight for his first two years there but by 1980 they were down in the Second Division. While Clark got a little of the first-team football he craved, making over 50 league appearances, it represented somewhat less than was originally bargained for.

At the end of his contract he was contacted by Docherty once again, this time with a view to him joining Third Division Preston and, preferring a return to the North-West, the offer of a contract guaranteeing him financial stability for a further three years was gratefully accepted. Then, when Docherty was sacked soon after, it appeared that the Derby scenario was going to repeat itself. Fortunately, things worked out to his satisfaction as new boss Gordon Lee thought highly of him and, as such, he remained a regular contender in the North End team, collecting four 'Player of the Year' awards in one particular campaign while becoming a firm fans' favourite.

He was later the victim of an injury and needed to be stretchered off the pitch with what was diagnosed as erosion of the pelvis, the problem proving so severe that he was sidelined for over a year. Brian Kidd pointed him in the direction of a top Harley Street surgeon but, even so, he was unable to train the same ever again. In March 1986, after Kidd and former Manchester City centre-half Tommy Booth both had spells managing the club, he was named as caretaker manager at Deepdale. Preston won their first five games under his charge, the first time they had achieved such a feat for 50 years, prior to John McGrath taking over the managerial reins. He left later that year having scored ten goals for North End in 110 Football League games.

Bury then came in with an offer and it took him just fourteen league games to realise that all at Gigg Lane wasn't as good as it had initially appeared. Harry Gregg then invited him to join Carlisle so as to add some experience to his young team and another half century of matches were added to his total at Blundell Park before Gregg was replaced. He then had brief flirtations at Northern Premier League outposts Morecambe and Southport, with the two spells adding up to twelve months in all.

Tommy Docherty once described Jonathan Clark as *'the best schoolboy footballer I have ever seen'*, as well as saying *'I didn't think he had to learn anything, and I would have mortgaged my house on him making it.'*

The subject of that lavish praise entered the licensing trade in early 1990 and currently manages a hotel in Blackpool.

MILLERCHIP, Lawrence (1968/69, 1969/70)

Born: Nuneaton, 29th January 1952
Height: 5ft. 6ins., **Weight:** 10st. 6lbs.
Role: Right full-back
Career: Middlemarch Primary School (Nuneaton)/ Arbury High School (Nuneaton)/ Nuneaton Boys/ Warwickshire Boys/ Birmingham & District Boys/ England Boys/ UNITED: App. March 1967 Pro. July 1969 to June 1971/ Altrincham/ Chorley/ Macclesfield Town August 1972/ Sandbach Ramblers September and October 1972

Laurie Millerchip made a total of six appearances for England Boys in 1967, which included, rather unfortunately, their record 6-0 defeat by West Germany in Berlin and a 0-0 draw against the same opposition in Saarbrücken. Also used in a 3-2 victory over Northern Ireland in Belfast and a 7-3 hiding of Wales in Swansea, his final international matches were against Scotland. The host nation lost 2-0 in London, a game in which he acquired the rather unwanted distinction of becoming the first ever representative of England Boys to be cautioned at Wembley, but he felt the elation of contributing towards a 3-0 defeat of their fiercest adversaries at Old Trafford.

Coming up against future United colleagues John McInally and Ian Donald in the Scotland fixtures, within the pages of one of the match programmes he was described as *'a hard tackling accomplished defender, with a good head and excellent distribution'*.

Millerchip grew up as an Aston Villa supporter and began his association in organised football on Saturday afternoons with Arbury Youth Club. Concurrently starring for his secondary school side, with whom numerous league titles and cup competitions were won, he was then promoted into a Nuneaton Boys side that secured successes locally. He captained Warwickshire as a schoolboy and was spotted by Joe Armstrong when assisting Birmingham & District Boys at the age of fifteen.

Clubs such as Nottingham Forest, Coventry, Arsenal, Spurs and Aston Villa monitored him and, while later invited to watch their respective first-teams in action, he didn't undergo formal trials with any of them. *'Me and my dad were invited to Old Trafford for a long weekend, but by then I had already been drawn towards United as they were well on their way to winning the First Division title,'* he explained. *'Also, I felt at ease with Joe Armstrong as I trusted what he told me about the club.'* Signing the necessary apprentice terms in March 1967, the move to Manchester was completed soon after he had secured his last England Boys cap.

He put in his first shift for the 'B' team in August 1967 and from then on usually found himself at that grade in his customary right full-back position. December came quickly, and with it the start of the Youth Cup, and despite still being a few weeks away from his 16th birthday, he was called into the squad as an unused substitute for a win against Huddersfield. Later given the number twelve shirt for both of the Fourth Round matches with Burnley, by the end of the term he had been present for around twenty games for the 'B' side as they finished third in the division.

There was an exhilarating end to the campaign in store for him when he was included in the side that won the Blue Stars tournament in Zurich and, as he revealed, upon returning to England his joy escalated even further, *'Because the first-team had reached the European Cup final, the youth squad flew from Switzerland to London to watch the game before attending a celebratory banquet at the Russell Hotel. The next day we travelled back north by train for a civic reception at Manchester Town Hall.'*

On the opening day of his second season, the 10th August 1968, he was given an initial sighting of the Central League when going on as a substitute in a 2-1 win at Everton. Gradually eased into the Reserves to share right full-back duties with Frank Kopel, the Youth Cup kicked-off at Blackpool in early December and he was utilised exclusively in that same position as the Reds went as far as the semi-final.

One of the gamest players on the payroll back then, Millerchip possessed a searing turn of pace, tackled forcefully and instinctively knew precisely the right moment to part with the ball. With those attributes, the hopes he carried of consolidating a place in the Central League side didn't appear to be misplaced.

It was around then that many of the background changes at Old Trafford started to take effect as Matt Busby had handed first-team responsibilities to Wilf McGuinness while Bill Foulkes was given the role of youth coach. Much to Millerchip's disappointment, when the 1969/70 term commenced he found himself back in the 'A' team and was unable to dent the Reserves as Shay Brennan occupied his position. He was made captain of the youth team, however, and again put in a full complement of eight games as the last four was reached for the second year in a row. It was mainly a year of discontent, though, as, while he was thrilled to be nominated as 13th man for the seniors' short trip to Manchester City in November, the remainder of the campaign was seen out on 'A' side chores.

It was a similar story all through the 1970/71 season, with him one of many who felt the effects of a shifting staff situation at the club. Recollecting his frustration at the situation he said, *'Things came to a head when Wilf McGuinness returned to his previous role of Reserves' coach after Busby resumed managerial duties. He discovered that I had been without match practice for nearly two months because I had been on the bench for all of that time.'*

He counted out time in the 'A' side and, unable to push his way into the Central League picture on a sustained basis, failed to win a new contract. Having appeared in over 100 competitive games for United, his official leaving date was in June 1971.

His availability was circulated by the Professional Footballers' Association, with the result being that Brighton manager Pat Saward was soon in contact. Travelling down to the south coast, terms were agreed with the Seagulls even though contract offers were also received from Aston Villa and Walsall. When he returned to Manchester to get married, a counter offer from Australia presented itself, but he turned the approach down only to hear that Saward had left Brighton and his deal was called off.

A trial at Doncaster Rovers lasted for a couple of months, even though in the end it came to nothing as no money was available, and following a one-game trial at Walsall he visited Bradford City where their manager was convinced that he was worth adding to the payroll. In a similar set of circumstances to those that had occurred at Brighton, the Bradford boss was sacked and the new man didn't want him.

After a merry-go-round that resulted in very little by way of a concrete outcome, and by now fairly cheesed off, he linked up with former Red John Cooke at Altrincham and also spent a short period at Chorley without seeing any first-team action at either outpost.

Unable to really settle, Millerchip was briefly hired by Macclesfield and Sandbach, the latter liaison curtailing through injury, and he then linked up with Grasmere Rovers for a couple of years or so.

Finally finding a spiritual home in the mid-1970's when signing for Urmston Town of the Manchester League, he remained with them for all of twelve years. During that time he worked for a government training board before moving into sales with Rank Xerox. In 1988, he started up his own office equipment and stationery supply company, the business venture coinciding with him joining Old Urmstonians in a veteran's league. He remained there until 1994 while also working in the telecom industry for nearly a decade.

Now employed as a sales and marketing manager for a clothes manufacturing company in the Manchester area, while unable to do too much running, his fitness is maintained by cycling and playing badminton. Married with two daughters, one of whom underwent trials for England at netball, Laurie Millerchip continues to take an interest in United's affairs and is a member of the Former Players' Association.

JONES, Paul Stanley (1971/72)

Born: Stockport, 10th September 1953
Height: 5ft. 9ins., **Weight:** 11st.
Role: Right full-back or left half-back
Career: St. Thomas' Primary School (Hillgate, Stockport)/ Dialstone Lane Secondary School (Stockport)/ Stockport Boys/ **UNITED**: Ass. Schoolboy July 1968 App. Pro. July 1969 Pro. December 1970/ **Mansfield Town** June 1973 to May 1974/ **Rochdale** (L) November and December 1973/ **Glossop** November 1974/ **Ashton United** August 1976 to March 1977/ **St. George Budapest** (Aus) March to August 1978

Question: When did Paul Jones make his Manchester United first-team debut? The answer would probably puzzle even some of the club's more knowledgeable amateur statisticians simply because his senior bow occurred in what has become recognised as a 'minor' competition and has therefore never been put properly recognised.

Regardless, Jones registered his solitary first-team appearance by substituting for Jim Holton when the Reds drew 1-1 with Fiorentina in a Group One clash of the Anglo-Italian Inter-League Clubs' Competition in front of 23,951 spectators at Old Trafford in February 1973.

He detailed the circumstances surrounding the event by saying, *'I had been a regular in the 'A' team and just broken into the Reserves when Frank O'Farrell told me I was to be given a free transfer at the end of the season, so I was pretty upset at the time. Then in the December, O'Farrell got sacked and Tommy Docherty came in. He got rid of a lot of the older players and told me I was reinstated and would be given a chance to prove myself until the end of the season. From then on I was a regular in the Reserves and United had just entered the Anglo-Italian Cup.*

There were a lot of friendlies going on and loads of players coming in and out. I think Docherty wanted to see us in Europe again and also wanted to try out a few of the younger players. So people like Frank McGivern, Pat Olney, Peter Fletcher and myself all got a run.

It was a great experience to play alongside Bobby Charlton, Willie Morgan, Brian Kidd and Martin Buchan, but at Old Trafford as well, it was just great! Then a few weeks later I was part of the squad that travelled to face Lazio in Rome and we had an audience with the Pope in the Vatican.'

The Reds contested a bitter 0-0 draw with a side that seemed happy with the result in the Italian capital and Jones wasn't required for what proved to be a dirty game in which the referee was carried off after an altercation with one of the home players.

Returning to Central League duty for the remainder of the campaign in one or other of the full-back positions, he worked especially hard to win the chance of a reprieve at the end of the term only to no avail.

'We played a trial match at the end of the season,' he recounted with much regret. *'Tommy Docherty told me that it was between Brian Greenhoff and myself who was going to be released and in the end I lost out.'* After spending four years at the club, his final curtain call was in the second string's 4-1 reverse at Hillsborough in May 1973.

Joining Mansfield a month later, an introduction to the Fourth Division in a 1-1 draw at Barnsley followed in September and later that month he scored his one and only goal at that standard with the winner against Darlington. Unable to force his way into the team on a regular basis, over the November and December period a loan spell with Rochdale left him no better off for the experience. He took part in a total of twenty Football League games for Mansfield over the course of the season only to be hit hard once more with the realisation that his contract wouldn't be renewed.

Disillusioned and unsure as to what his future held, he spent a month on trial at Chesterfield at the start of the 1974/75 term and within weeks had been fixed up in a more northerly location in the county of Derbyshire at Glossop. His first appearance for them was in an F.A. Vase tie, putting on a display which was described as *'cultured'* in the local press.

In August 1976 it was reported that he had signed for Bethesda until a change of mind by the player resulted in him instead joining Ashton United. Sometime during the following year he spotted a newspaper advertisement which offered the opportunity of vacancies for footballers in Australia and his subsequent application to join National Soccer League members St. George Budapest was accepted.

With the club paying for his flight to Sydney in the early months of 1978, by March he had tasted his first competitive action in the southern hemisphere in a home engagement with South Melbourne. Featuring in fourteen consecutive matches while the team was infected with a bout of inconsistency, when former Tottenham midfielder Ralph Coates arrived in June, Jones lost his place and took part in only two more league games.

His last appearance ended in a 4-1 victory over Fitzroy United in July 1978 and it brought an end to his days in football at the age of 24. Whatever disappointment he may have felt about the football side of things was balanced by the benefits of his new lifestyle down under, because the warm, sunny days of Sydney were in stark contrast to the cold and dark winter evenings of Greater Manchester.

Born in Stockport's Hillgate and raised at nearby Heaton Chapel, he was originally discovered by Joe Armstrong when representing Stockport Boys against Manchester Boys in the Manchester Trophy final at Edgeley Park, a curtain raiser to the Stockport County v. Derby County Friendly Shield match in April 1968. Lining up against his Stockport team that afternoon was Tony Young, another talented prospect who also took Armstrong's eye.

Jones made an inauspicious start in the opening match of the 1969/70 season when the 'B' team was dispatched 5-1 at Preston. He turned out in midfield or at full-back throughout the term, missing only eight games, as United went on to win the Lancashire League Division Two title by remaining undefeated from mid-September. Everton had led the title race for most of the campaign, until fourteen straight victories from the Old Trafford youngsters saw them overtake the Toffees in the home straight.

During the following season he made the transition to the 'A' team look comparatively easy. Originally a creative midfielder who operated in a style akin to that of an old-fashioned inside-forward, he was devastatingly quick over short distances. Also comfortable using either foot and renowned for his fluid passing game, he figured predominantly at left–back for the Lancashire League Division One team and was also named as a substitute for two of that term's Youth Cup ties. The major bright spot of his 1970/71 campaign occurred in April when he was included in the Reserves for a 1-1 draw at Aston Villa.

Continuing as a mainstay of the 'A' team, Jones was recalled to the Reserves for two matches in November and then led out the side that met Everton in the opening Youth Cup tie on the first day of December. Unfortunately, his time wearing the captain's armband only stretched to 180 minutes as the Reds were eliminated following a replay at Goodison Park.

He made a further four appearances for the Reserves in the second half of the season and was also involved in the Lancashire Senior Cup campaign, including a final in which United lost on a 5-2 aggregate to Burnley. There was more to shout about in the Lancashire Youth Cup, as he skippered the club's teenagers to a 5-3 aggregate victory over Bolton in early May.

The 1972/73 term proved to be topsy-turvy for him. Starting the term at right-back for the Reserves before settling down in central defence, by the middle of December he had featured in eight Central League matches at which point O'Farrell informed him that he was going to be released at the end of the season. *'There were lots of changes and many of the young players couldn't make it,'* he complained. *'I mean, I was one of the last Busby Babes and in four years I had played under four different managers. Coaching staff were coming and going, players were coming and going, it was a really difficult time.'*

After experimenting by giving numerous of the younger hopefuls the opportunity of impressing, Docherty decided to prune the playing staff by scrapping the 'B' team for the 1973/74 campaign and consequently he needed to see those of whom could make the grade and those who couldn't. So, through the medium of the Anglo-Italian Cup, the manager was able to blood a few who he felt might stand a chance.

After giving up football, Paul Jones worked in sales for many years before taking a job as an operations manager for a transport company. Nowadays living in Cronulla in Sydney's southern suburbs, while still not officially recognised in some quarters, he can at least claim that his modest career in the sport included an appearance in Manchester United's first-team.

O'NEIL, Thomas Patrick
(1968/69, 1969/70, 1970/71)

Born: St. Helens, 25th October 1952
Died: New Bold, St Helens, 1st May 2006
Height: 5ft. 6ins., **Weight:** 11st. 4lbs.
Role: Centre-half or right full-back
Career: St. Vincent's Primary School (St. Helens)/ St. Cuthbert's R.C. Secondary School (St. Helens)/ St. Helens Boys/ Lancashire Boys/ England Boys/ UNITED: App. Pro. July 1968 Pro. November 1969 to June 1973/ Blackpool (L) January to March 1973/ Southport August 1973/ Tranmere Rovers June 1978/ Halifax Town August 1980/ Altrincham July 1982/ Southport October 1982/ St. Helens Town July 1983/ Warrington Town July 1987/ Irlam Town season 1988/89/ Warrington Town season 1989/90/ Skelmersdale United July 1990 to c/s 1992

Tommy O'Neil was in the thoughts of many United supporters following his death in the spring of 2006. With 68 competitive senior games between May 1971 and December 1972 to his credit, long-term followers of the Reds recall him as the epitome of all-out commitment, a tough 'in yer face' defender who didn't know the meaning of giving less than his best. In the late 1990's he was back at the club where it all began for him, joining the coaching staff and gaining great satisfaction from working with various age groups at under-9 to under-16 stages.

Growing up in St. Helens, a hotbed of the pastime, it was no surprise that his first sporting affection was rugby league. He was involved with his school soccer side as a young boy but, because he had the twin distractions of watching his beloved Saints on Saturday afternoons, having already played for his school rugby side in the morning, it left little time for much else. Fortunately, St. Cuthbert's School was very much a sports-oriented establishment and he could satisfy both football passions without upsetting his teachers at all. About the time of turning twelve, O'Neil was selected to represent his town football team and two or three years later, during the 1967/68 season, further recognition arrived at his door when he was chosen for Lancashire Boys.

'My father was an Everton fan,' he said. *'There was a flicker of interest from Goodison Park, but it was actually Liverpool who took me on trial. I went over there but I scratched them off my list as I didn't take much of a liking to my Anfield experience. I heard from Burnley, Manchester City and Blackpool, and I had already received a very good offer from Wolves when Joe Armstrong came along. I completed a trial with United and I was a regular at The Cliff in my school holidays from then on.'* A right-sided midfielder back in the day, it was while with Lancashire Boys when he first teamed up with Tony Young and, situated just behind the Mancunian for the county team, they gained rave reviews for their performances.

Back in his rugby league exploits, he captained Lancashire prior to being awarded three England caps for his efforts at stand-off when touring France with the national squad. It was about then that he joined forces with St. Anne's Youth Rugby Football Club before turning out for a Sutton Heath under-18 side who were members of the Lancashire Combination.

Soon attending the north of England schools' football trials, his name appeared in the squad that was due to take on West Germany Boys at Wembley on the 27th April 1968. Nominated as a reserve, the match programme described him as *'a hard tackling player with boundless energy and an attacking flair'*. Despite not being required, two weeks later he won his solitary cap for England Boys in a 1-0 Victory Shield defeat by Scotland at Ibrox Park. A busy schedule ended in June when all of Lancashire Boys' Northern Counties Schools' Competition matches were completed and within weeks he became an apprentice professional at Old Trafford.

Because of the relatively short distance involved, and against his preference to move to Manchester, he was required to travel in each weekday for training. His first start for the Reds was in a 'B' team game in August 1968 and he made just one more appearance on the bottom rung before progressing to the 'A' side. Missing the opening two Youth Cup ties due to injury, by the turn of the year he was back to full fitness and gained inclusion in all of the later rounds.

A constant for the 'A' and youth teams right through the 1969/70 season, his consistency earned him a place in the Central League side before the decade was out as, when Nick Murphy was unavailable for the visit of Blackpool in December, he was seen as an ideal replacement. Keeping his place in the team for a trip to Anfield, in the aftermath of a 4-0 loss he returned to the 'A' team, albeit temporarily. For the second term on the spin, the young Reds almost went the full distance in the Youth Cup and, with his development going as he would have hoped for, the club offered him a new two-year deal. The most disappointing aspect of an otherwise superb period

biography

281

of development was that, after attending England Youth trials, injuries forced his withdrawal from the selection process.

He spoke about the events of the 1970/71 campaign, which proved to be landmarks for him in a number of ways, *'Because there were so many midfielders at the club, and with my height being a disadvantage in central defence, Bill Foulkes suggested that I give it a go at right full-back. We tried out a few experiments in the 'A' team in the first few weeks (of the term), and within a short time I felt really comfortable and confident there. I was also maturing physically and mentally and as a consequence I was used more regularly in the Central League over the course of the season.'*

Also given the captaincy of the Youth Cup side, unfortunately his reign didn't last as long as he would have hoped because the Reds took an early exit from the competition at the hands of Burnley.

He went on, *'My confidence was really at a peak and one morning I was training at The Cliff when Matt Busby informed me that I was going to make my first-team debut against Manchester City at Maine Road. I was so nervous that I couldn't remember getting home that evening.'* A day or two later, on the 5th May 1971 and in front of 43,626 fans, United recorded a memorable 4-3 victory that would live long in the memory of the eighteen year-old.

When Frank O'Farrell came in shortly after, a number of the playing staff were wary of what was in store for them but, as far as O'Neil was concerned, there was no need to worry. Missing only five senior matches in total, a great opening to the campaign took the Reds to the top of the table only for them to fall away spectacularly to a final position of eighth. He was then invited on a summer tour during which he was utilised against Mallorca, Panathinaikos and Tel Aviv.

The beginning of the 1972/73 term couldn't have been more different to the one before as United lost four and drew four of their opening eight fixtures, which resulted in him being dropped. As he was the only one to feel the axe fall, it indicated that O'Farrell wasn't confident about handling some of the senior personalities who should possibly have shouldered more of the responsibility. Nevertheless, by November he had forced his way back into the side as the Reds continued to struggle for form.

At the end of a sequence of three wins and three defeats, which disastrously culminated in a 5-0 reverse at Crystal Palace in December 1972, O'Farrell was sacked and when Tommy Docherty arrived the defender got just two games in which to prove himself. After being demoted again, this time there was no reprieve and within four weeks he was farmed out to Blackpool.

He explained, *'To say that I was dumbstruck would be stating the obvious. I just couldn't comprehend how I had gone from United's first-team to Blackpool in the Second Division in such a short space of time.'* However, and true to character, the Seasiders got one hundred per cent effort from their loan signing and saw enough of him over seven games to want to put in an offer for his transfer, a request that Docherty flatly refused.

Then detailing what was a perplexing situation, he continued, *'When I got back to Old Trafford at the end of March, Docherty made it clear I had no future with United and that I would be released at the end of the season. I was really baffled by that because I was now expected to tread water for a couple of months and could then leave for free when there was good money from Blackpool already sitting on the table.'* By now totally brassed off, he saw out the remaining fixtures in the Reserves, the last of which ended in a defeat at Sheffield Wednesday on the 3rd May 1973.

In a bid to maintain fitness, O'Neil trained with St. Helens and even considered signing on for their rugby league campaign. Soon offered a contract at Third Division Southport, his debut on the 1st September resulted in a 3-0 home win over Aldershot. A publication called *'The Complete League History of Southport F.C.'* noted that he was *'a ball winner with a granite-hard tackle....(but) occasionally fell foul of referees and would undoubtedly have made more appearances had his disciplinary record been better'.* It added, *'He was also useful upfront, being top scorer in 1977/78 with eleven goals, five of them penalties. He was voted 'Player of the Year' in three consecutive seasons'.*

Unbeknown to him, Crystal Palace, Reading and Fulham had all made enquiries about his availability at one time or another. With Southport unwilling to lose their prize asset, even his Herculean efforts weren't enough to prevent the club's relegation from the Football League. Present for Southport's final match at Watford in April 1978, in total O'Neil had registered 198 league games for them. He had spent almost five years at Haig Avenue and during that period it was widely considered the former Red was a class or two above those around him.

Then contacted by Tranmere while alternative offers from Reading, Southend and Crewe also came along, a two-year contract with the Prenton Park outfit was seen as the best option on the basis that he wanted to remain in the area. His first year there was a bad one as the Rovers finished second

Escorted by a number of the club's backroom staff, United's youth squad prepare to jet to Switzerland in 1970
Descending stairs (from top): Brian Greenhoff, Drew Harris, Kevin Lewis, Frank McGivern, Laurie Millerchip, Tommy O'Neil, Peter Fletcher, Bill Fairhurst
Standing (l-r): Willie Carrick, Ian Donald, Ken Ramsden (Ticket office manager), Damien Ferguson (hidden), Eric Young, Bill Foulkes (Coach), Jimmy Fleming, Ronnie Miller (hidden), Sammy McIlroy, Paul Jones, John Aston (Youth team manager), Unknown, Joe Armstrong (Chief scout), Joe Royle (Senior groundsman)

from bottom of the Third Division and were relegated. At the end of the next campaign, Tranmere found themselves just below mid-table and following his 74th league appearance for them it was seen as time for a change.

Rejecting offers from both Rochdale and Crewe, in 1980 he moved to Halifax. Early into his second term with the Town he suffered the misfortune of a bad leg break and missed the remainder of the final year of his contract. Not being in a position to add to his 40 Fourth Division games for the Shaymen, by the time he was fit again there were big questions being asked about how his leg would cope with the rigors of professional football.

Joining Bangor City for their pre-season preparations in 1982, Altrincham provided a brief home for his talents soon after. While at Moss Lane, Tranmere tried to lure him back but their offer was declined as he was still in some pain with his leg. By October 1982 he had returned to a former employer, Southport, and added 25 league games to his total while regaining full fitness with the Northern Premier League club.

A move closer to base followed in 1983 whereby he joined his local team, St. Helens Town, and after being installed as the skipper of the North-West Counties League side, four happy years were spent at Hoghton Road. St. Helens entered the F.A. Vase for the first time in the 1986/87 campaign and, against all the odds, reached the final at Wembley where they faced Warrington Town.

In what was his finest day in sport, and watched by proud daughters Kaylie and Lyndsey and wife Eileen, the vastly experienced O'Neil led his side to a 3-2 victory over their local adversaries. Following an open top bus parade around the town, the club captain recalled in a newspaper interview that the team was 3-0 behind in one of the early rounds only to bounce back and win the match 5-4.

A few weeks later he actually switched to Warrington Town before moving on once again to become Irlam Town's player/manager. Then reverting back to Warrington as player/manager of their second string, from 1990 onwards he spent two years with North-West Counties League side Skelmersdale United, once again as their player/manager, before making one last stop to join Beeches of the Mid-Cheshire League. While with Beeches he fractured his leg again and was forced out of the game at the age of 42.

Through those non-league days he held a variety of jobs in the building trade prior to obtaining teaching and coaching qualifications. From the early 1990's he was employed at Carmel Sixth Form College in St. Helens, where he taught essential skills and special needs until suffering a heart attack in 1996, at which point he took time off to recuperate. For the next seven years he continued working at Carmel College and also recommenced with United prior to requiring chemotherapy on his leg for cancer.

In May 2006, after a long fight against the disease, Tommy O'Neil passed away in his home town. On behalf of the club, Academy coach Paul McGuinness said of his former colleague, *'He was extremely enthusiastic about football, especially Manchester United, as he grew up at the club. He was a great character, who loved positive and aggressive football and enjoyed sharing his experiences of playing with Law, Best and Charlton. He'll be sorely missed.'*

HAGGETT, David Lyn (1977/78, 1978/79)

Born: Aberdare, near Merthyr Tydfil, 16th March 1961
Height: 6ft., Weight: 11st. 1lb.
Role: Midfielder or central defender
Career: **Abertaf Junior School (Abercynon, Mountain Ash)/ Mountain Ash Comprehensive School/ Cynon Valley Boys/ Glamorgan Boys/ Wales Boys/ Lostock High School (Stretford)/ UNITED:** Ass. Schoolboy October 1975 App. July 1977 Pro. March 1978 to April 1981/ **Jämsänkosken Ilves (Fin) (L) 1980/ Merthyr Tydfil** August 1981 to March 1982/ **Brecon Corinthians** August 1982 to September 1984/ **South Wales Police** mid-to-late 1980's

David Haggett was aged thirteen and playing local youth football for a team called Church Club when he undertook trials with Manchester City, Chelsea and Arsenal in his school holidays. Offered contract terms by all of those suitors, in addition to Queen's Park Rangers, he later came to the attention of Walter Robbins. United's scout in the Swansea area felt that the boy could be of some use to the club as a creative midfield option who demonstrated clean and clever distribution.

Haggett won selection for Wales Boys on three occasions in the 1975 school season, his first game resulting in a 2-1 victory over Scotland. That happy event was followed by an even greater margin of success, a 4-0 win against Northern Ireland, and, with England Boys also having won both of their games, that year's Victory Shield was decided by a meeting of the two teams in Cardiff. England scored four times to Wales' one goal, meaning the latter side were forced to settle for what was considered a highly creditable second place.

His consolation was to be offered a trial at Old Trafford and he arrived at precisely the same time and for the identical purpose as soon-to-be Liverpool stars Bruce Grobbelaar and Ronnie Whelan. Signing schoolboy terms in October 1975 while still in full-time education, further representative honours were gained the following year when he captained his country's under-15 team. The Welsh side included future professionals Mark Aizlewood and Kevin Ratcliffe, along with two other lads who were to later join United, John Lucas and Stuart Plunkett. Haggett played in a 2-2 draw with Scotland in the Welsh capital and a 1-1 draw against England at York, with his final Victory Shield appearance against Northern Ireland at Newport ending in a 2-0 victory for the home nation. Then taking part in a 4-1 friendly defeat staged at Wembley against England, his final schoolboy cap was awarded for another friendly, this one with France at Colwyn Bay.

'Before I got to Manchester it was arranged for me to attend Lostock High School in Stretford,' he noted. *'I must say, though, that my favourite part of the week was on Saturday mornings when I could play football.'*

His debut for United 'B' came in a 3-1 home win over Halifax 'A' in September 1976. A constant presence in the 'B' side throughout the campaign, there were, as is the norm, occasional tasters of action at 'A' standard and he was also drafted into the Lancashire Youth Cup team for both of the games against Oldham in March 1977.

During the 1977/78 term he became much more familiar in the 'A' team, ending at the head of their appearance table while missing only two matches, and he also participated as a central defender in all three Youth Cup ties as the Reds were unceremoniously dumped out of the competition at Middlesbrough. With the season drawing to a close he was chosen for both legs of the Lancashire Youth Cup final against Bolton and in between those ties he featured in the opening two fixtures of the Blue Stars tournament in Zurich.

Mainly continuing with the 'A' team throughout the 1978/79 campaign, he was required to count time for further promotion and said of that period, *'I played in both of that season's Youth Cup ties as captain and when I was leaving the pitch at the end of the Derby game, their manager Tommy Docherty gave me a wry smile as he had originally signed me for United two years earlier.'*

He then helped United to capture the one-legged Lancashire Youth Cup by scoring one of the goals in a 3-0 victory over Tranmere at Old Trafford, and at the end of the term his name topped the appearance list for the 'A' team again as he looked forward to pushing into second team contention in the near future. Within that period he also represented Wales Youth in two European Championship qualifiers against Norway.

With three years experience of junior football to call on, he finally broke through to the Central League side for a 1-0 defeat at Aston Villa in September 1979 and was used once more in the Reserves that same month. It wasn't the concentrated breakthrough hoped for, as he managed only one more appearance for the second string the following April.

His fourth and final season at Old Trafford was an almost total write-off because he was only able to put in seven starts in total. The reason for his long absences was a continuing back problem, which led to a great deal of frustration and not a lot of progress. He was loaned out to a Finnish club for a time and only managed sporadic matches for United between the end of October and Christmas. Returning on 24th January 1981 at Barrow, his last appearance for the 'A' team came in their 1-1 home draw against Port Vale Reserves on the final day of that month after which he admitted defeat and returned to Wales.

'The day I finished with United is easy to remember because it was the same one that Dave Sexton was dismissed,' he recollected. *'I had a contract which lasted until I was 21 and United wanted to pay it up because of my back. I was on my way up to Manchester to discuss things with Sexton when I heard about his sacking on the radio.'*

Haggett embarked on a new career in the Police Service in South Wales, as well as spending almost a full season with Merthyr Tydfil, and while with Welsh League club Brecon Corinthians he underwent a one-game trial for Swansea Reserves. Staged at Highbury against their Arsenal equivalents in September 1984, his task was to mark England international Graham Rix, who was returning from injury, and he then played out the rest of the decade for the South Wales Police team.

Upon completing a relevant qualification, he went on to coach under-11 and under-12 representative sides in the Cynon Valley, steering them to success in the Welsh Championships. He also managed Welsh League Division One side AFC Llwydcoed until 2006 and nowadays undertakes some coaching at Cardiff City's Academy.

Due to retire from the Police in 2012, David Haggett has a special reason for remembering United's Youth Cup defeat by Derby in February 1979. *'I lived in digs in Urmston and I was waiting at the bus stop after the match when I met my future wife,'* he explained. *'We've been together ever since.'*

it weren't for the inadequacies of Rochdale and Halifax, the 'B' team would have finished bottom of the league.

As the 1978/79 campaign got underway, the new apprentice made eight starts upfront for the 'B' side up to early November and was then rather alarmed to be asked to stand in at centre-half for the 'A' team at Stockport. The change came about because Syd Owen had been studying the youngster for some time and the coach felt that converting him to a defender would optimise his talents to better effect.

It was a superb assessment because the seventeen year-old was awash with the necessary attributes. He could certainly read the game, had excellent positional sense, was competent in the air and, with first-class distribution skills, possessed all the skill needed to move the ball out effectively from the back.

Taking to his new role like a duck to water, Keen was utilised in 21 out of the 'A' team's last 23 matches, mainly at right full-back. It was in the same position that he was stationed in both of that term's Youth Cup ties as United were knocked out of the competition in the early stages.

With the divisional title not realistically attainable, the only piece of silverware still up for grabs was the Lancashire Youth Cup and so in early May, having comfortably disposed of Manchester City in the semi-final, the young Reds faced Tranmere at Old Trafford in the last game of the season. The result was never really in doubt, so it was a case of celebrations all round as the trophy was won by a convincing 3-0 margin. A few weeks later he was in for some international glory when Roda JC Kerkrade of Holland were defeated 1-0 in the final of the Blue Stars tournament.

In his third campaign, Keen was situated in the heart of the 'A' team's defence alongside Chris Roberts before moving over to share right-back duties with Gareth Orritt. Then, in September 1979, he was called up for the Central League team at Aston Villa and, despite the Reds losing by a solitary goal, he felt able to hold his own against the tricky Brian Little. A model professional and consistent performer who was popular and respected by his peers, it was fitting that he should be entrusted with the captaincy of the Youth Cup team and his influence was a major reason they reached the semi-final for the first time in ten years.

In the opening tie against Chester, the skipper was given a torrid time by the emerging Ian Rush, who scored twice before United ran out 5-3 victors. Not troubled to anywhere near the same extent in the five ties that followed, by the end of the season he had made a significant breakthrough into the Reserves by taking part in twelve of their games in total.

During the following campaign he was aware that the final stages of his contract were drawing near, so he attempted to live up to his name by impressing Dave Sexton enough to obtain a new deal. Regularly taking a place in defence in the Central League side without seeming to get any closer to the first-team, on the 29th April he received the news from the manager of his release.

As it so happened, Sexton was sacked 24 hours later but the decision had already been taken and it was time to look for a new club. His last domestic game was for United's 'B' team at Liverpool on 18th May 1981 in the semi-final of the Knock-out Cup and his swansong came in Zurich, where he captained the under-18 team to victory against Slovan Bratislava to collect the Hermes Cup.

Officially released on a free transfer on the last day of July, after writing to more than 30 league clubs he was offered trials with only one, Burnley. Unfortunately, it came to nothing and he moved back to Barrow to join his local team, who were then members of the Conference.

He remained at Holker Street for the better part of three seasons as Barrow were relegated from the Alliance Premier League in 1983 only to bounce straight back by winning the Northern Premier League. In his final year with the Bluebirds, the defender was tempted over to South Africa to play for Arcadia Shepherds and upon returning to England in January 1985, Brian Kidd had been appointed as Barrow's new manager.

When Kidd moved to Preston he offered Keen the opportunity of a move to Deepdale. Following a year with North End he then spent a summer back in South Africa with Durban City before returning to England once again and deciding that a change of direction was required.

Because his professional career as a quantity surveyor was becoming more important, a move to London prompted a severance with full-time football.

Joining up with Enfield of the Football Conference, in 1988 he was a member of the team that took part in the F.A. Trophy final against Telford at Wembley. Following a 0-0 draw viewed by 20,161 spectators underneath the twin towers, the replay was staged at The Hawthorns where he collected a winner's medal as Telford were defeated 3-2. After completing nearly six years at The Stadium, the white jersey of Enfield was briefly swapped for the green and white shirt of Hendon.

Exiting the sport in the early 1990's so as to concentrate on his day job, Surrey-based Nigel Keen is responsible for the property division of the John Lewis Partnership and sits on the Waitrose board.

WARDROP, Michael John
(1971/72, 1972/73, 1973/74)

Born: Salford, 23rd December 1955
Height: 5ft. 8ins., **Weight:** 9st. 8lbs.
Role: Left full-back or midfielder
Career: St. James' Primary School (Salford)/ St. Lawrence's Secondary Modern (Salford)/ Salford Boys/ Lancashire Boys/ England Boys/ UNITED: Ass. Schoolboy August 1970 App. July 1971 Pro. December 1972 to January 1975/ New York Cosmos (USA) (L) April to August 1974/ Bury (L) September to December 1974/ Bury January to June 1975/ Kettering Town August 1975 to August 1976/ Droylsden (T) October 1978/ Droylsden November 1978 to March 1979/ Irlam Town early 1980's

Mike Wardrop's promise was first flagged up when Gordon Clayton watched him play for Salford Boys. The Reds' part-time coach was also a policeman and took it upon himself to call at the family home in Pendleton unannounced.

Because he was still on duty, the teenager's parents felt the horror of seeing a member of the constabulary on their doorstep making enquiries about their son, but the shock soon dissolved when the bobby explained who he was and that he only wanted to talk to them about young Michael joining United.

Wardrop was soon attending evening training sessions at The Cliff and, even though he took trials with the likes of Spurs, Burnley and Bury, as well as the Reds, the opportunity of rubbing shoulders with George Best, his boyhood hero, proved irresistible to him.

Signing schoolboy terms in 1970, his later international entrance resulted in a splendid 3-0 win for England Boys over Northern Ireland at Wembley. Also present as England racked up two big wins, a 5-0 mauling of Wales in Cardiff and a 5-1 thrashing of Holland back at Wembley, he then visited West Germany on football duty before starting in a 3-1 win over Scotland at Maine Road.

Originally joining United as a right-sided midfielder, his versatility allowed him to take up no less than five different positions in his first ten games. Debuting with one of the consolation goals in the 'B' team's 5-2 home defeat by Everton in August 1971, he explained how an enduring alternative sporting interest arose just about then, *'I took up golf at about the same time I went to Old Trafford. Along with Roy Morton, I used to play at either the Swinton Park or Davyhulme courses, often with Bill Foulkes.'*

By December he had commenced Youth Cup duty against Everton at Old Trafford and was also present for the replay six days later when the Reds lost 2-1. There were encouraging strides made throughout the campaign and in February 1972 he won an early call up to the Central League side, the 2-0 home defeat by Bury falling less than two months after his 16th birthday.

At the end of April he began to accumulate a few honours. Firstly, the 'B' team won their league by two points from second-placed Blackpool and on the 4th May they beat the Seasiders by a single goal to clinch the Supplementary Cup. Four days later he was chosen for a 3-2 defeat of Bolton at Burnden Park to ensure the Lancashire Youth Cup was won on a 5-3 aggregate.

Beginning a few early 'A' team games of the 1972/73 season at left full-back before moving into a preferred midfield role, he then made another appearance for the Reserves before being installed as the captain when United faced Leicester in a home Youth Cup tie in early December. Once the Foxes had been brushed aside, the young Reds should then have defeated Newcastle at St. James's Park but were made to settle for a 1-1 draw. It was off the pitch, though, that things were really happening just then as Frank O'Farrell was sacked and his replacement, Tommy Docherty, watched one of his first matches in charge when Newcastle were clobbered 4-1 in the replay.

Called upon for the Reserves again soon after, Wardrop was also used from the bench a few times from March onwards. Having experienced so much success in his first season he then suffered the disappointment of reaching a consecutive Lancashire Youth Cup final, only this time losing to Manchester City on aggregate. It appeared to be just a blip, though, as, on analysing the progress made during the campaign, at only seventeen he could claim the most appearances for the 'A' team while latterly pushing for a spot in the Central League side.

The early 1970's was a period of transition for Manchester United and, along with the widely publicised managerial changes, numerous players were bought and sold. For the young apprentices and professionals, often living miles away from home, it was an especially difficult time and on occasions they were left without any guidance, either in football or off-field matters. Fortunately for the local lad, at least he had the stability of his home life to fall back on.

Over the opening period of his third season at the club he was again used mainly on 'A' duties. Towards the end of 1973 he played in all three games of a Caribbean youth tour which resulted in the young Reds winning two matches and drawing the other. That season's Youth Cup commenced a few days later at Oldham, alas it ended with a juddering halt at Huddersfield the following March.

The dejection of falling at Leeds Road was especially hard on someone who held the honour of being the first person to captain United's Youth Cup side for two complete seasons. However, it was soon replaced by congratulations when a day or two later he was told of his involvement in a home first-team friendly against Glasgow Rangers on the forthcoming Saturday. Sent on as Gerry Daly's substitute for the last fifteen minutes against the Scottish artisans, it would prove to be his only exposure to football at that altitude and from then on he retained his place in the Reserves until being loaned to New York Cosmos for the summer.

Desperate to push his United career on, instead of remaining at Old Trafford he was encouraged to join Bury for a few months. Despite only performing at second team level for the Shakers, while on loan he chose to sign for them on a permanent basis on the second day of 1975 after reaching the conclusion that Docherty no longer wanted him. *'I didn't make it because I wasn't good enough,'* he claimed, *'but there were others, like Jimmy Kelly, who was a fantastic player, whose United careers were ruined by mismanagement.'*

He spent the remainder of the 1974/75 campaign at Gigg Lane and, still unable to secure a senior spot, underwent a trial at York City in the 1975 pre-season period. *'I felt like I was back to square one when (former United forward) Charlie Mitten got in touch to ask me did I want to join Johannesburg Rangers in South Africa,'* he bemoaned. *'The deal fell through two days before I was due to go.'*

During his spell in the United States, Wardrop had met Geoff Vowden, an ex-Birmingham City striker who was managing Kettering Town. Vowden convinced him to sign for the Rockingham Road outfit and his Southern Premier League debut for the Poppies took place in August 1975. He went on to make 53 appearances in all competitions, with two of his five goals for the club coming on their triumphant march towards claiming the Southern League Cup.

Best remembered by Poppies' supporters for scoring the winning goal against Northampton Town in the semi-final of the Northamptonshire Senior Cup, while he was resident at Rockingham Road the club famously organised the very first sponsorship deal in British football with Kettering Tyres. He returned to Manchester after just the one campaign there when a new manager was appointed.

Out of the game for over two years as his focus centred on running a pub in Cheadle, Wardrop then underwent a four-week trial at Droylsden before the Bloods signed him on full papers. He then put in a pre-season stint at Runcorn in the summer of 1979 prior to again spending more time away from the sport, Irlam Town proving to be his last association in football.

Nowadays the steward at Didsbury Golf Club, his son, Daniel, is a professional golfer on the tour circuit.

DUXBURY, Michael (1976/77, 1977/78)

Born: Blackburn, 1st September 1959
Height: 5ft. 10ins., **Weight:** 11st. 2lbs.
Role: Central defender
Career: Sacred Heart R.C. Primary School (Church, Blackburn)/ St. Mary's College (Blackburn)/ Accrington Boys/ Blackburn & Darwen Boys/ Lancashire Boys/ UNITED: Ass. Schoolboy May 1975 App. July 1976 Pro. October 1976/ Blackburn Rovers August 1990 to March 1992/ Bradford City (L) January to March 1992/ Bradford City March 1992 to May 1994/ Golden Electronics (Hong Kong) August 1994 to May 1996

A superb servant to the Reds, Mike Duxbury displayed a high level of performance over a prolonged period for the first-team in the 1980's, a decade in which the terms 'consistency' and 'Manchester United' didn't always go hand in hand. Starting in the days of Tommy Docherty, he remained with the club through the reigns of Dave Sexton and Ron Atkinson and into that of Alex Ferguson.

His very last game for United took place just fifteen days before the latter steered his side to victory in the 1990 F.A. Cup final, the Scot's first major trophy at Old Trafford. Duxbury's aggregate figures in competitive fixtures for the United senior side totalled 345 starts, 33 substitute appearances and seven goals.

Seven years previously, in November 1983 and at the age of 24, the first of his ten full England caps was awarded for a 4-0 home win over Luxembourg, with the last coming just eleven months later as Finland were defeated 5-0 at Wembley. The highlight of his international career took place in the Maracana Stadium in Brazil when England ran out 2-0 winners over their hosts, but his time at that standard was cut short due to the side going through a transitional stage, as well as him suffering a bad patch in which some of his former self-assurance disappeared.

He came into the world in Blackburn's Queen's Park Hospital and was raised at nearby Accrington. His father was a keen football fan and often took him to Turf Moor, Burnley then being resident in the old First Division.

Beginning as a striker for his primary school side, that same role was also fulfilled for a time at St. Mary's whereupon he was selected to represent the Accrington Boys (under-11) team. Along with his interest in football, the sports-mad youngster also represented Blackburn at hurdling and in the long-jump, and after becoming the Blackburn District cross-country champion he even ran for Lancashire.

Winning local cup honours at football with St. Mary's when moving back into a central midfield position, the rise from town to county level followed, at which point he came under the scrutiny of Gordon Clayton and Norman Scholes. Even though he trialled at Everton, Liverpool, Blackburn and Leeds, and despite receiving an offer from Arsenal, Duxbury instead elected to make his bed at Old Trafford and he first appeared for the 'B' team in August 1975, right at the outset of his solitary schoolboy season.

With a mere five 'A' and two 'B' games of the 1976/77 term gone he found himself on Central League duty when utilised as a substitute in a 2-1 defeat at Bury and signed professional terms at a salary of £16 per week just a week later. The following month he was in the Youth Cup team that crashed out at Bolton and he remained in the junior sides until the end of March when recalled to the Reserves. Seeing service with them for the last thirteen games of the campaign, there was no question that for a seventeen year-old he had made an excellent impression.

By showing that the rigours of second string standard could be handled he was involved in all bar four games of United's 1977/78 Central League campaign. On the knock-out scene he was selected for the three games in the national youth competition and also took part in a Lancashire Youth Cup final that was lost to Bolton.

Usually found at centre-half, his soccer education continued in the confines of Central League for the next two years and he ended with the most appearances for the Reserves in season 1978/79. Over the same period he also attended England Youth trials at Lilleshall but was overlooked for selection.

It was Dave Sexton who converted him into a full-back and from then on his promise positively blossomed into full flower. In April 1978, Sexton called him into the first-team squad for David Sadler's testimonial game at Preston where he was sent on to replace Gordon McQueen. When the fixture list had completed he was included in the seniors' party that undertook a tour to Norway and again took to the field as a substitute, this time against Brann Bergen.

His competitive first-team breakthrough finally came in August 1980 when he was called off the bench during a 0-0 draw at Birmingham City and he only needed to wait another month for his starting debut in a Manchester derby. Featuring for the seniors throughout the 1980/81 campaign, as the season unfolded he also became the recipient of four England under-21 caps. By now at a physical and mental level of maturity, it was in the 1982/83 term when his career really hit the heights as by then he had made the right full-back position his own.

Over the September and October of 1982 he was included in England's under-21 squad for the European Championships, but was unavailable for the quarter-final and semi-final ties. He had previously represented his country in three qualifying games and was recalled for the final against West Germany as England built up a 3-1 lead in the first leg at Bramall Lane. Scoring one of the goals in a 3-2 return defeat at Bremen, the aggregate meant that England were crowned as European under-21 champions.

Duxbury saw service in every one of United's senior matches that season, including the F.A. Cup final replay in which the Reds beat Brighton 4-0. The glory didn't stop there either, as it was followed with a Charity Shield success a few months later.

Over the next seven seasons there was no dislodging him from the first-team. Seemingly possessing the football equivalent of a Masters degree in adaptability, and even though he was challenged for his position at various times by signings such as John Gidman, Colin Gibson, John Sivebaek and Viv Anderson, as well as newcomers like Billy Garton and Clayton Blackmore, his displays as a no-frills midfielder, full-back or centre-back enabled him to retain his place.

A second F.A. Cup medal was collected in 1985 and four years later, at the outset of the 1989/90 term, his loyalty was rewarded when he was awarded a testimonial game against Manchester City. At all levels he had accumulated more than 600 competitive appearances for United, the last of which came for the senior side in their 4-0 defeat at Nottingham Forest on the 2nd May 1990, and the following month he was given a free transfer.

A number of offers were received upon his release, notably from Wolves and Barnsley, only for their advances to be declined in favour of joining Blackburn Rovers. Sadly, his eighteen months at Ewood Park was blighted by hip and ankle injuries and within that period he managed only 27 Second Division games. An initial loan period with Third Division Bradford City in 1992 led to a full contract offer, and he added another 65 league matches to his considerable total while at Valley Parade.

Then choosing to sign for Golden Electronics of Hong Kong, he and his family spent two years in Asia and while there the club won their national cup competition. Now aged 36, his final game on the 26th May 1996 was in the Hong Kong Golden Select XI's 1-0 defeat by England, which was viewed by 26,000 spectators at the Happy Valley Stadium.

Upon returning to Britain, he trained with Accrington Stanley for a short while and then decided to bid adieu to playing duties. He was later coaching at Blackburn Rovers' Academy when asked if he would be interested in doing some similar work at Bolton School and, remaining there to this day, his responsibilities encompass teaching cricket, swimming, athletics and football.

Living in the Blackburn area still, Mike Duxbury took up a role in Manchester United's Soccer Schools in July 2004 and from then until 2007 he coached in Hong Kong and Dubai for part of each year.

SMITH, Oswald George (1973/74)

Born: Kingston, Jamaica, 25th September 1956
Height: 5ft. 10ins., **Weight:** 11st.
Role: Midfielder or forward
Career: Stretford Grammar School/ Stretford Boys/ Lancashire Boys/ UNITED: Ass. Schoolboy November 1971 to January 1975/ Bolton Wanderers February to May 1975/ Aston University September 1975 to June 1979/ Wimbledon 1977/ Grays Athletic September 1977 to January 1978/ Curzon Ashton August 1978/ Altrincham July 1979/ Runcorn March 1980/ Altrincham July 1987/ Northwich Victoria July 1989/ Southport October 1989/ Fleetwood Town August 1991/ Winsford United March 1992 to January 1993

Ossie Smith was a gifted schoolboy footballer who possessed a seemingly endless amount of stamina. A judicious tackler who used the ball with unerring accuracy, his fine scoring record included many headed goals simply as a result of an ability to outjump defenders.

Joining the Reds in 1971, just a couple of months after turning fifteen, his playing spell with the club spanned a little over three years, although the number of games he took part in during that period totalled relatively few.

Smith eventually chose to commence a career path outside of the professional game and, on top of gaining caps for England at three different levels, instead he became one of the most respected non-league footballers of his era.

He arrived in the UK from the Caribbean in 1961 when only a toddler and grew up in Old Trafford. His initial association with the Reds began at the age of thirteen and while training twice a week at The Cliff he also played in the Cheadle & District League for Kingsfield United. He then went on to represent both Stretford Boys and the Cheadle & District League as well as, in the 1970/71 season, Lancashire Boys.

Soon offered trials by Manchester City and Blackpool, their advances were shunned in favour of penning schoolboy terms with United. Because his parents were insistent on him obtaining a professional qualification, he concentrated almost entirely on his studies until making a first start for the 'A' team in November 1973, which was a full two years after signing for the club.

A few weeks later he got his first sighting of the Youth Cup when named as an unused substitute for a 1-1 Third Round home draw with Bury. Drafted into the side for the replay at Gigg Lane, the number ten scored twice in a splendid 3-1 win and retained a place in the starting line-up for the next two games, the second of which saw the Reds knocked out at Huddersfield. A month after that Youth Cup exit he was elevated into the Central League team for a 2-1 defeat at Burnley.

Although the coaching staff were well aware that he carried no small amount of ability, even then they had hardly seen enough of him to be able to assess his true potential and a continued commitment to education throughout that period meant his football activities were always going to be a secondary priority.

Still not a regular in either of the junior sides when the following season got underway, as he was by then concentrating on his A-levels, Smith asked Frank Blunstone whether he was going to be taken on as a professional. *'Frank replied that it was too early to say,'* he remembers only too well. *'He explained that a judgement of that type should ideally be made over a complete season. It was then that I decided to focus fully on my studies.'* He quit United in January 1975, with the last of his twenty appearances for the club made for the 'A' team in their 1-1 home draw with Manchester City as long ago as the previous October.

Bolton Wanderers soon got wind of his departure from Old Trafford and gave him the opportunity to join them on a temporary basis. Happy to accept their offer to play on an ad hoc basis, his short stay at Burnden Park encompassed appearances in both legs of their aggregate Lancashire Youth Cup semi-final defeat by Everton and selection for both Greater Manchester and England at under-18 level, his solitary cap at the latter standard awarded for a 1-0 defeat against Wales at Hereford in April 1975.

He left Manchester soon after to commence a four-year degree course in quantity surveying in Birmingham, a time in which he assisted the Aston University team to reach the 1976 University final against Durham. The impression he made led to him being chosen for the England University side and he consequently took part in matches against similar teams from West Germany, Holland and all of the home nations.

As part of his degree course, Smith was required to spend some time in London and while residing in the capital he was connected with Wimbledon for three months without seeing service in their senior side. Later associated with Grays Athletic for just over a dozen games, one Essex newspaper described him as being *'particularly industrious'* while another match report claimed that his *'slinky skills'* impressed everyone.

In his final year at university he was nominated for the British Student team and it came as a great thrill for him to participate in the World Student Games in Mexico, even though the football part of the trip didn't live up to expectations as his side was knocked out in the group stages.

Later putting in just one 90-minute stint for Curzon Ashton while on home leave, the following year he joined Altrincham. While at Moss Lane he was utilised almost exclusively in the Robins' Reserve team prior to transferring to Runcorn in March 1980.

The marriage was made in football heaven, because over the next seven years the diamond-bright promise he had always threatened to display was polished to dazzling effect. Within weeks of his arrival at Canal Street the club succeeded in winning a Maine Road-staged Northern Premier League (NPL) Challenge Cup final, and that was only a foretaste of what was to follow.

In his first full term with the Cheshire outfit, they claimed the NPL Championship, the NPL Challenge Shield, the NPL Cup and he scooped their 'Player of the Year' award. Upon their promotion to the Alliance Premier League for the 1981/82 season, the Linnets finished at the top of the division while losing only five league games and they also retained the NPL Challenge Shield. Tasked with a central midfield responsibility, in the 1982/83 term Smith skippered the side as they added the Bob Lord Trophy and Gola Championship Shield to their recent haul of honours.

A further personal milestone followed in 1984 when he was chosen for the England semi-professional side for a match against Wales. Just a year later Runcorn again won the Bob Lord Trophy and in 1986 they reached Wembley only to lose by the solitary goal of the game to Altrincham in the F.A. Trophy final.

During an incredibly productive stay at Canal Street, he was present for more than 400 games and scored over a century of goals on his way to becoming a serial silverware magnet as the club scooped no less than fourteen trophies, which included capturing the Cheshire Senior Cup for three successive years.

It is no wonder that, even today, he is still regarded as a cult figure on the *'Linnets Legends'* page of the club's website where he is described as *'undoubtedly a great player and leader'*. Also noted as someone with *'boundless energy'*, the writer reminisces about *'those surging runs'* he once made and also mentions that his right leg *'appeared to be telescopic at times when he went into the tackle'*.

A change of management in 1987 led him to rejoin Altrincham where he remained for two years, a period that saw him sidelined for seven months with a ruptured achilles tendon.

With his best days coming to an end, he then meandered between numerous North-West clubs. Hitching up with Northwich for a few months, he also made over 50 appearances for Southport and was at Fleetwood for a time before signing for Winsford. Having been there for less than a year, a cartilage injury required surgery and, by now in his late 30's, he took it upon himself to retire from active duties.

Winsford's manager was sincere in his praise when telling the local newspaper that he had *'played a substantial part in our promotion by giving us much needed options in last season's run-in'* and summarised the thoughts of many when claiming *'he was a great player.'*

Remaining in the game by holding coaching and assistant manager roles at various venues such as Northwich, Winsford, Maine Road, Flixton and Cheadle, in recent years Ossie Smith has coached Stockport County's under-11's at their School of Excellence.

United babes on road to top

Chapter Five

HARRISON'S HOPEFULS

1981-82

1) Paul Hayward	9) Alan Arnold
2) Mark Bates	10) Craig Shakespeare
3) Lee Sinnott	11) Paul Smith
4) Colin Caddick	*12) Andy Shutt (for 5)*
5) Jonathan Chapman	
6) Wayne Farmer	
7) Andy Parkes	
8) Chris Wilson	

1) Philip Hughes	9) Norman Whiteside
2) Andy Hill	10) Mark Hughes
3) Grant Mitchell	11) Clayton Blackmore
4) Graeme Hogg	*12) Nicky Wood (for 7)*
5) Billy Garton	
6) Lawrence Pearson	
7) Sean Williams	
8) Mark Dempsey	

NOVEMBER 1981

WALSALL 1 v 3 MANCHESTER UNITED
Wilson — Pearson (2), Whiteside

Tuesday 24th
Kick-off 7.30 p.m.
Attendance 519

second round

Pearson is Reds' hero

The summer of 1981 saw a flurry of activity at Old Trafford, events which were kick-started by the not totally unexpected dismissal of manager Dave Sexton. Despite Sexton's achievements in steering the Reds to an F.A. Cup final and second place in the First Division during his four years in charge, as well as racking up seven straight victories at the end of the 1980/81 season, his lack of genuine charisma to a generation of fans brought up on the more flamboyant style of previous boss Tommy Docherty was a hindrance he never quite overcame. Early exits from the two domestic cup competitions and falling attendances almost certainly cost Sexton his job, and he was quickly replaced by someone who more closely mirrored Docherty's persona, the former occupant of West Bromwich Albion's hot-seat, Ron Atkinson.

While it could be said that very few United supporters would have objected to the change, they did, in fact, owe Sexton a great debt as it was he who had implemented huge improvements to the youth system at Old Trafford. Besides recruiting the highly regarded Syd Owen to oversee the club's junior set-up, the revamped scouting system he put in place yielded a number of hopefuls who would go on to serve United with distinction for many years to come. If any proof were needed that Sexton's methods were working, a look at the club's recent record in the Youth Cup, semi-finalists for the past two years, provided adequate evidence of the fact and of course, those consecutive last-four achievements meant that the 1980's had already offered up a greater degree of success in the tournament than did the whole of the previous decade.

Naturally, Atkinson wanted to choose his own backroom staff and one of those was former Everton youth coach Eric Harrison, a former defender whose 517 appearances were spent in the lower reaches of the Football League with clubs such as Barrow, Hartlepool and Southport.

It was said that, besides having already carved out an enviable reputation for himself as a coach who could consistently and correctly develop young players so as to realise their maximum potential, Harrison was enlisted to take on as much responsibility of the youth side of the club as possible in order that Atkinson would be in a position to concentrate his efforts on steering the seniors to success.

> *For the past nine years I have been fortunate to have been involved with a great club. Now, though, fortune has permitted me the opportunity to become involved with the greatest club of all.*
>
> *It is vitally important that young players feel comfortable on the ball, and by that I mean that they must be allowed to get on with their game without being forced to conform to rigid tactics and planning. My job is to encourage and develop the natural skills which players are gifted with and which have resulted in them being given the opportunity to make the grade at football's leading soccer academy.*
>
> *I had good success at Everton bringing a number of players through to the first-team, and if in the next year or two, Manchester United can boast similar continuity of progress from within our own ranks then the new youth policy which has started will prove of immense value and fire the imagination of everyone connected with Manchester United.*
>
> **ERIC HARRISON**

Grant Mitchell, who put in his only Youth Cup shift for United in their 3-1 win at Walsall's Fellows Park

Any thoughts of equalling or improving on those recent Youth Cup achievements by anyone with a United interest would have been comforted by the level of talent available to Harrison, who could continue to call on the powerful forward duo of Mark Hughes and Norman Whiteside, as well as the combative Graeme Hogg, a colossal presence at the centre of the Reds' defence.

For openers, Hogg was paired up with Billy Garton, a Salford lad who grew up as an ardent fan of the club almost within sight of Old Trafford, and filling the full-back berths were Andy Hill, formerly of Sheffield and Yorkshire Boys, and Mancunian Grant Mitchell.

Besides Hughes, Whiteside found himself accompanied further up the field by Clayton Blackmore, a youngster who made just the one Youth Cup start in the previous season's semi-final and could fill any number of roles, as well as midfielders Sean Williams, Lawrence Pearson and Mark Dempsey, the latter a locally-raised discovery.

Unusually, Harrison decided to spend the majority of the first few months of the season tutoring the 'B' squad who, as first year trainees were, like himself, adjusting to their new place of work. As a coach not known for cloaking his charges in cotton wool, early into his time in Manchester he expressed some forthright views on what was required of them when saying, 'Basically, they all need moulding. Soccer is the same game they played at school, but it is the organisation of the game that is different at professional clubs. The tempo is quicker.

They have less time on the ball and they must learn to play in their own position. Many of the youngsters have been star turns at school, doing everything and taking everything.

Here they have to be taught the United way. It's like going on a conveyor belt and coming off at the end a finished product and ready to drop into Ron Atkinson's first-team.

That is why one of the first lessons is to play for each other and remember it is a team game. Integration without disintegration.

1981-82

NOVEMBER 1981

'Get them young, and doing everything the United way, and it can only be for the benefit of the club and fans.'

An away tie at lowly Walsall, then plying their trade in the Third Division, meant that the Reds needed to negotiate unchartered territory in order to make further progress in the tournament. United's visit to Fellows Park didn't constitute the only Youth Cup tie at Walsall's humble surroundings that season because the Saddlers had already disposed of Nuneaton Borough in the First Round and during the course of a tight game, they decided matters with a solitary second half goal by Craig Shakespeare.

When United and Walsall faced up to one another there was much to admire in the contrasting styles of the two sides and a blank half-time scoreboard barely reflected the skill and enterprise displayed by the visiting artisans in addition to the more doggedly determined and direct efforts of the home eleven.

Plucky Walsall were hampered by the unfortunate loss of their commanding centre-back Jonathan Chapman following a clash of heads, an unfortunate hindrance which would soon prove to be one burden too many for them to cope with.

Just three minutes after the tea break, United forced home an opener when former Newcastle schoolboy starlet Pearson inflicted the damage after stealing through from the central area of the field to put the Reds 1-0 to the good. Far from lying down and feeling sorry for themselves, the Walsall lads fought back like a tetchy tiger with toothache to pull the tie around. In the 54th minute their endeavours paid off when Chris Wilson expertly curled a free kick over a United defensive wall and into the top of the net for what the Walsall Observer marked down as *'a truly delightful equaliser'*.

There was only a quarter of an hour left to play and the Midlanders still held designs on creating an upset until they found themselves rocked on their heels when, after being nicely teed up by Sean Williams, Lawrence Pearson scored a second for the guests, his shot deflecting over the goal-line by Wayne Farmer. In the 81st minute, the United lads assured themselves a victory. With Walsall consistently committing extra bodies forward in search of a leveller, their tactics came unstuck as Whiteside broke clear on his own to calmly shoot past Paul Hayward in the Saddlers' goal.

The win represented an encouraging start for the boy Reds, as well as to Eric Harrison's Youth Cup career with United, and there was fulsome praise for a number of the debutants, especially goalkeeper Philip Hughes. The Coleraine-born 'keeper coped with practically everything that was thrown at him with the maximum of composure and a minimum of fuss, and even at that early stage it seemed as though the club might have unearthed a prospect of real substance in the specialist position.

second round

A dozen of United's juniors from the 1981/82 season answer a photo-call at The Cliff
Back row (l-r) Clayton Blackmore, Billy Garton, Lawrence Pearson, Philip Hughes, Norman Whiteside, Mark Hughes, Andy Hill
Front row (l-r) Ken Scott, Peter Docherty, Graeme Hogg, Mark Dempsey, Sean Williams

1981-82

third round

JANUARY 1982

Monday 25th*

Kick-off 7.30 p.m.

Attendance 844

*This game was originally scheduled for Monday, January 4th and was postponed on two other occasions, Wednesday, January 6th and Monday, January 18th. In the latter case it was caused by a 'flu epidemic amongst United's youth squad

1) Philip Hughes	9) Norman Whiteside
2) Andy Hill	10) Mark Hughes
3) Ken Scott	11) Nicky Wood
4) Graeme Hogg	*12) Andy Robinson (for 9)*
5) Billy Garton	
6) Lawrence Pearson	
7) Clayton Blackmore	
8) Mark Dempsey	

1) Billy Stewart	9) Steve Gorst
2) Ronnie Kilshaw	10) Tony Kelly
3) Dave Martindale	11) Paul Jewell
4) Peter King	*12) Gary Ablett (for 9)*
5) Mark Warriner	
6) Dave Bleasdale	
7) Jimmy Comer	
8) Chris Seagraves	

MANCHESTER UNITED 0 v 0 LIVERPOOL

Over two months passed before the Reds' Youth Cup commitments resumed with Liverpool's visit to Old Trafford. In preparation for the arrival of the current European Cup holders' under-18 side, Eric Harrison instigated tweaks to the United line-up and Grant Mitchell was replaced by Ken Scott who, like Norman Whiteside, was another son of Belfast, while Oldhamer Andy Robinson was nominated as substitute.

Out, too, went Sean Williams, his place filled by switching Clayton Blackmore. The space vacated by Blackmore was occupied by Nicky Wood, whose brief showing in the earlier tie at Walsall helped to convince Harrison that he was ready for a starting berth.

In a scenario similar to the previous season regarding Whiteside's availability, schoolboy Scott was given leave of absence by his headmaster and flown over especially to bolster the defence. There was, however, a little matter of a fitness test to pass first, as Scott had injured his ankle in Ireland a couple of days before and was required to prove there were no lingering problems before taking his place in the side.

Because of a succession of minor knocks, the tie represented Whiteside's first game for several weeks and the decision to bring him back for such an important match was entirely down to Harrison, who admitted, *'We have been nursing him along for this game and he will definitely play.'* Of course, the coach was wise enough to know that the Reds' chances of getting past the Merseysiders were improved by playing at home, and by including Whiteside he sent out a message that defeating their opponents at the first time of asking was the most preferable option available.

As a prelude to the Youth Cup clash, the club's third teams faced up to each other in a Lancashire League Division One match just two days earlier, which caused Harrison to comment, *'We are expecting a game of good quality. We played the Liverpool 'A' team on Saturday and had a goalless draw, but the scoreline was no reflection of the football. It was a fine match, with chances at both ends, and I think we shall see the same high standard this evening.'*

What Harrison forgot to mention was that a league clash between the teams just eight weeks earlier had, despite a couple of goals from Mark Hughes, ended up 5-4 in Liverpool's favour. There was, then, no knowing whether the latest meeting would result in a similar goal glut, a goal drought, or something somewhere between the two.

Even though only Andy Hill, Lawrence Pearson, Robinson, Blackmore and Wood featured for the 'A' side on the Saturday just gone, the final outcome was exactly the same in the later cup contest when both sets of players did their dutiful best to cancel each other out.

Harrison seemingly gambled heavily in starting an obviously unfit Whiteside and there were mixed views as to whether the risk had paid off. The strapping teenager displayed a patent lack of mobility right from the kick-off but, with a tenacity that would soon install him as an idol of the Old Trafford crowd, he was still able to make an impact with some clever passes and neat flicks.

Indeed, it was the Irish striker who carved out the Reds' best chance of the game when intelligently putting Hughes in on goal on the hour. With just the goalkeeper to beat, and the outcome of the match seemingly at his feet, Hughes' progress was curtailed by a superb block tackle from Liverpool defender Peter King.

United were marginally the more progressive of the two teams for most of the second half during which winger Wood proved a constant source of inspiration down the right-hand side of the pitch. For the most part, though, the game was really quite dull and moments of genuine excitement were few and very far between.

An exhausted Whiteside was withdrawn fifteen minutes from time, at which point Liverpool appeared to sense that a replay might not be required after all. A number of breakaway attacks were repelled by United's defence in the later stages, which for many seemed to indicate a worrying threat of what was to come at Anfield. Ultimately, both camps were forced to make do with a draw and Eric Harrison later blamed nerves for the absence of the high-calibre football he normally expected from his players.

The Manchester Evening News marked an emphatic line under the contest when concluding '......*it was a disappointing match which neither side deserved to win*'.

Youth coach Eric Harrison (right) and assistant Jimmy Curran made up an essential part of manager Ron Atkinson's new order at Old Trafford

1) Billy Stewart	9) Gary Ablett
2) Ronnie Kilshaw	10) Tony Kelly
3) Dave Martindale	11) Paul Jewell
4) Mark Warriner	*12) Robert Sturgeon*
5) Peter King	
6) Dave Bleasdale	
7) Jimmy Comer	
8) Chris Seagraves	

1) Philip Hughes	9) Nicky Wood
2) Ken Scott	10) Mark Hughes
3) Andy Hill	11) Lawrence Pearson
4) Graeme Hogg	*12) Sean Williams (for 6)*
5) Billy Garton	
6) Andy Robinson	
7) Clayton Blackmore	
8) Mark Dempsey	

1981-82

LIVERPOOL 0 v 1 MANCHESTER UNITED
Pearson

FEBRUARY 1982

Monday 1st
Kick-off 7.00 p.m.

Reshuffled Reds rock Liverpool

As the Youth Cup 'to be played by' date for the Third Round was due on the following weekend, the Football Association would have been well within their rights to have insisted on the rematch between United and Liverpool taking place the very same week as the game at Old Trafford. Apparently due to logistical problems that wasn't possible, and so a compromise was agreed when the game was arranged to be staged two days after the official deadline had passed.

Inevitably, Norman Whiteside succumbed to his injuries and was never in contention for the replay. While his teenage colleagues were preparing to travel to Anfield, Whiteside was in hospital undergoing a manipulative operation on his troublesome knee.

There were no other significant injuries for Eric Harrison to concern himself about in the run-up to the game, despite five of the team taking part in a 3-2 win at Chester 'A' on the intervening Saturday, and so he promoted Andy Robinson from the bench and brought Sean Williams back into the reckoning when naming him as the substitute.

Robinson was one of three players booked in a keenly contested and high tempo 90 minutes, the other culprits being Liverpool's Chris Seagraves and United's Nicky Wood.

The match had already provided a greater quantity of entertainment than those unfortunate to be present at Old Trafford were witness to, when attempts were made on both goals within the opening five minutes. The Manchester Evening News reckoned that a *'reshuffled Reds, with Robinson taking over the injured Norman Whiteside's place, settled quickly and dominated the first half'.*

Certainly, United's forwards and midfielders, who were shackled to the point of total surrender in Manchester, looked much brighter. Out on the wing, Wood used his speed to greater effect and there was little to trouble a mostly unruffled back four.

Robinson made a key contribution towards the Reds' decisive goal, which came in the 37th minute. The execution of his fine cross into Liverpool's danger area was telling and gained a reward when Lawrence Pearson connected in order to divert a powerful downward header past Billy Stewart. Mark Hughes twice scorned further chances, as did fellow countryman Clayton Blackmore, and it seemed that Harrison's ploy in setting out to disrupt the home side's rhythm was a success so far.

Following the half-time interval, Liverpool's quality bubbled to the surface. Gary Ablett and Paul Jewell brought the best out of Philip Hughes with powerful drives, the Ulster custodian making stupendous stops in each case, and the home team followed up with shots from Seagraves and Kelly, both of which flew just wide of the mark.

In the emptiness of an almost vacant Anfield, shouted instructions from the two benches could clearly be heard by both sets of players, as well as most of the crowd.

Those in the United corner were comforted by the advantage held, although there were, as one reporter noted, occasions when *'Liverpool attacked strongly'* and the Reds did well to come through a couple of hairy moments when the one-goal leeway appeared decidedly fragile.

Throughout the later stages of the tie, United put the onus on Liverpool to make the running by contenting themselves in guarding their slender lead while simply utilising the odd breakaway in order to relieve some pressure from an increasingly overworked defence. There were determined performances from Garton and Hogg in the middle of the back four, the pair proving more and more hard-nosed as the prize of victory beckoned closer, whereas the full-back pairing of Ken Scott and Andy Hill attempted to sniff out and put a stop to any danger which might have emanated from the wide areas.

Scott earned enormous praise through dealing particularly well with the talented Paul Jewell, who gave the impression of being able to take a mile when only offered an inch.

Liverpool's inability to break down an obstinate rearguard totally justified Eric Harrison's clever tactical plans, and so Pearson's goal provided the lever which prised open the door to allow United's entry into the Fourth Round.

Well aware of the effort and commitment put in by his lads, Harrison claimed he was *'very, very pleased'* at the outcome.

> "You watch the first-team and the Reserves, but the F.A. Youth Cup brought the excitement to our level. Ron Atkinson would talk to us about the games, (and) come and watch us.
>
> I knew it meant something to the club, the team, and the other players who had come through the system. It was also the first year that Eric Harrison joined us, and he had a massive influence.
>
> Everyone was scared of Eric. He was a great coach but he ruled with an iron fist and that was his style. I couldn't see the method in his madness and I went head to head with him a few times.
>
> When we went to Liverpool, all of their players touched the 'This is Anfield' sign. Well, I wasn't having any of that. I really disliked Liverpool with a passion, and even though it was probably ignorant of me at the time, I spat on the sign as I ran out. It was my way of firing myself up, because there was no way on earth we were going to lose to Liverpool that night."
>
> **BILLY GARTON**

third round replay

293

1981-82

1) David Seaman
2) Tony Sharkey
3) Steve Livingstone
4) Robert Peel
5) Colin Thacker
6) Mark Hinchcliffe
7) Wayne Roebuck
8) Gerry Hill
9) Andy Nicholson
10) Mark Gavin
11) Scott Sellars
12) *Eamon Nolan*

1) Philip Hughes
2) Andy Hill
3) Ken Scott
4) Graeme Hogg
5) Billy Garton
6) Mike Rowbotham
7) Sean Williams
8) Mark Dempsey
9) Lawrence Pearson
10) Mark Hughes
11) Clayton Blackmore
12) *Andy Robinson (for 6)*

FEBRUARY 1982

LEEDS UNITED 0 v 0 MANCHESTER UNITED

fourth round

Thursday 11th*
Kick-off 7.30 p.m.
Attendance 794

When the draw was made for the next stage, it paired the Reds against Leeds. The two clubs hadn't met in the competition since December 1957 and much had changed in the interim period, particularly the stature of the Yorkshire club and the relationship between the cross-Pennine rivals.

While Leeds were hardly considered a 'big-time' outfit in those pre-Munich days, and couldn't boast much in the way of home grown talent, under manager Don Revie they went on to become a powerhouse on both the domestic and European scenes, and their many triumphs were achieved with the help of numerous personnel who were groomed through the Elland Road nursery, such as Paul Madeley, Peter Lorimer, Eddie Gray and Billy Bremner.

Leeds quickly earned a reputation as a physical and aggressive side under Revie and from the mid-1960's onwards clashes between the two United's developed into battles which weren't for the faint-hearted. The seeds of animosity were sewn as far back as 1965, a year in which Leeds ousted United from the semi-final of the F.A. Cup and the Reds turned the tables by pipping the Yorkshiremen on goal average for the First Division title.

The ill-feeling between the two sets of supporters reached a peak when Leeds again knocked United out at the last four stage of the F.A. Cup in 1970, following three mammoth matches, and it continued when the Reds again got the upper hand at the same round of the tournament in 1977.

Also, the fairly recent transfers of Joe Jordan and Gordon McQueen from Elland Road to Old Trafford still rankled with Leeds supporters, as did, to a lesser extent, a Frank Stapleton goal which gave the Mancunians recent bragging rights in their First Division encounters.

Against such a backdrop it was clear that the under-18 meeting would contain an above-average amount of spice than usual, and certainly much more than the two high-scoring affairs, which both went in United's favour, back in 1952 and 1957.

Despite arrangements which were already in place to play their Youth Cup Fourth Round tie on the following Monday, under a directive received from the Football Association, the Reds were press-ganged into the next stage just ten days after defeating Liverpool when the excursion over to the West Riding was made without the still recovering Norman Whiteside.

There were other injury woes for Eric Harrison to wrestle with, one being Nicky Wood's problem, a sore ankle meaning that he was another patient United's coach couldn't consider for selection.

Andy Robinson was deemed as being less than one hundred per cent fit, so he was given a spot on the bench while Mike Rowbotham and Sean Williams made the starting eleven due to the Reds' injury pile-up. Rowbotham was tasked with a midfield responsibility, which freed Clayton Blackmore up to bolster an attack weakened by the loss of Wood and Whiteside.

The latest contest was unlike those previous meetings as it was one almost bereft of scoring chances. Even so, the nil-nil result greatly pleased Tony Collins, who informed the press that Leeds would have much more to contend with in Manchester.

Fortune smiled on the Reds in the only two incidents of note at Elland Road, when headers from Leeds' Gerry Hill and Mark Hinchcliffe rebounded from the frame of the goal. Hill's effort came with only eighteen minutes left on the clock, and would most likely have brought about the conclusion desired by the home supporters.

Nevertheless, the breaks enjoyed by United's 'keeper were certainly well deserved. After taking an early clattering, the athletic and agile Hughes once again looked poised and confident, and it was noted that his handling was absolutely top-notch throughout the game.

The Reds' clearest chances fell to Mark Hughes and Clayton Blackmore, and their best efforts were repelled by a couple of marvellous saves from David Seaman.

The Evening News carried the following short summary:

Manchester United chief scout Tony Collins warned his old club Leeds today to expect a much rougher ride in Monday's F.A. Youth Cup replay at Old Trafford (7.30). Collins was delighted with the weakened Reds' achievement of holding out for a 0-0 draw at Elland Road last night. 'Considering we were without key players through injury, I was pleased with the result. We will do much more attacking in the replay' promised Collins.

Nicky Wood, who missed last night's game with ankle trouble, will be back to strengthen the attack on Monday, while Andrew Robinson, who was restricted to a brief appearance as substitute at Elland Road, will also be in at the start for the replay.

In a match of few opportunities the emergency all-Welsh strike force of Mark Hughes and Clayton Blackmore failed to breach a sound Leeds defence.

After restricting Liverpool to a goalless draw in the previous round and winning the replay at Anfield, the Reds are confident of beating Leeds at the second attempt to earn a Fifth Round visit to Birmingham City.

Philip Hughes, a key member of a solid defence that kept seven clean sheets during the 1981/82 Youth Cup campaign

*This game was originally scheduled for Monday, February 15th but was brought forward on the instructions of the F.A.

"We had a good defence that year and were very strong as a unit. We had Philip Hughes in goal who was a very steady 'keeper, not spectacular but really reliable. Billy Garton was a better ball player than me, but as centre-halves we would attack the ball while Ken Scott and Andy Hill would tuck in and sweep up behind us if we missed anything. We played a strong line and based our whole defence throughout the cup run on that system.

Eric used to drum it into us all the time to 'stay solid and don't let them score'. We had very basic set plays, which meant that if we won the ball we would give it to the midfielders. If we were in trouble then we played the percentage ball, knocking it diagonally into their corner and turning them. It proved to be very effective. That allowed us to go to places like Anfield and Elland Road and come away with good results."

GRAEME HOGG

1) Philip Hughes
2) Andy Robinson
3) Ken Scott
4) Graeme Hogg
5) Billy Garton
6) Sean Williams
7) Clayton Blackmore
8) Mark Dempsey
9) Norman Whiteside
10) Mark Hughes
11) Lawrence Pearson
12) Nicky Wood

1) David Seaman
2) Tony Sharkey
3) Steve Livingstone
4) Robert Peel
5) Colin Thacker
6) Mark Hinchcliffe
7) Wayne Roebuck
8) Gerry Hill
9) Andy Nicholson
10) Mark Gavin
11) Scott Sellars
12) Eamon Nolan

1981-82

MANCHESTER UNITED 1 v 0 LEEDS UNITED
Dempsey

FEBRUARY 1982

Monday 15th
Kick-off 7.30 p.m.

fourth round replay

Dempsey is the Reds' hero

With barely more than a weekend separating the match at Elland Road and the rematch, there was a welcome, if not rather surprising, return for Norman Whiteside.

It appeared there was more than a degree or two of risk involved in rushing the Reds' talisman back so soon after surgery because his inclusion hinged on whether or not he was able to successfully come through a late fitness test and, in doing so, Whiteside effectively edged out Mike Rowbotham entirely. The only other change was at right full-back, where the increasingly adaptable Andy Robinson deputised for thigh strain victim Andy Hill.

Events west of the Pennines were very different to those at Elland Road and in a far more open spectacle, Leeds slightly shaded the game in terms of possession and technique without being able to find the all-important goal their enterprise generally merited.

David Meek was present to record the details of a Reds' victory which didn't come easy, and he also divulged some interesting and little known facts about the match winner:

Mark Dempsey, the lightweight midfielder who once starred on children's television, was certainly the star of Manchester United's F.A. Youth Cup replay against Leeds United at Old Trafford. It was the pint-sized, curly-haired Dempsey who finally found a chink in a tough Leeds defence to score the only goal in two fiercely contested ties.

Mark Hughes, who took a lot of punishment from the visitors without complaining, put over a cracking centre from the left as the game headed towards extra-time with only ten minutes to go.

Dempsey, who seemed to have run himself into the ground, suddenly popped up in the goalmouth to head in the centre past David Seaman at point blank range.

The goal gave United a 1-0 win to make Dempsey the hero of the Fourth Round as the Reds now go through to the quarter-finals and a match with Birmingham City.

Dempsey appeared in the TV series 'Potter's Picture Palace' as a Manchester schoolboy before joining up at Old Trafford as an apprentice.

He signed professional last month but, though now aged eighteen, he is still struggling for height and weight.

It did not stop him running much of last night's match, with an outstanding performance in midfield, showing the kind of cheeky moves that first got him on TV playing the part of a mischievous schoolboy.

Norman Whiteside had two shots well saved by the Leeds goalkeeper but he could have done better with the second when he was through only to shoot rather tamely straight at the 'keeper.

The Leeds tackling upset a lot of home fans before Tony Sharkey, the visitors' right-back, was booked for one too many tackles on Hughes.

In addition to supplying the killer cross, the overall contribution from Hughes was telling. Totally committed from the first minute to the last, and fearless and brave when the going was at its toughest, the striker was content to suffer a few knocks on behalf of the team while carving out a couple of other wasted chances for his fellow Reds.

One goal was enough for victory, though, and the result meant that the Old Trafford kids had demonstrated a measure of tenacity by clawing their way through a couple of difficult rounds via the slenderest of margins.

Full of trickery and endeavour, Mark Dempsey's downward header put the Reds into the Youth Cup quarter-final

Norman Whiteside might easily have doubled United's advantage against Leeds

295

1981-82

1) Dave Coles	9) Duncan MacDowall	1) Philip Hughes	9) Lawrence Pearson
2) Tony McGarr	10) Brian Stewart	2) Andy Hill	10) Norman Whiteside
3) Nigel Winterburn	11) Derek McKay	3) Ken Scott	11) Mark Hughes
4) Glen Alzapiedi	*12) Martin Kuhl*	4) Graeme Hogg	*12) Nicky Wood*
5) Nigel Duce		5) Billy Garton	
6) Tony Knight		6) Clayton Blackmore	
7) John Whitehouse		7) Sean Williams	
8) Gary Fillery		8) Mark Dempsey	

MARCH 1982

BIRMINGHAM CITY 0 v 0 MANCHESTER UNITED

fifth round

Monday 1st*

Kick-off 7.00 p.m.

Attendance 635

This game was originally scheduled for Tuesday, February 23rd but was put back as Birmingham City had players on international youth duty

Two of United's rising stars, Graeme Hogg (left) and Mark Hughes, celebrate a special event

Despite performing admirably and not looking at all out of place in an unfamiliar defending role against Leeds, Andy Robinson vacated the right full-back spot when United's under-18's headed towards the West Midlands, and specifically St. Andrews, to meet up with possibly the most fancied of the sides that had already eased their way into the last eight stage of the competition. While Eric Harrison at last appeared to have the benefit of a fully fit squad at his disposal, the coach's final plans were required to be adjusted slightly as Robinson couldn't be considered for any position because of his requirement to participate in a school fixture.

An undecided outcome against Birmingham belied what was a thoroughly entertaining hour and a half of football for the small quota of Brummies in attendance. The Blues team contained a sprinkling of English and Scottish youth internationals in their ranks and with home advantage in their favour, they attracted short odds to curtail United's immediate Youth Cup interest.

Not for the first time that season, the Reds owed a debt of gratitude to Philip Hughes. The quickly maturing goalkeeper took to the field with an injured ankle which was tightly strapped up and despite the obvious hindrance he was easily United's top performer to end the match with some simply spellbinding stops to his credit.

Most of Hughes' best work came in the early section of the match. Within the first few minutes he was on hand to repel a long-range effort from Blues' Gary Fillery and almost before he could gather his thoughts, a header from Derek McKay needed to be turned behind for a corner.

In the Review, Joe Lancaster referred to the goalie as *'lion-hearted'* when noting that he had made *'jack-knife saves and then a rib-hammering save from a tremendous shot on the hour'*. Lancaster also noted that *'a few minutes later he dived again, this time to push another Gary Fillery drive around the post'*.

Not that Hughes was the only one busying himself that evening, because at the extreme end of the pitch Dave Coles needed to keep his eyes open and focussed on a mad scramble when he was handily placed to block attempts from Norman Whiteside and Sean Williams. Lawrence Pearson added to the second half pressure on Cole's goal when narrowly missing his intended spot and Clayton Blackmore was similarly off-target after being set up by a crafty piece of skill by the seemingly tireless Mark Hughes.

In an attempt to avoid a visit to Manchester, the Blues redoubled their efforts in the last ten minutes and Eric Harrison must have been delighted at the way Hill, Scott, Hogg and Garton stubbornly protected their penalty area. Called *'their best player'* by Joe Lancaster, Brian Stewart stood out as one for the future for Birmingham, even though on this occasion his skills floundered on the rock of United's unyielding back four.

The following day Harrison's opposite number, Birmingham youth coach Keith Bradley, commented, *'It isn't going to be easy (at Old Trafford) but we haven't given up all hope. We had our chances to win last night but their goalkeeper kept them in the game with some excellent saves.'*

Manchester United		Birmingham City	
1) Philip Hughes	9) Norman Whiteside	1) Dave Coles	9) Duncan MacDowall
2) Clayton Blackmore	10) Mark Hughes	2) Tony McGarr	10) Brian Stewart
3) Ken Scott	11) Lawrence Pearson	3) Nigel Winterburn	11) Derek McKay
4) Graeme Hogg	*12) Andy Robinson (for 7)*	4) Martin Kuhl	*12) Glen Alzapiedi (for 10)*
5) Billy Garton		5) Nigel Duce	
6) Sean Williams		6) Tony Knight	
7) Nicky Wood		7) John Whitehouse	
8) Mark Dempsey		8) Gary Fillery	

MANCHESTER UNITED 2 v 0 BIRMINGHAM CITY

Hughes M. (2)

1981-82

MARCH 1982

Saturday 13th*

Kick-off 2.00 p.m.

Attendance 1,649

fifth round replay

A replay date of seven days later was quickly earmarked with Birmingham until it was realised that the scheduling would bring huge disappointment to United's Welsh contingent, as both Mark Hughes and Clayton Blackmore were expected to be selected for a youth international against Holland in the European Championship Qualifiers.

Needing to act swiftly, Les Olive confirmed that City's officials were agreeable to a new date, reciprocating a similar favour the Reds had granted them for the game at St. Andrews, and the club secretary was at his persuasive best to obtain similar permission from the Football Association in order to stage the match later in the week than was originally planned.

Eric Harrison said of the predicament, *'I wouldn't have stopped our boys from winning international caps. They could have gone, but at the same time the last thing we wanted was to be without two of the team who have done so well in reaching this stage of the competition. I'm glad Saturday is confirmed as the new date.'*

And how grateful United were of Mark Hughes' availability for the return contest. After surviving some intense early pressure from Birmingham, which included facing three corners within the opening five minutes alone, the Reds' bustling striker instituted a turning of the tables by scoring on the quarter-hour mark.

Norman Whiteside was involved in the build-up when he took a throw-in on the right that reached Nicky Wood, who in turn crossed from the touchline. Hughes' reactions set him apart from those around him in the crowded penalty area and he swivelled smartly to thud the ball home from barely six yards out.

The goal completely transformed the game in United's favour and from the moment of Hughes' opener, the midfield looked unstoppable, the forwards menacing and the defence damn near impregnable. The first of Birmingham's only two real chances since going behind was in the 39th minute when Brian Stewart scorned the chance of an equaliser by blazing over what Joe Lancaster labelled *'a sitter'* in the Review.

The Blues' blood levels began to rise shortly after, and in one incident their centre-half Nigel Duce kicked out at Graeme Hogg while he was on the deck. Barnsley referee Trelford Mills then staggered the crowd by booking both players and further names followed into the official's notepad as the game moved from gently simmering to boiling point.

Duncan MacDowall and Derek McKay were Birmingham's other transgressors, and Mark Hughes blotted his copybook by also earning a bookable reprimand from Mr. Mills.

During the second period, all of United's boatmen continued to row in the same direction, which was the very least that was needed if they were to defeat a team that had previously demonstrated they knew their way to goal.

The final outcome hinged on two incidents, both of which involved the Hughes boys.

In a remote aberration on the part of the Reds' defence, Birmingham striker MacDowall was almost gifted a goal before Philip Hughes clutched hold of the ball just as it was about to cross the line. Then, in the 69th minute, United's other Hughes, the Mark version, scored for a second time. After manoeuvring around three City defenders, the number ten drove the ball between an advancing goalkeeper and the near post, his shot possibly taking the merest of deflections on its way home.

The Birmingham edition of the Express & Star newspaper noted *'Blues began as though they could take United apart'* and added *'With fifteen goals in the previous four ties they opened as though they would make amends for the goalless draw at St. Andrews'*.

The reporter also felt compelled to point out the away side's main failing when concluding *'Birmingham lost control of the midfield and the chance of their first F.A. Cup semi-final for fifteen years'*.

From United's point of view, it counted as a great victory over admirable and extremely durable opponents. The win also thrust them through to the last four stage for the 14th time, their third such feat in a row, and it constituted the club's best sequence in the tournament since those almost forgotten days of the 1958-1960 period.

MY BALL . . . United Youth's Graeme Hogg comes to the rescue and clears with this header as Birmingham pile on the pressure in the FA Youth Cup at Old Trafford today.

This game was originally scheduled for Monday, March 8th but was put back as United had players on international youth duty

1981-82

1) Philip Hughes	9) Norman Whiteside
2) Andy Hill	10) Mark Hughes
3) Ken Scott	11) Peter Docherty
4) Graeme Hogg	*12) Nicky Wood (for 11)*
5) Billy Garton	
6) Sean Williams	
7) Clayton Blackmore	
8) Mark Dempsey	

1) Mark Prudhoe	9) Paul Lemon
2) Barry Venison	10) Steve McDermott
3) John Gray	11) Nick Pickering
4) Martin Hamilton	*12) Paul Atkinson (for 3)*
5) Graeme Corner	
6) Simon Tait	
7) Stuart Sellar	
8) Patrick O'Donnell	

APRIL 1982

MANCHESTER UNITED   **1 v 0**   **SUNDERLAND**

Whiteside

Monday 5th
Kick-off 7.30 p.m.
Attendance 1,541

semi-final 1st leg

Young Doc makes his Reds debut

Switching their attention to the Youth Cup semi-final was a welcome relief for regular Sunderland seniors Barry Venison and Nick Pickering, as the Wearsiders were rooted at the foot of the First Division table and looking almost certainties for relegation. A demoralising home defeat for the Sunderland first-team against near neighbours Middlesbrough on the previous Saturday cast a depressing shadow over Roker Park and one local reporter remarked that Pickering *'looked jaded'* during the match.

Regardless, both boys were named in a squad that made the journey to Old Trafford for the first leg, Black Cats' manager Alan Durban reasoning, *'It will do them good to play in their own age group again.'* With staff morale clearly an issue at Roker Park, Durban went on to tell the Sunderland Echo that he hoped his teenage stars *'can restore some pride within the club tonight.'*

When the home side was named, the biggest surprise as far as United's fans were concerned was the axing of Lawrence Pearson for Peter Docherty, an amateur who could count on only a handful of appearances for the 'A' and 'B' teams as relevant experience. The youngest of former manager Tommy Docherty's three sons, Peter was reported as having previously trained with Burnley and it was also claimed he had only recently left his rugby-playing school in Altrincham. By coincidence, one of Peter's siblings acted as coach to United's latest Youth Cup opponents.

Following the passing of a late fitness test by leg strain victim Ken Scott, Eric Harrison returned Andy Hill to the line-up and Nicky Wood to the bench.

The outcome at the halfway mark went in United's favour, but only just, and in the Review, Joe Lancaster started his piece with a poser that seemed to occupy everyone's minds:

Will one goal be enough to take to Sunderland for the F.A. Youth Cup semi-final second leg on Monday, 19th April?

It should be on the cup record of 'keeper Philip Hughes, who has only let one through in seven previous outings. He never let it seem likely to be dented in a gripping first leg that brought one goal and a double standing ovation. It was a Cain and Abel situation, with Peter Docherty making a cup debut and laying it on the line against his elder brother Mike's team.

Schoolboy Docherty picked out Mark Hughes hovering in the box in the 33rd minute. Hughes flicked on the centre into Norman Whiteside's path and it was swept home. Hughes and Whiteside's double act brought the house down and should have floored Sunderland long before the goal.

As early as the fourth minute, 'keeper Mark Prudhoe answered a call to arms, saving a Clayton Blackmore volley. His heroic 'keeping kept the Roker Park club in the match.

He made spines stiffen when failing to hold a Hughes drive that bounced out to Whiteside but he managed to smother the ball on the line. United's crisp passing that found their men, and Whiteside beating three men and 'nut-megging' two of them had the crowd roaring.

Unfortunately, a knock reduced his mobility in the second half. Sunderland first-teamers Barry Venison and Nick Pickering took over and it was backs to the wall for the Reds. They stood firm and Nick Wood coming on for Docherty in the last twenty minutes eased the pressure.

A minute before the switch, Pickering cut in but Graeme Hogg hastily cleared and the ball just sneaked past his own woodwork. Philip Hughes saved a couple of headers from Paul Lemon who squeezed himself into a good position, then he held a fierce drive from striker Steve McDermott eighteen minutes into the second half.

There were more gasps when Whiteside dummied in the box, found space and tried to pick his spot. Prudhoe moved quickly and was alert to another chance from Mark Dempsey.

Both teams ran themselves into the ground but an unquenchable spirit for success made mind move muscle. Skill was not stifled as the youngsters chiselled into everybody's memory a match to be remembered.

In an alternative match summary, David Meek devoted some of his allotted print space to heap even more praise on a couple of lads who were beginning to stand out as the star turns of Harrison's team:

Manchester United have spent millions of pounds on strikers over the years, but in another season or so they could have a pair leading their attack who didn't cost a penny.

Norman Whiteside and Mark Hughes are forging a partnership at youth level that looks to me as promising as anything to come out of the junior ranks for years.

The pair of them have been outstanding in this season's F.A. Youth Cup team and they were the key men in last night's 1-0 victory in the first leg of their semi-final against Sunderland.

The way Hughes shields the ball and turns past opponents, along with the brilliant ball control of Whiteside, is a joy to watch.

The two of them bombarded the Sunderland goal in the first half with the whole team clicking into the kind of form that had hardened supporters declaring it was the best they have seen at Old Trafford all season.

Outside-left Peter Docherty made a significant contribution in creating the Reds' solitary goal against Sunderland at Old Trafford

1981-82

1) Mark Prudhoe	9) Paul Lemon	1) Philip Hughes	9) Norman Whiteside
2) Barry Venison	10) Steve McDermott	2) Andy Hill	10) Mark Hughes
3) Nick Pickering	11) Paul Atkinson	3) Ken Scott	11) Peter Docherty
4) Martin Kirsopp	*12) Graham Bassett (for 4)*	4) Graeme Hogg	*12) Nicky Wood*
5) Graeme Corner		5) Billy Garton	
6) Simon Tait		6) Clayton Blackmore	
7) Stuart Sellar		7) Lawrence Pearson	
8) Patrick O'Donnell		8) Mark Dempsey	

SUNDERLAND 1 (1) v (3) 2 MANCHESTER UNITED

Lemon — Hughes M., Whiteside

APRIL 1982

Monday 19th

Kick-off 7.30 p.m.

Attendance 6,174

semi-final 2nd leg

Just prior to the second leg, Eric Harrison told of his thoughts on how to tackle the recent Youth Cup conquerors of Aston Villa and Spurs on their home turf when he said, *'I never like sitting back trying to defend a lead. It gives the opposition too much of the ball and can put you under pressure. I told the lads at the start that we had got two games to win against Sunderland. We have won one and I am out to win the other. We will be doing our best to take the game to Sunderland looking for the goal that will kill them off.'*

A day later, the Sunderland Echo featured a match report which confirmed United's first Youth Cup final appearance for eighteen years:

Sunderland's battling youth side saw their dreams of F.A. Cup glory rise, fall, and finally die in a frenzied 45 minutes at Roker Park last night. A Paul Lemon goal put the Roker side well on the way to the F.A. Youth final but joy turned to despair with a double blast from Manchester United's twin strikers Norman Whiteside and Mark Hughes.

In an action-packed second half Sunderland battled hard but failed to match the skill and poise of United who took the game 2-1 for a 3-1 aggregate victory.

The drama began before the kick-off when thousands more than expected queued to get in. Neither the police nor Roker Park officials had planned for such a massive response and traffic jams caused all sorts of problems around the ground. Only fourteen turnstiles were opened at first but more were brought into operation as supporters clamoured to get inside in time for kick-off. Eventually the start was delayed for eight minutes, allowing everyone to get into the ground. Once inside, plans to house all supporters in the Main Stand were abandoned as thousands poured into the Roker and Fulwell Ends.

The official crowd was given as 6,174 but Sunderland secretary Geoff Davidson reckoned nearer 10,000 saw the game. The Fulwell End was eventually opened and fans allowed in free.

Both sides made a nervy beginning to the match with United's physical strength just giving them the edge as Sunderland strove to overcome the one-goal deficit from the first leg at Old Trafford. As the first half wore on United's strikers Hughes and Whiteside caused more and more problems and it was fortunate for Sunderland that goalkeeper Mark Prudhoe was again in top form. But the Roker side should have taken the lead after 35 minutes when Steve McDermott swung a superb ball across the United box, leaving little midfielder Martin Kirsopp with only the goalkeeper to beat. Unfortunately Kirsopp's control failed him and the sides went in level at half-time.

Five minutes after the restart the crowd went wild as Sunderland took the lead. A good ball by McDermott put Atkinson clear on the left and a gorgeous pass left Lemon to slide the ball home from ten yards.

If Atkinson was responsible for Sunderland's goal he was just as responsible for the 58th minute equaliser. A slack pass left Pearson with time to hit a long ball over the defence for Whiteside to latch onto and hit past Prudhoe.

Only six minutes later Sunderland could so easily have been back in the lead after a farcical bit of football. United had the ball in the net through Whiteside and the whole United team barring the goalkeeper joined in the celebrations on the touchline. But United hadn't noticed the offside flag and Sunderland raced upfield with their opponents still unaware of what was going on. Unluckily, the Roker side, too, were caught offside when a goal looked certain.

But with eighteen minutes left the brilliant Welsh youth international Mark Hughes scored a goal that marked him down as a star of the future. With his back to goal and all options seemingly closed, he turned and lashed a shot into the top corner giving United the all-important lead. Sunderland had moved Pickering and Venison into midfield from full-back after the United equaliser but they never took hold of the game.

Afterwards Geoff Davidson said the crowd response was 'unbelievable'. *'We thought fourteen turnstiles would be enough. I think there were nearly 10,000 here which is astounding when you consider we only had 11,800 for a First Division match with Ipswich,'* said Mr. Davidson.

Beaming Old Trafford boss Ron Atkinson couldn't disguise his feelings about the youngsters' feat of reaching the final when later saying, *'I'm delighted.......they are largely a new team comprised of first year apprentices and schoolboys but they have learned quickly.'*

Hands up if you want to play in the Youth Cup final: United's Andy Hill and Sunderland's Steve McDermott tussle for possession while Norman Whiteside (left) and Mark Dempsey (right) fix their gaze on the flight of the ball

299

1981-82

1) Philip Hughes	9) Norman Whiteside
2) Andy Hill	10) Mark Hughes
3) Ken Scott	11) Peter Docherty
4) Graeme Hogg	*12) Nicky Wood (for 7)*
5) Billy Garton	
6) Clayton Blackmore	
7) Lawrence Pearson	
8) Mark Dempsey	

1) Mike Potts	9) Jimmy Gilligan
2) Nigel Gibbs	10) Francis Cassidy
3) Neil Price	11) Dave Johnson
4) Neil Williams	*12) Gary Porter*
5) Colin Hull	
6) Paul Franklin	
7) Worrell Sterling	
8) Ian Richardson	

APRIL 1982

MANCHESTER UNITED 2 v 3 WATFORD

Blackmore, Dempsey — Gilligan, Sterling, Williams

final 1st leg

Monday 26th

Kick-off 7.30 p.m.

Attendance 7,290

> *"Norman Whiteside earned his (senior) promotion but what pleases me is that in two or three years time there are a number of other players who could be ready for first-team football.*
> *I have spent a lot of money since arriving at Old Trafford but it has not bought many players. Nowadays we need to bring through our own youngsters and that is really what tonight's final is all about."*

RON ATKINSON

Because the season's close was quickly drawing near, the opening leg of the final against Watford came just seven days after United's win at Sunderland and, as in the semi-final, the Reds were drawn to play their home leg first. It was documented that Eric Harrison wasn't particularly perturbed about which way round the final ties fell, as his boys had won as many of their previous ties on the road as those at home during the course of the current Youth Cup campaign.

The Hertfordshire club had never previously displayed any notable progress in the tournament until this particular season, which marked a dramatic upturn and was a creditable exception to that rule.

Following a First Round bye, the junior Hornets defeated Oxford United 2-0 at Vicarage Road. A trip to Loughton then brought a 4-0 win prior to further successive home victories, 3-0 against Southampton in the Fourth Round and 5-0 over Middlesbrough in the quarter-final. Watford then defeated Wolves, 2-1 at home and 5-1 at Molineux at the last four stage, in order to book their ticket to the final. The second leg of the semi-final win over the Wolverhampton club stood out as a personal highlight for Hornets' forward Ian Richardson, who was credited with causing them the most damage by producing a corking hat-trick.

Watford's fabulous win at Molineux was achieved without centre-half Colin Hull, an influential and respected captain who was forced to sit out the game through injury. Besides their obvious goalscoring prowess, it was clear that the young Hornets could also claim a sound defence, of which only Wolves of their previous Youth Cup opponents were successfully able to breach.

The Watford squad included attacking midfielder Neil Williams and lanky goal-getter Jimmy Gilligan, both of whom were recently included in the England Youth side during a contest in Yugoslavia. Gilligan and central defender Paul Franklin had also both made their senior debuts, along with exciting winger John Barnes. While he had only taken part in one previous Youth Cup tie, when participating for an hour in the concluding leg of the semi-final, Barnes was, even at such an early stage in his career, considered to be a major emerging talent. The reason he hadn't featured more than just the once in the Hornets' youth side was simply because he was a regular member of Watford's first-team, which resulted in his continued involvement in their promotion push. For that very reason, Barnes wasn't considered for the Old Trafford leg of the final as Watford were due to contest a crucial Second Division game against Crystal Palace on the following evening.

Prior to the action starting Watford's youth team coach Tom Walley stated, 'There will be no question of trying to hold them and bring them back to our place for the second leg. I watched them win 2-1 at Sunderland and go through 3-1 on aggregate on Monday night, and I fancy our chances. They have a couple of useful strikers but if we put them under pressure......well, I think we'll give them a better game than Sunderland did.'

Two days before Watford were due at Old Trafford, and while still aged only sixteen, Norman Whiteside made his First Division bow as a substitute at Brighton. The Ulster lad was always at the top of the class in terms of his physical maturity, and five goals reaped from the same number of his most recent Central League matches seemed to make up Ron Atkinson's mind that he was now capable of holding his own in a stiffer standard of soccer.

A Watford Observer scribe was on hand to record the details of a sizzling and scintillating showpiece for posterity:

Watford are budgeting for a gate of 10,000 when Watford Juniors take on Manchester United in the second leg of the F.A. Youth Cup final after leading 3-2 from Monday's first leg.

The Juniors make their record bid next Thursday evening at Vicarage Road and fans are warned to come early. Gates will open at 6.30 and, with a large contingent expected from Old Trafford, the club are opening all stands and terraces. Prices are £1 for the terraces (50p juniors and o.a.p's) and £1.50 for stand seats (£1 for juniors and o.a.p's).

And it promises to be a really exciting game if the first leg at Old Trafford is anything to go by. Before 7,290 fans, the Juniors stunned a Manchester United side bidding to win the trophy for the first time since George Best was a teenager. Against the run of play, the Juniors scored three times, leading 1-0 and 3-1 before United pulled one back with six minutes to go.

The Juniors never played to their potential on the dreadfully uneven Old Trafford surface and prompted Graham Taylor to comment later, 'I hope the Juniors have not used up all the luck due the first-team between now and the end of the season.'

The skills of first-team substitute Norman Whiteside and the clever Mark Hughes gave Colin Hull and Paul Franklin a torrid night and it was often left to the dapper Michael Potts and the luck of the bounce to withstand the pressure, notably in the second half.

Another player Watford will have to look out for in the return leg is the number six, Clayton Blackmore, who gave a great performance and produced several of United's best efforts. The tie is far from over yet, but Watford are not only a goal to the good but also know that they have to still strike their true form.

Potts was soon in action and halfway through the first half excelled to parry a goal-bound shot from Blackmore but Watford were always dangerous on the break with Johnson and Sterling working well on the flanks.

The young Hornets took the lead in the 34th minute after Gilligan and Hull contested a corner and the ball was half-cleared to Neil Williams who sent a bouncing shot into the net.

Whiteside broke back for United, drew Potts but slipped it wide before the Hornets, boosted by the goal, came close to increasing the lead when first Gibbs, on the overlap, sent a shot which hit the top of the bar and Sterling, from a Gilligan cross, hit the post with another effort.

Watford had just about earned their lead when United, boasting seven youth internationals, broke back on the stroke of half-time – Dempsey ghosting in on the blind side of the defence to score after a Pearson cross had been nodded on by son of 'The Doc,' Peter Docherty.

Whiteside had a close range effort parried by Potts early in the second half and Docherty went close as United took control over Watford's flagging midfield and snuffed out the visiting wingers.

But in the 56th minute Gilligan, a player with a penchant for spicing durable, steady performances with outstanding goals, shocked the home side when he rifled in a magnificent angled shot after Gibbs' free kick had been nodded on by Richardson, when everyone else was expecting a cross.

Price cleared off the line from Whiteside; Hughes went close before Watford broke away to score a third. Johnson hooked over a cross which the centre-half misjudged. Sterling read it well and as the ball bounced, he hooked it over the hesitant challenge from the goalkeeper to find the roof of the net.

United swarmed over Watford but after a series of unlucky breaks, they had to be content with an 84th minute goal to keep the tie alive.

Whiteside sent in the shot, Potts failed to hold and Blackmore, always near the action, was there to bring an extra edge to the second leg which, if half as exciting as the first, will prove excellent value for money.

Though the majority of spectators at Old Trafford were consumed with disappointment when the final whistle blew, just as equally they couldn't fail but to be impressed by a Watford side that simply refused to lie down and allow themselves to be steamrollered into defeat. In the Review, Joe Lancaster wrote *'under considerable pressure (Watford) were forced to show their defensive capabilities for most of the match. Clinical finishing on the few occasions they did break through brought them a 3-2 lead'.*

Below a banner headline proclaiming 'BOY REDS ARE DOWN BUT THEY'RE NOT OUT', David Meek argued that the club's teenage representatives put on such an outstanding performance *'it is impossible to write off their chances when they meet in the second leg at Vicarage Road'.* He then made a statement about both teams striking *'such a high note of superb soccer that clearly anything could happen in the return'.*

Both Meek and Lancaster made reference to United's last minute opportunity of drawing the tie level, Mark Dempsey lashing a shot over the bar when well placed to score. Dempsey reacted to the miss by holding his head in his hands, an indication of the anguish felt all around the stadium, but which definitely wasn't a reflection of the quality of football viewed.

1981-82

APRIL 1982

Seen from left to right, Ken Scott (number three), Mark Dempsey, Clayton Blackmore and Andy Hill stand and stare as Watford mount an assault on United's goalmouth

Billy Garton (number five) and goalkeeper Philip Hughes repel a Watford attack while Clayton Blackmore (far left), Andy Hill (left of Garton) and Norman Whiteside (right) await developments

final 1st leg

301

1981-82

1) Mike Potts	9) Jimmy Gilligan	1) Philip Hughes	9) Norman Whiteside
2) Neil Williams	10) John Barnes	2) Andy Hill	10) Mark Hughes
3) Neil Price	11) Dave Johnson	3) Ken Scott	11) Peter Docherty
4) Francis Cassidy	*12) Paul Candlish (for 11)*	4) Graeme Hogg	*12) Nicky Wood (for 6)*
5) Colin Hull		5) Billy Garton	
6) Paul Franklin		6) Sean Williams	
7) Worrell Sterling		7) Clayton Blackmore	
8) Ian Richardson		8) Mark Dempsey	

MAY 1982

WATFORD 4(7) v (6)4 MANCHESTER UNITED
a.e.t.

Garton (o.g.), Gilligan, Hill (o.g.), Johnson — Dempsey, Hughes M.(2), Whiteside

Thursday 6th
Kick-off 7.30 p.m.
Attendance 8,160

final 2nd leg

All dressed up and somewhere to go, the United youths get ready to board a coach for Watford to contest the second leg of the 1982 Youth Cup final
Back row (l-r) Mark Hughes (boarding coach), Mike Rowbotham, Andy Robinson, Nicky Wood, Graeme Hogg, Norman Whiteside, Lawrence Pearson, Peter Docherty, Billy Garton, Philip Hughes, Clayton Blackmore, Sean Williams, Andy Hill, Mark Dempsey, Ken Scott

For the concluding game there were just single changes to each side, one being no surprise at all while the other most certainly was. Because the Hornets' promotion to the First Division was assured over the preceding weekend, John Barnes was freed from senior chores in order to take a place in the Watford side at the expense of Nigel Gibbs.

In contrast to that expected development, there were more than a few eyebrows raised when Eric Harrison decided to bring Sean Williams back into United's starting line-up for the excluded Lawrence Pearson. The Pontypridd boy was one of eight players who had already been informed they were being given free transfers at the end of the season and he was as shocked as anyone by his surprise inclusion.

There was a monetary as well as a glory incentive for Reds' midfielder Mark Dempsey to get on the score sheet. Senior star Lou Macari promised Dempsey £100 for every goal he scored against Watford, albeit the cash would only change hands on the condition United won on aggregate. Macari had already shelled out bonuses of £10 and £20 for goals that Dempsey had registered in earlier rounds and he justified his actions when remarking, 'Losers get nothing in football and he might as well learn the lesson while he is young. He doesn't score many goals, which is why I decided to sponsor him. I am making him a hungry footballer.'

Dempsey lived up to his part of the bargain by scoring, but unfortunately he wasn't able to lighten Macari's pockets as the Reds were overtaken at the winning post in a game which even surpassed the excitement generated in the earlier tie at Old Trafford.

The Watford Observer recorded the conclusion of that season's tournament on what was a great day in the annals of the Vicarage Road club:

Watford captured the F.A. Youth Cup last Thursday evening in true Roy of the Rovers style, in probably the best game seen at Vicarage Road since the Southampton classic, writes Malcolm Vallerius.

Goals, excitement, breathtaking saves and a marvellous extra-time, cup-winning goal highlighted the second leg tie with Manchester United at Vicarage Road, which eventually finished at 4-4 for Watford to win 7-6 on aggregate.

The national press, raving about Watford's performance the following morning, dubbed the final as the most exciting in the competition's 30-year history and there could be few among the 8,160 crowd who would dispute that.

The game had everything. Both sides, committed to attacking, refreshing football produced a magnificent match, which will be long remembered by those who made the trip last Thursday.

Leading 3-2 from the first leg at Old Trafford, Watford could not have wished for a better start. After only ten minutes Jimmy Gilligan - destined for even greater glory later in the game - lost his marker on the right-hand side and drove in a hard, low cross to the near post. Defender Billy Garton, in his anxiety to clear the ball, could only manage to turn the ball into his own net, with goalkeeper Philip Hughes already committed to the cross.

United's youngsters, now two goals down on aggregate, would have been forgiven for dropping their heads. But five minutes later they were back in the game. The impressive Mark Hughes fired home Peter Docherty's cross from inside the box.

Both sides had chances to score then. Worrell Sterling, cutting in from the right, hit the side-netting and United's talented Norman Whiteside - this week called up for Northern Ireland's World Cup squad - shot across the face of Watford's goal.

1981-82

MAY 1982

However, ten minutes before the interval Watford regained the lead. Francis Cassidy sent over a long cross, Ian Richardson flicked on and David Johnson, arriving at the far post, crashed in a first-time shot against the inside of the post and into the net.

United, showing just brief glimpses of their class in the first half, came out after the break in a more determined mood and made it 2-2 on the night three minutes into the second half.

Whiteside, shielding the ball superbly on the half-way line, knocked a delightful ball into the path of Mark Dempsey, who only had to take it into the box and stroke it past goalkeeper Mike Potts. United then enjoyed their best period of the game. Watford were on the rack and the game seemed to be falling from their grasp before our eyes. United substitute Nicky Wood for Sean Williams and it was Wood's cross which led to United's third goal.

He centred and Hughes headed home to put United in front for the first time and level the scores on aggregate.

In the dying minutes, Watford, with several showing signs of fatigue, stormed back and as the game edged towards extra-time, Gilligan, allowed space and time on the right-hand side, drove a shot against the post from an acute angle and at the other end, Hughes exacted a marvellous save from Potts.

United seemed at the finish the stronger of the two sides as the referee blew the final whistle. They were leading on the night and several of the Watford youngsters had already been treated for cramp.

However, Lady Luck was on Watford's side. In the first minute of extra-time, Richardson, again showing considerable pace, chased a long, hopeful through ball. The United goalkeeper appeared favourite, but Richardson arrived first and managed to get a touch.

The ball cannoned off the goalkeeper, hit United defender Andy Hill, who had raced back with Richardson, and somehow ballooned up into an empty net. But no. They came back again. This time it was Whiteside who fired in a shot from just inside the box to make it 4-3 to the First Division club and 6-6 on aggregate.

Speculation in the press box then was on the destiny of the replay. But Gilligan had other ideas. After the tie had swung backwards and forwards in extra-time, Watford were awarded a corner on the left.

Cassidy trooped across to take the kick. He placed the ball, looked up and drove it across. Gilligan, unnoticed among a gaggle of players, rose superbly to crash a header home - and Watford had won.

We knew somehow, that this game, which had swung back and forth, was now safe and Watford survived United's attempts to make yet another comeback. Gilligan's goal, the sheer determination of Watford's play and the skills of Whiteside and Hughes stood out.

But, if sometimes United gave the impression of having outstanding individuals and some fine team work, the simple statistics tell the story - as ever. Watford had 30 goal attempts, United had 21, so once again, percentage football proved the point, as the sweat-stained Hornets lifted the trophy for the first time in their history and the fans went home equally breathless.

Various members of Watford's squad would continue to serve the club in their on-field escapades for some time, with only Mike Potts, Neil Williams, Francis Cassidy, Colin Hull and Paul Candlish failing to make it into their first-team. John Barnes, Worrell Sterling, Nigel Gibbs and Gary Porter progressed to put in over 1,100 senior divisional appearances for the Hornets and they and their colleagues additionally contributed towards in excess of 1,400 games for other Football League outfits.

Truly, they were an outstanding collection of individuals and worthy winners of that year's Youth Cup.

> We were confident that we would turn it on at their place in the second leg, but they proved a very resilient side, full of good headers and powerful runners. My partnership with Hughesy really gelled that night at the exceptionally high tempo we were forced to play in. I put us 4-3 up with about fifteen minutes of the added time to go, but despite our greater flair, we couldn't hang on. We were all shattered by the defeat and when you realise how many of our side went on to play in the First Division, it seems strange that we fell short.
>
> To this day it was one of the best games I have ever played in.
>
> **NORMAN WHITESIDE**

final 2nd leg

Norman Whiteside cracks in United's fourth goal of the night and the aggregate equaliser at Vicarage Road

1982-83

1) Trevor Campbell	9) Kevin Kent
2) Gary Leonard	10) Peter Frain
3) Andy Lacey	11) Martin Pike
4) Gary Robson	*12) Andy O'Connor (for 10)*
5) Mike Forsyth	
6) Wayne Ebanks	
7) Mickey Lewis	
8) Noel Luke	

1) Fraser Digby	9) Nicky Wood
2) Andy Robinson	10) Clayton Blackmore
3) Ken Scott	11) Lawrence Pearson
4) Andy Hill	*12) Simon Ratcliffe*
5) Billy Garton	
6) Willie Henderson	
7) Mike Rowbotham	
8) Gary Mills	

NOVEMBER 1982

WEST BROMWICH ALBION 0 v 1 MANCHESTER UNITED
Henderson

Monday 29th
Kick-off 7.30 p.m.
Attendance 1,200

second round

Reds call up boy keeper

Quite a lot had happened to one particular member of United's under-18 squad since he was last involved in a Youth Cup match. Having previously made only one senior competitive substitute appearance for the Reds, Ron Atkinson chose to give Norman Whiteside a starting place on the last day of the 1981/82 season when Stoke City were the visitors to Old Trafford. Whiteside put himself on the end of a superb Steve Coppell cross to register in the 2-0 win and not at anytime during the game did he look anything other than a fully-fledged first-teamer. Coming as it did just eight days after his 17th birthday, the feat installed him as Manchester United's youngest ever senior goalscorer.

That terrific achievement didn't escape the notice of Northern Ireland coach Billy Bingham, who promptly named Whiteside in his squad for the upcoming World Cup finals which were due to be held in Spain from the 13th June to the 11th July. Astonishingly, with just those two appearances for the Reds, Bingham elected to include him in the starting line-up for his country's opening group game, a 0-0 draw with Yugoslavia in Zaragoza, alongside former United Youth Cup participants Sammy McIlroy, David McCreery and Jimmy Nicholl. At only seventeen years and 41 days old, he broke the legendary Pele's record by 208 days to become the youngest player ever to appear in the World Cup finals.

Whiteside was chosen for all five of Northern Ireland's matches at España '82, including what is generally acknowledged as their greatest ever showing on foreign soil, a 1-0 win over the host nation in the Estadio Luis Casanova in Valencia. The Irish remained unbeaten, by also achieving draws with Honduras and Austria going into their fifth game, when a 4-1 defeat by France put them out. Nevertheless, for their accomplishments Whiteside and the rest of the squad returned to Ulster to be fêted as national heroes and their performances are still talked about in the province with a sense of pride.

Those accomplishments in Spain went a long way towards convincing Atkinson that the club's latest star pupil was ready for some more senior action, and since the start of the new season Whiteside had barely missed a minute of first-team football. As it so happened, Atkinson wanted him fresh for an upcoming midweek League Cup tie, which meant that for the Second Round of the Youth Cup, Eric Harrison was required to thrust Clayton Blackmore into a forward role.

Besides the absence of Whiteside, the usual plethora of ins and outs took place in the make-up of United's youth team for the commencement of the tournament, when an away tie at West Brom meant that Harrison's boys would come into direct competition with Gary Robson, the younger brother of current Reds' favourite Bryan Robson.

The inclusion of the two Andys, Hill and Robinson, as well as Billy Garton and Ken Scott, gave the defence a familiar look and they were supplemented by Fraser Digby, an England Boys' goalkeeper who was recruited from the Sheffield area.

The selection of Digby, then still at school, was practically forced on Harrison because of the actions of Philip Hughes. A prospect who appeared to possess most of the attributes needed to make it to the very top, and whose almost faultless displays between the posts in the Reds' Youth Cup ties of the previous season was considered as a major factor in them reaching the final, he found himself at loggerheads with the club and therefore had taken part in only four 'A' team games so far that campaign.

The offer of a new contract hadn't been exercised by the teenage custodian, the sticking point being that the term tabled was too short for his liking, and he then angered the Reds' management by announcing he was due to take part in a secret trial with a rival club. Hughes went on to inform the powers that be that he was withdrawing from the game at West Brom in order to ensure he wasn't cup-tied and it meant that Digby went into the match against the Baggies with only three junior appearances to his credit.

Further up the field there were competition entrances for Willie Henderson and Belfast-born Gary Mills. In some respects, the composition of the team was similar to many previous years, when the lads with experience outweighed those new to the side.

Ironically, in the face of United's latest goalkeeping fiasco, it was the Albion goalie who proved key to the Reds' progress into the next round. In an otherwise flawless performance, the Baggies' Trevor Campbell allowed a high and hanging Lawrence Pearson cross to slip from his grasp and drop behind him in the 14th minute. Campbell's gaff provided an early gift for Reds' midfielder Henderson, a local prospect from Marple, as he was on hand to exercise a simple task by knocking the ball over the line.

The goal was more than United might have expected at that stage and the effect on the home side was drastic, because from then until half-time West Brom looked totally without confidence and therefore offered little in the way of an attacking threat.

The majority of scoring opportunities came after the change around. Albion's Kevin Kent soon brought a flying save out of Digby, while at the other end chances were later spurned by practically all of United's midfielders and forwards.

There were one or two moments of indecision in the Reds' defence. However, in the main, the back four remained reasonably solid and as such it wasn't until the 88th minute when West Brom's best chance of equalising arrived. Kevin Kent was again the source of danger when he rifled a drive towards the target, Billy Garton deflecting the shot away with his head only for the ball to come flying back towards the top right-hand corner of the goal. It was left to Digby to save the day for United by acrobatically swooping through the air to catch the ball cleanly.

With the England Youth selectors reportedly in attendance in order to run the rule over Garton and Andy Hill, the former did his chances of possible international recognition no harm at all through snuffing out West Brom's last significant effort when putting in a superb challenge to block a shot from substitute Andy O'Connor.

Eric Harrison later expressed his feelings on the outcome by remarking, *'We could have just done with another goal. It is always dangerous in a cup tie when holding only a one-goal lead.'*

Fraser Digby's experience as a Red extended to only 270 minutes of football prior to making his first Youth Cup appearance at The Hawthorns

1) Fraser Digby
2) Andy Robinson
3) Ken Scott
4) Simon Ratcliffe
5) Andy Hill
6) Willie Henderson
7) Mike Rowbotham
8) Peter Docherty
9) Norman Whiteside
10) Clayton Blackmore
11) Lawrence Pearson
12) Nicky Wood (for 3)

1) Rob Palmer
2) Keith McCormick
3) Graham Harbey
4) Paul Blades
5) Shawn Ride
6) Jimmy Collins
7) David Collins
8) Paul Bancroft
9) John Ackroyd
10) Andy Garner
11) Mark Clifford
12) Andy Roberts (for 11)

1982-83

MANCHESTER UNITED 2 v 2 DERBY COUNTY
Blackmore, Ride (o.g.)   Garner (2)

DECEMBER 1982

Monday 20th

Kick-off 7.30 p.m.

Attendance 3,382

third round

Because of Philip Hughes' eventual decision to further his career at Leeds, Fraser Digby was again the obvious choice between the posts for Eric Harrison at the following stage, when the return of Peter Docherty and, more importantly, Norman Whiteside, gave United's forward-line a look of increased potency for the third pairing with Derby County in five campaigns. Whiteside's appearance record for the seniors was now up to 24 for the current season and his seven-goal tally really was quite exceptional for someone of his age.

The Derby Evening Telegraph produced a report for a match in which both sides could claim they *'gifted'* goals away to their opponents:

Derby County thoroughly deserved last night's F.A. Youth Cup Third Round draw at Old Trafford. Manchester United, last season's beaten finalists, included brilliant Northern Ireland striker Norman Whiteside, but they could still not overcome the gritty Rams challenge.

Derby were in superb form. Overall United had the better skills, but the Rams' fiercely competitive attitude made them value for a replay.

Skipper Graham Harbey produced a fine display at full-back, while Shawn Ride did well in the centre and Paul Blades contained Whiteside.

Tenacious John Ackroyd worried United and sixteen year-old Andy Garner showed his worth by scoring both Derby goals.

Derby opened in fine style and went ahead after six minutes. Mark Clifford laid the ball back to Jimmy Collins, who lifted a high ball forward from just inside the Derby half. Goalkeeper Fraser Digby made a complete hash of going for the ball and watched helplessly as it bounced over his head. Garner was left with a simple chance which he accepted gleefully.

Two minutes later it should have been 2-0. Ackroyd went past two defenders on the edge of the penalty area and fired in a low shot that Digby palmed away. Garner should have pounced to score easily, but he hesitated and United scrambled the ball away for a corner. Garner was booked soon after for a foul on Andy Hill and then United went close when a Hill header hit a post.

Palmer rescued Derby on several occasions with good saves, but he spoiled a fine performance with his complete lack of confidence on crosses. He stopped an almost certain equaliser after 31 minutes, though, when he flung himself across goal to push away a shot from Peter Docherty, son of former Derby County manager Tommy.

Jimmy Collins was cautioned for a foul on Docherty soon after and then in the second half things suddenly started to go wrong for Derby.

Lawrence Pearson's corner was allowed to fly across the face of the goal for Clayton Blackmore to score after 57 minutes. Blackmore headed in from almost on the line.

Worse was to come after 64 minutes. Pearson was running across the penalty area when Ride dived in for a desperate tackle, but he succeeded only in blasting the ball into the top corner for an own goal.

It seemed then that Derby were on their way out of the competition, but they battled back to earn a second chance.

Garner reacted quickly when a Ken Scott back pass fell short. Goalkeeper Digby was left stranded and Garner slid the ball coolly into the corner.

There was no denying the Rams. They defended well and conceded nothing to United who had expected to go through comfortably.

There was indeed a whole lot of expectation that the Reds were capable of progressing at Derby's expense, particularly with home advantage, and there was an overspill of frustration from a tightly-marshalled Whiteside when he was booked by Kirkby referee Mr. R. Guy. Whiteside wasn't the only United player who didn't get his own way, as County's plan of not allowing anyone in a red jersey to take too much time on the ball paid dividends by drawing a nervy and disjointed performance out of Eric Harrison's lads.

It was only after Garner had completed his brace and Derby appeared to tire markedly when United began to exploit a few holes in and about their opponents' penalty box. Following his earlier defensive mistake, Ken Scott made way for the introduction of Nicky Wood twelve minutes from time, his entrance adding fresh impetus to an attack which suddenly began to come up with a few constructive ideas.

Even though Simon Ratcliffe looked tidy and unruffled in his first appearance in the tournament, the absence of Billy Garton, whose armband passed to Andy Hill, brought about a measure of hesitancy and, occasionally, desperation at the back. Clayton Blackmore was easily United's most impressive forward and his equaliser was nothing more than he deserved for plugging away all throughout and right up until the end.

Unfortunately a win wasn't to be and the Reds' display was encapsulated in a moment five minutes from the final whistle when Whiteside incurred the wrath of the man in black by sending composed Derby captain Graham Harbey sprawling across the turf with a crude and dangerous tackle.

Andy Robinson (top) was only one of a number who were hard-pressed to contain a doggedly determined Derby while Nicky Wood sparked some late life into the Reds' search for a winning goal

305

1982-83

1) Rob Palmer	9) Andy Garner	1) Fraser Digby	9) Norman Whiteside
2) Neil Banks	10) Paul Bancroft	2) Ken Scott	10) Nicky Wood
3) Graham Harbey	11) David Collins	3) Clayton Blackmore	11) Lawrence Pearson
4) Mark Clifford	*12) Keith McCormick (for 4)*	4) Andy Hill	*12) Andy Robinson (for 6)*
5) Shawn Ride		5) Billy Garton	
6) Paul Blades		6) Willie Henderson	
7) Jimmy Collins		7) Peter Docherty	
8) John Ackroyd		8) Mike Rowbotham	

JANUARY 1983

DERBY COUNTY 0 v 1 MANCHESTER UNITED
Wood

Monday 10th*

Kick-off 7.00 p.m.

Attendance 516

third round replay

Both United and Derby were keen to settle their Third Round tie prior to the Christmas festivities, and the replay was hurriedly arranged for three days after the draw in Manchester until a heavy fall of snow kyboshed those plans and resulted in the game being put back until the New Year.

On the Saturday before the second clash, the reputation of Norman Whiteside took another giant leap forward when he claimed the prestigious 'International Discovery of the Year' award by the Sports Writers' Association. Over the very same weekend, Eric Harrison demonstrated one of the many attributes which made him such an outstanding coach over the many years of his tracksuited career, that of astute observation.

Casting a professional eye over Saturday's football highlights on television, Harrison logged a mental note of the soggy state of the Baseball Ground's playing surface. With more rain having fallen between then and kick-off, he decided to switch Clayton Blackmore into defence and re-introduce the quicksilver Nicky Wood to pair up alongside Whiteside in attack. The re-jigging was a masterstroke, with Wood scoring the Reds' winner and the Rams being restricted to the very minimum of chances.

The Derby Evening Telegraph reported on how it all went right for United:

Derby County fought bravely, but fell to superior opposition in this F.A. Youth Cup Third Round replay at the Baseball Ground last night.

The fierce competitive attitude of the young Rams kept them in touch with United and in the last fifteen minutes they pressed forward strongly and threatened to force extra-time.

But United, led by Northern Ireland's World Cup ace Norman Whiteside, were the better side and deserved to win.

Paul Blades had a fine match at the heart of the Derby defence and, along with Shawn Ride, contained Whiteside. Paul Bancroft did well in midfield and upfront John Ackroyd showed spirit and pace before he ran out of steam in the last ten minutes.

Graham Harbey was another Derby player who could be satisfied with his performance. Full-back Harbey has been hit by injury, but he is fast regaining the form that once put him on the verge of a first-team spot.

In goal Robert Palmer made a string of good saves to deny United. Palmer blocked a close range effort by Nicky Wood after 21 minutes, went down to stop a Ken Scott effort and in the last minute brilliantly tipped over a Whiteside effort that looked certain to hit the top corner until Palmer appeared.

But it always appeared inevitable that United would win on the muddy Baseball Ground pitch. The teams drew 2-2 at Old Trafford and Derby deserved a replay, but they rarely looked like scoring this time.

Perhaps their only real chance came after 82 minutes, when Andy Garner worked himself into a good position and had his ankles whipped from under him by Billy Garton. It looked a clear penalty but referee Gilbert Napthine waved aside appeals.

United's match-winner came after 52 minutes when full-back Clayton Blackmore won the ball on the left and sent a long, high pass over the Derby defence.

Wood reacted first and was well clear of defenders when he easily rounded Palmer and slid his shot neatly into the corner.

Derby sent on substitute Keith McCormick for Mark Clifford in a bid to add more punch in midfield, but the Rams could not unsettle this talented United team.

Last season United reached the final of the F.A. Youth Cup and they have a team good enough to repeat that feat. Their defence, with Garton the star, always looked solid and in midfield Peter Docherty, son of former Derby County manager Tommy, showed up well.

With Whiteside and Wood combining in attack, United have the potential for plenty of goals. It was a tribute to the Derby defence that they only managed one last night.

The main after-match point of discussion was the controversial decision by the Loughborough referee to ignore County's late penalty appeal. In the Review, Joe Lancaster pointed out that the official *'made a plunging sign with his hands in the closing minutes when big Billy Garton brought a Derby lad down in the box'*. Lancaster concluded the captain's challenge was legal *'....and the player's dive very ham-handed'*.

Manchester United goalkeeper Fraser Digby punches clear during this Derby raid. Paul Bancroft (left), Andy Garner (centre) and John Ackroyd are the Derby players pictured.

*This game was originally scheduled for Thursday, December 23rd but was postponed due to a snowbound pitch

1) Steven Crocker	9) Martin Allen	1) Fraser Digby	9) Nicky Wood
2) Fraser Allen	10) Kevin Edwards	2) Ken Scott	10) Gary Mills
3) Barry Prince	11) Alan Comfort	3) Clayton Blackmore	11) Lawrence Pearson
4) Doug McClure	*12) Stephen Scott*	4) Andy Hill	*12) Derek Murray*
5) Terry Evans		5) Billy Garton	
6) Andy Waddock		6) Willie Henderson	
7) David Kerslake		7) Mike Rowbotham	
8) Gary Cooper		8) Peter Docherty	

QUEEN'S PARK RANGERS 0 v 0 MANCHESTER UNITED

1982-83

FEBRUARY 1983

Thursday 3rd

Kick-off 7.30 p.m.

fourth round

Snapped at Timperley Cricket Club, Eric Harrison explains to the youngsters how best to approach their upcoming game at Loftus Road

United had undertaken several visits to the country's largest metropolis in their quest for Youth Cup glory down the years and their very first pairing with Shepherds Bush's finest certainly wore a cloak of novelty. By establishing themselves as England's pioneers of the synthetic soccer surface in 1981, Queen's Park Rangers were well into their second season of performing on a 'plastic' playing area.

The concept wasn't a new one, as American baseball clubs had used them from as long ago as the mid-1960's and many other sports in the United States, such as American football and field hockey, followed their lead over the next few years. One of the major benefits of synthetic pitches over natural ones was their low maintenance, as no trimming or irrigation was required, and so they cost almost nothing to maintain.

However, the greatest benefit of plastic pitches over grass was that they could be used constantly, because there wasn't the same wear associated with synthetic surfaces as with turf, and adverse weather conditions such as rain and snow had practically no effect on them.

There were negatives, though, as plastic surfaces caused the ball to bounce higher, and the risk of injury increased as there was less 'give' in a pitch which was most usually laid over a concrete base. They were known to affect knees, feet, ankles and the lower back area, as well as the 'burning' effect when a player 'skidded' their skin on it.

The prospect of performing on such a surface in a competitive match was certainly new to the United boys and so it was felt that the Londoners' experience of same might provide them with something of a slight advantage. The predicament wasn't lost on Eric Harrison who, for the second game in a row, was forced into considering how best to prepare his team for the conditions underfoot, and his thoughtful plans included ferrying the United squad over to Timperley Cricket Club for a spot of training and some practice matches on their all-weather pitch.

While the young Reds might not have looked quite as comfortable as the home team at certain times of the game, Harrison's wisdom was rewarded when his lads came away with a useful 0-0 draw.

The tie was marred by a growing problem that was rife throughout British football just then, that of hooliganism, and referee Tom Bune was faced with little choice other than to call a halt to the proceedings for approximately five minutes when about a dozen QPR and 'Cockney Reds' traded kicks and punches in an ugly brawl which spilled over from one of the seating areas and onto the pitch.

Stewards were quickly on the scene and did a good job in containing and eventually quelling the trouble in the absence of any further security presence. The unfortunate incident caused a reporter to observe, *'No police were inside the ground because it had never been thought necessary at a youth match. There were only about 500 spectators at the match but the small all-London crowd contained a noisy young element'.*

David Meek labelled it as *'a new low in hooligan behaviour'* and he bemoaned the fact that the Football Association was *'already in despair over recent outrages by Leeds United and Chelsea vandals'.*

Well known as a staunch supporter of the youth team, United senior star Lou Macari watched the match from the Main Stand as he was in London to take part in a taping of the popular television programme 'This Is Your Life', which was dedicated to Kenny Dalglish, his former Celtic team-mate and current Liverpool star.

As far as the football was concerned, the Reds were at their most vulnerable in the early minutes through taking an inordinate amount of time to settle against a team that required three attempts to defeat lowly London rivals Orient in the previous round.

Even so, they should have settled the matter without the requirement of a second game and a golden chance to do just that was spurned in the 58th minute when Peter Docherty sent Gary Mills in on goal with just Rangers goalkeeper Stephen Crocker to beat. Mills was felled by Crocker as he carried the ball past him, then to all of his colleagues' despair Ken Scott knocked the resultant penalty around the post.

1982-83

1) Fraser Digby	9) Norman Whiteside	1) Steven Crocker	9) Martin Allen
2) Ken Scott	10) Nicky Wood	2) Vince Tanner	10) Kevin Edwards
3) Clayton Blackmore	11) Lawrence Pearson	3) Barry Prince	11) Alan Comfort
4) Andy Hill	*12) Andy Robinson (for 11)*	4) Doug McClure	*12) Stephen Scott*
5) Billy Garton		5) Terry Evans	
6) Willie Henderson		6) Andy Waddock	
7) Mike Rowbotham		7) David Kerslake	
8) Peter Docherty		8) Gary Cooper	

FEBRUARY 1983

MANCHESTER UNITED 4 v 0 QUEEN'S PARK RANGERS

Blackmore, Rowbotham, Whiteside (2)

Monday 7th
Kick-off 7.30 p.m.

fourth round replay

Just four days after returning from London, Norman Whiteside, who was by now assisting the seniors in their quest for honours in both the F.A. and Milk Cups, came back into the youth side with Gary Mills making way in an otherwise unchanged combination. By applying their considerable skills and abundant aggression, United put on a vastly improved display to brush their way past QPR with some ease.

On a decidedly cool and snowy night in Stretford, which acted as an eerie reminder of the terrible events at Munich 25 years and one day previously, the pattern was set just past the fifteen-minute mark when the visiting goalkeeper was penalised for carrying the ball more than four paces for a second time. Clayton Blackmore blasted the free kick into the defensive wall and when Crocker was unable to clear the rebound effectively, despite ten of the Rangers team standing goal-side of him, and most of them in close proximity, Whiteside hammered the loose ball into the net.

With half an hour gone, Whiteside doubled his production for the evening. Bursting through from a deep position, the beefy Belfast boy wasn't tracked properly and he was allowed the space, carried the motive and kept his presence to drill the ball under Crocker to make it 2-0.

Old Trafford must have seemed like the coldest place on earth for the away team when Clayton Blackmore made it three without reply in the 62nd minute. Loitering at the far post with more than a little intent, Blackmore put away a header that was just too easy to miss. A decent victory then developed into a comprehensive one in the 77th minute, Mike Rowbotham capping a fine performance with a splendid individual goal.

There were a plentiful pile of printed plaudits for United's purring performance in the press, one summary giving the view that the southerners *'failed on the softness of the Manchester pitch and against the hardness of Whiteside'*. Nicky Wood was said to have led Rangers *'a merry dance'* while Blackmore's enterprise and class *'showed why he has been used as an emergency striker'*.

Knocking out a Loftus Road team containing three current England Youth internationals was considered something of a feather in their cap for Eric Harrison's charges. There was no disputing that Queen's Park Rangers looked an accomplished side on their own ground, though they were made to appear more like cannon fodder at Old Trafford.

Clayton Blackmore converted an easy chance to put United 3-0 up

All eyes are on the ball as Norman Whiteside (far right) rifles the Reds into the lead against Queen's Park Rangers

1982-83

1) Fraser Digby	9) Mark Mettrick	1) Andrew Pearce	9) Paul Clayton
2) Ken Scott	10) Nicky Wood	2) Daryl Godbold	10) Mark Metcalf
3) Clayton Blackmore	11) Lawrence Pearson	3) Tony Spearing	11) Neil Riley
4) Billy Garton	*12) Andy Robinson (for 6)*	4) Mark Crowe	*12) Austin O'Connor*
5) Andy Hill		5) Brendan McIntyre	
6) Willie Henderson		6) Jeremy Goss	
7) Mike Rowbotham		7) Louie Donowa	
8) Peter Docherty		8) Jon Rigby	

MANCHESTER UNITED 0 v 1 NORWICH CITY
Donowa

MARCH 1983

Monday 7th

Kick-off 7.30 p.m.

Attendance 1,234

United's starlets bow out

Brand new opposition was the order of the day for the second successive round when the Reds were instructed to tackle Norwich City by virtue of the draw. United were especially happy with their home advantage because it was fairly obvious from Norwich's progress that they would probably provide their most difficult opponents yet.

Whereas the Old Trafford youngsters were up to just eight tournament goals registered so far, the Norfolk club's total was a whopping twenty. Five goals alone came from Canaries' sharpshooter Paul Clayton while another four were registered by fellow marksman Jon Rigby. Despite being involved in a car accident just a few months before, and now thankfully fully recovered, Rigby had benefited from a summer spell in Norwegian football and was proving a constant menace to defences.

Norwich's Youth Cup run began with a comfortable 6-0 win over Southend at Carrow Road and they then disposed of Arsenal by four goals to two on the same ground after initially drawing 2-2 at Highbury. A couple of excellent home wins followed, with Aston Villa beaten 5-2 and, even more impressively, last season's winners Watford eliminated in the Fourth Round.

Norwich coach Dave Stringer was boosted by the return to fitness of youth team skipper Mark Crowe, and he revealed just how significant the trip to Manchester was to his team when telling the press, *'It's a marvellous occasion for us and if we can just clear this hurdle I'm sure we can go on and win the cup'.*

With a Sixth Round F.A. Cup match due to take place at Old Trafford on the following Saturday, manager Ron Atkinson pulled Norman Whiteside out of the Youth Cup tie because club captain Bryan Robson was already declared unfit for the showpiece game and the manager wanted the youngest member of his squad available for senior duty.

The Ulster lad's place in the youth team was taken by Mark Mettrick, and it was clearly asking a lot of the Glossop-based teenager to fill the boots of 'Big Norman' at that precise time as Whiteside's presence would have given an immense boost to United's chances of sealing a hugely creditable fourth consecutive appearance in the semi-finals. Unquestionably, there was something of a hint of desperation about Mettrick's inclusion, his record of a solitary goal in just three starts and one substitute appearance for the 'A' team hardly equipping him for a match of such importance.

Joe Lancaster gave his candid views on a disappointing outcome in the United Review:

Norwich, moving like an Inter-City express, deservedly reached the F.A. Youth Cup semi-final and a date with Luton Town after a 1-0 victory at Old Trafford.

They most likely will not stop at Old Trafford but go right on to the final. Manchester United certainly felt the draught and in the 33rd minute were in that precarious position of Stockport and Wilmslow passengers waiting to get on but not having time to pick up their bags. The Norwich Express was away leaving our boys stranded.

Classy striker Lou Donowa, an England Youth international, scored a brilliant individual goal, swivelling on the edge of the United box, beating two defenders and 'keeper Fraser Digby with a low shot. Three minutes later, Norwich almost added a second when Jon Rigby was put through but Clayton Blackmore came to the rescue. Blackmore nearly levelled the score in the 40th minute but his blast was deflected away.

An early chance by Mark Mettrick, a Loretto schoolboy making his youth team debut, having been set up in the 12th minute by Andy Hill, came to nothing. Welsh Youth international Blackmore struck a 22nd minute drive which Norwich 'keeper Andy Pearce turned aside but too often the young Reds were forced into defensive walls trying to cope with lively Norwich. It stopped United settling into a dominant rhythm.

To match those cutting attacks, the East Anglians had a solid defence and what more can be asked of any team, unless it is to keep injury free, and United did not. Willie Henderson, a midfielder, took a bang on the head and was replaced after 57 minutes by Andy Robinson. They were trying to seek inspiration and it almost came in the 73rd minute. Inevitably, it was Blackmore. This time he rattled the bar with a dipping volley and with that United's last chance of salvaging the game disappeared down the line.

There was still a flurry of late activity from central defenders Billy Garton and Andy Hill, who pushed forward in an effort to rescue the tie but Manchester United, beaten by Watford in last season's tremendous final, bowed out to a team who seem certain to win this year's competition.

The Canaries' angle was presented by the local Norwich newspaper:

Norwich City last night completed a marvellous hat-trick of victories to reach the semi-finals of the F.A. Youth Cup.

The Canaries denied the young Manchester United hopefuls a second successive final appearance thanks to a superb individual effort by Louie Donowa.

But it was a victory that owed more to a fine battling team performance – and saw Dave Stringer's lads emerge as one of the favourites for this season's competition.

City have now beaten original favourites Aston Villa, holders Watford and United in successive ties, but manager Dave Stringer still has his feet firmly on the ground after another memorable triumph which set up a semi-final clash with Luton.

'We gave a good all-round team performance and did well to beat United. But Luton are a good side and we must take each game as it comes.'

Stringer enthused about the flash of brilliance that took the Canaries into the last four – and delighted the large Norwich following in a disappointingly low crowd of just over 1,000.

'I thought Louie's goal was exceptional, a piece of real individualism. He took it really well.'

Donowa struck in the 34th minute in City's first genuine attack of the game. He gathered the ball on the edge of the area and waltzed past three United defenders before beating England Youth international 'keeper Fraser Digby with a beautifully judged shot.

That superb opener stunned the young Red Devils and watching manager Ron Atkinson, and although the home side battled gamely to get back into the match they only rarely threatened the resolute Norwich defence.

The back four of Crowe, McIntyre, Godbold and Spearing were outstanding and United's best effort came from outside the box.

Twice classy full-back Clayton Blackmore tested 'keeper Pearce but they were the only moments of anxiety and it was Norwich who looked the more likely to score again.

Obviously, Manchester United missed the influential presence of Norman Whiteside, who was rested for Saturday's F.A. Cup clash with Everton, but there was no denying the young Canaries deserved their moment of triumph.

City manager Ken Brown, one of the large Carrow Road contingent in the crowd, said afterwards he was delighted with the team.

Now he must be hoping his first-team can follow suit in the quarter-final of the F.A. Cup at Brighton on Saturday.

Norwich practically ensured their appearance in the final by defeating Luton 3-1 at Kenilworth Road in the opening leg of the last four stage, the teams later drawing 0-0 at Carrow Road.

Then, in a final which almost matched the United v. Watford epic of the previous season for goals, the teenage Canaries just edged past Everton by virtue of a 6-5 aggregate victory.

While Norman Whiteside might have seen his cup hopes dashed at junior standard, there was a major consolation prize waiting for him. In the same month that the club's under-18's lost to Norwich, he scored what proved to be a consolation goal when the senior Reds lost 2-1 to Liverpool in the Milk Cup final at Wembley.

His fortunes improved dramatically from then on, and in mid-April he blasted home an exquisite winner after United came from behind to defeat Arsenal by the same score in an absorbing F.A. Cup semi-final at Villa Park.

A stunning twelve months was completed for the Irishman when, following a 2-2 draw against Brighton back at Wembley, five days later Whiteside returned to the twin towers to score in the Reds' crushing 4-0 F.A. Cup final replay victory over the Seagulls.

fifth round

309

1983-84

1) Steve Harvey	9) Paul Barnes	1) Fraser Digby	9) David Platt
2) Simeon Hodson	10) David Kevan	2) Ken Scott	10) Nicky Wood
3) Gary Dilks	11) Dave Beaver	3) Pat Kelch	11) Gary Worthington
4) Paul Smalley	*12) Luke Betteridge ◊*	4) Andy Robinson	*12) Aidan Murphy*
5) Darren Davis		5) Simon Ratcliffe	
6) Dean Yates		6) Mike Rowbotham	
7) Mark Jones		7) Gary Mills	
8) Tony Daws		8) Martin Russell	

DECEMBER 1983

NOTTS COUNTY 0 v 3 MANCHESTER UNITED

Platt, Rowbotham, Wood

Saturday 17th*

Kick-off 11.30 a.m.

second round

In October 1983, shock news of the sudden death of Jack Pauline reached Old Trafford. One of the last remaining links from the days of the MUJACs, his association with United reached back as far as 1944 and lasted right up until 1978. A respected, much liked and approachable man, throughout his time at the club he was an unpaid volunteer who received only out of pocket expenses. For him, the satisfaction of seeing some of the club's younger element develop and progress towards better and greater successes was all he ever wanted.

Former youth coach Jimmy Murphy was naturally deeply saddened, and he said of the loss of his trusted friend and one-time colleague, *'A lot of players should be thankful Jack was around when they were just up-and-coming youngsters. Hundreds must have passed through his hands, but nothing was too much trouble for him. Jack ran the fourth team during the war and he was with the club when Sir Matt Busby and I arrived. He was a great help to us in arranging trials and running the Colts team before we had the staff to do it. He was a terrific asset to the club, especially in those early days.'*

Pauline grew up in Liverpool and during his formative years he played football in addition to indulging in a spot of refereeing. It was the organisational side of the game which held the most appeal for him, to the extent that while still a teenager he acted as his team's secretary and was also on their league committee. The sport obviously ran in the family, or at least as far as his brother, who at one time or another represented South Liverpool Football Club.

He came to Manchester quite soon into his career as an engineer with the GPO, later rising to the position of assistant executive engineer within the organisation, and while on their payroll he worked with, the then, part-time United scout Joe Armstrong. In the days when the off-field staff at Old Trafford could probably be counted on the fingers of a couple of hands, he carried out a multitude of tasks. The main one was in travelling with the side which was eventually called the 'B' team, and it was undoubtedly a labour of love for four decades.

In that regard Pauline frequently came into contact with those who were new to the club, and the impression he made, which was of a man who genuinely cared for them as individuals, was crucial in developing an ethos of benevolence Busby saw as fundamentally right and proper. He also paid the team's match expenses and ensured the players knew their travel arrangements as far in advance as possible. Because of his knowledge of the boys who came under his wing, his views were frequently sought from the club's coaches in relation to their ability, possible scope for development and, equally importantly, their overall character.

An integral member of the backroom staff when the club installed floodlights at The Cliff in 1950, from then on he headed straight from work in order to attend the evening training sessions held there. Because of his previous experience he was often called upon to referee the practice matches, thus freeing Murphy and Bert Whalley to play on one side each and so be in a position to coach the lads all through the games.

Pauline was also the secretary of whichever was United's most junior team, meaning he was required to attend any relevant meetings of the league they were in at any given time. Elected onto the management committee of the Eccles League in the 1950's, he served that body well and loyally for very many years.

It was around the same time when he began writing match reports in the 'With the Juniors.......' section for the United Review. As far as some of the Youth Cup games were concerned, his words represented the most comprehensive descriptions of those ties and without that input far less would be known about the club's exploits in the competition than is the case today.

For the record, his first acknowledged summary for a Youth Cup match was in December 1965, when the Reds defeated Manchester City, while his unaccredited accounts are believed to go right back to United's win over Barnsley in March 1953. To bring a magnificent period of service to an end, his last Youth Cup piece was penned for the defeat at Middlesbrough in March 1978 and he called time on soccer activities soon after.

The Liverpudlian often claimed football filled so much of his life that little time was left for any other hobbies, although in the summer months he managed to catch up on some gardening at his Fir Road home in Bramhall. Passing away as a result of a heart attack while out shopping, the 74 year-old left a son called David.

As far as current affairs were concerned, for Ken Scott, Andy Robinson, Mike Rowbotham and Nicky Wood, the 1983/84 season represented a third chance of Youth Cup glory, while for Gary Mills, Simon Ratcliffe and Fraser Digby, the campaign offered up their second crack at capturing the trophy.

Of the new boys, David Platt had joined the club after being spotted while playing for Chadderton Football Club in a pre-season friendly match against a United XI. The sixteen year-old failed to win an apprenticeship at school leaving time and his soccer prospects looked bleak until Eric Harrison's intervention, with

the club offering to take him on a Work Experience Scheme as a 'borderline' case. Through the benefit of full-time training and coaching, Platt was developing into one of the outstanding prospects of his class and his seven goals from a dozen 'A' team games had already earned him a start in the Reserves, for whom he figured alongside Wood and Rowbotham.

Donning the number eleven jersey for the Reds, freshman Gary Worthington was a nephew of the mercurial former Bolton, Leicester, Huddersfield and England striker Frank Worthington, and there were two other new names on the team sheet in the shape of defender Pat Kelch and midfielder Martin Russell.

An engagement with Notts County at Meadow Lane was the first obstacle the Reds were faced with overcoming in the new term's tournament, a game which held a special significance for one of the young Magpies. An ex-England Boys' international, Tony Daws was previously attached to United on associate schoolboy forms and he explained, *'I used to spend my holidays at Old Trafford and travel to Manchester every weekend to play for the junior sides. Most of the current United youth side are friends of mine, especially a couple of lads who played in the same Sheffield Schools team as me, so I'm really keen to do well.'* The youngster had asked to be released when his opportunities became limited at Old Trafford and he was immediately offered an apprenticeship by County, who were then a fixture in the First Division.

The original date pencilled in for the match was rescheduled when three inches of snow fell in Nottingham. The postponement only served to delay what was a reasonably easy entry point for the Reds as they cantered to a 3-0 win, all of the goals coming in a spell of just under half an hour in the second period.

Brain-box Nicky Wood, who had featured in the youth team as an Oldham schoolboy for the last two seasons, was now furthering his studies at Manchester University while simultaneously attached to United as a part-time professional.

Appropriately applying his thinking powers to put the Reds into the lead in the 50th minute, the move was instigated by Rowbotham with a pass to Platt and carried on when United's number nine directed the ball into Wood's path. The studious fellow out-thought two County defenders and he was able to cleverly poke the ball between 'keeper Harvey and the near post, despite initially appearing to drag it too far to the right of the goal.

Notts then entered into their best period of the game, when an equaliser wouldn't have shocked too many spectators, but the expectation level dropped dramatically inside the stadium through an error allowing the Reds to double their lead with 22 minutes remaining. A wayward pass from County's Dilks was snapped up by Rowbotham, who capitalised on the error by striking an accurate long ball to Wood. When Wood's attempt at goal was nudged away by Harvey, the poaching Platt couldn't have been situated any better to shove home the rebound.

After 79 minutes the workaholic Rowbotham was integral to a third United goal, only this time he acted as finisher rather than provider. From Mills' corner on the left, Platt rose to back-flick the ball across the Notts goalmouth and Rowbotham set the seal on a deserved victory when powering it in with his head. It made up for an earlier glaring miss, the midfielder smacking an effort straight at Harvey despite having practically all of the net to aim at.

The Reds had been required to overcome the twin obstacles of a heavy pitch and obstinate opponents, and it was certain their efforts would have greatly pleased Jack Pauline.

" It was my second season at the club and following the disappointment of the previous year we were keen to do well.
When we heard the draw against Notts County I thought that it was a great opportunity for us to progress in the competition.
We got up early to make the trip to Nottingham and for most of us it was our first experience using the senior team's coach.
We played in a 4-3-3 formation, as Eric was keen to mirror what they did in the first-team, so I played in centre midfield alongside Martin Russell and Mike Rowbotham with Gary Worthington and Nicky Wood playing wide of David Platt upfront.
The conditions were quite tricky so we were all on a high on the journey home and Eric Harrison was really pleased with the overall team performance. "

GARY MILLS

*This game was originally scheduled for Monday, December 12th but was postponed due to a snowbound pitch

1) Daryl Beeston
2) Phil Shirley
3) Darren Darwent
4) Neil Bailey
5) Stuart March
6) Steve Parsons
7) Mark Aherne
8) Andy Roberts
9) Andy Garner
10) Andy Irvine
11) Richard Danks
12) Mark Davey (for 7)

1) Fraser Digby
2) Ken Scott
3) Pat Kelch
4) Andy Robinson
5) Simon Ratcliffe
6) Mike Rowbotham
7) Gary Mills
8) Martin Russell
9) David Platt
10) Nicky Wood
11) Gary Worthington
12) Aidan Murphy

1983-84

DERBY COUNTY 0 v 9 MANCHESTER UNITED

Mills, Platt (3), Russell, Scott (2), Wood (2)

JANUARY 1984

PLATT-TRICK!

Saturday 21st*

Kick-off 2.00 p.m.

The draw for the Third Round meant that the Reds were matched up, yet again, with Derby County. A continuing spell of poor weather meant the game would become notable as one of United's most postponed Youth Cup ties ever, with no less than three dates scratched off the calendar before a ball was finally kicked. Even when the match did eventually go ahead, and after being in a saturated state for some time, the notorious Baseball Ground pitch was actually coated with frost and within the vicinity of Derby, proposed non-league games at Ilkeston, Alfreton, Belper and Heanor were victims of an overnight freeze.

The tie is also significant for two other reasons. For one, it represented the Reds' best win in the competition for over twenty years and the clash also stands as the highest margin of victory achieved by United in a genuine Youth Cup away fixture.

On paper at least, the names which comprised Derby's team gave the impression of a distinct lack of experience, with only Andy Garner a competitor in the games against the Reds just over a year ago.

That wasn't the case for Eric Harrison, because of the twelve teenagers who journeyed to the Baseball Ground, only Gary Worthington, Martin Russell and substitute Aidan Murphy were now lacking in Central League experience. Harrison had no hesitation in naming the same twelve who featured in the last round, and his faith in them brought a reward he could never have expected.

The Derby Evening Telegraph gave a round up of the events of an extraordinarily one-sided mismatch:

Derby County fell behind after only a minute of their F.A. Youth Cup Third Round tie against Manchester United at the Baseball Ground this afternoon.

On a hard surface, players often tried in vain to keep their feet, although United managed to play some good football at times. They always looked the stronger team.

They went ahead when Wood shot home after Derby defenders hesitated in making a clearance.

Soon afterwards, United went close when Scott fired a 25-yard shot just over.

The Rams included trialist full-back Darren Darwent from Newcastle in their line-up but they were without injured Mark Clifford and Richard Butler.

In attack, Andy Garner and Andy Irvine were Derby's big hopes for goals, but they were given little chance in the opening stages by a solid United back four.

David Platt almost added a goal for United when he went clean through, but his lob over the advancing Beeston went over the bar.

Rowbotham did make it 2-0 after eighteen minutes and only a few seconds later Russell was left with the easiest of chances when centre-forward Platt nodded down. Russell tucked the ball into the corner to leave the Rams three goals down and in real trouble.

Their biggest problem was that goalkeeper Beeston was showing no confidence and was partly at fault with all the early goals.

Rowbotham was taken off with an arm injury midway through the first half but he returned after treatment.

To their credit, Derby kept battling and created a couple of good moves. Irvine, in particular, worked hard and Parsons did well at the back.

But United's superior skills kept them going forward and slack marking by Derby allowed the visitors to retain the upper hand.

That was underlined after 36 minutes when Scott swapped passes with Wood on the edge of the penalty area. Scott was left completely unmarked and shot into the corner to make it 4-0.

More poor marking led to the fifth goal after 38 minutes. A kick by goalkeeper Digby found Wood on his own in the centre of the Derby penalty area and he shot into the roof of the net.

The Rams sent on Davey for Aherne at the start of the second half. Derby's attack did look a little more lively but still Manchester United looked by far the better side.

Scott knocked in his second goal of the match two minutes into the second period when his cross beat Beeston and flew into the corner.

Soon afterwards Scott went through again and crashed the ball high into the net but this time the referee disallowed the effort for offside.

Danks was having a good match on the wing, but it was a difficult game in which to judge the Derby players. United were totally in command on a slippery surface and the Rams were always struggling to make any impact.

They fell 7-0 behind after 56 minutes when Platt easily headed home from Worthington's cross.

Soon after Garner and Bailey swapped passes just outside the penalty area and Derby went close to a goal for the first time when Bailey's shot hit the bar.

Bailey went close again when he just failed to reach a Danks cross at the far post.

This was easily Derby's best spell. With Garner in midfield they managed some good football and held the powerful United attack.

But United added their eighth goal after 82 minutes when Platt touched home from close range.

The ninth was scored after 85 minutes when Mills, one of three unmarked players on the edge of the six-yard box, shot easily into the corner.

Joe Lancaster couldn't help poking a little fun at United's victims in the Review, claiming the Derby team were *'all timid of the conditions, and certainly not the same tigers that snatched a 2-2 draw at Old Trafford and then lost 1-0 in the replay in the same stage of last term's cup'*. That was unlike the Reds who, he noted, *'were keen to get on with the job'*.

Lancaster was particularly fulsome in his praise of two of the goalscorers when claiming *'there's nowt like Oldham lads when frost nibbles the kneecaps. They are brought up to believe it's the next best thing to a suntan. Nicky Wood and David Platt are no exceptions and enjoyed a holiday sharing five'*. Within that last sentence, United's correspondent corrected the Derby newspaper's scribe by identifying the Reds' number nine as the scorer of his team's second goal.

The report went on to reveal it *'became bitterly cold after the interval and many resolutions must have been to get backsides to radiators rather than to the wall'*. Lancaster also expressed some sympathy for goalkeeper Fraser Digby who, he reckoned *'needed thermals'* through being almost completely underworked.

David Platt was in a ruthless mood at the Baseball Ground

third round

*This game was originally scheduled for Thursday, January 5th but was postponed on three separate occasions due to a waterlogged pitch. The pitch had not recovered from the initial downpour for Saturday, January 7th and was again waterlogged on Tuesday, January 17th

311

1983-84

Barnsley	Manchester United
1) Wayne Thornton 9) Steve Agnew	1) Fraser Digby 9) David Platt
2) Heath Reynolds 10) Paul Cross	2) Ken Scott 10) Nicky Wood
3) John Deakin 11) Alan Semley	3) Alan McLoughlin 11) Gary Worthington
4) Craig Marshall *12) John Utley ‡*	4) Andy Robinson *12) Aidan Murphy (for 2)*
5) Mark Ogley	5) Simon Ratcliffe
6) Simon Jeffels	6) Mike Rowbotham
7) Adam Smith	7) Gary Mills
8) Ian Knight	8) Martin Russell

FEBRUARY 1984

BARNSLEY 2 v 2 MANCHESTER UNITED
Agnew, Smith — *Mills, Platt*

fourth round

Monday 6th
Kick-off 7.00 p.m.
Attendance 1,401

'There's no doubt it's going to be a very exciting tie and we're really looking forward to it,' enthused Barnsley coach Bobby Collins in the days leading up to United's next examination, and he added, 'We know they have got a couple of smashing strikers so we are going to have to be on our toes at the back. We've beaten one Manchester team – why not the other one?'

Collins was specifically referring to Barnsley's fine 3-1 win over Manchester City at the previous stage, a morale-boosting victory which followed on from earlier successes against Tranmere and Wolves in the First and Second Rounds respectively.

The Tykes' good form wasn't only confined to the Youth Cup, as their blossoming pool of talented teens were being hailed as the best the club had produced for some time and their marvellous run of form saw them unbeaten in the Northern Intermediate League since the previous November.

With no divisional commitments on the weekend preceding the cup clash, Barnsley's coach was able to name a full-strength side after initially harbouring injury doubts over centre-back Simon Jeffels, as well as forwards Paul Cross and Alan Semley.

In a match preview contained in the Manchester Evening News, mention was made of the inclusion of United's *'in-form teenage strikers David Platt and Nicky Wood'*, because not only did the aforementioned duo share five goals in the Youth Cup demolition of Derby, in just two 'A' team games since the turn of the year Platt had bagged five more while Wood claimed four at that standard plus another for the Reserves.

Eric Harrison touched on the very same subject when asked about his team's chances of making further headway. *'You never know what is round the corner, especially when it comes to scoring goals,'* he said only part-jokingly prior to revealing, *'At the same time I've got to say that I'm quietly delighted with the way things have been going.*

People have suggested that Derby couldn't have been very good to have been beaten by nine goals. But they knocked out Coventry City in the previous round so they were no mugs. On the day we played exceptionally well. We scored in the first minute, which always helps, and then went on from there with the whole team playing well.'

The United boys nosed in front in the 21st minute at Oakwell, Platt reacting quickly in a crowded penalty area to shoot home.

Reckoning the Reds' advantage led them into *'a false sense of security,'* the Manchester Evening News' views that Barnsley *'dominated the rest of the game'* by *'using the strength and skill of two or three outstanding individuals to great effect on a muddy pitch'* represented a fair assessment of the way the match developed from then on.

Stepping up the intensity of their attacks late in the first half, the Yorkshire team's break came four minutes prior to the whistle when, following a smart reaction save by Fraser Digby, Steve Agnew smacked home the rebound. The equaliser injected Barnsley with a powerful shot of self-belief and in the 50th minute Adam Smith deservedly sent them into the lead by powering home a cross from the marauding John Deakin.

The United lads were pinned back for a long stretch of the second half and several of them wore a desperate look at times. Fending off a third goal which would have surely killed them off, they then managed to equalise totally against the run of play.

A lung-busting run by Mike Rowbotham propelled him past three Barnsley players in the 70th minute only for his tantalising centre to be pushed out by 'keeper Wayne Thornton. The ball ran straight into the path of Gary Mills, who hardly needed to break stride in order to tuck it away effortlessly and make the score two-all.

Mills was surrounded in celebration by his team-mates, and the joy they displayed was only equalled by a sense of relief.

The Reds then elbowed their way into the game a smidgeon more than previously, and in a last minute breakaway Wood attempted to chip Thornton in an attempt to give United what would have been a wholly undeserved winner. It wasn't to be, and so North-East opponents, who awaited the victors at the next stage, were still no wiser as to whom they would be facing.

Several members of United's Youth Cup squad are snapped with their colleagues prior to a 'B' team match at Formby
Back row (l-r) Robert Philpott, Mark Mettrick, Aidan Murphy, Fraser Digby, Martin Russell, Paul McGuinness, Jonathan Hardy
Front row (l-r) David Platt, Andy Robinson, Alan McLoughlin, Andy Mathieson, Gary Worthington, Pat Kelch

1) Fraser Digby
2) Aidan Murphy
3) Pat Kelch
4) Andy Robinson
5) Simon Ratcliffe
6) Mike Rowbotham
7) Gary Mills
8) Martin Russell
9) David Platt
10) Nicky Wood
11) Gary Worthington
12) Paul McGuinness (for 7)

1) Wayne Thornton
2) Heath Reynolds
3) John Deakin
4) Craig Marshall
5) Mark Ogley
6) Simon Jeffels
7) Adam Smith
8) Ian Knight
9) Steve Agnew
10) Paul Cross
11) Alan Semley
12) John Utley (for 7)

MANCHESTER UNITED 0 v 1 BARNSLEY
Semley

FEBRUARY 1984

1983-84

fourth round replay

Wednesday 8th

Kick-off 7.30 p.m.

Attendance 657

● Striker Steve Agnew, who had hit the target in every Youth Cup match prior to Wednesday night, attempts to chip 'keeper Fraser Digby.

On the day of the replay Barnsley sacked their manager Norman Hunter, the 13th such victim of the season. The Oakwell directors chose to place Bobby Collins in temporary charge of team affairs and his first job was to accompany the best of his club's talented adolescents to Manchester.

Football's politics weren't confined to the news of Hunter's sacking either, as the daily newspapers were full of revelations in regards to United chairman Martin Edwards being a potential suitor to a £10million bid from Robert Maxwell to buy the club. A highly sensitive subject that reverberates around the corridors of the stadium to this day, the controversy caused by the possible purchase almost wholly overshadowed the young Reds' fate.

Meanwhile, out on the Old Trafford pitch, a little piece of history was made when Paul McGuinness, substituting for Gary Mills, emulated his father Wilf by appearing for United in the Youth Cup, a happy event which was soured somewhat surprisingly through the Reds falling to a goal scored by someone who chief scout Tony Collins later admitted was a current transfer target.

The Barnsley Chronicle's Melvyn Booth noted some of the circumstances behind United's exit:

Old Trafford, the stately home of Manchester United Football Club, has seen some glorious goals in its illustrious history – and the one which Alan Semley superbly created and finished just one minute from the end of Wednesday night's pulsating cup tie was a winner to rank amongst the best. It was just reward for a Barnsley side which battled every inch of the way against highly-rated hosts who had not been beaten in any competition this season and who were fortunate to go away from Oakwell on Monday night with a 2-2 draw.

But magnificent as Semley's effort was, this was not a match about one goal or one player. It was about a team which displayed courage and determination coupled with no little amount of skill, and there can't be any doubt they did themselves, the club and the town proud. The two pieces of action which decided this replay came right at the end, with both teams tiring and extra-time looking almost certain.

Just five minutes were left on the clock when United won a corner on the right. Martin Russell swung the ball over and Simon Ratcliffe's header beat 'keeper Wayne Thornton, but there was full-back Heath Reynolds to coolly clear off the line. Four minutes later, with the referee continually looking at his watch, came Barnsley's marvellous winner.

Ratcliffe was carrying the ball away from United's goal when he was robbed some 30 yards out by Semley who, ironically, had seemed to drift out of the game in the second half.

The lithe winger evaded two challenges as he advanced into the box and then unleashed a cracking drive which bulged the net beyond the diving Fraser Digby, Sheffield Schools' former 'keeper. It was a goal that gave Barnsley a deserved victory over the two matches and which presents them with a quarter-final tie against Sunderland at Oakwell.

The Oakwell youngsters looked purposeful from the off and almost took the lead after ten minutes when Paul Cross – who lead his side with character from the front – had a dipping volley tipped over the bar. United were restricted to only fleeting chances in the box but Thornton did well to turn away a curling drive from Michael Rowbotham and he was lucky to see a David Platt header bounce out off the foot of a post.

Barnsley's best effort of the first half came in the 45th minute when Semley had an angled shot parried and the ball just eluded the onrushing Simon Jeffels.

In the second half both sides had periods of dominance and it was United who opened the better. Nicky Wood, who had created all sorts of problems at Oakwell 48 hours earlier, cut inside from the wing in the 51st minute and rapped a shot against the upright.

The Manchester Evening News condensed all of the action into a few short paragraphs, remarking that *'Semley, switching from the wing into the middle'*, proved to be *'the difference between the two sides, because overall United had the better of the game'*.

The News additionally noted Reds Rowbotham and Simon Ratcliffe got themselves into hot water by being *'booked for late tackles trying to stop the pacey wingman and his dangerous crosses'*.

1984-85

1) Darrel Rose	9) Lyndon Simmonds
2) Mark Russell	10) Nigel Thompson
3) Terry Phelan	11) David Mehew
4) Stephen Scholes	*12) Darren Sheridan*
5) Peter Swan	
6) Steve O'Shaughnessy	
7) Jeff Clarke	
8) Lee Warren	

1) Fraser Digby	9) Nicky Welsh
2) Tony Gill	10) Gary Worthington
3) Jonathan Hardy	11) Drew McBride
4) Alan McLoughlin	*12) Paul Harvey (for 11)*
5) Aidan Murphy	
6) Andy Mathieson	
7) Robert Philpott	
8) Martin Russell	

DECEMBER 1984

LEEDS UNITED 3 v 2 MANCHESTER UNITED
Scholes, Simmonds (2)   Gill (pen), Russell

second round

Thursday 6th
Kick-off 7.00 p.m.

Young Reds in Cup crash

At the beginning of the 1984/85 season, Eric Harrison's bold plan to follow the Football Association's lead in establishing a Centre of Excellence for United's benefit was, to his great relief, given a resounding thumbs up. Pioneered by the then current England manager Bobby Robson, and despite the experiment not meeting with wholesale approval within the sport on top of attracting a lot of opposition from outside of it, the F.A. had already set up a similar project at the National Sports Centre in Lilleshall.

The new scheme allowed United to organise specialist sessions at The Cliff for approximately 35 boy footballers in the eleven-to-thirteen and thirteen-to-fourteen age groups on a couple of occasions each week with suitably qualified coaches.

Prior to the launch of the Centre, United were in a similar position to all other clubs in that they were unable to take youngsters under their wing until they reached the age of fourteen. A delighted Harrison revealed the motivation behind his plan when claiming of the fledgling development, 'Now we get the chance to pick them up as young as eleven and coach them in the Manchester United style.'

He expanded on the subject by saying, 'In the past, vital years have been lost with youngsters and while we can't actually sign them on schoolboy forms at eleven, we can teach them the correct football habits early. We concentrate on developing the basic skills of the schoolboys. Hopefully, we will improve their game and there is always the chance we will spot promising talents which in the end can only be for the good of the club.'

There were also other goings on behind the scenes that campaign, one being that Harrison's aide, Jimmy Curran, was now tied up much more than previously in the club's treatment room. Curran's decision to devote a bigger proportion of his time in assisting physiotherapist Jim McGregor in his remedial work with injured players meant that there would be even more coaching for Harrison to do than ever before, and he mentioned of the additional burden, 'It's hard work but it's worth the effort and when you produce a player who comes through, that's the icing on the cake.'

Another demonstration that there was no complacency lingering around The Cliff was evidenced just after the halfway mark of the season when it was announced the club was reintroducing a 'B' side to competitive action. Because Rochdale's 'A' team had been forced to withdraw from their division, Lancashire League representatives approached United with a view to fulfilling the Spotland outfit's remaining fixtures. The invitation clearly delighted Harrison, who explained, 'We don't mind at all because we were going to go in next season anyway. When I came to Old Trafford the club had dropped the 'B' team out of the league and were just playing friendly matches.

The club is now stronger at all junior and youth levels than at any time in my three and a half years here so the 'B' team will have no problems. The standard is good and when I was in charge of Everton Youth we had a team in the Second Division so I know what to expect. The youngsters making up the side will be associate schoolboys and trialists so it will be a taste of the big time for them meeting league clubs like Oldham and Blackburn.'

If those changes weren't enough to keep the seemingly inexhaustible Harrison busy, it was simultaneously announced that he was also intending to operate a Junior team. Mainly comprised of schoolboys who had attended midweek training stints at The Cliff, as well as taking part in a number of friendly games, United's youth coach went on to reveal the motivation behind the latest development by claiming, 'We had a few more lads down this season so I suggested they played some competitive matches and it has worked out well, giving us the chance to assess them in proper games rather than just friendlies.'

While most of those considerable and far-reaching moves were designed to improve the standard of the club's younger intake over the medium to long term, hopefully increasing their chances of winning as many of the honours open to them as possible while also providing better quality material for the first-team, Harrison was faced with solving a more immediate selection problem in the run-up to United's Second Round Youth Cup fixture at Leeds that December. Simon Ratcliffe was left with a sore ankle following his appearance for England Youth against their Scottish counterparts at Craven Cottage and his discomfort meant that he

United's superb training facility at Lower Broughton, where there was a huge leap in activity in the 1984/85 season

1984-85

DECEMBER 1984

second round

Making his Youth Cup bow at right full-back, Tony Gill's penalty wasn't enough to prevent a 3-2 reverse at Elland Road

couldn't be considered for duty at Elland Road. With nobody else standing out as an obvious replacement, Harrison's solution was to place midfielder Aidan Murphy into the centre-back's position in the absence of a better alternative.

There were plenty of new names on United's team sheet. Apart from Fraser Digby, who was making his eleventh consecutive Youth Cup appearance, Gary Worthington and Martin Russell, who had both figured in all four ties during the previous season, experience was somewhat threadbare. Only Alan McLoughlin, with a single start, and Murphy, with one full and another substitute appearance, were imbued with any past knowledge of the competition and therefore numerous debuts were inevitable.

A full-back from Bradford, Tony Gill took over from the capable Ken Scott while Jonathan Hardy, a Southport boy, occupied the opposite berth. There were also introductions for Drew McBride (Glasgow), Nicky Welsh (Swinton), Andy Mathieson (Belfast) and Robert Philpott (Stoke-on-Trent). Substitute Paul Harvey, a striker, was, like McBride, a Glaswegian.

Despite an obvious lack of savvy in the side, all of the other signs prior to the trip to Elland Road were positive ones. United's 'A' team headed the Lancashire League Division One and in the four games leading up to the Youth Cup tie, they had notched up wins in all of them by piling up an impressive twenty goals and conceding just once.

There was even a great start for the Reds at Leeds. Barely two minutes were on the clock when Dubliner Russell headed in a Welsh centre from close range and within the opening ten minutes another excellent scoring chance was carved open only for Gary Worthington to waste it. Sadly, Worthington's miss was loaded with the wrong sort of significance and from that point on it was practically all downhill for him and his colleagues.

Leeds equalised in the 17th minute when Stephen Scholes, situated in the centre circle, picked out Nigel Thompson who was loitering out wide on the left. Thompson delivered a wicked low cross which managed to evade all of United's defenders and it was turned into Digby's goal by the incoming Lyndon Simmonds.

Beating the Reds' offside trap, just three minutes later Simmonds looked odds on to score again until a superb block by Digby denied him. Digby later held a long-range drive from Thompson and other shots from David Mehew and Jeff Clarke were also saved by the busy United 'keeper prior to half-time.

The Manchester Evening News commented on this stage of the game with a view that *'Martin Russell tried manfully to supply the necessary creative play but too often United were simply overrun'*.

At the start of the second half, Leeds immediately picked up where they left off, in the ascendancy, and it was mildly surprising that they needed to wait as long as thirteen minutes to register their next goal. It was a self-inflicted injury that did for the Reds, a classic *'defensive misunderstanding'*, and it saw Simmonds grab his second goal when sweeping the ball home from a range of ten yards.

Following the shock of going behind, the Reds naturally began to look for a foothold. They gradually increased their tempo in a concerted effort to find a goal, but it was mainly just huff and puff and they were unable to create any really obvious chances until late on. In the 77th minute, their hopes of winning were more or less obliterated when Leeds grabbed a third, the enterprising Scholes again instigating the move when exchanging passes with two-goal Simmonds. From an inside-left position, and situated just inside the Reds' penalty box, Scholes also successfully ended the attack by slamming the ball hard and low and into the far corner of Digby's net.

Now tasked with pulling two goals back and with less than a quarter of an hour left to achieve their aim, United piled bodies forward in numbers. The pressure partly paid off in the 84th minute when a goalbound header from Aidan Murphy was met by a Leeds hand and Tony Gill, bravely soldiering on despite the handicap and pain of a broken nose, stepped up to convert the resulting penalty.

At the point where the 90 minutes was almost up, Philpott was desperately unlucky not to bring the Old Trafford side level when he cracked a near 30-yard effort that was superbly saved by Darrel Rose.

A few minutes of stoppage time were added on by referee Mr. D. Richardson of Blackburn, though there were no further incidents of note, and when the final whistle sounded United's interest in the Youth Cup needed to be parked in the long-stay bay for yet another twelve months.

Aidan Murphy moved upfront to try to help the Reds' cause late in the game

315

1985-86

1) Tony Woodworth
2) John Mercer
3) Peter Leebrook
4) Micky Southern
5) Darren Heesom
6) Stuart Darley
7) Steve Manton
8) Jason Harris
9) Malcolm Cope
10) Phil Devaney
11) Ashley Hoskin
12) *Mark Hazeldene (for 8)*

1) Gary Walsh
2) Aidan Murphy
3) Lee Martin
4) Ian Scott
5) Steve Gardner
6) Paul Harvey
7) Mark Todd
8) Drew McBride
9) Tony Hopley
10) David Wilson
11) Karl Goddard
12) *Russell Beardsmore (for 6)*

DECEMBER 1985

BURNLEY 0 v 2 MANCHESTER UNITED

Harvey, Hopley

Monday 2nd
Kick-off 7.15 p.m.
Attendance 543

second round

Hopley boosts United

Just two days prior to travelling to Turf Moor for a Second Round Youth Cup tie against Burnley, several members of United's under-18 side took part in an 'A' team away fixture during which local opposition UMIST were defeated 6-1. A convincing victory over obviously modest opposition made up from a section of Manchester's student population, it took their almost perfect performance record to fourteen wins and one draw from fifteen Lancashire League Division One fixtures fulfilled so far. There seemed to be a proper balance between attack and defence in the side, because of those games eleven were won with clean sheets and nine by a margin of two goals or more.

Of the side named to tackle the threat posed by the young Clarets, Eric Harrison nominated three who had tasted defeat at Leeds a year ago. One of them, Aidan Murphy, was making excellent progress as he had been utilised in most of that season's Central League matches, whereas Paul Harvey was a staple of the 'A' team and Drew McBride continued to learn his trade by flitting between both of the junior sides.

Included in the numerous new entrants was giant goalkeeper Gary Walsh, an outstanding capture from the Wigan area who had already made two winning appearances for the Reserves, and in front of him was Lee Martin, a full-back hailing from the town of Hyde on the eastern fringe of Greater Manchester. A resolute type of character, Martin could most often be found assisting the 'A' team on Saturday mornings.

There were also competition debuts for two Yorkshire lads, Karl Goddard (Bradford) and Ian Scott (Leeds), and Northern Ireland was represented by Mark Todd, a youngster who had already occupied five different places in the third team. Influential centre-back Steve Gardner, a Middlesbrough boy, was given the captaincy on his Youth Cup baptism while striker Tony Hopley, a prospect spotted on the club's doorstep, also made his bow in the tournament.

Even though the opening round of a new Youth Cup campaign normally counts as something out of the ordinary for most players, the opposition and venue made it an occasion never to be forgotten by one of the United team. As a Clarets fan from as long ago as he could remember, David Wilson was back at the ground where he had witnessed many a Burnley performance as a season ticket holder. Wilson came from a local family that contained a few footballers and they were out in force to cheer him on for all they were worth.

After scoring two of the goals against UMIST, Hopley distinguished himself still further by opening United's account against the Turf Moor teens. Gardner also made a significant contribution when preventing an equaliser midway through the second half by hacking a Steve Manton shot off the goal-line with Walsh well beaten.

By far the brightest light shining amongst the constellation of youthful talent on that evening in east Lancashire was home goalkeeper Tony Woodworth, who richly deserved the ovation he received at full-time. Mancunian Woodworth managed to keep the Clarets in the hunt with a list of tremendous saves, and the hopes of his team were only fully extinguished when the Reds notched their second goal at a late stage.

Acted out in front of a small crowd, which included United manager Ron Atkinson, the tie was keenly fought from start to finish. The visiting eleven looked the more able overall but Burnley, who included two with senior experience in their ranks in Ashley Hoskin and Darren Heesom, fought hard for a result right down to the wire.

The Reds almost extracted first blood as early as the ninth minute when a Hopley drive crashed against a post. Woodworth then pulled off a save which caused the United lads to curse and the crowd to gasp when tipping a Drew McBride screamer over for a corner.

In the 43rd minute, the Reds went ahead through an unforced and untimely error. Burnley's Mercer was at fault with a careless back pass, Hopley homing in on the mistake by shooting beyond an exposed Woodworth. Credit was due to Burnley for their battling qualities and no mean amount of skill although, the Manton effort apart, they weren't able to get the better of United's defenders too often or test Walsh as frequently as they would have liked.

The Reds eventually slipped into the next round when Harvey scored their second goal of the game. There were just two minutes of normal time remaining as Goddard carried out the spadework by dodging a couple of opponents and running into space out in a wide area. When his centre found Hopley, the ball was hooked back into the middle for Harvey to finally bring the curtain down on the plucky Clarets' aspirations.

The Burnley Express & News gave an honest appraisal of the match, noting the home eleven *'found it hard going'* against a side *'who were always the stronger'*. That newspaper's Manchester counterpart also carried a few paragraphs on the Reds' encouraging display, even if it was a trifle overexuberant at times, and a few lines of it read:

The United youngsters answered Burnley's commitment fiercely, too much so at times, with the result that Aidan Murphy, Steve Gardner and Mark Todd were all booked.

Burnley battled hard, but put no real pressure on Gary Walsh in the United goal. Nevertheless, it was a promising performance by a young side considerably changed from last season......

Full-back Lee Martin and his co-defenders formed a largely effective barrier in front of Gary Walsh at Burnley

1985-86

1) Simon Harrison	9) Andy Taylor
2) Andy Skelton	10) Andy Wood
3) Mark Hedley	11) Julian Curwen
4) Mark Wing	*12) Simon Duggins (for 2)*
5) Darren Wood	
6) Jamie Hewitt	
7) Jason MacDonald	
8) Andy Crowther	

1) Gary Walsh	9) Tony Hopley
2) Tony Gill	10) David Wilson
3) Lee Martin	11) Karl Goddard
4) Ian Scott	*12) Paul Harvey (for 8)*
5) Steve Gardner	
6) Mark Todd	
7) Aidan Murphy	
8) Drew McBride	

CHESTERFIELD 0 v 6 MANCHESTER UNITED

Hopley, McBride, Todd, Wilson (3)

JANUARY 1986

Monday 13th*

Kick-off 7.30 p.m.

Attendance 723

Wilson treble for Reds' kids

FA YOUTH CHALLENGE CUP — THIRD ROUND
Saturday, January 4,
Kick-off 3pm
CHESTERFIELD
v
MANCHESTER UNITED
Coalite stand £1 adults, 50p juveniles & OAPs
Sponsor, His Grace the Duke of Devonshire

Six weeks elapsed before the Old Trafford kids resumed cup action when they made the scenic trip down the A6 past Chapel-en-le-Frith and through the Peak District National Park to their destination, the Recreation Ground at Saltergate in Chesterfield.

The contest threw up some strange coincidences to the Youth Cup game at Derby some two years earlier. For starters, both matches were staged in Derbyshire at the same time of year and as a consequence, both were Third Round ties, the games eventually taking place after they were postponed on three occasions. Weirdest of all, though, both Derby and Chesterfield's line-ups contained no less than three players named Andy and they were consecutively numbered at eight, nine and ten in their respective line-ups.

Could United follow a slightly spooky sequence with the same successful score they achieved against the young Rams? The answer was an emphatic 'no', but they did manage to go two-thirds of the way towards it.

There was an air of disappointment around the Recreation Ground when the initially arranged date was forced to be rescheduled. Because Chesterfield's first-team was without a game, the Reds' visit was expected to produce a crowd approaching four figures. By already disposing of Cambridge United and Burton Albion from the competition, scoring nine times in the process, interest in the club's youth side was running high and so Chesterfield's officials arranged for their president, His Grace the Duke of Devonshire, to be introduced to both sides prior to the kick-off.

Fortunately, there was still a reasonable attendance when the game did finally get the go-ahead, despite it being set for what turned into a thoroughly miserable evening in terms of the weather.

The Spireites' best opportunities came in the minutes just after the break. Substitute Simon Duggins, with his very first touch of the ball, was barely inches wide of pulling the score back to 2-1 and within seconds the same player connected with a left-wing cross to direct a header against the post.

The United Review told most of the remainder of the story, the first sentence of which contained an accurate prediction:

United's unstoppable youngsters are winding themselves up for a serious tilt at the F.A. Youth Cup. Unbeaten in the league this season, they carried their fine form of late into this Third Round tie at Saltergate and left Chesterfield breathless.

There was a keenness about the whole side and they really took delight in banging home the six goals that made this visit a virtual formality.

Just ten minutes into the game and United were ahead through Drew McBride. Fifteen minutes later it was the turn of Mark Todd, he has recently forced his way into the Central League side, to hammer his shot past the unfortunate Spireites' 'keeper Simon Harrison.

The rain poured, the wind howled, but United in this mood wouldn't have batted an eyelid if the roof had fell in, for in the second half they really went to town with Tony Hopley grabbing the third before David Wilson took over to thunder home a hat-trick inside fourteen minutes.

Breathtaking stuff and the kind of ruthless finishing that could see the Reds making a concerted attempt to win the F.A. Youth Cup.

On a ground where United had already achieved a couple of memorable results in the national tournament, the prime example being their last-gasp final success there in the May of 1956, Wilson warmed up for his later goal feat by supplying the cross from which Todd converted the Reds' second.

Already with two goals to his credit, Wilson topped off a wonderful display when receiving a short ball in Chesterfield's penalty box before swivelling on a sixpence to smash home an unstoppable drive.

> *We worked on the shape of the team in the days leading up to the game. It was a very wet night and we played positively. I was striking the ball particularly well and after one good turn I hit it with my left foot and the ball smashed into the net.*
>
> *Eric didn't say too much about the game afterwards but we got the next day off, which was unusual, so we must have done okay. I was also allowed to go home with my parents that night, whereas normally we all had to go back on the team bus.*
>
> **DAVID WILSON**

*This game was originally scheduled for Saturday, January 4th but was postponed due to a snowbound pitch. The game was again called off on Monday, January 6th and Wednesday, January 8th for the same reason

third round

317

1985-86

1) Tim Teece	9) Richard Young	1) Gary Walsh	9) Tony Hopley
2) Wayne Fairclough	10) Robin Simpson	2) Tony Gill	10) David Wilson
3) Jonathan Chamberlain	11) Simon Baker	3) Lee Martin	11) Karl Goddard
4) David Kevan	*12) Keith Holmes ◊*	4) Aidan Murphy	*12) Denis Cronin (for 7)*
5) Paul Atkin		5) Steve Gardner	
6) Craig Jackson		6) Mark Todd	
7) Paul Barnes		7) Paul Harvey	
8) Stephen Lyons		8) Drew McBride	

JANUARY 1986

NOTTS COUNTY 0 v 3 MANCHESTER UNITED

Harvey (2), Todd

fourth round

Thursday 30th

Kick-off 7.00 p.m.

Attendance 516

The month of January wasn't even through before the young Reds renewed Youth Cup acquaintances with Notts County, the luck of the draw decreeing that the Magpies were handed home advantage against United for the second season out of three.

There was a feeling in Eric Harrison's camp that a good performance would be required at Meadow Lane for the desired progress to be achieved as County's youth side were currently leading the Midland Intermediate League and had lost only twice in fifteen outings.

Unfortunately from the home angle, Notts' youth coach Mick Walker was unable to select defender Dean Yates due to senior requirements, as well as regular midfielders Eddie Snook and Mark Harbottle. The loss of Snook through injury was an unavoidable problem, whereas Harbottle found himself outside of team plans through a suspension caused by being booked six times already that season. The void left by the pair provided Walker with a major selection problem in the lead up to the match and he went public in his condemnation of the latter, who he felt had let him and his colleagues down by a persistent lack of self control.

There were no such problems for Harrison. United's line-up had a settled look about it and only the absence of Ian Scott meant a repositioning for Aidan Murphy, with Paul Harvey taking over Murphy's previous spot. Harrison's team was now bolstered by the extra experience offered by defender Lee Martin, whose resounding success of his step up to the Reserves meant that he had figured in their last three matches. There was a similarly pleasing picture painted by the promotion of Mark Todd, the Ulster lad gaining two starts and a couple of substitute nominations for the second string over the past few weeks.

An indication that the Reds were about to end County's longest ever run in the Youth Cup came as soon as the second minute when the recalled Harvey notched the opener by taking advantage of an early misunderstanding in the Magpies' defence to force the ball into the back of Tim Teece's net.

There was little to choose between the sides from then until the break. The respective performers were certainly found wanting in terms of skill and finesse, even though the two coaches would have been well pleased with the commitment and focus applied by their charges.

From a spectator's point of view there was little to get excited about, although Gary Walsh was just about the busier of the two goalkeepers with a couple of catches to keep up his concentration level.

In the Review, the first half was called *'a tough, hard tackling contest which was definitely no place for the weak'* and it was also observed that *'Tony Hopley was lifted into the air by over-zealous County defenders so many times, he thought he was training for his pilot's licence'*.

Walsh was required to do his best work immediately the second period started and with Paul Barnes bearing in on goal, the Reds' custodian courageously threw himself at the feet of the County man when an equaliser seemed the most likely outcome.

Walsh's block from Barnes was the point at which the contest turned hugely in favour of the Reds, because in the 51st minute they doubled their tally when Harvey burst through a defensive cordon to rattle in a second. It was a particularly pleasing strike as the ball was confidently placed beyond Teece at the end of a delightful four-man move. The goal completely lifted the pressure off United and from then on their passage to the next phase was never seriously questioned.

A third goal was registered in the 55th minute, midfielder Mark Todd capping an excellent night's work for himself, and by the time brace hero Harvey limped off later in the game to the congratulations of the coaching staff, all of their thoughts were already turning to the next round.

Unfortunately no longer eligible for United's Youth Cup team, Bobby Charlton takes the opportunity of promoting his soccer school in front of (l-r) (Chairman) Martin Edwards, Gary Walsh, David Wilson and a marketing executive

318

1) Gary Walsh	9) Denis Cronin
2) Tony Gill	10) David Wilson
3) Lee Martin	11) Karl Goddard
4) Aidan Murphy	*12) Jon Bottomley*
5) Steve Gardner	
6) Mark Todd	
7) Paul Harvey	
8) Drew McBride	

1) Paul Heald	9) Clive Mendonca
2) Carl Fuller	10) Chris Marsden
3) Mark Russell	11) Jim Pearson
4) Darren Potts	*12) Mark Kelly (for 4)*
5) Kenny Geelan	
6) Simon Copeland	
7) Darren Lancaster	
8) Simon Grayson	

1985-86

MANCHESTER UNITED 3 v 0 SHEFFIELD UNITED

Cronin, Goddard, Todd

MARCH 1986

Monday 17th

Kick-off 7.30 p.m.

Attendance 922

Accompanied by youth development officer Joe Brown (back row, far left), coach Jimmy Curran (back row, far right) and manager Eric Harrison (front row, centre), the Reds' 1985/86 youth squad get a feel of the Old Trafford pitch

Players only, back row (l-r) Paul Harvey, Ian Scott, Lee Martin, Gary Walsh, Jim O'Donnell, Tony Gill, Aidan Murphy, Denis Cronin
Players only, front row (l-r) Russell Beardsmore, David Wilson, Drew McBride, Mark Todd, Steve Gardner, Tony Hopley, Karl Goddard, Phil Steer

fifth round

Old Trafford staged its first Youth Cup game for over two years when Sheffield United arrived there in mid-March. The solitary change in Eric Harrison's team from that which started at Notts County was the introduction of Denis Cronin, a speedy and predatory former Manchester schoolboy forward, who came in for the injured Tony Hopley.

Apart from a substitute appearance by David Wilson, there had been no further introductions to the rigours of the Central League from the ranks of the youth squad, but there were more glad tidings to report in regards to the progress of the 'A' side.

With 21 of their allotted 36 Lancashire League Division One fixtures completed, the third team's continued sparkling form was demonstrated by them being subjected to defeat just once, and that to an older and more experienced Tranmere second string. There were numerous Reserve sides in the 'A' team's division just then, though those of Crewe, Rochdale, Stockport, Barrow, Morecambe, Chester, Marine, Southport and Bury had all been defeated by the up-and-coming boy Reds, and some of them more than once, proving that all was well within the club's junior ranks.

In relation to the Youth Cup, and for the second time in succession, Harrison's lads got off to a flying start through Cronin making an almost instant impression by unsettling Blades' goalie Paul Heald with a fifth minute snapshot. Heald was unable to gather the ball and Karl Goddard exercised full advantage of his fumble by tapping home the rebound.

Charged with the incentive of being able to display their talents on home soil at last, United's youngsters rose to the task by giving the attendees a display which was both determined and assured. Apart from a couple of exceptions, Gary Walsh was barely troubled all night, and the general direction of the game was soon pointing towards just how many goals the Reds might be able to register.

Right on top of half-time, impressive livewire Cronin scored with a powerful right-foot shot from close range and in the 62nd minute Mark Todd made it a final score of 3-0 with his third goal in as many games.

Writing for the Review, Cliff Butler made a few of his considered views known:

The F.A. Youth Cup hasn't graced the Old Trafford sideboard since the days of Best, Sadler, Aston, etc, but if the attitude of this latest batch is reproduced in the semis then we could be in business. The 'Young Blades' of Sheffield United travelled over the Pennines with high hopes and they brought along a couple of coach loads of mums and dads to help them along.

Sadly for the Bramall Lane party, they caught United on the wrong night, for this was far and away their best performance of this season's campaign. They pushed the ball around with such confidence that the visitors were rarely, if ever, in with a shout. The defence was sound and commanding, the midfield imaginative and skilful and the forwards sharp and alert.

United's correspondent reckoned Todd's goal *'was worthy of clinching any game'* and he also shared an opinion that Goddard's opener gave his team *'the very boost they sought, and it enabled them to settle quickly and play a brand of football that was a delight to watch'.*

There were equally positive words emanating from the Evening News. Their reporter revealed the team *'have done better than coach Eric Harrison expected',* described the win as *'stylish',* and went on to inform the periodical's readers that the Reds *'got a good grip in midfield against similarly free scoring opponents who had knocked Everton out 5-2'.*

During the whole ninety minutes, Sheffield United were able to muster just two openings. A couple of minutes into the second half, Darren Potts was clean through before appearing to let the opportunity get the better of him and screwing his shot wide.

Then, with the Reds 3-0 up and seemingly coasting towards a last four berth, Simon Grayson caused a late scare before bringing a wonder save out of Walsh, who earned one of the loudest cheers of the evening after tipping his point-blank shot over the bar.

1985-86

Coventry City	Manchester United
1) Spencer Creedon	1) Gary Walsh
2) Howard Clark	2) Tony Gill
3) Shaun McGrory	3) Lee Martin
4) Tony Dobson	4) Ian Scott
5) Steve Sedgley	5) Steve Gardner
6) Terry Merriman	6) Mark Todd
7) Craig Dandridge	7) Aidan Murphy
8) Tony Mahan	8) Drew McBride
9) Steve Livingstone	9) Denis Cronin
10) John Hathaway	10) David Wilson
11) David Smith	11) Karl Goddard
12) Mike Cook (for 10)	12) Paul Harvey (for 10)

APRIL 1986

COVENTRY CITY 0 v 2 MANCHESTER UNITED
McBride, Todd

semi-final 1st leg

Monday 7th
Kick-off 7.00 p.m.
Attendance 3,331

Walsh the Reds hero

In order to reach their eighth Youth Cup final, the United lads were required to defeat Coventry City at the penultimate stage. Of course, the semi-final ties offered up the chance of some redress for those from the Old Trafford camp as the clubs had met at the same stage of the tournament in the 1969/70 season when the Sky Blues were the successful party.

It was a tremendous replay win at Spurs that earned Coventry a place in the last four and the mood in their camp was understandably bullish. During the build-up, skipper Steve Sedgley boasted, 'We are full of confidence and raring to go. Hopefully we will make up for the first-team losing to United on Saturday.'

Coventry's under-18 squad acted as ball boys for the visit of the Reds' senior side on the previous weekend in order to help them acclimatise to a big match atmosphere. United's 3-1 victory in the First Division clash was another bloody nose for relegation threatened City, yet youth coach John Sillett insisted the result would have no bearing on the cup contest. In the hours leading up to the opening leg, Sillett said of his charges, 'Tonight I've told them to relax and just go out there and enjoy the occasion. I have not even seen United play so all we can do is concentrate on our own performance.'

Ian Scott made a welcome return for the Reds, and Neville Foulger of the Coventry Evening Telegraph charted the main action contained within the 90 minutes:

The chips are down for Coventry City's F.A. Youth Cup battlers. To reach the final for the first time in sixteen years they now have to go to Old Trafford on Friday, give Manchester United a two-goal start – and win. It is a daunting challenge but coach John Sillett insisted, 'We can still do it – we're not out of the competition yet.'

There's no doubt however, that United are now firmly in command in this semi-final after their first leg victory in wet and miserable conditions at Highfield Road last night. Goals from Drew McBride in the 4th minute and Mark Todd in the 26th minute put United in the driving seat and despite fierce second half pressure, the Sky Blue babes could not snatch back a goal which could have given them a sporting chance.

Despite the fearful weather, however, a crowd of 3,331 turned up for the match and United director and former England star Bobby Charlton commented, 'It was a smashing match and a marvellous crowd on a night such as this.'

His thoughts would be echoed by most observers, despite the disappointment of City losing. Both sides gave everything they had in the conditions which grew worse as the match progressed and there was certainly no shortage of commitment and excitement.

City, however, never really recovered from the shock of conceding the early lead to United when McBride collected a through pass from Karl Goddard and coolly beat advancing goalkeeper Spencer Creedon. That quick strike set the pattern for the match and in the 13th minute the Sky Blues should have equalised. Big striker Steve Livingstone, put in the clear, had his shot blocked by 'keeper Gary Walsh and, when the ball came loose, Craig Dandridge struck the bar with his follow-up shot.

In the 23rd minute City seemed to have justifiable cause for complaint when a header from skipper Steve Sedgley appeared to have produced a goal until the referee changed his mind and awarded an offside decision instead. In a packed goalmouth, it seemed a strange decision to say the least. And three minutes later City's agony increased when Todd scored United's second goal with a low shot from 25 yards which flew past the diving Creedon.

With the wind at their backs in the second half, the Sky Blues fought hard to get back into the match but could not find the devil and bite they needed in and around United's penalty area. They had their chances – the best of them going to little John Hathaway in the 46th minute. But he was unable to find the target after a shot from Dandridge had only been half stopped. The lively Dave Smith chipped another opportunity wide and the inspirational Sedgley twice came forward to power in shots which were not far away from producing goals.

But in the end City were unable to breach United's organised and disciplined defence and now have it all to do at Old Trafford. Their outstanding performances at Newcastle and Tottenham Hotspur earlier in the competition, however, should give them hope that all is not yet lost.

While McBride's early strike understandably helped to settle any nerves amongst those on the United side, it was Todd's goal which really set the seal on a superb result. Making himself the toast of his team-mates after David Wilson chested down a Lee Martin free kick, Todd bulleted a shot that skimmed along the turf to give Creedon no chance of saving.

A kick square in the face a quarter of an hour from the end of the game laid out Gary Walsh for fully four minutes. A battered nose, some loose teeth and a bruised forehead was Walsh's undeserved reward for another fine performance, and he even recovered sufficiently to make another couple of stops, the upshot of which meant that United were now firm favourites for the final.

Left battered and bruised from his exertions at Highfield Road, Gary Walsh's performance ensured he kept a fifth consecutive Youth Cup clean sheet

" *The thing I remember most about that cup run was Gary Walsh. He went from one level to a completely different place. Something about the F.A. Youth Cup just ignited him.* "

STEVE GARDNER

1985-86

1) Gary Walsh	9) Denis Cronin
2) Tony Gill	10) David Wilson
3) Lee Martin	11) Karl Goddard
4) Ian Scott	*12) Jon Bottomley (for 10)*
5) Steve Gardner	
6) Paul Harvey	
7) Aidan Murphy	
8) Mark Todd	

1) Spencer Creedon	9) Steve Livingstone
2) Howard Clark	10) John Hathaway
3) Shaun McGrory	11) David Smith
4) Tony Dobson	*12) Mike Cook (for 7)*
5) Steve Sedgley	
6) Terry Merriman	
7) Craig Dandridge	
8) Tony Mahan	

MANCHESTER UNITED 1 (3) v (1) 1 COVENTRY CITY
Cronin — Dobson

APRIL 1986

Friday 11th

Kick-off 7.30 p.m.

Attendance 1,813

It's final date for boy Reds

In the days leading up to the second leg, Eric Harrison gave an interview during which he said of one of his star prospects, 'Gary (Walsh) really is a gem. I don't usually single players out but he has given the team a tremendous stability and confidence that is if anyone slips the net they've got him to beat. We had to defend for our lives at Coventry, and a measure of our back four is that once again we didn't give anything away.'

Going on to say he felt the club possessed more ability at youth level since the 1950's, and that his current squad was better than the one which reached the Youth Cup final four years earlier, Harrison added, 'In the 1982 side we had outstanding individuals in Norman (Whiteside) and Sparky (Mark Hughes) but this season we have no one player who stands out – we work as a team and as such we are a strong and determined unit with the ability to play high quality football. I'm on record as saying I didn't expect too much from the lads this season because most are first-year apprentices. But they have surprised me beyond all expectations. Even if we don't win the F.A. Youth Cup, the boys here are a success. They are the right type of players not just in ability but in temperament too.'

Coventry's central defender Tony Dobson had benefited from a few intense sessions of physiotherapy over the interim period and they allowed him to retain a place in the side at Old Trafford. There was no such luck for United's Drew McBride, though, as he was forced to sit the match out and watch Paul Harvey deputise for him. Coach Harrison repeatedly hammered home the point that the tie was far from over in the run up to the game and it was Dobson who took it upon himself to prove the Reds' coach was correct in his assessment of how events would unfold.

The Coventry Evening Telegraph's Neville Foulger was again on hand to provide the details of a ding-dong dust-up which had fewer than a couple of thousand Reds' followers cheering at its conclusion:

Coventry City's lion-hearted babes did the club proud at Old Trafford last night. They failed in their bid to reach the F.A. Youth Cup final for the first time since 1970 – but they failed gloriously. Trailing 2-0 after the first leg of this semi-final, the City kids took the fight to United, scored a superb goal in the 22nd minute and only conceded defeat four minutes from time when United snatched an equaliser on the night to make it 3-1 on aggregate.

As the final whistle went, coach John Sillett raced onto the pitch to congratulate every member of his brave but crestfallen team. And he had a special hug and handshake for central defender Tony Dobson, who typified both City's glory and dejection.

A niggling hamstring injury made Dobson touch-and-go for the match. But he not only played, he produced an inspiring performance at the heart of the defence – and scored the goal which had United on the rack. Dobson coolly controlled a long free kick from Howard Clark before turning to beat excellent goalkeeper Gary Walsh with a shot into the roof of the net. It was just the sort of start the Sky Blues needed and turned the game into a thrilling cliffhanger until a tragic error from Dobson finally ended City's hopes.

He mis-kicked an intended clearance in the 86th minute, making a gift of the ball to the dangerous Denis Cronin. The United striker raced through and, as Spencer Creedon advanced, calmly steered a low shot into the net. The relief on United's faces was there for all to see. City had taken them all the way and but for three fine saves from Walsh in the second half, the tie could easily have gone into extra-time. He tipped over the bar a lovely 30-yard chip from Tony Mahan and then twice denied striker Steve Livingstone with acrobatic leaping saves to his left.

A 2-0 win on the night and a draw over the two legs would have been no more than the Sky Babes deserved. Although United put together some neat, precise football they often flattered to deceive and City's sheer tenacity gave them control of the match for long spells.

Mahan worked tirelessly in midfield, Livingstone battled bravely upfront and defensively City did little wrong. If only they could have played as well as this for the 90 minutes at Highfield Road on Monday!

But watching manager Don Mackay will surely hope his first-teamers will at least emulate the spirit and determination shown by the kids last night. If they do, First Division survival can be achieved.

Coventry centre-forward Livingstone, whose father Joe occupied the same position and at the same venue in a Youth Cup tie for Middlesbrough in January 1960, was easily the most frustrated player on the pitch. Well marshalled by United skipper Steve Gardner for most of the game, the City marksman must have wondered what more he could have done to score when seeing Walsh reserve two of his finest stops to deny him.

As Coventry overstretched themselves in a vain attempt at squaring the scores, it was left to Cronin to purge the United team of their increasing dread of failure. Taking a threaded pass from substitute Jonathan Bottomley, who picked up Dobson's mistake of a clearance, Cronin sprinted into position prior to stroking the ball home.

It was a nicely executed goal, even if it had seemed like an eternity in coming.

Denis Cronin grabbed a late leveller against a gallant Coventry side

semi-final 2nd leg

321

1985-86

Manchester United	Manchester City
1) Gary Walsh 9) Denis Cronin	1) Steve Crompton 9) Paul Lake
2) Tony Gill 10) David Wilson	2) Steve Mills 10) Ian Scott
3) Lee Martin 11) Paul Harvey	3) Andy Hinchcliffe 11) David Boyd
4) Ian Scott *12) Tony Hopley (for 10)*	4) Ian Brightwell *12) Steve Macauley*
5) Steve Gardner	5) Steve Redmond
6) Jon Bottomley	6) Andy Thackeray
7) Aidan Murphy	7) David White
8) Mark Todd	8) Paul Moulden

APRIL 1986

MANCHESTER UNITED 1 v 1 MANCHESTER CITY
Harvey — *Lake*

Thursday 24th
Kick-off 7.30 p.m.
Attendance 7,602

final 1st leg

The celebrations surrounding United's achievement in reaching the 1986 Youth Cup final died down significantly with the news that neighbours Manchester City would be their opponents. The Maine Road outfit had arguably been the more progressive of the Manchester clubs at youth level over a period of several years, with the outcome being that it was they who were installed as the bookies' short-odds favourites to lift the trophy. It was easy to see why, because even though Eric Harrison's 'A' team could look back over a splendid season in the Lancashire League, when many of his squad displayed signs of real progress, a few too many draws meant that the divisional crown eventually ended up in Moss Side.

On the eve of an eagerly anticipated opening leg, the Evening News ran a suitable appetiser:

The kids from Old Trafford and Maine Road will be aiming to make up for the disappointment of their seniors when United and City meet in the first leg of the Youth Cup tonight. By battling through to the Old Trafford final tonight, Manchester's stars of the future have ensured that at least one trophy will be coming to the city to brighten a season which is destined to be barren of silverware for both clubs at senior level.

For the Boy Blues, tonight will represent part one of their bid to clinch the trophy for the first time and erase the memory of two successive defeats in the Youth Cup final in 1979 and 1980. The Reds, on the other hand, have an impressive record in this competition with the legendary Busby Babes sweeping all before them time after time as a prelude to greater glories.

The kids from Maine Road only booked their passage into the final on Tuesday night with a victory over Arsenal but youth team manager Tony Book had no hesitation in naming an unchanged side today. 'They are raring to go,' said Book. 'There won't be any reaction to Tuesday night's game. Every one of our lads will be going out at Old Trafford tonight willing to run until they drop. It will be the biggest night of their lives for many of them and more than anything I want them to go out and enjoy themselves. There should be a tremendous atmosphere. Getting through to the final is marvellous as it is for my lads. But to be meeting United is the icing on the cake.'

United's famous Busby Babes dominated the competition in the mid-1950's, winning it five times on the trot and drawing massive crowds to Old Trafford. They won it again in 1964 but their only final appearance since then was 1982 when they lost to Watford.

This season they have stormed through to the final, scoring seventeen goals and conceding only one – in the semi-final against Coventry. Mark Todd is their top marksman with four. The Reds are forced to make one change tonight. Karl Goddard is injured and Jon Bottomley, sub against Coventry, steps up.

The unavailability of the ever-present Goddard was a development Harrison could well have done without, despite it presenting an opportunity for the emerging Bottomley to make his full competition debut.

On the other hand, City were able to name exactly the same side that had carried them through seven consecutive Youth Cup matches. Two pre-Christmas wins of equal proportion, 7-1 against Tranmere at Prenton Park and Blackburn at Maine Road, gave early indications of their scoring capabilities, and a tough early January victory at Blackpool of one goal to nil showed they could also defend when required. Later that month, Tony Book's boys crushed Leicester 4-1 at home and followed up in March by defeating Fulham on their Craven Cottage ground.

City lost the opening leg of their semi-final, by a solitary goal at Highbury, but through winning 2-1 on home soil they took the tie into a goalless period of extra-time followed by penalties. Just as the clock was ready to strike ten o'clock, the Light Blues clinched a final spot when Ian Scott slammed home their fifth penalty to Arsenal's four. It really was that close.

With the novelty value of two Ian Scott's on the pitch, an exceedingly entertaining contest took place down Stretford way in the name of the first leg. Ominously for United, Tony Book's boys were the happier of the two parties at its conclusion and they got that feeling by extracting a hard earned draw from the den of their deadly foes.

By the following evening, most local football followers had read David Meek's match synopsis:

Manchester City are on course to win the F.A. Youth Cup for the first time in their history.

Gary Walsh gets down to block Paul Lake's 83rd minute spot kick.......

322

1985-86

APRIL 1986

final 1st leg

.......but can do little to prevent the City man tucking away the rebound

The Boy Blues came back from a goal down to force a 1-1 draw in the first leg of their semi-final against Manchester United at Old Trafford last night. But it was a cruel penalty that brought City their equaliser, and the advantage for Tuesday night's second leg at Maine Road.

The ball came up sharply off an opponent's boot to hit defender Lee Martin on the hand. The United full-back, who had played immaculately, had little chance to get his hand out of the way but referee Vic Callow gave a penalty. Goalkeeper Gary Walsh made a typically brilliant save from Paul Lake, but couldn't hold the shot and the Blues' dashing centre-forward slotted home the rebound.

The goal came as a huge relief to the City camp, who had watched their team squander many scoring chances. Although City are the stronger, speedier side in most positions, the young Reds put their game together with an excellence of passing that, early on, had their opponents struggling. They deserved their goal just after the interval when Paul Harvey flicked in a cross from David Wilson. But City finished strongly to merit their penalty equaliser, especially as they had played a storming semi-final only two days before.

As youth coach Tony Book said, 'I was delighted after what they had gone through against Arsenal. We could have done with a little more composure but the tie is in our favour now.'

United coach Eric Harrison said, 'We played some excellent football in the first half and I thought our lads gave everything.'

City certainly looked the better team at Old Trafford, totally dispelling the fear that the game might have come a little too soon after their gruelling exploits against the young Gunners, and they almost went into the lead in the first minute when David Boyd's cross nearly got the finish they desired from David White. In keeping with most of the Reds' Youth Cup matches that season, it was their midfielders who exerted a stranglehold on the contest, and efforts from Wilson and Scott in the opening half hour initially appeared to indicate they could achieve the lead needed to take to Maine Road.

A Lake attempt repelled by Walsh preceded a resurgence by City in the ten minutes prior to the break. Their best chances in that period both fell to Paul Moulden, who firstly shot wide and then followed up soon after when forcing Walsh into a superb save with a rasping drive from the edge of the penalty area.

Immediately upon the resumption, City's Hinchcliffe made an unchecked raid down the left wing which caught everyone by surprise, especially Moulden, whose hurried effort whizzed past a post. That miss was magnified in the 49th minute when United steamed ahead, Harvey gliding a left-footed shot beyond Crompton following a delicious centre.

The Reds nearly doubled their lead when the opposing goalkeeper made a hash of throwing the ball to a colleague. It was instead collected by the alert Harvey, who looked odds on to score until Crompton redeemed himself by thwarting his attempt at the expense of a corner.

With just over twenty minutes remaining, two of the games major incidents were still to come. The first occurred when Aidan Murphy clattered into Andy Thackeray and the two then acted out a 'handbags at ten paces' scene. Mr. Callow interpreted the set-to as a serious breach of the peace and so he meted out the severest of punishments by dismissing the two from the field.

The Solihull referee further irritated those of a United bent by awarding the Light Blues their rather fortunate penalty when for once Walsh's heroics weren't enough to deliver the result most inside the stadium would have wanted.

Coloured with a note of caution, City manager Billy McNeill's post-match view was that the outcome principally lay in their hands. *'We feel we now have the edge after that performance,'* he said. *'Derby clashes are so often games apart. Nothing can be taken for granted, as we know from experiences at senior level. What I can say, however, is that the fans are certain to get full value for money with the entire Manchester sporting public having every right to feel proud of the fine array of talent provided by both clubs.'*

1985-86

1) Steve Crompton
2) Steve Mills
3) Andy Hinchcliffe
4) Ian Brightwell
5) Steve Redmond
6) Andy Thackeray
7) David White
8) Paul Moulden
9) Paul Lake
10) Ian Scott
11) David Boyd
12) John Bookbinder

1) Gary Walsh
2) Tony Gill
3) Lee Martin
4) Ian Scott
5) Steve Gardner
6) Paul Harvey
7) Aidan Murphy
8) Mark Todd
9) Denis Cronin
10) Jon Bottomley
11) Karl Goddard
12) Tony Hopley (for 10)

APRIL 1986

MANCHESTER CITY 2(3) v (1)0 MANCHESTER UNITED
Boyd, Moulden

final 2nd leg

Tuesday 29th
Kick-off 7.30 p.m.
Attendance 18,158

City were able to name the same starting eleven for their ninth Youth Cup tie on the trot, though reports on United's injury situation was so-so. An ankle knock picked up in the Old Trafford leg of the final sank David Wilson's previously complete appearance record, but Karl Goddard returned to the side upon his recovery. Strangely, Jon Bottomley's continued presence escaped the attention of at least one match reporter, who mistook him for the absent Wilson.

On a mild, bright and breezeless evening, which provided almost perfect conditions for football, there was pandemonium outside the stadium in the 30 or so minutes leading up to kick-off. Despite the fact that City had proposed to open three sides of the ground, with the whole of the Platt Lane End and the visitors' enclosure of the Kippax Street earmarked exclusively for away fans, most of the crowd seemed to want to sit in the Main Stand.

Faced with a mass of spectators whose number swelled to over twice the size of that for the game which took place at Old Trafford, most of whom arrived less than an hour before the start, huge queues formed on the forecourt. The scene was one of some chaos and in order to solve the problem inside the ground, City officials acted quickly when relieving some of the pressure by allowing spectators to switch into some of Maine Road's less occupied areas.

Once the game got underway, the United lads were under the cosh almost from the off and only the imposing Gary Walsh appeared to stand between them and a result which could have stood as everlastingly embarrassing to United supporters. The junior Reds weren't defeated for the wont of trying, it was just that winning was never an option because City grabbed them by the throat and squeezed until they choked.

Under the clever heading 'FINAL-ly MADE IT!', the contours of the second leg were comprehensively tracked by the Manchester City match magazine:

After waiting 33 years for the privilege of parading the F.A. Youth Cup prize, another 84 minutes of patience shouldn't have mattered a great deal at Maine Road last Tuesday night. But it did. Because Manchester United, fluent at football but puny on power, wouldn't easily let go of their chance to be winners (it would have been the seventh time in Reds history) in this second and deciding leg of the final after a 1-1 meeting five days earlier.

As early as the second minute, the bonny Blues staked a claim to win this prestige competition for the very first time in club history. Moulden, who was a devastating routine in twists and tight turns, corkscrewed the United defence deep inside the penalty area on the right-hand side. His hither and thither jink opened the space and his cross looped over the goalmouth where David Boyd rose to it with a firm header which was well directed and just about one of the few things that threatened all night to beat the superb goalkeeping of Gary Walsh.

It was a thrilling send-off for City, hot favourites for the occasion. But they had to survive another 84 minutes, some of it edge of the seat stuff, before scoring the second goal that made them sure of the success for which they've worked so hard to achieve since the cup campaign was launched last November.

Appropriately, it was a classic finish. Moulden, the one City attacker always in the picture, played a deadly ball through to White bursting through the middle. The winger struck his shot fiercely, the defiant Walsh responded with more excellence as he blocked the ball – but Moulden's nimble mind had kept ticking over and the striker was streaking onto the loose ball and swiftly steering it low into the net from six yards out. For the first time there was no way back for United. And they knew it.

They were two glorious goals, taking the cup tally to 27 from nine games. Yet thousands of fans missed City's jubilation at the flying start. For twenty minutes into the match a huge queue of fans snaked out of the packed Main Stand to take seats in the North Stand, used as an overflow – but a constant flow of people being shepherded along the touchline must have been an unsettling sight for youngsters trying hard to calm early edginess. The response to this final occasion had been staggering: 18,158 watched the match, gate receipts approached £28,000, and while the tie never attained the classic standard of the first leg, it had plenty of 'oohs and aahs' for an enthusiastic audience.

In a nutshell, City looked the likelier winners because they had strength to go with their style. Moulden always looked a good leader of the line, especially in wider positions; Thackeray, later to pay a cruel price for being sent off in the first leg, provided substance in midfield; and rising head and shoulders above all the young performers was Brightwell at the heart of City's defence, a cavalier in action, a just eighteen year-old playing with the innocence of youth and displaying a certainty of mind and sure-footedness in everything he did.

It summed up the kind of presence he imposed in the 40th minute when he made one rampaging run of 40 yards which split United asunder. And Brightwell capped it with a blistering 25-yarder which the very wonderful Walsh tipped over the top.

City found left-winger Goddard a perplexing customer, prodding in passes and chipping in crosses which often unhinged the Blues. United's football was of better quality but the power didn't compare.

There were see-saw moments. Brightwell cleared a menacing Goddard cross (6th), Scott blocked a distance shot from the winger (13th) while at the other end Boyd headed over from a Mills cross (10th), White just failed to connect a spidery leg with Moulden's left flank cross (14th) and 'keeper Walsh got his arm to a Boyd attempt following a White cross from a quick free kick.

There were four serious occasions when City might have lost the lead. A bad goal kick from Crompton (18th) had Hinchcliffe grappling desperately to stop Wilson breaking clear and City's full-back was booked for spinning his opponent round......Cronin passed up a penalty area gift (30th) after being chipped in by Goddard, the striker slicing wide of the post......Mills whipped the ball off City's line (37th) after a deadly Wilson shot from a Cronin corner......and Mills again performed heroics in heading off his line from a Wilson attempt after Murphy had headed on from a corner.

Meanwhile, Walsh was putting up the shutters in United's goal. He got his arm to an effort from Boyd to deflect it wide (17th)......two minutes from the interval he blocked White's bid when Moulden's piercing pass got the winger through...... the 'keeper spread himself to great effect after Boyd homed in following Lake's very cute back-heel in the box (53rd)......and there were eye-catching snatch saves from dangerous crosses by Moulden (65th) and Hinchcliffe (72nd) at full-stretch. Additionally, White pushed off Martin to take control of a Moulden pass and rasped a shot which hit the side-netting and Scott's drive was stopped at the foot of the near-post by Walsh (72nd).

White, always capable of skipping the quite fantastic, found it difficult to maintain involvement while Boyd on the other flank was not firing effectively enough, either, as United's full-backs showed their passion.

Redmond led his lads into a period of supremacy as the second half wore on, though there was still a juddering shot from Goddard (80th) which rocked Crompton a few feet back on his heels. As he had been throughout the tournament, Crompton was safe and sound as proved by his record of only six goals conceded in the nine ties.

It was not vintage young Blues, but it was good enough, it was worthy enough to win the trophy which City started chasing back in 1953/54. United had made it a stiff test. As Redmond led his team to receive the trophy, cheered by ecstatic City fans, they were scenes to remember. But it was also a sad sight to see Thackeray refused the honour of collecting a medal, punishment for his dismissal from the first leg.

Thackeray was consoled by members of the City staff but they were painful minutes, a stricture too severe to be imposed on any player who had battled his heart out for the cause. Leaving a scar that may never be completely healed on a player so young, F.A. discipline at its barmiest one might think. City will apply for the midfielder to receive a medal without ceremony at a later occasion.

Thackeray was first to be handed the trophy as the players assembled for their well-earned lap of honour. Handshakes all round – and special memories for one man, youth and Reserve team coach, Tony Book, who had skippered City to same triumphs at the height of their post-war eminence in the late sixties. This Youth Cup achievement ended ten years of silverware famine (minor competitions apart) despite some close calls.

For Book, his coaching colleague Glyn Pardoe, youth team aide John Collins – the kind of backroom worker no club should be without – and even dressing room caretaker Jimmy Rouse, this was time for champagne, cheers and tears. Along with members of the scouting staff, led by chief scout Ken Barnes, City were back among the celebrations.

For the only time that season, the Reds were overrun in the centre of the pitch and they couldn't wrest the baton from a City side that conducted the majority of passages from a sweetly sounding symphony. Of Eric Harrison's side, only Karl Goddard and Gary Walsh were tuned up to the standard of the home eleven, most of the others merely making noises which were flat or out of time.

The crown of England's best youth side sat fairly and squarely on the heads of the City lads, and the accolades showered upon them came from far and wide and were justifiably merited.

For Harrison and his team of vanquished protégés, coming so near was no consolation and it meant that their wait to bring the Youth Cup back to Old Trafford would stretch at least another year longer.

1) Malcolm Roberts	9) Jamie Slater	1) Jim O'Donnell	9) Paul Harvey
2) Mark Dodd	10) John McCoy	2) Russell Beardsmore	10) Mark Robins
3) Graham Walker	11) Carl Thomas	3) Wayne Heseltine	11) Phil Steer
4) Russell Watson	*12) Dave Barton (for 3)*	4) Ian Scott	*12) Deiniol Graham (for 6)*
5) Darren Stanton	*14) Steve Haley (for 6)*	5) Derek Brazil	*14) Dyfan Williams (for 3)*
6) Tony Lee		6) Simon Hutchinson	
7) Robert Jones		7) David Wilson	
8) Mark Jones		8) Drew McBride	

WREXHAM 0 v 4 MANCHESTER UNITED
Harvey, Heseltine, Robins (2)

1986-87 — DECEMBER 1986 — second round

Tuesday 2nd
Kick-off 7.00 p.m.
Attendance 721

When United arrived at the Racecourse Ground in Wrexham to commence duty for what appeared to be a routine Youth Cup Second Round tie, the familiar faces of Walsh, Gill, Martin, Gardner, Murphy, Todd, Cronin, Bottomley and Goddard were all missing. On the plus side, Eric Harrison could still count on Ian Scott, David Wilson, Drew McBride, Paul Harvey and Russell Beardsmore while, for this opening encounter at least, Tony Hopley was sidelined through injury. To compensate, Harrison was able to call up Simon Hutchinson and Mark Robins, two recent graduates of the Football Association's School of Excellence.

The game in North Wales was marked by two historical features, one of which was almost inconsequential while the other was positively monumental. In terms of curiosity value, tackling Wrexham on their own patch meant that the Reds were required to compete in a Youth Cup game outside of the English border. In a much more significant context, the match represented the very first Youth Cup tie of the Alex Ferguson era, a period unparalleled in terms of success in Manchester United's magnificent history.

Ferguson had occupied the Old Trafford hot seat for less than a month and he was in the primary stages of assessing the club's strengths and weaknesses. By travelling to Wrexham, the new manager afforded himself an early opportunity to take a look at his under-18's in the major national tournament and the Scot made it known to the squad he would be in attendance by taking the time out to wish them good luck in their endeavours before they left Manchester.

The reality of football in the lower reaches of the professional game was once again brought into focus at the Racecourse. While United were making their bow in that season's Youth Cup, Wrexham had already been required to defeat Rhyl, Heswall, Crewe and Chesterfield in order to claw their way into the Second Round.

Idris Pike, the Robins' youth team manager, commented on the relatively small catchment patch that his scouting network operated within when admitting, *'Most of our players have been discovered by people from within the club. United have the pick of the whole country while we are only a Fourth Division side and have to look around the immediate area for our players to come to Wrexham, and perhaps our good run in the competition will help.'*

As a consequence of Hopley's absence, Eric Harrison switched Harvey from his normal wide position into the centre of the attack alongside Robins. Due to an alteration to the rules, United's coach was also able to name two substitutes and by coincidence both were Welsh internationals. Although born in Cannock, Deiniol Graham was brought up on the island of Anglesey and won caps for Wales Boys, and he was accompanied on the bench by Ruabon-based Dyfan Williams, who had also played for his country at schoolboy grade in addition to representing Wales at youth level.

There was little to choose between the two sides in the early minutes of the tie and it soon became clear that United would have to match their hosts in terms of effort and desire if they were to take anything out of the game. The first goalscoring opportunity fell to United's Harvey in the seventh minute and he was left anguished when Malcolm Roberts, a six feet, four inch tall goalkeeper from Liverpool, turned his close range shot over the bar. Roberts denied United again four minutes later, this time displaying his keen reflexes with a smart catch from Hutchinson's downward header. In the 22nd minute, Roberts was involved in what was the turning point of the match when he initially appeared to save a Robins' shot before allowing the ball to slip out of his grasp and roll over the goal-line.

To Wrexham's credit, they steeled themselves at the setback and from then until half-time their attacks posed a little more danger than before. Besides taking a few routine catches and crosses, goalkeeper O'Donnell was relieved to see a Tony Lee header sail over and a Carl Thomas in-swinging corner hit the crossbar.

In the 63rd minute, Harvey made it 2-0. Taking a pass on his chest inside the penalty area, he spun towards goal and drove the ball underneath the diving Roberts. A stray dog then amused the crowd for a few moments, the intervention causing the game to be stopped a couple of times before the canine culprit was captured by a club official.

However, there was now no catching United and when Robins fed a nicely weighted pass into the path of the onrushing Wayne Heseltine in the 71st minute, the marauding full-back obliged by drilling his shot into the back of the net. With the advantage of full-time training becoming much more telling in the later stages, Robins then completed a memorable tournament debut by tucking home a Phil Steer cross three minutes later to round off the scoring.

Alex Ferguson was sure to have been pleased at the result and the performance. The high level of skill and teamwork displayed by the Reds gave rise to some optimism, albeit against somewhat inferior opposition than they could expect to face further on down the track.

United's Dyfan Williams (right) renews aquaintances with Welsh Youth colleague and Wrexham captain Jamie Slater prior to kick-off at the Racecourse Ground

325

1986-87

1) Jim O'Donnell	9) Tony Hopley	1) Carl Muggleton	9) Steve Wilkinson
2) Ian Scott	10) Paul Harvey	2) Richard Toone	10) Robert Alleyne
3) Russell Beardsmore	11) Phil Steer	3) Steve Prindiville	11) Paul Williams
4) Derek Brazil	*12) Mark Robins (for 11)*	4) Sean Kimberley	*12) Andrew Ling*
5) Wayne Heseltine	*14) Deiniol Graham (for 8)*	5) Tony Brien	*14) Gary Torrance (for 11)*
6) Simon Hutchinson		6) Grant Brown	
7) David Wilson		7) Jason Garwood	
8) Drew McBride		8) Darren Williams	

JANUARY 1987

MANCHESTER UNITED 1 v 2 LEICESTER CITY
Hutchinson   Alleyne, Wilkinson

third round

Monday 26th

Kick-off 7.30 p.m.

Attendance 1,002

The Reds were grateful for the home advantage that the draw bestowed on them when learning that a fancied Leicester City side were to be their next opponents, the young Foxes' reputation mainly based on the inclusion of Robert Alleyne and Steve Wilkinson in their forward-line. Alleyne had already gathered some senior experience and Wilkinson was the current understudy to City's first-team star and current £1million Arsenal and Chelsea target, Alan Smith.

The contrast between the size of City's scouting net and that of the Reds' last Youth Cup opponents was demonstrated by the inclusion in their team of youngsters from as far away as Dublin, Sunderland and Harlow, as well as a couple of Leicester locals and a number of prospects who were spotted not so far away from Filbert Street, such as Birmingham, Dudley and Lincoln.

The Leicester boys prepared for the tie with a rearranged Midland Intermediate League match at Peterborough. Despite losing 3-0, it was their first outing for three weeks and a Posh team strengthened by the inclusion of a few senior men was considered by City's coaching staff as *'an ideal warm-up'* for the clash in Manchester.

While United had been required to negotiate a reasonably easy hurdle in the Second Round, the junior Foxes were busy knocking Shrewsbury out at the same stage. Following a hugely disappointing 0-0 draw at Filbert Street, they made no mistake at the second attempt by hammering the Shrews 6-0 at the Gay Meadow, the highlight of which was a Wilkinson hat-trick.

The Evening News recorded the details of a contest during which the efforts of the home side fell short of staving off their early exit:

Manchester United's youngsters woke up too late against Leicester City at Old Trafford last night.

They staged a spirited rally in the last half-hour, but overall Leicester were well worth their 2-1 win to put last year's finalists out of the F.A. Youth Cup.

Steve Wilkinson beat Derek Brazil for pace to put Leicester ahead, with a well-taken goal in the 36th minute of this Third Round tie.

A 61st minute replacement for Phil Steer, Mark Robins assisted in bringing about a United revival but couldn't produce a goal to prevent their elimination

Ten minutes after the interval, Robert Alleyne - who has had a couple of games in League football - headed home a centre from Jason Garwood.

With the arrival of Deiniol Graham as one of the substitutes, United got their act together. Simon Hutchinson scored with a good header from David Wilson's cross ten minutes from the end, but generally their finishing was as poor as their football had been in the first half.

Despite United 'keeper Jim O'Donnell going into the game with a dislocated finger, the club's medical staff deemed it was safe for him to take part in the game by strapping the sore digit to its immediate neighbour. While the former St. Pius High School and Manchester Boys' custodian might have felt inclined to sit out any other match, the discomfort he felt was easily outweighed by the never-to-be forgotten opportunity of making his first appearance on the Old Trafford pitch.

Leicester assumed command and gave O'Donnell his first proper test in the 12th minute with a Paul Williams effort. Harvey and Steer responded for the Reds, but City looked unruffled and their centre-back pairing of Grant Brown and Tony Brien caught the eye with assured displays. Just prior to the break, United's captain Scott produced a spectacular overhead kick to glance the ball onto and over Muggleton's bar only for Leicester to resume their dominance straight from the restart when Darren Williams fired a shot just over.

Six minutes after City's second goal, Eric Harrison withdrew the ineffective Steer and McBride and sent on both substitutes. There was a noticeable improvement, particularly upfront, and between the Reds' goal and the end of the game chances to equalise fell to Harvey, whose drive was caught by the cool Muggleton, and scorer Hutchinson, whose blasted shot flew well over Leicester's net when all present felt sure he was about to double his tally for the evening.

It was a depressing outcome for all concerned at Old Trafford, and things were destined to get a heck of a lot worse on the Youth Cup front before they got a darned sight better.

Named at left full-back, the offensively-minded Russell Beardsmore was one of many Reds who vainly chased after Leicester's fox cubs

1) Mike Pollitt
2) John Mortimer
3) Tony Jackson
4) Jason Lydiate
5) Wayne Heseltine
6) Simon Hutchinson
7) Paul Wratten
8) Mark Robins
9) Deiniol Graham
10) Simon Andrews
11) Craig Lawton
12) Wayne Bullimore (for 11)
14) Paul Sixsmith

1) Jason Pearcey
2) Gareth Price
3) Dave Parker
4) Paul Brogan
5) Mark Place
6) John Blair
7) Sean Hood
8) Dave Hodges
9) Steve Williams
10) Tony Gorman
11) Glen Wathall
12) Kevin Gray (for 9)
14) Shane Reddish (for 10)

1987-88

MANCHESTER UNITED 1 v 2 MANSFIELD TOWN

Graham — Gorman, Wathall

DECEMBER 1987

Tuesday 8th

Kick-off 7.00 p.m.

Attendance 561

Young Stags topple United

Any disappointment felt by Alex Ferguson, Eric Harrison, the players and backroom staff at Old Trafford to the premature exit from the 1986/87 episode of the Youth Cup would have positively paled into insignificance at the events on the evening of the 8th December 1987. Drawn at home to the under-18 side of a club entrenched in the Third Division, the newest version of the young Reds capitulated to an embarrassing defeat which undeniably remains as the ultimate low spot in United's long and illustrious participation in the tournament.

While there had been four other early knock-outs, at Everton in 1964 and 1971, to Bolton Wanderers in 1976 and Leeds United in 1984, none of those losses were suffered on home soil or to the level of opposition posed by modest Mansfield Town. On this occasion there was no escaping the fact that United's kids threw away their home advantage and let themselves and the club down with a painfully pitiful performance.

If any semblance of an excuse was to be offered, it could be pinpointed to the unusually high number of newcomers in the side, which totalled eight including a used substitute. There were also other factors to take into account, and they were placed on record by the Evening News:

Deiniol Graham's second half goal came about through an unforced error but wasn't enough to prevent a catastrophic loss to Mansfield

Paul Wratten was one of a number of Eric Harrison's team who failed to shine on their Youth Cup bow

Manchester United draft a third schoolboy into their team for tonight's F.A. Youth Cup tie at Old Trafford.
Craig Lawton lines up with goalkeeper Mike Pollitt and Jason Lydiate in a rebuilt young side. Paul Sigsworth, a third player from Bolton Lads Club, stands by as Simon Andrews and Tony Jackson face fitness tests.

In a later interview, Eric Harrison detailed one of the reasons for the dearth of junior talent at the club just then when explaining, *'Normally we'd take in twelve to fifteen apprentices in a season but this year we only took on nine, which is why we had to draft schoolboys in (against Mansfield). Our standards are high and in a barren spell like this it's no use signing youngsters on for the sake of it.'*

Managed by former Busby Babe Ian Greaves, the Stags' most memorable win in the national competition was plotted by youth coach John Jarman. An elated Jarman told a reporter that Town's win demonstrated just how successful his club's youth policy had become, and Greaves went on record as saying he was *'absolutely thrilled'* with the scoreline. Echoing everyone's thoughts when stating emphatically that the result was *'thoroughly deserved'*, the Field Mill boss added in a delighted tone, *'and we should have won by more'*.

For someone who knew more than most about the Reds' youth policy from his time at Old Trafford between May 1953 and December 1960, Greaves would also have been aware of the importance United placed on their showings in the Youth Cup, as well as just how much the deflating defeat would have hurt.

The Evening News claimed that Mansfield *'ran rings round a disappointing United'* while the Review chipped in by stating *'no-one could have any complaints'* at the outcome. Also noting that Town were a *'physically strong side containing four lads with first-team experience'*, the Review claimed the visitors *'approached the game with a no-nonsense attitude'*.

second round

1987-88

DECEMBER 1987

second round

The Mansfield Chad newspaper produced the following impression:

Mighty Manchester United were shaken by a little bit of Mansfield magic at Old Trafford on Tuesday night. John Jarman's youngsters dumped star-studded United out of the Second Round of the F.A. Youth Cup with two fine first half goals.

They outclassed and outwitted last year's finalists in front of their first-team manager, Alex Ferguson, and a crowd of almost 600.

Mansfield's teenagers, who have earned a reputation for their exploits in this competition in recent seasons, swept into a 19th minute lead when Glen Wathall rounded the goalkeeper to finish off a first time pass from right-back Gareth Price.

But it was midfielder Tony Gorman's goal just three minutes before half-time that eventually settled the tie. The seventeen year-old Eire Youth international unleashed a blistering twenty-yard drive that goalkeeper Mick Pollitt just couldn't hold onto. And it was only a defensive blunder that put United back in the contest eleven minutes after the interval.

Price's back-pass was far too strong for goalkeeper Jason Pearcey to hold and Deiniol Graham was presented with the easiest of chances from fifteen yards.

Graham, who played in United's first-team against Wimbledon recently, was Mansfield's biggest threat, but he was limited to long range efforts by central defenders Paul Brogan and Mark Place.

Even Lilleshall star Wayne Bullimore, from Sutton, failed to make an impression when he was asked to salvage United's cup hopes in the second half.

Mansfield, marshalled superbly from the centre of the park by David Hodges, could even have gone on to win by a greater margin. Wathall brought a fine close range save out of Pollitt in the opening stages when John Blair broke free down the right.

And it was one of Blair's jinking runs that should have earned him a penalty when he was upended inside United's eighteen-yard box six minutes from the end.

But by then the Stags were well on their way to yet another cup scalp and an away draw against Hartlepool United or Middlesbrough in the next round in the New Year.

For two of the United side, Burnley-born defender John Mortimer and Middlesbrough boy Paul Wratten, their inclusion against Mansfield represented a one and only appearance in the Youth Cup. In Deiniol Graham's case, the game gave him a solitary full start in the competition following on from his two prior substitute appearances.

While the management team at Mansfield could feel justifiably pleased with the relative success of their youth operation, the very opposite was now true of United. In many respects, the defeat acted as a catalyst and merely confirmed to Alex Ferguson what he already knew, that the club's supply line had been badly neglected and was now in as poor a state as it could be.

The same Manchester United that was once the torchbearer in respect of the scouting, recruitment and development of youthful soccer talent had, at least in the short-term, been unable to attract the quality of talent of days gone by. In truth, the type of young hopefuls who would once have walked over hot coals to get to Old Trafford were now being enticed elsewhere in search of a career in the game.

For the supervision of an almost complete rebuilding operation, United unquestionably possessed the right man for the job in Ferguson. Having been in charge of the club for just over twelve months, the Scot could point to achievements north of the border with St. Mirren and, most famously, Aberdeen, by establishing revamped youth operations for those outfits. As much as anything else, it was Ferguson's faith and nurturing of young talent at Pittodrie which did so much to help the Aberdeen club to smash the 'old firm' dominance of the two Glasgow giants, Rangers and Celtic, during the 1980's.

Even before the Mansfield game, Ferguson was already scrutinising the shoddy state of the scouting system at Old Trafford. United's manager was anxious to recruit helpers of the highest calibre in order to assist him in that respect and one of his primary objectives was to have a much greater 'spotting' presence in and around the Manchester conurbation. He felt, quite rightly, that many of the other North-West clubs, principally Manchester City, had been creaming the best talent off the top of the cake too often and for too long and one of his objectives was to attempt to reverse that trend as soon as possible.

With the backing of a board who was sympathetic to those requirements, under Ferguson's astute guidance and selective sowing of seeds, his aims would be achieved much sooner than anyone could ever have imagined.

> *Alex Ferguson went absolutely mad. Eric Harrison pulled me to one side and told me that both Ferguson and Bobby Charlton were disappointed with me personally.*
>
> *As captain of the team they had expected more leadership from me, to rally the lads, dish out a few rollockings and to do my job as captain. It was a real kick up the backside and what I probably needed to get my game back on track after the initial disappointment of going out.*
>
> *It was a very quiet dressing room that night.*

WAYNE HESELTINE

> *I don't mind if a team of mine is beaten after giving their best and competing for everything. But against Mansfield the lads just relied on their football ability to carry them through, and the result shows that wasn't good enough. They didn't mix it physically, and although at every level at Old Trafford we place emphasis on skill, you have to get stuck in as well and this team didn't. It was a devastating blow to go out this early in the competition but we didn't deserve to go through. I warned the players before the game that we only had one chance and I was very surprised and disappointed at the response. I had a few harsh words to say to them after the game and I haven't had to do that often at this level.*

ERIC HARRISON

1) Chris Errington	9) John Horner	1) Mark Bosnich	9) Jonny Rödlund
2) Ian O'Ware	10) Dale Anderson	2) Roger Sallis	10) John Shotton
3) Ian Darby	11) Darren Beales	3) Tony Jackson	11) Craig Lawton
4) Ian Gillies	*12) Michael Anderson*	4) Alan Tonge	*12) Simon Andrews (for 3)*
5) Martin Brace	*14) Nigel Gamblin*	5) Jason Lydiate	*14) Lee Sharpe (for 6)*
6) Jimmy Rodwell		6) Kieran Toal	
7) Derek Powell		7) Wayne Bullimore	
8) Nicky Southall		8) Darren Ferguson	

DARLINGTON 2 v 5 MANCHESTER UNITED

Anderson D., Horner — Bullimore (2, 1 pen), Rödlund, Shotton (2)

1988-89

second round

DECEMBER 1988

Tuesday 13th

Kick-off 7.00 p.m.

Attendance 885

FOOTBALL AT FEETHAMS
FA Youth Challenge Cup
Tuesday, December 13, 1988
DARLINGTON v MANCHESTER UNITED
Kick off 7.00 p.m
Adults £1.00 — Junior/OAP 50p
Free Admission to Paddock and Seated Area
ALL PAY

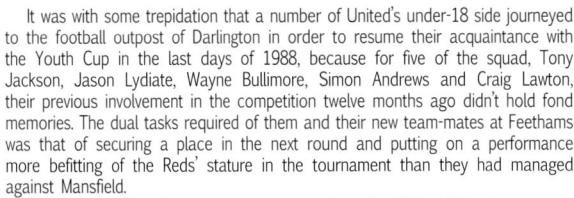

It was with some trepidation that a number of United's under-18 side journeyed to the football outpost of Darlington in order to resume their acquaintance with the Youth Cup in the last days of 1988, because for five of the squad, Tony Jackson, Jason Lydiate, Wayne Bullimore, Simon Andrews and Craig Lawton, their previous involvement in the competition twelve months ago didn't hold fond memories. The dual tasks required of them and their new team-mates at Feethams was that of securing a place in the next round and putting on a performance more befitting of the Reds' stature in the tournament than they had managed against Mansfield.

One of United's substitutes was a winger from the Midlands by the name of Lee Sharpe. Having already been blooded in Torquay's Fourth Division team during the 1987/88 season, the seventeen year-old was snapped up by Alex Ferguson for a fee believed to be around £185,000 soon after its conclusion. Initially viewed as 'one for the future', and following a spate of injuries within his senior squad, Ferguson was pressed into using Sharpe as an emergency full-back in First Division combat a couple of months prior to the game at Darlington and the youngster managed to hold onto a first-team place for several games.

There was an unusually international flavour about Eric Harrison's team. One of the new starters, goalkeeper Mark Bosnich, had joined the Reds on non-contract terms from the Sydney Croatia club in Australia while, from the northern hemisphere, Swedish forward Jonny Rödlund was spotted by United scouts at an international youth tournament.

Originating from much closer to home, full-back Roger Sallis came from the Derby area, midfielder John Shotton's birthplace was just up the road from Darlington at Hartlepool while Kieran Toal kept the Mancunian flag flying and defender Alan Tonge hailed from Bolton. The remaining member of the squad was first-year trainee Darren Ferguson. Acknowledged as an accomplished midfielder, the son of the club's manager attracted the interest of both Spurs and Nottingham Forest prior to signing for his father.

Memories of the Mansfield match manifested themselves during an opening period in which Darlington dominated most of the proceedings. Quakers' forward Darren Beales was prominent for the home eleven and both Ian Gillies and Dale Anderson tested Bosnich early on.

After looking the more likely team to concede a goal for 37 minutes, the Reds edged in front when Lawton gained possession in midfield and floated a measured ball over the advanced home defenders for Rödlund to gallop after. Sprinting on unchallenged, Rödlund kept his Scandinavian head typically cool and calculated to direct a shot past goalie Chris Errington and give his side an undeserved advantage.

With the gloves now off, the second half was a much more productive period, yielding a total of six goals, and it was barely a minute old before United were awarded a corner. Taken by the influential Bullimore, the ball was flicked on at the front post and Shotton was nicely situated to side-foot it home into a gaping goalmouth.

Buoyed by a 2-0 advantage, the Reds might have expected to see the game out without too much problem, but what they hadn't counted on was the resilience of a Darlington eleven who soon clawed their way back to equalise. An initial reply came in the 57th minute when Derek Powell's free kick was placed beyond the last United defender to the far post, Beales driving the ball back into the middle for Anderson to prod it into the net.

A minute later and a one-two down the right-hand side of the pitch between Anderson and John Horner was stupendously concluded when the latter arrowed an amazing overhead kick past Bosnich. Horner's incredible leveller brought the Quakers' supporters to their feet and later caused Darlington youth coach Phil Bonnyman to claim it was the best goal he had ever seen from a team he'd been involved with.

Of this period of play, the Review mentioned that the Reds *'suddenly looked very vulnerable and a repeat of last term's early exit to a lower division club loomed large'*. No wonder, for almost as soon as the scores reached 2-2 Darlington twice came close to nosing in front, Bosnich bringing off a good save from Beale's long-range shot before Southall walloped a ferocious free kick that almost snapped the crossbar in two.

It was another free kick in the 68th minute from which United found their salvation. Taken from just outside the Quakers' penalty area, captain Bullimore weighed up his options prior to bending the ball around a six-man wall and past a bemused Errington.

Seven minutes later, the Reds moved into the comfort zone again when they took a 4-2 lead, Shotton doubling his personal contribution by deflecting in a Sharpe effort. There were only three minutes left, and with the Darlington lads now completely out of steam, a flattering fifth was registered for United when Bullimore made easy work of converting a penalty.

> *I was already playing in the first-team before I got in the youth side, but to be honest I was still lacking quite a bit of confidence.*
>
> *When I was training with the likes of Wayne Bullimore, Kieran Toal and Lee Costa, they would be spraying the ball around so easily, 30 to 40-yard passes then killing the ball dead with their first touch. Their technique was amazing, I had never had that sort of coaching at Torquay, the drills and practice I mean. It was more physical there, we never trained like they did at United.*
>
> *I was being used as a left-back at senior level in my first year and occasionally on the wing so Eric Harrison slotted me in at full-back in the youth games as well, but I was still very raw.*

LEE SHARPE

329

1988-89

1) Mark Nightingale	9) David Lycett	1) Mark Bosnich	9) Jonny Rödlund
2) Nigel Downing	10) David Johnson	2) Roger Sallis	10) John Shotton
3) Ian Curry	11) Mark Dickinson	3) Tony Jackson	11) Craig Lawton
4) Graham Hyde	*12) Richard Holmshaw*	4) Alan Tonge	*12) Sean McAuley (for 7)*
5) David Wetherall	*14) Sam Goodacre (for 7)*	5) Jason Lydiate	*14) Simon Andrews (for 12)*
6) Kevin Elshaw		6) Lee Costa	
7) Jason Swann		7) Kieran Toal	
8) Jon Newsome		8) Darren Ferguson	

JANUARY 1989

SHEFFIELD WEDNESDAY 0 v 0 MANCHESTER UNITED

Monday 9th
Kick-off 7.00 p.m.
Attendance 538

third round

Young Fergie cops it!

'Livewire' Darren Ferguson was presented with a couple of opportunities to knock out Sheffield Wednesday at the first attempt

Because Wayne Bullimore was suspended for the Third Round tie at Sheffield Wednesday, themselves conquerors of Middlesbrough at the previous stage of the tournament, an opportunity arose for pint-sized Welsh midfielder Lee Costa to see if he could make an impression in the Youth Cup. Bullimore had been sent off during an 'A' team home defeat by Liverpool on the last day of 1988 and in his absence the captain's armband passed over to Darren Ferguson.

The game at Hillsborough was one of much perspiration and little inspiration and so the needle on the excitement scale never really climbed anything much above its 'lukewarm' mark. Even though both 'keepers were kept occupied, their work mainly consisted of dealing with crosses, back passes and organising their defenders rather than making saves.

The earliest chance fell to the home side as late as the midway point in the opening half, Wednesday's Kevin Elshaw rising highest to head home a corner, and even then the effort was ruled out by the referee, who adjudged that Bosnich was impeded in the process.

Ferguson should have opened the scoring for United in the 28th minute when, with only the goalkeeper to beat, his shot was saved by Mark Nightingale. The Reds then saw two other chances go begging. The first opportunity to be scorned occurred when Nightingale blocked a second Ferguson effort, and just after the interval a superb drive from John Shotton came back off a post with nobody about to knock the rebound into the net.

The following day, and because of those misses, reporter David Meek queried whether Ferguson might have had *'some explaining to do when he got home from football last night'*, though he did later go on to single the boss's son out as the team's *'livewire'*.

There were precious few incidents of note in the second half and consequently views were divided regarding the outcome. Over in Manchester, Meek continued his match report by reasoning that United *'deserved their replay,'* having *'outplayed bigger, stronger opponents'*, while the Review claimed *'the Reds just about had the edge over the 90 minutes'*.

In the *'Junior Report'* section featured in a later Sheffield Wednesday match programme, the Owls' commentator made a judgement that *'except for perhaps fifteen minutes, I think we were slightly on top'* before complaining *'had we put our chances away, we would already be in the next round'*. Then admitting *'United came into the game in the last period'*, the Hillsborough scribe defiantly declared *'the tie is by no means over'*.

By far the most unfortunate aspect of an otherwise acceptable trip over the Pennines was the injury to Sean McAuley. The Sheffield-born sixteen year-old had only just replaced Kieran Toal when he took a heavy bang to his chest in a collision with an opponent.

McAuley was immediately taken off and within an hour or so found himself diagnosed with a collapsed lung and on a hospital operating table. The injury was severe enough to keep him out of competitive action for a couple of months, after which he returned to the 'B' team, none the worse for wear, in mid-March.

John Shotton's piledriver, which cannoned against an upright early in the second half, could have saved United the trouble of a replay

330

1) Mark Bosnich
2) Roger Sallis
3) Tony Jackson
4) Alan Tonge
5) Jason Lydiate
6) Lee Costa
7) Wayne Bullimore
8) Darren Ferguson
9) Jonny Rödlund
10) John Shotton
11) Craig Lawton
12) Simon Andrews (for 9)
14) Lee Sharpe

1) Mark Nightingale
2) Marcus Hawley
3) Ian Curry
4) Graham Hyde
5) David Wetherall
6) Kevin Elshaw
7) Sam Goodacre
8) Jon Newsome
9) David Lycett
10) David Johnson
11) Mark Dickinson
12) Nigel Downing (for 7)
14) Richard Holmshaw (for 10)

1988-89

MANCHESTER UNITED 2 v 0 SHEFFIELD WEDNESDAY

Andrews, Bullimore (pen)

JANUARY 1989

Tuesday 17th

Kick-off 7.00 p.m.

Attendance 1,550

third round replay

The theme of youth was a topical talking point amongst the regulars at Old Trafford in the middle part of January 1989. Caused by a spate of injuries within the ranks of his star men, Alex Ferguson was forced into introducing a number of his young prospects to the senior set-up.

Lee Sharpe had been reinstated as a first-team regular over the past few weeks and others such as Russell Beardsmore, Mark Robins, David Wilson, Tony Gill, Lee Martin and Giuliano Maiorana were all asked to make contributions of some size or other in the cause of the seniors over the preceding two or three months.

In particular, a senior side with Sharpe, Gill, Martin and Beardsmore in the starting line-up, as well as Graham and Wilson utilised from the bench, put on a superb show in an F.A. Cup replay at Loftus Road to secure a morale-boosting 2-2 draw against QPR.

That splendid result was earned less than a week before Sheffield Wednesday's youth squad were due in Manchester, and if it wasn't enough to warm the hearts of all United fans, they were further elated on the intervening Saturday when the same four starters, plus Wilson and Maiorana as substitutes, crushed Millwall 3-0 in a one-sided First Division encounter at Old Trafford.

With first-team heavyweights such as Bryan Robson, Paul McGrath and Gordon Strachan missing from both of those games, the influx of junior talent acted as a huge mid-season fillip to Reds' followers. Because interest in the younger end of the club's staff was at a high, the attendance for the Youth Cup replay was probably slightly greater than it might have been, when Wayne Bullimore returned against the teenagers from Hillsborough and Kieran Toal found himself ousted from the side to make way.

As is often the case with rematches, the second instalment against the Wednesday kids was substantially more pleasing on the eye than had been the case in Sheffield. United experienced the better of the early exchanges, particularly in terms of territorial advantage, and it was their improved display in the middle of the pitch which in turn made life a little easier for the defence, as well as ensuring the forwards saw a great deal more of the ball than they did over in Yorkshire.

The young Reds began in a bright and breezy fashion and they kept chipping away at their guests until their persistence was rewarded just nine minutes prior to the interval, the point at which a chink in Wednesday's armoury was finally discovered.

An intricate build-up catapulted them into the lead after a switched-on John Shotton was put through the centre of the Sheffield back four. Faced with just the goalkeeper as a final obstacle, Shotton shimmied around him and it appeared that he only needed to roll the ball into an untenanted net to put his side into the lead.

It was then that Nightingale chose to perpetrate *'a rugby challenge worthy of Jonathan Davies'*, which brought the move to an end and United's number ten to the floor. Nightingale's action would certainly have caused his dismissal nowadays, and it got the punishment it deserved when, for the second time in three Youth Cup ties, Bullimore efficiently knocked in the ensuing penalty with a sweet left-foot strike.

The main talking point for United's supporters was the excellent showing from Lee Costa, who the Sheffield Wednesday lads were hardly able to contain. Costa was at the heart of practically everything the Reds created and his electric-charged performance was a sure sign he intended to keep his place in the side.

Still hampered by the effects of an earlier bout of 'flu, an ineffective Jonny Rödlund was withdrawn at the interval and it was down to his replacement to finally seal the Reds' win in the 80th minute, Simon Andrews' accurate glancing header from Craig Lawton's cross proving one of only a very few goalmouth incidents in the second half.

It was a period in which the Sheffield team was forced into making a greater attempt to get the ball forward and yet for all of their later possession, Mark Bosnich was hardly noticed in United's penalty box other than for the few mundane tasks required of him.

The following evening, David Meek contributed a few paragraphs on another super victory and a section of his piece read:

Manchester United's youth revolution marches on.
This time the real Babes of Old Trafford made their mark in a Third Round replay of the F.A. Youth Cup.
The United youngsters were dwarfed by the he-men from Hillsborough but stuck at it, none better than little Lee Costa, who was half the size of several opponents.
Wednesday's strength put them on top in the second half but Jason Lydiate, well supported by Alan Tonge, set an inspiring example in defence to turn the tide.

Roger Sallis (top) and Alan Tonge formed part of a defensive screen that Sheffield Wednesday found unbreakable

331

1988-89

1) Mark Bosnich	9) Simon Andrews	1) Chris Neville	9) Glyn Hooper
2) Roger Sallis	10) John Shotton	2) Aaron Gardiner	10) Neil Grice
3) Tony Jackson	11) Craig Lawton	3) Stephen Hyde	11) Andrew Banks
4) Alan Tonge	*12) Jason Lydiate (for 6)*	4) David Ellis	*12) Lee Boyle*
5) Lee Sharpe	*14) Jonny Rödlund (for 10)*	5) Chris Swailes	*14) Robbie Devereux (for 9)*
6) Lee Costa		6) Gavin Johnson	
7) Wayne Bullimore		7) Neil Currie	
8) Darren Ferguson		8) Lee Honeywood	

JANUARY 1989

MANCHESTER UNITED 4 v 1 IPSWICH TOWN

Bullimore, Lawton, Sharpe, Shotton — Swailes

fourth round

Tuesday 31st
Kick-off 7.00 p.m.
Attendance 1,834

Red kids rush into last eight

On the day Lee Sharpe was allotted a central defender's role in order to provide cover for a not entirely fit Jason Lydiate against Ipswich at Old Trafford, the versatile teenager was also named in an England under-21 squad which was due to travel to Greece to take part in a friendly fixture the following week.

Now in charge of the national under-21's, former United boss Dave Sexton had monitored Sharpe's meteoric rise over the course of the season and saw fit to recruit him into the squad alongside colleague Russell Beardsmore. England manager Bobby Robson said of the call-up, *'It's a great tribute to him to be in the under-21's at his age, and he's going to be a good player.'* Despite Sharpe being forced to limp out of the senior Reds' F.A. Cup win over Oxford on the previous Saturday, his substitution was purely precautionary and any worries about him being unable to face the Portman Road side were dispelled well in advance of the game.

Plainly happy with the side's showing in their tough home encounter with Sheffield Wednesday, Eric Harrison elected to grant the emerging Simon Andrews a starting berth in the forward-line.

Taking time out from preparing his players for the match, Ipswich coach Bryan Klug told a reporter, *'It is a great chance for the boys to play against one of the biggest clubs in the country. Old Trafford is not a venue we play at week-in, week-out and this has added to the occasion.'* Klug also claimed, *'We are not frightened of anybody'* while Town captain Gavin Johnson added, *'By the sound of things they are a good side, but hopefully we can do the business.'*

Following the game, Klug's tone was considerably changed. Remarking how disappointed he was in the performance of most of his boys, feeling superior finishing by United cost his charges the result, Klug claimed, *'In Gavin Johnson I thought we had the best player on the pitch, but the rest of the team did not enhance their reputations.'*

The Ipswich Evening Star's Nick Garnham provided an honest match appraisal:

IPSWICH Town bowed out of the FA Youth Cup at the hands of mighty Manchester United at Old Trafford last night.

But there was no disgrace in losing by three clear goals to an impressive United side in front of 1,834 supporters as Town put up a brave performance.

Ipswich battled gamely against their illustrious opponents and can hold their heads up high on a night when they gave as good as they got in the second half.

It was Ipswich who were first to threaten when they almost took the lead after two minutes. Neil Currie played in Andrew Banks and he side-stepped two challenges before bringing Mark Bosnich to his knees.

United then settled down and Wayne Bullimore began to stamp his authority on the midfield and spray the ball about.

It therefore came as no surprise when United went in front in the 20th minute. Simon Andrews held off Chris Swailes and put Craig Lawton in the clear for the winger to surge forward and finish with a crisp cross shot giving Chris Neville no chance.

Lawton almost made it two in the 23rd minute after David Ellis had been dispossessed by Bullimore, but this time his shot went wide of the near post.

United increased their lead nine minutes before half time after Swailes had fouled the lively Andrews 25 yards out from goal.

Bullimore stepped up to curl a delightful left foot shot over the wall and beyond Neville to put his side in the driving seat.

Lawton the fast raiding winger then struck the outside of the post as United threatened to overrun Ipswich after he again got behind the Town defence following a slip by Gavin Johnson.

Ipswich came close to reducing the deficit right at the start of the second half when Bosnich was forced to dive full length to parry away Lee Honeywood's shot after he had been set up by Glyn Hooper.

But Ipswich fell further behind in the 52nd minute to a splendidly executed goal which started with Bullimore's ball out to Lawton on the left and when he reached the by-line and whipped over a cross to the far post, the unmarked John Shotton buried a firm header past Neville.

It was a cruel blow to Town who responded by withdrawing Hooper three minutes later and replacing him with Robbie Devereux while Currie dropped back to allow Johnson to push forward.

Devereux almost pulled a goal back with his first touch, Bosnich turning his fierce shot aside for a corner after good work by Johnson, before the visitors deservedly reduced the arrears in the 64th minute.

Swailes rose high to head powerfully down from Devereux's corner and Banks swung a leg but did not make contact as the ball crept beneath Bosnich.

Bosnich redeemed himself when he arched backwards to tip over Johnson's rising 20 yard right foot drive as Ipswich continued to have the lion's share of the play.

But with four minutes remaining Lee Sharpe, who had pushed forward into the midfield to wrestle the initiative away from Ipswich, headed home from close range after Andrews had unlocked the Town defence.

In summarising the youth team's progress so far, David Meek noted *'despite their inexperience they have mastered varying styles ranged against them. They beat the man mountains of Sheffield Wednesday in the previous round, and last night gave the classier footballing team from Portman Road a lesson in passing and finishing. Coach Eric Harrison has produced a tidy team which is competitive but relies on building good basic football'.*

An Ipswich move comes to nought as Lee Sharpe (number five), Wayne Bullimore (right) and Alan Tonge (far right) watch on

332

1) Ashley Bayes	9) Kelly Haag	1) Mark Bosnich	9) Simon Andrews
2) Matthew Howard	10) Andy Driscoll	2) Roger Sallis	10) Jonny Rödlund
3) Khotso Moabi	11) Marcus Gayle	3) Lee Sharpe	11) Craig Lawton
4) Jason Cousins	*12) Peter Sim*	4) Alan Tonge	*12) Tony Jackson*
5) Robert Larkin	*14) Steve Small (for 3)*	5) Jason Lydiate	*14) Kieran Toal (for 10)*
6) Paul Buckle		6) Lee Costa	
7) Brian Cronk		7) Wayne Bullimore	
8) Rob Peters		8) Darren Ferguson	

BRENTFORD 2 v 1 MANCHESTER UNITED

Larkin, Moabi — Lawton

MARCH 1989

Wednesday 1st

Kick-off 7.00 p.m.

Attendance 2,567

1988-89 — fifth round

With the business end of the season now fast approaching, the Reds learned that their Fifth Round task was an away tie at the ground of Third Division Brentford. It had been as long ago as 36 years since United's youth team last visited Griffin Park but, with an unbeaten run of 27 games behind them, it was obvious that the modern day Brentford juniors would take some stopping.

Part of that superb sequence of results included the eight previous Youth Cup matches the Bees had been involved in. Successive home wins over Kingsbury Town (7-0), Uxbridge (6-2), Hampton (4-1) and Wokingham (4-1) gave Brentford the opportunity to finally pit themselves against Football League opponents. Bournemouth put up some stubborn resistance before being defeated 3-2 at Dean Court and the Bees then claimed a slender 1-0 win against Crystal Palace back on home turf. Their Fourth Round opponents were Stoke City and following a 1-1 draw at Griffin Park, Brentford nudged past the Potters with a splendid 2-1 win at the Victoria Ground. Of the 28 goals scored in the competition, hot-shot Kelly Haag was responsible for no less than a dozen of them.

There was a heightened belief among the United squad that reaching the Youth Cup final wasn't an impossibility and Eric Harrison made a couple of changes to the formation in an attempt to ensure his boys would gain a positive outcome. Because of the return to full fitness of Jason Lydiate, Lee Sharpe once again proved his versatility when asked to slot in as a full-back. Sharpe displaced the previously ever-present Tony Jackson, who was relegated to the substitute's bench, and Jonny Rödlund was recalled at the expense of John Shotton.

United completely dominated the opening ten-minute spell and the Griffin Park side were only too glad to come out of it unscathed. The most obvious chance of that period fell to Rödlund, whose shot from just outside the box whistled over the crossbar of England Youth international goalie, Ashley Bayes.

Brentford then began to peek out of their shell a little and only a spectacular diving header from Simon Andrews threatened Bayes' clean sheet from then until half-time. Over that same period the Bees almost scored when Marcus Gayle brought a save out of Bosnich and Andy Driscoll nearly managed to net the rebound. Brentford followed up with another clear chance, Brian Cronk failing in his attempt to meet a Gayle cross, and in the 38th minute a Haag drive was caught by Bosnich after Larkin headed down a free kick.

Goalmouth incidents were just as infrequent after the turnaround, though Harrison's lads always appeared in control of their own destiny. There was no shortage of a competitive edge and the names of Jason Cousins and Alan Tonge were scribbled in the referee's notebook following an affray. Just when a replay began to appear as the most likely outcome, and with many supporters already heading towards the exit gates, the evening's real action began to unfold.

There were less than six minutes of normal time remaining when a dipping cross into Brentford's penalty area was palmed out by Bayes. The ball rolled out to the feet of United's Craig Lawton who, faced with two defenders guarding the goalmouth, calmly placed it over their heads and into the net for what appeared to represent a late and highly prized winner. The young Reds were understandably ecstatic, and their extensive celebrations could partly explain the astonishing events which followed.

Only two minutes remained when a foul was given against United. A huge free kick taken by Paul Buckle was launched diagonally from the deep right-hand side of the pitch into the Reds' penalty box, the ball finding Brentford's centre-back and skipper Larkin among a crowded cluster of players. Because his determination was greater than those immediately around him, Larkin was able to direct a looping header over Bosnich for an equaliser.

Sixty seconds later, the Bees clinched a most dramatic victory when another Larkin intervention, this time a well-intentioned through ball, dropped to the feet of Khotso Moabi. A left-sided midfielder who had been moved up the pitch in a tactical reshuffle about twenty minutes earlier, Moabi outpaced a marker and calmly drew Bosnich off his line before stroking the ball past him.

If United's goal celebrations were considered to have been slightly overcooked, they were nothing compared to the home side's gleeful demonstrations. As the crowd showed their appreciation and he responded by saluting them, each and every one of the Brentford side converged on Moabi and he soon found himself at the bottom of a heap of overjoyed colleagues. However, whereas they returned to their own half of the pitch for the scant few seconds that remained of the contest, the scorer lay motionless on the pitch. In all of the excitement, Moabi had almost been crushed by his team-mates and in the process he sustained a cracked collarbone. While he was being led off the pitch in agony, the whistle sounded to cue a standing ovation for the home side from those spectators still remaining.

Brentford youth coach Colin Lee tempered his delight when later saying, *'I was very pleased with the result. To beat any Manchester United team is a bit of a feather in the cap. The injury to Khotso, however, has put a bit of a dampener on the evening.'*

The atmosphere in United's dressing room was a dark shade of black, which perfectly reflected the mood of an incensed Eric Harrison. It was no wonder, as the very least the Reds should have taken from the game was a draw, and even that would probably have constituted a disappointing result. Harrison couldn't contain his anger, and a number of those involved later revealed the after-match roasting the coach dispensed that night was the most severe they ever encountered in football.

If anything positive could be taken from the events at Griffin Park, it was that reaching the quarter-final was a much improved achievement when compared to those of the past two seasons, and despite the outcome in west London, the early signs were beginning to show that Alex Ferguson's youthful revolution was well under way.

Craig Lawton, whose late goal at Griffin Park was quickly surpassed by Brentford

> *This tie was a scrappy game, on a poor Griffin Park pitch, with not much happening until the 84th minute. I can remember Craig Lawton volleying the ball into the roof of the net and me turning back towards our goal, fists clenched, thinking 'we've bloody pinched it!'*
>
> *There was a flurry of pressure from Brentford, resulting in a goal from a free kick. I remember a lad broke through on his own, (Roger) Sallis got a rollocking from Harrison for trying to play offside, resulting in the ball being prodded past Bosnich for the winner. The ball seemed to take an eternity to roll in.*
>
> *Couldn't believe it, defeat snatched from the jaws of victory!*
>
> *After the game, Ferguson and Knox went bananas and said that only me and Simon Andrews had come out of the game with any credit. The hairdryer was turned on full blast and I recall 'Sharpey' copping a verbal bashing. Knox told him he wouldn't play in the first-team again!*

ALAN TONGE

1989-90

1) Alvin Isherwood
2) Matt Hilton
3) Kurt Whipp
4) Richard Kay
5) Neil Howarth
6) Taras Seals
7) John Oliver
8) Paul Douglas
9) Graham Lancashire
10) Steve Mercer
11) Steve Eyre
12) Dennis Hill (for 7)
14) Paul Pemberton (for 3)

1) Mike Pollitt
2) Alan McReavie
3) Sean McAuley
4) Alan Tonge
5) Jason Lydiate
6) Adrian Doherty
7) Lee Costa
8) Paul Sixsmith
9) John Sharples
10) Colin McKee
11) Ryan Wilson
12) Peter Smyth
14) Chris Taylor (for 9)

JANUARY 1990

BURNLEY 1 v 4 **MANCHESTER UNITED**

Lancashire   Costa (2, 1 pen), Sharples, Wilson

Wednesday 3rd*

Kick-off 7.15 p.m.

second round

Kitted out in their change strip, United's youths are ready to do battle at Turf Moor
Back row (l-r) Peter Smyth, Chris Taylor, Colin McKee, Mike Pollitt, Paul Sixsmith, Ryan Wilson, Sean McAuley
Front row (l-r) Alan Tonge, Jason Lydiate, Lee Costa, Alan McReavie, Adrian Doherty, John Sharples

A later than usual start to the competition saw Mike Pollitt returning between the posts for the Reds at Burnley following his two-year absence from the youth team. United's under-18's had already won at Turf Moor that season, by courtesy of a solitary goal victory in the Lancashire Youth Cup, and expectations of a similar outcome in the national tournament abounded in the Old Trafford camp.

Pollitt was assisted in defence by a new full-back, Belfast's Alan McReavie, and he and Sean McAuley lined up in a back four alongside Alan Tonge and Jason Lydiate, the latter named pair continuing to form the Reds' central defensive partnership. Lee Costa also remained from the last campaign, and other than that it was all change. Costa was joined in midfield by Paul Sixsmith who, like Pollitt, was from Bolton, as well as John Sharples, a Bury-bred boy.

Eric Harrison was able to name two dashing wingers of whom those in the know were predicting great things. They were Adrian Doherty, a tricky flyer from Northern Ireland who normally operated on the right flank, and Cardiff-born Ryan Wilson, while heading the attack was Glaswegian Colin McKee.

A lack of experience in the forward and midfield sections was certainly a concern to Harrison, whose options were somewhat limited through being forced to contend with injuries to Darren Ferguson and Craig Lawton.

In his report the following day, David Meek could hardly contain his admiration for one particular individual:

There have been a good few George Best pretenders hailed over the years at Manchester United.......sparkling youngsters who have looked to have the master's magic. But something has always happened to stop them. Either injury or loss of appetite for the game or they simply failed to develop.

I have always hesitated to predict a new Best, but I have got to report there is a schoolboy on the horizon who could make a splendid player.

Ryan Wilson, still at school in Salford and just sixteen, has electric pace and a graceful skill which makes him one of the most exciting prospects I have seen for a long time. The young left-winger rescued United in last night's F.A. Youth Cup Second Round tie at Burnley.

Burnley punished the Reds for a sloppy start with a goal from Graham Lancashire in the 18th minute. The tie was wide open until Wilson crossed for John Sharples to equalise five minutes before the interval.

Wilson put United in front with a spectacularly driven goal in the 75th minute and it was all over. The bubbly Lee Costa converted a free kick and a penalty to see the Reds win comfortably 4-1.

The Clarets were good value for their goal as they looked much the more progressive and committed in the opening quarter of the tie. Once the curtain closed on that period, the United lads appeared to gel more and more as the minutes ticked by and Burnley raids diminished accordingly.

Sharples' goal worked wonders in terms of lifting the spirit of Harrison's charges and following a few words of motivation from the coach at half-time, performances went up another notch. Such was their level of dominance, the major surprise of the second period was just how long it took for the Reds to actually push their noses in front.

Burnley's Alvin Isherwood produced some very fine work before Wilson gave him no chance of saving with his goal fifteen minutes from the end. Frustration then got the better of the Clarets' Neil Howarth, who was booked for his troubles, prior to Costa ensuring United's passage to the next round with seven minutes to go.

Eric Harrison was both pleased and encouraged, especially in the knowledge that a couple of the older boys would soon come back into the reckoning, and Costa made his coach's smile stretch just a touch wider by converting a spot kick in the 89th minute of the match.

This game was originally scheduled for Monday, December 11th but was put back due to Burnley's seniors being involved in an F.A. Cup replay

1) Saxton Brown
2) Tony Bennett
3) Nicky Bedson
4) Rob Myatt
5) Chris Gillard
6) Ryan Kidd
7) Paul Moore
8) John Johnston
9) Chris Boswell
10) Brian Mills
11) Matthew Beeby
12) Nick Craig (for 6)
14) Paul Llewellyn (for 7)

1) Mike Pollitt
2) Alan Tonge
3) Sean McAuley
4) John Sharples
5) Jason Lydiate
6) Adrian Doherty
7) Lee Costa
8) Paul Sixsmith
9) Colin McKee
10) Craig Lawton
11) Ryan Wilson
12) Peter Smyth
14) Chris Taylor

PORT VALE 0 v 3 MANCHESTER UNITED

Costa (pen), Wilson (2)

1989-90

JANUARY 1990

Wednesday 17th

Kick-off 7.00 p.m.

Attendance 1,614

Just fourteen days since returning from Turf Moor, Eric Harrison took his squad off to Staffordshire in search of further Youth Cup progress at the expense of hosts Port Vale. Harrison brought the now recovered Craig Lawton back into the reckoning and switched John Sharples into the back four in order to replace Alan McReavie.

Due to various knocks, Port Vale were denied the use of three of their usual youth team members, David Lowe, Ian Banks and Paul Llewellyn, although the last named did manage to make the bench in the absence of any other viable options.

The Vale Park club elected to use the contest in order to test their impressive new computerised turnstile monitoring system. Installed at a cost of £20,000, the equipment displayed the number of spectators entering the ground onto a screen and the trial run was staged in the hope that the attendance would top four figures. Having already ousted Crewe and Blackburn from the Youth Cup before crowds approaching the 1,000 mark, the Second Division outfit's expectation wasn't considered overly optimistic.

On the afternoon of the game, Valiants' youth coach Steve Hunt, who was present when the young Reds demolished Burnley, aired a few views on United's performance at Turf Moor. *'They were the stronger side with extra know-how and they have a couple of individuals who need watching,'* he noted before adding, *'It will be a tough task but if the crowd get behind the lads it will make a big difference.'*

David Meek produced a brief match insight:

Manchester United had their second player sent off in five days when they knocked Port Vale out of the F.A. Youth Cup last night.

Alan Tonge was dismissed fifteen minutes from the end for retaliating with a heavy late tackle after some wild exchanges.

Ironically, the dismissal might have helped the Reds clinch their 3-0 win in a hard fought Third Round at Vale Park.

For just a couple of minutes later referee Boulton, perhaps conscious of the need to be consistent, awarded United a penalty for a tackle by Rob Myatt on Colin McKee.

The dependable, always busy Costa smashed the penalty home to ease growing concern in the United camp.

For United's three-goal margin flattered them. They had missed several chances in the first half and almost went off at the interval a goal down.

Star man Ryan Wilson sped to the Reds' rescue in the 57th minute to take McKee's pass and put United ahead.

The penalty made the game safe and just before the end Wilson got into overdrive again to score one of his specials.

The youngsters may find it harder in the Fourth Round at home against Sheffield Wednesday.

Costa was unluckily denied an early breakthrough when his shot banged against a post. The Vale players later breathed a collective sigh of relief after a Lawton attempt was cleared from their goal-line and in one of the home side's better first-half moves, Paul Moore managed to inexplicably scoop a close range effort over Pollitt's bar. Barely seconds before the break, and more in hope than expectation, United's goalie stuck out a foot to deflect a Chris Boswell shot to safety.

In what the (Stoke-on-Trent) Evening Sentinel labelled *'a curiously heated spell'*, Lydiate and Sharples were cautioned just prior to Tonge's dismissal. Within a flash, there was no coming back for the Vale Park youngsters when United increased their lead.

The Sentinel's match reporter concluded that Vale *'were no match for the young Red Devils, who could even afford to have a player sent off and win in comfort'*. It was also noted that in the last minute *'Wilson again raced clear on the left from inside his own half to hit the goal of the game'*.

third round

Goalie Mike Pollitt punches away a Port Vale effort while Sean McAuley (falling), Jason Lydiate (number five), Paul Sixsmith and John Sharples (partly hidden) show concern

1989-90

1) Mark Bosnich	9) Colin McKee
2) Alan McReavie	10) Chris Taylor
3) Sean McAuley	11) Ryan Wilson
4) John Sharples	*12) Mark Gordon (for 6)*
5) Jason Lydiate	*14) Jimmy Shields*
6) Paul Sixsmith	
7) Adrian Doherty	
8) Lee Costa	

1) Brent Gillings	9) Nicky Robinson
2) Mark Smith	10) Leroy Chambers
3) Ian Curry	11) Gareth Dunn
4) Richard Holmshaw	*12) Tony Foster (for 9)*
5) Mark Dickinson	*14) Paul Newton (for 11)*
6) Paul Burton	
7) Nigel Downing	
8) Ryan Jones	

FEBRUARY 1990

MANCHESTER UNITED 3 v 1 SHEFFIELD WEDNESDAY
Costa, Doherty, McKee — *Holmshaw*

fourth round

Thursday 8th
Kick-off 7.00 p.m.
Attendance 1,017

The Youth Cup wins over Port Vale and Burnley had fallen in what history reveals as a pivotal month for Manchester United. As the occupier of the Old Trafford driving seat for over three years, Alex Ferguson was coming under increasing fire from fans and press alike for the failures of the first-team because they hadn't managed to win a game in their last eight attempts leading up to early January. When the seniors took on Nottingham Forest in an F.A. Cup Third Round clash at the City Ground on the seventh of that month, the media were almost universally labelling it as the Scot's last game in charge should United suffer the ignominy of an early exit.

Ferguson has recalled on many occasions about the reassurances he received from chairman Martin Edwards prior to the Forest game, in that he was promised his job was safe no matter what the outcome was on the day. However, in view of the pressure Edwards might have come under, no-one can say for sure that he would have been in a position to honour his pledge.

It is the belief of many contemporary observers that Edwards' continued support of the manager stemmed from the faith, time and effort Ferguson had invested into the affairs of the club below senior grade. A rejuvenated scouting operation was already bearing fruit and a fresh outlook about the Reserves, in which former and current youth teamers were being given their chance to replace some of the 'dead wood' men who previously clogged up the system by occupying places in the second string.

Adrian Doherty was just one of Ferguson's new breed, and he made a great impression in the Youth Cup against Sheffield Wednesday when waltzing around three defenders to lob a shot onto the bar in the ninth minute. Such was United's dominance, just eight minutes later they took the lead. The goal was scored from outside the penalty area by Lee Costa following some smart build-up play, his shot finding the corner of Brent Gillings' net despite the goalie's desperate left-hand dive to stop it.

Even though Richard Holmshaw equalised in the 35th minute, not even watching former United manager and current Wednesday boss Ron Atkinson could

The irrepressible Lee Costa blasted the Reds ahead against Sheffield Wednesday

have believed his team would survive the Reds' onslaught. The main feature of the match was the inspired display of Doherty, who continually lit up the ground with a bedazzling array of skills which the visitors were bemused and befuddled by.

With the team members still inwardly digesting Eric Harrison's half-time team talk, the Reds went ahead again two minutes into the second period when Doherty delivered a cracking cross from the right and Colin McKee's thudding header proved too much for Gillings. Nine minutes later, Doherty turned goalscorer rather than provider by pouncing on a mix-up in the Wednesday defence to execute a crisp drive and give the Reds a two-goal cushion.

The teenage Owls created only one further opening, in the dying minutes, when Paul Newton delivered a long throw-in to Nigel Downing, the latter neatly controlling the ball and crossing only for Mark Dickinson to head wide. The miss was of no great consequence because, as the Sheffield Star's report conceded, *'by then it was all over.'*

There were a few words of wisdom in the Evening News, the publication calling the performance *'impressive'* and *'entertaining'*, and they centred on the contrasting fortunes of the seniors and those of Eric Harrison's teenagers:

Manchester United's depressed fans should get themselves along to watch the youth team. Not only would they see a winning side, but one which has turned back the clock to play two clever, jet-propelled wingers.

It's like a breath of fresh air to see Ryan Wilson streaking down the left and the smaller, but equally fast, Adrian Doherty running at defenders down the right. Both are still only sixteen with great skills as well as pace, and they bring a refreshing dimension to the game. While it may be difficult to appreciate Alex Ferguson's work at first-team level at the moment, his impact is looking good at junior level.

Colin McKee's corking header edged United back into the lead

1989-90

1) Mark Bosnich	9) Colin McKee
2) Alan Tonge	10) Craig Lawton
3) Sean McAuley	11) Ryan Wilson
4) Jason Lydiate	*12) Steve Carter (for 9)*
5) John Sharples	*14) Jimmy Shields (for 2)*
6) Adrian Doherty	
7) Lee Costa	
8) Mark Gordon	

1) Paul O'Connor	9) Alan Weldrick
2) Andy Jeffrey	10) Jason Peake
3) Iain Duncan	11) Martin Williams
4) Des Lyttle	*12) Jason Lannin (for 11)*
5) Steve Holden	*14) Robert Vassall*
6) Des Linton	
7) Gary Fitzpatrick	
8) Chris Moore	

MANCHESTER UNITED 2 v 0 LEICESTER CITY
Lawton, McKee

MARCH 1990

Monday 5th

Kick-off 7.00 p.m.

Attendance 3,451

fifth round

In welcoming Leicester's juniors to Manchester for the Fifth Round, memories surfaced of United's rather limp display against the Foxes at Old Trafford three years earlier. City were at full strength, apart from the missing Scott Oakes, who was ruled out by a nasty whiplash injury caused in a recent car crash. Striker Oakes, who had made his senior bow earlier in the season, was seen as a leading light for the Filbert Street side and his enforced absence was considered a big blow to the visitors.

Because the game was scheduled to take place on a Monday, Leicester brought forward their Midland Purity Youth League fixture at Coventry from Saturday to Friday in order to give their squad an extra day to recover. The young Foxes warmed up for their excursion to Stretford by hammering the Sky Blues 5-0 to put them miles ahead at the top of their division and odds-on to finish as champions.

Steve Carter was nominated as one of United's substitutes after completing a long recovery period with a broken leg, and Eric Harrison took a gamble by naming Craig Lawton in the starting eleven, even though the teenager hadn't played competitively since returning from a hamstring strain. As it so happened, Harrison's faith in the two paid off handsomely, as Carter acted as provider for Lawton, who headed home what the Review described as *'an absolute dream goal for which he received a standing ovation'* to practically seal the team's passage into the semi-final.

The following report appeared in the Leicester Mercury:

City went out of the F.A. Youth Cup at Old Trafford last night to a workmanlike United side that made clear its intentions from the start, with wingers Doherty and Wilson putting the City defence under early pressure.

The home team were rewarded after 22 minutes when a through ball to the left found Wilson, who crossed for the unmarked Colin McKee to turn a header beyond Paul O'Connor.

Jason Lydiate did everything expected of him from a defensive viewpoint only to finish the match in some obvious discomfort

City pushed themselves more into the game – but were punished again in the 40th minute when a cross from Carter was glanced home by Craig Lawton to give the home side a two-goal interval lead.

The second half threatened to follow the same pattern with O'Connor being called into early action by the lively home forwards. On the hour, City replaced Martin Williams with Jason Lannin in an effort to turn the game around. His first touch fed Iain Duncan on the overlap, whose strong run carried him into the area only for his parting shot to hit the side netting.

Leicester were having the better of the exchanges with efforts from Duncan, Lannin and Jason Peake charged down by the now desperate home defence.

Although they continued to press forward, City failed to make the breakthrough and Manchester progressed to the semi-finals thanks to their first half show.

As if Eric Harrison didn't have enough injury problems to contend with, as the lay-offs of Darren Ferguson, John Shotton and Kieran Toal testified, United's coach watched with mounting concern as a number of his side began going down like ninepins in the later stages. Harrison needed to replace Colin McKee because of a badly bruised shin shortly after the Scot put the Reds into the lead and he was then moved to substitute a struggling Alan Tonge.

Shortly before the final whistle sounded, spectators in a crowd which was more than treble the size in attendance at United's last Youth Cup tie also observed Jason Lydiate and Lee Costa were limping heavily. While the dressing room later gave the appearance of a World War One hospital tent, it was at least a happy place to be as the boys celebrated their passage into the last four stage of the tournament.

Full-back Sean McAuley's fourth Youth Cup appearance produced a second clean sheet and a satisfactory outcome

339

1989-90

1) Ian Walker	9) Ollie Morah	1) Mark Bosnich	9) Mark Gordon
2) Neil Smith	10) Anthony Potts	2) Alan Tonge	10) Craig Lawton
3) Warren Hackett	11) Scott Houghton	3) Sean McAuley	11) Ryan Wilson
4) Ian Hendon	*12) Greg Howell*	4) Paul Sixsmith	*12) Steve Carter (for 11)*
5) David Tuttle	*14) Stuart Nethercott*	5) Jason Lydiate	*14) Colin McKee (for 6)*
6) Vic Hardwicke		6) Lee Costa	
7) Lee Fulling		7) Adrian Doherty	
8) Kevin Smith		8) Darren Ferguson	

APRIL 1990

TOTTENHAM HOTSPUR 2 v 0 MANCHESTER UNITED
Hardwicke, Houghton

semi-final 1st leg

Wednesday 4th
Kick-off 7.30 p.m.
Attendance 1,354

Semi-finals were a recurring theme around Old Trafford when March moved into April. Most of the publicity was centred around the senior side, their achievements in the F.A. Cup meaning that they were looking forward to a meeting with Oldham at neutral Maine Road on the forthcoming Sunday with a place at Wembley at stake.

A 3-1 home defeat by Manchester City at the last four stage of the Lancashire Youth Cup nine days before meeting Tottenham Hotspur in the semi-final of the national youth competition wasn't viewed as ideal preparation for the Reds and in particular, the leg injury which led to John Sharples being carried off didn't bode at all well. Sharples' misfortune heaped yet another selection poser onto Eric Harrison, whose decision was to recall Paul Sixsmith and utilise Lee Costa in the back four. Now back on the scene and raring to go, Darren Ferguson returned to stiffen the midfield and it meant that despite scoring in both of his last two Youth Cup appearances, Colin McKee was forced onto the substitutes' bench.

'*Spurs are fancied to win the competition and are a powerful side*', Harrison stated prior to the opening leg at White Hart Lane. When asked about United's chances of reaching the final he added bluntly, '*We will have to play a lot better than we did against Manchester City.*'

Harrison's assessment of Spurs posing strong opposition wasn't misplaced as midfielder Scott Houghton, goalkeeper Ian Walker and defenders David Tuttle and Ian Hendon were regulars in the England under-18 side, the latter also currently acting as the national team's skipper.

After keeping a tight lid on Tottenham's attack throughout most of the first half, United wilted twice with dire consequences soon after the restart. In the 51st minute, Houghton opened the scoring for Spurs when he controlled Walker's mammoth clearance on the right prior to carrying the ball along the Reds' eighteen-yard line and ramming a fantastic shot past Bosnich.

Just minutes later it was double trouble for the Reds as Tottenham's Hardwicke and Smith created danger by making inroads into United's defence. Shrugging off the close attention of at least one defender, Hardwicke tore into the danger area to beat Bosnich with an unstoppable drive.

The Evening News picked up the threads of the game's remaining highlights:

MANCHESTER United's hopes of reaching the FA Youth Cup final for the second time in five years were dented at White Hart Lane last night.

United were unable to find their rhythm and were always second best in this first leg of the semi-final.

Some solid defending kept the score down but United will certainly need to improve if they are to make up the deficit in the second leg at Old Trafford on Monday night.

Neither side were able to gain the early initiative but it was Spurs who threatened first and United goalkeeper Mark Bosnich had to be alert to save Kevin Smith's well directed header in the 12th minute. Seven minutes later, central defender Lee Costa was forced to stretch to intercept Lee Fulling's right wing cross with striker Ollie Morah closing in.

United's best chance came in the 27th minute when Craig Laughton created a good opening for himself but his 25 yard shot was well saved by Ian Walker.

Spurs' goals came in four minutes at the start in the second half from Scott Houghton and Vic Hardwicke.

United right back Alan Tonge was booked in the second half for a dangerous challenge on Houghton.

Eric Harrison brought Paul Sixsmith back into the fold for the trip to White Hart Lane

Mark Gordon filled the number nine shirt against Tottenham while the previous wearer of that jersey, Colin McKee, dropped out of the starting line-up

340

1) Mark Bosnich
2) Alan Tonge
3) Sean McAuley
4) Paul Sixsmith
5) Jason Lydiate
6) Lee Costa
7) Adrian Doherty
8) Darren Ferguson
9) Colin McKee
10) Craig Lawton
11) Ryan Wilson
12) *Steve Carter (for 9)*
14) *Mark Gordon*

1) Ian Walker
2) Neil Smith
3) Warren Hackett
4) Ian Hendon
5) David Tuttle
6) Vic Hardwicke
7) Lee Fulling
8) Kevin Smith
9) Ollie Morah
10) Anthony Potts
11) Scott Houghton
12) *Greg Howell (for 6)*
14) *Stuart Nethercott*

MANCHESTER UNITED 1 *(1)* v *(3)* 1 TOTTENHAM HOTSPUR
Doherty — Fulling

1989-90

APRIL 1990

Monday 9th

Kick-off 7.00 p.m.

Attendance 2,874

semi-final 2nd leg

Youths go down fighting

After building up what they viewed as a reasonably healthy lead to bring to Old Trafford, Tottenham secured the draw that booked the place they coveted in the 1990 Youth Cup final.

There was an urgent need for firepower on United's behalf and so Eric Harrison reinstated Colin McKee in the hope that the striker would be able to put a goal or two on the scoreboard.

On a rain sodden pitch, the Reds set about the Londoners with much gusto and on chances created they could have been at least back on level terms by half-time. Even a later Tottenham matchday magazine report noted that United *'dominated'* and *'played magnificently before the interval'*, a period in which the home side *'should have had two or three goals'*.

In the opening quarter of an hour alone, McKee missed a great chance when shooting over from only a few yards out and Ryan Wilson then held his head in his hands as his drive hit a post. McKee made amends after 24 minutes when threading a pass through for Adrian Doherty to latch onto. With so much open space in front of him, the Ulster boy was always going to be hard to catch, and he raced away to place the ball wide of Ian Walker and into the net just before Spurs' full-back Warren Hackett was able to get in a tackle.

Tottenham were certainly in all sorts of trouble at the back and they didn't look half the side that had made such easy work of beating the Reds at White Hart Lane. McKee could have significantly added to their problems when he spurned the opportunity of an equaliser from a position of promise but on this occasion, Walker came out on top through leaving his line quickly enough to smother the forward's goal attempt.

Of the early period of the match, former England goalkeeper and current Tottenham Reserves' coach Ray Clemence admitted, *'We were a little fortunate to be only one goal down at half-time because United could easily have been well ahead at that stage.'*

Spurs emerged a different side at the interval and rarely encountered much in the way of genuine danger after that. Indeed, from being under the cosh for most of the first 45 minutes, it was they who perhaps posed the majority of threats from then on. Sure, the Reds continued to search for a second goal, only their momentum was stifled by a more organised set of opponents and their attacks were much less potent.

Just six minutes from time, the visitors placed a definite reservation for the final with a fine equaliser. Following an excellent solo run by Anthony Potts, which saw him fly past three United defenders, a cross came in that Lee Fulling hit high and hard past Bosnich at the far post. With that, the outcome was all done and dusted.

Eric Harrison rightly showered his charges with prolonged and sincere praise for all of their efforts. Well aware of the disruption caused by so many injuries, as well as the lower than average age level of the squad, the coach was content in the knowledge that his lads couldn't have done much better.

As events transpired, the Reds were beaten by the eventual winners of the tournament, Spurs justifying their reputation as favourites by defeating Middlesbrough 3-2 on aggregate in the final.

Adrian Doherty was much too quick for the Tottenham defence prior to scoring for the Reds

Mark Bosnich was beaten by a late Lee Fulling goal which finally ended any hopes the United lads held of reaching the final

1990-91

1) Adrian Swan	9) Lee Ellison	1) Ian Wilkinson	9) Colin McKee
2) Darren Roulston	10) Francis Robinson	2) Alan McReavie	10) Ryan Giggs
3) Lynford Reynolds	11) Jason Weightman	3) Les Potts	11) Simon Davies
4) Sean Gregan	*12) Michael Priest (for 11)*	4) Mark Gordon	*12) Marcus Brameld*
5) Richard Cooper	*14) Vince Ravenhall (for 6)*	5) Jimmy Shields	*14) John O'Kane*
6) Tony Isaacs		6) John Sharples	
7) Kevin Bulmer		7) Adrian Doherty	
8) Simon Shaw		8) Peter Smyth	

NOVEMBER 1990

DARLINGTON 0 v 6 MANCHESTER UNITED

Davies, Giggs (4), McKee

Monday 26th
Kick-off 7.00 p.m.
Attendance 544

second round

Contained in his notes in United's 1990 Yearbook, chairman Martin Edwards mentioned that the previous season *'finished on a most satisfactory note'* because of the success of Alex Ferguson's seniors in capturing the F.A. Cup that May, and he went on to mention two of the club's youth products who had made big contributions towards the achievement.

Mark Robins got the show on the road with a fine headed winner at Nottingham Forest in January and added to his burgeoning reputation by firing the goal which pushed United into the final with an extra-time clincher in a marathon semi-final bout against Oldham. Lee Martin later indelibly wrote his name into the club's folklore when smashing in a 59th minute winner in a replayed final tie against Crystal Palace to give Ferguson his first major trophy in England, a triumph which opened up the floodgates for the glories of the next twenty-odd years.

Edwards rightly thanked Ferguson and all of those associated with the win at Wembley as they had *'suffered a great deal of criticism when things were going badly'*, and he added a few words about the F.A. Cup run being *'just reward for a tremendous amount of hard work, most of which has gone on quietly behind the scenes and has been directed on strengthening the club at all levels'*.

The chairman then went on to make specific mention of some of the fruits of Ferguson's labours:

Whilst naturally, all eyes have been focussed on the first-team players, we have seen a significant improvement in results with our Junior teams and I express special congratulations to the youngsters responsible for winning the Lancashire League Division One trophy – yet again.

The boys also won the Grossi-Morera International Youth Competition in Italy, the North-West Youth Tournament held locally, and finished runners-up in the Northern Ireland Milk Cup Youth Tournament.

Just a few weeks into the new season, an announcement was made about Joe Brown relinquishing his position of youth development officer in order to take up a part-time job which would see him shouldering the welfare needs of the many youngsters associated with the club. One of the first appointments made by Dave Sexton back in 1977, Brown's latest appointment followed on from his time as youth team coach and then as chief scout. The 61 year-old's previous position was filled by Brian Kidd, himself a distinguished former graduate of the youth team, who was to assume total responsibility for United's scouting and development affairs.

While also transferring from his duties with the 'B' side, it was stated that Kidd would remain as a director of the club's School of Excellence. Upon Kidd's elevation, another ex-Red, Nobby Stiles, took over the running of the 'B' team.

The changes demonstrated that Alex Ferguson placed great faith in the hard working and popular Kidd and his promotion was seen as a reward for all of the success he had achieved with his work in the community on United's behalf. It was also obvious the club were seeing numerous signs of progress as far as attracting top-notch junior talent was concerned and in view of how difficult it had been to set the wheels in motion in the first place, Ferguson was clearly intent on keeping them rolling.

Two years after making their first Youth Cup visit to Feethams, Eric Harrison's boys were again required to travel to the North-East home of Darlington Football Club, a game for which the coach seized the opportunity to introduce four rookie youngsters into a tie they were expected to win without something to spare. United's new goalkeeper was Ian Wilkinson, and he and Simon Davies were formerly of Cheshire Boys. Les Potts came to the club with the experience of representing Trafford Boys behind him while Peter Smyth (pronounced 'Smith') had featured on the international stage for Northern Ireland Boys.

There was also another new name on the team sheet, that of Ryan Giggs. Previously known as Wilson, it was the first time young Ryan appeared in the Youth Cup under his new surname. The change of moniker came about as a result of the Salford-based teenager taking his mother's maiden name after the divorce of his parents and so the tie against the Quakers actually represented his seventh appearance in the competition.

On the day of the match at Darlington, Giggs was only 72 hours away from his 17th birthday and the Old Trafford coaching staff were already talking in terms of them having unearthed a genuine diamond. Kidd and Stiles were both on record as saying he was the finest prospect they had seen since George Best and the manager demonstrated his complete agreement by convincing the board to tie the youngster to a long-term deal as soon as he was able to sign as a professional at the age of seventeen.

Ferguson couldn't contain his excitement at the development and claimed of the club's newest sensation, *'He is the best I have ever had at this age. If he keeps his head he has a marvellous chance and I have had no hesitation offering him a five-year contract.'*

Giggs certainly lived up to all that was expected of him, and more, at Feethams. Switched into a central striking role, he plundered a personal haul of four goals and constantly caught the eye with his pace, control and movement.

The opener came after just five minutes when a mammoth kick from 'keeper Wilkinson skidded along the soaked turf. Giggs demonstrated the quickest reaction, as well as the swiftest feet, and made the art of goalscoring look all too easy by knocking the ball past a wrong-footed Adrian Swan between the Darlington sticks.

Colin McKee later swivelled to shoot against a post, the home side responding likewise when Francis Robinson evaded the Reds' offside trap.

On the half-hour, Simon Davies looped a sweet effort past Swan from a distance of 25 yards and Giggs then put the Reds into an unassailable lead just before the break when he picked up another big clearance. The long punt put Darlington's defence in a tizz and Giggs pounced to round Swan and stroke the ball into the gaping net.

A few minutes into the second half, Giggs made it three for him when more misunderstanding in the Quakers' defence led to an opening he could hardly miss. Soon after, the home supporters were able to cheer a 'goal' by Lee Ellison, only the whistle was sounded for an offside decision several seconds before his effort crossed the line.

Twelve minutes from the end, Giggs registered again with what the Review called *'a virtuoso goal which brought applause from everyone in the ground'* and Colin McKee put the polish on a wonderful evening's work with a final goal to complete the scoring at 6-0.

A day later, the Northern Echo's headline proclaimed 'RYAN ROUTS QUAKERS', and the newspaper's view about the Reds enjoying practically *'complete superiority'* was certainly no exaggeration.

Once a Wilson, always a Giggs

1990-91

1) Ian Wilkinson	9) Colin McKee
2) Alan McReavie	10) Ryan Giggs
3) Les Potts	11) Simon Davies
4) Jimmy Shields	*12) Marcus Brameld*
5) John Sharples	*14) John O'Kane*
6) Mark Gordon	
7) Adrian Doherty	
8) Peter Smyth	

1) Ian Walsh	9) David Gouldstone
2) David Wilson	10) Chilton Coy
3) Iain Jenkins	11) Mike McDonough
4) John O'Neill	*12) John Doolan (for 6)*
5) David Unsworth	*14) Kenny Woods*
6) Brendan Turner	
7) Billy Kenny	
8) Chris Priest	

MANCHESTER UNITED 1 v 1 EVERTON
Doherty — McDonough

JANUARY 1991

Thursday 3rd

Kick-off 7.00 p.m.

Attendance 1,618

third round

Youth welfare officer Joe Brown holds court before several of the club's young prospects at The Cliff
Back row (l-r) Colin McKee, Jimmy Shields, John Sharples, Ian Wilkinson, Mark Gordon, Jonathan Stanger
Front row (l-r) Les Potts, Marcus Brameld, Peter Smyth, Alan McReavie

The United kids were forced into a much tougher assignment than the Darlington tie had posed when a 1-1 Third Round home draw with Everton was marked by tremendous strikes from both sides and as many as half a dozen bookings, including four for the visitors.

Unlike many seasons past, when the bulk of the Reds' youth team mainly consisted of personnel drawn from the ranks of the 'A' side, the under-18 squad was primarily selected from those mostly performing at Lancashire League Division Two grade for the visit of the Merseysiders. The 'B' team lads were experiencing a decent rather than outstanding campaign, with seven wins and five draws from their fifteen completed matches.

Of the three games in which no points were forthcoming, two were against the 'A' teams of Blackpool and Bury, which indicates they probably faced older and more knowledgeable opponents, as well as the 'B' representatives of their latest Youth Cup opponents.

Because there was seemingly little or nothing to find fault with in relation to the performance at Feethams, Eric Harrison stuck with precisely the same eleven who were in action there, and he also went as far as naming the same two substitutes.

United's goal came in the 19th minute when a mistake by Everton's Iain Jenkins resulted in him being dispossessed. The ball was picked up by Adrian Doherty, who sprinted fully 40 yards before blasting a fabulous shot past Ian Walsh to bulge the Toffees' net. Walsh despairingly managed to get a glove on the ball, only for the sheer force of Doherty's drive to take it past him.

There was much to admire from the two sets of players, with a few flashes of technical ability on display and bags of spirit and graft to indicate a desired level of commitment, though for most of a match curiously described as *'thrilling'* by the Liverpool Daily Post, there wasn't too much to get hot and bothered about in either penalty area.

One of the two main exceptions to that general rule occurred sixteen minutes after United's opener when Everton levelled with a goal which was practically a carbon copy of Doherty's. With full-back Les Potts caught in two minds just inside the Everton half, possession was forfeited to Blues' number eleven Mike McDonough.

Following a direct and determined run, and with three or four defenders in close pursuit, McDonough welded expert technique to a calculated presence of mind and chipped the ball calmly over an advanced Ian Wilkinson to notch a mightily impressive equaliser.

Right from the start of the second half, the marking from both sides tightened up yet another notch and for most of that period chances were thin on the ground. The majority of the rest of the action occurred in the final few minutes as United tried their hardest to avoid a replay they hadn't bargained for.

Described by one newspaper as *'a one-man show'*, the impressive Walsh provided a final barrier which the Reds were unable to breach as he pulled off superb late stops from John Sharples, Mark Gordon and Adrian Doherty. When he was finally beaten, a relieved Walsh got the rub of the green his performance perhaps deserved as Potts' shot was kicked off the line by the industrious David Wilson, who was singled out by Toffees' coach Jim Barron as *'the best player on the park'*.

The Manchester Evening News' David Meek produced his usual match summary, with his notes rather untypically ending on a note of pessimism, some of which read:

Manchester United's youngsters must have felt they were running into a brick wall in the F.A Youth Cup Third Round at Old Trafford.

Everton, a big strong side, used their muscle to good effect to bulldoze a draw. The Goodison giants gave the Red youngsters a rude awakening after their six-goal spree at Darlington in the last round.

United finished with commendable effort considering their younger team and created several chances. Everton are going to be a formidable side to beat in the replay at Goodison Park.

343

1990-91

1) Ian Walsh	9) David Gouldstone	
2) David Wilson	10) Chilton Coy	
3) Iain Jenkins	11) Mike McDonough	
4) John O'Neill	*12) Craig Dulson (for 7)*	
5) David Unsworth	*14) Kenny Woods (for 10)*	
6) Brendan Turner		
7) Billy Kenny		
8) Chris Priest		

1) Ian Wilkinson	9) Colin McKee	
2) Alan McReavie	10) Ryan Giggs	
3) Les Potts	11) Simon Davies	
4) Jimmy Shields	*12) Marcus Brameld (for 9)*	
5) John Sharples	*14) John O'Kane*	
6) Mark Gordon		
7) Adrian Doherty		
8) Peter Smyth		

JANUARY 1991

EVERTON 1 v 2 MANCHESTER UNITED
McDonough   Giggs, Smyth

Thursday 10th
Kick-off 7.00 p.m.

third round replay

Clearly sensing a need for the youth team to gel more effectively than they did against Everton at Old Trafford, Eric Harrison's solution was to turn out his entire under-18 side at 'B' standard less than 48 hours after the Merseysiders headed for home. The indications for a vastly superior performance and a favourable result in the Youth Cup replay were there for all to see when the 'B' team slammed Blackpool 'A' 3-0 with goals from Adrian Doherty, Mark Gordon and Colin McKee, and so Harrison took an identical thirteen to his former place of employment at Goodison Park the following Thursday.

While cup replays often offer up a different take than an initial knock-out tie, the game in Liverpool 4, which was noted as being *'tense'* in that city's Daily Post newspaper and *'a tight affair'* in the Review, proved that normal rule of thumb wasn't always the case.

It did, however, get away to a brilliant start for the Reds because with only five minutes gone, Ryan Giggs capitalised on a defensive error to slam the ball over goalie Ian Walsh's shoulder as he dived in vain to his right to block it. Only a few moments later, the same player missed an easy opportunity to put United 2-0 up when directing what appeared to be a simple header past an upright.

United's defence, which was superbly marshalled by a dominant captain in John Sharples, wasn't unduly troubled in the first half but came under increasing pressure after the tea break. The stand-off which had developed during the majority of the second half of the Old Trafford contest continued throughout most of the remainder of the match, and there was little in the way of genuine goalscoring prospects.

Then, just like the proverbial red buses, two came at once.

In the 81st minute, Mike McDonough punished United again when he nodded in an accurate cross to make the score 1-1. It appeared the contest might well go into extra-time, and with Everton buoyed by their equaliser, United's immediate prospects didn't appear that great.

Thankfully, the outlook of doom only lasted for a moment or two because immediately from the restart, the young Reds swept like a tidal wave to the other end of the pitch where a right-wing cross from an adrenalin-charged Doherty picked out fellow countryman Peter Smyth. Leaping like a salmon, the Ulster boy had everyone on the United bench on their feet and jumping up and down with delight when he headed firmly beyond Walsh for a cracking, dramatic winner.

All bar a couple of the Everton team moved forward in an attempt to bring parity back to the score, and when the whistle sounded several nail-biting minutes later, there were hugs and smiles amongst all of the Old Trafford delegation on what was a difficult job well done.

The Daily Mirror's cartoonist sees the funny side of Alex Ferguson's accent on youth in the United Review

344

1) Bob Holcroft	9) Andy Howard	1) Ian Wilkinson	9) Colin McKee
2) Steve Walsh	10) Stuart Gelling	2) Alan McReavie	10) Ryan Giggs
3) Dominic Matteo	11) Andy Roscoe	3) Les Potts	11) Simon Davies
4) Kevin Lampkin	*12) Robbie Fowler (for 7)*	4) Jimmy Shields	*12) Marcus Brameld*
5) Mark Kenny	*14) Rod McAree (for 8)*	5) John Sharples	*14) Andy Noone*
6) Barry Brownbill		6) Mark Gordon	
7) Alex Russell		7) Adrian Doherty	
8) Ian Horrigan		8) Peter Smyth	

1990-91

LIVERPOOL 1 v 3 MANCHESTER UNITED

Kenny (pen)   Giggs, Gordon (pen), McKee

FEBRUARY 1991

Tuesday 5th

Kick-off 7.00 p.m.

Attendance 1,155

fourth round

Boy Reds storm in

United's reward for their success on a tough trip to Merseyside was.......another tough trip to Merseyside, where Eric Harrison was able to name an unchanged side for the fourth successive time.

The Reds had already fulfilled all of their Lancashire League fixtures against Youth Cup opponents Liverpool and remained undefeated, the 'A' team drawing their away match 1-1 while slamming the Merseysiders 5-1 at The Cliff. The 'B' side had played out a stalemate during their home fixture before managing to pick up maximum points by securing a welcome 2-0 away victory.

Even so, Eric Harrison would have made it quite clear to the players that the form book never won a game for anyone and those past achievements would be of absolutely no assistance at all to them at Anfield.

A Manchester Evening News staff reporter was on hand to make a record of another rewarding piece of work carried out by the Reds:

Manchester United swept into the quarter-finals of the F.A. Youth Cup last night.

The scoreline barely did justice to United's massive control and superior teamwork, even though they struggled briefly in the second half after Liverpool had scored a penalty. United had match-winners in strikers Colin McKee and Ryan Giggs, who grabbed a goal apiece. And central defender John Sharples was a towering obstacle for the Liverpool forwards.

McKee shot United ahead in the 24th minute after Sharples had back-headed an Adrian Doherty corner. It was no more than United deserved after a bizarre, 16th minute incident when Giggs was denied a goal by a linesman after his shot, half saved by Bob Holcroft, appeared to trickle over the line.

United emphasised their superiority 40 seconds into the second half when Barry Brownbill handled and Mark Gordon slammed a penalty past Holcroft.

Liverpool could offer little in reply, although Alex Russell went close after a long, tricky run and Ian Wilkinson saved from Andy Roscoe.

But, in the 56th minute, Andy Howard went down under a Sharples challenge. Ian Horrigan's penalty was saved but it had to be retaken and Mark Kenny made no mistake.

Liverpool sensed an upset and briefly United became disjointed. But they pulled themselves together and sealed victory in the 84th minute with a Giggs solo goal.

Even the Liverpool Echo identified United were *'powerful'* at Anfield before singling out Colin McKee as *'ever-threatening'*. The Echo's sister newspaper, the Daily Post, gave an indication that United could have inflicted more damage than they did on the home side when recording Liverpool were *'indebted to 'keeper Bob Holcroft'*.

> *I had a good partnership with John Sharples, who would run through brick walls, attack the ball and win headers. I was more of a technical player, bringing the ball out of defence and covering for John.*
>
> *As a United fan from a young age, I always knew about the rivalry with Liverpool and even at youth level we didn't want to lose. We fancied our chances as we had a decent team, were doing well in the league and also in the Lancashire Youth Cup, so we certainly didn't fear them.*
>
> *Eric Harrison just told us to get stuck in, win our individual battles and that our teamwork would get the result.*
>
> **JIMMY SHIELDS**

While United's goalscorers were accorded most of the praise for the win at Anfield, the performances of goalie Ian Wilkinson (top) and midfielder Peter Smyth were no less impressive

345

1990-91

1) Colin Hopkins	9) Christian White	
2) Kevin Phillips	10) Gareth Taylor	
3) Nicky Good	11) Steve Roast	
4) Paul Tisdale	*12) Neil McKilligan (for 4)*	
5) Jason Peters	*14) Scott Wright (for 9)*	
6) Matthew Bound		
7) Lee Powell		
8) Neil Selby		

1) Ian Wilkinson	9) Colin McKee	
2) Alan McReavie	10) Ryan Giggs	
3) Les Potts	11) Simon Davies	
4) Jimmy Shields	*12) Marcus Brameld (for 7)*	
5) John Sharples	*14) Andy Noone*	
6) Mark Gordon		
7) Raphael Burke		
8) Peter Smyth		

MARCH 1991

SOUTHAMPTON 0 v 2 MANCHESTER UNITED

Giggs, Smyth

Friday 22nd
Kick-off 7.00 p.m.
Attendance 1,976

fifth round

It's Ryan's slaughter!

Way back in 1957, Southampton were the first team to defeat Manchester United in the Youth Cup and 34 years further on their current youth coach, Dave Merrington, attempted his utmost into talking the newest batch of teenage Saints into another famous victory.

Merrington's mood was bullish when telling his local newspaper, *'We won't worry about United – let them worry about us. This is our game, our big night at The Dell and we are going all out to win it. You can have all the tactics in the world but I am more interested in seeing our players go out and put into practice everything they have worked at. They have put in a huge amount of work and tomorrow night they will all know their jobs.*

If we don't win no-one will be able to say we have not had a right go. We won't talk about United or their set pieces or how they play. If we are right, we can do them. But win, lose or draw, United will have a hard game.' Merrington ended defiantly by saying, *'If we can just get through this tie, the cup is there for the taking.'*

Southampton hopes rested heavily on the scoring prowess of Neil Selby, already with 21 goals to his credit, and striking partner Christian White. Winger Lee Powell, whose form had merited call-ups to the Saints' first-team squad, as well as a substitute spot for the Wales 'B' team, was expected to provide a plentiful supply line for Selby and White.

There was a massive blow for United on the injury front. Apart from Eric Harrison being unable to travel due to illness, Adrian Doherty had suffered a wicked knee injury since the Youth Cup tie at Anfield and his place was taken by Bristol-born Raphael Burke. It was a serious setback for Doherty, one of the leading lights of the youth side throughout the season, as he wasn't expected to regain full fitness for some considerable time.

The Dell crowd witnessed a rather drab opening half which was mainly notable for the monotonous offside trap employed by the home side along with their inability to turn the vast majority of possession into more than one scoring opportunity. Such was United's resolute defensive barrier, the only save Ian Wilkinson needed to make was from an overhead shot by Southampton's White.

Events started to turn United's way soon after the break, and just four minutes into the second period they were handed the lead on a platter when a clumsy collision between Saints' defenders Kevin Phillips and Jason Peters resulted in the ball running loose. Colin McKee was only required to beat the goalkeeper but instead unselfishly stroked the ball into the path of the overlapping Ryan Giggs, who calmly rolled it into the empty net. Despite vehement Southampton protestations that the scorer was offside, the goal was allowed to stand.

The Saints continued to see more of the ball than United, yet worthwhile chances still continued to elude them. Then, with the electronic scoreboard displaying time played as one minute over the allotted allocation, Giggs was fouled by Nicky Good barely a few feet outside Southampton's eighteen-yard box and perhaps feeling somewhat downhearted by this stage, a number of the home side reluctantly formed a human wall near to the penalty spot. It was left to Peter Smyth to curl a low free kick around their screen of five and just inside the far post to give the Reds a somewhat flattering 2-0 winning margin.

Saints' coach Dave Merrington encapsulated his side's efforts when later commenting, *'I couldn't have asked for greater commitment but we couldn't unlock the door in the last third of the pitch.'* Summing up the Southampton angle, the Southern Evening News noted, *'After scoring seventeen goals in four games to reach the quarter-finals, the young Saints became shot-shy and ended up losing a match they could have won'.*

John Sharples (number five), Simon Davies (centre, facing), Jimmy Shields (jumping) and Colin McKee (right of centre, facing) in action at The Dell

1990-91

MARCH 1991

fifth round

United skipper John Sharples puts in a tackle while Alan McReavie (left) tracks back

John Sharples (far left), Marcus Brameld (left), Mark Gordon (number six) and Simon Davies (right) surround Southampton's Christian White

1990-91

1) Paul Robinson	9) Nicky Robinson	1) Ian Wilkinson	9) Colin McKee
2) Brian Linighan	10) Leroy Chambers	2) Alan McReavie	10) Marcus Brameld
3) Gareth Dunn	11) Richard Curzon	3) Les Potts	11) Simon Davies
4) Ronnie Simpson	*12) Jonathan Flint*	4) Jimmy Shields	*12) John O'Kane (for 7)*
5) Simon Stewart	*14) Mark Simmonite (for 4)*	5) John Sharples	*14) Ben Thornley (for 10)*
6) Paul Burton		6) Mark Gordon	
7) Michael Rowntree		7) Raphael Burke	
8) Ryan Jones		8) Peter Smyth	

APRIL 1991

SHEFFIELD WEDNESDAY 1 v 1 MANCHESTER UNITED
Curzon — *Sharples*

semi-final 1st leg

Monday 8th
Kick-off 7.00 p.m.

By the time the Youth Cup semi-final rolled around, the United boys were already assured of a place in the Lancashire Youth Cup final and in order to make another showpiece appearance in the national tournament, they would have to overcome Sheffield Wednesday.

Wednesday hadn't been blessed with the best of fortunes against United in the Youth Cup and, in fact, could count only one previous victory over the Reds, which was back as far as 1963 at Hillsborough. United were also able to brag of good recent form against their opponents as they had eliminated the young Owls from the competition in each of the last two seasons. If the Reds could complete a hat-trick of successive wins over their foes from the steel city, a place in the final against either West Ham United or Millwall was theirs.

During their current cup run, Wednesday had beaten Bury by four goals to one at home in the Second Round prior to knocking out Aston Villa 3-2 in Birmingham. A Fourth Round defeat of West Brom, by 2-1 at Hillsborough, then saw Wednesday enter into something of a marathon with Hull. A 1-1 home draw was followed by an identical scoreline at Boothferry Park, and a third game back in Sheffield finally saw Wednesday through by a convincing 5-1 margin.

After the unwanted news of Adrian Doherty's fitness woes prior to the match at Southampton, Eric Harrison was further rocked by the realisation that Ryan Giggs would be unavailable against Sheffield Wednesday due to a hamstring injury picked up in training. Giggs' deputy was Marcus Brameld, whose starting role followed on from his two previous Youth Cup appearances as a substitute.

The Sheffield Star printed the main aspects of the action, most of which was reserved for the tail-end of the proceedings:

Sheffield Wednesday last night came within inches of taking a two-goal lead into their F.A. Youth Cup semi-final second leg at Old Trafford on April 18.

They hit the post in the last minute when leading 1-0 and Manchester United survived that scare to score an injury-time equaliser which makes them favourites to reach the two-leg final.

Wednesday led with a 70th minute goal at the Leppings Lane End by left-winger Richard Curzon, who forced the ball home at the near post after a tremendous run and cross by danger man Leroy Chambers.

There was an exciting finish to an evenly fought tie which was watched by League Cup final rivals Ron Atkinson and Alex Ferguson.

United substitute John O'Kane had a header cleared off the line by left-back Gareth Dunn in the 89th minute, then striker Chambers burst through to hit the post in the last minute.

And in the first minute of time added on for stoppages, United's Peter Smyth played a free kick to the edge of the box and captain and centre-half John Sharples hooked a dipping shot onto the roof of the net.

Still the drama was not over. In the third minute of injury-time another goal-line clearance by Dunn kept out a second header by O'Kane.

There was a chance for each side in the first half, United midfield player Smyth side-footing over the bar and Wednesday centre-forward Nicky Robinson heading wide from a cross by the bustling Chambers.

United striker Colin McKee made one brilliant run in the second half to be denied by 'keeper Paul Robinson. The forward then poked the rebound wide.

Flying winger Raphael Burke, reminiscent of a young Danny Wallace, proved a handful at times but, despite flashes of quality from United, the Owls looked a tidy outfit and cannot be written off yet.

The Review reckoned the Reds were *'livelier and more purposeful than a Wednesday team packed with young giants'* and also remarked *'our youngsters, with a slice of luck, could have made Thursday's second leg a formality'.*

Then noting that it *'seemed inconceivable'* United could end up losing *'a match which for so long they had controlled'*, the Review correctly viewed the draw *'as an excellent result at this stage of the competition'.*

All prepared and hungry for a place in the Youth Cup final, pictured above is the team that took on Sheffield Wednesday at Hillsborough
Back row (l-r) Jimmy Shields, John Sharples, Ian Wilkinson, Mark Gordon, Simon Davies, Colin McKee
Front row (l-r) Raphael Burke, Peter Smyth, Les Potts, Marcus Brameld, Alan McReavie

1990-91

1) Ian Wilkinson	9) Colin McKee	1) Paul Robinson	9) Nicky Robinson
2) Alan McReavie	10) Ryan Giggs	2) Brian Linighan	10) Leroy Chambers
3) Les Potts	11) Simon Davies	3) Gareth Dunn	11) Richard Curzon
4) Jimmy Shields	*12) Marcus Brameld*	4) Ronnie Simpson	*12) Jonathan Flint*
5) John Sharples	*14) Ben Thornley (for 7)*	5) Simon Stewart	*14) Mark Simmonite*
6) Mark Gordon		6) Paul Burton	
7) Raphael Burke		7) Michael Rowntree	
8) Peter Smyth		8) Ryan Jones	

MANCHESTER UNITED 0 (1) v (2) 1 SHEFFIELD WEDNESDAY
McReavie (o.g.)

APRIL 1991

Thursday 18th

Kick-off 7.00 p.m.

semi-final 2nd leg

Two days after the first leg of the Youth Cup semi-final, United's 'B' team drew their last Lancashire League match of the season with Crewe. Only one member of the squad who had extracted a draw from the Hillsborough tie was involved against the Railwaymen, midfielder Simon Davies joining the fray as a substitute.

It meant that the majority of them were allowed ten days to prepare for the crunch meeting with the young Owls, a game that would decide which of them was to claim a place in the final.

With Ryan Giggs declared fit once more and home advantage seen as crucial, the Reds were heavily favoured to achieve their objective but, against all the odds and to their eternal credit, the Wednesday lads stuck at their task to secure the outcome they craved in a most dramatic fashion.

On a pitch which proved heavy going, honours were fairly even for the first fifteen minutes, a period in which there was quite a bit of shadow boxing and both sides won a couple of corners. United then gradually gained the upper hand until the visitors rallied to make their own imprint on the match.

In the 27th minute, a Brian Linighan centre was collected by Ian Wilkinson, who was challenged by Sheffield's Ryan Jones. Wilkinson spilled the ball into the net on contact with the Wednesday player only for the referee to rule that a foul had been committed. The away side then began to look the more potent for a time and efforts from Leroy Chambers and Richard Curzon were only just off the mark, United replying with an attempt by Giggs which was competently saved by a steadfast Paul Robinson.

The Reds again came to the fore after the intermission and scoring opportunities started to fall their way more and more frequently. Colin McKee headed a Ben Thornley cross over the top when finding the net appeared to be a mere formality and Robinson was then called on to make further stops from Sharples and Giggs.

Wednesday were unable to make any inroads into United's defence throughout this section of the game and it was fifteen minutes from the end before they won their first corner of the second period. After 83 minutes, Owls' defender Simon Stewart made a superb sliding tackle to thwart Giggs in a dangerous situation and then, with the seconds ticking away, Simon Davies was similarly denied as the Reds frantically searched for an elusive winner.

Whether those openings represented chances missed or attacks repelled depends on whether they were viewed from a defensive or offensive viewpoint, yet within a short period of time any distinctions didn't count a jot.

With three minutes of added time already passed and both sides mentally preparing themselves for another half an hour of toil, Wednesday's Nicky Robinson accepted a pass from colleague Chambers. Striding forward unchallenged for ten yards before attempting a hopeful shot, his effort appeared harmless enough before cannoning off a United defender. The deflected direction of the ball completely wrong-footed 'keeper Wilkinson before it nestled in the back of the net, and as the stark reality of defeat hit them like a hammer blow, a number of the young Reds dropped to their knees in anguish. With barely enough seconds on the clock for the restart, the referee blew for full-time and the groans echoing around the ground told the sorry story that United were out.

There were the expected quotes in the press of the Reds being *'cruelly robbed'* and such like but, in all fairness, Wednesday were due some praise for standing up to United's prolonged onslaughts and based on the two legs as a whole, they had carved out a number of openings for themselves.

Ritchie Barker, assistant manager at Hillsborough, could do little other than to admit the deciding goal was lucky before hinting at the cause of the Reds' defeat when advising that scorned chances aren't always down to bad fortune. David Meek concurred with Barker when writing *'the United youngsters have only themselves to blame for wasting a string of golden opportunities'*.

On the following Sunday, Alex Ferguson's seniors were beaten 1-0 by Sheffield Wednesday in the Rumbelows Cup final at Wembley courtesy of a John Sheridan strike. It represented a magnificent result for the Yorkshire club but later, in the national youth final, the Hillsborough juniors were defeated by three goals to nil over two legs by Millwall.

There was some consolation for the boy Reds later that month as nine of those who started against the young Owls conquered Preston by a 2-0 margin at Deepdale to secure the Lancashire Youth Cup, the goals coming from Brameld and McKee.

The often polarising fortunes of footballers was demonstrated within a short period of time when the match against North End acted as a parting gesture for a number of the Old Trafford youths. While Ryan Giggs added to an earlier senior substitute appearance by marking his full first-team debut with the deciding goal in a home encounter with Manchester City in early May, just weeks later his erstwhile team-mates Marcus Brameld, Alan McReavie, Les Potts, Jimmy Shields and captain John Sharples found their names on the club's annual list of released personnel.

Ben Thornley, who made substitute appearances in both legs of the semi-final

> Having managed to draw the first leg we were confident of progressing to the final. We dominated the game and just couldn't deliver that killer goal. We hit the post, the bar, had shots cleared off the line and I felt extremely nervous because of what was at stake. Many youth teams before us had failed to deliver and this was our chance to not only make a bit of history but also to help secure our contract extensions.
>
> It was the last minute of normal time and their winger delivered an early cross from the right, our back four moved up just outside the eighteen-yard box. The cross struck Alan McReavie's heel and buried itself in the bottom corner of our goal. It felt like an emptiness that I had never experienced before. I felt alone and deflated. The ball was respotted and the referee immediately blew the final whistle. For most of us this signalled the end of our contracts and dreams. That goal has haunted me throughout the years and I have always pondered....... 'What if?'

LES POTTS

349

HOGG, Graeme James (1980/81, 1981/82)

Born: Aberdeen, 17th June 1964
Height: 6ft. 1in., **Weight:** 12st. 4lbs.
Role: Central defender
Career: Woodside Primary School (Aberdeen)/ Powis Academy (Aberdeen)/ St. Machar Academy (Aberdeen)/ Aberdeen & District Boys/ **UNITED**: App. July 1980 Pro. June 1982 to August 1988/ **West Bromwich Albion** (L) November and December 1987/ **Portsmouth** August 1988/ **Heart of Midlothian** August 1991/ **Notts County** January 1995/ **Brentford** January to May 1998/ **Linlithgow Rose** November 1998 to May 1999

It took three years and six months from the time Graeme Hogg originally signed for United for him to be given a first-team berth and over the next four and a half seasons he compiled 109 appearances in all senior competitions. Biding his time in the Reserves over the first half of the 1983/84 campaign, the pendulum swung dramatically in his favour after Gordon McQueen was crocked in a game at Anfield and with Paul McGrath also on the injured list, in January 1984 he was finally handed a first-team jersey for a surprise Third Round F.A. Cup defeat at Bournemouth. He did enough to retain his place, and over that month and the next he was taken on separate trips with the seniors for challenge matches in Algeria and Libya.

A brave, willing and dependable stopper, his style could accurately be described as strongly competitive, and he was particularly difficult to beat in the air. Now and again lacking grace on the deck, nevertheless the left-footer's burly, no-nonsense approach was usually appreciated by those around him.

By the age of fourteen he had joined Aberdeen Lads Club and quickly attracted the attention of Harry Yorston, the ex-Aberdeen and Scottish international forward, and Jack Buchanan, United's scout in North-East Scotland. Present for trials on three occasions in Manchester while also training at Pittodrie in the evenings from Monday through to Thursday, his ability came under the scrutiny of Dons' coaches Bobby Clark and Lennie Taylor. No formal offer ever came from Aberdeen, who were then managed by a certain Alex Ferguson.

Chosen for Aberdeen Boys, the solid-framed defender trialled at Middlesbrough, for whom he competed in a game against Durham Juniors. United eventually made their move to obtain his services late in the day, by offering him an apprenticeship shortly after his 16th birthday.

Beginning like so many before and since, his competitive club debut for United 'B' heralded the opening day of a new season, the 16th August 1980, and following a scoreless draw at Bury he was promoted up a step after taking part in just one further 'B' team fixture. In early December he was invited into the Youth Cup squad, seeing action in each and every tie as the Reds reached the semi-final, and also got in a full complement of five Lancashire Youth Cup appearances.

The 1981/82 term was similar to the last in the respect that he was mainly utilised at 'A' level. During the campaign he was named as captain of the Youth Cup team that reached the final where, after a titanic struggle, they succumbed to Watford. Alongside the exciting cup run, the young Scot put in some masterful displays in the junior sides and was pegged up to the Central League in March 1982 for a 3-1 win at Stoke.

Partnering Billy Garton for most of the time, he started the challenge of the 1982/83 season in the Reserves. However, with defenders of the calibre of McGrath, McQueen, Martin Buchan and Kevin Moran all hustling for first-team places, it was clear he still had some impressing to do in order to make further progress. Even so, the lad was moving forward and he felt privileged to be involved at a level where his football education could only improve by performing alongside the likes of a masterful old hand like Buchan.

The benefit of his dedication and the lessons learned paid off when Ron Atkinson gave him his senior baptism at Dean Court, and in just his third league game Hogg scored his one and only goal for the Reds when toe-poking a corner into Birmingham's net at St. Andrews.

Less than two months after his first-team debut, in a 2-0 European Cup Winners' Cup defeat at Barcelona in March 1984, he had the misfortune to turn a cross from Carrasco into his own goal while otherwise putting in a solid performance.

Again demonstrating great defensive qualities as the Reds went on to retrieve the tie in the second leg by way of a famous 3-0 victory at Old Trafford, he also came up against Juventus in both legs of the semi-final when the Reds were unluckily defeated 3-2 on aggregate. He was involved in first-team affairs until the end of the 1983/84 campaign and his expanding success story gained another chapter when he was selected for Scotland's under-21 side which faced Yugoslavia in the European Championships.

By now a first-team regular, barring injury he was a constant presence at number six throughout the 1984/85 term while on the international scene, three additional Scottish under-21 caps were awarded for his efforts against West Germany, Iceland and Spain. Disappointingly, that extended spell of achievement was spoiled when a groin injury sustained in the penultimate league game at Queen's Park Rangers kept him out of the 1985 F.A. Cup final, even though he had helped out in most of the previous rounds.

Hogg performed in the Charity Shield and the opening nine games of the following season when, firstly, his back was injured and he then damaged knee ligaments. Sidelined throughout most of the first three months of 1986, upon recovering he found himself in the Reserves again while either Garton or Mark Higgins took one of the senior central defensive roles alongside McGrath.

He registered three appearances for the Reserves at the start of the 1986/87 campaign and had forced his way back into the senior side when, in November 1986, Ferguson replaced Ron Atkinson. The new man gave him just five games before dropping him for what remained of the term.

The situation was unchanged in his final season with United as he was seemingly not rated by Ferguson and needed to rely on injuries in order to get a sniff at senior grade. In a bid to gain some first-team football, a month's loan was arranged at West Brom and he contributed seven league appearances while at The Hawthorns. With the Albion keen to take him on a permanent basis, the next major development occurred back at Old Trafford when Steve Bruce arrived in December 1987.

The Scot realised then that his United prospects had disappeared entirely and despite seeing service in nine further league and three cup matches in the second half of the term, he was now considered a fringe player and even featured as far down as the 'A' team.

His last appearance for the Reds generated mixed emotions. Used as a substitute in a 4-1 home win over Portsmouth on the 7th May 1988, there was much sadness and an equal amount of relief on his part.

Numerous clubs wanted him, but his previous injuries proved a hindrance. He was offered terms at Manchester City, failing the medical because of a problem with his pelvis, and then discussed a move to Sheffield Wednesday. Even after passing a medical at Hillsborough, the Owls considered the asking price was too high.

In the early part of August 1988, a £150,000 deal was agreed with Portsmouth and under manager Alan Ball he enjoyed the best period of his career. At the end of his three-year contract with Pompey, for whom he made precisely a century of Second Division appearances, Hearts came in with a £200,000 bid and, ignoring the defender's preference to remain on the south coast, the chairman rubberstamped the deal when taking a shine to the size of the cheque.

Commencing in August 1991, his spell in Edinburgh wasn't particularly pleasing from a personal perspective because he couldn't retain a place in a side in which Scottish internationals Craig Levein and Davie McPherson vied with him for places.

He was persistently dogged by an achilles injury for much of his time at Tynecastle and in 1994 he was involved in the infamous 'double red card' incident, which came about when his criticism of Levein during a pre-season friendly at Raith prompted a violent reaction. Levein responded by breaking his nose in an ensuing brawl and the pair were then dismissed, Hogg leaving the pitch on a stretcher. Both earned hefty bans from the Scottish Football Association, with the Aberdonian's extending to ten games over three months, and that sorry situation signalled the end of his relationship with the Jam Tarts.

Charlton Athletic showed some interest in signing him until, with discussions regarding terms well underway, a recurrence of his achilles injury necessitated an operation. Upon regaining fitness, in January 1995 Notts County agreed to buy him for a £70,000 fee. Still plagued by injury, mustering only 66 league games in three years, his days at Meadow Lane were one constant struggle for fitness and when Sam Allardyce took over, the manager's mission to minimise the wage bill meant that he found himself surplus to requirements.

In January 1998, Brentford agreed to take over the remainder of his contract. He squeezed in 25 games at Griffin Park and, after winning the 'Man of the Match' award on three consecutive Saturdays, the club offered him a one-year deal, despite their relegation. Unfortunately, before the contract could be signed, the controversial Ron Noades took over and Hogg was again without a club.

A trial at Northampton in the summer of 1998 proved a waste of time so he went back to Scotland and began training at Falkirk. With his professional career at an end, part-timers Linlithgow Rose provided him with a modest platform for six months. Described as *'immense'* by a local scribe, his competitive streak was still to the fore for the Rose, which resulted in three dismissals as the club captured the East Region League.

Now working as a heavy goods driver, an article in the United Review in September 2010 mentioned that his son, Connor, was involved at Falkirk's Academy.

FERGUSON, Darren (1988/89, 1989/90)

Born: Glasgow, 9th February 1972
Height: 5ft. 10ins., Weight: 11st. 10lbs.
Role: Midfielder
Career: **Culter Primary School** (Aberdeen)/ **Cults Academy** (Aberdeen)/ **Aberdeen**/**Wilmslow High School**/ **UNITED**: Trainee July 1988 Pro. July 1990/ **Wolverhampton Wanderers** January 1994 to March 2000/ **Cosenza Calcio** (It) (L) December 1998/ **Sparta Rotterdam** (Hol) (L) January to April 1999/ **Wrexham** (L) September 1999 to March 2000/ **Wrexham** March 2000 to January 2007

Alex Ferguson was offered the job of managing Manchester United in November 1986, a development which didn't only change his and the Reds' future, but also that of his wife and three sons.

When Cathy Ferguson bore twins in the winter of 1972, Darren was smaller than Jason as he had a touch of jaundice and required the support of an incubator for a short period. All three boys would show ability as footballers, although Darren was considered to be easily the most talented. Eldest son Mark, a centre-forward who possessed an above average technique, had featured in Aberdeen's second string while Jason also preferred to operate upfront. More robust, in the mould of his father, after representing Scotland Boys Clubs, Jason featured in United's junior teams without any real success.

Darren was styled in a completely different fashion to that of his brothers and he allied calm composure with a passing style which married accuracy and creativity. A highly dependable midfielder who leaned heavily towards the constructive rather than destructive side of the game, at a young age he played for Culter Boys Club in the Aberdeen & District Juvenile League and was also on the books of Aberdeen. Having lived in the 'Granite City' since he was six, his father's new job forced him to leave the area he had known for most of his life at a time when he was working through the later stages of high school education and another major consequence of moving from Scotland was his omission from international schoolboy trials.

It wasn't long after venturing south that he began to attract the interest of a number of English clubs. With one newspaper noting that Nottingham Forest had made a move for the fifteen year-old who was described as *'a player of great potential with local Cheshire side, Wilmslow Sports'*, he undertook a trial at Spurs before the opinion of senior United backroom staff duo Archie Knox and Brian Kidd convinced his dad that keeping him in Manchester was the right thing to do.

His first effort for the Reds was as a substitute in the 'B' team's 5-2 home victory against Formby 'A' on the 12th September 1987, with an opening start following against Crewe two weeks later. The latter match threw up a club curiosity, as part-way through it he was replaced by none other than his twin Jason. Taking part in another nine games as the 'B' team finished second in the division, he then signed as a trainee in the 1988 holiday period.

During his first full campaign with the club he alternated between United's junior teams, starting out with the 'A' side in August and then dropping a level from October through to February. In the middle of that period with the 'B' team he was drafted into the Youth Cup side for an opening round tie at Darlington. With Wayne Bullimore unavailable for the following game against Sheffield Wednesday, he acquired the armband for the night, although it was swiftly relinquished for the replay upon the regular captain's return.

The young Scot returned to 'A' team duties in March and less than two weeks later he made a significant leap up to the Central League when replacing Simon Hutchinson in a 2-1 home victory over Liverpool. Then taking at least some part in five out of the Reserves' remaining eight fixtures, and while not quite in overdrive, his United career had certainly shifted up a couple of gears.

Like many aspiring footballers before and since, following a splendid previous term he found the 1989/90 season much more of a slog as, following a return to the Reserves, injury woes set him back to the extent that he was forced to spend October in the 'A' team. One particular medical problem grew more serious and the surgery it necessitated sidelined him until mid-March. As a consequence he missed most of the Youth Cup campaign, returning to face Spurs in a semi-final that was lost on aggregate.

The breakthrough many expected of him came in the next term when his displays in the Reserves resulted in him knocking hard at the first-team door. With United's midfield failing to achieve any type of consistency, in February 1991 he was named as a substitute for a First Division match at Sheffield United and replaced an immobile Neil Webb on the half-hour mark. Despite losing the game by the odd goal in three, his contribution warranted a full debut against Everton the following week and on this occasion, in front of 45,656 fans at Old Trafford, the Reds were defeated 2-0.

It was also during that season when he was selected for Scotland's under-21 side for matches against the USA, Poland and Yugoslavia, while three more senior appearances were added in an exceptionally fertile period in his development.

Ferguson was a member of the first-team squad that toured Norway prior to the 1991/92 campaign and while over there he took part in all three matches against Strømsgodset, Viking Stavanger and Molde. Also utilised in a full complement of four senior friendlies that August, it came as no surprise when he was selected for the opening First Division fixture, a home engagement with Notts County. One further first-team appearance was added before he returned to the Reserves but, most annoyingly, injury sidelined him again from October right through to February. Finding it tough to get back into the senior reckoning as the Reds aimed to claim the league for the first time in over a quarter of a century, once the title challenge had fallen away he was recalled in late April.

He was commandeered for all bar one of United's warm-up fixtures prior to the 1992/93 term and then found himself a regular for the seniors as they set out in the newly-formed Premiership, doubly determined to make up for the disappointment of the previous season. Present for the first fifteen league games before making way for the returning Bryan Robson, the Glaswegian could hardly contain his disappointment as he felt that his form warranted keeping a place in the team. By the end of the campaign his appearances tally ensured that he collected a winner's gong, while the curse of not capturing the league title for so long was finally laid to rest.

Also adding to his Scottish honours with games against Switzerland and Malta at under-21 standard, all wasn't as rosy as it seemed because, after being dropped earlier in the term, he had experienced some difficulty by being under the control of his father. Competing with Robson and Paul Ince for a midfield place was hard enough and, in the days before squad rotation, the signing of Roy Keane in the summer of 1993 didn't auger well for his prospects. It was then when he informed Ferguson senior of his requirement for a change of environment and it soon became common knowledge that he was on the lookout for new employment.

Rangers were reportedly on the verge of offering him the chance of a fresh start after Archie Knox informed the Glasgow giants that he was available for transfer. 'Gers manager Walter Smith watched him in the opening of the Reserves' 1993/94 fixtures at Blackburn, where an untypically under par performance meant that the opportunity was destined to pass him by. Despite collecting another medal as a non-playing substitute for the Charity Shield win over Arsenal, he gamely continued in United's Reserves while remaining on the periphery of the senior scene.

When Wolves manager Graham Turner approached him with a view to moving to Molineux, it appeared that the chance he desperately wanted had finally come. The Wanderers were flying high at the top of Division One and most observers felt that it was only a matter of time before they would return to the top flight. So, in January 1994, a transfer fee of £250,000 made him Wolves' property.

His time at Molineux didn't get off to the best of starts as Turner was replaced just two months after the new signing's arrival. Initially a regular in the Wolves midfield under new boss Graham Taylor, with the team struggling to put up the strong promotion challenge anticipated, the natives began to get restless. In November 1995, Taylor was replaced by a temporary appointment and just a month later Mark McGhee took over. Having to serve four managers, all with their own styles and in a spell of only eighteen months, didn't help him to integrate and it was hardly surprising that results were equally inconsistent.

Ferguson was forced to undergo a hernia operation in January 1997 and soon resumed in the club's second side. His relationship with McGhee had become a little strained by then, and when Colin Lee took over the reins in late 1998, with well over 100 appearances for the Wanderers behind him, he decided to seek out new territory.

Surprisingly joining Italian Serie 'B' side Cosenza on a trial that ran to a week and a half, it began in bizarre circumstances as he needed to flee for his life when a mob of angry supporters stormed the club's training ground on his very first day. The fans were incensed about the dismissal of coach Juliano Sonzongni, the man who had invited him over, and riot police were called in as the training session ended in complete farce.

Still out of favour at Molineux, in January 1999 his continued thirst for regular first-team football led a Dutch agent to organise a three-month loan to Sparta Rotterdam for him and he arrived in Holland in early February. His Sparta debut against F.C. Utrecht took place eleven days later and he went on to participate in twenty league and cup games for the club.

Now out of contract, a trial with Preston in September 1999 resulted in him playing for their Reserves at Burnley and later that same month he dropped into Division Two to join Wrexham, initially on loan. Robins boss Brian Flynn had been chasing him before his Dutch excursion and finally secured his signature on a two and a half year contract in March 2000.

By the following January the Welsh club had rejected a £400,000 offer that would have taken him to Wigan and the very next month they handed him a two-year contract extension. He assisted the Robins to a Division Three promotion in 2003 and captained them in an LDV Vans Trophy final triumph over Southend at the Millennium Stadium a couple of years later.

Looking to the future by getting involved at Wrexham's School of Excellence, in early 2006 he took over the coaching of their under-14 side having carried out similar work with their junior teams for four years. He also negotiated all of his UEFA coaching qualifications while often being labelled the *'best player outside the top two divisions'*.

Now nearing the end of his playing days, he craved a new challenge rather than suffering a style of football that often bypassed the midfield altogether, and his last game for Wrexham, of over 300, was an F.A. Cup tie at Derby in January 2007.

When a managerial vacancy arose at Peterborough that month, and his 35th birthday within touching distance, Ferguson was ready, willing and able to take the task on. Following a telephone interview with the Posh's chairman which lasted for an hour and a half, the Aberdonian took over the reigns at London Road with the security of a four-year contract.

His achievement in guiding Peterborough to two successive promotions and into the second tier of English football was described by former Posh owner Barry Fry as *'miraculous'*, though it didn't prevent his dismissal in November 2009 with the club at the foot of the Championship table.

Placed in charge at Preston two months later, he was sacked for the second time in just over a year in December 2010 following a string of poor results. Only two weeks went by before Ferguson was reinstated at Peterborough and he steered the club back up to the Championship in 2011 via a 3-0 play-off victory over Huddersfield at Old Trafford.

SHARPLES, John Benjamin (1989/90, 1990/91)

Born: Bury, 26th January 1973
Height: 6ft. 1in., **Weight:** 11st. 3lbs.
Role: Central defender or midfielder
Career: Holcolme Brook Primary School (Bury)/ Woodhey High School (Ramsbottom)/ Bury Boys/ Greater Manchester Boys/ UNITED: Ass. Schoolboy February 1988 Trainee June 1989 to June 1991/ **Sheffield Wednesday** (L) May to June 1991/ **Heart of Midlothian** July 1991/ **Ayr United** July 1994/ **York City** March 1996 to August 1998

A big, strong physical force out on a football field, John Sharples was renowned for his inherent leadership qualities and a tireless work ethic on behalf of the team cause. While proficient enough in aerial combat, he was much better known for his robust tackling, an asset that made him a serious customer to come up against. In possession his preference was to seek advantages by bringing the ball under control so that he could pass it on to a colleague.

Having come to the attention of Joe Brown, he joined United's School of Excellence when aged eleven, from which point he trained at The Cliff twice weekly. Attached to the club for the next seven years, fitness issues hampered his progress to the extent that he was released in 1991 through failing to bridge the gap from the 'A' team to the Reserves.

Sharples had been involved in competitive football via a link with Ramsbottom United in the Bury Amateur League, his talent ensuring that he was selected to represent Bury Boys at the under-11 grade. As captain of the town team he lined up alongside future professionals Chris Makin and Trevor Sinclair and continued with Ramsbottom in Sunday morning fixtures, usually in a central midfield position, until school leaving time. Gaining further football honours with Bury Boys at under-14 and under-15 levels, he also represented Lancashire at cricket from under-13 to under-15 stages.

When speaking of his early experiences as a Red, he recalled, *'I played for a United junior side against a touring China Youth XI in March 1988 and the following season I was chosen for Greater Manchester Boys. That same season I played six times in United's 'B' team and we won Division Two of the Lancashire League.'*

Taken on as a trainee in 1989, the sixteen year-old was soon assisting the youth team to the final of the Milk Cup. A groin strain forced him to exit the match early and the condition was severe enough to cause his absence from the start of the new term. The set-back seemed to be nothing to lose any sleep over, though later events would show that it was an early manifestation of the problems which were to follow.

When the Youth Cup draw paired United with Burnley in January 1990, he was given the chance to prove his adaptability. *'I wore the number nine shirt at Turf Moor but actually played in midfield'*, he pointed out. *'I was put back in defence in the later rounds and I then got an ankle ligament injury in an 'A' team game which prevented me from playing in the semi-final matches against Spurs.'* That initial campaign was considered to be one of reasonably steady progress, with annoying lay-offs preventing him from showing any true consistency.

The 1990/91 term was to be another mixed one for the Bury teenager because it turned into a constant battle against ankle, hamstring and groin problems. Beginning the second and third games in the 'B' side, Sharples was soon back in the reckoning for the 'A' team and when a new assault on the Youth Cup started in November, he was bestowed with the captaincy. Creditably ousting some top sides en route to the semi-final, not making it a step further was a massive personal disappointment as he relished the honour and responsibility of leading the team. With the 'A' side already crowned as Lancashire League champions, he lifted the Lancashire Youth Cup following a victory at Deepdale, although any immediate joy was tinged with regret as by then he was aware that his association with United was at an end.

When discussing about how events panned out from then on, he revealed, *'Eric (Harrison) contacted the F.A. in a bid to find me a new club and I went for a trial at Sheffield Wednesday. I got a run out in a few of their 'A' team games as well as accompanying them on a tour of Switzerland. Even though I had another knee injury, I was offered a two-year contract by their manager, Ron Atkinson. Peterborough, Barnsley and Bury were all interested in me, but I accepted a better deal at Hearts. (Manager) Joe Jordan had seen me in action and matched Wednesday's offer of a two-year deal.'*

With yet another knee problem to contend with in the build-up to the campaign, he soon began featuring regularly for Hearts' Reserves. Unfortunately, things didn't go according to plan for the Edinburgh club under Jordan and when he was replaced in May 1993, Sharples found himself even further away from senior action. Having never appeared in Hearts' first-team, and unable to create a suitable impression on the new manager, by the 1994 close season he had returned home to Lancashire.

That July, Ayr United came up with a two-year professional contract for him. The 21 year-old was installed as the Scottish Division One club's captain and spent nearly two years at Somerset Park before York City targeted him with a £75,000 transfer bid. Needing a swift injection of cash, Ayr accepted the offer, which was a club record for a defender at that time.

Signing for York on deadline day and once more named as the team's skipper, a continuation with his knee problem necessitated an operation and meant that he was required to spend the summer of 1997 on crutches. Despite regaining his fitness for the pre-season preparations, another breakdown caused him to miss most of the following campaign and, unable to recover sufficiently, in August 1998 he was forced to call it a day.

In an attempt to give his life new impetus he enrolled at college and qualified as a training instructor. Also completing his UEFA 'B' coaching badge at Leeds United, for a time he worked as a personal trainer in a gym.

One last crack at football came about when he undertook a trial at Telford in July 1999. Sadly, after just one pre-season friendly, the realisation that his knee wouldn't stand up to the strain of regular competition was obvious and in order to continue in some type of sporting activity he began participating in local cricket around York. John Sharples moved to Falkirk to commence employment in a gym in 2002 and was last heard of working for the local council, as well as studying to be a social worker.

GARTON, William Francis (1981/82, 1982/83)

Born: Salford, 15th March 1965
Height: 5ft. 11ins., **Weight:** 11st. 8lbs.
Role: Central defender
Career: Trafford Road Junior School (Ordsall)/ Ordsall High School/ Salford Boys/ Lancashire Boys/ UNITED: Ass. Schoolboy April 1980 App. May 1981 Pro. March 1983 to May 1990/ **Birmingham City** (L) March and April 1986/ **Salford City** June 1992/ **Witton Albion** November 1993 to May 1994/ **Hyde United** October 1994 to May 1998/ **Salford City** November 2000 to May 2001

Of all those who have made the grade at Manchester United, Billy Garton's story is unique. Not because of what he did or didn't achieve in the game, but where he came from allied to the era in which he played. While there have been a few Salford lads who have developed through the ranks at Old Trafford in the post-war period, the likes of Eddie Colman, Harold Bratt, Peter Jones and Phil Bardsley were all present during eras of success, whereas he suffered through a time of domination by Liverpool.

'I can't remember the first game I went to as a kid, but I recall matchdays vividly,' he claimed. 'Because I lived in Ordsall, people would park their cars in our street. I used to ask, 'Can I mind your car, mister?' in an effort to scrape together enough money to get into the game. Sometimes I could and sometimes I couldn't, but I could see the lights of the stadium from our house and I knew what the score was by just listening to the crowd. Then I would sneak in with twenty minutes to go when they opened the gates.'

Now able to look out over the beach and Pacific Ocean from his home in San Diego instead, he went on to say, 'I was born in Hope Hospital and lived all my life in Salford. My uncle, Henry, was a very good footballer and played for Salford Amateurs. They say he could have been a professional but he was happy to play locally. At first I just played for Trafford Road Juniors and then when I was about nine I joined Salford Lads Club. It was a good team and I knew everyone as we played on the streets together. I wasn't a defender in those days, I played in midfield or upfront. I suppose I must have been half decent because the really good sides kept asking me to join them.

Barr Hill and Deans Youth were the best teams about, but I was happy just to play with my mates. Then when I was about fourteen, I joined Barr Hill just for one season and also got selected for Salford (Boys). A few clubs became interested in me, Everton, Birmingham City, and I also had two weeks at Blackpool. Then one day after a match for Salford, (coach) Eric Walker introduced himself to my dad and asked if I fancied joining United. My father wasn't a football man but he was incredibly supportive, so when he told me about United I was so excited. It was just beyond my wildest dreams.'

The Reds' interest came in 1979/80, a term in which United at last put in a realistic challenge to take the First Division title away from Liverpool. Garton was taken on as an associate schoolboy in the April of that campaign and, now part of the family, he could hardly contain himself at the prospect of meeting his great idol, Martin Buchan.

With all the enthusiasm that a Red Salfordian could muster, his first effort for the club came in August 1980 when, wearing the number four shirt while lining up at centre-half, his 'B' side kept a clean sheet in a draw at Bury. 'I hadn't played much at centre-half as a kid,' he noted. 'When you are young you tend to play anywhere in order to get a game. I enjoyed my first season playing in defence and always thought I was comfortable in that position. I was a thoughtful player, quite big for my age but also fast and athletic with good control. I was never into raw-boned crunching tackles. The coaching staff saw me more as a sweeper and that's why they put me in defence.'

The following week he was drafted into the 'A' side, only to experience the difference between local or schoolboy football and the professional game when Bolton defeated the Reds 5-2. Turning out solely for the 'B' team from then on, predominantly in central defence or on a handful of occasions at left full-back, they finished the term in the lower part of the league table.

He impressed in the opening 'B' fixture of the 1981/82 campaign, a 3-2 win at Southport, and to his astonishment, the following week he was yanked up to the Central League for a clash against Wolves, his first game on the Old Trafford pitch. His recollections of that experience were understandable, 'I was just in shock! I had just signed as an apprentice and was told I was going to look after Martin Buchan. I mean, he was my hero and I wanted to play just like him. It was just a dream come true. Here I was, this snotty-nosed Salford lad, who had a very poor, impoverished upbringing, when sometimes my parents couldn't even afford electricity in the house and my dad was out of work and I was living on hand me downs.

As I looked at the team sheet, it was filled with internationals on both sides. I was in awe of some of my own team-mates. Back then you know you are a long way from the Reserves and here I was lining up against John Richards, one of the most experienced forwards in the First Division. At first I didn't think I was good enough, but that game gave me self-belief as we won 3-0 and I had stopped Richards from scoring. It was a real feather in my cap.'

Over the next few months he became a fixture in the 'A' team and was also drafted in for a Youth Cup tie at Walsall. As the season progressed he started to gain invaluable experience in the Reserves alongside Mike Duxbury, Paul McGrath and Gordon McQueen, and by the time the better weather was due he had established himself in the second string by starting in ten out of eleven fixtures over March and April. Also cementing a formidable partnership with Graeme Hogg in the under-18 team, the side conceded only two goals in nine games on their way to reach the final.

'I remember the Youth Cup run very clearly,' he said. 'It was an exciting time. We would travel to away games and play in the big stadiums, stay in hotels, it was a new experience for us all and I loved it.'

United faced Watford in the two-legged final only to hand the initiative to the Vicarage Road side by losing on home turf. A pulsating conclusion in Hertfordshire resulted in an astonishing 4-4 draw, which meant that the Reds were edged off the winners' podium by the narrowest of margins.

Garton recalled, 'Atkinson said it was the best game of football he had seen. To be fair it had everything and it could have gone either way. People often talk about my own goal, but it was just a frantic contest that neither team deserved to lose. It was a fantastic experience and I felt it was the making of Eric Harrison. That was the foundation of what happened later and it was proof that he was the right man.' Although terribly disappointed, it was an otherwise marvellous campaign for the defender as he had taken part in 44 matches and his stock was clearly on the rise.

He started six consecutive games for the Reserves over the September and October of 1982 prior to dropping down to the 'A' team where he remained for the following three months. In the meantime he resumed in the Youth Cup as West Brom, Derby and QPR were all felled before a classy Norwich side ended United's hopes of any further progress in early March. By now back in the Reserves, his luck in the Lancashire Youth Cup was only marginally better as the Reds lost out in the final to Manchester City in the May. Injured the following day in an 'A' team fixture, it caused him to miss a post-season youth tour to Holland.

He was still absent for the opening couple of weeks of the 1983/84 term before turning out for the 'A' team at Stockport in mid-September. However, he featured in only two further games in the first half of the campaign as he struggled for fitness and was out of action entirely for four months from October. That period should have seen him pushing for a first-team place, a fact which was borne out when Hogg forced his way up to make sixteen senior appearances.

His resumption with the Reserves came in early February although, unfortunately, it was obvious he had returned too quickly and was sidelined for another five weeks. He started a dozen games as the season drew to a close, which included the last eight Central League fixtures. Then afforded a place on the bench for Lou Macari's testimonial, a game in which he went on for Mike Duxbury against Celtic, a week later he was included in the first-team squad that flew out to Hong Kong and Australia. Despite not getting a run out in the match in the Far East against Bulova, nor in the opening match in Australia versus the national team, for the final two games against Nottingham Forest and Juventus he took the right full-back spot.

'I really enjoyed my time in Australia as I had suffered a stop-start season and was looking forward to getting fit,' he claimed. 'It was good to be involved in the first-team and still be in the manager's thinking.

I remember the match against Juventus at the Sydney Cricket Ground particularly well. The ground was pretty good, but every now and then you ran across a piece of turf and it was like an ice rink. It took me a little while to realise it was the actual cricket pitch that had been rolled thousands of times and we tried to keep the ball away from it after that. Your boots would go 'click, click, click', it was like Bambi on ice!'

His breakthrough was edging nearer, and he did himself a power of good by scoring twice in three games for the Reserves in September 1984. Then, as he was walking down a corridor at The Cliff one day, Atkinson casually asked if he would 'Fancy playing tomorrow night?' to which Garton replied naively, 'Fancy playing where?' It was only then that it dawned on him the manager was referring to a League Cup tie at Old Trafford.

Still without a car at that stage, his normal route to the ground was on the No. 58 bus down Ordsall Lane to Trafford Bar. On the seat in front of him on that memorable day was a man reading a newspaper, which carried a back page headline that blazed 'Billy the Kid' in reference to his promotion.

As he walked to the stadium, his boots in a plastic bag, he went unrecognised when crossing the forecourt and into the players' entrance.

The outcome was exactly as required, a 4-0 victory over Burnley, and once all the commotion was over he celebrated with a pint in the Jubilee Pub on the council estate where he had been raised. Six weeks later he went on as a substitute against PSV Eindhoven at Old Trafford, then finally got a First Division start at Filbert Street when United came away with a 3-2 victory.

Now brimming with confidence, although recording only one further first-team game that campaign, he went on to become a mainstay of the Reserves' defence and such was his form that he scored in each of the last three of his 29 Central League appearances.

He made further progress by performing in twelve first-team matches in the 1985/86 term. However, with McGrath and Moran the preferred partnership in the heart of the defence, Atkinson saw fit to loan him out to Birmingham, for whom he made five league starts in a one-month stopover.

With the first-team down at the wrong end of the table and results becoming critical, Atkinson favoured the experience of McGrath, Moran and, to a lesser extent, Hogg in the opening months of the 1986/87 season. That poor run led to Atkinson's demise and new manager Alex Ferguson took over in the November. Keeping with the old guard initially, it didn't take Ferguson long to identify some of the problems and he dropped McGrath a month later. Garton was elevated for eight consecutive league and cup fixtures from late December into February before McGrath was reinstated.

He was present for nine senior league and cup matches through September and October 1987 until injury sidelined him once again. A few weeks later Steve Bruce joined from Norwich, a development that spelled the beginning of the end for the local lad.

He bemoaned, *'At first I was constantly getting these hamstring problems. It would be okay for a few weeks and then it suddenly flared up. It was really frustrating as the physio couldn't find anything wrong. I'm sure people started doubting me and thinking I was some sort of hypochondriac. I just couldn't get fit, so in the end I saw a doctor. I was told I had a sciatic nerve problem, where there was a protrusion on one of the discs in my back. It was pressing on my nerves, causing my hamstring problems. I had back surgery to shave my disc and was told I would make a full recovery. But I still felt terrible and discovered I had glandular fever and was out once again. After my injury and illness, Alex Ferguson brought in Steve Bruce and Gary Pallister and I knew I was never going to get back into the first-team.'*

If the previous year wasn't bad enough, his last campaign with the Reds was even worse. After trying to get fit in the summer, he made an appearance in the Reserves' second game, a solitary goal defeat at Manchester City on the 6th September 1988. Without realising it, he had already put in his last stint for United.

'I missed virtually the whole season and was resigned to moving on,' he sighed. *'There was some interest from John Bond at Birmingham where I had enjoyed a decent loan spell and Forest were also interested, but I wanted to stay local. So when (Manchester) City came in for me I agreed to join them.*

I signed forms and everything, then Mel Machin phoned up and said the deal was off as I had failed the medical. In the end the doctors identified that I had ME. I had no idea. Then after being told about the illness everything fell into place about why I was struggling so much. I was gutted because I knew it was the end of my career, but I was also relieved that I had finally got to the bottom of the problem.'

Even though his condition had finally been diagnosed, Garton was depressed as he was without a job and had a young daughter to support. There was talk of a testimonial, though chairman Martin Edwards didn't support the idea and it was left to his friends to organise something without United's help. In the end, on a cold and rainy night, some 4,000 fans turned up at Salford RLFC to give him a send-off that seemed hardly appropriate.

His next move was to enrol on an F.A. coaching course which, ironically, was held at The Cliff, and he also spent hours at Manchester's Central Library in order to research articles about his illness. He got involved in sports promotional work, and by 1992 his health had improved to such an extent that he took up the manager's job at Salford City. When breaking the news, the local Reporter newspaper revealed that he had been attached to Doughty Rangers in the Eccles Sunday League, while a club spokesman said that with his *'reputation and standing in the football world, we are hoping he will be able to bring players to us and generate more interest.'*

'It was a challenge being a manager but I loved it. I was playing, too, but I got sent off in my first game for fighting,' he admitted. *'A big crowd had come to watch as the papers had been building up the game all week. Things weren't going well on the pitch and I was getting more wound up. Then one of their players tackled me and I took offence and threw a punch. I wasn't fit enough to play full games and I didn't play every week, but I was just pleased to be back in the game.'*

He spent only seventeen months at Salford City before being offered better terms by Vauxhall Conference outfit Witton Albion. He told a reporter of the move, *'If I can get through games at that sort of level I might as well be playing a higher standard of football.'* Employed on a full-time basis, in the 1993/94 term he took part in 23 matches there. The following term he was installed as player/coach at Hyde United and in almost four years at Ewen Fields he turned out in nearly 150 league and cup games.

During that period he undertook a university degree in PE and Teaching and soon began working in schools on a voluntary basis. In 1994, he was offered a teaching job at St. Vincent's School in Altrincham and quickly worked his way up to the position of deputy head. It was then that he met his future wife, and they often travelled to the USA to visit her family. While in the States he crossed paths with Jeff Illingworth, a former PE teacher at Ordsall High School, and began helping out by coaching children.

After being out of the game for a couple of years, in 2000 he took over the reins once again at Salford City. Putting in a few more appearances for the Moor Lane side before receiving an invite to join Illingworth in California to start a 'Soccer Club', because his wife was entitled to a green card, they decided to emigrate there. Salford's chairman publicly thanked him for his efforts by saying that he *'had brought a lot of professionalism to the club.'*

Today, Billy Garton runs 'Carmel Valley Manchester Soccer', a club which accommodates over 600 children and fields nearly 30 teams, while his wife operates a thriving dance studio.

Casting his thoughts over his time in football, he concluded, *'I sometimes look back at my career and wish that I had done the weights and built myself up more. I was always good on the ball but I didn't always win those physical battles. But I played for Manchester United and I will always be proud of that. I will never lose sight of where I came from, what I have worked hard to achieve, and I consider myself a lucky guy.'*

HILL, Andrew Rowland (1981/82, 1982/83)

Born: Maltby, South Yorkshire, 20th January 1965
Height: 5ft. 11ins., **Weight:** 12st.
Role: Defender
Career: Longley Primary School (Sheffield)/ Herries Secondary School (Sheffield)/ Sheffield Boys/ South Yorkshire Boys/ UNITED: Ass. Schoolboy October 1979 App. May 1981 Pro. January 1983/ Bury July 1984 to March 1991/ Manchester City (L) December 1990/ Manchester City March 1991/ Port Vale August 1995 to May 1998

When Andy Hill reminisces about his time in football, memories of signing for Manchester United as a junior, playing for his country at under-18 level, becoming the youngest ever captain of Bury at the age of nineteen and representing Manchester City in the Premiership are fondly recalled. Even the best of those highlights don't even come close to what he considers the pinnacle of this career as, having spent thirteen years as a professional, the Yorkshireman stepped out at Wembley with head held high as a member of the Port Vale team that faced Genoa in the 1996 Anglo-Italian Cup final.

Following his rejection of a new contract at Manchester City, Hill had only been with the Valiants for seven months during which he spent most of the interim period trying to help them gain a respectable mid-table position in the third tier of England's league hierarchy.

On the cup front, Vale had excelled in the Anglo-Italian competition, with two wins and two draws in the group stage before seeing off Ipswich and West Brom to reach the final. The fact that Genoa comfortably won 5-2 in front of 13,000 supporters now seems immaterial because, having dreamed of playing under the twin towers for as long as he could remember, recollections of the occasion tend to overshadow the result.

Remaining at Vale Park for a further couple of years before undergoing an operation on an injured ankle, the end of the 1997/98 campaign brought the curtain down on approximately 500 career appearances for the 33 year-old.

Coming from a clan of Sheffield Wednesday supporters, his family moved from Rotherham to the steel city when he was three. Big for his age, as young as six he was knocking in loads of goals for Owlerton Juniors in the Sheffield & District Junior League on Saturday mornings and did much the same for his school team in the week. During his formative years in the 1970's he often watched a Sheffield United side containing the likes of Alan Woodward, Eddie Colquhoun, Tony Currie and Len Badger.

By age twelve he was operating in midfield or defence for Sheffield Boys and occupied either of those roles when introduced to the county side two years later. Holding his own academically, school wasn't considered a main priority as he confessed to being *'driven and totally focused on playing football'* at that point. Of his continued progress he later said, *'My name was put forward for England Boys trials and I also went for trials at Wednesday and (Sheffield) United. They both offered me terms, but were a bit slower than (Manchester) United as their scout Ron Cattell had already watched me, and I didn't need convincing when they said they wanted me.'*

Missing from the start of the 1980/81 term while in recovery from an ankle break suffered with Owlerton, he was fit again by September and made his bow for United 'B' in their 1-1 home draw with Blackpool that same month. In those early days at Old Trafford, Hill would travel to Manchester on Fridays and, donning the left full-back jersey the following morning, his experiences that season encompassed nineteen games. Powerful and fiercely determined, not easily beaten in the air, the lad also meant business when he tackled and wasn't embarrassed in possession.

Upon leaving school he soon progressed up to the 'A' team. Nominated either at left full-back or occasionally at centre-half, for the opening Youth Cup tie of the 1981/82 campaign at Walsall he was named at number two. It proved to be a tremendous, if arduous, attempt at glory as the young Reds needed nine games, including three replays, to reach the last stage.

Missing from two earlier ties through injury, in late April he took his place in the team that faced Watford at Old Trafford to contest the first leg of the final. On the following Saturday his first game for the Central League side ended in a stalemate at Preston and five days later he rejoined his Youth Cup colleagues for a coach trip down the M1 they all hoped would finish in a cup triumph. It wasn't to be. With the players reflecting on their own contributions and what could have been during a return journey which was filled with a stony silence, he later reflected on those games by saying, 'They were the highlight of my career at United. But after scoring an own goal at Vicarage Road I just felt absolutely devastated.'

Hill finished the 1981/82 term on a positive note by retaining his place in the Reserves for their final three games, and he then tasted his first experience of Zurich. It was a chance for many of the team to put the Watford memory to rest and the junior Reds responded by dishing up some scintillating soccer to capture the Hermes Cup when defeating Israeli side Hapoel Tel Aviv in the final.

He began the next season by making the occasional step up to the Reserves and was also used in a full set of six Youth Cup ties in central defence, usually alongside Billy Garton. His displays were noted by Graham Taylor, who called him into the England Youth team, and most encouragingly of all, from February to the end of the campaign he retained a place at Central League standard.

Enjoying a great relationship with Eric Harrison, who was a firm believer in his capabilities, it was a black day when Ron Atkinson informed him of his release a year later, especially as he had solidified his place in the second string at centre-half or in either of the full-back slots.

The development was tough to take, as he later recalled, 'It was a massive shock. I was progressing well and thought I had done enough to earn a new contract.' Whatever the reason, and there was conjecture that perhaps Atkinson felt he lacked the required polish for a First Division footballer, his free transfer followed the Reserves' 2-1 home victory over Bolton in May 1984.

Hill was then involved in talks with numerous clubs, including Derby and Halifax, and his agreement to sign for Bury was based on manager Martin Dobson's promise not only of regular first-team football, but also the captaincy. The versatile defender enjoyed a superb first year as the club gained promotion into Division Three in 1985 and he would go on to feature in almost all of Bury's successes and failures in the late 1980's and early 1990's. Initially placed on the left or in the centre of their back four due to the presence on the right-hand side of Trevor Ross and, later, Lee Dixon, he made his mark as someone who very rarely had a bad game.

When Dixon moved on he switched to right full-back and held the position for the rest of his stay at Gigg Lane. Ever-present for just one term with Bury, in virtually all his time there he figured in over 40 games per season. In 1990, the Shakers even threatened to make it up to the Second Division, eventually settling for fifth place, and twelve months later they ended up seventh.

A most unusual incident occurred when his 50-yard back pass soared over a despairing 'keeper and into Bury's net in a Littlewoods Cup tie against Preston at Deepdale. Fortunately, his blushes were spared as the Shakers went on to win the match, although the moment won't easily be forgotten by the culprit or, indeed, anyone else who witnessed it.

Following 264 league games as a Shaker, his lengthy tenure at Gigg Lane was eventually ended by Bury's financial troubles in 1991 when the entire squad was put up for sale. With Sheffield United apparently interested, just a few weeks after Sam Ellis moved to Manchester City his former boss moved in to sign him. An initial loan spell in Moss Side proved encouraging and so City concluded his transfer for a fee of around £200,000.

Finally in the First Division, he established himself in the 1991/92 season until being sidelined with a series of injuries, including pelvic and double hernia problems that kept him in rehabilitation for nearly a year and a half. Offered what he considered to be a poor contract in 1995 due to City's own money problems, as a consequence he decided to move on with six goals in 100 league games to look back over.

There were suggestions that Sunderland and Middlesbrough were interested in signing him, so it was a little surprising when he joined Second Division Port Vale on a three-year deal. During his first two years at Vale Park he was involved in most games, including their cup exploits which paved the way to Wembley. A serious ankle knock required an operation in the 1997/98 campaign and, despite Bury tempting him with a two-year contract to return to Gigg Lane, quitting altogether appeared to be the healthier option.

At first undecided about his future, an eighteen-month period of relaxation encompassed plenty of golf, keeping fit and coaching his son's football team. It ended in 1999 when an offer to coach Bury's under-16 side at their Centre of Excellence was accepted, and in 2001 he was promoted to Director and Head of Youth at Gigg Lane.

Relocating to America in 2003, Nevada Wanderers initially employed him as a coach and he was then put in charge of their Olympic Development Program as Academy Director.

Andy Hill returned to the UK in 2005, settling into a job as a site manager at a local primary school, and by August 2007 he had initiated a soccer school based at Hopwood Hall College in Middleton called Pro-Vision North-West. The establishment is basically a 'second-chance academy' which caters for the development of fourteen to eighteen year-olds who have, in the main, been released by professional clubs. Alongside that venture he is also currently Head of Player Development at Bacup Borough.

SHARPE, Lee Stuart (1988/89)

Born: Birmingham, 27th May 1971
Height: 6ft., Weight: 12st. 13lbs.
Role: Left full-back
Career: **St. Francis Xavier Primary School (Oldbury)/ Hagley High School/ Halesowen & Stourbridge Boys/ Birmingham City** Ass. Schoolboy July 1986 to May 1987/ **Torquay United** YTS July 1987 to May 1988/ **UNITED:** Pro. June 1988/ **Leeds United** August 1996 to June 1999/ **Sampdoria** (It) (L) December 1998 to March 1999/ **Bradford City** (L) March to May 1999/ **Bradford City** June 1999 to August 2002/ **Portsmouth** (L) February to May 2001/ **Exeter City** August 2002/ **Grindavik** (Ice) May to July 2003/ **Garforth Town** September 2004

Whether at an airport, in a hotel, or simply just walking down the street, people from all over the world recognise Lee Sharpe. They see him in fashion magazines, mentioned in gossip columns, and he has even judged the Miss Manchester Contest while also dating numerous celebrities and actresses.

Having starred in hit television shows such as Celebrity Wrestling, Dancing On Ice, Coronation Street and, most famously, Celebrity Love Island, additionally he played the part of a roving reporter on Footballers' Wives and a commentator on Football Italia, Score, Football Focus and Match of the Day 2. He launched his own fashion collection, has acted as an ambassador for sportswear brand Sergio Tacchini in the UK, manages a property development business, undertakes engagements as an after-dinner speaker, and has presented the FHM Music TV Show on top of promoting hair care products.

His charity, the Lee Sharpe Foundation, helps needy children in Africa and South America, and he even climbed Mount Kilimanjaro to increase awareness of their plight. He has set up and been involved in the Homeless World Cup, a global football competition that set out to bring dignity back into the lives of homeless people, and while the sum total of all the above activities seem extraordinarily time consuming, he has still found time to appear on the Legends Football circuit for Manchester United, a commitment which takes him all over the world.

Growing up on a council estate in inner-city Birmingham, his love of, and in-built ability for, many sports included cricket and basketball, though his aspirations centred on one in particular. 'All I wanted to do was be a footballer,' he admitted. 'I used to dream of playing in front of big crowds, taking people on and scoring goals. I was lucky I suppose as I had pace, good balance and it all came natural to me. My mum wanted me to do better at school, but my dad said someone has to be a professional footballer, so why not me. My PE teacher at school, Mr. Shannon, was brilliant because he would make me believe I could do anything. He really gave me confidence, something that stayed with me when I got older.'

His road to the top began at eight years of age on Saturday mornings with the local Cubs side, and three years later, after scoring a winning goal against them, he joined Stourbridge Falcons. By now living in Halesowen, his Falcons team won plenty of local competitions and their star player soon started to attract the attention of Football League clubs in the area.

An Aston Villa follower back then, the youngster fantasised about performing at a packed Villa Park as Gary Shaw or Tony Morley. However, it wasn't the Claret and Blues who came calling but rivals Birmingham City, and it was they who convinced him to sign associate schoolboy terms.

Upon reaching the last year of high school he joined Stourport Wednesday.

Soon elevated into their senior team, who operated in an open-age Sunday League, at the same time he won his first representative honour when turning out for Halesowen & Stourbridge Boys.

Just as he was about to leave school, Birmingham City informed him that he was being released, which meant that other avenues needed to be explored. Assessments with West Brom and Wolves were lined up, and he even considered joining the Army until a couple of his friends encouraged him to go for a trial with Torquay United.

Undertaking three games in as many days, which included a first-team minor cup match against Exeter, the impression he made was enough to gain him the chance of a YTS apprenticeship. The offer hinged on Torquay remaining in the Fourth Division, and that meant they required a result against Crewe in the last game of the 1986/87 campaign. His hopes looked to be in tatters as the Devon club were two-nil down at one point until rallying to draw the game. The young Midlander had his contract and he moved into rooms soon after to prepare himself for what he expected would be a lengthy spell of learning the ropes in Torquay's second team.

'The pre-season was like boot camp and I had experienced nothing like it,' he recounted. 'I started in the Reserves at first, playing at centre-forward, and then in October I was drafted into the first-team to play against Exeter when someone was injured. The following week I was on the bench for a League Cup tie at White Hart Lane. I went on fairly early and was marking Gary Stevens. I mean, it was fairytale stuff.

I was still only sixteen, had virtually no training or coaching to speak of, and there I was playing in front of 20,000 people. I loved it straight away and from then on I was in the first-team squad. I was a sub mainly in the first half of the season, but after Christmas I started getting a few more starts. I had a really good game against Stockport and then played in a bruising match with Hereford in early April. The following week we had Colchester and it was a tough game that ended scoreless. I was getting kicked all over the place.'

Given his opportunity by manager Cyril Knowles, who called him 'a natural', it wasn't long before the local newspaper began to heap praise on the dashing teenage prospect. Following the Colchester match, Knowles was walking away from the ground when he noticed a large Jaguar car appear and inside was none other than Alex Ferguson. One of the Reds' scouts had been at the Hereford game and, then reporting his findings back to the Old Trafford hierarchy, it prompted the Scot to want to take a look for himself.

After seeing the lad in action, Ferguson was convinced he had what it took to make an impression at a higher grade and actually refused to leave Torquay without his signature. The next day, United's manager secured his target on a four-year deal for an initial fee of £180,000 that included additional payments which would take the deal up to £300,000 and also included a friendly match.

Because he was on YTS terms, the Reds' newest capture wasn't able to transfer immediately and so remained at Plainmoor until the campaign ended. With Knowles keen to ensure that his prize asset wasn't injured, Sharpe was used sparingly in the final matches. 'I felt like Willy Wonka clutching his golden ticket', he gleefully recalled. 'I mean, Manchester United. Fergie liked the fact that in a really rough game, where I was getting battered, I kept getting up and asked for the ball. It wasn't my pace or skills he liked but my hard work. I then scored twice for Torquay in a 6-1 win over Newport and caught the train up to Manchester. I was expecting a cab or a car to be waiting, but Ferguson was there himself. I was really impressed.

I stayed with Wayne Heseltine in digs and then went to training at The Cliff on Thursday. It was all so unreal, I was in the dressing room with all my own kit and passing the ball to people like Bryan Robson. Their first touch was absolutely amazing, they could all kill the ball dead without even trying. I was concentrating so hard not to make mistakes.

Fergie showed me around and introduced me to everyone. He also told me I would be in the Reserves for the first couple of years. On the Friday I trained with the Reserves before Archie Knox drove me to Tranmere to meet up with the Torquay lads who had a game that night.'

He took part in eight consecutive second string friendly matches at outside-left in the build-up to the 1988/89 term until filling in at left-back in a 1-1 draw with Swindon at The Cliff. With numerous defenders carrying injuries, as early as the 6th September he was asked to resume in the role rather than his customary wing position for a Central League clash at Manchester City. During training the following day, Archie Knox requested him to take up the defensive role again and called Ferguson over to watch.

Just three days after that session he was named on the bench for a senior home match against Middlesbrough and then found himself accorded a substitute role the following week at Luton. On the 21st September, Sharpe made his first-team debut in the semi-final of the Mercantile Credit Football League Centenary Trophy against Newcastle and retained the left-back berth on the following Saturday for a 2-0 win over West Ham at Old Trafford. It had certainly been a meteoric rise for him and, with little experience to call upon, he was now turning out alongside seasoned internationals on one of the biggest league stages of them all.

With eight appearances in the First Division behind him, and just 24 hours after putting in another 90-minute stint for the seniors at Coventry, he replaced Kieran Toal in a Youth Cup tie at Darlington. He reappeared on the bench for the Third Round Replay against Sheffield Wednesday and then assumed the captain's armband for later Youth Cup clashes with Ipswich and Brentford.

Featuring in 30 first-team games in total, mainly at full-back, in February he was also called up for England under-21's 1-0 defeat by Greece in Patras. By the end of the season the strains of full-time football had taken their toll, at which point he was admitted to hospital for a hernia operation.

The prelude to the 1989/90 campaign saw him included in the senior squad for a tour to Japan. Nominated in the starting eleven for the opening league match, a sensational 4-0 thumping of Arsenal, he made eighteen First Division appearances leading up to Christmas before experiencing fitness problems once again. Rested for a spell just into the New Year, following just one more Reserve game he was back in hospital for a double hernia operation. It ruled him out for all of the remaining fixtures and he couldn't be considered for an F.A. Cup final, and consequent replay, in which the Reds defeated Crystal Palace to win Ferguson his first trophy while in charge at Old Trafford.

The 1990/91 term saw a fully fit Sharpe take his place on the bench for a Charity Shield clash with Liverpool. A regular in the first-team from then on, this time in his preferred position out on the wing, it was for his League Cup exploits that he made headline news. After notching a goal against Liverpool in the Third Round, United were paired away to Arsenal and he chose the occasion to have a field day.

'That's the night everyone remembers about my career. Football wasn't all over the telly then so it made a big impact. A hat-trick against the England goalkeeper and the current League Champions? I couldn't believe it. We were wearing a blue and white away kit that didn't last long, and we were two-nil up when I nicked the ball off Lee Dixon and curled a 25-yard right-footed shot that hit the crossbar and went in.

Arsenal came out in the second half and pulled two goals back before I scored my second, a header. I don't usually score headers, but Denis Irwin knocked one high into the box and I ran from midfield with no-one around me and headed it down into the left-hand corner. That's when I did the famous 'hands' celebration. Danny Wallace then put me through on a one-on-one with Seaman. I ran onto it and again with my right foot just hit it past him. I went delirious celebrating with the fans. I was as high as a kite.'

Sometime after the game, Lawrie McMenemy, who was then one of England manager Graham Taylor's support staff, made a determined effort to congratulate him. Little did he suspect the significance that meeting would bring a short time later.

Sharpe scored in both legs of the League Cup semi-final against Leeds in February and, at the end of the following month, while still only nineteen years-old, won his first full England cap when replacing Tony Adams in the second half of a 1-1 draw with the Republic of Ireland at Wembley.

Fixtures were coming thick and fast by this stage and in early April he travelled to Poland where United took on Legia Warsaw in the semi-final of the European Cup Winners' Cup. A splendid team performance resulted in a 3-1 victory and eleven days later he lined up as the Reds faced Sheffield Wednesday in the League Cup final. Sadly, United didn't play anywhere near to their potential and lost by a solitary goal.

Whatever disappointment felt from the defeat at Wembley was soon forgotten as the team had unfinished business against Polish adversaries in late April and, with the in-form Sharpe registering just before the half-hour mark, the Reds' passage to the final was assured. Over the next fortnight he was rested before being brought back in time for the biggest game of his life when, on a soggy night in Rotterdam, United came up against the mighty Barcelona in the European Cup Winners' Cup final.

Speaking of that showcase match, he said, 'I don't remember all the details, except that we had to work really hard. They were a class side and kept the ball well. I was asked to do a much more defensive job than normal, tracking back all the time and helping Clayton Blackmore out.

When we won, it just went mental, everyone jumping all over each other. At the party afterwards I was talking to Robbo and saying I didn't think I played that well, but he told me that I had a really good game. He felt I had done an important job by sticking with my man on different runs and had shown a lot of experience for my age. It was just such a great night. I always gave all my medals to my dad and never had memorabilia around the house, but I've kept this rolled up poster of the teams lining up. It's tatty now but it's there in my living room all the time.'

In the final weeks of the season he claimed the 'Barclays Young Eagle of the Year' award and was included in the England under-21 squad that travelled to France to participate in the Toulon Tournament in late May. Collecting another four caps by featuring against Portugal, France, the CIS and Czechoslovakia, his last effort of a sensational spell of success came in the final when England defeated the latter 2-1 to win the competition.

For all of the positives of the previous campaign, the 1991/92 term wasn't quite as plain sailing for the likeable Brummie. Around that time there were many rumours about his lifestyle, although the reality was much less controversial, as a groin injury suffered in pre-season resulted in him being ruled out until late September when he returned for the Reserves.

His re-introduction to senior status was in the infamous 4-1 home defeat by QPR on New Year's Day, after which he gradually regained his match fitness. His confidence continued to grow by scoring in the League Cup semi-final against Middlesbrough as United returned to Wembley, this time to face Nottingham Forest. Joining the action when replacing Andrei Kanchelskis, he added another medal to his dad's collection when a tight game was won 1-0. The campaign then ended on a massive low as the Reds lost out in the battle with Leeds for the First Division championship and were required to settle for second place.

The start of the 1992/93 term brought numerous changes, with the most obvious being that the First Division had now morphed into the Premiership, but he had contracted viral meningitis and once again missed the opening months of the season. Fully recovered by November, after which he featured regularly in the team while contesting the left wing position with an up-and-coming starlet called Ryan Giggs.

His reward for consistent performances was a recall to the England squad in late March when claiming a second full cap for his efforts in a 2-0 win over Turkey in Izmir. Two months later, following 26 years of hurt, United were finally crowned as England's top-flight champions and, with domestic commitments over, Sharpe made four more England appearances, three of which were on an American tour.

The following year was almost certainly his finest as he had filled out a little, without losing any of his searing pace, was strong and, for a change at the opening to a campaign, 100 per cent fit. He returned to international duty to win the last two of his eight full caps in World Cup Qualifiers against Poland and Holland and, later forced to forfeit a spell of the action with another hernia problem, his honours list grew by two when United achieved a Premiership and F.A. Cup double.

In his final two years at the club, Sharpe remained a key member of the squad and despite breaking his ankle in a League Cup tie against Newcastle, he featured frequently as the Reds completed the double again in 1996.

To all intents and purposes, everything on the surface seemed great, apart from the fact that he wasn't enjoying his football as much as he would have liked. So, completely out of the blue, he requested a transfer. The crux of his problem was caused by the manager asking him to fill different roles, and often within changing formations. With scant knowledge or experience of what was required, his usually-robust confidence began to drain and he got involved in a few arguments with Ferguson. While the manager made it very clear that he wanted him to stay, his mind was set on getting away. Having given United good service in return for their modest outlay eight years earlier, the club had gained over 260 senior appearances out of him.

There was interest from Deportivo in Spain and Lens in France before he finally agreed to join Leeds for £4.5 million. Things went well initially, despite missing two months with a groin problem, until his fortunes worsened when a snapped cruciate ligament in the pre-season period caused him to miss the entire 1997/98 term. When David O'Leary took over, his career nosedived even further as the new appointment was keen to promote youth players into the first-team and told him he had no future at Elland Road. The Yorkshire club certainly hadn't benefited much for their huge outlay because they got only 30 league appearances and five goals from their expensive capture over a three-year period.

He claimed, *'I got a call from David Platt at Sampdoria and went out there for a spell, but it didn't work when he was sacked. I stayed for a couple of months but couldn't speak the language and the new manager brought in new faces. I spoke with Joe Royle at Manchester City and then ended up going to Bradford on loan until the end of the season.*

It was good to be playing again and I helped get them into the Premiership. I had a year left on my contract, United were winning the treble at the time and Leeds just didn't want me back. I went on holiday and both Manchester City and Bradford were keen to sign me. Bradford were in the Premiership so I decided to sign for them. It was the worst decision of my career.'

Joining the Valley Parade club in a cut-price £200,000 deal, loss of form and niggling injuries meant he couldn't get a decent run in the team. Over the next couple of years, new managers, an influx of new players and interference from the board room meant that he was forced to earn his money in the Reserves. Towards the end of the 2000/01 campaign he got a lifeline with a four-month loan move to Portsmouth. Unfortunately, Bradford's chairman wouldn't sanction a permanent move to the south coast outfit, so he again spent the final year of his contract in the Bantams' second string with the odd cameo for the first-team.

Following trials at Grimsby and Rotherham in the summer of 2002 and a four-game link-up with Exeter that August, he entered into a short-lived seven-game affair with Icelandic League side Grindavik in 2003 and once back home announced his retirement from the professional game. In 2004, Lee Sharpe briefly connected to North-East Counties League side Garforth Town and even put in an appearance for a Wetherby pub team called the Half Moon. Following a couple of years when things got him down a tad, his highly lucrative transition from ex-footballer to celebrity got underway.

Currently a resident of Leeds, in 2009 he reflected on his time at Old Trafford by saying, *'I wished I'd had the chance to develop the technical skills like the younger lads as I never had that grounding. I was just thrown in and everyone thought I could handle it, but every next step up was a totally new experience and I didn't know how to prepare myself for it. I just wanted to go out and play the game with a smile on my face. I remember we had such a good team spirit, a great bond. It was a good team wasn't it?'*

McLOUGHLIN, Alan Francis (1983/84, 1984/85)

Born: Fallowfield, Manchester, 20th April 1967
Height: 5ft. 8ins., **Weight:** 10st. 10lbs.
Role: Left full-back or midfielder
Career: St. Ambrose Primary School (Chorlton-cum-Hardy)/ St. Mark's R. C. Secondary School (Didsbury)/ Chadderton F.C./ Manchester Boys/ **UNITED:** App. May 1983 Pro. April 1985/ **Swindon Town** August 1986 to December 1990/ **Torquay United** (L) March to August 1987/ **Torquay United** (L) August and September 1987/ **Southampton** December 1990 to February 1992/ **Aston Villa** (L) September and October 1991/ **Portsmouth** February 1992/ **Wigan Athletic** December 1999/ **Rochdale** December 2001 to May 2002/ **Forest Green Rovers** July 2002 to June 2003

Born of Irish parents, Alan McLoughlin was spotted by Eric Harrison while playing for Chadderton against a United junior team in August 1982. The coach was so taken with the boy's performance that he immediately put up the offer of a trial when sensing that the prospect possessed the necessary wherewithal to make a living out of the game. Harrison's judgement was once again right on the button, so much so that the raw teenager went on to appear in two World Cup finals and would later be the subject of a seven figure transfer fee.

Explaining his Plan B, McLoughlin said, *'I had no other offers as I was considered too small by other clubs. In fact, I had already planned to take a course at Xaverian College if I didn't make the grade as a footballer.'* Training regularly on Monday and Wednesday nights from then on, he was involved in numerous friendly matches over the next few months and inadvertently ended an era in United's history in May 1983 by signing the very last apprenticeship contract at the club prior to the new Youth Training Scheme being brought into operation.

His first competitive game for United 'A' came in a 3-0 home win over Southport Reserves in the November of that year and a period of only two or three weeks passed before he was informed to prepare himself to join up with the Central League squad for a match at Everton. *'I didn't even own a sports bag,'* he recalled with just a twist of embarrassment. *'I really panicked and had to make a mad rush to the Arndale Centre in Manchester to buy one. It was worth it, though, because we got a 1-0 win at Goodison Park.'*

He was overlooked for the first two Youth Cup ties of that season, but by February 1984 he had been blooded in the tournament by replacing Pat Kelch at Barnsley in the left full-back position. Following selection for the final Central League game of the term, by coincidence the return fixture against Everton, his first club honour came about when the 'A' team won the Lancashire League.

He spent the 1984/85 campaign consolidating a place in the 'A' side, mainly at full-back, and even at that stage was confident enough to ask if he could captain the side. The seventeen year-old was selected in midfield for the Reds' only Youth Cup game of that season, a 3-2 defeat at Leeds, and he gained a few more matches for the Reserves as his 'A' team went on to head their division for the second successive year.

Over the course of the 1985/86 term, McLoughlin totalled nineteen appearances for the Reserves as they finished in second place in the Central League and he was then offered a further one-year contract. Of how the next stage of his career unfolded, he said, *'No-one could give me any assurances about my chances of first-team football, so I decided that I had to look away from Old Trafford for an opening.'* In April 1986, West Brom accommodated him for a week-long trial and he returned to play his last game for United 'A' in their 6-0 home win over UMIST early the following month.

He then joined Stoke City on trial, travelling to France with them to participate in a youth tournament, and despite performing well enough to win the 'Player of the Tournament' award, the Potters failed to table a permanent deal. A further assessment followed, at Oldham, and he then had the chance of another with Doncaster before manager Lou Macari offered him an identical opportunity at Swindon. Accompanying them for a pre-season tour to Malta on an initial appraisal period, he signed for the newly-promoted club in August 1986.

McLoughlin was unable to get into the Swindon side as they charged to a second promotion in a row in 1987 and he even found himself farmed out to Torquay, experiencing 24 senior league games there over two loans spells. Following his return to the County Ground he became a regular in Swindon's midfield under manager Ossie Ardiles, chalking up 106 league appearances while scoring nineteen times, and towards the end of that period he was capped at full international level for the Republic of Ireland in a 3-0 friendly win in Malta. Already chosen for the Italia '90 Irish World Cup squad, just nine days after the game in Valetta he was sent on as a substitute for a 1-1 draw against England in Cagliari.

In the latter part of 1990, manager Chris Nicholl made him a costly capture for Southampton at a cool £1,000,000 and in doing so beat off interest from Sheffield Wednesday's Ron Atkinson, the very same manager who had sanctioned his Old Trafford release over four years earlier.

His relationship with Southampton was disjointed, because Nicholl was sacked and when Ian Branfoot took over the reins he elbowed the Mancunian out of his future plans. McLoughlin spent a short loan spell at Aston Villa over the September and October of 1991. Taking part in a Zenith Data Cup tie against Coventry, as well as being chosen for bench duty a few times, he didn't appear in Villa's league team.

By February 1992 Southampton had transferred him to Portsmouth, where the opportunity of regular first-team football presented itself again. At the last eight stage of the 1992/93 F.A. Cup campaign he scored the winning goal against Nottingham Forest to set up a semi-final meeting with Liverpool, a game that Pompey were extremely unlucky to lose.

He became a national hero in the Republic of Ireland in November 1993 when utilised from the bench to score the equalising goal in a 1-1 draw with Northern Ireland in Belfast, a result which took the Republic to the 1994 World Cup finals in America. The midfielder wasn't used in the tournament and returned to spend a further five years at Fratton Park. While amassing 309 league games and 54 goals for Portsmouth, the club's captain also collected the last of 42 full Eire caps.

A stay at Wigan which commenced in December 1999 was brim full of frustration as he added only 22 Division Two appearances to his tally in a period of two years. Firstly he slipped a disc in his back, his only major injury to that point, and was then fed a diet of football in their Reserves.

While training to improve his fitness back at the County Ground, there were overtures from Swindon and Swansea, but he chose to take up a counter offer from Rochdale. During the five months he spent at Spotland, the 'Dale were defeated by Rushden & Diamonds in the 2001/02 Division Three play-offs.

The sun went down on his career at Conference club Forest Green Rovers, where he gained a Football Association 'B' coaching qualification. Another slipped disc forced him to have an operation on his back and it acted as the catalyst that made him give up the playing side of the game in 2003. He continued to act as youth team coach at Forest Green Rovers and also co-commentated on football matches for a now defunct Portsmouth-based radio station called The Quay.

In February 2011, Alan McLoughlin joined BBC Radio Solent as a co-commentator for games involving Portsmouth and, now the owner of a UEFA 'A' licence, in the July of that year he was appointed as Pompey's Senior Academy Coach.

BULLIMORE, Wayne Alan (1987/88, 1988/89)

Born: Sutton-in-Ashfield, Nottinghamshire, 12th September 1970
Height: 5ft. 9ins., Weight: 12st. 1lb.
Role: Midfielder
Career: Hillocks Primary School (Sutton-in-Ashfield)/ Quarrydale Secondary School (Sutton-in-Ashfield)/ Sutton-in-Ashfield Boys/ Mansfield Boys/ Idsall School (Shifnal)/ UNITED: Ass. Schoolboy September 1985 Trainee May 1987 Pro. September 1988/ Barnsley March 1991/ Stockport County October 1993/ Scunthorpe United November 1993/ Bradford City December 1995 to March 1997/ Doncaster Rovers (L) September and October 1996/ Peterborough United March 1997/ Scarborough August 1998/ Grantham Town May 1999/ Barrow August 2000/ Wakefield & Emley September 2003/ Stalybridge Celtic October 2003/ Belper Town December 2003/ Bradford Park Avenue February 2004/ Ilkeston Town March 2004/ Stocksbridge Park Steels March 2004 to 2005/06 season

Wayne Bullimore's time at Old Trafford ended when Alex Ferguson brought to his attention that Barnsley had made a second approach regarding his availability, the Oakwell club having contacted United with an initial enquiry the previous summer. Whether it was as a consequence of his fractured relationship with the manager of the Reserves, or that he lacked the pace or other attributes necessary to make it to the top can only be speculated on, but with the transfer deadline fast approaching, a move appeared to be the best option. Checking out by converting a penalty, his last game concluded in a 3-2 defeat by Everton Reserves at Goodison Park in March 1991.

Headway into the Tykes' first-team affairs came a couple of months after the 1991/92 campaign began. He was initially named as a substitute for a Rumbelows Cup match in late October, and his Second Division entrance in November yielded a 1-0 victory at Oxford.

Bullimore was used only sporadically in Barnsley's senior team over the following term and when Viv Anderson took charge in the summer of 1993, an agreement made with the previous boss was negated and forced him to look for a new club. Over two and a half years, his appearance record at Oakwell amounted to just 35 league matches.

Stockport County provided a temporary refuge by taking him on board on non-contract terms, when out of nowhere he was offered a two-year deal by Scunthorpe. In 1995, towering displays singled him out as the club's midfield organ grinder and earned him a place in the PFA's 'Third Division Team of the Year'. Having gained 67 league appearances out of him, in the December of that year Scunthorpe accepted a £40,000 offer from Bradford City for his services.

At first the move appeared to be all he expected, because Bradford were a club with a progressive attitude. Unfortunately, 60 seconds into his debut, torn cruciate ligaments in his left knee caused him to miss the remainder of the season. By the time his fitness returned, new players had arrived at Valley Parade and with the likes of Chris Waddle and Gordon Cowans holding down midfield roles, he was once again resigned to the obscurity of second team football.

Developments in September 1996 resulted in him taking a loan spell at Doncaster in a bid to get some serious action. His injury hoodoo resurfaced only four games into his association with the Rovers, when a cartilage damaged in training sidelined him for another four months.

He had originally signed an eighteen-month contract with Bradford, and it came up for renegotiation with him having participated in only two league games. Bullimore was highly embarrassed about the lack of value he had given the Yorkshire club as they had done their utmost to support him. Nevertheless, the desire for first-team football led him into joining Barry Fry's

Peterborough. Even though the Posh were relegated to the bottom tier a few weeks later, and with only eleven starts and fifteen substitute appearances in a little less than a year and a half to speak of, overall he found his Peterborough experience an enjoyable one.

Then agreeing to sign for Scarborough, a move he later described as *'an absolute nightmare'*, during the 1998/99 campaign the club lost its manager and couldn't afford to meet its wage bill while spiralling towards an exit from the Football League. To top it all, further injury woes required him to undergo a hernia operation.

After leaving Scarborough he combined his football with a role on the Leeds United coaching staff, working within the 'Leeds Soccer in the Community' scheme for three months of the 1999/00 term before becoming the assistant community officer at Barnsley. Twelve months later he was promoted to community officer at Oakwell and held the position for two years.

Between 1999 and 2006, no less than eight non-league clubs held his registration papers. They were mainly Northern Premier League outfits, and he continued until his mid-30's when the effects of numerous knocks began to take their toll. One notable achievement during that period was when he scored a hat-trick of penalties for Stocksbridge Park Steels against Belper Town in September 2004. All three goals came in a five-minute spell, although they still didn't prevent his former club from recording a 4-3 win.

Still working at Barnsley Football Club, he has relinquished his previous role as coach to their Under-10 Academy squad and now acts as the chief executive of their Sports and Education Trust.

It was around the same age of his former charges when his association with football began with Sutton Dale Boys Club in his home town. A left-footed central midfielder who was difficult to shake off the ball, his reading of the game helped to counterbalance a lack of defensive inclination. The main weapon in his armoury was a marvellous range of passing skills, which were frequently employed in dictating the pattern of play.

He later represented Sutton Boys and Mansfield Boys, and it was while building up a reputation in the latter team that he was spotted by Ron Cattell. The United scout gave him the chance of attending trials at The Cliff and while doing so he stayed in the Halls of Residence at Salford University.

Bullimore was pursued by numerous clubs and spent time with Arsenal, Nottingham Forest, Sheffield Wednesday and Sheffield United while also attracting interest from Manchester City, Leeds and Everton. All other advances were ignored as, once the scene at Old Trafford had been surveyed and terms were forthcoming from Ron Atkinson, there was only one place he wanted to be.

Then offered a two-year placement at Lilleshall, leaving home at the age of fourteen meant that he was denied the opportunity to play for East Midlands Boys. He was one of only the second intake at the newly-established F.A. National School and while in Shropshire he won ten caps for England Youth. The most memorable match of his England Youth period was staged at Wembley against France prior to the 1984 Charity Shield showpiece, and he also took part in international tournaments in Italy and France.

In August 1986, while in his second year at Lilleshall, his involvement with United began when scoring in a 6-0 'B' team victory over Chester, and he then added just six more appearances in that season.

Signing as a trainee, in his first full campaign with the Reds he resumed with the 'B' side. Some glory was secured as early as September 1987, with a 6-3 aggregate Supplementary Cup final victory over Crewe, and he waited only a couple of months longer before being slipped up a couple of grades in a 1-1 away draw against Sheffield Wednesday Reserves.

Following a brief introduction to the 'A' team, he was drafted into the Youth Cup squad in December to face his local team, Mansfield Town, at Old Trafford. Sent on from the substitute's bench, his best efforts couldn't prevent the Reds from suffering a defeat which sent shock waves through the club that could be measured on the Richter Scale.

The game was a pivotal moment in Alex Ferguson's reign and following his reading of the riot act to the team after the match, the manager set about completely overhauling the club's ailing youth system in order to pave the way for the bountiful rewards that would follow in the years ahead. However, those on duty that night almost certainly didn't appreciate the significance of their failings or, indeed, the roasting they received. By the end of the term, Bullimore's world seemed much brighter as the 'A' team won their division after sitting at the top of the table for most of the time.

For the first few months of the 1988/89 season he was used in the Reserves, despite not getting on with coach Brian Whitehouse, who limited his appearances. As the Youth Cup campaign got underway that December, he was honoured to skipper the side for the visit to Darlington and repaid the faith shown in him by notching two goals in a 5-2 victory. Having been sent off in a 'A' team game against Liverpool on New Year's Eve, and forced into serving a ban, the armband passed to Darren Ferguson for the following tie at Sheffield Wednesday. He resumed the role of captain for the replay at Old Trafford, but when Lee Sharpe was drafted into the team for the Ipswich and Brentford matches, he lost the responsibility again.

A couple of months after the Youth Cup exit at Griffin Park he was welcomed into the first-team squad for a friendly match against Histon, which had been arranged as part of the Guiliano Maiorana transfer. His brief, solitary senior appearance came when replacing Maiorana from the bench.

After turning out in six of the Reserves' opening eight matches of the 1989/90 term, it was February of the following year before he made any further inroads at that standard. He continued to score with some regularity for the 'A' team throughout the winter, and the third team eventually topped their division again.

Despite signing a one-year extension to his contract at the beginning of his fourth year at the club, the 1990/91 season proved to be one long struggle to force his way back. Russell Beardsmore and Darren Ferguson blocked his way to a central midfield spot in the Reserves and there were no signs that he was capable of putting pressure on those above him. Realising that the predicament wouldn't get any easier, it was then that he chose to drop to a level where his chances would be that much greater.

ROBINSON, Andrew Craig
(1981/82, 1982/83, 1983/84)

Born: Oldham, 10th March 1966
Height: 5ft. 9ins., **Weight:** 12st.
Role: Defender or midfielder
Career: St. Paul's Primary School (Royton)/ North Chadderton Comprehensive School/ Oldham Boys/ Greater Manchester Boys/ England Boys/ **UNITED**: Ass. Pro. October 1981 App. May 1982 Pro. March 1984 to January 1986/ **Burnley** (L) October and November 1985/ **Bury** January 1986/ **Carlisle United** March 1987/ **Wycombe Wanderers** August 1988/ **Aylesbury United** July 1991/ **Chertsey Town** October 1993/ **Chesham United** July to November 1995

With the financial divide between professional footballers and the average supporter constantly widening, it is hardly surprising that many of the former have a surplus of funds with which they look for ways to invest. When Gary Neville launched his own property development business, the ex-Reds' full-back hired builders to convert and renovate barns in the Rossendale Valley and similarly, when another United star decided to act the investment tycoon, some of his capital was ploughed into real estate in Dubai.

A former member of United's youth team from the early 1980's might have harboured the same intentions but, alas, didn't enjoy the luxury of Premiership wages to support him. With a modest Football League career that spanned less than three years already over, Andy Robinson attended a college course to equip himself with a new trade and now has his own property company. Rather than employing someone else to do the hard graft, unlike Neville, he does a lot of it himself.

Alongside David Platt, he was with Royton Youth Club when their name changed to the more recognisable and respected Boundary Park Juniors. He excelled at cricket, golf and tennis, as well as winning representative honours in athletics, and it wasn't long before similar recognition at football followed. Seen competing for Oldham Boys in a match at Tottenham, Harry McShane and Joe Brown relayed back glowing reports of his ability to Old Trafford immediately after.

He was normally used in midfield, but there was no discernible dilution of effectiveness when he was asked to stand in at centre-half, full-back or sweeper. That versatility and his other traits soon attracted the attention of many, and trials at Crystal Palace and Arsenal were completed while Manchester City and Oldham also got in touch. After hearing repeated recommendations from United's scouting network, Dave Sexton visited the Robinson household with the intention of persuading him to join the Reds.

In February 1981, with honours for Greater Manchester behind him, the fourteen year-old was selected for England schoolboy trials at Lilleshall. Sailing through the selection process with flying colours, his international debut came in the opening Victory Shield match against Northern Ireland at Wembley on the 28th March. He contributed to a comfortable 4-0 victory and retained his place for the next game against Wales when England returned over the border from Cardiff after a 1-0 win. The following month he travelled to Switzerland for a two-match tour, helping England to hammer the home side 7-1 at Interlaken and 4-0 in Burgdorf.

At the end of April he faced Scotland at Old Trafford, where a hard fought 1-0 success ensured that the home side lifted the Victory Shield. On his travels once again soon after, England defeated Holland 4-1 in Gouda before suffering their first reverse of the campaign when beaten 3-0 by France in Auxerre. The schoolboy season culminated with two matches against West Germany, England losing the first game 2-1 at Wembley prior to gaining revenge with a 4-0 drubbing of the Germans in Poole.

'Funnily enough, I was chosen for all nine of England Boys' matches that season and yet I was the only player who wasn't attached to a Football League club,' he said. 'I finished off my A-levels and a little later on that year I got the offer to join United.'

First pulling on a United shirt in a 2-1 'B' team victory at Wigan in October 1981, only eleven days passed before he became an associate professional. Just over three months later he substituted for Norman Whiteside in a 0-0 home Youth Cup draw with Liverpool and despite being unable to push his way into a strong side, due mainly to the fact that he was still at school and therefore not in full-time training, Eric Harrison made good use of his adaptability by placing him in midfield for the replay at Anfield. He then substituted for Mike Rowbotham at Leeds and later filled in for regular right full-back Andy Hill against the Yorkshire side at Old Trafford. Used once again as a substitute in the 2-0 Fifth Round home replay against Birmingham, Harrison overlooked him for the semi-final and final ties.

He featured in a pre-season friendly for the Reserves in 1982, but it was his only sighting at that standard all term as he predominantly turned out for the 'A' team. Robinson was stationed at centre-half or sweeper for them on the odd occasion, although a lack of inches dictated that he was utilised in midfield or, more usually, at full-back. Beginning the Youth Cup run in that very same role, he was then demoted to substitute for three of the remaining four ties only to then finish the season with the most number of appearances for the 'A' team as they completed their fixtures in sixth place.

Once again a mainstay of the 'A' team during the 1983/84 term, he was drafted into the Central League side for their home game against Derby in November. It was noted that the number three put on a decent performance in the 1-0 reverse and he was then told he was to be made captain of the team for the forthcoming Youth Cup tie at Notts County.

Proudly leading the side in all four matches as the Reds were knocked out by Barnsley, over the remainder of the campaign he featured in five further Reserve games without really looking likely to establish himself in the team. However, he only missed one of the 'A' team's fixtures as they collected the Lancashire League Division One title and was also called up for England Youth trials.

He appeared in the majority of the Reserves' pre-season friendlies in 1984 and played at left full-back in the opening eight Central League games before losing his place to Clayton Blackmore. Reverting back to the 'A' team from then on, the third team captured the league title for a second time in succession.

The 1985/86 term represented the last year of his contract and he was determined to do everything in his powers to secure an extension. Things looked to be going to plan when he was put on Central League duty for the opening six games of the campaign until a loan request was unexpectedly received from Burnley manager Martin Buchan, who approached Ron Atkinson with a view to taking him to Turf Moor for a month. Within a few days of the deal being finalised, the former Scotland captain resigned and his assistant, former United coach Tommy Cavanagh, took charge.

Any negative repercussions about the change were dismissed almost immediately as, within a week of joining the Clarets, he made his Fourth Division debut in a 2-0 home defeat by Swindon and retained a place in the side for the next four matches before his loan term expired.

Unable to get back into the Reserves at Old Trafford, it was obvious that he hadn't ticked enough boxes as far as Atkinson was concerned. Even though he read the game well and demonstrated excellent passing ability, the necessary pace and aggression required to make it to the top was absent. His final game for United 'A' was in their 3-1 home victory against Barrow Reserves in December 1985 and he was released a little while later.

Wilf McGuinness heard of his availability through his son, Paul, who was then on United's books. McGuinness senior was coaching at Bury and advised Shakers' manager Martin Dobson to run the rule over the Oldhamer. Bury were delighted to capture him on a free transfer in January 1986, even though his time at Gigg Lane didn't turn out the way either party hoped for as he made only nineteen Third Division appearances, nearly half of which were from the substitute's bench.

When Carlisle approached Bury for his signature on transfer deadline day in 1987, a one-year contract was quickly agreed and he was included in their remaining eleven matches as the Cumbrians were relegated to the Fourth Division. During the 1987/88 season, Robinson was a regular in the Carlisle team that finished second from bottom of the lower echelon, with only a woefully poor Newport County side preventing their almost certain relegation to the wastelands of non-league football.

Despite accumulating 46 first-team league games at Brunton Park, Carlisle's offer of a new contract was rejected in favour of a move to Football Conference members, Wycombe Wanderers. From then on no longer a full-time professional, he also worked for the Wycombe chairman while learning carpentry. In the first of his three terms there, the club completed a divisional placing of fourth and in the second they reached the Bob Lord Trophy semi-final, as well as winning the Berkshire & Buckinghamshire County Cup.

When Martin O'Neill took over the Loakes Park managerial post in August 1990, the Wanderers' success continued with a placing of fifth in the Conference, a 3-1 F.A. Trophy final win over Kidderminster Harriers at Wembley, and a second consecutive appearance in the Berks & Bucks County Cup final. Getting regular games became harder in his last campaign at Wycombe, so he joined Isthmian Premier League outfit Aylesbury United in July 1991 and within five months they had reached the Second Round Proper of the F.A. Cup, going out 3-2 to Hereford.

After making 75 appearances for Aylesbury, Chertsey Town became his next port of call in October 1993. Two very rewarding seasons were spent at Alwyns Lane as they were promoted by finishing second in the Ryman League Division Two, while in the 1994/95 term ex-England stars Kenny Sansom and Ricky Hill helped the Town up to the Ryman Premier Division.

In the summer of 1995, he answered Chesham United's call to become their player/assistant manager, retaining the dual tasks for the Isthmian League club only until that November when he left the game for good.

Over the ensuing years, Buckinghamshire-based Andy Robinson has worked as a self-employed builder, refurbishing houses and developing a property business that still provides his livelihood. Married to his school sweetheart, he has taken his F.A. coaching badges and still actively follows the Reds from his season ticket seat in the Sir Alex Ferguson Stand.

HESELTINE, Wayne Alan (1986/87, 1987/88)

Born: Bradford, 3rd December 1969
Height: 5ft. 10ins., Weight: 11st. 1lb.
Role: Left full-back or central defender
Career: St. Antony's Primary School (Clayton, Bradford)/ Sir Edmund Campion Junior School (Bradford)/ St. Bede's High School (Bradford)/ Bradford Boys/ West Yorkshire Boys/ Yorkshire Boys/ UNITED: Ass. Schoolboy November 1984 Trainee June 1986 Pro. December 1987/ Oldham Athletic December 1989/ Bradford City August 1992 to June 1994/ Guiseley August to October 1994

There often comes a time in a young footballer's career when they find themselves caught in a corridor of uncertainty, as they are clearly talented enough to hold their own in the Reserves yet unable to force their way into the first-team. The reason for not being able to make an impression at the higher level could be down to a basic lack of technique or speed, a shortage of confidence, or it might be that there are simply too many others with better credentials blocking the way forward.

In December 1989, Wayne Heseltine found himself in such a situation and many years later he described how later events unfolded for him when saying, 'I'd been at United for three years, I was in my first full season as a professional and playing regularly in the Reserves. But at the back of my mind I wondered if I would ever get a chance because there were quite a few players ahead of me.

I was offered another year at the start of the 1989/90 season and was playing really well. Then, when I was training at The Cliff one day, someone said that the gaffer wanted to see me. The manager told me that a handful of clubs had been interested in me over the last few months and one of them was Oldham. The manager mentioned that he had a lot of time for Joe Royle, and he also said that Oldham played the game the right way and that I should have a word with him.

He explained that I was behind Lee Martin and Lee Sharpe in his plans, but thought I had a future at the club. He then told me that if I wasn't happy with what Oldham had to say then he would see me at training the next morning. He told me what I should ask for in term of wages, which was more than I was on at United. I was in digs with David Wilson and he reckoned that all the other lads couldn't believe that I hadn't been given a chance in the first-team. So I spoke to Joe Royle and Willie Donachie, they named a few games when I had played well and offered me a three-year contract.'

The young Yorkshireman put pen to paper in a £40,000 transfer deal just three days before Christmas and made his first Football League appearance at Swindon in January 1990. Unfortunately, with Denis Irwin, Neil Adams or Andy Barlow all preferred by Royle, the opportunity of senior football never again presented itself at Boundary Park.

In December 1990, while competing in a second string match, a freak challenge four minutes from time resulted in a broken ankle and leg which sidelined him for over seven months. 'I made my comeback for the Reserves against Burnley, but the constant pounding on Oldham's plastic pitch didn't help at all,' he said. 'I was jumping for headers from a different leg, it was always on my mind and it probably took fifteen months before I was back to normal.'

It was a favour from Athletic team-mate Andy Ritchie at the end of the 1991/92 term that paved the way for his next move. Ritchie telephoned ex-United colleague and current Bradford City manager Frank Stapleton and

biography

it was agreed that Heseltine could trial at Valley Parade in the close season.

He explained, 'I trained on my own all summer to get back to fitness. I also had a week at Hull City who wanted me to sign terms. But Bradford needed a left-back, and after playing in a few local cup matches they offered me a two-year deal. I knew Stuart Pearson, Mike Duxbury, as well as Stapleton, and Bradford was on my doorstep so I decided to join them.'

It meant that the local lad had gone full circle in footballing terms, and it was hoped that the benefit of performing in familiar surroundings would provide the impetus he desperately needed to get his career back on track.

Raised in the Clayton district of Bradford, he learned about the game from his father and uncles, all of whom had been involved in amateur football around the locality. By the time he reached the age of eleven, a multi-talented Sunday side by the name of St. George's had given him the chance to display his talents to the full. Suffering only one defeat over the next five years while picking up various trophies, St. George's were clearly the best side in the district in their age group and it was inevitable that some of those who made up the team would attract the attention of the scouting fraternity.

'I played in central midfield for my school and representative teams,' Heseltine revealed. 'All of my schools were big into football and most of the lads who went to St. Bede's all played for Bradford Boys. I suppose I was about thirteen when I got invited to visit different clubs, Bradford, Huddersfield, Sheffield Wednesday, Leeds, York, and I also went down to Arsenal a few times in the school holidays.

The United scout, Ron Cattell, had also been watching me play at King George II Playing Fields on and off for a couple of years and he asked me to go to Old Trafford. He spoke with my dad and I went over there. I liked going to United, it was close to home and I already knew Karl Goddard and Tony Gill, and so the following year I signed terms with them.'

Moving across the Pennines in the 1985 seasonal break, the new recruit made up a rooming quartet with Gill, Goddard and Phil Steer in Lower Broughton. He appeared for the 'B' side in a 3-0 home victory over Blackburn that August and it wasn't long before Eric Harrison moved him from his customary midfield role into defence. While the boy was initially a little in awe at his surroundings, his confidence soon grew and he finished the term with the experience of 24 'B' team matches under his belt.

He was promoted into the 'A' side after only six games of the 1986/87 campaign, featuring regularly at that level as a left full-back, and Harrison also selected him for both Youth Cup ties, the run ending sooner than everyone would have liked at the hands of Leicester.

Notable for being comfortable with the ball at his feet, Heseltine possessed an excellent first touch and tackled keenly. He was particularly strong in the air, and seldom beaten when jumping for the ball, and while he lacked a yard of pace, his positional sense often got him out of trouble.

Within a few weeks of his third season at Old Trafford, he substituted for Joe Hanrahan in a 1-0 Central League defeat at Huddersfield and skippered the 'B' team to a 2-1 second leg Supplementary Cup final win at Crewe four days later to tie up a 6-3 aggregate victory. The Bradford lad was involved in the opening thirteen 'A' team games, either in central defence or at full-back, prior to gaining much more exposure in the Reserves as the term developed.

The joy of turning professional on the 7th December 1987 was well and truly dampened 24 hours later, when he had the inauspicious honour of leading United's under-18's to their most embarrassing Youth Cup defeat ever at the hands of lowly Mansfield. The Reds lost by the odd goal in three and the watching Alex Ferguson was spitting feathers at the final whistle.

Heseltine continued to put in solid performances for both the 'A' team and Reserves, and by the end of the campaign he had taken part in 44 games. Other than the Youth Cup humiliation, it would have been a reasonable season, because the Reserves finished in mid-table while the 'A' side galloped away to a second successive Lancashire League title triumph.

From then on he settled down to Central League football, with 27 games for the second string in the 1988/89 term and a further thirteen matches during the first half of 1989/90 campaign. It was then that Ferguson approached him about transferring to Oldham, and he signed off in the Reserves' single goal victory at Manchester City on the 9th December 1989.

After his tribulations at Oldham, it was assumed that brighter days lay ahead with his hometown club. 'I was pleased with my first season at Bradford,' he mentioned. 'I played in nearly every game as left-back or sweeper and just missed out on becoming their 'Player of the Year'. In my second year, I fell out with Stapleton and found it hard to get back into the team, although the people on the local phone-in's couldn't believe I wasn't playing. Then Stapleton got sacked and eight or nine players were released on free transfers. After that I spent a few months at Guiseley, but basically I just fell out with football and decided to get a job.'

Wayne Heseltine began working for a friend who owned a flooring business and he eventually managed three shops before moving over to the commercial side in 1999. Continuing to live in the Bradford area, he now operates his own company which employs over 40 people and supplies flooring products to retail outlets all over Europe.

SCOTT, Ian Richard (1985/86, 1986/87)

Born: Horsforth, Leeds, 4th March 1969
Height: 5ft. 11ins., **Weight:** 12st. 1lb.
Role: Defender
Career: Yeadon Westfield Junior School (Leeds)/ Leeds Grammar School/ Leeds Boys/ West Yorkshire Boys/ Yorkshire Boys/ UNITED: Ass. Schoolboy May 1983 App. Pro. May 1985 Pro. March to June 1987/ Stockport County September 1987 to December 1988

Ian Scott was being utilised as a centre forward for Leeds Boys under-11's in a match against Newcastle Boys when he was spotted by a scout who later approached his father. United's representative had witnessed a display in which the youngster appeared comfortable on the ball, distributed it well and possessed a vision way beyond his years.

Later upgraded up to the Yorkshire Boys team, the county combination also contained future Red Karl Goddard and a soon-to-be England star in David Batty. 'I had trials with Leeds and Nottingham Forest,' he said. 'I went for another at Barnsley, a club I was very impressed with, and I also generated some attention from Arsenal and Manchester City. I received an offer from Elland Road, but my father convinced me to accept schoolboy terms with United as Leeds were then languishing in the Second Division. I was only twelve when I first went to Manchester. Eric Harrison took me under his wing at Old Trafford and he had a huge influence on my development.'

While still at school, he represented the Reds in numerous friendly matches over the duration of the 1984/85 season, making his competitive debut for the 'B' team in February 1985 in their 1-1 home draw with Oldham. After developing physically, some of his earlier pace disappeared and he was moved back into midfield.

Stepping up and into the 'A' team as early as August 1985, most of his football that term was played in an even deeper position, as a defender, and it was at the back where he was initially used in the Youth Cup. Because it was felt that someone tall and who could read the game well was required for the opening tie at Burnley in the December, Harrison selected him at centre-half. As was usually the case, the coach was proved right when the Reds left Turf Moor with an encouraging 2-0 win to their credit.

As a result of injuries to Mark Higgins and Graeme Hogg, barely a month had passed before Scott was introduced to the Reserves for the first time, the Reds losing 2-0 to Newcastle at Old Trafford, and a couple of days later he was present for a Youth Cup Third Round game at Chesterfield.

During the early months of 1986 he was in and out of action because of a hamstring injury, consequently missing the Youth Cup ties against Notts County and Sheffield United, as well as an England under-17 Youth trial, but was then included in all of the Youth Cup semi-final and final ties and the last Central League fixture of the campaign. He was unfortunate to miss out on three gold medals that season as, not only did the Youth Cup final result in failure, the 'A' team finished second to Manchester City in their division while the 'B' side ended level on points and goal difference with Oldham only to lose the title on the number of goals scored.

At the end of the campaign he was involved in a remarkable experience when United's youngsters took part in the 15th International Salem Youth Tournament. Accompanied by elder statesman Bobby Charlton, they flew to Zurich prior to completing the journey to Munich by coach, whereupon the Yorkshire teenager was chosen for all five matches. He explained, 'On our way home we were involved in a friendly fixture against Zurich Blue Stars Youth and Charlton, who I believe was then aged 48, played for us under the assumed name of Newman. We won an easy game 9-0 and 'Newman' scored two of our goals. One of them was from a ferocious shot that screamed into the net from near the half-way line!'

Scott continued his education throughout the 1986/87 term while training on Tuesdays, Wednesdays and Thursdays. On most Fridays he would return to Leeds to study for his A-levels and then attend school on the Monday prior to returning to Manchester for another 'three-day week'. He was soon captaining the 'A' side and making occasional appearances in the Reserves, although all wasn't rosy for him as around this time he suffered from continual hamstring and back problems due to growing quickly.

In November 1986, he came up against his former Yorkshire Boys team-mate Batty, who was in the Leeds Reserve side when the Reds ran out 3-0 winners on the night. However, the major happening at the club that month was undoubtedly the introduction of Alex Ferguson as United's new manager.

At the beginning of the following month Scott captained the Youth Cup team to a 4-0 win at Wrexham, which in turn set up a Third Round home tie against Leicester. With United putting on a poor performance, the Foxes were good value for their 2-1 win and the watching Ferguson made it known that he was totally underwhelmed by the side's display.

Signing professional terms in March 1987, the April of that year saw his participation in the Real Sociedad Youth Tournament in Spain, where the Reds lost the final 8-7 on penalties to Italian side Torino.

The next development in his career was the one he truly dreaded, that of his release. *'Because my form had dipped due to injuries, Ferguson's decision to let me go couldn't really be questioned and I simply had to take it on the chin,'* he reflected ruefully. *'The manager praised my attitude and application and also reassured me that I was good enough to carve out a future at another club. It was left to me to decide whether to stay or not for what little remained of the season.'* Electing to see out his contract so as to put himself in the shop window, in early May he invested his last 90-minute shift for United when scoring once in a 3-0 win at Manchester City 'A'.

Port Vale trialled him in July 1987 and he duplicated the process at Notts County immediately afterwards. Receiving offers from both of them, a contract at Stockport showed itself to be much more beneficial and following his Fourth Division debut for County a little while later, constant injury set-backs, which included a hernia operation, restricted him to only 25 league games for the club. When he developed a stress fracture in his back in 1988, a surgeon advised him to quit.

Upon that recommendation he returned to Leeds early in 1989 when career advice was sought from his former grammar school economics teacher. Joining the insurance division of Barclays Bank, he learned the ropes for four years before switching to another company in the same field.

Ian Scott has been an insurance broker for approximately twenty years and was last heard of managing a sales team based in the north of England.

LYDIATE, Jason Lee (1987/88, 1988/89, 1989/90)

Born: Manchester, 29th October 1971
Height: 5ft. 11ins., **Weight:** 12st. 4lbs.
Role: Central defender
Career: Barton Moss Primary School (Eccles)/ Eccles Secondary Modern School/ Eccles Boys/ Salford Boys/ North-West County Boys/ UNITED: Ass. Schoolboy January 1987 Trainee July 1988 Pro. June 1990/ Bolton Wanderers March 1992/ Blackpool March 1995/ Scarborough August 1998 to May 1999/ Rochdale (L) February to May 1999/ Finn Harps (Ire) August and September 1999/ Winsford United September 1999/ Hyde United February to April 2003

While the media are keen to portray the lives of professional footballers as being full of flash cars, WAGs and 'loadsa money', it can often be a precarious one, because an injury could wreck a career in a instant and tactics or unfamiliar formations can make them an instant hit or a total flop with supporters. Changes at the helm often create uncertainty around a club's entire playing and backroom staff and, in fact, the movement of most individuals between locations is directly related to the sport's managerial merry-go-round.

However, while a recent change of personnel in the Old Trafford hot-seat may have spelt the end for some, in the early months of 1987 it actually worked in one person's favour. *'I'm not sure how it came about,'* Jason Lydiate puzzled. *'I was playing for Salford Boys one Saturday morning when Joe Brown asked my dad if I fancied coming down for trials. Well, I was a keen United fan and couldn't wait to try out. I had already been down to see Blackburn and Manchester City, and there were numerous other clubs showing interest at the time.*

I was offered schoolboy terms by United and I signed them, and then it was coming to the time when we were due to be told if we were going to be offered a YTS place. Ron Atkinson wasn't going to offer me a place but later on Alex Ferguson saw me in training and wanted to sign me. It was then that I was offered a two-year YTS deal with a two-year professional contract to follow.'

Growing up in Eccles, where he began playing football for his school team in the week, by the age of ten he was representing Eccles Boys on Saturday mornings. Upon moving to secondary school he joined a productive Salford Sunday League side, Barr Hill, and over the next few years was party to league and cup honours with them while also advancing into the Salford Boys under-14 and under-15 teams.

Further progress was made when he was selected for North-West County Boys and also received an invite to England trials at Lilleshall. Already five feet, ten inches tall at the age of fifteen, his bodily credentials and mentality matched those required of a centre-back as he was powerful in the air, a superb tackler, quick, highly aggressive and almost allergic to fear.

He made it through to the last 40 candidates at Lilleshall and was included in the international 'shadow squad', whose purpose was to act as cover should any of those selected get injured or become unavailable. Any disappointment felt at missing out for England Boys was soon put to one side as he was ready to join United and thereby follow in the footsteps of his uncle Gerald, who had been a junior with the Reds in the 1956/57 season.

Lydiate was still a pupil at Eccles Secondary Modern School during the 1987/88 term but, being local and also physically mature beyond his years, he was immediately thrust into the thick of things when chosen for the opening 'B' team fixture of the campaign, in which Crewe were defeated 4-2 in the first leg of the Supplementary Cup final.

After only ten more 'B' team games he was unexpectedly beckoned into the Youth Cup squad that faced Mansfield at Old Trafford where, on a night best forgotten, the Reds were second best all over the pitch. Losing the tie 2-1, the team were told a few home truths by Eric Harrison at its conclusion.

He had taken part in over 30 matches by the end of that season at which point, with schooling now over, he could give football his full attention while working with one of the games best ever youth coaches. *'Eric was a really hard man but I have to say I never had a problem with him,'* he claimed. *'He was really fair and everyone knew where they stood. I suppose being a 100 per cent type player actually helped me and, although I was never the best technically, I knew that I could learn a lot from him in that area.'*

It was somewhat of a pleasant development when, just a month after signing as a trainee, he was required for the Reserves as Barnsley visited on the opening day of the 1988/89 term. With Derek Brazil and Wayne Heseltine holding down the centre-back positions, he slotted in at right full-back and performed admirably in a 4-2 success. Mainly featuring in both of the junior sides throughout the term, his experience also expanded to ten Reserve games and all five Youth Cup ties.

Lydiate totalled seven appearances in the second string, as well as making a major contribution towards the 'A' team topping the Lancashire League in the 1989/90 campaign, and he was also designated as captain of the Youth Cup team as the young Reds once again reached the semi-final.

With Steve Bruce and Gary Pallister at their collective peak in the first-team, competition in the Reserves was intense with Brazil, Mal Donaghy and Neil Whitworth all challenging him for a place in the middle of the defence. Nevertheless, the 1990/91 season turned out to be one of his best for, not only did he make 25 appearances, the nineteen year-old also took the 'Denzil Haroun Reserve Team Player of the Year' award.

Recalling that time, he commented, *'I was really happy with my form and all the coaching staff were saying just to keep it up. I knew I was well thought of and I often trained with the first-team.'*

He kick-started the 1991/92 term with a couple of 'A' team matches before rejoining the Reserves in early September. Soon out of action through injury, he featured only once over the next three months before returning to the 'A' team in mid-December. Forcing his way back into the Reserves in the New Year, the defender spoke of a conclusion he had reached, *'In my last season I started to get a problem with my back. I never got to the bottom of it, but it would flare up from time to time and I was out of action for a few months. I was in the last year of my contract and when I got back in the team I started to give my future some thought. I went to see the manager and just asked him what my chances were of breaking into the first-team.*

We were going well at the top of the league and, although Steve Bruce was 31, he was playing out of his skin while Gary Pallister was still only 27. Fergie told me that he couldn't see me breaking up that partnership, certainly not in the short term. So I had a really big decision to make, either sign a new contract and wait it out in the Reserves or try my luck elsewhere.'

Dressing himself in a United strip for the last time in March 1992, within a couple of hours the second string had drawn 0-0 at Rotherham.

Bolton manager Phil Neal quickly came up with the offer of a three-year deal and immediately drafted him into the Trotters' first-team for a defeat at Preston. By the end of the campaign he had started a total of three games and just when things were going tickety-boo, Neal was dismissed only for Bruce Rioch to take over. Unfortunately for Lydiate, Rioch had an alternative agenda for the Bolton defence and over the next three seasons he averaged only about ten matches per term.

It was no surprise, then, when a fall-out ensued and he moved to another Lancashire destination in March 1995. After three years and 86 league appearances for Blackpool, the end of his contract and a change in manager forced him to join Scarborough. Straight away realising his mistake as the long travelling hours took their toll, in the end it was agreed that he could link up with Rochdale on loan until his deal expired.

In the summer of 1999 his availability generated little interest from Football League clubs so he spent a two-game spell with Finn Harps in Ireland before helping out an ex-Bolton colleague by putting in just 90 minutes for Winsford. Then deciding to take a rest from the game while working in Hope Hospital, two years later he undertook a plastering course prior to starting his own business.

From February to April 2003, Jason Lydiate figured in ten games for Hyde United while continuing in the building trade for the next couple of years. Now employed by a company that undertakes repair services, he is currently working towards his UEFA Level Three coaching badge with a view to getting back into the game as a coach or manager at some stage.

GARDNER, Stephen George (1985/86)

Born: Middlesbrough, 3rd July 1968
Height: 5ft. 9ins., **Weight:** 11st. 8lbs.
Role: Central defender
Career: Sacred Heart Junior School (Middlesbrough)/ St. Paul's Secondary School (Teeside)/ Middlesbrough Boys/ Cleveland Boys/ **UNITED:** Ass. Schoolboy March 1983 App. Pro. May 1984 Pro. July 1986/ **Burnley** July 1987 to June 1990/ **Glossop North End** February to May 1991/ **Bradford City** August to November 1991/ **Bury** October 1992 to January 1993/ **Witton Albion** March 1993/ **Rossendale United** June 1993 to May 1994/ **Bacup Borough** August 2000 to c/s 2001

Some football careers are defined by championship or cup-winning goals, whereas others are altered by serious injury, loss of form, a dip in enthusiasm or a fall-out with a coach or manager. However, rarely are they changed on the whim of a football club chairman just days after putting in a 'Man of the Match' display against the current leaders of the Premiership.

It was January 1993, with a cold, blustery wind chilling both spectators and players alike, when an ex-United junior returned to Old Trafford in the white jersey of Bury. Little did he know that it would be his last game as a professional footballer, despite winning his personal battle against one of the Premiership's most effective strike forces.

Steve Gardner told how he came to be involved in that match when explaining, *'A Bury scout had been in contact with me before Christmas to suggest I come down for a trial. I wasn't playing for anyone at the time, but my fitness was still good because I used to do a lot of martial arts. I had a trial, and I joined them on a pay-per-game basis as we couldn't agree terms. Bury were drawn against United in the Third Round of the F.A. Cup and I was thrown straight in. I had a great game marking Eric Cantona and Mark Hughes, and neither of them scored so I was really happy with my performance.*

I went into work on the following Wednesday as normal and the Bury chairman called me to say that the club wanted to offer me a permanent contract. He also said that I needed to sign it right away, which I did. I then found out that five Premiership clubs had showed an interest in me so I went straight back to the chairman and told him what I had just heard.

Basically, Bury wanted money, and before I signed for them they wouldn't have got a penny. I asked the chairman to let me talk to the other clubs and release me, but he refused and decided to hold my registration. It wasn't like they paid any money for me, or had spent years developing me, it was just a way of making money out of me. So I walked out and never played for them again.'

A resident of Croft Street in Middlesbrough all through his formative years, he came from a family with sporting inclinations, because his father was a notable boxer in the Army and an uncle showed enough football ability to be trialled at Huddersfield. By the time he was twelve, Gardner was a key member of a Nunthorpe Athletic under-12 side that was associated with Middlesbrough Football Club. Making a name for himself on Saturday mornings either at centre-half or centre-forward, it wasn't long before scouts began attending Nunthorpe's matches with increasing frequency.

'When I was twelve, we went on holiday to Tenerife and there was an under-18 tournament going on,' he recalled. 'I ended up playing and a scout from Ipswich Town saw me and invited me for trials. I played for Middlesbrough Boys from under-12's right through to under-15's and I was also in the Cleveland County team from the age of thirteen to fifteen, as well as turning out for my school and going for trials. Middlesbrough Boys were a very good side and we did quite well. My stepfather, Tommy, was great. He took me everywhere and I wouldn't have got anywhere without him. I made the last 22 in trials for England Boys, but I needed to get signed up with a professional club like most of the other lads.'

Middlesbrough Boys defeated Southampton in the quarter-final of the 1982/83 English Schools' Trophy and met South London at the last four stage. With future professionals Stuart Ripley and Colin West in fine form, the Teesiders navigated the tricky tie and then faced Sunderland in a two-legged final. A 4-4 aggregate score meant that both sides shared the trophy and Gardner had collected his first significant honour.

He was assessed by numerous clubs up and down the country, including his beloved Middlesbrough, and eventually bowed to the lure of Manchester United in the spring of 1983. During his last year at school, the prospect made numerous trips to Manchester in the 1983/84 season and was used in fourteen friendly matches over the period. While naturally a little homesick in his stays at Salford University's Halls of Residence, that feeling was more than outweighed by the thought of becoming a professional footballer.

Moving down to the North-West in 1984, after which he shared a place with Norman Whiteside and Paul McGrath in Chorlton-cum-Hardy, he commented of his room-mates, *'I know a lot has been written about those guys, but they were fantastic with me. I was Bryan Robson's 'boot boy' and the senior players made it feel like a big family. If there were any problems Robbo was just brilliant, he would sort everything out for you. He went way above just being the team and club captain, he was a mentor to every player and everyone looked up to him.'*

In the September of his first full term, Gardner was utilised in the Reserves' friendly with Abbey Hulton Suburban and continued playing in junior friendly matches until Burnley informed the Lancashire League that due to financial pressures they were unable to fulfil their divisional obligations. United were asked if they would be willing to take over the Clarets' outstanding matches and after reaching an agreement, the 'B' team suddenly had fifteen fixtures to squeeze in between February and May. Subsequently, and with a dearth of young talent available, the defender was required for competitive action and he ended the campaign with the most appearances for the 'B' side as they finished up second to Blackburn.

By that stage he had also been elevated up to the 'A' team, for whom he acted as one of their back four and team captain in 33 out of 36 fixtures. Scoring three times in the first six games as the Lancashire League Division One side went on an unbeaten eighteen-match start to the 1985/86 season, when the opening round of the Youth Cup came along in December, there was a huge fillip in store for him. *'Eric Harrison pulled me to one side and told me that I was going to made captain,'* he said proudly. *'He predicted that I was going to take the team all the way to the final and win the Youth Cup for the club. Eric was the greatest coach that I ever worked with. He had amazing vision and knowledge of the game. He could have done anything he wanted.*

It was a fantastic experience. The senior pro's treated us like superstars playing in the World Cup. Most of the first-team would watch us and there was a great buzz about the place when we played Youth Cup matches.

In the semi-final against Coventry I had to mark Steve Livingstone, one of my mates from Middlesbrough. That was one hell of a battle. Unfortunately, we came up against a really strong Manchester City team whose players were all in the Reserves and pushing into the first-team.'

Gardner ended the term at the top of the 'A' side's appearance table and when domestic responsibilities were finally completed, he and his teenage colleagues participated in the Salem Youth Tournament in mid-May as their campaign finally came to a close.

Now in his third year with the club and looking for a new contract, the 1986/87 season was one where he needed to impress new manager Alex Ferguson. He continued to captain the 'A' side over the opening weeks, his consistency at that grade earning him a call up to the Reserves in November for a 3-1 defeat at Liverpool. Later featuring in a few more Central League matches, there was also the matter of stiff competition for a centre-back place from Billy Garton, Graeme Hogg and Simon Ratcliffe, all of whom were ahead of him in the pecking order.

He went on to score five times in six 'A' team games through March and April as the Reds raced away to the league title by six points from Everton, and in the latter month he registered one of the goals in a 2-2 draw with Torino in the final of the Real Sociedad Youth Tournament final, the United boys eventually losing out 8-7 on penalties.

A stylish, well-balanced and naturally two-footed ball player who possessed decent pace, his main defensive qualities consisted of being strong in the air and powerful in the tackle when necessary. A late developer, which was a view Eric Harrison passed on to Alex Ferguson, his form and potential prompted the manager into tabling a new deal. It wasn't the end of the matter, though, as the subject of Ferguson's offer disclosed, *'I loved it at United. Training every day with some of the world's greatest players, it was just fabulous. But when I was offered a new contract the wages weren't that great. I was getting married, with a child on the way, and thought that at eighteen I could get a better deal somewhere else. Crystal Palace were interested, but when Burnley came in it just made sense.'*

Gardner's last game for United 'A' ended in a 3-0 win at Manchester City in May 1987 and he joined the Fourth Division outfit in July.

He made an impressive start at Turf Moor, notching up 85 appearances while winning the 'Young Player of the Year' award in both of his first two terms, and he also assisted Burnley to reach the Sherpa Van Trophy final at Wembley. At the beginning of the 1989/90 campaign, his hot form turned ice cold when he broke his leg in training and was unable to regain a place in the side under a new manager. While there was some interest from Celtic, a lack of match practice together with his injury resulted in his contract expiring.

Without a club, he began working as a contract manager for a building company and was asked to help out at Glossop for the final few months of the 1990/91 season. He then underwent a six-week trial at Bradford City, whose management tabled a one-year deal. However, early into the new term, Frank Stapleton and Colin Todd took over the reins and decided the recent recruit was surplus to requirements. The club then chose to pay up

Gardner's contract in full before the Christmas period and once again he was out of work. Still only 23 years-old, with a solid body of relevant experience behind him, he felt disappointed that so little interest was shown from Football League clubs and so, when the opportunity to join Bury presented itself, the chance was grasped with both hands.

He revealed how the direction of his life has changed since when mentioning, *'I worked at Phillips as a supervisor in Padiham for the next eight years or so until my wife was offered a job in Texas. She works for a medical company and they offered her a very good role in their US operation. I played for a year at Rossendale and turned out a few times for Bacup, just doing a favour for a friend, but there was no reason to stay in the UK. So we moved over in 2003 and I got a job with my wife's company.'*

Steve Gardner still lives in Mission, Texas, and is currently studying for his UEFA badges. Also involved in coaching South Texas Academy's nine-to-eighteen year-old age groups at MLS club Houston Dynamos on a part-time basis, he sums up his earlier time in the sport when claiming, *'I still tell people that my first game as a professional was for Manchester United and my last was against Manchester United.'*

TONGE, Alan John (1988/89, 1989/90)

Born: Bury, 25th February 1972
Height: 5ft. 8ins., **Weight:** 11st. 11lbs.
Role: Central defender or right full-back
Career: Mytham Road Primary School (Bolton)/ Little Lever Secondary School/ Bolton Boys/ Greater Manchester Boys/ UNITED: Ass. Schoolboy January 1987 Trainee July 1988 Pro. July 1990 to June 1991/ Horwich RMI August 1991/ Exeter City December 1991/ Elmore July 1994/ Clyst Rovers July to December 1995

It goes without saying that determination is one of the major factors required to make it in the game, but it probably takes just as much will-power and grit to build an alternative career after being released by arguably the world's most famous football club, on top of then needing to deal with a debilitating back injury that puts an end to one's career in sport.

In the spring of 1991, Alan Tonge was told that he wasn't good enough to make it with the Reds and he managed the disappointment stoically by continuing to assist the club's 'A' team. Later chosen for four out of five games in a Blue Stars Tournament effort which ended in a 2-1 final defeat by Spartak Moscow, at the end of May he was one of the squad who undertook a short two-match tour to Trinidad.

In the July of that year he was assessed for potential employment over a three-week period by Bolton Wanderers before joining Rochdale for the same purpose. When nothing materialised from his seven-day stay at Spotland, Horwich RMI took him on board until a call was received out of the blue from Exeter City boss Alan Ball in November. The former World Cup winner was aware of his release and, remembering the defender's performances on a trip to Russia, offered him a two and a half year contract.

Even though the nineteen year-old eventually totalled fourteen starts and five substitute appearances in the league for Exeter, severe disc problems in his back required two major operations, the first of which was extremely serious and needed four screws and two plates to be inserted in the affected area. It transpired that he had been born with a bone missing from his back, and years of competitive football had aggravated it to such an extent that it threatened his well-being. After spending about a year and a half trying to regain full fitness, and with his mobility practically gone and hardly able to touch his toes, it was at that point when a surgeon suggested he think about doing something else for a living.

Not wanting to give up football completely, Tonge signed for Western Football League members Elmore for a year before transferring to Clyst Rovers in the Western Football League Premier Division for a spell.

Unfortunately, his back issues resurfaced and forced him to give up the game for good at the age of just 23. During the period spent in non-league circles he was also employed as a driver for an agency and so decided to move back to Bolton to join the White Arrow Group in the same capacity.

A three-year stint as a warehouseman/driver with TNT in Rotherham provided a solid if unsatisfying living and, feeling that he could achieve much more, in September 2000 he took control of his future by enrolling for a three-year degree course in Sports Science at the Bolton Institute. Creditably obtaining a 2:1, another twelve months spent studying to be a teacher paid off in July 2004 when he obtained a post at a school in Manchester.

Born in Bury's Fairfield Hospital, a route into competitive football initially came via his primary school side and he then joined Farnworth Boys at age eleven prior to moving to Moss Bank in the Bolton Boys Federation. A central midfielder in those days, at thirteen he linked up with Bolton Lads Club and was then selected for Bolton Boys.

It was while attached to the former that Reds' scout George Knight spotted him and from then on he attended training sessions at the School of Excellence on Monday and Thursday evenings at The Cliff. The youngster went for trials with Manchester City and Oldham, and was also offered schoolboy terms by Bolton but, influenced by his personal allegiance towards the club, once United had shown an interest he was determined to join the ranks at Old Trafford. By then situated at full-back, Tonge went on to win further honours by playing for Greater Manchester Boys at under-14 level prior to penning schoolboy terms for the Reds early in 1987.

Debuting in the number two jersey for the 'B' side on the opening day of the 1987/88 season against Marine Youth, he was used in eighteen of their 26 league fixtures and also took part in friendly matches against Canterbury under-17's of New Zealand and an F.A. School of Excellence combination at The Cliff, as well as Chinguacousy of Canada at Ayrshire Road.

He commenced the following term in the 'A' team and clocked up eleven matches for them in addition to starting another nineteen games for the 'B' side. Selected in central defence for a 5-2 Youth Cup win at Darlington in December 1988, he then made his first two appearances on the Old Trafford pitch within the space of 48 hours as, following the Youth Cup win over Sheffield Wednesday on the 17th January, by the 19th of that month he had been sent on as a substitute in a 7-1 thrashing of West Brom Reserves. He later featured in a Youth Cup tie with Ipswich before he and his under-18 colleagues were eliminated by Brentford in a shock Fifth Round defeat.

Even so, his form was such that he was called on to travel to Moscow with a Football League under-18 representative team that was managed by Lawrie McMenemy and Alan Ball. Situated at centre-half and acting as captain, his side swept to a 2-1 victory. Upon returning to England he continued to help out a 'B' team that cruised to a Lancashire League title by a cool eleven points while conceding only a miserly twenty goals during the whole campaign. At the end of that season he was included in the first-team squad for a friendly against Histon at Cambridge United's ground and while there Alex Ferguson used him as a replacement for Lee Martin in the 3-1 win.

He became an 'A' team stalwart in the 1989/90 term and was selected to participate in the Grossi-Morera Youth Tournament in September. The tour got off to an interesting start when an unfamiliar moniker unexpectedly cropped up, and all of the squad members were stunned to hear that the former Ryan Wilson had recently assumed his mother's maiden name. Tonge said of that incident, *'As part of the referee's checks, an official read out your name and you had to stand up. It came to Ryan and the official read out 'Ryan Giggs'. All the lads were looking at one another thinking 'Ryan who?' Mine got read out as Alan Tonj, the 'ge' pronounced as a 'j', and Brian Kidd took great jest in calling me that for the rest of the trip.'*

With the Reds defeating the likes of AC Milan, Napoli and Torino over in Italy, they faced Auxerre in a final in which a wonderful performance saw Eric Harrison's team win by a 4-1 margin.

After the turn of the year he once again occupied a role in central defence for a Youth Cup match at Burnley before moving to right full-back for the next stage. However, a bad tackle with fifteen minutes to go at Vale Park resulted in a red card which saw him banned for the Fourth Round win over Sheffield Wednesday. Of that transgression he said, *'I was silly, I shouldn't have done it. Their left winger was giving me verbals, so I decided to sort him out. It was the crowd that got me done, they started chanting 'off, off, off.'*

He reclaimed his place in the side as United then defeated Leicester to reach a semi-final in which they came up against a handy Tottenham Hotspur team. There was no great concern in the camp when the Reds lost the first leg at White Hart Lane, because it was felt that the tie could be turned around in Manchester. Unfortunately, a solitary Adrian Doherty goal wasn't enough to overturn a 2-0 deficit and United were eliminated 3-1 on aggregate, although Tonge's disappointment was slightly offset as his 'A' team had already been crowned Lancashire League champions.

He continued in the 'A' team through most of his final season at the club and also saw service in four of the Reserves' fixtures. A no-nonsense character who was useful on the ball and built up a reputation for putting in consistent displays, his problem lay in the fact that senior stars such as Viv Anderson and Mal Donaghy blocked his path to the second string. With his 'A' side on their way to pipping Manchester City by one point to take the divisional title for the second successive year, it was then that Alex Ferguson explained his contract wasn't going to be renewed.

While disappointed, especially as he felt that another one-year deal would have been appropriate, the decision was out of his hands. At least his last domestic game for the Reds ended in a victory, when the Reserves won 4-2 at Sheffield United on the 1st May 1991.

Still living in Bolton, Alan Tonge now teaches BTEC Sports Science for sixteen-to-eighteen year-old students at Wright Robinson Sixth Form College in Manchester. He recently claimed of his time at Old Trafford, *'I was fortunate to train and play with some brilliant footballers. One of the saddest things I carry to this day was that I didn't get any first-team appearances, apart from the friendly at Histon. Sadly, that wasn't meant to be.'*

United babes wing way to glory

Chapter Six

HARRISON'S HEROES

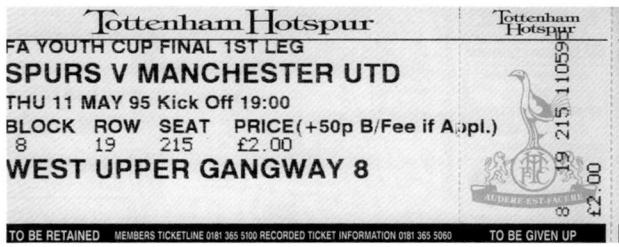

1991-92

1) Sean Musgrave	9) Craig Russell	1) Kevin Pilkington	9) Colin McKee
2) Paul Gate	10) Ian Lawson	2) Mark Gordon	10) Robbie Savage
3) Paul Harwood	11) Martin Smith	3) George Switzer	11) Ben Thornley
4) Paul Jeffrey	*12) David Carr (for 2)*	4) John O'Kane	*12) David Beckham (for 7)*
5) Andrew Scothern	*14) David Ferry (for 10)*	5) Gary Neville	*14) Chris Casper*
6) Gareth Cronin		6) Keith Gillespie	
7) Dean McGee		7) Nicky Butt	
8) Michael Gray		8) Simon Davies	

NOVEMBER 1991

SUNDERLAND 2 v 4 MANCHESTER UNITED
Lawson, Russell (pen)   Gillespie, McKee (2), Savage

Wednesday 27th
Kick-off 7.00 p.m.

second round

Red babes top the hit parade

In light of the relative successes of the past three seasons, when one quarter-final and two consecutive Youth Cup semi-final appearances were achieved, it was blindingly obvious that the club was now firmly back on track as far as their youth policy was concerned.

Encouragingly, the many whispers emanating from those die-hard United supporters who were in regular attendance for Lancashire League matches at The Cliff and Littleton Road gave rise to indications about the stock now coming through the system as being the best for some considerable time.

With the opening Youth Cup game approaching, the recent form of the juniors was encouraging as the 'A' team had secured one draw and eight wins from their eleven fixtures while Blackpool were already accounted for in the Lancashire Youth Cup. Emerging strongly from a shaky start to their season, the 'B' squad's revival saw them stringing seven straight victories together.

Despite Eric Harrison fielding a largely new line-up in a tough looking tie at Sunderland, the fresh batch of cadets came away with a morale-boosting win. Of the twelve who took part in the second leg of last season's semi-final, only Davies, McKee, Thornley and Gordon were selected for the match at Roker Park.

In view of Alex Ferguson's long-since stated intention about the club needing to claim a much greater share of the locally available talent, it was heartening to see that four of the newcomers to the starting eleven were from Manchester or its surrounds. Left-back George Switzer was a Salford recruit while Ben Thornley and Gary Neville both came from only slightly further afield at Bury. Midfielder Nicky Butt, in the opinion of many observers the best prospect of them all, was a bona fide Mancunian from the High Bank area of Gorton.

Signs that United weren't restricting their recruitment drive exclusively to the immediate locality were evidenced with the capture of goalkeeper Kevin Pilkington (Derbyshire), Keith Gillespie (Northern Ireland) and Robbie Savage (Wrexham).

Unusually, Alex Ferguson overruled Harrison's request to include Ryan Giggs in the side at Sunderland. The Welsh under-21 international, whose 18th birthday fell two days later, was now considered a fully fledged first-teamer and the manager wasn't prepared to expose his young protégé to injury or fatigue. Ferguson said of his decision, *'We want Ryan fresh for the first-team on Saturday. We've also kept him out in fairness to the youth strikers.'*

Colin McKee, whose hat-trick helped to secure a 6-1 win for the Reserves over Manchester City on the previous Saturday, took hardly any time to keep his scoring run going through registering the opener against Sunderland in only 80 seconds. A cross from the right by newcomer Butt was just too great an invitation for McKee, whose sweet connection resulted in his looping header sailing over Sean Musgrave.

The early goal provided a considerable fillip and United further increased their lead in only the tenth minute when another centre, this time from Gillespie, was headed downwards and into the net by an unmarked Savage. The goal was one of terrific teamwork and culminated a move involving eleven passes which stretched the home defence to breaking point. Just a minute later, Sunderland countered with a brilliant reply from Ian Lawson, his header from Martin Smith's superb cross from the left wing beating Pilkington with some style.

The gulf in quality between the two sides was proven when United stepped up the pace to all but kill off their opponents with just a couple of effective attacking moves. In the 24th minute Gillespie released McKee, who produced a lightning burst of speed to gain possession. McKee's pace took him away from Sunderland's rearguard and he then completed a reasonably simple task by placing the ball past Musgrave. Three minutes later, the compliment was returned when Gillespie took on the Scot's pass and ran from a deep position before hammering a fierce shot home to make it 4-1.

Straight after the change of ends there was something of a transformation from the host eleven who were helped by a sprinkling of snow which began falling immediately prior to the break. With the downfall continuing throughout the interval and just into the second period, the home team were fortunate to be able to change their footwear, or possibly just utilise longer studs, whereas the Reds were simply forced to make do with the boots they were wearing.

Added to the feeling they had no option other than to employ an all-out attacking policy, Sunderland were infused with a passion to set about their deficit and they pinned United back for almost all of the concluding half. During that spell, Martin Smith hit a post and Pilkington later made a splendid save from Michael Gray's long-range attempt.

Sunderland were rewarded in the 72nd minute when Craig Russell was sent tumbling in the penalty area only to dust himself down and convert the resulting spot kick with great composure. In the very last minute, Smith mustered up a rasping drive and watched as his attempt again came back off the woodwork.

Speaking of the team's contrasting performance on either side of the interval, Eric Harrison sounded exasperated when saying, *'They took me to the heights and depths both on the same evening, but overall I'm very pleased with the result.'*

The Review's correspondent felt the youngsters were *'brilliant'* in the first half as they oozed *'sheer class in every department'*, and the same reporter also claimed that it had been *'many a long year since a United youth team displayed such beautiful football'.*

Savage by name, humorous by nature, the Welsh teenager headed United into a two-goal lead at Roker Park

366

1) Kevin Pilkington	9) Colin McKee	1) John Norris	9) Danny Donovan
2) Mark Gordon	10) Robbie Savage	2) Richard Knight	10) Steve McManus
3) George Switzer	11) Ben Thornley	3) Keith Russell	11) Martin Butler
4) John O'Kane	*12) Chris Casper*	4) Chris Demetrios	*12) Wayne Instone*
5) Gary Neville	*14) Ryan Giggs (for 10)*	5) Richard Brown	*14) Steve Vaughan*
6) Keith Gillespie		6) Stuart Ryder	
7) Nicky Butt		7) Steve Winter	
8) Simon Davies		8) David Edwards	

1991-92

MANCHESTER UNITED 2 v 1 WALSALL

Butt, Thornley — Winter

DECEMBER 1991

Tuesday 17th

Kick-off 7.00 p.m.

Attendance 5,410

third round

With the first-team capturing the European Super Cup by defeating Red Star Belgrade courtesy of a one goal to nil margin at Old Trafford just a month ago, and sustained successes by the seniors in the Barclays League and Rumbelows Cup, it was hardly surprising that the visit of Walsall was greeted by United's biggest Youth Cup attendance for five years.

At the same stage of the competition in the previous season, the Reds played out a draw with Everton before a crowd of just over 1,600 spectators, yet for the visit of the Saddlers just eleven months later, the gate had swollen to almost three and a half times that number.

United's starting line-up was identical to the one that returned victorious from Sunderland and Eric Harrison was even afforded the luxury of naming Ryan Giggs as a substitute. Gigg's inclusion in the squad caused Alex Ferguson to comment, *'He is keen to play with the boys he is growing up with, (although) Eric wants to keep faith with the team who have been playing while Ryan has been in the first-team. So we will get him involved and keep him in reserve if things are not going our way.'*

Walsall experienced the misfortune of finding star striker Neil Tolson ruled out through suspension, an absence caused by his dismissal in a junior game. Forced to miss the glamour trip to Manchester while serving out a three-match ban, the prolific Tolson had only recently scored an extra-time winner for the Saddlers to clinch a 3-2 victory at West Brom and put his side into the semi-final of the Midland Youth Cup, an achievement made all the more remarkable as Walsall were actually trailing 2-0 at one stage.

The Bescot Stadium juniors also included a West Country boy called Steve Winter in their ranks, a midfielder who earned the Saddlers their right to meet United when coming off the bench in the last round of the national competition and firing in a last-minute winner against Ipswich.

David Meek put together some notes on the Reds' close call:

Manchester United were lucky to squeeze through to the Fourth Round of the F.A. Youth Cup by 2-1 against Walsall at Old Trafford last night.

The Reds started well and were 2-0 up in half an hour. By the end, though, they were hanging on in the face of a plucky revival.

Walsall, who reckon they have their best youth team for some years, surprised United with the quality of their play and determined response in the second half.

Ben Thornley, former Salford schoolboy team-mate of Ryan Giggs, gave United the lead in the 17th minute with a fifteen-yard shot. Ten minutes later, Nicky Butt drove in number two.

Walsall gave the first indication of a revival just before the interval when Mark Gordon did well to block a shot from Chris Demetrios.

Simon Davies had a chance to make the game safe for United early in the second half after a brilliant run and a shot which beat the goalkeeper only for Richard Knight to clear off the line.

United found the waterlogged pitch more of a handicap than did the visitors and Steve Winter returned after being carried off to take a rebound off the goalkeeper in the 62nd minute.

The goal inspired Walsall's bid for a replay. Thornley hit a post for United, but it was they who came under the greater pressure as David Edwards and Martin Butler went close to an equaliser.

United brought on Giggs as a substitute for the last ten minutes to help clinch their escape.

On a surface described in the press as resembling *'a lake in parts',* the result of *'a heavy downpour in the hour prior to kick-off,'* the West Midlanders grew in confidence after scoring whereas the Reds were deemed to have *'just managed to hang on'* to their lead.

As well as a large measure of relief from the home support, there was also a genuine feeling of sympathy for the Saddlers within Old Trafford. The Review was even moved into making a comment about United's under-18's being *'made to fight every inch of the way'* for their win prior to adding that spectators would *'never have guessed Walsall were the youth section of a Fourth Division club'.*

The Review's judgement was invariably clouded by the 76th minute effort from Walsall's Butler, whose *'brilliant shot'* cannoned off the bar with Kevin Pilkington stranded, and Edwards' off-target header three minutes earlier, which was deemed as a *'gilt-edged chance'.*

It was those close calls which prompted coach Harrison into finally utilising Ryan Giggs. A late surge by the Reds demonstrated their capabilities more accurately, when Ben Thornley's strike rebounded from an upright and a Giggs shot skidded inches past a yawning goalmouth.

Simon Davies (top) scorned an opportunity to put the result beyond doubt while John O'Kane and his co-defenders were often stretched to keep Walsall at bay

1991-92

1) Richard Bibby	9) Jim Whitley
2) Gary Sliney	10) David Kerr
3) Rae Ingram	11) Scott Thomas
4) Richard Edghill	*12) Joe McLean (for 7)*
5) Nev Riches	*14) Micky Beirne (for 12)*
6) Steve Lomas	
7) Sean Harkin	
8) Adie Mike	

1) Kevin Pilkington	9) Robbie Savage
2) John O'Kane	10) Raphael Burke
3) George Switzer	11) Ben Thornley
4) Chris Casper	*12) David Beckham (for 6)*
5) Gary Neville	*14) Mark Gordon*
6) Keith Gillespie	
7) Nicky Butt	
8) Simon Davies	

FEBRUARY 1992

MANCHESTER CITY 1 v 3 MANCHESTER UNITED

Thomas *O'Kane, Thornley (2)*

Thursday 6th
Kick-off 7.00 p.m.
Attendance 5,424

fourth round

Of the last four Youth Cup meetings with Manchester City, United hadn't won a single one of them and so the news that an excursion to Maine Road was in the offing didn't exactly represent a preferred draw for Eric Harrison or his boys. The senior Reds were reeling from the effects of a devastating cup loss and a similar outcome in the junior tournament was the last thing anyone at the club could contemplate just then.

Caused by an injury to Colin McKee, Harrison gave Raphael Burke a start, as well as introducing Burnley-born Chris Casper to the defence, while Mark Gordon was elbowed out to make way for him.

Writing for the Evening News, City correspondent Paul Hince provided a taster for the clash:

Manchester City are plotting another cup upset for their arch rivals from Old Trafford. The kids from City and United lock horns in the Fourth Round of the F.A. Youth Cup at Maine Road tonight......24 hours after Alex Ferguson's senior side suffered a shock defeat against Southampton in the F.A. Cup.

Although the brilliant Ryan Giggs is still eligible for the Old Trafford youth team he has not been included in tonight's squad after playing against Southampton last night. Instead the Reds will be looking to their promising young wingers, Ben Thornley, who earned schoolboy honours with England, and Raphael Burke, who is a product of the F.A. School of Excellence at Lilleshall.

The Boy Blues have reached the Fourth Round stage with victories over Doncaster and West Brom and will rely heavily tonight on the penalty area menace of Old Trafford-born Adrian Mike who is the club's leading scorer at junior level.

City will be skippered by Northern Ireland schoolboy international Steve Lomas who, along with seventeen year-old Richard Edghill, has been in sparkling form during the Blues' run in the Youth Cup.

Says City's youth team coach Terry Darracott, 'Tonight's match should be a cracker. All derby games are fiercely contested because there is so much local pride at stake and that applies to the juniors every bit as much as to the seniors. United always have a strong youth team but I was impressed by the way our lads beat West Brom.'

City will open up the Main Stand for tonight's tie which kicks off at 7 p.m. Admission prices will be £2 for adults and £1 for juniors.

The same scribe also produced the following match report a day later:

United babes in the mood

MANCHESTER United's super kids have brought the smile back to the face of manager Alex Ferguson.

The Old Trafford boss was positively beaming after watching the Rookie Reds avenge their 1986 F.A Youth Cup final defeat with a richly-deserved victory over the Boy Blues in a pulsating fourth-round tie at Maine Road.

Roared on by a crowd of almost 5,500, the Reds drew first blood after 17 minutes when the all-action John O'Kane crashed in a close-range shot.

Eight minutes later the Old Trafford starlets were handed goal number two when an under-hit back-pass from Nev Riches landed straight at the feet of the impressive Ben Thornley, who skipped around the stranded Richard Bibby before stroking his shot into the empty net.

But the Maine Road kids are short of neither talent nor determination and Thornley's goal sparked a spirited revival inspired by their driving skipper Steve Lomas.

With striker Adie Mike threating to run riot, the Reds were suddenly under siege and the Blues scored the best goal of the game after 30 minutes following a dazzling, right-wing run from Mike followed by an inch-perfect cross headed home expertly by Scott Thomas.

The final nail in City's coffin was hammered in by the quicksilver Thornley 15 minutes from time when he cut in from the left to whip a ferocious shot into the bottom corner.

Said the happy Ferguson: "This makes up a little bit for the Southampton result. Both sets of kids did their clubs proud but we took control in the second half and were worthy winners in the end."

Ferguson's thoughts were mirrored by Blues boss Reid who conceded: " United were just too strong for us. I thought we were in with a chance at half time but they dominated after the interval."

In a scenario similar to that seen at the Youth Cup final six years before, the kick-off at Maine Road was delayed by ten minutes to allow a number of the crowd to gain entrance prior to the game commencing and the two teams then spent at least the same amount of time probing for their opponents' weak spots.

Once United slipped into a slick passing game, there was little the home side could do to contain them, and an observation from the Review regarding the Reds having *'turned the clock back to again display the tremendous one-touch football which had destroyed Sunderland inside 30 minutes in the Second Round at Roker Park'* was completely in tune with events on the pitch.

Apart from a spell of pressure either side of the half-hour mark, Kevin Pilkington was easily the least busy of the two goalkeepers on view at Maine Road

1991-92

1) Kevin Pilkington
2) John O'Kane
3) George Switzer
4) Chris Casper
5) Gary Neville
6) Colin McKee
7) Nicky Butt
8) Simon Davies
9) Robbie Savage
10) Ryan Giggs
11) Ben Thornley
12) *David Beckham (for 6)*
14) *Raphael Burke (for 11)*

1) Danny Coyne
2) Tony Draper
3) Marcus Richardson
4) Gary Jones
5) Michael Foster
6) Ian Cooke
7) Mike Edwards
8) Jon Kenworthy
9) Eddie McCullagh
10) Alan Morgan
11) Mike Smith
12) *Phil Johnson ◊*
14) *Paul Smith ◊*

MANCHESTER UNITED 2 v 0 TRANMERE ROVERS
Giggs (2)

FEBRUARY 1992

Thursday 13th

Kick-off 7.00 p.m.

Attendance 8,708

fifth round

Just a week separated the Reds' splendid victory at Maine Road and the visit of unfamiliar Youth Cup foes to Old Trafford for the Fifth Round. A point blank save from goalie Danny Coyne at Rotherham helped to ensure Tranmere's passage into the quarter-finals for the very first time and the Birkenhead club's march through the rounds also included a tremendous win at Anfield, as well as the elimination of a strong Oldham team.

Such was the importance placed on the game by United's management that Eric Harrison was given the thumbs up to include Ryan Giggs from the kick-off. Now a fully fledged Welsh international, Giggs wore the number two shirt for the seniors on the Saturday just gone but he was back in the under-18's forward-line for the eagerly anticipated Youth Cup contest.

The strength of Tranmere's youth set-up just then was such that they had enjoyed the better of the meetings between the two clubs at junior level so far that season and in retrospect, it was viewed as fortunate Giggs was available for the knock-out competition because it was his contribution that ultimately tipped the balance of fortune in United's favour.

Tranmere's 'A' side inflicted a crushing 5-0 defeat on United's third team at The Cliff on the opening day of the campaign and they proved the result was no fluke by following up that victory with a 1-0 winning margin on the Wirral in mid-December. The Prenton Park outfit's 'B' side won 2-0 at Littleton Road in September only for United 'B' to avenge their loss by securing a later 2-1 away win with goals from Ben Thornley and first-year trainee Paul Scholes.

Giggs was unquestionably the main attraction for a superb crowd of over 8,700 spectators and he rewarded their patronage with a goal in each half. However, his opener really belonged to Thornley, whose skill and speed was applied to a move which followed a superb tackle on the halfway line by Nicky Butt seven minutes before half-time. Butt sent Thornley on his way, and the winger then carried possession for more than 30 yards before darting inside and hammering a low cross-shot past the highly impressive Coyne. As the ball was just about to

Pictured fending off the attention of a Tranmere opponent, Nicky Butt won a challenge which eventually led to United taking the lead

cross the goal-line, Giggs, whose acceleration took him flying past a number of defenders, applied the finishing touch.

Tranmere were never entirely out of the running until the 61st minute, a point at which Giggs doubled his tally for the night. For the second time in the game, Coyne was given no chance of saving when his former international youth colleague converted a cross from the industrious Simon Davies.

The Evening News' reporter was full of praise for the visitors and noted *'Warwick Rimmer, the former Bolton midfielder, has put together a skilful side and only a particularly good performance by the United youngsters swung the game their way'*. The article also offered the opinion that *'United would have had more goals but for the excellence of Tranmere 'keeper Danny Coyne. The Welsh youth international was in brilliant form early on and continued to make great saves all night and keep Tranmere's talented team battling to the end'.*

Still unable to claim a starting berth, David Beckham made his third Youth Cup substitute appearance against a game Tranmere team

> *Everyone warned me that we would be in for a hard game and they were right. I thought it was going to be one of those nights when we would never score. Their goalkeeper was saving everything and I think it inspired them to hit back hard.*
>
> *But we played some decent football and I was pleased with everyone's performance. I think we have some very useful players in this season's team. They have good futures if they keep working at it.*

ERIC HARRISON

1991-92

1) Kevin Pilkington
2) John O'Kane
3) George Switzer
4) Chris Casper
5) Gary Neville
6) Colin McKee
7) Nicky Butt
8) Simon Davies
9) Robbie Savage
10) Ryan Giggs
11) Ben Thornley
12) David Beckham (for 8)
14) Raphael Burke (for 6)

1) Chris Day
2) Andrew Marlowe
3) Kevin Jordan
4) Paul Mahorn
5) Neil Young
6) Kevin Watson
7) Darren Caskey
8) Nick Barmby
9) Lee Hodges
10) Jeff Minton
11) Danny Hill
12) Sol Campbell (for 6)
14) Del Deanus (for 11)

MARCH 1992

MANCHESTER UNITED 3 v 0 **TOTTENHAM HOTSPUR**

Giggs (2), Jordan (o.g.)

Saturday 7th
Kick-off 2.00 p.m.
Attendance 7,633

semi-final 1st leg

Magic of Giggs

Recollections of the last four stage of the tournament two years ago bubbled to the surface as Tottenham Hotspur barred the path between United and a coveted ninth Youth Cup final. The earlier two-legged affair had slipped away from the Reds during the opening match in London, only on this occasion the draw decreed it was they who would be given the initial opportunity to stamp their authority on home soil.

A glance at the honours held by the personnel in the Tottenham squad made it quite obvious that the fabric of the opposition was now made up of considerably better quality than had been the case earlier in the competition. Representing Spurs were seven professionals; Andrew Marlowe, Paul Mahorn, Darren Caskey, Jeff Minton, Lee Hodges, Nick Barmby and captain Neil Young, while Del Deanus was capped by England as a schoolboy and Hodges currently represented England Youth. Additionally, Danny Hill, Sol Campbell, Caskey, Marlowe, Barmby and squad member Andy Turner had all worn the shirt with the three lions emblem at both schoolboy and youth levels.

The Tottenham boys were currently perched at the head of the South-East Counties League Division One table and apart from their run in the national tournament, Spurs' cup prowess was further highlighted by their achievements in reaching the finals of both the South-East Counties League Cup and Southern Junior Floodlit Cup.

Raphael Burke went on for Colin McKee to inflict further torment on an already beleaguered Tottenham defence

It was clear the United lads faced their sternest test of the campaign and the general feeling around Old Trafford was that if they could edge out their immediate foes, there could be no more difficult opponents than Spurs in the final.

Because Alex Ferguson's seniors were inactive that weekend, the game was scheduled a Saturday afternoon slot and the timing was a major contributory factor in ensuring yet another fabulous attendance.

The availability of Ryan Giggs provided a major boost to all of a red persuasion, and with his inclusion United utilised their home advantage to the full by surging into pole position.

The details of Giggs' 13th and 14th Youth Cup goals, and how Tottenham managed to shoot themselves in the foot on at least three occasions, were noted in David Meek's synopsis:

Manchester United are heading for their first F.A. Youth Cup final for seven years.

The young Reds put themselves in the driving seat with a 3-0 first leg win in the semi-final at Old Trafford.

Ryan Giggs scored twice with Spurs a shambles in the first half. The 7,633 crowd could hardly believe their eyes as the fancied Londoners stumbled from one disaster to another.

Spurs put through their own goal, gifted a second goal with a back pass mix-up and then had a man sent off for abusing a linesman.

The nightmare started for the visitors in the seventh minute when Robert Savage crossed from the left wing and saw full-back Kevin Jordan head high into a corner of his own goal.

The Londoners produced a stinging drive from Kevin Watson but schoolboy Kevin Pilkington tipped the shot over his bar.

Giggs produced a moment of magic in the eleventh minute to put his team further ahead. He twice lost the ball as he cut in from the left but won it back with deft footwork to lash home a low drive from the narrowest of angles.

The United first-teamer grabbed his second goal in the 23rd minute but only with the help of a back pass from Paul Mahorn, who put the ball past his own goalkeeper for Giggs to run through and tap over the line.

Tottenham were in tatters in the 39th minute when they had Nick Barmby sent off after he had been penalised for a foul. The youngster clearly spoke out of turn to the linesman close to the scene who flagged to bring referee Vic Callow over to him and the official immediately dismissed Barmby.

Although Spurs had cut their own throats, United had also produced some fast, flowing football with Simon Davies outstanding in midfield, Giggs always a threat, several nice touches from Ben Thornley and some biting tackles from George Switzer.

United certainly now hold all the aces for the second leg at White Hart Lane on Tuesday, March 24, but they should have applied themselves better in the second half.

They allowed ten-man Tottenham back into the game, with Lee Hodges testing Pilkington with a header and Watson shooting close.

Spurs also had a goal disallowed.

Tottenham coach Pat Holland later complained, 'We started the match as if we had never played the game in our lives and certainly never played together before. We seemed to have the jitters, whether it was the big occasion or the crowd, I don't know.

Certainly the back four were guilty of not playing sensible football and we were made to pay for it. I don't know what it was that caused the transformation in the second half but with ten men we dominated the rest of the match. We created chances which we should have put away. Had we come in 3-1 or even 3-2, it would have been a fairer reflection.

As it is we have got a mountain to climb in the second leg but I am still fairly confident that we can at least make a go of it and maybe even nick the tie.'

1) Chris Day	9) Lee Hodges	1) Kevin Pilkington	9) Colin McKee
2) Neil Young	10) Jeff Minton	2) John O'Kane	10) Robbie Savage
3) Kevin Jordan	11) Andrew Marlowe	3) George Switzer	11) Ben Thornley
4) Paul Mahorn	*12) David Culverhouse (for 4)*	4) Chris Casper	*12) Joe Roberts (for 10)*
5) Del Deanus	*14) Andy Turner (for 6)*	5) Gary Neville	*14) Leonard Taylor (for 11)*
6) Kevin Watson		6) David Beckham	
7) Darren Caskey		7) Nicky Butt	
8) Sol Campbell		8) Simon Davies	

1991-92

TOTTENHAM HOTSPUR 1 (1) v (5) 2 MANCHESTER UNITED

Turner

Butt, Thornley

MARCH 1992

Wednesday 25th*

Kick-off 7.00 p.m.

Attendance 967

semi-final 2nd leg

The pessimism of Tottenham supporters in their side's chances of making yet further progress was reflected in the woefully small attendance at White Hart Lane for the second leg of the semi-final.

Eric Harrison promised nothing less than a positive performance from United and he brought his tactics into the open when revealing to the press, *'We have a good lead but we have no intention of playing defensively. It would be a disservice to our lads to ask them to go for safety first. It's no way to bring up youngsters and I don't think they would know how anyway.'*

While Ryan Giggs was in preparation for a first-team game at Queen's Park Rangers on the following Saturday, Harrison gave a full competition debut to gifted midfielder David Beckham. A sixteen year-old apprentice who hailed not a million miles away from Spurs' ground at nearby Leytonstone, Beckham was courted by Tottenham before instead deciding to sign for United and he had spent his first year at Old Trafford alternating between the 'A' and 'B' sides.

As a consequence of their dysfunctional early showing in Manchester, Spurs' formation was considerably different from that at Old Trafford, although there were only two personnel changes, with Sol Campbell brought in for the banned Nick Barmby and Del Deanus deputising for an axed Danny Hill.

Tottenham opened with a purpose which stressed the obvious, that they needed a quick goal to put them back in contention, and so they began the match in a mood so energetic that it initially suggested they could provide United with a few problems. Just at the point when their early whirlwind was coming to an end, the Reds scored twice in only 56 seconds to place them five goals in front overall and well out of sight of the Londoners.

In the 15th minute, the maturing Ben Thornley beat a hasty path down the left wing, put a centre straight onto Nicky Butt's ginger head and the ball flashed into Chris Day's net. In the very next United attack, Thornley was nicely placed to head home a measured centre from Colin McKee.

Now benefiting from an unassailable lead, the Reds relaxed somewhat in the second half. Despite being required to put up with incessant rain, both sides created numerous chances and Kevin Pilkington made several stops prior to being beaten with three minutes to go by Andy Turner's bullet shot from twenty yards.

After-match comments were plentiful, and they were unanimous about United's victory being reasonably comfortable. The Manchester Evening News felt the *'defeat of Tottenham was more convincing than the scoreline suggests'* and, when noting their merited early two-goal advantage, it was claimed the Reds *'could have doubled that margin by half-time'.*

The Review was full of appreciation and after heralding another *'brilliant performance by our juniors'*, its report heaped praise on Eric Harrison who, it was claimed, *'could have been excused for adopting a safety first approach to the game'.* The Review reckoned the coach's *'attacking principles not only went a long way to making the second leg as entertaining as the first, it also paid early dividends in terms of goals'.*

It was certainly a case of 'mission accomplished' by the lads and the upshot was that United were now in their third Youth Cup final under Harrison's tenure. The feat was also the first of its kind during Alex Ferguson's reign and it gave yet another indication that the club's progress graph was pointing in an acutely upward direction.

United's line-up for the second leg of the 1992 Youth Cup semi-final at White Hart Lane
Back row (l-r) John O'Kane, Nicky Butt, Simon Davies, Kevin Pilkington, Chris Casper, Gary Neville
Front row (l-r) Ben Thornley, George Switzer, David Beckham, Robbie Savage, Colin McKee

* This game was originally scheduled for Tuesday, March 24th but was put back by 24 hours for reasons unknown

1991-92

1) Jimmy Glass	9) Niall Thompson	1) Kevin Pilkington	9) Colin McKee
2) Tim Clark	10) Grant Watts	2) John O'Kane	10) Robbie Savage
3) Scott Cutler	11) George Ndah	3) George Switzer	11) Ben Thornley
4) Mark Holman	*12) Stuart McCall (for 9)*	4) Chris Casper	*12) Joe Roberts (for 10)*
5) Russell Edwards	*14) Paul Sparrow (for 6)*	5) Gary Neville	*14) Leonard Taylor*
6) Andy McPherson		6) David Beckham	
7) Mark Hawthorne		7) Nicky Butt	
8) Simon Rollison		8) Simon Davies	

APRIL 1992

CRYSTAL PALACE 1 v 3 MANCHESTER UNITED

McCall — Beckham, Butt (2)

Tuesday 14th
Kick-off 7.30 p.m.
Attendance 7,825

final 1st leg

UNITED READY TO END 28-YEAR WAIT FOR CUP
Red-hot kids on the brink

Two days before the opening leg of the Youth Cup final, United's first-team defeated Nottingham Forest by courtesy of a 14th minute Brian McClair goal at Wembley to win the Rumbelows (League) Cup for the first time. The downfall of Brian Clough's Forest gave a lift to everyone connected to the club, despite the seniors' faltering assault on the Barclays League title, and it also kept Alex Ferguson's recent succession of cup wins flowing.

The youths were again without Ryan Giggs, a recent winner of the 'PFA Young Player of the Year' award, as they looked to secure the type of result at Crystal Palace which would put them in the most advantageous position possible for the second leg in Manchester.

Palace could boast a fine pedigree in the tournament, a fact demonstrated by their achievement as the most recent club to retain the Youth Cup. Having captured the trophy in 1977 and 1978, the young Glaziers made their way to the 1992 final by way of victories almost exclusively over London opponents.

A 2-0 win against Charlton at Welling United's ground got them off to a good start, but an identical defeat of Chelsea at Stamford Bridge in the next round was so much more impressive. Crewe were the next to fall, by a two to nothing scoreline at Plough Lane, and a month later West Ham were beaten by the recurring margin at the same venue.

The semi-final pairing of Palace and Wimbledon threw up an odd situation as the latter, having decided their former ground wasn't up to First Division standards, were currently staging their senior games at Palace's Selhurst Park stadium. It was agreed that both Youth Cup games would take place at Wimbledon's Plough Lane enclosure, Palace winning their away leg 2-1 and drawing 3-3 at 'home' a week later to enable them to take a place in a third final.

Although born in Birmingham, Palace striker Niall Thompson was raised in Canada and thereby earned the distinction of captaining that country's youth side prior to linking up with the Selhurst Park club. Going into the final, Thompson topped Palace's Youth Cup 'goals scored' column with three while Stuart McCall, Mark Holman and Grant Watts had registered two each.

After naming a full-strength team, Palace youth coach Stuart Scott noted in the match programme that four of his squad, McCall, Scott Cutler, Andy McPherson and Simon Rollison, were being released by the club and he wished them all the best for their futures.

The Croydon Advertiser's David Groves covered the opening leg:

Nearly 8,000 fans braved the awful elements at Selhurst Park for this fine F.A. Youth Cup final first leg clash on Tuesday.

Palace's Main Stand was packed as enthusiastic supporters gave the youngsters the first-team treatment with a balloon welcome, accompanied by 'Glad All Over' on the public address system.

Heavy rain did not dampen their spirits, even in defeat, and the 'Eaglets' were given a great ovation at the end for a battling performance.

Without question Palace had more of the play and more chances than the young Manchester United stars – all youth internationals – but the difference was the visitors' slicker passing and clinical finishing.

Trailing to two first half goals, Palace fought bravely after the break and gave themselves hope for the second leg with a late goal – only to be caught by United, who are chasing the cup for a record seventh time.

They took the lead in the 17th minute when impressive winger Ben Thornley was given far too much space and crossed for the unmarked Nicky Butt to fire first time under Jimmy Glass.

Three minutes later Palace nearly equalised when top scorer Grant Watts' far post shot was kicked off United's goal-line.

Further sloppy defending led to United's second goal on 29 minutes. Andy McPherson's poor back pass went straight to Thornley at the far post and he worked the ball back for David Beckham to shoot inside the far corner from eighteen yards for a spectacular goal.

McPherson was harshly hauled off four minutes later, with first-year boy Paul Sparrow replacing him as Palace abandoned their sweeper system and moved right-back Tim Clark into midfield.

Palace nearly scored after 41 minutes when Mark Hawthorne saw his fine 25-yarder fumbled by Pilkington at the far post, but the ball refused to cross the goal-line.

Tempers became frayed after 59 minutes when United's John O'Kane and Palace's Niall Thompson were both booked by referee Alf Buksh following a fracas.

Substitute Sparrow was then booked for a foul on 63 minutes as Palace became physical and United's George Switzer was cautioned in the 74th minute for a foul on Watts.

Speedy winger George Ndah, who had moved into the centre for the final fling, looked certain to score following a great run but Pilkington saved with his outstretched legs.

And there was more agony for Palace when Simon Rollison saw his long shot snake into the goal only to discover a colleague was offside.

'Super-sub' striker Stuart McCall, who had replaced injured Niall Thompson on 76 minutes, had the home fans roaring with a deserved 86th minute goal, heading home superbly from Watts' fine cross.

However, United replied a minute from the end when Beckham broke away on the right and his low cross was met by unmarked Butt who shot home his second goal.

Palace's joint coach Dave Garland summed up, 'Their goals were given away rather than created. But United played to their potential and we didn't. We must now hope that United are more relaxed next time, thinking they've won it. This might give us the opportunity to get back at them and score early. Then, who knows?'

The next day's Evening News also contained a report on the game, a section of which went:

United are firm favourites to win the F.A. Youth Cup for a record seventh time after their emphatic success in the first leg of the final last night.

Teeming rain made conditions something of a lottery, but United mastered them early on.

Palace never came to terms with their pace on the break and were trailing by two goals at half-time.

Nearly 8,000 saw the match last night at Selhurst Park and at least double that is expected at Old Trafford for the second leg, the date of which is still to be decided.

It was no surprise when Eric Harrison told the press he was delighted at the outcome. Harrison tried to ensure his lads would remain focussed when sounding a simple but logical public warning to them with the words, *'We won 3-1 on their ground and now we have to make sure they don't repeat that scoreline at Old Trafford.'*

1991-92

APRIL 1992

John O'Kane (left) attempts to stand his ground against a Palace attack while Chris Casper (second from right) chases back to help

Chris Casper slides in to block a Palace attempt on goal at a rain-soaked Selhurst Park

final 1st leg

373

1991-92

1) Kevin Pilkington	9) Colin McKee
2) John O'Kane	10) Ryan Giggs
3) George Switzer	11) Ben Thornley
4) Chris Casper	*12) Keith Gillespie (for 11)*
5) Gary Neville	*14) Robbie Savage (for 8)*
6) David Beckham	
7) Nicky Butt	
8) Simon Davies	

1) Jimmy Glass	9) Stuart McCall
2) Paul Sparrow	10) George Ndah
3) Scott Cutler	11) Tim Clark
4) Mark Holman	*12) Sean Daly (for 8)*
5) Russell Edwards	*14) Grant Watts (for 6)*
6) Andy McPherson	
7) Mark Hawthorne	
8) Simon Rollison	

MAY 1992

MANCHESTER UNITED 3 (6) v (3) 2 CRYSTAL PALACE

Davies, McKee, Thornley — McCall, McPherson

Friday 15th
Kick-off 7.30 p.m.
Attendance 14,681

final 2nd leg

Red rookies roll back years with cup of magic

As was universally expected, Ryan Giggs was made available for the concluding leg of the Youth Cup final, which took place a whole month and a day after United's impressive win at Selhurst Park. Giggs displaced another Welsh boy, the extremely unfortunate and previously ever-present Robbie Savage, and he also took the captain's armband off Davies upon his return to the side.

'I am very thrilled with this team,' beamed Eric Harrison, 'It's the best youth side I have had and the bonus is that they are mostly first-year trainees which means they are eligible next season. It is most unusual to have such a good side from a first-year intake.'

He went on, 'They wouldn't know how to play for a draw. We don't teach them that kind of football. When we look at a boy to come to United we won't look for strength either. We go for technical ability and hope they will develop physically.'

Commenting on his eleven years at the club, Harrison admitted, 'Perhaps we should have done better in the F.A. Youth Cup. Tonight we hope to put that right.'

Alex Ferguson demonstrated some knowledge of the game's historical context when he added, 'We don't like to go overboard about young players but this lot are very exciting. With their ability and desire to play they should go far. Winning the F.A. Youth Cup can be significant. When Manchester United last won it in 1964 it triggered the best period in the club's post-Munich history.'

With Niall Thompson unavailable through his involvement with the Canadian under-21 side, Palace youth coach Stuart Scott also took Grant Watts out of the side and brought in Paul Sparrow and Stuart McCall, both of whom had made an input of sorts in the first leg.

Costumed in a snazzy Brazil strip, the visitors got off to a great start by scoring from a corner soon after the opening whistle. It was later revealed that during the considerable time in-between the two legs, the young Reds were made to practice at defending such set pieces as they were identified as Palace's main threat to their ambitions.

Even though it was discomforting for the home supporters for a while, the Londoners' lead didn't last.

The Evening News was represented by David Meek for the second leg, just as it was the last time United claimed the trophy back in the days when Beatlemania was at its height, and he recorded the outcome every United follower of a certain age had waited almost a football eternity to see:

Manchester United's magnificent youngsters rolled back the years last night.
Alex Ferguson's whizkids – under the guidance of coach Eric Harrison – won the F.A. Youth Cup for the first time in 28 years.
And in doing so they brought back reminders of the glory days of the Busby Babes of the 50's and their last win in the swinging 60's, when they launched George Best and entered their last great period of success.
The beauty of the second leg of the final against Crystal Palace at Old Trafford was their terrific teamwork, studded with magical play by creative players.
They delighted a bumper 14,681 crowd as they romped home 3-2 for a 6-3 aggregate. They twitched with nervousness early on to give Palace the encouragement of a first minute goal, an Andrew McPherson header.
But slowly but surely, United's midfield got to grips, not least the athletic Simon Davies, who played an inspiring captain's role to turn the game round.
Individuals like winger Ben Thornley and left-back George Switzer stamped their ability on the game.
Thornley scored a superb equaliser in the 33rd minute when he cut in from the left to dummy and measure a perfect shot past the goalkeeper. The Bury-born winger and former England schoolboy showed a great range of skills and won a standing ovation when he was substituted because of injury late in the game.
But Switzer emerged the fans' favourite with his steely but skilful approach.
Five minutes after the interval he got forward in a great move with Davies which saw the midfielder put the Reds into the lead.
Stuart McCall pulled a goal back in the 62nd minute when he powered through, but Palace were largely a spent force and Colin McKee headed home the Reds' third at the far post.

And so the F.A. Youth Cup could at last be returned to where all true United supporters feel is its spiritual home, the Old Trafford trophy cabinet. Through their victory, the team which will eternally be referred to as 'the class of '92' had emulated the seniors' success of two years before by defeating Crystal Palace in a national final.

Selhurst Park officials were gracious in defeat, and former United wing favourite and current Eagles' manager Steve Coppell remarked, 'The performance of the United boys is a pointer for a very healthy future. It's clear the conveyor belt producing young players is rolling again at Old Trafford. There is quality in the team and they have certainly struck a rich seam with the side which played against us.'

It was later revealed that Palace's goalkeeper Jimmy Glass had broken the little finger on his left hand. Glass fractured the digit in attempting to keep out Simon Davies' 50th minute effort which put United into a 2-1 lead on the night and by a 5-2 margin overall. The goal might even have been considered as a first-team contribution because Davies later told an interviewer he had borrowed senior star Paul Ince's boots for the game.

A euphoric Alex Ferguson spoke of the team's composition when revealing, 'I had to make some hard but common sense decisions soon after I arrived with our scouting set-up. Brian Kidd at local level has been a tremendous influence with the scouting of youngsters. We saturated the Manchester area and the result is that seven of last night's team all come from the Greater Manchester or Lancashire area.'

A few last words on the happy event were left to chairman Martin Edwards, who penned the following lines for the 1992 United Yearbook:

The success and quality of our young players is now there to be seen by all. Everyone within the club has known for some time exactly what the manager and his staff have been working towards at youth level and I couldn't be more pleased for them – they thoroughly deserve the acclaim.

> *I was very proud to be made captain of the youth team and that season was very special, not just because we won it but because of the impact it had on me personally. It taught me how to act as a person, about honesty, desire, endeavour and respect. It all came under the banner called 'standards'.*
>
> *The team spirit was fantastic and we all wanted to win. We all wanted to play for each other and so after training we would all get together and practice for hours. Eric set the tone with those standards, but he would often have to forcibly send us home from training. We were having such a great time and it seemed so easy when we worked together. We actually worked just as hard in training as we did in the matches.*
>
> *In the final against Crystal Palace they scored first early on and as we lined up for the restart we all looked at each other. We just knew there was no way we were going to lose that game.*

SIMON DAVIES

374

1991-92

MAY 1992

final 2nd leg

Ryan Giggs looks elated while showing off a trophy which holds such historical significance for Manchester United and was last won by the club nine years before his birth

375

1992-93

Manchester United
1) Darren Whitmarsh
2) John O'Kane
3) Steven Riley
4) Chris Casper
5) Gary Neville
6) Keith Gillespie
7) Paul Scholes
8) David Beckham
9) Joe Roberts
10) Robbie Savage
11) Ben Thornley
12) *Richard Irving (for 10)*
14) *Mark Rawlinson (for 7)*

Blackburn Rovers
1) Alec Ridgway
2) Ian Berry
3) Danny Goodall
4) Josh Metcalf
5) Andy Scott
6) Jon Pickup
7) Darren Grassby
8) Lee Moss
9) Steve Grunshaw
10) Lee Hitchin
11) Jim Berry
12) *Paul Ainscough (for 7)*
14) *Chris Bardsley (for 10)*

DECEMBER 1992

MANCHESTER UNITED 4 v 1 BLACKBURN ROVERS

Gillespie, Irving (2), Scholes — Ainscough (pen)

Tuesday 8th*

Kick-off 7.00 p.m.

Attendance 1,268

second round

*This game was originally scheduled for Wednesday, December 2nd but was postponed due to a waterlogged pitch

By the time United's under-18's entertained Blackburn in their opening defence of the Youth Cup in December 1992, the 'A' team's supremacy of the Lancashire League Division One was already established as they had given themselves a great opportunity to claim the divisional championship by reeling off a fantastic ten straight wins. That impressive run included some terrific scoring totals, the Reds achieving a 7-2 win over Marine Reserves, 6-0 victories against Oldham and Bolton's 'A' sides, and a 5-1 mauling of Crewe Alexandra Reserves.

Significantly in respect of the Youth Cup draw, they had also given Blackburn 'A' a chasing with a 5-0 win at The Cliff.

Even without the abrasive edge offered by midfielder Nicky Butt, who was ruled out with a pulled calf muscle, United defeated Rovers in the knock-out competition without overextending themselves and the benefit of having so many members of last season's triumphant side still available was an obvious help towards Eric Harrison's quest to retain the trophy. A youngster with no experience in the competition, Paul Scholes found himself slipped into Butt's position, which meant that Harrison was required to give starting roles to just two other fresh faces.

Besides lively Crewe-born Joe Roberts, who donned the number nine jersey after previously appearing twice as a substitute, full-back Steven Riley was, like Scholes, from the Middleton area. The only position causing Harrison undue concern was the last line of defence, and his decision to use a trialist was picked up on by the press:

Manchester United sent an SOS to Ireland in an emergency rush for a new youth team goalkeeper.

Old Trafford is bursting with young talent except in goal, and coach Eric Harrison still hasn't found a regular to succeed Kevin Pilkington.

Pilkington was in the team which won the F.A. Youth Cup last season, but he is now over-age. The Reds have tried out several youngsters in their junior sides and give a debut tonight to seventeen year-old Darren Whitmarsh of Larne.

It was, however, an identically aged former England schoolboy cap and latterly F.A. School of Excellence graduate called Richard Irving whose contribution inflicted the most damage on Blackburn. Substituting for Robbie Savage with only half an hour remaining while the score stood at 2-1, the West Yorkshire lad hit two goals in only seven minutes to apply a more realistic sheen on the scoreline.

The match began slowly, with the main incident of note during the early period occurring when Roberts headed a David Beckham cross against Blackburn's bar. The next major talking point occurred on the half hour when Rovers lost Ian Berry after he intentionally clattered Scholes. A rather silly thing to do for someone already on a yellow card, the defender's second bookable offence triggered an automatic dismissal.

United made their guests pay for Berry's stupidity almost immediately, Keith Gillespie capitalising on a lack of concentration by a visiting forward and racing unchecked into the Blackburn penalty area where he thumped away a tremendous right-foot drive into Alec Ridgway's net. With the Reds' numerical superiority increasingly beginning to tell, Rovers experienced a let-off just before the interval as Savage slammed a shot against the woodwork.

Blackburn were forced to substitute achilles strain victim Darren Grassby with Paul Ainscough at the break and shortly after the restart they went 2-0 down. The scorer of United's second goal was Scholes, whose opportunism allowed him to take full advantage of an easy chance to slot the ball home from close in.

Five minutes later, following a handball decision in Whitmarsh's penalty area, Blackburn's Ainscough drilled home the resulting spot kick to bring his side back into contention for a while.

The young Reds then did enough to keep themselves out of trouble, and Irving's later goal burst came at a time when a flagging ten-man Rovers were required to push extra bodies forward in search of an equaliser.

United's performance earned rich praise from the opposing camp as Blackburn youth coach Jim Furnell reckoned the Reds were in a *'different class'* prior to disclosing *'there were no complaints from the staff at the result'*. Furnell felt the game *'gave us an insight into the standard players have to reach to become competitive at this level and progress further in their careers'* and he even went as far as predicting that United would win the Youth Cup for a second year on the trot.

Accompanied by both substitutes, pictured above is the United side that defeated Blackburn in a rearranged Youth Cup match at Old Trafford
Back row (l-r) Mark Rawlinson, Joe Roberts, Chris Casper, Darren Whitmarsh, Keith Gillespie, John O'Kane, Richard Irving
Front row (l-r) Steven Riley, Robbie Savage, David Beckham, Gary Neville, Ben Thornley, Paul Scholes

1) Darren Whitmarsh
2) John O'Kane
3) Philip Neville
4) Chris Casper
5) Gary Neville
6) Keith Gillespie
7) Nicky Butt
8) David Beckham
9) Richard Irving
10) Robbie Savage
11) Paul Scholes
12) Mark Rawlinson (for 8)
14) Joe Roberts (for 10)

1) Malcolm Rigby
2) Jody Malpass
3) Eddie Lawley
4) Ian Ridgway
5) John Beale
6) Brian Horseman
7) Matthew Dodson
8) Mick Galloway
9) Ben Needham
10) James Muir
11) Paul Smith
12) Alvin Henry (for 9)
14) Jon King (for 10)

1992-93

MANCHESTER UNITED 3 v 1 NOTTS COUNTY

Irving, Neville G., Scholes *Dodson*

JANUARY 1993

Tuesday 12th

Kick-off 7.00 p.m.

Attendance 2,565

third round

■ HIT MAN... Richard Irving, scorer of the first goal, gets in a volley as United go forward again

With Nicky Butt returned to full fitness and Keith Gillespie recovered from a spell of feeling unwell over the previous weekend, both were included in the team named by Eric Harrison to face Notts County at Old Trafford. The coach implemented other changes, one of which was an injury issue, as Ben Thornley couldn't take part in the tie through damaging his knee ligaments in training. The intense competition for youth team places was underlined when Richard Irving's brace against Blackburn earned him a spot in preference to Joe Roberts and Gary Neville's younger brother, Philip, was placed in the back four at the expense of Steven Riley.

Even though they were boosted by a 3-0 home win against Wolves in a Midland Purity Youth League fixture over the preceding Saturday, and travelled to Manchester with an unchanged eleven from their victory, the Notts County team suffered an identical fate to that experienced by all of their predecessors in past Youth Cup clashes between the two clubs.

Both sides settled their nerves early on, but it was United who drew first blood in the 19th minute when Irving justified his inclusion by teasing the County goalkeeper before cheekily chipping the ball over him to edge the Reds in front.

The Magpies' best opportunity to draw level came in the 57th minute when a thunderous free kick from James Muir was repelled by a splendid acrobatic save from Darren Whitmarsh, who tipped his flashing effort over the bar.

It was unlikely that Harrison would have been even remotely satisfied with the team's showing as the Reds hadn't displayed their usual form up to then and there was hardly a hint of the free-flowing football they were capable of.

In the 67th minute, captain Gary Neville made his way into County's penalty box just as David Beckham was preparing to take a corner. Neville had been in good form with both his head and his feet all evening, and he capped a decent performance by powering the ball past Malcolm Rigby after Beckham's flag kick was glanced across the goalmouth by Robbie Savage.

Paul Scholes made the outcome of the game a foregone conclusion in the 74th minute when registering with a fine piece of skill that the Review noted had *'brought the house down'*, and the Evening News added to the midfielder's increasing reputation by observing he *'outshone the youngsters who have been appearing on the first-team scene'*. Scoring with practically the last kick of the game, County's Matthew Dodson pegged United's winning margin back down to two goals and ruined Whitmarsh's clean sheet.

Later that month, Alex Ferguson instigated a pivotal decision on the club's behalf when he took the bold step of signing David Beckham, Keith Gillespie, Nicky Butt, Gary Neville, Chris Casper, Paul Scholes, John O'Kane and Ben Thornley on four-year professional contracts. It was an unprecedented move, because never in the history of Manchester United was so much faith shown in so many young players at any one time.

The perseverance of the club's board and the work Ferguson and his staff had invested in the youth system was now revealing more genuine contenders for senior status at Old Trafford than at any time for three or four decades. Ryan Giggs was already well on his way to becoming a first-team superstar while Ferguson's son Darren was also making a telling contribution at senior level. By then, Beckham, Gillespie, Butt and the older Neville brother had all taken on at least some first-team responsibility and with the manager prepared to back his judgement by offering terms which were designed to keep them all at the club for the foreseeable future, it appeared that they, as well as a few others, were the shape of things to come.

As someone who was better placed than anyone to comment on the proliferation of youth promotions into the seniors, Eric Harrison pointed out, *'They have been in the spotlight and I have been telling them it can work one of two ways for them. They can either blossom as people predict, or they can crumble. It's not my style to push these boys but the fact is they are being talked about and, as a result, they are now under pressure to deliver. I'm confident that they won't let all the publicity go to their heads but it's still a big challenge for the lads.'*

377

1992-93

1) Darren Whitmarsh	9) Richard Irving
2) John O'Kane	10) Joe Roberts
3) Philip Neville	11) Ben Thornley
4) Chris Casper	*12) Mark Rawlinson (for 10)*
5) Gary Neville	*14) Steven Riley*
6) Keith Gillespie	
7) Paul Scholes	
8) David Beckham	

1) Neil Fairbairn	9) David Mosley
2) Danny Brooker	10) Kieron Swift
3) Gavin Fell	11) Jason Cunningham
4) Marc Cable	*12) Shaun Fleming (for 3)*
5) Paul Stephenson	*14) Vinnie John (for 9)*
6) Mark Thomas	
7) Peter Lingley	
8) Franco Di Rubbo	

FEBRUARY 1993

MANCHESTER UNITED 3 v 0 WIMBLEDON

Beckham, Irving, Scholes

Tuesday 2nd
Kick-off 7.00 p.m.
Attendance 3,225

fourth round

Reds' tall order

The Reds came up against the latest in a lengthening line of sizeable Youth Cup opponents when they were pitted with Wimbledon at Old Trafford. In view of the fact that a number of the Dons' personnel measured in at over six feet tall, it was perfectly clear the club's youth squad was modelled along similar lines to those of their senior team.

Well aware that the Selhurst Park tenants were in the hunt for the South-East Counties Division Two title and had also reached the Youth Cup semi-final a year ago, Alex Ferguson commented prior to their arrival, *'They are a tough, strong side.......and are top of their junior league.'*

Eric Harrison was forced into bringing back Ben Thornley and Joe Roberts as a result of knocks to Robbie Savage and Nicky Butt. Savage's injury was by far the most worrying of the two as he had been taken to hospital at half-time during a game against Blackburn Rovers 'A' with a suspected broken leg. Mercifully, the Welsh boy was cleared of a fracture but he was subsequently ruled out of further involvement in the game for a few weeks with a severely damaged ankle. Butt's problem wasn't nearly as bad as that of his team-mate, a sore ankle sustained in a convincing 7-1 win over Tranmere at The Cliff meaning that he was only expected to be out of action for around a week or so.

Despite the absence of Savage and Butt, the Reds cruised to a 3-0 win and the display they delivered caused Wimbledon's youth coach Ernie Tippett to sing their praises with some conviction. *'Manchester United really are something special, I don't see anybody being able to beat them,'* he said. *'They pass the ball extremely well, their movement off the ball is a different class and they were better than us in every department. They really are one tasty team.'*

The Manchester Evening News came up with a match overview which added further substance to Tippett's claims:

Manchester United's super kids said 'thank you' for their handsome new contracts.
They turned on the style brilliantly to show exactly why manager Alex Ferguson has given them such a massive vote of confidence.
His bright boys rang rings around the big, strong Wimbledon side to cruise into the quarter-finals of the F.A. Youth Cup.
A crowd of 3,225 – bigger than some Wimbledon first-team gates – saw why Fergie's Fledglings are being hailed as the best since the 60's and right out of the Busby Babes drawer.
Rated the best team in London, Wimbledon made their presence felt and had three players booked, but they were left chasing the game as the Reds moved the ball with authority and great vision.
Paul Scholes, the Middleton boy who is the tiger in midfield, scored the opening goal in the 23rd minute after a scramble from Keith Gillespie's cross. He stuck out a foot and the ball trickled over the line.
Kieron Swift gave United a fright when he hit a post just before the interval, but it was only momentary as the Reds came out to put their visitors under tremendous pressure.
Joe Roberts and Gillespie combined to send Richard Irving in for a 55th minute goal, while David Beckham beat the offside trap to score the third (62).
United missed several chances, extravagantly so at times, but they still left the feeling that had it mattered they could have gone up another gear.

A brief mention of the match in the Review contained an observation about the youths achieving their win by way of *'some sparkling football'.* Then noting the visiting team was a *'strong and robust outfit'* who *'managed to hold United'* for a while, the summary went on to point out *'there was only going to be one winner'* once the Reds had forged a lead for themselves.

Providers both: Keith Gillespie (top) sent over the cross for United's opener while he and Joe Roberts combined to set up the team's second goal

378

1) Darren Whitmarsh
2) John O'Kane
3) Steven Riley
4) Chris Casper
5) Gary Neville
6) Keith Gillespie
7) Mark Rawlinson
8) David Beckham
9) Richard Irving
10) Paul Scholes
11) Ben Thornley
12) Karl Brown (for 2)
14) Robbie Savage (for 7)

1) Andy Warrington
2) Mick Gosling
3) Eammon Dooley
4) Lea Thomlinson
5) Paul Mockler
6) Scott Jordan
7) Steve Roberts
8) Graeme Murty
9) Darren Falk
10) Lee Medforth
11) Elliott Simpson
12) Andy Bowker (for 9)
14) Jamie Davison

1992-93

MANCHESTER UNITED 5 v 0 YORK CITY

Beckham, Irving, Neville, O'Kane, Savage

MARCH 1993

fifth round

Monday 8th

Kick-off 7.00 p.m.

Attendance 4,937

United dish out lesson in finishing

The 1992/93 campaign was certainly proving a lucky one in terms of the draw, a tie against brand new Youth Cup opponents York representing the fourth time in succession that the Reds benefited from a home engagement.

Even though he was fully recovered from his ankle problem, Nicky Butt was still unavailable to help United contest a place in the semi-finals because he was on the other side of the world in Australia in his capacity as a member of England's youth squad.

Another absentee against York was Philip Neville. International duty also beckoned for him as he was in line for a place in the England under-16 team that was scheduled to meet Holland on the forthcoming Wednesday.

Back into the side came Steven Riley, with Mark Rawlinson gaining a promotion and Karl Brown, whose return to full recovery mode followed a lengthy injury lay-off, was installed as one of the substitutes.

As for United's opponents, York had never progressed past the Third Round of the Youth Cup before and by defeating Carlisle, Orient, Newcastle and West Brom along the way, their accomplishment in reaching the final eight stage represented an infrequent attainment for a club of their stature.

The events at Old Trafford spelled the end of their party, though, as Malcolm Huntington of the Yorkshire Evening Press noted:

York City's dreams of creating an upset against F.A. Youth Cup holders Manchester United came to an abrupt end when they were crushed 5-0 in the quarter-final at Old Trafford last night.

The young Red Devils were too quick and skilful for battling City, who fought hard but were quite simply outclassed.

It will be a major surprise if United don't retain the trophy on the evidence of this superb team performance.

Despite being without two internationals, the team – eight were in the winning side last year – tore City apart with some inventive attacking football as the visitors were left chasing shadows.

Unless I am very much mistaken, most of the thirteen United names mentioned will go on to make their marks at a high level in two or three years time.

City youth coach, Ricky Sbragia, said afterwards, 'Manchester United are almost certainly the best youth team in Britain and they were much too good for us. We had one good spell when we were 2-0 down just after half-time and if we had scored then, we might have had a boost to our confidence. I was a bit disappointed, to be frank. We had worked very hard to get to the last eight, but I didn't feel we performed on the night.

Perhaps the occasion was a bit too much for most of the players. United had the quality, awareness, pace and skill and we failed to get close enough to stop them doing what they are good at. Having said that, perhaps we were not allowed to. In short, they controlled the game at their pace from the first minute to the last.

I hope we can learn something from the game because they are premier players and our players will now know how far they have got to improve if they are to try to match them.'

Goalkeeper Andy Warrington, who handled well and made a number of good saves, was City's best player. He hadn't the slightest chance with any of the goals, four of which were magnificent efforts, a brilliant build up finishing with stunning efficiency. City always found it difficult to put any sort of pressure on their opponents and didn't manage a single shot on target.

United went ahead after sixteen minutes when Gary Neville headed home at the far post after David Beckham's corner had been flicked on by Chris Casper.

Paul Scholes, who showed remarkable skills throughout along with Beckham and has already played for the first-team, hit the bar before United went 2-0 up after 33 minutes.

Ben Thornley's run down the left saw Scholes make a superb turn in little space and when he fed the ball across goal, John O'Kane whipped the ball low past Warrington.

Substitute Robert Savage, who had been on the field for only three minutes, increased United's lead after 64 minutes, Scholes, Beckham and Richard Irving making a sweeping move which ended in Irving passing low across goal for Savage to sidefoot home – a classic goal.

Irving, receiving Thornley's pass, thundered a low shot just inside Warrington's left-hand post from twenty yards for number four in the 76th minute and six minutes from time Savage provided the chance for Beckham to score another spectacular goal with a shot which flew into the roof of the net from fifteen yards.

Besides the comments made earlier, York coach Ricky Sbragia later admitted 'nothing could have prepared us for the skill and pace of the Manchester United youth side' prior to adding 'United obviously have the cream of young England. They were very impressive with a skill, technique and an awareness way beyond what we could handle. I am sure that in a few years we will be comparing them with the Busby Babes.'

The praise lavished on the teenage Reds wasn't only restricted to the observations of Sbragia and Huntington, because the Review also chipped in when boasting they 'were never really troubled as they lived up to their billing as favourites for the trophy'.

David Meek joined in with the accolades and also noted United's 'defence figured in the attack as much as the forwards' before claiming that the team 'even seemed to have a gear to spare as they piled up the score'.

Captured on film against York, Steven Riley impressed on his recall to the side

379

1992-93

1) Darren Whitmarsh
2) John O'Kane
3) Philip Neville
4) Chris Casper
5) Gary Neville
6) Keith Gillespie
7) Nicky Butt
8) David Beckham
9) Richard Irving
10) Paul Scholes
11) Ben Thornley
12) Jovan Kirovski (for 8)
14) Steven Riley

1) David Wietecha
2) Dean Francis
3) Colin Luckett
4) Danny Chapman
5) Ben Thatcher
6) Matt Middleton
7) Mark Beard
8) Neville Gordon
9) Mark Kennedy
10) Geoff Pitcher
11) Jermaine Wright
12) Robert Morey
14) Brett Smith

APRIL 1993

MANCHESTER UNITED 1 v 2 MILLWALL
Thornley   Gordon, Kennedy

Tuesday 6th
Kick-off 7.00 p.m.
Attendance 7,678

semi-final 1st leg

Reds Den-ted!

The matching up of United with Millwall in the semi-final meant that the Reds were required to take on unfamiliar Youth Cup opponents for the third consecutive tie.

While the south London club's senior side might only have been plying their trade down in the second tier of English football, albeit in a healthy top-third of the table spot, their terrific efforts at junior level over the past few years weren't without their rewards. The teenage Lions had captured the Youth Cup twice, in 1979 and as recently ago as 1991, a remarkable feat which meant their record of final victories in the tournament was one greater than that of financially better resourced near neighbours West Ham and equal to those of cross-capital competitors Chelsea.

Comforted in the knowledge that, bar the crocked Robbie Savage and Joe Roberts, the pool of players he could pick from appeared confident, fit and ready to tackle the task in hand, Eric Harrison seemed rather unfazed when telling the press in the lead up to kick-off, *'I've watched Millwall and they have an impressive Irish striker who scores a lot of goals. We are going well, too, and I think it will be an entertaining game.'*

Going well they certainly were. The United boys had grasped the Lancashire League Division One title over the preceding weekend by spanking Marine Reserves 10-0, and an outstanding campaign at that standard placed the 'A' team a huge thirteen points clear of their nearest rivals with an incredible goals tally of 122 scored and only 36 conceded in their allotted 30 games.

Due to the absence of Savage and Roberts, Harrison drafted in Jovan Kirovski as a substitute. A sixteen year-old American of Yugoslav parentage, Kirovski was cleared to play for the club after starting school in Salford and earned his chance in the under-18's squad through catching the eye in several 'B' team matches.

One of the main men in the Millwall side was Swindon-born centre-half or left-back Ben Thatcher, a renowned practical joker whose skills had clinched him a place at the F.A. School of Excellence, as well as England caps at under-15, under-16 and under-18 levels.

Shouldering most of the Lions' scoring responsibility was Dubliner Mark Kennedy. Already with over 40 goals claimed in his first season at The Den, and a clutch of appearances for the Republic of Ireland schoolboy team on his record, the six feet tall Kennedy was still a few weeks away from his 17th birthday and appeared a genuinely outstanding prospect.

Lining up for the start, the United lads could well have been forgiven for

Ben Thornley (number eleven) appears to be dancing as (l-r) Philip Neville, Gary Neville, Keith Gillespie and Chris Casper appear bemused by his gyrations

380

APRIL 1993

thinking they were facing a prison team as the visiting squad had decided to adopt a 'mean' look by cropping their hair short for the contest. All of the travelling Millwall party, right down to the coach driver, were treated to a shearing session with Thatcher's clippers prior to their arrival in Stretford and the Lions tried to live up to their image, especially early in the game, by attempting to rough the home team up a little.

Wingers Ben Thornley and Keith Gillespie featured well for the Reds in the opening period by consistently outpacing their markers. The quicksilver Gillespie looked particularly potent when racing past defenders almost at will to provide numerous telling crosses.

It was through the efforts of one of those wide men that United struck a decisive blow just before half-time as Thornley scored with a super shot. The goal came just after the 43rd minute booking of Millwall's Danny Chapman for a foul and was the culmination of a brilliant run during which the winger sidestepped three attempted tackles. Chapman almost made amends for giving away the free kick which led to Thornley's goal when he later watched his powerful header blocked on the line.

There were a number of reasons for the Reds surrendering their initial supremacy. For starters, they appeared to run out of gas in the second half whereas the Millwall players continued to give the impression they were in training for a marathon. The Old Trafford kids additionally made far too many unforced errors, for which they would soon pay a hefty price.

David Meek also picked up on another major factor in the Reds' untypically unconvincing showing:

(United) were not helped by injuries which saw Paul Scholes playing as an emergency striker to leave the midfield without his drive, but overall they fell below their usual standard.

Based purely on the events after the break, the home camp could have no arguments as Kennedy levelled the score on 62 minutes and later, when Neville Gordon clinched the result with a brilliantly executed winner. Kennedy's goal climaxed a move in which Millwall defender Dean Francis carried possession for almost the full length of the pitch prior to executing a superb cross that the Irishman delighted in taking full advantage of.

There were a few more scares in store for the crowd, for example when Gordon directed a header inches over Darren Whitmarsh's crossbar and a Geoff Pitcher effort was booted clear in a mad scramble. Millwall wrapped up a gutsy comeback when Gordon latched onto a poor clearance and smacked a 25-yard drive which zoomed through the air and beyond Whitmarsh to nestle in the back of the net.

An unexpected reverse, nevertheless it meant the United lads had finished on the losing side in the competition for the first time in almost two years. Their visit to The Den would surely prove a tremendous test of character, and one newspaper ominously recorded that the match represented a *'king-size challenge'* for them to progress to the final.

The Lions' win was well received on the other side of the Thames, the South London Express claiming *'Battling Millwall roared to victory'* and *'silenced'* the Old Trafford faithful. Also airing a view about the result keeping the Den's *'young braves on course for a final place'*, the newspaper awarded Wietecha, Thatcher, Middleton and Gordon nine marks out of ten for their performances while the rest of the team were given eight apiece.

Faced with a Millwall challenge, Philip Neville (number three) attempts to clear as Nicky Butt (centre) and David Beckham (right) look to assist him

1992-93

Millwall
1) Glen Knight
2) Dean Francis
3) Colin Luckett
4) Danny Chapman
5) Ben Thatcher
6) Matt Middleton
7) Mark Beard
8) Neville Gordon
9) Robert Morey
10) Geoff Pitcher
11) Jermaine Wright
12) *Paul Irvine*
14) *Brett Smith*

Manchester United
1) Darren Whitmarsh
2) John O'Kane
3) Steven Riley
4) Chris Casper
5) Gary Neville
6) Keith Gillespie
7) Nicky Butt
8) David Beckham
9) Richard Irving
10) Paul Scholes
11) Ben Thornley
12) *Jovan Kirovski (for 9)*
14) *Colin Murdock*

APRIL 1993

MILLWALL 0 (2) v (3) 2 MANCHESTER UNITED
Butt, Kirovski

semi-final 2nd leg

Tuesday 13th
Kick-off 7.30 p.m.
Attendance 6,276

For the second leg of the semi-final, Millwall were forced into a couple of changes. One was in their defence, because giant six foot, five inches tall goalkeeper David Wietecha picked up an injury at Old Trafford and needed to be replaced by understudy Glen Knight. Much more significant for the Lions was the absence through suspension of deadly forward Mark Kennedy, and there were also suggestions that several of the team were suffering the after-effects of a bout of 'flu.

While reintroducing Steven Riley at full-back for Philip Neville, Eric Harrison voiced a few words about the earlier tie as well as the upcoming one. United's coach felt the young Reds *'allowed themselves to be knocked out of their stride'* at Old Trafford and he went on to say, *'It's the first time I have seen them so shaken and they didn't play the football they are capable of. They can perform a lot better and I think they will. They know what to expect this time.'*

If United had been shaken in Manchester, they were certainly stirred in London. Required to show patience in possession at The Den, eventually their superior technique, especially in midfield where the likes of David Beckham and Nicky Butt looked every inch the cut of future first-team material, shone over the park like a beacon. A lethal weapon during their successes in the earlier rounds, it was actually the Reds' finishing which prevented them from equalising sooner than they did, and even in the opening 60 seconds, a flying header from Paul Scholes flashed just wide of Millwall's goal frame.

Two of the most decisive moments fell between the 52nd and 62nd minutes of the match, the first of which was when Danny Chapman stroked a defence-splitting pass through United's back four to an unmarked Neville Gordon. In an eyeball to eyeball situation with Darren Whitmarsh, Gordon almost had too much time to think and he was unable to hold his nerve, with the 'keeper spreading himself to make an absolutely crucial stop. Had the Millwall number eight converted the chance, United would have been required to score twice in less than 40 minutes in order to gain parity.

Ten minutes later, the Reds were level on aggregate and would go on to wrap up a place in the final just in time to evade the requirement of extra-time.

Peter Cordwell of the *Lewisham & Catford Mercury* was positively glowing in praise of United's superb performance in his compact, colourful and highly perceptive match report:

What a delight!
It took a bunch of kids to restore this spectator's faith in football. Dave Bassett wasn't among the 6,276 people entranced at The Den on Tuesday night, but maybe someone will mention it to him.
This marvellous Manchester team weren't clones closing down, they were artists opening up.
Remember skill? Remember ability? Remember flair? Remember passing to feet? If you've forgotten, try and get to the two-legged F.A. Youth Cup final (against Norwich or Leeds) and savour the style of these likeliest of lads, reckoned to be the best United crop since the Busby Babes.
And not an overdeveloped thigh in sight. Just footballers. All of them could play. All were comfortable on the ball. A free kick, for example, was just another pass, not a Wimbledon punt forward.
There's much to admire about Millwall's ultra-commitment, with some sharp passing thrown in. Youth coach Tom Walley is producing good players who will never shirk the issue. But is there another level, another plane? United's kids proved there is.
The wonder was that Millwall were 2-1 up from the first leg at Old Trafford and were still in front after an hour. Then two rapier strikes restored reality.
Winger Ben Thornley weaved some more magic down the left and rolled a ball inside for midfielder Nicky Butt to score with a stunning shot into the top left-hand corner. Thornley then combined with centre-forward Paul Scholes – the magnet in most of United's moves – and sub Jovan Kirovski sent a bullet header into the same part of the net.
They should play the final at Wembley. United would grace the place.

Cordwell's suggestion in regards to staging the final under the twin towers echoed back to Joe Richards' identical view on the matter exactly forty years before and although well meaning in its intention, was still seen as impractical.

Even so, his theories on United's display weren't wrong and the Reds scored numerous chances prior to drawing level. Besides Scholes' first minute miss, the same player's close-range effort was blocked by Knight following a slick three-man move involving Thornley and Beckham, and in the minutes prior to his goal, Nicky Butt twice headed over the crossbar when advantageously positioned.

A determined David Beckham exits the tunnel at The Den immediately followed by Keith Gillespie

> *I think United knew about me from playing in the Northern Ireland Milk Cup and they weren't happy with their other 'keepers at the time so asked me to come across and play in the F.A. Youth Cup matches. They would fly me over before each tie and I would play in the odd Lancashire League game to get used to everyone.*
>
> *When you look back at what all those players achieved it was an amazing team, Scholes, Butt, Savage, Gillespie, Beckham, Phil and Gary Neville.*
>
> *We should have won the home game against Millwall but made a few mistakes at the back and we were very disappointed to be a goal down. We then travelled down by bus to London and trained at Charlton Athletic's ground before the second leg.*
>
> *I knew it was going to be a tough game at The Den but Nicky Butt was great that night and we managed to come away with a win that put us in the final. On the way back to Manchester we knew we would be playing Leeds United, who were a good side, but we were confident that we could win it.*
>
> *Everyone was just buzzing and looking forward to the final.*

DARREN WHITMARSH

382

1992-93

APRIL 1993

semi-final 2nd leg

A Millwall attack wrong-foots Chris Casper (number four) and Keith Gillespie (number six)

Darren Whitmarsh prepares to smother a Jermaine Wright shot while Gary Neville (number five) and Ben Thornley (right of Neville) await the outcome

383

1992-93

1) Darren Whitmarsh	9) Richard Irving
2) John O'Kane	10) Paul Scholes
3) Steven Riley	11) Ben Thornley
4) Chris Casper	*12) Colin Murdock (for 9)*
5) Gary Neville	*14) Robbie Savage (for 8)*
6) Keith Gillespie	
7) Nicky Butt	
8) David Beckham	

1) Paul Pettinger	9) Noel Whelan
2) Andy Couzens	10) Simon Oliver
3) Kevin Sharp	11) Jamie Forrester
4) Mark Tinkler	*12) Alex Byrne*
5) Kevin Daly	*14) Steve Tobin*
6) Rob Bowman	
7) Matthew Smithard	
8) Mark Ford	

MAY 1993

MANCHESTER UNITED 0 v 2 LEEDS UNITED

Forrester, Whelan

Monday 10th

Kick-off 7.30 p.m.

Attendance 30,562

final 1st leg

The outcome of Jovan Kirovski's sweet 83rd minute winner at The Den meant that the only barrier now standing between the Reds and the honour of retaining the Youth Cup for the first time since 1957 was Leeds United.

The Yorkshire club weren't able to boast of any significant accomplishments for their efforts in the tournament, their best previous performances amounting only to reaching the quarter-finals in 1954, 1964, 1966, 1970, 1981 and 1987. It had been a different matter throughout this particular season, as they demonstrated skill, nerve and durability in liberal quantities in their drive to the final.

Leeds commenced their Youth Cup campaign with a 2-1 win at Sheffield Wednesday and then knocked Stoke for six, with two in reply, in the Potteries. At the Fourth Round stage, Queen's Park Rangers were massacred 5-1 at Elland Road before a return to Sheffield, this time to Bramall Lane, resulted in a 2-2 draw with the Blades. Leeds then used home advantage to good effect by winning 2-1 in the replay.

Now breaking new ground, they were well on their way in the semi-final when triumphing 3-0 at Norwich, but it was a more fraught affair for them at home where the Canaries almost turned the tables with a 2-0 victory.

By a single goal advantage, Leeds were in the final at last.

It had also proved to be a reasonably good season for the Elland Road youngsters in the Northern Intermediate League as they managed to secure third spot behind champions Barnsley. Over the course of the campaign, Noel Whelan scored 22 goals in 24 games, Jamie Forrester notched seventeen times in eighteen matches while Steve Tobin registered fifteen goals from two dozen appearances.

Meanwhile, on the west side of the Pennines, these were indeed happy days at Old Trafford. After being pipped into second place in the championship race a year ago, ironically by Leeds, the seniors clinched the F.A. Premier League title in the days leading up to the Youth Cup final. Only a week before the visit of the Yorkshire lads, the Reds' senior squad were presented with the trophy which signified an end to the club's divisional barren spell of 26 years.

In his introductory page in the match programme, Alex Ferguson was full of praise for the junior Reds:

I would like to congratulate the boys on reaching the final as they defend the crown they won so handsomely last season, and I wish both teams the best of luck in what promises to be an entertaining match.

Leeds have a good team, the result of Howard Wilkinson taking stock some time ago of his youth set-up at Elland Road, just as I did soon after my arrival at Old Trafford.

They are building an organisation and system to challenge us, as I am sure we will see tonight and in the second leg in Leeds on Thursday.

But it will take a couple of very good performances by Leeds to stop our team who are an exceptionally gifted group of boys. I have never known their like before. They stand apart in my experience as a manager and play with a great sense of team without deserting their individual ability.

They are being recognised internationally with six of them currently in England's under-18 squad and the bonus is that they are a bunch of pleasant, well disciplined boys who will be able to handle success in professional football.

For the opening leg, Eric Harrison's preference was to nominate the same side that had secured victory over Millwall in south London. United's youngsters were made fully aware by their coach that they were up against a completely different class of opposition to those faced on a week-in, week-out basis in the Lancashire League but, nevertheless, Harrison's warnings seemed to go unheeded when the teenagers failed to generate their usual level of quality in a nervous display.

David Meek recorded the events of an occasion which soon turned sour on the Reds:

Manchester United's young dream turned into something of a nightmare against Leeds at Old Trafford last night.

Hopes of seeing the Reds' talented juniors keep the F.A. Youth Cup they won last year look slim after a 2-0 defeat in the first leg of their final against powerful and purposeful opponents.

Leeds used a good mix of strength and skill right from the start. And United were still struggling to get their game together when Jamie Forrester scored on the line from Rob Bowman's flicked header to give Leeds a 16th minute lead.

The shock spurred the Reds more into the form which has seen them complete a Lancashire League and Cup double this season.

But they were still unable to find an accurate finish on target.

They knocked the ball about better and five minutes before the interval their 'Young Player of the Year', Paul Scholes, had a goal disallowed for offside following a corner.

Richard Irving nearly got through after the interval but fluffed the advantage given him by the referee after being held back.

Then United cut their own throats in the 62nd minute with a freak goal, conceded when the normally impeccable Gary Neville smashed a clearance against Noel Whelan for the rebound to sail from the edge of the box into the net.

It looked as if the United youngsters were overwhelmed by the amazing crowd of 30,000 who had clearly come expecting to see the kids match the achievement of the first-team.

Manager Alex Ferguson believes they still will and is confident his boys can win the second leg at Elland Road on Thursday.

'They looked tired and nervous. Full credit to Leeds who defended well but we didn't see our team play anything like their normal game. They will be more relaxed next time and they can still pull it back on Thursday,' he said.

The visitors' opening goal was something of a tragedy for Darren Whitmarsh, who was caught in no-man's land and failed in his attempt to punch the ball away from the lurking Bowman. When Bowman nodded it on, Forrester would have been hard pushed to miss the target from where he was standing, which was almost next to a post.

That incident cloaked the stadium in a drab atmosphere for the rest of the proceedings and when Richard Irving, who was stood in a patch of open space, failed to beat Paul Pettinger from just ten yards out late on, all in the United camp were acutely aware of the size of the coming task in Yorkshire.

Richard Irving scorned a guilt-edged chance to peg a goal back for a disjointed United in their home defeat to Leeds

384

1992-93

1) Paul Pettinger	9) Noel Whelan	1) Darren Whitmarsh	9) Richard Irving
2) Andy Couzens	10) Simon Oliver	2) Philip Neville	10) Robbie Savage
3) Kevin Sharp	11) Jamie Forrester	3) Steven Riley	11) Ben Thornley
4) Mark Tinkler	*12) Alex Byrne (for 6)*	4) Chris Casper	*12) Colin Murdock (for 9)*
5) Kevin Daly	*14) Steve Tobin (for 10)*	5) Gary Neville	*14) Mark Rawlinson*
6) Rob Bowman		6) Keith Gillespie	
7) Matthew Smithard		7) Paul Scholes	
8) Mark Ford		8) David Beckham	

LEEDS UNITED 2(4) v (1)1 MANCHESTER UNITED

Forrester, Smithard — Scholes (pen)

MAY 1993
Thursday 13th
Kick-off 7.30 p.m.
Attendance 31,037

final 2nd leg

Three days later Leeds announced an unchanged side for the second instalment whereas Eric Harrison was hindered in his selection choices by a foot injury to Nicky Butt and John O'Kane's ankle problem. Harrison was thankful there was a ready made replacement for O'Kane in Philip Neville, who was available again after featuring for England's under-16 side in Turkey, while Robbie Savage came in for Butt. It was a particularly opportune event for Savage, who was excluded from the Manchester leg of the final a year ago to make way for the returning Ryan Giggs.

Harrison was still hopeful of the right result at Elland Road and told a press man of the home encounter, 'I think the lads were shocked to find 30,000 had come to watch them at Old Trafford and the expectations after the championship success got to them.' He added, 'I had never seen so many white faces before. They were overwhelmed, but it was a priceless experience and I'm sure they will have learned from it. It was the first time this season that they have failed to score. They came back against Millwall to win after losing the first leg at home and we can do it again.'

Sadly, despite Harrison's optimism, it wasn't to be and it was left to David Meek to detail how the major prize of the season eluded United's kids:

Manchester United finally met their match, with Leeds worthy winners of this season's F.A. Youth Cup.

The Reds were always going to have a hard time in last night's second leg of the final at Elland Road after a shock 2-0 defeat at Old Trafford.

And that's exactly how it worked out, especially when Leeds added to their lead with a spectacular overhead goal from the brilliant Jamie Forrester after only twelve minutes.

United levelled on the night just before the half hour with a penalty from Paul Scholes after Mark Tinkler had tripped Keith Gillespie.

But Leeds took just a minute for Matthew Smithard to wipe out the goal when he raced onto a header from Noel Whelan to give the home club a 2-1 advantage on the night and a handsome aggregate victory by 4-1 in front of another bumper crowd of 31,047.

It was bitterly ironic for United that two of their biggest problems were once on their schoolboy books.

Forrester and full-back Kevin Sharp were both due to come to Old Trafford from the F.A. School of Excellence but chose to join Auxerre in France in a more rewarding deal.

Leeds signed them for £200,000 after they had become homesick.

But even on a disappointing night for United, there was at least one starlet shining through the gloom.

Scholes, United's 'Young Player of the Year' from Middleton, had an outstanding game in midfield combining a tigerish appetite for the ball with good control and clever switches of attack.

United certainly played better than in the first leg but they found Forrester and Whelan a handful upfront while failing to press home their attacks.

Scholes missed a couple of chances early on and they were finally doomed to defeat and the loss of the trophy they won last season when Ben Thornley blazed over the bar after a good move between Gillespie and Robert Savage.

Coach Eric Harrison was disappointed but after a Lancashire League and Cup double believes the experience will be a valuable education for his young charges.

Manager Alex Ferguson said, 'I'm not worried. They are good players and you can't win every match. They have had a super season.'

The Reds' chance of ultimate victory was vastly reduced when Forrester's fantastic bicycle kick arrowed into the back of Whitmarsh's net. So eye-catching was the effort, at least two newspapers compared the goal to Denis Law's scoring acrobatics of years gone by.

Immediately following his penalty conversion, and despite realising it might only count as a consolation, Paul Scholes raised a smile from the travelling United fans when he wagged a mischievous finger at the massed bank of home supporters behind the goal. As if to indicate 'you'll be hearing from me again', it was a prophetic gesture from the midfielder.

The Yorkshire Post put the wraps on the occasion when noting Leeds were the first club from the White Rose county to capture the trophy and also mentioned the jubilant home squad paraded the silverware around the pitch in full view of the vast crowd.

The sign above Paul Scholes' head tells its own tale as his short-range attempt on goal is blocked by Paul Pettinger at Elland Road

385

1993-94

1) Brendan Murphy	9) Scott Jackson
2) David Blair	10) Graeme Tomlinson
3) Neil Grayston	11) Tony Carss
4) Des Hamilton	*12) Jimmy Proctor*
5) Wayne Benn	*14) Chris Richardson*
6) Andy Stuttard	
7) Craig Midgley	
8) Mike Lynch	

1) David Pierce	9) Richard Irving
2) Philip Neville	10) Jovan Kirovski
3) Matthew Monaghan	11) Philip Whittam
4) Mark Ryan	*12) Lee Barnes*
5) Ashley Westwood	*14) David Johnson (for 11)*
6) Terry Cooke	
7) Michael Appleton	
8) Gary Twynham	

NOVEMBER 1993

BRADFORD CITY 2 v 0 **MANCHESTER UNITED**

Hamilton, Westwood (o.g.)

Monday 22nd
Kick-off 7.00 p.m.
Attendance 739

second round

The front cover of the match programme for the tie at Valley Parade included an image of Graeme Tomlinson who later signed for United

After all of the many notable triumphs that United had enjoyed in the Youth Cup over the last few years, the outcome of their tie at Bradford City in November 1993 was neither welcome nor expected and the young Reds' performance proved to be one of the most disappointing and direst of the decade.

United had visited Valley Parade on Youth Cup duty only once before, in October 1958, when a 3-1 win launched them on their way to a semi-final appearance. The junior Bantams then went on to become the Reds' whipping boys in the competition in the early 1960's, suffering three comprehensive defeats at Old Trafford in as many seasons.

Philip Neville, Richard Irving and Jovan Kirovski represented a trio of survivors from the 1992/93 campaign and they were nominated to start against a side that had already knocked local rivals Barnsley out of the tournament. None of the other eight starting participants, or either of the two substitutes, possessed any previous Youth Cup experience.

United's line-up at Valley Parade radiated a decidedly local appearance as, of the new boys, goalkeeper David Pierce and Gary Twynham originated from Manchester while Mark Ryan and Michael Appleton came from Salford. Philip Whittam was recruited from the Bolton area and in respect of the remainder, centre-back Ashley Westwood called Astley his home whereas striker Terry Cooke was born on the far outskirts of Birmingham at Marston Green. Defender Matthew Monaghan was another from outside of the locality because he had travelled to Old Trafford from Bangor in North Wales in search of a career in football.

The result of the match was virtually decided when Bradford, who were then managed by ex-United centre-forward Frank Stapleton, scored twice in the opening eight minutes. Displaying an abundance of aggression, skill and adventure right from the first whistle, City killed off the Reds' chances of a win, and thereby a third successive final appearance, without experiencing the type of response which would have been expected.

The opener came inside five minutes when Bradford midfielder Des Hamilton, who impressed throughout the whole duration of the contest with his acceleration and trickery, raced through United's ranks and fended off a couple of defenders before striking a powerful rising shot past Pierce.

The Bantams struck again soon after, this time fatally as far as their Lancastrian visitors were concerned. Bradford's second goal was credited to Reds' defender Westwood who, in attempting to clear a cross from Tony Carss while holding off a forward's rigorous challenge, unintentionally headed the ball over Pierce and into his own net.

Now more than a little shell-shocked, United were collectively unable to lift themselves sufficiently in order to force their way back into contention. Just prior to half-time the home side almost scored again, Hamilton razoring a pass through a porous defence only for Graeme Tomlinson to shoot above the bar from a good position.

The Reds' best period of the game came at the opening of the second half, but they wasted their pretty approach work with an abject lack of finishing power. In the 55th minute, Whittam was substituted by David Johnson as Eric Harrison attempted to breathe more fire into United's attack and the coach was mightily disappointed soon after when the replacement missed a sitter by contriving to blast a Neville centre over the top from close range.

City soon reverted to the quality of their first half performance level, leaving their opponents with too little possession to make any further noticeable impression. The Reds' only other serious scoring opportunities during the second period were a Westwood header which missed the target and a Johnson effort that flashed outside a post. Those attempts were easily matched by Bradford, for whom Tomlinson could, and should, have comfortably ended the game with a bagful of goals.

The Manchester Evening News match report stated the Old Trafford side *'made a bad start'* and that they *'never looked like saving the game despite a second half fightback'*, whereas the Bradford Telegraph & Argus correctly claimed it *'was a richly deserved victory and, with better finishing, the scoreline would have been more emphatic'*.

Mancunian Gary Twynham, whose only Youth Cup appearance concluded in a dismal defeat at Valley Parade

LANCASHIRE F.A. YOUTH CUP

1970 - 1985 & 1989 - 1998

Manchester United have competed in numerous local cup tournaments for over 100 years, with the first-team taking part in the Manchester Senior Cup since their Newton Heath days and the Lancashire Senior Cup prior to the outbreak of World War One.

Mainly because of the diminishing appeal of those competitions, and the broader attraction of the F.A. Cup and other national and international tournaments, over a period of time it became the norm for the club's Reserves to participate in these competitions. At youth level, the 'A' side entered the Gilgryst Cup from 1932 onwards and they and the 'B' team fought for supremacy in the Lancashire Supplementary Cup for decades while simultaneously fulfilling divisional obligations in the Lancashire League.

So, when the Lancashire F.A. introduced a county version of the Youth Cup, the Reds were invited to participate. Originally labelled the 'Youth Floodlit Competition', the tournament was conceived with a number of objectives in mind.

Firstly, as the title suggested, it provided an opportunity for youngsters to further their experience of playing competitively under floodlights while also giving them an additional taste of knock-out football. The latter point was particularly important for some of the smaller clubs, whose teenage representatives were often eliminated early from the national competition and there was, therefore, the chance for participating clubs to avail themselves of a 'second chance' of cup soccer. Also, the Lancashire F.A. wanted to raise awareness of youth football within their jurisdiction and demonstrate that they were keen to take an active role in same.

The concept was relatively simple. Each team took part in a qualifying tie, the winner progressed through to the last four stage and the victors of the semi-finals then met in the final. With the same age restrictions applying as in the national competition, the majority of clubs simply entered their usual youth team and so familiar names were found on the relevant match team sheets. United's first ever tie was at Turf Moor on the 17th November 1970 but, as the United Review noted, it actually turned into a false start:

A further interest has been added to the youth scene by the introduction of a Youth Floodlit Competition by the Lancashire F.A. Unfortunately, our first venture in the new tournament ran foul of the weather when our game at Burnley was rained off with the teams level at one-all 30 minutes after the start.

The game finally took place the following February, when the Reds ran out 3-1 winners only to be knocked out by Bolton in the semi-final.

The format of the competition altered for the 1971/72 term, with home and away ties introduced for the semi-final and final stages. The change seemed to suit the young Reds because they triumphed at their second attempt with a 5-3 aggregate victory over Bolton.

United won the trophy again in 1975, 1976, 1979 and 1981, and the competition often provided an opportunity for other youngsters, who were injured or out of form during F.A. Youth Cup campaigns, to experience some quality knock-out action. Additionally, with the final often staged in May when the league season was over, a number of players made their last appearance for United in the competition. For example, Gary Micklewhite captained the Reds to victory over Tranmere Rovers in 1979 only to then be transferred in the close season.

For the 1985/86 to 1988/89 terms inclusive, the Reds decided not to compete at all while they experimented with international youth tournaments in Italy, Germany and Holland. However, their name was back in the hat for the 1989/90 season and following success at Lancashire League level throughout the late 1980's and 1990's, it was no surprise that the Reds added further titles in 1991, 1993, 1994, 1996 and 1997. As the Football Association introduced their Academy initiatives across the country, the 1997/98 campaign brought an end to United's participation in the competition, which ended with them reaching a one-game semi-final only to be knocked out by Tranmere.

While the Reds never achieved a 'double' of both F.A. Youth Cup and Lancashire F.A. Youth Cup victories in the same season, there were a host of players who managed to collect gold medals in both tournaments.

Despite United only being involved in the Lancashire Youth Cup for some 24 seasons, their ten victories proved useful in the development of many of the club's juniors who never experienced any other cup glories. Nowadays, the Manchester Senior Cup is frequently used as a testing ground for youth players as they make the step up from Academy to Reserve football.

A joyous United squad celebrate winning the 1994 Lancashire Youth Cup immediately after their victory at Burnley
Back row (l-r) John Hudson, Mark Ryan, Michael Appleton, David Pierce, Ashley Westwood, Ian Hart
Front row (l-r) Richard Irving, David Johnson, Philip Neville, Philip Whittam, Jovan Kirovski, Terry Cooke, Neil Mustoe

1994-95

1) Paul Gibson	9) David Johnson	1) Gareth Hughes	9) Mike Bignall
2) Philip Neville	10) Terry Cooke	2) Stuart Rock	10) Gareth Wilson
3) Philip Whittam	11) David Hilton	3) Paul Jones	11) Lewis Coady
4) Ashley Westwood	*12) John Hudson*	4) Mark McGregor	*12) Neil Wainwright (for 7)*
5) Ronnie Wallwork	*13) Heath Maxon GK*	5) Andrew Thomas	*13) Dave Walsh GK*
6) Neil Mustoe	*14) Des Baker*	6) Richard Rawlins	*14) Robert Williams (for 6)*
7) David Gardner		7) Mike Cody	
8) Paul Heckingbottom		8) Stephen Futcher	

NOVEMBER 1994

MANCHESTER UNITED 4 v 1 WREXHAM
Cooke (2), Johnson (2) — *Bignall*

second round

Monday 28th
Kick-off 7.00 p.m.
Attendance 1,240

Bearing in mind the grief felt in the Old Trafford camp through the under-18's fall at the opening Youth Cup hurdle twelve months ago, in November 1994 Eric Harrison's need was to construct an almost new side for a fresh assault on the tournament. Building his team around skipper Philip Neville, Harrison also included Ashley Westwood and Philip Whittam, two of the other defenders who experienced such a foul tasting defeat at Bradford.

Joining Neville, Westwood and Whittam in the back four was Ronnie Wallwork, a sturdily-built Mancunian, and situated directly behind them was Paul Gibson, who wasn't the first of the club's goalkeeper captures from Sheffield. Caused by an extension to the number of substitutes the Reds' coach was able to name, Poole-born Heath Maxon became the first United 'keeper to occupy a place on the bench for a Youth Cup fixture.

Harrison named another Valley Parade survivor, Terry Cooke, to lead the search for goals alongside David Johnson, who had substituted for Whittam in that same match. Making up the team were industrious midfielder Neil Mustoe, Salfordian David Gardner, and two Barnsley boys, Paul Heckingbottom and David Hilton.

United's opening opponents had negotiated no fewer than five rounds already, scoring 29 goals in the process, and they were positively relishing their glamour trip to Manchester after making Youth Cup visits to the more modest outposts of Mansfield, Stalybridge Celtic and Port Vale, on top of acting as hosts to Rochdale and Burton Albion.

Wrexham's youth development officer, Cliff Sear, said of his players, *'Tonight is a big, big occasion for them. Playing at Old Trafford is going to be special for them and when you look at youth policies, United's is the best in the country.'*

Taking into account the manner of the Reds' exit at the hands of Bradford, where two goals were conceded in the early minutes of the contest, the last thing Harrison would have wanted was a bad start to the game. Nevertheless, it was precisely what he got.

In only the third minute of the match, Wrexham's Michael Cody made a swift dash down the right flank from inside his own half and his perfect centre was just too inviting for the prolific Mike Bignall, who flashed a header past Gibson to send the two hundred or so visiting supporters wild with delight.

The Reds responded twice within a few minutes and both attacks could easily have yielded a reward. Johnson was the first to be denied, when his arched header rebounded off the woodwork, and Cooke then drove in a shot which appeared to have beaten Gareth Hughes until the 'keeper clawed the ball back into his grasp just as it was about to cross the goal-line.

United's equaliser came in the 16th minute, with the damage done to the visitors largely self-inflicted. When Wrexham were awarded a free kick midway inside their own territory, it was knocked out to Lewis Coady on the left wing. Coady failed to react properly, and his hesitation allowed Johnson to steal the ball away from him with all the skill of a sneak thief. Retaining possession over a distance of some 40 yards, Johnson finished the job off himself by taking the ball past Hughes and rolling it into the net.

In the 32nd minute, United scored a second. The goal was credited to the energetic Cooke, whose advance took him into the danger area from the left. Cooke's powerful drive took a wicked deflection off the Robins' Stephen Futcher for the ball to curl over a static goalie and drop into the empty net.

Further decent chances fell to both parties prior to the interval. Westwood's powerful header came back off a post and Wrexham's Bignall, plumb in front of goal and unmarked just a few yards out, scuffed his attempt to let the Reds off the hook.

Hughes was alert when making an early second half stop from Cooke prior to the Welsh boys settling into something of a purple patch. A 25-yard drive from Stuart Rock was the most they could make of a goodly amount of possession, but at the other end of the pitch, the pace and skill of Johnson and Cooke continually threatened the Wrexham defence.

Johnson plundered his second goal at the conclusion of a swift break in the 73rd minute by powering the ball home with an eye-catching diving header and seven minutes later, co-striker Cooke wrapped up the scoring by slamming away an absolutely superb angled drive.

The Review made a point of mentioning that *'anything other than a United victory seemed unlikely'* and concluded its match report by observing the result *'was achieved by a more than acceptable performance for this stage of the competition'.*

David Hilton attempts to create some space for himself on the edge of Wrexham's eighteen-yard box

388

1994-95

NOVEMBER 1994

David Johnson tricks his way past a stranded Gareth Hughes to create the Reds' equaliser

Terry Cooke looks aghast as one of his first half efforts fails to find the back of Wrexham's net

second round

389

1994-95

MANCHESTER UNITED 1 v 1 **CHARLTON ATHLETIC**

Hudson — Dowson

Manchester United:
1) Paul Gibson
2) Danny Hall
3) Paul Lyons
4) Ashley Westwood
5) Ronnie Wallwork
6) David Gardner
7) Philip Neville
8) Paul Heckingbottom
9) David Johnson
10) Terry Cooke
11) David Hilton
12) *John Hudson (for 11)*
13) *Heath Maxon GK*
14) *Des Baker (for 6)*

Charlton Athletic:
1) Dean Lee
2) Les Burt
3) Stuart Reynolds
4) Andy Larkin
5) Jamie Stuart
6) Danny Edwards
7) Joe Baker
8) Lee Bowyer
9) Keith Dowson
10) Darren Morley
11) Jamie Garnish
12) *Marc Godbold*
13) *Justin Lomakin GK*
14) *James Way (for 9)*

DECEMBER 1994

third round

Wednesday 21st
Kick-off 7.00 p.m.
Attendance 1,430

Hero Hudson rescues Reds

A much sterner test than the one posed by Wrexham was expected by a long chalk when the Third Round draw resulted in a pairing of United with Charlton Athletic. The main threat posed by the Addicks was sure to be their twin-striking partnership of Keith Dowson and Joe Baker because with Christmas just a few days away, and including all competitions, both of them were already into double figures as far as goals were concerned.

In their Youth Cup campaign, Charlton had eliminated Woking (8-0, away) and Cardiff City (2-1 at home) and, despite the apparent size of the task ahead of them, were confident enough to make noises about extending their progress prior to reaching Old Trafford.

As far as the Reds were concerned, Eric Harrison deemed that changes were required at the back. Since the Wrexham tie just a month ago, Phil Whittam had been the unfortunate recipient of both a broken leg and a dislocated ankle so his place was filled by Paul Lyons. The Leigh-born full-back's partner for the evening was another debutant, Danny Hall, a first-year trainee who had been recruited from up in the North-East.

The reason for Hall's inclusion was specifically due to an experimental change of position for Philip Neville, as it was felt within United's management circle that he was capable of exerting a greater influence over the team's pattern of play. Neville's progress had previously slowed down somewhat due to the dual problems of a knee injury and a cartilage operation, but he was now revealing the broader extent of his potential and it appeared to be the correct time to test the theory.

Harrison explained that Neville's new midfield duty was *'something manager Alex Ferguson and myself want to have a look at'*, the repositioning meaning there was no place available for Gloucester teenager Neil Mustoe.

With some late, late drama somewhat masking a poor start to United's second consecutive tie, Steve Dixon of the Greenwich & Eltham Mercury noted specifically how and precisely when they escaped defeat:

Ninety-two minutes. Ninety-two!
Can you believe it? The Charlton players certainly couldn't. They had led mighty Manchester United at Old Trafford in the F.A. Youth Cup Third Round from the early exchanges until deep into second half injury-time, composed defending combining with blind luck to keep the home side out.

Charlton youth coach Neil Banfield was confident that his young side were properly prepared for their biggest ever test and it showed, as the visitors settled much quicker than their opponents.

From the sixth minute they had something to defend, Keith Dowson latching onto a through ball that had been misjudged by the United defence to beat 'keeper Gibson with a crisp low shot.

Thus Charlton had the better of the opening quarter-hour, with their confidence boosted by that early goal. However, United gradually began to impose themselves, with stocky centre-forward David Johnson causing major problems with his pace.

First Jamie Stuart and then Danny Edwards had to be alert to prevent Johnson from scoring and the young striker wasted two glorious opportunities before half-time, one hitting the crossbar and the second blazed wide with only Dean Lee to beat.

Charlton 'keeper Lee had already excelled himself to push away a free kick from the outstanding Terry Cooke – like Johnson and Neville an England Youth international – and Lee had to be assured in his handling as United won plenty of corners to test the visitors' defence.

Half-time came and went and the United players grew more impatient, introducing substitutes Des Baker and John Hudson into the forward-line in a last-ditch attempt to save the game.

And almost immediately Les Burt had to make a vital tackle to prevent Baker from closing in on goal.

United continued to waste chances, Wallwork blazing over from underneath the crossbar. And although Dowson had to go off injured with a badly strained ankle, James Way proved an able deputy. He created an immediate chance for Darren Morley, whose shot was smothered by Gibson.

With United's increasingly desperate attempts to salvage the game continually thwarted by Lee, it seemed Charlton would survive.

But in the second minute of injury-time, Cooke set off again down the left-hand side, leaving a tired Jamie Garnish in his wake. His deep cross was headed past Lee by substitute Hudson, who was immediately engulfed by delirious team-mates.

It was almost the last kick of the game and the Charlton lads were left to dream of what might have been as they left the field heads in hands.

There was no need to be despondent, however, after a magnificent display, and Banfield was full of praise. 'They have been a credit to themselves, their families and the club,' he said. 'There are a few bumps and bruises in there, but it's mainly broken hearts. However, we will look forward to beating Manchester United at The Valley, hopefully with a decent crowd to cheer us on.'

Missed opportunities were again a feature of the Reds' performance and, added to those squandered by Johnson, who was *'in with a few chances but it wasn't his night for accuracy,'* according to one source, another account of the match contained an accusation about Terry Cooke firing *'wastefully into the side netting'* when well positioned.

The Manchester Evening News report described the home goalscorer as *'footloose'*, because his boot flew off while he was in the act of equalising. The News' summariser also reasoned *'despite making hard work of it, United are optimistic about their replay chances'* and claimed in mitigation that *'the slowly freezing pitch was against their ball-players'*.

Meanwhile, the Review rightly reasoned that *'Charlton were well organised and, despite United making several decent openings, they never looked comfortable in front of goal'*.

John Hudson (hand on post) and Paul Heckingbottom await the delivery of a Charlton corner kick

1) Dean Lee	9) Keith Dowson	1) Paul Gibson	9) David Johnson
2) Les Burt	10) Darren Morley	2) Philip Neville	10) Terry Cooke
3) Stuart Reynolds	11) Jamie Garnish	3) Danny Hall	11) Paul Heckingbottom
4) Andy Larkin	*12) Dean Blain (for 2)*	4) Ashley Westwood	*12) John Curtis (for 3)*
5) Jamie Stuart	*13) Justin Lomakin GK*	5) Michael Clegg	*13) Heath Maxon GK*
6) Danny Edwards	*14) Jamie Kyte (for 9)*	6) Neil Mustoe	*14) David Gardner (for 11)*
7) Joe Baker		7) John Hudson	
8) Lee Bowyer		8) Grant Brebner	

CHARLTON ATHLETIC 2 v 5 MANCHESTER UNITED

Edwards, Stuart — Cooke, Heckingbottom, Hudson, Johnson (2)

JANUARY 1995

Thursday 12th*
Kick-off 7.00 p.m.
Attendance 3,515

REDS STORM BACK TO BOOK ARSENAL YOUTH TIE

Boys' night out!

Not for the first time, or even the last, in relation to a Youth Cup game involving United, there was pandemonium outside the stadium prior to and just after the kick-off at the replay.

With over 3,500 spectators to contend with at The Valley, the decisions made by home officials to set the kick-off for 7 p.m. rather than slightly later, attempting to accommodate a swelling crowd in a stand large enough to seat only 3,000 people and refusing to sell tickets in advance, were widely criticised by the Charlton Athletic Supporters' Club. It was estimated that as many as 400 spectators didn't gain entry until after 7.35 p.m., while a number of fans scrambled under a gate and others simply gave up in frustration and went home.

Stadium manager Roy King admitted the club were slow to put contingency plans into force, which included opening an exit gate to allow latecomers entrance. King claimed as many as 2,000 arrived just a few minutes prior to the start and he blamed the police for their refusal to put the normal match traffic management system into operation.

The majority of those inside the stadium during the opening half would have been well pleased with what they saw. With Philip Neville reverting to his familiar full-back role and Neil Mustoe restored to midfield alongside new starter Grant Brebner, United were 2-0 down inside 33 minutes. Sporting a change strip of yellow and green, the Manchester boys defended benevolently and looked as if they were on a crash course to catastrophe. They also appeared to have totally ignored Eric Harrison's pre-match order that he was *'looking for a big improvement in performance'* after reasoning *'it was not good in the first game'*.

Danny Edwards opened the scoring for Charlton in the 15th minute when he thumped a blistering 30-yard drive past Gibson and Jamie Stuart later punished the Reds by turning a Darren Morley free kick into their net. One newspaper was scathing of the first half display offered up by the visitors, claiming that in the opening 45 minutes *'United's gormless devotion to pointless kick and rush had a sizeable crowd blinking in disbelief'* before pronouncing that the *'proud tradition of Busby's Babes seemed to be in criminally careless hands'*.

But what a transformation there was to follow.

Only three minutes had ticked away after the resumption when United grasped at a lifeline. On a foray in support of the forwards, Neville's attempt on goal was charged down and the rebound fell kindly for Terry Cooke, whose quick wits instructed him to hit home the loose ball while his skills allowed him to execute the task.

Just four minutes later, United scored another when the Cooke/Neville combination clicked again. The former completely fooled Charlton's rearguard when sent on his way by his skipper and Cooke then delivered a skimming cross along the mouth of the goal which Paul Heckingbottom nonchalantly tapped in at the far post.

The United lads were now taking on the very responsibilities they seemed to shirk in the first half, causing Charlton's attacking threat to slowly fade and then disappear from view entirely. In the 67th minute, John Hudson made it 3-2 to the visitors when he headed home a Heckingbottom left wing corner and, in putting a previously profligate performance in terms of finishing behind him, David Johnson then scored twice in the 71st and 73rd minutes to complete one of the club's most impressive Youth Cup comebacks.

The Reds' resurgence was so remarkable that the Review made a tongue-in-cheek comment about the coaches replacing *'the entire eleven players with another set they had been keeping under wraps in the dressing room'*.

The Greenwich & Eltham Mercury exercised a view that the *'chief architect of (United's) revival was thrustful winger Terry Cooke'*. The Mercury also noted that Charlton were left *'choking on (United's) expensive exhaust fumes'* and then pointed out the Addicks' best chance of making progress *'disappeared in the 92nd minute at Old Trafford'*.

United's Paul Gibson saves while Michael Clegg (far left), Paul Heckingbottom, Ashley Westwood (falling, centre) and Philip Neville (right) can only hold their breath

1994-95

third round replay

*This game was originally scheduled for Thursday, January 5th but was postponed due to a frozen pitch

1994-95

1) Paul Gibson	9) David Johnson	1) Noel Imber	9) Isaiah Rankin
2) John Curtis	10) Terry Cooke	2) Orlando Hollingsworth	10) Timmy Griggs
3) Philip Neville	11) Philip Mulryne	3) Ross Taylor	11) Robbie Drake
4) Ashley Westwood	*12) Ronnie Wallwork*	4) Jamie Howell	*12) James McDonald (for 11)*
5) Michael Clegg	*13) Heath Maxon GK*	5) Chris Coffey	*13) Lee Richardson GK*
6) Neil Mustoe	*14) Des Baker (for 11)*	6) Jeff Woolsey	*14) Greg Tello (for 2)*
7) John Hudson		7) Michael Black	
8) Grant Brebner		8) Albert Clarke	

JANUARY 1995

MANCHESTER UNITED 2 v 1 ARSENAL
Hudson, Mustoe — *Woolsey*

Tuesday 31st
Kick-off 7.00 p.m.
Attendance 2,701

fourth round

> *"It will be a difficult game for us. Arsenal were impressive in winning the competition last season and they still have seven players from that side eligible to play this year.*
> *However, we are going into the game with more confidence after showing a big improvement in performance when we played Charlton in London."*
>
> **ERIC HARRISON**

Their amazing victory over Charlton gave the Reds what was commonly considered a plum home draw against Arsenal, the current Youth Cup holders. There had only been one previous pairing of the two clubs in the competition, which occurred a couple of decades ago in the 1972/73 season, and it ended in a victory to the Gunners following a replay at Highbury.

While those such as United, Wolves, Chelsea and Blackburn might have stolen a march on the London outfit in terms of organising their youth development programmes in the 1950's and early 1960's, by 1966 Arsenal were themselves holders of the Youth Cup. In 1995 they were up to four such triumphs, three behind United and, added to their other victorious campaigns in 1971, 1988 and 1994, plus a final defeat in 1965, those achievements meant that they were rightly acknowledged as the second most successful club in the tournament.

In order to bolster the Reds' defence, Philip Neville, who did everything expected of him and much more during his senior entrance in a home F.A. Cup tie against Wrexham on the Saturday just gone, switched to left-back in order to make way for Nuneaton lad John Curtis.

On the eve of the game, David Meek shone a spotlight on the former England schoolboy captain, whom everyone in the know was predicting a great future for: Still only sixteen, Curtis will be on special leave from the F.A. School of Excellence at Lilleshall. He was pursued by all the big clubs when he was at school in the Midlands, but signed associated forms at Old Trafford before going on to the F.A. School, run for the country's best youngsters.

The Lilleshall boys are not allowed to play for their professional clubs except in the F.A. Youth Cup, and even then it is unusual for them to be selected to play with an older age group. But Curtis was on the bench for United's replay in the last round at Charlton and is credited with a major role in helping to pull back from two goals down to win the tie 5-2.

Michael Clegg, a defender from Ashton-under-Lyne, retained his place in the under-18's as a result of his steady debut showing at The Valley and as well as Curtis, another making his bow in the tournament was Phil Mulryne, a skilful winger from Belfast whose serious thigh strain had caused him to miss most of the season so far.

Possibly mindful of the succession of early goals conceded in the previous games, the Reds commenced with an early barrage on Arsenal's goal. In a pattern that persisted almost throughout the tie, Mulryne, Brebner and Johnson each scorned useful openings early on.

It took Terry Cooke to unravel the mystery of how to unlock the Gunners' defence in the 22nd minute when he delivered a top class centre which zipped along the edge of the visitors' six-yard line. A work-hungry Neil Mustoe broke forward from his midfield duties to beat a desperate Arsenal defender to the ball, knocking it past goalkeeper Noel Imber's left hand and just inside the post to make it one-nil to United.

Even though the Reds then wasted a couple of chances to double their lead immediately after, and were enjoying a period of almost complete dominance, a resilient Arsenal struck back to equalise only seven minutes later. It was a simple task required of defender Jeff Woolsey, as he climbed higher than all around him in order to loop a header past Gibson from a corner taken by Orlando Hollingsworth.

Neil Mustoe squeezes the ball past Noel Imber to give the Reds an advantage over their teenage Highbury adversaries

392

1994-95

JANUARY 1995

fourth round

That winning feeling! John Hudson looks overjoyed just a second or two after claiming United's clinching goal against Arsenal

The contest slowly evolved into an even affair in terms of both possession and enterprise but the Reds definitely manufactured by far the better goalscoring chances. Particularly in the later stages of the first half, Gunners' goalie Imber was easily the busier of the two custodians and he produced good work in a bid to keep his team's hopes afloat.

The winner came four minutes past the hour mark and went to United's John Hudson. It came about when Johnson tried his luck with a hard drive at the target and, for once, Imber was unable to hold the ball cleanly. Sensing the opportunity in a flash, Hudson beat him to the rebound by the merest fraction of a second to steer the ball home.

A tense finish followed, during which the Reds could easily have been made to curse their earlier slack finishing. As Robbie Drake's effort missed Gibson's goal frame by a matter of inches in the very late stages, it served once again to summarise the slender difference between progress and elimination in a knock-out competition.

Arsenal coach Pat Rice later remarked that United *'hit us hard in the first 25 minutes'* and he continued by saying, *'Our goalkeeper was absolutely superb. He kept us in the game in the first half......when we could easily have been four goals down.'*

Various media reports made mention of the Mustoe/Brebner midfield partnership working effectively, while Neville and Curtis were credited as solidifying the defence.

The Evening News gave a different opinion to all of the others, offering a view that *'the hero at the back was Ashley Westwood. Not the most sophisticated looking player, he nevertheless dominated the centre of defence against a muscular attack seeking to use strength'.*

1994-95

1) Stuart Brock	9) Richard Walker	1) Paul Gibson	9) Des Baker
2) Jonathan Miley	10) Darren Byfield	2) Philip Neville	10) Terry Cooke
3) Leslie Hines	11) Lee Hendrie	3) Ronnie Wallwork	11) Philip Mulryne
4) David Moore	*12) Alan Kirby (for 6)*	4) Ashley Westwood	*12) Danny Hall*
5) Ben Petty	*13) Adam Rachel GK*	5) Michael Clegg	*13) Heath Maxon GK*
6) Tommy Jaszczun	*14) Andy Mitchell (for 7)*	6) Neil Mustoe	*14) Michael Twiss (for 11)*
7) Richard Burgess		7) Grant Brebner	
8) Lee Burchell		8) Paul Heckingbottom	

FEBRUARY 1995

ASTON VILLA 2 v 3 MANCHESTER UNITED
Burgess, Walker   Cooke, Mulryne, Wallwork

Tuesday 28th
Kick-off 7.00 p.m.
Attendance 4,323

fifth round

Dyna-mites

Even though the month of February wasn't quite over, United's 'A' team were already assured of the Lancashire League Division One title while their esteemed quarter-final opponents, two times Youth Cup winners Aston Villa, were looking odds-on to be crowned champions of their equivalent competition.

The Villa youngsters had completed 22 Midland Purity League games so far that campaign and were able to boast an immaculate divisional record by winning every single one of them. With home advantage going Villa's way in the national cup tie, it was safe to suggest that United might be required to answer some searching questions in order to further themselves in the competition.

The under-18's task caused Alex Ferguson to comment, *'It's a big game for our boys and they will need to perform if they are to beat this Villa team. They should have been well on top in their replay at Charlton Athletic but wasted their scoring opportunities to end up with a real battle.'*

Ronnie Wallwork returned in defence for the Reds because John Curtis had taken part in a junior international against Greece over the previous weekend and was unable to obtain the necessary leave from the F.A. School of Excellence. An injury victim who couldn't be considered again for some weeks following a cartilage operation, David Johnson was replaced by Des Baker and Paul Heckingbottom came back into the side while the winning goal hero against Arsenal, John Hudson, dropped out.

Resplendent in an outfit of blue and white and kicking towards the newly all-seated Holte End, United were quickly into their stride and delivered the first, devastating body blow after just four minutes. Obviously out to make an impression back in his native Birmingham, Terry Cooke flighted a hanging corner over from the right which was helped on by Michael Clegg, and when the claret and blue shirted defenders failed to clear, Wallwork hooked the loose ball into the top corner of the net from fifteen yards out.

The Villa were momentarily stunned only to then bounce straight back off the ropes on eight minutes with a telling counter-punch. A smart move down the right side of midfield saw the ball at the feet of Lee Burchell who, in turn, stroked an inch-perfect pass behind United's back four, the scintillating sequence ending with Richard Burgess guiding home a quite superb equaliser.

After such an explosive start to the game, both sides then settled into a period of searching out their opponents' weaknesses, though it all represented plentiful excitement as far as the crowd was concerned. Just on the half hour mark, United landed another punch to the jaw of their hosts when a long cross from the right was delivered into Villa's penalty box. Philip Mulryne connected cleanly with his head and the ball sailed into the corner of the net with the home 'keeper left flat-footed.

For the remainder of the first half, the junior Villains pressed with all their might in an attempt to draw level while United continued to look marginally the more dangerous with confident counterattacks of phenomenal pace and penetration.

The second period started in a similar fashion to the first when United grabbed a goal after just three minutes, another slick move coming to fruition with Cooke smashing home a square pass from Baker. Villa may have been battered, bruised and on the canvas but thoughts of throwing in the towel were never entertained. Four minutes after Baker's goal, the resilient Brummies were back in the game once again as a measured cross from defender Leslie Hines was turned into the net by Richard Walker.

For the final 38 minutes of the tie, the entranced spectators were treated to a soccer spectacular which perhaps even surpassed the events of earlier. There were super stops from both goalkeepers, stylish forward movement, dogged defending, and dynamic and powerful midfield enterprise.

Even in the dying minutes, Villa's Walker headed what seemed a certain goal only for Paul Gibson to pull off a wonder save, and Cooke then went close twice for United with barely seconds remaining.

When the final bell sounded, every single person in attendance at the famous old stadium was of the same opinion – that they would be hard pressed to see a better game of football at any level that season. So ended a truly marvellous match in which neither team deserved to lose. As it was, United were the honoured party and they progressed to their 20th Youth Cup semi-final appearance as a result.

Rightly so, the game was variously described as *'superb,' 'thrilling'* and *'enthralling'* by the press. Claiming United *'went looking for goals from the start and Villa adopted the same attitude'*, the same reporter recorded the Reds *'were pushed all the way by a Villa side who kept battling until the final whistle'*.

Villa coach Tony McAndrew later bemoaned the outcome when saying, *'We didn't play particularly well in the first half. Manchester United were very direct but they knew what they were doing with the two front men having plenty of mobility and making runs through the midfield. But in the second half our lads played better and showed tremendous character and effort.'*

A day later, the Evening News carried a summary which was full of praise for the contestants, and a section of it read:

Manchester United are on course for their third F.A. Youth Cup final in four years. The latest batch of young hopefuls clinched their place in the last four of this season's competition with a brilliant performance at Villa Park last night.

Hotly-tipped to take the trophy and unbeaten in league and cup this season, Villa were expected to present United with a severe test and they didn't disappoint in a cracking match that had the 4,500 crowd roaring their approval.

Both sides put the emphasis on attack and it made for a breathtaking match which swung from end-to-end at a relentless pace.

It was a pity that one of the sides had to bow out of the competition for, on the strength of this contest, they were both worthy of lifting the trophy.

Captain Philip Neville vainly attempts to fend off an attack in a five-goal thriller at the Villa

1994-95

FEBRUARY 1995

Midfielder Neil Mustoe (right) attempts to restrict a Villa man's options

Centre-back Ashley Westwood (right) is for once outnumbered in United's tremendous victory at Villa Park

fifth round

1994-95

1) Paul Gibson	9) Des Baker
2) Philip Neville	10) Terry Cooke
3) Ronnie Wallwork	11) Philip Mulryne
4) Ashley Westwood	*12) David Johnson (for 7)*
5) Michael Clegg	*13) Heath Maxon GK*
6) Neil Mustoe	*14) Danny Hall (for 8)*
7) Grant Brebner	
8) Paul Heckingbottom	

1) Steve Mumford	9) Carl Cort
2) Kevin Board	10) Jason Euell
3) Andy Futcher	11) Stacey Joseph
4) Clement Owusu	*12) Danny Lyons (for 7)*
5) Iain Laidlaw	*13) Justin Cameron GK*
6) Danny Hodges	*14) Richard O'Connor (for 11)*
7) Lenny Griffiths	
8) Len Piper	

MARCH 1995

MANCHESTER UNITED 2 v 1 WIMBLEDON

Cooke, Neville — Cort

semi-final 1st leg

Saturday 25th
Kick-off 2.00 p.m.
Attendance 6,167

Neville's Reds let chances slip by

When the opening leg of the last four stage came around almost a month after the Reds' stunning win at Villa Park, Eric Harrison named the same starting eleven to face Wimbledon who were responsible for eliminating the young Villains. David Johnson, who hadn't been involved in a competitive game since undergoing surgery, impressed Harrison in training to win himself a place on the bench. Harrison took a view that Johnson was just fit enough to gain inclusion in the squad and that his firepower might be utilised in an emergency, if required.

Wimbledon, who were still groundsharing with Crystal Palace, and whose side included former England schoolboy international Andy Futcher and current England Youth star Danny Hodges in their ranks, were required to endure a couple of replays to reach this stage. Winning 2-1 with a minute to go at West Ham in their opening tie, the Dons conceded a penalty and needed to defeat the Hammers 4-2 in the rematch.

Ipswich were crushed 4-0 in the Third Round, after which Wimbledon sank Stoke City 1-0 in the Potteries. At the quarter-finals, another late incident occurred when Sheffield United scored in the eight minutes added on by the referee to draw level at 3-3, the Blades then wasting their luck entirely by losing 3-2 on their home patch in the replay.

There was no senior action taking place over that weekend, so it was possible to stage the youth game on a Saturday p.m. slot. A combination of the timing of the game and the venue, as well as the fine weather, meant there was yet another demonstration of the superb support frequently afforded to the junior Reds at Old Trafford over the years.

The United faithful saw a keenly fought encounter, which proved frustrating in terms of the end result, and it was ultimately left to the captain of the side to save the day.

Derek Walker was on hand to report on the sequence of events for the major Manchester newspaper:

Phil Neville's 54th minute strike gave Manchester United's teenagers a deserved 2-1 win over Wimbledon in the F.A. Youth Cup semi-final first leg at Old Trafford today.

But the United skipper's delight at scoring the winner was tempered by the fact that he knows his side should have claimed more than the slender one-goal advantage that the Reds will take to Selhurst Park in a fortnight for the deciding leg.

United dominated a one-sided first half and were unfortunate not to take a lead into the break.

The boy Reds peppered Dons' 'keeper Steve Mumford's goal but he pulled off a string of saves to keep out United until the 40th minute. All-action striker

Paul Heckingbottom (right) appears to have left it a fraction too late when attempting to tackle a Wimbledon opponent at Old Trafford

1994-95

MARCH 1995

Paul Heckingbottom (left) wraps his foot around the ball while Michael Clegg (right) keeps an eye out for any developments

Terry Cooke had a supercharged half, creating a string of chances only to be denied on several occasions by fine work from Mumford.

It was only justice Cooke should stroke United in front when he curled a super 25-yard effort over the despairing 'keeper.

But Wimbledon shocked United by hitting straight back with virtually their first authentic attack. Carl Cort caught the Reds' defence napping with a snap-shot equaliser from the edge of the box.

Cooke and Mumford met again early in the second half when the 'keeper dallied with a back pass. Cooke robbed him but Mumford spared his own blushes by smothering the teenage striker's shot.

The confrontation between the pair proved the key to the match and another clash between them led to United's second. A goalmouth scramble involving both players saw the ball break to Neville who was presented with a simple tap-in.

The 54th minute strike delighted the 6,167 crowd, an attendance higher than Wimbledon's first-team average.

Neil Mustoe felled Danny Hodges with a shot the Dons' defender caught full in the face.

It was, indeed, a match of missed chances as far as the Reds were concerned. Baker, Westwood and Mulryne all failed to hit the target with opening half headers, an unwanted trend which continued through most of the concluding section of the tie, both before and after Neville's winner.

The deciding goal came about when Paul Heckingbottom sent the speeding Baker away down the right. Baker hit his cross to the near post and there resulted a face-off between Cooke and Mumford. Neville was the fastest to respond to the uncertainty and he casually side-footed the ball past the Wimbledon goalkeeper to give United the win they felt entitled to.

Dons' Ernie Tippett defiantly told reporters after the final whistle, 'We are more than capable of getting through to the final' and despite the uneasy time his lads had endured, the youth coach went on to say, 'It's just disappointing that we didn't come away with the draw our display deserved.'

His opinions weren't shared by the majority of paying customers and the common consensus among the crowd was that United's place in the final could already have been booked. It was a view which seemed to be endorsed by the Review's correspondent, who wrote that the Reds 'should have been taking a healthier lead to Selhurst Park. They piled up the chances in this first leg, but they only converted two of them and Wimbledon showed that given the opportunity they can be a bit of a handful'.

Tradition heavily favoured the Reds at this point because in nineteen previous Youth Cup semi-finals, progress was made on each and every occasion they were able to claim a first leg lead.

Based on their showing on this particular day, there was no reason to believe the newest batch of United teenagers would fail in their quest to sustain that fabulous sequence.

semi-final 1st leg

1994-95

1) Steve Mumford
2) Kevin Board
3) Andy Futcher
4) Clement Owusu
5) Iain Laidlaw
6) Danny Hodges
7) Richard O'Connor
8) Len Piper
9) Carl Cort
10) Jason Euell
11) Luke Longman
12) *Stacey Joseph (for 11)*
13) *Justin Cameron GK*
14) *Danny Lyons (for 7)*

1) Paul Gibson
2) Philip Neville
3) Ronnie Wallwork
4) Ashley Westwood
5) Michael Clegg
6) Danny Hall
7) Neil Mustoe
8) David Johnson
9) Des Baker
10) Terry Cooke
11) Philip Mulryne
12) *John Curtis*
13) *Heath Maxon GK*
14) *Grant Brebner*

APRIL 1995

WIMBLEDON   0 (1) v (5) 3   MANCHESTER UNITED

Cooke (2), Mulryne

Saturday 8th
Kick-off 2.00 p.m.
Attendance 4,441

semi-final 2nd leg

Harrison gives aces a shuffle

As a prelude to the London episode of the semi-final, Wimbledon's charismatic owner, Sam Hamman, invited the parents of all the United players to lunch prior to kick-off. Alex Ferguson later applauded the move as a *'splendid gesture'*, feeling Hamman's actions added a *'nice touch'* to the occasion.

By an ironic twist of fate, while the youth team were at Selhurst Park to face the stadium's tenants, United's seniors were readying themselves to take on the ground's landlords in an F.A. Cup semi-final at Villa Park a day later.

There were changes from the encounter at Old Trafford, Richard O'Connor and Luke Longman deputising for Lenny Griffiths and Stacey Joseph in the Dons' line-up while David Johnson and Danny Hall returned for the Reds to leave Paul Heckingbottom and Grant Brebner out in the cold. Johnson's inclusion allowed Terry Cooke, who was freshly back from winning England under-18 honours in Budapest, to take up a more familiar wide role.

When asked about his team's chances of reaching the final, Eric Harrison replied bluntly, *'It all depends on the mood of the players......because their form varies so much from game to game. It has been like this from day one of the season. I suppose I should be used to it by now but I still can't accept it.*

Performance is what is important to me and I hope to see them playing more football in the second leg.'

Put simply, and on a personal level for Harrison, a win or a draw meant that the coach would be responsible for guiding a United side to the Youth Cup final for a fifth time.

On a gloriously sunny day south of the River Thames, the game got underway with the visitors defending the Holmesdale Road end of the ground, where a brand new, fully-seated stand was under construction.

The Reds attacked from the start, with only a couple of last-ditch tackles and good covering work from the Wimbledon defence stopping them from scoring before the latecomers were settled in their seats.

As it was, just eleven minutes had elapsed when Des Baker supplied a killer pass to put fellow striker Cooke completely in the clear. Cooke raced almost half the length of the pitch to leave himself face to face with Wimbledon's goalkeeper and without breaking stride, he nonchalantly knocked the ball around Mumford and then calmly walked it into an empty net.

Johnson then spurned two half-chances prior to Cooke raiding another goal in

Michael Clegg (centre) finds himself in the thick of the action at a sun-drenched Selhurst Park

398

Wimbledon's Luke Longman hammers in a free kick against a United wall comprising (l-r) Danny Hall, Neil Mustoe, Philip Mulryne and Terry Cooke

the 23rd minute. The United striker was provided with a second gift opening by Baker, who watched in disappointment when his fierce drive was parried by Mumford. The ball ran kindly to Cooke, who made no mistake to put the Reds 2-0 up on the day and 4-1 to the good overall. Cooke's goals meant that the Dons' aspirations of reaching their first Youth Cup final had now been completely detonated.

On the stroke of half-time, the Reds nearly chalked up another goal following a brilliant piece of individual skill by the in-form Baker. The tricky Dubliner chased a long clearance to the left-hand corner of Wimbledon's penalty area where he moved the ball over to his right foot. Baker proceeded to smash a dipping shot over Mumford, barely inches above the bar, and his dazzling effort caused both the home fans and the small number of United supporters in attendance to applaud in unison.

The second half was a much more even affair. The Reds needed to soak up some concerted pressure from the young Dons in the concluding 45 minutes, though they still posed a few problems for their hosts with quicksilver raids out of defence.

The game was over as a contest in the 61st minute when the smart thinking Neil Mustoe sent Johnson away from a free kick. Johnson's pass picked out Philip Mulryne, who promptly executed an excellent finish after cleverly waiting for the 'keeper to commit himself.

A memorable moment in a generally entertaining game, Mulryne's effort arguably represented the best goal of the collection.

Wimbledon weren't completely done for and they carved out a couple of chances for themselves late in the game. Ashley Westwood cleared one of them off the goal-line and in the very last minute, Paul Gibson brought off a great save to repel an Iain Laidlaw shot from the left-hand side of the box and preserve his clean sheet into the bargain.

It was a task ably accomplished by the Reds and the width of the winning margin didn't flatter them in the slightest.

1994-95

1) Simon Brown	9) Peter Gain	1) Paul Gibson	9) Des Baker
2) Stephen Carr	10) Neale Fenn	2) Philip Neville	10) Terry Cooke
3) Ross D'Arcy	11) Rory Allen	3) Ronnie Wallwork	11) Philip Mulryne
4) Kevin Maher	12) James Bunn (for 11)	4) Ashley Westwood	12) John Curtis (for 9)
5) Simon Wormull	13) Aaron Shave GK	5) Michael Clegg	13) Heath Maxon GK
6) Simon Spencer	14) Mark Janney	6) Danny Hall	14) David Gardner (for 11)
7) Stephen Clemence		7) Neil Mustoe	
8) Mark Arber		8) David Johnson	

MAY 1995

TOTTENHAM HOTSPUR 2 v 1 MANCHESTER UNITED

Allen, Wormull — Cooke

Thursday 11th
Kick-off 7.00 p.m.
Attendance 3,503

final 1st leg

Terry cooks up a grand finale

The 1990's was proving to be a fantastic period for Manchester United in their Youth Cup exploits and even though the decade wasn't quite halfway through, the club was in its third final in four years, a truly remarkable achievement in the modern era and easily their most successful run since the glory days of the 1950's.

Their opponents were the much fancied Tottenham Hotspur, and for the first leg at White Hart Lane, Eric Harrison was keen to select exactly the same side as that which had defeated Wimbledon at Selhurst Park. However, there was a big question mark posed by the fitness of big centre-half Ashley Westwood, who had returned from an international match with a badly twisted knee which confined him to the sidelines over the last two weeks. Eric Harrison said of Westwood, 'He's trained a couple of times in the past few days and I'll have a look at him again today. But at the moment Ashley's only 50-50.'

Harrison also shared his views on United's opponents, as well as passing on some forthright opinions on his own team's chances when commenting, 'Spurs have won the South-East Counties League and have proved an outstanding, high-calibre outfit. I watched them against Manchester City at Maine Road and they are physical but also a good footballing side. It is going to be tough.

My team do tend to be erratic but tonight isn't a night for being erratic. We need everyone up to form. We've done better as the competition has gone along but you never know with this lot. But we've reached the final, so we must be capable. I'm looking for a good performance and I hope they do justice to themselves.'

En route to the final, Spurs defeated a Sutton Coldfield side by the name of Boldmere St. Michaels with a whopping 10-0 margin in the Second Round on home territory and then beat Wolves 4-2, again at home, before drawing 1-1 with Southend. Spurs edged the Shrimpers out 2-1 in the replay in Essex before winning by exactly the same margin in the Fifth Round at Bristol City. In the opening instalment of the semi-final, Tottenham secured their most impressive win by hammering Manchester City 5-0 in Moss Side and they then completed the double over the Citizens by taking the second leg by two goals to one.

The main threats as far as United was concerned were sure to be Spurs striker Neale Fenn, with nine Youth Cup goals to his name, and midfielder Peter Gain, whose total numbered six. Spurs also included Stephen Carr, already credited with first-team experience, and Stephen Clemence, capped by England at schoolboy and youth levels, in their ranks. Clemence, a former pupil at the F.A. School of Excellence, was the son of former Liverpool, Spurs and England goalkeeper, Ray Clemence. There was another family connection in the side as utility player Mark Arber's father was Bob Arber, Tottenham's youth coach.

A small crowd, which was due in part to the game being screened live on Sky television as well as the notorious difficulty of reaching White Hart Lane on a midweek evening of London congestion, witnessed what commentator Martin Tyler described as some 'early nervous moments' on the part of both teams.

The Reds certainly weren't in tune at the beginning of the tie because Spurs came out on top of practically all of the early skirmishes. The result was that they initially went close to scoring in the seventh minute and actually edged in front just 60 seconds later.

The first inkling of the quality of their opponents occurred to the United lads soon after Carr took a throw-in on Tottenham's right. The ball was controlled by Fenn, and the stylish striker cushioned it back to Carr who then delivered a telling cross into Gibson's penalty box. With four United defenders standing off, Rory Allen volleyed the ball and was aghast to see it drift a couple of feet past Gibson's post.

In Spurs' next attack, another throw-in, which was taken by Simon Wormull almost from the same spot as the earlier one, was again returned to Carr. The defender chipped the ball accurately to the corner of United's box where it was headed on to Allen by Fenn. Allen, who was facing away from goal, played an exquisite pass on his instep and around his marker, and it fell like an open invitation to the advancing Wormull who slotted it under Gibson from twelve yards out. The move was so swiftly and expertly executed that most of the visiting defenders appeared to be frozen to the ground as it developed around them.

For the next twenty minutes or so, Spurs dominated the proceedings almost entirely and the general flow of the game was in the direction of Gibson's penalty area. When the realisation dawned that there were still plenty of minutes on the clock and a trophy at stake, the Reds slowly started forcing their way back into contention.

Philip Neville was prominent in the revival and all throughout the game he gave a masterful demonstration of how to captain a side across stormy waters. The Reds' skipper appeared completely unruffled as he went about his business and could be seen supporting the midfield and forwards almost as often as he was tidying up at the back. Scoring chances were almost absent for United, though, and Spurs held a deserved lead to half-time.

Two minutes after the restart, disaster struck. The Reds seemed to have left their defending instincts in the dressing room when Tottenham's England Youth international Simon Spencer whipped a pinpoint centre straight into United's six-yard zone. Standing almost in front of a woefully exposed Gibson, the highly impressive Allen stooped to beat him with a spectacular diving header.

The game was now a real slog for United. The host team held all of the available aces and they simply allowed the Reds as much possession as they wanted while contenting themselves by defending deep in their own territory and launching counter offensives whenever possible.

Soon after Eric Harrison sent on John Curtis for Des Baker in the 69th minute, Gibson's reflexes came to United's rescue when he made a near miracle save from Spencer's shot. Gibson's heroics were crucial in keeping the Reds' hopes alive because at that moment it could have been all over for Harrison's kids.

A goal looked a highly unlikely occurrence for the Mancunians and only six minutes were left to play when they were gifted a golden chance to reduce their deficit. Fortuitously, it fell to just the person they would have wanted it to.

When a promising Spurs attack broke down on United's eighteen-yard line, the otherwise immaculate Spencer dallied and the ball was nicked off his toes by David Johnson. Picking up possession, Johnson hit a defence-splitting pass over 30 yards towards Terry Cooke who was stationed in the inside-right position. Tottenham's Ross D'Arcy looked odds-on favourite to intercept Johnson's through ball until somehow allowing it to squirm under his boot. Cooke latched onto it in an instant and took the ball on before confidently slipping it past Simon Brown's left hand for his eighth goal of the cup run.

Eric Harrison was all too aware of the significance of Cooke's consolation, claiming it 'has given us a lifeline', but, even so, he admitted disappointment at both the result and the performance when remarking, 'We didn't do ourselves justice. We made it difficult for ourselves by conceding a goal at the start and another just after half-time. Spurs closed us down very well and we couldn't pass the ball around like we can do.'

> I was in good form around the time we played Spurs. I had just been called into the England Youth set-up for the first time for the European Qualifiers against Hungary. I picked up a knock on my knee in a really tough return game at Walsall and thought I might miss the Spurs game but luckily was passed fit.
>
> We weren't too sure what to expect from Spurs, but they set off like a house on fire and a few tackles were flying in. Eric Harrison yelled at me to start mixing it with them. I was known to be a hard player and he wanted me to go in stronger on some of their players, to win the physical battle.
>
> We had a lot of the possession but made two bad errors for their goals which came at bad times. Eric had a massive pop at all of us after the game because he had taken us down to White Hart Lane fully expecting to win and was really unhappy about the way we played. Even so, we were pretty confident and after seeing Spurs in action in the first leg we knew we had enough in the tank to turn things around at our place.

ASHLEY WESTWOOD

1) Paul Gibson	9) Des Baker	1) Simon Brown	9) Peter Gain
2) John Curtis	10) Terry Cooke	2) Stephen Carr	10) Neale Fenn
3) Philip Neville	11) Philip Mulryne	3) Ross D'Arcy	11) Rory Allen
4) Ashley Westwood	*12) David Hilton (for 11)*	4) Kevin Maher	*12) Stephen Clemence (for 5)*
5) Ronnie Wallwork	*13) Heath Maxon GK*	5) Simon Wormull	*13) Aaron Shave GK*
6) Danny Hall	*14) David Gardner (for 6)*	6) Simon Spencer	*14) Sammy Winston (for 11)*
7) Neil Mustoe		7) Garry Brady	
8) Grant Brebner		8) Mark Arber	

1994-95

MANCHESTER UNITED 1 (2) v (2) 0 TOTTENHAM HOTSPUR

Cooke

United win 4-3 on pens a.e.t.

MAY 1995

Monday 15th

Kick-off 7.30 p.m.

Attendance 20,190

The United eleven who entertained Tottenham Hotspur for the second leg of the 1995 Youth Cup final
Back row (l-r) Ronnie Wallwork, Des Baker, Paul Gibson, Ashley Westwood, Neil Mustoe, Philip Mulryne
Front row (l-r) John Curtis, Philip Neville, Terry Cooke, Grant Brebner, Danny Hall

final 2nd leg

The day before the second leg of the final was one of great disappointment for all United followers as, in the final fixture of their Premiership season, the seniors failed to defeat West Ham at Upton Park and thereby lost the title by one point to Blackburn. Despite the despondency, over 20,000 spectators turned out to see if the youth side could pull off a result which seemed only remotely possible with a few minutes to go at White Hart Lane.

In his programme notes, Eric Harrison commented:

I would like to welcome Tottenham Hotspur to Old Trafford this evening and, at the same time, congratulate the boys of both teams on reaching the final of the F.A. Youth Cup. It is no mean achievement because this is a hard fought competition requiring young players to perform to a high standard.

Players at this level have to deliver on two counts. We naturally ask them to win their matches, but at the same time we want them to play the kind of football which will see them develop into first-team footballers. The priority at Manchester United is to bring the youngsters through to the top level and I am sure Spurs have the same objective. So we will be looking for them to play the kind of constructive, attacking football which both clubs are renowned for playing, which in a pressure game like a cup final is not easy.

I will still be looking to the future tonight. I have always said that about my work with the junior sides and I have not changed tack, be it an 'A' team fixture or the kind of exciting occasion we have on show this evening.

My boys have a hard act to follow with the class of '92 who won the Youth Cup three years ago now making such an impact at first-team level. That's the target and hopefully we shall get a good representation through again.

To a certain extent this year's team has surprised me because early season they trained well, but did not play particularly well in actual games. Frankly they

were driving me mad, but I think we are over that hump now. They have had some excellent performances and good results and certainly came away from Aston Villa and Wimbledon with flying colours.

Now their form is a truer reflection of their proper ability because basically they are a talented bunch of lads. They have settled down and came out of the first leg at White Hart Lane with the kind of result to see them in with a fair chance of bringing this coveted trophy to Old Trafford again.

Spurs are a very strong and skilful side in keeping with their club's tradition and I find it heartening that two footballing sides have come through to the final. That is something that is not only good for the clubs concerned, but for the future of football.

Following his sending off in the semi-final of the Lancashire Youth Cup, David Johnson was suspended and the development forced Harrison into shuffling his side. John Curtis was brought in at right-back, Philip Neville was switched to left-back and Michael Clegg was omitted as Grant Brebner won back a place in the starting eleven.

There was much less disruption to the Spurs side, and their solitary change saw Garry Brady taking over in midfield from the demoted Stephen Clemence.

With thousands still seeking entrance to Old Trafford at the proposed kick-off time, the start of the match was put back by twenty minutes.

The Reds looked a far more accomplished side for the concluding chapter of the competition than they had at White Hart Lane. United's vastly improved performance by no means undermined the contribution made by Tottenham, as the Londoners once again displayed what a fine side they were.

There were numerous chances at both ends throughout the 90 minutes but the overriding impression of the game left on most observers present was the

401

1994-95

MAY 1995

final 2nd leg

many number of tremendous saves made by visiting goalkeeper Simon Brown. Spurs' number one was many times busier at Old Trafford than in the corresponding game on his home patch and positively revelled in the action while excelling himself in what were much more trying circumstances.

With barely seconds to go, and the game still scoreless, a great number of spectators had already left for home in the knowledge that Spurs would be claiming the Youth Cup for the fourth time when Curtis chested down a high ball near to the right-hand touchline approximately 40 yards from goal. He chipped in a diagonal pass towards the fringe of Spurs' penalty box where Ronnie Wallwork back-headed the ball to Terry Cooke, who had defenders Carr and Maher in close attention. United's newly crowned 'Young Player of the Year' brought it under control with his right foot before swivelling and, from a distance of fourteen yards, smashed the ball with his left past the despairing Brown to put the Reds level at last.

There then followed a barren period of extra-time and the game ended with the aggregate score locked at two-two which meant, of course, that the destination of the trophy needed to be decided on penalties.

Now the drama really began.

The Reds were under real pressure almost straight away when Neale Fenn's successful spot kick preceded Philip Neville blasting his against the outside of a post with Brown beaten. United's skipper looked as though the weight of the world was on his shoulders as he turned to his colleagues but one of them, goalkeeper Paul Gibson, then brought off a great save down to his right to keep out Simon Spencer's effort.

The next three penalties all found the back of the net by, in turn, Neil Mustoe for United, Garry Brady for Spurs and the Reds' Ronnie Wallwork.

Tasked with taking Spurs' fourth penalty, and the shoot-out poised at two-apiece, Stephen Carr cruelly and crucially missed the target. After Des Baker rammed his kick home to shift the pressure over and onto the visitors, Kevin Maher was able to keep his head in order to slot his kick away and bring the scores level again.

United had one penalty remaining and up to the marker stepped Terry Cooke, who looked like coolness personified as he placed the ball down carefully on the white spot. Taking only a short run up, he ended it by striking the ball cleanly to arrow it past Brown. The celebrations following United's first ever Youth Cup shoot-out began immediately as Cooke chased away with all of his team-mates in hot pursuit and the crowd cheered as much in relief as approval.

It had been so, so close.

Anyone with any grain of compassion must have felt some sympathy for a gallant Spurs side that had given their all over 210 minutes of football and were finally felled by a single-goal margin in the lottery of a penalty sequence.

A captain all through the tournament in both name and attitude, a smiling Philip Neville led the squad up the steps to receive the cup. In claiming a winners' medal, he emulated his elder brother Gary, who had experienced the same achievement three years earlier.

The events of the Reds' victory were later condensed into three words by Eric Harrison on United's Clubcall telephone service as *'a fantastic night'*, and he later jokingly told the Manchester Evening News, *'I would have slashed my wrists if we hadn't scored in normal time.'*

Harrison summarised his feelings when pointing out, *'Possibly this success was even better than '92 because three years ago the side was full of outstanding players. These are good players and they have had a lot to live up to.'*

Eight members of the United squad display various states of emotion in the seconds after Paul Gibson repelled Simon Spencer's penalty

1994-95

MAY 1995

Philip Neville and match-winner Terry Cooke look delighted as they show off their glittering prize

Players and backroom staff alike share the moment of the Reds' triumph over Spurs

final 2nd leg

1994-95

MAY 1995

final 2nd leg

Like seven others before him, Philip Neville joins the illustrious list of United Youth captains who felt the elation of lifting the famous trophy

404

1) Nick Culkin	9) Jonathan Macken	1) Craig Davis	9) Robert Pell
2) John Curtis	10) Des Baker	2) Kevin Trower	10) Gary Duffty
3) Paul Teather	11) Michael Twiss	3) Danny Hobson	11) Paul Dillon
4) Tommy Smith	*12) David Hilton (for 9)*	4) Richard Ashcroft	*12) James Gordon (for 9)*
5) Ronnie Wallwork	*13) Heath Maxon GK*	5) Chris Kelly	*13) Chris Sedgwick (for 10)*
6) Stuart Brightwell	*14) Robert Trees (for 4)*	6) Andy McIntosh	*14) Dale Spiby (for 7)*
7) Grant Brebner		7) Phil Parkin	
8) Philip Mulryne		8) Danny Hudson	

1995-96

MANCHESTER UNITED 3 v 1 ROTHERHAM UNITED

Baker, Brebner, Wallwork — Duffty

NOVEMBER 1995

Tuesday 21st

Kick-off 7.00 p.m.

Attendance 1,222

second round

A *'mixture of the old and new'* was how the Manchester Evening News' United correspondent Stuart Mathieson described the side that took on Rotherham to defend the Youth Cup trophy which a number of them helped to win six months earlier. Mr. Mathieson was himself fairly new, having recently taken over from the long serving and highly respected David Meek as the Reds' local scribe. For the record, Meek was accredited for writing his very first Youth Cup match report when United met Everton at Old Trafford way back in November 1958.

Because Philip Neville was now over the age threshold, Ronnie Wallwork was handed the captaincy of the team while John Curtis, who had made an excellent impression during his intermittent appearances in last season's cup run, took up his favoured right-back position. Three other Youth Cup gold medal-holders, Grant Brebner, Philip Mulryne and Des Baker, were included along with Michael Twiss who, with one previous substitute appearance to his credit, edged his way into the starting eleven.

On the eve of the game, Eric Harrison explained to Mathieson about some of the factors he was required to take into account in relation to his charges' prospects when saying, *'Expectations are high and that's not a bad thing. The young kids have to realise what they have to live up to and it's no good coming to Manchester United if you haven't got belief in yourself.*

I have said to the players that lads like Gary Neville, Nicky Butt, Paul Scholes and David Beckham in the first-team now who enjoyed success at this level in '92 always had belief in themselves.

Temperament is just as important a quality as passing the ball, heading the ball and whatever. Without doubt you have to have temperament at our club and the Youth Cup finds a lot out. I'm always excited and very keen when the Youth Cup comes around because it is a yardstick for me. It gives me a good idea to see how they handle things.

You've got to get over nerves. You can't play at our place if you're nervous. It's a very big factor and they've got to overcome it. For some this will be their first time before a crowd at Old Trafford and I'll be looking to the survivors from last year to give the others a lead.'

Nerves may very well have been a factor in United conceding an early goal to Rotherham, with some sloppy defending twenty yards out punished when Gary Duffty hit a corking shot just out of arm's reach of new goalkeeper Nick Culkin, a recent capture from York City. There were only six minutes gone, so it wasn't a good start, and the setback echoed some of the events of the earlier rounds in the previous campaign. Things could have turned even worse two minutes later when a dipping 30-yard free kick from Rotherham's Chris Kelly just cleared Culkin's crossbar by what appeared to be the thickness of a couple of sheets of paper.

Thankfully, the lead wasn't to last and the Millers were pegged back as early as the 14th minute. When Craig Davis made a splendid save from Reds' newcomer Stuart Brightwell, little did the Millers' goalie know that he was only delaying what the majority of the crowd considered was the inevitable as Wallwork climbed high to the resulting corner to flick a looping header accurately over a host of watchers and into the net.

Rotherham asserted themselves again over the last twenty minutes of the first half and looked particularly dangerous a number of times through that period of the match. On one occasion goalscorer Duffty steered a deft through ball into space to give Danny Hobson a sight of goal, and a veil of impending doom appeared to descend around Culkin's goalmouth until Hobson's shot was blocked for a corner.

Duffty and Hobson saw further efforts thwarted prior to team-mate Andy McIntosh directing a goalbound header that was blocked on the line following another corner. The impressive Duffty then zeroed in on the loose ball, only he was unable to force it home.

Obviously motivated by a calm discussion with coach Harrison at the break, the Reds stepped up their effort rate considerably thereafter and in the 56th minute the increase yielded a further goal for them.

On at half-time for the injured Tommy Smith, Droylsden youngster Robert Trees provided the initial inspiration when whipping over a super centre from the right to pick out Brebner, whose bullet header flashed past the Rotherham 'keeper and into the far corner of the net.

Another Brebner effort was saved later on, and Mulryne then rattled the Millers' bar with a shot from distance. Former Rotherham schoolboy star Paul Teather later tested the reflexes of the visiting goalkeeper prior to the Reds sealing the result in the last minute of normal time.

Ghosting into a huge void in Rotherham's penalty area, Des Baker coolly stroked the ball over the line to conclude the scoring and the Reds' rather uneasy passage to the Third Round.

Tommy Smith started against Rotherham prior to being.......

.......substituted by Robert Trees, who set up United's second goal

1995-96

1) Michael Johnston
2) Elliott Dickman
3) Neal Parker
4) Darren Holloway
5) Greg Knight
6) John Provan
7) Stephen Peters
8) Paul Thirlwell
9) Paul Beavers
10) Michael Bridges
11) Paul Richardson
12) Michael Barton (for 7)
13) Gary Lloyd (for 6)
14) John Sommerville (for 11)

1) Nick Culkin
2) John Curtis
3) Danny Hall
4) Andy Duncan
5) Ronnie Wallwork
6) Stuart Brightwell
7) Grant Brebner
8) Philip Mulryne
9) Des Baker
10) Mark Wilson
11) Michael Twiss
12) Tommy Smith
13) Heath Maxon GK
14) David Brown (for 7)

JANUARY 1996

Wednesday 10th

Kick-off 7.00 p.m.

third round

SUNDERLAND 1 v 4 MANCHESTER UNITED

Bridges   Baker (2 pens), Brown, Wilson

Fergie's kids too hot for Roker Youths
Devilishly good

As is occasionally the case, the draw for the next stage of the Youth Cup brought United's under-18's together with opponents who also shared a current first-team interest.

Sunderland's senior side had recently held their United counterparts to a draw in the F.A. Cup in Manchester and the replay at Roker Park was set for the Tuesday after the Youth Cup contest. Former York and current Black Cats' youth coach Ricky Sbragia made fighting talk when telling a local reporter, *'We want this to be a double – us winning and the first-team winning next week. We have done our homework, we have been watching a video of them and Pop Robson has told us about their strengths.*

But the first-team have showed us the way at Old Trafford. Last year we reached the last eight in the competition and I think we have a better side this year.'

On the day of the match, Sunderland assistant manager Paul Bracewell added, *'The whole place is a buzz at the moment and the youth team is no exception. Ricky Sbragia has prepared them well and will have them up for the game, and I think the young players will be looking forward to it.*

With it being Manchester United it adds to the spice, and it should be a good game. Every club likes to see their kids coming along and there will be some good players out there tonight.'

Eric Harrison brought Danny Hall back for the trip up north and also handed competition debuts to Hexham-born Andrew Duncan and a Scunthorpe boy by the name of Mark Wilson. On the other side of the fence, the home team was bolstered by the inclusion of former United apprentice Elliott Dickman in their back four.

The Sunderland Echo summarised an excellent win for the Reds, a success which was marred only by the stretchering off of Grant Brebner, a victim of multiple stud lacerations sustained in an accidental collision with opposing skipper Darren Holloway after 31 minutes, and the conceding of yet another early goal:

First blood to Manchester United in the first of their two cup clashes with Sunderland at Roker Park in the space of six days.

Sunderland were outpowered by the F.A. Youth Cup holders at Roker Park last night.

Michael Bridges headed the Roker youngsters into a seventh minute lead, but any hopes of providing a shock result and making progress were soon dashed.

Two minutes later, youth international Des Baker equalised from the penalty spot, Mark Wilson took advantage of a Darren Holloway mistake to put the Reds ahead and substitute David Brown's first touch of the ball made it 3-1 by the 35th minute.

Holloway's misery was completed in 71 minutes when he conceded a second penalty and Baker again beat Michael Johnston from the spot.

Sunderland stuck to their task throughout with Johnston rarely tested but the visitors always had the edge.

Bridges beat £100,000 signing Nick Culkin with a far-post header from first year Y.T.S. Stephen Peters' centre.

Holloway, however, nudged Wilson and the referee had no hesitation in awarding a penalty and the lead was wiped out almost instantly.

Wilson took advantage of a casual headed back pass from Holloway to finish in style and give United a 26th minute lead.

Stuart Brightwell, no relation to the Manchester City pair, proved a constant threat and he set up Brown to score from close range in the 35th minute.

Sunderland rallied briefly but lacked penetration. Brown twice missed from good positions to put the issue beyond doubt.

Baker accepted the chance to increase the lead and book his side a deserved place in the Fourth Round.

Back over in Manchester, reactions to the win were unanimous in their praise of the Reds' mature and commanding display, and parallels were drawn to the tie at Roker Park in November 1991 which set the 'class of '92' on their way to Youth Cup glory.

While the Review chose to call it a *'highly efficient performance'* and added *'there could be no complaints about the outcome'*, the publication's correspondent, in relation to the forthcoming F.A. Cup clash, went on to predict that *'if Alex Ferguson's stars can match this assured display by the juniors then there should be no problems'.*

The Evening News claimed United had *'marched confidently into the last sixteen......despite slipping behind to an early goal'* and also noted that the second half *'failed to reach the heights of the first'* before concluding the Reds *'did enough to maintain overall control'.*

Pick on someone your own size: Mark Wilson shields the ball from a rather larger Sunderland opponent at Roker Park

1) Nick Culkin	9) Des Baker	1) Paul Barber	9) Damien Hilton
2) John Curtis	10) Mark Wilson	2) Chris Wigger	10) Steve McCullough
3) Paul Teather	11) Michael Twiss	3) Darren Kenton	11) Tom Ramasut
4) Andy Duncan	*12) Stuart Brightwell (for 6)*	4) Che Wilson	*12) Drewe Broughton (for 9)*
5) Ronnie Wallwork	*13) Heath Maxon GK*	5) Joe Green	*13) Adrian Coote (for 8)*
6) Danny Hall	*14) Grant Brebner (for 10)*	6) Wesley O'Connor	*14) Adrian Forbes (for 7)*
7) Ryan Ford		7) Craig Bellamy	
8) Tommy Smith		8) Sammy Winston	

1995-96

MANCHESTER UNITED 1 v 0 NORWICH CITY

Wilson

FEBRUARY 1996

Tuesday 13th

Kick-off 7.00 p.m.

Attendance 2,545

fourth round

An injury to one of his key personnel posed a problem for Eric Harrison while the Reds prepared to meet their next obstacle at Old Trafford. The stylish Philip Mulryne was the victim of a strained knee ligament several days before the tie and his injury didn't respond to treatment quickly enough for him to be considered. *'It's a big blow for us'* admitted the coach, *'because Philip controls everything in midfield and we do rely on him heavily.'*

Then asked about the progress made by the youth squad so far that season, Harrison responded by saying, *'We've done quite well so far. We were very ordinary against Rotherham. It was our first match at Old Trafford and it always seems to affect us. Hopefully we've got that out of our system now.*

We improved dramatically in the last round at Roker Park. We were tight in defence and looked like we could score goals again. We were good going forward against Sunderland and that's what we encourage throughout the club.'

Later going on to speak about United's immediate opponents, the coach claimed, *'Norwich are a good, strong outfit. They have a couple of big lads upfront and a very fast left winger so it will be a very difficult task.'* Harrison finished the interview by making a comparison between his current batch of starlets and those of the previous campaign by pointing out, *'We are around about the same standard as we were last year when the lads went on to win the (Youth) Cup. If we could do the same again it would be nice but you never know with the kids.'*

On the balance of play, Norwich could feel aggrieved at not securing some sort of favoured result against the Reds and the outcome the visitors desired proved beyond them simply because of an abject failure to score on the occasions when well placed to do so.

In front of the watching Sir Bobby Charlton, Alex Ferguson and former Carrow Road favourite Steve Bruce, City were quick to register their early intentions when Nick Culkin was alert in grabbing Darren Kenton's near-post cross away from the lurking Sammy Winston. Norwich's number eight was taking his second shot at the Reds in the competition after representing Spurs as a substitute in the Old Trafford leg of the Youth Cup final less than a year before.

Tom Ramasut then brought a save out of Culkin with a bending free kick and Damien Hilton caused United hearts to skip a beat, his drive from the edge of the box missing the target by the slenderest of margins.

An energetic Michael Twiss supplied the killer pass which allowed Mark Wilson to score United's winner

One bright spot for the Reds during the first half was the form of Michael Twiss on the left flank. The young winger was in an effervescent mood and he consistently teased and tested Norwich's full-back Chris Wigger, who was eventually booked for a succession of fouls. Twiss' persistence paid off in the 63rd minute when he ghosted past Wigger for the umpteenth time and released Mark Wilson, who cracked a shot which glanced off an opponent. The deflection completely bamboozled Paul Barber between the Norwich posts and the ball whistled beyond him and into the net. It was a wretched piece of bad luck for the Canaries and proved to be the decisive moment of the game.

When Adrian Coote saw his smart lob from eight yards out sail over Culkin to land on the roof of United's net with only seven minutes remaining, City's last opportunity to salvage the result had passed them by.

An East Anglian publication called the game *'a tale of two Wilsons'*. Noting that *'the impressive home striker Mark's hopeful effort from 25 yards looped off the shoulder of young Canary Che'*, the writer felt it *'was rough justice'* on the latter because he and Steve McCullough *'formed a creative and combative midfield partnership that did much to keep Norwich on top in the first half'*.

There was a feeling in the City camp that they should have come out of the game with greater credit than the score suggested and comments in the Norwich press regarding them being *'undaunted by the imposing arena and swaggering style of the cup holders'* lent substance to those opinions.

The general view was that the Reds were a long way from playing to their full potential and one reason for the lacklustre performance was put down to what Stuart Mathieson labelled the *'Old Trafford Syndrome'*. Mathieson's description of the affliction was given in his match report as *'the awesome surroundings and the cross to bear of being the cup holders'*.

The reporter felt it *'almost choked the life out of Eric Harrison's relatively new crop'* and the coach himself said of the symptoms, *'It has happened before in cup runs where we have been poor, especially at Old Trafford. We can't bury the jinx. It just won't go away.'*

Nick Culkin needed to be especially vigilant early on against Norwich

407

1995-96

1) Roy Naylor	9) Jamie Cassidy	1) Nick Culkin	9) Des Baker
2) Lee Prior	10) Jon Newby	2) John Curtis	10) Mark Wilson
3) Phil Brazier	11) Michael Owen	3) Paul Teather	11) Michael Twiss
4) Eddie Turkington	*12) Andy Parkinson*	4) Andy Duncan	*12) David Brown (for 6)*
5) Gareth Roberts	*13) Ian Dunbavin GK*	5) Ronnie Wallwork	*13) Heath Maxon GK*
6) Stuart Quinn	*14) Paul Proctor (for 10)*	6) Stuart Brightwell	*14) Tommy Smith*
7) David Thompson		7) Grant Brebner	
8) Jamie Carragher		8) Philip Mulryne	

MARCH 1996

LIVERPOOL 3 v 2 MANCHESTER UNITED
Owen (3, 1 pen) — Brebner, Twiss

Tuesday 5th
Kick-off 7.00 p.m.
Attendance 5,221

fifth round

Kids on the skid

There would be no 'Old Trafford Syndrome' at the next level, simply because the teenage United were set a testing task away from their home ground at the more unwelcoming venue of Anfield.

United had generally come out on top over their Merseyside rivals in the Youth Cup and victories in 1954, 1960 and 1982 were only blemished with a solitary away defeat in 1966. Never having won the Youth Cup, Liverpool remained the only one of the 'big' clubs not to do so.

When asked whether they were confident about lifting the trophy this time around, Liverpool youth team coach Hugh McAuley responded, *'Why shouldn't we be? We like to feel we've got good, hard working youngsters and with this being a quarter-final your thoughts tend to progress towards bigger and better things.*

While we still say the aim is to produce players who will do well at a higher level, we are playing Manchester United and we will be up for this game. It will be the biggest crowd most of our lads have played in front of. The fact that this game is against United and that our lads will have support from family will add to the occasion.'

Injuries to Michael Moore, David Lamour and Michael Johnson meant that McAuley would once again entrust the goalscoring responsibilities to Michael Owen, an F.A. School of Excellence student, and Jon Newby, a Crosby schoolboy.

Owen had scored two of Liverpool's goals in their 3-2 win over Sheffield United in the last round of the Youth Cup and McAuley claimed that *'great things are expected'* of him.

Also described by his mentor as *'a real predator'*, Owen's inclusion for Liverpool brought about something of a family coincidence because his father, Terry, had actually lined up twice against United for Everton in the Youth Cup in December 1966.

Liverpool turned the occasion into a 'Fun Night' by asking the Speke-based Rockettes Majorettes to provide the pre-match entertainment with some music and dance, and there were also a number of boys from war-torn Bosnia in attendance. Liverpool invited the Bosnians to the youth game after they had earlier enjoyed a kick-about at their Melwood training ground and, aged between twelve and sixteen, the lads were all members of the Locomotiva Football Club.

United put on a dazzling display during the majority of the opening half at Anfield and besides showing glimpses of their true capabilities at last, they should have reserved themselves a place in the semi-final within the first half an hour or so.

Only three excellent saves by goalkeeper Roy Naylor and some wayward shooting by the Mancunians kept the home side in the contest but, as the break approached, Liverpool began to assert themselves with an ever so slightly greater purpose than they had managed in the earlier exchanges. With every member of the United side well aware of the importance of the fixture, Eric Harrison wasn't required to provide too much in the way of pre-match motivation and apart from the lack of a goal or two, by the interval he was reasonably satisfied with the way events were panning out.

The opening goal of a see-saw second session came in the 56th minute when a great run from the game's main protagonist, Michael Owen, saw him gatecrash through the middle of United's defence to direct the ball accurately past Nick Culkin.

Harrison's boys drew level just seven minutes later, with Grant Brebner ramming home a low cross from Mark Wilson, and United then stunned the Anfield crowd by edging in front in the 76th minute as Michael Twiss scored a goal not too dissimilar to Owen's earlier effort.

The home side dragged themselves back into contention almost immediately through United defender Paul Teather upending Liverpool substitute Paul Proctor in the area. Prior to hitting the deck Proctor hadn't even touched the ball, a piece of trivia which cut no ice with Owen, who doubled his production when making no mistake from the spot with a confidently placed penalty.

Two minutes into stoppage time, Proctor was again involved in a crucial incident and after winning a tackle on the left wing, the ball ran to Owen. The sixteen year-old, who displayed penalty area instincts which were as slick as a streetwise alley cat, nervelessly made space for himself before sending his shot beyond Culkin to give the game a most dramatic finish and Liverpool a berth in the semi-final.

The Review contained the following comments:

United released their grip on the F.A. Youth Cup after a terrific tussle against Liverpool at Anfield last Tuesday evening.

Our youngsters left the field at the end with their heads held high and rightly so, for they had played to the full their part in a wonderful cup tie.

The Evening News reckoned the visitors were *'shattered'* by losing a match that could just as easily have gone their way. Then adding the outcome was harsh on *'a United side which had contributed greatly to a marvellous evening's entertainment'*, the News identified the Reds' major shortfall when viewing *'but for some wretched finishing in the opening twenty minutes, they could have had the tie wrapped up by half-time'*.

The game did much to enhance the reputation of the emerging Michael Owen, who by the end of the season had assisted Liverpool to lay their Youth Cup bogey to rest with a 4-1 defeat of West Ham in the final.

Ronnie Wallwork (number five) goes one way, Michael Twiss (right) another, while Liverpool's David Thompson takes a tumble

1995-96

MARCH 1996

fifth round

Ronnie Wallwork does his upmost to get to grips with Liverpool hat-trick hero Michael Owen

Skipper Wallwork repels another attack with the back-up of team-mates Paul Teather and Andy Duncan (number four)

409

1996-97

1) Adam Sadler	9) David Brown
2) Ryan Ford	10) Alex Notman
3) Danny Higginbotham	11) Gavin Naylor
4) John Curtis	*12) Jamie Wood (for 9)*
5) Wes Brown	*13) Leon Mills (for 2)*
6) Stuart Brightwell	*14) David Healy (for 6)*
7) Mark Wilson	
8) Richie Wellens	

1) Leigh Edwards	9) Jamie McNeil
2) Paul Taylor	10) Julian Pepper
3) Rob Morris	11) Andy Griffiths
4) Gareth Shone	*12) Steve Hopkins (for 4)*
5) Steve Roberts	*13) Phil Melarangi (for 7)*
6) Barry Ellison	*14) Darren Nall (for 6)*
7) Steve Rishworth	
8) Andy Davies	

NOVEMBER 1996

MANCHESTER UNITED 7 v 0 WREXHAM

Brightwell, Naylor, Notman (4, 1 pen), Wood

Monday 25th
Kick-off 7.00 p.m.
Attendance 941

second round

It was now just a few days shy of ten years since United's kids travelled across the border to Wrexham where they recorded a respectable 4-0 win which will always be remembered in the context of the Youth Cup as the start of Alex Ferguson's incredible reign.

The manager's record now showed two cup-winning seasons, one other final appearance, two semi-finals and two quarter-finals, so Ferguson could be justifiably proud of his achievements in overseeing such a remarkable record at junior level, particularly in view of the effort required in reviving the youth operation. Ferguson would, no doubt, be the first to acknowledge the contribution made to those improvements by a number of his staff, one of whom was Eric Harrison and included many capable and dedicated scouts such as ex-youth team member Terry Beckett.

For the Second Round visit of the Robins in November 1996, Harrison was once again forced to assemble a new side from the ashes of the old. Now beginning his third and final Youth Cup campaign, John Curtis was nominated as the team's skipper and he was accompanied by only three survivors, Stuart Brightwell, David Brown and Mark Wilson, who were present for the Reds in their defeat at Liverpool earlier in the year. Of the debutants, Wes Brown, Danny Higginbotham and Richie Wellens were doorstep discoveries as all three of them were born and bred Mancunians.

The match turned into a personal triumph for one of the newcomers to United's side, an under-18 starlet from north of the border by the name of Alex Notman. The visiting camp might well have put up a case for Leigh Edwards taking the laurels as the game's most important individual, because despite conceding seven goals more than he would have liked, the goalkeeper put on an outstanding display of agility and bravery and at times it appeared his efforts alone prevented the Reds from running up a cricket score.

Unlike many past campaigns, when United required some time to get their sporting juices flowing, it took only three minutes for Wilson to test Edwards and barely seven more for the team to break their duck. A splendid goal it was, too, with Stuart Brightwell racing all of 40 yards before seeing his ground shot take something of a deflection and scooting over the back of Wrexham's net.

Edwards then made saves from Brightwell and David Brown as the Robins found themselves largely penned in their own half. They did temporarily escape from

Alex Notman registered four goals, the first time anyone had achieved such a feat for United in the Youth Cup since Ryan Giggs six years before

their confines soon after, when Steve Roberts headed just wide, but the response from United was merciless as they quickly scored twice to settle the outcome.

On 21 minutes, Notman was handily placed to guide the ball over the line from close in and when the same player was felled in the box just a few moments later, he gathered his thoughts prior to nonchalantly knocking in the resulting penalty.

That was it as far as the first half went, and the crowd had to wait until nine minutes after the restart before Notman produced a slide-rule finish just as Edwards vainly attempted to close him down.

A misunderstanding in United's penalty area almost led to Wrexham scoring when Curtis headed the ball past the oncoming Adam Sadler. Typical of the visitors' luck on the night, it bounced well wide of a post and away for a corner.

There then occurred a spate of substitutions, with Eric Harrison sending on Salford teenager Jamie Wood for David Brown and the Robins attempting to boost their presence with two fresh pairs of legs. Wood made the most profound impact by scoring from short-range a little while after, and the crowd was then treated to what was by far the best goal of the night.

Brightwell was again the instigator when making another surging run through the middle of the park. His fantastic drive was parried by Edwards right into the feet of Notman, who executed the simple task of side-footing the ball calmly over the goal-line. United's opponents were now completely demoralised and it came as no surprise when Gavin Naylor put the Reds in seventh heaven to conclude the scoring in the 82nd minute.

A look at the two teams as they trooped off the pitch at full-time told its own story. While the Wrexham eleven and their entourage hung their heads in utter dejection, the United lads appeared happy with their evening's work as well as the outcome. And rightly so, because the win represented the club's highest winning margin in the competition since the defeat of Derby in January 1984 and their best start to a Youth Cup campaign for 33 years.

The Wrexham Evening Leader's reporter condensed the action into a few words with the view that the Racecourse boys *'did not do themselves justice on the night, but the gulf between the two sides was enormous'*.

Danny Higginbotham put on a steady performance on his Youth Cup debut

410

1996-97

Liverpool	Manchester United
1) Roy Naylor	1) Adam Sadler
2) Neil Murphy	2) Ryan Ford
3) Danny Williams	3) Danny Higginbotham
4) Steven Gerrard	4) John Curtis
5) Stephen Wright	5) Wes Brown
6) Sean Hessey	6) Stuart Brightwell
7) Andy Parkinson	7) Richie Wellens
8) Nicky Rizzo	8) Mark Wilson
9) Michael Owen	9) David Brown
10) Jon Newby	10) Jamie Wood
11) Sean Friars	11) Alex Notman
12) Matthew Cass (for 4)	12) Gavin Naylor (for 10)
13) Ian Dunbavin GK	13) Paul Rachubka GK
14) Richie Partridge (for 10)	14) Leon Mills

LIVERPOOL 1 v 2 MANCHESTER UNITED

Owen (pen)   Brown D., Notman (pen)

JANUARY 1997

Tuesday 7th

Kick-off 7.30 p.m.

Attendance 4,931

Reds spot on...

The outcome of the draw for the next round was indeed an intriguing and mouth-watering prospect, through the Reds being given a swift chance to revenge their elimination from the Youth Cup just ten months previously by trophy-holders Liverpool.

Even with his concerns over the free-scoring Alex Notman, who was on the mend after recently suffering a 'dead leg' with bleeding complications, Eric Harrison said of the possible absence of the marksman, 'It would be a blow but you don't have to get anxious and paranoid about it. I'm not a doom and gloom merchant.' Practically ruled out of contention at one stage, Notman took part in a training session on the morning of the game and by successfully demonstrating his fitness, he was given the nod to start from Harrison.

Over in the Anfield camp, youth coach Hugh McAuley was still able to call upon the services of a number of the team who had defeated United in such dramatic circumstances during the previous campaign. In view of the earlier events on Merseyside, there was a strong suspicion that Harrison's lads would need to contain the threat of Michael Owen, who acted as their chief tormentor on that occasion. Already the recipient of a senior squad number, Owen could look forward to the prospect of being shadowed by John Curtis for 90 minutes.

The tie failed to live up to expectations as far as the quality of football on offer was concerned and a lack of fluidity from both teams was attributed to a scarcity of recent match practice. The absence of minutes on the pitch certainly affected the two sets of strikers, especially United's, with practically all of their offensive thrusts petering out well before reaching the danger areas. Even when the visiting team did manage to venture far enough forward to create a goalscoring or crossing opportunity, their shooting and centres were woeful.

While the amount of possession was fairly evenly shared over the duration of the first section of the match, Liverpool unquestionably scorned the two best chances. The first of them arrived in only the seventh minute when a tantalising through ball executed by Sean Hussey gave Owen an uninterrupted sight of goal. While the near 5,000 spectators held their breath in expectation of the ball ending up in the back of Adam Sadler's net, Owen disappointed the bulk of them by crashing it straight at the 'keeper.

Hearts were in United mouths once more just after the half-hour mark, another Liverpool raid suddenly turning menacing when a delicious pass from Jon Newby allowed the quicksilver Owen to run beyond the visitors' back four. Once again benefiting from the time and space required to fire his team ahead, Owen contrived to hit his shot against the outside of a post.

Despite the level of technique on show only increasing a degree or two in the second half, the concluding period did at least contain a few more incidents of note, three of which yielded goals.

Liverpool carved out the lead they just about deserved in the 49th minute as a result of a blatant penalty. The move which led up to the awarding of the spot kick developed when impressive Australian midfielder Nicky Rizzo cleverly picked out Owen on the right-hand side of the field and sparked the latter off on a jinking run.

Owen was tracked every inch of the way by Curtis towards the Kop end of the ground and there, just to the left of Sadler's goalmouth and only a yard or two in from the bye-line, United's skipper bundled the forward off the ball with a clumsy challenge unbecoming of an England Youth international. The outcome was inevitable, with Owen rising to his feet before sticking the ball away and thrusting Liverpool in front.

There was a little less than half an hour to go when Eric Harrison felt a change was required and sent on winger Gavin Naylor. It was a shrewd decision, because United's threat down the left side of the pitch had previously been non-existent and all of a sudden that strip of the field was transformed into their most fertile area. Full of running and displaying a desire to make life as difficult for the Anfielders as he could, the substitute's speed and silky skills quickly turned the overall balance of play in favour of the away team.

Eight minutes after Naylor's introduction, Liverpool skipper Neil Murphy was rather harshly adjudged to have fouled David Brown in the penalty area and Notman took on the responsibility of executing the spot kick to draw United level. The impetus swung still further over to the team kitted out in all-white, and they capitalised on the 73rd minute withdrawal of Liverpool's gifted Steven Gerrard and their late superiority with a wonderful winner.

Naylor's continuing threat down the left gained the reward it deserved with only three minutes remaining after his cross was flicked on by Notman. Liverpool's defence was momentarily wrong-footed because of Notman's subtle intervention and Brown weighed up his options before heading the ball in at the far post.

In the seconds remaining, Brown could have increased United's advantage and Owen wasted an opening which would have taken the tie to a replay.

Cliff Butler, who was on hand to record the proceedings for the Review, noted, 'This was not one of United's great F.A. Youth Cup performances, but there can be no doubting that it was a memorable and important result. And that's what will be written into the record books'.

The loss was acutely felt by Liverpool, causing Hugh McAuley to say, 'United are a pedigree team, but we felt we should have won. Michael (Owen) missed two chances he would normally have put away, but there was a real threat to us until a dubious penalty was awarded against Neil Murphy. We always needed a second goal and we lost some discipline and bite in midfield. It didn't help to lose Steve Gerrard with an injury. We were punished for a moment of slackness. The ball went beyond our central defenders and we lost to a looping header in the top corner.'

By winning against such a powerful and highly rated side such as Liverpool, there was a growing feeling that the newest batch of Reds were developing sufficiently to warrant the 'favourites' tag they had now acquired.

> *Eric Harrison didn't overplay Michael Owen's inclusion. He was mentioned as a danger but we believed we were good enough to go there and win.*
>
> *To go to Anfield and beat Liverpool at any level is an amazing feeling, especially when they had such a strong team, but we always had a lot of self-belief.*
>
> **ALEX NOTMAN**

Adam Sadler dives at the feet of Liverpool's Michael Owen while John Curtis attempts to clear the stray ball

third round

411

1997-98

1) Gareth Stewart
2) Leam Richardson
3) Peter Murphy
4) Garth Scates
5) Martin Taylor
6) Keith Brown
7) Andy McAvoy
8) David Dunn
9) Craig Woodfield
10) Gary Hamilton
11) Ciaron Ryan
12) *Patrick Connolly (for 9)*
14) *Paul Forsyth (for 11)*
15) *Jonathon Topley*

1) Paul Rachubka
2) Lee Roche
3) Stephen Rose
4) Michael Ryan
5) Wes Brown
6) Wayne Evans
7) Richie Wellens
8) John Thorrington
9) David Healy
10) Alex Notman
11) Luke Chadwick
12) *Kirk Hilton (for 4)*
13) *Adam Sadler GK*
14) *Paul Wheatcroft (for 8)*

DECEMBER 1997

BLACKBURN ROVERS 1 v 1 MANCHESTER UNITED
Hamilton   Healy

Tuesday 2nd

Kick-off 7.30 p.m.

Attendance 1,257

second round

Healy spares blushes

There were a couple of interesting international inclusions in the United youth team that took on Blackburn Rovers at Ewood Park on a dark December evening in 1997.

Despite being raised in Stockport, new goalkeeper Paul Rachubka was born in the infinitely warmer climate of California while midfielder John Thorrington came from sunny South Africa. By way of a contrast, and in keeping with Alex Ferguson's stated policy of cornering as much of the local market in young talent as possible, a number of others who made up the side originated from within a short travelling distance of Manchester Town Hall.

Previous participants Wes Brown and Richie Wellens were, of course, both Manchester lads as were outfield substitutes Kirk Hilton and Paul Wheatcroft. Lee Roche hailed from Bolton while his full-back partner, Stephen Rose, came from the Salford conurbation. Michael Ryan was, like Rachubka, from Stockport, one of the club's most fruitful recruitment areas over the years.

Wayne Evans gave the midfield a South Wales tint while further up the field, David Healy, from Downpatrick in Northern Ireland, was accompanied by Luke Chadwick, an exciting and slippery winger from Cambridge whose name appeared on Arsenal's books as a schoolboy.

It had been five years since United last crossed paths with Blackburn in the national youth tournament, but in the county competition the Reds held something of a recent curse over the Ewood Park boys. In the previous two Lancashire Youth Cup finals, United had defeated the Rovers in both of them, being victorious with a 3-2 margin at Blackburn in the 1995/96 season and by a 3-1 scoreline at Old Trafford during the 1996/97 campaign.

The sparse crowd that braved the numbingly cold conditions must have wondered why they had bothered as the seconds ticked increasingly slowly away in the first half. United were simply shocking, such a poor display making them appear like a set of actors suffering from opening night nerves, and their only moves of note prior to facing Eric Harrison at the interval were tame attempts at spoiling Stewart's clean sheet by Thorrington and Healy.

Blackburn weren't that much better, though they looked more up for the fight than the Reds, and at least they benefited from the efforts of the most influential individual on the pitch. Just back from a knee injury, the tigerish David Dunn formed a business-like midfield partnership with Garth Scates and, while putting in a marvellous midfield display, for a very long time it appeared that the former's contribution would probably be the difference between the two sides.

It was Dunn who came closest to scoring in the opening 45 minutes when his clever chip appeared to spell danger prior to sailing fractionally over Rachubka's crossbar.

For most of the rest of the half, the two contestants mainly slugged it out in the centre of the pitch with neither of them able to make much headway going forward.

Shortly into the second session, Rovers again went close when a Keith Brown header clipped the top of United's goal frame. It was the point at which Blackburn took almost entire control of the match and only for some wayward shooting, they could easily have forged ahead much sooner than they did.

Rovers' goal stemmed from a corner taken by Dunn in the 69th minute. Jumping as if on springs, Gary Hamilton managed to avoid all of United's defensive attentions and decisively headed the ball into Rachubka's net.

The Reds' forward-line remained a timid bunch for most of the game and two more weak efforts, from Thorrington and Healy again, did little to suggest they were capable of saving face. United's only glimmer of hope was that, for all of their territorial advantage, the Ewood Park juniors weren't able to create too many goalscoring chances and at only one-nil down, there was always a chance for them to retrieve the situation.

And that is just what happened, when they forced an equaliser only five minutes from full-time.

Understandably considered a let off under the circumstances, the origin of United's goal was formed just inside Blackburn's half, where Wellens took control of the ball. He ran with it unchecked before slotting a searching pass through a gap in Blackburn's back four to Healy, who, racing onto the ball at great speed, kept his focus and expertly slotted it into the corner of the net.

The Manchester Evening News report gave an honest appraisal of the contest, and in commenting on the equaliser, included an opinion that *'it was a reprieve which United barely deserved after a poor display against a more adventurous Rovers side'*.

A summary in the Lancashire Evening Telegraph accurately viewed it *'an evenly-fought opening period'* after which *'Rovers' youngsters took command of the game and dominated their rivals'.*

The Telegraph reckoned the Reds would be *'keen to make the most of their escape'* in the second instalment and added a remark about Healy's leveller being *'rough on Rovers, but they needed to sharpen up their work in the final third of the pitch to reap their just rewards'.*

Ulster boy David Healy came to United's rescue with an 85th minute equaliser at a freezing Ewood Park

Manchester United		Blackburn Rovers	
1) Paul Rachubka	9) David Healy	1) Gareth Stewart	9) Craig Woodfield
2) Lee Roche	10) Alex Notman	2) Leam Richardson	10) Gary Hamilton
3) Stephen Rose	11) George Clegg	3) Peter Murphy	11) Paul Forsyth
4) Michael Ryan	*12) Kirk Hilton*	4) Garth Scates	*12) Jonathon Topley*
5) Wes Brown	*14) Ian Fitzpatrick (for 6)*	5) Martin Taylor	*14) Ciaron Ryan (for 11)*
6) Wayne Evans	*15) Paul Wheatcroft (for 7)*	6) Keith Brown	*15) Patrick Connolly (for 9)*
7) John Thorrington		7) Andy McAvoy	
8) Richie Wellens		8) David Dunn	

MANCHESTER UNITED 2 v 3 BLACKBURN ROVERS
a.e.t.
Healy, Roche — Hamilton, Ryan M. (o.g.), Scates

1997-98

DECEMBER 1997

Monday 8th

Kick-off 7.00 p.m.

Attendance 3,170

second round replay

Eric Harrison with Youth Cup substitutes Paul Wheatcroft (left) and Ian Fitzpatrick at The Cliff

In dodging a bullet while obtaining a result at Ewood Park, the Reds could equally have no complaints at their defeat in the replay at Old Trafford. The fact that Blackburn needed to rely on a tragic yet spectacular own goal by United's Michael Ryan sixteen minutes into extra-time was merely incidental and couldn't in any way detract from their overall superiority over the two games.

Blackburn did, however, go about their victory the hard way and at 2-0 up, they let the Reds back in to force an additional half hour of play.

Only eight minutes had gone when Gary Hamilton fired the Rovers in front following a mistake in United's defence and nine minutes later the Reds perpetrated another defensive howler, this time through 'keeper Paul Rachubka placing a clearance straight to the feet of Garth Scates. The midfielder reacted brilliantly, cracking a searing 25-yard shot into the back of the net before Rachubka was able to regain his position.

Alex Notman and David Healy found opposing goalie Gareth Stewart alive to their first half efforts, but with Keith Brown marshalling a tenacious back four, the visitors looked comfortable with their lead. The Rovers made two good openings shortly after the resumption, Craig Woodfield firing wide after producing a scintillating run and Scates then going close to adding to his earlier goal.

United's unlikely recovery began in the 64th minute. Following the award of a free kick five or six yards outside Blackburn's penalty area, Healy acted with a sniper's instincts to find the top corner of Stewart's net with an outstanding drive. Seven minutes later, Reds' supporters were cheering with delight when an incisive move tore the Rovers' defence wide open and full-back Lee Roche was on hand to poke the ball home.

David Dunn twice went close for Blackburn near the end but, for all their efforts, extra-time was required to separate the two sides.

The opening period passed without any notable incidents. Then, just a minute after the sides had swapped ends for the third time, Rovers finally claimed the winner they undoubtedly deserved when their industrious captain, Leam Richardson, provided the inspiration by knocking a probing ball to the fringe of United's eighteen-yard box.

A number of players from both sides attempted to win possession, and a crucial touch was made by Ryan. In an effort to whack the ball upfield, the defender's attempted clearance looped high into the air, dipped over the helpless Rachubka, and then, like United's prospects of further progress, plummeted. After the ball had finally nestled in the vacant net, all of the Blackburn team celebrated gleefully, an act they repeated at the final whistle.

There was no denying, their obvious superiority had prevailed in the end.

Commenting on the manner of the victory, the Lancashire Evening Telegraph reckoned that *'Rovers should not have had to rely on such unorthodox means'* and that the boys in blue would *'not care how the game was won, just that it was'*. The Telegraph's reporter also felt that effort often displaced quality by stating, *'considering the scoreline, it wasn't a ding-dong battle. The best period of the game from an entertainment point of view was probably the last fifteen minutes of normal time with the score 2-2 and both teams looking for a winner'*.

For the many-talented Rovers side, their success over the Reds was the beginning of a fantastic run of results in the Youth Cup that only came to an end when they were defeated 5-3 by Everton in the final.

As far as most of the United lads were concerned, the defeat served to demonstrate that they weren't up to the standard required, and it either hastened their departure from the profession or caused a demotion to a level more suited to their talent.

DAVIES, Simon Ithel (1990/91, 1991/92)

Born: Davenham, Cheshire, 23rd April 1974
Height: 6ft., **Weight:** 11st. 11lbs.
Role: Midfielder
Career: Park Road Junior School (Middlewich)/ Middlewich High School/ Middlewich Boys/ Mid-Cheshire Boys/ Cheshire Boys/ UNITED: Ass. Schoolboy June 1988 Trainee July 1990 Pro. July 1992 to August 1997/ Exeter City (L) December 1993 to February 1994/ Huddersfield Town (L) October and November 1996/ Luton Town August 1997 to December 1998/ Macclesfield Town December 1998 to August 2000/ Rochdale August 2000/ Bangor City July 2001/ Total Network Solutions May 2003/ Bangor City August 2004/ Rhyl January to April 2005

With two high profile players controversially sold in the summer of 1995 and another about to be off-loaded, Alex Ferguson elevated six youngsters for United's opening day match at Villa Park in August, three of whom were on the pitch from the kick-off. When the new-look Reds left Villa Park on the wrong end of a 3-1 scoreline, it caused Match of the Day pundit Alan Hansen to famously claim *'You never win anything with kids.'* The ill-judged comment rebounded on him a million times as the 'kids' helped to bring about a Premiership and F.A. Cup double that season and all bar one of them went on to forge out careers in the game which included winning full international caps.

What Hansen failed to pick up on was that many of those young players were blooded during the previous term. In fact, for a home Champions League Group tie against Galatasaray in December 1994, not only did Ferguson name four former youth team outfield members in the starting line-up, there were another four sitting on the substitutes' bench, including one who was still eligible for Youth Cup duty. Giving 'kids' their chance in the first-team was nothing new to the manager, and it certainly didn't represent anything revolutionary as far as Manchester United was concerned.

While a 4-0 win over the champions of Turkey was down to a superb team effort, one of the side made headlines by firing the Reds into the lead after only three minutes. Chesting down a cross was twenty year-old Simon Davies and, with perfect timing, the number eleven hit a low, hard left-footed drive into the far corner of the net to set the Reds on their way. It was a moment to savour for him, one which was probably the apex of his time at Old Trafford, and he said of the experience, *'I remember the goal really well, not so much the build-up but straight afterwards the first person to come over to me was Eric Cantona. He was my hero, even though he pronounced my name 'See-mon', which always had the lads taking the mick.'*

Brought up in the leafy Cheshire countryside, Davies' first taste of organised football was with Middlewich Red Star under-10's, a team coached by his father, Ithel, a staunch Manchester United fan and proud Welshman. A couple of years later the boy began an association with Lostock Lions, a club whose coach was connected to Manchester City. Because of the link-up with the Maine Road outfit, an invitation to train at Platt Lane for a spell was received and he also underwent trials with a few other local clubs.

As he detailed, it was while representing Mid-Cheshire Boys in 1988 when someone with ties to Old Trafford first noticed him, *'We were playing Salford Boys at Littleton Road in a cup-tie and although we lost 2-1, I scored our goal and played quite well. Then a United scout came over and asked me to come to The Cliff for a trial on the Monday evening. Normally they would train on a Monday, but they swapped things around so that I could play in a trial game and I must have done okay because the following night Alex Ferguson and Joe Brown came to my house and asked me to sign for United. I was really blown away. I mean, it's not like the postman or milkman calling, it was Alex Ferguson, the manager of Manchester United, and he was offering me a five-year contract.'*

With the proposal of the persuasive Ferguson proving too powerful a pull, the prospect penned the required paperwork on the following Saturday and so began a nine-year association with the club. From then on the England schoolboy triallist went running every morning so as to maintain his fitness and keep him in the best possible condition for when he finally left education to begin as a full-timer at Old Trafford.

Still in his last year at school, his time as a Red got off to an encouraging start when Oldham were defeated in the final of the North-West Youth Tournament in August 1989. Later that month, with his parents cheering him on, a goal on his debut for the 'B' team wasn't enough to prevent a 4-2 defeat at Chester City.

Slight of build back then, that season he totalled seventeen appearances for the Lancashire League Division Two side and increased that number by one in the 1990/91 term while also featuring occasionally in the 'A' team. The pacy wide midfielder registered a Youth Cup goal at Darlington in November 1990 and was ever-present as the under-18's reached the semi-final only to be eliminated by Sheffield Wednesday in unfortunate circumstances.

The campaign ended on a two-pronged high when, just over a week after the Youth Cup defeat to the boys from Hillsborough, he was elevated into the Reserves for a 1-0 home win over Nottingham Forest. Success at Preston in the Lancashire Youth Cup final two days later brought the domestic curtain down in splendid conclusion as the club's juniors started to make supporters sit up and take notice that something extraordinary was going on behind the scenes.

He became joint-highest appearance maker and top goalscorer for the 'A' team in the 1991/92 term and was also handed the skipper's armband when the new Youth Cup campaign began at Sunderland in November. Again present for a full quota of matches in the competition, he relinquished the captaincy of the side when Ryan Giggs was named in the starting eleven, which included the second leg of the final.

Turning professional in July 1992, his efforts over the next two years were mostly spent in the Reserves' divisional commitments. He watched on while the likes of Gary Neville, Nicky Butt, Keith Gillespie and David Beckham made headway into the first-team, desperately hoping that a similar chance would come his way, although a loan at Exeter was useful in providing him with the experience of eleven league games.

By the time the 1994/95 season arrived, Ferguson was confident that Davies was ready. Named on the bench for a Champions League clash with Gothenburg at Old Trafford in mid-September, a week later he started a Coca-Cola Cup tie at Port Vale. He took part in two more Coca-Cola Cup matches in October and was also named as a substitute for both Champions League ties with Barcelona.

Finally breaking through to the Premiership when nominated a place in the starting line-up at home to Crystal Palace in November, it was the beginning of a six-match run that also encompassed two Champions League appearances and three further Premiership games, including the scoring success against Galatasaray. Although there was a considerable wait until the following spring for his next involvement, an Old Trafford engagement with Chelsea, the ambitious youngster was pleased with his development.

After making what was a significant breakthrough he was confident of further progress but, with Ryan Giggs and David Beckham excelling in the wide positions throughout the Reds' double winning campaign, his opportunities were limited to just two first-team starts. A second Reserve League triumph was scant consolation for him as competition for places intensified amongst the crop of outstanding juniors at the club. While his career may have been stalled at club level, Davies was included in the Welsh squad that travelled to Lugano in late April and won his only full international cap against Switzerland when leaving the bench at the Stadio Cornaredo.

'When I look back I probably lacked the consistency needed at the very highest level,' he admitted. *'You don't realise it at the time, but all those players at United were incredibly consistent. They set the bar so high, that was the standard. Although I could hold my own in most situations, doing it week in and week out was tough.'*

With Jordi Cruyff and Karel Poborsky added to the payroll in 1996, and now even further back in the pecking order, it was clear the time was right for him to move on. Still managing to take part in six first-team friendly matches, including a couple of clashes with Inter Milan, the nearest he got to competitive senior action was two substitute appearances in the Coca-Cola Cup, a sure sign he wasn't in Ferguson's plans for the future. A short loan spell at Huddersfield in the autumn allowed him to add three league matches to his tally and he made his 239th and last appearance for United in the 0-0 draw with Stoke's Reserves the following May.

Even though there was a year remaining on his contract, he elected to go through a two-week trial with League Two side Luton Town, who were undertaking some pre-season matches at Lilleshall. Despite some interest shown by Stockport, joining the Hatters on a three-year deal and concurrently costing his new employers a £150,000 transfer fee seemed the better option. Unable to nail down a place at Kenilworth Road, and with only 24 league appearances to count on, twelve of which were made from the bench, his contract was only half-way through when he returned north to join Macclesfield.

Eighteen months later he switched to Rochdale for a season before moving into coaching, something he had wanted to do for some time. Later linking up with Welsh League side Bangor City in order to keep in shape and allow him time to finish his coaching studies, as the 2001/02 term drew to a conclusion, further honours came his way when he was included in Wales' semi-professional squad for the Four Nations Tournament. To his great surprise, he claimed the 2002/03 'Welsh Premier League Player of Season' award and twelve months later he was selected in the 'Welsh Premier League Team of the Season' alongside ex-Red Clayton Blackmore.

Over the next couple of years he moved around the Welsh non-league scene while also coaching Wrexham's under-14 team with Darren Ferguson. A member of the TNS squad that came up against Manchester City in the UEFA Cup in August 2003, he went on to reach the Welsh Cup final with them in 2004.

In the summer of 2006, Davies joined the youth set-up at Chester City and in March 2007 was promoted to Head of Youth Development there. He took over as caretaker manager in March 2008 and impressed the club's hierarchy enough to be offered the job full-time. However, just four months into the 2008/09 term, a string of poor performances led to his demotion back to youth team manager.

He remained at Chester during a period of significant turmoil before finally exiting in the autumn of 2009. Within a few short months he was back in the game, this time taking up a coaching role at Eastlands, and, having attained his pro-licence, Simon Davies continues to work with Manchester City's under-16 Academy side.

When looking back over his early days in the national under-18's competition, he mentioned in 2011, *'I have really fond memories of the F.A. Youth Cup, it really saved me. When I first came to United I was in digs in Lower Broughton with Mark Bosnich and Giuliano Maiorana and, even though I enjoyed the banter, I just couldn't settle. I had come from the quietest part of Cheshire to one of the busiest parts of Manchester and so I moved back home and travelled in by train and bus each day. I was still playing in the 'B' team, but when Paul Gough couldn't play in the Darlington (Youth Cup) tie I was drafted in. I had a really good game and built up a great partnership with Peter Smyth. It was the first time that I had that sort of relationship on the pitch and I basically learnt what it was like to be a footballer.'*

BROWN, Wesley Michael (1996/97, 1997/98)

Born: Longsight, Manchester, 13th October 1979
Height: 6ft. 1in., Weight: 13st. 11lbs.
Role: Central defender
Career: St. Chrysostom's Primary School (Longsight)/ Burnage High School (Manchester)/ Manchester Boys/ Greater Manchester Boys/ Idsall School (Shropshire)/ England Boys/ UNITED: Trainee July 1996 Pro. November 1996/ Sunderland July 2011 to present

Beginning at the age of nine, Wes Brown's association with Whalley Range-based Fletcher Moss Rangers lasted until he was fourteen, a period in which he was spotted by two local United scouts and former players, Harry McShane and Tommy O'Neil. Having previously taken part in trials with Manchester City, the thirteen year-old instead joined United's Academy in 1993. A pupil of Burnage High School, an establishment that also produced previous Old Trafford connections in Roger Byrne and Peter Coyne, his astonishing sporting talents resulted in him particularly excelling at football and basketball.

He took part in four out of five matches when United won the 1994 Sunderland (under-16) International Football Festival by defeating Sheffield United in the final by two goals to nil before attending the F.A. School of Excellence at Lilleshall. Rated as one of the top prospects in the country, during the 1994/95 campaign he represented England Boys on eight occasions.

He was a member of the United team that reached the final of the Northern Ireland Milk Cup only to lose 1-0 to Middlesbrough in July 1995 but, because he was still attending Idsall School in Shropshire, his contributions for the Reds were minimal in the 1995/96 season. Nevertheless, while on a visit back to Manchester in September 1995, Brown substituted for Andy Duncan in the 'A' team's 1-1 home draw with Blackburn and later added four more 'B' team appearances over the Christmas and Easter periods prior to signing on as a trainee in July 1996.

Throughout the 1996/97 term he was mainly involved with the 'A' team and made his Youth Cup entrance in a 7-0 thrashing of Wrexham in the November. He was also chosen for the following three ties of the campaign as the Reds were eliminated by Watford in a replay. By the end of the season his 'A' team had been crowned Lancashire League Division One champions and his reputation was further boosted when chosen as the 'Jimmy Murphy Young Player of the Year'. In order to complete a quick hat-trick of honours, the under-18's then defeated Blackburn at Old Trafford in the Lancashire Youth Cup final.

His exploits followed a similar path over the following year as he normally figured for the 'A' side and participated in both the county and national Youth Cup competitions.

He was initially called up for the Reserves in February 1998 and, alongside securing another Lancashire League medal and four England under-18 caps, his performances then earned him a place on the bench for a senior home match against Leeds in May. Sent on as a substitute in the 60th minute as United strolled to a 3-0 win, just seven days later he was included in the starting line-up for the first time when the Reds defeated Barnsley 2-0. It concluded a great period for the talented Mancunian, whose abundant promise was there for all to see.

Now regarded as a first-teamer of the future, his performances in the 1998/99 term again caught the eye. By then an accomplished central defender, Brown edged his way into the senior set-up by deputising at full-back when Denis Irwin was injured. Alert to danger, quick-footed and well able to make surging forays down the wing, football pundits marvelled at his potential and they often likened him to a young Paul McGrath.

He then assisted England's under-21's in matches against Sweden (twice), Bulgaria (twice), Luxembourg, the Czech Republic and Poland. Receiving a first full cap under manager Kevin Keegan as a result of taking part in a 1-1 draw against Hungary in Budapest in April 1999, the best moments of an incredible campaign were still to come as, firstly, he became the recipient of an F.A. Premier League championship medal by virtue of the Reds defeating Spurs 2-1 at Old Trafford to narrowly pip Arsenal to the title. While not involved in the F.A. Cup final victory over Newcastle at Wembley six days later, his name did appear in the substitutes' column for the historic Champions League win over Bayern Munich at Barcelona's Nou Camp stadium.

After forging such a solid grounding as a professional, a cruciate ligament knee injury picked up on the training ground meant that his career needed to be put on hold for the entire 1999/2000 season. Back in time for the commencement of the following term, before long he was a regular in Alex Ferguson's starting eleven. A composed individual who always appeared very relaxed on the ball, his displays alongside Dutch international Jaap Stam soon saw him pushing to regain a full international place.

He went on as a substitute for the injured Sol Campbell after only 29 minutes of England's World Cup Qualifier against Albania in March 2001 and comfortably settled into the side alongside Rio Ferdinand. At club level, the shock departure of Stam to Lazio in August 2001 prompted Ferguson to go on record as saying that Brown was *'a world-class defender and it is now time for him to prove it'*.

Sadly for the Longsight lad, the twin plagues of injury and loss of form struck at exactly the wrong time because he was hit by another knee injury and only returned at the end of the campaign.

He regained a semblance of form at the end of the 2001/02 season to win a place on the plane to Japan and Korea for the World Cup finals but, following a couple of shaky showings in England's pre-tournament friendly fixtures, his efforts in the Far East extended only to watching the tournament from the bench.

biography

417

His injury woes returned at the start of the 2002/03 term when he fractured his ankle and was ruled out for three months. Bouncing back to oust both the in-form John O'Shea and veteran defender Laurent Blanc to partner Ferdinand in the centre of United's defence, in February 2003 he also returned to the England team as a second half substitute against Australia and displayed a consistently high standard during course of a campaign in which the Reds again clinched the Premiership title after an exciting race with Arsenal. Sadly, his wretched luck hadn't completely gone away and in the final game of the season at Everton in May 2003, the 23 year-old suffered yet another knee knock.

Undergoing another operation to solve what was diagnosed as anterior cruciate ligament damage, Brown gradually rebuilt his strength and fitness. Then, with just the lack of fortune that he was now accustomed to, in early 2004 he returned to action much sooner than he would have liked in order to replace the suspended Ferdinand. Lacking match practice, his performances were laboured and United's league aspirations crumbled, although he recovered some form and confidence just in time to help secure victory in the F.A. Cup final against Millwall.

During the 2004/05 season he shuttled in and out of the side. Finding himself unable to hold down a place as Ferdinand and Mikaël Silvestre occupied the central defending roles, instead he often covered the right full-back spot when Gary Neville was injured. After signing a new three-year contract in October 2004, improved performances in the interim period were rewarded by Sven-Göran Eriksson four months later when he was recalled to the international team for a 0-0 draw with Holland at Villa Park. He occupied a regular place for United throughout the remainder of the term and was a member of the side that lost the F.A. Cup final on penalties to Arsenal.

He then travelled to the United States for a series of international friendly matches and was present when England secured a 2-1 victory over the host nation in Chicago in late May. It brought a satisfying end to a period in which, for a welcome change, his time on the treatment table had been minimal.

The signing of Nemanja Vidic in January 2006 limited his opportunities in the senior side and, with Gary Neville mostly out of the picture, it wasn't until the 2007/08 campaign that he established himself at right-back. That season saw him produce arguably his best ever football and it concluded in a blaze of glory with Premier League and Champions League successes.

Brown penned a new five-year deal in April 2008 and his immediate future seemed assured. Unfortunately, injury and loss of form came back to haunt him in the following term and caused him to lose his place in the team. Over the next couple of years he was in and out of the side while Jonny Evans acted as the preferred back-up to Vidic and Ferdinand.

Still feeling he was capable of performing in the Premier League on a regular basis, the 31 year-old joined Sunderland on a four-year contract in July 2011. It ended a liaison with United which had yielded five Premier Leagues, two F.A. Cups, three League Cups, four Community Shields and a couple of Champions League triumphs. Besides those fabulous achievements at club level, his experiences as a full international had stretched to 23 caps prior to him announcing his retirement from England duties in August 2010.

For many, Wes Brown's cultured style of play, which combined attributes such as a strong tackling and exceptional positional sense, made him one of the most gifted central defenders of his time. Alas, intermittent fitness issues restricted his development and meant that he was never able to fully maximise his early potential.

NEVILLE, Gary Alexander (1991/92, 1992/93)

Born: Bury, 18th February 1975

Height: 5ft. 11ins., **Weight:** 12st. 7lbs.

Role: Centre-half

Career: Chantlers Primary School (Bury)/ Elton High School (Bury)/ Bury Boys/ Greater Manchester Boys/ UNITED: Trainee July 1991 Pro. January 1993 to February 2011

The eldest son of parents who had always been avid Manchester United supporters, Gary Neville sat with his father in the old 'K' stand at Old Trafford from being just four years-old. By the age of seven he was turning out for the Bury-based St. Stephen's under-10 side before moving on to play for Ice Juniors at under-11 standard. It was around that point when a letter was received from United by his primary school enquiring if they felt any of their pupils were good enough to attend a trial. From amongst hundreds of schoolboys across the region, he was one of only sixteen chosen who went on to represent the Reds' School of Excellence at the under-11 stage and it constituted a wish come true for someone who only ever wanted to be involved with the club he had always followed.

Originally a goalscoring midfielder, he then represented Bury Boys from under-12 through to under-15 levels while also training every Thursday at The Cliff under the watchful gaze of Brian Kidd and Nobby Stiles. His stock rose still further when later winning honours for Greater Manchester Boys, by which time he was occupying a more familiar central defensive role. A naturally athletic, all-round sporting type who was also chosen for Lancashire Schools at cricket, around the age of fifteen he was attached to the highly-regarded Oldham-based Boundary Park Juniors football team that operated in the Bury & Radcliffe League.

By then he had done enough to convince the Reds' coaching staff that he was ready to be tested further and his club debut proper came in a 'B' team game at Carlisle in November 1990. Already on schoolboy terms at the club, he substituted for Pat McShane in a 3-1 win and then took part in a handful of additional games for the fourth string as the season progressed, all of them at full-back. Neville was simultaneously winning league and cup honours with Boundary Park Juniors, including the 1991 Lancashire under-16 Soreen Youth Cup, in a stellar side that also included Nicky Butt, Karl Brown, Paul Scholes and his younger brother, Phil.

After signing on at Old Trafford in the summer of 1991 and picking up the princely wage of just £29.50 per week, the new school leaver hoped with all his might that he could make a living out of the game. Even though that sum would be considered pocket money by today's standards, there was still the temptation of spending his new found wealth with his friends. However, on his father's advice, he instead elected to concentrate on his football career and from the age of sixteen, for a period of about two years, his choice was to become a virtual recluse after dark, shunning pubs and clubs and foregoing alcohol while learning his chosen trade as a professional sportsman.

Within days of becoming a trainee he got into a winning habit when captaining his side to success in the Northern Ireland Milk Cup. After he tucked away a penalty in a semi-final victory over Motherwell, the Reds defeated Hearts 2-0 in the final to pick up the prestigious trophy for the very first time. Neville was then utilised in the 'A' team for most of the campaign and in November he was drafted straight into the Youth Cup eleven as United notched up a 4-2 victory at Sunderland. During the home defeat of a plucky Walsall side in the Third Round a couple of weeks before Christmas, he and Chris Casper already looked to have formed a decent defensive partnership.

Such were his commanding performances in United's junior sides that he was elevated into the Reserves for a 3-2 home win over Manchester City in February 1992. Five days later, the Reds locked horns with City once more, this time at Maine Road in the next round of the Youth Cup, when United again scored three times to send their local adversaries crashing out of the competition.

The teenagers' progress took them all the way through to a final in which Ben Thornley, Colin McKee and Simon Davies scored the all-important second leg goals before nearly 15,000 spectators and Neville and his co-defenders did enough to ensure that the trophy made its way home for the first time since 1964. A fabulous maiden season ended in Switzerland when skippering the youth team to a Blue Stars Tournament final in which they fell to a solitary goal from Spartak Moscow.

The start of Alex Ferguson's accent on youth was now underway and, together with Nicky Butt, the Bury native was in the vanguard as the 1992/93 term started. He completed two 'A' team games and made a couple of starts for the Reserves before being placed on the bench for the opening UEFA Cup tie against Torpedo Moscow at Old Trafford. With the game fizzling out towards a 0-0 draw and only a couple of minutes remaining, a long-held ambition was realised when he made his first-team debut by substituting for Lee Martin.

His displays for United inevitably drew the attention of the England Youth selectors and by late September he had participated in the Genoa Youth Tournament, as well as going on to make numerous appearances in the UEFA Youth Championship Qualifiers as the campaign unfolded.

During his second full year at the club he captained the 'A' team to success when they won their league by thirteen points from second placed Everton and also led the side to a 3-0 Lancashire Youth Cup final victory over Blackburn at Old Trafford. It wasn't all smiles and cheers, though, as he then experienced his first major disappointment when skippering the under-18's to a 4-1 aggregate Youth Cup final defeat by Leeds.

He received further honours by competing in all four games for an England under-18 team that participated in the European Championship finals in July 1993, including a final in which Turkey were beaten 1-0 at Nottingham. It was certainly another momentous season for him as he had progressed from United's 'A' team to become a European Youth Championship winner in a period spanning less than twelve months.

The eighteen year-old continued his winning ways when captaining United's youth team to a City of Sunderland Challenge Cup final win over Feyenoord. By the October of 1993 he had cemented a place in the Reserves, operating equally as efficiently at full-back or central defence, and went on to make another substitute appearance for the first-team in

November, this time on European Cup duty in the cauldron of the Ali Sami Yen Stadium against Galatasaray. By the end of that term United's Reserves had been crowned as champions of the Pontin's League, ten points clear of Aston Villa, and he finished on top of their appearance table. On the last day of the campaign, and with the Reds having already retained their Premiership title, he achieved another boyhood dream by starting a senior match at Old Trafford when wearing the number 23 jersey in a 0-0 draw with Coventry.

Under the influence of Eric Cantona and United's coaching staff, the club's young professionals learned the importance of welding hard work to their in-built talents and Neville, who lived, slept and ate football, needed little encouragement in that respect. Often staying behind after training to put in hours of additional practice in a bid to perfect his craft and realise his aim of becoming a regular in the senior side, that dedication and unquenchable desire to continually keep improving began to pay off in the 1994/95 term as he contested the right full-back slot with David May and Roy Keane.

Because Paul Parker was injured for most of the time, the chance to stake his claim was made with a number of solid performances. As the proceedings began to draw to a close, the right-back berth was claimed as his own and by the April he had helped United defeat Crystal Palace to reach the F.A. Cup final. Keeping a place in the side for the Wembley showpiece, Everton caused a shock by winning 1-0. Then, in June 1995, his pain turned to pride when he was called into the full England team for a 2-1 win over Japan in the Umbro Tournament.

The defender enjoyed much success over the next ten years. With the Reds achieving a Premier League and F.A. Cup double in 1996, a few weeks later he assisted England to reach the semi-finals of Euro '96. He shared in the sweetness of a further league title in 1997 and was then selected as the regular right full-back throughout England's 1998 World Cup campaign in France.

Party to the winning of a trio of major trophies in 1999, that achievement culminated in United edging a nerve-jangling finale against Bayern Munich in Barcelona, an experience he described as *'the greatest night of our lives'*. A further league title followed in 2000, a year in which he participated for England at the European Championships in Holland and Belgium, and it was followed up with another divisional triumph twelve months later.

Following a disappointing 2001/02 season with United, he anguished when injuring his ankle, a problem which caused him to miss England's 2002 World Cup campaign. Upon regaining his fitness, Neville contributed towards United reclaiming the Premier League title in 2003 and winning the F.A. Cup in 2004.

As the 2004/05 term drew to a close he had already taken part in over 300 league games and remained as the number one choice for both club and country in the right full-back position. Articulate, intelligent and often forthright, those attributes stood him out as the ideal candidate to act as United's PFA representative, though his views have occasionally resulted in controversy.

While never as elegant as Rio Ferdinand, as quick as Ashley Cole or as strong as John Terry, he possessed an uncanny ability to read the game, could cross a ball accurately with either foot and was blessed with an almost bottomless reservoir of energy which meant that constantly getting up and down the pitch was never a problem. Also ingrained with a never-say-die attitude, it is little wonder that Alex Ferguson and no less than six England managers consistently selected him over a period spanning something near to a decade and a half.

Taking into consideration the honours he amassed in that time, his credentials were unarguable. Ferguson once said of him, *'If he were only two inches taller he would be the best centre-half in the world'* and also called him *'the best English right-back of his generation'*.

Even when an established star, his regularity in arriving at Carrington before most of his colleagues would inevitably begin with him taking a swim. Also usually one of the last to leave, when football training was over he concentrated on building his stamina with a few boxing routines.

The beginning of the end of his time out on the pitch occurred in March 2007 when he again injured an ankle in a home win over Bolton, a knock which was originally supposed to keep him out for just three weeks. Forced to watch the remaining fixtures on crutches, over the course of the following campaign he got in just nine minutes for the senior team.

As a result of spending long periods in the treatment room, his career continued to stutter until February 2011 when he announced his retirement just a couple of weeks away from his 36th birthday. Of that event he said, *'I have been a Manchester United fan all my life and fulfilled every dream I've ever had. Obviously I'm disappointed that my playing days are at an end. However, it comes to us all and it is knowing when that time is, and for me that time is now.*

I have played in the most incredible teams, with some of the best players in the world, as well as against them, and I have been lucky to have been part of the club's great success.'

Having clocked up over 600 first-team games for the Reds, many consider him to be one of the most accomplished defenders the club has ever possessed. While most of his admirers assumed the 85-times capped former international would take up a full-time coaching role, a change of direction occurred when he instead joined Sky Sports as a soccer pundit for the start of the 2011/12 season.

Going on to receive numerous positive reviews from viewers and industry professionals alike for his ability to analyse games and deliver accurate viewpoints, he was then asked by manager Roy Hodgson to assist England as a coach at the 2012 European Championships.

In his spare time, Gary Neville plays the guitar. If he applies the same work ethic to his music and his TV responsibilities as he did to his football, he could very well become either one of the greatest commentators of all time or the next Eric Clapton.

NEVILLE, Philip John (1992/93, 1993/94, 1994/95)

Born: Bury, 21st January 1977
Height: 5ft. 11ins., **Weight:** 12st.
Role: Full-back or midfielder
Career: Chantlers Primary School (Bury)/ Elton High School (Bury)/ Bury & Radcliffe League/ Bury Boys/ Greater Manchester Boys/ England Boys/ UNITED: Ass. Schoolboy February 1991 Trainee July 1993 Pro. June 1994/ Everton August 2005 to present

Phil Neville excelled at many sports from a very young age, particularly soccer, cricket and athletics. He began in competitive football for St. Stephen's F.C. at under-10 and under-11 stages prior to moving to Ice Juniors when aged eleven. After twelve months with Ice he joined Bury Juniors for three or four years prior to signing for the esteemed Boundary Park Juniors.

Also the recipient of numerous representative honours when occupying a central midfield position, he captained the Bury & Radcliffe League under-12 and under-14 teams, as well as Bury Boys at under-14 and under-15 standard for two successive years. A quite superb schoolboy career continued when he skippered Greater Manchester under-15's before winning selection for England Boys.

A Bury F.C. fan as a youngster, Neville originally attended Blackpool's School of Excellence until United offered him the chance to follow in his elder brother Gary's footsteps. Initially joining the Reds' School of Excellence in September 1988, whereas Phil's pre-United days were similar in some respects to that of Gary, his pedigree at representative level was actually far greater.

Besides football, the younger Neville won numerous honours at cricket and captained the Lancashire Schools' side from the under-11 stage right through to under-16 level. He was also named as skipper for the North of England under-14 and under-15 teams and went on to captain the England Schools' Cricket XI at the same stages. Additionally becoming the youngest cricketer to represent Lancashire CCC's Second XI when stepping out against Middlesex at just fourteen years-old, his record as the youngest batsman to score a century for the county's Seconds at the age of fifteen remains unsurpassed.

During the 1991/92 football season he represented England Boys on eight occasions. Debuting for his country with a goal in a 2-2 draw with Wales at Burnley, his appearances took in two matches in Germany and one in France. He also visited Wembley on a couple of occasions with the national side, once for a stalemate with Holland and also for a 2-2 draw with Italy in front of 45,000 spectators, and he additionally managed to register the only goal of the game when England met Scotland at Ibrox.

Neville got in a friendly for United against Stoneclough at Littleton Road before occupying the number three shirt for all five matches as his side reached the final of the Sunderland International Football Festival in August 1992, and he retained it when jumping straight into the 'A' team on the opening day of the new season. Featuring predominantly in the Lancashire League Division One side throughout the term, in January 1993 he was drafted into the Youth Cup team for a Third Round home tie against Notts County because of an injury to Steven Riley.

Situated alongside brother Gary in what was a family first for the club, no two brothers had ever previously lined up in the same Youth Cup team for United. The younger sibling went on to make a total of four competition appearances that season, including the second leg of the final at Elland Road, and he collected three caps when chosen for England in the European under-16 Championship finals in Poland.

The Lancastrian was one of a squad of eighteen who jetted over to Northern Ireland to participate in the Milk Cup in July 1993 and he then completed just three games for the 'A' team prior to forcing his way into the Reserves in early October.

He won a first under-18 international cap for his efforts in a 3-3 draw with France at Yeovil in mid-November, although some of the delight he felt with his England honour faded a few days later when captaining an inexperienced United side that crashed out of the Youth Cup to Bradford City at the first hurdle.

It was the only real black mark on his season, because in early April he helped the club's teenagers to reach the final of the Bellinzona Youth Tournament and later that month he rifled in one of the Reds' goals when the Lancashire Youth Cup trophy was claimed with a 4-2 success at Burnley. With only eight games for the Reserves behind him, a period of rapid progress was crowned when he completed the full 90 minutes in Mark Hughes' testimonial match against Celtic at Old Trafford in May.

Kicking off the 1994/95 season in great style by collecting two additional under-18 caps for his efforts against Norway in late July, there were a couple of first-team friendly matches to get his teeth into before continuing in the 'A' team or the Reserves. He won his fourth England Youth cap in September 1994 when competing against France at Reading and by the year end his consistent displays had caught the eye of Alex Ferguson. The Bury boy got the nod from the manager to make his competitive first-team entrance in a home F.A. Cup Fourth Round tie against Wrexham in January and three days later he was part of a superb team effort when holders Arsenal were knocked out of the Youth Cup.

In February 1995, Ferguson again made use of his defensive qualities in a 3-0 Premiership win at Manchester City and by the end of that campaign Neville could look back over a contribution of nine games for the Lancashire League Division One champions and also a dozen appearances for the Reserves.

However, his main achievement that season was skippering the under-18 side to a Youth Cup final in which they faced Tottenham Hotspur. The Reds were fortunate to be only one goal in arrears from the first leg at White Hart Lane, where only a favourable rub of the green and Terry Cooke's superbly taken strike kept them within touching distance. In the Old Trafford instalment, another Cooke goal scored almost at the death took a tight game to a penalty shoot-out and, after Spurs succeeded to find the back of the net with their initial spot kick, United's captain stepped up to take his side's first penalty only to hit a post. Fortunately, Paul Gibson saved Spurs' next effort and the Reds went on to clinch a positive outcome. It was a particularly rewarding achievement for Neville who tirelessly covered almost every blade of grass while leading the side by example.

In early June he gained further international experience when taking part in four games for England's under-21's at the Toulon Tournament in France. Coming up against the host nation, Brazil, Malaysia and Angola, it completed a hectic year filled with a few nice memories.

By the time the 1995/96 season got underway he was considered a first-team squad member and Ferguson often entrusted him with one of the full-back positions. In the first half of what would turn out to be a fabulous campaign, he collected two additional under-21 caps for his appearances against Portugal and Norway and went on to play a major part in United completing a domestic double of Premiership and F.A. Cup triumphs.

In May 1996, the nineteen year-old became a full England international when present for a 3-0 win over China at Wembley. Starring alongside Gary, they were the first brothers to represent the national side together since Bobby and Jack Charlton in the 1960's.

Always displaying a professional attitude, and a fine role model for any boy wanting to make a career out of the game, over the next few years his exploits could accurately be described as patchy. He was part of another Premiership success in 1997 but, with United failing to win any significant honours over the next twelve months, England manager Glenn Hoddle omitted him from the World Cup squad for France '98. There were times when observers commented that his confidence seemed jolted during the 1998/99 campaign and it took several months for him to recover his usual form. Operating at left-back or in midfield, though frequently used as a substitute, his consistent streak eventually returned and by the end of that glorious season he had made a contribution of 43 appearances towards United winning an unprecedented trio of major trophies.

Well able to carry out a number of roles with equal effectiveness, his obvious versatility was probably more of a hindrance than a blessing because he was never able to call any one position his own. Nevertheless, Alex Ferguson clearly considered him a valuable asset and he was equally highly thought of in the new-look England set-up.

After assisting United to yet another Premiership title in 2000, England fans made him a scapegoat for the team's inadequacies when he gave away a penalty against Romania in the European Championships. Over the next five years he helped win two more Premiership titles and was an unused substitute for the 2004 F.A. Cup final victory over Millwall. Nevertheless, and despite numerous solid displays in midfield, he was still looked upon as a trusty squad member rather than a regular for the seniors. Then losing his place in the England squad again, in the 2004/05 season he managed a mere dozen Premiership starts for the Reds.

During the 2005 close season, in a bid to get more first-team football, his agreement to transfer to Everton for a fee reported as *'in excess of £3.5million'* ended a seventeen-year link with the Reds. While United's supporters were sorry to see him go, none could begrudge him the opportunity of a regular game, and all of them had numerous reasons to thank him for his considerable efforts on behalf of the club.

A fixture in Everton's senior set-up over the last seven seasons, manager David Moyes handed him the captaincy in 2007, the same year he won the last of 59 full England caps. He led the side to the 2009 F.A. Cup final, defeating Manchester United in the semi-final at Wembley, and has since gone on to total over 270 first-team appearances for the Toffees.

In February 2012, the Football Association announced that he was to assist Brian Eastwick to look after England's under-21's against Belgium as they seek to develop quality home-grown managers of the future.

An ambassador of Bliss, the special baby care charity, and a patron of the Royal Manchester Children's Hospital, Phil Neville and his family now occupy a luxury apartment in the 47-storey Beetham Tower on Manchester's Deansgate.

CURTIS, John Charles Keyworth
(1994/95, 1995/96, 1996/97)

Born: Nuneaton, 3rd September 1978
Height: 5ft. 10ins., **Weight:** 11st. 7lbs.
Role: Right full-back or central defender
Career: Weston-in-Arden Primary School (Bulkington)/ George Elliot School (Nuneaton)/ Nuneaton & District Boys/ Warwickshire Boys/ Midlands Boys/ England Boys/ Idsall School (Shropshire)/ **UNITED**: Trainee July 1995 Pro. September 1995 to May 2000/ **Barnsley** (L) November 1999 to May 2000/ **Blackburn Rovers** May 2000 to August 2003/ **Sheffield United** (L) March to May 2003/ **Leicester City** August 2003/ **Portsmouth** February 2004 to February 2005/ **Preston North End** (L) September to November 2004/ **Nottingham Forest** February 2005/ **Queen's Park Rangers** July to December 2007/ **Worcester City** January and February 2009/ **Wrexham** February 2009/ **Northampton Town** July 2009/ **Gold Coast United** (Aus) June 2010 to September 2011

John Curtis' reputation was such that in his early to mid-teens he attracted the attention of a veritable galaxy of scouts and consequently found himself trialled at virtually every First Division/ Premier League club, as well as undergoing an assessment with Glasgow Rangers.

Beginning as a midfielder for Coventry Sunday League side Chetwynd Squirrels at only six, by the age of eleven he had moved to Bulkington Boys Club and joined Stoke City's School of Excellence, which was based at nearby Arley. It was while appearing for Stoke at a tournament in Ayr that he was moved into central defence and from then on he began to acquire the skills and know-how that would win him an incredible 48 international caps by the time he was eighteen.

He remained with Bulkington for a couple of years before joining Grove Farm of the Nuneaton & District Sunday League. During that period he severed his association with Stoke in order to join the School of Excellence at Aston Villa and, having won county and regional honours, it was then that he came to the attention of United talent-spotter Geoff Watson.

His magnificent liaison with England Boys began with an appearance against the Republic of Ireland at Reading and he then took part in another seven games for his country in the 1992/93 season, two of which were at Wembley and included others in Switzerland, Swansea and Northern Ireland.

With United already assured of their first top-flight title success in 26 years, in May 1993 he and his family watched in awe as 40,447 spectators celebrated an event that many thought would never arrive at the last home game against Blackburn. The fourteen year-old then agreed to join the club on schoolboy terms and, if he was pleased with the outcome, Alex Ferguson was doubly so as the boy was arguably that year's hottest ticket.

Curtis' initial contribution towards his new club's cause came a couple of months later, when the Reds lost in the semi-final of the Northern Ireland Milk Cup to Rangers, and he then left home to move to the F.A. School at Lilleshall only to be promptly installed as captain of England Boys. That campaign unfolded into a fantastic adventure as the national side recorded eight straight victories, which included capturing the Victory Shield and took in wins in Holland, Germany and Switzerland. Claiming France's scalp at Wembley was rewarding, though not nearly as much as beating the Germans 2-1 in view of 65,000 at the Olympic Stadium in Berlin.

The youngster had no involvement with United during that spell as he was also busied by appearing for England in the Faroe Islands-based Nordic Cup, as well as the European under-16 Championships in Dublin.

He eventually reconnected with the club in January 1995 for a Youth Cup Third Round replay at Charlton where, to his utter surprise, he replaced Danny Hall as the Reds snatched a 5-2 victory when a defeat had looked the most likely outcome for a large part of the game. At the end of a memorable month he found himself performing on the Old Trafford pitch for the first time by starting a Youth Cup clash with Arsenal.

That period was also notable for his accumulation of another ten England under-16 caps, one of which was awarded to him for the rare distinction of skippering the team that took on Brazil at Wembley, and he was then drafted back onto the United scene to feature in the second leg of the Youth Cup semi-final against Wimbledon at Selhurst Park and both legs of a dramatic final against Spurs. Curtis left Lilleshall after completing his formal education and gaining county honours at both cricket and athletics.

He took up 'A' team residency in the following term, usually at left full-back but also in the middle of the back four on occasions. In November 1995, he wore the number three shirt for the visit of Rotherham in the Youth Cup and also resumed his impressive international career when chosen for England's under-18 side against Latvia and Sweden. With John O'Kane and Michael Clegg holding down the full-back positions in the Reserves, he had to bide his time until early April before making the step up. Named as a substitute for a Pontin's League fixture at Notts County, he replaced Paul Parker in United's 1-0 victory and then returned to an 'A' team that went on to become champions of the Lancashire League Division One.

His first experience of a senior game was when appearing as a substitute in Brian McClair's testimonial against Celtic in August 1996. Then splitting his time fairly evenly between the 'A' team and the Reserves, it was an especially fruitful period because both sides won their respective league titles and he also skippered the under-18's to a Lancashire Youth Cup final triumph. The major blemish of the season came in the national Youth Cup when, as captain and central defence partner of Wes Brown, the side were edged out in the Fourth Round.

Also named as United's 'Young Player of the Year', at the end of the campaign he took part in all three of England's qualifying games against the Ivory Coast, the UAE and Mexico in the World Youth Cup finals in Malaysia. England reached the last sixteen, after which a loss to Argentina saw them exit the competition.

The 1997/98 term heralded another notable achievement, as in the October he began training with the first-team prior to winning a call up for a 2-0 League Cup defeat at Ipswich on the 14th of that month. Eleven days later he made his first Premiership start, and the conclusion was infinitely better when stationed alongside Gary Pallister at the heart of the Reds' defence in a 7-0 whitewash of Barnsley at Old Trafford. He featured in seven further league games, mostly as a substitute, as United finished second to Arsenal in the title race.

Even though he travelled to Scandinavia for the seniors' pre-season tour, opportunities were strictly limited in the treble-winning term and the majority of his senior appearances were made in the Worthington Cup. While he was used purely as cover for Gary Neville or Denis Irwin, on the international front he was integral to the England under-21 set-up and added yet another domestic honour when United defeated Oldham 3-0 in the Manchester Senior Cup final.

While largely happy at the club, like most young professionals he thirsted for first-team football. Curtis travelled with the Reds' squad on their summer tour of Australia and the Far East in 1999, making an appearance as a substitute against the Socceroos and also competing against China, but as the new campaign got going he was once again stuck at second string standard. He had taken part in two additional senior games when, in the November, an opportunity arose to join Barnsley for the remainder of the season. Charged with a need to prove himself consistently at a higher level than United's Reserves operated at, the move was beneficial to the tune of 28 appearances.

Once back at Old Trafford, it became obvious that he wasn't going to displace Neville or Irwin and so he assented to a £2,250,000 transfer to Blackburn. It was a somewhat unfortunate turn of events, in that someone of his promise was at Old Trafford when the full-back positions were so reliably covered by two of the finest defenders the club has ever had.

He was an ever-present in the Blackburn side that made an immediate return to the Premiership in his first term at Ewood Park. Strangely, Rovers' manager Graeme Souness then largely froze him out of his plans and over the next couple of years the Midlander was chosen for barely a dozen matches. Loaned out to Sheffield United for a short period in 2003, while at Bramall Lane he took part in an F.A. Cup semi-final against Arsenal at Old Trafford and also in a Championship play-off final at Wembley against Wolves, albeit both games ended in defeat.

After leaving Blackburn at the age of 24, his fortunes tumbled dramatically. Over the next eight years his decline encompassed a spell without a club, having his contract cancelled by Queen's Park Rangers, putting in a couple of appearances for non-league Worcester City, and even a fifteen-month stretch in Australian football. Each move seemed to represent yet another step down a ladder he appeared to be heading to the very top of in his teenage years.

Aside from his fading on-field exploits, he acted as Notts County's under-16 coach from February 2008 to May 2010, and from June to December 2011 he was head coach and development manager of the Genova International School of Soccer in Northern Italy, an establishment which provides a pathway into European leagues for non-European nationals.

For a period of approximately four months beginning in October 2011, John Curtis was employed as West Bromwich Albion's senior Italian scout and in January 2012 he set up as a self-employed soccer coach/consultant with a view to helping young players find a way into professional football.

WALLWORK, Ronald (1994/95, 1995/96)

Born: Manchester, 10th September 1977
Height: 5ft. 10ins., Weight: 12st. 2lbs.
Role: Central defender or left full-back
Career: Briscoe Lane Primary School (Newton Heath)/ Manchester Boys/ Failsworth High School/ Oldham Boys/ Idsall School (Shropshire)/ England Boys/ UNITED: Ass. Schoolboy October 1991 Trainee July 1994 Pro. March 1995 to June 2002/ Carlisle United (L) December 1997 to February 1998/ Stockport County (L) March to May 1998/ Royal Antwerp (Bel) (L) January to May 1999/ West Bromwich Albion July 2002 to January 2008/ Bradford City (L) January and February 2004/ Bradford City (L) February and March 2004/ Barnsley (L) November and December 2006/ Huddersfield Town (L) September 2007 to January 2008/ Sheffield Wednesday January to June 2008

Ronnie Wallwork joined United's Centre of Excellence as a young boy after previously playing for his junior school. Initially selected for Manchester Boys when just twelve years-old, at the age of thirteen he took up with a local Sunday side called Newton Heath Juniors prior to progressing into the club's adult team around a year later. At that time he also represented Oldham Boys at under-15 level, his family having moved to Failsworth in the town's catchment area, and was soon offered a chance to attend the F.A. School of Excellence at Lilleshall in Shropshire.

He had firmly committed himself to the Reds some time earlier and as a consequence showed no interest in attending trials with any other clubs. Wallwork felt privileged to be selected for England Boys at the Faroe Islands-staged Nordic Cup competition in August 1993 and while there he took part in games against Denmark, Norway, Sweden and Finland.

During the 1993/94 campaign he participated in a further five games for England in their European (under-16) Championship Qualifiers. Taking to the field in home and away fixtures against Italy and Holland, alongside an engagement with the Republic of Ireland at Lilleshall, in April he was chosen for the tournament finals in Eire and gained selection for three of England's four group games versus the Ukraine, Portugal and the host nation.

He featured for United in the Northern Ireland Milk Cup in July 1994 and on the 13th of the following month found himself utilised in the 'B' team's 4-1 win at Liverpool. Wallwork continued at that grade for most of the season and at the end of November he was selected in central defence for a one-sided Youth Cup victory over Wrexham at Old Trafford. Retaining his place for the home draw with Charlton in December, he was overlooked for the replay but was put on the bench when United defeated Arsenal to progress into the Fifth Round.

The Mancunian was then drafted back into the side and he made a major contribution towards steering the Reds into the semi-final by scoring one of the goals in a scintillating 3-2 win at Villa Park. He remained in the team for the rest of the competition, with United accounting for Wimbledon at the last four stage and then going on to defeat a gallant Tottenham team in the final. As the penalty shoot-out unfolded in the concluding leg against Spurs, his conversion of the Reds' second spot kick went a long way towards ensuring the trophy was won 4-3 on penalties.

He continued to make progress and pick up silverware while the 1995/96 term unfolded. In early September, after completing only two 'A' team games, there was an early promotion in store when he was chosen for the Reserves against Liverpool at Anfield. A few more opportunities presented themselves during the campaign, but with Pat McGibbon, Chris Casper, David May and Colin Murdock all vying for places, competition was fierce.

Predominantly used in the 'A' team, and honoured with the captaincy throughout a Youth Cup run which was ended by Liverpool in the quarter-final, he found greater fortune in the Lancashire Youth Cup when skippering the Reds to a 3-2 victory at Blackburn on the last day of April. As the season unfolded he was selected for England's under-18 team on five occasions and by its conclusion United 'A' had captured the Lancashire League Division One title.

The 1996/97 term saw him become established in a second string that went on to secure a Pontin's Reserve League championship. He also contributed to the 'A' team's cause as they took their title for the second successive year while simultaneously demonstrating his versatility by contributing as much in defence as in midfield. With the campaign drawing to a close he was selected as a substitute for Brian McClair's testimonial match against Celtic and eventually got a run out when replacing Roy Keane.

Wallwork travelled to Malaysia with the England under-20 squad for the World Youth Championships in June 1997. Figuring in all three qualifying games against the Ivory Coast, the UAE and Mexico as England topped their group, a 2-1 defeat at the hands of Argentina saw them knocked out of the competition.

The following season provided him with a steep learning curve. Starting it with the Reserves, in the October his name appeared as a substitute for a Premier League game in which United acted as hosts to Barnsley. On the 64-minute mark, with the Reds comfortably up by six goals to nil, he replaced Gary Pallister to make his senior league bow before another goal concluded the score at 7-0.

In a bid to give him some additional first-team minutes, Alex Ferguson arranged a three-month loan spell at Carlisle which began in December. Back at base camp by the following February with ten league games behind him, after just one further appearance for the Reserves he linked up on loan with Stockport.

Those periods spent at Carlisle and Stockport provided him with much-needed experience and the process was repeated during the 1998/99 term. Tasked with assisting the Reserves over the opening half of the campaign before joining Antwerp in January, his efforts in trying to help them reach the Belgian First Division were soon thrown into turmoil when he and fellow Red Danny Higginbotham decided that the referee's decisions warranted some debate at the conclusion of one particular game.

An incident occurred which culminated with Wallwork manhandling the official, an act that resulted in him being banned from Belgian football for life. The sanction should have been ratified worldwide and looked set to end a promising career until United's lawyers uncovered a loophole that saved his fate. They discovered that because he was a registered British player, the defender came under the jurisdiction of Lancaster Gate and not the Belgian football authorities. The outcome was that his punishment could only be meted out by the English Football Association and so he received a suspension rather than a life ban.

In January 2000, just five months after thinking that his prospects were dead and buried, a remarkable recovery was completed at the World Club Championships in Brazil when he was included in a United side that took on South Melbourne. Even so, and despite being a consistent performer for the Reserves, over the next two and a half years he skirted around the fringe of Alex Ferguson's first-team squad while never really threatening to carve out a permanent place in the side.

At the end of the 2000/01 season, a Premier League winner's medal came into his possession by virtue of appearing in twelve games, eight of which were as a substitute. He only managed three games over the course of the next term and it was then when the stark realisation set in that a move was required in order to find first-team football. With his contract up and a number of clubs making approaches, including Portsmouth, West Brom, Birmingham, Dundee United and Bradford, his last game for United was at Altrincham's Moss Lane ground in the Reserves' 2-1 home defeat by Leeds in May 2002.

Following some deliberation he decided to join newly-promoted West Brom, whose opening fixture was against United at Old Trafford. After an encouraging initial period in which he established himself in an Albion side doomed to relegation, he then found it difficult to retain a starting place. In search of regular football, and despite West Brom heading for promotion again, he spent two loan spells at Bradford City in the early part of 2004. When Bryan Robson took over as the Baggies' boss in November 2004, Wallwork found himself back in contention and he repaid his new manager by finishing the campaign as Albion's 'Player of the Year'.

He was again a regular for West Brom in the 2005/06 season, but was in and out of the team under Tony Mowbray. Loaned out once more, this time to Barnsley, his spell in Yorkshire was curtailed when he was sensationally stabbed in a nightclub incident in Manchester.

The 2007/08 term proved to be his swan song as a footballer. Still unable to force his way into the Albion's senior side, he joined Huddersfield for a few months as a prelude to transferring to Sheffield Wednesday in the January. He failed to enhance his reputation at Hillsborough, by adding only seven appearances prior to being released in the summer, and then couldn't impress while on trial at Carlisle.

Ronnie Wallwork ran his own clothes business in Manchester over the next couple of years or so before being charged with concealing criminal property in January 2011. He pleaded guilty to three counts of handling stolen goods in July 2011 and was given a fifteen-month custodial sentence in the December of that year.

WILSON/GIGGS, Ryan Joseph
(1989/90, 1990/91, 1991/92)

Born: Canton, Cardiff, 29th November 1973

Height: 5ft. 11ins., **Weight:** 11st.

Role: Left-winger or forward

Career: Hwyell Dda Primary School (Ely)/ Grosvenor Road Primary School (Swinton)/ Ambrose Barlow High School (Swinton)/ Moorside High School (Swinton)/ Salford Boys/ Greater Manchester Boys/ England Boys/ UNITED: Ass. Schoolboy February 1988 Trainee July 1990 Pro. November 1990 to present

Described in a 2012 issue of a periodical as *'a walking milestone nowadays'*, Ryan Giggs has established records and achieved successes that will probably stand for generations, and some of them possibly forever.

When he signed for United as Ryan Wilson way back in 1988, little could anyone have guessed that twenty years later he would be required to perform an act that would write another glorious chapter in Manchester United's history.

The 2008 Champions League final took place on a soaked pitch in Moscow, where the Reds were battling it out with Chelsea for European supremacy, and with the game deadlocked at 1-1 and an additional half hour looming, Alex Ferguson sent him on in place of Wayne Rooney with only four minutes of normal time remaining. That development in itself was significant, because in joining the action the Welshman notched up his 759th appearance for the club and in doing so broke Sir Bobby Charlton's total which was set 35 years previously.

Charlton later commented, *'I have known Ryan since he was fifteen and he is just a credit to himself and the club. We are very proud of his achievements and if anyone was going to break my record, I am delighted that it was him.'* In an age when footballers rarely commit themselves to the same employer for very long, a squad system is utilised, fewer league games are played and numerous substitutes are allowed, such a marvellous spell of longevity speaks volumes for his skill and character.

Back in Moscow, with extra-time unable to separate the two teams, the game needed to be decided by a penalty shoot-out. The spot kick count stood at 5-5, both teams having missed one each, when Giggs stepped forward to take United's seventh attempt. Using all his experience to calmly place the ball in the bottom right-hand corner of the net, it proved the winning strike as Chelsea's Anelka then saw his penalty blocked by Edwin van der Sar and the Reds were crowned as champions of Europe for the third time.

Great triumph as that was, the modest Worsley resident had already become the most decorated player in the history of the British game and his collection of awards includes the following:

1992 – Rumbelows (League) Cup, European Super Cup, F.A. Youth Cup, PFA Young Player of the Year
1993 – Premier League, Charity Shield, PFA Young Player of the Year
1994 – Premier League, F.A. Cup, Charity Shield
1996 – Premier League, F.A. Cup, Charity Shield
1997 – Premier League, Charity Shield
1999 – Premier League, F.A. Cup, UEFA Champions League, Inter-Continental Cup
2000 – Premier League
2001 – Premier League
2003 – Premier League, Charity Shield
2004 – F.A. Cup
2006 – Carling (League) Cup
2007 – Premier League, Community Shield
2008 – Premier League, Community Shield, UEFA Champions League, FIFA Club World Cup
2009 – Premier League, Carling (League) Cup, PFA Player of the Year
2010 – Carling (League) Cup, Community Shield
2011 – Premier League

A League Cup winner at eighteen years-old, a Premier League champion at nineteen and party to an F.A. Cup final victory at twenty, together with 64 full caps for Wales, his exploits have entailed him criss-crossing the globe on football duty and in doing so he has met presidents and queens.

So where did it all begin?

Born in Cardiff's St. David's Hospital and growing up in Ely, a working class suburb to the west of the Welsh capital, in those early years much of his time was spent at his maternal grandparents' home in Pentrebane where he played football on the street outside. The son of a well known rugby union player, Wales captain Danny Wilson, the family moved to the Salford area when he was seven years-old because his father switched to the professional game and signed for Swinton RLFC. Missing family and friends and finding it difficult to settle at first, after losing his Welsh accent and watching his father in action at every opportunity, things gradually began to improve.

Such was his talent that the boy also represented Lancashire at rugby and it is quite feasible that he could have carved out a name for himself in the game before concentrating on football.

He became aware of his natural ability in the school playground where, upon receiving the ball on the wing, he found he could skip past opponents almost at will. By the age of about ten, while playing for Grosvenor Park in a local schoolboy match, his ability caught the eye of Dennis Schofield and he was asked to join Deans Youth, a club he was attached to until he was fourteen.

By the time he was in his early teens, Wilson had become the talk of local football circles and was selected to trial for Salford Boys. After making the final cut he was chosen to play in the Salford 'B' side and, netting six goals for them in an 8-1 victory, his reward was immediate elevation into the city's 'A' team.

He went on to establish himself as a regular for Salford Boys while also attending coaching sessions with the Manchester City-affiliated Junior Blues. Later recalling that his involvement came about *'because City were the only club in the area who did anything like that'*, the United follower also claimed he *'was never going to sign for them'* and often upset the Maine Road club's coaching staff at their Platt Lane complex by continually wearing a red shirt, despite all their warnings.

Another reason there was no chance of him joining City was because the man chaperoning the promising youngster to those sessions was Harold Wood, himself a United fan and chief steward at Old Trafford. Following a tip-off from Wood, Brian Kidd made it his business to see the prodigy in the

Then known as Wilson, the teenage future Ryan Giggs gets acquainted with an alternative sport while on a trip to the continent as a United junior

flesh and in December 1986, the teenager was watched by Alex Ferguson when attending a week-long trial at The Cliff. At the end of the assessment period, Salford were pitted against a United Youth XI and Wilson conjured up a hat-trick in their 4-3 victory. Ferguson viewed the proceedings through his office window and so, when Manchester City failed to follow up their initial interest, the manager took the opportunity to visit the lad's Swinton home along with Joe Brown in order to sign him on schoolboy terms just a few days after his fourteenth birthday.

He captained Salford to victory over Blackburn in the 1987 Granada Schools' Cup final, a game which was staged at Anfield, and the trophy was presented to him by Liverpool chief scout, Ron Yeats. Impressed by the boy's performance, Yeats would have recommended him to the Liverpool management had the wispy youngster not already been picked up by United.

Over the course of the 1988/89 schools' season, Wilson was one of the leading lights of a Salford side that also included future United trainees George Switzer and Ben Thornley. In their quest to capture the English Schools' Trophy, Salford defeated Manchester before drawing 1-1 at Islington in the quarter-final and were required to meet the southerners again for a replay staged at Broughton Lane.

Islington held out until the end of normal time, when Wilson changed the game in a way that millions have since watched him do under the name Giggs. The Manchester Evening News reported that he *'glided past two markers to crack home a fifteen-yard shot and then cleverly floated the ball over the goalkeeper's head to score the third goal'.*

The Salfordians faced Plymouth in the semi-final, with their talisman scoring three times in the opening 50 minutes to set up a comfortable 6-1 victory, and he was also present when they won 2-1 at St. Helens only to fall 2-0 in the second leg of the final at a virtually empty Old Trafford.

Qualifying for England Boys selection trials at Nottingham Polytechnic due to being educated in Greater Manchester, he captained the national schoolboy side nine times during the period that Salford were making progress in the English Schools' Trophy. England's campaign kicked off with one of his goals contributing towards a 5-0 Victory Shield win over Northern Ireland at Craigavon and subsequent successes against Belgium, at Wembley, France and Holland came prior to England suffering their first defeat of the term to Scotland at Old Trafford. Following another win, over Switzerland at Leeds, the winger found himself in an uncomfortable position when being required to sing the English national anthem in Swansea in the lead-up to their final Victory Shield match with Wales. The concluding two games saw a strong West Germany team defeat England 3-1 at Wembley before the home nation turned the tables with a 2-0 result in Birmingham a few days later. In the course of that last appearance for England, the skipper rattled in his fourth international goal and also fluffed a penalty.

In early August 1989, he helped the club's juniors to win the North-West Youth Tournament before competing in the 'A' team's 4-0 win over Bolton two weeks later. He was then included in the squad that won the Grossi-Morera Youth Tournament by beating Auxerre 4-1 in the final in mid-September, and it was while over in Italy that his colleagues discovered he had assumed his mother's maiden name following his parents' separation. However, his original name continued to be used until the end of the season when he could then re-register under a moniker that would become famous all over the world.

As a result of making an encouraging early impression, on the morning of the 23rd September, while still a pupil at high school, the fifteen year-old went on as a substitute for the 'A' team at The Cliff and then replaced Giuliano Maiorana in a 2-1 Central League home defeat by Everton that very afternoon. He made frequent appearances for the club's junior sides throughout the opening period of the 1989/90 campaign and scored against Burnley in his first Youth Cup tie in January. A satisfactory period of progress was marked by the under-18's reaching the Youth Cup semi-final and the club's third team clinching the Lancashire League Division One title by two points over Manchester City.

The 1990/91 term proved a very busy one for him. Giggs scored seven goals in as many 'A' and 'B' team matches, including four for the latter side at home to Carlisle in September, and was then reinstated in the Reserves for most of the campaign. He rifled four goals in a Youth Cup stroll at Darlington in December and went on to hit the back of the net in successive rounds at Everton, Liverpool and Southampton as the Reds reached the last four stage for the second consecutive year.

Three weeks prior to the game at The Dell, his meteoric rise culminated when he substituted for Denis Irwin in a 2-0 home First Division defeat by Everton. After appearing in the Youth Cup semi-final second leg in April, he was called into a Welsh Youth team that was defeated 1-0 at Wrexham by an England side containing a number of the lads who he had lined up alongside as a schoolboy two years previously.

That minor blip was soon put to one side when he scored the only goal of the game on his starting debut for United's seniors against Manchester City at Old Trafford. While Ferguson decided against including him in the squad for the European Cup Winners' Cup final with Barcelona eleven days later, a hectic end to the season concluded when he took part in the Blue Stars Tournament in Switzerland and then put in a couple of appearances for Wales Youth and one for the Welsh under-21 side.

A player with an almost faultless temperament, superb balance, a penchant for chipping in with a goal or two, wonderful dribbling skills, a phenomenal burst of speed and a winning frame of mind, those traits alone would almost certainly have seen him established as a first-team star. However, it is his willingness to track back on defensive duties and shed sweat on behalf of the team cause that has equally endeared him to Ferguson and the Old Trafford faithful over the years.

Those numerous attributes helped to gain him a foothold in Ferguson's side in the 1991/92 campaign, a period in which his career gathered further pace with Rumbelows Cup, international and PFA honours. Also a term in which he contributed towards the young Reds' achievement in bringing the Youth Cup back to M16 for the first time in 28 years, it was he who famously bridged that gap when hoisting a trophy held dear by United supporters and last claimed on behalf of the club by Bobby Noble in 1964.

Further triumphs followed, with a Premiership title in 1993 and league and F.A. Cup doubles in 1994 and 1996. It has been a career studded with unforgettable moments on the pitch, none more so than in 1999 during the last-ever F.A. Cup semi-final replay, when he conjured up an astonishing winner by running directly at the heart of an Arsenal defence hailed as the best in the game. Bursting past four opponents prior to unleashing a fierce shot into the roof of the Gunners' net, there were those who proclaimed it the greatest goal of all time, and many United fans feel it gave the team the confidence and impetus they required to go on and win an unprecedented trio of major trophies.

Having made his first full international appearance against West Germany in 1991, and in doing so becoming the youngest ever debutant for Wales, Giggs was installed as his country's captain in 2004. During one of their matches, in September 2006, the Welsh took on Brazil in a friendly at White Hart Lane and such was his display that Dunga, the South American side's coach, paid him a compliment when stating that he wouldn't have looked out of place by playing for the five-time world champions alongside those such as Kaká and Ronaldinho. Announcing his retirement from international football in May 2007 at a press conference held at the Vale of Glamorgan Hotel, it brought the curtain down on a sixteen-year term in the international arena. His last game for Wales, as skipper, was in a Euro 2008 Qualifier against the Czech Republic in Cardiff that June.

He has been the recipient of numerous other awards, including 'BBC Wales Sports Personality of the Year' in 1996, 'Wales Player of the Year' for 1996 and 2006 and 'Inter-Continental Cup Man of the Match' in 1999, as well as being included in the 'Premiership Team of the Decade' in 2003, 'PFA Team of the Century' in 2007 and inducted into the English Hall of Fame in 2005. Additionally awarded an OBE in 2007, an honorary Master of Arts degree from Salford University in 2008 and bestowed with numerous 'PFA Team of the Year' inclusions and monthly awards, his association with the premier English knock-out tournament was acknowledged when he was named in the 'F.A. Cup Team of the Century'.

Now holding the record appearances tally for United with an aggregate total of over 900, he is the only person to have scored in twelve successive Champions League tournaments and has also registered at least one goal in each and every Premier League campaign since the division was rebranded in 1992.

Chosen by his contemporaries as the 'PFA Player of the Year' and a wider television-watching public as the 'BBC Sports Personality of the Year' in 2009, despite United winning two major trophies that year, the sour taste of defeat in the Champions League final at the hands of Barcelona rankled and caused him to claim, *'Next year we will come back stronger and look forward to the challenge.'*

He was awarded the Freedom of the City of Salford at a ceremony at the Lowry in January 2010 and exactly twelve months later found himself voted as the greatest ever Manchester United player. Yet another landmark followed that year when he was honoured with the 2011 'Golden Foot' award. His prediction regarding a return to the Champions League final was only out by twelve months, when the Reds once again had to deal with a loss at Wembley where Barcelona's midfield of Xaxi, Iniesta and Messi proved too strong.

Away from the pitch, Ryan Giggs champions campaigns such as 'Kicking Racism out of Football' and the UNICEF landmine cause. He has also been involved with the 'Five Star Scanner Appeal', an organisation that raises money for cancer research and treatment for children.

When asked how he would like to be remembered, and in tribute to the city he has known as home since being a young boy, the answer came back, *'It would be someone who grew up in Salford, died in Salford and excited people at Old Trafford, near Salford.'*

Chapter Seven

GLOBAL STRATEGY

1998-99

Manchester United		Everton	
1) Paul Rachubka	9) Paul Wheatcroft	1) Dean Delany	9) Carl Howarth
2) Mark Lynch	10) Ian Fitzpatrick	2) John Wright	10) Francis Jeffers
3) Kirk Hilton	11) Luke Chadwick	3) George Pilkington	11) Kevin McLeod
4) Lee Roche	*12) Dominic Studley*	4) David Knowles	*12) Gary Dempsey (for 9)*
5) John O'Shea	*13) Allan Marsh GK*	5) Peter Clarke	*14) Damien Logan*
6) George Clegg	*14) Stephen Cosgrove (for 6)*	6) Tony Hibbert	*15) Joe McAlpine (for 11)*
7) Wayne Evans	*15) Danny Webber*	7) Keith Southern	*16) Matt McKay (for 8)*
8) Michael Stewart	*16) Jimmy Davis*	8) Leon Osman	*17) Eddie O'Brien*

DECEMBER 1998

MANCHESTER UNITED*   2 v 2   EVERTON

Chadwick (2)   Hibbert, Jeffers

Saturday 19th

Kick-off 2.00 p.m.

Attendance 271

* Played at Gigg Lane, Bury

third round

Red kids live to fight again

When the team bus carrying a party of United players who were eager to do Youth Cup battle with Everton rolled up at Gigg Lane in the later days of 1998, Eric Harrison wasn't one of the passengers. Having reached the age of 60 earlier in the year, Harrison decided to retract from the day-to-day involvement in the game that had kept him in gainful employment for all of his adult life.

During his time in charge of various under-18 squads, the Reds had taken part in 87 Youth Cup matches and he was missing from only one of them, at Southampton in March 1991, due to illness. Within that period Harrison made a major contribution in shaping the careers of countless hopefuls who went on to serve the club and, in a wider sense, the sport, with great distinction.

He had, of course, been involved in five Youth Cup finals, winning two of them, and also managed to steer his boys to a couple of semi-finals in addition to quarter-final appearances in 1983, 1989 and 1996. There were a few disappointments, as well as a couple of disasters, although they mainly came about at times when the club's reservoir of teenage talent had almost evaporated.

Overall, it was a record Harrison could be extremely proud of and his input towards the grooming of potential stars, some of whom developed into world class performers, was unanimously praised when it was announced he was leaving his position. While those such as Bobby Charlton and Alex Ferguson were quick to express their gratitude for his efforts and speak of their admiration of the coach's value over the last couple of decades, commendations for his work on the training pitch were also heard from many of the footballers whose careers were shaped from the common sense principles and high standards preached by the Yorkshireman during their adolescent years.

There have been innumerable occasions over the years where a team has lost a cup tie they should have won at a canter and, indeed, one or two of Harrison's youth sides had sometimes been the beneficiaries and victims of such outcomes.

The game against Everton in December 1998 was a typical case in point. Staged at Bury's ground due to the precarious state of the Old Trafford pitch, the Reds had only themselves to blame for not making progress at the expense of the Merseyside Blues at the first time of asking. While they never totally dominated the match, the young United certainly held the balance of possession and they spent long enough in Everton's half of the pitch to have made absolutely certain of their passage to the next round.

Once it was decided not to stage the tie at Old Trafford, Gigg Lane became the obvious choice of venue because United's Reserves had contested their home matches there for a number of seasons. Much more controversial than the choice of stadium was the decision to coincide the fixture on the same afternoon that the senior side were in action at home to Middlesbrough. Without the presence of the club's hardcore of youth team followers to support them, the clash of fixtures means that the attendance is ranked as one of the lowest in United's seven-decade participation in the competition.

Due to a change in the Football Association's rules, the Reds' opening tie was now at the Third Round stage of the competition. The last occasion they had entered the tournament at anything other than the Second Round was as far back as September 1961 when, coincidentally, they faced Everton in the Preliminary Round.

As is usual, new United youth coach Dave Williams looked to the more experienced members of his side in order to assist the newcomers in bedding into the team. Nevertheless, the five-times capped Wales international and

Paul Wheatcroft evades a challenge during United's draw with Everton at Gigg Lane

426

1998-99

DECEMBER 1998

third round

Pictured (l-r) George Clegg, Michael Stewart, Wayne Evans and Luke Chadwick form a defensive wall as Everton prepare to take a free kick

former Bristol Rovers, Norwich and Bournemouth midfielder would have reminded all the squad of the enormity of the task ahead because Everton were still able to field four of the team who had lifted the Youth Cup earlier that year, namely Francis Jeffers, Dean Delany, Leon Osman and Tony Hibbert.

The tie was evenly balanced in the early minutes, with just a couple of hopeful crosses for the respective 'keepers to see to, and the action started in earnest following the opening of the heavens bang on the quarter-hour mark when a Hibbert free kick for the visitors was meekly headed into Paul Rachubka's hands by Keith Southern.

In the 20th minute, an excellent ball from George Clegg helped to put the Reds ahead. Luke Chadwick gathered Clegg's pass on the left-hand touchline prior to cutting a track along the border of Everton's eighteen-yard area and, after leaving a couple of defenders for dead, he unleashed a great shot into the corner of Delany's net.

Five minutes later, Chadwick's hero status turned sour when the winger lost possession in a dangerous defensive area. The ball ended up at the feet of Jeffers and in a one-to-one with Rachubka, the unfazed Evertonian striker placed it under the diving goalkeeper to level the scores.

After Everton's Carl Howarth was cautioned for a foul on Clegg, the visitors took the lead in the 32nd minute. Coming at a time when United were firming up their grip on the match, the goal was a real body blow. Hibbert's long-range scorcher seemed to arrive out of nowhere but, as the ball flew like a bullet into the top right-hand corner of United's net, it was enough to give his side the lead come half-time.

The quality of the Reds' performance went up a number of levels following Williams' gee-up and an improvement could be seen immediately from the restart through slicker passing and greater co-ordination. There was also a higher degree of commitment from some of the United lads, one or two of whom were more or less anonymous previously. The increased determination was further evidenced when Clegg was booked for a foul seven minutes into the second period, and the next incident of note nearly resulted in a goal for the Reds just four minutes further on.

When set free in Everton's penalty area, Chadwick cleverly dribbled past the exposed Delany before appearing to lose his balance slightly. An unguarded net beckoned, only for Chadwick to be tackled by stocky Blues' defender John Wright before he was given the chance to recover.

In the 65th minute, Chadwick was again United's main source of inspiration when some nice interplay eighteen yards from goal resulted in him being released at speed. The winger did well to control the ball while in full flight, and his momentum thrust him into some space whereupon he calmly stroked a right-foot shot into the rigging to make it 2-2.

Everton then made two substitutions before Wright, the full-back who had been given a roasting all afternoon by Chadwick, finally fouled his tormentor once too often and was booked.

With just under twenty minutes left, an inviting centre by United's Wayne Evans was met by Paul Wheatcroft, whose acrobatic attempt on goal was brilliantly stopped by Delany. The Reds probed relentlessly for a winner from then until the final whistle, though the cup holders wouldn't readily release their grasp on the trophy. There was certainly little for anyone to complain about United's performance since the start of the second half, even though a mountain of pressure actually translated into a mere molehill of chances.

Just before the 90 minutes were totally spent, there was a great opportunity to avoid the necessity of a rematch when a searching centre into Everton's box was met full on by Wheatcroft. His header appeared to have a 'winning goal' label attached to it until Delany performed more heroics by leaping to fingertip the ball onto a post. While both blue and red-shirted players alike stood and watched as if they were waiting for a cue, it trickled back along the goal-line and into the grateful arms of a relieved 'keeper.

/ 1999-00

1) Ben Williams	9) Danny Webber	1) Barry Roche	9) Andy Reid
2) Mark Lynch	10) Jimmy Davis	2) Niall Hudson	10) Matt Turner
3) Mark Studley	11) Neil Wood	3) Keith Foy	11) Niall McNamara
4) Gareth Strange	*12) Ashley Dodd*	4) David Prutton	*12) Martin Kearney GK*
5) Marek Szmid	*13) Alan Tate*	5) John Thompson	*14) Robert Gill (for 7)*
6) Josh Walker	*14) Danny Pugh*	6) Jermaine Jenas	*15) Ben Sherwood*
7) Ben Muirhead	*15) Daniel Nardiello (for 6)*	7) Brian Cash	*16) Richard Dell*
8) Michael Rose	*16) Gary Sampson*	8) Gareth Williams	*17) Nicky Carter*

DECEMBER 1999

MANCHESTER UNITED* 1 v 2 NOTTINGHAM FOREST

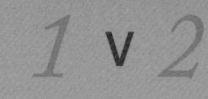

Webber   Jenas, Reid

Thursday 2nd

Kick-off 7.00 p.m.

Attendance 210

* Played at Gigg Lane, Bury

third round

The side that United's youth coach Dave Williams fielded for the home Third Round tie against Nottingham Forest at Gigg Lane in December 1999 was notable as being the most inexperienced eleven ever to represent Manchester United in the Youth Cup.

Apart from Danny Webber, who gained just 45 minutes as a substitute against Everton at Goodison Park during the previous campaign, and Mark Lynch, who played a part in both games against the Toffees, the remaining nine starters were completely untested in the competition.

There was a continuing strong mix of locals amongst United's teenage intake. Between the sticks for the Reds stood Ben Williams and he, along with the aforementioned Webber and Lynch, was joined by Mark Studley and Neil Wood, all five of whom originated from Manchester. Michael Rose was a Salfordian while Gareth Strange counted as the latest in a growing list of discoveries from the fruitful acres of the Bolton locality.

Midlanders were three-fold in the Reds' line-up. An accomplished midfielder who had represented England at schoolboy level, Marek Szmid was a Nuneaton lad whereas midfielder Josh Walker came from Sutton Coldfield and forward Jimmy Davis lived at nearby Redditch. Making up the eleven was Ben Muirhead, a dashing winger who originated from Doncaster.

In contrast, Forest were able to name a number of personnel whose efforts took them as far as the quarter-finals during their last assault on the Youth Cup, a fine run which came to an end when they lost 3-2 at home to Newcastle. Included in Forest's ranks was England Youth defender Jermaine Jenas and he lined up with David Prutton, a current first-teamer who had, that very week, signed an extension to his contract with the club. The Nottingham boys were well supported by the City Ground powers that be, as ex-United youth team player and current Forest manager David Platt, assistant manager Steve Wigley, and the club's major benefactor, Nigel Doughty, were all present at the game.

If ever the conditions dictated that a football match should be devoid of any entertainment value, this was it.

From a charcoal-coloured sky, and accompanied by a wind that must have bordered on the gale force scale, rain positively cascaded down for hours before and all throughout the 90 minutes. The weather even posed the possibility of the game's postponement until the all-clear was given a couple of hours prior to kick-off.

Fortunately for the tiny band of die-hards dotted around Gigg Lane's Main Stand, the football didn't mirror the prevailing conditions and they were witness to a match of top quality which contained some marvellous individual performances.

The tie began with plenty of huff and puff from both sides, and the ball wasn't allowed to stray too far from the middle of the pitch while the players adjusted to the soggy state of the surface.

In only the eighth minute, Forest gained a somewhat lucky advantage when an Andy Reid shot nicked off an opponent, the ball skidding along the sodden turf and underneath 'keeper Williams. Two minutes later, the Reds rode their luck after a mazy dribble from Brian Cash took him to the outskirts of United's penalty box from where his bending drive powered through the rain before rattling the crossbar.

The Reds' best chance of a result appeared to lie in the twin attacking force of Webber and Davis. Both were able to put their pace to good use and in turn they created goalscoring opportunities which were thwarted by Barry Roche in the Forest goal. It was in midfield where United's real problems lay, with Nottingham's Prutton and Williams constantly catching the eye, and the determined duo demonstrated much more skill and force than anything produced in the engine room of the home side.

As the half progressed, it was clear that the City Ground kids carried the overall greater class and experience while most of the United lads appeared tentative, lacking confidence and in one or two cases even a shade or two overwhelmed. If there were any positives to be found, it was that the Reds kept their aspirations alive through sheer hard work and occasional threats posed by their front two.

Eleven minutes into the second period, United's prospects took a dramatic tumble when Forest forged further in front. A free kick awarded way out on the right was taken by goalscorer Reid and as a static defence stood and watched, the unmarked Jenas leapt to connect with his head and the ball was in the back of Williams' net for goal number two. With just over half an hour to go, it now seemed as though a miracle of biblical proportions was required to save the Reds from defeat.

To the credit of the United boys, the further setback jolted them into their best spell of the game and only a minute or so went by when a shot from Michael Rose whizzed inches wide of the target.

Further pressure followed from United, but the clear-cut openings they badly required proved elusive. With just six minutes remaining, Forest's John Thompson handed the Reds a lifeline when he fiddled and fluttered in a defensive situation, and in carelessly giving away possession he allowed Danny Webber to profit by hammering home a fierce drive.

Two fatigued teams then fought out a frantic last few minutes, only the opportunity of an equaliser never presented itself to the Reds.

Several minutes after the match, Forest's Academy director Paul Hart was clearly elated when saying of his side, *'We were very tired towards the end but we kept our shape and our composure and came through with flying colours. The game was played in dreadful conditions but the pitch stood up to it very well indeed. It played magnificently and luckily we were able to see the game through to a conclusion.'*

Forest's nerves were undoubtedly settled by an early goal described by the Nottingham Post as *'fortunate'*, and the Manchester Evening News responded with a view about the Reds being *'forced to chase the game'* from then on.

For United, the defeat represented a third consecutive exit at the opening stage of the competition, and the glories that the Youth Cup had brought to the club through the early to mid-1990's were now beginning to seem like something of a distant memory.

Of the members of the side who participated against Forest, almost half of them would soon fast-track into football obscurity with Studley, Walker, Strange, Rose and Szmid all released within eighteen months.

In common with most of his colleagues, Josh Walker struggled to make an impact in the Reds' defeat to a lively Forest side

430

1999-00

DECEMBER 1999

Skipper Marek Szmid (left) and Mark Lynch (right) give chase while Ben Muirhead (behind) watches on

Szmid puts in a crunching tackle on Forest playmaker Andy Reid

third round

431

2000-01

1) Simon Cox	9) Joey Alcott	1) James Jowsey	9) Daniel Nardiello
2) Craig Brown	10) Scott Williams	2) Steven Clegg	10) Neil Wood
3) Michael Tonna	11) Alex Stanley	3) Kris Taylor	11) John Rankin
4) Matt Birnie	*12) Stuart Kurton (for 8)*	4) Gary Sampson	*12) Andy Taylor (for 11)*
5) Declan O'Hara	*13) Mark Brown GK*	5) Alan Tate	*13) Nick Baxter GK (for 1)*
6) Ricky Allaway	*14) Tom Hodgkiss (for 11)*	6) Paul Tierney	*14) Marc Whiteman (for 12)*
7) Adam Campion	*15) Adam Theo*	7) Ben Muirhead	*15) Chris Humphreys*
8) Mark Boddy	*16) Gary Middleton*	8) Matty Williams	*16) David Fox*

NOVEMBER 2000

READING 0 v 1 MANCHESTER UNITED
Nardiello

Wednesday 29th
Kick-off 7.45 p.m.
Attendance 8,894

third round

Twelve months further on from United's worst ever Youth Cup sequence, Dave Williams accompanied a squad to Berkshire where the teenage Reds were due to pit their attributes against those of Reading at their superb Madejski Stadium.

It was, of course, a first meeting between the two clubs in the tournament and, with a 6-0 away win over Bristol Rovers in the last round to cheer, the home supporters were full of the expectation that their youngsters would be able to pull off a giant killing act over illustrious adversaries. As a thoughtful exercise in public relations, Reading gave away hundreds of free tickets to local schoolchildren and that gesture, allied to the advanced publicity surrounding the match, ensured a competition record crowd for the club.

Williams' side was again lacking in suitable tournament experience because only Ben Muirhead and Neil Wood had undertaken the full 90 minutes against Nottingham Forest a year ago whereas Coventry-born striker Daniel Nardiello made a substitute appearance at Gigg Lane. Two of the unused substitutes from that game, Easington boy Alan Tate and Mancunian Gary Sampson, were in from the start this time around and the former was given the responsibility of leading the team.

Defender Steven Clegg, from Ashton-under-Lyne, and midfielder Paul Tierney, a Salford lad, completed the local representation while Matty Williams, who was to partner Nardiello in the quest for goals, hailed from North Wales. Gritty competitor Kris Taylor had been secured from Wolves, and forming the last line of defence was James Jowsey, a goalkeeping prospect so highly regarded that the club had been prepared to shell out £200,000 to Scarborough for his services.

The Reading team contained a couple of promising international youth players. Goalkeeper Simon Cox, who was included against the Reds despite recently having nine stitches inserted in his left knee, represented the Republic of Ireland at under-18 level while Declan O'Hara was the current captain of Northern Ireland's youth side.

Commenting on how he intended to approach United's visit in the match programme, Royals' coach Kevin Dillon revealed, 'We have decided to prepare for tonight's match in the same way that we did for the trip to Rovers, with a training session at Sonning followed by a pre-match meal back at the stadium and a video for the players to watch. There will also be a chance for us to have a chat about Manchester United with the tactics board because we had them watched last week, then it will be time to go downstairs and get ready for the game.'

In conditions which were almost opposite to the ones experienced against Forest a year ago, those at Reading were practically perfect and a flat, manicured surface along with a dry, almost breezeless evening boded well for a side prepared to persevere with cultured football.

The Royals kicked-off and made their attacking intentions apparent as early as the third minute when Scott Williams centred for Joey Alcott to head weakly into the hands of Jowsey.

The proceedings were then held up for a time from the sixth minute onwards because of a nasty head injury to United's John Rankin. After receiving some fairly lengthy treatment on the field, the concussed midfielder was assisted onto a motorised buggy and transported to the dressing room for even more attention. It was obvious that the Bellshill-born youngster could take no further part in the game and so Dave Williams sent on Andy Taylor as a replacement.

James Jowsey takes a catch as Paul Tierney (number six) helps out. Meanwhile, Neil Wood (far left) and Alan Tate (right of Wood) look on

2000-01

NOVEMBER 2000

Just after the delay, Matty Williams came near to opening the scoring by outpacing Reading's defence in a chase for a long punt and he was only denied by the quick thinking of 'keeper Cox, who sensed the danger just in the nick of time to fractionally beat the striker in pursuit of the ball.

With the midway point of the opening half approaching, the Reds' most eye-catching individual, winger Ben Muirhead, featured in a promising move. When a Reading attack broke down in an advanced position, Jowsey quickly threw him the ball and Muirhead, who was lurking near to the halfway line, carried possession at lightning speed towards the home side's penalty area. His squared pass was cleared out of play by a quick-thinking defender and from the resulting corner, Muirhead himself glanced a header over the bar when he could just as easily have hit the target.

There was a discomforting sight for the large crowd on 32 minutes when the injured Rankin was transported around the perimeter track to a waiting ambulance which was stationed in one of the corner tunnels. Unable to receive the attention he required at the ground, United's medical staff decided that he should be transferred to a local hospital as a precautionary measure.

Later the recipient of a neat pass from Wood, Muirhead scorned another opening by driving a powerful shot three feet over the Royals' bar. A minute later it was Reading's turn to almost break the deadlock, Adam Campion's corner kick curling menacingly towards the Reds' goalmouth, and with Jowsey, Tate and Tierney all rooted to the line, the ball slapped against the crossbar prior to being scrambled away to safety.

Reading ended the opening section of the game on a high note when Williams produced a smart piece of trickery which opened up enough space for him to hammer in a left-foot effort that was well blocked by Jowsey. It was practically the last task Jowsey was required to perform as he was carrying a knock and Nick Baxter took over the gloves for the second half.

The Reds resumed with Tierney blazing the ball over the woodwork just after the restart and Muirhead soon found himself stopped by a finely timed tackle by opposing captain Ricky Allaway. Cox later saved at the feet of Muirhead and Nardiello then had a goal disallowed after a push on a defender, the Royals responding in kind when O'Hara went close with a header that flashed just wide.

In the last 60 seconds of normal time, O'Hara was a fraction away from connecting with a corner which would surely have delivered the desired victory for the home side. However, with most spectators in agreement about the evenness of the two teams, the major incident of note was still two minutes away.

Catastrophe struck for Reading in time added on after Tate launched a free kick from deep inside United's half. As the ball dropped from a great height, O'Hara hesitated momentarily and it reached Nardiello. The Reds' number nine initially failed to gain proper control, but once he got the ball out of his feet his instincts pointed him towards goal. Despite defenders situated in close proximity to his left and right, Nardiello appeared the calmest person in the ground as he nudged the ball home to claim the Reds' latest of late winners.

One lapse in concentration proved expensive for the home side and the circumstances were such that they would probably have kept the Reading players awake with nightmares. Royals' youth team boss Dillon summarised the feelings of the home camp by complaining, *'We just went to sleep and it's cost us.'*

third round

Despite the unwanted attention of Reading's Joey Alcott, Kris Taylor attempts to keep things moving in United's midfield

2000-01

1) David Moran	9) Daniel Nardiello	1) Neil Collins	9) Andy Parton
2) Steven Clegg	10) Neil Wood	2) Matt Baxter	10) Dave Burraway
3) Danny Pugh	11) John Rankin	3) Steve Ridley	11) Danny Mulchinock
4) Gary Sampson	12) Craig Coates (for 8)	4) Andy Butler	12) Stuart Preston (for 8)
5) Alan Tate	13) Tom Heaton GK	5) Jamie McCombe	13) Gavin Chapman GK (for 1)
6) Paul Tierney	14) Kris Taylor	6) Danny Masson	14) Kirk Shrimpton
7) Ben Muirhead	15) David Fox (for 4)	7) Scott Brough	15) Richard Hawcroft
8) Matty Williams	16) Chris Humphreys (for 9)	8) Terry Barwick	16) Sean Singh (for 5)

MANCHESTER UNITED 8 v 0 **SCUNTHORPE UNITED**
Butler (o.g.), Nardiello (4), Rankin, Williams, Wood

JANUARY 2001

Monday 22nd*
Kick-off 7.00 p.m.
Attendance 2,357

fourth round

REDS SEND IN THE CLONES

"We measure success by getting players through to the first-team and after that by making a career for a player who can make money for the club on a sale, like Danny Higginbotham, John Curtis or David Healy. Our target is to get them into the first-team and we will only do that if they can do the things that the first-team players have to do.

The standards are exceptionally high, so there are not a great number who are actually capable of going through, after three of four years, to our first-team. But we hope we can give them a good education, a good grounding, good technique and understanding of the game."

DAVE WILLIAMS

Following a couple of postponements over at Gigg Lane, it was finally decided that the Fourth Round home tie against Scunthorpe would be staged at Old Trafford. Due to United's increased usage of their pitch, caused through a regular involvement in European competition, it had now been over three years since a Youth Cup tie was seen there. For most of Dave Williams' side, it provided a first chance to show off their skills in the club's stadium and, besides looking forward to the opportunity, they were also determined to make it an occasion to remember.

In terms of United's line-up, a unique feature was the selection of two entirely new goalies. James Jowsey hadn't recovered from his injury at Reading, so he was replaced by David Moran, and Tom Heaton found himself accorded the substitute 'keeper's job at the expense of Nick Baxter. Other than that, the only change was for Danny Pugh to be brought in at number three for bench-bound Kris Taylor while John Rankin reclaimed his place after recovering from the blow to his head at the Madejski Stadium.

The contest actually represented a maiden competitive meeting between the clubs at any level. The visitors brought approximately 200 supporters, a couple of directors and three journalists to taste the atmosphere, and one of those scribes penned a piece in the Scunthorpe Telegraph below a 'THEATRE OF NIGHTMARES' banner which spelled a stark outcome for the Lincolnshire juniors:

It was supposed to be a glory night as Scunthorpe United made their first appearance at the Theatre of Dreams – but it quickly turned into a nightmare.

The Iron Juniors were never expected to win at Old Trafford against a home side packed full of future stars whose passing and movement were a joy to watch.

But even the thrill of appearing in England's premier club stadium was soured by the manner of this defeat, with the eventual eight-goal deficit including four catastrophic individual howlers.

Manchester United were awesome in the first half, their under-18's a mirror image of the way the first-team play under the guidance of Sir Alex Ferguson.

All the players supported each other, they snapped into challenges to win the ball back on the rare occasions they lost it and there was breathtaking pace and skill throughout the team.

The names might not mean much now but the sizeable Scunthorpe contingent in the 2,000 plus crowd may have had their first glimpse of tomorrow's household names. Left-back Danny Pugh has already played for the Reds' Reserves while centre-back Alan Tate, the captain with more than a touch of Nicky Butt about him, impressed throughout.

Going forward they had far too much pace for the Iron defence. John Rankin was excellent, Ben Muirhead exciting on the right and the front two of Matthew Williams and Daniel Nardiello linked and moved superbly. Nardiello – son of ex-Coventry player Don – ended up with four goals though in truth three were gifted to him, including two in the opening 38 minutes' six-goal blast.

5 minutes: Rankin lifts the ball over a static defence allowing Williams to run clean through from what looked to be an offside position and scuff a shot across Neil Collins and in off the post.

20 minutes: A flick from Williams puts Rankin in on the left and he drills a low cross along the six-yard line where Scunthorpe central defender Andy Butler inadvertently slices a thunderbolt into the top corner of his own net.

28 minutes: Rankin unleashes a 30-yard fizzer into the bottom corner for the goal of the game.

33 minutes: An overhit cross from Muirhead is spectacularly volleyed goalwards by Nardiello but squirms under the body of Collins.

35 minutes: Pugh gallops clear on the left and pulls it back to Neil Wood whose effort is well saved by Collins before the same player cracks in the rebound.

38 minutes: Another long pass puts Nardiello away on the left but his low shot unbelievably again goes straight through the unhappy United 'keeper.

Half-time, Manchester were 6-0 up from just six shots on target (after 35 minutes, they had been 4-0 up from just three!). Scunthorpe, meanwhile, had seen Andy Parton sky a seventh minute half-chance six yards out, Jamie McCombe glance a header wide from a free kick and Butler have the ball in the net only for the referee to disallow it for a clear foul on the 'keeper.

Mercifully, the home side eased off after the break for a while but the warnings were still there when a wonderful one-two between Pugh and Williams saw the former drill a shot across the face of goal and inches wide.

On 64 minutes, Nardiello turned home a Muirhead cross to complete his hat-trick and added his fourth on 66 minutes with a low shot that Collins made another complete hash of.

That was the inconsolable Collins' last action as he signalled for his own substitution, apparently because of a shoulder injury, and headed for the tunnel.

Gavin Chapman got thrown into the deep end and managed to keep a clean sheet in front of an empty Stretford End – without actually making a save.

Muirhead chipped a good chance over, Butler rescued his 'keeper with a

Daniel Nardiello tormented Scunthorpe with a superb personal tally of four goals

This game was due to be played at Gigg Lane on Tuesday, January 9th and then again on Wednesday, January 17th but was postponed on both occasions due to a waterlogged pitch

2000-01

JANUARY 2001

fourth round

Goalkeeper David Moran (centre) stays on his toes while Alan Tate (number five) keeps Scunthorpe at bay with a clearing header

goal-line clearance and Danny Masson did likewise to deny Muirhead again after uncertainty between Chapman and Steve Ridley. To add to the Iron's woes, key midfielder Terry Barwick was stretchered off and skipper McCombe limped off.

It was a shame that so many of the Scunthorpe youngsters froze on the big stage but they still have the honour of appearances both at Wembley and Old Trafford in the last nine months to treasure forever.

The Manchester Evening News' Stuart Brennan added the following humorous comments as part of his match report:

The mad scientists working on the first human clone are too late.......Manchester United have already perfected it. In Dr. Fergenstein's football labs, deep in the bowels of Castle Carrington, the fiendish Reds are busy moulding new young footballers in the likeness of the all-conquering first-team.

It's all part of a masterplan aimed at world domination. And the latest creations announced themselves last night with a monstrous 8-0 mutilation of poor Scunthorpe. The performance of David Williams' youth team had all the Red hallmarks – it was easy to imagine you were seeing raw copies of the outstanding first-team out on the Old Trafford turf.

The same neat 4-4-2 formation, the same pass-and-move philosophy, the same work ethic, the same team effort – and oodles of individual talent to set it all off.

Sir Alex watched from the stands, and what he saw represented what may prove to be his greatest legacy to United – and to English football.

The glories of the last ten years will live with United fans forever, but the Reds cannot afford to revel in such memories. And the youth set-up at Old Trafford, revamped and revolutionised by Fergie and his staff, will remain a key element.

The boss insists that anyone who pulls on that red shirt, from under-11 upwards, plays in the style of the first-team. Winning is not all-important at this level. Performance and experience are all, but to win well in the F.A. Youth Cup is always satisfying.

2001-02

1) Matt Ramsey	9) Dennis Oli	1) James Jowsey	9) Colin Heath
2) Irvin Alexander	10) Brian Fitzgerald	2) Lee Sims	10) Darren Fletcher
3) Sam Scully	11) Kerry Butler	3) Lee Lawrence	11) Kieran Richardson
4) Marcus Bean	12) *Martyn Williams (for 11)*	4) David Fox	12) *Kalam Mooniaruck (for 7)*
5) David Wattley	13) *Jake Cole GK*	5) John Cogger	13) *Tommy Lee GK*
6) Marien Ifura	14) *Chris Mills (for 5)*	6) Phil Bardsley	14) *Eddie Johnson (for 8)*
7) Dean Lodge	15) *Daniel Lewis (for 7)*	7) Mads Timm	15) *Ben Collett (for 11)*
8) Wes Daly		8) Chris Humphreys	16) *David Jones*

DECEMBER 2001

QUEEN'S PARK RANGERS 1 v 3 MANCHESTER UNITED

Lodge   Heath (2), Timm

third round

Tuesday 4th

Kick-off 7.00 p.m.

Attendance 2,330

None of the squad members who Dave Williams assembled for the opening tie of the 2001/02 campaign had even been born the last time United took on Queen's Park Rangers in the Youth Cup back in 1983. Williams was again required to put together a practically new team because only James Jowsey had started a game in the competition before, while the experience gained by Chris Humphreys, Colin Heath and skipper David Fox amounted merely to substitute appearances.

However, the majority of the team were regulars in the under-17 Academy League during the 2000/01 season, meaning that some form of understanding of each others play would have existed between them, though whether that knowledge was deep enough to carry them far in the national knock-out competition was a matter of conjecture and remained to be seen.

For the tie at Loftus Road, the full-back positions were taken by Lee Sims (Manchester) and the lightning fast Lee Lawrence (Wigan), while in the centre of the defence John Cogger (Sunderland) was assisted by Phil Bardsley (Salford). In midfield, the Stoke-born, Devon-raised Fox was flanked on the right by the workaholic Darren Fletcher (Edinburgh) and on the left by the exceptionally gifted Kieran Richardson (Greenwich). Most of the goals were expected to come from forwards Heath (Chesterfield), Humphreys (Manchester) and the terrifically talented Mads Timm (Odense, Denmark).

On a dry and exceedingly mild evening for the time of year, when there wasn't the faintest hint of cold in the air, many of the crowd who descended on Loftus Road arrived only just before the proposed kick-off time. There was so much congestion outside the stadium that, with not an earthly hope of getting everyone in the ground for the start, it forced the authorities into taking a quick decision to delay the start by fifteen minutes.

If the temperature wasn't cold at the start of the match, more is the pity that the Reds were because, inside four minutes, Rangers went ahead with a superb move and excellent finish combination. The goal stemmed from a throw-in on United's left which reached the feet of Brian Fitzgerald in the inside-right position. Fitzgerald placed the ball out wide to Irvin Alexander, who measured an inch-perfect pass into a pocket of space occupied by Dean Lodge. The last named managed to evade three defenders when running on to take possession before he sidestepped Cogger and blasted a marvellous cross-shot past Jowsey and in off a post.

As it transpired, there was no need to despair as it soon became obvious that the Reds had the measure of their hosts. Unless the R's were to score again, an event which appeared more and more unlikely as the game unfolded, it only seemed to require the exercising of a little patience before United would haul themselves back onto level terms.

Humphreys was at the centre of the next three main incidents of note. Almost equalising in the eleventh minute when hitting a ferocious volley that skimmed Rangers' crossbar, within 60 seconds he had inflicted an injury to Kerry Butler by way of a heavy tackle. Obviously in some distress, Butler was forced to leave the field for some fairly lengthy treatment and it was only a couple of minutes after returning when he was substituted.

Just beyond the midway point of the half, Humphreys stroked an accurate long ball from the centre of the pitch up to his striking partner Heath. From an unlikely position just outside the home side's penalty area, and despite a defender looking over his shoulder, Heath struck a left-foot shot that was acrobatically finger-tipped onto the right-hand post and out of play for a corner by Matt Ramsey.

On 33 minutes, the match was lit up by a foraging run down the left by the adventurous Lawrence. Keeping possession for some considerable distance, Lawrence's endeavour took him deep into enemy territory where he executed a cross positively laden with danger. As the ball slashed across Ramsey's six-yard area, Humphreys failed by a whisker to get the touch required which would have forced it into the net. Just a few moments after, the same player attempted a speculative long-range effort that sailed over the bar by some distance.

Since going a goal behind, the Reds had enjoyed an almost complete monopoly of control and when half-time arrived it was expected that their overwhelming superiority would probably be exchanged for a goal or two before much longer.

Thankfully, that was precisely what happened because it took United just four minutes to equalise after the break with a goal registered by the scavenging Heath. When a high ball launched downfield from the centre circle by Cogger was passed from Humphreys to Richardson, the number eleven casually cushioned a deft pass through to Heath who, completely unmarked, blasted the ball past Ramsey from a distance of about twelve yards.

There were further openings for Timm, Richardson and Heath before the former accepted a simple chance on 73 minutes to bring about almost total silence inside Loftus Road. Another venture down the left by Lawrence developed when the defender rounded his marker and headed for the bye-line, from where he put Heath in possession. Rather than attempting a shot himself, Heath simply delivered the ball into the feet of the unmarked Timm, who slotted it home comfortably to make the score 2-1.

Rangers at last responded when Dennis Oli and Martyn Williams both made attempts to convert the same dangerous cross while later, an in-swinging corner needed to be touched over the bar by Jowsey.

The QPR revival didn't last long as such, and the Reds confirmed their win with a third goal ten minutes from time. It was a terribly bad one from Rangers' point of view as Richardson, stationed on United's left, was alive to the opportunity when a dithering defender failed to properly control a routine pass from his goalkeeper. Richardson cheekily pinched the ball off his toes, and he sped into the penalty box before riding out a lunging tackle and unselfishly squaring a pass to Heath. The number nine was stationed barely five or six yards out, and with no opponent able to react quickly enough to the danger, he could hardly miss the target.

The victory was now seemingly assured and so Dave Williams made a double substitution six minutes before the end, sending on Kalam Mooniaruck for Timm and Eddie Johnson for Humphreys, and he then replaced Richardson with Ben Collett in stoppage time.

All in all, it was an excellent opening exercise for the Reds and their performance, particularly in coming from behind in an away fixture, was heartening. It also demonstrated that despite the side being a relatively young one, there seemed to be a measure of resilience about it which boded well for the future.

Colin Heath raises his arm in triumph after putting the Reds on level terms

2001-02

DECEMBER 2001

third round

David Fox (left) and Darren Fletcher double up on a lone Ranger at Loftus Road

Speedy Lee Lawrence slides in to make his presence felt during United's super 3-1 win over QPR

439

2001-02

1) Neil Barnes	9) James Martin		1) James Jowsey	9) Colin Heath
2) Chris Cottrill	10) Andrew Barrowman		2) Lee Sims	10) Chris Humphreys
3) Steve Luckett	11) Carl Motteram		3) Lee Lawrence	11) Kieran Richardson
4) Mat Sadler	12) Paul Longthorn (for 6)		4) David Fox	12) John Cogger
5) Robert Hipkiss	13) Colin Doyle GK		5) Phil Bardsley	13) Tommy Lee GK
6) Sam Alsop	14) Jon Cartledge		6) Kris Taylor	14) Eddie Johnson
7) Darren Carter	15) Duane Courtney (for 5)		7) Kalam Mooniaruck	15) David Jones
8) Mark Allen	16) Peter Till (for 9)		8) Darren Fletcher	16) Mads Timm (for 7)

JANUARY 2002

BIRMINGHAM CITY 2 v 3 MANCHESTER UNITED

Allen (pen), Carter — *Heath, Humphreys (2)*

Wednesday 23rd
Kick-off 7.00 p.m.
Attendance 1,789

fourth round

Forty-eight hours after United's win in Shepherd's Bush, the Fourth Round draw was made by the F.A.'s chairman of the Youth Committee, Maurice Armstrong, and his vice chair, John Waterall, whereupon the young Reds were handed a tie at Birmingham. When the game was staged three weeks into the New Year, Dave Williams included Kalam Mooniaruck in place of Mads Timm with Kris Taylor, one of the game's central characters, coming in for John Cogger.

Birmingham, who went to the trouble of selling tickets in advance and producing a full match programme, were disappointed when an anticipated attendance of 5,000 actually fell below 1,800. Because they were facing United, the Blues decided to stage the tie at St. Andrews rather than at their normal Youth Cup venue, Damson Park, the home of Solihull Borough Football Club.

In the hours leading up to the game, Birmingham's Academy Director Brian Eastwick told the club's official website, *'Undoubtedly Manchester United is one of the top football clubs in the world and their development programme over the years has continually produced players who invariably go on to become household names. However, our boys were delighted when they heard the draw as they know it will be a good yardstick to measure themselves against possibly the very best. Undoubtedly, we now have some talented players within our Academy system, but I think it is fair to say that United will have a greater depth in quality.'*

Two of the talents Eastwick mentioned were Mat Sadler, current captain of England's under-17 side, and midfielder Darren Carter, another England junior star.

The Reds heeded Dave Williams' advice to be more alert in the opening section of the match than they had been at Loftus Road and with their concentration levels at the correct pitch, they looked solid at the back and managed to forge in front just before the quarter-hour mark. Kieran Richardson provided the assist when he gained possession in an advanced position on the left, took a few strides forward and laid an exquisite pass into the unbroken stride of the shaven-headed Chris Humphreys, whose clean strike zipped under the Blues' goalie.

There was a gap of only four minutes before the Reds doubled the trouble for the Brummies. Taylor served up the chance by belting a long clearance from inside his own half straight up to Colin Heath, who appeared unconcerned as Robert Hipkiss made a poor attempt at shadowing him. Heath simply waited for the ball to drop to his feet, making goalscoring look all too easy as he slid a left-foot shot beyond a shamefully exposed 'keeper. Somebody then appeared

Chris Humphreys proved effective by plundering a couple of goals at St. Andrews

to push the panic button in Birmingham's dugout, because eight minutes later Hipkiss was replaced by Duane Courtney as they sought to shore up a creaking excuse for a defence.

The substitution helped the Blues to recover their composure to the extent that they managed to halve the deficit ten minutes from the break. When Carl Motteram found a yard or two of space in United's area, James Jowsey came out to deal with the danger, at which point the City player clipped the ball over him. Taylor, who was stationed only a yard or so from the goal-line as he attempted to clear, was adjudged to have handled it when he clearly used his head.

The referee waved away all of United's protestations and under the circumstances Taylor was fortunate not to receive his marching orders. Mark Allen took his time before sending the ball to Jowsey's left and, despite the Reds' goalkeeper getting a firm hand in the way, sheer power took it over the line.

United responded in the 39th minute when a corner from Mooniaruck was spectacularly volleyed just over Birmingham's crossbar by Fox. Both sides carved out numerous chances to increase their tally, though it was the Blues who unarguably forced the pace after the interval, and in that regard they could be viewed as the unfortunate party when going behind still further in the 67th minute.

Humphreys provided some short relief by bundling the ball into City's net following some trickery by Richardson on the left, but the two-goal cushion lasted barely three minutes. United's defence cleared a corner only for the home side to regain possession and return a high ball into Jowsey's area. It was headed into the path of Carter and Birmingham's captain tapped home with his left-foot to bring the game, and the crowd, back to life.

The best chances fell to the home side thereafter. In their next attack of note, another hoisted ball spread confusion in United's ranks, and with the goal at his mercy just six yards from the target, Motteram missed his kick and with it the easiest opportunity of an equaliser simply evaporated.

Even when the referee added on two minutes of stoppage time, keeping a number of the away bench standing nervously near to the touchline, a teasing cross from the left managed to elude three of the Birmingham side positioned in or around the six-yard box. The Reds were through, with United's website later rightly claiming there had been a *'nerve-jangling finale'* to the match.

Kalam Mooniaruck deputised for Mads Timm with credit against Birmingham

440

1)	James Jowsey	9)	Colin Heath
2)	Lee Sims	10)	Chris Humphreys
3)	Lee Lawrence	11)	Kieran Richardson
4)	David Fox	12)	*John Cogger (for 2)*
5)	Phil Bardsley	13)	*Tommy Lee GK*
6)	Kris Taylor	14)	*David Jones*
7)	Kalam Mooniaruck	15)	*Ben Collett (for 3)*
8)	Darren Fletcher	16)	*David Poole (for 10)*

1)	Kevin Duncan	9)	Antony Sweeney
2)	Andy Watts	10)	Steve Manson
3)	Matty Robson	11)	Marc Batey
4)	Stuart Dixon	12)	*Stephen Flockett (for 7)*
5)	Darren Craddock	13)	*James Winter GK*
6)	John Brackstone	14)	*Jamie Oldroyd (for 8)*
7)	Lee Peachey	15)	*Chris Pearson*
8)	Colin McKenzie	16)	*Andy Hill (for 11)*

2001-02

MANCHESTER UNITED 3 v 2 HARTLEPOOL UNITED
Heath, Poole, Richardson *a.e.t.* Manson, McKenzie

FEBRUARY 2002

Wednesday 6th

Kick-off 7.00 p.m.

Attendance 3,732

fifth round

When Hartlepool arrived in Manchester on the 44th anniversary of the Munich air disaster, they became United's 66th different opponents in the Youth Cup. In remembrance of the tragedy, both sets of players wore black armbands and the stadium flags were lowered to half-mast.

While Sir Alex Ferguson watched the game's fluctuations intently, sitting alongside him was former Reds' goalkeeper and current Hartlepool manager Chris Turner. The tie was staged at Old Trafford following a request by Turner to his former boss, even though Gigg Lane was originally earmarked as United's venue of choice, and the occasion prompted an appeal in the local Mail newspaper from Hartlepool youth coach Martin Scott, who said, 'I know it is a bit of a trek over to Manchester but it is not very often you get to see a Hartlepool team play there. It would be a tremendous boost to the lads if people made the effort to go over there and cheer them on.'

Despite going into the tie saddled with the label of rank underdogs, the teenage representatives of the away club performed admirably and even managed to hold the Reds at bay until well past the interval. Appearing highly organised, very mobile and extremely 'up for it,' particularly during the early section of the match, they restricted United to just four clear openings in the first half, the best of which fell to Colin Heath in the 33rd minute when he crashed a shot at goalie Kevin Duncan in a one-on-one scenario. Prior to Heath's miss, Darren Fletcher forced a firm, one-handed stop from the 'Pool 'keeper and the young Scot found a similar response when shooting from distance a little while later. With six minutes to the break, Mooniaruck's driven attempt was repelled by Duncan and Kieran Richardson was wide of the target with his follow up.

The belief that a result could be obtained was now quite a bit higher in the Hartlepool camp than prior to kick-off, so coach Scott sent on striker Stephen Flockett in place of midfielder Lee Peachey at the intermission and altered a five-man midfield to a more offensive 4-4-2 system. There were just eleven seconds of the new half gone when the switch paid out an immediate jackpot, defender Darren Craddock picking out Steve Manson who gleefully curled a shot around Jowsey and into the right-hand corner of the net.

Raids on the visitors' goal suddenly intensified, and in attempting to get his team back on level terms, Fox rattled Hartlepool's bar from a Richardson cross.

The scoreboard showed 61 minutes had elapsed when the Reds equalised through a defensive error. After Mooniaruck swung a cross in from the right for it to be only partly controlled by Craddock just four yards from his goal, Heath swiftly homed in to steal the ball and promptly smash it over the line.

Just six minutes later, United sneaked ahead. It was another cross that unhinged Hartlepool, again from right to left, and with Duncan exposed and the ball running loose, Richardson capitalised by firing home from close quarters.

If Dave Williams thought his lads were now on the home straight, it was an entirely wrong assumption to make because the 'Pool levelled within a minute when Kris Taylor made a misjudgement through being caught in possession. It was Colin McKenzie who pinched the ball before darting towards goal and, coming up against Jowsey, he looked in complete control of the situation to knock it past him with some aplomb.

United's best opportunity to clinch the result within normal time fell to Richardson in the 83rd minute. Bringing a long clearance under control in a dangerous position, Duncan claimed the accolades by saving bravely at his feet.

The goal that finally separated the sides was credited to substitute David Poole, who had been introduced for Humphreys in the 80th minute. Poole had earlier hit a post, and with only two minutes of the second period of extra-time gone, he managed to find space by outpacing Hartlepool's back four. Duncan reacted by sprinting to the edge of his area, only his action in ballooning the ball to safety backfired when it hit Poole on the leg and flew into the unmanned net to give the Reds a most fortunate winner.

In an attempt to re-energise a fading forward-line, the visitors introduced Jamie Oldroyd as a replacement for McKenzie and the substitute was involved in the final action of note when almost capitalising on another Taylor mistake just before the end. The Victoria Ground juniors probably felt aggrieved at the manner of their exit, though the match statistics revealed United's dominance included winning nine corners to only one against, while also managing no less than 26 attempts on goal with the visitors claiming just four. However, while Hartlepool's performance in defeat was rightly viewed as a spirited one, the Reds' victory was universally perceived as laboured.

Alex Ferguson told the Hartlepool Mail, 'You should be proud of them up there, it was a terrific game and very hard for our lads. They did very well and everyone in Hartlepool should be pleased with them.' Ferguson then joked, 'In fact, I hope you are going to knight them all and give them the freedom of the town!'

A gaff by Kris Taylor (top) resulted in an equaliser for Hartlepool whereas Lee Sims put in a more assured performance than his colleague

441

2001-02

1) James Jowsey	9) Colin Heath	1) Craig Parry	9) Griff Jones
2) Lee Sims	10) Chris Humphreys	2) Grant Black	10) Ashley Scothern
3) Lee Lawrence	11) Kieran Richardson	3) Robbie Williams	11) Nicky Wroe
4) David Fox	12) *John Cogger (for 2)*	4) Calum Selby	12) *Tom Baker (for 10)*
5) Phil Bardsley	13) *Tommy Lee GK*	5) David Coulson	13) *Marc Shackleton GK*
6) Kris Taylor	14) *Kalam Mooniaruck (for 7)*	6) Adam Oldham	14) *Gary Meecham (for 4)*
7) Danny Byrne	15) *Eddie Johnson (for 10)*	7) Chris Cox	15) *Dale Tonge (for 11)*
8) Darren Fletcher	16) *David Poole*	8) Richard Carrington	16) *Thomas Harban*

MARCH 2002

MANCHESTER UNITED 3 v 3 **BARNSLEY**

Heath (2, 1 pen), Johnson — *Barnsley win 3-1 on pens a.e.t.* — Coulson, Jones (2, 1 pen)

Friday 1st
Kick-off 7.00 p.m.
Attendance 3,538

sixth round

Take that, says Robbie

A second home tie of the season brought one of United's oldest Youth Cup adversaries to Manchester and the outcome of a thrilling tussle signalled the Reds' au revoir to the competition for another year. Visitors Barnsley displayed bags of spirit, as well as no mean amount of talent, and there were few arguments about the validity of their victory come the end of an extended match packed with incident.

The game started ever so well for United. Kicking towards the Scoreboard End, Danny Byrne, who was drafted in as a replacement for Kalam Mooniaruck, got things going by cracking a shot from distance over the top and soon after, a Kieran Richardson drive was well saved by Craig Parry.

It didn't take long for the tide to turn, and in the 17th minute Nicky Wroe sparked Barnsley's attack into life when screwing his shot wide from the left-hand corner of United's eighteen-yard box. Only two minutes passed before the visitors were awarded a penalty after Lee Lawrence brought down Chris Cox, Griff Jones rattling in the spot kick to put his side 1-0 up.

The young Tykes, who were kitted out in an eye-catching yellow shirts and blue shorts Brazil-type outfit, were obviously well prepared for such a development and they performed a prolonged celebration routine over towards, and even involving, a corner flag.

Just as in the last round, when the Reds went in arrears to Hartlepool, their response was positive and over the next ten minutes they swarmed in and around the Oakwell kids' box. A decent effort from Chris Humphreys zoomed just over Parry's crossbar and then Richardson and Colin Heath, twice in the case of the

Midfielder Danny Byrne's negligible contribution ended on 78 minutes when he was replaced by Kalam Mooniaruck

A picture of total concentration, James Jowsey prepares to face up to one of Barnsley's spot kicks

latter, placed shots straight into the grateful goalie's arms.

For all of their considerable territorial advantage, it counted for zilch when the Reds suffered a further blow eight minutes from the break as Barnsley added another goal to their total.

It wasn't a pretty sight for Dave Williams to behold, and United's coach must have grimaced when a simple pass from the right landed perfectly at the feet of the unmarked Jones and he executed a relatively easy task by guiding the ball beyond Jowsey.

Still United pressed on, and in the 41st minute their clearest opening so far came from a terrible back pass from Barnsley's number three. It looked all over a goal for United until Heath, for the third time, knocked the ball weakly and straight towards Parry. Kris Taylor then moved up to join the attack for a corner, and he got enough power, but nowhere near the correct direction, when meeting the flag kick head on.

There was much for Williams to put right at the break. His team's midfielders were largely out of sorts, the full-backs had rarely ventured forward and, most disconcerting for United's followers, there were far too many long balls out of defence.

The coach's immediate action was to replace Lee Sims with John Cogger, and the substitute took only two minutes to make his presence felt when measuring a superb cross from the right. It landed plum on the head of Heath and the lanky

2001-02

MARCH 2002

striker cushioned the ball home to make the score look a little more respectable.

Heath remained the centre of attention when he walloped a magnificent 25-yard drive which was tipped over by Parry. From the resulting corner, Barnsley hearts were sent fluttering again before a scramble ended when the ball was ballooned from out of their six-yard area.

The action soon switched to the opposite end of the park, where Jones was cautioned for a crude challenge on Jowsey, and then Cox and Scothern added to the excitement by going close for Barnsley. Cox's was a particularly spectacular attempt, because his header from Richard Carrington's cross appeared to be well on its way to the top corner prior to Jowsey arching his back far enough to bring off a quite superb save.

From the 73rd to the 80th minutes there was a spate of substitutions. Eddie Johnson was sent on in place of Humphreys and at almost the same time Barnsley replaced Wroe with Dale Tonge. Kalam Mooniaruck was then sent on for Byrne and the Tykes hooked off Scothern to make way for Tom Baker.

Just at the point where it seemed the Reds were going out of the tournament, a second penalty was awarded, this time for the home team, when the referee spotted a debatable handball offence. There were less than two minutes left on the clock as Heath kept his nerve to send a hard shot low across the turf and beyond Parry.

Four minutes of stoppage time then followed, and at the end of it the two sides took a little respite before preparing to continue their battle for another half an hour.

On United's website, Cliff Butler identified that *'the game appeared to lose a little of its oomph in the opening spell of extra time'* and he added a comment about the Reds' revival moving *'into another phase'* in the 100th minute. In what was arguably the most pleasing move of the match from a home standpoint, a measured pass from the midfield area picked out the loitering Johnson and from just inside the boundary of the penalty box, the burly marksman blasted a tremendous shot to edge United ahead for the first time.

Despite the setback, Barnsley's faith never wavered and they continued to press at every opportunity. The Reds did themselves no favours and their continued and annoying habit of hoisting high balls forward at a time when as much possession as possible was required seemed to play right into their opponents' hands.

There was one last substitution for the Yorkshire side, with Gary Meecham sent on for Calum Selby at the change round, and only a couple of minutes into the concluding period they levelled.

Jones added to the theory that finishers often act as the best providers when he delivered a floated corner kick for David Coulson to power a thunderous header into Jowsey's net. That was it as far as goals from open play went, and so the tie was required to be settled by a series of spot kicks. The Tykes might have felt they held a slight psychological advantage at that point, because they had defeated Wycombe Wanderers by five penalties to four in their last Youth Cup outing.

The sequence started badly for Barnsley as Carrington's penalty was saved by Jowsey, a potential advantage to United that was immediately discarded when Parry got in the way of a poor effort from Mooniaruck. Meecham then converted for Barnsley while Heath, who was the next in line for the Reds, completely missed the target.

Jones made it two out of three for the visitors prior to United's third attempt, taken by Johnson, cannoning off the bar. Cox's kick was repelled by Jowsey to give the Reds a measure of hope, which increased when Fox was successful with his turn.

The result was then settled once and for all when Robbie Williams slotted away the Tykes' winner to commence even more celebrations in the Barnsley camp, plus a number of Take That jokes from all others.

United's stay in the tournament would have ended about three quarters of an hour earlier than it did only for a fortunate stay of execution that Barnsley's official website described as a result of *'a disgraceful penalty decision'*. The site further explained that *'Kieran Richardson's low cross hit Grant Black on the arm from no more than three yards but referee R. Lewis interpreted a deliberate obstruction of the ball and gave the spot kick'.*

Even though the site's terminology might have been considered a little on the strong side, few would have disagreed that the penalty award was indeed a harsh one.

Barnsley were defeated by Aston Villa in the semi-final, the Villains going on to win the Youth Cup at the last stage by defeating an Everton side containing a certain Wayne Rooney by four goals to two.

All of United's ten outfield players show concern as the penalty shoot-out drama unfolds
(l-r) Kalam Mooniaruck, Kris Taylor, Phil Bardsley, Eddie Johnson, Lee Lawrence, Kieran Richardson, David Fox, Colin Heath, Darren Fletcher, John Cogger

sixth round

443

2002-03

1)	Adam Collin	9)	Guy Bates	1) Luke Steele	9) Eddie Johnson
2)	Martin Brittain	10)	Calvin Zola-Makongo	2) Lee Sims	10) Kieran Richardson
3)	Kris Gate	11)	Phil Cave	3) Lee Lawrence	11) Ben Collett
4)	Chris Carr	12)	*Lewis Guy (for 9)*	4) Mark Howard	12) *Phil Picken*
5)	Steven Taylor	13)	*Adam Bartlett GK*	5) Paul McShane	13) *Tommy Lee GK*
6)	James Beaumont	14)	*Danny Howe (for 3)*	6) David Jones	14) *Adam Eckersley*
7)	Alan O'Brien	15)	*Chris Shanks*	7) Chris Eagles	15) *Sylvan Ebanks-Blake (for 8)*
8)	Ross Gardner	16)	*Carl Finnigan (for 7)*	8) Ramon Calliste	16) *Callum Flanagan (for 9)*

DECEMBER 2002

NEWCASTLE UNITED* 1 v 3 MANCHESTER UNITED

Gardner — Eagles, Richardson, Taylor (o.g.)

Wednesday 4th**

Kick-off 7.00 p.m.

Attendance 847

Played at Kingston Park

> *It's a tough draw for the Third Round but we know we've got a good enough team to beat them. Although our record recently hasn't been that good (against Newcastle), now I think we're ready to take them on.*
>
> *Always in big games you've got to see if you can handle the pressure and the occasion and (coach) Jim Ryan said to us to play the match, not the occasion. So hopefully we can do that and come out on top.*

DAVID JONES

Because of the departure from Old Trafford of Academy coaches Dave Williams and Neil Bailey in the summer of 2002, the task of guiding the youth side now fell to Brian McClair. The Reds' former striker and crowd favourite had made a magnificent impression throughout the previous season when steering United's second string to their first F.A. Premier League (North) title by just one point from North-East rivals Newcastle and Middlesbrough. By coincidence, the Magpies presented the Reds with their opening Youth Cup task in his tenure as the club's new Academy coach.

In an interview with MUTV prior to kick-off, McClair made no attempt to hide his intentions for the match when revealing that the usual criteria of quality of performance over the result would be shelved. He declared, *'If it turns out to be a good game as well then that's a bonus for people, both for the television and for those who are going to be there, but on this particular occasion we're not really interested in that. It's about have we got the desire to win the game.'*

Striker Eddie Johnson suggested the game might answer some questions about the side's resolve when explaining, *'If you are playing for the first-team in front of 65,000 people you can't go into your shell, you've got to be on top of your game and some players thrive on the big stage and some don't. This is like a test for everyone. It's quite good that we've got Newcastle because they are obviously one of the favourites……it's good that we get them in the early stages, because whoever wins means either team has got a good chance of going on and progressing, maybe all the way.'*

Some of the United boys might have been forgiven for thinking there was a score to settle with their hosts. Goalkeepers Luke Steele and Tommy Lee, along with outfield players Phil Picken, Lee Lawrence, Lee Sims, Ben Collett, Chris Eagles, Kieran Richardson, as well as Johnson and Jones, were all at least partly involved in the unsuccessful two-legged Academy League under-17's final at the end of the 2001/02 season. Having lost both of those matches, a mood hung over the United camp which suggested a reversal of that outcome was high up on their wish list.

There were so many newcomers to the side, and it meant that much responsibility rested on the shoulders of Sims, Lawrence and Richardson, the only regulars remaining from United's last Youth Cup campaign. The remainder of the squad comprised a mixture of those currently frequenting the club's under-17 and under-19 teams.

If revenge was on the agenda for the Reds at the home of RFU club Newcastle Falcons, an eleventh hour venue change, it was exactly what they got and precisely what they deserved.

third round

**This game was originally scheduled to be played at St.James's Park at 7.00 p.m. and was then brought forward to 12 noon. The venue and kick-off time were then changed again to allow for floodlight repairs at St.James's Park.*

Reds' full-back Lee Lawrence tries to escape a Newcastle challenge at Kingston Park

444

DECEMBER 2002

United's Ramon Calliste makes an unorthodox attempt at squashing the threat of Calvin Zola-Makongo

In a display which beamed confidence, cohesion and craft, McClair's charges hardly ever looked in danger and once Eagles blasted a free kick around a defensive wall and into the bottom corner of Adam Collin's goal eight minutes from half-time, it was hard to envisage the Magpies staging a comeback.

During a largely drab opening half hour, the Hertfordshire-born Eagles struck a post with a corking volley following a clearance from a corner, and once they gripped Newcastle by the throat, United never let go to finish the first period in total domination.

Just sixteen seconds after the break, the Reds gave the Magpies another choking when the first-team experienced Richardson, who was situated in a midfield position, passed the ball out to Lawrence on the left. The full-back knocked it long to Eagles and from almost on the bye-line, he crossed it to where Richardson had darted forward to take up a position in the centre. Thereupon taking custody of the ball, Richardson's initial shot was charged down, but he made a rapid response when rasping the rebound into the roof of the net to put clear light between the two sides.

Martin Brittain later cleared an attempt out of Newcastle's goalmouth prior to Steele smothering a Carl Finnigan attempt in a rare breakaway at the other end.

Six minutes from time, another goal arrived which proved terminal as far as the Geordies' prospects for progress were concerned. The forceful Johnson created room on the right-hand side of the field before flipping over a cross that caused concern amongst the home rearguard. Eagles then nodded the ball on, and in a misunderstanding with his goalkeeper, England Youth captain Steven Taylor diverted a header into his own goal to the dismay of watching Newcastle manager Sir Bobby Robson.

Another mix-up, this time at the United end, led to the Magpies clinching a consolation goal with just three minutes remaining, Ross Gardner sidestepping Steele to roll the ball over the line. A recent £500,000 capture from home town club Peterborough, Steele made a right hash of a hopeful high ball as a result of which he forfeited both possession and his clean sheet.

The following day, Newcastle's Taylor went on record as saying, *'We didn't perform on the night. We've been playing well all season but were disappointing last night. Manchester United were fantastic. They ran the show in midfield, which is where it counts, and we were second to most balls.'*

Magpies' coach Kenny Wharton added to the accolades afforded to the Reds by conceding, *'They deservedly won the game. The pitch was difficult but Manchester United passed the ball well compared to us. The second goal knocked the wind out of our sails, with it coming as early as it did in the second half, and it was an uphill battle after that.'*

The pleasure Brian McClair took from the game was immense. Having seen a tremendously assured and committed display, which was more akin to a side that had benefited from an extended run in the competition rather than one which contained eight full Youth Cup debutants, the canny Scot was well aware of the confidence his youngsters were certain to derive from such a convincing victory.

> *At the start (of the game) we thought it was quite difficult but we just overpowered them. Then the goals just started to flow in and they couldn't cope with us.*
>
> **CHRIS EAGLES**

2002-03

1) Luke Steele	9) Eddie Johnson	1) Rob Poulter	9) Mason Palmieri
2) Lee Sims	10) Kieran Richardson	2) Matt Hill	10) Liam Needham
3) Lee Lawrence	11) Ben Collett	3) Luke Foster	11) Lewis McMahon
4) Mark Howard	*12) Phil Picken*	4) Richard Wood	*12) Keeron Stone*
5) Paul McShane	*13) Tom Heaton GK*	5) Scott Lowe	*13) Jordan Yorath GK*
6) David Jones	*14) Danny Byrne*	6) Marcus Orlik	*14) Aaron Callaghan (for 7)*
7) Chris Eagles	*15) David Poole*	7) Ross Greenwood	*15) Ian Douglas*
8) Mads Timm	*16) Ramon Calliste (for 8)*	8) Laurie Wilson	*16) Tom Marsden*

JANUARY 2003

MANCHESTER UNITED* **2** v **0** SHEFFIELD WEDNESDAY

Collett, Richardson

Tuesday 21st

Kick-off 7.00 p.m.

Attendance 428

*Played at Moss Lane, Altrincham

fourth round

He hoots, he scores

For the home engagement against Sheffield Wednesday which followed the young Reds' excellent win on Tyneside, a decision was taken to stage the tie at the home of Altrincham Football Club. United's Reserves were playing their home games at Moss Lane, so the option to utilise the stadium for the Youth Cup clash was an obvious one.

There was only one change to the Reds' formation from the Newcastle match, Brian McClair electing to include the more experienced Mads Timm as a replacement for Ramon Calliste.

During the 2001/02 season, Timm managed eight goals from fourteen appearances for the under-17 side before missing most of the latter part of the campaign due to injury. Despite that potentially damaging setback to his development, the Dane was afforded his senior debut when taking to the field as a second half substitute in a Champions League tie against Maccabi Haifa in neutral Cyprus and his pace and trickery were seen as useful additions to the youth team's armoury.

Wednesday's Academy director, Jimmy Shoulder, admitted he viewed the game with a mixture of *'excitement and apprehension'*. Shoulder, whose youngsters were eyeing a clash against city neighbours Sheffield United should they come out on top against the Reds, commented, *'They're one of the best teams in the country. At whatever level you play Manchester United, from first-team down to under-9's, there's always a buzz.*

The players have been looking forward to it since the draw, which was before we played Reading in the last round. It's a great incentive to have a local derby to look forward to.'

Sheffield Wednesday's website gave a preview to the tie, a section of which read:

The Owls earned the prize with a comeback victory at Reading in Round Three, even though the glamour has been somewhat removed from the occasion by the Red Devils' decision to switch the match to Altrincham's Moss Lane ground.

For the first time this season, the Academy director has a full squad of outfield players to choose from, although a broken finger suffered by first choice goalkeeper Adam Ogden means former England schoolboy international Rob Poulter will deputise for him between the sticks.

It probably wouldn't have mattered who was in goal when the Owls went behind in the 33rd minute as the outcome would have been exactly the same. A mazy run by the crafty Timm ended on the left-hand side of Wednesday's penalty area where he was dispossessed. With his back to goal and some twenty yards out, Ben Collett turned on the loose ball to drill an incredible left-foot shot past Poulter and into the top corner.

Until that point it had been quite a tough tussle. As the rain lashed down, Timm might have put United one ahead as early as the fifth minute but hammered his drive wide, and just a couple of minutes later Eddie Johnson went close with another effort. The visitors then created the most obvious opening of the early exchanges when Laurie Wilson looked on in amazement as Luke Steele brought off what the United Review described as *'a fantastic save'*, low down to his right, from the Wednesday number eight. Sheffield's best chances of the first period resulted from two sliced clearances by Steele, but on both occasions he was helped out of trouble by alert defending.

Collett's goal cued a spell of intense pressure on the Wednesday defence and included a Johnson attempt that hit the side-netting, as well as a shot from Eagles which was fumbled by Poulter. When the referee signalled the break, relief was visible on the faces of the Sheffield lads as they trooped off in search of a little tea and a lot of encouragement.

Poulter produced a memorable save in the 57th minute by readjusting his footing to deflect Collett's drive across the face of goal. United, who had entered into what one report described as *'a passing groove'*, continued to hold the lion's share of the ball while Wednesday looked at their most dangerous from set pieces. Over on the touchline, McClair sensed the need to make a slight adjustment, so he sent on Calliste for Timm in the 69th minute to bring about an immediate injection of vitality with his speed and verve.

The next major point of discussion came eight minutes from time when Collett was dismissed for his second bookable offence, which was a foul committed on Owls' defender Matthew Hill. Cautioned in the first half for a mistimed rather than malicious tackle, an act of clumsiness which was described by a reporter as *'Scholes-esque'*, Collett left the referee with little scope other than to send him for an early bath.

If Wednesday felt that an opportunity to force a replay was staring them in the face, they were dealt a final blow with just three minutes left on the clock. Calliste was a central figure in the proceedings when collecting a pass out of defence down United's right-hand side. Upon gaining possession, the Cardiff teenager turned to leave his marker for dead and after carrying the ball diagonally across the Sheffield half of the pitch, put a precision pass at the feet of Kieran Richardson. Bringing the ball instantly under control, Richardson charged through Wednesday's penalty area to blast home at the near post from a tight angle.

It represented another tidy win for the Reds who, with David Jones in both creative and industrious form, stifled almost all attacking intentions out of the Wednesday side, despite leaving it late to confirm their place in the next round.

While the United Review's observation that *'the outcome remained in the balance until the final few minutes'* was true enough, by the same token the Reds never looked in too much trouble after emerging unscathed from the middle section of the first period when the graft of Wilson, McMahon and Needham presented them with a brief troublesome spell.

Winger Ben Collett scored a fabulous opener for United prior to seeing red later in the game

1) Luke Steele	9) Eddie Johnson	1) Tom Lindley	9) Kevan Hurst
2) Lee Sims	10) Kieran Richardson	2) Rory Beanes	10) Billy Sharp
3) Lee Lawrence	11) David Poole	3) Ricky Howarth	11) Jonathan Forte
4) Mark Howard	*12) Adrian Nevins*	4) Adrian Harper	*12) Danny Longmore*
5) Paul McShane	*13) Tommy Lee GK*	5) Dominic Roma	*13) Danny Haystead GK*
6) David Jones	*14) Danny Byrne*	6) Nicky Ellis	*14) Ryan Gyaki (for 8)*
7) Chris Eagles	*15) Phil Bardsley*	7) Colin Marrison	*15) Danny Platel*
8) Mads Timm	*16) Ramon Calliste (for 11)*	8) Ian Ross	*16) Jake Speight*

MANCHESTER UNITED 1 v 1 SHEFFIELD UNITED

Johnson — United win 4-3 on pens a.e.t. — Sharp (pen)

FEBRUARY 2003

Wednesday 5th

Kick-off 7.00 p.m.

Attendance 416

fifth round

Young United keep their dream alive

Because Ben Collett was required to serve a one-match ban for his sending off in the previous tie, Brian McClair elected to pitch David Poole into the fray for the Fifth Round contest against Sheffield United. Reds' goalkeeper Luke Steele turned down the opportunity of an international cap by electing to face the Blades, as he was in line for an appearance in the England under-20 team. Preferring instead to assist his Old Trafford team-mates in their quest to prolong the Youth Cup run even further, little could he have known just how central he would be to those aspirations.

The Reds had already fulfilled three out of their four Academy fixtures against the Bramall Lane club that season. While the under-19's succeeded by a 2-0 scoreline in Yorkshire, the under-17's were defeated in both of their matches with the Blades, 3-1 at Carrington and 5-2 in Sheffield.

Sir Alex Ferguson, Rio Ferdinand and the Neville brothers were among the crowd and they viewed the proceedings with an understandable interest as Sheffield United launched their first attack in the early moments. Blades' number nine Kevan Hurst claimed possession in the centre circle and measured a cute pass into the inside-left position for colleague Billy Sharp to chase. Sharp turned to slide the ball almost onto United's penalty spot where England Youth international Jonathan Forte was waiting.

When the move broke down, Chris Eagles took the ball from Kieran Richardson and ran 30 yards to give Eddie Johnson the opportunity to show what he could do, the stocky striker rather wasting the approach work by hitting a soft effort that took a slight deflection before being picked up by the Sheffield 'keeper.

Despite a lack of sting in Johnson's shot, much was expected of the Chester boy because he had carved out something of a name for himself through his hugely impressive contributions in the previous rounds. With his powerful and willing runs, both on and off the ball, Johnson's main responsibility was in creating pressure on the opposing centre-backs, a task he positively thrived on.

The next notable incident resulted in the Reds going behind in only the 13th minute. The threat developed down United's left when Sheffield's Colin Marrison squirmed around Lee Lawrence and attempted to charge into an area of empty space. Just as Marrison entered the penalty box, Lawrence clumsily clattered him from behind and the referee gave no second thoughts as to the awarding of a penalty. Sharp accepted the responsibility of taking the kick and, with the ball going one way and Steele the other, the Yorkshire side were 1-0 up.

By and large, United's display in the first half didn't come up to expectations, although they managed to create one decent chance to draw level before facing McClair in the dressing room. Lee Sims got the move underway when he stroked a pass down the right flank into the feet of Eagles. The winger's attempt to cross was thwarted, but after some untidy play he was given another chance. From an inside-right position, and with four defenders lined up almost square twenty yards from goal, Eagles threaded the ball between two of them. Johnson read his intention and by remaining just onside, he was okay to latch onto the pass. Given a clear sight of goal, and faced with only Lindley to beat, he appeared to slip slightly and his scuffed shot was easily caught by the 'keeper.

A rather more difficult task later fell to Richardson, whose shot from eighteen yards was snatched and consequently sailed over the crossbar.

The United website match report made a note about the Reds being *'out-muscled by a physical Sheffield United'* for much of the first half and another that Richardson and Timm *were hustled and bustled off the ball'*. With the break drawing close, MUTV commentator Joe Evans felt that Sheffield's lead was *'thoroughly deserved'* and almost before he had finished talking, Sharp wasted a glorious chance to double the advantage by blasting across the Reds' six-yard area when a goal appeared much the more likely outcome.

The later instalment was an entirely different kettle of fish, and the United boys raised their performance considerably to draw level just eight minutes into the second half. The equaliser was a real belter, Mads Timm instigating it when moving up the gears and down the centre of the pitch. His short pass went to Richardson who, with five opponents around him, nudged a measured diagonal pass through to the onrushing Johnson. Without waiting to gain control, Johnson was rewarded for an unselfish performance by guiding the ball past Lindley to bring parity to the score.

The Reds might have racked up several more goals thereafter, only a giant list of lost chances prevented them from doing so, and when Lawrence headed the most obvious one against the bar from an unmarked position just six yards out, it seemed that further progress in the tournament might not be forthcoming after all. One particular report claimed the second half *'turned into shooting practice for the Reds'* and added that *'the surrounding gardens were showered with stray footballs rather than the echoes of cheers'*.

In the last minute of normal time, the Blades' Marrison brought the folly of United's wasted opportunities into focus when he sliced a shot off target in a classic 'open goal' situation. Previously, Sharp had the ball in Steele's net and was about to begin celebrating until the referee ruled the effort out because of the striker's push on Paul McShane.

The game went into extra-time with both teams understandably weary from their exertions. Ramon Calliste, who had been sent on for the lacklustre Poole, showed his usual zest and, with electric pace and quick feet, he looked the most capable of breaking the deadlock.

Timm was presented with the last real chance of a winner from open play, but he rolled his attempt meekly past Lindley and the ball was hacked away just before it reached the goal-line.

After the miserable experience of losing to Barnsley in a penalty shoot-out a year ago, there was some pessimism amongst those die-hard United youth team followers in the crowd at what was to come and the edginess felt by the home supporters was only lessened after the first round of kicks was completed.

Electing to re-spot the ball, David Jones showed the way by feigning before striking it. The technique worked, because the skipper slashed his effort to the left while Lindley dived in the opposite direction. Rory Beanes' reply for the Blades was an extremely poor effort that Steele stopped with ease.

Johnson was next up for United. His penalty kick against Barnsley the previous March had dirtied the bar and he managed to fail again, this time through his kick being saved by the Sheffield custodian. When Kevan Hurst thumped home his turn, the game was all-square once more.

Five more penalties were then converted in succession. Spot kicks from, in turn, Calliste, Howarth, Eagles, Marrison and Richardson all found their way into the back of the net.

In order to keep his side in the game and take the penalty sequence to a sudden death stage, Billy Sharp, arguably Sheffield's most potent forward, was given the responsibility of their last kick. Standing in the United goal, Steele entered into a little gamesmanship by stretching his arms as high and wide as he could in an attempt to appear as big an obstacle as possible while also pulling on the crossbar to make the target look smaller.

The trick worked a treat. While Steele leapt to his left, Sharp looked to have him beaten only for the shot to drift inches wide and with that miss, the Reds were clear through to the quarter-final.

McClair later revealed he had introduced some spot kick drills into recent coaching sessions and added, somewhat tongue in cheek, that it was his intention to do something similar in respect of finishing from open play before the next round came along.

> *We went in at half-time a goal down, so we told the players that once we'd got an equaliser we'd feel comfortable and get on a roll. What happened instead was the players decided they would teach the coaches a lesson and miss all their chances! As a result the game went to a penalty shoot-out.*
>
> *We had spent a bit of time with our players practising penalties but you can't account for the pressure of taking them in a cup tie and I have to say they did take them fantastically well.*
>
> **BRIAN McCLAIR**

2002-03

1) Luke Steele	9) Ramon Calliste	1) Philip Palethorpe	9) Chris Dagnall
2) Lee Sims	10) Kieran Richardson	2) Ollie James	10) Paul Martin
3) Lee Lawrence	11) Ben Collett	3) Neil Ashton	11) Paul Brown
4) Phil Bardsley	*12) Mark Howard*	4) Alan Griffiths	*12) Thomas Rooney (for 7)*
5) Paul McShane	*13) Tom Heaton GK*	5) Carl Tremarco	*13) Ross March GK*
6) David Jones	*14) Sylvan Ebanks-Blake (for 9)*	6) Ged Scott	*14) Gary Pinch (for 2)*
7) Chris Eagles	*15) Danny Byrne*	7) Gareth Hooper	*15) James Vaughan*
8) Mads Timm	*16) Phil Picken*	8) Steve Jennings	*16) Adam Dickinson*

MARCH 2003

MANCHESTER UNITED* **3 v 1** TRANMERE ROVERS

Eagles, Ebanks-Blake, Timm — Dagnall

Thursday 6th

Kick-off 7.30 p.m.

Attendance 913

**Played at Moss Lane, Altrincham*

sixth round

Just magic from Mads

Following the only other meeting between United and Tranmere Rovers in the Youth Cup, eleven years ago, the Reds went on to win the trophy with the aid of Ryan Giggs, then a budding first-teamer. That home meeting was also at the last eight stage and, with the further inclusion of rising star Kieran Richardson, the midfielder having already been blooded in both senior European and domestic competition by Alex Ferguson, further similarities to the earlier match existed.

Joined by the reintroduced Ben Collett, Ramon Calliste was brought in for double groin operation casualty Eddie Johnson while Phil Bardsley, whose long absence was caused by a fractured cheekbone, replaced Mark Howard.

The Birkenhead side had been required to win two games more than United to reach the same stage of the tournament, plundering eighteen goals along their journey. The main threat to the Reds was likely to come from Chris Dagnall, a striker with an enviable record of 30 goals in all competitions for the season, six of which were claimed in the Youth Cup. The Prenton Park club's junior section was certainly one to be admired and respected just then, and their lifting of the Lancashire Youth Cup for the past two years gave ample demonstration of the quality of their pool of teenage talent.

The pitch was a problem common to both teams and there must have been some doubt as to whether the game would go ahead. As the temperature plummeted after sundown in Altrincham, the Moss Lane surface slowly glazed over and when the teams came down the tunnel, the sound of their studs clattering on concrete could clearly be heard. What disturbed those within earshot the most was that the noise hardly altered as they began running around the pitch. Even though the ground staff at Altrincham took the precaution of heavily sanding a playing area which looked quite bare in patches, it was obvious the sides would be required to take just a little more care than normal if they were to remain on their feet.

A detailed match report was posted on the Rovers' website:

Tranmere's dreams of lifting the F.A. Youth Cup for the first time are over, for this season at least! A 3-1 defeat at the hands of Manchester United ended their interest in the competition, but as the only non-Academy or non-Premiership side still in the cup they did themselves and the club proud.

Events could so easily have been different had Rovers taken their early chances and as it is the scoreline still seems harsh as United were forced to go all the way to see off the plucky challenge of John McMahon's men.

Up against a side including one player with Premiership experience and several other internationals, Tranmere did themselves proud in front of a star-studded crowd including Sir Alex Ferguson, Gary Neville, Roy Keane and Denis Irwin.

John McMahon named the same starting XI that beat Port Vale in the last round, with Paul Martin once again partnering Chris Dagnall in attack with fit-again Thomas Rooney named amongst the subs.

Dagnall had the chance to give Rovers the lead with less than a minute on the clock but he wasn't clinical enough in front of goal to make United pay. Paul Brown also went close for Rovers, screwing a shot just wide before Mads Timm brought a great save out of Phil Palethorpe with seven minutes on the clock.

The United midfielder found himself through on goal but a great block from Palethorpe saw the danger averted. The young 'keeper got down well after a good through ball from Calliste split the Rovers defence apart.

Tranmere should have taken the lead on fourteen minutes through Paul Brown. Good play from Dagnall saw Rovers' leading scorer take it past two before laying it off for Brown, who opened the scoring against Vale in the last round, but he fired wide off the outside of his left boot.

Rovers were left rueing their missed chances on 23 minutes when Manchester United took the lead. A good attacking move saw Chris Eagles left free on the left and he made no mistake, firing past Palethrope into the roof of the net.

Paul McShane was the first player booked for the home side on 27 minutes for a late tackle but the caution count was evened just before the break when Carl Tremarco was shown the yellow card, a decision that surprised most Rovers fans inside Moss Lane.

Paul Brown had another good chance on 29 minutes after a good move centred around Chris Dagnall. He played in Martin, who pulled the ball back for Jennings to play in Brown, but his snap shot flew wide when maybe he had time to compose himself.

Tranmere went close again five minutes later. Dagnall and Martin combining well before letting the ball roll for the advancing Ged Scott, who fired over the bar.

Despite a hard fought first half, Tranmere found themselves in an unfamiliar position of a goal down at the break.

Mads Timm was certainly the danger man for United as the blonde midfielder ran the show for the home side. His touch, pace and ability was electric and certainly proved the difference between the two sides, so certainly a name to keep an eye on in the future. He thought he'd doubled United's lead on 54 minutes when his 30-yard effort beat Palethrope before cannoning back off the bar, the United number seven picked up the rebound but Palethrope scrambled across his goal-line to make the save.

Brian McClair made his first change on the hour when Sylvan Ebanks-Blake replaced Ramon Calliste.

A well worked corner for Rovers a minute later almost got a goal when Ashton crossed for Jennings at the far post and his header back in was just cleared from the head of Paul Martin.

Mads Timm did get the second on 63 minutes, scoring an excellent solo goal, and it was nothing more than he deserved, even if the side didn't, after being at the centre of everything the home side created.

John McMahon made his first change on 70 minutes with Thomas Rooney replacing Gareth Hooper as Tranmere went for broke with three in attack. Despite being two goals down Rovers continued to press and, barring the odd United break, the game was largely played in the United half.

Tranmere finally got the break they deserved on 79 minutes, Chris Dagnall the scorer. An excellent tackle by Neil Ashton on Timm as the United midfielder shaped to shoot started the move before Ashton played the long ball over the top for Dagnall, who fired under Steele in the United goal.

While the Super White Army were hopeful of seeing their side take the game to extra-time, United went further ahead a minute later, Ebanks-Blake scoring despite a strong suspicion of handball as he controlled, but he made no mistake firing past Palethorpe.

Paul Brown brought a good save from Steele after the restart when he curled a free kick goal-bound after Timm was booked for a foul on Rooney. Ollie James was forced off with three minutes remaining with what looked like cramp, replaced by Gary Pinch.

So Rovers' cup run has come to an end. They may have been beaten but certainly not disgraced by Manchester United who had several players who could well become household names.

In Mads Timm they have an ideal replacement for Ryan Giggs as he tore Rovers apart single-handedly but the United boys will know they've been in a game tonight. Rovers certainly gave them a scare but on the night luck was not on our side as half chances and 50/50 balls seemed to have a habit of falling for the Reds.

With millions of pounds worth of infrastructure separating the youth development programmes of the two contestants, the main difference between them at the end of 90 minutes was some exceptional finishing.

Apart from Timms' mesmerising exhibition, there were further encouraging displays in the Reds' ranks. David Jones never once shirked a tackle in what was at times a ferocious midfield battle, and United's Southport-born skipper put on another mature performance which added further substance to his expanding reputation. In defence, Wicklow boy McShane formed an effective portcullis with Bardsley that went a long way towards propelling the Reds into yet another semi-final. The two certainly needed to be in top form, because right from the word go Tranmere adopted a direct approach in an attempt to disrupt United's rhythm.

A major factor in the Reds' success was the introduction of Ebanks-Blake, with the no-nonsense forager ruffling a few feathers to make Tranmere's back four look much less sure of themselves than previously. His goal represented a quick reply to Dagnall's and it curtailed any thoughts the Rovers might have held about staging a comeback.

2002-03

MARCH 2003

Mads Timm celebrates scoring his and United's second goal with a great individual effort at Moss Lane

sixth round

2002-03

1) Jack Delo	9) Sebastian Ndombe	1) Luke Steele	9) Eddie Johnson
2) Bob Thanda	10) Alex Varney	2) Lee Sims	10) Kieran Richardson
3) Chris Nunn	11) Stacy Long	3) Lee Lawrence	11) Ben Collett
4) Barry Fuller	*12) Adam Gross (for 3)*	4) Phil Bardsley	*12) David Poole*
5) Osei Sankofa	*13) Rob Elliot GK*	5) Paul McShane	*13) Tom Heaton GK*
6) Simon Jackson	*14) Fred Wilson (for 8)*	6) David Jones	*14) Mark Howard*
7) Lloyd Sam	*15) David Evans (for 11)*	7) Chris Eagles	*15) Danny Byrne*
8) Karl Beckford	*16) Stephen Tucker*	8) Ramon Calliste	*16) Sylvan Ebanks-Blake (for 8)*

MARCH 2003

CHARLTON ATHLETIC 1 v 1 MANCHESTER UNITED
Beckford (pen) Richardson

Saturday 29th

Kick-off 3.00 p.m.

Attendance 9,074

CAPITAL RETURN

semi-final 1st leg

David Jones leads United out at The Valley closely followed by Luke Steele

Mindful of the last time United contested a Youth Cup tie at The Valley, when a degree of chaos was present outside the stadium both prior to and after the start of the game, hosts Charlton Athletic went to great pains to organise themselves more efficiently this time around because, with a Saturday afternoon start and admission pegged at only £3 for adults and £1 for concessions, a crowd of some proportion was inevitable. It was also something of a special event for the home club, as it had been all of sixteen years since they last reached a Youth Cup semi-final.

Charlton's operations director Mick Everitt said, 'It's going to be a great occasion and as it's a free weekend, we are expecting lots of supporters to come and watch the match. The problem for the club is that it's difficult to gauge just how many people will turn up. If three or four thousand people arrive at The Valley just before kick-off and expect to enter the stadium in time to watch the entire match, then we will have real problems.

So we are trying to encourage as many fans as possible to either buy their tickets in advance or turn up at The Valley slightly earlier than normal. It's a chance to see some of our own brightest prospects take on some of the most highly rated youngsters in the country, with players like Kieran Richardson having already played for United in the Champions League this season.'

One of the 'brightest prospects' Everitt referred to was Barry Fuller. Ashford-born and skipper of the young Addicks, he was described in the match programme as 'mobile, fierce in the tackle and boasting a never-say-die attitude'. Stretchered off in an Academy game just a week before with what initially appeared a bad injury, Fuller's dogged determination invariably played a part in him winning a desperate race for fitness to face United.

Other stars in the Athletic squad included England under-18 internationals Osei Sankofa and Stacy Long, as well as Bob Thanda, Fred Wilson and Sebastian Ndombe, who hailed from the Republic of Congo, Australia and Angola respectively.

Forward Alex Varney marked Charlton's Youth Cup start in great style by claiming a hat-trick between the seventh and the 27th minutes at Cardiff to help the Addicks to a 3-1 win. The Valley kids had their hands full at the next stage against a strong Wolverhampton Wanderers side but, with home advantage and the benefit of a penalty scored by Karl Beckford ten minutes from time, they squeezed through to the Fifth Round.

MARCH 2003

The Athletic then succeeded in two away ties. Their prospects looked bleak at Sunderland, where they were 2-0 down after half an hour, until clawing their way back with goals from Stacy Long and Lloyd Sam. In a replica of United's penalty shoot-out against Sheffield United, Charlton ended Sunderland's run in the spot kick sequence by exactly the same margin. By reaching the semi-final, the Addicks surprised a few when triumphing at Leeds with a single goal from Ndombe.

In regards to the event, Charlton Academy director Mick Browne committed his thoughts to paper via the medium of the match programme:

Today's encounter is the first of two legs and it will be a format that none of our players will have experienced before. You could argue that United have the advantage by being at home in the second leg, but I am actually pleased that we are playing at home first. I firmly believe that the boys will respond well to playing at Old Trafford and feel that we are capable of winning there.

Mark Robson and myself have worked hard all week to ensure that the boys are organised and prepared for the game, but our fate will be decided by how our young players respond to playing in a semi-final at The Valley in front of a big crowd. United will be most people's tip to reach the final, but if we believe in ourselves and don't freeze on the day, we are more than capable of causing an upset.

Brian McClair named a squad which was almost the same as that for the tie against Tranmere, with Eddie Johnson returning for Mads Timm while David Poole replaced Phil Picken on the bench. Having advanced through the earlier stages on the less than perfect surfaces of Kingston Park and Moss Lane, McClair's lads were delighted at the prospect of performing on a beautiful lush pasture at The Valley.

Ndombe found himself with an opportunity of opening the scoring against United in the early minutes when he headed a dangerous cross from Sam over the bar from only six yards out. The Reds replied with a long range effort from David Jones, and Johnson then wasted an absolute gift by back-heading a long ball over the stranded Charlton goalie from just inside the penalty area. Johnson's miss caught Athletic in a vulnerable position, as they needed to substitute hamstring victim Chris Nunn and were in the process of rearranging their defensive formation.

Charlton went ahead in the 22nd minute through some carelessness when the Reds lost possession in the middle of their opponents' half. The home side built up a move down the right in which Ndombe served up an intelligent pass to Sam, who darted between Lee Lawrence and Paul McShane in order to make his way into the box. Lawrence was pronounced guilty of nudging Sam over while in full flow and Karl Beckford hammered a superb penalty past Steele to punish the indiscretion.

The Addicks then appeared to settle back on their lead, allowing United to keep hold of the ball for the majority of the time while they satisfied themselves by counterattacking at speed. If it was a deliberate act, the tactic soon proved to be a gross error of judgement because from then on the Reds pushed forward almost at will, with half-chances falling to Eagles and Johnson in quick succession.

It was during the later stages of the first half when the increasing maturity of some of the United lads became apparent. McShane and Bardsley were as solid as rocks at the heart of a defence that had conceded a miserly two goals from open play in their four previous ties while outside of them, Lawrence and Sims

United's Phil Bardsley and Charlton's Alex Varney are both focussed on claiming a loose ball

semi-final 1st leg

2002-03

1) Ross Turnball	9) Anthony Peacock	1) Luke Steele	9) Eddie Johnson
2) Tony McMahon	10) Gary Liddle	2) Lee Sims	10) Kieran Richardson
3) Alan Harrison	11) Chris Brunt	3) Lee Lawrence	11) Ben Collett
4) Matthew Bates	12) *Peter Masters*	4) Phil Bardsley	12) *Mark Howard*
5) Andrew Davies	13) *David Knight GK*	5) Paul McShane	13) *Tom Heaton GK*
6) David Wheater	14) *Jason Kennedy (for 9)*	6) David Jones	14) *David Poole*
7) James Morrison	15) *Danny Reed*	7) Chris Eagles	15) *Ramon Calliste*
8) Andrew Taylor	16) *Tom Craddock*	8) Mads Timm	16) *Sylvan Ebanks-Blake (for 8)*

APRIL 2003

MIDDLESBROUGH 0 v 2 MANCHESTER UNITED

Collett, Richardson

Tuesday 15th

Kick-off 8.05 p.m.

Attendance 8,310

final 1st leg

With United and Arsenal's seniors going neck and neck for the Premiership crown and a showdown between the two set for the following evening at Highbury, the best equipped youth side available to Brian McClair lined up at the Riverside Stadium to face Middlesbrough.

Of the 333 teams that entered the Youth Cup at the beginning of the season, the United squad to a man were quietly confident that they would be the last ones standing at the conclusion of the final.

There was a word on the grapevine that Middlesbrough were satisfied simply in making it through to the final. Feeling the achievement was more than they could have hoped for at the outset of the competition, any further victory was apparently something beyond their wildest expectations. With five sixteen year-olds in the side and three others just a year older, reaching the last two stage represented a marvellous feat for such a young team, most of whom were still eligible for the following season's tournament.

A 3-1 Third Round home victory over Bury represented an encouraging start for the 'Boro and they then continued their winning ways by defeating Barnsley via a single goal at Oakwell. With the sides locked 1-1 at the end of 120 minutes of football at Luton, a 4-3 penalty shoot-out conquest over the Hatters preceded a 1-0 win at Spurs. In the semi-final, Manchester City were defeated 2-1 after extra-time in the concluding leg following a 1-1 draw at the Riverside.

Middlesbrough's best previous effort in the Youth Cup was in 1990, a year in which they were defeated 3-2 by Spurs in the final.

The two 'Boro boys who were expected to cause United the most problems were local forward Anthony Peacock and midfield maestro, James Morrison. The man responsible for the recruitment of Middlesbrough's trainees, Ron Bone, said of Peacock, *'He's a fantastic talent. Although he's small, he's got body strength and his footballing brain is one of the best I've come across.'*

Morrison, a Darlington lad, was one of the aforementioned sixteen year-olds whose tender age hadn't prevented him from already appearing for 'Boro's Reserves. Bone revealed of Morrison, *'He's quick and can go past people and score goals.'* Middlesbrough's defence was formed around Billingham-born Andrew Davies, and when asked about the team's skipper, Bone replied, *'What can you say? He's a colossus. He can play at the back or upfront and has got everything, physical presence, he's technically good, strong in the air and quick.'*

The 'Boro trio of Morrison, Andrew Taylor and Tony McMahon were current members of England's under-17 Youth side while Davies had recently received a call-up into the national under-20 squad. Adding further quality to the team, goalkeeper Ross Turnbull held the distinction of featuring at every England level up to under-18.

With the evening calm and dry, and on a surface that looked so perfect it appeared more suited to a snooker match, Hampshire referee Rob Styles got the proceedings underway. Respective managers Steve McClaren and Sir Alex Ferguson were in attendance, and also present was former Reds' first-teamer Jonathan Greening, along with ex-United youth team goalkeeper Stephen Pears, the latter a member of Middlesbrough's coaching staff.

Despite the obvious pedigree within their ranks, and the backing of the majority of an 8,000-plus crowd behind them, Middlesbrough weren't allowed the lengthy settling in period they might have preferred by suffering the blow of going in arrears in only the fourth minute of the game.

The move started when the home side carelessly lost the ball on the halfway line and Richardson then ran at their defence prior to passing out to Timm on the left. Faced by the presence of nine 'Boro players in the last third of the pitch, initially there didn't appear any immediate danger to the home side. Timm returned the ball to Richardson, who had his back to goal and was stationed some twenty yards out. Then turning at speed, the midfielder struck a superb right-foot shot that caught Turnbull and almost everyone else by surprise to enter the net barely six inches inside the foot of the post.

It was a tremendous show of skill and represented Richardson's fifth goal of the cup run from open play, as well as being his third in consecutive matches. The development provided a great boost for McClair's team and considerably assisted in removing some of the nervous energy from the side so that they could now better demonstrate their fluent passing game.

From then on 'Boro were restricted in the amount of possession United were prepared to concede, with the second clear-cut chance of the match falling to the Manchester side in the 17th minute. A slick exchange of passes between Jones, Collett and Timm ended with the former left facing only Turnbull at a distance of just eight yards. To Middlesbrough's relief, they were let off the hook when Jones' shot was deflected away by the 'keeper's left leg, and Eddie Johnson later frightened the home defence by turning outside the area to drill a powerful shot past Turnbull's right-hand post.

Clearly affected by conceding so early, Middlesbrough's qualities became increasingly more obvious as the interval approached. Their best, and only, opening of the first period came about with six minutes of the half remaining and developed when Alan Harrison processed a plum 30-yard pass along United's right, though Paul McShane looked odds-on favourite to cut it out until slipping as Morrison raced past him. Luke Steele reacted by steaming out to meet the 'Boro man and as Morrison tried to chip him, the goalkeeper got a slight yet vital touch on the ball, propelling it several feet in the air. As it fell, Morrison was only required to help the ball into the empty net but, as he waited, Lee Lawrence somehow got a foot in to deflect it for a corner. It was a fantastic piece of defending from the consistent full-back and Steele clapped as much in relief as appreciation before giving him a hug as a thank you gesture.

The most worrying aspect from McClair's perspective just then was that Timm appeared to be injured as he was seen limping slightly. Timm's woes could be traced back to when he was caught by Davies in the lead up to an off-target strike by Collett.

If McClair told his troops *'more of the same'* in the dressing room for the second game running, he wasn't to get it because the dominance and comfort United had enjoyed for most of the first session largely disappeared upon the change of ends. Whether the cause stemmed from Timm's withdrawal in the 58th minute was a matter of conjecture, although the Reds' attacking options were severely restricted thereafter.

Peacock was at the heart of his team's best work and he was described in one match report as being *'like a pesky fly which cannot be swatted away'* when driving at United's defence.

Middlesbrough's Chris Brunt caused hearts to flutter on United's bench with an hour showing on the clock. Initially winning a tackle in the centre circle, Brunt sprinted on until he was about twenty yards from goal before hitting a left-foot shot across Steele and just wide of his intended target. The scare caused a few recriminations, because all around there were defenders who were left wondering how Brunt was allowed to travel so far without being properly challenged.

United threatened momentarily when substitute Ebanks-Blake brought a save out of Turnbull. Middlesbrough came back again from a set piece when McMahon

Chris Eagles tracks back on defensive duties at the Riverside

456

2002-03

APRIL 2003

(l-r) David Jones, Paul McShane, Kieran Richardson and Lee Lawrence attempt to form a barrier around Middlesbrough's James Morrison

shaped as if he was going to deliver his free kick from the left across the penalty area. Instead finding Brunt, his downward header flitted across the six-yard line without a home foot able to make contact.

Three minutes later, the ever-willing Johnson had his name taken after losing the ball to McMahon and bringing him down from behind.

A dose of controversy was injected into the match in the 71st minute when Harrison drilled a low cross into United's danger area. The pace of the ball deceived Morrison, who was practically stood on the penalty spot, and he failed to gain proper control. It flew up to hit Lawrence, who was standing nearby, and Morrison reacted by appealing for a penalty, as did most of the crowd.

The referee was in a perfect position to view the incident from just seven or eight yards away and he immediately waved away the claim. Co-commentating for MUTV, Old Trafford legend Paddy Crerand correctly spotted that Lawrence had deflected the ball away with his knee.

Throughout all of Middlesbrough's pressure period, the United player who caught the eye more than any other was undoubtedly David Jones. Rarely wasteful, ever willing to get stuck into the hard work while showing deft touches of skill when appropriate, the skipper provided a mammoth presence at a time when his team's difficulties were at their greatest.

United were given a glimpse of goal late on by hunting in and around 'Boro's box, a point at which the home side temporarily struggled to hold onto possession. Middlesbrough were almost made to pay when Johnson smartly stepped over a pass along the outskirts of their area and Ebanks-Blake read his intention to squeeze between three defenders and power in a drive that Turnbull palmed away to his left. 'Boro responded through Morrison, whose attempted long-range effort contained neither the power nor the accuracy to cause Steele concern.

There were less than 60 seconds remaining when United racked up a second, and potentially killer, goal. The move evolved down United's right and included participation from Johnson, Eagles, Bardsley and Sims. Eagles cut inside with the ball at his feet and as Ebanks-Blake smartly took a defender out of the picture

with a dummy run, he crossed it into the area. Jones was just unable to control the centre and the ball bounced past him to the unmarked Collett. Ignoring Jones' request to square it to him, the winger instead slammed an unstoppable shot into 'Boro's net.

The game was called to a halt soon after and the upshot of Collett's goal meant that United would now go into the second leg as firm favourites.

Middlesbrough Academy director David Parnaby neatly summarised the perspective of the Riverside camp when saying, *'They scored early, which was disappointing, but we recovered well and had our moments. The second goal was a blow.'* Parnaby also predicted, *'The scorer of the first goal at Old Trafford will be crucial. If we score it will be game on, if United score we will have a mountain to climb.'*

One reporter felt that even though Middlesbrough *'always presented something of a threat, the truth is that United were too quick, too slick and a touch too strong throughout'.* A different scribe was of the opinion that the Reds were *'within touching distance'* of another Youth Cup triumph, adding they *'must only avoid an embarrassing three-goal defeat......to clinch the trophy many of United's illustrious names have won in the past'.*

> *" To come away here and play against a good quality, good passing and strong side means it's a satisfying result. What pleased me most was that we defended so well. Goalkeeper Luke Steele had to come to collect a lot of crosses, which is one of (Middlesbrough's) major strengths. And we did that so well that, in the last five minutes, we gave ourselves a platform to score a breakaway goal, Ben Collett finishing a lovely move. "*
>
> **BRIAN McCLAIR**

final 1st leg

2002-03

APRIL 2003

final 1st leg

Sylvan Ebanks-Blake and Boro's Andrew Davies go up for a high ball while Ben Collett (left) readies himself to pick up any scraps

A typically wholehearted tackle from Eddie Johnson demonstrates his commitment at the Riverside

1) Luke Steele	9) Eddie Johnson	
2) Lee Sims	10) Kieran Richardson	
3) Lee Lawrence	11) Ben Collett	
4) Phil Bardsley	*12) Mark Howard (for 5)*	
5) Paul McShane	*13) Tom Heaton GK*	
6) David Jones	*14) David Poole (for 10)*	
7) Chris Eagles	*15) Ramon Calliste (for 8)*	
8) Sylvan Ebanks-Blake	*16) Phil Picken*	

1) Ross Turnball	9) Anthony Peacock
2) Tony McMahon	10) Gary Liddle
3) Alan Harrison	11) Chris Brunt
4) Matthew Bates	*12) Peter Masters (for 11)*
5) Andrew Davies	*13) David Knight GK*
6) David Wheater	*14) Niklas Nordgren (for 9)*
7) James Morrison	*15) Danny Reed (for 3)*
8) Andrew Taylor	*16) Jason Kennedy*

2002-03

MANCHESTER UNITED 1 (3) V (1) 1 MIDDLESBROUGH
Johnson — Liddle

APRIL 2003

Friday 25th

Kick-off 8.05 p.m.

Attendance 14,849

final 2nd leg

Coming as it did just two days after one of the greatest European games ever seen at Old Trafford, the Reds' incredible 4-3 win over Real Madrid in the quarter-finals of the Champions League, the youth team were again supported by a quite fantastic turn out from the Manchester public.

Despite the seniors ultimately going out to the Spaniards on aggregate, they were within a handful of points of tying up yet another Premiership title and capturing the Youth Cup would have added further gloss to an already fabulous season.

Prior to the concluding game of the final, Brian McClair was keen to deflect the glory onto others, saying modestly, *'I've done very little. There are a lot of people who deserve pats on the back for these players – scouts, coaches who have had players from a young age, and parents who have had to make sacrifices to give them an opportunity to become professionals.*

This isn't about the last six or seven months. This has been worked on by a lot of people for a long time. Everyone thinks that football is glamorous, and it is to a certain extent, but the lads have worked very hard and sacrificed a lot.'

As a result of the injury he sustained at the Riverside, Mads Timm was unavailable to McClair. His absence wasn't unexpected, allowing United's coach to plan accordingly and in good time, and with five substitute appearances in the competition to his credit, the improving Sylvan Ebanks-Blake was installed as the Dane's replacement.

Middlesbrough lined up as per the first game, but with an altered formation in order to allow Andrew Davies to take up an attacking role. It was essential that 'Boro made inroads into United's lead and with one of their leading lights switched from the back to upfront, it seemed as if they were prepared to gamble to do so.

Present once more to support the club's teenagers, Sir Alex Ferguson was accompanied in the stands by first-team stars David Beckham, Roy Keane, the Neville brothers, Paul Scholes, Quinton Fortune, John O'Shea, Ryan Giggs and Ole Gunnar Solskjaer. Because he was currently the subject of intense media speculation about joining Real Madrid, Beckham was given the loudest welcome of all as the Old Trafford following wanted to let the former Youth Cup winner know they preferred him to remain in Manchester.

With an air of expectation hovering over the stadium, those same spectators were left in little doubt that the Youth Cup would end up in the club's trophy cabinet only a quarter of an hour after kick-off. The Reds displayed a typical attacking attitude right from the word go, and in the ninth minute Kieran Richardson struck a warning shot just over Middlesbrough's bar while hundreds of supporters continued to stream into the stadium.

Eddie Johnson fired the Reds ahead by putting the finishing touch to an assault which began when Luke Steele punted a long ball downfield. It landed a few yards away from the opposite box, the bounce causing Middlesbrough's defence to flap as Ebanks-Blake put in a challenge, and Johnson claimed the stray ball when it came within his vicinity. From just outside the eighteen-yard line, he turned to blast a shot of some velocity past Ross Turnbull and the 'Boro goalie was only able to stand and gaze as it whistled to his right.

Now with his dander up, Ebanks-Blake soon glimpsed another opening when set up by David Jones. Richardson then cheekily attempted to repeat the goal he scored at Charlton when bending a free kick from the right-hand touchline towards the net, his 26th minute attempt missing the angle of crossbar and post by a whisker. Later, at the climax of a sequence of thirteen passes, a long shot

David Jones made life as difficult as possible for Middlesbrough in the second leg of the final

459

APRIL 2003

final 2nd leg

from Eagles flashed just past Turnbull's goal as the custodian responded by diving full-length to his left.

The young Reds were clearly out to impress and the advantage held meant they were able to confidently demonstrate the full range of their skills to the Old Trafford crowd. Jones, Johnson and Eagles were further denied by Turnbull as the first half continued and Ebanks-Blake almost added to Middlesbrough's torment by cracking a short-range drive over the bar a few seconds before it drew to a close.

To 'Boro's credit, they maintained faith in the passing principles that had brought them thus far in the tournament and those present were delighted with the goods on show from two superb sets of talented young artisans. Obviously, United's task was much the easier and the feeling was that if they could keep possession for long enough, the trophy would be theirs.

Middlesbrough made a switch at the interval, withdrawing Anthony Peacock in favour of Swedish midfielder Niklas Nordgren, and the alteration changed their outlook for a time as they piled forward in an attempt to claw a goal back. Gary Liddle tested Steele with a 30-yard blockbuster, while Chris Brunt later smashed a free kick into a five-man wall.

Displaying his inherent attacking instincts, Ebanks-Blake assumed he had further increased United's total when turning a great Richardson assist into the net, only for the 'goal' to be disallowed by a linesman who spotted the provider pulling at a defender's jersey in the build-up.

There were only a quarter of an hour left when Ebanks-Blake was withdrawn in a double substitution, Ramon Calliste going on as his replacement while Mark Howard deputised for McShane at the back.

Middlesbrough gained a consolation three minutes later and an excellent goal it was, too. A four-man move down the right suddenly became dangerous when Davies was set free in space, and from a position level with the six-yard line, he put over an almost undefendable cross which curled slightly away from goal as it reached Liddle. 'Boro's number ten was stationed directly in front of Steele, who was caught in no-man's land with an absence of defensive cover, and he bulleted a great header high into the net to make the score 1-1 on the night. There were practically no celebrations from the Middlesbrough boys, who instead made haste back to the halfway line in order for the game to be restarted as quickly as possible.

Richardson went off almost immediately to a standing ovation as McClair sent on another pair of fresh legs in the shape of David Poole.

'Boro then almost scored again when Morrison was found by a clever pass from Danny Reed, his run carrying him past Jones towards United's penalty area. Once there, he blasted hopefully at Steele, who couldn't hold onto the shot. The goalkeeper blocked the loose ball as Davies tried to force it home and, as it rolled around, Jones rescued his defence with a desperate clearance.

On MUTV, commentator Steve Bower felt Middlesbrough's latest attempt on goal represented a *'wake up call'* and that was exactly what it proved to be because the Reds then concentrated until the end to preserve their spoils. During that period, Calliste wasted the chance to start the party early as he was sent through all alone by a crafty pass from Poole and as Turnbull made rapid strides to narrow down the angles, the substitute flicked the ball to the 'keeper's left only for it to slowly trickle away from the target. It was a smart piece of work by Turnbull, as Calliste looked the favourite to cash in on the space he had created for himself.

That was the last of the serious action. When full-time was signalled, the United lads embraced each other while onlookers showed their appreciation by cheering and clapping, and judging by his expression, there was no-one happier than Alex Ferguson. Sitting next to the manager were former youth team coaches Wilf McGuinness and Eric Harrison, neither of whom were able to hide their feelings as both beamed with the broadest of wide smiles.

Steve Bower claimed the Old Trafford boys had *'joined the history books that are steeped in tradition......and they have earned the F.A. Youth Cup for Manchester United for a record ninth time in their history.'*

Following numerous handshakes and an obligatory soaking for coach McClair from the popping champagne bottles, a gallant Middlesbrough squad collected their losers' medals. The 'Boro lads then clapped the triumphant United team as they made their way to the podium while supporters made their approval known once more.

Joined by several of the club's backroom staff, the United squad are pictured in a jubilant mood following their victory over Middlesbrough

APRIL 2003

David Jones was the last to collect his medal, but the first to get his hands on the trophy and, holding it aloft for all to see, the Reds' captain created a successful link to his 1953 predecessor, Ronnie Cope, which stretched back exactly half a century.

Ever economical with his well chosen words, Brian McClair had the last say when declaring, *'Manchester United want young players who want to win and this cup competition has given them the chance to show us that they do want to win. They really wanted it, that's shown right through. I'm delighted for them.'*

Skipper David Jones poses for the cameras with United's latest piece of silverware

final 2nd leg

2003-04

third round

1) Karl Daniels	9) Eric Manangu	1) Tom Heaton	9) Sylvan Ebanks-Blake
2) Ricky Clark	10) Simeon Jackson	2) Phil Picken	10) Chris Eagles
3) Eugene Burndam	11) Scott Wark	3) Adam Eckersley	11) Ramon Calliste
4) Steven Grant	12) *Ashley Stevens (for 14)*	4) Mark Howard	12) *Ritchie Jones*
5) Magnus Okuonghae	13) *Iyad Ahmed (for 10)*	5) Paul McShane	13) *Lee Crockett GK*
6) Chibuzor Chilaka	14) *Ross Watson*	6) Jonathan Spector	14) *Callum Flanagan*
7) Marcus Kelly	15) *Daniel Grainger*	7) Floribert N'Galula	15) *Phil Marsh (for 6)*
8) Tom Shaw	16) *Oliver Wilkinson*	8) Steven Hogg	16) *Danny Simpson*

NOVEMBER 2003

RUSHDEN & DIAMONDS 1 v 2 MANCHESTER UNITED
Manangu · Calliste, Howard

Tuesday 25th

Kick-off 7.30 p.m.

Attendance 5,214

On the Division Two club's website, it was reported that *'Rushden & Diamonds are looking forward to a carnival atmosphere in this evening's keenly anticipated F.A. Youth Cup match against Manchester United.'* Rushden's operations manager told the website, *'We had sold over 4,500 tickets when I arrived for work this morning and we fully expect more sales throughout the day. In fact, it is questionable whether we will have any space left for cash sales tonight. I would advise anyone who is thinking about attending this match to contact the ticket office urgently.'*

He went on to explain that the ground's capacity needed to be reduced slightly because MUTV wanted to screen the game live, and when quizzed about the development he replied, *'They contacted us last week to ask if they could cover the match and (they) originally wanted to erect camera platforms on the North and South Stands. Of course, these areas were pretty much sold out by then, so we settled upon a commentary platform and cameras on the Peter de Banke Terrace, which is less than ideal for them but the best we could offer at short notice.*

Coverage by MUTV will give us invaluable national and international exposure and further assist our current efforts to raise awareness of Rushden & Diamonds Football Club at this crucial time in the club's history.

I fully expect to see Manchester United shirts throughout the stadium tonight, and I hope that, whatever supporters' allegiances this evening, they can enjoy each other's company. In fact, our supporters have an ideal opportunity this evening to help us show what a wonderful club this is and convince these newcomers to come back again soon.'

For the trip to Northamptonshire, Brian McClair was fortunate in being able to recall five of those who had taken part in the Youth Cup final triumph over Middlesbrough just seven months ago. Of the remainder of his squad, goalkeeper Tom Heaton understudied Luke Steele for six out of eight of last season's Youth Cup ties while defender Phil Picken finally got his big chance after occupying a place on the bench four times previously. In keeping with the recent trend of parading imported foreign prospects, Belgian Floribert N'Galula and American Jonathan Spector were drafted in alongside the locally-based pair of Adam Eckersley and Steven Hogg.

It was plain to see that the Diamonds had made recent improvements to their youth set-up. Having recruited Neville Hamilton in the summer of 2003, the youth coach was delighted to watch two of his squad, Magnus Okuonghae and Eric Manangu, make a contribution towards Rushden's 4-0 win over Colchester on the previous Saturday.

Hamilton told a reporter of United's visit, *'The boys are really up for the game but what I have to do is try and keep them nice and focussed. If I can keep them low key and relaxed then I believe that will help on the day.*

We have continued to do what we have been doing all season in training. We have been working a lot on free kicks and set pieces, which could be important on the day.

It's an important game for the boys and for the football club. It's the biggest game ever in my career.

The publicity for this match has been fantastic and the lads have showed maturity when they have been required to do media interviews.

I'm hoping they don't freeze and just enjoy the atmosphere of the whole match. It's a great chance for my players to play in front of a big audience.'

The trophy holders were certainly tested by the minnows and they were behind for a long time before wiping out their hosts' hopes with a late flourish. Apart from looking physically stronger, fitter and much more skilful than the young Diamonds, United were able to count on the experience of Chris Eagles, as the winger had been blooded in a Carling Cup win at Leeds just a few weeks before when substituting for his former youth team colleague, Kieran Richardson.

The Reds began brightly enough and N'Galula tested Rushden goalie Karl Daniels with a low drive after foxing three defenders in the fourth minute. Eagles looked sharp when exposing the Diamonds' defence with penetrating bursts of speed or accurate passes and he and his team-mates soon developed a rhythm that suggested it might turn into a most uncomfortable night for the home side in front of their fantastic and highly vocal support.

For all of their overwhelming early superiority, it counted for absolutely zero on ten minutes when Rushden bloodied United's nose from their first corner. There was certainly nothing complicated about the goal, as Marcus Kelly belted a corner to the far post where Okuonghae's header was blocked by Heaton before being bundled over the goal-line by Manangu.

Far from allowing the setback to erode their confidence, the Reds actually used it as a springboard to launch yet more attacks. Calliste was thwarted by a brave save from Welsh under-17 international Daniels, who dived near his feet, and Eagles then found some space in an offensive position prior to hoisting his effort over Rushden's crossbar.

With Manangu often isolated upfront for the home team, McClair knew there was plenty of time for his boys to get themselves back in the frame and when a close-range effort from Calliste almost did the trick, it seemed to confirm what the Reds' coach was probably thinking.

In the 34th minute, N'Galula presented Ebanks-Blake with a free header from just six yards distance, which he wasted by directing it wide of the mark, and just prior to the interval, Spector found himself attacking a corner kick only for his headed effort to land on the roof of the net.

In view of the amount of possession United had claimed, former youth team sharpshooter and current MUTV pundit Andy Ritchie observed, *'We've just got to step it up a gear, just that little bit. We've just got to be more decisive in the last third.......to be more ruthless in front of goal.'*

Nevertheless, when the whistle for half-time sounded shortly after, the scoreline shone brightest for the Diamonds.

There was no let-up for Rushden, and Daniels in particular, as the 'keeper continued to impress with quick stops from Calliste and the marauding Eckersley. Four minutes into the second period, Daniels again earned the cheers of the majority of the crowd when somehow managing to get his body behind a low shot from Calliste.

United's number eleven was enjoying a fine game and looked to be living up to the high standards expected of him as he largely made the opening for himself by ghosting through the home defence in comparative ease. It would only have taken a goal or two to cap an excellent night's work for the Welsh boy, only he was once more denied by some safe handling by Daniels in the 56th minute.

By that point the Diamonds appeared to be rapidly running out of steam, so they threw on Iyad Ahmed for Simeon Jackson just a couple of minutes after a snaking and unchallenged run by Eagles ended with his attempt at goal flashing over the bar and into the crowd.

Even though the home team were hardly able to muster an attack, they again almost confounded over 5,000 onlookers when another corner from Kelly set off a panic attack amongst United's defenders before being dealt with by the determined Heaton.

The Reds continued to keep Daniels occupied, and the goalkeeper once again demonstrated his alertness by blocking a powerful on-target effort from Eagles in the 74th minute.

The save seemed to nudge the Diamonds even further towards what would have been a famous victory, and it was at that juncture when Brian McClair sent on Phil Marsh to add some extra punch to the forward-line. Within moments, Marsh's introduction seemed to have done the trick until Daniels added to an already lengthy litany of heroic deeds by casually catching a short-range shot from the scavenging Ebanks-Blake.

While McClair continued to look concerned on the touchline, blessed relief arrived on 79 minutes with the award of a corner. Eagles floated the flag kick across Rushden's six-yard box, from where Mark Howard powered a majestic diving header into the net with Daniels for once rooted to the spot.

If that wasn't bad enough for the Nene Park teenagers, only just over three minutes passed before the Reds underlined their superiority by taking the lead. Following a couple of corners that Heaton handled confidently, a typically smooth move saw the ball worked into the feet of Calliste, who coolly directed it past Daniels. As was perfectly understandable, his goal sparked a lengthy celebration from a mightily delighted United team.

The Diamonds piled forward as often as possible from then until the end, a period in which they took the unusual step of substituting a substitute, but their efforts ultimately proved futile.

The brief match summary posted on United's website made mention that the Reds had *'scraped'* through the tie and it went on to mention they were *'given a scare by their unfancied hosts'*.

Just over a week later, it was announced that Simeon Jackson was to be taken on trial at Old Trafford, Brian McClair admitting that his scouts had watched the Jamaican-born, Canadian-raised prospect *'three or four times'* prior to the Youth Cup clash and were suitably impressed with what they saw. Jackson had only been at Nene Park for three months and, having scored eleven times in as many games for Rushden's junior sides, was signed on YTS forms.

During a period lasting just over a fortnight, Jackson subsequently made one full and another substitute appearance for United's under-17 team prior to returning south.

462

1) Tom Heaton	9) Sylvan Ebanks-Blake	1) Kasper Schmeichel	9) Karl Bermingham
2) Mark Howard	10) Ramon Calliste	2) Danny Warrender	10) Stephen Ireland
3) Steven Hogg	11) Adam Eckersley	3) Paul Collins	11) Carlos Logan
4) Floribert N'Galula	12) Jonathan Spector (for 6)	4) Nathan D'Laryea	12) Phil Reilly (for 7)
5) Paul McShane	13) Tommy Lee GK	5) Nedum Onuoha	13) Laurence Matthewson GK
6) Ritchie Jones	14) Phil Marsh (for 8)	6) Ian Bennett	14) Ishmael Miller (for 11)
7) Phil Picken	15) Callum Flanagan (for 10)	7) Marc Laird	15) Kelvin Etuhu (for 9)
8) Lee Martin	16) Graeme Port	8) Jonathan D'Laryea	16) Micah Richards

MANCHESTER UNITED 2 v 0 MANCHESTER CITY
Calliste, Flanagan

2003-04

JANUARY 2004

Tuesday 13th

Kick-off 7.30 p.m.

Attendance 5,547

fourth round

When the Reds resumed their interest in the Youth Cup seven weeks after their win at Rushden & Diamonds, a famous name from the club's past was there to face them.

The draw paired United up against neighbours Manchester City for their 13th meeting since 1954, and kitted out in the number one jersey for the Light Blues was a certain Kasper, son of arguably the Reds' greatest ever goalkeeper, the incomparable Peter Schmeichel.

On the eve of the game, the Evening News carried a lengthy preview which covered the angles of both camps. When quizzed about his team's chances, City Academy chief Jim Cassell responded by saying, *'Personally, I hope that we can come out on top but I really believe that this game is too close to call. There is nothing between the two sides, although Manchester United will be favourites because they have home advantage and they are also the holders. That could give them the edge.'*

Then asked a question about City's exit from the Youth Cup in last season's semi-final, Cassell replied, *'People said that last year we should have got to the final but that is doing a disservice to Middlesbrough. They came with a game plan and stuck to it well, so you have to give them credit for that. As for United winning the trophy, well again, they deserve all the praise they got.*

Win, lose or draw tonight, I will go and shake hands with everyone from United. It is all part of developing the young kids and showing them how to be proper sportsmen.'

Over on the south side of town, Brian McClair gave his take on the clash when observing, *'In my time at this level City traditionally have had better results in the games we have played in Academy matches. But the Youth Cup is a totally different situation.*

At Academy level we are not preparing teams to win games. We are looking for performances and trying to push players on. But this game we are preparing to win. It is not because it is City, it is because it is the Youth Cup. In other matches the result is not top of the list.

We are trying to get them to play well, get some form and progress through the ranks. But this is the one competition where we can prepare to win the game like the first-team. The fact that it is City adds to it all. Derbies are derbies at any level.'

United's coach was also asked about Lee Martin, a recent recruit from Wimbledon, who he intended to include in the side. *'Lee is a nice, quiet, confident lad,'* McClair said prior to adding, *'He was watched on numerous occasions before we invited him up here for a two-week trial and he showed enough potential then to persuade the manager to pay a fee for him.'*

City started slightly the stronger of the two teams, both of whom appeared somewhat on the tentative side. That mood manifested itself in the tenth minute when Steven Hogg's intended pass fell to City's Ireland, whose thunderous drive whizzed a fraction over. Martin then burst through the City defence until the powerful Onuoha nudged him off the ball.

The Reds slowly began to probe for weaknesses and when Ebanks-Blake controlled a long ball from Tom Heaton, the marksman cut inside to force Schmeichel to deal with his fiercely struck effort. There was no respite for City and the impressive Martin, who had already covered a fair amount of acreage, helped to inflict the first significant damage on them by playing an exact 30-yard pass to Ebanks-Blake down the right-hand side of the away team's penalty area in the 22nd minute.

Onuoha was unable to get to Ebanks-Blake, so United's centre-forward was able to whip a cross over. Schmeichel made a rash decision to run off his line, ending up in no-man's land, and the error left Ramon Calliste free to tap home an easy chance and give his side a crucial breakthrough.

There were calls for a penalty four minutes later, when Martin went down under a challenge from Onuoha on the bye-line, and more action followed, Karl Bermingham bringing an excellent low save out of Heaton through putting his head on a long swerving cross.

Adam Eckersley responded by crashing a curling free kick against Schmeichel's crossbar and City then struck the inside of a post, with Onuoha's following header scrambled away by Paul McShane.

Schmeichel vacated his line with more success than earlier to deny Phil Picken and down at the other end there was only a minute to the break when McShane again helped to preserve United's lead with a great block to stop Marc Laird from shooting.

The second half was almost a mirror image of the first, with City again beginning marginally the brighter while the Reds later upped their presence considerably. Martin continued to delight the home support with penetrating runs from deep positions, and with City seemingly losing their grip, they took off Laird for Reilly just after the hour mark and substituted Carlos Logan for Ishmael Miller four minutes later.

Brian McClair waited just a little while longer than his counterpart, sending on Callum Flanagan for Calliste in the 69th minute only to then have to replace Martin through cramp.

United reserved themselves a place in the Fifth Round with thirteen minutes to the end and again Schmeichel looked at fault. A huge punt from Tom Heaton caused the goalie and defender Nathan D'Laryea to get into what was later described as *'a hesitant mix-up'* and Flanagan *'bravely took advantage of the misunderstanding'* to head home the Reds' second goal and concurrently seal City's fate.

Reilly did his level best to retrieve what appeared to be a hopeless situation for the visitors with a short-range pop at goal and City's misery was completed in the last minute as Bermingham was stretchered off in some pain with knee ligament damage.

Just before the final whistle was blown, the heavens opened to shower the players and officials with hailstones.

The Manchester Evening News was full of praise for the dashing performance of Lee Martin, who it was felt *'inspired'* the Reds to their junior derby victory. Noting that the sixteen year-old was secured *'for a downpayment of £200,000'*, an amount which *'could rise sharply'*, the newspaper claimed the midfielder's Youth Cup bow *'certainly suggested United will have to send more cheques down to London'.*

Brian McClair rounded off the Reds' success by admitting, *'It was an ugly win. But there was a possibility of it being like that, with the occasion at Old Trafford and the heavy pitch.'*

Looking purposeful and dangerous throughout, Sylvan Ebanks-Blake's unorthodox pose appears to bewilder a City opponent

463

2003-04

1) Tom Heaton	9) Sylvan Ebanks-Blake	1) Joe Lewis	9) Lee Howlett
2) Mark Howard	10) Chris Eagles	2) Olly Willis	10) Danny Crow
3) Steven Hogg	11) Adam Eckersley	3) Adam Smith	11) Robert Eagle
4) Jonathan Spector	*12) Ramon Calliste (for 7)*	4) Jake Osborne	*12) Matt Watts (for 11)*
5) Paul McShane	*13) Tommy Lee GK*	5) Matthew Halliday	*13) Shane Herbert GK*
6) Ritchie Jones	*14) Markus Neumayr (for 10)*	6) Andrew Fisk	*14) Andrew Cave-Brown (for 9)*
7) Phil Picken	*15) Callum Flanagan*	7) Nicky Howell	*15) Seb Muddel (for 7)*
8) Lee Martin	*16) Graeme Port*	8) Lee Blackburn	*16) Ardavan Djahansouzi*

FEBRUARY 2004

MANCHESTER UNITED 4 v 2 NORWICH CITY

Calliste (pen), Halliday (o.g.), Howard, McShane — Howell, Smith

Tuesday 17th

Kick-off 7.00 p.m.

Attendance 2,958

fifth round

Norwich City's arrival at Old Trafford brought back memories of the Canaries' superb 1983 youth team, a combination which ranks as one of the most accomplished visiting under-18 sides ever to grace United's palatial home. That City side went on to clinch the Youth Cup for the only time in the club's history, and there were those on the Carrow Road side of the fence who might have felt another such visit to Manchester represented something of an omen.

Norwich youth coach Sammy Morgan recorded his disappointment at not being able to utilise first-team fringe player Ryan Jarvis through injury, and despite that loss he didn't feel a favourable result was beyond the scope of his charges. '*As you would expect, Manchester United are a very good footballing side who like to pass it around and are solid all over the pitch*,' he explained. '*There's a lot of quality in there and they have been able to attract players from way beyond their borders. They have got one or two they have paid a few bob for, so we are really looking forward to matching ourselves against them.*'

The game's dull opening chapter closed on ten minutes when Paul McShane glanced over a perfectly placed free kick from Eckersley. Norwich then continued the match's more entertaining second phase by taking the lead three minutes later, and what a fine goal it was. Sweeping upfield after clearing a corner, the Reds were left exposed with only Phil Picken back to mark two City forwards. The ball was controlled by Nicky Howell, and he displayed ice-cold nerves to firstly round Picken and then twist past Heaton before guiding it between the posts.

Commenting on MUTV, Gary Neville gave an accurate assessment about the goal being something of a blessing in disguise for two of the home team. United's star full-back based his view on the fact that both Picken and Heaton made attempts to bring the Norwich lad down, and if he had fell to either challenge, one of them could very well have been red-carded.

McClair's boys were lucky to survive another couple of close calls, one of which was a Danny Crow drive that almost deflected over Heaton after hitting Spector's outstretched leg. The Reds' main problem was City's pace, which the visitors used to great advantage by counterattacking whenever possible.

Half-time was only three minutes away when United got the break they so badly needed. Picken was the instigator of the equaliser when he lofted a fairly aimless cross into Norwich's penalty area, and with three defenders stationed on the six-yard line and no home player posing any type of threat, Halliday unbelievably headed it into his own net.

Crosses continued their curse on the Canaries in the 50th minute, as Mark Howard forced himself between two defenders to head the Reds into the lead.

There were only twelve minutes remaining when City's Blackburn blasted a superb cross-shot that missed a post by inches and, as so often happens, United went down to the other end to score. Jake Osborne was booked for bringing down Calliste close to the corner flag and McShane acted out a captain's part by nodding in the resulting free kick. Calliste then made a couple of more telling contributions in the 84th minute, initially when he was felled in the box by Crow and then by rising to convert the spot kick. There was no way back for Norwich, but their consolation came in stoppage time with the best goal of the game as Adam Smith whacked a twenty-yard diagonal fizzer past Heaton.

In a familiar 'we wuz robbed' outburst, City coach Morgan later claimed, '*The lads never gave up and it took a ridiculous decision from the referee to kill us off. That was never a penalty in a month of Sundays.*'

There was a completely different take emanating from the report on the Reds' website, which noted that '*Despite a poor start and a couple of subsequent scares, United deserved to progress to the next round*'. Then judging the performances of Martin, Eagles and Jones as '*superb*', it was also noted that '*the crowd were excited by Ramon Calliste's twenty-minute contribution*'.

United's Adam Eckersley gets a close-up of Nicky Howell's size nine's

464

1) Steven Drench	9) Clark Walsh	1) Tom Heaton	9) Sylvan Ebanks-Blake
2) Gavin Peers	10) Keith Barker	2) Mark Howard	10) Ramon Calliste
3) Andy Taylor	11) Joel Byrom	3) Adam Eckersley	11) Lee Martin
4) Paul Weaver	*12) Bryan Hodge*	4) Jonathan Spector	*12) Phil Picken*
5) Luke Jones	*13) Zak Jones GK*	5) Paul McShane	*13) Tommy Lee GK*
6) Craig Barr	*14) Andy Reid*	6) Ritchie Jones	*14) Markus Neumayr*
7) Sergio Peter	*15) Joe Garner (for 9)*	7) Chris Eagles	*15) Steven Hogg (for 6)*
8) Gary Stopforth	*16) Ralph Welch*	8) Floribert N'Galula	*16) Jami Puustinen (for 10)*
	17) Adam Thomas		

BLACKBURN ROVERS 2 v 0 MANCHESTER UNITED

Barker, Byrom (pen)

MARCH 2004

Saturday 6th

Kick-off 2.00 p.m.

Attendance 3,206

Now installed, yet again, as the tournament favourites, the Reds made the short jaunt up to Ewood Park where they faced old foes in the form of Blackburn. Because United's seniors were entertaining Fulham in an F.A. Cup quarter-final tie, it meant that two of the club's sides were contesting a last four spot on the same day.

The Rovers were required to come through a bruising encounter at the previous stage of the Youth Cup when defeating Gillingham at Morecambe's Christie Park. The 2-1 win came at a price, as the tricky Tareck Sakali was left with cruciate knee ligament damage and striker Matt Derbyshire's season also ended when he seriously damaged an ankle. Added to the absence of influential midfielder Peter Corvino, it meant that coach Rob Kelly needed to rearrange his resources to tackle the force of United's young guns.

There was no shortage of discussion points resulting from the early section of the match, a period in which it probably dawned on the Reds that they faced a tough fight and also needed to match Blackburn's high work rate. The name Luke Jones went into the referee's notebook for fouling Lee Martin on the left-hand side of the home penalty area on eleven minutes and Craig Barr suffered an identical punishment through rashly clattering into Chris Eagles with a late challenge three minutes later.

Within moments, the action switched to the opposite end of the pitch, where a direct run from German winger Sergio Peter came to a sudden halt when he was upended by a clumsy Martin tackle. The first penalty to be awarded at Ewood Park all season, Joel Byrom placed it left-footed to Heaton's right with the goalkeeper going in the opposite direction.

It took the Reds another quarter of an hour to really get back into the swing of things and they then created two quick chances. Firstly, Ebanks-Blake threatened in the Blackburn box until Andy Taylor blocked his progress and from the resulting corner, Martin volleyed a right-footer off-target from sixteen yards out.

There was yet more incident as the half drew to a close, Peter severely testing Heaton after performing a little trickery and Eagles replying with a shot on the turn. The referee then felt compelled to caution a third member of Blackburn's back four, with Gavin Peers booked for bringing down Calliste.

The Reds were awarded the latest in a lengthy parade of free kicks three minutes into the second half when Eagles was pulled back on the edge of the box. Eckersley hit it low, Drench getting down swiftly in order to palm the ball to safety.

Heaton needed to catch a through ball from Clark Walsh which was intended for the onrushing Peter and the German then cheekily pinched it from him. Peter was just about to strike it into the net when the referee blew for the infringement and in Rovers' next attack of note, United survived a penalty shout as Keith Barker went down just as he attempted to get a shot in.

The best opportunities then fell almost exclusively to the hosts. Walsh smartly back-headed a free kick to Barker, whose attempt was directed straight at Heaton, and Peter then drew a more exacting save out of the Reds' goalie. Heaton later produced his best work by tipping an on-target header from Jones over the bar. The game was over as a contest eight minutes from time when Rovers' Byrom curled in a free kick from the left wing and Barker got above his marker to bullet home a header.

In the dying seconds of normal time, Blackburn's Taylor launched a long ball upfield and Barker unselfishly squared it to substitute Joe Garner, whose scuffed shot prevented him from adding to his side's advantage.

Eagles scorned a late chance for an under par United, but by then the Rovers had earned their right to a semi-final spot. There was a brief mention about the defeat on United's website, which included a statement that the Reds *'rarely reached their usual high standards and were deservedly beaten'*.

Jonathan Spector (left) watches on as Mark Howard looks pained while shielding the ball at Ewood Park

2004-05

1) Lee Crockett	9) Jami Puustinen	1) Chris Sanna	9) Keith Thomas
2) Jonny Evans	10) Giuseppe Rossi	2) Adam Kirkpatrick	10) Martin Paterson
3) Ryan Shawcross	11) Jamie Mullan	3) John Quigley	11) Matt Hazley
4) Ritchie Jones	*12) David Gray*	4) Scott Musgrove	*12) Eric Graves (for 15)*
5) Gerard Piqué	*13) Ben Amos GK*	5) Danny Hughes	*13) Robert Garrett (for 11)*
6) Darron Gibson	*14) Sean Evans (for 9)*	6) Matt Swift	*14) Robert Duggan GK*
7) Lee Martin	*15) Danny Simpson (for 5)*	7) Danny Smith	*15) Francino Francis (for 9)*
8) Phil Marsh	*16) Fraizer Campbell (for 8)*	8) Carl Dickinson	*16) Norbert Zsivoczky*

DECEMBER 2004

MANCHESTER UNITED* 0 v 1 STOKE CITY

Paterson

third round

Thursday 16th

Kick-off 7.30 p.m.

Attendance 307

*Played at Ewen Fields, Hyde

He might have gone on to become a soccer superstar who has won a clutch of the sport's top honours, including a couple of Champions League winner's medals, Copa del Rey and La Liga titles, as well as the game's greatest team honour, a World Cup final triumph. He may also have been fêted as one of the most assured central defenders on the planet whose girlfriend is acclaimed pop diva Shakira, but Gerard Piqué's one and only appearance in the F.A. Youth Cup lasted just over half an hour and ended in grief at a murky Ewen Fields in Hyde.

Fielding the club's most internationally diverse youth team line-up so far, starting berths were given to American/Italian striker Giuseppe Rossi, Ulster lads Jonny Evans and Darron Gibson, Finnish forward Jami Puustinen and the Catalonian Piqué, while Edinburgh's David Gray was nominated for one of the five bench spots.

However, the most striking aspect of the influx of foreigners was the appointment of 63 year-old Francisco Filho, United's very first, and as yet only, non-UK born Youth Cup coach. The Brazilian had joined the club in time for the start of the 2002/03 season and upon his appointment chief executive Peter Kenyon remarked, *'To have someone of Francisco's calibre here is fantastic. The youth team is an integral part of Manchester United, especially if we are to continue developing the football of the future.'*

Having expressed concern at the lack of home grown youngsters promoted to senior status in the recent past, Alex Ferguson was able to place his faith in a coach who had spent almost 30 years working at the French Football Academy at Clarefontaine, where he helped to develop such renowned talents as Thierry Henry and Jean-Pierre Papin.

Filho had been involved with United's Academy for the past two years and it was felt that the time was right for him to take over the reigns of the Youth Cup team from Brian McClair. Because the club had entered both the Barclays Premiership Reserve League North and the lesser standard Pontin's Holidays League Division One (West), McClair was required to assist fellow coach Ricky Sbragia with those heavier than usual second string commitments.

If the Brazilian required a boost going into the clash, it was gained on the previous Saturday when United's under-18's secured an excellent 4-2 away win

One of three United centre-backs, Gerard Piqué was substituted at Ewen Fields

against their Youth Cup adversaries with two goals each from Phil Marsh and Puustinen. Midfielder Jamie Mullan, who was credited with a couple of assists in the Potteries, told MUTV, *'It was good to win because we were 3-1 up against them in our league game earlier in the season and they came back. This was a good result and hopefully we can beat them in the Youth Cup during the week. This result gives us great confidence.'*

For Filho's maiden test in the tournament, the conditions at Hyde were just about as far removed from the sunny climes of São Paulo as it was possible to imagine. Dark, cold, extremely blustery and teeming down with rain, nevertheless the pitch looked in remarkably good condition as the Reds got the game underway.

In a preview of what was to follow, United managed to scorn two gilt-edged chances in the early stages. On three minutes, it looked like Puustinen was about to continue his recent scoring run against the Potters until the Finn somehow contrived to blast the ball over the bar from inside the six-yard box. Six minutes later, a terrific cross from the industrious Mullan was met by the unchallenged Rossi, whose close-range header went more or less the same way as Puustinen's previous effort.

One of the game's major turning points came dead on the quarter-hour mark when Piqué was injured in a clash with Stoke's Thomas. Leaving the field for treatment, a full three minutes passed before the former Barcelona junior was able to return. It was immediately clear that Piqué was still in some distress and judging by his restricted mobility, it also appeared fairly obvious the injury wasn't one he would be able to 'run off'. As the seconds ticked by, almost every one of the small number of supporters present were questioning why the lad wasn't taken off and, looking at his pained expression, so was he.

In the 20th minute, the Reds' problems increased tenfold when they went behind to a goal that would have had the watching Alex Ferguson fuming. Running with the ball down Stoke's inside-right channel, Keith Thomas knocked it into the middle of United's area and, with two or three opponents around him, Martin Paterson demonstrated a passion to get on the end of it. He managed to scramble the ball past Crockett and across the goal-line, and Paterson wouldn't

This game was originally scheduled to be played at Moss Lane, Altrincham

Giuseppe Rossi had no luck in front of goal against Stoke

2004-05

DECEMBER 2004

have minded one bit about a member of the press corps later describing his effort as *'scruffy'*.

Piqué's continuing fitness issue again came to the fore in the 33rd and 35th minutes. On the first occasion, a long hopeful ball from the Stoke half of the field led to a misunderstanding between him and his 'keeper. The Spaniard seemed to expect Crockett to come and claim it, and the indecision prompted the lurking Paterson to nip in and chip the stranded goalie.

Luckily for the embarrassed defensive duo, there wasn't enough power in the attempt and the ball was cleared to safety. Soon after, Piqué allowed Paterson to wriggle free from his attention and Crockett was forced to save the City striker's shot with his legs.

A couple of minutes later, and to everyone's great relief, United's distressed number five was at last substituted by Danny Simpson. A bit of reorganising then took place, as Simpson heeded instructions to take up a midfield role while Ritchie Jones was ordered to fill in at the back for the departed centre-half.

The opening period concluded with chances at both ends. United's occurred through the prompting of Mullan who, cutting in from the left flank, rifled the ball right along Stoke's six-yard line only for Rossi to fractionally fail to make the crucial contact. Shawcross was then cautioned for a bad foul on City's Hughes and he almost paid a further price from the free kick that followed. Placing the ball just a few yards inside United's half, Stoke's Carl Dickinson smashed an outrageous attempt on Crockett's goal. It nearly paid off, too, because the Reds' 'keeper was off his line and the flight of the ball forced him to make a quick shuffle back to catch it.

Those hardy souls present thought Filho had sent on a goalkeeper replacement for the start of the second half until it was realised that Crockett was now wearing a different jersey. Asked to change his grey one because it clashed with City's similar looking silver shirts, the Peterborough-born custodian was supplied with a black top.

Encouragingly, United resumed in a much brighter mode and only four minutes in Mullan grimaced as his near-post drive was pushed away for a corner. The Reds then wasted three decent openings in the space of as many minutes, and Puustinen was again in the dock through being accused as the main culprit. Drawing a save from Sanna in a one-on-one showdown when it looked much easier to score, he hit the ball against a defender who was stood on the goal-line from the resultant corner. Mullan lifted spirits momentarily by making a great run through the Stoke defence, only his good work went kaput when Gibson leathered his squared pass yards over the bar.

In the 64th minute, the players were subjected to a near-typhoon scale downpour and as the rain cascaded down, it prompted a couple of substitutions from the visitors.

The Reds almost got the equaliser their enterprise deserved in the 70th minute, the much-vaunted Rossi at last managing to find the back of the net off City's Matt Swift only to be denied by an offside decision. Just after Filho sent on Fraizer Campbell for Phil Marsh, Darron Gibson floated over a terrific cross from the right wing only for Mullan to fluff his header and, according to MUTV, that miss represented United's 13th effort on goal to Stoke's three.

The Potters increased that figure to four when, in a quick counter, Paterson stroked an exquisite pass to the feet of Francis, who disappointed his team-mate by directing a scoring attempt directly at Crockett.

Going into the final ten minutes, United's need for a goal was now one of some desperation. Mullan appeared to be their best hope of salvation and some tricky wing play by him provided another chance for the flat-footed Rossi. A fresh pair of legs was introduced when Sean Evans replaced Puustinen and a minute or two later, Gibson planted a direct free kick right into Sanna's arms.

Just before normal time elapsed, there was an unfortunate clash of heads and through it Stoke were forced to take off the livewire Francis. The referee added on an extra four minutes, during which United's Martin allowed his simmering frustration to boil over and he found himself booked for dissent.

It was certainly a great win for Stoke and the look of sheer joy on the faces of their players and staff told its own story. For United, and coach Filho in particular, the result was a shocker and few of the Reds came out of the game with any credit in a collectively woeful performance against distinctly average opposition.

United's website provided the most telling observations by claiming, *'Credit must go to Stoke who, having gone 1-0 up, were tactically well-organised; a corner for the Potters in the dying stages saw not one Stoke player in United's penalty area, so eager were the team to claim United's scalp in the prestigious youth tournament. The Reds can take solace in an energetic performance from midfielder Lee Martin, and the promising passing skills of Darron Gibson in the middle of the park, even if this season's campaign ended much earlier than expected'.*

Along with coach Francisco Filho (back row, far left), the majority of United's 2004/05 youth squad pose at a sunny Carrington
Back row, players only (l-r) Floribert N'Galula, Ryan Shawcross, Darron Gibson, Lee Crockett, Chris Backhouse, Lee Martin, Jami Puustinen, Jonny Evans
Front row (l-r) Kyle Moran, Aaron Burns, Kieran Lee, Danny Simpson, David Gray, Danny Rose, Michael Lea, Sean Evans, Fraizer Campbell

third round

2005-06

third round

1) Jake Meredith	9) Nathaniel Howell		1) Ron-Robert Zieler	9) Fraizer Campbell
2) Michael Howell	10) James McPike		2) Kieran Lee	10) Sean Evans
3) Craig Davies	11) Sone Aluko		3) Michael Lea	11) Danny Rose
4) Jamie Price	*12) Lewis Green (for 10)*		4) Craig Cathcart	*12) Jamie Mullan (for 8)*
5) Mark Hall	*13) Joel Skeldon GK*		5) Jonny Evans	*13) Ben Amos GK*
6) Darren Campion	*14) Amadou N'Diaye*		6) Darron Gibson	*14) Aaron Burns (for 9)*
7) Nick Wright	*15) Jared Wilson*		7) David Gray	*15) Ryan Shawcross*
8) Brett Hinks	*16) James Johnson (for 7)*		8) Sam Hewson	*16) Corry Evans (for 7)*

DECEMBER 2005

BIRMINGHAM CITY 0 v 2 MANCHESTER UNITED

Evans S. (2)

Thursday 15th

Kick-off 7.00 p.m.

Attendance 459

For the Reds' excursion to Birmingham in December 2005, new youth coach Paul McGuinness selected Reserve regulars Darron Gibson, Jonny Evans and Fraizer Campbell while a number of others chosen could also claim at least some exposure to second string standard. The appointment of McGuinness meant that he was now the third such incumbent of the position in as many seasons, although with his appearance against Barnsley in 1984, it meant that he had emulated his father for a second time by not only playing but also coaching United's Youth Cup side. Allied to that brief exposure in the competition 21 years before, and his and his dad's extensive knowledge of the club's long and distinguished traditions in the tournament, there was a groundswell of feeling that the under-18 squad was in the care of a capable steward.

Speaking to MUTV about the possible starting line-up at St. Andrews, McGuinness revealed, *'(For) the last couple of (Academy) games we've been able to play one or two of the boys who've normally been in the Reserves to give us a little bit of consistency and teamwork together before the Youth Cup, so that's been useful, and we've also had one or two practice matches with the Reserves which gets all the players together. So we're hopeful it all gels well.'*

The plans McGuinness put in place paid off with a polished performance from a team consisting of numerous newcomers, including German goalkeeper Ron-Robert Zieler and a Belfast native called Craig Cathcart.

There was little to set the pulse racing in an edgy opening seventeen minutes, at which point Campbell smashed a left-footed shot into the side-netting of Jake Meredith's goal at the Tilton Road end of the ground. From then on it was pretty much United all the way as Birmingham's chances of a result seemed to submerge deeper and deeper with every passing second. Campbell tested Meredith to the full with a dipping drive which bounced awkwardly in front of the 'keeper and the Huddersfield-born schemer then hit a glorious shot from well outside the box that only just whistled past the angle of post and crossbar.

With a fraction over two-thirds of the first half gone, MUTV's Steve Bower remarked that United were stretching their hosts and co-commentator Arthur Albiston responded in the affirmative. There followed another passage of forgettable play, during which Reds' skipper Jonny Evans and the Blues' Jamie Price were cautioned for fouls, and it ended in the 40th minute through United striking a decisive blow.

Birmingham appeared in no danger while probing for a chink in United's armoury on the left-hand corner of Zieler's penalty area until carelessly losing possession and allowing the Reds to break away with a delightful interchange of passes between Hewson, Rose, Campbell, Gibson and Lee. The latter guided an inch-perfect pass along the right flank to David Gray, who cleverly dummied his marker to make some elbow room for himself. Gray ran on before sliding a low cross to the feet of Sean Evans, whose shot from sixteen-yards distance flew into the right-hand corner of Meredith's net. Standing in and around the away dug-out, there was a quiet air of satisfaction emanating from the club's coaching quartet of McGuinness, Jimmy Ryan, Brian McClair and John Cooke and it was based on the fact that all of the opening half's chances had fallen to United while Zieler wasn't once required to make a save.

The second period began in a similar fashion to the first and, apart from long-range efforts from Sean Evans and Campbell, it was all cat and mouse stuff, with the Reds keeping the ball for lengthy passages of play. United were still more feline than rodent in the 71st minute, when Evans doubled his night's output with a supremely executed goal. Situated ten yards inside his own half, the highly impressive Campbell set him up with a searching long ball that sailed between two City defenders. The Ludlow-based poacher brilliantly chested it down on the run and drove on with a defender running alongside him until situated about twelve yards out. From there, Evans drilled a lovely shot under the outstretched Meredith to put United 2-0 up.

Based on the Reds' domination of their opponents, Arthur Albiston felt the goal was *'maybe a wee bit longer coming than we would have hoped for'* and he went on to predict with some confidence, *'I would feel that is game, set and match now.'*

United fairly cruised through the remainder of the game. Only a 'goal' disallowed for pushing from Danny Rose, a cut-back from the bye-line by substitute Corry Evans which managed to evade all of his colleagues, and a free kick from Sean Evans that missed the target by a few inches to deny him a hat-trick, was the sum total of the remaining action.

Even though it wasn't the most entertaining of cup ties, the game got McGuinness' reign as Youth Cup coach off to a flyer and he would have been delighted with the performances of some of the team's individuals, particularly Campbell and the rock-like centre-back pair of Cathcart and Jonny Evans.

Fraizer Campbell gets on the ball at St.Andrews

Who's a happy boy then? Sean Evans shows his delight at scoring a superb second goal against Birmingham City

468

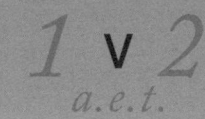

1)	Trevor Carson	9)	Dave Dowson	1)	Ron-Robert Zieler	9)	Fraizer Campbell
2)	Luke Ball	10)	Robbie Weir	2)	Craig Cathcart	10)	Sean Evans
3)	Liam Connolly	11)	Craig McFarlane	3)	Kieran Lee	11)	Jamie Mullan
4)	Michael Allan	*12) Jamie Chandler (for 10)*		4)	Jonny Evans	*12) Aaron Burns (for 8)*	
5)	Gavin Donoghue	*13) Chris Backhouse GK*		5)	Ryan Shawcross	*13) Ben Amos GK*	
6)	Richard Smith	*14) Lee Chapman*		6)	Danny Rose	*14) Febian Brandy (for 4)*	
7)	Kevin Davison	*15) Michael Kay (for 2)*		7)	David Gray	*15) Chris Fagan (for 10)*	
8)	Jake Richardson	*16) Michael Liddle (for 11)*		8)	Sam Hewson	*16) Tom Cleverley*	

2005-06

SUNDERLAND*   1 v 2   MANCHESTER UNITED
McFarlane   *a.e.t.*   Brandy, Hewson (pen)

JANUARY 2006

Wednesday 18th

Kick-off 7.00 p.m.

Attendance 390

Played at the Archibalds Stadium, Durham

On the same evening when former United Youth Cup participants Giuseppe Rossi, Ryan Giggs and Kieran Richardson supplied four of the five goals to dump Burton Albion out of the F.A. Cup in a Third Round replay, the club's current collection of under-18's were hard pushed to progress into the next stage of the national knock-out tournament. There were two personnel changes from the side that had totally outmanoeuvred Birmingham, with Paul McGuinness bringing in the giant Ryan Shawcross and the rather smaller Jamie Mullan for Michael Lea and Darron Gibson. Shawcross lined up with Jonny Evans in the centre of the defence while Craig Cathcart switched into Lea's place at full-back.

Kitted out in an all-blue strip, United got the event underway in a light drizzle, and on hand to record the majority of the game's relevant incidents was a Sunderland Echo representative:

Sunderland took Manchester United all the way in last night's F.A. Youth Cup tie, only to go down to an extra-time defeat. It was heartbreaking for the Wearsiders, who had put up a tremendous battle at Durham.

They fell behind after fifteen minutes to a debatable penalty. There was no signal from the second official and referee Hewitt was yards behind play as Sunderland's 'keeper Trevor Carson clashed with striker Fraizer Campbell, who was on the bench for the first-team against Burton in the recent F.A. Cup tie. However, a spot kick was awarded and Sam Hewson easily beat Carson with a low shot to the 'keeper's right.

Only two brilliant saves, denying Danny Rose and Jamie Mullan, prevented the lead from being increased, but Sunderland recovered with Craig McFarlane driving narrowly wide. Then full-back Liam Connolly, up for a corner, hammered in a goalbound shot on the back post, only to see the strike deflected over the top from three yards.

Kevin Ball's side carried the pressure into a second period that lacked goalmouth incidents for long periods, but was exciting for the 390-strong crowd nevertheless.

Sunderland had grown stronger as the half progressed, with midfield powerhouse Michael Allan, ably supported by first Jake Richardson and later Jamie Chandler, providing the impetus.

On 79 minutes, a Dave Dowson header was just tipped over by United 'keeper Ron-Robert Zieler, but, in the 85th minute, the young Black Cats did get the leveller their efforts fully deserved.

It was scored by Craig McFarlane, who cut in from the left and let fly with a tremendous drive that Zieler got a hand to but couldn't prevent from crossing the line.

The game went into extra-time and in the second period, sub Michael Liddle had two golden chances to score, one with a header inches over the bar and the second side-footed wide from an open goal which would have taken the tie into penalties.

But it was United who grabbed the winner six minutes from the end when Sean Evans broke and squared the ball for sub Febian Brandy to side-foot home.

It had been a fine effort of great commitment and skill by the Wearsiders. Northern Ireland international Trevor Carson was outstanding in goal and is a great prospect. Central defender Gavin Donoghue held the defence together, with Allan gradually taking over in midfield with his tackling and distribution.

The attack was well led by Dave Dowson, who showed deft control and looked better when Sunderland switched to 4-4-2 with Kevin Davison supporting in the second half.

United seem to have unearthed another Ryan Giggs in winger Jamie Mullan. Two-footed and pacy, with a good shot and full of tricks, he gave both Sunderland full-backs, Luke Ball and Connolly, a hard time as he switched flanks.

But, in the final analysis, it was a game that could so easily have ended in glory for the hosts. But, as with many games at the club this season, it was another good performance that ended with no reward.

There really should have been no need for an extra half an hour. With just less than ten minutes to go of normal time, the scintillating Mullan craftily dodged the attentions of three of the home team to play a pass to Campbell, who was twenty yards out and in a central position. He sidestepped a defender and cracked a wicked right-foot drive towards Carson, whose parried save bounced kindly for Brandy, and the substitute planted the ball home with a smart header. A linesman had flagged before the ball hit the back of the net, despite video evidence later showing that Brandy was level with the last defender when Campbell thumped his attempt on goal.

Despite that, it still represented a fine win against a much better organised and skilful set of opponents than those faced in the last round. Paul McGuinness had every reason to feel pleased with the result, even though there might just have been a concern regarding the lack of goals in relation to the amount of possession his boys had held in the two cup ties so far.

Kieran Lee (right) tries to close down Sunderland's Kevin Davison in full view of Sean Evans

fourth round

2005-06

fifth round

1) Ron-Robert Zieler	9) Febian Brandy	1) Joe Woolley	9) James Walker
2) David Gray	10) Fraizer Campbell	2) Lawrie Wilson	10) Chima Orelaja
3) Kieran Lee	11) Sean Evans	3) Grant Basey	11) Myles Weston
4) Craig Cathcart	12) Aaron Burns (for 11)	4) Harry Arter	12) Dane Springer (for 11)
5) Ryan Shawcross	13) Ben Amos GK	5) Jani Tanska	13) Kieron Thorp GK
6) Danny Rose	14) Sam Hewson (for 9)	6) Aswad Thomas	14) Kieran Murtagh
7) Jamie Mullan	15) Chris Fagan	7) Alistair John	15) Onome Sodje (for 10)
8) Darron Gibson	16) Tom Cleverley	8) Rashid Yussuff	16) Michael Carvill (for 8)

FEBRUARY 2006

MANCHESTER UNITED **2 v 1** CHARLTON ATHLETIC

Brandy, Campbell   Walker

Tuesday 7th

Kick-off 7.00 p.m.

Attendance 874

The decision as to whether or not the club's youngsters would once again be allowed to strut their stuff on the hallowed Old Trafford turf hinged on the first-team's potential requirement of a replay to get past Wolves in the F.A. Cup on the prior Saturday. Fortunately, the seniors secured their passage at the first time of asking, with a great 3-0 win at Molineux, and so the Youth Cup match against Charlton didn't need to be switched to Hyde.

There was some great news for Craig Cathcart 24 hours prior to the Addicks' visit, as he celebrated his 17th birthday with the offer of a professional contract to consider. The delighted Ulsterman began his 18th year by being asked to fill in for the injured Jonny Evans and the enforced alteration meant that David Gray was pushed into the problem right-back spot. Only Darron Gibson had made an appearance in the stadium previously and he took up the captaincy in the absence of his fellow countryman.

Charlton arrived with a young side, a couple of whom were still at school, but tournament wins at Walsall and Wolves indicated they were far from immature in football terms. An hour before kick-off, the Valley kids were out on the pitch in their tracksuits in order to take a look around and get a feel for what was to come. Aware that most, if not all, of them might never be presented with the opportunity of playing at the ground again, they were in a buoyant mood and spent several minutes happily snapping each other on their cameras and phones.

It was another wet and windy night in M16 and the Reds got the game underway on a heavy surface by kicking towards the Scoreboard End. United began with what Stuart Mathieson called *'a touch of the Old Trafford jitters as they made their bows on the big stage'* and they failed to create more than one noteworthy chance in the opening 45 minutes.

On the other hand, the Athletic lads were unfortunate not to be more than one goal to the good. They ripped the Reds apart with a speedy counterattack in the 15th minute, when a cross from Weston put United's outnumbered defence all at sea and only just evaded the reach of a couple of supporting team-mates.

Five minutes later, the Londoners' beglowed Harry Arter, easily the best midfielder on the park to that point and for some time after, came out with the ball from a crunching tackle in the right-half position and set a move in motion down that side of the pitch. Chima Orelaja whipped the ball across early, a foot or two above the leaping Cathcart and in the direction of James Walker, and Charlton's main striker obliged by flicking the ball with his head into the corner of Zieler's net.

On MUTV, Gary Neville remarked of the setback, *'It's a big test now for our lads. Obviously, that wouldn't have been in the script.'* The club captain then shared his views on what he felt might happen next by saying, *'But this is where they will show (they are) Manchester United players, because over the years we have had a habit of conceding goals and I'm sure the lads will come back from it'.*

Speaking as someone who had been in the same position himself, Neville added, *'The good thing for us is that they have scored early enough for us to do something about it.'*

The Reds' woeful showing then deteriorated still further simply because they were hopeless in possession. Continually poor at passing and frequently running into trouble when carrying the ball, they made Charlton's high effort rate and quick tackling tactics work to a tee.

Stuart Mathieson wasn't the only one in the ground to notice an instant improvement from the restart, and he took up the story in his match review:

.......it was a different United who came out after the interval intervention of coach Paul McGuinness. The previously inhibited Reds came out of their shell with a storming start to the second half that suddenly made Charlton look cumbersome.

Nobody made them more on edge than the pint-sized Febian Brandy.

It took Brandy just two minutes and 49 seconds to square the scores up. Through better pressing from the Reds' midfielders and forwards, the slippery seventeen year-old intercepted a pass intended for the Addicks' Tanska and he ran clear to plant the ball through the legs of a bewildered Joe Woolley.

Just after, Gibson crashed a trademark long shot at Woolley and it was obvious that attitudes were already changed. The United lads now felt they could go on and win the tie, whereas the Charlton boys knew that rather than dictating the flow of the game, they would now be required to paddle hard against the fast-moving current.

The next obvious chance fell to Sean Evans in the 63rd minute when he was put through on goal in a similar position to where Brandy had scored from. With Woolley advancing well off his line, and to gasps of despair from the crowd, Evans made a mess of a golden opportunity by lofting a left-footer over him and about two feet wide of a post.

Despite the change round in fortunes, the Londoners refused to cave in and they upheld the fine traditions of their club by trying to play with the ball on the floor and to feet whenever possible. Their problem stemmed from a reduced capacity of steam, with the amount of effort expended in the first half resulting in a total lack of firepower from the Addicks' forward-line.

United were now in full stride, though, and Mullan was the instigator of the next chance when measuring a cross towards Fraizer Campbell. The number eleven cushioned the ball invitingly into the 'D', from where Danny Rose volleyed a deflected shot that Woolley palmed away to his right.

When the Reds did finally seal their victory, it was in fortunate circumstances and came in the 78th minute. Campbell was approximately 22 yards out and chasing the ball as it drifted away from Charlton's penalty area. Collecting it on his right foot, he turned back towards goal and slap bang into a tackle by the powerful Thomas. As the ball fell loose, Campbell reacted rapidly when swivelling to hit it with his left foot. The ball struck the giant Tanska, and time seemed to stand still as it looped up in the air only to bounce behind the advanced Woolley and into an untenanted net.

The Addicks made three substitutions in the last seven minutes of normal time in a last-ditch attempt to save a game they might well have felt was winnable at the interval, only for the Reds to keep their composure and see the match out.

Besides all of those in the away dressing room, another person who wasn't particularly happy at full-time was the club's head groundsman. The pitch had taken a severe hammering and appeared badly cut up by the end, and it was probably due to the damage done to the surface in the Charlton game that most of the early rounds of United's Youth Cup matches have since been staged away from Old Trafford.

Febian Brandy struck soon after half-time to make the score 1-1 against Charlton

470

1)	Laurence Matthewson	9)	Kelvin Etuhu
2)	Curtis Obeng	10)	Daniel Sturridge
3)	Shaleum Logan	11)	Karl Moore
4)	Sam Williamson	12)	*Ched Evans (for 10)*
5)	Garry Breen	13)	*David Vadon GK*
6)	Paul Marshall	14)	*Scott Evans*
7)	Ashley Williams	15)	*Clayton McDonald*
8)	Michael Johnson	16)	*Christian Mouritsen*

1)	Ron-Robert Zieler	9)	Fraizer Campbell
2)	David Gray	10)	Sam Hewson
3)	Kieran Lee	11)	Sean Evans
4)	Craig Cathcart	12)	*Michael Lea*
5)	Ryan Shawcross	13)	*Ben Amos GK*
6)	Danny Rose	14)	*Febian Brandy (for 10)*
7)	Jamie Mullan	15)	*Aaron Burns*
8)	Darron Gibson	16)	*James Chester*

2005-06

MANCHESTER CITY 1 v 0 MANCHESTER UNITED

Etuhu

FEBRUARY 2006

Thursday 23rd

Kick-off 7.30 p.m.

Attendance 6,492

When United's website led with a headline which claimed 'REDS' EXIT IN YOUTH CUP MUGGING,' it perfectly encapsulated their first under-18 clash at Manchester City's Eastland's stadium. On top for the vast majority of the time, the Reds appeared to want to succeed much more than their opponents and, but for a lack of penetration where it really matters, City would have been dead and buried long before the interval.

The Light Blues earned the right to entertain their cross-town foes by winning their last two Youth Cup ties on the road, at Nottingham Forest and West Ham, as well as at home to Coventry.

Academy manager Jim Cassell claimed City were approaching the game as they would any other and added that everyone concerned with the club was aware of the importance of the junior meeting. *'Irrespective of anything, if you get to the last eight of a national competition you must be doing well, and we are pleased with the way things are going,'* he said.

With a place in the semi-final against Newcastle or Brighton at stake, Paul McGuinness observed, *'Obviously there's a little more pressure on (City). They're playing at home, so there's more expectation on them to do well. It's a local derby and they're all the same through the age groups. It's very tight, very competitive and I'm sure it will be no different this time.'*

Speaking in front of the MUTV cameras, Gary Neville shared his experience of such occasions when remarking, *'These lads will have played each other probably since the age of thirteen or fourteen for town teams, counties (and) England schoolboys. They will be very aware of one another, the strengths, they will have played against each other on Saturday mornings.......they'll know all about each other before the game.'* When asked by Steve Bower about the effect of a win over their neighbours, Neville responded, *'To get through tonight, the confidence they will get, either team, will be absolutely enormous and make them think they can win (the cup).'*

As far as team selection went, coach McGuinness preferred Sam Hewson to Febian Brandy while over on the City side of the divide, captain Micah Richards was injured and so Cassell handed the job to Michael Johnson.

Seconds after kick-off, MUTV's Steve Bower described the scene by stating, *'It's a horrible night.......a strong wind, it's been raining for some time, although that will give a little bit of zip to the surface.'* He then posed the question, *'Is it one of the better playing surfaces out there Gary?'* to which Neville replied, *'It is a good playing surface, it's an open stadium and it gets plenty of sunlight to it.'* The club skipper then joked, *'The conditions shouldn't surprise us Steve, (for) the last two years in the Youth Cup every time I've commentated it's bucketed down.'*

United began purposefully and nearly passed City to death before Fraizer Campbell almost put the visitors ahead in the 13th minute by only just failing to make proper contact with a dangerous in-swinging free kick from Jamie Mullan. The Eastlands lads looked rigid in their formation and a tendency to give the ball away at every opportunity suggested a nervousness that the Reds weren't able to convert into a mark up on the scoreboard.

Easily the most controversial incident of the match occurred on 26 minutes, when City once again couldn't find a way forward and a long pass back was sent to 'keeper Matthewson. Campbell was enthusiastic enough to chase hard after it and the Blues' goalie, who was at least ten yards outside his zone, made a monumental error by slamming the ball straight at the United striker. As Campbell tried to latch onto the stray ball, Matthewson simply barged into him before clearing to safety. There was no whistle from the man in charge, which caused Neville to remark sarcastically, *'Well done ref.'*

The match was then interrupted for several moments while a few mindless idiots were cleared off the pitch and during the lull, Bower commented that Paul McGuinness would have been happy with the way his lads were performing but perhaps a bit disappointed that *'they haven't made their entire domination of this game count with a goal.'* He then turned his opinions towards the home bench and made a valid point about City's coaching staff being *'mightily relieved to still be in this at 0-0.'*

In the 41st minute, the Old Trafford side came the closest yet to changing the barren scoreline when a fast break ended with a cracking 20-yard drive from Campbell fizzing just wide and Matthewson diving at full stretch. The chance caused Neville to gasp slightly and he quickly remarked to his co-commentator, *'We should be winning this game Steve, we look a better team, we look like we've got players who can control the ball and pass the ball and are comfortable....... (can) handle the situation better.......and you just hope that doesn't switch around in the second half.'*

Throughout the intermission there was further discussion about what the rest of the game might bring. Bower viewed that the message from the respective coaches to their charges would be very different, to which Neville responded, *'It certainly will. City, I would imagine they will say 'get into the game, start playing'....... Paul, I'm sure he'll be saying 'Lads, you've got to capitalise on this play, you're playing fantastically well. You're getting into the right areas of the pitch but now you've got to make it count.' If it goes like this for another twenty minutes, maybe (Paul) has to be brave and take a chance and make a change. I'm sure he won't want to do that, I'm sure he will hope the lads who are out there continue to play like they have and get that goal in the first ten (or) fifteen minutes.'*

City were livelier in the second period of the match, but only just, and the Reds continued to spray the ball around while constantly probing for that elusive breakthrough. It nearly came in the 55th minute, with David Gray directing a free header well wide from a corner right in front of the 1,500 or so United fans massed in the corner of the South Stand.

City finally created something worthwhile seven minutes later when a long ball from the halfway line was chased by Etuhu until Cathcart intervened to clear it for a corner. The Blues then caused themselves a problem on the boundary of their penalty area as a terrible defensive header fell to Sean Evans. Sizing up the situation in a jiffy, Evans noted there were those in a better position to so he knocked the ball sideways for Campbell, whose crashing volley zoomed above Matthewson's head and caused Neville to mention excitedly, *'He's hit it like a rocket. He's the man who can win it for us. We want the chance to fall to him if we do get one.'*

There were only eighteen minutes left to go when Brandy was introduced for Hewson as McGuinness decided to gamble on sacrificing some midfield industry for a greater forward presence. The change fell inside City's best spell, a period which saw them test the Reds' defence with four quick set pieces.

As chants of *'United, United'* rang out from the away support, Campbell covered half of the perimeter of the Blues' eighteen-yard line prior to striking another terrific shot that Matthewson parried. The ball was eventually worked back to Mullan, whose attempt on goal carried nowhere near the same power or threat as Campbell's.

Neville piped up again to say, *'It will be cruel if we don't win this match tonight. But football is cruel at times, particularly for young players who won't understand that this can happen to them. It's a game that really we have deserved to win. City are tired. We just have to show that cutting edge. (A goal has) got to be coming, I can feel it coming.'*

Campbell made another great burst only to be denied by Breen and United kept up the pressure with a shot by Gibson that was charged down as well as a teasing centre from Gray. The Blues broke away to win a corner and, not having cleared it properly, substitute Ched Evans was allowed to play a ten-yard pass to the unmarked Etuhu and he turned to slam home a completely undeserved 85th minute winner.

Bower exclaimed, *'With only (City's) second shot on target, United are behind.'* A dejected Neville brought to his co-commentator's attention that a couple of Reds failed to follow the ball out when it was initially knocked away, inadvertently creating the space for Etuhu to occupy.

McGuinness acted straight away by instructing Shawcross to take up an offensive role for the last few minutes and United actually packed ten players into City's box for a late corner. Then, with 91 minutes on the clock, Mullan floated over an inviting cross from the left to Shawcross, who placed his back post header about a foot away from its intended target. The miss caused Neville to groan loudly, and for the benefit of MUTV's viewers Bower got right to the point by remarking, *'When you get a chance like that in stoppage time, you have to take it.'*

And with that, the Reds were out.

In a post-match analysis, Neville reckoned the Old Trafford boys would, quite rightly, be hurting badly at the manner of their exit. *'They'll be down for a considerable amount of time now I would think,'* he noted before adding, *'It takes years to get over those defeats. I lost in a similar way in '93 and you never forget it......you put so much into it.'* Bower then made a comment with regards to the score being hard to stomach because City hadn't threatened and Neville summarised the loss by saying, *'We just dominated the game in possession, in passing, in movement, in authority, and we handled the conditions and the nerves better. But City have gone through, that is what will be remembered and it's difficult to take.'*

There was at least one individual in the Eastlands camp genuine enough to admit that a travesty of justice had taken place, as manager Stuart Pearce told City's website, *'It was probably the worst that (our lads) have played, but they have beaten the best team they have played. That's just the nature of football at times. We were a little bit fortunate if I am honest, but that happens in football.......'*

sixth round

471

2006-07

1) Ben Amos	9) Febian Brandy	1) Craig Turner	9) Ryan Damms
2) Richard Eckersley	10) Chris Fagan	2) Joe Wilcox	10) Ben Porter
3) Tom Cleverley	11) Danny Welbeck	3) Niall Canavan	11) Peter Winn
4) James Chester	*12) Corry Evans (for 6)*	4) Jack Webster	*12) Jason Moxon*
5) Craig Cathcart	*13) Sam Filler GK*	5) Jack Francis	*13) Michael Redgritt GK*
6) Danny Drinkwater	*14) Danny Galbraith (for 11)*	6) Dan Robinson	*14) John Leonard*
7) Magnus Eikrem	*15) Conor McCormack*	7) Matt Smith	*15) Jonathan Walton (for 11)*
8) Sam Hewson	*16) Anton Bryan (for 10)*	8) Andrew Culshaw	*16) Joel Barnett (for 7)*

DECEMBER 2006

MANCHESTER UNITED* 3 v 0 SCUNTHORPE UNITED

Brandy (2), Cathcart

*Saturday 16th***

Kick-off 2.00 p.m.

Attendance 238

* Played at Ewen Fields, Hyde

third round

There was a huge amount of disappointment felt over in Lincolnshire when United's officials chose to reschedule and re-site the club's first Youth Cup tie of the 2006/07 season at short notice. Caused by a spell of heavy rain in the days leading up to the game, and with further downpours predicted, it was felt best to protect the fragile fabric of the Old Trafford pitch by once again staging the match at Hyde.

Scunthorpe youth coach Tony Daws, himself a Youth Cup opponent of the Reds for Notts County back in 1983, revealed the problems he faced and the reaction from his squad when news of the rearrangement broke by saying, *'There were one or two expletives when I told them. All our preparation has been organised for two weeks and it means we've got to change it. The players have been on a two-week training programme with the aim to peak on Thursday. Now we've got to alter it so they don't peak on Thursday. It changes our planning because I've got two days to fill. It's very disruptive.'*

Paul McGuinness selected a side that was more locally orientated than the one defeated by Manchester City during their last stab at the competition. Because long-term injury casualty Zieler was out of contention, Macclesfield-based Ben Amos filled in for net-minding duties while four of the other new starters hailed from the North-West, with Danny's Drinkwater and Welbeck coming from Manchester, Richard Eckersley from Salford and James Chester from Warrington. Forward Chris Fagan, a third-year trainee, was tempted across the Irish Sea from Dublin, Tom Cleverley called Bradford his home whereas Magnus Eikrem, a blossoming midfielder of whom especially high hopes were held, had been recruited from Ole Gunnar Solksjaer's soccer school in Norway.

Despite his Academy side not faring too well on divisional duty just lately, McGuinness anticipated that their fortunes would improve in the knock-out tournament and he told a reporter, *'It's important to get through because you get another opportunity to show what you can do. If you don't get through it's a missed opportunity, so we'll be giving it everything we've got.*

Last year we started slowly against Birmingham but got better and played really well against Manchester City and were just lacking the final killer touch. Hopefully we have learned the lesson that we need to be more ruthless.'

Below a banner which read 'CUP OF STIFF BRANDY IS TOO STRONG FOR IRON', the Scunthorpe Telegraph spilled the beans in regards to what went on at Ewen Fields:

> SIR Alex wasn't there and neither was Sir Bobby to see Manchester United's wannabe stars of the future take on the young fledglings from Glanford Park in the third round of the FA Youth Cup.
>
> Indeed, while they were mostly second best to what is arguably the best young talent in the country, the final 3-0 scoreline was harsh on the Iron youngsters.
>
> They worked their socks off to stay in the game. If only they had been able to find a bit more in the final third, then it might have been a different story.
>
> Manchester were good, but nothing that special, as they opened the scoring on the half hour mark, added a second just after the interval and then grabbed a third in the closing minutes when fatigue had set in for Scunthorpe, who had nothing left in the tank.
>
> The difference between the two teams was the quality in their attacking play.
>
> Manchester strutted while the Iron lads had to fight for scraps.
>
> Star man for the home side was No 9 Febian Brandy, a youngster in style and stature very similar to that of former Old Trafford favourite Dwight Yorke.
>
> He was the one man who most troubled a Scunthorpe defence excellently marshalled by skipper Jack Francis, himself a former schoolboy on the books of Chelsea.
>
> Goalkeeper Craig Turner also showed his ability with two terrific first half saves.
>
> First he produced a terrific reaction save at his far post to keep out a close range header from Brandy.
>
> Then he arched to turn over the top an excellent 20-yard drive from Danny Welbeck.
>
> He was also unlucky with Manchester's opener in the 31st minute when Brandy's pace took him clear through the middle and into the box.
>
> Turner spread himself well and got a touch to the shot, but could not stop it squeezing under his body and into the back of the net.
>
> Turner pulled off another great save to deny Magnus Eikrem before Brandy made it 2-0 in the 52nd minute with a shot that the Iron 'keeper could only help on its way into the back of the net.
>
> Scunthorpe stuck admirably to their task, with Jack Webster and Andrew Culshaw toiling manfully in the middle of the park.
>
> They began to get the ball down and pass it but could not find a chink in a home defence in which classy centre-back Craig Cathcart was always a commanding figure.
>
> It was a Cathcart header from a left wing corner that completed the 3-0 scoreline in the 88th minute – producing a final scoreline that was a little harsh on Scunthorpe.

**This game was originally scheduled to be played at Old Trafford on Thursday, 14th December but was put back and switched to Hyde due to concerns over the pitch

Two-goal hero Febian Brandy gets in a header while United's (l-r) Danny Welbeck, James Chester, Craig Cathcart and Chris Fagan are frozen in anticipation

472

1) Ben Amos	9) Febian Brandy	1) Matej Rondos	9) Matt Paterson
2) Richard Eckersley	10) Chris Fagan	2) Ian Jones	10) Jake Thomson
3) Tom Cleverley	11) Danny Galbraith	3) Joseph Mills	11) Jamie White
4) James Chester	12) Corry Evans (for 11)	4) Michael Byrne	12) Kayne McLaggon (for 9)
5) Craig Cathcart	13) Sam Filler GK	5) Oliver Lancashire	13) George Ellis GK
6) Danny Drinkwater	14) Danny Welbeck (for 7)	6) Jamie Hatch	14) Oscar Gobern (for 8)
7) James Derbyshire	15) Conor McCormack (for 6)	7) Aristotles de Carvalho	15) Craig Read
8) Sam Hewson	16) Anton Bryan	8) Andrew Giallombardo	16) James Mackay

MANCHESTER UNITED* 2 v 0 SOUTHAMPTON

Drinkwater, Hewson

JANUARY 2007

Wednesday 17th

Kick-off 7.00 p.m.

Attendance 332

Played at Ewen Fields, Hyde

fourth round

2006-07

James Chester (left) and goalscorer Danny Drinkwater combine to thwart Southampton's Andrew Giallombardo

Nearly sixteen years had passed since the Reds last crossed Youth Cup swords with Southampton and it was the better part of half a century ago when United forfeited their near five-year unbeaten run in the tournament to the south coast club. Saints' youth coach Georges Prost approached the game in the knowledge that he was unable to utilise transfer target Gareth Bale, who might even have been in Alex Ferguson's sights according to some reports, though there was some better news on the selection front with the news that skipper Oliver Lancashire was able to play with a lightweight cast protecting his recently fractured wrist.

Prost said of the choice of venue, *'It is a shame it is not at Old Trafford. That is disappointing for the boys – and for the coach. I wanted to go out and score a goal there! It would have been more of an occasion, but it is still a huge game for us wherever it is played. It is one of the toughest draws we could have had, (but) this is a chance to make a name for ourselves. Beating Manchester United at any level is something to remember. They are fifth in their division, like us. They have some good players, but so do we and it should be a good game.'*

Having defeated Stockport 2-0 with goals from Michael Byrne and Jamie Hatch at their Staplewood training ground in the last round, County conceding home advantage because Edgeley Park was persistently waterlogged, Southampton's recent record in the Youth Cup was really something to be admired. Narrowly beaten by Ipswich in the 2005 final, a year later the young Saints suffered more heartache and were only eliminated in a penalty shoot-out at the semi-final stage by eventual winners Liverpool.

Born in Manhattan and raised in Brooklyn, former USA under-17 captain and current Saints' defensive midfielder Andrew Giallombardo told his local newspaper of what the game meant to him when enthusing, *'Manchester United have such a great reputation all over the world. They were one of the few English teams I could watch on ESPN back in the States so it's very exciting. This game is all we can talk about at the moment.'*

Paul McGuinness, who was *'hopeful we can get a few fans along'* in order that *'they'll see we have some talented footballers in this team'*, was without Eikrem and dropped Welbeck to the bench. Their absences created voids for a couple of new lads to fill, with Warrington youngster James Derbyshire stepping in for the Norwegian while Scottish forward Danny Galbraith took over Welbeck's spot.

Scribe Simon Walter was present to record the goings-on for the Southern Daily Echo and a truncated version of his match report read:

.......last night Saints began with the belief that they could knock the Red Devils out of the competition for the first time in three attempts since it was conceived in 1953.

Both Jamie White and Jake Thomson, the two most dangerous Saints players last night, tested goalkeeper Ben Amos before Hewson gave nine-times F.A. Youth Cup winners United a 23rd minute lead.

Hewson reacted quickest to the rebound after the dangerous Febian Brandy had been denied by Saints goalkeeper Matej Rondos, a Slovakian youth international.

Saints were given a let-off when Chris Fagan failed to convert at the far post following another dangerous right-flank run and cross from striker Brandy, a seventeen year-old local boy. But, in the 42nd minute, Drinkwater converted Salford-born right-back Richard Eckersley's cross to double United's lead at the far post.

Harefield's White was again denied by Amos on the stroke of half-time and had a header deflected over the crossbar on the hour. Then Thomson launched an audacious 45-yard chip that sailed beyond Amos but dipped just over the bar.

But Saints were lacklustre by the high standards they have set themselves in the F.A. Youth Cup in recent seasons and lacked power in attack to complement the skills of White and Thomson.

United could even have extended their lead in the latter stages. Drinkwater missed the target after a slick United move and Saints right-back Ian Jones, a former Welsh team-mate of Gareth Bale, headed off the line from Irish striker Fagan. But United held on and will be at home again in the Fifth Round against Crystal Palace.

473

2006-07

1) Ben Amos	9) Febian Brandy	1) Martin Pearson	9) Ben Kudjodji
2) Richard Eckersley	10) Chris Fagan	2) Matt Fish	10) Victor Moses
3) Tom Cleverley	11) Danny Galbraith	3) Lee Hills	11) James Dayton
4) James Chester	*12) Corry Evans*	4) Anthony Straker	*12) Tom Lyons*
5) Craig Cathcart	*13) Ron-Robert Zieler GK*	5) Moses Swaibu	*13) Kieron Thorp GK*
6) Danny Drinkwater	*14) Anton Bryan (for 10)*	6) Ryan Carolan	*14) Sean Scannell (for 3)*
7) Danny Welbeck	*15) James Derbyshire*	7) Jerahl Hughes	*15) Michael Kamara*
8) Sam Hewson	*16) Conor McCormack*	8) Jamie Smith	*16) Joe Sweeney*

JANUARY 2007

MANCHESTER UNITED* 2 v 0 CRYSTAL PALACE
Brandy, Hewson

fifth round

Tuesday 30th

Kick-off 7.00 p.m.

Attendance 332

* Played at Ewen Fields, Hyde

At the conclusion of United's only other brush up against Crystal Palace in the national under-18's knock-out tournament, the legendary 'class of '92' claimed the trophy for the club for the first time in nearly 30 years and began a sequence which saw Eric Harrison's lads reach the final three times in just four attempts.

For the 2007 clash, the stage was much less modest, paying viewers were far fewer in number, and the prize on offer not nearly as glamorous. Nevertheless, there was still a place in the quarter-finals up for grabs and in order to ensure the Reds claimed one of them, Paul McGuinness brought Danny Welbeck back into the youth team's forward-line.

Welbeck had made a decent contribution towards the Academy side's 'goals scored' column, with five claimed from fifteen appearances so far, however, in seven of those games the striker was used as a substitute, including his first five matches. Considering the Mancunian only turned sixteen in the November just gone, and that he was almost exactly two years younger than team-mate Sam Hewson, it was apparent his progress was really quite something and that he might be someone to look out for.

Top scorer for the Academy side was Febian Brandy, the in-form striker already having notched up ten goals in what was proving to be a stuttering season for the club's pool of teenage talent.

As far as an overview of the youth match went, the Evening News reckoned *'United's youngsters moved into the last eight with a comfortable 2-0 Fifth Round win over Crystal Palace at Hyde's Ewen Fields last night'* and opined that the Reds *'always looked capable of winning, although Palace also had their moments in an entertaining game'*. Stung by a goal in each half, it was busy bees Brandy and Hewson who inflicted the most serious pain on the Selhurst Park kids.

The game started evenly and there was little to choose between the sides during the first quarter of the allotted time. There was also sufficient skill and effort from the two sets of midfielders and the upshot of all of their graft meant that the ball wasn't seen too often in either penalty area.

The Reds' best chances of the first half fell to Brandy and Welbeck, the former heading against a post while the latter unleashed a swerving shot at Martin Pearson's goal as the search for an opener intensified. At the opposite end, the Eaglets thought they had scored when Moses Swaibu placed the ball in the net only to be denied for offside and Jamie Smith was unlucky to see his attempt go wide when shooting on the turn.

By the 36th minute, the game was badly in need of a goal and, fortunately, it went United's way. Welbeck was pivotal to the move through putting in some good work out on the wing and when he found Hewson loitering about eighteen yards out from Palace's net, the midfielder obliged by cracking in a strong low drive past Pearson.

Palace began the second half as the better side and Reds' goalie Ben Amos was pressed into action when dealing with many more routine catches and crosses than had been the case prior to the interval. For all of their drive and passion, the south Londoners just couldn't find a way through United's miserly defence, although with only one goal in it the final outcome remained in the balance.

The last meaningful act of the match came in the 71st minute and it stemmed from a mistake by one of the visitors. A through ball was knocked into Palace's box, where Pearson managed to make a mess of collecting it while colliding with a colleague, and the fumble let in Brandy, whose shot appeared to be saved. There then followed a few looks of confusion on the faces of most of the players until the referee signalled a goal upon receiving an instruction from a linesman that Brandy's effort had in fact crossed the line.

Certainly a messy goal to secure the result with, but none of the United boys were complaining and it would have to do in the circumstances. The Reds then managed to keep out of trouble for the remaining minutes, a task made relatively simple through their opponents' lack of guile and cutting edge in the last third of the field.

Despite the in and out form of the Academy side, the win against Palace continued what was developing into an encouraging Youth Cup run during which the youngsters had now scored seven times without reply.

Danny Welbeck, already looking a hot ticket for further progress

Tom Cleverley's high work rate helped to keep the Palace lads at bay

1) Ben Amos	9) Febian Brandy	1) Artur Krysiak	9) Jamie Sheldon
2) Richard Eckersley	10) Chris Fagan	2) Jared Wilson	10) Sone Aluko
3) Tom Cleverley	11) Danny Galbraith	3) Darren Campion	11) Dean Lea
4) James Chester	*12) Corry Evans (for 10)*	4) Ryan Burge	*12) Sean Hunt*
5) Craig Cathcart	*13) Ron-Robert Zieler GK*	5) Krystian Pearce	*13) Dean Lyness GK*
6) Danny Drinkwater	*14) Anton Bryan (for 7)*	6) David Joyce	*14) Jack Rutter*
7) Danny Welbeck	*15) James Derbyshire*	7) James McPike	*15) Shaun Timmins*
8) Sam Hewson	*16) Conor McCormack*	8) Lewis Green	

MANCHESTER UNITED 2 v 0 BIRMINGHAM CITY

Hewson (2, 1 pen)

2006-07

FEBRUARY 2007

Wednesday 21st

Kick-off 7.00 p.m.

Attendance 834

sixth round

Now into the last eight section of the competition, United's good fortune with the draw continued when familiar opponents Birmingham City were required to travel to Stretford. It was the third time in just six seasons that the Reds found themselves paired with the St. Andrews' boys and if past performances were anything to go by, United could feel confident in the knowledge that in five meetings since the 1981/82 campaign, they had drawn one and come out on top in all of the others.

A 2-0 scoreline suggested a rather routine win for the Old Trafford kids, but that wasn't how it actually panned out and the Blues, conquerors of Chesterfield, Charlton and Barnsley in the earlier rounds, managed to create a fine impression and fashion a few openings while more than holding their own for long periods of the match.

Demonstrating their desire to claim a place in the semi-finals, Paul McGuinness' charges threatened to blow their opponents away in the early minutes and only a couple of superb saves from Polish goalkeeper Artur Krysiak kept out efforts from Danny's Welbeck and Galbraith.

Just when it seemed as if Birmingham had weathered the storm, the Reds struck hard and decisively in the 15th minute. Just like in the last round, Welbeck acted as provider-in-chief for the opener when displaying some neat footwork out on the right wing before crossing. City's defenders were presented with two opportunities to clear the danger, only for Sam Hewson to ignore the attention of a trio of opponents in close proximity and slam the ball high into Krysiak's net from a place near to the penalty spot.

Despite the loss of a goal, Birmingham impressively managed to keep their composure and for an extended time stretching either side of the interval, they looked the most likely to score next.

Stepping on the gas almost immediately, a James McPike header was only just off-target from a Darren Campion free kick, when the ball should really have found the back of the net, and Campion himself almost produced an equaliser by nodding wide from a Ryan Burge corner.

Shortly before half-time, the Blues nearly secured a leveller through Sone Aluko, whose fantastic 25-yard drive looked to be flying towards the top corner of Ben Amos' net until the United 'keeper matched the effort by diving at full-length to tip the ball over his crossbar.

While the Reds had begun the first half in the ascendancy, Birmingham swung the tables round and grabbed the initiative right from the restart to force a succession of corners. There was an unfortunate occurrence at one of the flag kicks, when McPike was left prostrate on the turf after receiving a nasty bang on the head in the penalty box, but fortunately, following a few minutes of treatment, the number seven felt well enough to resume.

It was obvious there were some tactical changes implemented by the visitors during the early section of the second period as, besides employing a higher line in order to press United's defence, the Blues were closing down much quicker, far harder and more frequently.

The Reds made certain of their win in the 70th minute and a second goal in their favour was largely due to the ball skills of the diminutive yet determined Febian Brandy. The inventive striker went on a jinking run right into the heart of the Birmingham defence, with his progress only halted through an unfair challenge by Blues' centre-back and captain Krystian Pearce. It was left to Hewson to seal the result, by sending his penalty kick to Krysiak's right as the goalie gambled incorrectly and moved in the opposite direction.

The Brummies refused to throw in the towel and they almost got themselves back into the game late on when Pearce was only inches away from redeeming his earlier transgression by smashing a fierce drive onto the top of Amos' bar with the 'keeper well beaten.

There was some frantic action in the dying minutes, during which Birmingham's Ryan Burge was booked, and when the final whistle sounded the Reds certainly knew they had been in a game.

There were similar views expressed in the newspapers local to the two sides, with the Manchester Evening News noting that United *'were matched all the way'* by the Midlanders while the Birmingham Mail correctly claimed the kids from St. Andrews *'wouldn't give up'* and made the Reds *'work for the right'* to earn their passage.

Blues' coach Terry Westley felt *'2-0 was a bit harsh on us'* and he went on to say that *'we clawed our way back into it'* after going behind. Westley couldn't disguise his disappointment when observing, *'People say about scoring at the right time and United did just that'* before adding one of the harsher realities of the sport into the interview by remarking, *'We've had a good run and now the players have to try and get a career out of football.'*

Richard Eckersley helped the Reds to a fourth consecutive Youth Cup clean sheet

Like all of his colleagues, Danny Galbraith worked hard against Birmingham

2006-07

1) Martin Hansen	9) Craig Lindfield
2) Stephen Darby	10) Lee Woodward
3) Michael Burns	11) Ray Putterill
4) Jay Spearing	*12) Steven Irwin*
5) Robbie Threlfall	*13) David Roberts GK*
6) Charlie Barnett	*14) Sean Highdale*
7) Jimmy Ryan	*15) Ben Parsonage*
8) Ryan Flynn	*16) Nathan Eccleston (for 10)*

1) Ron-Robert Zieler	9) Febian Brandy
2) Richard Eckersley	10) Chris Fagan
3) Corry Evans	11) Danny Galbraith
4) Kenny Strickland	*12) Conor McCormack*
5) James Chester	*13) Gary Woods GK*
6) Danny Drinkwater	*14) Anton Bryan (for 6)*
7) Danny Welbeck	*15) Matty James (for 9)*
8) Sam Hewson	*16) Scott Moffatt*

APRIL 2007

LIVERPOOL 1 v 2 MANCHESTER UNITED
Lindfield   Hewson (pen), Threlfall (o.g.)

Monday 16th
Kick-off 7.45 p.m.
Attendance 19,518

final 1st leg

Hewson strike gives United aces the edge

Due to the Irish centre-back's senior commitments, which were caused by a spate of injuries at first-team level, Paul McGuinness was forced to find a replacement for Craig Cathcart for the opening leg of the final at Anfield and he chose Ormskirk-born Kenny Strickland for the job. Cathcart had occupied the bench for United's F.A. Cup semi-final victory over Watford at Villa Park on the Sunday just gone and Alex Ferguson required him for the Premiership visit of Sheffield United 24 hours after the youth clash on Merseyside.

Nominated as the team's stand-in skipper, Sam Hewson could only see good in his colleagues promotion. *'Craig has been playing well and the manager has noticed that and given him the opportunity,'* he said. *'It's great because the rest of this team know if we play as well as Craig has this season, then the manager might look at us.'*

Allied to the enforced absences of Ben Amos and Tom Cleverley, it meant that three of the most promising of McGuinness' team were only able to view the match from the sidelines.

In Amos' case, his injury continued a list of such goalkeeping problems for United in the competition that could be traced back to Gordon Clayton's fractured wrist prior to the 1954 final.

As the Manchester Evening News' correspondent observed, those changes, possibly added to a few nerves, definitely had a detrimental effect on United in the early stages:

The young Reds had arguably saved their poorest performance of the tournament for the opening 45 minutes on Merseyside.

Against the experienced 2006 winners, who had seven of the squad that beat City in last season's final on duty, United looked a shadow of the side who had enthralled Old Trafford in the extra-time defeat of Arsenal just a fortnight ago.

United youth coach Paul McGuinness must have been content at least that there was only one goal to chase down after the first half.

Liverpool's breakthrough came on sixteen minutes from the head of Craig Lindfield and, taking into account United's stuttering start, it appeared to provide the Anfielders with a springboard with which to aim for ultimate success. It developed through some wizardry from winger Ray Putterill, who tormented Richard

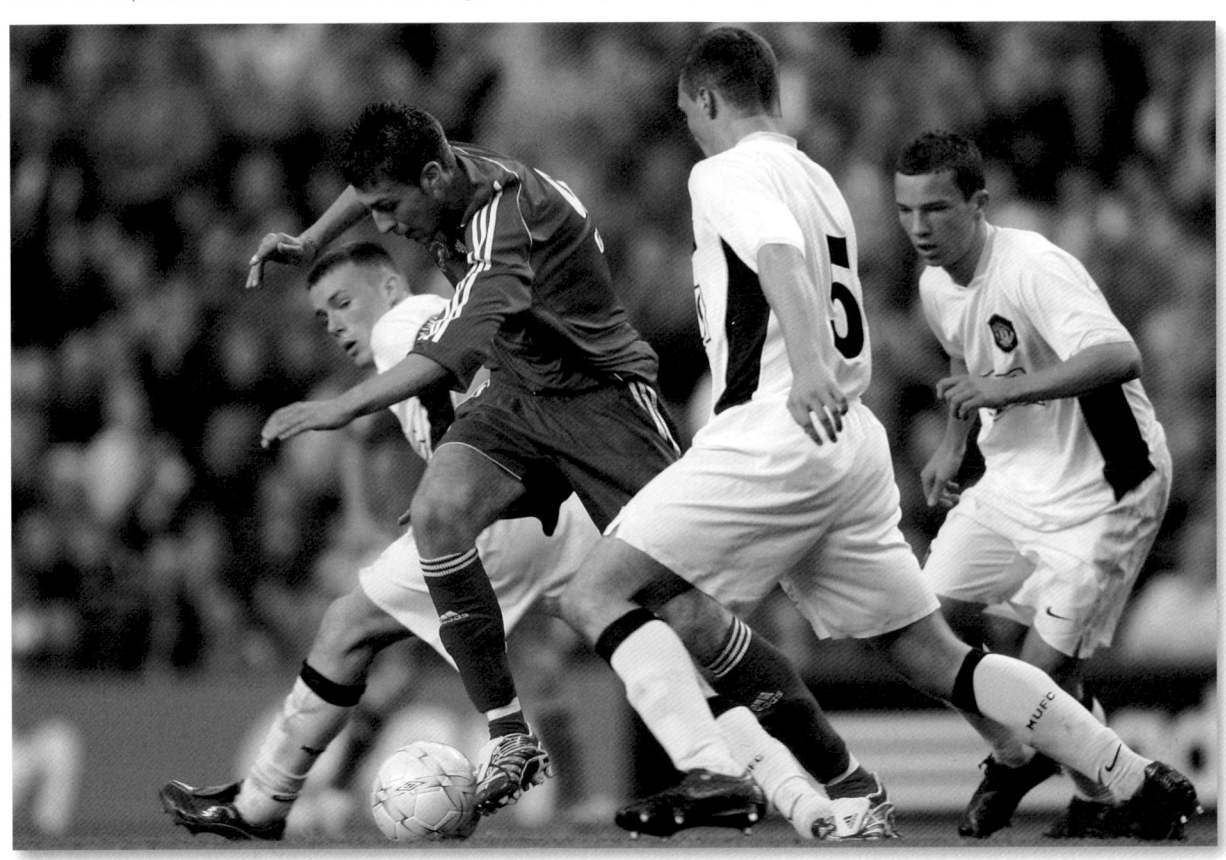

Sam Hewson (left), James Chester (number five) and Danny Drinkwater hunt down Liverpool's Craig Lindfield

478

APRIL 2007

Sam Hewson hammers home a penalty at the Kop end of Anfield to give United an advantage for the second leg

final 1st leg

Eckersley before cutting inside on his right foot. The recipient of a terrific centre from Putterill, Lindfield outjumped his marker and managed to escape Zieler's charge to nod home from a distance of five yards.

Brandy could lay claim to being United's best performer in what was a rocky spell for the visitors and either side of going behind he blasted recklessly wide, as well as attempting to beat 'keeper Martin Hansen with an ambitious bicycle kick. The only other chance that fell to the Mancunians before the intermission resulted from Chris Fagan's skimmed drive, which was competently caught by Hansen.

Liverpool caused United plenty of problems in the wide areas and had Lee Woodward managed to convert an almost identical centre from Putterill that produced their goal, McGuinness' pep talk might have been delivered in an entirely different tone.

Despite being under the cosh for most of the time so far, United eventually got their act together, and of their revival the Evening News commented:

But the Red teenagers have proved they have a deep well of courage and resilience and they didn't let their disappointing early showing wreck their confidence.

They showed more purpose and more skilful passing in the second half and five minutes after the interval Daniel Galbraith sent in the kind of crosses Liverpool had been delivering in the first half.

It was the first major onslaught Liverpool's defence had faced and Robbie Threlfall made a pig's ear of it in front of the 19,518 crowd as he met the ball on the bounce to head past his own 'keeper.

Even the Liverpool Echo was forced into admitting United *'vastly improved after the break'* as the Kop kids *'lost their grip'* on the proceedings, and the periodical also observed *'eventually, they benefited from Liverpool's self-destruction'*. There were pockets of resistance from the home team, with the hard working Jimmy Ryan driving a shot wide from a distance of 25 yards and Putterill continuing to cause havoc on United's right-hand flank, but their almost blanket coverage of previously was now cast off.

The goal that decided the matter in hand arrived in the 74th minute, with the infectious Brandy breaking into Liverpool's box where Jay Spearing's mistimed tackle sent the trickster tumbling to provoke the award of a penalty by referee Mark Clattenburg. Subjected to a barracking from the facing Kop supporters, Hewson drew strength and composure from the captain's armband to coolly send the spot kick beyond Hansen for a welcome winner and his fifth goal of that season's tournament.

There was an expected late surge by Liverpool as they sought to square the scores, only for them to be foiled on several occasions by a towering granite-like wall comprising of Strickland and Chester.

Anfield youth coach Steve Heighway said of the result, *'It's still all to play for. We felt we would have needed to score at Old Trafford anyway to win the cup, so we've still got to do that.'*

> *There were boos and whistles but you expect that, and I was just glad to put (the penalty) away. I thought we did well, and we defended well throughout. I think we probably made just one mistake all night for their goal. We created chances and we got the ball down and passed it which was pleasing.*
>
> *We're now hoping for a big crowd in the second leg, we want as many fans behind us as possible and hopefully we can finish the job at Old Trafford.*

SAM HEWSON

2006-07

1) Ron-Robert Zieler	9) Febian Brandy	1) David Roberts	9) Craig Lindfield
2) Richard Eckersley	10) Chris Fagan	2) Stephen Darby	10) Ryan Flynn
3) Corry Evans	11) Danny Galbraith	3) Michael Burns	11) Ray Putterill
4) Kenny Strickland	*12) Conor McCormack*	4) Jay Spearing	*12) Steven Irwin (for 8)*
5) James Chester	*13) Gary Woods GK*	5) Robbie Threlfall	*13) Josh Mimms GK*
6) Danny Drinkwater	*14) Anton Bryan (for 6)*	6) Charlie Barnett	*14) Sean Highdale*
7) Danny Welbeck	*15) Magnus Eikrem (for 7)*	7) Jimmy Ryan	*15) Ben Parsonage*
8) Sam Hewson	*16) Scott Moffatt (for 3)*	8) Astrit Ajdarevic	*16) Lee Woodward (for 7)*

APRIL 2007

MANCHESTER UNITED 0 (2) V (2) 1 **LIVERPOOL**

Liverpool win 4-3 on pens a.e.t.   Threlfall

Thursday 26th*

Kick-off 7.45 p.m.

Attendance 24,347

'I just hope now that our support gets behind these young lads at Old Trafford,' Alex Ferguson told Manchester United Radio. 'They deserve a big crowd because they've done a fantastic job getting there and it's not been an easy ride for them. They've played some good teams to get where they are. They didn't play that well in the first game but it was a very difficult game in front of a passionate crowd at Anfield. I hope they can now seal the result.'

Paul McGuinness was another to be interviewed on the subject, and he revealed the team's preparation, 'We played our under-16's against Sheffield United on Saturday and they did very well, winning 4-0. That gave our boys a bit more rest. We've been training and looking at the first leg.' Later asked about the loss of one of his most consistent defenders, who was ruled out through a knee knock picked up in training, the coach responded, 'Craig (Cathcart) missed the first leg because he was involved with the first-team. But to miss the final at Old Trafford, where he would have hoped to lead the team to victory, will be a big disappointment.'

McGuinness declared, 'We'd like to play a bit more football than we did in the first leg and we are capable of that, especially if we can get a big support behind us. We want to put Liverpool under a bit more pressure and have more control of the game. We hope to be taking the game to them.'

Alas, the continued loss of key personnel proved a bridge too far for the United lads, most of whom were well below their best, and it was up to Stuart Mathieson to summarise the Reds' faded conclusion to what was an otherwise superb cup run:

UNITED'S Class of 2007 heartbreakingly failed in their quest to write their name into Old Trafford's illustrious Youth Cup Hall of Fame last night in a cruel penalty-shoot out.

Sir Alex Ferguson is rarely wrong with his assessment of anything United, but the Reds boss didn't believe that this crop of kids would make an impact on the coveted trophy this campaign.

The boy wonders have made him eat his words time and time again after he publicly admitted his misgivings about their chances and, despite this agonising defeat at the final hurdle, Fergie will surely still happily consume a slice of humble pie.

They have made a courageous and thrilling fist of it in the competition and once more were involved in typical Old Trafford drama.

Coach Paul McGuinness has said that even losing is a vital part of their soccer education. Try telling the distraught teenagers last night that they had just had a vital lesson. But in the cold light of day perhaps they will realise that even their famous predecessors from 15 years ago – David Beckham, Gary Neville, Paul Scholes and Nicky Butt – suffered the depression of final defeat after winning the trophy 12 months earlier.

But this was an agonising and tear-jerking finale as United's Magnus Eikrem and captain Sam Hewson missed their spot kicks in front of the Stretford End and holders Liverpool had a 100 per cent record to retain the trophy.

The Red youngsters had played in front of 38,000 at Arsenal, 19,000 at Liverpool, but the 24,347 willing them on in their own backyard initially seemed to freeze some.

The one player who appeared unaffected by the sirens and horns that echoed around the stadium was Febian Brandy. Not surprising since he was the striker who as a 12-year-old was blowing kisses and doing somersaults after scoring when he was player of the tournament in Barcelona!

The diminutive Mancunian is an elusive forward and cup holders Liverpool struggled to keep him quiet. He was in cahoots with gangly schoolboy and fellow local Daniel Welbeck who warmed to the task as well.

Welbeck is most pundits' favourite to be the mystery player who Fergie privately believes has a great chance of being a star in the future. But neither he nor Brandy could find the final touch to add to the Reds' 2-1 first-leg lead.

When the visitors finally came to the fore last evening it was the impressive Craig Lindfield who began to chip away at United's confidence.

Red keeper Ron-Robert Zieler had to pull off a splendid one-handed save on to his post to deny the striker in the second half but three minutes later after 55 minutes it was defender Robbie Threlfall who thrashed in an unstoppable opener to level the tie on aggregate.

United were visibly wilting as the Anfielders began to turn the power on but they couldn't break down the Reds' defence who gallantly stood firm to take them to the nerve-shredding ending of a brave adventure.

As with numerous other big soccer occasions, the two teams came at the match from a cagey standpoint and United even took the precaution of frequently 'doubling up' on Liverpool's wide men. There were openings for both sides to score just before Threlfall's goal, with Brandy escaping the shackles of marker Jay Spearing only to fail to beat replacement goalie David Roberts in a one-on-one face-off and Ryan Flynn unable to direct a rebound past Zieler after Lindfield's header came back off a post. Lindfield also contrived to hit an upright in extra-time with a low drive and Anton Bryan should have done better from close quarters in the last fifteen minutes.

And so it went to penalties.

United won the toss only to immediately lose the advantage, when a nervous looking Magnus Eikrem saw his kick saved by Roberts, and Putterill responded by firing his into the back of Zieler's net. In turn, Fagan, Lindfield, Chester, Flynn, Galbraith and Threlfall all converted to make it four penalties to Liverpool and three to United. It meant that Hewson needed to score, and his failure to do so handed the trophy to the jubilant Merseysiders, who were the better team in many of the match's key aspects.

> *We missed the experience of Craig Cathcart at the back to start our attacks. Tom Cleverley is another natural ball player at the back and we missed the composed play to start our moves going forward.*
>
> *That has been the message in the dressing room to all the lads, this is about experience. It's shown tonight that they weren't quite ready, so they have to go and hone their skills so that when they get the chance again everything will come automatically and they can handle it. They'll be back.*
>
> **PAUL McGUINNESS**

final 2nd leg

*This game was originally scheduled to be played on Thursday, 19th April but was put back a week for reasons unknown

Ron-Robert Zieler made a superb stop to deny Liverpool's Craig Lindfield just prior to Robbie Threlfall's leveller going in

2006-07

APRIL 2007

Febian Brandy caused a few problems for the visiting defence but was unable to find the back of David Roberts' net

All of United's outfield players look transfixed as Ron-Robert Zieler prepares to face another Liverpool penalty in the spot kick shoot-out

final 2nd leg

481

2007-08

1) Ben Amos	9) Danny Welbeck	1) Josh Pelling	9) Liam Upton
2) Scott Moffatt	10) Federico Macheda	2) Steve Cook	10) Kane Louis
3) Joe Dudgeon	11) Danny Galbraith	3) Ruben French	11) Dan Royce
4) Matty James	*12) Oliver Gill*	4) Lee Bryant	*12) Zac Beda (for 5)*
5) Kenny Strickland	*13) Gary Woods GK*	5) Andy Pearson	*13) Mitch Walker GK*
6) Corry Evans	*14) Anton Bryan (for 11)*	6) Lewis Ide	*14) Ollie Rowe*
7) Magnus Eikrem	*15) Cameron Stewart (for 7)*	7) Steve Brinkhurst	*15) Peter Martin (for 9)*
8) Danny Drinkwater	*16) Conor McCormack*	8) Kane Wills	*16) Lewis Dunk*

DECEMBER 2007

MANCHESTER UNITED* 2 v 1 BRIGHTON & HOVE ALBION

Bryan, Macheda — Bryant

Thursday 13th**

Kick-off 7.00 p.m.

Attendance 306

* Played at the Victoria Stadium, Northwich

third round

Due mainly to the better facilities on offer, particularly in regards to a far superior playing surface, United's Reserves found themselves at yet another new location for the start of the 2007/08 campaign, so it was somewhat inevitable that when Youth Cup time rolled around in the December of that season, the under-18's would be required to perform at the same venue. There was something of a surprise when the club's management initially decided to stage the Third Round tie against Brighton at Old Trafford, though it didn't come as a complete shock when they switched it to Northwich's Victoria Stadium just three days prior to the Seagulls' arrival.

Bolstered by a convincing 3-0 win at Bristol Rovers in their last Youth Cup contest, on the day before their meeting with United the Brighton squad travelled up to the Midlands, where they took part in a workout at Wolves' training ground, and they then went through another light session just before journeying up to Cheshire.

United fielded a side not wholly dissimilar to the one defeated by Liverpool just eight months ago, with only Scott Moffatt (Manchester), Joe Dudgeon (Leeds), Matty James (Bacup) and Federico Macheda (Rome) as new starters and Ben Amos returning in goal. In view of the depth of experience in the side, as well as the potential offered by the new blood, everything seemed to bode well for a prolonged run in the tournament.

A combination of a chilly, misty evening and the distance involved in travelling from Manchester for Reds' followers contributed towards a depressingly low crowd, about a quarter of whom were Brighton supporters. Even so, they viewed a super game in which the Reds put in a two-faced performance, which was largely subdued in the first half and saw them overwhelmingly on top in the second.

Obviously pumped up for the clash, the junior Seagulls showed they were far from overawed, especially during the early section of the match, and they managed to find plenty of space down the left where Dan Royce caught the eye with his craft and pace. United captain Corry Evans claimed the home team's first effort on goal from a corner when nodding the ball into Josh Pelling's hands and Moffatt went near with a header as a result of Eikrem's tremendous cross.

The Albion came away from those scares to create a couple of their own openings, the first of which was when Liam Upton fired over. The south coast youngsters were much more satisfied at the conclusion of their next chance, when a combination involving three of their defenders resulted in them taking the lead on 29 minutes. Their goal came from a classic set-piece move, with Ruben French swinging over a corner from the right, the ball then taking a flick on by fellow full-back Steve Cook and centre-back Lee Bryant ending the sequence by turning the ball over the line at the far post.

The Reds only threatened to equalise just once over the remaining minutes before the interval, Danny Welbeck scorning that opportunity by screwing his effort wide following a super-fast break up the pitch.

United were a different proposition thereafter and approximately 60 seconds after the restart Danny Drinkwater bashed a shot against a post. Then breasting the ball down on the perimeter of Brighton's box, Drinkwater struck a sweet left-foot volley against the other upright on 53 minutes.

The Seagulls impressively tried to continue knocking the ball about and they occasionally probed for weaknesses in the Reds' defence without really threatening to increase their lead. The match now resembled a cavalry charge, only there were no horses to be seen in United's half of the pitch.

The Reds' exertions earned an initial reward in the 74th minute as Brighton's resistance finally began unzipping, and the Albion only had themselves to blame because there were ample chances to clear their lines. When none of them were accepted, Anton Bryan took aim from about twenty-yards distance and his deflected drive somehow managed to wind its way through a cluster of opponents and beyond Pelling.

Completely dousing Brighton's lights just six minutes later, the winner developed when Bryant lost possession and the classy Macheda stormed towards goal only to be felled by the visiting 'keeper. Dusting himself down prior to claiming responsibility for taking the spot kick, Macheda's initial effort was kept out by a terrific save from Pelling only for the Roman, in true gladiatorial style, to mercilessly slay the goalie's hopes of keeping his team in the hunt by blasting in the rebound. Not the prettiest of goals, nevertheless it sealed a victory which always seemed inevitable once the Reds saw fit to increase their effort rate.

Immediately after the match Paul McGuinness pointed out, *'In the first half they caused us a few problems but in the second half we were much better. We were in control of the game, had far more possession and put the pressure on until we finally got the goals to win the game.'*

**This game was originally scheduled to be played at Old Trafford

Corry Evans (left), Danny Drinkwater (right) and Kenny Strickland (far right) appear to show only minor concern as Joe Dudgeon races ahead of Brighton's Liam Upton

1) Ben Amos	9) Danny Welbeck	1) Alex Mitchell	9) Gary Madine
2) Scott Moffatt	10) Federico Macheda	2) Matthew Brown	10) Andy Cook
3) Cameron Stewart	11) Anton Bryan	3) Matt Duffy	11) Connor Tinnion
4) Matty James	*12) Conor McCormack*	4) Jonny Blake	*12) Ged Dalton (for 11)*
5) Oliver Gill	*13) Gary Woods GK*	5) Dan Wordsworth	*13) John Jamieson GK*
6) Corry Evans	*14) Danny Galbraith (for 3)*	6) Tom Aldred	*14) Simon Lakeland (for 8)*
7) Magnus Eikrem	*15) Oliver Norwood (for 7)*	7) Steve Hindmarch	*15) John Seaton (for 4)*
8) Danny Drinkwater	*16) Joe Dudgeon*	8) Matthew Wood	*16) Michael Dowson*

MANCHESTER UNITED* 1 v 2 CARLISLE UNITED

Welbeck   *Hindmarch, Madine (pen)*

2007-08

JANUARY 2008

Wednesday 16th**

Kick-off 7.00 p.m.

Attendance 330

* Played at the Marston's Arena, Northwich

fourth round

With Federico Macheda and Danny Welbeck having totalled fifteen of the under-18's league and cup goals for the season, Paul McGuinness' immediate target of getting past Carlisle hinged to an extent on their ability to find a way to the Cumbrians' net. Prior to the match, the coach was complimentary of their individual and collective abilities when speaking to a representative of the club's website.

'They are very good players,' he pronounced. 'Danny is still only young and has a year left at this level (and) Federico is a very good technical player. He's a good finisher, makes good decisions and some clever runs. His English is coming on, he's a bright boy. He understands what we're after and he has fitted in well with the culture of the club.

Federico and Danny are on a really good wavelength. When you see them in training and you look at the likes of Rooney and Tevez and the way they link up, these two lads are capable of doing similar sorts of combinations.'

Unfortunately, McGuinness' plans were wrecked by an efficiently marshalled and stubborn set of opponents who refused to wave a white flag no matter what his talented teenagers threw at them. Added to the fact that there was a sprinkling of below-par performances from within United's ranks, it caused their expectations to slip irretrievably between the cracks at the newly-named Marston's Arena.

There was even a decent start for the Reds. In the eighth minute, Anton Bryan revealed a glimpse of his searing pace down the left wing and he cut inside on his right foot to blast a rasping shot over the bar and raise hopes of a satisfying outcome. It was, therefore, quite a shock to the small crowd when, just four minutes later, Carlisle's Gary Madine situated himself on the end of an exquisite pass into the Reds' eighteen-yard zone and attempted to dribble his way past Ben Amos.

The big goalie brought him down in full flow and no-one could question the referee's next action in awarding a spot kick, although it was something of a puzzle as to why the 'keeper wasn't dismissed.

The yellow-carded Amos then infuriated those occupying the away dug-out by tying his laces, noisily banging his studs against an upright and generally play-acting before taking his position to face the penalty. Seemingly unconcerned about those exaggerated actions, Madine side-footed an accurate kick into the corner of the net to give his side the advantage.

United quickly went on full alert and during a fertile period in terms of chances created, Moffatt dragged a left-footed attempt across Carlisle's goalmouth and inches wide of a post, Macheda's twenty-yard drive was parried by Alex Mitchell and Corry Evans toe-poked the ball onto an upright. The last thing that anyone expected was for the Brunton Park boys to score again, but that is exactly what happened in the 34th minute. And what a goal it was too.

A huge goal kick from Mitchell seemed to get lost in the blackness of the night sky until dropping in the vicinity of team-mate Madine. Heading it down the right-hand side of the field and directly into the path of Steve Hindmarch about 25 yards out, the ball sat up nicely and was almost begging to be hit, so Carlisle's number seven obliged by smashing an unstoppable swerving right-footed stunner that ripped past Amos to bulge the far corner of the net.

Realising the task ahead of them was now classed as enormous, the Reds retained possession almost entirely from then until the break. Easily United's brightest spark on the night, Welbeck earned a free kick which Eikrem wasted by thumping into the Carlisle wall, and the former then took it upon himself to improve his team's fortunes by swivelling to fire in a shot that found the bottom corner of Mitchell's net and half his side's deficit on 42 minutes.

The goal spurred the Reds on and they cut through their blue-shirted opponents like razor wire all through the second half, only the opening they sought never materialised.

Paul McGuinness threw on another attacking option in Danny Galbraith thirteen minutes after the turnaround as wave upon wave of pressure floundered on the Cumbrian's defence. There was only a quarter of an hour left when Macheda tasked Mitchell with a drive from distance as all bar one of the opposing side were now situated between him and the goal-line.

A smooth move for United saw the ball knocked into the feet of Galbraith, with his conversion ruled out through slightly mistiming his run to be caught offside. The Reds conjured up two or three passages of short passing in Carlisle's penalty area, though there was always someone on hand to knock the ball away for the visitors.

The Evening News recorded *'United's moments of danger were fleeting, despite a constant flow towards Carlisle's goal'* and, whereas their opponents *'limited themselves to breakaways'*, the Reds' danger men *'struggled to conjure up anything to seriously threaten'*.

The unexpected defeat to Carlisle spelt the end of the Youth Cup line for Corry Evans (top) and Danny Drinkwater

**This game was originally scheduled to be played at Old Trafford

485

2008-09

1) Gary Woods	9) Federico Macheda	1) Niclas Heimann	9) Fabio Borini
2) Ryan Tunnicliffe	10) Danny Welbeck	2) Nikki Ahamed	10) Gael Kakuta
3) Joe Dudgeon	11) Robbie Brady	3) Rohan Ince	11) Frank Nouble
4) Scott Wootton	*12) Kenny Strickland*	4) Jeffrey Bruma	*12) Billy-Joe King*
5) Oliver Gill	*13) Conor Devlin GK*	5) Ben Gordon	*13) Jan Sebek GK*
6) Matty James	*14) Davide Petrucci (for 8)*	6) Daniel Philliskirk	*14) Conor Clifford (for 7)*
7) Ravel Morrison	*15) Cameron Stewart (for 11)*	7) Jacopo Sala	*15) Billy Knott (for 10)*
8) Oliver Norwood	*16) Nicky Ajose (for 9)*	8) Jacob Mellis	*16) Josh McEachran (for 8)*

NOVEMBER 2008

MANCHESTER UNITED 2 v 3 CHELSEA
Morrison, Welbeck — *Borini, Kakuta, Nouble*

Thursday 27th
Kick-off 7.00 p.m.
Attendance 1,246

third round

Having not met Chelsea since a semi-final victory in 1955, the Reds went into their latest Youth Cup meeting against the southerners in splendid form. With 4-0 divisional wins over Bolton and Blackburn on the last two weekends, and only one defeat suffered all season so far, there was a tempered expectation that they might be able to claim the scalp of their multi-international opponents.

In his pre-match jottings, Mail Online correspondent Ivan Spark revealed that eight of Chelsea's starting eleven cost the club a fee, including left-back Ben Gordon and midfielder Jacob Mellis, who 'fetched around £400,000 each for Leeds and Sheffield United respectively'. Later pointing out that John Terry was the last youngster to fully establish himself for the Blues, his senior debut coming ten years ago, it appeared that owner Roman Abramovich was prepared to splash his cash in order to make Chelsea's Academy the best around. With an appearance in last year's Youth Cup final, a defeat by Manchester City, it looked as though the seeds planted by the club's benefactor were well on the way to fruition.

Aware that Paul McGuinness was forced into handing full competition debuts to five of his side, Spark mentioned that United 'believe a hardcore of local youngsters is essential for protecting the club's values' and added that nine of the sixteen squad members 'were born within 35 miles of Old Trafford'. Then going on to write that 'Chelsea, by contrast' included a French boy, a couple of Italians, a German goalie and a Dutch lad, Spark stated, 'The one certainty is that given the head starts that life in the Academies of Manchester United and Chelsea give them, most of these players should forge successful careers' before querying 'in which team's colours is altogether trickier to predict'.

Chelsea youth team manager Paul Clements took Spark's last statement a step further when saying, 'Hopefully, some of the boys on show will get the opportunity to play at Old Trafford again, ideally at senior level, but they have to understand that for some of them it may be the biggest moment in their career. That's the way it is, unfortunately.'

When asked about his take on the draw, McGuinness responded, 'We go into the game with confidence, as our recent form in the league has been very good and our training and preparation for this game has been spot-on. We certainly feel that we have some very talented players, but we know from experience that the team grows with each success in a Youth Cup run.

If we get past this big hurdle, it will be a great boost to everyone's belief that they could go all the way. The aim of the Youth Cup for us is to gain a simulation of first-team experience, therefore playing Chelsea at Old Trafford is as close to that as you can get.'

Well impressed by at least one of the club's fresh faces, the Evening News' scribe pencilled the following words:

There was nothing like the ambitious 40,000-strong crowd United had hoped would show to watch the next generation of talent at Old Trafford – but for the handful that braved a wintry November night, one name will have been tattooed on their brains.

The little-known and even littler-framed Ravel Morrison produced a performance of such showmanship in the first half of this F.A. Youth Cup Third Round tie that at times he looked capable of beating Chelsea all by himself.

It is a measure of the winger's display that he even overshadowed Danny Welbeck, who has made such impressive strides in the United first-team over the last month. Morrison scored one and later produced such a sublime piece of footwork that the entire crowd was on its feet, while half of Chelsea's defence were on their backsides. He could be forgiven for failing to maintain such high standards after the break – after all, at the tender age of fifteen, it was probably close to his bedtime.

Robbie Brady and Chelsea's Jeffrey Bruma tussle for possession

Oliver Gill put on a fine performance in defeat against Chelsea

486

NOVEMBER 2008

third round

With time almost up, Danny Welbeck strikes a second goal for the Reds

For all his brilliance, it wasn't enough to inspire United to victory, with Chelsea turning the game on its head late in the first half.

Gael Kakuta poked Chelsea's first shot on target past Gary Woods three minutes before the break, and then Frank Nouble crashed a twenty-yard effort into the top corner in first half injury-time.

Fabio Borini killed the game off as a competition as United pushed for an equaliser in the second half, with Welbeck's injury-time volley proving only a consolation.

But it was Morrison who did more than anyone to light up Old Trafford. After Welbeck had fluffed his lines early on when one-on-one with Niclas Heimann, Morrison showed a much more ruthless streak, coolly lifting a shot over the Chelsea goalkeeper after only eight minutes.

He should have added a second shortly after when showing tremendous composure to round Heimann twice, as well as lead Chelsea's defenders a merry dance before laying off to the impressive Matthew James, whose shot was cleared off the line.

In truth Morrison was guilty of over-embellishment and should have taken one of several chances to shoot himself – but he was handed another bite of the cherry when James' shot rebounded to him six yards out only for him to blast over.

It proved to be particularly costly with Chelsea's double blast just before half-time.

At a time when the likes of Welbeck, Jonny Evans and Darron Gibson are making inroads into the senior side, this was a chance to see the next generation of United starlets. Included were chief executive David Gill's son, Oliver, and Italian striker Davide Petrucci, who has been labelled the next Roberto Baggio in his homeland, a second half substitute.

And despite chances after the break for Welbeck and James in particular, it proved to be the end of the road for United in a competition they have won a record nine times.

The Review began its match report by noting 'Football's most painful lessons are often the most valuable', and there were additional claims made regarding United being in 'full control' prior to scoring the first goal, as well as the Londoners striking 'out of nowhere' to edge themselves in front.

2009-10

1) Conor Devlin	9) Will Keane	1) Jack Butland	9) Jake Jervis
2) Michele Fornasier	10) Davide Petrucci	2) Jamie Dunphy	10) Ashley Sammons
3) Sean McGinty	11) Nicky Ajose	3) Luke Rowe	11) Akwasi Asante
4) Tom Thorpe	*12) Larnell Cole*	4) Jordon Mutch	*12) Nathan Redmond*
5) Scott Wootton	*13) Sam Johnstone GK*	5) Will Packwood	*13) Glenn Daniels GK*
6) Ryan Tunnicliffe	*14) Jesse Lingard*	6) Dan Preston	*14) Jakub Hronec*
7) Ravel Morrison	*15) John Cofie*	7) Luke Hubbins	*15) Omar Bogle (for 8)*
8) Paul Pogba	*16) Alberto Massacci (for 4)*	8) Mitchell McPike	*16) Brice Ntambwe*

DECEMBER 2009

MANCHESTER UNITED* 2 v 0 BIRMINGHAM CITY
Ajose, Pogba

Thursday 10th

Kick-off 7.00 p.m.

Attendance 635

Played at Moss Lane, Altrincham

third round

In a match preview devoted to the Reds' latest attempt at re-capturing the national under-18's knock-out trophy, the Evening News included a few paragraphs which mentioned the composition of Paul McGuinness' squad:

United's core of locals will ensure the Reds' foreign legion understand the importance of the F.A. Youth Cup. Old Trafford's youngsters start their assault on the prestigious trophy tonight against Birmingham City at Altrincham's Moss Lane.

And a collection of Europe's stars of the future has had United's followers buzzing. The likes of French sixteen year-old midfielder Paul Pogba, fellow midfielder Davide Petrucci from Rome and Italian defender Michele Fornasier have added an exotic touch to the Reds wannabes.

However, there remains a heavy accent on local talent in United's Academy.

Tom Thorpe, Ravel Morrison and Larnell Cole are from Manchester, Jesse Lingard is from Warrington and Bury's Nicky Ajose and Ryan Tunnicliffe are among the heart of the squad.

McGuinness explained, *'The local lads have been here since they were eight and nine years old. They are well versed in the importance of the tournament. They know the history of it and they know this is their chance to become a part of the club's history if they are successful.*

At this moment in time it is the be-all and end-all. However, if the tournament doesn't work out for them that doesn't mean they won't progress. A few years ago we had a group who lost in the First Round to Stoke City and that team contained Jonny Evans, Darron Gibson, Gerard Piqué, Ryan Shawcross and Fraizer Campbell. Now look at how well all those players are doing.

So it doesn't mean the end of the world if things don't go right – but I won't be telling them that yet!'

As for Birmingham, they included Mitchell McPike, whose brother James appeared against the Reds in the 2006/07 competition, and Jordon Mutch, a midfielder whose loan to Hereford allowed him to take part in City's second string and youth matches whenever he wasn't required by the Edgar Street outfit. Mutch went into the game with first-team experience for both Hereford and the Blues, and was actually the second youngest senior debutant after club legend Trevor Francis at St. Andrews.

A link-up between a local lad and a foreign import got United away to a great start after only 57 seconds when Pogba nodded in an Ajose free kick struck from out on the wing. Just like they did at Old Trafford nearly three years ago, the Midlanders then tried to make life difficult for the Reds and, giving as good as they got, McPike squandered a presentable opening by blazing wide following a nice piece of approach work on the left by Jake Jervis.

United were required to shuffle their back line on 21 minutes as Thorpe, who was unable to shake off the effects of a knock sustained in a robust tackle earlier, was replaced by Alberto Massacci. After the Italian was placed in his normal position of left full-back, and Fornasier moved into the centre of the defence, Conor Devlin found himself pressed into action by making a couple of easy saves from Jervis and Asante.

Coming at a time when Birmingham were in the ascendancy, the Reds' second goal brought some much needed relief and coincided almost exactly with the half-hour mark. In a fast break, Petrucci weighted a delightful pass to Will Keane about twenty or so yards out. Keane stroked the ball first time to the in-rushing Ajose, who took it under control in an instant prior to walloping a powerful low drive across England under-17 goalkeeper Jack Butland and into the far corner of the rigging. Now more than a mite dismayed at the scoreline considering their earlier input, Birmingham faded like an old pair of jeans and Butland needed to make saves from Morrison, Petrucci and Ajose in quick succession.

The visitors' chances of progressing took another huge jolt eight minutes into the concluding period when the red-headed Devlin eclipsed the heroics performed by his opposite number with a simply incredible penalty save. The Blues were awarded the spot kick because Pogba was adjudged to have brought down Jervis, and Birmingham's number nine looked to have yanked his side back into contention by blasting a powerful shot towards the bottom corner of the goal. Correctly guessing the ball was going to his right, Devlin gave the impression of stretching like elastic as he flung himself at full-length to touch it away to safety.

Scoring openings fell to both teams during the last half an hour, a time in which the Reds were fortunate to escape punishment from a goalmouth mêlée and Birmingham almost conceded to a Sean McGinty header from close in. The mercurial Morrison chanced his arm with two long-range, off-target drives and as even more Blues players charged forward in their forlorn need of a goal, Keane hit a post in the 80th minute.

Following their earlier rearrangement, United's back four looked composed and compact, usually confining their opponents to shooting from distance, while Devlin continued to impress with his confident demeanour and secure handling. All told, the win represented a pleasing first step on what the young Reds expected would develop into a lengthy cup road.

Conor Devlin (top) was unbeatable against Birmingham while Paul Pogba hit the target within a minute of the kick-off

488

1) Danny McDonald	9) Dom Knowles	1) Conor Devlin	9) Will Keane
2) Ed Williams	10) Liam Newman	2) Alberto Massacci	10) Davide Petrucci
3) Jake McEneaney	11) Michael King	3) Nicky Ajose	11) Josh King
4) Dave Lynch	*12) Josh Cooke GK*	4) Scott Wootton	*12) Michele Fornasier (for 2)*
5) Tom Anderson	*14) Steve Edwards (for 11)*	5) Sean McGinty	*13) Sam Johnstone GK*
6) Curtis Woods	*15) Joe Jackson (for 10)*	6) Ryan Tunnicliffe	*14) John Cofie (for 11)*
7) Ross Wilson	*16) James Taylor (for 7)*	7) Larnell Cole	*15) Etzaz Hussain*
8) Joe McKee	*17) Steve Hewitt*	8) Paul Pogba	*16) Jesse Lingard (for 10)*

BURNLEY 1 v 5 MANCHESTER UNITED

McKee

Keane (2), King (2), Petrucci

2009-10

JANUARY 2010

Wednesday 13th

Kick-off 7.00 p.m.

Attendance 1,036

Just like in 1957, 1968, 1971, 1985 and 1990, the United kids were required to travel the 25 or so miles north in order to tackle a teenage Burnley combination at their Turf Moor home. Because of the consequences of one of the severest winters on record, with all of their Academy games called off in the interim period, the young Reds hadn't kicked a ball in anger since the Youth Cup defeat of Birmingham. However, they were able to avail themselves of the superb facilities at Carrington and, through pitting themselves against the club's Reserves on an almost full-size indoor pitch, as well as taking part in sessions on the undersoil-heated grass there, they were able to maintain a maximum level of fitness.

Paul McGuinness revealed the thinking behind his squad's preparation and what lay ahead for them by saying, *'When you play the Reserves you're up against bigger, stronger and faster opposition than you're used to. It's a bit like sparring in boxing – when you prepare for a fight you train against bigger and quicker opponents. So it's been really useful.*

Youth Cup ties are like a fight. It's a battle. Teams are fired up to play (us) and I think Burnley will be really pleased that such a big tie will be played at Turf Moor. I know the coaches at Burnley and they're steeped in the history of the club. They'll have their boys really fired up but also playing good football.'

Whatever the outcome, the day was always going to be an exceptionally sad one for all of those concerned with Manchester United. The recent death of Albert Scanlon, the scorer of the Reds' very first Youth Cup goal in October 1952, cast a dark shadow over Old Trafford and the Salfordian's funeral took place on the same day of his beloved club's latest match in a competition he did so much to enhance all those many years before. Although none of United's younger supporters had seen Scanlon's considerable on-field attributes, many of them were introduced to him through his appearances as a perceptive and popular pundit on MUTV and so there was, therefore, a genuine feeling of loss experienced at his passing by a large section of the club's following.

The latest generation of United's talented tots did him proud at Turf Moor, with a skilful yet merciless masterclass of finishing power and a liberal sprinkling of class all over the pitch which was simply too much for the hosts to take. With the powerful Josh King introduced upfront for Ravel Morrison, the Reds were practically home and dry within half an hour and they went on to double their two-goal lead either side of the break.

United began in a mood that indicated they were itching to get stuck into the Clarets and apart from a speculative 30-yard shot from Michael King, Burnley were unable to make many inroads towards Devlin's goal in addition to forfeiting possession for most of the time.

The Reds' opener was a collectively superb affair. Coming as a result of a move involving numerous passes in the 21st minute, when Josh King's shot was blocked Petrucci homed in on the stray ball to stroke it just inside an upright. Just six minutes later, King accepted a pass from Larnell Cole on the left and moved forward into some space to bend a tremendous effort inside the far corner of Danny McDonald's net.

The Burnley lads were visibly shell-shocked and their confidence was further eroded in the 33rd minute as Nicky Ajose won the ball in midfield and reclaimed it a couple of passes later. Sliding it perfectly into the feet of Will Keane, the Stockport-born hit-man threw gallons of petrol onto the flames of Burnley's troubles by nervelessly lobbing the ball over McDonald and snugly into its intended target from just less than twenty yards out.

The Clarets' website reporter recorded *'but for a couple of wayward efforts and some good goalkeeping from McDonald, we could have been much further behind by half time'* and soon after the restart they actually did concede again. King once again inflicted the damage when claiming a misplaced pass and he punished the error by blasting home an unstoppable shot. Injured soon after, King was replaced by Ghanaian John Cofie, a striker who was captured from Burnley during the last summer break.

The Clarets' task moved from highly improbable to mission impossible twenty minutes from the end as defender Tom Anderson picked up two yellow cards in quick succession, giving the referee no option other than to send him for a lonely bath. At times it seemed that all that stood between the Reds and a monumental total was McDonald, who kept out Cofie twice, caught a crafty back-heel attempt from Keane, and watched helplessly as efforts from Cole and Tunnicliffe whizzed past him and off-target.

An error by Devlin let in Joe McKee for a consolation goal with 84 minutes gone, only for United to respond when Pogba and Cofie linked to set up the deadly Keane, whose left-footed finish with two minutes to go would surely have brought a broad smile from Albert Scanlon.

fourth round

Davide Petrucci squeezes between two home defenders to register the first of five United goals at Burnley

2009-10

1) Josh Swann	9) Tom Hitchcock	1) Conor Devlin	9) Will Keane
2) Jackson Ramm	10) Michael Potts	2) Reece Brown	10) Davide Petrucci
3) Dami Ajagbe	11) Jason Banton	3) Zeki Fryers	11) Josh King
4) Jason Lowe	12) Gearoid Morrissey (for 11)	4) Scott Wootton	12) Alberto Massacci
5) Grant Hanley	13) Matthew Urwin GK	5) Sean McGinty	13) Sam Johnstone GK
6) Phil Jones	14) James Knowles (for 9)	6) Ryan Tunnicliffe	14) Ravel Morrison (for 2)
7) Micah Evans	15) Matthew Pearson	7) Nicky Ajose	15) Etzaz Hussain (for 10)
8) Jordan Bowen	16) Osayamen Osawe (for 7)	8) Paul Pogba	16) John Cofie (for 3)

JANUARY 2010

BLACKBURN ROVERS **3** v **0** MANCHESTER UNITED

Hanley, Lowe (2)

Thursday 28th
Kick-off 7.00 p.m.
Attendance 874

fifth round

END OF THE ROAD FOR RED KIDS

If Turf Moor sometimes proves a happy Youth Cup hunting ground for the young Reds, the home of their neighbours, Blackburn Rovers, has never provided them with so much as a solitary victory.

A graveyard for Jimmy Murphy's boys in 1959 and Brian McClair's kids in 2004, Ewood Park had also yielded two hard-fought draws for United's under-18's, and both of those preceded knock-outs for the Old Trafford teenagers.

Not only was it once again on the cold and wet side at the Rovers' stadium, rain cascading down for the whole duration of the game, with less than 900 people fitted into the Jack Walker Stand, it was also pretty desolate. On a soggy surface which was lacking grass in places due to a senior fixture having been staged there 24 hours earlier, United's display could similarly be described as 'patchy' and it was an inability to score when on top that proved their downfall.

There were two changes to the starting eleven who defeated Burnley, Reece Brown taking over from Alberto Massacci and Zeki Fryers coming in for Larnell Cole. There could be no excuses as far as confidence was concerned, as the United squad was buoyed by their most recent result at Academy level over the weekend just gone, when goals from Nicky Ajose, John Cofie and Etzaz Hussain turned around a 2-0 deficit to overcome Stoke City at Carrington.

While Will Keane (left) and Ravel Morrison look on, Ryan Tunnicliffe keeps his eyes firmly on the ball as the Reds are overpowered by a strong Rovers' combination

490

Having just conceded a penalty, Nicky Ajose indicates that Tom Hitchcock went down a little theatrically

Tightly marked on the night, striker Josh King was unable to provide the goals required against Blackburn

That form wasn't carried over to the following Thursday and it was Blackburn who posed the greater threat early in the floodlit match, with Jason Banton testing Devlin early in the game and the goalie proving equal to the task by beating away the attempt. Soon becoming obvious that extracting a result out of the contest required both teams to roll their sleeves up, the teenage Rovers looked more willing and able in regards to the physical aspect of the game.

It was the middle section of the first half when the Reds could have booked their place in the last sixteen and Blackburn were indebted to 'keeper Josh Swann for his alertness as he produced a terrific stop after Ajose found the head of Paul Pogba from a free kick. Davide Petrucci later conjured up a little piece of magic by tricking his way past Jackson Ramm, only to then place his chipped effort onto the roof of the net.

United's clearest opportunity of the contest came in the 33rd minute. A deflected shot from Ryan Tunnicliffe again reached Pogba and the French boy reacted by nodding it in the direction of Josh King. Situated only about six or seven yards out, the Norwegian forward rose a good two feet above his marker only to get his direction all wrong and head the ball well wide.

That miss signalled a rapid downturn for the away team and only six minutes later they were behind. It was a contentious goal, because it stemmed from a corner which was given when Devlin appeared to be impeded by Tom Hitchcock as he attempted to deal with a cross. Rather than giving the foul most of the players expected, the referee caused a few heads to be scratched by awarding a flag kick. The corner delivered in by Michael Potts from the right spelt problems and they increased significantly when the ball was flicked on towards the far post.

There, rushing in, was Jason Lowe, who kept his composure to knock it between a rooted Devlin and a static King and over the goal-line.

The Rovers seemed to redouble their efforts in the second half and Devlin demonstrated what makes a fine goalkeeper with some quite outstanding stops to keep the Reds in contention. When a Potts free kick was headed goalwards by Grant Hanley, Devlin frustrated him with a great right-handed save and then managed to top that super piece of work by parrying a blistering drive from Hitchcock.

United were largely under the thumb by this time and a Scott Wootton header that found the side-netting, in addition to a chance Sean McGinty side-footed wide, provided only isolated scares for the home defence.

Devlin continued to keep Blackburn at bay by repelling a Hitchcock volley in the 68th minute and he brought off another tremendous save from a Hanley effort a few moments later. This time, though, the Blackburn captain wouldn't be denied and he bravely headed in the rebound from under the crossbar to make the score 2-0.

Ravel Morrison was introduced in the 73rd minute and John Cofie followed him on five minutes later in an attempt to add some sparkle to a jaded forward-line. With the result by then practically a lost cause, just before the end Ajose was harshly judged to have brought down Hitchcock to concede a penalty. Hitchcock's spot kick was brilliantly parried by Devlin only for the loose ball to be knocked into the net by the alert Lowe.

Even though there were five minutes of time added on, the majority of them were spent in the half of a totally dispirited United side.

2010-11

Manchester United		Portsmouth	
1) Sam Johnstone	9) John Cofie	1) Tom Fry	9) Ryan Williams
2) Michael Keane	10) Will Keane	2) Lewis Tallack	10) Carl Walshe
3) Tyler Blackett	11) Gyliano van Velzen	3) Dan Butler	11) Andy Higgins
4) Tom Thorpe	12) *Zeki Fryers (for 7)*	4) Billy Tsovolos	12) *Alex Grant (for 11)*
5) Michele Fornasier	13) *Liam Jacob GK*	5) Dan Bennett	14) *George Colson (for 7)*
6) Ryan Tunnicliffe	14) *Jesse Lingard (for 2)*	6) Sam Magri	15) *Ashley Harris (for 8)*
7) Larnell Cole	15) *Alberto Massacci (for 5)*	7) Elliot Wheeler	16) *James Seeley*
8) Paul Pogba	16) *Luke Hendrie*	8) Lewis Stockford	21) *Matt Gledhill GK*

JANUARY 2011

MANCHESTER UNITED* 3 v 2 PORTSMOUTH

Fry (o.g.), Keane W., Pogba — Williams (2)

Monday 10th**

Kick-off 7.00 p.m.

Attendance 414

* Played at Moss Lane, Altrincham

Of the players available to Paul McGuinness for Youth Cup duties in January 2011, two of them, goalkeeper Sam Johnstone and striker Will Keane, were included in the second string's opening fixture of the season back in September. In addition, forward John Cofie was used off the substitute's bench during that same game whereas Ravel Morrison, who began it, was currently unavailable. Encouragingly, numerous other members of McGuinness' squad, including Tom Thorpe, Zeki Fryers, Ryan Tunnicliffe, Paul Pogba, Michael Keane, Sean McGinty, Jesse Lingard, Tyler Blackett and Gyliano van Velzen were already acquainted with football at Reserve standard.

Added to the Youth Cup experience in the party, which extended to numerous of them taking their second shot at the tournament, as well as Tunnicliffe and Morrison entering into a third such attempt at capturing the trophy, it meant that there could be no excuses regarding a lack of relevant know-how from the club's current crop of starlets.

There was also a significant pointer as to what might have been expected from United's teenage pool of talent when, in the second team's last outing, a cracking 5-1 win over Newcastle was secured by way of two goals from Will Keane, a single from Tunnicliffe and a brace from Morrison. Their achievements against the Magpies certainly shouted a statement of intent from the trio, because rarely has such a combination of current under-18's been felt in such a positive way at Reserve level.

Portsmouth passed up on the opportunity to play the game at Old Trafford when failing to agree on the original date of the 14th December suggested by United. Insisting instead on an earlier meeting, and following two postponements, the match eventually went ahead about a month later.

The Fratton Park kids travelled north with few people giving them any chance of bagging a favourable result. Pompey's under-18's were currently anchored at the bottom of their division, having picked up a measly four points from a possible 39, and club manager Steve Cotterill was moved to sack Academy boss Paul Smalley just a couple of weeks prior to the Youth Cup contest. It meant that the south coast outfit's junior squad were required to undertake the journey without a permanent man in charge, and Cotterill couldn't have done much for their confidence when saying about his need for a new appointment, *'It's not about getting everything sorted for Manchester United because whoever goes in is going to be on a hiding to nothing in that game anyway.'*

Considering the amount of snow and rain that had fallen in the Manchester area over the past few weeks, and it continued to pour in buckets through most of the match, the Moss Lane pitch was in good shape and the smooth surface helped United to quickly get into their pass-and-move stride.

Despite the Reds' early possession, it was actually Pompey who carved out the initial chances and Billy Tsovolos almost caused a shock when firing over after being teed up by Carl Walshe. Portsmouth's Lewis Stockford watched as his drive flashed past a post and Ryan Williams then attempted an audacious long-range shot which Johnstone caught comfortably.

Slowly but surely, the Reds began to pose an increasing amount of danger to their guests and in the 29th minute they got their trophy campaign underway in high style with a quite stupendous strike. Will Keane played a major part in the build-up, by making a lengthy dash from near to the centre circle and down the inside-left channel towards the perimeter of Pompey's penalty area. Chased most of the way by Stockford, Keane moved the ball onto his right foot only to have a shot obstructed by centre-back Dan Butler.

An interchange of passes then took place between Cole, Cofie and Pogba before the latter, from all of 30 yards out, whacked an astonishing blockbuster which moved from right to left, arching over 'keeper Tom Fry and just under the crossbar to bulge the back of Portsmouth's net. On MUTV, commentator David Stowell exclaimed, *'That's an absolute stunner. What a way to get the F.A. Youth Cup run going'* before adding excitedly that the goal was *'ridiculously good'*.

Pogba's opener dampened Pompey's enthusiasm considerably and with United exercising a tightening stranglehold on the match, Dan Bennett earned the wrath of the referee through ploughing into Will Keane.

The Reds as good as sewed up the result when scoring twice between the 59th and 61st minutes, though their second goal was nowhere near as pleasing on the eye as their first or third and it constituted a real howler as far as Fry was concerned. The pink-jerseyed goalie seemed to be all at sea when jumping for a Cole corner, the Reds' tenth of the game, and instead of knocking the ball away, he instead managed to punch it into his own net at the near post with a stiff right-hander.

Portsmouth were later in a state of disarray when a high ball was claimed by Tunnicliffe almost exactly in the middle of their half of the field. Tunnicliffe ran into space as the ball landed at the feet of Will Keane, who spun away from a marker prior to hammering the ball left-footed and high into Fry's goal from a distance of sixteen yards.

Even though United were three ahead, there was still plenty of action to savour over the remaining half an hour, during which Will Keane controlled a long ball from his twin, Michael, only to have another 'goal' ruled out for offside. At the other end, Johnstone saved from Williams and Will Keane found himself flagged for offside again after slotting in a close-range opening that was carved out for him by Cole.

The Reds later missed a penalty which was awarded when Sam Magri fouled Will Keane, Gyliano van Velzen slotting the spot kick away only to be ordered to re-take it due to some encroachment. The Dutch winger failed at his second attempt, with Fry making amends for his earlier mistake by leaping to his right to make a decent catch.

McGuinness then instigated a triple substitution and the changes may have slightly disrupted United's concentration as Pompey bit back to score twice. Initially inking a mark up on the score sheet as Williams outpaced Fryers to stuff a cross-shot past Johnstone, the same player was on hand to accurately ram the ball between the legs of the Reds' goalie from a most unlikely angle to double his team's total.

Portsmouth's goals made for a twitchy time of it in United's dugout over the final moments of the match, but overall the young Reds could feel reasonably pleased at the outcome of what was, despite their late lapses, quite an easy victory.

Better known for a superb level of skill with the ball at his feet, goalscorer Paul Pogba demonstrates a useful heading ability against Pompey

**This game was postponed on Monday, 6th December and Thursday, 9th December 2010, on both occasions due to a frozen pitch

third round

492

1)	Sam Cowler	9)	Dylan Tombides
2)	Filip Modelski	10)	Dominic Vose
3)	Callum Driver	11)	Blair Turgott
4)	Paco Craig	12)	Sebastian Lletget (for 11)
5)	Sergio Sanchez	13)	Deniz Mehmet GK
6)	Eoin Wearen	14)	Matthias Fanimo (for 10)
7)	Robert Hall	15)	Daniel Potts
8)	George Moncur	16)	Declan Hunt

1)	Sam Johnstone	9)	John Cofie
2)	Michael Keane	10)	Will Keane
3)	Tyler Blackett	11)	Gyliano van Velzen
4)	Tom Thorpe	12)	Zeki Fryers (for 11)
5)	Michele Fornasier	13)	Liam Jacob GK
6)	Ryan Tunnicliffe	14)	Jesse Lingard
7)	Larnell Cole	15)	Alberto Massacci
8)	Paul Pogba	16)	Luke Hendrie

2010-11

WEST HAM UNITED 0 v 1 MANCHESTER UNITED

Keane W.

JANUARY 2011

Wednesday 19th

Kick-off 7.00 p.m.

Attendance 1,405

fourth round

United's starting eleven are ready for action at the Boleyn Ground
Back row (l-r) Tyler Blackett, John Cofie, Sam Johnstone, Tom Thorpe, Michael Keane, Gyliano van Velzen, Paul Pogba
Front row (l-r) Ryan Tunnicliffe, Larnell Cole, Michele Fornasier, Will Keane

Caused by the earlier tie against Portsmouth taking place rather later in the calendar than would normally be the case, there was only a nine-day interlude before the Reds were required to take on West Ham in the Fourth Round.

The two United's hadn't crossed swords in the Youth Cup for almost 54 years, when the Old Trafford lads of 1957 defeated the junior Hammers over the two legs of the final by an 8-2 aggregate to win that season's competition.

The current batch of West Ham boys were enjoying a fine run of form, winning five games on the spin, which included victories over Arsenal and Chelsea. Caused by home advantage going the Hammers' way, the tie was seen as a tough assignment from a Manchester perspective and the Londoners were viewed as marginally the favourites to go through.

A week before the Reds were due at the Boleyn Ground, West Ham defeated Hamburg at the last four stage of the inaugural Youth Championship of Football tournament in Abu Dhabi before losing 1-0 to host club Baniyas in the final. Academy coach Tony Carr called the venture a 'great experience' and reckoned it to be 'the perfect preparation' prior to meeting their northern opponents. The lead-up wasn't quite as exotic for the personnel from Old Trafford, although a 4-3 Academy win over Wolves at Carrington, a game for which some of the Youth Cup squad were rested, wouldn't have done morale any harm at all.

There were no changes to the Reds' starting line-up from the last round, and they made a first impression at Upton Park in the fourth minute when a Pogba free kick, given for a foul on Cofie, forced Sam Cowler into making a smart save to his left. A similar length of time passed before Cofie aimed a shot which flew straight at Cowler and the same player then saw his effort blocked for a corner.

The away side began to increase the tempo after the quarter-hour point. Will Keane drove a shot into the side-netting for starters, Larnell Cole fed Gyliano van Velzen only for the winger's cross-shot to be deflected, and Cole then went nearest by volleying a Tyler Blackett cross over the bar from ten yards out. The improving van Velzen then displayed some trickery down the left to turn past his marker and his right-foot shot was beaten down by West Ham's 'keeper before a defender hacked the ball away for a throw-in.

Under the glow of a full moon, which acted as supplementary floodlight, the game was shaping up quite nicely as a spectacle, with superiority slightly tilted in the Reds' direction when, in the 35th minute, the pendulum swung decisively in their favour.

There seemed hardly any threat to the Hammers as Tunnicliffe contested a high ball with his opposite number approximately 35 yards out from goal. Gaining a decisive touch to head it on for Cole, the flanker performed a spot of ball-juggling with his back to goal before turning to strike it on the volley. Sensing that something might come of it, the predatory Will Keane had sprinted past Cole and into the penalty area, where the ball bounced awkwardly in front of Cowler prior to deflecting off his chest.

It came up at a perfect height for Keane who, despite being tracked all the way by Paco Craig, was fractionally quicker and headed it powerfully downwards and past the stranded goalie. In addition to getting United off the mark, Keane's opportunist goal also set up a fairly obvious 'HOWLER FROM COWLER' headline for the watching press men.

The action continued when Cole outwitted Callum Driver with a neat flick only

493

JANUARY 2011

to be brought down by his marker. Tunnicliffe couldn't make anything of the free kick and West Ham were then handed an identical award at the far end of the pitch, George Moncur hitting the ball cleanly only for Johnstone to react quickly when it dipped over the defensive wall and tip it over the frame of the goal. From the Hammers' following offensive, there was some pinball played out in front of Johnstone before the attacking team lost the initiative through an offside flag.

If the Reds' half-time advantage was merited, from then on things evened up. Immediately seizing the initiative, West Ham kept Johnstone on his toes by making him deal with crosses from Driver and Hall, as well as a tepid shot from Blair Turgott. The second period was only ten minutes old when Michael Keane bombed forward to deliver a low ball across the Hammers' six-yard area and, eluding the touch of Cofie, in addition to bypassing Cowler, Pogba knocked the ball back in only for Driver to clear in desperation.

There was a little over an hour gone when van Velzen should have put the Reds two-up. Having swapped flanks with Cole, he received a centre from his fellow winger and instead of taking the time available to bring it under control, he instead hurriedly volleyed wide. That miss could have proved costly a few minutes later as Dylan Tombides made his way to the dead-ball line and pulled an inviting ball back for Lletget, whose subsequent attempt was only just off-target.

The first two of three increasingly controversial incidents occurred in the 78th minute and in all cases the decisions weren't what the home team would have chosen. When Tombides was scythed down just outside the Reds' penalty box, play was waved on because the advantage remained with the Hammers and so Robert Hall carried possession a few paces where he was met by Blackett. With Hall going down under the full-back's challenge, appeals for a penalty went up only for an unimpressed referee to again signal that play should continue.

Cofie later let fly with a strong twenty-yard drive which Cowler pushed aside to his right and soon after the latest incident an announcement was relayed over the public address system that a minimum of three minutes were to be added on. Time was almost over when substitute Matthias Fanimo burst past Michael Keane and cut a pass back from the bye-line for Hall to strike what was almost certainly going to be West Ham's last chance of sending the tie into extra-time. Situated no more than three or four feet away from Hall, Michele Fornasier's left arm got in the way of his shot and, once again, the referee gave the defender the benefit of the doubt prior to blowing for full-time just a few seconds later.

It was certainly a fortunate escape for United, the man in black seemingly ruling Fornasier was too close to get out of the way of the ball while also taking into account that the Italian's arm was down by his side.

Naturally, the Upton Park contingent weren't at all impressed by the official's action and Tony Carr summarised his opinions on the match by declaring, *'I think we shaded it in terms of territory, possession and chances created in the second half, and I thought we had two penalty claims that looked very legitimate.'*

It was never going to be an easy exercise from the Reds' point of view and their slender win displayed what the club's website correspondent noted was *'an impressive level of maturity'* in securing the spoils.

> *We have a decent team with one or two excellent players. I think we're strong in the strikers' department for example, where we have William Keane and John Cofie. Then we've got Paul Pogba and Ravel Morrison.*
>
> *We have a chance this year, we're hopeful........*
>
> **SIR ALEX FERGUSON**

Ryan Tunnicliffe hoists the on-target Will Keane onto his shoulder while West Ham goalkeeper Sam Cowler lies despondent on the Upton Park turf

1)	Sam Johnstone	9)	Gyliano van Velzen	1)	Jak Alnwick	9)	Dan Taylor
2)	Michael Keane	10)	Ravel Morrison	2)	Alex Nicholson	10)	Adam Campbell
3)	Tyler Blackett	11)	Jesse Lingard	3)	Michael Riley	11)	Michael Hoganson
4)	Tom Thorpe	12)	*Alberto Massacci*	4)	Ben Sayer	12)	*Ryan McGorrigan (for 10)*
5)	Michele Fornasier	13)	*Liam Jacob GK*	5)	Remie Streete	13)	*Ben Robinson GK*
6)	Ryan Tunnicliffe	14)	*Tom Lawrence*	6)	Louis Storey	14)	*Marcus Maddison (for 7)*
7)	Larnell Cole	15)	*Sean McGinty*	7)	Aaron Spear	15)	*Lee-Ryan Toland*
8)	Paul Pogba	16)	*Jack Barmby*	8)	Patrick Nzuzi	16)	*Brandon Miele (for 4)*

MANCHESTER UNITED* 1 v 0 NEWCASTLE UNITED

Morrison

FEBRUARY 2011

Wednesday 16th

Kick-off 7.00 p.m.

Attendance 657

* Played at Moss Lane, Altrincham

In welcoming long-time and respected Youth Cup adversaries Newcastle to Altrincham, Paul McGuinness was faced with some injury problems. A scorer in the last two rounds, Will Keane was ruled out with a 'dead-leg' while John Cofie had undergone an operation on his knee within the last few days. McGuinness was fortunate in that Ravel Morrison was back in contention again, the midfielder having been off the radar for a couple of months prior to regaining his match fitness with a couple of outings for the Reserves, so the coach placed him and Jesse Lingard in the starting line-up. The Reds' makeshift attack comprised of ex-Ajax trainee van Velzen utilised as the main forward and Morrison employed in a roving brief just behind him.

Newcastle were somewhat lucky to still be in the competition as they only managed to scrape past Grimsby by the tune of two to one in the last round at St. James's Park. With their first-team then sitting in ninth place in the Blue Square Premier League, the junior Mariners missed a penalty and then suffered further when an intended cross by Ben Sayer sailed into the back of their net to give the Geordies a lucky 110th minute winner.

The young Magpies looked about as comfortable as a cat at Crufts down Moss Lane way and there must have been an almighty inquest into why the Reds only managed to put one goal past them, even though they registered 35 attempts of which 21 were on target.

McGuinness' tactics worked a treat and his boys carved out a trio of obvious opportunities in the opening period, the first of which was created by Larnell Cole for Lingard in the tenth minute. Cole displayed a neat piece of skill before executing a nice pass to his colleague, who was aghast when wastefully firing over from just eight yards out. Ten minutes later, the bubbly Morrison shook off the attentions of a couple of defenders only to then slam a shot a millimetre or two off its intended destination.

The Reds had been in almost total command right from the off and it only seemed like a matter of time before they would break through the Magpies' rather flimsy barricade. Revelling in the responsibility and freedom of his role, Morrison impressed again when setting up the increasingly influential Ryan Tunnicliffe on the boundary of Newcastle's eighteen-yard box, only for the midfielder to aim the ball straight down the throat of the opposing 'keeper.

The Geordies put up slightly more of a fight of it in the second half and they even managed to create a clear-cut opening when substitute Ryan McGorrigan's looping header was collected by Sam Johnstone. Newcastle followed up shortly after when central defender Remie Streete almost beat Johnstone with an even more dangerous header.

Those fluffed chances set the alarm bells ringing as far as the Reds were concerned and in the 64th minute they surged ahead with a simply splendid strike by the superb Morrison.

When a cross from the right was over-hit to the far side of Newcastle's box and was miscontrolled by Alex Nicholson, Tyler Blackett took the ball past him and centred into the middle. There, Paul Pogba breasted it into the path of Morrison, who evaded three defenders in one movement by switching onto his left foot, and Newcastle's goalie never moved as the Reds' number ten slashed it hard and into the net via the underside of the crossbar.

There were further chances to make the game safe, particularly those that fell to Tunnicliffe and Cole, the latter's effort skimming diagonally across Newcastle's goalmouth and the wrong side of a post, but Morrison's *'moment of magic'*, as the Review called it, was all that separated the two teams at the end of a one-sided mismatch.

There were numerous comments of praise posted on several of the internet message boards in regards to the Reds' performance. One contributor noted that *'Lingard and van Velzen caught my eye'* while another viewed Tunnicliffe to be *'a powerhouse player'* who possessed *'skill in abundance'*.

Ravel Morrison hits a powerful left-footed drive past Magpies' goalie Jak Alnwick to give the Reds a deserved victory at Moss Lane

fifth round

2010-11

2010-11

1) Tyrell Belford	9) Adam Morgan
2) Jon Flanagan	10) Krisztian Adorjan
3) Brad Smith	11) Suso
4) Andre Wisdom	12) *Matthew McGiveron (for 8)*
5) Stephen Sama	13) *Jamie Stephens GK*
6) Conor Coady	14) *Toni Silva (for 9)*
7) Raheem Sterling	15) *Henoc Mukendi*
8) Craig Roddan	16) *Michael Ngoo (for 11)*

1) Sam Johnstone	9) Gyliano van Velzen
2) Michael Keane	10) Ravel Morrison
3) Tyler Blackett	11) Jesse Lingard
4) Tom Thorpe	12) *Alberto Massacci*
5) Michele Fornasier	13) *Joe Coll GK*
6) Ryan Tunnicliffe	14) *Tom Lawrence (for 11)*
7) Larnell Cole	15) *Sean McGinty (for 9)*
8) Paul Pogba	16) *Jack Barmby*

MARCH 2011

LIVERPOOL 2 v 3 MANCHESTER UNITED

Morgan (2) — Cole (pen), Morrison (2)

Sunday 13th
Kick-off 12.00 p.m.
Attendance 10,199

sixth round

'Dramatic'. 'Absorbing'. 'Intoxicating'.

Those were some of the words applied by various observers to describe United's eighth and most incident-packed Youth Cup clash against Liverpool at Anfield. And they weren't wrong either.

Still without his two main strikers, Will Keane and John Cofie, Paul McGuinness was restricted in his team selection and so chose to go with an identical eleven starters who ushered Newcastle out of the tournament a month ago. Rather refreshingly deciding to stage the tie on a Sunday, the host club were rewarded with a superb gate, of which about 500 were United fans situated in the lower section of the Anfield Road enclosure.

Finalists as recently ago as 2009, the Merseysiders had comprehensively caned Southend in the Fifth Round. Scoring nine times without reply against the Essex side, the star of that particular show was a £600,000 capture from QPR called Raheem Sterling, whose five goals established a club record in the Youth Cup.

One website felt the meeting represented *'the biggest F.A. Youth Cup tie in years'* and also claimed that Liverpool's Academy coach Rodolfo Borrell reckoned his side *'are now becoming a big draw for Reds' fans starved for success'.*

Pushing the almost atomic level of competition between the two clubs at senior level to one side, which included a heated 3-1 Premier League home win for the Anfield club as recently as the previous weekend, it was clear there was a definite mutual respect at junior level. Speaking to the club's TV channel, Liverpool Academy director Frank McPartland admitted, *'The rivalry between the two clubs is very intense but if you asked me to pick a side to go up against at youth level, I would always plump for Man. United. It's simply because of the way they work with their youngsters. They aim to play good football and their philosophy is similar to ours. They have a true winning mentality and that is what we want to instil throughout our own system.'*

Beginning by facing the Kop end of the stadium, the Merseysiders sparkled in the spring sunshine during the early stages and on four minutes Sterling's surging run was halted through a foul committed by Paul Pogba, who received a booking for his troubles. Sam Johnstone was required to deal with the resultant free kick and United's 'keeper later saved a powerful drive from the number seven. Morrison offered some resistance to Liverpool's raids when linking up with Pogba, only to then fire over Tyrell Belford's bar, but that rare sortie was soon forgotten as Johnstone was again called on to save from Spanish flyer Suso.

The home team took a deserved lead in the 33rd minute when Sterling picked up possession about 30 yards out and in a central position. Faced by a couple of defenders, he threaded an inviting pass through the legs of Fornasier and into the stride of Adam Morgan. On the score sheet in each of his last eight outings, Morgan's intelligent run ensured he remained onside and the in-form hit-man passed Blackett and Thorpe to leave himself an easy job of jabbing the ball beyond Johnstone. United's problems were almost doubled just before the break, only for the dependable Johnstone to again come to the rescue by repelling the foraging Sterling.

Liverpool were all over United like a rash in the early minutes of the second half and the pressure they applied meant that a second goal for them was almost inevitable. It came in the 53rd minute when a break down the left suddenly changed from routine to highly dangerous as Hungarian Krisztian Adorjan measured a wonderful pass between Larnell Cole and Michael Keane for Brad Smith to gallop onto. Smith's fabulous low cross zipped across the six-yard box

Paul Pogba receives a second yellow card and his marching orders by David Coote for what the referee deemed as unsporting behaviour in the taking of a penalty kick

2010-11

MARCH 2011

sixth round

United full-back Michael Keane climbs high to head clear from Liverpool winger Raheem Sterling

to the far stick where Morgan evaded Blackett's challenge to tap in a simple second. On MUTV, Arthur Albiston noted that Smith's inviting ball *'had a lot of pace on it'* and further claimed *'it was just asking one of his strikers to get in there and finish it'.*

Up to the hour point, United appeared somewhat disjointed and could even be excused at appearing a trifle dispirited, with the lack of an out-and-out front man finding them wanting when it came to causing problems for Liverpool's back four. What happened next was nothing less than an incredible transformation and the events of the last 30 minutes would surely have tested the skills of even the most experienced of clairvoyants.

The catalyst for what was to follow stemmed from a surging run from ten yards inside his own half of the field by Ryan Tunnicliffe. Knocking the ball forward for Morrison, the never-say-die midfielder sprinted forward as Larnell Cole aimed it towards Liverpool's eighteen-yard line. As full-back Flanagan and goalkeeper Belford appeared to be singing from different hymn sheets in relation to whose responsibility it was to deal with it, Tunnicliffe almost escaped from them both before being bundled over from behind by Stephen Sama. MUTV's David Stowell concluded that the subsequent penalty was earned by the *'sheer desire'* displayed by Tunnicliffe, and as he spoke, referee David Coote brandished a red card to Sama for denying a clear goalscoring opportunity.

Because regular penalty taker Will Keane was watching from the sidelines, Paul Pogba volunteered to take the spot kick and following a short run up, he checked his stride in order to commit the 'keeper before sending Belford the wrong way. However, under a recent FIFA directive, that method of executing penalties was seen as a form of ungentlemanly conduct and so Mr. Coote ordered the kick to be retaken while also showing Pogba a yellow card. The referee seemed to have overlooked that the French lad's name was already in his book until he was reminded by one or two of the opposition, and it meant that Pogba became the second player to receive his marching orders within the space of a couple of minutes. Under those very trying circumstances, Cole did exceptionally well to remain calm and tuck away a super penalty that Belford could only watch.

From then on the game wore a completely different complexion and Liverpool suffered most from the absence of a man by losing both their shape and composure. The dramatic changes in circumstances prompted Stowell to ask of his TV audience, *'What will happen next in this crazy game?'* and he was answered just three minutes later when United sensationally equalised.

Tunnicliffe was again at the heart of a move in which he was allowed to slide a pass out to Cole on the right wing. Cole shimmied past Smith before delivering a cross which bore a similarity to the one that Liverpool's full-back used to create Morgan's second goal. The ball bounced past five home defenders in reaching Morrison eight yards out, and his first-time rocket shot whooshed under Belford to level the scores in full panoramic view of a silenced Kop.

United's appetite for the fight was now insatiable and from being a team that could barely squeak as loud as a mouse until well into the second period, they were now roaring like a pride of lions and went on to become kings of the Anfield jungle with just four minutes remaining.

Liverpool had nine players back as Cole prepared to take a corner and he floated it just past the near post where Adorjan beat Tom Thorpe to clear the ball rather unconvincingly to a point just beyond the penalty spot. As it began to drop, and with two opponents rushing out to close him down, Morrison arched himself to hit a Mark Hughes-type missile that whistled through a crowd of bodies and bounced once before rippling Belford's net. It was a quite magnificent goal and provided the match with a stunning kiss-off in United's favour.

Just before the end, Blackett and Liverpool skipper Conor Coady got into a tangle and the two angrily squared up to one another. The referee held red cards up at them both, and that was the same colour as Coady's face as he departed the field with blood streaming from his nose.

Naturally, the win meant a lot to the United lads and the feeling of elation was in evidence at full-time when all of the non-playing members of the squad and some of the coaches made their way onto the pitch to congratulate them on a stupendous recovery. David Stowell summarised the win perfectly when informing his viewers that the Old Trafford boys had shown *'the character and determination they are famous for'* in the den of their fiercest foes.

Most sections of the media delighted in reporting the four sendings off and yet many of the multitude of match overviews failed to mention that there was only one really serious flashpoint in the whole game. Additionally emphasising that some inappropriate chanting had emanated from the away support while totally ignoring similar actions by a minority of Liverpool followers, that regrettable behaviour in the United end was confined to about a dozen morons, three of whom were arrested and six ejected.

All things considered, it was a super day to be a United fan and those in attendance bore witness to what could arguably be described as the club's greatest ever Youth Cup comeback.

> *I thought Liverpool were the better team until they scored the second goal, thereafter we were the better team.*
>
> *When we lost the second goal it seemed to force a reaction from the players and they started to play better. As the game got to that important stage, they got their finger out.*
>
> **SIR ALEX FERGUSON**

2010-11

1) Jamal Blackman	9) Milan Lalkovic	1) Sam Johnstone	9) Will Keane
2) Todd Kane	10) Josh McEachran	2) Michael Keane	10) Jesse Lingard
3) Tomas Kalas	11) Adam Nditi	3) Sean McGinty	11) Gyliano van Velzen
4) Nathaniel Chalobah	12) *Archange Nkumu (for 8)*	4) Tom Thorpe	12) *Charni Ekangamene*
5) Aziz Deen-Conteh	13) *Matt Tomlinson GK*	5) Michele Fornasier	13) *Joe Coll GK*
6) George Saville	14) *Ben Sampayo (for 7)*	6) Ryan Tunnicliffe	14) *Tom Lawrence (for 10)*
7) Bobby Devyne	15) *Lewis Baker (for 11)*	7) Larnell Cole	15) *Mats Daehli (for 9)*
8) Rohan Ince	16) *Alex Davey*	8) Paul Pogba	16) *Jack Rudge*

APRIL 2011

CHELSEA 3 v 2 MANCHESTER UNITED

Chalobah (2), Devyne   Lingard, Pogba

semi-final 1st leg

Sunday 10th
Kick-off 12.30 p.m.
Attendance 5,518

For two of United's under-18 squad, Ravel Morrison and Ryan Tunnicliffe, their earliest exposure to Youth Cup football came about when Chelsea paid a visit to Manchester in the 2008/09 season. Along with Tyler Blackett, Morrison was forced to sit out the first leg of the 2010/11 semi-final against the Blues through suspension and with John Cofie still not recovered from his earlier surgery, Will Keane's return couldn't have been better timed. To compensate for the loss of the consistent Blackett, capable deputy Sean McGinty was asked to fill the left full-back spot.

In the build-up to the match on MUTV, Lou Macari said of the occasion, 'You only needed to be in our hotel last night to see how important it is, mothers and fathers there, grandads, grandmothers, children related to the families, aunts and uncles, all down for the game. They want to see their son on the pitch performing exceptionally well.' When asked about how the club's most gifted teenagers might respond to playing in front of another big crowd, Macari replied, 'I think it helps them if they're going to be footballers and play eventually at Old Trafford in front of 76,000. Days like today test their temperament.'

With the prospect of welcoming illustrious visitors and confidence in the home camp reported as high, Chelsea coach Dermot Drummy was happy to tell the press that his squad was practically at full-strength. Drummy also shared his first-hand experience of meeting up with the Reds in the Youth Cup and what he expected of the initial tie when saying, 'I was the assistant at Arsenal when Manchester United knocked them out a few years ago, and the one thing about them is they never know when they are beaten. They stay in the game, at first-team level right down to youth team level.

They're a magnificent club with a fantastic Academy and we envisage two top class games, but I'm very hopeful that we get the right result. The tie will not be settled on one leg, but we have got to go out and play our football the way we know and hopefully take something up to Old Trafford.'

While a healthy turnout of fans was expected, there was never any chance of the attendance topping that of the previous round at Anfield. Because of the additional cost of closing the thoroughfares around Stamford Bridge, the crowd was capped, variously reported at between 7,000 and 8,000, and all of the spectators were housed at right-angles in the Shed and East Stand sections of the stadium.

Within the ranks of the current Youth Cup holders, one to pay attention to was unquestionably Josh McEachran, a constructive midfielder already with fifteen senior appearances to his name, including six in the Champions League. The premier European club competition was very much in the minds of both sets of supporters, because United's seniors had secured an excellent 1-0 win at Stamford Bridge in the opening leg of the quarter-final just four days before.

The Chelsea boys comprised a mixture of English and overseas-born talents, with the balance of the starting eleven tipped slightly in favour of the latter, and those not of domestic origin were Tomas Kalas (Czech Republic), Nathaniel Chalobah and Aziz Deen-Conteh (Sierra Leone), Bobby Devyne (Kenya), Milan Lalkovic (Slovakia) and Adam Nditi (Tanzania).

On one of the most beautiful of spring days imaginable, neither side was able to hold onto possession for more than a few touches until United almost conceded on three minutes when Kalas put over a testing centre for an unmarked Lalkovic to head straight at Sam Johnstone. Just over sixty seconds later, Will Keane demonstrated he wasn't feeling any untoward effects of his lengthy lay-off when trying a hopeful long shot that flew into the empty seats at the back of Jamal Blackman's goal. Jesse Lingard then showed up to good effect with a similar attempt and the Blues responded by getting the ball into United's box where Johnstone and McGinty paired up to foil Lalkovic.

Both teams began to see their fair share of the ball, and the pattern of the game hadn't quite emerged, except for the feeling that there were always going to be goals in it, when the first went Chelsea's way almost bang on 30 minutes.

There were plenty of United bodies back to defend a corner which was whipped over by McEachran, and it was a case of too many cooks spoiling the broth when Johnstone was unable to catch cleanly as a number of them crowded around him. The ball fell kindly to England under-17 captain Chalobah, whose position three yards from the goal-line meant that he only needed to prod his foot

Paul Pogba (left of centre, front), Tom Thorpe (right of centre, behind) and Will Keane (far right) await the delivery of a corner along with a number of Chelsea opponents

498

at the ball to force it over.

Will Keane scorned a great chance to even the scores a short while later when a crafty lob by his twin brother was back-headed towards Blackman by Chalobah. The Chelsea defender hadn't realised United's number nine was loitering behind him and as Keane wafted a leg at the loose ball, Blackman whipped it away. MUTV's David Stowell said of the incident, *'That has to go down as a golden opportunity'* to which co-commentator Arthur Albiston responded, *'(The ball) just wouldn't come down for him. He's (Keane) probably surprised, thinking what a chance I've got here. He just tries to flick his foot out, unfortunately he doesn't make a connection with it.'*

That miss was viewed as twice as costly when Chelsea increased their lead three minutes from the interval. The Reds were scuppered by another corner, this one executed by George Saville, and when Chalobah rose higher than Paul Pogba, Tom Thorpe and Michael Keane twelve yards out, his majestic header looped spectacularly over Larnell Cole who was guarding the far post.

In the sanctuary of the dressing room, Paul McGuinness would have been correct in telling his lads there was still a game and a half to pull the tie around and that they had never at any time looked second best. The coach might also have reminded them of the later events at Anfield as to what they were capable of, and a shot score of five to four in Chelsea's favour pointed to them not being very far off the pace on the current day's play.

It didn't take the Reds long to even up that count when a surging run from the magnificent Tunnicliffe provided them with a goalscoring opportunity. The midfielder's progress took him from the halfway line to within twenty yards of Chelsea's goal, where Lingard knocked a square pass to van Velzen, the winger then whipping a beautiful shot around a defender only for Blackman to leap to his right to keep it out.

United were committing more players forward than in the first half and their grip in midfield began to have a detrimental effect on Chelsea, whose time and composure on the ball was reduced accordingly. A McGinty cross that managed to evade everyone's attention made things warm for the Blues, a brilliant 25-yard piledriver from Pogba that Blackman flicked over the crossbar kept the match simmering, and when Lingard swept in at the far upright to score in the 56th minute, the tie went white hot.

Arthur Albiston said of the breakthrough, *'Well, if the strike from Pogba didn't deserve a goal, Lingard made sure (by) getting on the end of the subsequent corner. It's a dangerous corner.......drifted into the near post. It's very hard for defenders to climb and get anything on them. (Lingard) has done well to keep that down, six yards out, on the half-volley. It's no more than (United's) play deserved since the start of the second half.'*

Appearing less affected by the sunny conditions than their hosts, the Reds' momentum was maintained by Will Keane and Pogba testing Blackman in turn.

In the 71st minute, Chelsea took off Nditi for Lewis Baker and with his very first touch, the substitute was involved in his team's third goal. Taking a pass from McEachran on the left wing close to the halfway line, Baker laid it inside for Lalkovic and the Czech knocked it back outside for Deen-Conteh, who galloped forward a few paces prior to shifting the ball all the way across Johnstone's penalty area. Steaming in like an overdue express train at the far side of the six-yard box, Devyne was all by himself and ready to clip in a simple finish with his right foot.

Keane and Pogba were both presented with chances to score during a mad scramble in the Reds' next attack and there wasn't long to wait until their overall superiority delivered another dividend. From yet another flag kick, this time taken by Lingard, Chelsea cleared only as far as Tunnicliffe, who fed it back out to where it originally came. Lingard was afforded all the time he needed to consider his cross, and it found the head of Pogba amongst a host of others. The French boy was up highest to butt the ball down powerfully, and it took one bounce, escaping the clutch of Blackman, before entering the net.

Having scored one goal and created another, Lingard then almost made it three for the Reds. There were eight United players within 25 yards of Blackman when four of them constructed an intricate move, and van Velzen became the provider by rolling a pass straight at Lingard, whose side-footed attempt crept past the woodwork.

For the nine remaining minutes, both teams seemed happy to settle for what they held and the two goalkeepers turned into virtual spectators. Chelsea claimed the benefit of a slender lead to take to Old Trafford, whereas the Reds were satisfied to still be in with a shout, especially considering they were two goals behind on a couple of occasions.

Asked about his views on United's showing, Lou Macari stated, *'That was a big*

United substitute Tom Lawrence attempts to steal possession from Chelsea's number six George Saville

test for them. (They) went in at half-time 2-0 down and it was always going to be interesting to see how they reacted in the second half. I thought in the first ten, fifteen minutes of the second half they played brilliant. Lots of through balls into the box, (they) just got cut out at the last moment.

Will Keane with the ball at his feet was twisting and turning, Pogba got better and better as the game went on, and you were just looking for them to get that break to get back in the game. The response was brilliant, the response is what you expect from Manchester United. All credit to them, I do believe that if they play as well at Old Trafford as they played today, they're going to go through.'

While the Review reckoned the under-18's *'produced another second half show of character to put themselves firmly back in the frame'* for the second leg, the club's website added to the feeling about their being a way through to the final by noting that the two goals scored in the capital *'gave United's youngsters a chance of completing the job'* in M16.

> *The atmosphere from the United fans was incredible, they really lifted us by singing songs all through the game. I couldn't believe how hot it was, Jesse (Lingard) was actually sick in our penalty box in the first half, we just weren't used to playing in those conditions.*
>
> *Paul Pogba got us back in the game with the second goal and we thought our attacking mentality of scoring more than them would see us through on the day. That didn't happen, but we felt confident of winning the second leg at Old Trafford.*

WILL KEANE

2010-11

1) Sam Johnstone	9) Will Keane	1) Jamal Blackman	9) Milan Lalkovic
2) Michael Keane	10) Ravel Morrison	2) Todd Kane	10) Josh McEachran
3) Sean McGinty	11) Gyliano van Velzen	3) Tomas Kalas	11) Bobby Devyne
4) Tom Thorpe	*12) Alberto Massacci*	4) Daniel Pappoe	*12) Ben Sampayo*
5) Michele Fornasier	*13) Joe Coll GK*	5) Aziz Deen-Conteh	*13) Matt Tomlinson GK*
6) Ryan Tunnicliffe	*14) Jesse Lingard (for 8)*	6) Nathaniel Chalobah	*14) Lewis Baker*
7) Larnell Cole	*15) Tom Lawrence (for 10)*	7) George Saville	*15) Adam Nditi (for 8)*
8) Paul Pogba	*16) Tyler Blackett (for 11)*	8) Rohan Ince	*16) Philipp Prosenik (for 11)*

APRIL 2011

MANCHESTER UNITED 4 (6) V (3) 0 **CHELSEA**

Keane W. (3, 1 pen), Morrison

semi-final 2nd leg

Wednesday 20th
Kick-off 7.00 p.m.
Attendance 9,124

The unrelenting and ferocious level of competition for places at Old Trafford was brought into sharp focus when Paul McGuinness announced the team to take on Chelsea for the right to play in the Youth Cup final.

Despite putting on a wonderful performance at Stamford Bridge and winning the votes of many as the Reds' unsung hero down in London, Jesse Lingard found himself relegated to the substitutes' bench for the returning Ravel Morrison while Tyler Blackett couldn't wrest his place back from the steady and dependable Sean McGinty.

As well as Morrison and Blackett, Chelsea's influential skipper Daniel Pappoe was also free from serving a suspension. A young man who was filled with a special incentive to get past United, Pappoe had missed out on an appearance in the 2010 Youth Cup final through being subjected to a similar such ban.

There were no discernable signs of nerves as the two sets of players lined up in the tunnel prior to kick-off. Many were happy to share a few words with their opponents whereas one or two took in some last-minute liquid refreshments and others adjusted various items of their kit. The 22 players and three main officials stepped out to a great welcome from a crowd of over 9,000 and the captains stood for the toss of a coin, which Pappoe duly won.

It was mostly a case of 'feel your way as you go' while the teams attempted to be the first to settle into a rhythm. The main piece of action for the crowd to savour early on was when the Blues' Jamal Blackman was a little slow in clearing with his feet, and he was closed down by Will Keane only for the ball to ricochet off the striker and end up flying behind the goal for a dead-ball kick.

On the club's television channel, Gary Neville noted on more than one occasion that Chelsea's back four were utilising a high line, a tactic he felt was *'so dangerous'* under the circumstances. Blackman's misjudgement aside, the Stamford Bridge boys bedded down slightly the faster of the two sides, although they only threatened once, and that chance occurred when Milan Lalkovic delayed striking for too long after being set up by a crafty pass from Deen-Conteh to allow Sam Johnstone to save with his feet.

Morrison gave a glimpse of his expanding capabilities when picking up a pass from Tunnicliffe in the centre circle. Jinking his way past one blue shirt prior to sprinting past another while defenders backed off him, Morrison didn't require a written invitation to belt a shot that swerved slightly in flight for Blackman to clutch securely down to his right.

Just seconds after Blackman threw the ball out, Tom Thorpe robbed Lalkovic just in front of the dug-outs and there was a passage of eighteen passes between the United lads prior to van Velzen claiming possession out wide on the left. Exercising some nifty footwork there to elude three defenders, the Dutch boy crossed towards Pogba, who stood within a foot or two of the penalty spot. Pogba was just about to be challenged when laying off a short pass to Morrison, whose drive glanced off George Saville and spun over and past Blackman to restore parity on aggregate.

According to the Manchester Evening News, the goal came *'slightly against the run of play'* and scribe Cliff Butler went on to record that *'Chelsea couldn't believe their luck'*, because *'four minutes later they suffered another blow when full-back Sean McGinty crossed from the left for William Keane to score the Reds' second goal with a towering header'*. While that report was right to infer that United were late arrivals to the party, with three minutes left until the break, they were now the life and soul of it.

Tom Thorpe stretches into a tackle in an attempt to stave off a Chelsea attack

500

APRIL 2011

semi-final 2nd leg

The predatory Will Keane prods the ball home from close range to put the Reds 3-0 up and thrust them into a two-goal overall advantage

At 2-0 down on the night, the requirement of a goal now rested with Chelsea, and in their initial attack of note of the concluding section of the game, Johnstone was equal to a splendid drive from Lalkovic. There then followed a lengthy period during which an abundance of quality football was seen and yet a paucity of genuine chances produced.

In his capacity as an observer on MUTV, Neville said of the end of that period, *'They're just starting to make a few mistakes at the back Chelsea, just giving the ball away in bad areas. You don't want to be doing that, particularly as the legs get more tired, you don't want to create your own problems.'*

And sure enough, the Blues did get themselves in a pickle in the 76th minute. A misplaced pass from Todd Kane came back to haunt him as Morrison ghosted through the middle of the park while to his left, no-one had convincingly tracked the overlapping Tyler Blackett. Morrison's pass was controlled by the substitute, and Blackett's squared ball found Will Keane in a position to bundle it through the legs of the prostrate Blackman and over the goal-line.

There was one last scare for United to survive when Johnstone was impeded as he tried to catch a high centre from Kane. As the floored goalkeeper looked to the referee for a decision, Lalkovic, from no more than ten feet out, smashed the ball towards goal only for Thorpe to get in the way. Gary Neville said knowingly of the centre-back's superb defensive intervention, *'That's when you know it's your night'.*

The Reds guaranteed their passage five minutes from time when Will Keane completed his hat-trick, a splendid feat which was made all the more remarkable considering it was only his second game in two months. From an historical perspective, the achievement also installed him as the club's first scorer of three goals in a Youth Cup semi-final since Albert Kinsey inflicted precisely the same punishment on Manchester City in April 1964.

Again breaking through the middle, Tunnicliffe inched the ball forward to his right where Keane was clipped by the outrushing Blackman as United's leader tried to round him. Raising himself to take the penalty, Keane walloped it past the offending goalie to complete the score at 4-0, the Reds' best winning margin in the home leg of the last four stage of the competition since 1954.

In the Evening News, Cliff Butler's views about the Reds' *'outstanding and disciplined display'*, which was *'allied to boundless determination'*, matched a comment on the Football Association's website that in coming back from their defeat in London, *'United's youngsters showed the never-say-die attitude so often linked to their senior side'.*

The Telegraph's conclusion that the Stamford Bridge boys were made to endure *'an emphatic drubbing'* appeared above an observation that United's one-sided victory *'will have been especially painful for Chelsea owner Roman Abramovic, who is determined that his side start producing youngsters capable of graduating to the first-team'.*

2010-11

1) George Long	9) Joe Ironside
2) Ben Montgomery	10) Jordan Slew
3) Aaron Barry	11) Callum McFadzean
4) Matt Harriott	*12) Carlos Pomares (for 5)*
5) Harry Maguire	*13) George Willis GK*
6) Terry Kennedy	*14) Liam Wilkinson (for 7)*
7) Corey Gregory	*15) Connor Martin (for 9)*
8) Elliott Whitehouse	*16) Porya Ahmadi*

1) Sam Johnstone	9) Will Keane
2) Michael Keane	10) Ravel Morrison
3) Sean McGinty	11) Gyliano van Velzen
4) Tom Thorpe	*12) Alberto Massacci*
5) Michele Fornasier	*13) Joe Coll GK*
6) Ryan Tunnicliffe	*14) John Cofie (for 11)*
7) Jesse Lingard	*15) Zeki Fryers*
8) Paul Pogba	*16) Tom Lawrence*

MAY 2011

SHEFFIELD UNITED 2 v 2 MANCHESTER UNITED

McFadzean, Slew — Keane W., Lingard

final 1st leg

Tuesday 17th
Kick-off 7.30 p.m.
Attendance 29,977

RavelMorrison49 Ravel Ryan Morrison
United to win the league todayy - and then win the fa youth cup tuesday :)
14 May

RyanTunnicliffe Ryan Tunnicliffe
Bangers and Mash for tea! Great food, preparation for the game starts now!!
16 May

JohnCofie9 John Cofie
RT @edf92: @SMcGinty22 @RyanTunnicliffe @JohnCofie9 @sam_j39 rise and shine playas! The final has arrived... @gamehead >> leggooo xx
17 May

WillKeane48 William Keane
FA Youth Cup Final day ... Come on boys!
17 May

SMcGinty22 Sean McGinty
Let's put a show on tonight for the sell out crowd and not forgetting @GNev2!
17 May

RavelMorrison49 Ravel Ryan Morrison
Fa youth cup final 2dayy manchester united v sheff united first leg 7:30 kick off fill u in with more info after the game
17 May

RyanTunnicliffe Ryan Tunnicliffe
Big game tonight. Youth cup final first leg. 30,000 sell out?? Let's av it!!!
17 May

JohnCofie9 John Cofie
@RyanTunnicliffe the time has come brother !! Leggggggoooooo xx
17 May

RyanTunnicliffe Ryan Tunnicliffe
On the way to bramall lane now. Game time. #focused !!!
17 May

SMcGinty22 Sean McGinty
Game time is fast approaching... Buzzin for it now!!
17 May

Excitement for the big day grows among the away squad as some of them make comments on the social media website Twitter in the build-up to the first leg

When Sheffield United greeted the Reds for the first leg of the Youth Cup final, it was against the backdrop of their recent demotion to the third tier of English football. Nevertheless, that development could not in any way detract from the splendid achievement of their under-18 side, whose efforts in going further in the tournament than any of their predecessors deserved every praise going.

In reaching the last two, from an initial entry of 460, the junior Blades chalked up wins over Cheltenham (4-1, away), Millwall (3-0 at home), Blackpool (3-1 at home), Leicester (2-1, away) in addition to away and home victories of 1-0 and 2-0 respectively over 2010 finalists Aston Villa. Top goalscorer in the competition was skipper Elliott Whitehouse with four, while three of the side, Harry Maguire, Matt Harriott and Jordan Slew, were charged with at least some knowledge of senior standard soccer. Even though the club's relegation might have been hard to stomach for Sheffield United's supporters, as far as their production line was concerned, things had never looked brighter at Bramall Lane.

In the match programme, Blades' Academy manager John Pemberton, himself a junior at Old Trafford in the early 1980's, committed a few of his thoughts and the Sheffield club's objectives to paper:

A lot of teams have spent a lot of money on facilities and bringing in players from all over the world, whereas we have a lot of home grown boys. That's the route we're trying to go down, looking at progressing these players into our first-team and getting some local talent in the side. They've certainly done themselves no harm by getting to the F.A. Youth Cup final.

I came to the club last May and decided to target the core group of what has been our Youth Cup team this season. They've been very receptive to what we've done. They've worked very hard and they all get on fantastically well. We don't have any outstanding stars but what we do have is a group of players who work hard for each other, have a great spirit and a great discipline.

The F.A. Youth Cup is massive for young players at every club. Some clubs don't even play their Reserve games at their home now, so this gives younger players a rare chance of playing at proper stadiums and in front of bigger crowds.

Pemberton was quite right in bringing up the subject of how beneficial it can be for teenage talents to perform in front of large crowds, and how pleased he must have been when almost 30,000 turned up to make the attendance by far the biggest seen at Bramall Lane all season. In what was a superb exercise in public relations, Sheffield United guaranteed every season ticket holder free entrance to the match and then made it an occasion for families to enjoy by charging no more than three quid for every other available seat. The massive attendance was, therefore, a just reward for the Yorkshire outfit's enterprise.

Because Larnell Cole had become the young Reds' second 'dead-leg' victim of the season, Paul McGuinness brought Jesse Lingard back into his team and fit-again John Cofie provided another useful option for the coach from his place on the substitutes' bench. Ten days before arriving in the steel city, McGuinness' team signed off their Academy commitments with a resounding 5-0 win over Leeds at Carrington, one of their best results of the campaign, and the game brought a first goal for the club from Gyliano van Velzen.

To the home fans' much-amended signature tune of John Denver's 'Annie's Song', the Manchester side, resplendent in an all-white strip with red and black trimmings, got the showpiece underway to earn two corners in as many opening minutes only for the Blades to hit back as Slew's terrific centre was headed over by Corey Gregory. MUTV's David Stowell commented that both teams had *'started brightly'* and he went on to inform the channel's viewers about there being a vast body of supporters who were still trying to gain entry into the ground.

In the 13th minute, McGuinness' charges put together a move which took them down the right-hand side of the pitch, where Sean McGinty wrapped his left foot around the ball to put over a tempting cross for Lingard. The Blades hadn't properly cleared their lines from the latest Manchester offensive when Paul Pogba drilled over a tantalising centre from the opposite side of the pitch. The French boy's cross arched around three defenders and bounced on the six-yard line, where Lingard darted in to meet it. The ball deflected off the goalkeeper and struck the underside of the bar before flying out of the danger area following what appeared to be a clear case of intentional arm against ball by Sheffield's Maguire.

When Stowell asked, *'Oh, was that a handball? Was it off the line? What's been given?'*, co-commentator Arthur Albiston replied, *'Well, the linesman has flagged right away David.'* Confusion reigned as a few Reds appealed for a penalty, but on receiving a signal from assistant Gary Beswick, referee Michael Oliver awarded a goal, a decision which inferred that Maguire had handled the ball only after it crossed the line.

There were two ways of looking at the goal from the Blades' perspective. Of course, it meant that they were now behind, but the consequences could have been much worse for them because had their number five been penalised for handball, a penalty and a subsequent sending off would have seen the home team reduced to ten men and without Maguire for the second leg in Manchester.

As the midway point of the first half approached, Ravel Morrison displayed clever feet and a tidy turn of pace by carrying possession for over 50 yards prior to guiding the ball under George Long only for Maguire to boot it out of the goalmouth. By far and away the most flamboyant piece of skill shown so far, Morrison was only one of a number of Reds who looked totally at ease with their surroundings. The move prompted Albiston to observe, *'Great piece of play. First of all from Tunnicliffe winning the ball, that's what he's all about.......releasing Morrison. He's done everything right, slips it past the 'keeper. Unfortunately, it's cleared off the line.'*

502

2010-11

MAY 2011

To the acclaim of his team-mates, Tom Thorpe saved a certain goal at the other end by heading a fine Whitehouse effort over the crossbar, a slice of action which caused Stowell to declare, *'You could say, right there in an instance, that showed you why they are both captains.'* Other than that chance, the Blades hadn't posed the Reds too many problems and with Tunnicliffe marshalling the midfield from a defensive perspective, and Pogba, Lingard, van Velzen, Morrison and Will Keane roaming further up the pitch to good effect, the Old Trafford lads were well in control.

Just when everyone thought the visitors would be able to enjoy a half-time cuppa with a 1-0 lead, Sheffield dragged themselves back on level terms with a platinum-standard goal which was good enough to grace any game. During a build-up that began on the fringe of the Reds' penalty area, Whitehouse undertook some of the donkey work by holding off stern challenges from Lingard, Pogba and Tunnicliffe, leaving Callum McFadzean to pick up the mantle in the centre circle as the referee motioned for play to continue. With his head up and eyes focussed on the target, McFadzean raced on unchecked until bringing the majority of the vast Bramall Lane crowd to their feet by executing a shot that contained enough power to overtake a thunderbolt as it screamed just inside Johnstone's right-hand post.

The goal moved Albiston to state in undisguised admiration, *'Fantastic hit. Twenty-five yards out, clean as a whistle with his left foot…….what a strike. In fact, Johnstone got his hand to it, but he just couldn't keep it out.'* Albiston added, *'The ironic thing is Johnstone's not had a lot to do the whole game really. Long has been the far busier 'keeper but Sheffield United have got themselves back in this tie.'*

Both sides displayed a burning desire to gain an advantage for the second leg throughout the second half and van Velzen was the first to show when twisting and turning a couple of defenders prior to testing Long. The Sheffield side hit back when Slew's shot was edged over the bar by Johnstone to bring about a great roar from the home support and Whitehouse was desperately unfortunate in the Blades' next attack. Directing an effort under Johnstone only for Fornasier to sky the ball up in the air in an attempt to clear, his goalkeeper managed to assist by picking himself up off the floor and punch it out for a corner. Stowell described the scene as *'pandemonium in the box for a moment'* while Albiston commented, *'Good play by Sheffield United, wasn't it? Another deep cross in, headed down, Johnstone took the right option, just get it out of play.'*

The Reds weren't to be outdone and Morrison ventured on another great run from the halfway line to the point where he could see the whites of Long's eyes. Cheekily taking a defender out with a dummy run, van Velzen opened up the space to leave Morrison with a free shot, which brought a fabulous save out of Long down low to his right. Michael Keane tried a similar exercise a little later, only without the same accuracy, and with the action bubbling up nicely while Sheffield posed a much greater attacking threat than in the first half, the goals that everybody anticipated arrived almost together in the 70th and 72nd minutes.

When the Blades cleared an attack out of their area, Sean McGinty swept a pass to Thorpe, who kept the move flowing by inching the ball to Tunnicliffe. He in turn played it out to Michael Keane, the full-back then laying the ball off to Pogba. By this time the Blades were inclined towards a 'what we have we hold' policy and eight of them were positioned within fifteen yards of the midfielder, who was

Jesse Lingard stabs the ball goalwards at Bramall Lane to provide the visitors with an early opener

final 1st leg

503

2010-11

MAY 2011

final 1st leg

Gyliano van Velzen slips the attention of an opponent in order to make some space for himself at Bramall Lane

positioned just outside their penalty box. Standing on the right-hand side of the area with his arm raised was Lingard, so Pogba obligingly chipped it to him over a number of opponents. Lingard occupied what seemed like acres of free space, yet instead of waiting he volleyed across the box for the ball to escape the clutches of a flailing 'keeper and Will Keane was on hand to steer it into a gaping net.

'Great ball from Pogba to pick out Lingard.......and what a great ball into the six-yard area', said Albiston. '(Lingard) just helps that into the box and says somebody go and finish that off, and Keane will oblige all day long.' Stowell countered, 'Well, you could say he couldn't miss, but you have to be there to tuck them away and he usually is.'

The familiar strains of 'There's only one Keane-o' had barely died down from the jubilant Manchester following when Sheffield replaced Gregory with Liam Wilkinson. The substitute hadn't even touched the ball before Slew slashed a shot from 20 yards which nicked off Thorpe's heel and zoomed past a diving Johnstone to square matters once again. There was a hint of good fortune about the goal, 'but if you're positive that's what happens' Albiston pointed out.

There were gesticulations aplenty from the two coaches down by the touchline, and they made a few substitutions between them in the last quarter of an hour as the pace never looked like slacking. The best of the half-chances remaining fell to the Reds, when Morrison went on a 30-yard dribble prior to seeing his short-range effort stopped by Long, and Tunnicliffe experienced a similar blocked effort from an almost identical position.

Stowell and Albiston made numerous references to the amount of effort that had been expended by the contestants and in summarising, the latter noted,

'Fantastic game of football.......we've been fortunate this season to see United play very well down at Chelsea, Liverpool as well, but that was right up there with them. Either team could have won at the end, they were both going hammer and tongs to get a winner. Nobody was settling for a draw and it probably would have been a little unjust if either team had lost that game.'

Stowell wrapped up the after-match chat perfectly when crystallising the thoughts of many by saying, 'These two sides started level and they end level tonight. There was so much to enjoy about this first leg and there is so much to look forward to in the second.

The only bad thing about tonight's game is that it had to end.'

> "The most important thing is that these lads go on and play professional football, and hopefully at Manchester United.
>
> I think this is the best group of young players that I've seen in the last ten or fifteen years, so for me I think you will see a few of these in the next twelve to eighteen months getting introduced into the first-team and to see whether they can handle first-team football. I think they deserve it, they're at a really good level."
>
> **GARY NEVILLE**

2010-11

MAY 2011

final 1st leg

Will Keane looks overjoyed as he points towards the Manchester following moments after putting United 2-1 in front

505

2010-11

1) Sam Johnstone	9) Will Keane	1) George Long	9) Joe Ironside
2) Michael Keane	10) Ravel Morrison	2) Ben Montgomery	10) Jordan Slew
3) Sean McGinty	11) Gyliano van Velzen	3) Aaron Barry	11) Callum McFadzean
4) Tom Thorpe	*12) Tyler Blackett (for 11)*	4) Matt Harriott	*12) Carlos Pomares (for 5)*
5) Michele Fornasier	*13) Joe Coll GK*	5) Harry Maguire	*13) George Willis GK*
6) Ryan Tunnicliffe	*14) Larnell Cole (for 7)*	6) Terry Kennedy	*14) Liam Wilkinson (for 9)*
7) Jesse Lingard	*15) John Cofie (for 10)*	7) Corey Gregory	*15) Connor Martin (for 7)*
8) Paul Pogba	*16) Alberto Massacci*	8) Elliott Whitehouse	*16) Porya Ahmadi*

MAY 2011

MANCHESTER UNITED 4(6) v (3)1 **SHEFFIELD UNITED**

Keane W. (2, 1 pen), Morrison (2) — Ironside

Monday 23rd
Kick-off 7.30 p.m.
Attendance 24,916

final 2nd leg

As the North Stand begins to fill up in the background, the United boys take a second to face the cameramen
Back row (l-r) Sean McGinty, Gyliano van Velzen, Sam Johnstone, Tom Thorpe, Michael Keane, Paul Pogba
Front row (l-r) Ryan Tunnicliffe, Ravel Morrison, Will Keane, Michele Fornasier, Jesse Lingard

If the support for their under-18's hadn't already been amply demonstrated at Bramall Lane, over 6,000 Sheffield United fans journeyed over the Pennines to cheer on the club's young heroes and boost the aggregate attendance for the two legs of the final to nearly 55,000. In the run-up to the match, Blades' Academy coach John Pemberton commented on his squad's performances so far, as well as what he hoped might happen next, by explaining, *'All the way through this run we've had to the final they have displayed bundles of character, spirit and resilience – not to mention ability. For the first twenty minutes against United we looked a bit nervous against a very good side in front of a big crowd. But, once the lads came to terms with what they were up against and got used to the atmosphere, they were magnificent.*

I am so pleased with the way they performed and, after that display, we certainly won't be going to Old Trafford with any fear. We went all out for a win in the first leg and we shall be doing exactly the same in the return game and, if everything goes well, our supporters will be able to see a group of lads who do themselves and the club proud.'

Paul McGuinness named the same eleven who started the game in Yorkshire, ten of whom were either past or approaching their 18th birthday and prepared for the match in the knowledge that it represented their last in the Youth Cup. None of them was more determined to ensure the trophy ended up at Old Trafford than Ryan Tunnicliffe, one of the young Reds' leading lights who was a recent recipient of the club's 'Academy Player of the Year' award.

There was a spot of pageantry prior to the kick-off, with both teams entering from the tunnel side by side before meeting dignitaries from the Football Association and the competition's sponsors to the sound of a musical fanfare. The 22 starters looked like they were desperate to get to work as 'God Save the Queen' was relayed around the ground and, following the obligatory photos, the referee indicated for the game to start.

The large number of Sheffield supporters ensured there was a piece of Bramall Lane inside Old Trafford and the Blades' fans were in good voice, doing much to provide the match with an atmosphere deserving of the occasion. Their presence caused MUTV co-commentator Gary Neville to state, *'It's probably the biggest I've ever seen for an away following in a Youth Cup game. It's all credit to them.'*

The only starter on the home side eligible to play in the competition in the 2011/12 season, Dutch maestro van Velzen was the first to show for the Reds, snaking inside from the left to hold off a couple of defenders before striking the ball wide from just outside the penalty area. The home side also won a couple of free kicks in advanced parts of the pitch, the second of which cannoned off a defender to deny Pogba an almost certain goal.

When discussing the tactics he felt would help the Reds' cause, Neville advised, *'I think it is key that we don't run with the ball. That is what Sheffield United want, they want you to run with it so they can get close to you. We need to keep passing the ball, particularly in this first half an hour.'*

The Yorkshire side then constructed a terrific move down their left in which Callum McFadzean slid a pass towards Aaron Barry to shift three Reds out of the picture. Barry's centre reached Jordan Slew and, facing away from the goal with

506

2010-11

MAY 2011

Sean McGinty pressed up behind him, he swivelled to hammer in a shot that flew wide of Sam Johnstone's left-hand post by about two feet. Slew indicated that a great chance had gone to waste by holding his head in his hands as Johnstone began remonstrating with his defence for their lack of concentration.

Looking at the incident from a defender's angle, Neville observed, *'Good play by Sheffield United. Good ball into the box. There's no doubt that Jordan Slew is the danger man. Fantastic turn, the way he holds off Sean McGinty, rolls him. He's very unlucky, just pulls it past the post with his left foot.'*

The Reds began heeding Neville's instructions to move the ball between them in the 20th minute when Paul Pogba, one of the Reds' finest exponents of the art of passing, stretched his legs a few paces before playing Morrison into the Blades' penalty box. Morrison was able to hold off a strong challenge from Barry, and goalkeeper Long needed to block the ball to prevent the livewire midfielder from causing his team any significant damage.

The Sheffield side came closest to opening the scoring in the 34th minute, when a corner was headed onto the roof of Johnstone's net by Joe Ironside, and they continued to make life difficult for the Reds by knocking the ball about when it suited them and employing a more direct approach every now and again. Then, just at the point when their game plan seemed to have taken some of the heat out of the Reds' fire, Paul McGuinness' boys stole a march on their gritty opponents by forging in front.

The move that led to the goal started with a throw-in taken by Michael Keane on the right-hand touchline deep inside his own half and it concluded exactly 32 seconds later. His twin received the throw and played a pass back to Michele Fornasier, who moved the ball to McGinty out on the left. Passes then took place between Tunnicliffe and Fornasier for the former to send Michael Keane down the wing. The full-back's cross wasn't cleared effectively and when Will Keane's scuffed attempt at goal landed in a patch of space, Morrison killed the ball prior to knocking it past a rooted Long and just inside an upright.

Neville said of the opening, *'Yes, we've just got the ball down and played. It's the first time I've seen the full-back go on an overlap. Great pass by Ryan Tunnicliffe, the defender doesn't deal with it at the near post. Will Keane makes a little bit of a mess of it but he keeps his composure. (Ravel) sent the 'keeper the wrong way, showed him the eyes. He's been a star player throughout this Youth Cup run. I just hope the general performance of the team can settle down and they can play the way which we know they can.'*

As David Stowell rightly called it on MUTV, the goal gave the Reds the *'shot in the arm'* they needed and from then on, isolated incidents apart, the Blades never quite posed the same threat as previously. Jesse Lingard almost made it 2-0 in first half injury-time only for his cross-shot to be headed off the line by Terry Kennedy, and a minute later the referee awarded a penalty when the same defender inexplicably undid his earlier good work by needlessly handling a Morrison cross.

Stowell felt Kennedy's action was *'a silly thing to do'* and then added that *'Sheffield United have committed suicide in the F.A. Youth Cup final'* as the spot kick sped past Long. Neville responded, *'Will Keane kept his head, sends the 'keeper the wrong way.......and you just feel for Terry Kennedy, he's just not going to forget that in a hurry. He'll be carrying that with him all the way through the summer.'*

Pogba tested Long with a fantastic strike from 30 yards in the 50th minute and in doing so provided a flashback to his goal against Portsmouth which kick-started the Reds' road to the final. A minute later Morrison and Maguire came together for an unfortunate clash of heads and the Sheffield United defender left the pitch on a stretcher following a lengthy spell of treatment.

With Pogba's influence increasing by the second, he sent Morrison clean past the Bramall Lane club's back four only for the number ten to astound everyone by missing his target. Morrison then attempted an overhead kick from a corner and later escaped all of the Blades' attentions when going around the outside of their defence in trying to set up Lingard at the far post.

Describing the Mancunian's ability in glowing terms, Neville claimed, *'When you see Ravel like that, there's no-one better, he just glides past people. It's a rare talent, to be able to do that from a central midfield player. He's always involved in the best moments we have.'*

Keane and Pogba managed to get in each other's way when attempting to

final 2nd leg

Floating like a butterfly, Ravel Morrison went on to twice sting like a bee against the Blades

507

Will Keane places his spot kick past Sheffield United goalkeeper George Long to put the Reds well in command

head in a Lingard cross and Sheffield found an immediate response as Slew made a powerful charge through the Reds' eighteen-yard area. The requirement of a goal lay very squarely inside the Blades' court and just as they were preparing to make a change, the destiny of the Youth Cup was taken out of their hands with twenty minutes remaining.

Tom Thorpe made a burst through the middle and he got Morrison involved while continuing his run. Morrison moved diagonally forward to his right and in doing so evaded one defender and then another. His movement opened up a gap wide enough to tempt him to shoot, and in a split second the ball crashed past Long and into the far corner. 'A majestic goal looks like it just may well have sealed it' was how Stowell described the Reds' position as Neville gushed 'Fantastic strike. Absolutely brilliant play.'

The Sheffield team gained a measure of reward for their efforts in the 73rd minute when countering at speed. Slew made tracks down the left and hit a wonderful precision pass away from Thorpe and Fornasier for Ironside to control with only Johnstone between him and the goal. As the 'keeper came out in the absence of any cover, Ironside stuck the ball under him as the away support increased the volume level inside the stadium by ten-fold.

The Blades were committed to almost all-out attack when the Reds finally dashed their hopes in the 82nd minute. A Sheffield move broke down at the East Stand side of the ground only for the recently-introduced Larnell Cole to breakaway and put him and Will Keane in a two-on-two situation at the opposite end of the pitch. Cole's pass to his colleague was only partly intercepted and Keane pinched the ball off McFadzean before escaping Kennedy's intended tackle to hammer it beyond Long.

Johnstone was forced into making a firm two-handed save from Connor Martin in the dying minutes, though the result of the match was now a foregone conclusion. Sixty seconds into the seven minutes of added time, which was mainly due to Maguire's injury, Morrison was substituted to a standing ovation. As the striker made his way over to the touchline, Stowell was moved to say, 'Two goals for a hugely talented player. Massively influential in this F.A. Youth Cup run, and he now gets the applause his performances on the pitch this season have very much deserved.'

Will Keane was only denied another Youth Cup hat-trick because his on-target shot was cleared for a corner by Barry, and when the final whistle blew just after, the United lads embraced each other as their achievement in capturing the trophy began to sink in.

While the celebrations got underway on the pitch, Stowell said of the achievement, 'The F.A. Youth Cup fairytale has the best possible ending. United have powered their way to victory here tonight, they've shown grit, they've shown guts, they've shown determination and they've scored some cracking goals along the way as well. Will Keane at the double to add to his goal in the first leg at Bramall Lane, Ravel Morrison popping up with two sumptuous finishes.......

This is a very talented bunch of players and they finish the season with silverware.'

Later adding, 'Like father, like son, Paul McGuinness joins Wilf in the F.A. Youth Cup winners' enclosure,' Neville responded to Stowell's comments by saying, 'I'm pleased for Paul, he's been waiting for this moment for years and years and he's been so close. But this year you could see it in the earlier rounds, this team was something different, they had power and strength.......

It's one of the best teams I've seen at youth level for a long time.'

The younger McGuinness understandably looked delighted during an on-pitch interview with MUTV, an undertaking that was prematurely curtailed when the club's youngsters charged over and began chanting 'Championes' as they surrounded him. Besides adding to his family's distinguished record in the competition, the name of Paul McGuinness could now be etched alongside those of Jimmy Murphy, Eric Harrison and Brian McClair in the annuals of the club's history as a winning F.A. Youth Cup coach, a truly fabulous achievement which maintains Manchester United's reputation of producing players of quality for themselves and the wider football world.

Tom Thorpe hoists the famous trophy high as Manchester United claim the F.A. Youth Cup for a record tenth time

2010-11

MAY 2011

final 2nd leg

509

JONES, David Frank Llwyd (2002/03)

Born: Southport, 4th November 1984
Height: 5ft. 11ins., **Weight:** 10st. 5lbs.
Role: Central midfielder
Career: Rofft Primary School (Wrexham)/ Darland High School (Rossett)/ Wales Boys/ UNITED: Trainee July 2001 Pro. July 2003 to January 2007/ Preston North End (L) August 2005 to January 2006/ NEC Nijmegen (Hol) (L) January to April 2006/ Derby County (L) November 2006/ Derby County January 2007/ Wolverhampton Wanderers June 2008 to May 2011/ Wigan Athletic August 2011 to present

Possibly the most academically gifted of any individual ever involved with the Reds, Lancashire-born David Jones juggled his studies to secure ten GCSE passes at school while concurrently making three trips a week to United's Academy. His exams resulted in a full complement of straight 'A' grades, seven of which were 'A*', and he then went on to acquire A-levels in maths and sports science.

He grew up in Gresford, near Wrexham, and as such qualified to win schoolboy honours with Wales. Linking up with the Academy section of his local professional club at the age of eight, he was spotted while playing for the Robins by United scout David Nicholas. Jones was trialled by Liverpool, Aston Villa and Everton and, despite supporting Sheffield Wednesday while holding a particular admiration of the mercurial Chris Waddle, he fulfilled an ambition to sign for United by joining the club's Centre of Excellence sometime in 1995.

Then working his way through the junior section of the Academy system, he was only fifteen when taking part in the Milk Cup in July 2000. Towards the end of a campaign in which he was a mainstay for the under-16's, the industrious playmaker was present for the semi-final and final wins at the Bludenz Youth Tournament in Austria.

The 2001/02 season saw him involved in three overseas competitions and it began once again with the Milk Cup. Three weeks later he was included in the squad that journeyed to Germany for the Coca-Cola Cup and he then settled into the under-17 side for all bar four of their fixtures, two of which were when he was claimed by the under-19's. Precisely a month after his 17th birthday he was named as a substitute for a Youth Cup win at Queen's Park Rangers and he remained on the bench for the next two rounds against Birmingham and Hartlepool. In early March he made a substitute appearance for England's under-18's during a 3-0 victory over Italy and later participated for the Reds in the Nokia Debitel Cup tournament in Düsseldorf.

Despite being only slightly built back then, his natural ability was beginning to burst out of him. Well able to keep a match moving with an intelligent long or short passing game, his technique allowed him to make space when receiving the ball.

He shone for the most part as a provider, and the youngster wasn't averse to doing more than his fair share of covering, tackling and tracking back in order to influence the result of a game. Additionally blessed with a maturity way beyond his years, early into the 2002/03 term he and club-mates Luke Steele and Eddie Johnson were members of an England Youth team that defeated Hungary 3-1 in Budapest.

Each and every one of those qualities and many more were evidenced by anybody who viewed United's progress in that campaign's Youth Cup ties during which he imposed himself as the team's midfield organ grinder by providing a strong link between a solid back four and a frequently dangerous forward-line.

Just five days after the Fifth Round win over Sheffield United, Jones substituted for Darren Fletcher to make his first appearance for the Reserves and a few weeks later he became the ninth United skipper to lift the Youth Cup trophy.

The praise heaped on him following the away section of the Youth Cup final was wholesome, with one newspaper commenting that he was responsible for *'breaking up sporadic Middlesbrough attacks while also creating numerous United chances with his exceptional vision and neat passing'*. The same report added that he *'glued this side together and, while lacking the pace and verve of Richardson, or the eye-catching artistry of Timm, he is vital to the functioning of the team'*.

Following the home leg, the Manchester Evening News described him as being *'at the heart of everything'* before adding *'in front of a big, boisterous crowd he blossomed. He knows when to keep it simple, to keep play ticking, and threads little passes through the tightest of spaces'*.

Commenting on how the next stage of his development unfolded, he admitted, *'It is fair to say that I struggled with the more aggressive approach of the senior professionals in the pre-season friendlies in 2003 and so I began to work out regularly in the gym at Carrington as well as attending yoga classes from then on. I also took up Tai Chi to build up my tendons because this was hopefully going to make me quicker over the first five yards.'*

Named as a substitute for a Carling Cup tie at West Brom that December, by adapting to the greater physical demands of second string football he went on to become United's joint highest appearance maker in the Premier Reserve League (North).

As that chapter of his development closed he was able to look back on a Manchester Senior Cup final triumph, selection for the England under-21's 2-2 draw with Sweden in Kristiansund and the honour of captaining the young Reds to yet another Blue Stars final victory.

Jones was simply outstanding for both of United's Reserve teams in the 2004/05 season, his displays in the middle of the park completely bewildering onlookers as to why he couldn't get a prolonged look in at senior level. The break he so thoroughly deserved arrived in December 2004 when he was sent on as a 79th minute replacement for Kleberson in a 1-0 home Carling Cup quarter-final victory over Arsenal and a week later he was one of four unused substitutes for a Champions League game against Fenerbahce in Turkey.

The following month he at last made the starting line-up for an F.A. Cup Third Round home tie against Exeter after which his performance prompted a passage in the United Yearbook to claim that he *'grew in confidence as the game progressed and was one of the few players to come out of the game with significant credit'*.

By the end of the campaign he had captained the Reds to the top of the Barclays Premier Reserve League and a National Play-off final win at Charlton, as well as making a substitute appearance in the Pontin's League Cup final.

Many supporters were anticipating a big push from him as the 2005/06 term approached, and it got off on the right foot when Alex Ferguson named him in the party for the pre-season visit to the Far East. He played twice on the tour, in the opening game versus Hong Kong and also against Kashima Antlers in Tokyo.

In early August, before a competitive ball had been kicked, it was announced that Preston had obtained his services on a proposed campaign-long loan and on the sixth of that month he was introduced to the Championship as a 75th minute substitute in a 2-1 victory at Watford. Despite impressing at Deepdale, his loan spell was terminated early, at which point he joined Dutch First Division side NEC Nijmegen.

While his time with North End was a useful experience in many ways, it was felt that a purer form of football would be a greater benefit to him in the long term and Jones later claimed he had *'seen more of the ball in my first training session in Holland than I had in my whole time at Preston.'* Finishing the Dutch term with six goals from seventeen appearances, a knock led him to returning to Manchester in April 2006 whereupon he confidently informed Alex Ferguson, *'I'm ready for the first-team.'*

The manager was able to make an early assessment of his progress when the Reds entertained UEFA Cup winners Seville in a home pre-season friendly that August and the 21 year-old rose to the challenge of his recall by scoring one of United's three goals. With Ferguson having only recently bolstered the midfield by splashing out £14million for Michael Carrick, Jones then made six appearances for the Reserves and started both of that season's Carling Cup ties, at Crewe and Southend, before Derby claimed him on a loan signing in November.

Within a month of his arrival at Pride Park he gave an indication that a permanent move there would be to his liking as he felt that they were *'a club going places.'* He got his wish a few weeks later when £1,000,000 changed hands to make him a Derby County employee and he realised another at the end of the campaign when the Rams gained promotion into the Premier League.

Jones was unable to maintain a regular place in a struggling County side, making only fifteen appearances for them in the top-flight, and he then flickered on and off new manager Paul Jewell's radar.

He was put out of his Pride Park misery when penning a three-year deal with Championship club Wolves in June 2008. Used in most of their games initially, fitness issues slowed his progress as the Molineux outfit topped the division to climb into the Premier League. Again afflicted by injury woes early in the 2009/10 term, his invaluable contribution from then on assisted the club's survival in the top echelon. Despite being offered a new contract, he left Wolves as a free agent to eventually sign for Wigan after making a good impression during a pre-season trial.

Still able to represent either England or Wales as a full international, David Jones has been the subject of much praise from many quarters in respect of his unstintingly positive attitude and dedicated application. Former Wolves manager Mick McCarthy said of him, *'He's been an absolute pleasure to deal with…….he's always on time, always pleasant and always supportive'* while Alex Ferguson is reputed to have remarked that United sold him far too cheaply.

CATHCART, Craig George (2005/06, 2006/07)

Born: Glengormley, Belfast, 6th February 1989
Height: 6ft. 1ins., **Weight:** 11st. 6lbs.
Role: Central defender or right full-back
Career: Ballyhenry Primary School (Belfast)/ Glengormley High School (Belfast)/ County Antrim Boys/ Northern Ireland Boys/ UNITED: Scholar July 2005 Pro. February 2006 to August 2010/ **Royal Antwerp** (Bel) (L) August 2007 to January 2008/ **Plymouth Argyle** (L) August 2008 to May 2009/ **Watford** (L) September to December 2009/ **Blackpool** August 2010 to present

For some, Craig Cathcart was something of a 'nearly man' while at Manchester United. He never won a domestic trophy with the Reds, he missed out on playing in the 2007 Youth Cup final and he also came close to making a breakthrough into the first-team. Sadly, when he left Old Trafford in the summer of 2010, while many of his contemporaries could look back on league and cup successes, the only silverware he took with him was a winner's trinket from the 2007 Champions Youth Cup. In fact, following that accomplishment in Malaysia, the young Ulsterman featured in only eleven more matches for the Reds over the next three years.

While a Febian Brandy goal may have been the difference between United and Juventus in the Champions Youth Cup final, it was the pairing of Cathcart and James Chester in the heart of the Reds' defence which provided the bedrock for progress throughout the tournament. The former was on the top of his game, causing many pundits to predict a brighter future for him than that of his fellow compatriot, Jonny Evans.

Upon returning to Manchester he was soon packing his bags once more, this time for a five-month loan spell at Antwerp, which was common practice at the time for the club's juniors. Gaining invaluable experience in Belgium over the early months of the 2007/08 term, by January 2008 he was back in digs in Sale and went on to feature in seven of the Reserves' games up to May.

Although not originally included in the travelling squad, Cathcart was flown over to South Africa for part of the first-team's 2008/09 pre-season tour. He made his senior debut by putting in a full 90 minutes in the Reds' 4-0 win over Kaizer Chiefs and while out there he also featured in a friendly against Nigeria. With his short spell in Belgium regarded as a useful exercise, United's coaching staff felt that a further loan period would benefit his development and so he was packed off to Plymouth for six months, a time period which was later extended to encompass the whole campaign.

Making his debut for the Pilgrims in the Carling Cup at Luton, he clocked up regular appearances for the Home Park club and as the term came to a close he was one of nine uncapped players who were called into the full Northern Ireland squad to face Italy in June. Even though his services weren't required, the development was a firm indication of how highly he was thought of by his country's management team.

After featuring in two of the Reserves' friendlies at the start of the 2009/10 season, an injury to Nemanja Vidic in the Audi Cup in Germany led to another first-team start in the semi-final against Boca Juniors, as well as a substitute appearance in the final defeat by Bayern Munich. Unfortunately, after spending a big chunk of two years away from Old Trafford, the central pairing of Rio Ferdinand and Vidic were firmly established, with Jonny Evans preferred as their back-up, and Cathcart was no nearer to disrupting the status quo regardless of the knowledge he had gained.

A number of Championship clubs showed an interest in signing him permanently, with Plymouth and Ipswich both making bids, but the Old Trafford hierarchy weren't keen to part with their young asset, at least not in the short-term.

He scored within three minutes of the Reserves' league season opener at Bolton and competed in a 5-0 win over Bury in the Manchester Senior Cup three days later before going out on loan again, this time to Watford. He picked up an injury while at Vicarage Road and returned to Manchester in early December, curtailing his loan by a few weeks, and it was probably during the period of convalescence that the young Irishman realised his future lay away from Old Trafford. Playing one final game in a red shirt when Stockport were defeated in the Manchester Senior Cup in early March, by the end of the campaign he was ready to move on.

Raised in a football family, with his father a notable player in Northern Ireland soccer circles, he had started out with Carnmoney Colts before switching to St. Andrew's Boys Club when he was eleven. By the time he had turned twelve, the defender was attending Manchester United's School of Excellence in Belfast and later left St. Andrew's to join Greenisland Boys Club. He went on to gain representative honours for both Antrim and Northern Ireland as a schoolboy, and despite receiving offers from Arsenal and Chelsea, they were rejected in favour of a career at Old Trafford in 2005.

His initial start was at right-back in the under-18's 2-0 win over Milton Keynes Dons in August and on the last day of October he won a promotion into the Reserves for a Manchester Senior Cup match with Oldham. In December he paired up in the middle of the back four with Jonny Evans when the young Reds defeated Birmingham in the Youth Cup and was then moved to right full-back for the Fourth Round tie at Sunderland. With Evans out of the picture, he and Ryan Shawcross formed a central defensive barrier for the later Youth Cup matches against Charlton and Manchester City.

The 2006/07 term saw significant improvement in his game and the development was such that he was used in eight of the Reserves' opening dozen league games. Already a youth international, in November 2006 the seventeen year-old was selected for Northern Ireland's under-21 side that faced Germany in Torgau.

A composed and polished performer who possessed the necessary pace, read the game well and could compete in the air, his physical and mental maturity stood him out as a natural leader and it was no surprise when he was named as captain of the Youth Cup team. In the February of that season a further representative honour came his way when he was selected in the European squad for the 2007 UEFA-CAF Meridien Cup, a competition between two 'all-star' under-18 teams from Europe and Africa.

Over the next few weeks he sat on the bench for an F.A. Cup tie with Middlesbrough and was then similarly named as an unused substitute for a Champions League tie with Roma, an F.A. Cup semi-final against Watford and a Premier League clash with Sheffield United. While those elevations were well merited, they also brought disappointment because after helping the young Reds to success over Arsenal at the last four stage of the Youth Cup, a couple of mouth-watering clashes against Liverpool were set to give supporters a real treat and him the opportunity of playing in a national final.

Unfortunately, the team's skipper was unable to take part in the opening leg due to his first-team commitments and he then missed out on the concluding match through suffering a knee injury in training, a knock which finished his season entirely. Not only had the chance to make his senior competitive entrance been lost, but he was forced to watch from the stands as the under-18's missed out on some glory by losing a penalty shoot-out to their Merseyside rivals. Nevertheless, a string of fine performances throughout the term deservedly earned him the Jimmy Murphy 'Young Player of the Year' award.

Fit again by August 2007, he travelled to Kuala Lumpur to contest the inaugural Malaysian Youth Cup, helping the team navigate past Porto, Boca Juniors, Inter Milan, Barcelona and Flamengo to set up a meeting with

Juventus. Little could he have known that the triumph in Asia would prove to be the high watermark of his five years at the club.

Making the inevitable move away from Old Trafford in August 2010 when joining Premier League newcomers Blackpool on a three-year deal, a few weeks later he was awarded a full Northern Ireland cap for his appearance in their 1-0 win against Slovenia in Maribor. A late call up for the injured Jonny Evans and playing out of position at left-back, his cross set up the winning goal for Corry Evans.

On the domestic scene, his 2010/11 campaign was one of disappointment. Even though he managed to score a 15th minute opener for the Tangerines in their 3-2 defeat by United at Bloomfield Road in January, Blackpool were relegated on the last day of the fixture list, ironically at Old Trafford.

A classy operator in his younger days, Craig Cathcart didn't develop sufficiently enough to cope with top-flight football in the Premier League and Champions League. While his attributes are undoubtedly many, for the 'nearly man' they simply didn't add up to enough.

ROCHE, Lee Paul (1997/98, 1998/99)

Born: Bolton, 28th October 1980
Height: 5ft. 10ins., **Weight:** 10st. 10lbs.
Role: Right full-back or central defender
Career: Mytham County Primary School (Little Lever)/ Little Lever High School/ Bolton Boys/ Greater Manchester Boys/ **UNITED:** Trainee June 1997 Pro. February 1999 to June 2003/ **Wrexham** (L) July 2000 to May 2001/ **Burnley** July 2003/ **Wrexham** July 2005 to May 2007/ **Droylsden** October 2007 to February 2011

Born into a Manchester United supporting family, Lee Roche grew up in Little Lever and began his interest in football at primary school. At the age of ten he joined up with Little Lever Sports Club in the Lancashire Amateur League and it was while with them that talent-spotter Harry McShane first viewed him when representing a Bury League side in a match against Salford. McShane later invited the young boy to attend a trial at The Cliff, a request Roche wasn't unaccustomed to because he had already been assessed by Bolton, Bury and Manchester City. The crucial factor in this case was that as a Reds' convert, he was so much keener on joining United than any other club.

By the time he turned fourteen, the defender was attached to Bolton Lads Club and had been selected to represent Bolton Boys at both under-15 and under-16 levels as well as making appearances for Greater Manchester Boys. He trained regularly with United after school and was waiting to undergo England trials until a stress fracture of the back sidelined him for over twelve months. Upon returning to football at the age of sixteen, Roche linked up with Charlestown Football Club in the Salford League and assisted them to a divisional and cup double in the 1995/96 season while concurrently appearing in United's Centre of Excellence under-15 and under-16 sides at full-back or in central defence.

On the opening day of the following term he was called off the bench during a 3-2 'B' team victory at Liverpool and then went on to establish himself in the under-16 side. Utilised in all six matches when the Reds surged to victory in the Bludenz Youth Tournament in March 1997, three months later he was taken on as a trainee.

He scored the Reds' consolation goal when they were defeated 2-1 by Middlesbrough in the Northern Ireland Milk Cup final prior to the commencement of the following campaign and later split his time fairly evenly for either the 'A' or 'B' teams as the former went on to take the Lancashire League Division One title. It was also during that season when he appeared at right full-back in both of the Youth Cup ties against Blackburn as the Reds were knocked out at the first hurdle.

Before the 1998/99 term started he was called into an England Youth team that faced the Republic of Ireland in Dublin and, after missing out on schoolboy honours through injury, he was especially proud to represent his country in a superb 5-0 success. It was then a case of returning to Academy action for a few weeks prior to marking up a first appearance for the Reserves when replacing Wes Brown in a 1-0 victory against Nottingham Forest. A fortnight later he claimed a second England Youth cap through his involvement in a 4-2 win over Italy in Rome.

Going on to regularly captain the under-19 Academy team, he was chosen as United's skipper and in central defence for the youngsters' attempt at recapturing the Youth Cup during that campaign. Sadly, it was a case of history repeating itself as United lost by four clear goals to Everton following a 2-2 draw in their opening tie. Nevertheless, on a purely personal level, the lad seemed to be progressing well enough.

In March 1999, a month after turning professional, he was included in an England under-18 squad that journeyed to Rota in southern Spain to contest the European Championships.

While seen as an important competition in its own right, it was felt that the tournament would also provide suitable preparation for the FIFA Youth World Cup, which was due to be staged in Nigeria the following month. Used in an 8-0 win against Andorra, as well as a 2-1 victory over Israel in Spain, upon returning to England he was informed that he would be one of the Youth World Cup party which included Ashley Cole, Andy Johnson, Peter Crouch, Matthew Etherington and United's own Paul Rachubka. Roche appeared in one additional match for the Reserves before he was set to join up with the England squad in late March but, unfortunately, the elation felt by his selection soon nosedived into despair when a tackle in training left him with medial knee ligament damage and a subsequent four-month lay-off.

Fit again for the start of the 1999/00 season, he claimed a place in sixteen out of the Reserves' 24 league matches and was a member of the team that won 2-0 at Oldham to claim the Manchester Senior Cup in May.

In a bid to further test his capabilities, Alex Ferguson sent him on a season-long loan to Wrexham, then of League One. He proved an instant hit at the Racecourse Ground, making 41 appearances as the club finished in tenth place, and his form for Wrexham also earned him further international honours when he won an under-21 cap in a European Championship Qualifier against Finland at Barnsley in mid-March, England winning the game 4-0. After then helping Wrexham to bag the Welsh Premier Cup, a great term was concluded when he claimed the Robins' 'Young Player of the Year' award.

Usually found in United's Reserves over the next couple of years, in November 2001 he finally got his chance of first-team football in a Worthington Cup tie at Arsenal. Even though the experience was priceless, the result was somewhat less favourable as the Reds were comprehensively beaten 4-0. At the end of that campaign he was integral to another success story when the club's second string won the Barclaycard Reserve League title.

Roche was later given two further senior opportunities, the first of which came in November 2002 when substituting for Laurent Blanc in United's 5-3 Premiership defeat of Newcastle. Performing for his boyhood heroes in front of 67,625 fans at Old Trafford provided him with a great thrill, and he gained another by taking part in a 2-0 Champions League defeat by Deportivo La Coruna at the Estadio Riazor the following March.

Fast, strong, dependable and infused with an above-average level of concentration, the Boltonian was also a decent passer of the ball and a particularly accomplished tackler. Ultimately, however, he was unable to dislodge the incredibly consistent Gary Neville from the first-team and therefore found himself the subject of a free transfer soon after playing his last game for the club, a 1-0 defeat by Middlesbrough Reserves in May 2003.

Later the recipient of numerous offers from potential employers, amongst them Watford and Bradford City, he instead decided to sign for Championship side Burnley as a result of receiving an introduction through one of the Neville brothers. Despite blasting in a spectacular 25-yard volley on his debut, a regular place in their first-team initially eluded him. In his second season at Turf Moor he looked to have hammered down a more lasting spot in Burnley's senior side, but when manager Stan Ternent was fired he was used less frequently and sometimes out of position.

He linked up with Wrexham again in 2005 and added a tally of 45 league appearances for the Welsh club before being released two years later. Unable to find employment of a similar standing, Lee Roche joined Droylsden in the autumn of 2007 and remained with the progressive Blue Square Bet League outfit until February 2011.

EVANS, Jonathan Grant (2004/05, 2005/06)

Born: Belfast, 2nd January 1988
Height: 6ft. 2ins., **Weight:** 12st. 2lbs.
Role: Central defender
Career: Belfast High School/ Belfast Boys/ Northern Ireland Boys/ **UNITED:** Trainee July 2004 Pro. July 2006 to present/ **Royal Antwerp** (Bel) (L) August 2006 to January 2007/ **Sunderland** (L) January to May 2007/ **Sunderland** (L) January to May 2008

United have been farming out youngsters ever since John Connaughton went to Halifax in 1969. However, it has only been in Alex Ferguson's reign that the loan system has been strategically used for player development, with season-long spells away from Manchester now a regular occurrence. Unfortunately for the majority, their loans are more commonly followed by an exit from the club as they fail to display the necessary wherewithal. A rare exception to that general rule is Jonny Evans, and such was his rapid development, from youth team to the seniors' tour of South Africa made within a six-month period, that Ferguson and his staff felt a brief spell away from Old Trafford might benefit the Northern Ireland prodigy.

The centre-back figured against Orlando Pirates and the Kaizer Chiefs in South Africa in July 2006, a month in which he registered his first senior goal in a friendly match against Celtic at Parkhead. Soon sent on his travels once again, this time to Belgium to join Royal Antwerp on a five-month loan, his mid-December return to Manchester coincided with the start of the Belgian League's winter hibernation.

During that period he joined a select group of Manchester United youngsters in experiencing a full international appearance before making his league debut when named at left full-back for Northern Ireland's European Qualifier against Spain at Windsor Park in early September. It was a sensational night for the Irish, with a hat-trick from former Red David Healy sealing a memorable 3-2 victory, and by October Evans had added to his cap collection with further run-outs against Denmark and Latvia.

Following a short Christmas break he was sent out on loan again, this time to Sunderland, and he assisted them to the Championship title while also collecting a further two international caps to consolidate a place in his country's back four. Even though he had featured before at full-back as a United junior, it was when representing Northern Ireland and Sunderland that he developed the versatility which would make him an important member of Alex Ferguson's squad in later years.

The 2007/08 term was almost a carbon copy of the previous one, with Evans participating in another senior pre-season tour, this time in Asia. He missed the opening weeks of the campaign due to a minor injury but was fit enough to be included in the Carling Cup eleven who faced Coventry at Old Trafford. It turned out to be a baptism to forget as the Reds were given the runaround by a more determined Sky Blues outfit and ended up on the wrong end of a 2-0 scoreline. Nevertheless, he remained in first-team contention and featured in Champions League ties with Dynamo Kiev and Roma as Christmas approached.

Rejoining Sunderland early in the New Year to get in much needed Premier League experience by adding fifteen further appearances to his tally, there was also the added bonus of a few more starts for his country.

As far as United were concerned, his loan spells were considered an unqualified success and a number of clubs began making enquires in regards to obtaining his services. Going on to collect his first major honour when United won the Community Shield at the start of the new season, by September 2008 the young Ulsterman had made his first Premier League start for the Reds in a 1-1 draw at Stamford Bridge. A couple of months later, Rio Ferdinand picked up a back injury and he slotted effortlessly into central defence alongside Nemanja Vidic.

He remained in the team over the second half of the campaign and must have felt he was dreaming when the Reds secured victory over Spurs in the Carling Cup final. A Premier League winner's medal landed in his lap come May, and there was also a Champions League final to look forward to against Barcelona. Named on the bench for the meeting with the Catalans in Rome, he didn't get a run-out as the Reds were swept away by the Spanish giants but, even so, it had still been a magnificent first full season and at just 21 years of age it appeared that nothing other than many trophy-laden years lay ahead of him.

Brought up on the hard streets of the Rathcoole Estate in Belfast, Evans started his soccer career at Greenisland Boys Club. Coached by his father Jackie, who was once on Chelsea's books as a youngster, it wasn't long before United's representatives spotted his potential and he was invited to join the club's Belfast Centre of Excellence when aged just nine years-old. He came over to England for trials a year later, but after the F.A. introduced the '90-minute rule', his family moved to Manchester in order to assist his prospects.

Curiously first appearing in a United shirt back in his home country when participating in the 2004 Northern Ireland Milk Cup, he was a mainstay of the under-18 Academy side throughout the season. He also found himself as one of a trio of central defenders in a back three for the home Youth Cup defeat by Stoke and made one start in the Barclay's Reserve League and four appearances in the Pontin's Reserve League to give him a steady, if unspectacular, start to his time at the club.

Continuing to impress for both the Academy and second string throughout the 2005/06 term, by the end of it he had contributed towards the winning of the Reserves' division in addition to the Manchester Senior Cup. He also made two more appearances in the Youth Cup, the first two of which, against Birmingham and Sunderland, was as captain.

Although clearly possessing potential, there were those who felt he lacked concentration, either positionally or in the tackle. Little could any of those doubters foresee the rapid strides he would make over the next couple of years, which led to him occupying a place on the bench for the Champions League final. The three loan periods had certainly helped to turn the rough and raw prospect into a more cultured and mature footballer, though just like many youngsters before and since, the acid test wasn't how success and praise is dealt with but the way in which loss of form and criticism is handled.

The 2009/10 season was a mixed one for him. A regular over the first half of the campaign, his displays were often inconsistent and it appeared to some that the Irishman might even be struggling for confidence on occasions. The situation wasn't helped when some of the crowd and certain sections of the media appeared to focus on any mistake he made only to ignore the better aspects of his game, nevertheless he was included in the team that retained the Carling Cup in a hard fought win over Aston Villa. Filling in either at left full-back or central defence, it seemed that he was slowly recapturing his 2008 form.

In the 2010/11 term, most of the Old Trafford faithful agreed that he was back to something like his true self. His distribution, an aspect of his game which was subjected to most criticism, showed a marked improvement and his confidence seemed restored. Naturally left-footed, and therefore sometimes asked to cover for Patrice Evra, as the season drew to a close he deservedly collected his second Premier League gong.

Over the summer of 2011, Alex Ferguson drafted Blackburn's Phil Jones into his squad and, because Chris Smalling had arrived the previous year, it appeared that Evans might struggle to get games. Even so, with Wes Brown and John O'Shea moving to fresh pastures, and Rio Ferdinand now considered a veteran, the club's former junior has all the attributes needed to remain a valued member of the senior squad, a fact evidenced when he was allocated the number six jersey for the 2011/12 campaign. His form over the last six months of that term was probably his finest to date.

While they might not work for everyone, his loan periods didn't spell the end but actually provided a solid foundation for the future.

TATE, Alan (2000/01)

Born: Easington, Co. Durham, 2nd September 1982
Height: 6ft. 1ins., Weight: 13st. 5lbs.
Role: Central defender
Career: **Easington Primary School/ Murton County Secondary School (Seaham)/ Seaham Boys/ East Durham Boys/ Durham Boys/ UNITED**: Trainee July 1999 Pro. July 2000 to February 2004/ **Royal Antwerp** (Bel) (L) December 2001 to April 2002/ **Swansea City** (L) November 2002 to May 2003/ **Swansea City** (L) October to December 2003/ **Swansea City** February 2004 to present

Brought up in Murton, a village in Durham, by the age of nine Alan Tate was already attending Sunderland's School of Excellence and playing for his school's under-11 side. He was later attached to a couple of Sunderland junior outfits, the Roker Rookies and Kennek Roker, while concurrently winning numerous league and cup honours with his secondary school team. Such was his reputation that clubs such as Leeds, Chelsea, Ipswich, Newcastle United and Nottingham Forest all trialled him at some point or other.

At the age of eleven he began to interest United and was offered a place at the Reds' School of Excellence, an establishment which was based at the McEwan Centre in nearby Houghton-le-Spring. Despite his preference to remain with Sunderland because he was a dyed-in-the-wool fan of the Black Cats, it was well known that United's facility was far superior as prospects were given greater attention there. Sunderland then catered for 36 youngsters whereas United facilitated only sixteen with the same number of coaches.

Having previously captained all his schoolboy teams, reaching as far as county level, rank bad luck caused him to be injured while undertaking trials for England Boys.

A safety-first stopper, he was constantly alive to the defensive side of the game where his height gave him a huge advantage in the air. Never afraid to physically impose himself against opponents, his laid back demeanour often reminded observers of a young Gary Pallister as even in the most intense battles he was rarely ruffled.

When he was fourteen, a coach at United's North-East Centre of Excellence called Ged McNamee suggested that he travel down to Old Trafford for an initial assessment. Two years later, having already represented the Reds in the 1998 North Tyneside Youth Tournament, Tate began to make frequent trips to Manchester and appeared at both under-16 and under-17 levels during the following season. Offered terms soon after debuting for the under-17's in March 1999, just four months later he was resident in Salford and ready to begin life as a trainee footballer.

A regular for the under-17 side that ended the 1999/00 campaign just a point behind Academy League champions Crewe, in the December of that season his progress led to him being named as an unused substitute for the Youth Cup tie against Nottingham Forest and he then lined up against Oldham in a Manchester Senior Cup group game late in the season.

He faced up to Dutch, Swedish, German and Russian opposition in the Bayern Munich Youth Tournament as a warm up for league duties prior to the beginning of the following term and was then included in the opening Premier Reserve League (North) fixture against Bradford City at Gigg Lane.

An obvious choice to skipper that term's Youth Cup side, as such he took part in the three-tie rout which ended when United were eliminated by Nottingham Forest in February. Over the Easter period he appeared in the Düsseldorf Youth Tournament, during which the boys were defeated on penalties by Stuttgart at the semi-final stage. Even so, it was still a memorable competition for him as he was awarded the prestigious title of 'Defender of the Tournament'. With the campaign drawing to a close, Tate was bestowed with the captaincy of the side that was defeated by Manchester City in the Manchester Senior Cup final, but after winning the 2001 'Young Player of the Year' award he was more than happy with the strides that he had made.

He continued with the under-19's throughout the first part of the 2001/02 season and made occasional appearances in the Reserves before being offered the chance to join Royal Antwerp on loan. Realising it was a great way to further his experience, in December 2001 he got a first peek at senior football for the Belgians before recommencing in the under-19's as the term drew to a close.

Following just half a dozen games for the Reserves at the start of the 2002/03 campaign, the giant defender then spent a large part of the next thirteen months on loan at Swansea. Commencing with the Welsh club in November 2002, his debut ended in a 2-0 defeat at Scunthorpe later that month and he notched up another 26 appearances before making his way back to base camp.

Towards the end of a second loan spell later in the year, Swansea manager Brian Flynn asked about his availability on a permanent basis. Alex Ferguson originally refused, even offering him a further one-year extension to his contract but, having acquired a taste for first-team fare as well as contending with the likes of Rio Ferdinand in Manchester, the target accepted that it would be almost impossible to penetrate the first-team at Old Trafford in the foreseeable future.

He had certainly paid his dues, with around 100 competitive games for the Reds to speak of, and a two and a half year contract provided him with a clear way to progress his career.

Tate has since notched up over 300 appearances for the Swans, often at full-back and on numerous occasions as captain, as they have climbed from League Two up to their present status in the Premier League. His adaptability has seen him operate in midfield and every defensive position, which even includes two stints as a stand-in goalkeeper. Named as the club's 'Player of the Year' for the 2005/06 season, that same term Swansea also defeated Carlisle in the Football League Trophy final at the Millennium Stadium.

He figured in 43 league games in the 2010/11 term and set up two of the goals in a Wembley Play-off win over Reading that secured promotion to the top flight. Unfortunately, following just one Premier League match in August 2011, his leg was broken in a freak accident when he was trapped between a tree and a golf buggy. His injury kept him sidelined until March 2012, after which he figured in four senior games, the last of which was as a substitute against United at Old Trafford in May.

PETRUCCI, Davide (2008/09, 2009/10)

Born: Rome, Italy, 5th October 1991
Height: 6ft. 2ins., Weight: 13st. 7lbs.
Role: Midfielder or forward
Career: Instituto Poliziano (Rome)/ AS Roma (It) July 2002 to June 2008/ UNITED: Scholar June 2008 Pro. October 2009 to present

While Manchester United have long held an enviable record of attracting soccer talent from all over the British Isles, in relatively recent years F.A. restrictions have forced the Reds to look further afield for potential stars of the future. So, when club scouts saw Davide Petrucci impress for one of the Italian youth teams, and knowing a loophole exists in that country's football system, they made their move to secure him, although no-one could have guessed at the furore they were about to create.

It had been very different with the likes of Mads Timm, Floribert N'Galula, Jonathan Spector, Marcus Neumayr, Magnus Eikrem and Jami Puustinen because they came from much smaller clubs that were happy to accept a provisional fee and allow their youngsters a chance to shine at Old Trafford. For others such as Giuseppe Rossi and Gerard Piqué, different circumstances prevailed, while Federico Macheda was about to be released by Lazio and so the Italian outfit could hardly complain when he ended up in Manchester.

However, Roma is a proud and successful Serie A club, with a fine pedigree of developing young talent, and so when United decided to exploit the rule which forbids domestic clubs from signing their own players until they reach seventeen, their actions made back page headlines all around the world.

'It's a nightmare! Manchester United have dealt us another low blow, stealing Petrucci from under our noses, probably the best product of our youth system. In three to four years, he will be worth 100 times as much,' reported Il Romanista, the Italian capital's leading newspaper. 'They are stealing him from us,' claimed Roma's Technical Director Bruno Conti, while incensed Roma supporters screamed, 'It's poaching!'

Legally at least, no rules had been broken. Nevertheless, United were seen to be manipulating the situation to their advantage and as such were painted as the 'English enemy' by the Italian press.

Speaking to a newspaper at the time, Petrucci explained, 'A month ago Roma offered me a contract at the minimum rate, without clarifying whether it would be for three or five years. I asked for a bit of time to think about it, Manchester United had already made their proposal, but Roma only gave me three days and left me out of the squad. To a certain extent they closed the door on me while United opened a big door. They (Roma) could have valued me more highly.

You can't just forget six years at Roma. I was born a Roma fan and I will be one for the rest of my life, but this is a great opportunity, I'm going to the strongest club in the world. It was difficult to say no, even if I would have been very happy to spend my whole career at Roma. United have offered my father, Stefano, a job as a gardener and he will accompany me. I will go over on June 30 and start in United's Academy the next day.'

In the end United were willing to offer Petrucci, who had scored fourteen goals from nineteen games in Roma's youth team, a salary of £95,000 a year compared to the £16,000 being offered by the Rome club. Bruno Conti revealed that an aggrieved Roma were unwilling to improve the terms because it would upset other youth team players who had already penned similar deals and added that the want-away teenager would have been given opportunities to show his value the following season.

Regardless of what might have eventuated in his native country, the boy elected to relocate to Manchester and sign a three-year contract while United paid £200,000 in compensation to conclude the deal.

Having started out with his local club, San Basilio, from age seven to nine, he was then selected to undertake trials for Roma from amongst hundreds of other boys before joining them the following year and concurrently attending a school attached to the football club known as the Instituto Poliziano. After working his way through their junior ranks, in October 2006 he was called into the Italian team for a youth clash with France.

It was while operating alongside Macheda in a match against Holland in Sardinia when he was first seen by United scouts and after twelve appearances at the younger level he moved up to the under-17 team in August 2007. Then, in an Italy versus Ukraine match at the Pordenone Youth Tournament that November, representatives from Old Trafford watched with interest as he made passes which consistently split the opposing defence wide open. Compared to a young Francesco Totti at Roma, the scouting team had seen enough and decided to act.

With eight Italian under-17 caps to his name upon arriving in England, he made an immediate impact in the 2008 Northern Ireland Milk Cup when a comfortable 3-0 defeat of South Coast Bayern of the USA in the final resulted in him capturing his first piece of silverware on behalf of the Reds.

Petrucci then went straight into the under-18 Academy side, making his entrance in a 0-0 draw at West Ham. Originally a central midfielder, the coaches were keen to link him up with Macheda and so moved him into a more attacking midfield role. He made a further seven appearances before being drafted in as a substitute for the Reserves in a 2-1 defeat at Hull in November. Just over a week later the Italian once again left the bench for a 3-2 Youth Cup home reverse against Chelsea and from December until February he featured for both the under-18's and the Reserves.

Tall, elegant, blessed with an even temperament, excellent ball control and the ability to prise open the most hard-nosed of defences, it appeared that all the trouble taken to capture him was worth it.

It was just then when he began suffering from annoying groin and back injuries that were diagnosed as 'growth spurts', whereby the body tissue, muscles, tendons and bones all grow at different paces, thus putting undue stress on the body of the young athlete. Having started only sixteen games, rest was ordered and he missed the remainder of the season.

Such was the acute nature of his problem, the seventeen year-old was unable to train throughout the summer and found himself sidelined for nigh on eight months. Returning in the October of the 2009/10 term, he was named as captain of the Youth Cup team and led them to victories over Birmingham and Burnley before Blackburn not only curtailed the Reds' run at Ewood Park but also his campaign. Inclusive of an appearance for the Italian under-19 side in a 3-0 win over Turkey, he had only featured in twelve matches all season as his injury concerns reappeared.

In what must have been an incredibly frustrating time for him, he continued to work hard on his fitness and also returned home to Italy at regular intervals in order to maintain his morale. A year after breaking down for the second time, in February 2011 he returned to action for the Reserves in a Lancashire Senior Cup tie with Oldham. He went on as a substitute and put in a further five appearances from the dugout before making his first start of the term in early April.

'It's a great feeling and I'm feeling each time better and better,' he enthused. 'It's very positive at the moment and I'm looking forward to playing more games, even though the season is nearly over now. We can always play better than we play the week before. The more you play, the more you feel better. I feel quite close now to my best. I just need games to play and to show what I can do.'

Going on to take part in a few more matches before the campaign closed, the coaching staff ensured that he took things steady as they were keen not to rush him back, and there was some form of reward in his penultimate game when the Reds defeated Bolton 3-1 in the final of the Manchester Senior Cup.

Highly regarded by all at Old Trafford, Davide Petrucci lost a lot of altitude during his extended lay-off. However, following a slow start to his 2011/12 season, he not only demonstrated that he was back to full fitness, his displays in the centre of midfield had coaches and fans alike in agreement that his prospects were fully back in the ascendancy.

A young man whose on-field attributes include exceptional vision, a flair for executing passes at speed, tenacity in the tackle and a high work rate, his most recent reward came when he was called up for Alex Ferguson's first-team squad that toured South Africa in the summer of 2012.

JAMES, Matthew Lee (2006/07, 2007/08, 2008/09)

Born: Rochdale, 22nd July 1991
Height: 6ft., Weight: 11st. 9lbs.
Role: Midfielder
Career: Brittania Community Primary School (Bacup)/ Fearns Community Sports College (Bacup)/ England Boys/ UNITED: Scholar July 2007 Pro. July 2009 to May 2012/ **Preston North End** (L) February to May 2010/ **Preston North End** (L) July 2010 to January 2011/ **Leicester City** May 2012 to present

In the summer of 2011, when England's under-21 side toiled at the European Championships before being eliminated at the group stage, many pundits were critical of their almost non-existent midfield. With Arsenal's Jack Wilshere unavailable, the country's press began to put the team's performances under the spotlight and *'pedestrian'* was probably the most frequent word levelled against them. Numerous names were bandied about in terms of who else could have made a difference, only no-one mentioned Matty James. Missing the second half of the 2010/11 season through achilles and calf injuries, his previous displays for Championship side Preston were more than encouraging, and with 34 international youth caps under his belt, maybe his positive passing style was exactly what England required.

North End had taken him on loan during the second part of the 2009/10 campaign and the Lancastrian made a dream league start for them when scoring after only ten minutes against Sheffield United at Deepdale to trigger a 2-1 victory.

Impressive contributions throughout the remainder of the term caused Preston's management team to negotiate a further six-month loan deal for the first half of the 2010/11 campaign until injury limited his progress and he tracked back to Carrington beset with a couple of niggling problems.

An established under-19 international captain who led England to the European Championship semi-finals in Normandy in the summer of 2010, he already owned three caps at under-20 level and a promotion into the under-21 set-up seemed the next logical step.

Growing up in Bacup, where it soon became clear that he possessed a natural talent for most sports, James won league and cup honours when representing Rossendale at under-8 and under-9 levels and was soon invited to join Blackburn Rovers' Academy. Captain of his school team, he also swam for Rossendale & Rochdale District as well as playing cricket for Bacup. After two years with Blackburn he joined the Manchester United Academy at under-12 standard and made rapid progress.

Introduced into the Academy team against Bolton at Leyland in October 2005 when replacing Chris Fagan, little did most of the crowd know that the fourteen year-old was almost certainly the youngest player ever to feature for the club's under-18 side. Unfortunately, a broken ankle curtailed much of that campaign, though he would soon bounce back.

Fully fit by August 2006, James was a member of the Nike Cup squad and went on to make two substitute appearances for the under-18's in the autumn. Then, in early November, he was called into the England under-16 Victory Shield squad as they prepared to face Northern Ireland in Ballymena.

Coming off the bench during a comfortable 3-0 win to get his international career underway, he was used a few times in the Academy side in March and was selected for his country once again, this time at the Montaigu Tournament in France. Upon his return, the midfielder was surprisingly named on the bench for the first leg of the Youth Cup final at Anfield and with just a few minutes remaining he became one of a relatively few Reds who have taken part in the competition prior to reaching their 16th birthday when replacing Febian Brandy.

James started to appear more often for the under-18's in the 2007/08 term but was out of action for a few weeks in September when undergoing minor heart surgery. Still only sixteen, he stepped up to the second string in November for a 2-1 win at Middlesbrough and was party to his first club success when named as a non-playing substitute in the Manchester Senior Cup victory over Bolton the following May.

It was also during this season that he was named as captain of England's under-17 team, for whom he scored three times in twelve appearances, and also started both Youth Cup games as the Reds fell at the second hurdle to Carlisle. Normally found in central midfield, his versatility allowed him to fill in at centre-half or full-back when required.

The 2008/09 term began on a bright note when he led the youth team to victory in the Northern Ireland Milk Cup and after spending the first three months with the under-18's, he was named as captain of the Youth Cup team that faced Chelsea at Old Trafford. Unfortunately, the Londoners knocked the young Reds out at the first hurdle, which was a huge personal disappointment to him, although he started to appear more frequently for the Reserves in December and remained in the second string from then on. By the end of the campaign he was able to add another Manchester Senior Cup triumph to a growing collection of honours and his last taste of action came in the form of three appearances for England's under-19's in UEFA Championship matches against Bosnia, Slovakia and Scotland.

The coaching staff wanted to continue his development and explored the possibility of loan opportunities in order to improve his game still further. Experiencing a mild setback in July 2009, when falling ill during the under-19 European Championships in the Ukraine, after only two games he returned to the UK for rest.

Back in action for the Reserves' opener in August, a victory in the held-over Lancashire Senior Cup final win over Bolton, he featured in a dozen matches before the opportunity of a suitable loan move became available. Coming under the wing of Alex Ferguson's son Darren, who had recently taken over the reins at Deepdale, less than a year later the younger Ferguson was sacked by Preston at which time James was recalled to Old Trafford.

A player of much poise and promise, he was unable to make the leap into United's senior squad and so decided to accept Leicester City's offer of a three-year deal in May 2012.

JONES, Richard Glynn (2003/04, 2004/05)

Born: Stockport, 26th September 1986
Height: 6ft., Weight: 11st.
Role: Midfielder
Career: **Ladybrook Primary School (Bramhall)/ Bramhall High School/ Stockport Boys/ England Boys/ UNITED**: Trainee July 2003 Pro. July 2004 to July 2008/ **Royal Antwerp** (Bel) (L) January 2006/ **Colchester United** (L) October and November 2006/ **Barnsley** (L) February to May 2007/ **Yeovil Town** (L) August to December 2007/ **Hartlepool United** July 2008/ **Oldham Athletic** July 2010/ **Bradford City** July 2011 to present

There is a saying in football that when an opportunity comes along you have to take it, and for a two-month period beginning in October 2005, a former United Youth Cup captain was presented with his chance. With the senior Reds' midfield decimated by injuries and Alex Ferguson keen to promote from within, Ritchie Jones, who had impressed many with his displays in the club's second team, was drafted into the Carling Cup side to face Barnet. Starting in central midfield alongside Liam Miller, the local lad lasted the full 90 minutes and made a telling contribution in a 4-1 victory. A week later he was placed on the bench for a Champions League game in Lille and over the next few weeks featured in a home Carling Cup tie with West Brom, was named as a substitute for a Premiership clash at Aston Villa and took part in another Carling Cup match, this time at Birmingham.

So, when United were drawn away to Burton Albion in an F.A. Cup Third Round tie in early January, the nineteen year-old once again found himself named in the starting line-up. Sadly, an inept display saw the Reds struggle and although he was well placed to score the winner in the last minute, Burton's 'keeper saved what seemed like a certain goal. Ferguson was fuming that so many of his team had failed to put in a performance worthy of the club and it seemed that heads would roll. That was exactly what happened as far as Jones was concerned, because the following week he was debuting for Royal Antwerp in the Belgian Second Division.

The original plan was for him to join Antwerp in early January for a six-month loan spell, but after only two games he returned to Manchester and spent the remainder of the term in the Reserves.

It was certainly a tale of two halves. The first section of the season promised much, with the concluding part ending in a lot of disappointment as far as his first-team prospects were concerned. Nonetheless, he made 26 appearances in all competitions for the second string as they secured the Barclays Premier Reserve League North championship, won the National Play-off against Spurs and also captured the Manchester Senior Cup.

Jones then spent the first couple of months of the 2006/07 campaign in the Reserves before being recalled to first-team duty for a Carling Cup tie at Crewe where, despite setting up the Reds' opener for Ole Gunnar Solskjaer, he was mainly inconspicuous. Two days later he was loaned out to Colchester and then undertook another loan spell, this time at Barnsley.

Once again a first-team chance had come and gone, and unfortunately it proved to be his last to impress on the bigger stage.

Brought up in the leafy confines of Bramhall, a location renowned more for footballer spotting than for soccer playing, he joined United's Centre of Excellence at nine years of age while also attached to Mountfield Rovers in the Stockport Metro League. He went on to play for Stockport Boys and first came to prominence in the 2001/02 term when featuring regularly in the Reds' under-16 team. Soon catching the attention of the international selectors, in early November he won his first cap for England Boys in a Victory Shield win over Wales and additionally made three substitute appearances for United's under-17 Academy side. As the season drew to a close he was recalled into the international fold and took part in another four matches for the young Lions.

During the following campaign he appeared in all bar five of the under-17's fixtures as they finished in second place in their division and also made the step up at international level by featuring in games against the Faroe Islands, Sweden, Norway and Iceland when the England under-17's captured the Nordic Cup in late summer.

The next two years saw him progress quickly through the junior ranks and the 2003/04 term started positively when he scored the winning goal in the Northern Ireland Milk Cup final against Preston. Also used in the Youth Cup team that was eventually eliminated by Blackburn, his breakthrough to the Reserves occurred on the final day of the season in a 2-1 home win over Newcastle.

At junior level, the 2004/05 campaign will always be remembered for the disastrous home Youth Cup match with Stoke when the Reds were surprisingly knocked out at the first attempt. Named as captain for the night, the distraught Jones was captured by MUTV cameras with his head in his hands and tears streaming down his face at full-time. Nevertheless, the season picked up considerably as the second string won the Pontin's Holiday League Division One (West) title and League Cup and he was voted 'Man of the Tournament' in Zurich, as well as scoring in the final, when United were victorious in the Blue Stars competition against AIK Stockholm.

A powerful tackler with a good engine, who earned a reputation for his ability to retain the ball and pass it simply to the front men, although lacking true pace, his energy levels were such that he appeared able to get up and down the pitch without much effort. That combination of attributes assisted him to collect eleven England under-19 caps in the period prior to Ferguson deciding it was time to blood him against Barnet.

By failing to grasp a second opportunity, his long-term prospects at the club were, for intents and purposes, over. Sent out on loan once again in August 2007, this time to Yeovil, he only managed a handful of starts for United's Reserves in the second half of the campaign and was then released.

With a solid grounding behind him and possessing a decent pedigree, it wasn't long before potential employers began to show an interest and he rebooted his career by joining League One club Hartlepool in 2008. A regular in the 'Pool side over the next couple of years, he joined Oldham for the 2010/11 term. Despite being offered a one-year extension to his contract at Boundary Park, in July 2011 it was reported he had joined Bradford City.

In 2010, the Football Association's director of football development, Trevor Brooking, cited him in a newspaper article regarding promotions into the full national team. Brooking stated, *'A classic example is the 2005 England under-19 tournament team, none of whom is anywhere near the full national team now at the age of 24. Typical is skipper Ritchie Jones, who was then at Manchester United but is now a midfielder at Oldham. One crucial reason is that Premier League clubs are not willing to trust in local youth in the way that other countries do.'*

While that might be the case at some soccer locations, Jones was given a few sightings of the senior scene at Old Trafford only to find the high demands of being a Manchester United first-team regular too much of a stretch for his capabilities.

McSHANE, Paul David (2002/03, 2003/04)

Born: Dublin, 6th January 1986
Height: 5ft. 11ins., Weight: 11st. 8lbs.
Role: Central defender
Career: St. Kevin's Community Boys' School (Arklow, Co. Wicklow)/ St. David's Secondary School (Greystones, Co. Wicklow)/ UNITED: Trainee July 2002 Pro. January 2003 to August 2006/ **Walsall** (L) December 2004 and January 2005/ **Brighton & Hove Albion** (L) August 2005 to May 2006/ **West Bromwich Albion** August 2006/ **Sunderland** July 2007 to August 2009/ **Hull City** (L) August 2008 to January 2009/ **Hull City** August 2009 to present/ **Barnsley** (L) February to May 2011/ **Crystal Palace** (L) January to May 2012

Raised in the north of County Wicklow, Paul McShane comes from a family with a strong sporting history. His father, Sean, played Gaelic football and hurling for both Raleny and Dublin while his grandfather, Bob Mockler, was a famous Irish hurler. The young McShane was an accomplished Gaelic footballer himself and had a connection with Newtownmountkennedy GAA Club, as well as captaining the Wicklow under-14 side, before deciding to concentrate on football. A United supporter from as long ago as he can remember, his knowledge of the physical side of the game was learned as a young boy at school and also by *'playing on the green'* in Kilpedder with his older brother.

Distinguished by a shock of spiky ginger hair, at the age of eight he linked up with the local Greystones soccer team. Then moving to Newtownmountkennedy F.C., at the age of thirteen he joined St. Joseph's Boys Club in Dublin and was spotted by United scout Geoff Watson while starring for Eire Boys under-14's.

Over a period of time no less than eighteen English clubs showed their interest in signing him and he visited a number of them, including Leeds, Leicester, Manchester City, Sunderland, Wolves and Blackburn, before attending a trial at Old Trafford in 2002 that proved pivotal to his immediate future. Recalling how the club captain came to influence his decision, he revealed, *'I was considering an offer from Leeds when Roy Keane convinced me that the only place to learn my trade was with United. Of course, I accepted his advice. When I got to Manchester I shared living accommodation in Sale with Tom Heaton, but I was actually suffering from a stress fracture in my back.'*

As his new team-mates prepared themselves for the oncoming season, McShane was confined to the treatment table and while receiving attention he began to adjust to life at a football club by getting involved in the normal banter with Gary Neville, Rio Ferdinand, Quinton Fortune and David May, who were all also recovering from various injuries. Absent from the opening three fixtures, his qualities were evidenced in his first outing for the under-17's, a 2-1 win at Liverpool. If anyone expected him to ease his way back to full fitness, they would have underestimated the teenager's resolve as he thoroughly deserved the 'Man of the Match' nomination. An unrepentant yet honest performer who was consistent, constantly committed and relished a battle, after only five games he was placed in the under-19 team.

Forming a formidable barrier with either Phil Bardsley or Mark Howard as an ever-present for that season's victorious Youth Cup team, his potential was recognised when he was drafted into the Reserve squad towards the end of the term.

The 2003/04 campaign was one of consolidation on both domestic and international fronts and he began it by captaining the young Reds to victory in the Northern Ireland Milk Cup. He had made just four starts for the under-19's when chosen for his Premier Reserve League debut, a 3-1 home win over Birmingham on the second day of October, and the following month he was installed as the skipper of the Youth Cup side that defeated Rushden & Diamonds. As injuries sustained on a regular basis curtailed his progress to some extent, they didn't prevent him from continuing with the captaincy until the Youth Cup run ended at Blackburn the following March, nor did they stop him from representing the Republic of Ireland at youth level on occasions.

With international call-ups and knocks ruling out some of Alex Ferguson's senior stars, in July 2004 he got the nod to join a United senior party that travelled to America as part of their pre-season preparations. He acquitted himself well in front of 58,000 fans against Bayern Munich in Chicago and was invited off the bench partway through the next game against Celtic in Philadelphia.

McShane had made ten starts in the Reserve League North before being named as a substitute for a Champions League tie with Fenerbahce in Turkey in early December and, while not called on during the 3-0 defeat, it was a taster that would hold him in good stead.

Just before Christmas arrived, Walsall player/manager Paul Merson snapped him up on a loan deal that would yield four League One appearances. In relation to the signing, a delighted Merson claimed, *'I'm well pleased because he's a good player. Manchester United think very highly of him and I've got no worries (about) throwing him in against Sheffield Wednesday.'* Still aged only eighteen, he went straight into the Saddlers' squad that travelled to Hillsborough on Boxing Day. It proved to be a game of mixed fortunes, though, as Walsall's five-match unbeaten run ended with a 3-2 defeat and the rookie was cautioned before pulling a goal back with a header at the far post.

Then featuring for Eire's under-21 side for the first time during a 3-1 defeat by Israel in Tel Aviv in March 2005, two months later he took part in four cup finals in the space of just eleven days. Kicking off with a Pontin's League Cup victory on the 2nd May, three days later he was with the young Reds when they won the Blue Stars tournament in Zurich. By the ninth of the month he had been active in a Premier Reserve League Cup final and just 72 hours after that defeat he added a third winner's medal as the Reserves licked Charlton in a National Play-off head-to-head at The Valley.

With the encouragement of a very successful campaign behind him, McShane was utilised in numerous pre-season friendly games in 2005 and he caught the attention of a number of clubs, including Swindon and Falkirk. In the end he agreed to a loan deal with Brighton & Hove Albion that was supposed to stretch to the last day of the year until later being extended to encompass the whole term. Clocking up 40 games for the Seagulls, and despite them finishing bottom of the Championship table, he gained the 'Player of the Season' and 'Away Fans' Player of the Season' awards. Considering it was improbable that he would sign for the club on a permanent basis, those achievements spoke volumes for his attitude.

While he was forging such a good impression on the south coast, Alex Ferguson signed Nemanja Vidic. It spelt out the bare fact that he was never going to make the manager's A-list and, now surplus to requirements, West Bromwich Albion stepped in when he was made available on a free transfer. The Baggies made use of him in 32 Championship matches as they ended the season in fourth position, only to then make a vast profit by selling him to Sunderland for an initial £1,500,000 fee which could eventually have cost them another £1milllion. By the time that manager Roy Keane was moved to call his new capture *'a terrific character,'* he was more usually found in the right full-back position because his height was probably an inch or three short of what was required from a central defender at that standard.

He did his reputation no harm at all when winning a first full cap for the

Republic of Ireland in October 2006. With the Irish gaining a creditable draw against the Czech Republic in a Euro 2008 qualifier, once again he won the 'Man of the Match' award.

The Guardian newspaper carried an article about him in April 2007, which was penned by Steve Claridge. The former Leicester, Birmingham and Portsmouth striker was glowing in his praise by claiming that he *'does not hide from his responsibilities on or off the ball'* and that the Irishman represented *'the type a manager appreciates because he knows exactly what he's going to get every week.'*

Hull City took him on loan at the beginning of the 2008/09 term and he was one of the players that did so much to get their inaugural Premier League campaign off to such a good start. The personal highlight of his nineteen outings for the Tigers was undoubtedly when scoring the opening goal in a 2-2 draw at Anfield in December 2008. A month later he was recalled to the Stadium of Light as Sunderland struggled in their attempt to sign a defender in the transfer window.

In August 2009, he transferred to Hull City for an undisclosed fee believed to be £1.5million and, even though he has been farmed out to Barnsley and Crystal Palace for spells, Paul McShane remains with the Yorkshire club to this day.

EVANS, Corry John (2005/06, 2006/07, 2007/08)

Born: Newtownabbey, Belfast, 30th July 1990
Height: 5ft. 11ins., Weight: 11st. 8lbs.
Role: Midfielder or defender
Career: Covenant Christian School (Whiteabbey, Belfast)/ Monkstown Secondary School (Belfast)/ Ashton-on-Mersey School/ UNITED: Scholar July 2006 Pro. July 2009 to July 2011/ Carlisle United (L) October and November 2010/ Hull City (L) January to May 2011/ Hull City July 2011 to present

'A star was born in Maribor and that star's name was Corry Evans. When you look at Corry you simply see a boy — and he's just a boy aged twenty — but look deeper and you'll understand some of the sacrifices Northern Ireland's best young footballing talent have to make to hit the big time'. So ran a section of an article in the Belfast Star newspaper after Corry Evans had gone on as a substitute to score the winning goal on his competitive full international debut against Slovenia in September 2010. It represented a fourth appearance for his country and a solitary strike from him proved enough to give Northern Ireland the points in what was an important European Championship Qualifier.

The goal was set up by debutant and ex-Red Craig Cathcart, a late replacement for Evans' older brother Jonny who had failed a fitness test, and as the ball was crossed low into the box, Corry was on hand to place the ball confidently into the back of the net with his first touch. While the joyous visiting supporters sang *'There's only one Corry Evans'*, he gave his reaction after the game by saying, *'I didn't know what to do to be honest as I don't score many goals. It was just a great moment for myself and also all my family and all the fans.'*

His road to international fame started in the modest north Belfast family home of Jackie and Dawn Evans. His father had been a junior at Chelsea and later plied his trade at Barnet before returning to Ulster to work at airplane builders Short Brothers while also turning out for Crusaders at weekends.

Like his older brother, Corry starred for Greenisland Boys Club. When Jonny was offered an opportunity to sign for Manchester United it was too good a chance to turn down and so Corry was forced into leaving high school in his first year when the family relocated over to England. Jackie, who had just lost his job at Shorts before bringing the boys to Manchester to chase their footballing dreams, always believed in their talents and was willing to risk uprooting the whole family in order to give them the best chance of making the grade.

Due to rules in force there, had he remained in Northern Ireland the younger Evans wouldn't have been able to sign forms for any club, but United got his signature on their under-14 Academy forms and effectively fended off all competition for him until he reached the age of sixteen. The confidence held in him by the Old Trafford coaching staff was further demonstrated when he received a trainee contract on his 16th birthday.

It wasn't only at the club where he experienced a settling in period because, as he detailed, there was also the matter of his continued education to consider, *'It was hard when we first moved. Having to move across to a different country and a new school was my biggest concern. My dad had confidence in my ability, but he said that either way it was going to be good for my football. He said that I would improve because I would get better coaching and that wouldn't happen at just any Academy. I would be playing more times a week and at a better standard. He tried to reassure me and looking back it has helped me a lot being at United from such an early age instead of only moving at sixteen. With a manager like Sir Alex Ferguson and a club like Manchester United, you know that down the years they have always given young players a chance.'*

His first competitive match came in the under-18 Academy side's third match of the 2005/06 season. Five more starts saw him impress enough to get a place on the bench for the Reserves' Manchester Senior Cup tie against Oldham and even though the Reds were losing heavily, it was a significant moment for the fifteen year-old schoolboy when he substituted for Sam Hewson. His development continued six weeks later, this time when replacing David Gray in a Youth Cup tie at Birmingham, and he also played three times for Northern Ireland Boys in the Victory Shield that term, his last minute goal providing a 1-0 win over England at Chester.

The following season saw him increase his appearances for the under-18 Academy side from eight to seventeen and he was also included in the squad that entered into an exciting and prolonged Youth Cup run. Named as a substitute for the opening rounds, he was drafted into the team at full-back for the semi-final second leg meeting with Arsenal in place of the injured Tom Cleverley. A fabulous victory set up a final clash with Lancashire rivals Liverpool and, commencing both ties, the Belfast boy had to content himself with a runner's up medal on this occasion.

In August 2007, United were invited to send a youth team to Malaysia to participate in the inaugural Champions Youth Cup. Starting every game as the young Reds defeated Juventus 1-0 in the final to record a prestigious victory, once back in Manchester he was named as captain of the Academy under-18 team and his versatility allowed him to take up a variety of roles in midfield and across the back four. In the October of that season he made his Reserve League debut at Middlesbrough and despite a disappointing early Youth Cup exit to Carlisle, a full international bow against Italy in the June provided ample compensation. Having already represented Northern Ireland at under-17, under-19 and under-21 levels, his elevation into the big time was due reward for all of his previous efforts and sacrifices.

Going on to become practically a permanent fixture for the Reserves over the next couple of years, once again showing his adaptability by playing in every position except goalkeeper and striker, his level-headed approach on the pitch resulted in him being named as captain for the second half of the 2008/09 term, a period during which he led the side to victory in the Manchester Senior Cup as well as being nominated as a first-team substitute at Hull on the last day of the campaign. Lancashire Senior Cup and Barclays Premier Reserve League titles were added in the 2009/10 season, and he was also named on the bench for the seniors in the Carling Cup at Barnsley.

His progress was acknowledged with inclusion on the seniors' tour to the USA in July 2010 and while there he took part in his one and only first-team match when competing in a friendly against Philadelphia Union. However, the competition for senior places in Manchester United's midfield was as stiff as ever and in October he spent a one-month loan at Carlisle, making a solitary appearance for the Cumbrians at Bristol Rovers. Loaned out again in January 2011, this time to Hull, because former Reds James Chester and Cameron Stewart were already at the club, he settled quickly to become an important member of the side. With his thirst for regular first-team football one of urgent necessity, it was announced in the April that he would be joining the Tigers permanently in the close season.

Corry Evans was a credit to the Reds both on and off the pitch throughout his time with the club, and his positive, determined attitude and professionalism for someone so young stood him apart from a number of his peers. With those and many other attributes, it seems that he is set for a long career in the game.

HEWSON, Sam (2005/06, 2006/07)

Born: Bolton, 28th November 1988
Height: 5ft. 6ins., Weight: 11st. 8lbs.
Role: Midfielder
Career: Brandwood Primary School (Bolton)/ Westhoughton High School/ Bolton Boys/ UNITED: Scholar July 2005 Pro. 2007 to June 2010/ Hereford United (L) January to April 2009/ Bury (L) February to May 2010/ Altrincham September 2010 to March 2011/ Knattspyrnufélagið Fram (Nor) July 2011 to present

It is said that players don't need to be told when they are performing well because everything they try seems to come off and as a consequence their confidence increases. For an eight-month period between January and August 2007, Sam Hewson was probably playing the best football of his career. Little did anyone know at the time but he had reached the peak of his powers and despite going on to appear in the Football League while on loan, he never came near to attaining the same level again.

A mainstay of the club's under-18 Academy side, the midfielder's impressive form at the beginning of the 2006/07 season secured him a place in England's under-19 squad for the regional stages of the European Championships in Austria. Leaving the bench to make his international bow in a 1-1 draw with Spain and then starting the following match against the host nation, it was a surprise call-up, if only because he had been omitted from youth squads at under-16 and under-17 levels in the past.

As Christmas came and went, Hewson mined a rich vein of form for United's under-18's in both the Academy and the Youth Cup. Finding the net in the latter competition against Southampton and Crystal Palace in the Fourth and Fifth Rounds respectively, his brace in a 2-0 win over Birmingham set up a classic semi-final clash with the young guns of Arsenal. With the Reds a goal down after the first leg, his industry in the middle of the park went a long way towards supplying the ammunition for a stunning comeback in what ranks as one of the greatest youth games ever seen at Old Trafford.

United then faced Liverpool in the final, and with Craig Cathcart unavailable, Paul McGuinness nominated him as captain. Delivering a commanding performance at Anfield in the first leg, the stand-in skipper kept his nerve to give the Reds an advantage by knocking in a spot kick at the Kop. However, he turned from hero to villain during the second leg when, with the teams level after extra-time, his miss in the penalty shoot-out was a major factor in Liverpool retaining the trophy.

With a total of seven under-19 caps under his ownership, Hewson was included in the United squad that travelled to Asia to participate in the new Champions Youth Cup at the beginning of the 2007/08 term. His displays in Malaysia were, quite simply, superb. Taking a role in front of the back four, behind the lone striker or in a more traditional central midfield role, his drive and tenacity was key to the Reds' success while two goals against Flamengo in the semi-final capped one of his finest showings in a red shirt. Whatever disappointment he may have felt at losing the F.A. Youth Cup was put to the back of his mind when collecting a winner's medal after facing some of the world's best youth teams.

It had been a wonderful 2007 so far. Unfortunately, emulating or building on that triumph would prove to be easier said than done.

The native Boltonian was first discovered by United scouts while attached to AFC Walkers and he joined the Academy as an eight year-old. A sporting all-rounder who represented Bolton at both football and cricket as a schoolboy, he was subsequently the recipient of an 'Outstanding Award for Individual Sporting Success' from his school.

While progressing through the junior ranks at Old Trafford, his small size belied his ability on the ball and fiercely competitive nature. First appearing in the under-17 side in the 2003/04 campaign, because the Academy structure was changed for the 2004/05 season he was only able to make a solitary appearance for the under-18's before cementing his place at that grade and in the Youth Cup team during the following term.

It was then when his performances started to be noticed and led up to his eight 'purple patch' months of impressive displays, which culminated with the success in Malaysia.

Over the next eighteen months he seemed to stagnate in the Reserves. The Bolton Wanderers season ticket holder continued to collect silverware, though, as the second string defeated his hometown club to lift the Manchester Senior Cup in May 2008 and the Lancashire Senior Cup with a win over Liverpool three months later. His place came under pressure, because both Matty James and Danny Drinkwater were pushing hard for a place from the under-18's and Rodrigo Possebon was trying to stake his claim after obtaining international clearance. Loaned out to League Two club Hereford early in 2009, the Edgar Street club benefited from ten of his appearances before the end of campaign.

While some have found that a loan period acts as a springboard to greater things, Hewson lacked his usual fire at the commencement of the 2009/10 season. Taking part in another Lancashire Senior Cup final win in August only to then find himself in and out of the Reserves, his goal against Bury in the Manchester Senior Cup led to them asking for his services and he duly signed a loan agreement with the Gigg Lane club in January 2010. His last game for United was, ironically, against Bolton's Reserves on the 28th of that month and, with his time at Bury yielding only one start and six substitute appearances in the league, the spell did little to further his now faltering prospects.

With little interest shown by any potential new employers, and his form over the last couple of years or so largely underwhelming, the midfielder was released and eventually signed for Altrincham. However, without being able to break into the Conference team on a regular basis, and unwilling to spend his time on the bench, he left them a few months later.

In the summer of 2011, Sam Hewson was trialled by Fram and the Norwegian club later gave him the chance to revive his career by offering him a two-year contract.

FOX, David Lee (2000/01, 2001/02)

Born: Stoke-on-Trent, 13th December 1983
Height: 5ft. 9ins., Weight: 12st. 2lbs.
Role: Central midfielder
Career: **East Budleigh Primary School (Devon)/ Exmouth Community College (Devon)/ East Devon Boys/ Devon Boys/ England Boys/ UNITED**: Trainee July 2000 Pro. December 2000 to January 2006/ **Royal Antwerp** (Bel) (L) July 2003 to January 2004/ **Shrewsbury Town** (L) October and November 2004/ **Blackpool** January 2006/ **Colchester United** June 2009/ **Norwich City** June 2010 to present

If attitude, application and dedication were the only attributes required to become a top footballer, David Fox would today be sitting at the apex of the soccer tree and only a couple of vital ingredients in his make-up have prevented him from doing so.

A hard working and conscientious individual who benefits from an acute sense of what is going on around him on the pitch, the midfielder demonstrates equal ability when making either long or short passes and, seemingly always with time to spare, he is constantly available to support his colleagues. Despite lacking pace and a little tenacity, some think his style is cast from the same mould of former United favourite Ray Wilkins.

While appearing to possess many of the credentials required for further progress within the club, he started the first five games of the Reserves' 2004/05 Barclays Premiership campaign with a clear understanding that his long-term future was going to be away from M16. An opportunity to join League Two club Shrewsbury arose in early October and, upon agreeing to a month-long loan deal, his commencing game for the Shropshire club was against Rushden & Diamonds on the eighth of that month.

Once back he alternated between both of United's Reserve teams and was often named as captain, which offered up the responsibility of lending support to the younger players around him. He was later utilised in Rotherham's second string while taking a trial at Millmoor in early March, and the Championship club's attempt to sign him prior to the transfer deadline was thwarted only because he had already committed to undergoing an assessment with a Dutch Eredivisie side, ADO Den Haag. Nothing came of his trip to the Netherlands and, despite making a huge contribution towards the Reds' two Reserve sides exercising a virtual clean sweep of trophies, first-team status was as far away as ever.

With his contract due to expire at the end of the 2005/06 term, once it got underway he needed to seriously consider his future direction. By January 2006 he had accepted League One Blackpool's offer of an eighteen-month contract and his last game for the Reds was in a 5-1 win over Leeds Reserves soon after.

Spending his early schooldays in the Potteries, he found himself in Devon when his well-known goalkeeper father, Peter Fox, left Stoke City for Exeter City in 1993. Aside from his involvement with school football, the youngster also played for Budleigh Salterton, a local boys club that participated in the Devon League. Going on to win honours for East Devon Boys and Devon Boys, he was then capped at both under-15 and under-16 levels for England and put in one trial appearance for United's under-15 side in April 1999.

'I was attached to Exeter City's School of Excellence at a time when I was too young to sign schoolboy terms for them,' he explained. 'While I was at Exeter, United's Academy Director, Les Kershaw, got to know about me because he owned a holiday home in the area. I had been spending a few weekends with Arsenal before I got Les' invitation to have a trial at Old Trafford. I joined the Academy in April 2000 and a few days later I was playing at the Bludenz Youth Tournament in Austria.'

At the outset of his first full season, Fox was plunged into action in the Northern Ireland Milk Cup and as early as September the newcomer gained selection for the England (under-17) Youth team in matches against the Czech Republic, Sweden and Poland.

Nominated one of the places on the bench for all three of that campaign's Youth Cup ties, his only run out came in the 8-0 slaughter of Scunthorpe. He was present for all bar one under-17 Academy matches as the Reds topped the table by two points over Aston Villa and added two further England Youth caps to his haul by facing France and Holland.

Then making the natural progression into the under-19 Academy side at the beginning of the 2001/02 term, just several games in, on the 25th October, he substituted for Philip Neville to make his Premier Reserve League debut in a 1-0 victory against Aston Villa. It was a fabulous opening to the season for him as he had also featured twice for England at under-19 level earlier that month against Iceland and Russia. While making the occasional appearance from the substitute's bench for the Reserves, his maturity and respect from his fellows stood him out as the obvious candidate to skipper that campaign's Youth Cup team. The four-game run was curtailed by Barnsley when a poor shoot-out performance saw him as the only one of the home side to convert a penalty.

By April 2002 his under-19 side had finished second in the league, equal on points with Liverpool, only to miss out on a place in the play-offs. He was later capped twice more for England, having featured in both European Youth Championship Qualifiers against Lithuania, and with enough appearances to qualify for a Reserve League winner's medal, on the last day of the term he and his team-mates were honoured on the Old Trafford pitch.

His 2002/03 season looked very similar to the last, with him predominantly turning out for the under-19's and getting a few games in the Reserves. Over the duration he also piled up no less than nine youth caps at under-20 level, the first being for his inclusion against Germany in October and the last for an appearance against Japan in June.

Shortly after being loaned out to Royal Antwerp with Colin Heath, he was again called on to represent the England under-20's. The contest against Wales took place in Stoke, the city of his birth, and resulted in a 2-0 win to the host nation. The following month he was selected to represent England in the World Youth Championships in the United Arab Emirates and clocked up minutes on the pitch in group games against Japan and Columbia. All told, his appearances at youth level for England had now swollen to 22.

Following his return from Belgium at the turn of 2004, Fox figured in seven games for the Reserves and secured another domestic honour when taking part in United's 3-1 victory over Manchester City in the Manchester Senior Cup final. He would remain at Old Trafford for another twenty months but, while greatly respected, his failure to crack through the senior barrier led to his eventual transfer to Blackpool.

He helped the Tangerines to League One success in the 2007 Play-off final when they defeated Yeovil to reach the Championship. However, in June 2009 he was one of eight players released by new manager Ian Holloway but was quickly snapped up by Colchester. Making his first start for them in their 7-1 opening day defeat of Norwich, when manager Paul Lambert joined the Canaries in the summer of 2010 he took the creative midfielder with him.

A superb first season with Norwich saw him make 32 appearances, and he capped off the term with an inch-perfect cross for Simeon Jackson's match-winning goal against Portsmouth in May 2011 which secured the Carrow Road club's return to the Premiership. On the maiden day of the 2011/12 campaign, David Fox picked up the unenviable record of the fastest booking on a Premiership debut when collecting a yellow card within 60 seconds of the start of a match against Wigan. Six weeks later he returned to Old Trafford for the first time since his transfer five years earlier.

THORPE, Thomas Joseph (2009/10, 2010/11)

Born: Manchester, 13th January 1993
Height: 6ft. 1in., **Weight:** 11st. 7lbs.
Role: Central defender
Career: Denton West Primary School/ Audenshaw High School/
UNITED: Scholar July 2009 Pro. July 2010 to present

Despite captaining United's victorious 2011 Youth Cup side, Tom Thorpe didn't receive anywhere near the number of accolades afforded to some of his more exalted colleagues. On first viewing, the centre-back might appear to be lacking a little height or speed in relation to some of those he is expected to mark. However, those who have seen him a number of times will willingly testify that the lad isn't often beaten in the air, his positional sense is such that he is rarely lacking when the ball is on the deck, and his tackling technique is so clean and crisp that he is hardly ever penalised for free kicks.

Consequently, by the time Sheffield United had been dismantled in the second leg of the Youth Cup final, his communication skills, increased strength, on-field intelligence and natural ability as a leader were drawing comparisons to Martin Buchan, the club's legendary captain of the 1970's and early 1980's.

When the club's teenagers travelled to Anfield for the Youth Cup quarter-final tie against Liverpool, a back injury put his place in doubt and those in the know felt his absence would represent a major loss. While the likes of Paul Pogba, Ryan Tunnicliffe and Ravel Morrison had been getting lots of positive publicity, his form in the heart of the Reds' defence was still largely unnoticed. Yet for the hardy souls who frequent Carrington at weekends he had been one of the most consistent performers in the under-18 team for the previous twelve months and fortunately he was just about fit enough for the game on Merseyside, where the Reds secured a fantastic 3-2 victory.

While a pupil of Denton West Primary School, his football skills were developed when turning out for West End Boys on Saturday mornings. Originally a right winger who scored a mammoth 65 goals in his first season, they included eleven in a match against Mossley. Around the same time he attended a Friday night 'football clinic' at Denton's Egerton Park School with Lincoln Delve, a local scout and coach. Only six years-old, Thorpe was asked to come back for a few weeks, a time period which was eventually extended to twelve months and encompassed regular visits to The Cliff on Sunday afternoons. By the time he moved to Audenshaw High School, Thorpe had been selected for Tameside Boys. Unfortunately, every time the town team came calling the dates clashed with his training schedule at United and so the chance of securing representative honours escaped him.

He skippered the club's under-15 team to the quarter-finals of the 2008 Nike Premier Cup and after then appearing in a few games for the under-16's, the defender gained a first international sighting in a 6-0 win over Northern Ireland at Ballymena. Also featuring in a 2-0 win over Scotland at Lincoln to help England Boys lift the Victory Shield, his promotion into United's Academy under-18 side followed in December.

A mainstay and captain of the Reds' under-16 team for most of the 2008/09 season, the Mancunian also managed a total of six under-18 appearances and collected further international honours when England's under-16 side defeated Germany to win the Montaigu Tournament in April.

The first year scholar made the transition into the under-18's look seamless during the 2009/10 campaign. Getting off to a great start when leading the youth team to success in the Northern Ireland Milk Cup final with a 2-1 victory over Sheffield United, the following month he was elevated into the England under-17 set-up for a friendly against Turkey at Northampton.

Thorpe made his Youth Cup bow in a victory over Birmingham in December. Substituted due to picking up a knock early in the game and subsequently sidelined for several weeks, by the time he had recovered the teenage Reds were out of the competition.

Upon returning, he was ever present in the Academy side until the season drew to a close as the under-18's topped Group C. Later included in the national under-17 squad that competed in the European Championships in Liechtenstein, a progressive year ended on a fabulous high when England defeated Spain 2-1 in the final to become champions for the first time.

The 2010/11 term saw him mature into a calm and collected centre-back who distributes the ball well out of defence and looks composed in possession. Present for all eight matches on a fabulous Youth Cup run, Tom Thorpe is definitely someone to look out for, a fact evidenced when he was named as England's under-19 captain for the European Championship finals in Estonia in July 2012.

While he may not capture many headlines, the local boy is set for a bright future in the game and his many admirers are keeping their fingers crossed that he turns out to be one of the best central defenders the club has produced in many years.

GIBSON, Darron Thomas Daniel
(2004/05, 2005/06)

Born: Londonderry, 25th October 1987
Height: 6ft., Weight: 13st.
Role: Midfielder
Career: **Holy Family Primary School (Londonderry)/ St. Columb's College (Londonderry)/ Londonderry Boys/ Northern Ireland Boys/ UNITED**: Trainee December 2003 Pro. July 2004 to January 2012/ **Royal Antwerp** (Bel) (L) August 2006 to June 2007/ **Wolverhampton Wanderers** (L) October 2007 to April 2008/ **Everton** January 2012 to present

It might have taken a long time, but during the 2010/11 term Darron Gibson finally made enough headway into Manchester United's first-team to qualify him for a Premier League championship medal and in doing so became the only Red from Derry to win such an honour.

Over the previous two years he was on the periphery of the senior squad. Mainly involved in cup ties while often gaining exposure to league football from the bench, Gibson put in 91 minutes in the 2009 Carling Cup final win over Spurs and went on to make a cameo appearance in the same competition's showpiece a year later when Aston Villa were put to the sword.

While some may have complained about the lack of opportunity, the midfielder had been at Old Trafford long enough to understand how United's squad system operated and, as he detailed at the time, he was also young enough to take a longer term view, *'The spirit is so good within the squad and everyone is so tight together, no-one wants to upset it. This is a great club and we have a great manager who knows what he is doing and how to keep players happy. We have a good group at the minute. Hopefully it will stay like that for a long time.*

Sir Alex Ferguson is probably the greatest manager ever, so it does give you confidence when he talks to you and tells you that you can win him a game. But when you are a younger player, you have to wait for your chance. When it comes along you have to take it. There is a little extra pressure because you have to prove you can do as well, if not better, than the players who are in every week. Luckily for me this season, when I came back from injuries, there were a few others who were out as well. I got my chance, have kicked on from there and played a few games since.'

The eldest son of John and Liz Gibson, who hail from the Hazelbank area of Ballymagroarty, in 1999 he won the Derry & District Primary Schools' 'A' league and cup double with Holy Family under the management of Mr. John Meehan. Holy Family then went on to claim the Northern Ireland Primary Schools' title and, just for good measure, the prestigious Walker's seven-a-side tournament with Gibson captaining the side. Remaining unbeaten throughout the year, it was during Holy Family's Northern Ireland Cup run when the team's skipper was first spotted by a number of scouts representing English Premiership clubs.

He travelled over to Aston Villa on numerous occasions from the age of twelve and Arsenal took him to a summer tournament in Holland. Besides the interest of those two heavyweights, the hot prospect went through trials with Newcastle, Leicester, Leeds, Charlton, Manchester City and Sunderland as well as Manchester United. Having furthered his knowledge of the sport under the tutelage of his uncle and former Derry City under-21 manager Paul 'Oxo' McLaughlin, the player became involved with the local Maiden City Soccer School where he represented Institute F.C. at underage level.

Despite winning schoolboy caps for the country of his birth, a dispute in obtaining a release from their squad to play for United led to him changing allegiance and creating a few ripples on the west side of the Irish Sea. The holder of an Irish passport, he switched to representing the Republic of Ireland and debuted for their under-17 side in the Four Nations tournament in Hungary in August 2003.

During his trial period in Manchester, the Ulster lad was utilised in the under-17 Academy side when they drew 1-1 at Crewe in December 2003. He then added a further four appearances at that level and gained one outing for the under-19's prior to joining the Reds on a full-time basis in the 2004 shutdown period.

In his first full term in England he featured predominantly for the under-18's and also gathered up a handful of starts in the Pontin's West Reserve League. He additionally made significant progress in international terms by representing Eire at under-18 and under-19 levels. Consequently named in the Republic of Ireland side that faced England in a friendly international at Cork in September 2004, while there he came into competition with United team-mates Tom Heaton and Ritchie Jones.

He was used as a substitute when the Reserves opened their 2005/06 campaign with a 3-0 away win over Bolton. Gibson went on to finish with 21 league appearances at that standard, on top of turning out eleven times for the Academy side, and because of an injury to Jonny Evans, the captaincy of the Youth Cup side was thrust upon him for the ties against Charlton and Manchester City. Equally comfortable with both feet, technically proficient, possessed of an alert mind and known for an ability to strike the ball with incredible force, with that season's 'Jimmy Murphy Young Player of the Year' award situated on his mantelpiece, there was talk even then that he seemed to have all the makings of future first-team material.

With a view to accelerating his development, it was decided to send him out on loan. He spent a full season at Royal Antwerp and then the majority of another at Wolves, though whether the experiences gained at those locations benefited him to the extent expected is questionable. During the short time spent back at Old Trafford in the middle of those loan periods, he broke into the full Eire side for a 4-0 defeat by Denmark in August 2007.

Over a period of three years his exposure to United's senior scene increased steadily. Called from the bench only once in the 2007/08 term, he was given nine starts and made six substitute appearances in the 2008/09 campaign, while twelve starts and eleven substitute showings ratcheted up his experience considerably in the 2009/10 season.

He turned down a move to Sunderland in the 2011 recess, apparently because of a failure to agree personal terms, after which Alex Ferguson kept him on the outer fringes of his plans.

With over a half century of appearances to his name in United's senior team, as well as a full cap count which runs well into double figures, Darron Gibson decided his future lay away from Old Trafford in January 2012 when opting for a switch to Everton that gives him the security of a four and a half year contract and the prospect of more minutes on the pitch.

SZMID, Marek Andrzej (1999/00)

Born: Nuneaton, 2nd March 1982
Height: 5ft. 8in., Weight: 11st. 6lbs.
Role: Central defender
Career: **Our Lady of the Angels Primary School (Nuneaton)/ St. Joseph's R.C. Middle School (Nuneaton)/ Higham Lane High School (Nuneaton)/ Nuneaton Boys/ Nuneaton & District Boys/ Warwickshire Boys/ England Boys/ UNITED**: Trainee July 1998 Pro. September 1999 to June 2001/ **Southend United** November 2001/ **Sutton Coldfield Town** August 2002/ **Nuneaton Griff** August 2003/ **Nuneaton Borough** July 2004/ **Nuneaton Griff** October 2004 to May 2005/ **Vauxhall Motors** July to September 2005

Explaining the origins of his roots, Marek Szmid said, *'Our family is of Polish descent on my father's side while my mum is from Staffordshire. My dad is from Manchester and he only moved to Nuneaton to take up a teaching post after graduating.'* About his early days in football, he revealed, *'I played for Chetwynd Squirrels on Sunday afternoons in the Coventry League when I was seven and three years later I joined Coventry City's School of Excellence. I was only ten when I was picked for the Nuneaton Boys under-12's and I was then selected for the (Nuneaton &) District side from under-13 up to under-16. I also represented the county for three years. I played for Coventry from under-10 to under-12 before playing for Aston Villa's School of Excellence under-12's to under-14's.'*

In 1996, at the end of Villa's under-14 campaign, Geoff Watson, the Reds' scout who had initially discovered him, made arrangements for Szmid, Josh Walker and Jimmy Davis to move to United en bloc and in return the Birmingham club received some measure of financial compensation.

What would develop into a terrific involvement on the international scene began for him in the 1997/98 season when representing England Boys against Belgium in Brussels. He then played against Wales at Bury and Northern Ireland at Barnsley, but by far the most indelible memory of that period came when he faced up to Brazil at Wembley. The Midlander performed against the South Americans again at Middlesbrough and then added six more appearances to his record by participating in the Montaigu (under-15 World Cup) Schoolboy Tournament in France where England defeated Italy in a third/fourth place play-off.

Also seeing service against Hungary at Old Trafford, that fruitful passage of his career was rounded off when England Boys scored a single goal victory over Germany in Berlin in front of a crowd that numbered 67,000.

A versatile type who could do himself justice at right-back or centre-back, his best position was undoubtedly as a holding midfielder. As someone who tackled fiercely, was highly industrious, read the game well and passed the ball accurately, he possessed all the attributes required to excel in the role.

Commencing on divisional duty for the Reds in September 1998 while stationed on the right-hand side of midfield, he missed only three league games for the under-17's that term, one of which came when he was aired at under-19 level. The others were as a result of him being required by England again, as he took part in two European Championship under-16 Qualifiers against Turkey and squeezed in a friendly against Scotland prior to resuming in another Euro Qualifying match against Cyprus in Paphos.

United's under-17's ended their campaign as league champions, but he was unavailable for the opening two play-off games because there were still international obligations to fulfil. The national side made quite a fist of it at the European Championship finals in the Czech Republic by topping their group table. While there the Nuneaton teenager picked up three additional caps for his appearances against Sweden, Hungary and the host nation, with the Czechs eventually defeating England during extra-time in the quarter-final via a 'golden goal' decider.

He returned to feature in the Reds' unsuccessful semi-final play-off against Blackburn and after a highly eventful year he was glad of a break.

Szmid made the transition to the older age group when installed as the captain of the under-19's. His superb attendance record continued as he missed only four matches out of their 1999/00 season, and for three of those games he was on the bench.

In the December of that term he was situated out of position when skippering the Youth Cup team that crashed out of the tournament at the opening hurdle against Nottingham Forest and he also got the nod to play for England against Luxembourg before withdrawing through injury.

The going was certainly proving tougher, because he felt the club weren't maximising his full capabilities. *'I wasn't very happy,'* he shrugged. *'I was being utilised all across the back four but mostly in the centre of defence. The year before I had been situated on the right side of midfield and I didn't feel that either of those roles really suited me. I was a regular in central midfield for England and I felt that I was missing out on the opportunity to develop in that position. It was, after all, the role I was more likely to make a career out of.'*

He started by sitting on the bench all the way through the Reserves' opening eight fixtures of the following term. At the same time now and again used in the Manchester Senior Cup, following a start in the Premier Reserve League North defeat by Manchester City in December 2000 he disappeared off that scene completely through picking up an injury a few weeks later.

If the news of his free transfer was bad, there was more in store when an avenue of opportunity closed on him before it had fully opened. *'I was offered a contract by one particular club only for them to withdraw it while I was still recovering,'* he said ruefully. Szmid was soon to regret rushing back before recovering properly as, over the 2001 close season while on trial at Rotherham, torn medial ligaments in his right knee caused him to break down again just as the warm-up matches were about to start.

There was a lull for a few months before he was assessed by Southend prior to being fixed up with a deal at Roots Hall until the end of that campaign. Even though he was delighted to have found employment again, his first-team contributions amounted to less than two matches. In February 2002, his Division Three entrance as a substitute concluded in a 5-1 defeat at Hartlepool and a few weeks later he found himself on from the kick-off for a 2-1 loss at Leyton Orient.

With the Shrimpers unwilling to extend his contract, in July 2002 he spent three weeks on trial at Peterborough. However, when the proposed ITV deal fell through, manager Barry Fry revealed that there was no spare money to sign him. Now at a juncture where a completely new career path was seen as the way forward, he took a U-turn into academic life by enrolling for a university degree in Liverpool. At the same time signing for Sutton Coldfield Town on a non-contract basis, he made himself available for the Southern League Western Division club from time to time while on home leave.

By August 2003 he had begun an ad hoc relationship with his local side, Nuneaton Griff, who were members of the Midland Combination Premier Division, and in a bid to maintain his fitness he also trained with Marine of the Unibond Premier Division.

Far from his association with football petering out, in January 2005 he was unexpectedly recalled back to the international arena when drafted into the England futsal squad. A five-a-side game which was originally developed in South America in the 1930's but is now played globally and is recognised by FIFA, it was put into the Football Association's strategy in 2001 and since then has been promoted throughout the United Kingdom.

Szmid marked his first appearance by scoring for the England futsal team in a 5-2 defeat by France in Lille and, adding further caps to his tally, he also played for his university side and Vauxhall Motors in the Conference North.

It was while appearing for the university team in September 2005 that he suffered a double fracture of his fibula and tibula which resulted in two operations to repair. Despite attempting a comeback, continual breakdowns and a knee operation forced him into calling it a day two years later. By then he had graduated with a 2:1 (Hons) in Sport Development & PE and that achievement was followed in 2008 with a teaching qualification.

Taking up the story to date, he mentioned, *'I was then employed as a PE teacher at Ashton-upon-Mersey School until I started working at the Manchester United Academy. During my time at the school I coached the Trafford and Greater Manchester representative teams and twice helped them to success in the ESFA National Cup. In addition, I had a sixth form team at the school that won the County Cup two years running and reached the last four of the National Cup.'*

Marek Szmid currently manages the Greater Manchester under-16 side, although he was forced to give up all other sporting commitments due to his United responsibilities. He carries the title of assistant head of education & welfare at Carrington and his main task is to co-ordinate the education programme for the club's under-18 Academy squad.

UNITED AT THEIR BEST

Chapter Eight

SONS OF UNITED

BECKETT, Terence (1954/55, 1955/56)

Born: Ancoats, Manchester, 17th October 1938
Height: 5ft. 6ins., Weight: 9st. 6lbs.
Role: Inside or outside-right
Career: St. Patrick's School (Collyhurst)/ Manchester Boys/ England Boys/ UNITED: Am. May 1954 to June 1956/ Manchester City August 1956/ Altrincham July 1957 to January 1959

Terry Beckett was a pupil at a school which was once noted for supplying players to Manchester United. St. Patrick's, in Collyhurst, also produced, most notably, two members of the Reds' 1968 European Cup winning team, namely Brian Kidd and Nobby Stiles.

Arriving at Old Trafford with a superb pedigree as a free-scoring forward, Beckett had been a member of the Manchester Boys side that lost 4-1 to Liverpool in the quarter-final of the English Schools' Trophy in 1953. That year also saw him chosen for his international debut in Belfast, which yielded a goal for him in an emphatic 7-0 win over Northern Ireland Boys. Selected as a reserve for a contest against Wales Boys at Watford in March 1954, a second England appearance came in that same year when another of his goals assisted towards a 3-3 draw with Eire Boys in Cork.

Silky skilled, the striker was equally effective operating in a wide role or as an inside-forward. Undoubtedly, though, his main attribute was that of a fox-like cunning in the penalty area and throughout an all too brief career his name was frequently found on the score sheet.

Not surprisingly, there was a queue of clubs willing to offer him an opening upon his leaving school and among the interested parties were Burnley, Preston and Spurs. Wolverhampton Wanderers was another suitor that craved him, so much so that one day their famous manager, Stan Cullis, travelled to Manchester with contract papers at the ready, in anticipation of securing a highly prized signature. Cullis turned up unexpectedly at his target's house in a black cab, a rare sight in a working class suburb of the city during the early to mid-1950's but, unfortunately from Wolves' point of view, the journey was a wasted one because the boy had committed himself to United just 24 hours earlier.

A 2-0 home win over a Rochdale side made his entrance to club affairs a satisfactory one and he went on to spend the majority of the 1954/55 season in the Colts, predominantly in his favoured inside-right position. With his goals a contributory factor, which included a haul of four against Stockport in late November, the Colts dropped a mere two points from their opening twenty fixtures.

It was that splendid form which gained him his introduction to Youth Cup affairs at Barnsley in December 1954. It was destined to be a sensational start as he notched the Reds' first two goals in a 4-2 victory after they had trailed 2-0 at half-time. Scoring in the next two Youth Cup games, against Sheffield Wednesday and Plymouth, his opener in the second leg of the final against West Brom at The Hawthorns made the destiny of the trophy a foregone conclusion. It was certainly a fabulous end to the term, because he also experienced the joy of winning both the Lancashire League and Supplementary Cup.

Beckett started the 1955/56 season with the Colts once again and was elevated to the 'A' team at outside-right in October. A knock meant that he was unavailable for the opening Youth Cup tie at Preston and upon returning to action he remained in the third string throughout November and December before resuming with the 'B' team thereafter.

He took part in four Youth Cup games that term, bagging goals against Newcastle and Bexleyheath & Welling, before losing his place for the second stage of the semi-final and the final games against Chesterfield.

In the summer of 1956 he was overlooked for the youth squad's tour to Switzerland and shortly after elected to join Manchester City on amateur forms. Making around seventeen appearances for City's 'A' team in a solitary season at Maine Road, he scored three times.

He then made the move to Cheshire League side Altrincham and it was something of a coup for the ambitious Robins to capture both him and another ex-Red, Noel McFarlane, for the start of the 1957/58 season. Just a couple of months later, the club's former United contingent increased to three when Tommy Littler arrived from Stockport County.

It took him only fifteen minutes of his first game to register a goal for Altrincham, in a win over Mossley at Moss Lane, and four days later a victory at Congleton caused the local newspaper to record that *'the speed and craft was still there with top honours going to McFarlane and Beckett'*.

Three months further on National Service suddenly interrupted, and he managed only two further appearances for Altrincham, both in the December of that term. While in the military he was stationed in Cyprus, amongst other places, where he regularly turned out for the Middle East Army side.

While enjoying a stretch of home leave in the early part of 1959, he made his final appearance for Altrincham against Chester Reserves at Moss Lane, typically scoring the opening goal on the two-minute mark as the home side cruised to a 7-0 win. On the following Tuesday he returned to Cyprus, unaware that he had played his final game on British soil.

Subsequently the victim of a serious back injury, whereupon he was never again able to run 'flat out', at just twenty years-old his football career, which had promised so much in the early days, came to an abrupt and premature end. The back problem sustained during his period of Army service not only curtailed his sporting activities, it later became progressively more debilitating over a period of time.

An electrician by trade, Terry Beckett can sometimes be seen around Old Trafford on match days. Retaining his United links by scouting for the club, he has performed the task continuously since way back in 1983.

MADDISON, Ray Wilfred (1956/57)

Born: Manchester, 13th June 1939
Height: 5ft. 11ins., Weight: 11st. 7lbs.
Role: Left full-back
Career: Plymouth Grove School (Longsight)/ UNITED: Am. May 1956 to April 1958/ Manchester City Am. 1958/ Nantlle Vale December 1958 to September 1960/ Hyde United 1961/62 season

Like the vast majority of boys of the immediate post-war generation, Ray Maddison learned how to play games such as cricket and head tennis out in the street. As far as football was concerned, the many countless hours spent on the cobbles helped him to develop into a two-footed, adaptable type who opponents didn't find easy to get past. He also excelled at dribbling, was difficult to beat in the air and distributed the ball precisely.

Attending a school that fielded three soccer sides of varying ability, a juniors, a shield team and a cup eleven, his talent for the sport ensured that he progressed through all the grades from the former and into the latter. Also trialled for Manchester Boys, his absence from a schools' cup final was caused through a family vacation to Canada which lasted for five months. At the age of fifteen he linked up with Gorton Lads Club for a couple of years and his contributions for them were acknowledged when he was chosen to represent the Manchester Boys Club League against their counterparts from Sheffield.

Maddison signed on at Old Trafford just a day after United's under-18's captured the Youth Cup by drawing at Chesterfield in the second leg of the 1956 final, by which time he was already part-way through an apprenticeship as a mechanical engineer at Fairey's in Heaton Chapel. His versatility was a godsend as far as the club's coaches were concerned, as they could use him in almost any given role, and he eventually filled no less than seven outfield slots for them.

He scored from the inside-right position in the Juniors' 9-0 thumping of Broadheath on his first appearance for United in the September of that year and grabbed another goal a week later before being upped into the Colts. Remaining at the higher level for the next three months at left full-back, within that period he also occupied the number three shirt for the home Youth Cup ties with Burnley and Sunderland and another at Huddersfield. Of the game in Yorkshire he said, *'We got changed there in a wooden hut. We were 2-1 down at half-time and Matt Busby came in to see us. He went round to each and every one of us individually and gave us a few words of encouragement.'*

Over the second half of the season he occupied either the right-half or centre-half spots for the Colts while his place in the under-18 team was forfeited to Stuart Gibson. With Gibson ruled out through injury, Maddison was recalled for the Youth Cup final matches against West Ham, and he mentioned of the game at Upton Park, *'In order to motivate us, Jimmy Murphy conducted what I would call a 'wind-up session' before the kick-off by saying things like West Ham were the favourites. Bert Whalley told us that the first-team were going to win the F.A. Cup so we needed to win the Youth Cup. Harold Bratt was in front of me for that match and he was just outstanding. He made it a very easy 90 minutes for me.'*

The Reds returned to Lancashire with the cushion of a one-goal lead and the Hammers faced a team brimming with confidence at Old Trafford. *'We were good value for our win over the two ties and never at any time did I think that we could lose,'* he claimed. *'My father and uncle were in the crowd for the home game and it was the best I ever played for the youth team.'*

Rewarded with a close season tour to Switzerland and Germany, he began the 1957/58 term in the Colts and was promoted up to the 'A' team in late September. The local prospect was back in the Colts in November but then stepped up again to captain the 'A' side from the right-back slot from February through to April.

Now just a couple of months away from his 19th birthday and the owner of a Lambretta scooter, it was then that his outside commitments began to have a detrimental effect on his football aspirations. Because he was required to attend technical college on Monday, Wednesday and Friday evenings, besides training with United on Tuesday and Thursday nights, the burdensome schedule caused him to ask for his ties to be cut with the club, at which point his amateur contract was terminated.

Later that year he was trialled by Bury and followed up the experience by spending a period of *'nine or ten weeks'* with Manchester City, a time in which he gained some exposure in their 'B' side. In December 1958, he joined up with Welsh League Division One club Nantlle Vale for a spell lasting just under two years and then hitched up with Hyde United for the entire 1961/62 season, though he wasn't utilised at senior grade by the Tigers.

Just about then he was employed on the construction of a nuclear power station in Somerset and his workload down there effectively brought an end to his football activities. Over the ensuing years, Ray Maddison has lived in Northamptonshire, Worcestershire, Berkshire and Suffolk while acting as a director for numerous engineering companies.

Currently residing in Colne, he owns an engineering firm which employs over 50 workers and supplies components to the aircraft industry.

FIDLER, Dennis John (1954/55, 1955/56)

Born: Stepping Hill, Stockport, 22nd June 1938
Height: 5ft. 9½ ins., Weight: 10st. 2lbs.
Role: Outside-left
Career: **North Reddish Junior School (Stockport)/ Stockport School/ Stockport Boys/ Cheshire Boys/ UNITED**: Am. August 1953/ **Manchester City** Am. November 1956 Pro. January 1957/ **Port Vale** June 1960/ **Grimsby Town** October 1961/ **Halifax Town** April 1963/ **Darlington** October 1966/ **Macclesfield Town** April 1968/ **Altrincham** May 1971/ **Macclesfield Town** July 1972 to c/s 1973/ **Witton Albion** July 1974 to May 1975/ **New Mills** November 1975

Dennis Fidler played football for a Stockport School side that fulfilled a whole season of fixtures undefeated. Later chosen for Stockport Boys, it was as a result of a hat-trick he scored for them in a 4-1 English Schools' Trophy win over Salford Boys that he came to sign for the Reds. Most of the United scouts watched the game, and the very next day Joe Armstrong was knocking on the door of his home at Barlow Fold Road in Reddish.

Naturally left-footed and possessing a fast and direct style, full-backs found him a nuisance. His preference was to pass them along the touchline and, while undoubtedly possessing an eye for goalscoring opportunities, he could also provide chances with a superb crossing technique.

In early September 1953 he lined up alongside Bobby Charlton and Wilf McGuinness for the opening Juniors' fixture of a new season and, despite not scoring, a number of his assists contributed to an 11-1 thrashing of Lancashire Dynamo. Because his school objected to his United attachment, two games later he disappeared off the radar altogether.

He started the 1954/55 term in the 'B' team and just half a dozen games in, it was felt that he lacked the experience for Lancashire League football so was then mainly used in the Juniors. By the following January he had been given a short run in the 'A' side and claimed five goals in his first two games at the higher level, three of which came in a 15-1 destruction of Miles Platting. Fidler was unable to force his way into the youth team, though, because the left-wing job was taken by either Charlton or Ken Morgans.

That was, until the final.

His Youth Cup call-up came at the expense of Morgans in the Old Trafford leg of the final against West Brom in April 1955 when, in front of over 16,000 spectators, United made easy work of the Albion by winning four goals to one. There was no change to the Reds' line-up three days later at The Hawthorns, where a 3-0 score gave them an emphatic aggregate victory and the local lad a treasured Youth Cup plaque after just two appearances in the tournament.

The following term was one of contrast as he managed only six games for the 'B' side and double that for the 'A' eleven due to various knocks. It was a completely different story in the Youth Cup, however, as he was included in the team right from the start, and as the early rounds went by he and his colleagues seemed determined to keep increasing their winning margins. A 5-2 victory at Preston and respective 4-0, 7-1 and 11-1 home wins over Sunderland, Newcastle and Bexleyheath & Welling had the teenagers in devastating goalscoring form, the result of what he later described as *'a magical attacking formula'*. Registering his first Youth Cup goal against the Magpies, it was matched with another against Bexleyheath & Welling.

Following an uncompromising battle against Bolton in the opening leg of the semi-final, the Reds won a famous victory at Burnden Park. His major contribution to the 3-0 success was to smash home the crucial second goal when running onto *'a perfectly weighted pass from Bobby (Charlton)'*.

Even so, his greatest feat in the Youth Cup was still to come. Opponents in the final, Chesterfield, managed to keep the score down to 3-2 at Old Trafford and when they scored to level the tie in the second leg, there looked to be a real danger that the trophy would be residing in Derbyshire after the presentations were made. Then, in the dying seconds of time added on, Fidler hit the winner past a despairing Gordon Banks to win the cup for United. Scoring with the last kick he ever made in the competition, amazingly, the ball was struck with a right foot which he has always maintained was *'normally used just for standing purposes'*.

It was a great personal milestone in his career and, with the onset of the 1956/57 season, it would have been reasonable to assume that he could have moved up the promotion ladder a rung or two. That looked probable as, after three 'B' team games, he was resituated in the 'A' side, and as early as October was tried in the Central League. The 2-2 draw against Bury Reserves at Gigg Lane represented the peak of his progress at Old Trafford and soon after, barely six months since his glory night at Chesterfield, he was allowed to leave.

Manchester City came up with a firm offer and he subsequently made the short trip across to Maine Road. He joined briefly as an amateur before becoming a professional two months later and in between those signings he was installed in City's Central League side. Gaining his first start in their second string at Villa Park in December 1956, by the following October he had made his Football League debut in a 2-2 home draw against Luton. He spent three and a half years with City and amassed five first-team appearances, scoring once, 90 starts for their Reserves, finding the net 29 times, and just over a dozen 'A' team games.

Leaving Maine Road on a free transfer to link up with Port Vale, the Potteries outfit gained excellent service from him as he managed to score fourteen goals in 43 league and cup games. The Valiants made a nice profit on him, too, when selling him on to Grimsby for £2,000 in October 1961.

He wasn't a regular for the Mariners and in an eighteen-month period commenced just nine league games, scoring three times. Two of those goals came in a 3-3 draw at Halifax during his first month at the club and that very feat could well have influenced the Yorkshire outfit's decision to bid for his services when he was made surplus to requirements at Blundell Park at the close of the 1962/63 season.

Remaining at The Shay for three fruitful years, his 142 league appearances for Halifax brought him a super tally of 40 goals, whereupon a move to the northerly outpost of Darlington followed. Fidler played both his first and last games for the Quakers in London, as he debuted at Leyton Orient in October 1966 and wound up his contribution for them at Brentford in late February 1968. The game at Griffin Park wasn't simply his last for Darlington; it was also his final appearance in the Football League.

An announcement in a Cheshire newspaper a few weeks later revealed that he had been snapped up by Macclesfield, the same report further stating his decision to give up full-time soccer was made so that he could concentrate more time on his family's fish business, which was situated in his home town of Stockport. He was within a few weeks of his 30th birthday and was, quite sensibly, making arrangements for the time when his football days came to an end. What he couldn't have known was that far from being the winding down process that many ex-professionals go through when dropping into non-league circles, some of his finest moments in the game were just around the corner.

The Macclesfield side of the late 1960's and early 1970's was unquestionably one of the greatest to have ever graced the non-league scene and had the pyramid system which is now in operation been in force back then, the club would almost certainly have gained entry into the Football League many years sooner than they did. When he walked through the entrance door at the Moss Rose in April 1968, Macclesfield were already on the last leg of winning the Cheshire League championship.

The Silkmen then became founder members of the newly-formed Northern Premier League and in a memorable first full campaign the wide man immediately struck up an almost telepathic understanding with his unrelated namesake, centre-forward Brian, as Macclesfield stormed to the title, won the Cheshire Senior Cup and reached the final of the North-West Floodlight League Cup.

Macclesfield had set a superb standard for the new league and in the 1969/70 term they were the side that all the others wanted to beat. Building on their success of the previous campaign with nerve, flair and consistency, they retained the Northern Premier League, as well as capturing the Northern Premier League Challenge Cup and the North-West Floodlight League Cup.

But that wasn't all......

That season saw the introduction of the F.A. Challenge Trophy, which was instigated as a national knock-out competition for non-league clubs and, after beating Burscough, Gainsborough and Bangor City in the early rounds, Macclesfield k.o'd Burton Albion in the quarter-final and Barnet at the last four stage to put them into the final against Telford. Staged on the 2nd May 1970 before a crowd of 28,000 at Wembley, Fidler savoured his proudest day in football as the Silkmen were victorious by two goals to nil.

In the following term even more silverware arrived at the Moss Rose, with the club regaining the Cheshire Senior Cup and retaining the Northern Premier League Challenge Cup, on top of reaching the final of the North-West Floodlight League Cup once more.

Departing after three fabulous years in the summer recess of 1971, he moved the short way to nearby Altrincham before returning to his spiritual home just over a year later. While on the books at Moss Lane, in February 1972, Altrincham were prepared to grant him a free transfer so that he could apply for the player/manager position at Northwich Victoria. The local newspaper claimed that he had impressed when interviewed by the Northwich board, only the job offer didn't materialise.

In his second engagement at Macclesfield he was made club captain and, while the glory days were largely gone, the Cheshire Senior Cup was won for the third time in five years. It was to be his final fling as a player for the Silkmen, and he left them with many good memories and quite a stash of medals. He had been involved in over 200 matches for the club and scored, on average, a goal every four games, an outstanding record for one who operated principally in a wide position.

Then voluntarily absent from the game, a full year elapsed before he joined Witton Albion for a season. He was later picked up by another Cheshire League club, New Mills, although his efforts for the Church Lane outfit amounted to only two appearances.

Now able to devote much more time to interests outside of football, he eventually branched out of the family business to open a fishmonger's shop of his own in Bramhall. His involvement in soccer continued by way of a playing association with Bramhall Football Club and he later managed the Mid-Cheshire League side in the period around 1987. For a time Macclesfield Town also engaged him in some coaching work.

Dennis Fidler now resides in Italy, where he has operated a business renting out holiday apartments.

FULTON, Bryce (1952/53)

Born: Kilwinning, Ayrshire, 7th August 1935
Died: Eccles, 20th December 1975
Height: 5ft. 8ins., **Weight:** 11st.
Role: Right full-back
Career: Eccles Grammar School/ Eccles Boys/ UNITED: Am. May 1952 Pro. March 1953/ Plymouth Argyle August 1957/ Exeter City July 1964 to June 1966/ Stockport County January to June 1967

Bryce Fulton spent his formative years in the Ayrshire coastal town of Irvine, which is situated approximately twenty miles south-west of Glasgow. The Fulton family moved to Eccles before he had reached his teens when his father, who was an electrician in the coal mining industry, secured a job at a colliery in nearby Swinton.

Besides showing signs of early sporting promise, he was also a highly intelligent type and qualified, through entrance exams, to attend Eccles Grammar School. It was while at the school that he began to develop as a footballer, initially in a goal-getting capacity.

Representative honours were bestowed on him through his selection for Eccles Boys. One of the town team's games was staged at The Cliff against Salford Boys, the opposing side including his future Reds' team-mate Eddie Colman in their line-up, and it is highly probable that United were monitoring both of them at that time.

During his schooldays he also played for an Eccles & District League outfit which went by the unusual name of Ex-Roffians. Notching a useful tally of goals, the amateurs employed him exclusively as an inside-forward.

He passed several exams while at Eccles Grammar and because of his academic prowess it was always assumed within the family circle that he would further his potential by going to university.

That was until the offer to join United came along.

While Mr. Fulton was ecstatic at the thought of his son playing for Manchester United, both his mother and headmaster were less than pleased that he could contemplate the precarious and, in those days, not especially well-paid life of a professional footballer. In particular, his mother was of the opinion that he could have achieved much more had he followed the scholarly route into adult life. Ultimately, the teenager felt the chance was too good to waste and he signed on at Old Trafford with a youthful confidence that he could eventually make the grade.

Immediately converted to full-back, progress came fast while success wasn't far behind. Following an appearance for the Colts in a 3-1 victory at Dukinfield Town in August 1952, within a month he was up to 'A' team standard. He was used in both full-back positions over the rest of the season, and also switched between the third and fourth elevens. Helped by a quick turn of pace, and as a result of his experience of forward play, he provided a highly constructive link between the defence and half-back line.

One of the outstanding prospects in United's junior ranks, Fulton was an automatic choice in the 1952/53 Youth Cup team. In the week leading up to the Fifth Round tie against Barnsley at Old Trafford he was awarded a paid contract, and between then and the end of the campaign no less than four honours landed in his lap. Besides the Colts and the 'A' team heading their respective leagues, the Scot was party to the taming of Wolves in the Youth Cup final in addition to being present at The Cliff when Ashton United were defeated in the Gilgryst Cup final.

Within three weeks of the 1953/54 term starting he was hoisted up to Central League grade for a 1-0 defeat at Leeds. Limited to only half a dozen or so games for the second team thereafter, his Manchester League side headed their division once again and the defender's season ended in Switzerland where he took part in all five ties in the Blue Stars tournament.

His appearances in the Central League became more frequent in the following season, rising to over twenty, and he was also nominated a place in the side that defeated Oldham 5-0 in the Manchester Senior Cup final.

Over the August and September of 1955 he took part in the Reserves' opening five fixtures when the team stormed to the top of the Central League with a full complement of ten points and a 'goals scored' column of 21. Then picking up a knock, with so much superb talent on the books he was unable to regain his place and, upon reverting to third team grade, the coaches again tried him in his previous role as an inside-forward for a spell before the experiment was abandoned. He completed nine games in the Central League, missing out on a championship medal by just one appearance, although alternative glory showed itself in a 6-3 Supplementary Cup final victory over Blackpool.

Despite the distraction of National Service, his progress was not untypical of what was expected. There was a concern, however, that over time he had 'filled out' to the extent that his weight increased by the best part of two stones.

In his final campaign at United, Fulton waited until October 1956 before being chosen for a Reserve game, and even then he was handed the centre-forward shirt. Breaking back on a more sustained basis in November, apart from a period out of action around the turn of the year he remained with the second string until the end of the term. With the quality of full-backs United had on their books just then, such as Roger Byrne, Bill Foulkes, Geoff Bent and Ian Greaves, getting a look-in at first-team level seemed unlikely.

In August 1957, he and half-back Tommy Barrett were prised away from Old Trafford by ex-United goalscorer extraordinaire and newly-installed Plymouth manager, Jack Rowley. Enduring a slow start at Home Park, by the following February he had made his Football League entrance and when the Pilgrims ran off with the Third Division title in his second season, the number of starts he made qualified him for a championship souvenir.

Spending almost seven years at Home Park, he proved to be a wonderful acquisition for the Devon club and in consecutive campaigns, 1960/61 and 1961/62, was missing from only two league games in total. Going on to rack up a sum of 176 league, four F.A. Cup and nine Football League Cup appearances in the senior side, as well as making 57 starts in the Football Combination for Argyle's second eleven, when it was time to move on from Plymouth, the best of his playing days were undoubtedly behind him.

Life in the West Country obviously suited him as, on his release from the south coast club in 1964, employment was found with county rivals Exeter City. While with the Grecians he was affectionately known by the home supporters as the *'Red Barrel'* due to his now rather stocky appearance in the club's red and white striped shirt.

Following a period out of contract, during which Wigan Rovers made a failed attempt to sign him in September 1966, a last move in football circles brought him back to the North-West with Stockport. Only on their books for five months without featuring in County's first-team picture at all, after his contract expired in June 1967 he took employment as a van driver, combining the job with a little scouting work for Plymouth.

Sadly, at only 40 years of age, Bryce Fulton's life was suddenly and tragically cut short, an inquest into his death which mentioned *'alcoholic poisoning'* gave the cause as *'misadventure'*.

ELMS, James Brian (1956/57, 1957/58, 1958/59)

Born: Ardwick, Manchester, 16th September 1940
Height: 5ft. 6ins., Weight: 10st. 7lbs.
Role: Outside-left or left half-back
Career: Nansen Street Primary School (Ardwick)/ Central Grammar School for Boys (Manchester)/ Manchester Boys/ Lancashire Boys/ UNITED: Am. July 1956 Pro. April 1958/ Crewe Alexandra October 1960/ Ashton United July 1961/ Llandudno August 1963/ Hyde United October 1963/ Radcliffe Borough August 1969 to April 1972

The subject of possibly the most unusual approach made to any potential United prospect, in 2009 Jimmy Elms revealed how he came to join the club when saying, *'I had just taken part in a game and I was making my way home on the bus when Bert Whalley started chatting to me. Bert got off at the same stop and we walked back to our house because he wanted to speak with my parents. My dad was a United follower and he wanted me to join them, so I agreed to sign as an amateur.'*

His association with football had commenced at primary school and he later represented Central Grammar at both rugby and cricket. He was forced to wait a year or two to play soccer for Central, though, until a teacher by the name of Mr. Panter started a team there.

As a result of a recommendation by another of his teachers, Ted Whetton, he attended trials for Manchester Boys at Nell Lane in Chorlton. With the selectors suitably satisfied with his qualities, Elms represented Manchester at under-14 and under-15 stages in the left-half position and then gained selection for Lancashire. Upon leaving school he trained with United through the football season and also joined the ground staff at Lancashire Cricket Club. He was utilised as LCC's first-team 12th man on occasion during his time with the Reds and additionally competed against a few minor counties.

Making his debut for United's Juniors on 1st September 1956, the game resulted in a 9-0 battering of Broadheath. He was situated at that level for most of the rest of the campaign, but by November he had contested in the 'B' team at left-half. It was in that very position where he gained an early look-in at the Youth Cup when deputising for Harold Bratt in the home tie against Sunderland a few weeks later. That was it for him as far as the Youth Cup went that term, although he was recognised as the team's standby thereafter.

He won the first of four England Youth caps in October 1957 for his contribution to a win over Holland in Amsterdam and went on to take part in games with Luxembourg, Yugoslavia and Belgium, in each case alongside legendary future full international captain, Bobby Moore.

That same month he was included in United's Youth Cup team in the number eleven jersey for a win at Burnley and retained his place right through a run which ended at the last four stage at Molineux the following April. Elevated to the 'A' team much more often in the wake of the Munich tragedy, he remained with them for the vast majority of the next three and a half years.

His memories of that awful day remain clear, and he said of it, *'I was at Old Trafford with Nobby (Stiles) and we were cleaning the boots and mopping out the gym when one of the trainers told us what had happened. I went home and was just glued to the television, I never thought about jumping up the ladder or anything like that. The next day we all went back to the ground and did some work with Bill Inglis and Jack Pauline.'*

Elms was ever-present in the Youth Cup team as they reached the semi-final again in the 1958/59 campaign, and within that period he made his Central League baptism in a home game with Huddersfield in December 1958.

Noted for his versatility, one of his main priorities was working hard at closing down opponents. When in possession he could be a tricky customer and was always looking to pass defenders with the aim of presenting quality crosses for the strikers to feed off.

Speaking about why he failed to graduate to the Reserves on a regular basis, he explained candidly, *'I took my foot off the pedal once I signed as a professional and I simply didn't train hard enough. Just before I left I was fighting Harold Bratt, Jimmy Nicholson and Wilf McGuinness for a place in the Central League side.'*

He put in seven appearances for the 'A' team and even a couple for the 'B' side at the commencement of the 1960/61 season. His last contribution resulted in a scoreless home stalemate with Bury 'A' in October 1960 and blessed relief was at hand when Crewe came calling for his signature soon after.

There were three major reasons for leaving United. Firstly, his progress had completely stalled, and he really wanted to establish himself at left-half, something that proved beyond him at Old Trafford. There was also the not insignificant matter of his marriage to Ann the following June and, from a financial standpoint, it would have been far preferable to be playing first-team football.

Unfortunately, it soon became clear that he was much better suited to Ann than Crewe as, with only one Fourth Division start in a 1-1 home encounter against Doncaster in December 1960 to speak of, his release followed about six months later.

He went on to enjoy a fruitful two-year association with Ashton United, who were then operating in Division Two of the Lancashire Combination. Much success came the club's way in that period as they topped their league without dropping a single home point in the 1961/62 campaign and also claimed the Combination Cup. In the following term, Ashton won the Manchester Intermediate Cup, as well as finishing third in the top tier of the Lancashire Combination.

Following a short stopover at Llandudno which encompassed just one or two games, he joined his third United, on this occasion the Hyde version. The Cheshire League outfit benefited from his constructive ideas and consistency for nearly six years, with match reports variously using adjectives such as *'tireless'*, *'imaginative'* and *'effervescent'* to highlight his contributions. Throughout his stay at Ewen Fields, described by the man himself as his *'best time as a player'*, he worked in a sales role for a wallpaper company while also running an off-licence. He was later employed in the clothing trade and as a sales agent in textiles, and sometime after he established his own company in the same line of business by selling on behalf of firms based in Hong Kong and Portugal.

In May 1968, Hyde United organised a testimonial game against Oldham for their loyal servant. The following season saw them enter the Northern Premier League as founder members and when it ended he had seen service in approximately 200 matches for the Tigers. He then transferred to Radliffe Borough and also gave them fine service for the next three years.

With a cousin joining as a business partner, their company, Elms Marketing, took off when they moved into leisurewear. Securing a licence to sell products for Euro '96, in 1997 they obtained similar rights for the 2000 World Cup. By 1999 the business had been sold at a handsome profit, which allowed him to retire at just 59 years of age.

Jimmy Elms has held an unbroken association with Longsight Cricket Club since the age of fourteen and, whereas most of his efforts for them have been on-field, he has even served as their president. He also continued with football until the age of 50 in the Stockport Sunday League.

Nowadays splitting time between living in Cheshire and sunning himself at his property in Majorca, his continuing interest in sports extends to watching cricket at the 'other' Old Trafford while serving on the committee of United's Former Players' Association.

BESWICK, Ivan (1953/54)

Born: New Moston, Manchester, 2nd January 1936
Died: Guernsey, 4th June 2012
Height: 5ft. 8ins., Weight: 10st. 2lbs.
Role: Right full-back
Career: St. Mary's Central School (Newton Heath)/ UNITED: Am. October 1952 Pro. October 1954 to June 1957/ Nantlle Vale August 1958/ Oldham Athletic August 1958/ Stalybridge Celtic August 1961 to c/s 1963 and seasons 1964/65 and 1965/66

After captaining his school football team for two years, Ivan Beswick was attached to Moston Lads Club in local Manchester circles when he and a number of others from the side were invited to the summer training sessions, which United held at the Manchester University playing fields in Fallowfield, known as The Firs.

Recalling those times, he said, 'At the end (of the workouts) they would call out the names of those who they wanted to come back the next week for the next training get-together. I was chosen for several consecutive weeks until one day, right out of the blue, a telegram arrived at our house informing me I'd been selected for one of the United junior sides.'

What had caught the eye of the coaches was his effective use of the ball with either foot and his ability to combine guile with electric speed in order to minimise his opponents' options. Only slightly built, he was considered a 'classy' defender who was often likened to Roger Byrne, the Reds' great club captain of the period, and he was frequently 'paired' against winger Albert Scanlon in training as the two were perfectly matched for pace.

He made the Juniors' right full-back slot his own in the 1952/53 season as the Altrincham Junior League was won at a canter. Then stepping up to the Colts in his second term at the club, his entrance in the Youth Cup came at Everton in October 1953. Even though the vocal Goodison Park crowd got right behind their team to create a great atmosphere that autumn morning, it wasn't enough to stop United winning by a decisive strike from Eddie Colman. Beswick was present for all of that campaign's ten Youth Cup ties when the Reds retained the trophy for the first time.

Barely two months of the 1954/55 season had passed when he broke into the 'A' team and an external honour also came his way when he was distinguished by being chosen for Lancashire Youth in a game staged at Blackpool. On the back of his performance at Bloomfield Road the host club offered him professional terms, but when United got wind of the Seasider's interest they quickly changed his amateur forms for a paid contract.

In November 1954 he started to appear at outside-right and a little later on the opposite flank, a switch of roles which was made in order that he could add another string to his bow. By the end of the term he was considered a versatile member of the Colts or 'A' team who could be relied on in both full-back places or on either wing.

He graduated into the Central League side in September 1955 as a replacement for Scanlon, who was away on representative duty, and the first of his eight appearances for the Reserves that campaign saw Burnley blitzed 7-1 at Old Trafford.

Unable to stake a regular claim in the second string in the 1956/57 season due to the form of Scanlon and Colin Webster, his efforts were concentrated instead in the Lancashire League. Over the later stages of the term he began to experience severe fatigue after playing or exercising and, convinced he had a fitness problem, attempted to counteract his tiredness by training even harder. What he wasn't aware of was that the cause of his symptom was a duodenal ulcer. The problem surfaced with painful consequences when the ulcer burst while he was returning from the United versus Aston Villa F.A. Cup final in May 1957. It was immediately apparent that he wouldn't be able to participate in any type of sport for some time and was released by United a few weeks later.

Spending a month in hospital and a further year convalescing before feeling able to resume football activities, the recovery period was used to study towards a degree in engineering electronics. Having worked for the Ferranti Company during his early days at Old Trafford, the qualifications would prove to be a valuable asset to him in future years.

Now ready to pick up the threads of his soccer career, in August 1958 the defender conditionally agreed to join Welsh League club Nantlle Vale as he was awaiting the result of a trial game at Boundary Park. That assessment involved him playing for Oldham Reserves against their first-team counterparts and, after he had subsequently taken part in a second trial, manager Norman Dodgin tabled a three-year contract.

Nantlle Vale immediately cancelled his registration and because of their co-operation in the matter, it was agreed that Athletic would visit Penygroes for a friendly fixture. The proposed game was suggested as a gesture of goodwill between the two clubs but was never actually fulfilled.

The late 1950's were dark days indeed for Oldham. They finished 21st and 23rd respectively in the Fourth Division in 1959 and 1960 and were forced to apply for re-election on both occasions. The Mostonian's Football League debut was one of the rare bright spots of the period, when the Latics defeated Crewe 2-1 at Boundary Park in November 1958, and he chalked up a further 35 Football League and a couple of F.A. Cup starts before Dodgin was sacked in the summer of 1960.

The man who was given the unenviable job of reviving Athletic's fortunes was ex-United hero, Jack Rowley. Beswick began the opening eleven games of the 1960/61 campaign, but it was a bad start for the new man in charge with only one victory to speak of. Rowley then began to rebuild the team by replacing existing personnel with his own men and the full-back left Boundary Park when his contract expired.

After then joining near neighbours Stalybridge Celtic, the majority of his senior team appearances were made in his opening year with the club and he then alternated between Celtic's first and second sides in the 1962/63 season. The problem with his ulcer still hadn't entirely subsided and so he took another year out of the game when voluntarily undertaking further corrective surgery. He returned to Stalybridge for two more terms, though from then on he was exclusively involved with Celtic's Reserves, then members of Division One of the Manchester League.

Considering his medical complications, he could be considered as having done really well to reach the age of 30 before finishing with the game.

Ivan Beswick became a chartered engineer when his football days were over and in October 1988 he formed a company that manufactures metal detectors for the food industry. It became the largest organisation of its kind in the world, employing hundreds of people across the globe, and even after selling the firm to a Swiss buyer in 1997, he remained in charge as its managing director for a time.

WHELAN, Anthony Michael
(1968/69, 1969/70, 1970/71)

Born: Salford, 20th November 1952
Height: 5ft. 10ins., **Weight:** 11st. 8lbs.
Role: Outside-left or centre-forward
Career: St. Chad's Primary School (Cheetham Hill)/ St. Ambrose Primary School (Chorlton-cum-Hardy)/ St. Anthony's R.C. Secondary School (Blackley)/ St. Paul's Secondary Modern School (Stretford)/ Stretford Boys/ **UNITED**: Ass. Schoolboy 1967 App. Pro. July 1968 Pro. December 1969 to February 1973/ **Manchester City** March 1973/ **Rochdale** July 1974 to March 1977/ **Los Angeles Skyhawks** (USA) (L) April to August 1976/ **Fort Lauderdale Strikers** (USA) April 1977/ **Atlanta Chiefs** (USA) April 1980 to October 1981/ **Philadelphia Fever** (USA) November 1981 to April 1982/ **Fort Lauderdale Strikers** (USA) November 1982 to November 1983/ **Witton Albion** December 1983 to March 1984

When George Best signed for the Los Angeles Aztecs in early 1976, it was seen as a major boost in regards to the popularity of the North American Soccer League. The development helped to change soccer in that country, with the likes of Pele, Franz Beckenbauer, Johan Cruyff and Eusebio generating interest and excitement on, and sometimes off, the pitch.

Georgie wasn't the first ex-United junior to try his luck in the States, though, as former Reds Freddie Goodwin and Dennis Viollet were among the original flag-bearers when the first leagues started there in 1967. That year, two professional soccer divisions got underway in America, the FIFA-sanctioned United Soccer Association, which consisted of entire European and South American teams imported into the US and given local names, and the unapproved National Professional Soccer League. The latter even managed to secure a national television contract with the CBS network. However, the viewing ratings proved unacceptable and resulted in the arrangement being terminated, which led to the leagues merging to form the North American Soccer League (NASL) in 1968.

So, while Best was creating newsprint for the Aztecs in the NASL, across town 23 year-old Tony Whelan joined the newly founded Los Angeles Skyhawks of the expanding and competing American Soccer League (ASL) in the spring of 1976. The club staged their games at the impressive 10,000 capacity Birmingham High School Stadium, where manager Ron Newman welded together a team comprising of little known American college players and experienced professionals from the lower divisions of the English Football League.

By the end of that campaign, the Skyhawks boasted the best record in the league and despite struggling through difficult play-off matches, they reached the ASL Championship final. A goal in arrears and down to ten men through having a man sent off against New York Apollo, the Skyhawks scored a last minute penalty to win the title. Whelan, who was dubbed 'Wheels' through a combination of his surname and speed across the grass, quickly became a fans' favourite and finished as the team's third highest goalscorer.

He returned to England for most of the 1976/77 season and featured in 34 Fourth Division games for Rochdale before heading back to the States for an indefinite period. 'It took some lengthy negotiations to get released from Rochdale, but I really liked playing in America and was keen to go back,' he said before adding, 'I attended a tribunal in London when I was trying to get my release from Rochdale. Sir Matt Busby sat on the panel and assured me afterwards that everything would be okay. He was true to his word because I was allowed to go to the States without a fee being paid, although Rochdale retained my registration.'

Ron Newman left the Skyhawks after winning the title and had been offered a job with Fort Lauderdale Strikers in Florida. I was given a chance to go back full-time, so I took it.'

Leaving the relative obscurity of the ASL to link up with the big boys in NASL, whereupon he rubbed shoulders with the likes of Gordon Banks, Fort Lauderdale won the Eastern Division in his first term only to miss out in the Divisional play-off. It was quite some feat to capture the league title as they were required to fend off a formidable New York Cosmos side containing mega-stars such as Pele, Beckenbauer and Alberto Carlos.

The following year he lined up alongside Best and Ian Callaghan and was ever-present as the team went one better to reach the 1978 American Conference final. Around then he was also made an honorary citizen of Plantation in Florida in recognition of his services to the youth of the community, a fine accolade in view of the fact he had been in the area for less than two years. Repositioned as a sweeper during his time in Florida, and even with the addition of Gerd Muller, a crack at the 1979 title was just beyond the Strikers.

Having already taken his USSF 'A' and 'B' coaching licences in the States earlier that year, in April 1980 he linked up with the Atlanta Chiefs, spending two campaigns with the Georgia-based club and teaming up for a while with ex-United striker Brian Kidd there. Successfully captaining the Chiefs to a double of indoor and outdoor league championships in 1981, he then signed for Philadelphia Fever of the Major Indoor Soccer League (MISL).

The MISL was a national indoor five-a-side league that operated in the NASL shut-down from December through to March. With the new NASL calendar some way off restarting, in July 1982 he made his way back to England to complete a full F.A. coaching licence at Lilleshall prior to returning to Fort Lauderdale, this time to combine playing with youth coaching. Just before completing his second spell in Florida, he was included in the Fort Lauderdale Sun-Sentinel 'All-Striker' team, a combination that included such luminaries as Best, Muller, Kidd and the Peruvian Teofilio Cubillas.

Of Nigerian/English descent, Whelan mostly grew up in Partington before his family moved to Wythenshawe in 1965, and it was while assisting Stretford Boys over a period of two years when he found himself attracting attention from the representatives of professional football clubs. Joe Armstrong invited him to train on a couple of evenings a week at The Cliff and because the set-up was to his liking the fourteen year-old signed associate schoolboy forms prior to being taken on as an apprentice in 1968.

He made an inauspicious start for the club when the 'B' team were on the wrong end of a 5-0 thrashing by Stockport 'A' that August. Elevated to the 'A' side in October, two weeks later he hit three in the 'B' team's 7-0 whitewash of Bury. For the remainder of the term he turned out for both junior sides, mainly at inside-left or on the left wing, and in April there was a surprise call-up into the Youth Cup squad while they prepared for a semi-final clash against West Brom. Used as a replacement for the crocked Damien Ferguson, it wasn't a good day for the teenage Reds as they lost 2-1 at Old Trafford and the tie 5-3 on aggregate.

As he noted, it was soon after that defeat to the Baggies when a compensating success charged him with confidence, 'I was in the team that won the Blue Stars youth tournament in Zurich in May 1969. It was a major turning point in my career because I played well and I then really started to believe that I could go on and become a professional footballer.'

The following campaign started promisingly when he notched five goals in his first seven 'B' team games. By mid-September 1969 he had climbed back up to 'A' standard and more or less remained there for all of the remaining fixtures. Having sat on the bench for the opening Youth Cup tie at Oldham, in December he was drafted into the Central League side for a 3-1 home victory against Leeds and then went on to take part in all of the later Youth Cup ties, scoring goals against Sheffield United at Old Trafford and at Coventry, as the side reached the last four for the second successive year.

At the end of that season, shock and delight came over him in equal measures when told of his inclusion in the senior squad that was to tour Bermuda, Canada and America. Because five of United's senior men were on World Cup duty in Mexico, when the team was announced for the opening fixture against a Bermuda XI in Hamilton at the end of April, his name was in the starting line-up.

Taking the left wing spot and acquitting himself well as the Reds came in at half-time two goals to the good, his replacement in the second half was none other than George Best. Four days later Whelan went on to replace Willie Morgan in a 6-1 win over the Bermuda Football Union. He missed out on being selected for the Toronto Cup matches against Bari and Glasgow Celtic, only to then manage a full 90 minutes in the match against Eintracht Frankfurt in San Francisco and return home with three first-team appearances under his belt.

By the time the 1970/71 term started, the striker was considered a staple of the Reserves and often appeared alongside those such as Morgan, Alex Stepney, Pat Crerand and Nobby Stiles. Whelan was selected at centre-forward for the opening two matches and then turned out across the forward line during the campaign. When May rolled around he could boast his best goalscoring season to date, which meant hitting double figures for the first time.

Despite starting the following term in the Reserves, after only three games he was relegated to the 'A' team in a bid to find some form. Following an eight-match run with the third team from August to October, he forced his way back into the second string and scored in the Lancashire Senior Cup final when the Reds battled out a 2-2 draw with Burnley in late April, the Turf Moor club winning the replay 3-0.

It seemed that he had now reached something of a plateau. A regular for the Reserves yet unable to force his way into contention for the seniors, by the time Tommy Docherty arrived he was found back in the 'A' team again. With his immediate prospects now in doubt, a chat with the new manager confirmed that he wasn't part of the club's blueprint for the future and his contract was terminated on the 10th February 1973.

He summed up his initial spell at the club by saying, 'During my apprenticeship I witnessed four different managers take charge. Looking back it probably did affect my progress, but there were a lot of very good players around at the time. Although I finished as the leading goalscorer in the Reserves one year, my first-team chance never came. When Tommy Docherty released me I was mortified, but in the end I bounced back and got back in the game at Manchester City of all places.'

He had already been offered terms by Third Division Bolton when Malcolm Allison stepped in to take him to Maine Road for a one-month trial. Within three weeks he had broken into City's senior side at West Ham and his career looked as though it was about to lift off. Unfortunately, three months later Allison left for Crystal Palace and his contract was cancelled by mutual consent after he made only five further appearances in sixteen months.

Whelan ended up at Rochdale, where he spent three productive seasons. Voted their 'Player of the Year' in 1975, twelve months later he and Cardiff City's Clive Charles were the first two black players to receive a PFA award. His attributes were noted far and wide, with Rochdale even rebuffing an approach from up-and-coming Cambridge manager Ron Atkinson for his services.

It was then that his seven and a half-year American adventure began. With his experiences in the States proving almost entirely positive, towards the end of 1983 he returned to England for good.

In the hope of working his way back into the Football League he joined Witton Albion, and while with them he was selected to play for an F.A. Non-League XI against a Universities' team. Tragically breaking his leg in two places during the match, by the time he had fully recovered his career was finished at the age of 31.

Over the next twelve years he spent time as an education and welfare officer and turned out for both United and City's old boys' teams. Also involved at Bobby Charlton's Soccer School, following a spell on Manchester City's community programme he was invited to return to Old Trafford in 1990. Initially taken on a part-time basis by Brian Kidd and Nobby Stiles, eight years later he went full-time.

Over the years he has gained several coaching qualifications, as well as a Bachelors degree in Humanities from the Open University and a Masters degree in Sociology from Manchester Metropolitan University. He also wrote the foreword to 'The First Black Footballer: Arthur Wharton 1865-1930 - An Absence of Memory' (1998) and is the author of 'The Birth of the Babes: Manchester United Youth Policy 1950-1957', an acclaimed book which explores the impact of youth development in football and the building of the Busby Babes by Matt Busby.

In March 2008, in recognition of his work developing elite young players, The Voice listed him as one of the 30 most influential black people in English football, and by the October of that year he had received an award at the House of Lords from the organisers of the 'Kick It Out' anti-racism campaign.

Today the deputy assistant Academy director for the under-9 to under-16 age groups, Tony Whelan may have been forced to leave the club in order to secure regular first-team football, but his contribution to United's cause on the junior stage is incalculable and his reputation as an intelligent, innovative coach is well merited and widely acknowledged.

JONES, Ernest Peter (1954/55, 1955/56)

Born: Salford, 30th November 1937
Height: 5ft. 10ins., Weight: 11st. 8lbs.
Role: Centre-half or left full-back
Career: **Wellington Street School (Salford)/ Salford Boys/ Lancashire Boys/ UNITED:** Am. December 1952/ **Wolverhampton Wanderers** Am. 1953/54 season/ **UNITED:** Am. May 1954 Pro. April 1955/ **Wrexham** March 1960/ **Stockport County** July 1966/ **Altrincham** July 1968/ **Chorley** August 1970/ **Radcliffe Borough** July 1972 to February 1973

An honest, conscientious and gutsy defender who was rugged and reliable, Peter Jones made just one appearance in United's senior side, at left full-back, against Portsmouth in October 1957. Shortly after the 3-0 defeat at Old Trafford he was conscripted for his National Service and was never again called on by Matt Busby.

During his spell in the Ordnance Corps he was a regular in the British Army side and got in games for the Reds on most weekends. Not long after his release from the military, in March 1960, he was allowed to join Wrexham for what was reported as a *'four figure fee'*.

The Salfordian gave Wrexham full value for their shillings, featuring in 226 Football League matches for them over a six-year duration, and within that period he experienced a promotion to the Third Division, a relegation and a couple of appearances in the Welsh Cup final. Wrexham finished at the bottom of the Fourth Division in 1966 and were made to apply for re-election for the first time in their history. It was no surprise that a number of the staff paid a price for the failure and Jones, following a wage dispute, found himself transferred to Stockport County.

Remaining at Edgeley Park for two years, he was part of another promotion success and this time it came with the Fourth Division championship. The defender added another 54 league games to his total at which point he took up with Altrincham, who beat Macclesfield for his signature, in July 1968.

Used in a number of positions by the progressive non-leaguers, and present when they captured the North-West Floodlit League Cup, Altrincham also went as far as the 1969 semi-final of the Northern Premier League Cup.

In the 1969/70 season, he contributed towards the Robins' triumph in the Northern Premier League Cup final and their achievement in reaching the Cheshire Senior Cup final.

Over the next two years he assisted Chorley, who were newly-promoted hopefuls of the Northern Premier League, and Radcliffe Borough, then of the Cheshire League, prior to quitting at the age of 35.

Having represented Salford and Lancashire while at school, in November 1952, at the age of fifteen, he took up work as a trainee miner at Newtown Colliery in Swinton and at almost the same time signed amateur forms for United. Unable to get a game over the next few months, at the end of the 1952/53 campaign he was tempted away by what appeared to be a better opportunity offered by Wolverhampton Wanderers. His stay at Molineux lasted just the one term, during which he figured in Wolves' Worcestershire Combination team, and it was curtailed by homesickness.

Upon rejoining the Reds in 1954, Jones began employment in a steelworks and, skipping the Juniors entirely, was most often found in the middle of a Colts half-back line while frequently flanked by Eddie Colman and Wilf McGuinness. In the October of that season he helped to keep Liverpool's forwards quiet in a Youth Cup match at Anfield and went on to take part in all of the other ties bar one, when injured for the visit of Plymouth, as the United youngsters swept through the rounds to defeat West Brom in the final. With his Lancashire League side topping their division, as well as capturing the Supplementary Cup with a 6-1 hammering of Preston, the campaign was a memorable one for him. At its conclusion he was made a professional and gave up his job as a cabinet maker in the process.

He resumed in the Lancashire League side for the start of the next term and his greatest honours in the game followed just a few months later when, in the October and November of 1955, he was capped for England Youth for a 9-2 win over Denmark at Plymouth and a 3-1 victory against Holland at Norwich. During that spell he was tried out at left full-back for the first time in the Colts and just two days later found himself occupying the same position when the under-18's secured a Youth Cup victory at Deepdale. The role obviously suited because he remained there throughout another glorious run in the competition.

On the opening day of the 1956/57 season he was situated at right full-back for the Reserves' 3-2 defeat at Stoke and hung onto the spot for a 6-0 home win over Preston. Three weeks later he was given a run of four consecutive games at left full-back in the Central League team before returning to a lesser standard until the tail-end of the campaign.

From August 1957 to his senior debut two months later he was almost ever present in the number three shirt for the Reserves. After his National Service kicked in, his appearances were generally made for either the second or third teams, though they were understandably reduced for a while because of his Army commitments.

Then entering into a consistent run in the 'A' side in January 1959, Jones was back in the Reserves by the end of the term. While young bucks Barry Smith or Frank Haydock were usually chosen at centre-half for the second team in the 1959/60 season, and Tommy Heron, Ian Greaves and Reg Holland normally shared the full-back responsibilities, his stuttering prospects were finally rejuvenated with a transfer to the Racecourse Ground. His last game for United was on 12th March 1960 in the 'A' team's 1-1 home draw with Burnley.

Since his days in the professional game ended, Peter Jones has turned his hand to window cleaning and running a fish and chip shop before joining a textile company and then moving to a chemical firm.

He kept up a connection with football by managing Norweb Villa in the Manchester Accountants' League and, still living in Salford, remained active with an interest in golf.

KENNEDY, Patrick Anthony (1952/53)

Born: Dublin, 9th October 1934
Died: Trafford, 18th March 2007
Height: 5ft. 9ins., **Weight:** 11st. 7lbs.
Role: Left full-back
Career: Johnville (Dublin)/ Eire Boys/ UNITED: Am. July 1951 Pro. February 1953/ **Blackburn Rovers** September 1956/ **Bangor City** 1959 (registration cancelled)/ **Southampton** July 1959/ **Oldham Athletic** July 1960 to June 1961

Initially spotted for the Reds by ace Irish scout Billy Behan, Paddy Kennedy played for a renowned Dublin junior club called Johnville prior to winning international caps for Eire Boys.

Kennedy participated in a little hurling in his younger days but was much more accomplished at Gaelic football, and he actually experienced the thrill of representing Dublin as a schoolboy at the mecca of the sport, Croke Park, which is situated in his home city.

His first taste of soccer in England came when Eire Boys secured a sensational 8-4 win over the home nation at Goodison Park in 1951. The defender was also involved in another high scoring victory for the Republic's young guns when Northern Ireland Boys were hammered seven goals to one in Belfast.

In each of those international schoolboy appearances he lined up alongside future United colleagues, as Noel McFarlane was a member of the side that starred on Merseyside while Tommy Hamilton was in action against their opponents from north of the border.

It was as a result of the game at Goodison Park that he came to sign for United, coach Bert Whalley having been given the task of running the final rule over him. His display ensured that he went to Old Trafford that July and, residing with Albert Scanlon's family for a while, he made an entrance at centre-half when his Red side won 2-1 in a 'Reds v. Blues' trial match.

The Dubliner was always viewed as a centre-half prior to joining United and he continued in that position during his early days with the club. By the start of his second season he had been repositioned at left full-back for the Colts before returning to his original position. Later elevated into the

Manchester League side, and following a handful of appearances at number five, he was again switched to left full-back.

Commenting on the change of roles, he said, *'As I began to progress through the junior ranks, I felt less and less dominant as a centre-half. It was agreed with the coaches that I could alter my position to left full-back and straight away I felt an increase in my confidence.'*

The move was a resounding success and as such he became an important member of a rearguard that conceded only five goals in nine Youth Cup ties. A solid sort who proved extremely steadfast, he later claimed to be *'naturally right-footed, and comfortable enough with my left foot that I could take free kicks with it.'* Because of his earlier experience as a pivot, his capabilities in the air were well above average.

He had earned no less than three honours by the end of the 1952/53 campaign for, as well as the Youth Cup achievement, his 'A' team defeated Ashton United in the Gilgryst Cup final while a 3-0 win at New Mills in April 1953 clinched the Manchester League title. At the conclusion of a marvellous domestic season, he took part in all three of the tour matches in Ireland.

The following term was also one of some glory. Again a regular in the 'A' team, they repeated their trophy double of the previous campaign by topping the Manchester League and retaining the Gilgryst Cup via a 3-2 final victory over Stockport County 'A'.

On the opening day of the 1954/55 season, Kennedy played for the Reserves at Derby and six weeks later gained his First Division baptism at Wolves. Even though he was selected for a first-team friendly at Clyde in the week leading up to the game at Molineux, he was still somewhat thrown in at the deep end because the Reds were without regular full-backs Roger Byrne and Bill Foulkes, as well as goalkeeper Ray Wood, through international call-ups.

Despite being on the wrong end of a 4-2 defeat, the general consensus was that the young Irishman hadn't let anyone down at Wolverhampton and he went on to make over 30 appearances in the second string as they went on to finish second in the Central League championship.

The 1955/56 season proved much more difficult for him. After missing the early months through injury, he returned for the Colts in mid-November before immediately jumping back up to the 'A' team a week later. Finding it almost impossible to dislodge Ian Greaves or Geoff Bent from their full-back positions in the Central League team, he was brought back into the senior fold for another friendly game when the Reds travelled to Dens Park to take on Dundee in April 1956.

There were still two First Division fixtures remaining, but United already had enough points in the bag to be certain of the title. The day in Scotland was something of a disaster for Matt Busby's men, who lost by five goals to one. Needing to contend with having Ray Wood taken off with an ankle injury in the 18th minute, the team was already two to nil in deficit when Kennedy donned the green jersey for the remainder of the game.

With only four games of the next season completed and little scope for further senior opportunities, relief came his way in September 1956 when he was signed for a *'small fee'* by Blackburn manager Johnny Carey. It was thought that the 21 year-old was viewed as a long-term replacement for Rovers and England full-back Bill Eckersley, but a first-team call-up came much quicker than expected as, having only been at Ewood Park a week or two, he assisted them in a night match at Barnsley.

Three days later, with one scribe stating that he was *'very sure in defence'*, his bow before the Ewood Park crowd came in a victory over Derby. Those two encouraging displays were quickly noted by the Irish selectors, who were planning for forthcoming games against Denmark and West Germany. On the following weekend Blackburn won at Swansea and it was later reported he had picked up *'a back injury that has not responded to treatment'*.

His place in the Rovers side went to Dave Whelan, the current chairman of Wigan Athletic, and he never again got the chance to build on those early performances.

Then relegated to Blackburn's Central League side for the remainder of his three-year contract, within that time he sustained a serious thigh strain. The problem worsened drastically after being incorrectly treated and it continued to dog him from then on.

Courted by non-league Bangor City in 1959, the Welsh club was owned by a wealthy Liverpool jeweller. The Blackburn board then made it clear they wanted a fee for his services and were only prepared to waive it if he joined a club from outside the confines of the Football League.

With no suitor apparently willing to meet their financial requirement, Kennedy initially felt that with a day job and the match fees received from Bangor, he would have been financially better off than by joining a professional outfit. Travelling over to Merseyside, the necessary forms were inked at the jeweller's shop premises. Then, at the eleventh hour, Southampton offered to stump up the cash required to make him their property and after some deliberation he contracted himself to the Saints.

His actions earned him a reprimand from the Football Association, who fined him two guineas (£2.10) for simultaneously entering into contracts with two clubs.

He was with the south coast club for exactly a year, his tenure at The Dell commencing on the 4th July 1959. His Saints debut was made on the 28th of the following month in a home draw with Norwich and two days later he was present for a defeat at Chesterfield.

The injury he had suffered at Ewood Park soon surfaced again and he then only ever featured for Southampton at either Reserve or third-team levels.

His last football port of call was at Oldham, the Latics securing his services for £500. Unable to stake a claim in their first-team, after a year at Boundary Park he drifted out of the game completely.

There were offers from non-league clubs upon his release from Oldham, only by then it was thought that enough was enough. A highly promising career had been ruined by a recurring injury, which ultimately restricted him to just six senior starts with four different clubs.

Paddy Kennedy lived in Urmston for many years and he passed away in Trafford General Hospital at the age of 72.

BRATT, Harold (1956/57, 1957/58)

Born: Salford, 8th October 1939
Height: 5ft. 11ins., Weight: 12st.
Role: Left half-back
Career: Liverpool Street School (Salford)/ Salford Boys/ Lancashire Boys/ England Boys/ UNITED: Am. May 1955 Pro. November 1957/ Doncaster Rovers May 1961/ Altrincham October 1963 to December 1964/ Northwich Victoria October 1966 to c/s 1967 and January to May 1968

An industrious and energetic wing-half, Harold Bratt progressed from representing both Salford Boys and Lancashire Boys before crowning his school football honours by winning an international cap, his solitary appearance for England Boys coming in a resounding 6-0 win over Northern Ireland Boys at the Baseball Ground, Derby in April 1954.

Vigorously pursued by Wolverhampton Wanderers as he prepared to leave school, their scout for the Manchester area regularly entertained his father over pints of beer at his local while attempting to obtain young Harold's signature. The boy did, in fact, play one game for a Wolves junior side while still at school, which was almost certainly either a trial or an 'unofficial' appearance.

It is possible that his brief relationship with Wolves may have cost him further honours for his country because in those days the English Schools' F.A. was totally opposed to giving recognition to any boy who had even the merest of connections with professional clubs.

Two factors contributed to him becoming a United player. Firstly, his headmaster, a Mr. Davies, held strong links with the club and, secondly, on his commitment to signing on at Old Trafford he was guaranteed a job at Morris & Jones, a firm of wholesale grocers near to his Salford home. The purpose behind securing him employment was that he would join the Reds on amateur forms, training twice a week in the evenings and playing on Saturdays, prior to gaining paid terms.

His career at Old Trafford was jolted by a setback even before it had started in earnest, which was due to a serious foot injury sustained while at Morris & Jones. Taking part in a kick-about game of football one day in his lunch break, the ball sailed over a fence only to land in an electricity substation, and when Bratt went to retrieve it, he stood on a spiked piece of metal that pierced his foot.

The accident was an extremely painful experience and it caused his absence from the entire 1954/55 season, although fortunately the injury healed completely and had no long-term effect on his ability.

Once recovered he soon made up for lost time, completing his debut as United 'B' were beaten 6-3 by Blackburn on the opening day of the 1955/56 campaign. Moved down to the Juniors shortly after, the side won the Altrincham Junior League and defeated Trafford Park Youth 10-2 in the Whitaker Cup final.

Shortly into his second term with the club, in October 1956, he was given his Youth Cup baptism against Burnley at The Cliff and then began to appear in the 'A' side. Also present for every Youth Cup game bar one, his solid and consistent performances were a cornerstone of the Reds' progress as they claimed the Youth Cup for a fifth time with a final victory over West Ham.

He participated in the First and Second Round ties against Burnley and Blackpool respectively at the beginning of the following season's Youth Cup run before giving up his job at the grocery company to become a professional in November 1957. Then making the transition into the 'A' side a successful one, Jeff Whitefoot's transfer to Grimsby meant that only Wilf McGuinness stood in his way of scaling even further up the ladder.

When McGuinness suffered a serious injury in January 1958, Bratt's initial call up for the Reserves ended in a 2-2 draw at Bolton. His second game in the Central League was a 4-3 home win over Wolves on the 1st February and his third came when the Reserves resumed their fixtures after the Munich tragedy at Sheffield Wednesday. He also featured in all of that season's remaining Youth Cup games when the Reds finally tumbled out of the competition as a result of their defeat by Wolves, the club that had tried so hard to sign him.

A regular spot in United's Central League side ensued over the next year before he found himself displaced at that standard by Jimmy Nicholson. Nevertheless, in November 1960 his first-team breakthrough came in a Football League Cup tie at Bradford City.

It was the inaugural League Cup competition, a tournament which generally held little attraction for the Reds in its early years. Even so, despite a poor team performance and being required to contend with an absolute quagmire of a pitch, a 2-1 reverse to the Third Division side was still a major shock.

He had actually waited ten months for the chance to play for the seniors after being selected to replace Freddie Goodwin for an F.A. Cup game at Derby in January 1960. Informed that he was to be included in the side the day before the game, Goodwin unexpectedly recovered from injury and so that particular chance went up in smoke. The game at Valley Parade was his only showing in United's senior side and when the 1960/61 campaign ended he was allowed to leave.

His credentials ensured that a number of clubs pursued him, among them Oldham Athletic, but he chose instead to join Fourth Division Doncaster. One of the main conditions which influenced his decision to sign for the Rovers was that he was allowed to continue living in Salford.

Making his Doncaster debut at Gillingham in August 1961, over that opening term at Belle Vue he amassed 36 Football League, one F.A. Cup and two Football League Cup starts. Clocking up a further two dozen league and cup appearances during his second season in Yorkshire, the last of them was in a home game against Barrow in March 1963.

At the beginning of the next campaign he was restricted to just three matches for Rovers' Reserves before departing in the October. Having been at Doncaster for two and a half years, ultimately the constant journeying backwards and forwards over the Pennines forced his decision to leave.

After refusing offers to remain in the Football League from Chesterfield and Plymouth, a professional contract was quickly arranged with Altrincham, his bow for the Robins following just a few days later against Wrexham Reserves at the Racecourse Ground.

With the burden of travelling long distances to play football removed, the pleasure he derived from the game increased dramatically. Enjoying a settled spell in Altrincham's first-team, the wing-half was an extremely popular figure both on and off the pitch at Moss Lane. In a period lasting just over a year he made approaching 50 appearances for them whereupon, in December 1964, an article appeared on the sports page of the Altrincham Guardian which stated, *'Harold Bratt, one of the finest club-men ever to pull on boots at Moss Lane, is to revert to playing as an amateur! Harold will shortly be joining the Salford City Police........'*

Following that press report he never represented Altrincham at first-team standard again.

Commencing as a bobby on the beat, he served Salford Police in various capacities before moving into C.I.D. and other police work. In the by now merged Greater Manchester Police Force, for the remainder of his time under their employment he acted as a physical training instructor.

In the early days of his new career he represented Salford Police, Greater Manchester Police, Lancashire Police and the British Police at football.

Out of the paid game for almost two years, in October 1966 he joined up with his old friend Ronnie Cope at Cheshire League outfit, Northwich Victoria. Spending two spells with the Vics before departing along with his former United colleague, the Salford man clocked up approximately 40 starts for the Drill Field club.

Harold Bratt retired from the Police Force in the mid-1990's at the age of 55. He continued to work on a part-time basis for the Home Office, by supervising physical training for juveniles in Bolton and Salford, and various charities have since benefited from his unpaid work on their behalf.

LOWRY, Brian Thomas (1953/54)

Born: Ancoats, Manchester, 12th December 1936
Height: 5ft. 4ins., **Weight:** 9st. 7lbs.
Role: Outside-right
Career: St. Anne's School (Ancoats)/ Manchester Boys/ Lancashire Boys/ **UNITED**: Am. May 1953/ **Grimsby Town** August 1954/ **Aldershot** July 1956/ **Scarborough** July 1957/ **Droylsden** August and September 1958

A member of the same Manchester Boys team as Wilf McGuinness, and the same Lancashire Boys side as Eddie Colman, Brian Lowry joined United straight from school. He had been an inside-forward in the St. Anne's team that won the Daily Dispatch Schools' Shield, a competition open to all of the schools in the Manchester area, and the success qualified them to compete against similar winners from all over Lancashire.

St. Anne's reached the final of the county stage, which ultimately ended in a draw over two legs, and as a result the trophy was held for six months each by the Ancoats school and the other finalists.

After then playing for a talented Ardwick Lads Club side, United were soon on the scent and Bert Whalley was the club representative who made initial overtures to his parents regarding him becoming a member of the Old Trafford staff.

As an added incentive to sign for the Reds, Lowry was offered an administrative position and so he penned amateur forms for football purposes while concurrently working in the club offices. One of his tasks was to answer the telephone and during that time it would have been likely that anybody who dialled TRAfford Park 1661 would have heard his voice on connection.

His first appearance was for the Juniors in August 1953 and, while mainly utilised as a two-footed winger, he infrequently found himself as an inside-forward or in the half-back line. Quite a nippy lad who could go past defenders with some ease, even at age sixteen he was an intelligent reader of the game and showed mature vision.

In November 1953, he was given the right-wing berth on his Youth Cup bow at Goodison Park. Five others also made their debuts in United's youth eleven that morning and, in a game where the margin of victory hardly did justice to their superiority, a 1-0 win over Everton put them into the Second Round.

Scoring in his next Youth Cup match against Wrexham at The Cliff, he was then chosen for the Bradford Park Avenue tie and both games against Rotherham. Retaining his place by putting in some sterling performances while on duty for the Colts, in amongst his exploits was a four-goal haul against Dukinfield Town in February 1954, a game in which Bobby Charlton also netted four times in a 10-1 win.

The local boy's final start in the Youth Cup was at Bexleyheath & Welling and he then stood down for the later stages of the tournament, principally because of Albert Scanlon's return from injury.

When he had signed for the Reds on non-paid forms, it was with a view to eventually becoming a professional. However, at the outset of the 1954/55 season, the management were only prepared to extend his amateur terms, at which point Grimsby came in with the offer of a two-year professional contract. Feeling that their deal was a better option than the one United had proposed, the seventeen year-old packed his bags and set off for Blundell Park.

Within a matter of days of signing for the Mariners he was present for a home Third Division (North) fixture against Tranmere and then played in a further nine consecutive games for Grimsby which, incredibly, were all sandwiched into the month of September 1954. Resigned to Town's seconds from then on, with only two exceptions, it was around that period when he also commenced his stint of National Service. The compulsory absence from Blundell Park caused by his term of duty couldn't have helped his chances of regaining a senior spot and following a final first-team home match with Halifax in October 1955, no extension was offered when his contract elapsed.

Upon departing Grimsby, Lowry immediately signed for Aldershot as he was serving in the Royal Army Ordnance Corps at the nearby Farnborough camp. He failed to win a senior berth at the Recreation Ground, but did play a number of times for their Reserves, and at the close of the 1956/57 term he was given a free transfer.

With National Service behind him, he then headed for a coastal football outpost for the second time. On this occasion joining Scarborough, the Midland League club's officials had noted the winger's performances against them when he was a member of Grimsby's Reserves. Not for the first time, soccer was combined with administrative work and throughout his association with Scarborough he held a clerical job in their Supporters' Club office. Following 35 appearances and eight goals, in the spring of 1958 he was surprisingly allowed to leave and, by now a little cheesed off with football, he tracked back to Manchester.

Soon picked up by Lancashire Combination club Droylsden for the start of the 1958/59 season, his departure came after only about half a dozen games.

His only active involvement thereafter was with the Bull's Head, a highly progressive Gorton & District Sunday League side, and by the age of 22 his links with the sport were over due to recurring chest problems.

He then worked as, amongst other things, a dyer and bleacher. Still residing in the Greater Manchester area, in 1991 he retired from the Post Office, to whom he had given fourteen years service as a sorter.

LAWTON, Norbert (1956/57, 1957/58)

Born: Newton Heath, Manchester, 25th March 1940
Died: Manchester, 22nd April 2006
Height: 5ft. 9½ ins., **Weight:** 11st. 8lbs.
Role: Inside-right or centre-forward
Career: Christ the King School (Newton Heath)/ St. Gregory's Technical School (Ardwick)/ Manchester Boys/ Lancashire Boys/ **UNITED**: Am. July 1955 Pro. April 1958/ **Preston North End** March 1963/ **Brighton & Hove Albion** September 1967/ **Lincoln City** February 1971 to July 1972

Bert Whalley and Jimmy Murphy made up an Old Trafford deputation of two who initially approached Nobby Lawton in respect of him joining United. The astute coaches had been impressed with his performances for a Manchester Boys side that reached the 1955 final of the English Schools' Shield, only to lose to Swansea Boys. Equally at home in a wing-half or inside-forward role, his polished displays did much to propel Manchester into the last stage, and he was also chosen to represent Lancashire Boys prior to signing for the Reds.

From the inside-right position, he scored on his club bow that August when the Juniors blasted YCW for six without reply. A regular at that grade throughout, his side completed their Altrincham Junior League fixtures undefeated while he also claimed a brace in the Whitaker Cup final when Trafford Park Youth shipped ten goals and could respond with only two. Because Mark Pearson was a year ahead of him, Lawton was used only once in the Colts and couldn't get near the Youth Cup team.

Mainly featuring for the Juniors until the November of the following term, by then the local lad had taken part in Youth Cup wins over Burnley and Huddersfield. As the season went on he was seen more often in the Colts and also claimed Youth Cup goals against Sunderland, Everton and Blackburn. Nicknamed *'Blind Pew'* by team-mates due to his short-sightedness, on his ninth consecutive appearance in the tournament he stroked home another into West Ham's net in an Upton Park victory which eased the way for a convincing second leg final win at Old Trafford.

The 1957/58 campaign began with him in the 'B' team, and by late September he was up to 'A' level, albeit for odd matches here and there. Tried in all forward positions in the junior sides, with Pearson and newcomer Johnny Giles taking the inside roles while Alex Dawson was involved on first-team affairs, he was given the number nine jersey for a Youth Cup tie at Burnley. He managed a goal at Turf Moor but was exposed to the harsh realities of football when discovering his spot was to go to Dawson for the next round at Blackpool.

With playing staff in short supply following the Munich crash, his name appeared more frequently in the 'A' side and at the end of March he was drafted in for a Central League home win over Stoke. He scored against the Potters and hung onto his place for the Reserves' next fixture at West Brom.

Then regaining a position in the Youth Cup side because Dawson was needed for more pressing requirements, Lawton marked his return against Doncaster with one of the goals in a 6-2 victory and soon after gave up his job as a coal merchants to sign as a professional. Suddenly, that was the end of the road in the Youth Cup as far as he was concerned as, by the time of the unsuccessful semi-final against Wolves, a bout of double pneumonia caused him to temporarily lose the use of his legs.

He was still finding his feet in the 'A' and 'B' teams in the 1958/59 term without overly impressing in any one position. By February he had once again been given a gallop in the Central League, though his appearances for them weren't that frequent.

One of the mainstays of a struggling 'A' side in the 1959/60 season, he occasionally reacquainted himself with the Reserves until March when situated at that standard for a stretch of six matches. The three goals he claimed in those games suddenly brought him a call-up for the first-team's 3-2 win at Luton in early April and Matt Busby then allowed him another couple of games to see what he could do before returning him to the Reserves.

His progress had been painstakingly slow, but in his sixth campaign at the club he finally established himself at Central League level while predominantly replacing Tommy Spratt. Starting the opening seven games in one or other of the inside-forward positions, from mid-September onwards he was moved to right-half for the first time for over a dozen matches. He then went back to inside-forward and over the course of the term was also used twice in the senior side.

As the 1961/62 season got going he resumed at wing-half for the Reserves, this time on the left, and later won a recall to the first-team when Mark Pearson picked up a knock. Following four starts at left-half over the months of September and October 1961, he returned to the forward-line in the December of that year to score six times in 23 league and cup contests, matches which included the Reds' F.A. Cup semi-final defeat by Spurs. Never a prolific goalscorer at any level, even so he captured the headlines on Boxing Day by blasting a hat-trick in a 6-3 home victory over Nottingham Forest.

He was injured in the spring of 1962, only to regain a left-half berth shortly into the following campaign when beginning another twelve First Division contests, the last of which was a sparkling 5-1 home win, once more against Nottingham Forest, in December.

After waiting as long as he had to get his chance, a dose of realisation set in and when Matt Busby plunged into the transfer market for Pat Crerand, having already spent big on Denis Law, it was obvious to him that it heralded the end of his time at the club. He certainly hadn't been helped by a succession of set-backs and it is certain that the Old Trafford crowd never saw him at his best.

The Soccer Star magazine, dated the 16th June 1962, pinpointed just why when revealing:

One could easily name half a dozen players still in the game who have had long careers without a serious injury, but look at all that has happened to Manchester United('s) 22 year-old inside-forward Nobby Lawton in the short time he has been a professional. He has had double pneumonia, cartilage trouble, pleurisy, appendicitis, and now a cracked shin bone!'

On the 9th March 1963, he was included in the team that lost a Central League match at Villa Park and was then sold to Second Division Preston for a sum of £14,000.

With the confidence of playing regular first-team football, and free from all of his previous fitness issues, he finally developed into something like the finished article. Now able to repay his transfer fee with continually high levels of creativity, craft and commitment to North End's cause, it was in their colours that he reached the pinnacle of his football career when, in May 1964, he skippered them to the F.A. Cup final. Despite losing 3-2 to West Ham, the achievement represented a tremendous feat for the underdogs.

He became a much admired figure at Deepdale and over the next three years continued to add more and more games to his growing total while also chipping in with an occasional goal or two. His final game for Preston was a 1-0 win over Norwich in August 1967 and, in all, he had made 162 appearances for the Lilywhites.

North End transferred him to Brighton for a fee of £10,000 that September and manager Archie Macaulay soon bestowed the captaincy of the club on him. Operating as the cog in Albion's midfield engine room for the next three and a half years, in addition he earned great respect from his kindred sportsmen by the manner in which he performed his duties on the executive committee of the Professional Footballers' Association. In his role at the PFA, he diligently fought for improved terms for his fellow professionals.

He served on the club's team selection committee for two matches in November 1968 prior to the appointment of new manager Freddie Goodwin. There was an almost instant improvement in Brighton's fortunes with Goodwin's arrival, of which the contribution from his old United club-mate was a major factor.

Lawton made an indelible mark on the memories of those Albion supporters present at the Goldstone Ground in February 1969. Hitting an incredible shot, which went like a missile into Shrewsbury's net from a distance all of 40 yards, those Brighton fans whose memories stretch that far back still claim it was one of the best goals ever seen at the old stadium.

During the 1969/70 season the Albion dished up some marvellously entertaining football, but their push for promotion eventually failed. Events on the field took a downturn in the following term and he requested a transfer after losing his place.

Leaving Brighton to join Lincoln on a free transfer in February 1971, it was obvious he was already carrying the knee injury which would soon end his career. In the nine months between his signing for Lincoln and November 1971, the Mancunian made twenty Football League starts and one Football League Cup appearance before regretfully conceding that his knee couldn't take the strain demanded of a professional footballer any longer. The blow of being forced out of the game was softened ever so slightly when he was granted a benefit by his employers in March 1972, a game in which a Lincoln City XI met an All-Star XI.

He moved back to the Manchester area when his football days were over and was, for more than twenty years, the sales director of an export packaging company based close to where he grew up.

Sadly, Nobby Lawton died from cancer in 2006. As a person he will be missed by many, while the comments of former United and Preston team-mate Alex Dawson, that he was a footballer who possessed *'the rare combination of class and bite,'* act as a testimony to the attributes he displayed to thousands on Saturday afternoons all those years ago.

PEARCE, Peter Derek (1953/54)

Born: Audenshaw, Manchester, 26th April 1936
Height: 5ft. 10½ ins., **Weight:** 11st. 7lbs.
Role: Centre-forward
Career: Fairfield Road Junior School (Droylsden)/ Ducie Avenue Secondary School (Moss Side)/ UNITED: (NC) January 1954 Am. May to November 1954/ **Stalybridge Celtic** September and October 1956/ **Glossop** December 1956/ **Stalybridge Celtic** August and September 1957/ **Ashton United** March 1958/ **New Mills** August to November 1958/ **Droylsden** December 1958 to c/s 1959

A lean, fair haired centre-forward who was hungry for goals and would chase any seemingly lost cause in search of one, Peter Pearce was born in one of the more well-to-do suburbs of Manchester.

A City follower from an early age, he was something of an all-rounder at sport and won a Manchester Athletics Championships medal as a youngster, in addition to representing both of his schools and Manchester at cricket.

As a footballer, he was an out-and-out striker who got a fair number of goals with his head and, even though naturally right-footed, was so adept with the ball on his 'wrong' foot that he was occasionally utilised as an outside-left.

In 1951, he was a member of the Ducie Avenue team that defeated Didsbury Central in the Manchester Area final of the Daily Dispatch Schools' Shield. Pearce scored one of the Ducie goals which then put them into the county stage final, where they were defeated by Stamford Secondary School of Ashton-under-Lyne at Ashton United's Hurst Cross ground.

Leaving school a year later, his working life began at the now long-gone Federated Insurance Company in Manchester. Around the same time he also joined up with a highly talented boys' football team, Ryder Brow, and it was his goalscoring achievements for them that would soon bring him to United's attention. Ryder Brow had already forged links with the Reds via Roger Byrne, who was a member of their side prior to going to Old Trafford in 1949.

Spending a couple of years with the Gorton outfit, they were packed with activity and achievement. His team reached the final of the Manchester Federation of Lads Clubs Cup, in which they came up against a Benchill eleven who included Bobby Harrop amongst their number. In October 1953, he was selected to represent Manchester County Youth along with Harrop and two other United juniors, Sammy Chapman and Alan Rhodes, in a game against Cheshire Youth at the Butcher's Arms, home of Droylsden Football Club.

Early in 1954, the Reds were forced to release Chapman, who was desperate to return home to Northern Ireland, and their search for a replacement led them to Ryder Brow where Pearce was banging in the goals. Taking up the story, he said, *'United wanted me to sign amateur forms, but I said 'no'. If I had agreed, I wouldn't have been able to play for Ryder Brow or the Manchester Federation of Lads Clubs team and they were both doing really well at the time.'*

Opting instead to pen non-contract papers, his club debut was in the Youth Cup replay against Rotherham at The Cliff. The Reds had drawn with the Millers in Yorkshire earlier in the month and he was drafted into the side without knowing most of his United team-mates. Jimmy Murphy was aware that his young charge's preference was to home in directly on goal, so he gave instructions that the ball should be carried out to either of the flanks if possession was held in an advanced position.

'I wasn't sure as to exactly why I was being asked to do this, but I soon found out,' he explained. *'When I got a chance to carry out the directions, I charged towards the wing only to hear someone calling for a pass just inside me. I turned to see Duncan Edwards running into position and when my pass fell at his feet, he walloped the ball into the net with a shot of such ferocity that it could have seriously damaged Rotherham's goalkeeper if he'd managed to get in the way.'*

He wasn't called on for the Fifth Round and only took part in one game for the Colts prior to returning for the semi-final matches against West Brom. He then put in just one more appearance, smashing a hat-trick in a 6-0 win over Heywood St. James at The Cliff, before registering his one and only Youth Cup goal against the Baggies in the second leg at Old Trafford.

While the Reds were heading for another Youth Cup showpiece, the Manchester Federation of Lads Clubs side had progressed into a final of their own, that of the National Lads Clubs Cup. Staged at Upton Park on the morning of the 1954 F.A. Cup final, Manchester defeated their London counterparts 2-1, with him and another Ryder Brow boy grabbing the

Peter Pearce (left) fixes his focus on the ball before dispatching it into the net in a junior match at The Cliff

decisive goals, and later that day the victorious team watched as West Brom beat Preston at Wembley.

He was chosen to represent England at Boys Club level shortly after, with the match against Northern Ireland taking place at the ground of Cliftonville Football Club. The visitors lost the game by three goals to two, although he experienced the honour of scoring both of his country's goals.

Unable to force his way into the Reds' line-up for the Youth Cup final against Wolves, as a mark of his earlier contributions United officials invited him to travel to Switzerland for the close season tour. Despite not being used in any of the continental games, it had been a whirlwind few months for him in a football sense, as he was successful in a national final, represented his country and had also been associated with the Reds at home and abroad.

He signed amateur forms for United upon returning from Switzerland and moved up as far as the Colts team. In September 1954, he was conscripted into the Army and from the December of that year was fed on a diet of 'khaki' football for nearly two years, the call-up practically ending any ambitions he held of progressing any further at Old Trafford.

On his release from the military in September 1956, he signed for Stalybridge Celtic of the Cheshire League and in only his third game for them, a bang on the ankle caused him to leave the field. It was the first sign of a problem that would plague him from then on and it ended his initial spell at Celtic within weeks.

Shortly after departing Bower Fold, he joined Manchester League club Glossop and scored no less than eight times in just less than a dozen appearances for the Surrey Street side. Out of action for a couple of weeks following one of Glossop's matches, the local newspaper reported *'twinkle-toed Peter Pearce left the field with an ankle injury caused by a fall in a tackle'*. Later that season he scored Glossop's second goal in a 2-0 victory in the Manchester Junior Cup semi-final against Newton Heath Loco and, despite him knocking in another in the final, his side lost to Brindle Heath Lads Club.

The beginning of the 1957/58 campaign saw him return to Stalybridge. He appeared to be back to full fitness when claiming a hat-trick in a pre-season trial game and followed up that feat by scoring Celtic's goal in a 1-1 draw away to Bangor City on his second 'debut' for them.

Out of action for much of the remainder of the term, by March 1958 he was on Ashton United's payroll. By coincidence, Ashton needed a replacement for another former Manchester United youth team forward, Alan Blakeman, who had gone to Rotherham.

In August 1958, he moved to New Mills and the Church Lane outfit must have been absolutely delighted with his contribution as he piled up eight goals in only nine games. Choosing to leave the Millers in order to sign for a club that was practically on his doorstep, he played just four games for Droylsden's first-team, the last of which was against Horwich in January 1959, and then turned out for their Reserves before quitting. The ankle knock he had carried for some time showed no signs of improving and he realised that he could have subjected himself to permanent damage by continuing. His decision to finish more or less coincided with his 23rd birthday.

Outside of football and still employed in the financial services industry, he became a life inspector for a well known insurance company and later opened an insurance brokerage in Rochdale.

In the early 1970's, he was integral to the formation of a respected local junior football club, Brendon Bees, and was even charged with looking after one of their teams for a period. His family held a long association with the Bees, as his son and his grandson have both been on their books.

Peter Pearce currently lives in the Tameside area of Manchester and retired from the insurance business after the greater part of 40 years service in 1989.

McGUINNESS, Paul Edward (1983/84)

Born: Wythenshawe, Manchester, 2nd March 1966
Height: 5ft. 9ins., Weight: 11st. 6lbs.
Role: Midfielder
Career: St. Hugh's Primary School (Timperley)/ English Martyrs Primary School (York)/ Nunthorpe Grammar School (York)/ Altrincham Grammar School/ Trafford Boys/ Greater Manchester Boys/ UNITED: (NC) 1983 Pro. July 1984 to May 1986/ Loughborough University/ Crewe Alexandra August 1986 to July 1987/ UNITED: Pro. July 1989 to March 1991/ Brighton & Hove Albion (L) October and November 1990/ Bury (NC) March to May 1991/ Chester City July 1991 to May 1992

Paul, the son of ex-manager Wilf McGuinness, is one of three who have appeared in the Youth Cup for the Reds and whose fathers also sat in the Old Trafford hot-seat; Peter Docherty and Darren Ferguson being the others. One record he holds uniquely, though, is that of being the only person to play for and manage United's Youth Cup team, and in only his second season in charge he guided them to the final against Liverpool.

Taking over as the young Reds' coach at the start of the 2005/06 campaign, his most pressing requirement was to rebuild in the wake of the disaster of the previous term, when Stoke knocked Francisco Filho's boys out of the national cup competition at the opening hurdle. One of his first moves was to instigate an immersion into the club's culture, because he felt it imperative that his charges should have an understanding of the rich tradition of youth development at Old Trafford, especially in terms of the Youth Cup and the Blue Stars tournament.

He explained, *'They've seen tape after tape of all the great games and players here. It gets in the blood. The spirit becomes engrained in them. Learning about the history of Manchester United and all about the players is part of the youth education policy here. They learn from what they see and imitate them. They watch clips of World Cups with Brazil and Argentina. We show them Barcelona and how Arsenal play as well. But they are some of the luckiest lads in football because they can watch United every week. That's great because they are picking stuff up from the best.'*

McGuinness spent his formative years in Timperley and first connected to the sport through an involvement with his school side. He also turned out in local football circles, but felt that his time would be better spent with his father. In recalling those early days he said, *'I only played briefly for a couple of Sunday League teams as I preferred school football and I practiced on a Sunday, often with my dad on the fields near our house. I didn't enjoy the Sunday League games as much as representative schools football, and the service for my practice was after all from an ex-England international!'*

Having a parent with such an illustrious association in the game might have turned other lads off football altogether, but he revelled in his father's experience. Expanding on the subject, he mentioned, *'It goes without saying that without my dad I wouldn't have played football, not because he pushed me but because I fell in love with the sport around the age of eight. I was then in an environment where football was everywhere. I would go to training with my dad and join in with the apprentices when I was twelve years-old, or with the first-team at different clubs when I was fourteen or fifteen.*

We would go to watch games together and through being exposed to professional football you begin to understand it and love it even more. My dad didn't coach me in a formal sense, he talked to me, and I learned the principles of the game through basic football sayings that he had been taught by the likes of Jimmy Murphy.'

When his father was appointed as York City's manager in February 1975, the family remained in Manchester for a spell before moving across the Pennines in the September of the following year. Continuing to play for his school side in the interim period, the young McGuinness returned to Manchester in 1980 and was selected for both Trafford Boys and a Greater Manchester under-15 team that was then joint national champions.

He stated of that period, *'I then had trails at Middlesbrough, Leeds, Burnley, Forest and Blackburn, but I waited, hoping for a chance at United. A year or two later I played for the Greater Manchester under-18 side that won the Inter-County final.'*

When the opportunity to join the Reds presented itself he didn't need much time to deliberate, however, while most of those in his age group signed apprentice terms, he elected to continue with his studies. After agreeing to turn out on a non-contract basis, his first game for United was on the opening day of the 1983/84 campaign when sent on as a substitute for Mark Mettrick in the 'A' team's 3-0 home win over Crewe.

He claimed a regular peg in the 'A' side's dressing room throughout most of the term, though the majority of November and December was lost due to school commitments. The following February saw him make his one and only appearance in the Youth Cup when replacing Gary Mills in a home defeat by Barnsley, and on the final day of the campaign his progress was confirmed when he was named as 12th man for the Reserves' game against Everton at Old Trafford.

Completing his 'A' levels at college in 1984, and following some *'gentle persuasion'* from Eric Harrison, he agreed to sign professional terms. Once again predominantly used in the 'A' team, another crack at second string football presented itself in September when he went on as a substitute in a 2-1 home reverse against Liverpool, and he was then involved with the second string for seven full appearances from October through to December. In addition, he missed four out of 36 Lancashire League Division One games, all due to commitments with the Reserves, as the 'A' side headed every one of their competitors for the second consecutive year.

He was placed on Central League duty on the opening day of the 1985/86 season and retained his place for the next five fixtures as a result of putting in some sterling performances in the heart of the Reds' midfield. Such was his form that he was then included in the senior squad for the first time in early October, Ron Atkinson naming him as 13th man for the trip to Luton. United went into the game having won their previous ten games in the First Division, with the excited youngster required to cancel his driving test once he heard of his inclusion, and for the remainder of the term he equally represented the 'A' team and the Reserves.

Experiencing professional football at close quarters from an early age, and thereby truly appreciating the precarious nature of the industry, it was as a result of wanting to protect his future as much as possible that he decided to renew his education. A bright lad, who was just as comfortable in a classroom as out on a football field, he elected to enrol on a P.E. and Sports Science course at Loughborough University. Even though his studies were never neglected, he has since admitted that it was impossible to keep away from football activities for too long when saying, *'In my first year I didn't play for the university, apart from one friendly, as I was still with United. I started playing for them in my second year and we won the U.A.U. Championship in each of the three years I was with them.'*

Somewhere around then he attracted the interest of Crewe manager Dario Gradi and, being a free agent, agreed to join the Gresty Road club for the 1986/87 season. His Football League debut occurred when he left the bench in a 1-1 home draw against Wolves on the 13th September and he then took part in twelve successive games until November when academic duties were given preference. Figuring alongside future England internationals David Platt and Geoff Thomas, only one further appearance was added to his tally, in a home game against Cardiff in late March, and over the next couple of years he continued to represent Loughborough University alongside working towards his qualification.

In January 1989, he visited Eric Harrison and Brian Whitehouse at The Cliff. Harrison suggested his experience could be useful to the Central League team because they faced possible relegation after a very poor campaign. McGuinness agreed to sign non-contract papers for the second time and on the 19th of that month he made a welcome return in a 7-1 home win over West Brom Reserves. He then accumulated a further five Central League appearances, including a 4-0 home win over Coventry on the last day of the term. Harrison had asked him to fill in at full-back when concluding that his influence would help steady the defence, and with a decisive victory the drop was avoided.

By then his university course had ended and in the 1989 close season he was offered a two-year professional contract with a view to him assisting the younger players by providing some much needed know-how. It could reasonably be said that his coaching experience was now about to start in earnest.

He began the next season as an unused first-team substitute for Mike Duxbury's testimonial game against Manchester City after which his experience in the centre of midfield assisted the Reserves up to fourth position in the league. Missing only six games all season while additionally helping out on thirteen occasions for the 'A' side, he was *'under no illusions'* as he knew that he *'would never be able to make it into the senior set-up'* and was content to see out his contract while focusing attention on his long-term prospects.

The 1990/91 campaign proved a complete contrast as he found it difficult to maintain his status in the Reserves and managed only four substitute appearances at that standard during the entire term. Joining Brighton on a month-long loan in October, the Seagulls utilised him at second team level while he also gained selection as a substitute for their senior side on no less than five occasions without being called on.

Then featuring mainly in the 'A' team after returning to Old Trafford, his last game on the 13th March 1991 ended in a 5-1 home defeat by Bolton and two days later his contract was cancelled by mutual consent. He had accumulated enough games to qualify for his fourth Lancashire League Division One championship medal and it is thought that he probably holds the club appearance record at that level.

Signing for Bury for the remainder of the campaign, and seeing service in a handful of matches for the Shakers' Reserves, he transferred to Chester for the 1991/92 season but only played seven games, four as a substitute, at Third Division grade.

It was while he was on the look-out for another opening when Alex Ferguson offered him the chance to work with the younger element at Old Trafford in a dual welfare/coaching role and so, at the age of 26, all playing ambitions were permanently shelved in order to pursue a career from the touchline. In October 1993, he became the Centre of Excellence director and later Academy assistant director at Carrington, his responsibility extending to looking after all the junior teams from under-9's up to under-16's.

Remaining in that role for over ten years before taking responsibility of the under-18 Academy and Youth Cup teams in 2005, as always he is keen to pay his respects to those who have helped him. *'I feel very honoured and privileged to have been entrusted with this important job by Sir Alex Ferguson, the greatest manager in the history of the game'* he said. *'It fills me with pride to work alongside Jimmy Ryan and Tony Whelan, two great servants of the club over a long period of time, as well as following in the footsteps of my father and some of the great youth coaches at Manchester United, most notably Jimmy Murphy and my old mentor, Eric Harrison.'*

On a football pitch, Paul McGuinness revelled as an organiser and leader who often captained the sides he was involved with. A perceptive, predominantly right-footed, ball-winning midfielder who grafted hard between penalty boxes and rarely gave away possession, as a coach he conducts himself in a thoughtful and determined yet approachable manner, totally befitting someone with his level of responsibility within the club.

While keen to point out the assistance received when guiding the young Reds to their tenth Youth Cup final triumph in 2011, it is clear the sacrifices he has made, the dedication and knowledge applied to his chosen profession and the deep-rooted traditions of the club he instils in his charges will surely bring him further such successes in the future.

GIBSON, Stuart (1956/57)

Born: Broughton, Salford, 23rd December 1938
Died: Torquay, 2nd July 2008
Height: 5ft. 9ins., **Weight:** 10st. 12lbs.
Role: Left full-back
Career: St. Clare's School (Higher Blackley)/ Manchester Boys/ Northern Nomads/ Cheshire Youth/ UNITED: Am. May 1955 to October 1957/ Altrincham November 1957 to February 1958/ Charlton Athletic January 1959 to March 1960/ Torquay United April and May 1960/ Brixham United August 1960/ St. Blazey August 1962/ Falmouth Town August 1964/ St. Blazey August 1965 to c/s 1966

Although born on the Salford side of the River Irwell, Stuart Gibson lived in Dorwood Avenue in the Higher Blackley area of Manchester until he was called up for National Service duty at the age of nineteen. His father, Bill, was a former professional footballer who operated as a full-back for Leeds, Blackpool, Southend and Macclesfield prior to the Second World War. There was plenty of paternal encouragement when it came to participation in sporting activities, but it was son Stuart, one of three brothers, who was the most natural when it came to ball games and he progressed to play football, cricket and table tennis at a skilled level.

In divulging how contact came to be made with United, he explained, *'I captained my school football team for two years and I also played for Manchester Boys. One of my teachers, a chap called Mr. Grissdale, felt that a professional club should take a look at me and so he arranged for me to have a trial at The Cliff. I was fifteen at the time and I was only five feet, five inches tall and weighed around nine stones. After the trial, Jimmy Murphy advised me to contact the club twelve months later in order to give me the chance to fill out and possibly grow by an inch or two.'*

He left school shortly after to become a clerk at the National Boiler & General Insurance Company, which was situated in St. Mary's Parsonage in Manchester city centre, and about the same time signed up for Northern Nomads, a top-class amateur outfit. Scoring for them three times on his debut, a 10-3 victory over landlords Stalybridge Celtic, he shared the company of no less than seven amateur internationals while occupying the outside-right position. During the period spent with Northern Nomads, Gibson also won a number of Cheshire Youth caps.

Over the summer months he played for Broughton Cricket Club on Saturdays, as well as in midweek for his work's side, and at the age of sixteen hit his first century for National Boiler & General in an evening fixture against East Levenshulme.

Particularly accomplished at table tennis, his talent with the paddle won him the All-England Knight's of St. Columbia under-21 championship at age sixteen and he retained the title twelve months later. He also starred for Manchester at table tennis under the critical eye of coach and England international, Benny Kosophski.

'I held Jimmy Murphy to his word and United signed me as an amateur in 1955,' he revealed. *'I had to change jobs, though, because the insurance company I was working for weren't at all sympathetic to my new football commitments. Luckily, Joe Armstrong was able to fix me up at Lever Brothers in Lever Street where I became a furrier.'*

In the 1955/56 term he established himself at left-full back for the Juniors, and also got a few games at right full-back and even at inside-right. Despite previously being deployed as a winger for Northern Nomads, the transition to a defensive role caused him no problems whatsoever because his speed into the tackle and exact distribution with either foot meant that he could impress in a variety of roles. Also, with his experience as a wide man, there was the advantage of him often being able to read the intentions of the winger he was designated to mark.

Missing the first half of the 1956/57 season entirely, his reappearance in January 1957 was in the 'B' team. Gibson displayed great form in the 2-2 Youth Cup draw at Everton a month later and held his place for a replay which resulted in a 5-2 victory. He then featured in a 6-0 Youth Cup win over

Blackburn and both semi-final ties against Southampton, but just when everything was pointing in the right direction he was hit with a sporting tragedy of mammoth proportions.

'In the week leading up to the away leg of the Youth Cup final against West Ham, the youth squad and the first-team were training together on the Old Trafford pitch,' he recalled. 'Obviously they (the seniors) were preparing for the F.A Cup final at Wembley on the Saturday and in a completely innocent goalmouth incident, their big centre-half Mark Jones accidentally toppled over me. Most of Jones' weight fell on my toes and within twenty minutes I had hobbled off to get some help in the medical room where I was placed on a bed between Duncan Edwards and Dennis Viollet.

The blood clots under my big toe nails were released and the whole of the nail area was then sprayed with penicillin. By the following morning infection had set in and I was in so much pain that both of my big toe nails had to be removed. It meant that I missed the two legs of the Youth Cup final and my injury almost certainly cost me an England Youth cap.'

The set-back was a major turning point in his career, although he was regarded highly enough to be taken on that year's trip to the Blue Stars tournament. Following approximately ten more games for United, one of which was made during the Swiss tour when Chur were defeated 6-0 in the Reds' second game, his story then took another twist. 'In August 1957 I asked United if they would put me on a paid contract and the response I got was pretty negative,' he claimed. 'They wanted me to wait a little while longer because the club felt that they had a full complement of professional players. It was a bit frustrating as I saw it as something of a snub, so I left soon after to join Altrincham.'

Gibson was initially utilised by Altrincham against Winsford at Moss Lane, quickly reverting to playing at number seven again in a forward-line that also contained Tommy Littler and Noel McFarlane. The Robins secured a 3-0 win and he was given a good write-up in the local newspaper, whose reporter reckoned the newcomer was *'extremely willing'*, as well as noting that he *'had a foot in all three goals'*.

There was more praise in store when plundering his first goal for the club in a victory at Macclesfield, which caused one reviewer to state that he had *'slashed his way past two defenders and cracked home a great solo goal'*. The time spent at Moss Lane was short and sweet, however, and his final game for Altrincham fell in February 1958 whereupon he commenced Queen's service with the First Battalion Grenadier Guards.

While with the Guards he was stationed at Chelsea Barracks, and in his very first game for their football side was spotted by George Robinson, Charlton's assistant manager. Robinson asked him to a trial at The Valley, where he made a sufficiently good impression for the Addicks to sign him.

Between January 1959 and March 1960 he racked up five appearances for Charlton's Reserves in the Football Combination, in addition to clocking up an equal number for their third team in the Aetolian League. Utilised principally as an inside-forward, of his ten starts, nine were actually made away from home. The high point of that period came when he performed in front of a crowd of over 10,000 for Charlton's Reserves against Arsenal's second string at Highbury.

Later winning four Army caps while on National Service, as well as captaining the Household Brigade team, he also represented the latter at cricket and was once chosen to play in a benefit game against the famous Surrey side of the 1950's. While stood at the crease he faced the bowling of Tony Lock, who sent balls down the track alternatively with his left hand and then his right.

Upon his demob, Gibson was offered what he felt were meagre terms by Charlton and instead of taking up their offer he chose instead to move to the Torbay area as his parents were in semi-retirement there. Still aged only 21, Torquay United snapped him up and he subsequently got in a handful of games for their third team.

In May 1960, he hit a hat-trick in a 7-2 win over Ottery St. Marys in the Devon Senior Cup final, a game which was staged at Exeter City's ground. Now working in the family business, which consisted of operating a mackerel fishing boat and hiring out floats and pedalos on Paignton beach, his decision to leave Torquay United was made on a matter of principle over their selection policy.

His next move was to Brixham United, a Plymouth & District League side. It was an excellent choice of club as he enjoyed two fabulous years at the Wall Park ground and scored goals by the bagful. Brixham were crowned league champions in 1961 and he managed a hat-trick in the game that clinched them the title.

That success was only a prelude for what came next, because twelve months later Brixham retained the league title and won the Senior Victory Cup, the Arthur Little Memorial Trophy and, with one of his shots providing the only goal of the game, the Devon Senior Cup. Additionally gaining representative recognition with selection for the Plymouth & District League side, the Devon County F.A. also saw fit to cap him.

Following all of the unprecedented triumphs at Brixham, Gibson then agreed to match professional terms with South Western League outfit, St. Blazey. Described in the local newspaper as *'a fast raiding winger with some very clever touches'*, the period spent at St. Blaize Park was another fruitful one as the club followed Brixham's example by winning their particular division two years in succession, and still more representative honours came his way when he was included in a South Western League XI.

Moving to rivals Falmouth Town in August 1964, his reputation was such that one newspaper correspondent referred to him as *'undoubtedly one of the finest wingers in the West'*. The 1964/65 season came to a conclusion for Falmouth with second place in the South Western League and a Cornwall Senior Cup final appearance against one of his former clubs, St. Blazey. A 0-0 draw before a 4,000 crowd preceded a 2-1 win in the replay, Falmouth's winner coming ten minutes from time when his corner kick was headed home by a forward colleague.

He rejoined St. Blazey in August 1965 only to make another appearance in the Cornwall Senior Cup final. That term brought his football activities to a premature end as, through tearing the tissues around his spine, he was forced to accept a physician's advice to cease his involvement in the game.

When the family business was sold in 1970 he attended St. Luke's Teacher Training College in Exeter, where an Honours Degree in Education Philosophy and Theology was obtained. Thereafter teaching at the Cuthbert Mayne School in Torquay, that particular establishment achieved fame as the first ever joint Roman Catholic and Church of England comprehensive school in the country.

As well as coaching children at football and cricket and winning selection for Devon at over-50 cricket standard, during the 1980's he supervised the Devon Schools' cricket team and assisted a number of youngsters to obtain under-15 England caps. A love of the summer sport also led him to continue participating in cricket circles around Torquay, his main club being Cockington Corinthian, for whom he played until in his 60's and was proud and honoured to become their president.

Sadly, having seemingly beaten cancer five years previously, Stuart Gibson succumbed to the illness in 2008, just a few months short of his 70th birthday.

ADAMS, Kenneth (1954/55)

Born: Warrington, 19th January 1937
Height: 5ft. 7ins., **Weight:** 9st. 7lbs.
Role: Outside-right
Career: Hamilton Street Junior School (Warrington)/ Boteler Grammar School (Warrington)/ Lancashire & Cheshire Grammar Schools/ Merseyside Grammar Schools/ Winsford United April 1954/ UNITED: Am. September 1954 to c/s 1955/ Birmingham University XI/ Hednesford February 1958 to c/s 1958

A supporter of Warrington RLFC as a boy, Ken Adams found his particular talents were better suited to the round ball code of football. Bearing in mind that rugby league was king in the Warrington locality, he was fortunate to attend a secondary school which was a soccer playing establishment. A flair for football won him representative honours for both Merseyside and Lancashire & Cheshire at grammar school level, and it led to him being recommended to Winsford United by the father of a school friend who happened to be a scout for the Cheshire League club.

His first appearance for them came in a Good Friday fixture at Macclesfield in April 1954 and it was an especially 'good' day, both personally and collectively, when he starred in a resounding 4-1 victory. It caused a local scribe to write that there was *'a new right-wing on view in Ken Adams, a Warrington grammar school player. Adams, only seventeen years-old, made a satisfactory debut. He figured in two moves that brought goals and displayed good ball control'*. The newcomer then made the Winsford number seven spot his own until the end of the term.

At the commencement of the next season he took part in the traditional Winsford trial game between the 'Blues' and the 'Reds'. Finishing on the winning 'Red' side, his contribution earned him the right to continue with the first-team. In one of their early fixtures, this time a 5-0 trouncing of Northwich, another reporter commented that *'the full-backs were beaten far too often by Adams'*.

United soon picked up on the reviews he was receiving and they acted by signing him on amateur forms at the end of September 1954.

A quick player, who could beat a man, he favoured 'cutting' inside his marker to do so. Predominantly right-footed, he packed a fierce shot which he wasn't afraid to use. He put down an early marker in a 10-2 Lancashire League victory over Oldham in early October and was then chosen for the opening rounds of the Youth Cup, with all four games proving memorable for different reasons.

In the First Round against Liverpool, he made a dream start by scoring within a minute of the kick-off and his next appearance was in the infamous 'fog' game against Manchester City at Maine Road, the Reds trailing until midway through the second half after which two goals from Duncan Edwards saw them through. Speaking of the conditions that day, he said, *'The weather was so bad that I took the precaution of telephoning Manchester to check the game would go ahead before setting off from Warrington.'*

At the Third Round stage, another deficit, this time 2-0 to Barnsley at Oakwell, was turned into a 4-2 win and in his final Youth Cup game United routed Sheffield Wednesday 7-0.

He was then elevated into the 'A' team, but an indifferent performance against Lancashire Steel meant that he lost his Youth Cup place to the emerging Ken Morgans.

Towards the end of a campaign which yielded a Lancashire League title, he was offered a place at Birmingham University, an opportunity that would ultimately shape the rest of his life. He recalled of that period, *'I saw at close hand the attributes needed to succeed in professional football and I felt that I didn't possess enough of them. On my last day at Old Trafford I bumped into Jimmy Murphy and he shook my hand and wished me good luck for the future.'*

He didn't see too much football over the next couple of years as, apart from representing the university, the demands of study took precedence on his time and it wasn't until the early part of 1958 before Hednesford tempted him back into competitive action. Then members of the Birmingham League Second Division, his first appearance for them was on the 15th February 1958 and it prompted the local newspaper to comment that he *'showed some classy touches'*.

Before the game against Moor Green at the now demolished Cross Keys ground in March 1958, a party of Girl Guides were present to make a collection for the Manchester United Disaster Fund. Their actions must have seemed a sad reminder to him as his former youth team colleagues, Duncan Edwards and Eddie Colman, had tragically lost their lives at Munich just a month before.

The winger made just thirteen appearances for the Pitmen, scoring once, as they finished in sixth position in the table. Reports of those games stated that *'the Hednesford right-wing was its most valuable asset'* and how he *'looked booked for a higher grade of football'*. Alas, when the season came to an end, a nagging cartilage problem was the catalyst that made him place football as runner-up to his career for the second, and final, time.

Ken Adams became a biology teacher after graduating from Birmingham University. Later progressing to head of biology prior to rising to deputy head at a comprehensive school in Sutton Coldfield, he retired in 1993 after 34 years in the profession.

CAROLAN, Joseph Francis (1955/56)

Born: North Stand, Dublin, 8th September 1937
Height: 5ft. 10ins., **Weight:** 11st. 4lbs.
Role: Right half-back
Career: St. Peter's School (Dublin)/ Home Farm (Dublin)/ UNITED: Pro. February 1956/ Brighton & Hove Albion December 1960 to June 1962/ Tonbridge September 1962/ Canterbury City July 1968/ Sheppey United player/manager May 1969/ Tonbridge player/manager January 1970 to March 1971

Like many other of his compatriot sportsmen from the Republic of Ireland, as a youngster Joe Carolan was almost equally skilled at soccer, hurling and Gaelic football. Playing his early soccer for a Dublin side, Banneville Juniors, he was connected to the esteemed Home Farm club and had already begun an apprenticeship as a cabinet maker before coming to United's attention.

In some respects he followed a similar path to Old Trafford as his fellow countryman, Billy Whelan. Having attended the same school in the Cabra district of Dublin, even though Whelan was the older of the two by a couple of years, they had competed together in a hurling final as boys. Whelan had also been associated with Home Farm prior to joining the Reds and, naturally, the two continued their friendship once Carolan arrived in England in February 1956.

Getting off to a splendid start later that month in the 'B' team's 13-2 annihilation of Stockport County 'B', his Youth Cup call-up came just two months later as, fortuitously, his 18th birthday had fallen just the right side of the eligibility deadline date. Just like Whelan's debut in the competition, it was in crucial circumstances.

The Reds had been held to a 1-1 draw at Old Trafford in the opening leg of the Youth Cup semi-final by a Bolton side that had much more to offer in physical terms than in football ability. The Dubliner was given the right-half slot for the second instalment at Burnden Park in preference to Bobby English, helping the Reds to secure a great 3-0 win which projected them into the final.

He retained a place for the home section of the showpiece when the Reds' cause was greatly assisted by his goal. The slender lead established in Manchester was pegged back at Chesterfield, where a late winner gave United the trophy and the newcomer a winning feeling barely ten weeks after arriving in England. Amazingly, all three of his Youth Cup appearances had taken place within the space of just fifteen days.

He was utilised in both half-back places and at left full-back in the following term, mainly for the 'A' side, and within the first couple of months of the 1957/58 campaign his elevation to the Central League side was celebrated with a 3-0 win at Burnley. He returned to the 'A' side immediately thereafter, and within a few weeks of the air crash was recalled to second team affairs.

The Irishman was used in all bar one of the opening eighteen Central League fixtures of the 1958/59 season. With a period of over two and a half years of steady progress behind him, his first-team debut resulted in a 2-1 home win over Luton in November 1958. He proved to be something of a lucky charm as, in the games completed prior to his introduction, only five had been won, eight were lost and five drawn, but once he was on board the seniors went on a run of seven straight victories and eventually finished second in the table.

The Reds weren't quite as successful in the 1959/60 term, when slipping down to seventh position. It was, nevertheless, undoubtedly his best ever in terms of appearances when participating in 44 league and cup matches at left-back. Only Bill Foulkes, who was ever-present and started just one league game more, surpassed his total for the campaign.

In November 1959, superb form earned him full international recognition when he figured in a 3-2 win for Eire over Sweden in Dublin. One of Eire's goals came courtesy of club-mate Johnny Giles, who was also making his full Irish debut. Again alongside Giles, his second appearance for the Republic saw them sweep to a 2-0 home win over Chile the following March.

If that season was considered one of some considerable progress, the following one couldn't have been any more different for him.

After United lost their opening two league fixtures in August 1960, the second of which was a 4-0 thumping by Everton at Goodison Park, Matt Busby dropped him in favour of Shay Brennan. Dutifully returning to the Reserves, when Busby captured Noel Cantwell in the November the development brought an end to any thoughts he may have held of reclaiming a senior place. He then took part in a 3-1 defeat by Liverpool Reserves at Anfield and his transfer to Brighton & Hove Albion was completed soon after.

The fee Brighton splashed out to get him was around £13,000, a massive investment for the south coast club as they were battling against relegation from the Second Division. Carolan's composure brought some stability to a previously badly leaking defence and the Albion escaped the drop with their star signing registering 22 appearances before the end of the term.

Once more, though, things were to change drastically. The defender lost favour almost immediately with new manager George Curtis and, restricted to just eleven league starts during his second year at the Goldstone Ground, the club allowed him to leave when his contract expired in 1962.

Now aged almost 25, and still within the period when the confines of the maximum wage for footballers was a major restriction on their earning potential, he broke from the professional game in order to set up a window cleaning business. Shortly after, Southern League outfit Tonbridge took him on board and so began a marvellous relationship that was of benefit to all concerned.

Financially far better off by switching to part-time football while working for himself, his experience and ability proved tremendous assets to the Kent club. Tonbridge had been forced to endure almost nothing but hard knocks for quite some time and normally couldn't have hoped to land someone of such quality with the potential of his best years ahead of him. A cool character who had a certain poise about him, he was soon made club captain and in 1964 promotion from the Southern League First Division was secured.

Then leading the side to the Kent Senior Cup in 1965, Carolan was promptly named their 'Player of the Year'. He remained at the Angel Ground for a further three years, turning in consistent displays week in and week out, before eventually moving to Canterbury City in July 1968.

His one and only campaign at Canterbury was notable for an exciting F.A. Cup run, during which all the qualifying hurdles were successfully negotiated to put the club into the First Round Proper. Paired away to Swindon, City's gallant efforts were halted when the home team scored a last minute penalty for a 1-0 win.

In May 1969, Sheppey United installed him as their player/manager. Remaining at Botany Road for only eight months, the three times per week journeys were cited as the underlying reason for his eventual resignation.

He was immediately re-engaged closer to home by his old club, Tonbridge. Given the same playing and managerial duties as he had enjoyed at Sheppey, and with the restriction of long and wasteful travelling times now over, he was able to put much more effort into his new responsibilities. Displaying an uncanny knack of simultaneously improving the club's fortunes and quality of football, everything was accomplished on a shoestring budget and he became much admired and respected in Kent football circles for his achievements in what were patently trying circumstances.

During his second spell at the Angel Ground he passed the 400 appearances mark for Tonbridge. Then, in March 1971, an article that made disappointing news for local football fans appeared on the sports page of the local newspaper, part of which read, *'Joe Carolan, player/manager of Tonbridge F.C. has resigned. The announcement was made to shocked supporters just before the Salisbury match on Saturday'*. A spokesperson told the newspaper that, *'Joe's departure was a real shock to everyone connected with the club. The reason is he has extra business activities and would not be able to devote so much time to football. He has done a lot for the club after recent doleful seasons and will be a hard man to follow.'*

Upon leaving Tonbridge any ties with football were cut entirely, although his two sons, Ian and Neil, both enjoyed spells with the club in the 1980's.

LEWIS, Edward (1952/53)

Born: Davyhulme, Manchester, 3rd January 1935
Died: Johannesburg, South Africa, 2nd May 2011
Height: 5ft. 11ins., **Weight:** 11st. 9lbs.
Role: Centre-forward
Career: Burgess Street Primary School (Harpurhey)/ North Manchester Grammar School/ Manchester Boys/ Lancashire Boys/ MUJACs/ Bolton Wanderers/ Goslings/ **UNITED:** Am. November 1949 Pro. January 1952/ **Preston North End** December 1955/ **West Ham United** November 1956/ **Leyton Orient** June 1958/ **Folkestone Town** July 1964/ **Ford United** player/manager July 1966 to May 1968

Sometime during the middle part of the 1940's, Eddie Lewis engaged in competitive football for the very first time when turning out for his primary school and so began an association with the sport which continued for over 65 years.

Brought up from the age of two at number 58, School Street in Harpurhey, by 1947 he had already passed through a regional 'feeder' team, the Manchester Northern Area XI, and into the inside-left berth in a Manchester Boys side whose captain and inside-right was future United star Dennis Viollet. Because of his age, he was able to feature in the Northern Area team for a record four consecutive seasons.

Elevation into the Lancashire Boys side followed, his debut in county colours coming at outside-left in a fixture against Cheshire at Tranmere Rovers' Prenton Park ground. After spending three years in the Manchester Boys team, a fourth was denied to him because of interference from his secondary school. He had almost certainly lost the opportunity to captain the city side for the same reason and his school's high-handedness additionally cost him a number of appearances for both Lancashire and England Boys.

Later selected to represent England Boys against Northern Ireland in 1949, unfortunately, while competing in a 'North against South' final trial game at Rotherham's Millmoor ground, a whack received from future Wolves star Eddie Clamp meant that he had to settle for travelling to Belfast as a non-playing reserve.

When recalling how his link-up with the Reds came about, Lewis divulged, *'I was initially associated with United due to playing for the MUJACs. My father felt that I wasn't given proper recognition by their manager and so I played a couple of games in Bolton's junior sides before signing for a very progressive local club called Goslings, who were funded by three wealthy grocers named Abe, Fred and Cliff Gosling. They staged their matches at the Newton Heath Loco ground and were members of the same Manchester League as United's 'A' (third) team.*

In only my fourth game at Goslings, I scored the winning goal when we beat United 'A' 4-3 and so (club chief scout) Louis Rocca invited me to join the staff in November 1949.'

A consistent and deadly opportunist goalscorer, who was capable of taking chances with either feet or head, he initially performed in a number of friendly games alongside the likes of Mark Jones, Jackie Blanchflower and Jeff Whitefoot, and shortly after becoming a United junior his family settled at 44, Nicolas Road in Chorlton.

Living closer to Old Trafford held obvious advantages for the young hopeful, one of which was being able to walk to the ground with senior star Allenby Chilton.

He spent the bulk of his first full campaign at the club with the 'A' team, the side winning the Manchester League, and gained his Central League spurs in April 1951 in a 3-1 defeat at Chesterfield. Remaining with the third eleven during the 1951/52 term, from August to November 1952 he crashed home ten goals in seven appearances for them, which included a haul of four against Ward Street Old Boys.

Because of those accomplishments, Lewis was in fine fettle when chosen to lead the forward-line against Leeds in United's inaugural Youth Cup game. By the Second Round he had written his name on the score sheet in fine style by claiming four of the opening six goals against Nantwich and at the next stage he registered twice against Bury.

Of his Youth Cup achievement against the Shakers, he pointed out, *'It was those two goals that got me into the first-team on the following Saturday at West Brom. I was only seventeen at the time. My parents and sister made their way to The Hawthorns on the train and I scored after just seven minutes. It was a really great day, even though we went down 3-1.'*

Following that appearance against the Baggies he briefly faded out of the senior picture only to reappear a month later against Blackpool at Old Trafford. Scoring again as the Seasiders were defeated 2-1, Matt Busby kept faith with him all through January and most of February 1953.

Back in the Youth Cup, his next goal came in the home leg of the semi-final against Brentford and he then finished with a flourish in the final ties by grabbing three of United's total of nine at the expense of Wolves. His first-team season ended with a tally of fourteen league and F.A. Cup starts, which included a mightily impressive total of nine goals.

Of his spell as a young hopeful at Old Trafford, he remarked, *'There were about fifteen of us all about the same age and we had a great team spirit. It was all for one and one for all. On Mondays we normally had the day off, except that anyone who had an injury needed to report for treatment or they would be disciplined. We would normally go to the (Davyhulme) golf club, usually for a game of snooker or table tennis, and later on we'd often end up at the cinema.*

On Tuesdays we would have a practice match. They were what you might call 'colourful' because we took them very seriously and we could kick lumps out of each other. Our first-team goalkeeper, Jack Crompton, would take us on Wednesdays and he would have the whole youth squad running down the canal bank which is situated alongside the ground. There and back, we'd probably cover ten miles. One of the times we were out running some of the lads were attacked by a flock of geese.

On other occasions we would play seven-a-side matches on the asphalt surface just outside the stadium. This was after I signed as a professional. Before that I worked for six months at the Manchester Ship Canal Docks Office and just trained at Old Trafford on Tuesday nights and at The Cliff on Thursday nights.'

At the commencement of the 1953/54 campaign he scored once in five out of the opening seven First Division games and then needed to wait until April 1954 to get another opportunity in a home defeat by Cardiff. In between he was utilised in the Reserves either at centre-forward or one of the inside-forward positions.

The 1954/55 term was one of highs and lows for him as he recorded a hat-trick for the Reserves at Derby on the opening day and went on to claim a brace in their next fixture. Then finding the back of the net only once more up to November, a demotion to the 'A' side resulted in him totalling nine goals in just three matches, which included five against Radcliffe Borough and three against Stockport. Lewis was reinstated to Central League duty in early December and remained with the Reserves for the rest of the season, collecting 27 goals in 33 starts for them.

On the first day of the 1955/56 campaign he scored twice in a 4-2 Central League home victory over Derby and regained a place in the first-team on the following Saturday for a 3-1 win over West Brom at Old Trafford. Retaining it for a further three games without scoring, his last match as a United senior came in a 2-1 home win over Everton in September 1955 and three months later he was sold to Preston.

While he possessed commendable attributes, such as strong shooting, abundant enthusiasm and an ability to run and run, there was clearly no chance of him ever being able to dislodge forwards of the calibre of Tommy Taylor.

It was obvious almost immediately that the move to Deepdale wasn't a good one for him. The decision to sign for North End was based largely on the fact that it was close to his Manchester home and it came as some relief when, just under a year later, having scored just twice in twelve league games, he was on his way to West Ham, with future Manchester United manager Frank O'Farrell travelling in the opposite direction. His move to the Boleyn Ground marked the start of a much happier period for him and just a few months after his arrival the Hammers were promoted to the First Division. Within a period of just over eighteen months at West Ham, the striker bagged a creditable twelve goals in 31 appearances.

In the summer of 1958, Lewis made the short journey across London to link up with Second Division Leyton Orient and it was while with them that their wily manager, Alec Stock, took him out of the forward-line and converted him into a left full-back. The move undoubtedly transformed his fortunes and the six years spent at Brisbane Road were much the best he enjoyed in the Football League.

Almost certainly at his playing peak in Orient's promotion winning side of 1962, within a term that ended with the club's promotion to the First Division he missed just one game through injury. His contribution to the achievement was acknowledged in football's halls of power when he was picked to represent the Football League, who were due to meet their Dutch counterparts in a prestige fixture in Amsterdam until it was postponed due to fog.

During Orient's one and only season in the top flight he made 28 appearances and in the 1963/64 campaign, following their swift demotion, that figure was topped by two. Representing the homely London club for the last time in February 1964 with a total of 164 league and cup starts behind him, in the latter part of his time at Brisbane Road he sustained a serious knee injury and was put in charge of the club's Reserves. It was around then that he also began supplementing his income from football by selling life assurance on a part-time basis.

In the 1964 close season, and by now approaching the age of 30, Lewis joined Folkestone Town and was immediately handed the club captaincy. Folkestone had won promotion to the Southern League Premier Division just prior to his arrival and over the next two years they proceeded to consolidate their place in the higher sphere while also winning the Kent Senior Shield in consecutive terms.

In the 1965/66 campaign, Town enjoyed a splendid F.A. Cup run that ended at the hands of Crewe in the Third Round after they had previously beaten Gillingham and Wimbledon, both away from home. After leaving Folkestone it was proposed that he should move back to Orient in a coaching capacity, until at the eleventh hour a fresh manager was installed at Brisbane Road and the vacancy was suddenly filled by one of new man's own appointments.

He instead took over the dual role of player/manager at Greater London League Premier Division outfit Ford United, a club which formed part of the sports section of the car manufacturer's massive Dagenham plant. His managerial career got off to a perfect start in August 1966, when Ford scored in the opening minute of the first match of their season, a game which ended in a 3-1 victory over Barkingside. Playing in a variety of positions for them over the next two years, he also introduced a youth policy for the betterment of the club and, with one eye on the future, it was around then when he passed a preliminary coaching course in London.

In May 1968, he received a couple of interesting offers. Turning down the manager's job at Hornchurch in order to take up a coaching position with Clapton Football Club, he spent about eighteen months with the amateur Isthmian League outfit famed for its Spotted Dog ground. Over the latter part of the 1960's he gained further formal experience when awarded a full coaching badge after attending a course in Durham and then added an MCC Youth Cricket Coach's Certificate to his list of achievements in 1969.

The following year he, his wife Shirley and two daughters emigrated to South Africa where there was an expanding soccer scene with a shortage of experienced coaches. Settling on the coast in East London, he initially worked in insurance for Africa Life.

Within a year of his arrival he had moved his family to Johannesburg and linked up with National Football League club Jewish Guild, who soon established themselves in the First Division under his management. Since that time his résumé reads like a veritable who's who of South African football as he has been involved at some point or other with a number of the top sides there.

He managed Highlands Park in 1972 and moved on to coach both Lusitano and Germiston Primrose in 1973. Best known for his association with two of the country's most famous clubs, Kaizer Chiefs and Wits University (University of Witwatersrand), it was while with the latter that he initiated a mixed race junior set-up, a move which went against the grain in a country gripped by a culture of apartheid. As a relative newcomer to the country, it was known that his views on social integration were not widely accepted and as such he was subject to covert police surveillance for some considerable time.

While acting as Wits University's coach/director of soccer in the mid-to-late 1970's, Lewis was responsible for introducing future Manchester United and England goalkeeper Gary Bailey to professional football and was also involved in launching the career of future Scotland captain Richard Gough.

By 1978, he had assisted Wits University to claim the Mainstay Cup before an estimated crowd of 35,000 at the Rand Stadium. He also coached the Kaizer Chiefs on three different occasions, the Chiefs winning the Datsun Challenge Cup in 1983 as well as being crowned Champion of Champions. Lewis then guided amateurs Jeppe Quondam to a Transvaal League championship in 1986 and steered Giant Blackpool to a promotion from the Second Division in 1988 while also acting as the OK League team manager.

In a contemporary magazine article, it was noted he 'would send his players on long fitness runs before getting down to the technicalities of the game. The epitome of the friendly, fatherly figure, he ambled into the Blackpool club and taught a bunch of raw, but keen black youngsters the art of winning'. That same piece also mentioned that he was 'a kind coach, but a strict and feisty disciplinarian and something of a fitness freak'.

Voted 'Adidas Manager/Coach of the Year' in 1989 while with Bob Save Super Bowl winners Moroka Swallows, his three years with the club saw them win the same competition again in 1991. He then moved to D'Alberton Collies in an identical capacity in July 1993.

Switching to Durban-based club Manning Rangers in March 1994 before re-engaging as a coach with Moroka Swallows in the June of that year, a later return to Wits University lasted for a period of two or three seasons. There were numerous other clubs prepared to pay for his expertise over the ensuing years, and he combined his work on the training grounds and in the stadiums of South Africa with appearances on radio and television as a no-punches pulled pundit. A much respected expert in the media, he also wrote numerous press articles on soccer.

His vast football knowledge was recognised on the very highest of global stages when he was appointed tactical advisor to the Bafana Bafana (South Africa) national side at the 1998 World Cup finals in France, an honour that followed on from others gained when coaching a South African Continental XI in 1974 and his appointment as South Africa's joint national team manager/coach in 1979.

Lewis had a busy 1999. Appointed caretaker coach of the Free State Stars in the March, that August he was placed in charge of a Nelson Mandela XI who took on a World XI at Ellis Park and then spent some time back at Manning Rangers.

There is no doubt that he did much to improve the quality and standing of the sport in a part of the world which was regarded as a football backwater when he arrived there in 1970. He fondly recalled that in those early days, many of the players he came into contact with were not even fully familiar with the rules of the game.

Latterly resident in the Lyndhurst district of Johannesburg, the Mancunian was appointed as Moroka Swallows' technical adviser in 2007, a year in which he was one of 50 recipients of a Certificate of Meritous Award for African Football at a ceremony in Cape Town. Within twelve months he had been asked to set up and run a youth academy for the Swallows, a development which took him full circle to the times when he initially came under the wing of Jimmy Murphy and Bert Whalley at Old Trafford in the late 1940's.

Eddie Lewis later took up a role within the club as an adviser in first-team affairs, and a career of incredible longevity and wonderful accomplishments was ended in the spring of 2011 with his death at the age of 76.

Bert Whalley supervises a coaching session at Old Trafford in which Eddie Lewis is shown how to strike a ball correctly

CLAYTON, Gordon (1952/53, 1953/54, 1954/55)

Born: Chadsmoor, Cannock, Staffordshire, 3rd November 1936
Died: Stretford, Manchester, 29th September 1991
Height: 5ft. 11ins., Weight: 12st. 6lbs.
Role: Goalkeeper
Career: **Central School (Cannock)/ Cannock & District Boys/ Staffordshire Boys/ Birmingham & District Boys/ England Boys/ UNITED**: Am. June 1952 Pro. November 1953/ **Tranmere Rovers** November 1959/ **Sankeys of Wellington** March 1961/ **Radcliffe Borough** August to December 1963

Deemed to be one of the best goalkeepers in the country for his age, Gordon Clayton won a solitary cap for England Boys when the home nation defeated Wales 5-1 at Birmingham's St. Andrews ground in 1952. The newspaper local to his Cannock home recorded that he *'showed great confidence'* against the Welsh while adding he was the first schoolboy international from the town.

A polished individual who rarely made costly mistakes, he used his size to maximum effect and was particularly adept at dealing with high balls and crosses. Universally known by his nickname, 'Big Gordon' joined the club on the same day as Duncan Edwards, the two having previously been team-mates for Birmingham & District Boys, as well as their country, and they remained firm friends thereafter.

Amazingly, in August 1952 his competitive club debut was for United Reserves in a 4-0 Central League defeat at Derby. Then alternating between third and fourth teams throughout the season, both won their respective league championships. His form ensured that he became an automatic choice for the under-18 team and it wasn't until their fifth Youth Cup tie, against Barnsley in the quarter-final, that he was forced to pick the ball out of the net. So solid were the Reds in defence that only five goals were conceded during the whole competition, and when the trophy was collected at Molineux after the second leg of the final, he was only a few miles away from his Staffordshire birthplace.

He moved up to share Central League duties with Jack Crompton in the 1953/54 term while continuing as the youth team 'keeper, the young Reds' progress carrying along similar lines to the previous campaign. It was again five matches before he was beaten, this time against Rotherham, and United then brushed Bexleyheath & Welling and West Brom aside to reach their second Youth Cup final. It was then that he was hit by a wretched piece of bad luck, when a broken arm sustained just prior to the visit of Wolves prevented him from claiming his rightful place in the side.

Sharing 'A' team duties with Tony Hawksworth in the 1954/55 season, when Youth Cup places came up for grabs he reclaimed his for the opening three ties. Then, on the back of an uninspiring first half team performance at Barnsley, his place went to Hawksworth and with the younger custodian managing to keep a clean sheet in a romp over Sheffield Wednesday, he was unable to dislodge him thereafter. There was a major consolation for him, though, as he won an international youth cap when England were defeated 4-3 by Holland in Arnhem.

He also lost his 'A' team berth to Hawksworth during the 1955/56 term, which forced him to settle for mainly 'B' fare. The following campaign was totally different because, with Hawksworth on National Service and Crompton about to retire, a huge revival in his fortunes saw him leapfrog into the Reserves to make over 30 Central League appearances.

In March 1957, with the Reds leading the First Division championship, a knock to Ray Wood gave him a glimpse of the big time at Wolves. Doing his reputation no harm at all in the 1-1 draw, with one reporter noting that *'Young Gordon Clayton came through his senior baptism in goal almost without fault'*, his return to the first-team on the last day of the league calendar ended in another 1-1 draw, this time with West Brom at Old Trafford. Because of Wood's later injury in the F.A. Cup final, he travelled on the seniors' end of season tour to the continent and was chosen for fixtures against a Copenhagen XI and Staevnet, which ended in respective 3-2 and 4-3 victories for the Reds.

Unable to repeat his achievement of reaching first-team status over the next two and a half years, in the 1957/58 term he was overtaken by David Gaskell, who regularly made it into the Reserves at his expense. Clayton was hindered by ongoing problems with his knees throughout that period and needed to undergo surgery for two 'cleaning' operations.

Having remained mostly in the 'A' team throughout the 1958/59 campaign and the early weeks of the 1959/60 season, and with no sign of further progress in sight, he was transferred to Tranmere along with Bob Harrop. His last game for United was on the final day of October 1959 in the 'A' side's 4-3 Supplementary Cup win over Manchester City.

Rovers signed him as a potential replacement for George Payne, who was nearing the end of a long and distinguished career. His first senior appearance for the Third Division club came in January 1960 at Reading and his last was in a home match against Walsall in February 1961, with just two more starts made in-between. When a new 'keeper was signed, the 24 year-old moved into non-league circles with Sankeys of Wellington, a professional Cheshire League club. Clayton was no stranger to the area as he had been stationed at nearby Donnington camp during his National Service days.

At the end of the 1961/62 term, during which he often gained the highest marks out of ten for his performances, Sankeys won their very first Shropshire Senior Cup final. A year later he was what the local newspaper remarked *'somewhat surprisingly'* released in a staff clear-out which probably came about as a cost-cutting exercise.

He was soon fixed up with Lancashire Combination club Radcliffe Borough, his association with them lasting only just above a dozen games. Making his first appearance at Accrington in August 1963, his last was at Padiham in November at which time he joined the Manchester Police Force.

In April 1969, he was temporarily tempted out of football retirement to play for an 'All-Stars' team which included a few former Reds, such as Wilf McGuinness and Dennis Viollet. The charity game was against hosts Altrincham and raised money to send Manchester Boys on a tour to America.

United's new manager McGuinness re-employed him on part-time terms soon after in order to help with some scouting work and assist with the junior teams on Saturday mornings. When McGuinness was dismissed, Clayton became a part-time talent spotter for Huddersfield.

He was brought back to Old Trafford as a full-timer by Tommy Docherty, initially as a coach and equipment manager and later as Norman Scholes' assistant chief scout. Throughout his second and third spells at Old Trafford he was responsible, or at least partly responsible, for the recruitment of many of the youngsters who went through United's youth system.

A few months after the appointment of Dave Sexton as the club's new manager, he was enticed away by Docherty. Upon appointing him to head up Derby's scouting operations, Docherty said, *'I rate Gordon one of the best judges of ability, and he knows exactly what I want. Gordon has always expected to get the chief scout's job at Old Trafford, Norman Scholes is in his 60's, but he has been unsettled by reports that Harry Haslam is in line to join United as chief scout.'* Just four months later, Docherty lost his job and the former 'keeper quickly followed him out of the Baseball Ground exit door.

Some eighteen months passed before he was back in the game in an identical capacity at Burnley. In early 1983, with the Clarets floundering near the foot of the Second Division table, Frank Casper was appointed as caretaker manager and Clayton became his assistant. Reverting back to scouting responsibilities a few months later following Burnley's relegation, he was dismissed almost immediately upon the appointment of John Bond as manager.

He scouted for Bury in the middle part of the decade and was then installed as manager of Bass North-West Counties League club, Cheadle Town. He won a 'Manager of the Month' award in November 1987 and remained at Park Road until sometime during the following year. Three years later, having already applied for the manager's job at Northwich, he was appointed as the Vic's number two to Sammy McIlroy. The press reported that he had recently been managing a snooker hall in Manchester's Piccadilly.

Tragically, barely three months after linking up with the GM Vauxhall Conference side, he suffered a fatal heart attack at the age of 54. In his column in Northwich's matchday programme, McIlroy wrote:

Events on the pitch have been overshadowed by the sudden death of my very good friend and colleague, Gordon Clayton; he was well liked by all who knew him and will not be forgotten. His warm personality soon endeared him to the many friends he made at the club, all of whom will miss him very much indeed. I am sure you will all join me in extending our sincere condolences to his wife Pat, and to his son and daughter, David and Theresa.

BLAKEMAN, Alan (1954/55)

Born: Oldham, 2nd November 1937
Height: 6ft., Weight: 11st. 7lbs.
Role: Centre-forward
Career: **Denton Lane School (Chadderton)/ Oldham Athletic** August 1952/ **Junction Lads Club** 1953/54 season/ **UNITED**: Am. May 1954 to April 1955/ **Oldham Athletic** September 1955/ **Bolton Wanderers** August 1956/ **Ashton United** April 1957/ **Rotherham United** May 1958/ **Workington** January 1959/ **Southport** July 1959/ **Ashton United** October and November 1959/ **Stalybridge Celtic** September and October 1960/ **Ashton United** September 1967 to May 1968

Born and raised at Foxdenton Farm, Chadderton, barely a few pitch lengths distance from Boundary Park, Alan Blakeman was denied the honour of representative schoolboy football due to his involvement with Oldham Athletic from the age of fourteen. The reason given for his omission from the town boys' team was because the authorities felt it was unfair on the other candidates as he had been the beneficiary of professional training.

Big and strong for his age, he preferred to utilise his physical attributes in the centre-forward role, although it wasn't unknown for him to operate at inside-forward or even on the wings. Nevertheless, his major contribution to whichever side he belonged to, or whatever position he filled, was that rare gift of being able to score goals consistently. Possessed of a hard running style, an in-built sniper's instinct allowed him to find the net with shots from distance, and he could also poach from short range with either his boot or his head.

His association with the Latics began when he assisted their Colts side in the Blackley Amateur League in 1952/53, a season when the local boy was also introduced into Athletic's 'A' (third) eleven. The following term saw him alternate between both teams, but part way into the fixture list he left after a disagreement to link up with a side known as Junction Lads Club.

It was while connected to the Middleton Youth League team that he was talked into joining United by coach Bert Whalley. Signing in good time for pre-season training in 1954, he made a dramatic entrance in the newly-formed Altrincham Junior League by cracking six goals past Hale Road in an 11-0 whitewash and a week later he blasted four more as the Juniors annihilated Stretford Youth 13-2.

He was soon elevated into the Lancashire League side and once again demonstrated a canny knack for goal-getting when claiming another four in a 10-2 humiliation of Oldham. Having then been off the radar for a while, in February 1955 he was chosen to face Sheffield Wednesday for a Fourth Round Youth Cup match at Old Trafford and, not wanting to waste the chance, distinguished himself by scoring a terrific hat-trick in a 7-0 win.

When the Youth Cup clash with Plymouth came around a month later, Bobby English was preferred to lead the line. Quite understandably, and considering his exploits against Sheffield Wednesday, the development didn't go down well and his spell with the Reds lasted only a few games longer. He typically went out with all guns blazing and a hat-trick against Knutsford in the semi-final of the Altrincham Junior League Cup was followed with a brace in a terrific 5-0 final win over Stamford Lads.

A few months later he returned for another period with Oldham and just over a week after re-signing Blakeman took part in another Youth Cup tie, on this occasion against Liverpool at Boundary Park. Despite Athletic conceding twice late on to lose the game 5-3, astonishingly he hit all three of the home side's goals and also saw two of his efforts cannon back off the bar, one of which was from a distance of 40 yards. It is highly improbable that any other participant in the history of the Youth Cup has ever scored separate hat-tricks for different clubs in only two appearances.

Operating in the club's Reserves throughout his second engagement at Boundary Park, in January 1956 he was offered a professional contract. He declined the opportunity to become a full-timer because of commitments to the family poultry business and all through his time in football the farming side of his life was always given top priority.

That August he penned part-time forms for Bolton. The Trotters were one of the footballing powers of the land in the mid-1950's and over a span of eight months at Burnden Park he was tried at both second and third team levels. With the legendary Nat Lofthouse an automatic choice at centre-forward for the Wanderers' senior side just then, there was some considerable merit in his making headway into Bolton's Central League team.

By April 1957 the nineteen year-old had moved to Lancashire Combination club Ashton United and later that month the local newspaper described him as 'a well built youth of distinct possibilities' while also commenting that he was 'a powerful lad and needs some moving off the ball when in possession'. Within weeks of his arrival at Hurst Cross he was the recipient of an Ashton Challenge Cup final medal when neighbours Stalybridge were crucified 11-4 in a goal festival.

With his goal average better than one every other game while at Ashton, it wasn't long before scouts from Football League clubs began circling and in December 1957 a reporter revealed that he had been invited for a trial with Bournemouth. His form also excelled when winning representative recognition as, during his stay with Ashton, he registered four goals in two appearances for the Manchester County F.A.

In March 1958, Ashton entertained Second Division Rotherham for a Monday evening friendly fixture and in front of a crowd of 4,000 he managed a brace in a 6-5 defeat. Following the game, Rotherham manager Andy Smailes told the press, 'This lad could get goals in any company' and then promptly invited him to travel to Upton Park on the following Saturday because he planned to include him in the Millers' side against West Ham. However, the striker politely declined the offer as he had an even bigger match to attend - he was getting married that very same day.

At the conclusion of some protracted negotiations, Smailes did eventually secure the desired signature and in September 1958 he gave Blakeman his first Football League start at inside-left in a defeat at Charlton. Just over a month later the Oldhamer was situated at left-half for a home draw with Leyton Orient, but when it became apparent that a regular spot was in doubt he was released from his contract.

On leaving Millmoor he was immediately snapped up by Fourth Division Workington. Figuring in a first-team friendly at Scunthorpe on the day he signed, a week later he was chosen at number nine for a win at Chester. For his first home game, Watford were the visitors to Borough Park and he took the opportunity to show his artistry to the Workington supporters by netting a hat-trick in a 3-1 victory. Scoring seven times in fourteen starts for the club, his final league appearance was at Walsall in April 1959. His departure was largely due to the distance involved in travelling from Oldham to Cumbria and back along with the subsequent time spent away from his business.

He was then accommodated nearer to home by Southport, another Fourth Division outfit. Following his involvement in the 1959 pre-season 'Probables v. Possibles' trial game at Haig Avenue, he went on to score three goals in ten Lancashire Combination league and cup games but was unable to break into the Sandgrounders' senior eleven. In October 1959, he asked Southport to cancel his contract, once more citing the reason that he couldn't combine work with football.

Immediately rejoining Ashton, his second period at Hurst Cross spanned merely four matches and he was then out of the game entirely for almost a year before resurfacing at Stalybridge. His interest in the game seemed to have almost evaporated by then as he made only two appearances for the Bower Fold club before disappearing from the soccer scene entirely.

Practically seven years had elapsed before his connection with football was renewed when returning for a third spell at Ashton. Over the course of a season in which he passed his 30th birthday, he demonstrated to the Hurst Cross crowd that none of his ability had been lost. Getting off the mark on his third 'debut' by scoring against Wigan goalkeeper and former Red David Gaskell, he ended the campaign having trawled a couple of dozen successful strikes from less than 30 appearances, at which point he decided to clock off from the sport.

Alan Blakeman operated a milk retail business in Oldham for a number of years. His son, David, is well known on the local football scene and played in the same Chadderton side as a young David Platt in the early 1980's.

COOKE, John (1965/66, 1966/67)

Born: Sheffield, 4th October 1948
Height: 5ft. 6ins., Weight: 9st. 10lbs.
Role: Inside or outside-right
Career: St. Mary's Primary School (Sheffield)/ St. Peter's Secondary School (Sheffield)/ Sheffield Boys/ Yorkshire Boys/ UNITED: Ass. Schoolboy October 1963 App. May 1964 Pro. October 1965 to May 1968/ Nottingham Forest August to November 1968/ Altrincham November and December 1968/ Sligo Rovers (Ire) February 1969 to May 1970/ Wigan Athletic January 1971/ Goole Town July 1971/ Altrincham February 1972/ Droylsden May 1973/ Macclesfield Town April 1975/ Hyde United October 1975/ Radcliffe Borough August 1977/ Droylsden January 1978/ New Mills July 1979/ Ashton United March 1980 to May 1981/ Droylsden March and April 1983

'I trained twice a week at Sheffield United from the age of twelve and I was only thirteen when I first went to Old Trafford,' said John Cooke. 'I was playing for Sheffield Boys when I was scouted by a fellow called Walter Jones. I made the final 22 in the England Boys selection process and I was wanted by both of the Sheffield clubs, (Aston) Villa and West Brom. I went to Leeds but I preferred what I saw at United and initially signed as a schoolboy in 1963.

I used to come over now and again, including the school holidays, in order to train with the apprentices. At that time I stayed with Jimmy Nicholson and Dennis Walker in Stretford, and when I started my apprenticeship the following year I shared with Ian Brough.'

A tricky ball merchant who could dribble his way into the heart of most defences, Cooke was known to work tirelessly for the team effort and often appeared to cover every blade of grass on the pitch. Predominantly right-footed, for someone of his size he was competent in the air.

He made a great start for the Reds by scoring an eye-catching goal in a 10-1 'B' team home win over Rochdale in August 1964. Continuing by making constant additions to his goal tally throughout the campaign, mainly from the outside-left position, as time went by he also gained an isolated start for the 'A' side. His main objectives in that first year, which he conclusively achieved, were to establish himself and *'become familiar with the United way of life.'*

'Before my second year began I moved into Carlo Sartori's house,' he revealed. *'Mrs. Sartori was a fantastic cook and I ate like a king.'* Besides experiencing the delights of Italian cuisine at its best, the 1965/66 season also turned out well for him in a football sense as he moved up to 'A' grade and just three games into the fixture list claimed his first hat-trick when Bury were beaten 4-2. With his continued fine form noted, and only four weeks after his 17th birthday, he was summoned up for a Central League 1-1 home draw with Derby.

Six weeks later he made a tremendous impact in the Youth Cup at Maine Road where, besides setting up goals for Frank McEwen and Brian Kidd, he directed a coolly taken header into Manchester City's net from a centre by the former just before the interval.

The following January, United were drawn against Liverpool in the next round and he claimed of that match, *'When we arrived at Anfield the pitch was totally frozen. We expected the game would be postponed and it was a bit of a shock when it was given the go-ahead.'* Little went right for the Reds on the treacherous surface and, despite having the majority of the possession, they went out on a three-goal margin.

He continued in the junior sides at outside-left, outside-right and, occasionally, in his favoured position of inside-forward, and before the term concluded he had gained another appearance with the Reserves.

His 1966/67 campaign began with a bang when he registered seven goals in his first five starts for the 'A' side, which included a hat-trick in a 4-1 victory at Blackburn. As a consequence, he was immediately drafted back into the Central League team and also took part in all of the Youth Cup ties during a run that saw the Reds' progress ended by Sunderland.

From Christmas onwards he made only half a dozen appearances for the 'A' side because by then he was usually with the Reserves. Just three days after the Youth Cup defeat at Roker Park, in one of his rare 'A' team starts, he scored five times in an 8-0 win at Oldham and at only eighteen years-old, Cooke could reflect on his contribution with some degree of satisfaction.

'I was given a place on the wing at the start of the next season but I didn't like it as it wasn't my best position,' he remarked. Continuing to alternate between 'A' standard and the Reserves without establishing himself in the latter, a number of others were now beginning to press him for a place. With competition from the likes of Jimmy Ryan, Alan Gowling and Sartori to contend with, a disappointing term turned into a disaster when, just prior to the European Cup final in May 1968, he was informed that he was being released on a free transfer. After averaging a goal every two games in four years at Old Trafford, he made his last United appearance that same month.

He soon managed to get fixed up with a trial at Nottingham Forest where Johnny Carey, the ex-United captain, was manager. Earning himself a month-by-month deal, he made appearances for Forest's Reserves until Carey was sacked and then filled in with a brief spell at Altrincham before returning home.

Of that time he mentioned, *'I had only just turned twenty and I was kicking my heels for a couple of months in Sheffield before Cliff Lloyd (of the PFA) got in touch to ask if I was interested in signing for Sligo Rovers of the Irish League. I said 'yes' as I wanted to resume my career as quickly as possible.'*

Associated with Sligo for about fifteen months, there were some complications arising from his stay in Ireland. A newspaper report claimed that he had to win *'a High Court action to allow him to leave'* and that *'he will be unable to return to a Football League club unless (Sligo) get a fee of £3,000'.* While the report wasn't entirely accurate from a financial angle, Cooke was forced to take the matter to court where he succeeded in obtaining an early Bosman-type ruling on the principle of restraint of trade.

He hitched up with Wigan when the legal complications had finally been ironed out and while at Springfield Park he took part in a successful Lancashire F.A. Floodlit K.O. final. By then he had concluded it would be difficult to secure a professional contract and that he would have to look for other employment. Goole Town were next to obtain his services and his competitive debut for them in August 1971 was actually their first match in the Northern Premier League. The time he spent at Goole was useful from another viewpoint as it was they who managed to fix him up with an opening to learn carpentry and joinery.

For the next few years he wandered between numerous North-West clubs and in 1978 commenced a second spell at Droylsden. Later that year the Bloods qualified for the First Round Proper of the F.A. Cup for only the second time in their history and he was in the team that caused a minor upset by defeating Rochdale with a single goal at Spotland.

He moved on to New Mills and was then contracted to Ashton United when, in March 1981, an article in a Manchester newspaper mentioned that he was taking his coaching badges with a view to assuming charge of Ashton's Reserves. Those plans had altered within two months when he was handed the assistant manager's job at nearby Stalybridge Celtic.

Going back to Droylsden in March 1983 to assist on the playing side for the final couple of months of the term, that October another report revealed that he had been appointed as their manager, having *'been in charge of training and coaching at the club this season'.*

In November 1984, he quit Droylsden to become assistant manager to Brian Kidd at Barrow and then followed his former United team-mate to Preston in July 1985. Reports stated that Kidd had been installed as second in command at Deepdale and that Cooke's position of youth team coach was on a full-time basis.

When Kidd left Preston, the Yorkshireman began coaching for Manchester City on a couple of evenings each week in their community development area and also spent short spells as assistant boss at Altrincham and managing Mossley. He rejoined Manchester United in the early 1990's when Kidd offered him the opportunity of working with the juniors.

John Cooke has operated a joinery firm in Tameside for approximately 25 years. Nowadays comparing his release from Old Trafford in 1968 as *'like having your legs cut off'*, he continues to coach all age groups at United's Academy while acting as assistant to Paul McGuinness on match days.

MORTON, Alan (1952/53)

Born: Morpeth, Northumberland, 22nd November 1936
Height: 5ft. 5ins., **Weight:** 9st. 11lbs.
Role: Outside-right
Career: Newminster Secondary Modern School (Morpeth)/ East Northumberland Boys/ Northumberland Boys/ England Boys/ UNITED: Am. June 1952 to May 1953/ **Sunderland** November 1953/ **Berwick Rangers** July 1955 to c/s 1956/ **Morpeth Town** October 1956/ **Ashington** November 1957/ **Northleach Town** 1958/ **Banbury Spencer** September 1960 to c/s 1962

Alan Morton enjoyed a brilliant spell as a schoolboy footballer, by winning local and county recognition before being selected for England Boys in a 7-1 win against Northern Ireland in Belfast in 1951.

Further schoolboy caps came into his possession a year later for his appearances in 4-1 and 1-0 wins against Scotland, the latter at Wembley, a 5-1 victory over Wales and a 1-0 defeat in Dublin against Eire. Accompanied by Duncan Edwards in all of those games, even though they were poles apart in terms of build, the two became good pals and while rooming together at the legendary Mrs. Watson's house during his time at United, they regularly enjoyed a few frames of billiards.

An instinctive and direct winger who was principally right-footed, in order to become adept on either side he practised constantly with his left. While certainly not the most technically gifted amongst the younger element at the club in those days, he could usually be counted on to make a contribution and certainly didn't have too many problems finding his way to goal.

Morton's initial appearance was in a friendly against Belvedere Works in August 1952, when scoring once in a 6-1 win, and his competitive start came two weeks later as another of his goals counted towards the Juniors' 11-0 thrashing of Sharston. A regular on the bottom rung for the opening part of the season, during which he scored about thirteen times, he was mainly with the Colts for the second half of the term. As well as his appearance in the Juniors' 3-1 win over Linotype in the Altrincham Junior Cup final, his two sides topped their respective leagues and enough appearances were accumulated for him to qualify for medals on both fronts.

His Youth Cup bow came against Nantwich in the November of that campaign when Jimmy Murphy's faith in him was repaid with two of United's huge total of 23 goals. Retaining his place on the right wing for the following ties against Bury and Everton, by the time of the quarter-final against Barnsley he had dropped out of the reckoning.

His abiding memory of the game against Everton under-18's remains something of a sore one. *'I caught the ball full in the face when a defender tried to clear it'*, he recounted, *'and there was blood flying everywhere.'* Those three appearances were the sum total of his Youth Cup career because he was effectively kept out of the side before and after those ties by the preferred number seven, Noel McFarlane.

Having failed to progress beyond the fourth team, he had been with the Reds for just less than twelve months when a chance of returning closer to home presented itself. With United recommending him to Sunderland, and following his release from Old Trafford, there was a stagnant pause until he was offered a professional contract with the Roker Park outfit and within the waiting period he was chosen for the Newcastle United N's (Junior) side in a fixture at Greenock Morton's ground.

His transfer to Sunderland represented one of progress initially but, whereas the policy of promoting young talent into the first-team wasn't unusual at Old Trafford, the same couldn't be said at his new place of employment. Finding himself in the company of some gifted teenagers, alas it was almost unheard of for any of them to reach senior status and so when his contract ran out, he moved again.

In July 1955, he was given the option of joining Lincoln City or Berwick Rangers. A newspaper reported he was to spend a week in Lincoln, a time in which he would look at lodgings, meet the staff and consider a job offer. As he was courting at the time, and not being too impressed with his Sincil Bank experience, his stay lasted only 24 hours. Choosing to go part-time with Berwick, the same newspaper mentioned that while at Sunderland he had *'played in 26 consecutive matches in the Reserve side'* and was *'apprenticed to a firm of joiners in Newcastle'*.

Mid-1955 was an historic period for Berwick Rangers because, when Morton arrived, they had just been elected from the 'C' to the 'B' Division, then the Scottish equivalent of stepping up from non-league to league football. Following a couple of trial games in which he was described as a *'progressive, bustling winger'*, he was included in the Borderers' first game in the higher sphere and went on to score their second ever goal at the new level against Stranraer. While attached to Rangers he also worked at Linton Colliery alongside Bobby Charlton's father.

After completing something like 30 games for Berwick, he joined his local club, Morpeth Town, with whom he shared an on-off relationship all throughout his time in football.

Moving to Ashington a year or so later, in his first four games he scored eight goals for their Reserves in the Northern Alliance. His tenure at Portland Park was then interrupted from June 1958 onwards by time spent on National Service duty in the Ordinance Corps.

Having been back in Northumberland for almost seven years, he next popped up in a most unlikely location when transferring to Cheltenham & District League Division One club, Northleach Town. He remained in the area for about three years after marrying into a farming family, during which time Banbury Spencer of the Birmingham League were the next to obtain his signature. Scoring on his debut in September 1960, the tie-up with Banbury lasted for approximately eighteen months.

Then returning north when the marriage dissolved, his football resumed with a successful side known as Hartford while he also took work as a lorry driver. Around the autumn time of 1964 he was playing for the Morpeth St. George's Hospital team.

Still living in the former pit town, Alan Morton remarried in 1982. He was made redundant by the National Coal Board at the age of 50 and was unable to find work thereafter.

CHAPMAN, Samuel Edward Campbell
(1953/54)

Born: Belfast, 16th February 1938
Height: 5ft. 10ins., Weight: 10st. 7lbs.
Role: Inside-right or centre-forward
Career: **Templemore Avenue School (Belfast)/ Belfast Boys/ Northern Ireland Boys/ UNITED**: Am. June 1952 to January 1954/ **Glentoran** (NI) April 1954/ **Glenavon** (NI) November 1955 to c/s 1956/ **Mansfield Town** October 1956/ **Portsmouth** February 1958/ **Mansfield Town** December 1961 to June 1964

One of United's earliest schoolboy recruits from Ulster, Sammy Chapman came to Old Trafford after previously appearing twice for Northern Ireland Boys. Making his international debut in a 3-3 draw against Wales Boys at Belfast's Grosvenor Park in April 1951, at the same venue two weeks later he scored the only Irish goal in the home nation's 7-1 loss to an England side containing future Reds Duncan Edwards and Alan Morton.

A discovery of United scouts Bob Bishop and Bob Harpur, he was lured over to England a little over twelve months later, although circumstances dictated that he would spend only just over a year and a half on the club's books.

As the school leaving age in Northern Ireland was then fourteen, and in order to comply with the different education rules in this country, he was required to attend a school in Stretford until reaching the age of fifteen.

He made his first contribution for the club in an 11-1 hammering of Sharston in early September 1952 and then contributed goals at regular

Matt Busby holds court while (l-r) Colin Webster, Walter Whitehurst, Sammy Chapman, Bert Whalley and Alan Morton hang on every word

From National School he obtained a one-year scholarship to Sandymount High until forced to leave in order to earn a living that supplemented the family finances. His soccer aspirations took a huge leap when he was selected for Dublin Boys in their only fixture of the 1957/58 season, a 0-0 away draw against Belfast Boys. For a while he considered joining the British Army, instead becoming a messenger boy, and for a year he cycled around the highways and byways of Dublin, earning the princely sum of £1.1s. (£1.05) a week while also receiving tips in the form of cigarettes from the American Embassy.

He won recognition at a higher grade still when selected at inside-forward for the Eire Boys team that faced Wales Boys in Cork in April 1960. While Ireland didn't fare too well against the Welsh, losing 3-1, his luck changed three weeks later when lining up against England Boys in Dublin where, with his influence crucial, the home side registered twice in a keenly contested draw. Future United pal Jimmy Keogh was also in the Irish team that day while soon-to-be Red Barry Fry donned a white shirt for England.

By then his displays were beginning to attract the attention of numerous scouts. Billy Behan had been aware of his progress for some time and recommended that Jimmy Murphy pay a visit to the fair city to take a look for himself. Liverpool also had him watched and, while United only suggested a trial, Bill Shankly upped the ante by tabling a contract.

However, as a result of the Reds' scouting system having been established for some years in Ireland, well before other clubs saw the potential there, he was swayed towards Manchester and so, in August 1960, together with Hugh Curran and Keogh, he accompanied Johnny Giles across the Irish Sea for his assessment. Giles was returning to England following a home vacation, while in Dunphy's case he was reaching out into the big, wide world for the first time and hoping with all his might that he could, like his fellow passenger, successfully swap the blue and white of Stella Maris for the red and white of Manchester United.

Many years later he made some interesting observations about the state of affairs at Old Trafford on his arrival. 'It was heavy with atmosphere,' he claimed, 'because the Munich disaster had changed United from a club into a cult. Busby watched 45 minutes of the match that changed my life. I did okay and they offered me a contract. They had 45 pros and creamed off the prodigies from all over Britain and Ireland. I was a timid teenager from Dublin's Northside. It was a mind-blowing experience.'

Within the space of a month all three of the Irish triallists were signed up on apprenticeships.

Initially selected to play in United's fifth team, then members of the Altrincham Junior League, his first start was in an abandoned home match against Irwin Rangers and he was required to wait until the following Saturday before being able to make his full official debut when scoring in a 7-1 victory at Cheadle. He then completed a handful of games for the Juniors before being selected for the 'B' team, for whom he appeared regularly in both inside-forward positions, and by the end of the term he also had the experience of a few 'A' team matches under his belt.

In the 1961/62 season he reversed his work of the previous one by becoming an 'A' team member while turning out for the 'B' on the odd occasion. He became acquainted with the Youth Cup in a home tie against Everton in September 1961 and during that term went on to score four goals in a run that ended when United were ousted by Newcastle. In January he sampled a spell in the 'B' side for a month, but within two weeks of being recalled into the 'A' team he was elevated to the Central League eleven for a 1-1 draw at Leeds and, in total, five Reserve team opportunities came his way throughout the campaign.

The Irish boy signed professional terms right at the start of the 1962/63 season. Again named in the 'A' team in his usual inside-forward role, only a few weeks passed before a switch to the half-back line occurred and he remained there for the majority of the time. Dunphy was included in the 'B' side that won the Supplementary Cup with a 4-3 aggregate win over Liverpool and for the second year in a row he played in all five Youth Cup ties, all at left-half, as the Reds were knocked out at Sheffield Wednesday. With injuries ruling out Bobby Smith and Jimmy Nicholson, in early April he got a run of five games in the Reserves.

The continued breakthrough desired came at the dawn of the 1963/64 term when he began in the Reserves and managed to hold down a regular place from then on. In mid-October he was named as 12th man in the first-team squad that travelled to Nottingham Forest and by the end of the campaign he had notched up 30 Central League appearances, scoring six goals in the process. A United Review of the period likened him to Denis Law for *'his natural ability, fair hair, lean build and willingness to tackle hard'*. While most of that description rang true, the subject of the piece always felt that he possessed about as much strength as a milkshake and with a thin frame, wasn't overly fond of winning the ball.

A highly literate and often vocal person, his abrasive personality occasionally found him out of favour with some of his senior colleagues. Leading a bachelor's lifestyle and frequently found out and about in Manchester after dark, he said of that time, *'I wasn't going to make it. I wasn't living like a footballer should. I was down at Jimmy Saville's club, watching the Beatles and Wayne Fontana & the Mindbenders.'*

He found himself relegated to the 'A' team in his fifth and final season at Old Trafford, representing them in the opening nine games before being recalled into the Central League side in October. On the 12th December 1964 he was again named as the seniors' travelling understudy, this time for a trip to The Hawthorns, and those two incidences against Forest and West Brom would be as near as he ever came to gaining selection for the first-team.

Bad weather resulted in numerous games being postponed over the Christmas period, but he was back in the 'A' side by the middle of January. Despite managing a hat-trick in a 6-0 home win over Tranmere, with the emergence of John Fitzpatrick and Albert Kinsey from the youth team, and Graham Moore unable to hold down a senior berth, Dunphy was squeezed out of the second string. He remained with the third eleven for the rest of the season and, although his performances were reasonable and he also scored a few goals, his efforts weren't enough to warrant continued promotion. It was plain, especially to him, that his time with United was coming to an end.

Whether it was down to his way of life, the conflicts with some of the other personnel, a lack of ability or a combination of those factors, he was unable to break back into the Reserves and in April 1965 asked for a transfer. Even though Matt Busby wanted him to stay for another year, the Dubliner's mind was set on getting away.

Despite an £8,000 offer from Birmingham City soon landing on his table, Busby curiously sold him to York City for only half that amount. Upon walking through the entrance at Bootham Crescent in August 1965, Dunphy found himself around the familiar faces of Dennis Walker, John Pearson and his old room-mate, Ken Morton. He was immediately drafted into York's senior team and within three months had the honour of becoming their first ever full international when capped in a World Cup Qualifier play-off against Spain in Paris. With only 22 Third Division appearances for the Minstermen to his credit, they cashed in on his potential by transferring him to Millwall for £8,000, precisely the same sum that Busby was offered by Birmingham.

With the Lions only recently elevated into the Third Division, his debut for them at Workington in January 1966 came just a few months before they went up another rung. He spent nearly eight years at Cold Blow Lane and they were exciting times as the club more than held their own in the higher sphere, almost making it into the top flight when agonisingly finishing third in 1972.

He went on to become Millwall's most capped player, and 22 of his 23 full international appearances were made while earning £35 per week and living in a club house. In serving Eire he performed in places as far away as Ankara in Turkey, Poznan and Katowice in Poland, as well as Prague, Valencia, Copenhagen, Budapest, Berlin, Florence and Stockholm, with a last start for his country staged in his home city against Austria in May 1971.

Following an argument with Millwall's manager in October 1973, he was left out of the side and a month later agreed to join Charlton. He had taken part in over 300 games for the Lions in what was certainly his most satisfying spell as a professional footballer.

Charlton's style of play caused him to struggle for a while and manager Theo Foley was sacked just at the time when he was often sidelined with a back injury. While not always seeing eye to eye with the new incumbent, nevertheless he felt that he had made a worthwhile contribution towards the Addicks winning promotion to the Second Division in 1975. The gratitude he got was to be dropped for the last game of the campaign and given a free transfer. While at The Valley, his number of league games had increased by 42.

Fourth Division Reading was his next stopover and, despite still hampered by continuous back trouble, he played his part as an influential captain as they, too, won promotion in 1976. The club was unable to consolidate its position in the higher sphere and, having added 77 more Football League matches to his total, the midfielder was released in May 1977.

During his time with the Berkshire club he began coaching the London University team and guided them to third position in the British University Tournament, their best placing for a decade. Despite gaining good grades in his F.A. coaching qualification, no-one was interested in his credentials when applying for management jobs and so he elected to join Johnny Giles' Shamrock Rovers as player/youth team coach. Simultaneously holding down a coaching role with the Irish national side, while at Shamrock Rovers he became the recipient of a FAI Cup medal in 1978, an event which caused the (Dublin) Evening Herald to comment on the player's *'delight'* at *'collecting his first cup medal since he scored a penalty to win a Paddy Thunder Cup final as a fourteen year-old with Stella Maris'*. Because of the interest created by *'Only A Game?'*, two years later it was felt that the time was right to give up football in order to focus his attention on book writing and journalism.

Currently the host of his own programme called 'The Breakfast Show,' it is aired from a Dublin radio station every weekday morning.

YOUTH PROGRAMMES

There are two issues numbered sixteen in the 1962/63 season, which are United Youth v. Sunderland Youth (27/2/63) and United Reserves v. Blackpool Reserves (2/3/1963), with the first named printed minus a date while the latter was dated. This situation came about because of the long delay in staging matches that winter due to poor weather conditions and the uncertainty as to when the games would eventually be played. The Youth Cup programme was almost certainly prepared well in advance in readiness for the eventual thaw, but why the same number was duplicated is anybody's guess.

The practice of numbering in sequence with Reserve issues was resurrected in the 1985/86 campaign and continued up to and including the 1997/98 term, with the two exceptions being the single sheets produced for the games against Mansfield Town in 1987/88, which should have carried the number four, and Sheffield Wednesday in 1988/89, which logically should have been number ten. These numbers appear to have been omitted in error.

The last time that a home issue was numbered was for the visit of Blackburn in December 1997 after which they carried the words 'Special Edition' up to and including the game against Stoke in December 2004. This differentiates them from Reserve issues, which continue to be numbered. Incidentally, the words 'Special Edition' or 'Special Issue' were used on all home Youth Cup four-pagers prior to the 1960/61 campaign while all of the single sheets from this period went unnumbered. Also, the programmes for the home ties of the finals of 1982, 1986, 1992, 1993 and 1995 carry the words 'Special Edition'.

United have issued single sheets only for Youth Cup matches since the 1966/67 season. The only exceptions to this have been the finals against Watford in 1982 and Manchester City in 1986, when four-pagers were on offer, or the finals of 1992, 1993, 1995, 2003, 2007 and 2011 when programmes with at least twelve pages were produced.

If you have a copy of the single sheet for the Old Trafford leg of the semi-final against Sunderland in 1982, unless you actually purchased one at the game, it is probable that you own a forgery as literally dozens of fakes flooded the programme market soon after the match. There are genuine ones that have some notes on the reverse but, just to confuse matters, there are also legitimate copies with no notes. It is easy to spot the counterfeit production as the paper used is noticeably whiter, has a distinctly grainy texture and is thicker than the one produced by the club. It is believed that at least one Reserve issue from the same season (against Aston Villa) was also reproduced.

The vast majority of the readers of this publication will be specifically interested in the history of Manchester United Football Club while some may have purchased it because they have a more general fascination for football. By their very nature, historians are frequently collectors of club memorabilia, particularly match programmes, and because of this interest it seemed a useful exercise to include some detail on the subject in respect of Youth Cup issues relating to United.

What can be stated with absolute certainty is that a match programme or single sheet has been made available for each and every home game that the Reds have staged in the tournament, either at Old Trafford, The Cliff, Gigg Lane, Altrincham's Moss Lane, Hyde United's Ewen Fields or the Marston's Arena/Victoria Stadium in Northwich.

Firstly, it would be useful to differentiate between a programme and a single sheet. The latter publication, by definition, consists of a single, unfolded sheet of paper and carries simple details, such as the team line-ups, although there may be other information provided on occasions. Single sheets are often utilised for Youth Cup matches as it is not considered particularly cost-effective to produce anything more substantial for a game which might only attract a fairly modest gate.

In the early years of the Youth Cup, United tended to make single sheets available for the early rounds and four-page efforts for the semi-finals and finals, though there are some exceptions as, for example, there was only a single sheet printed for the home leg of the semi-final against Chelsea in 1955. On the other hand, four-page issues were produced for the Fourth Round tie against Newcastle United in January 1958 and the quarter-final matches against Barnsley in 1953, Bexleyheath & Welling in 1956, Blackburn Rovers in 1957 and Doncaster Rovers in 1958.

All of the four games staged at The Cliff between 1952 and 1956 resulted in single sheets being issued. For the 1958/59 to 1963/64 seasons inclusive, every one of United's Youth Cup home games saw programmes of four pages on sale. The trend, therefore, was for the club to offer Youth Cup issues in comparison to what was currently available for Reserve games, although the regular issuing of four-page programmes came into being a couple of years earlier for Youth Cup ties.

In the 1960/61 campaign, the first of six consecutive terms that four-pagers were the norm for second string home fixtures, the Youth Cup programmes against Liverpool (7), Bradford City (13), and Sunderland (23) were numbered for the one and only time in sequence with first-team home programmes. For terms 1961/62 to 1969/70 inclusive, they were numbered in sequence with the Reserves' issues.

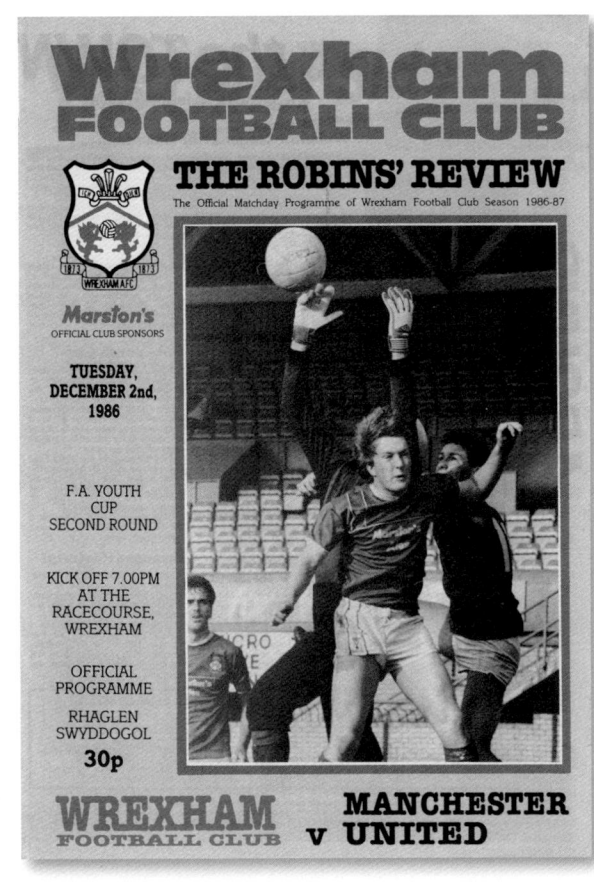

For the two home matches in the 1973/74 campaign, against Bury and Derby County, simple black and white sheets were on sale and these are the only two occasions when no colour has been utilised for a Youth Cup programme or single sheet at Old Trafford. Caused by restrictions on the printing trade in force at that time, it is almost certain that they were produced 'in-house'. The only other occasion in recent times that no colour has been used for a home fixture was when a glossy A5-sized single sheet was distributed when Nottingham Forest were the Reds' guests at Gigg Lane in December 1999. All home final programmes since 1982 have been printed in colour.

For the 'away' games against Nantwich in 1952 (played at The Cliff), Morecambe in 1959 and Wigan Athletic in 1961 (both staged at Old Trafford), United provided the single sheet/programmes rather than the 'home' clubs. Conversely, when the Reds played their 'home' game at the City Ground in Nottingham in 2001, a Forest produced black and white single sheet was made available.

For the Everton v. United clash at Anfield in November 1958, the 'home' side issued a single sheet rather than the host club.

In respect of away games, it is absolutely certain that nothing was published for the games at Preston in 1955, Huddersfield in 1956, Bolton in 1976 and Walsall in 1981.

Until fairly recently it was assumed that Sunderland failed to produce anything for their leg of the semi-final in April 1982 but a single sheet has since come to light. Because of its scarcity, the probability is that it was only made available in the press area and/or directors' box.

Information has also been received from a prominent Chester collector that it is extremely unlikely any type of production exists for the game at Sealand Road in December 1979. Similarly, a Leeds collector of some repute has claimed that the Yorkshire club did not issue for Youth Cup matches until the early 1960's, which seems to rule out anything for the Reds' visit to Elland Road in December 1957.

Curiously, Arsenal issued two different sized single sheets for the Fourth Round replay in February 1973.

For every away leg of the finals United have appeared in, programmes of at least four pages have been provided. This trend has generally been extended to the semi-final away legs, the exceptions being the single sheets at Wolves (1958), Blackburn (1959), Preston (1960), West Brom (1969), Manchester City (1980), Sunderland (1982), Coventry (1986) and Chelsea (2011 and 2012). The extremely small number of single sheets available at Stamford Bridge in 2011 and 2012 were supplemented with similar, though not identical, issues which could be downloaded from their website.

There was only one programme on offer at the two legs of the final in 2003 and, for the final matches in 2007, both programmes were the same except for the cover and the four innermost pages. The programmes for the respective legs of the final in 2011 were also largely similar.

In the early years of the tournament a couple of 'pirate' programmes were circulated. This type of counterfeit souvenir was fairly commonplace in the late 1940's and 1950's, particularly at big games such as internationals and cup finals, and they were sold to an unsuspecting soccer public around football stadiums as the genuine article. At least two pirate issues exist for United Youth Cup games from that era, for the home leg of the 1954 final and the tie at Anfield in October of the same year.

Many years after the practice was thought to have died out, informative and attractively produced four-page pirates were issued for the home games against Stoke in December 2004, Scunthorpe in December 2006 and Southampton in January 2007. All three matches took place at Hyde and it is obvious that the publications emanated from the same source as they are quite similar in appearance.

For the under-18's trip to West Ham in January 2011, an excellent 'unofficial' sixteen-page programme was available outside the ground in addition to a black and white A4 sheet given away on the gate.

There is only one known issue for a postponed game and that was for the intended visit of Blackburn to Old Trafford for the Second Round tie on the 2nd December 1992.

Because most clubs have the facility to either print or photocopy on-site nowadays, it isn't unusual to find both single sheets and programmes at Youth Cup games. The programmes are invariably put together by a production team/ printing firm off-site in the days leading up to the match while a single sheet is then printed at the stadium when the teams are known. An example of this occurred in January 2002 when Birmingham City sold programmes at the gate and then distributed (incorrectly dated) black and white sheets for free in the stands close to kick-off. There are other instances of programmes and single sheets being made available for Youth Cup ties, such as at Reading in November 2000 and at Rushden & Diamonds in November 2003.

A number of the recent finals and semi-finals have also seen the availability of both programmes and single sheets, although the latter are usually found only in restricted areas such as the press box.

Single sheets were issued for the Tomlinson Trophy games at Old Trafford in 1953 and at Anfield in 1954 while for the 1955 game against Bedfordshire Luton Town provided a large four-pager.

Youth Cup and Tomlinson Trophy programmes and single sheets are keenly sought by collectors, with some now extremely hard to find. Examples of scarce Youth Cup issues would be those at Everton in 1957, Sunderland in 1963, Oldham in 1973 and Liverpool in 1982, as even some of the most avid and long-standing United memorabilia collectors have never seen anything from these matches, and there are those who even question the existence of one or two of them.

The single sheets produced for the four games played at The Cliff are very difficult to obtain, as are the productions for the matches at Bexleyheath and Rotherham in 1954, Burnley and Blackpool in 1957, Coventry in 1970 and Middlesbrough in 1978.

A number of the rarer and more significant Youth Cup and Tomlinson Trophy issues have been reproduced in this book.

561

YOUTH COACHES

JIMMY MURPHY *1952/53 to 1963/64* - Unquestionably the most successful youth coach ever in this country, Jimmy Murphy oversaw the winning of six Youth Cups and three Tomlinson Trophies, seven Blue Stars tournament titles and a Bavarian Youth tournament triumph. In respect of the Youth Cup, his twelve seasons in charge also saw the club reach three semi-finals and two quarter-finals, and his record of 93 games included 73 wins and thirteen draws, an absolutely remarkable achievement that no-one has ever come near to matching.

Of course, Murphy's accomplishments weren't only confined to the junior stage as he also guided Wales to a World Cup quarter-final spot in 1958 and acted as assistant to Matt Busby throughout all of United's domestic and European glories of the 1940's, 1950's and 1960's.

From when he joined the club in 1946 until stepping down as youth coach in 1964, over 60 juniors made it into the first-team, with a third of those going on to represent their country.

Murphy continued to support Busby until his retirement in 1971 and was then enticed back to carry out some scouting work for Tommy Docherty later in the decade. A dedicated and passionate teacher whose tactical and technical tuition aided many a budding teenage talent to attain their full potential, he passed away in November 1989.

JOHNNY ASTON Senior *1964/65 to 1969/70* - An original MUJAC, Aston uniquely became the only member of that initial group who progressed into the club's senior side. Going on to win league, F.A. Cup and international honours, he represented England at the 1950 World Cup finals in Brazil.

After illness forced his retirement, Aston joined the coaching staff in October 1958 to replace the deceased Bert Whalley as Murphy's aid, specifically in order to help develop the club's younger element. He continued in that role until Murphy stood aside following the Youth Cup final victory over Swindon in 1964.

While his record of reaching two Youth Cup semi-finals might appear modest, Aston was responsible for bringing more than a dozen youngsters through to the first-team. A coach who bonded well with his pupils, he rarely bawled at them, preferring instead to use a gentle explanation to get his point across.

He went on to head up United's scouting operation following the retirement of Joe Armstrong only to lose his job when manager Frank O'Farrell was dismissed in December 1972.

BILL FOULKES *1970/71* - Making his first-team debut in 1952, United's stalwart defender finished his career with nearly 700 appearances to his credit. Foulkes was initially offered a job as a trainer and later managed the youths prior to taking charge of the Reserves. Neither brought much success and he later managed Witney Town for a spell before moving across the Atlantic to become the manager of Chicago Sting, Tulsa Roughnecks and the San Jose Earthquakes.

While at Chicago, Foulkes arranged for a number of United's juniors to join them on loan and thereby gain much-needed experience. He later took charge of clubs in Norway and Japan prior to settling back in the UK in 1992.

PAT CRERAND *1971/72 and 1972/73* - In charge of United's under-18's for two seasons, the team's Youth Cup runs finished at Goodison Park in 1971 and Highbury in 1973. Crerand was later promoted to second-in-command under Tommy Docherty at Old Trafford, a relationship which ended in much acrimony when the Reds' former wing-half and Scottish international left to manage Northampton in 1976.

As popular now in his role as a commentator with MUTV as he was in his playing days, Crerand's often humorous and occasionally biased views about United are tempered with numerous insightful observations based on his many years spent at football's coalface.

FRANK BLUNSTONE *1973/74 to 1976/77* - Former Crewe, Chelsea and England winger Blunstone made over 300 appearances for the Stamford Bridge club before moving into coaching upon hanging up his boots in 1964. Innovative and enthusiastic, he operated as a member of Chelsea's backroom staff under Tommy Docherty and then Dave Sexton and was appointed as manager of Brentford in 1969.

Frustrated by Brentford's lack of depth, as they operated without a Reserve or youth side, he accepted Docherty's offer of a coaching job with United in 1973 with the remit to *'recreate the days of the Busby Babes'*. His appointment was delayed by three months due to the serious injuries he sustained in a car accident, but once up to speed his methods were well liked by both management and players. Following Docherty's dismissal in 1977, Blunstone joined him at Derby a few months later.

JOE BROWN *1977/78* - A professional with Middlesbrough, Burnley, Bournemouth and Aldershot, Joe Brown's on-field exploits ended in 1961, after which he returned to Turf Moor to join the coaching set-up there. Over the years he graduated from looking after the youth team and Reserves and then became first-team coach and assistant manager prior to taking over the club's hot-seat in 1976.

During the following year he replaced Frank Blunstone at Old Trafford and after just the one term in that role he was placed in charge of scouting operations. Remaining in the job until June 1982, Brown's supportive nature was put to good use when he became the club's first youth development officer, a role he ably fulfilled until the early 1990's.

SYD OWEN *1978/79 to 1980/81* - A Luton legend who clocked up more than 400 appearances while at Kenilworth Road, Owen appeared in an England World Cup squad that journeyed to Switzerland in 1954 and five years later was named 'Footballer of the Year' while also leading the Hatters to an F.A. Cup final.

He was a valued member of Don Revie's coaching staff at Leeds prior to taking up a similar role at Old Trafford. Following a period of mediocrity for United's under-18's, Owen steered them to successive Youth Cup semi-finals in 1980 and 1981 in addition to securing two Lancashire Youth Cup triumphs.

ERIC HARRISON *1981/82 to 1997/98* - *'As I settled in at Old Trafford, I thought many, many times about the Busby Babes. My mission was to try to develop a generation of players to be just as good.'*

So said Eric Harrison, who succeeded in his aim by moulding one of the most exciting group of youngsters ever to play soccer. Members of the 'Class of '92' would go on to win practically every honour in the game open to them and dozens of his lesser talented former charges have served their profession with distinction.

Harrison learnt the basics of coaching while he was still a player at Hartlepool, watching on as manager Brian Clough dispensed large doses of common sense and discipline. He took up a backroom role at Everton before becoming one of Ron Atkinson's first appointments in the summer of 1981.

Guiding his sides to a couple of Youth Cup triumphs from five finals, with two semi-finals also on his record, the Yorkshireman currently scouts for Blackburn.

DAVE WILLIAMS *1998/99 to 2001/2002* - After retiring as a footballer, Dave Williams spent time as a coach at Newport, Bournemouth, Everton and Leeds prior to joining United as Harrison's understudy in 1997. Assuming control of the under-18's a year later, his exploits in the Youth Cup included two first hurdle k.o's and a quarter-final spot in 2002.

Leaving United that same year, he later managed Norwich's youth Academy and also coached the Welsh international youth sides.

BRIAN McCLAIR *2002/03 and 2003/04* - McClair graced Old Trafford over eleven years, firstly as a free-scoring centre-forward and then as a midfield linkman. A deep thinker who is highly intelligent and well spoken, he won domestic and European honours with the Reds before becoming Brian Kidd's number two at Blackburn in 1998.

In 2001, McClair was appointed as United's second string manager and promptly steered them to the Premier Reserve League title at the first time of asking. The 2002/03 term was marked by his achievement in guiding the under-18's to the club's ninth Youth Cup triumph and, after shadowing Les Kershaw, then United's Academy supremo, he replaced him in 2006 and remains in that role to this day.

FRANCISCO FILHO *2004/05* - Beginning his football career in 1957, it encompassed spells in his native Brazil, Venezuela, Portugal and France. Filho then embarked on a 29-year career as a coach, most notably in France, and landed in Manchester in 2002.

His time in charge of United's under-18's was infinitely shorter, lasting just over 90 minutes, and was marked by him sending out a formation against Stoke which, untypically for United, included a defence comprising of a trio of centre-backs.

He said of his aims, *'Little by little I am going to try to change certain habits; for example, to teach them to pass the ball more and use the spaces. They have a tendency to look for the final pass straight away. Manchester United are a Latin club with English characteristics. We pass, we play with the ball on the floor, but we also have the English mentality to fight.'*

After just one season in charge as the youths' boss, he retired until being tempted back into the game four years later when accepting a director's role with an American club, AC St. Louis.

PAUL McGUINNESS *2005/06 to present* - One of the most respected coaches in the modern game, Paul McGuinness has built up an impressive record in the Youth Cup. Taking the side to finals in 2007 and 2011, he has also experienced success in the Northern Ireland Milk Cup, the Claudio Sassi Memorial Trophy and has won the F.A. Premier Academy League North.

Within his seven years in charge of the under-18's, over a dozen players have reached the first-team with many having gained full international honours.

His side reached the 2012 Youth Cup semi-final, a particularly impressive feat given that the majority of the squad were still first-year scholars or younger. With the club's youths in such capable hands, the future looks secure for some considerable time to come.

TALENT of TOMORROW

Certain aspects of the game of professional football have changed beyond all recognition since the MUJACs were formed in August 1938. In respect of Manchester United's development of young players, what was once a local initiative prompted by a Salfordian philanthropist who put up a few thousand pounds to save the club now represents just a small part of the global strategy of a PLC today worth hundreds of millions of pounds under foreign ownership.

Regarding youth football, the basic infrastructure has undergone a major transformation over the last decade or so. When the junior Reds operated in the Lancashire League in the mid-1950's, youngsters commonly joined the club at the age of fifteen upon leaving school and learned their chosen trade against the likes of Rochdale's second string and Stockport County Reserves, often coming up against seasoned professionals.

The usual path to the first-team in those days began when the boys linked up with the Juniors and later progressed from the 'B' team into the 'A' side. Then gaining experience alongside first-team players in the Reserves, once the coaching staff thought they were ready they would then be blooded in the senior side. During this process boys would 'find their level', with some never making the necessary step up due to injury, lack of physique or limitations with their natural abilities. In other instances, exceptionally talented lads, such as Norman Whiteside in the 1980's, would spend very little time in the junior sides and found themselves elevated through the youth team and into the first eleven with meteoric acceleration.

When the F.A. introduced the Academy system at the outset of the 1998/99 term, the face of youth development altered significantly. Children began joining clubs as young as six or seven years of age and the traditional way of scouting players from the schools' system soon became defunct. Under-17 and under-19 age groups and leagues were introduced to replace local divisional competitions and that set-up has since been superceded with under-16 and under-18 leagues in which juniors only compete against opponents in their own age group.

In comparison, the Reserve team became a virtual under-21 side, with players over eighteen unable to play in the Academy due to F.A. restrictions but frequently not deemed ready for the rigours of the first-team. It seems a long way from the days when Bryan Robson was asked to put in appearances in the Lancashire League as part of his recovery from injury, a process which not only aided the England captain by giving him a gentle reintroduction to competitive football, it also provided a priceless experience in the development of the young hopefuls around him.

Because senior stars are rarely seen anywhere near the second string these days, those beneath them are never able to test their capabilities against better opposition. Thus, the new under-21 set-up has become something of a 'holding pen', in which numerous young players wait to be loaned out to a lower league club or hope for a permanent transfer away.

In the last ten years alone, Alex Ferguson has loaned out over 70 players to other league clubs, predominantly those in the lower divisions, in a bid to give them a taste of senior football. This strategy has paid major dividends as the likes of Jonny Evans, Tom Cleverley and Danny Welbeck have all returned to the club after loan spells with invaluable experience behind them and are now established in Ferguson's first-team squad. Rather than suffering the often stale atmosphere of a second string match, they were able to play week-in and week-out in either top of the table promotion clashes or in relegation dogfights. Those named also made the journey home with silverware in their pockets and an increased desire to forge a career at Old Trafford.

The loan system has also aided those players who perhaps just weren't quite up to the highest standards set by Ferguson and his coaching staff, by providing them with opportunities at other clubs. While former Red Ryan Shawcross has been on the verge of international selection through his displays for Stoke City, ex-United prospect Fraizer Campbell went one better, with the under-21 forward selected by Stuart Pearce for the full England squad that faced Holland at Wembley in February 2012. A dream came true for Campbell that night as he went on as a substitute to become the 90th Manchester United youth player to win international honours.

However, for the vast majority, the loan system has been inestimable in helping youth players to forge a career in the game, and at the start of the 2012/13 campaign there were 51 former United youth players on the books of other English league clubs. In addition, there are scores of other former juniors plying their trade in different leagues around the globe, from Richard Eckersley in Canada, Grant Brebner in Australia, Sam Hewson in Norway and, most famously of all, Gerard Piqué in Spain.

A further development has been the formation of alliances with overseas clubs such a Royal Antwerp, whereby juniors not only clocked up minutes in the Belgian club's first-team, but also benefited from the experience of regular football on foreign fields. The original scheme was first established in November 1998 and, although results have been mixed, for the likes of John O'Shea and Jonny Evans, the time spent on the continent proved a worthwhile part of their development. The relationship still exists, and even if United send over fewer hopefuls than in the past, there is no reason why further success cannot be achieved via this route.

A decade later, in November 2008, a novel negotiation was announced between United and Desportivo Brasil, a youth club owned by Traffic Football Management. The agreement gives United first option on more than 120 teenagers being groomed for European football in the São Paulo Academy. This enables the club to peruse the pool of Brazilian products within the set-up, and once a potential star turns eighteen, they are invited to train at the Carrington Training Centre alongside home grown hopefuls. Rafael Leao has acted as the original flag-bearer over the last couple of seasons, while Galdstony and Agnaldo were involved in the Reserves' pre-season matches in the summer of 2012.

Additionally, Paul McGuinness took the opportunity of utilising some of the local talent as 'guests' during the Belo Horizonte Youth Tournament in Brazil in November 2011.

Whether the relationship results in United discovering a future Ronaldo, Ronaldinho or Neymar remains to be seen, but it clearly illustrates the club's ambitions in South America.

In terms of finding young talent, locally we see completely different trends. After the F.A. introduced the '90-minute rule', all clubs were limited by geographical boundaries as to whom they could sign and so a potential talent in Carlisle could only join the Carlisle United or perhaps the Preston North End Academy, regardless of how good their operation was. Consequently, a coach with only limited credentials might train the most promising youngster in the country simply because of where the latter was born or lives.

During the early years of the Academy system, the Reds fell foul of breaking the geographical rules on occasion while, on the flip side of the coin, if United wanted to sign a player at age thirteen or fourteen, they were forced to pay 'compensation' to the 'owning' club. In a bid to circumnavigate the process, the Old Trafford talent-spotters now look further afield for talented youth products and the club has subsequently developed a global scouting network that continues to search for future Fergie Fledglings.

Resultantly, the percentage of foreigners joining United at junior level has increased significantly in recent years. While Scots, Welsh and Irish nationals have been recruited in some capacity since the early 1930's, United broke new ground when Australian Ray Baartz joined in October 1964. Together with Doug Johns and, later, Col Curran, what started originally as a three-month 'work experience' soon turned into a professional contract for Baartz, who remained at the club for two years before returning to Australia to win international honours.

It was another twenty-odd years before the likes of Jonny Rödlund and Mark Bosnich joined the ranks, both of whom enjoyed long club careers, albeit not in Manchester, and also represented their respective countries. Up to the introduction of the Academy system only a few juniors had landed in Manchester from outside the British Isles, yet from 1998 to the start of the 2012/13 season, there have been 24 foreign youth imports, a significant indication of possible future direction.

To be sure, trials at The Cliff on Tuesday nights have long gone!

There have been plenty of additional signs of progress over the last ten to fifteen years as United followed the F.A. guidelines and constructed a state of the art facility at Carrington, leading the way with numerous facets of football and player development.

One aspect of innovation was the appointment of René Meulensteen as a coach, one of the first foreign appointments at that level within the club. Meulensteen was hired fundamentally for his knowledge of the 'Coerver Method', a set of coaching techniques developed by Dutchman Wiel Coerver, which is a model greatly admired by Alex Ferguson. While the intention was to develop the skills of those in the Academy, such was its success that it has since been adopted by the entire first-team.

The focus on skill development over the last ten years was highly visible when the under-18's captured the F.A. Youth Cup in 2011, with a number of small yet technically gifted players such as Ravel Morrison, Jesse Lingard and Larnell Cole excelling throughout the competition.

As far as global travel is concerned, it is not uncommon now to see junior teams fly to America and Asia, as well as across Europe, to gain experience in a range of different international youth tournaments, and while the Blue Stars Tournament still holds a special place for many at the club, for sure it does not possess quite the same prestige as in years gone by.

Things have also changed significantly at a financial level, because from 1940 to 1990, United rarely reaped monetary benefit from their youth system. However, over the last twenty years, tens of millions of pounds have been recouped by the club from the sale of their former juniors, who weren't deemed good enough for the high standards at Old Trafford but were capable of performing lower down the league rankings.

It would be fair to say that with United performing at such a high level in world football, the requirements to make it as a first-team regular are now incredibly challenging. Throughout the last 60 years it hasn't been untypical to see nine or ten juniors in the same senior line-up, with at least one or two individuals joining the first-team ranks each year.

Over the last few seasons, the conveyor belt has undoubtedly slowed and, while the likes of Luke Chadwick, Kieran Richardson and Darron Gibson were given clear opportunities to make the grade over time, only Jonny Evans and Darren Fletcher have become regulars in the senior set-up. Encouragingly, Tom Cleverley and Danny Welbeck forced their way into contention in the early part of the 2011/12 term, though whether they turn out to be stalwarts over the next decade or fade away, only time will tell.

In the last twelve months, further changes have been felt at youth level with both the EPPP (Elite Player Performance Plan), an F.A. sponsored youth development scheme, and The NextGen Series, an international knockout tournament for youth teams, being introduced. While United made changes to achieve accreditation at Tier One level in the former, to date they have elected not to enter the latter.

The EPPP has six major principles:
1. Increase the number and quality of 'home grown players' gaining professional contracts and playing first-team football at the highest level.
2. Create more time for players to play and be coached.
3. Improve coaching provision.
4. Implement a system of effective measurement and quality assurance.
5. To positively influence strategic investment into the Academy system and demonstrate value for money.
6. Seek to implement significant gains in every aspect of player development.

In addition, changes from the previous Academy system include the abolition of the '90-minute rule', the introduction of a four-tier Academy system and a fixed tariff for transfers of players who are under eighteen years of age.

United have been designated as a Tier One Academy and as such they will be able to access the most promising boys and supply the best coaching. Finally, while the club always seem to pay over the odds for junior talent, a tariff-based system will allow much needed equality in transfer dealings.

These are all welcome developments as far as United are concerned, as the club has forged an enviable reputation for innovation with youth development, something that started through the input of Louis Rocca, Walter Crickmer and James Gibson over 80 years ago.

It is always difficult to predict what problems any future alterations to the rules might present, but with youth development so intrinsically built into the brickwork at Old Trafford, if any club has the history, culture, infrastructure and philosophy to best evolve with these changes, it will be Manchester United.

ROLL of HONOUR

Abbott	Peter Ashley	1970/71
Ackerley	Ernest Nicol	1960/61, 1961/62
Ackerley	Stanley	1958/59, 1959/60
Adams	Kenneth	1954/55
Ajose	Nicholas Olushola	2008/09, 2009/10
Albiston	Arthur Richard	1972/73, 1973/74, 1974/75
Amos	Benjamin Paul	2006/07, 2007/08
Anderson	William John	1962/63, **1963/64**, 1964/65
Andrews	Simon Paul	1987/88, 1988/89
Appleton	Michael Anthony	1993/94
Armfield	John Christopher	1980/81
Ashworth	Ian	1976/77
Aston	John	**1963/64**, 1964/65
Atherton	Alan	1959/60, 1960/61
Ayres	Kenneth Edward	1971/72, 1972/73
Bailey	George Ernest	1975/76, 1976/77
Baker	Desmond Patrick	**1994/95**, 1995/96
Bardsley	Philip Anthony	2001/02, **2002/03**
Baxter	Nicholas Peter	2000/01
Beardsmore	Russell Peter	1985/86, 1986/87
Beckett	Terence	**1954/55**, 1955/56
Beckham	David Robert Joseph	**1991/92**, 1992/93
Bernabeu	Gerard Piqué i	2004/05
Best	George	1962/63, **1963/64**
Beswick	Ivan	**1953/54**
Bielby	Paul Anthony	1972/73, 1973/74, 1974/75
Blackett	Tyler Nathan	**2010/11**
Blackmore	Clayton Graham	1980/81, 1981/82, 1982/83
Blakeman	Alan	1954/55
Bosnich	Mark John	1988/89, 1989/90
Botham	Raymond Paul	1974/75, 1975/76
Bottomley	Jonathon Derek	1985/86
Bradley	David	1974/75, 1975/76[†]
Brady	Robert	2008/09
Brameld	Marcus James	1990/91
Brandy	Febian Earlston	2005/06, 2006/07
Bratt	Harold	**1956/57**, 1957/58
Brazil	Derek Michael	1986/87
Brebner	Grant Ian	**1994/95**, 1995/96
Brennan	James	**1954/55**
Briggs	William Ronald	1959/60, 1960/61
Brightwell	Stuart	1995/96, 1996/97
Brooks	David	1972/73
Brough	Ian James	1966/67
Brown	David Alistair	1995/96, 1996/97
Brown	Karl David	1992/93
Brown	Reece	2009/10
Brown	Wesley Michael	1996/97, 1997/98[†]
Bryan	Antonio Stefan	2006/07, 2007/08
Bullimore	Wayne Alan	1987/88, 1988/89[†]
Burke	Raphael Edward	1990/91, 1991/92
Burns	Aaron Tyrone Stewart	2005/06
Burns	Francis	1964/65, 1965/66, 1966/67[†]
Butt	Nicholas	**1991/92**, 1992/93
Byers	Alexander James	1996/97
Byrne	Daniel Thomas	2001/02
Calliste	Ramon Thomas	**2002/03**, 2003/04
Campbell	Fraizer Lee	2004/05, 2005/06
Carolan	Joseph Francis	**1955/56**
Carrick	William Francis	1969/70, 1970/71
Carter	Stephen George	1989/90
Casper	Christopher Martin	**1991/92**, 1992/93
Cathcart	Craig George	2005/06, 2006/07[†]
Chadwick	Luke Harry	1997/98, 1998/99
Chapman	Samuel Edward Campbell	1953/54
Charlton	Robert	**1953/54**, **1954/55**, **1955/56**
Chester	James Grant	2006/07
Chisnall	John Philip	1958/59, 1959/60, 1960/61
Clark	Jonathan	1974/75, 1975/76, 1976/77[†]
Clarke	Robin Thomas	1972/73
Clarkson	Alan Paul	1971/72, 1972/73, 1973/74
Clayton	Gordon	**1952/53**, 1953/54, 1954/55
Clayton	Joseph Anthony	1961/62
Clegg	George Gerald	1997/98, 1998/99
Clegg	Michael Jamie	**1994/95**
Clegg	Steven John	2000/01
Cleverley	Thomas William	2006/07
Coates	Craig	2000/01
Cofie	John Erzuah	2009/10, **2010/11**
Cogger	John Sidney	2001/02
Cole	Larnell James	2009/10, **2010/11**
Collett	Benjamin Luke	2001/02, **2002/03**
Colman	Edward	**1952/53**, **1953/54**, **1954/55**[†]
Connaughton	Patrick John	1966/67, 1967/68
Conroy	William John	1972/73
Cooke	John	1965/66, 1966/67
Cooke	Terence John	1993/94, **1994/95**
Cope	Ronald	1952/53[†]

Cork	David	1977/78
Cosgrove	Stephen	1998/99
Costa	Lee Anthony	1988/89, 1989/90
Coyne	Peter David	1976/77
Crockett	Lee Adam	2004/05
Cronin	Denis Vincent	1985/86
Culkin	Nicholas James	1995/96
Cummings	Leslie Walter	1957/58
Curtis	John Charles Keyworth	**1994/95**, 1995/96, 1996/97[†]
Daehli	Mats Møeller	2010/11
Daniels	Bernard Joseph	1968/69
Davies	Alan	1978/79, 1979/80
Davies	Simon Ithel	1990/91, **1991/92**[†]
Davis	James Roger William	1999/00
Dawson	Alexander	**1955/56**, **1956/57**, 1957/58
Dempsey	Mark James	1981/82
Derbyshire	James Jeffrey	2006/07
Devlin	Conor Patrick	2009/10
Digby	Fraser Charles	1982/83, 1983/84, 1984/85
Docherty	Peter	1981/82, 1982/83
Doherty	Adrian John	1989/90, 1990/91
Doherty	John Peter	1952/53
Donald	Ian Richard	1969/70
Donaldson	William Hugh	1958/59, 1959/60, 1960/61
Drinkwater	Daniel Noel	2006/07, 2007/08
Dudgeon	Joseph Anthony	2007/08, 2008/09
Duff	Alan William Robert	1961/62, 1962/63, **1963/64**
Duncan	Andrew	1995/96
Dunphy	Eamon Martin	1961/62, 1962/63
Duxbury	Michael	1976/77, 1977/78[†]
Eagles	Christopher Mark	**2002/03**, 2003/04
Ebanks-Blake	Sylvan Agustus	**2002/03**, 2003/04
Eckersley	Adam James	2003/04
Eckersley	Richard Jon	2006/07
Edwards	Duncan	**1952/53**, **1953/54**, **1954/55**
Edwards	Paul Francis	1965/66
Eikrem	Magnus Wolff	2006/07, 2007/08
Elms	James Brian	1956/57, 1957/58, 1958/59
Emmerson	Wayne Edward	1965/66
English	Robert Harold	1954/55, 1955/56, **1956/57**
Evans	Corry John	2005/06, 2006/07, 2007/08[†]
Evans	Jonathan Grant	2004/05, 2005/06[†]
Evans	Sean William	2004/05, 2005/06
Evans	Wayne Andrew	1997/98, 1998/99
Fagan	Christopher Joseph	2005/06, 2006/07
Fairhurst	William Anthony	1969/70, 1970/71
Farrar	David	**1963/64**, 1964/65[†]
Ferguson	Damien Paul	1968/69, 1969/70
Ferguson	Darren	1988/89[†], 1989/90
Fidler	Dennis John	**1954/55**, **1955/56**
Field	Paul Stanley Thomas	1976/77
Fitzpatrick	Ian Matthew	1997/98, 1998/99
Fitzpatrick	John Herbert Norton	**1963/64**
Fitzpatrick	Kenneth John	1973/74, 1974/75
Flanagan	Callum Andrew	2002/03, 2003/04
Fleming	Michael	1966/67
Fletcher	Darren Barr	2001/02
Fletcher	Neville Stuart	1962/63
Fletcher	Peter	1970/71, 1971/72
Ford	Ryan	1995/96, 1996/97
Fornasier	Michele	2009/10, **2010/11**
Fox	David Lee	2000/01, 2001/02[†]
Fryers	Ezekiel David	2009/10, **2010/11**
Fry	Barry Frank	1960/61, 1961/62, 1962/63
Fulton	Bryce	**1952/53**
Galbraith	Daniel William	2006/07, 2007/08
Gardner	David Scott	**1994/95**
Gardner	Stephen George	1985/86[†]
Garton	William Francis	1981/82, 1982/83[†]
Gaskell	John David	**1956/57**, 1957/58, 1958/59
Gibson	Darron Thomas Daniel	2004/05, 2005/06[†]
Gibson	Paul Richard	**1994/95**
Gibson	Stuart	1956/57
Giggs/Wilson	Ryan Joseph	1989/90, 1990/91, **1991/92**[†]
Giles	Michael John	1957/58, 1958/59
Gill	Anthony Dean	1984/85, 1985/86
Gill	Frank	1966/67
Gill	Oliver David	2007/08, 2008/09
Gillespie	Keith Robert	**1991/92**, 1992/93
Gilmour	Thomas	1975/76, 1976/77
Givens	Daniel Joseph	1966/67
Goddard	Karl Eric	1985/86
Goodeve	Kenneth George Alfred	1967/68, 1968/69[†]
Gordon	Mark	1989/90, 1990/91, 1991/92
Graham	Deiniol William Thomas	1986/87, 1987/88
Gray	David Peter	2005/06
Grayson	Barry John	1962/63
Greenhoff	Brian	1968/69, 1969/70, 1970/71
Griffiths	Clive Leslie	1970/71, 1971/72, 1972/73
Griffiths	John Stuart	1976/77
Grimshaw	Anthony	1974/75, 1975/76
Haggett	David Lyn	1977/78, 1978/79[†]
Hall	Daniel Jonathan	**1994/95**, 1995/96
Hall	James	1967/68, 1968/69, 1969/70
Hamilton	Thomas Joesph	1952/53
Hardy	Jonathan Robert	1984/85
Harris	Andrew Laverty	1970/71
Harrop	Edward	1962/63, 1964/65
Harrop	Robert	1952/53, **1953/54**
Harvey	Paul Edward	1984/85, 1985/86, 1986/87
Hawksworth	Anthony	**1953/54**, **1954/55**, **1955/56**
Haydock	Frank	1958/59
Healey	Daniel Kevin	1971/72
Healy	David Jonathan	1996/97, 1997/98
Heath	Colin	2000/01, 2001/02
Heaton*	Thomas David	2003/04
Heckingbottom	Paul	1994/95
Henderson	William Alexander	1982/83
Hennessy	John	1957/58
Heseltine	Wayne Alan	1986/87, 1987/88[†]
Hewson	Sam	2005/06, 2006/07[†]
Higginbotham	Daniel John	1996/97
Hill	Andrew Rowland	1981/82, 1982/83[†]
Hilton	David	**1994/95**, 1995/96
Hilton	Kirk	1997/98, 1998/99
Hogg	Graeme James	1980/81, 1981/82[†]
Hogg	Steven Roy	2003/04
Holland	Eric Reginald	**1955/56**, **1956/57**, 1957/58[†]
Hopley	Anthony Bernard	1985/86, 1986/97
Howard	Mark James	**2002/03**, 2003/04
Howe	Richard David	1980/81
Hudson	Vincent John	1994/95
Hughes	Leslie Mark	1980/81, 1981/82
Hughes	Philip Anthony	1981/82

565

Humphreys	Christopher Norman	2000/01, 2001/02
Hunter	Geoffrey	1977/78
Hunter	John Reginald	**1956/57**
Hussain	Etzaz Musafar	2009/10
Hutchinson	Simon	1986/87, 1987/88
Ikin	David John	1962/63
Irving	Richard James	1992/93, 1993/94
Jackson	Anthony James	1987/88, 1988/89
Jackson	David Patrick	1976/77
James	Matthew Lee	2006/07, 2007/08, 2008/09[†]
James	Steven Robert	1966/67, 1967/68[†]
Jeffrey	David	1979/80, 1980/81
Johnson	David Anthony	1993/94, **1994/95**
Johnson	Edward William	2001/02, **2002/03**
Johnstone	Samuel Luke	**2010/11**
Jones	David Frank Llywd	2002/03[†]
Jones	Ernest Peter	**1954/55, 1955/56**
Jones	Richard Glynn	2003/04, 2004/05[†]
Jones	Paul Stanley	1971/72[†]
Jones	Stephen Francis	1977/78, 1978/79
Jowsey	James Robert	2000/01, 2001/02
Keane	Michael Vincent	**2010/11**
Keane	William David	2009/10, **2010/11**
Keen	Nigel John	1977/78, 1978/79, 1979/80[†]
Kelch	Patrick Joseph	1983/84
Kelly	James William	1972/73, 1973/74, 1974/75
Kelly	Michael Edward	1967/68
Kennedy	Patrick Anthony	**1952/53**
Keogh	James William	1961/62
Keough	Daniel Peter	1978/79, 1979/80, 1980/81[†]
Kidd	Brian	1965/66, 1966/67
King	Joshua Christian Kojo	2009/10
Kinsey	Albert John	1962/63, **1963/64**
Kirkup	Alan Richard	1973/74, 1974/75
Kirovski	Jovan	1992/93, 1993/94
Kopel	Frank	1965/66, 1966/67
Latham	David Colin	1959/60, 1960/61, 1961/62
Lawrence	Lee Anthony	2001/02, **2002/03**
Lawrence	Thomas Morris	**2010/11**
Lawton	Craig Thomas	1987/88, 1988/89, 1989/90
Lawton	Norbert	**1956/57**, 1957/58
Lea	Michael Robert	2005/06
Lee	Kieran Christopher	2005/06
Lester	Gordon	1953/54
Lewis	Edward	**1952/53**
Lewis	Kevin William	1968/69, 1969/70, 1970/71
Lingard	Jesse Ellis	2009/10, **2010/11**
Littler	Thomas	**1953/54**
Loftus	Robert	1967/68
Lorimer	Michael David	1960/61, 1961/62
Loughnane	Peter Brian	1975/76
Lowey	John Anthony	1974/75, 1975/76
Lowry	Brian Thomas	1953/54
Lowther	Shaun	1979/80
Lucas	Peter John Stucley	1977/78
Lydiate	Jason Lee	1987/88, 1988/89, 1989/90[†]
Lynam	Christopher Anthony	1978/79, 1979/80
Lynch	Mark John	1998/99, 1999/00
Lyons	Paul	1994/95
Macheda	Federico	2007/08, 2008/09
Macken	Jonathan Paul	1995/96
Maddison	Raymond Wilfred	**1956/57**
Maneely	James Alfred Mervyn	1961/62, 1962/63
Marsh	Phillip	2003/04, 2004/05
Marshall	Bernard John	1964/65
Martin	Lee Andrew	1985/86
Martin	Lee Robert	2003/04, 2004/05
Massacci	Alberto	2009/10, **2010/11**
Mathieson	Andrew John	1984/85
McAuley	Sean	1988/89, 1989/90
McBride	Andrew	1984/85, 1985/86, 1986/87
McBride	Peter Patrick	**1963/64**, 1964/65
McCormack	Conor James	2006/07
McCreery	David	1973/74, 1974/75, 1975/76
McDermott	John Charles	1976/77, 1977/78
McDermott	Kel Warnock	1980/81
McEwen	Francis Kevin	1963/64, 1964/65, 1965/66[†]
McFarlane	William Noel	**1952/53**
McGarvey	Scott Thomas	1979/80, 1980/81
McGinty	Sean Andrew	2009/10, **2010/11**
McGivern	Francis	1971/72
McGuinness	Paul Edward	1983/84
McGuinness	Wilfred	**1953/54, 1954/55, 1955/56**[†]
McIlroy	Samuel Baxter	1970/71, 1971/72
McInally	John Stewart	1968/69
McKee	Colin	1989/90, 1990/91, **1991/92**
McKelvey	Brendan Patrick	1972/73, 1973/74
McKeown	Isaac Lindsay	1973/74, 1974/75
McLoughlin	Alan Francis	1983/84, 1984/85[†]
McMillan	Samuel	1959/60
McMurdo	Ian Thomas	1967/68, 1968/69, 1969/70
McReavie	Alan Steven	1989/90, 1990/91
McShane	Paul David	**2002/03**, 2003/04[†]
Mettrick	Mark Richard	1982/83
Micklewhite	Gary	1977/78, 1978/79
Miller	Ronald George Bissett	1969/70
Millerchip	Lawrence	1968/69, 1969/70[†]
Mills	Leon James	1996/97
Mills	William Gary	1982/83, 1983/84
Mitchell	Grant Stanley	1981/82
Moffatt	Scott Lee	2006/07, 2007/08
Moir	Ian	1958/59, 1959/60, 1960/61
Monaghan	Matthew Shaun	1993/94
Mooniaruck	Kalam Yusuf	2001/02
Moran	David	2000/01
Morgans	Kenneth Godfrey	1954/55, **1955/56, 1956/57**[†]
Morris	David Maurice	1975/76
Morrison	Ravel Ryan	2008/09, 2009/10, **2010/11**
Mortimer	John David	1987/88
Morton	Alan	1952/53
Morton	Kenneth	1962/63, 1963/64, 1964/65
Morton	Roy Steven	1971/72, 1972/73
Mountford	Raymond	1975/76
Muirhead	Ben Robinson	1999/00, 2000/01
Mukendi	Floribert N'Galula Mbuyi	2003/04
Mullan	Jamie John	2004/05, 2005/06
Mulryne	Philip Patrick Steven	**1994/95**, 1995/96
Murdock	Colin James	1992/93
Murphy	Aidan Joseph	1983/84, 1984/85, 1985/86
Mustoe	Neil John	**1994/95**
Nardiello	Daniel Anthony	1999/00, 2000/01
Naylor	Gavin Edward	1996/97
Neville	Gary Alexander	**1991/92**, 1992/93[†]
Neville	Philip John	1992/93, 1993/94[†], **1994/95**[†]

Neumayr	Markus Martin	2003/04
Nicholl	James Michael	1972/73, 1973/74, 1974/75†
Nicholson	James Joseph	1958/59, 1959/60, 1960/61†
Noble	Robert	1962/63, **1963/64**†
Norwood	Oliver James	2007/08, 2008/09
Notman	Alexander McKeachie	1996/97, 1997/98
O'Donnell	James Alexander	1986/87
O'Kane	John Andrew	1990/91, **1991/92**, 1992/93
O'Neil	Thomas Patrick	1968/69, 1969/70, 1970/71†
O'Shea	John Francis	1998/99
O'Sullivan	Peter Anthony	1966/67, 1967/68, 1968/69
Olney	Patrick Anthony	1972/73
Orritt	Gareth	1979/80, 1980/81
Paterson	Steven William	1975/76
Pearce	Peter Derek	1953/54
Pears	Stephen	1978/79, 1979/80
Pearson	John	1962/63, 1963/64, 1964/65
Pearson	Lawrence	1981/82, 1982/83
Pearson	Mark	**1955/56, 1956/57**, 1957/58
Pegg	David	**1952/53, 1953/54**†
Petrucci	Davide	2008/09, 2009/10†
Philpott	Robert Brian	1984/85
Picken*	Philip James	2003/04
Pierce	David Edward	1993/94
Pilkington	Kevin William	**1991/92**
Platt	David Andrew	1983/84
Plunkett	Stuart Edward	1977/78
Pogba	Paul Labile	2009/10, **2010/11**
Pollitt	Michael Francis	1987/88, 1989/90
Poole	David Andrew	2001/02, **2002/03**
Poole	Bernard	1957/58, 1958/59
Poole	Terence	1966/67
Poppett	Kevan	1976/77
Potts	Leslie Andrew	1990/91
Prophet	Paul	1971/72
Pugh	Daniel Adam	2000/01
Puustinen	Jami Petteri	2003/04, 2004/05
Queenan	John	**1954/55, 1955/56**
Rachubka	Paul Stephen	1997/98, 1998/99
Rankin	John Gibson	2000/01
Ratcliffe	Simon	1982/83, 1983/84
Rawlinson	Mark David	1992/93
Reynolds	Michael Andrew	1979/80, 1980/81
Rhodes	Alan	**1953/54, 1954/55**
Richardson	Kieran Edward	2001/02, **2002/03**
Riley	Steven	1992/93
Rimmer	John James	**1963/64**, 1964/65, 1965/66
Ritchie	Andrew Timothy	1977/78, 1978/79
Robbins	Gordon	1952/53
Roberts	Christopher Owen	1978/79, 1979/80
Roberts	Joseph Edward	**1991/92**, 1992/93
Robins	Mark Gordon	1986/87, 1987/88
Robinson	Andrew Craig	1981/82, 1982/83, 1983/84†
Roche	Lee Paul	1997/98, 1998/99†
Rödlund	Jonny Erik Gunnar	1988/89
Rogers	Martyn	1975/76, 1976/77, 1977/78
Rose	Daniel Stephen	2005/06
Rose	Michael Charles	1999/00
Rose	Stephen Derek	1997/98, 1998/99
Rossi	Giuseppe	2004/05
Rowbotham	Michael Grant	1981/82, 1982/83, 1983/84
Russell	Martin Christopher	1983/84, 1984/85
Ryan	David Peter	1972/73, 1973/74, 1974/75
Ryan	Mark	1993/94
Ryan	Michael Stuart Patrick	1997/98
Sadler	Adam	1996/97
Sadler	David	1962/63, **1963/64**
Sallis	Roger John	1988/89
Sampson	Gary James Frank	2000/01
Sartori	Carlo Domenico	1965/66
Savage	Robert William	**1991/92**, 1992/93
Scanlon	Albert Joseph	**1952/53, 1953/54**
Scholes	Paul Aaron	1992/93
Scott	Ian Richard	1985/86, 1986/87†
Scott	Kenneth	1981/82, 1982/83, 1983/84
Sharpe	Lee Stuart	1988/89†
Sharples	John Benjamin	1989/90, 1990/91†
Shawcross	Ryan James	2004/05, 2005/06
Shields	John James	1989/90, 1990/91
Shotton	John Matthew	1988/89
Simpson	Daniel Peter	2004/05
Sims	Lee Michael	2001/02, **2002/03**
Simmonds	Melvyn Robert	1967/68
Sixsmith	Paul	1989/90
Smith	Barry	**1956/57**, 1957/58, 1958/59†
Smith	Miles Graham	1957/58
Smith	Oswald George	1973/74
Smith	Robert William	1959/60, 1960/61, 1961/62†
Smith	Thomas Edward	1995/96
Smyth	Peter William	1990/91
Spector	Jonathon Michael Paul	2003/04
Spratt	Thomas	1957/58, 1958/59, 1959/60
Steele	Luke David	**2002/03**
Steer	Phillip James	1986/87
Stevenson	Alan	1979/80, 1980/81
Stewart	Cameron Reece	2007/08, 2008/09
Stewart	Michael James	1998/99
Stiles	Norbert Peter	1957/58, 1958/59†, 1959/60†
Storey	Raymond David	1974/75, 1975/76
Strange	Gareth Albert	1999/00
Strickland	Kenneth Andrew	2006/07, 2007/08
Studley	Dominic Peter	1998/99
Studley	Mark Lee	1999/00
Sutcliffe	Peter David	1973/74, 1974/75
Switzer	George	**1991/92**
Szmid	Marek Andrzej	1999/00†
Tate	Alan	2000/01†
Taylor	Andrew James	2000/01
Taylor	Christopher	1989/90
Taylor	Kris	2000/01, 2001/02
Taylor	Leonard Alexander	**1991/92**
Teather	Paul Anthony	1995/96
Thornley	Benjamin Lindsay	1990/91, **1991/92**, 1992/93
Thorpe	Thomas Joseph	2009/10, **2010/11**†
Thorrington	John Gerard	1997/98
Tierney	Paul Thomas	2000/01
Timm	Mads	2001/02, **2002/03**
Toal	Kieran Michael	1988/89
Todd	Mark Kenneth	1985/86
Tonge	Alan Michael	1988/89, 1989/90
Tranter	Wilfred	1960/61, 1961/62, 1962/63†
Tunnicliffe	Ryan	2008/09, 2009/10, **2010/11**
Trees	Robert Victor	1995/96
Twiss	Michael John	1994/95, 1995/96

Twynham	Gary Steven	1993/94		Williams	Ben Philip	1999/00
Van Velzen	Gyliano	**2010/11**		Williams	Dyfan Howard	1986/87
Walker	Dennis Allen	1960/61, 1961/62, 1962/63		Williams	Matthew	2000/01
Walker	John	1954/55		Williams	Anthony Sean Morgan	1980/81, 1981/82
Walker	Joshua George	1999/00		Wilson	David Graham	1985/86, 1986/97
Wallwork	Ronald	**1994/95**, 1995/96†		Wilson	Mark Anthony	1995/96, 1996/97
Walsh	Gary	1985/86		Wood	Jamie	1996/97
Wardrop	Michael John	1971/72, 1972/73†, 1973/74†		Wood	Neil Anthony	1999/00, 2000/01
Watson	William	1965/66, 1966/67, 1967/68		Wood	Nicholas Antony	1981/82, 1982/83, 1983/84
Webber	Daniel Vaughn	1998/99, 1999/00		Woods	Gary	2008/09
Weir	David	1965/66, 1966/67, 1967/68		Woods	Peter Anthony	1967/68
Welbeck	Daniel Nii Tackie Mensah	2006/07, 2007/08, 2008/09		Wootton	Scott James	2008/09, 2009/10
Wellens	Richard Paul	1996/97, 1997/98		Worrall	Garry George	1978/79, 1979/80
Welsh	Stephen Nicholas	1984/85		Worthington	Gary Lee	1983/84, 1984/85
Westwood	Ashley Michael	1993/94, **1994/95**		Wratten	Paul	1987/88
Wheatcroft	Paul Michael	1997/98, 1998/99		Wray	Andrew Phillip	1978/79, 1979/80
Whelan	Anthony Michael	1968/69, 1969/70, 1970/71		Wright	Brian Edward	1961/62
Whelan	William Augustine	**1952/53**		Wylie	Michael	1970/71, 1971/72
Whiteman	Marc Christopher	2000/01		Wynn	David	1979/80, 1980/81
Whiteside	Norman John	1980/81, 1981/82, 1982/83		Yeomans	David George	1957/58
Whitmarsh	Darren Martin	1992/93		Young	Eric Royston	1968/69, 1969/70, 1970/71
Whittam	Philip Richard	1993/94, 1994/95		Young	Thomas Anthony	1968/69, 1969/70, 1970/71
Wilkinson	Ian Matthew	1990/91		Zieler	Ron-Robert	2005/06, 2006/07

Bold season = Winner's medal received   * Received winner's medals as non-playing substitutes for the 2002/03 season   † Youth Cup captain

DREAM TEAM
Steve & Tony's all-time greatest Manchester United Youth XI

1
Gary WALSH

2 Gary NEVILLE   **5** Wes BROWN   **4** Nobby STILES   **3** Bobby NOBLE

7 George BEST   **6** Duncan EDWARDS   **8** Paul SCHOLES   **11** Ryan GIGGS

9 Bobby CHARLTON   **10** Alex DAWSON

Subs: Norman WHITESIDE, Jimmy RIMMER (GK), Johnny GILES, Eddie COLMAN, Arthur ALBISTON

1938/39 MUJAC line-up from the back cover; Back row (l-r) Arthur Powell, Tom Cookson, John Phoenix, John Aston, Higgins, Charlie Stafford, Harry Haslam, Mickey Mears, James Hall, Jimmy McClelland. Front row (l-r) Jack White, Geoffrey Lockwood, John Healey, Harry Howcroft, Arthur Brennan, Unknown